CHILTON'S

FORD

FORD ESCORT AND MER
1981-95 REPAIR MANUAL

President, Chilton Enterprises	David S. Loewith
Senior Vice President	Ronald A. Hoxter
Publisher & Editor-In-Chief	Kerry A. Freeman, S.A.E.
Executive Editors	Dean F. Morgantini, S.A.E., W. Calvin Settle, Jr., S.A.E.
Managing Editor	Nick D'Andrea
Special Products Manager	Ken Grabowski, A.S.E., S.A.E.
Senior Editors	Jacques Gordon, Michael L. Grady, Debra McCall, Kevin M. G. Maher, Richard J. Rivele, S.A.E., Richard T. Smith, Jim Taylor, Ron Webb
Project Managers	Martin J. Gunther, Will Kessler, A.S.E., Richard Schwartz
Production Manager	Andrea Steiger
Product Systems Manager	Robert Maxey
Director of Manufacturing	Mike D'Imperio
Editor	Jaffer A. Ahmad

CHILTON BOOK COMPANY

ONE OF THE **DIVERSIFIED PUBLISHING COMPANIES,**
A PART OF **CAPITAL CITIES/ABC,INC.**

Manufactured in USA

Chilton Way, Radnor, PA 19089
ISBN 0-8019-8675-3
Library of Congress Catalog Card No. 94-069435
1234567890 4321098765

Contents

Contents

SAFETY NOTICE

Proper service and repair procedures are vital to the safe, reliable operation of all motor vehicles, as well as the personal safety of those performing repairs. This manual outlines procedures for servicing and repairing vehicles using safe, effective methods. The procedures contain many NOTES, CAUTIONS, and WARNINGS which should be followed along with standard procedures to eliminate the possibility of personal injury or improper service which could damage the vehicle or compromise its safety.

It is important to note that the repair procedures and techniques, tools and parts for servicing motor vehicles, as well as the skill and experience of the individual performing the work vary widely. It is not possible to anticipate all of the conceivable ways or conditions under which vehicles may be serviced, or to provide cautions as to all of the possible hazards that may result. Standard and accepted safety precautions and equipment should be used when handling toxic or flammable fluids, and safety goggles or other protection should be used during cutting, grinding, chiseling, prying, or any other process that can cause material removal or projectiles.

Some procedures require the use of tools specially designed for a specific purpose. Before substituting another tool or procedure, you must be completely satisfied that neither your personal safety, nor the performance of the vehicle will be endangered.

Although information in this manual is based on industry sources and is complete as possible at the time of publication, the possibility exists that some car manufacturers made later changes which could not be included here. While striving for total accuracy, Chilton Book Company cannot assume responsibility for any errors, changes or omissions that may occur in the compilation of this data.

PART NUMBERS

Part numbers listed in this reference are not recommendation by Chilton for any product by brand name. They are references that can be used with interchange manuals and aftermarket supplier catalogs to locate each brand supplier's discrete part number.

SPECIAL TOOLS

Special tools are recommended by the vehicle manufacturer to perform their specific job. Use has been kept to a minimum, but where absolutely necessary, they are referred to in the text by the part number of the tool manufacturer. These tools can be purchased, under the appropriate part number, from your local dealer or regional distributor, or an equivalent tool can be purchased locally from a tool supplier or parts outlet. Before substituting any tool for the one recommended, read the SAFETY NOTICE at the top of this page.

ACKNOWLEDGMENTS

The Chilton Book Company expresses appreciation to Ford Motor Company for their generous assistance.

1 GENERAL INFORMATION AND MAINTENANCE

HOW TO USE THIS BOOK

Chilton's Total Car Care Manual for 1981-95 Ford Escort/Mercury Tracer, 1982-86 EXP, 1981-87 Mercury Lynx and 1982-83 LN7 is intended to teach you about the inner workings of your car and save you money on its upkeep.

The first two sections will be used most frequently, since they contain procedures to carry out maintenance and tune-up information. Studies have shown that a properly tuned and maintained engine can get at least 10 percent better gas mileage (which translates into lower operating costs) and periodic maintenance will catch minor problems before they turn into major repair bills. The other sections deal with the more complex systems of your vehicle. Operating systems from engine through brakes are covered. This book will give you detailed instructions to help you change your own brake pads and shoes, tune-up the engine, replace spark plugs and filters, and do many more jobs that will save you money, help you avoid expensive problems and give you personal satisfaction.

A secondary purpose for this book is a reference guide for owners who want to understand their vehicle and/or their mechanics better. In this case, no tools at all are required. Knowing just what a particular repair job requires in parts and labor time will allow you to evaluate whether or not you're getting a fair price quote and help decipher itemized bills from a repair shop.

Before attempting any repairs or service on your vehicle, read through the entire procedure outlined in the appropriate section. This will give you the overall view of what tools and supplies will be required. Read ahead and plan ahead. Each operation should be approached logically and all procedures thoroughly understood before attempting any work. Some special tools that may be required can often be rented from local automotive jobbers or places specializing in renting tools and equipment.

All sections contain adjustments, maintenance, removal and installation procedures, and overhaul procedures. When overhaul is not considered practical, we tell you how to remove the failed part and then how to install the new or rebuilt replacement. In this way, you at least save the labor costs. Overhaul of some components (such as the alternator or water pump) is just not practical for do-it-yourselfer's; but the removal and installation procedure is often simple and well within the capabilities of the average owner.

Two basic mechanic's rules should be mentioned here. First, whenever the LEFT side of the vehicle or engine is referred to, it is meant to specify the DRIVER'S side of the vehicle. Conversely, the RIGHT side of the vehicle means the PASSENGER'S side. Second, all screws and bolts are removed by turning counterclockwise, and tightened by turning clockwise (left loosen, right tighten).

Safety is always the MOST important rule. Constantly be aware of the dangers involved in working on or around any vehicle and take proper precautions to avoid the risk of personal injury or damage to the vehicle. See the section in this Section, Servicing Your Vehicle Safely, and the SAFETY NOTICE on the acknowledgment page before attempting any service procedures.

Always read carefully the instructions provided. There are three commonly made mistakes in mechanical work:

1. **Incorrect order of assembly, disassembly or adjustment.** When taking something apart or putting it together, doing things in the wrong order usually just costs you extra time; however, it CAN break something. Read the entire procedure before beginning disassembly. Do everything in the order in which the instructions say you should, even if you can't immediately see a reason for it. When you are taking apart something that is very intricate (for example, a carburetor), you might want to draw a picture or use an instant camera to record how it looks when assembled at one point in order to make sure you get everything back in its proper position. We will supply exploded views whenever possible, but sometimes the job requires more attention to detail than an illustration provides. When making adjustments (especially tune-up adjustments), do them in order. One adjustment often affects another.
2. **Overtightening (or undertightening) nuts and bolts.** While it is more common for overtightening to cause damage, undertightening can cause a fastener to vibrate loose and cause serious damage, especially when dealing with aluminum parts. Pay attention to torque specifications and use a torque wrench in assembly. If a torque figure is not available, remember that if you are using the right tool to do the job, you will probably not have to strain yourself to get a fastener tight enough. The pitch of most threads is so fine that the tension you apply with the wrench will be multiplied many times in actual force on what you are tightening. A good example of how critical torque is can be seen in the case of spark plug installation, especially when you are putting the (steel) plug into an aluminum cylinder head. Too little torque can fail to crush the gasket, causing leakage of combustion gases and consequent overheating of the plug and engine parts. Too much torque can damage the aluminum threads or distort the plug, which changes the spark gap at the electrode. Since more and more manufacturers are using aluminum in their engine and chassis parts to save weight, a torque wrench should be in any serious do-it-yourselfer's tool box.

➡There are many commercial chemical products available for ensuring that fasteners won't come loose, even if they are not torqued just right (a very common brand is Loctite®). If you're worried about getting something together tight enough to hold, but loose enough to avoid mechanical damage during assembly, one of these products might offer substantial insurance. Read the label on the package and make sure the product is compatible with the materials, fluids, etc. involved before choosing one.

3. **Cross-threading.** This occurs when a part or fastener such as a bolt is forcefully screwed into a casting or nut at the wrong angle, causing the threads to become damaged. Cross-threading is more likely to occur if access is difficult. To avoid cross threading, it helps to clean and lubricate fasteners, and to start threading with the part to be installed going straight in, using your fingers. If you encounter resistance, unscrew the part or fastener and start again at a different angle until the threads catch and it can be turned several times without much

effort. Keep in mind that many parts, especially spark plugs, use tapered threads so that gentle turning will automatically bring the item you are threading to the proper angle if you don't force it or resist a change in angle. Don't put a wrench on the part or fastener until it has been turned in a couple of times by hand. If you suddenly encounter resistance and the part or fastener has not seated fully, do not force it. Pull it back out and make sure it is clean and threading properly.

Always take your time and be patient; once you gain some experience, working on your car will become an enjoyable hobby.

TOOLS AND EQUIPMENT

➧ See Figures 1, 2, 3, 4, 5, 6, 7, 8 and 9

Having the right tools for the job is essential. Without the proper tools and equipment it is impossible, or at least unnecessarily frustrating, to properly service your vehicle. It would be impossible to catalog each and every tool needed to perform every procedure in this book. It would also be unwise for the amateur to rush out and buy an expensive set of tools on the theory that he may need one or more of them sometime.

The best approach is to proceed slowly, gathering together a good quality set of those tools that are used most frequently. Don't be misled by the low cost of bargain tools. It is far better to spend a little more for quality. Forged wrenches, 6 or 12-point sockets and fine tooth ratchets are by far preferable to their less expensive counterparts. As any good mechanic can tell you, there are few worse experiences than trying to work on a car with bad tools. Your monetary savings will not be worth the consequent cost of frustration and mangled knuckles.

Certain tools, plus a basic ability to handle tools, are required to get started. A basic mechanic's tool set, a torque wrench, and a Torx® bit set. Torx® bits are hex lobular drivers which fit both inside and outside on special Torx® head fasteners used in various places on Ford and Mercury vehicles.

Begin accumulating those tools that are used most frequently: those associated with routine maintenance and tune-up.

In addition to the normal assortment of screwdrivers and pliers, you should have the following tools for routine maintenance jobs (your car uses some metric fasteners):

- Metric wrenches, sockets and combination open end/box end wrenches in sizes from 3mm to 19mm; and a spark plug socket. If possible, buy various length socket drive extensions. One break in this department is that the metric sockets available in the U.S. will all fit the ratchet handles and extensions you may already have (1/4 in., 3/8 in., and 1/2 in. drive).
- Jack stands for supporting the raised car.
- Oil filter wrench.
- Funnel for pouring oil.
- Grease gun for chassis lubrication.
- Hydrometer for checking the (non-sealed) battery.
- A container for draining oil.
- Many rags for wiping up the inevitable spills and mess.

In addition to the above items there are several others that are not absolutely necessary but handy to have around. These include oil-absorbing material in case of spills, a long funnel for filling the transaxle and the usual supply of lubricants, antifreeze and fluids. This is a basic list for routine maintenance, but only your personal needs and desires can accurately determine your list of necessary tools.

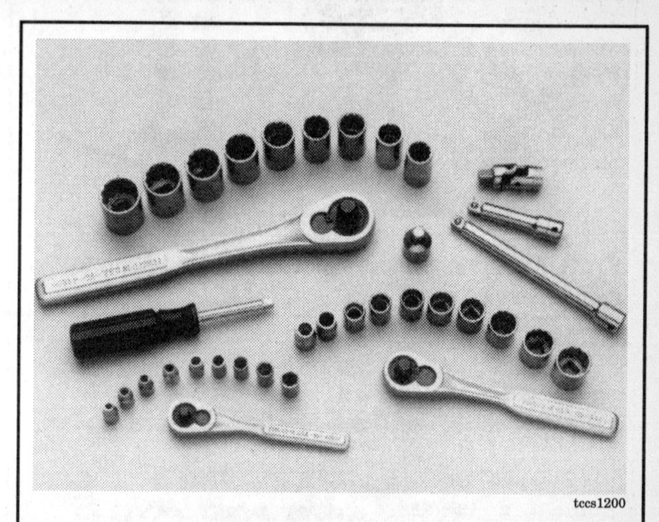

tccs1200

Fig. 1 All but the most basic procedure will require an assortment of ratchets and sockets

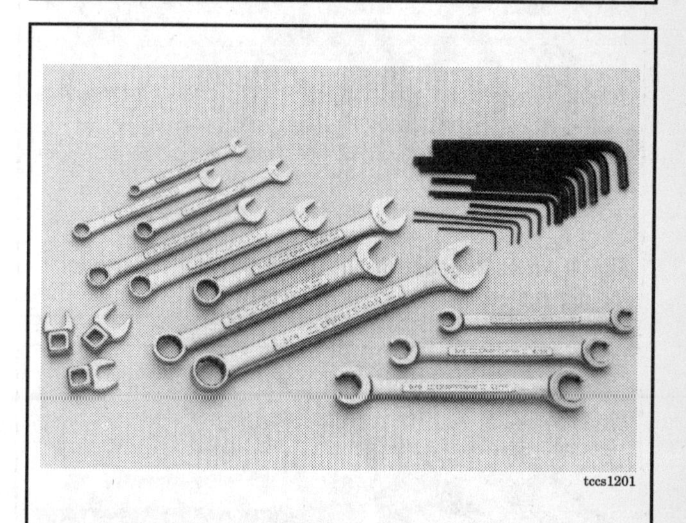

tccs1201

Fig. 2 In addition to ratchets, a good set of wrenches and hex keys will be needed

The second list of tools is for tune-ups. While the tools involved here are slightly more sophisticated, they need not be outrageously expensive. There are several inexpensive tach/dwell meters on the market that work every bit as well for the average mechanic as an expensive professional model. Just be sure that the tachometer scale reads to at least 1200 rpm (preferably 1500 rpm), and that it works on 4-cylinder engines.

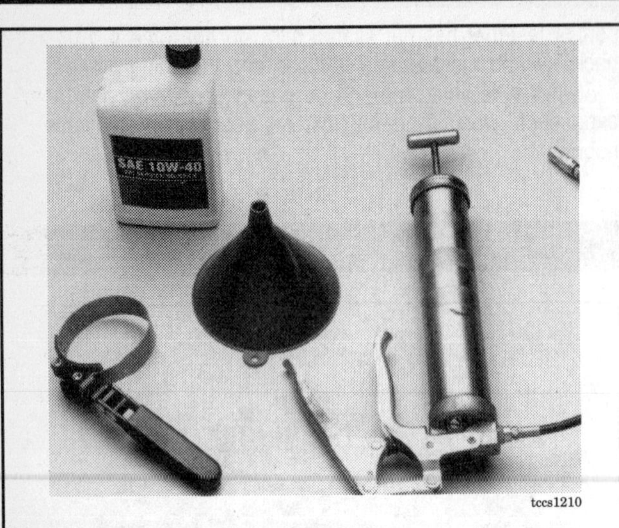

Fig. 3 A few inexpensive lubrication tools will make regular service easier

A basic list of tune-up equipment could include:

- Tach/dwell meter.
- Spark plug wrench or socket.
- Timing light (a DC light that works from the vehicle's battery is best, although an AC light that plugs into 110V house current will suffice at some sacrifice in brightness).
- Wire-type spark plug gauge and plug adjusting tools.
- Set of feeler blades.

In addition to these basic tools, there are several other tools and gauges you may find useful. These include:

- A compression gauge. The screw-in type takes longer to use, but eliminates the possibility of a faulty reading due to escaping pressure.
- A manifold vacuum gauge.
- A test light.
- An induction meter. This is used for determining whether or not there is current in a wire. These are handy for use if a wire is broken somewhere in a wiring harness.

As a final note, you will probably find a torque wrench necessary for all but the most basic work. The beam-type models

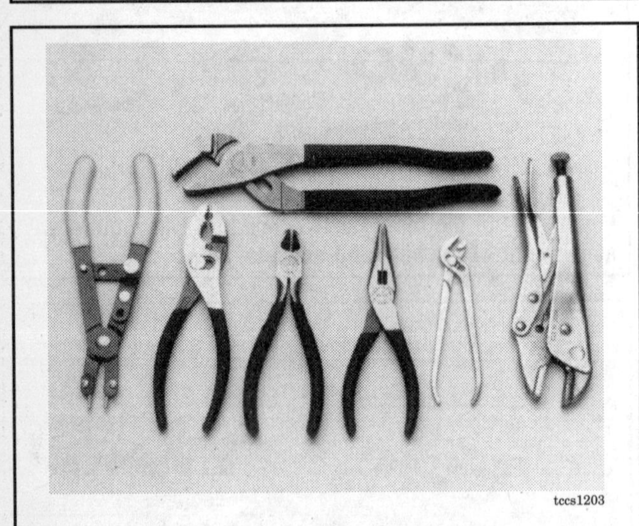

Fig. 4 An assortment of pliers will be handy, especially for old rusted parts and stripped bolt heads

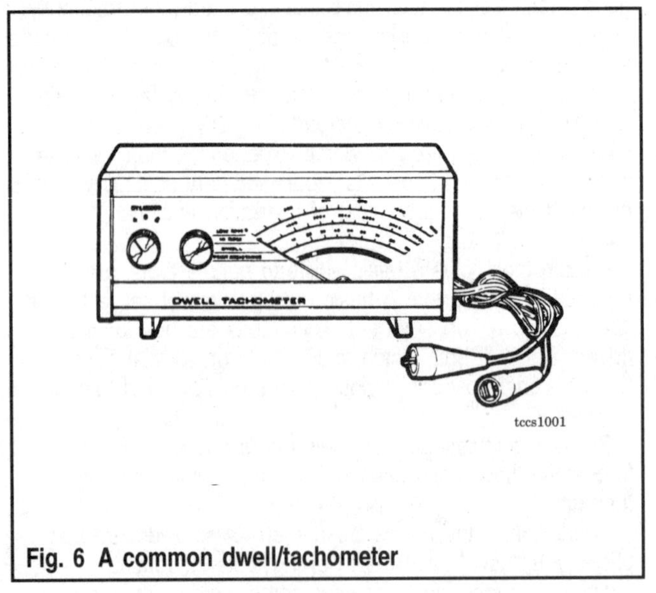

Fig. 6 A common dwell/tachometer

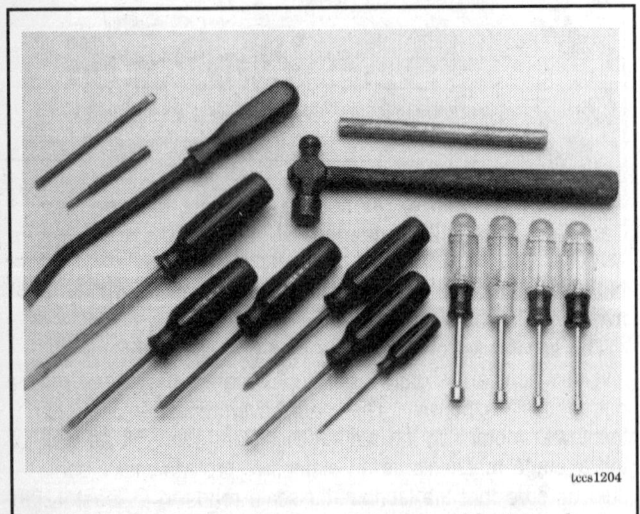

Fig. 5 Various screwdrivers, a hammer, chisels and prybars are necessary to have in your tool box

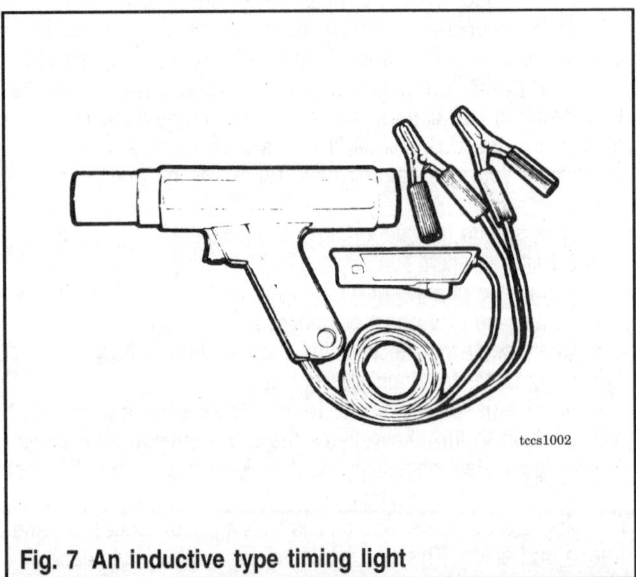

Fig. 7 An inductive type timing light

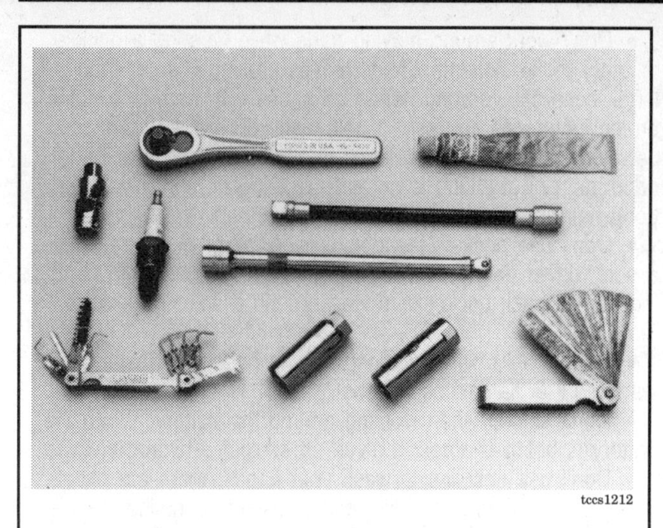

tccs1212

Fig. 8 A variety of tools and gauges are needed for spark plug service

are perfectly adequate, although the newer click (breakaway) type are more precise and you don't have to crane your neck to see a torque reading in awkward situations. Breakaway torque wrenches are more expensive and will need to be recalibrated periodically.

A torque specification for each fastener will be given in the procedure in any case that a specific torque value is required. If no torque specifications are given, use the following values as a guide, based upon fastener size:

Bolts marked 6T

- 6mm bolt/nut: 5-7 ft. lbs.
- 8mm bolt/nut: 12-17 ft. lbs. (16.25-23 Nm)
- 10mm bolt/nut: 23-34 ft. lbs. (31-46 Nm)
- 12mm bolt/nut: 41-59 ft. lbs. (55.5-80 Nm)
- 14mm bolt/nut: 56-76 ft. lbs. (76-103 Nm)

Bolts marked 8T

- 6mm bolt/nut: 6-9 ft. lbs.
- 8mm bolt/nut: 13-20 ft. lbs. 17.5-27 Nm)
- 10mm bolt/nut: 27-40 ft. lbs. (36.6-54 Nm)
- 12mm bolt/nut: 46-69 ft. lbs. (62-93.5 Nm)
- 14mm bolt/nut: 75-101 ft. lbs. (103-137 Nm)

➡Special tools are occasionally necessary to perform a specific job or are recommended to make a job easier. Their use has been kept to a minimum. When a special tool is indicated, it will be referred to by a manufacturer's part number, and, where possible, an illustration of the tool will be provided so that an equivalent tool may be used.

Some special tools are available commercially from major tool manufacturers. Others can be purchased through your Ford and/or Mercury dealer.

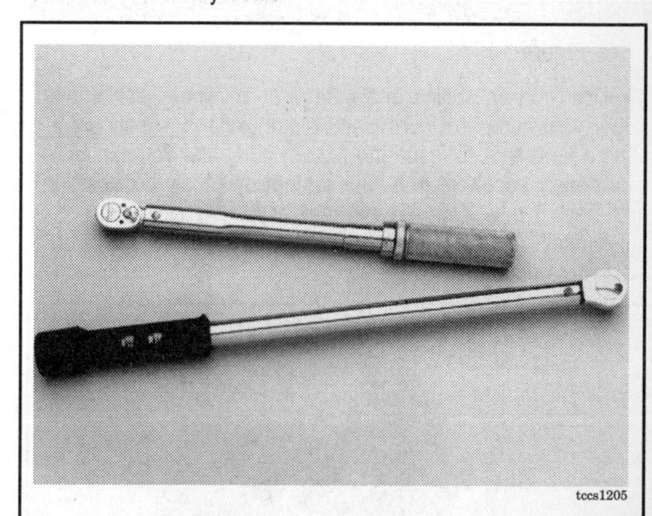

tccs1205

Fig. 9 Many repairs require the use of a torque wrench to assure that components are properly fastened

SERVICING YOUR VEHICLE SAFELY

It is virtually impossible to anticipate all of the hazards involved with automotive maintenance and service, but care and common sense will prevent most accidents.

The rules of safety for mechanics range from "don't smoke around gasoline," to "use the proper tool for the job." The way to avoid injuries is to develop safe work habits and take every possible precaution.

Do's

- Do keep a fire extinguisher and first aid kit within easy reach.
- Do wear safety glasses or goggles when cutting, drilling or prying, to prevent debris or foreign matter from getting in your eyes. If you wear prescription eyeglasses, wear also safety goggles or compatible safety glasses over your regular glasses.
- Do shield your eyes whenever you work around the battery. Batteries contain sulfuric acid; in case of contact with the eyes or skin, flush the area with water or a mixture of water and baking soda and get medical attention immediately.
- Do use safety stands for any under-car service. Jacks are for raising vehicles; safety stands are for making sure the vehicle stays raised until you want it to come down. Whenever the vehicle is raised, block the wheels remaining on the ground and set the parking brake.
- Do use adequate ventilation when working with any chemicals. Also, the dust from certain aftermarket brake linings may contain asbestos, and should not be breathed into the lungs. Even trace amounts of this hazardous material is known to cause cancer and lung disease following a lengthy incubation period.
- Do disconnect the negative battery cable when working on the electrical system. The secondary ignition system can contain extremely high voltage.
- Do follow manufacturer's directions whenever working with potentially hazardous materials. Both brake fluid and antifreeze are poisonous if taken internally.
- Do properly maintain your tools. Loose hammerheads, mushroomed punches and chisels, frayed or poorly grounded

electrical cords, excessively worn screwdrivers, spread wrenches (open end), cracked sockets, slipping ratchets, or faulty droplight sockets can cause accidents.

- Do use the proper size and type of tool for the job being done.
- Do when possible, pull on a wrench handle rather than push on it. Adjust your stance to prevent a fall.
- Do be sure that adjustable wrenches are tightly adjusted on the nut or bolt and pulled so that the face is on the side of the fixed jaw.
- Do select a wrench or socket that fits the nut or bolt. The wrench or socket should sit straight, not cocked.
- Do strike squarely with a hammer — avoid glancing blows.
- Do set the parking brake and block the drive wheels if the work requires that the engine be running.

Don'ts

➧ **See Figure 10**

- Don't run an engine in a garage or anywhere else without proper ventilation — EVER! Carbon monoxide is poisonous; it takes a long time to leave the human body and you can build up a deadly supply of it in your system by simply breathing in a little every day. You may not realize you are slowly poisoning yourself. Always use power vents, windows, fans or open the garage doors.

Fig. 10 A hydraulic floor jack and a set of jackstands are essential for lifting and supporting your car

- Don't work around moving parts while wearing a necktie or other loose clothing. Short sleeves are much safer than long, loose sleeves and hard-toed shoes with neoprene soles protect your toes and give a better grip on slippery surfaces. Jewelry such as watches, fancy belt buckles, beads or body adornment of any kind is not safe working around a vehicle. Long hair should be kept under a hat or cap.
- Don't use pockets for toolboxes. A fall or bump can drive a screwdriver deep into your body. Even a wiping cloth hanging from a back pocket can wrap around a spinning shaft or fan.
- Don't smoke when working around gasoline, cleaning solvent or other flammable material.
- Don't smoke when working around the battery. When the battery is being charged, it gives off explosive hydrogen gas.
- Don't use gasoline to wash your hands; there are excellent grease-cutting soaps available. Gasoline contains chemicals that are harmful to body, it removes protective natural oils from the skin, leaves it dry, flaking and ready to absorb more oil and grease.
- Don't service the air conditioning system unless you are equipped with the necessary tools and training. If necessary to discharge the refrigerant system, a recovery/recycling station must be used. The refrigerant is extremely cold and when exposed to the air, will instantly freeze any surface it comes in contact with, including your eyes. Although the R-12 refrigerant (used on models before 1994) is normally non-toxic, it becomes a deadly poisonous gas in the presence of an open flame. One good whiff of the vapors from burning R-12 refrigerant can be fatal.
- Don't allow R-12 to enter a R-134a system, or vice versa. Never mix parts between systems as they are not compatible. This includes O-rings and refrigerant oil.
- Don't use screwdrivers for anything other than driving screws! A screwdriver used as a prying tool can snap when you least expect it, causing injuries. At the very least, you could ruin a good screwdriver.
- Don't use a bumper jack (that little ratchet, scissors, or pantograph jack supplied with the vehicle) for anything other than changing a flat! These jacks are only intended for emergency use on the road; they are NOT designed as a maintenance tool. If you are serious about maintaining your vehicle yourself, invest in a hydraulic floor jack of at least 1½ ton capacity, and at least two sturdy jack stands. Do not use cinder blocks which can crumble and suddenly crush under the weight of the vehicle while you are working on it.

MODEL IDENTIFICATION

➧ **See Figures 11 and 12**

The vehicle can be identified by the 6th and 7th character of the Vehicle Identification Number (VIN). This 2-digit identification code will provide such information as body type, series and line.

1FABP [18] F2LZ100001

VIN Code	Line	Series	Body Type	Body Code
Make — Ford				
90	Escort	Pony	2-Dr. Sedan Hatchback	DAZ
91	Escort	LX	2-Dr. Sedan Hatchback	DAZ
93	Escort	GT	2-Dr. Sedan Hatchback	DAZ
95	Escort	LX	4-Dr. Sedan Hatchback	HCZ
98	Escort	LX	4-Dr. Wagon	FFW

86751011

Fig. 11 Common line, series and body type identification codes — 1981-90 models

IFAPP [14] 82MW100001

Code	Line	Series	Body Type	Body Code
Make — Ford				
10	Escort	Pony	3-Door Hatchback	PY3
11	Escort	LX	3-Door Hatchback	LX3
12	Escort	GT	3-Door Hatchback	GT3
14	Escort	LX	5-Door Hatchback	LX5
15	Escort	LX	4-Door Wagon	LXW

86751012

Fig. 12 Common line, series and body type identification codes — 1991-95 models

SERIAL NUMBER IDENTIFICATION

Vehicle

➧ **See Figures 13, 14 and 15**

The Vehicle Identification Number (VIN) is located on the instrument panel close to the windshield on the driver's side of the vehicle. It is visible from outside the vehicle. This 17 character label contains such information as manufacturer name, month and year of manufacture, type of restraint system, body type, engine, etc. The VIN is used for title and registration purposes.

A Vehicle Certification Label (VCL) is also affixed on the left front door lock panel or door pillar. This label contains such information as gross vehicle weight, paint code, tire pressure, transaxle and axle type, etc. The VCL is also used for warranty identification of the vehicle.

The 10th character of the VIN designates the year the vehicle was built. For example, the code indicating the model year for a car with the VIN 1FAPP1482MW100001 would be the 10th character "M." The model year M indicates is 1991. Each year covered by this manual has a different letter-based code beginning with "B" in 1981. The model codes proceed in order through the alphabet: "C" is for 1982, "D" is for 1983, "E" is for 1984, etc. The exceptions to this rule are letters such as I, O or Q which are not used to avoid confusion with numbers.

Engine

The 8th character of the VIN designates the engine type installed in the vehicle. An engine identification label is also attached to the engine timing cover.

Transaxle

▶ See Figures 16 and 17

The transaxle code is found on the Vehicle Certification Label (VCL), affixed to the left (driver's) side door lock post. The code is located in the lower right-hand corner of the VCL. This code designates the transaxle type installed in the vehicle. A transaxle identification tag is also affixed to the transaxle assembly.

Drive Axle

The drive axle code is found in the lower right-hand corner of the vehicle certification label. This code designates the transaxle ratio.

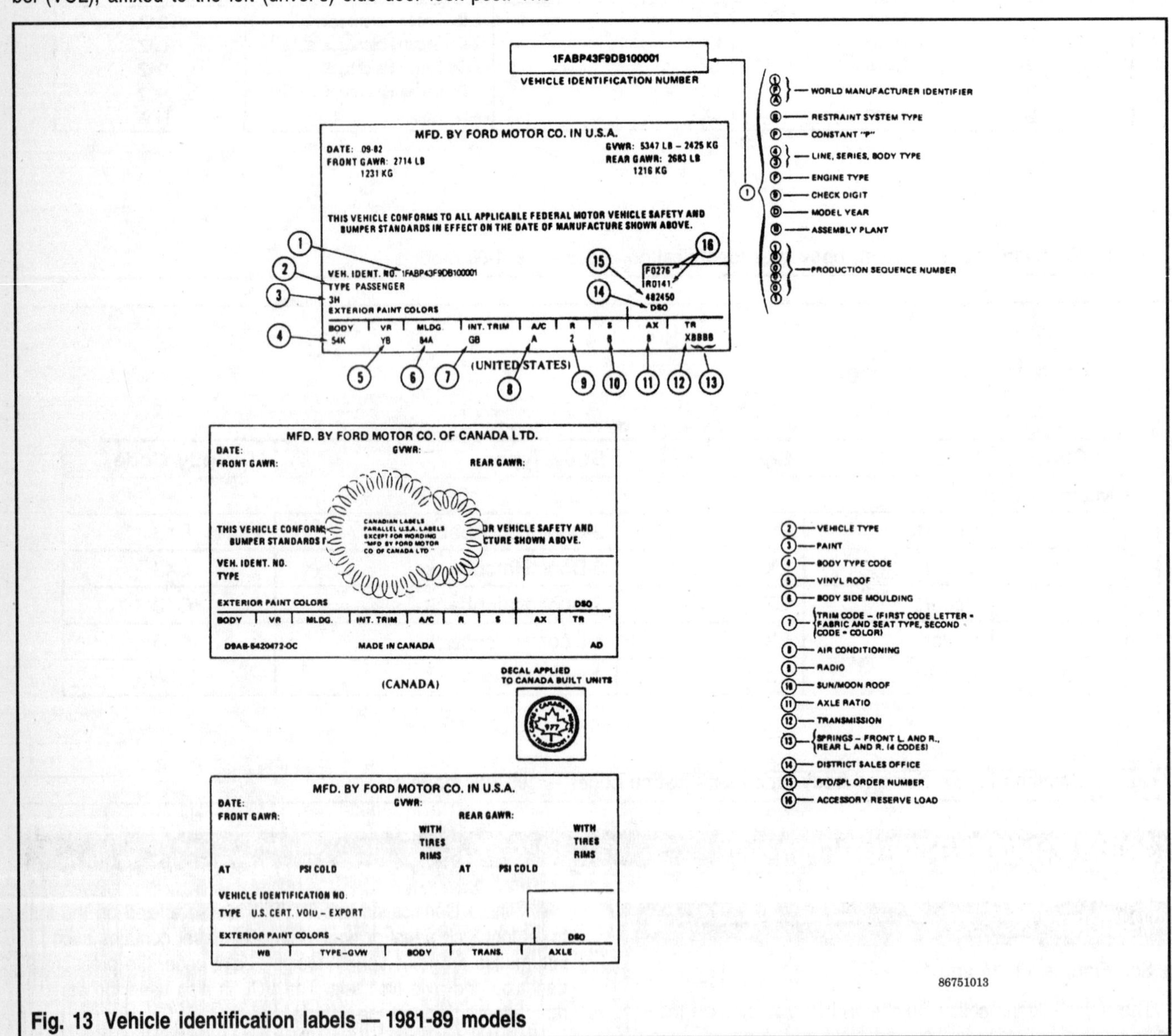

Fig. 13 Vehicle identification labels — 1981-89 models

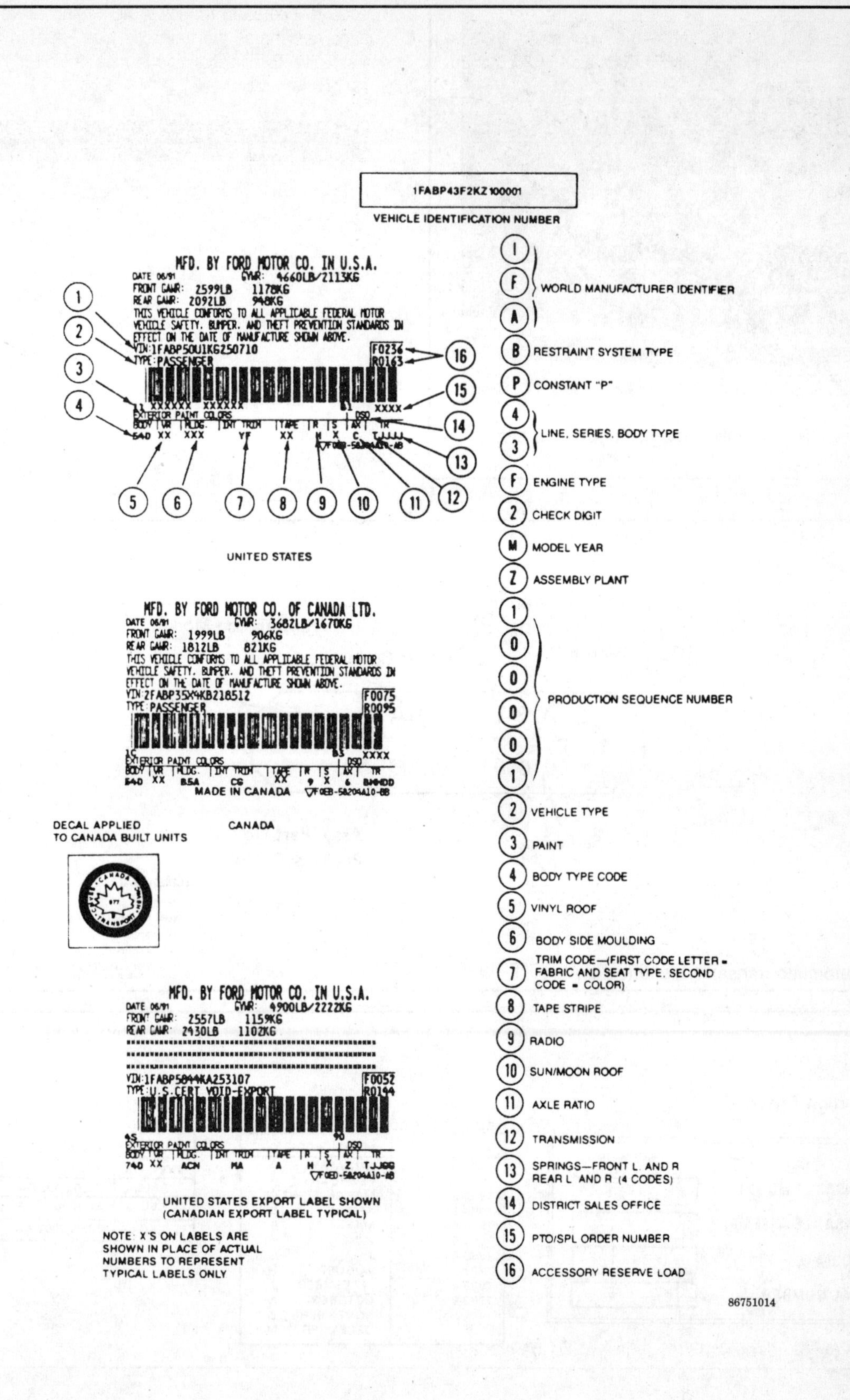

Fig. 14 1990-95 Vehicle identification and certification labels

86751305

Fig. 15 The VIN is visible through the driver's side windshield

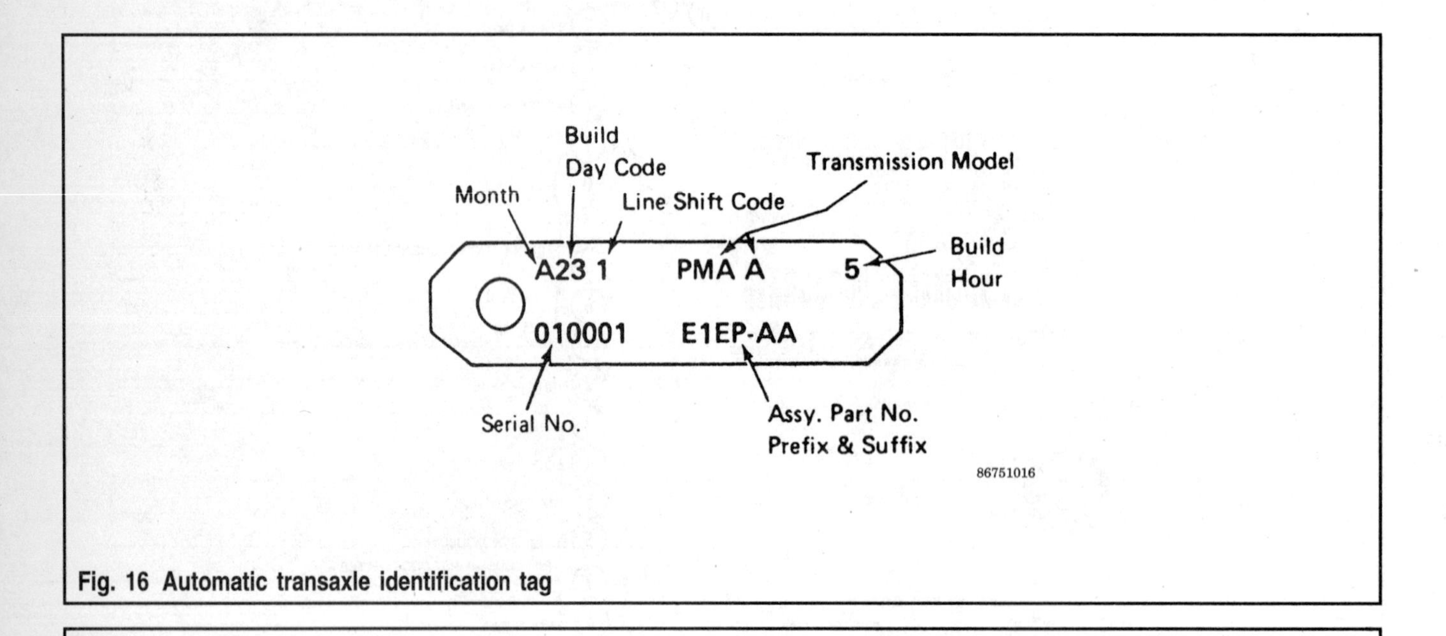

Fig. 16 Automatic transaxle identification tag

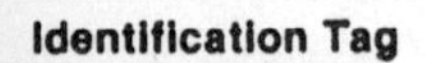

Identification Tag

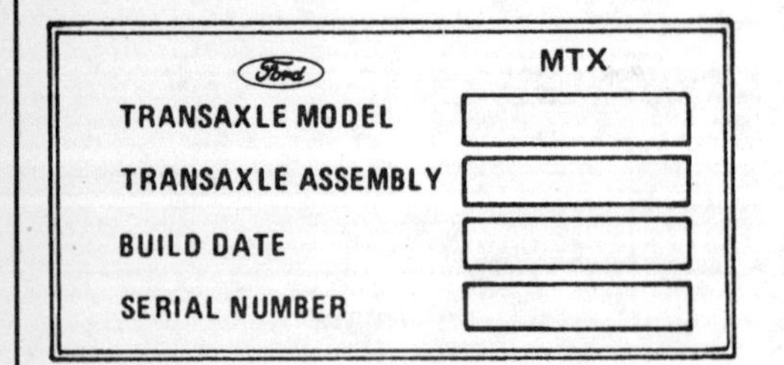

BUILD DATE CODES

YEAR-CODE	MONTH-CODE	
1980-0	JANUARY	A
1981-1	FEBRUARY	B
1982-2	MARCH	C
1983-3	APRIL	D
1984-4	MAY	E
1985-5	JUNE	F
1986-6	JULY	G
1987-7	AUGUST	H
1988-8	SEPTEMBER	J
1989-9	OCTOBER	K
	NOVEMBER	L
	DECEMBER	M

COLOR REFERENCE		
TYPE T/A	MODEL	BACKGROUND
1.6L	EIER-7002-DA	YELLOW
1.6L	EIER-7002-CA	LT. BLUE
1.6L	E2ER-7002-AA	RED

86751015

Fig. 17 Manual transaxle identification tag

ENGINE IDENTIFICATION

Year	Model	Engine Displacement Liters (cc)	Engine Series (ID/VIN)	Fuel System	No. of Cylinders	Engine Type
1981	Escort/Lynx	1.6 (1606)	2	2BBL	4	SOHC
1982	Escort/Lynx	1.6 (1606)	2	2BBL	4	SOHC
	EXP/LN7	1.6 (1606)	2	2BBL	4	SOHC
1983	Escort/Lynx	1.6 (1606)	2	2BBL	4	SOHC
	Escort/Lynx (1)	1.6 (1606)	4	2BBL	4	SOHC
	Escort/Lynx	1.6 (1606)	5	MFI	4	SOHC
	EXP/LN7	1.6 (1606)	2	2BBL	4	SOHC
	EXP/LN7 (1)	1.6 (1606)	4	2BBL	4	SOHC
	EXP/LN7	1.6 (1606)	5	MFI	4	SOHC
1984	Escort/Lynx	1.6 (1606)	2	2BBL	4	SOHC
	Escort/Lynx (1)	1.6 (1606)	4	2BBL	4	SOHC
	Escort/Lynx	1.6 (1606)	5	MFI	4	SOHC
	Escort/Lynx (2)	1.6 (1606)	8	MFI	4	SOHC
	Escort/Lynx (3)	1.6 (1601)	7	2BBL	4	SOHC
	Escort/Lynx	2.0 (1998)	H	DSL	4	SOHC
	EXP	1.6 (1606)	2	2BBL	4	SOHC
	EXP (2)	1.6 (1606)	4	2BBL	4	SOHC
	EXP	1.6 (1606)	5	MFI	4	SOHC
	EXP (2)	1.6 (1606)	8	MFI	4	SOHC
1985	Escort/Lynx	1.6 (1606)	2	2BBL	4	SOHC
	Escort/Lynx (1)	1.6 (1606)	4	2BBL	4	SOHC
	Escort/Lynx	1.6 (1606)	5	MFI	4	SOHC
	Escort/Lynx (2)	1.6 (1606)	8	MFI	4	SOHC
	Escort/Lynx (3)	1.6 (1601)	7	2BBL	4	SOHC
	Escort/Lynx (4)	1.9 (1901)	9	2BBL	4	SOHC
	Escort/Lynx	2.0 (1998)	H	DSL	4	SOHC
	EXP	1.6 (1606)	2	2BBL	4	SOHC
	EXP (1)	1.6 (1606)	4	2BBL	4	SOHC
	EXP	1.6 (1606)	5	MFI	4	SOHC
	EXP (2)	1.6 (1606)	8	MFI	4	SOHC
	EXP (4)	1.9 (1901)	9	2BBL	4	SOHC
1986	Escort/Lynx	1.9 (1901)	9	2BBL	4	SOHC
	Escort/Lynx (1)	1.9 (1901)	J	MFI	4	SOHC
	Escort/Lynx	2.0 (1998)	H	DSL	4	SOHC
	EXP	1.9 (1901)	9	2BBL	4	SOHC
	EXP (1)	1.9 (1901)	J	MFI	4	SOHC
1987	Escort/Lynx	1.9 (1901)	9	CFI	4	SOHC
	Escort/Lynx (1)	1.9 (1901)	J	MFI	4	SOHC
	Escort/Lynx	2.0 (1998)	H	DSL	4	SOHC
1988	Escort	1.9 (1901)	9	CFI	4	SOHC
	Escort (1)	1.9 (1901)	J	MFI	4	SOHC
1989	Escort	1.9 (1901)	9	CFI	4	SOHC
	Escort (1)	1.9 (1901)	J	MFI	4	SOHC

86751C10

ENGINE IDENTIFICATION

Year	Model	Engine Displacement Liters (cc)	Engine Series (ID/VIN)	Fuel System	No. of Cylinders	Engine Type
1990	Escort	1.9 (1901)	9	CFI	4	SOHC
	Escort ①	1.9 (1901)	J	MFI	4	SOHC
1991	Escort/Tracer	1.8 (1844)	8	MFI	4	DOHC
	Escort/Tracer	1.9 (1901)	J	SEFI	4	SOHC
1992	Escort/Tracer	1.8 (1844)	8	MFI	4	DOHC
	Escort/Tracer	1.9 (1901)	J	SEFI	4	SOHC
1993	Escort/Tracer	1.8 (1844)	8	MFI	4	DOHC
	Escort/Tracer	1.9 (1901)	J	SFI	4	SOHC
1994	Escort/Tracer	1.8 (1844)	8	MFI	4	DOHC
	Escort/Tracer	1.9 (1901)	J	SFI	4	SOHC
1995	Escort/Tracer	1.8 (1844)	8	MFI	4	DOHC
	Escort/Tracer	1.9 (1901)	J	SFI	4	SOHC

BBL - Barrel (carburetor)
CFI - Central Fuel Injection
DOHC - Double Overhead Camshaft
DSL - Diesel
MFI - Multi-port Fuel Injection
OHV - Overhead valve
SEFI: Sequential Electronic Fuel Injection (same as SFI)
SFI - Sequential Fuel Injection (a form of Multi-port Fuel Injection)
SOHC - Single overhead camshaft
VV - Variable Venturi carburetor
① High output
② Turbo
③ Methanol high output
④ Introduced as a 1985 1/2 model

86751C11

ROUTINE MAINTENANCE

Air Cleaner

The air cleaner element should be replaced every 30 months or 30,000 miles (48,000 km). More frequent changes are necessary if the car is operated in dusty conditions.

REMOVAL AND INSTALLATION

Carbureted and CFI Engines

➧ See Figures 18 and 19

➡The crankcase emission filter should be changed each time you replace the air cleaner element.

1. Remove the wingnut that retains the air cleaner assembly to the carburetor or throttle body. Remove any support bracket bolts (engine to air cleaner). Disconnect the air duct tubing, vacuum lines and heat tubes connected to the air cleaner.
2. Remove the air cleaner assembly from the vehicle.

➡To avoid dirt from falling into the carburetor, removing the air cleaner as an assembly.

3. Remove the spring clips that hold the top of the air cleaner to the body. Remove the cover.
4. Remove the air cleaner element. Disconnect the spring clip that retains the crankcase filter to the air cleaner body, and remove the filter.

To install:

5. Before installing, clean the inside of the air cleaner housing as needed by wiping with a rag. Check the mounting gasket (or gaskets, if the car is equipped with a spacer). Replace any gasket(s) that show wear.

6. Install a new emission filter and a new air cleaner element.

7. Install the air cleaner element. Reconnect the spring clip that retains the emission filter to the air cleaner body, and install the filter.

8. Install the spring clips that hold the top of the air cleaner to the housing. Install the cover. Attach the air cleaner assembly to the carburetor/throttle body.

9. Install the wingnut that retains the air cleaner assembly. Install any support bracket bolts (engine to air cleaner). Reconnect the air duct tubing, vacuum lines and heat tubes connected to the air cleaner.

Diesel Engines

1. Loosen the clamp that attaches the resonator outlet tube to the engine and disconnect the resonator outlet tube from the intake manifold.

2. Unfasten the air cleaner cover retaining clips and remove the air cleaner cover resonator and tube assembly.

3. Remove the air filter element.

4. Remove the three screws and washer assemblies located in the bottom of the air cleaner tray at the fender apron.

5. Disengage the air cleaner tray from the resonator assembly and remove.

To install:

6. Attach the air cleaner tray to the resonator and install the air cleaner body-to-fender apron retaining screw and washer assemblies. Tighten to 1.5-6.0 ft. lbs. (2-8 Nm).

7. Install the air filter element.

8. Install the air cleaner cover and air resonator and tube assembly. Fasten the air cleaner cover retaining clips.

9. Attach the fresh air tube to the engine intake manifold with clamp. Tighten to 12-20 ft. lbs. (1.4-2.3 Nm).

FILTER ELEMENT ONLY

See Figure 20

If only replacement of the air filter element is necessary, use the following procedure:

1. Unfasten the air cleaner cover retaining screws.

2. Lift the air cleaner cover away from the tray.

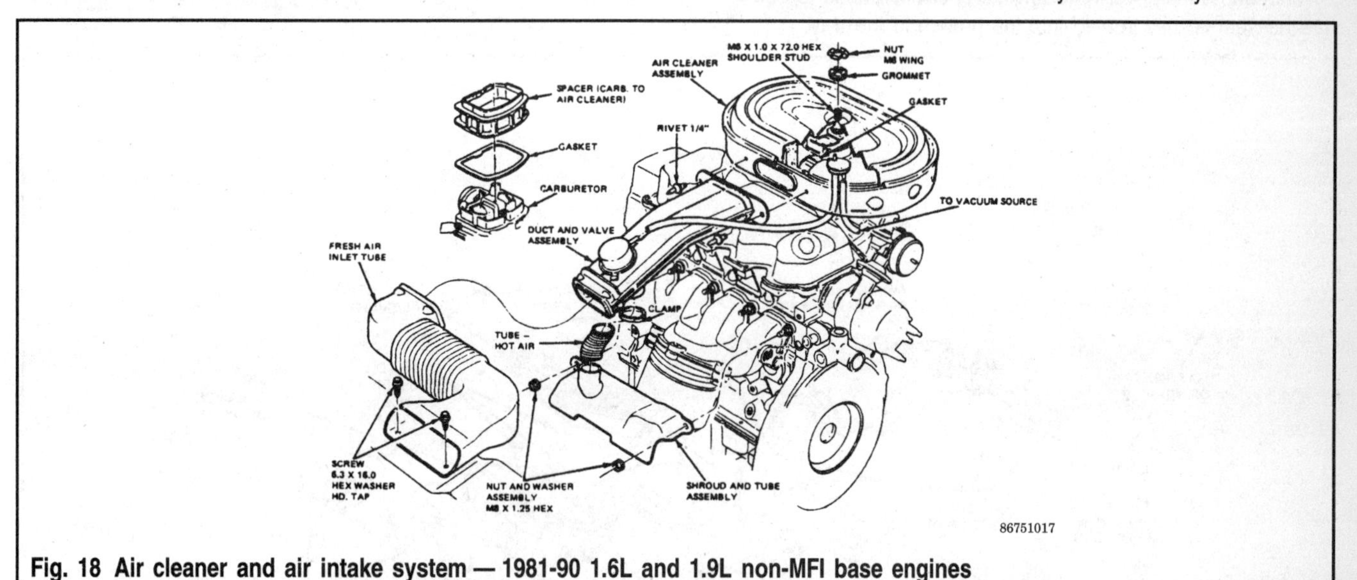

Fig. 18 Air cleaner and air intake system — 1981-90 1.6L and 1.9L non-MFI base engines

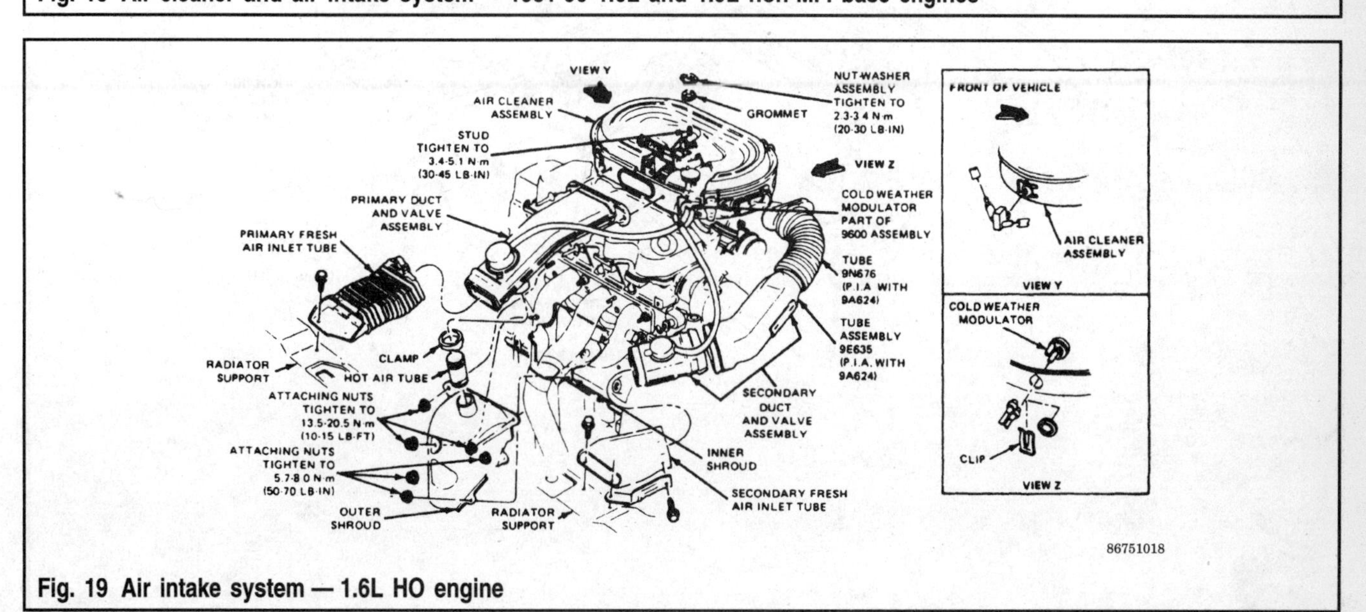

Fig. 19 Air intake system — 1.6L HO engine

3. Remove the air filter element.

To install:

4. Wipe the inside surface of the air cleaner tray and cover. Install the air filter element.
5. Install the air cleaner cover on the body and fasten the retaining clips.

1983-90 MFI Engines

➧ **See Figures 21, 22, 23, 24, 25, 26 and 27**

1. Unclip the air intake tube and remove the tube from the air cleaner tray.
2. Unclip the air cleaner tray from the air cleaner assembly.
3. Pull the cleaner tray out to expose the air cleaner element.
4. Pull the air cleaner element from the tray. Visually inspect the air cleaner tray and cover for signs of dust or leaking holes in the filter or past the seals.

To install:

5. Place the air cleaner element in the tray making sure the element is installed in its original position. Check to see that the seal is fully seated into the groove in the tray.
6. Clip the air intake tube to the air cleaner tray.
7. Reconnect the negative battery cable.

1.8L Engines

1. Loosen the resonance chamber attaching clamp at the vane air flow meter and disconnect the chamber from the vane air flow meter.
2. Disconnect the vane air flow meter electrical connector.
3. Position the resonance duct inlet hose attaching clamp free from the resonance duct.
4. Remove the air cleaner assembly retaining bolts and nut. Remove the air cleaner assembly.

To install:

5. Place the air cleaner assembly into its mounting position and connect the air intake duct to the assembly.
6. Connect the resonance duct inlet hose to the resonance duct and install the attaching clamps.
7. Install the air cleaner assembly mounting bolts and nut. Tighten to 14-19 inch lbs. (19-25 Nm).
8. Connect the vane air flow meter electrical connector.

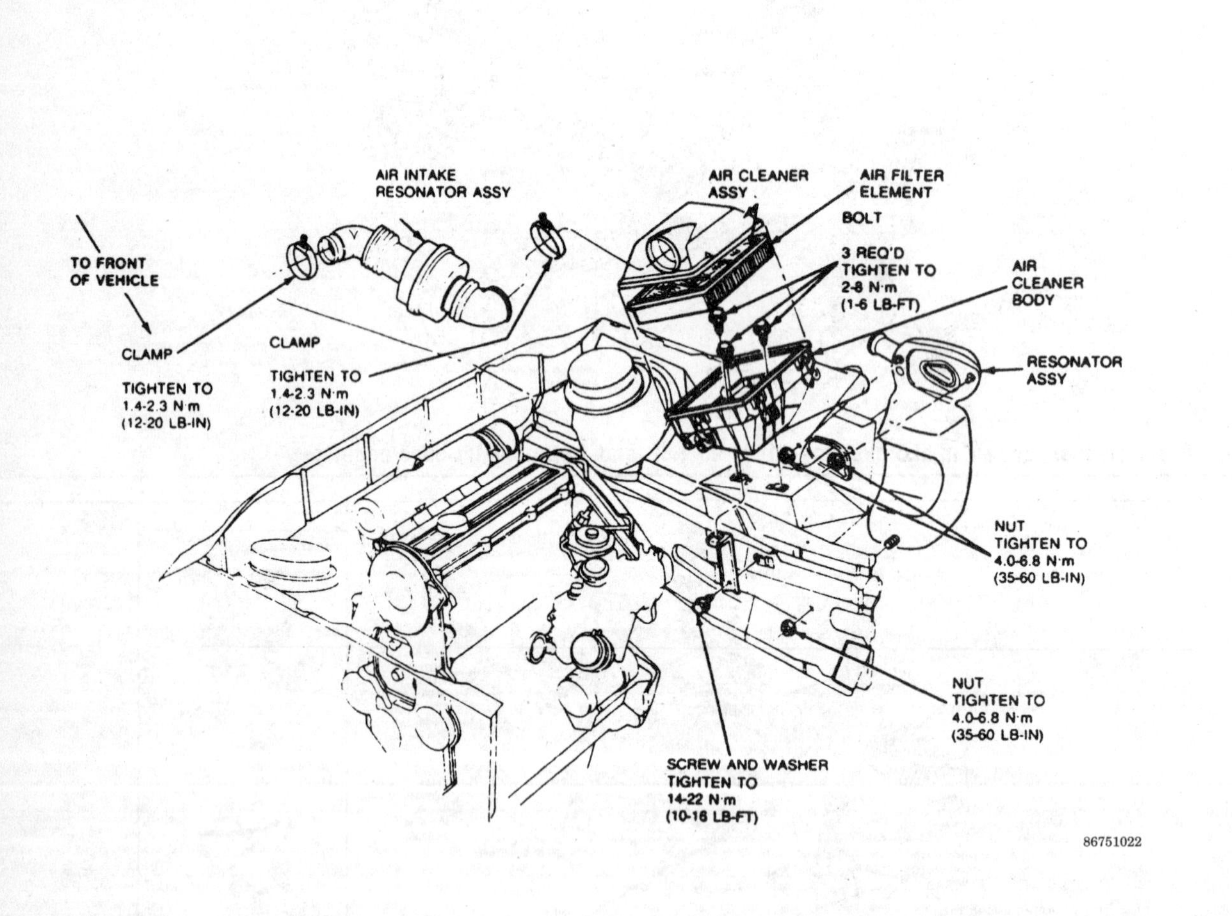

Fig. 20 Air intake system — 1984-87 2.0L diesel engines

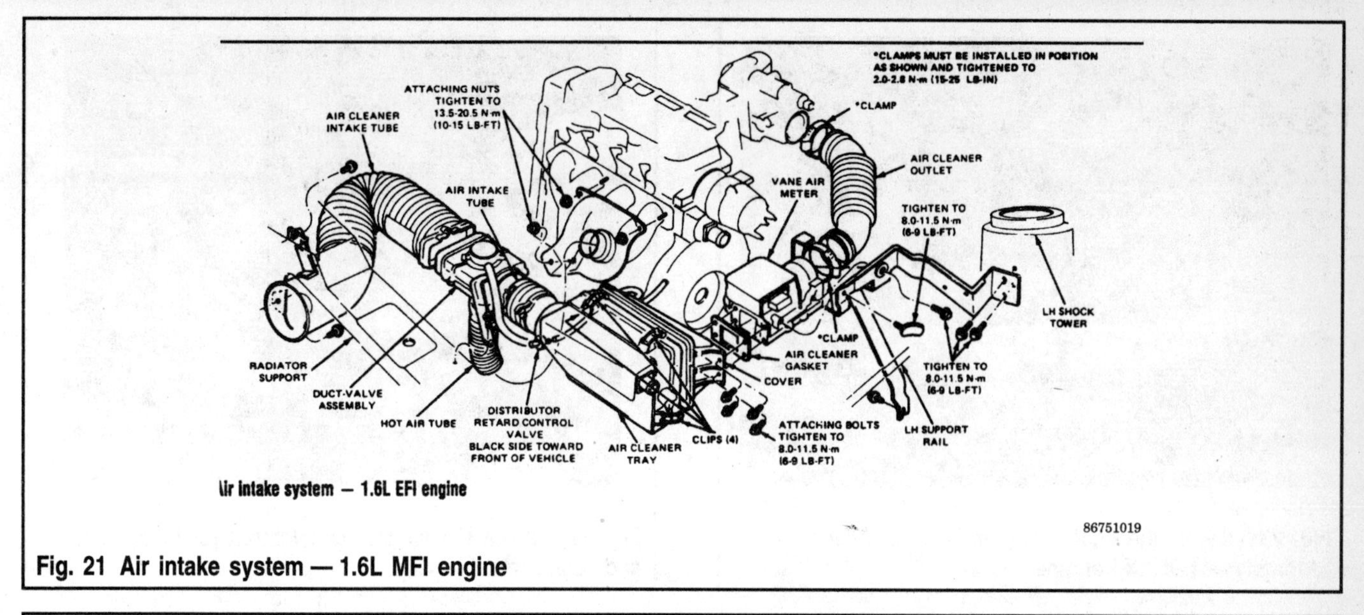

Fig. 21 Air intake system — 1.6L MFI engine

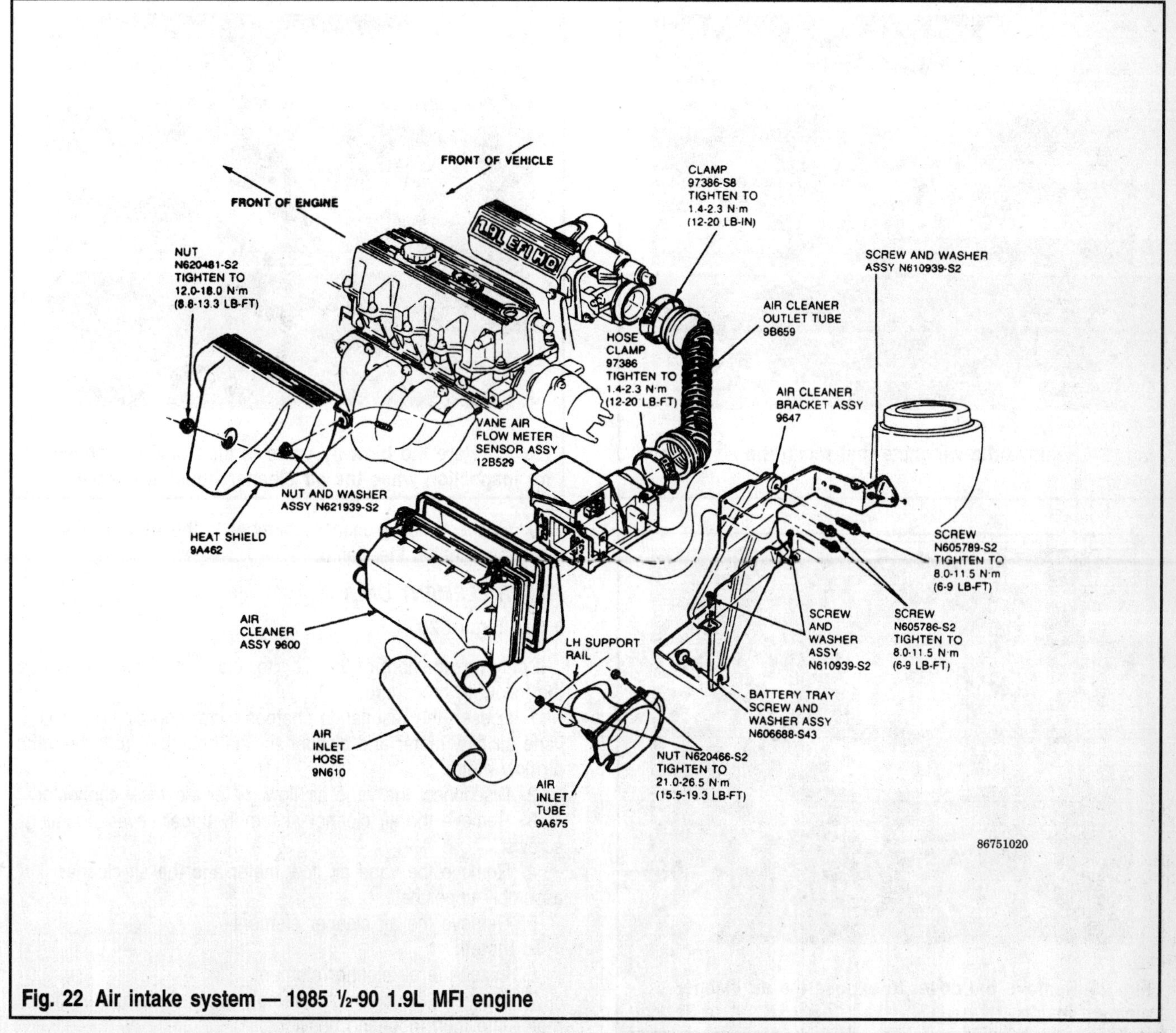

Fig. 22 Air intake system — 1985 ½-90 1.9L MFI engine

86751300

Fig. 23 View of the engine bay and the air filter assembly — 1.9L CFI engine

86751301

Fig. 24 Remove the wingnuts that retain the air cleaner cover

86751302

Fig. 25 Remove the cover to expose the air cleaner element inside

86751303

Fig. 26 Lift out the air cleaner element for inspection and replacement

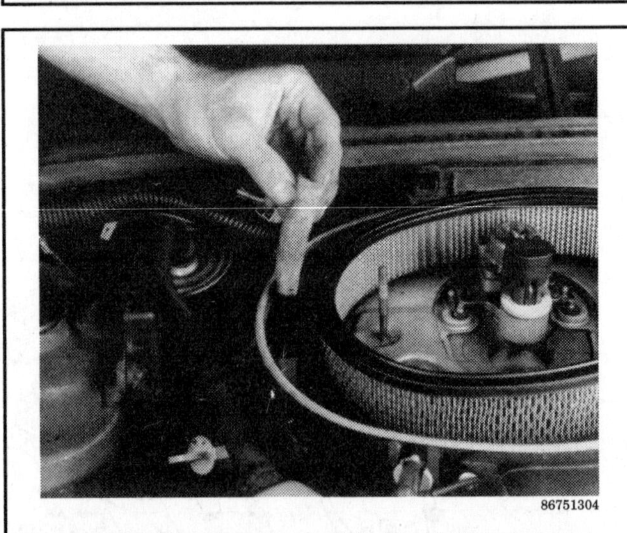

86751304

Fig. 27 Here the blow-by valve is also being removed for inspection while the air cleaner housing is open

9. Connect the resonance chamber to the vane air flow meter and tighten the clamp.

FILTER ELEMENT ONLY

➧ **See Figure 28**

If only replacement of the air filter element is necessary, use the following procedure:

1. Loosen the resonance chamber attaching clamp at the vane air flow meter and disconnect the chamber from the vane air flow meter.
2. Disconnect the vane air flow meter electrical connector.
3. Remove the air cleaner assembly upper cover mounting screws.
4. Remove the vane air flow meter and the air cleaner assembly upper half.
5. Remove the air cleaner element.

To install:

6. Install the air cleaner element.
7. Place the air cleaner assembly cover and vane air flow meter into their mounting positions.

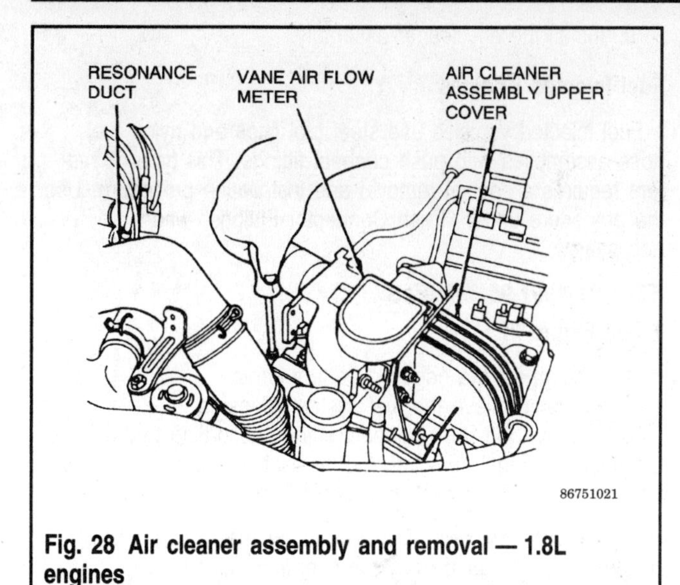

Fig. 28 Air cleaner assembly and removal — 1.8L engines

8. Install the air cleaner assembly cover retaining screws. Tighten to 69-95 inch lbs. (8-11 Nm).
9. Connect the vane air flow meter electrical connector.
10. Connect the resonance chamber to the vane air flow meter. Install and tighten the attaching clamp.

1991-95 1.9L Engines

1. Loosen the tube clamps at both ends of the air intake tube.
2. Carefully remove the air intake tube. A gentle twisting motion will release the tube from its mounting surfaces.
3. Disconnect the MAF sensor and the ACT sensor electrical connectors.
4. Remove the crankcase vent hose from the bottom of the filter housing.
5. Remove the two mounting bolts and one retainer nut.
6. Remove the air cleaner assembly.

To install:

7. Place the air cleaner assembly into position. Make certain the assembly is positioned properly on the top of the air intake duct.
8. Install the mounting bolts and retainer nut.
9. Install the crankcase vent hose.
10. Reconnect the MAF and ACT sensor electrical connectors.
11. Position the tube clamps on both ends of the air intake tube.
12. Install the air intake tube on the throttle body and the MAF sensor. Tighten the tube clamps to 12-20 inch lbs. (1.4-2.3 Nm).

FILTER ELEMENT ONLY

If only replacement of the air filter element is necessary, use the following procedure:

1. Release the four air cleaner lid clamps.
2. Lift the lid assembly from the filter housing and remove the filter element.

To install:

3. Hold the air cleaner lid aside and install the filter element in the filter housing.
4. Position the air cleaner lid on the filter housing. Be certain the lid is firmly seated.
5. Engage the air cleaner lid clamps.

Fuel Filter

The fuel filter should be replaced, immediately, upon evidence of dirt in the fuel system. Regular replacement of the fuel filter should be every 30,000 miles (48,000 km). If the engine seems to be suffering from fuel starvation, remove the filter and blow through it to see if it is clogged. If air won't pass through the filter easily, or if dirt is visible in the inlet passage, replace the filter.

➡A backup wrench is an open end wrench of the proper size used to hold the fuel filter or fitting in position while the fuel line is removed. A flared wrench is a special hex wrench with a narrow open end allowing the fuel line nut to be gripped tightly. A regular open end wrench may be substituted if used carefully so as not to round the fitting.

The fuel filter on the non-MFI models contains a screen to minimize the amount of contaminants entering the carburetor via the fuel system. The fuel filter on the non-MFI models is located in the carburetor.

The MFI model fuel filter provides extremely fine filtration to protect the small metering orifices of the injector nozzles. The filter is a one-piece construction which cannot be cleaned. If the filter becomes clogged or restricted, it should be replaced with a new filter. The filter is located downstream of the electric fuel pump, and is mounted on the dash panel extension in the right rear corner of the engine compartment on 1981-90 vehicles. On 1991-95 vehicles, a replaceable inline fuel filter is located inside the engine compartment between the fuel tank and fuel rail. A serviceable fuel filter screen is located inside the fuel tank at the fuel pump inlet.

✱✱WARNING

Do not smoke or carry an open flame of any type when working on or near any fuel-related component. Highly flammable mixtures are always present and may be ignited, resulting in possible injury.

REMOVAL & INSTALLATION

Gasoline Engines

If the vehicle is equipped with a pressure relief valve, install an MFI/CFI fuel pressure gauge T80L-9974-B or equivalent and depressurize the fuel system. If the vehicle is not equipped with a pressure relief valve, the fuel filter connection should be covered with a shop rag or towel to prevent the fuel from spraying during the removal procedure. It is also possible to reduce the amount of pressure in the fuel system by locating the inertia switch (usually located in the luggage compartment) and disconnecting the electrical connection on the inertia switch. Next crank the engine for 15 seconds to reduce the system pressure.

Carbureted Engines

➧ See Figures 29, 30 and 31

1. Remove the air cleaner assembly.
2. Use a backup wrench on the fuel filter inlet hex nut (located in the carburetor inlet). Loosen the fuel line nut with a flare wrench. Remove the fuel line from the filter.
3. Unscrew the filter from the carburetor.

To Install:

4. Apply a drop of Loctite® Hydraulic Sealant No. 069, or equivalent, to the external threads of the fuel filter.
5. Hand start the new filter into the carburetor, then use a wrench to tighten the fuel filter to 6.5-8 ft. lbs. (9-11 Nm).
6. Apply a drop of engine oil to the fuel supply tube nut and flare, and hand start the nut into the filter inlet approximately two threads.
7. Use a backup wrench on the fuel filter to prevent the filter from rotating while tightening. Tighten the nut to 15-18 ft. lbs. 20-25 Nm).
8. Start the engine and check for fuel leaks.

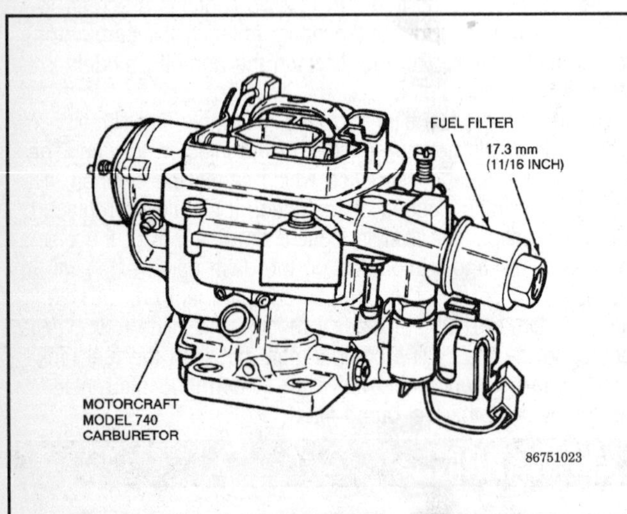

Fig. 29 Fuel filter mounting — carburetor equipped engines

Fig. 30 Here the hairpin-type clip is being removed from the push connector to access the fuel filter

9. Install the air cleaner assembly.

Fuel Injected Engines

Fuel injected vehicles use steel fuel lines and nylon fuel hose assemblies with push connect fittings. This type of system requires a special removal and installation procedure. Use the procedure under "Push Connector Fittings" when necessary.

EXCEPT 1991-95 MODELS

➧ See Figure 32

1. Disconnect the negative battery cable.
2. Properly relieve the fuel system pressure.
3. Remove the push connect fittings according to the "Push Connector Fittings" removal and installation procedure. Install new retainer clips in each connector fitting.

➡The flow arrow direction should be noted to ensure proper flow of fuel through the replacement filter.

4. Remove the filter from the bracket by loosening the filter retaining clamp enough to allow the filter to pass through.

To install:

5. Install the filter in the bracket, ensuring the proper direction of flow, as noted earlier. Tighten the clamp to 15-25 inch lbs. (1.7-2.8 Nm).
6. Install push connect fittings at both ends of the filter.
7. Connect the negative battery cable.
8. Start the engine and inspect for leaks.

1991-95 ESCORT

➧ See Figure 33

1. Properly relieve the fuel system pressure.
2. Disconnect the negative battery cable.
3. Position a suitable container below the fuel filter to collect any excess fuel that may leak from the filter and lines.
4. Remove the retaining clip from the fuel filter upper hose.
5. Disconnect the upper hose from the fuel filter and drain any excess fuel into the container. Plug the hose.
6. Loosen the fuel filter mounting clamp.
7. Raise and safely support the vehicle.

Fig. 31 Make sure to install the filter right side up

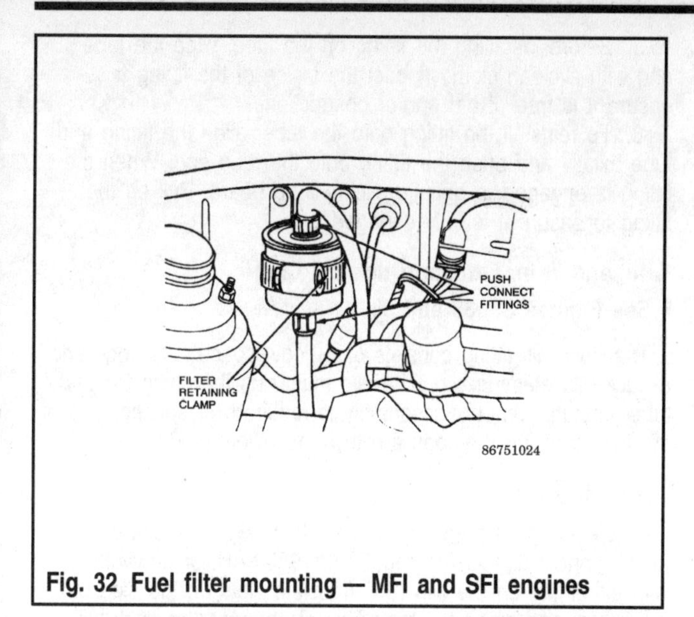

Fig. 32 Fuel filter mounting — MFI and SFI engines

8. Remove the retaining clip from the fuel filter lower hose.
9. Disconnect the lower hose from the fuel filter and drain any excess fuel into the container. Plug the hose.
10. Lower the vehicle.
11. Remove the fuel filter.

To install:

12. Position the fuel filter and tighten the filter mounting clamp.
13. Connect the filter upper hose to the filter and install the upper hose retaining clip.
14. Raise and safely support the vehicle.
15. Connect the filter lower hose to the filter and install the lower hose retaining clip.
16. Lower the vehicle.
17. Connect the negative battery cable.
18. Start the engine and check for leaks.

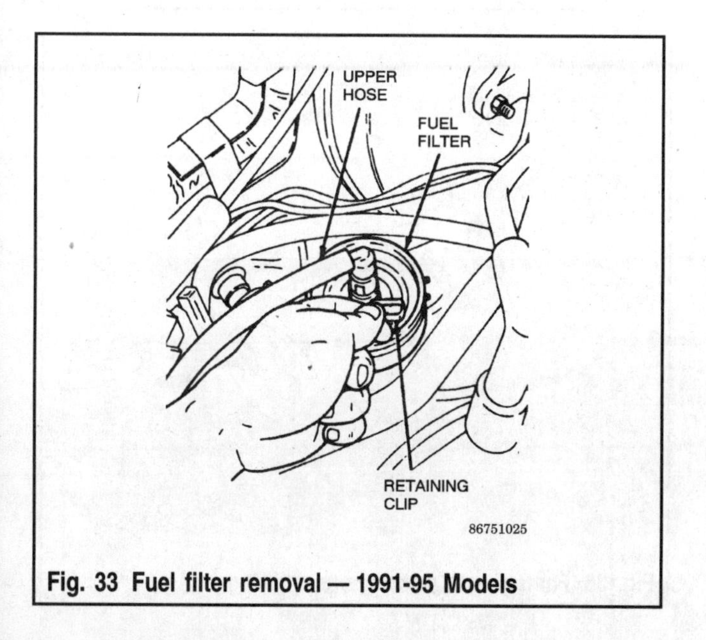

Fig. 33 Fuel filter removal — 1991-95 Models

Diesel Engine

See Figure 34

The fuel filter/conditioner must be serviced (water purged) at each engine oil change (7500 miles/12,000 km) interval. To purge water from the system:

1. Make sure the engine and ignition switch are **OFF**.
2. Place a suitable container under the fuel filter/conditioner water drain tube under the car.
3. Open the water drain valve at the bottom of the filter/conditioner element 2½-3 turns.
4. Pump the prime pump at the top of the filter from 10 to 15 strokes, or until all of the water is purged from the filter, and clear diesel fuel is apparent.

➡If the water/fuel will not drain from the tube, open the drain valve one more turn or until the water/fuel starts to flow.

5. Close the drain valve and tighten.
6. Start the engine and check for leaks.
7. Whenever the fuel filter is replaced, or system service performed, the filter must be air bled as follows:
   a. Loosen the fuel filter air vent plug.
   b. Pump the head of the filter in an up and down motion.
   c. Continue to pump until the fuel flows from the air vent plug hole in a steady stream free of air bubbles.
   d. Depress the head of the filter and close the air vent plug.
   e. If the engine should run out of fuel during this operation or the system is opened allowing air to enter, bleed the air from the fuel filter first.
   f. Pump the head of the filter repeatedly until it becomes hard to pump (approximately 15 times) to force air from the system.

To install:

8. Make sure that the engine and ignition are **OFF**.
9. Disconnect the module connector from the water level sensor located at the bottom of the filter element.
10. Using a strap-type filter wrench, turn the filter element counterclockwise to loosen from the top mounting bracket. Remove the element from the mount adapter.

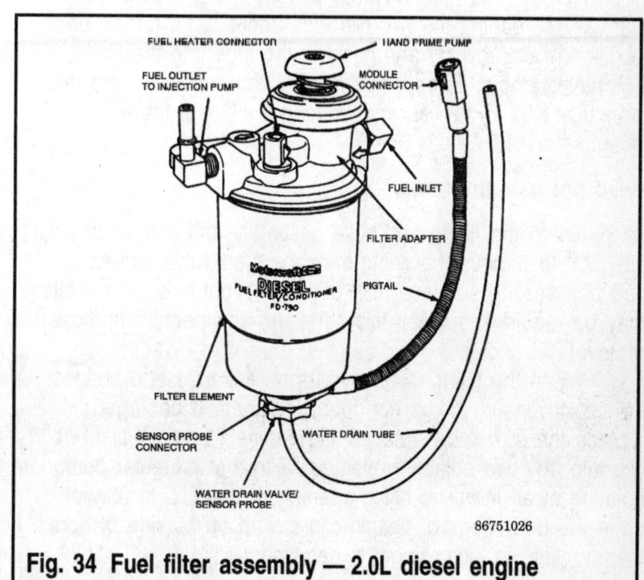

Fig. 34 Fuel filter assembly — 2.0L diesel engine

11. Remove the water drain valve/sensor probe from the bottom of the element. Wipe the probe with a clean dry cloth.
12. Unsnap the sensor probe pigtail from the bottom of the filter element and wipe with a clean dry rag.
13. Snap the probe onto the new filter element.
14. Lubricate the two O-rings on the water sensor probe with a light film of oil. Screw the probe into the bottom of the new filter element and tighten.
15. Clean the gasket mounting surface of the adapter mount.
16. Lubricate the sealing gasket of the filter element with oil. Screw the filter element onto the mount adapter. Hand tighten the element, then back off the filter to a point where the gasket is just touching the adapter. Retighten by hand and then an additional ½-⅝ turn.
17. Reconnect the water level sensor module connector.
18. Prime the fuel system by pumping the primer handle until pressure is felt when pumping.
19. Start the engine and check for fuel leaks.

Push Connect Fittings

Push connect fittings are designed with two different retaining clips. The fittings used with 5/16 in. (8mm) diameter tubing use a hairpin clip. The fittings used with ¼ in. (6mm) and ½ in. (12.7mm) diameter tubing use a "duck bill" clip. Each type of fitting requires different procedures for service.

Push connect fitting disassembly must be accomplished prior to fuel component removal (filter, pump, etc.) except for the fuel tank where removal is necessary for access to the push connects.

REMOVAL & INSTALLATION

5/16 in. Fittings (Hairpin Clip)

See Figures 35 and 36

1. Inspect internal portion of fitting for dirt accumulation. If more than a light coating of dust is present, clean the fitting before disassembly.
2. Remove the hairpin-type clip from fitting. This is done by manually spreading the two clip legs about ⅛ in. (3mm) each to disengage the body and pushing the legs into the fitting. Complete removal is accomplished by lightly pulling from the triangular end of the clip and working it clear of the tube and fitting.

Do not use any tools.

3. Grasp the fitting and hose assembly and pull in an axial direction to remove the fitting from the steel tube. Adhesion between sealing surfaces may occur. A slight twist of the fitting may be required to break this adhesion and permit effortless removal.
4. When the fitting is removed from the tube end, inspect the clip to ensure it has not been damaged. If damaged, replace the clip. If undamaged, immediately reinstall clip, insert clip into any two adjacent openings with the triangular portion pointing away from the fitting opening. Install clip to fully engage the body (legs of hairpin clip locked on outside of body). Piloting with an index finger is necessary.
5. Before installing the fitting on the tube, wipe the tube end with a clean cloth. Inspect the inside of the fitting to ensure it is free of dirt and/or obstructions.
6. To reinstall the fitting onto the tube, align the fitting and tube axially and push the fitting onto the tube end. When the fitting is engaged, a definite click will be heard. Pull on the fitting to ensure it is fully engaged.

½ in. and ¼ in. Fittings (Duck Bill Clip)

See Figures 37, 38 and 39

The duck bill fitting consists of a body, spacers, O-rings and a duck bill retaining clip. The clip maintains the fitting to steel tube juncture. When disassembly is required for service, one of the two following methods are to be followed:

¼ IN. FITTINGS

To disengage the tube from the fitting, align the slot on the push connect disassembly tool T82L-9500-AH, or equivalent, with either tab on the clip (90° from the slots on the side of the fitting) and insert the tool. This disengages the duck bill

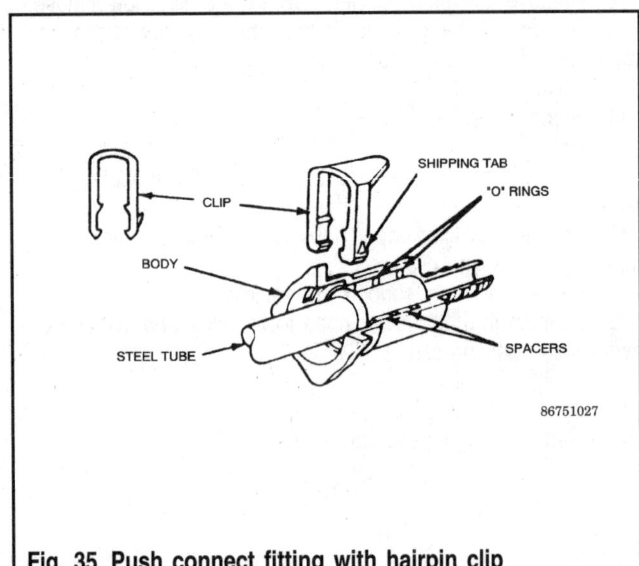

Fig. 35 Push connect fitting with hairpin clip

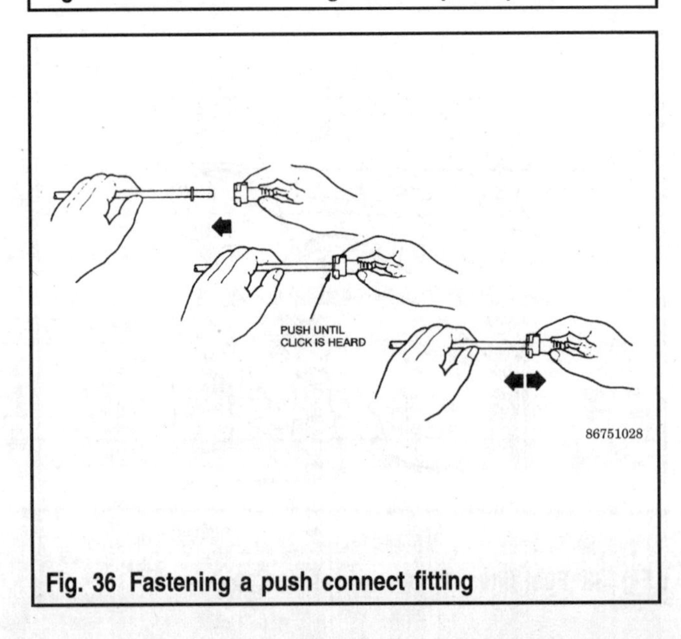

Fig. 36 Fastening a push connect fitting

from the tube. Holding the tool and the tube with one hand, pull the fitting away from the tube.

➡Only moderate effort is required if the tube has been properly disengaged. Use hands only. After disassembly, inspect and clean the tube sealing surface. Also inspect the inside of the fitting for damage to the retaining clip. If the retaining clip appears to be damaged, replace it. Some fuel tubes have a secondary bead which aligns with the outer surface of the clip. These beads can make tool insertion difficult. If there is extreme difficulty, use the disassembly method following:

1/2 IN. FITTING AND ALTERNATE METHOD FOR 1/4 IN. FITTING

This method of disassembly disengages the retaining clip from the fitting body.

Use a pair of narrow pliers, (6 in. locking pliers are ideal). The pliers must have a jaw width of 0.2 in. (5mm) or less.

Align the jaws of the pliers with the openings in the side of the fitting case and compress the portion of the retaining clip that engages the fitting case. This disengages the retaining clip from the case (often one side of the clip will disengage before the other. It is necessary to disengage the clip from both openings). Manually pull the fitting off the tube.

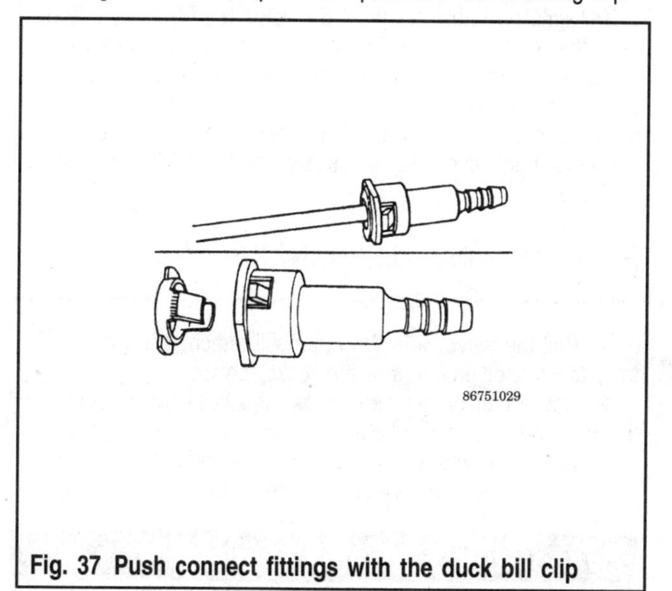

Fig. 37 Push connect fittings with the duck bill clip

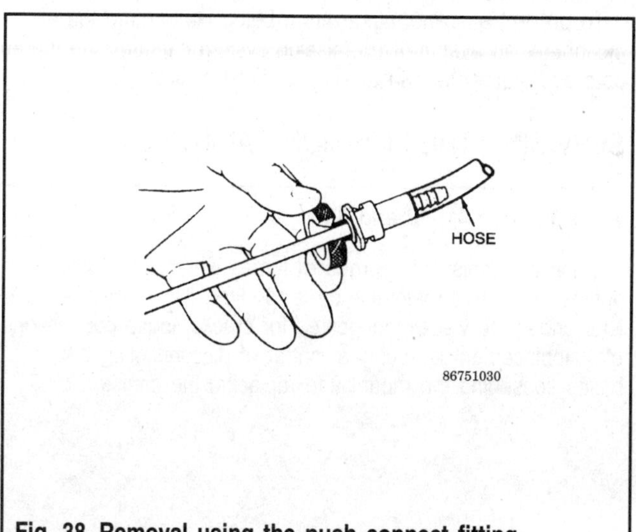

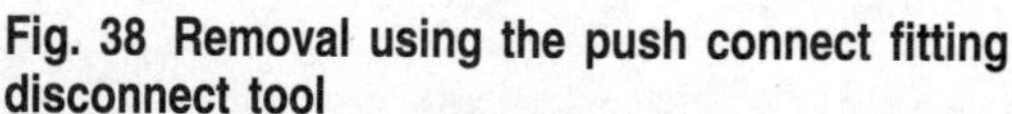
Fig. 38 Removal using the push connect fitting disconnect tool

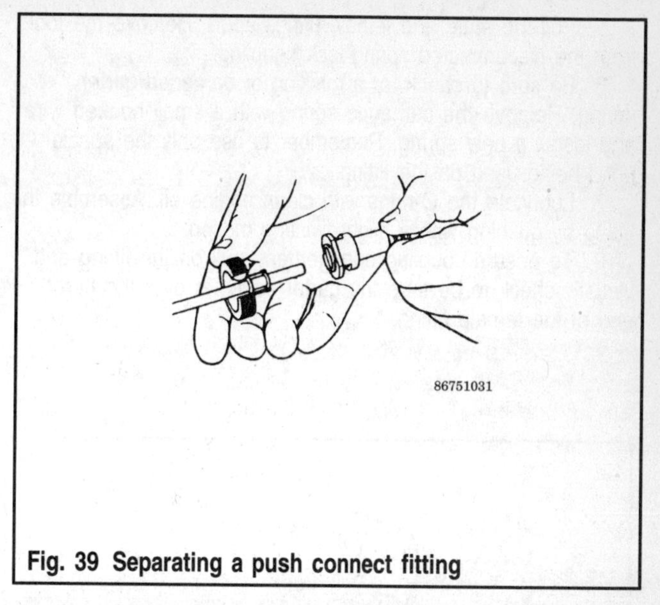

Fig. 39 Separating a push connect fitting

➡Only moderate effort is required if the retaining clip has been properly disengaged. Do not use tools to attempt to increase pulling force.

The retaining clip will remain on the tube. Disengage the clip from the tube bead and remove. Replace the retaining clip if it appears to be damaged.

➡A slight "ovalness" of the ring of the clip will usually occur. If there are no visible cracks and the ring will pinch back to its circular configuration, it is not damaged. If there is any doubt, replace the clip.

Install the clip into the body by inserting one of the retaining clip serrated edges on the duck bill portion into one of the window openings. Push on the other side until the clip snaps into place. Slide fuel line back into the clip.

SPRING LOCK COUPLING

▶ See Figure 40

The spring lock coupling is a fuel line coupling held together by a garter spring inside a circular cage. When the coupling is connected together, the flared end of the female fitting slips behind the garter spring inside the cage of the male fitting. The garter spring and cage then prevent the flared end of the female fitting from pulling out of the cage.

Two O-rings are used to seal between the 2 halves of the coupling. These O-rings are made of special material and must be replaced with an O-ring made of the same material. To disconnect the coupling do the following:

1. Discharge the fuel from the fuel system.
2. Then fit Spring Lock Coupling Tool D87L-9280-A (3/8 in.), D87L-9280-B (1/2 in.) or equivalent to the coupling.
3. Fit the tool to the coupling so that the tool can enter the cage opening to release the garter spring.
4. Push on the tool into the cage opening to release the female fitting from the garter spring.

5. Pull the male and female fittings apart. Remove the tool from the disconnected spring lock coupling.
6. Be sure to check for a missing or damaged garter spring. Remove the damaged spring with a small hooked wire and install a new spring. Remember to use only the special O-rings being used on the fitting.
7. Lubricate the O-rings with clean engine oil. Assemble the fitting by pushing with a slight twisting motion.
8. To ensure coupling engagement, pull on the fitting and visually check to be sure the garter spring is over the flared end of the female fitting.

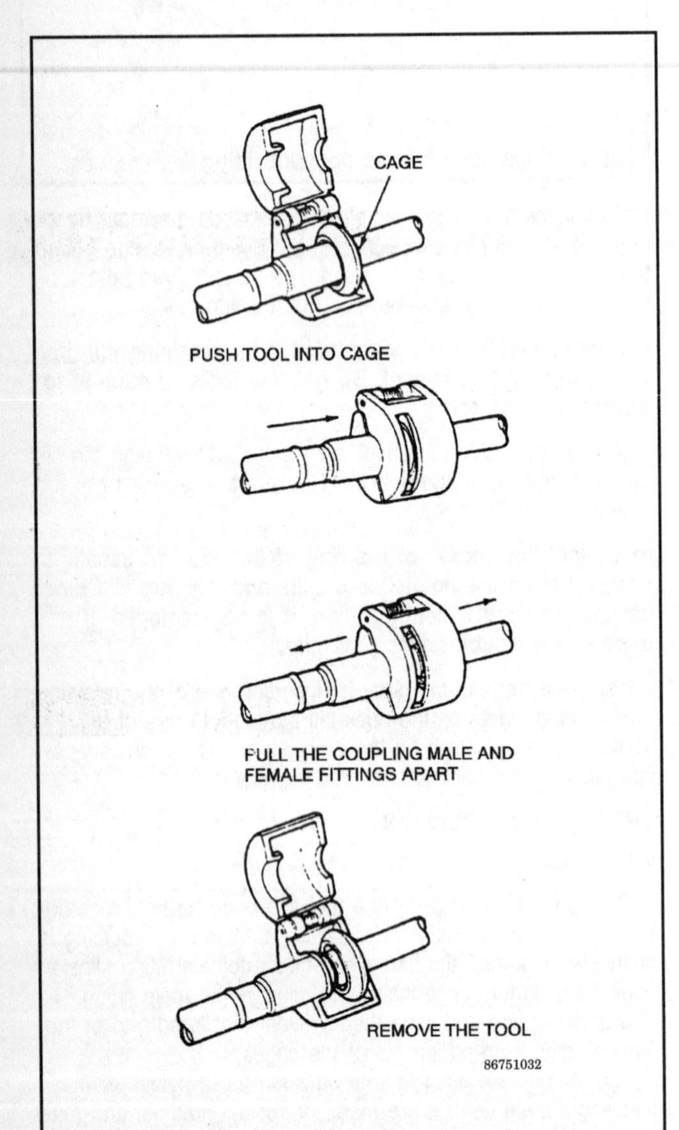

Fig. 40 A special tool is required to unlock the spring lock coupling

PCV Valve

OPERATION AND INSPECTION

➡Most 1981-90 models do not use a positive crankcase ventilation (PCV) valve. Instead, an internal baffle and an orifice control the flow of crankcase gases. (See Section 4 for more details on emission controls).

For models that do have a PCV valve, it is located on top of the valve cover or on the intake manifold. Its function is to purge the crankcase of harmful vapors through a system using engine vacuum to draw fresh air through the crankcase. It provides a way to burn crankcase vapors, rather than exhausting them. Proper operation of the PCV valve depends on a sealed engine.

Engine operating conditions that would indicate a malfunctioning PCV system are rough idle, oil present in the air cleaner, oil leaks or excessive oil sludging.

The simplest check for the PCV valve is to remove it from its rubber grommet on top of the valve cover and shake it. If it rattles, it is functioning. If not, replace it. In any event, it should be replaced at the recommended interval whether it rattles or not. While you are at it, check the PCV hoses for breaks or restrictions. As necessary, the hoses should also be replaced.

REMOVAL & INSTALLATION

1. Pull the valve, with the hose still attached to the valve, from the rubber grommet in the rocker cover.
2. Use a pair of pliers to release the hose clamp, remove the PCV valve from the hose.
3. Install the new valve into the hose, slide the clamp into position, and install the valve into the rubber grommet.

Evaporative Emission Canister

To prevent gasoline vapors from being vented into the atmosphere, an evaporative emission system captures the vapors and stores them in a charcoal filled canister.

SERVICING THE EMISSION CANISTER

➧ **See Figures 41, 42 and 43**

Since the canister is purged of fumes when the engine is operating, no real maintenance is required. However, the canister should be visually inspected for cracks, loose connections, etc. Replacement is simply a matter of disconnecting the hoses, loosening the mount and replacing the canister.

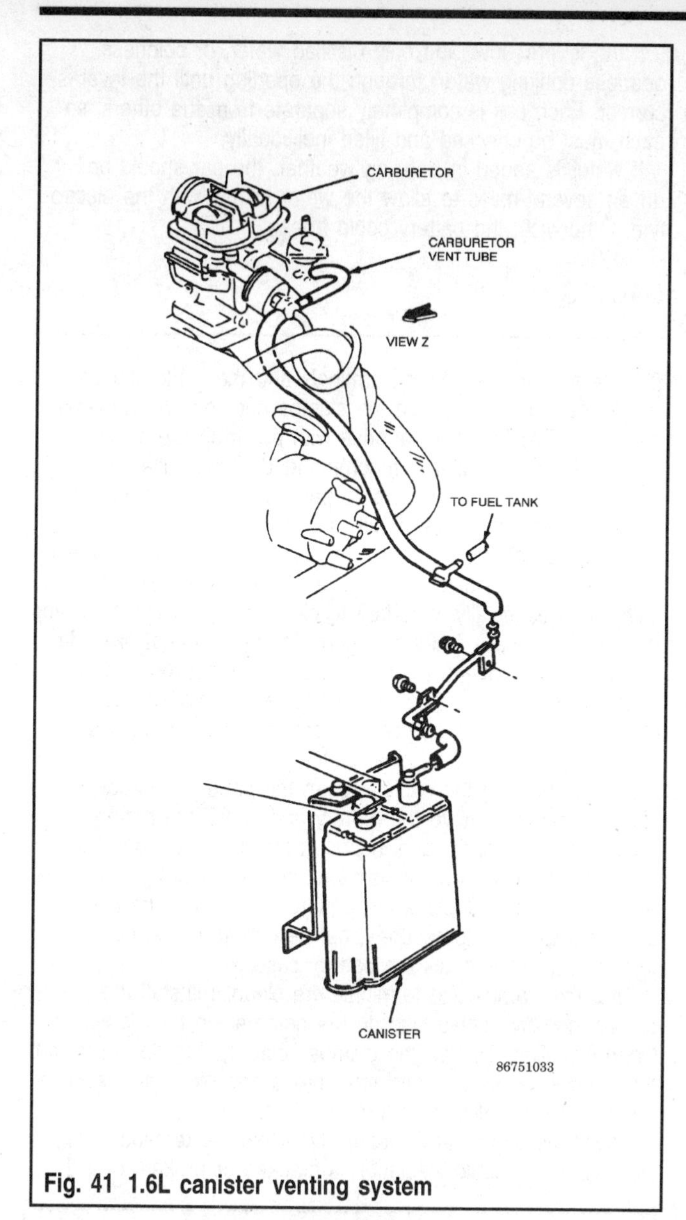

Fig. 41 1.6L canister venting system

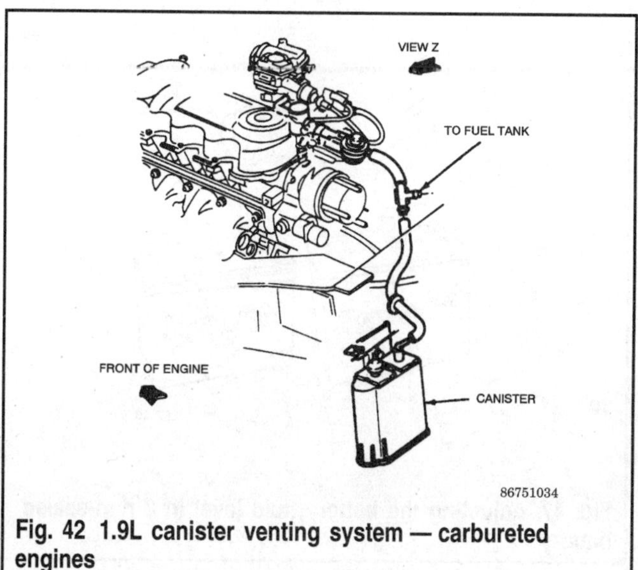

Fig. 42 1.9L canister venting system — carbureted engines

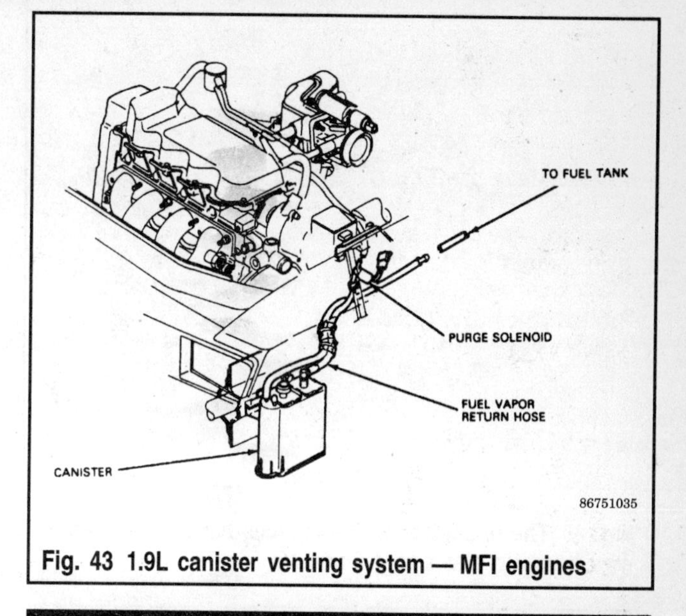

Fig. 43 1.9L canister venting system — MFI engines

Battery

GENERAL MAINTENANCE

See Figures 44, 45 and 46

Your vehicle was originally equipped with a maintenance-free battery, which usually eliminates the need for periodic checking and adding of fluid.

Keeping the battery top clean and dry reduces service problems and extends the battery life.

➡Batteries normally produce explosive gases which can cause personal injury. Therefore, do not allow flames, sparks or lighted tobacco to come near the battery.

****CAUTION**

Always shield your face and protect your eyes. Always provide ventilation.

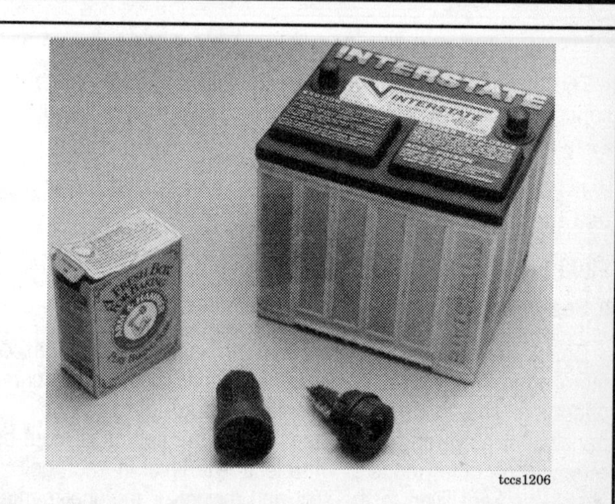

Fig. 44 Maintenance is performed with household items (baking soda to neutralize spilled acid) or with tools such as this post and terminal cleaner

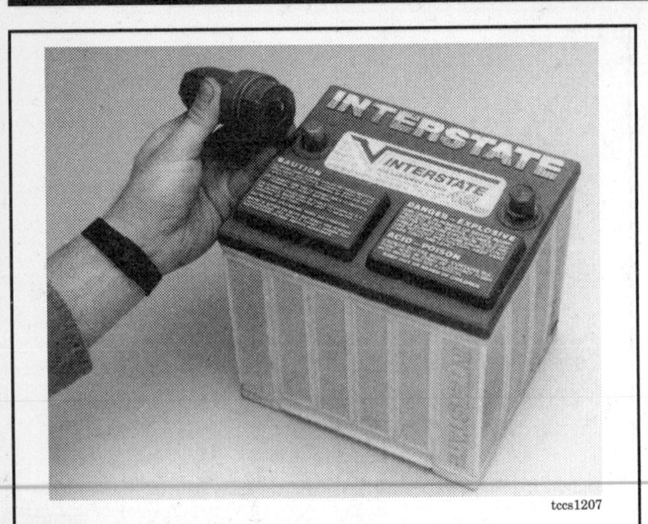
tccs1207

Fig. 45 The underside of this special battery tool has a wire brush to clean post terminals

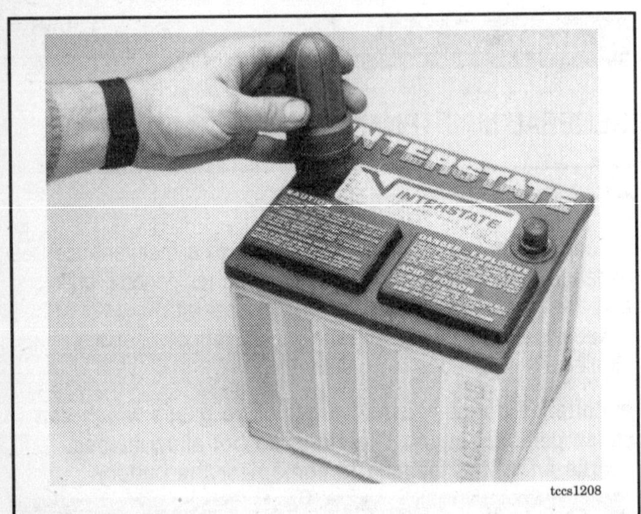
tccs1208

Fig. 46 Place the tool over the terminals and twist to clean the post

FLUID LEVEL

The original battery in your vehicle was a sealed maintenance-free battery. It does not require addition of water during its normal service life.

➡If you replace your battery with a non-sealed battery, use the following procedure.

Fluid Level (Except Sealed Batteries)

See Figure 47

Check the battery electrolyte level at least once a month, or more often in hot weather or during periods of extended car operation. The level can be checked through the case on translucent polypropylene battery cases; the cell caps must be removed on other models. The electrolyte level in each cell should be kept filled to the split ring inside, or the line marked on the outside of the case.

If the level is low, add only distilled water, or colorless, odorless drinking water, through the opening until the level is correct. Each cell is completely separate from the others, so each must be checked and filled individually.

If water is added in freezing weather, the car should be driven several miles to allow the water to mix with the electrolyte. Otherwise, the battery could freeze.

CABLES

Once a year, the battery terminals and the cable clamps should be cleaned. Loosen the clamps and remove the cables, negative cable first. On batteries with posts on top, the use of a specially made puller is recommended. Such pullers are inexpensive, and available in auto parts stores. Side terminal battery cables are secured with a bolt.

Clean the cable clamps and the battery terminal with a wire brush, until all corrosion, grease, etc. is removed and metal is shiny. It is especially important to clean the inside of the clamp thoroughly, since a small deposit of foreign material or oxidation there will prevent a sound electrical connection and inhibit either starting or charging. Special tools are available for cleaning these parts, one type of conventional batteries and another type for side terminal batteries.

Before installing the cable, loosen the battery hold-down clamp or strap, remove the battery and check the battery tray. Clear it of any debris, and inspect it for structural soundness. Rust should be wire brushed away, and the metal given a coat of anti-rust paint. Replace the battery and tighten the hold down clamp or strap securely, but be careful not to overtighten, which will crack the battery case.

After the clamps and terminals are clean, reinstall the cables, negative cable last; do not hammer on the clamps when installing. Tighten the clamps securely, but do not distort them. Give the clamps and terminals a thin external coating of grease after installation, to prevent corrosion.

Check the cables at the same time that the terminals are cleaned. If the cable insulation is cracked or broken, or if the

86751039

Fig. 47 Adjusting the battery fluid level in a non-sealed battery

ends are frayed, the cable should be replaced with a new cable of the same length and gauge.

➡Keep flame or sparks away from the battery; it gives off explosive hydrogen gas. Battery electrolyte contains sulfuric acid. If you should splash any on your skin or in your eyes, flush the affected areas with plenty of clear water; if it lands in your eyes, get medical help immediately.

TESTING

Tests are made on a battery to determine the state of charge and also its capacity or ability to crank an engine. The ultimate result of these tests is to show that the battery is good, needs recharging or must be replace.

Visual Inspection

Before attempting to test a battery, it is important to give it a thorough examination to determine if it has been damaged.

To inspect the battery, remove the cable clamps. Disconnect the negative cable first. Check for dirty or corroded connections and loose battery posts. Also, check for broken or cracked case or cover. If a defective, loose or broken post or cracked case or cover is found, replace the battery.

The battery contains a visual test indicator which gives a green signal when an adequate charge level exists, and a white signal when charging is required.

Battery Capacity Test

The battery capacity test should follow the Visual Inspection. A high rate discharge tester (Rotunda Battery Starter Tester 02-0204 or equivalent) in conjunction with a voltmeter is used for this test. Follow the instructions supplied with the tester. If the battery is below minimum voltage for the capacity test, charge the battery for 20 minutes at 35 amperes and repeat the capacity test. If the battery fails a second time, it must be replaced.

CHARGING

If the test indicator is white, the battery should be charged. When the dot appears or when maximum charge is reached, charging should be stopped.

Charging Rate

The following specifications should be used as a general guideline when battery charging is necessary:

- 5 amps — not to exceed 15 hours
- 10 amps — not to exceed 7.5 hours
- 20 amps — not to exceed 3.75 hours
- 30 amps — not to exceed 2.5 hours

When charging is performed at 5 amps, charging is virtually 100% three hours after the indicator changes from white to green.

➡Use fast charging only in an emergency.

If the battery indicator does not turn to green after the battery has been charged a sufficient length of time, the battery should be replaced. Do not overcharge.

Specific Gravity

➧ See Figure 48

➡If your battery is not a sealed maintenance-free battery, a specific gravity test can be performed.

At least once a year, check the specific gravity of the battery. It should be between 1.20 and 1.26 at room temperature.

The specific gravity can be checked with the use of an hydrometer, an inexpensive instrument available from many sources, including auto parts stores. The hydrometer has a squeeze bulb at one end and a nozzle at the other. Battery electrolyte is sucked into the hydrometer until the float is lifted from its seat. The specific gravity is then read by noting the position of the float. Generally, if after charging, the specific gravity between any two cells varies more than 50 points (.050), the battery is bad and should be replaced.

It is not possible to check the specific gravity in this manner on sealed maintenance-free batteries. Instead, the indicator built into the top of the case (on some batteries) must be relied on to display any signs of battery deterioration. If the indicator is dark, the battery can be assumed to be OK. If the indicator is light the specific gravity is low, and the battery should be charged or replaced.

REPLACEMENT

When it becomes necessary to replace the battery, replace it with a battery of equivalent capacity.

1. First, disconnect the negative battery cable; then disconnect the positive cable.
2. Remove the battery hold-downs and heat shields, as required.
3. Remove the battery from the vehicle.

To install:

4. Install the replacement battery into the vehicle.
5. Install the battery hold-downs and heat shields, as required.
6. Reconnect the positive (+) cable first; then reconnect the negative cable.

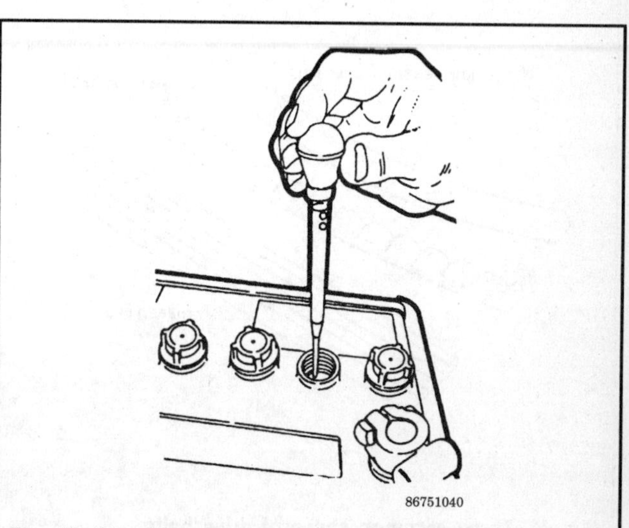

Fig. 48 Checking the battery specific gravity with a hydrometer — non-sealed type battery

7. After installing the cables, apply a small quantity of grease to each battery post to help prevent corrosion.

Belts

▸ See Figure 49

Your vehicle may be equipped with a 4-rib, 5-rib, or conventional 1/4 in. (6mm) V-belt, depending on accessories. These belts must be properly adjusted at all times. Loose belt(s) will result in slippage which may cause noise or improper accessory operation.

INSPECTION

Inspect all drive belts for excessive wear, cracks, glazed condition and frayed or broken cords. Replace any drive belt showing the above condition(s).

➡If a drive belt continually gets cut, the crankshaft pulley might have a sharp projection on it. Have the pulley replaced if this condition exists.

ADJUSTING

The following should be observed when belt tension adjustment and/or replacement is necessary:

- Due to the compactness of the engine compartment, it may be necessary to disconnect some spark plug leads when adjusting or replacing drive belts. If a spark plug lead is disconnected it is necessary to coat the terminal of the lead with silicone grease (part number D7AZ19A331A or the equivalent).
- On vehicles equipped with power steering, the air pump belt tension cannot be adjusted until the power steering belt has been adjusted.

➡Proper adjustment requires the use of the tension gauge. Since most people don't have the necessary gauge, a deflection method of adjustment is given.

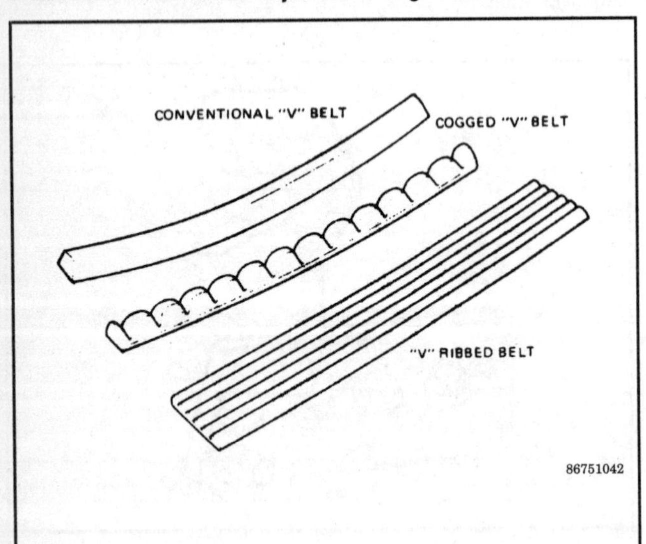

Fig. 49 Three common styles of drive belts

1. Locate a point on the belt midway between the two driven pulleys.
2. The deflection of the belt should be:
   - For all belts with a distance of 12 in. (305mm) between pulley: 1/8-1/4 in. (3-6mm).
   - For all belts with a distance greater than 12 in. (305mm or less) between pulley: 1/8-3/8 in. (3-6mm).
3. Correctly adjust the belt deflection and tighten all mounting bolts. Start the engine and allow it to reach normal operating temperature. Shut the engine **OFF** and recheck belt deflection. Readjust if necessary.

1981-86 Alternator Belt With Modified Bracket

▸ See Figures 50 and 51

Some later models are equipped with a modified alternator bracket (high mount alternator). The bracket incorporates a slot that will accommodate a tapered prybar, such as a lug wrench, to give a place to apply leverage.

Insert the tire lug wrench into the slot opening. Pry on the alternator until the correct belt tension is reached.

While maintaining belt tension, first tighten the 3/8 in. adjusting bolt to 24-30 ft. lbs. (32-40 Nm), then tighten the pivot bolt to 45-65 ft. lbs. (61-88 Nm).

All 1987-88 Except V-Ribbed Belts

▸ See Figures 52, 53 and 54

1. Loosen the accessory adjustment and pivot bolts.
2. On the 2.0L diesel engine, loosen the shake brace nut and bolt.
3. Using the proper prytool, pry against the necessary accessory in order to gain the proper belt tension.
4. Tighten the adjustment bolts. Release the pressure on the pry bar. Tighten the pivot bolt.
5. Tighten the shake brace nut and bolt on the 2.0L diesel engine.
6. Check the belt tension and reset it if not up to specifications.

1987-90 1.9L Engines With V-Ribbed Belts

▸ See Figures 55 and 56

It is necessary to adjust the power steering belt prior to the air pump belt as follows:

1. From above the vehicle, loosen the pivot bolt and upper adjustment bolt.
2. From below the vehicle, loosen the lower adjustment bolt and apply pressure with a 1/2 in. drive. Tighten the lower bolts to 30-45 ft. lbs.
3. From above the vehicle, tighten the pivot bolt to 30-45 ft. lbs. (41-61 Nm) and the upper adjustment bolts to 30-45 ft. lbs. (41-61 Nm).
4. To adjust the alternator belt on the 1987-88 models, loosen the pivot bolt and upper adjustment bolt.
5. Using the proper pry tool, pry against the necessary accessory in order to gain the proper belt tension.
6. Tighten the pivot bolt to 15-22 ft. lbs. (20-30 Nm) and the adjustment bolt to 24-34 ft. lbs. (33-46 Nm). The alternator through-bolts are tightened to 45-55 ft. lbs. (61-75 Nm).

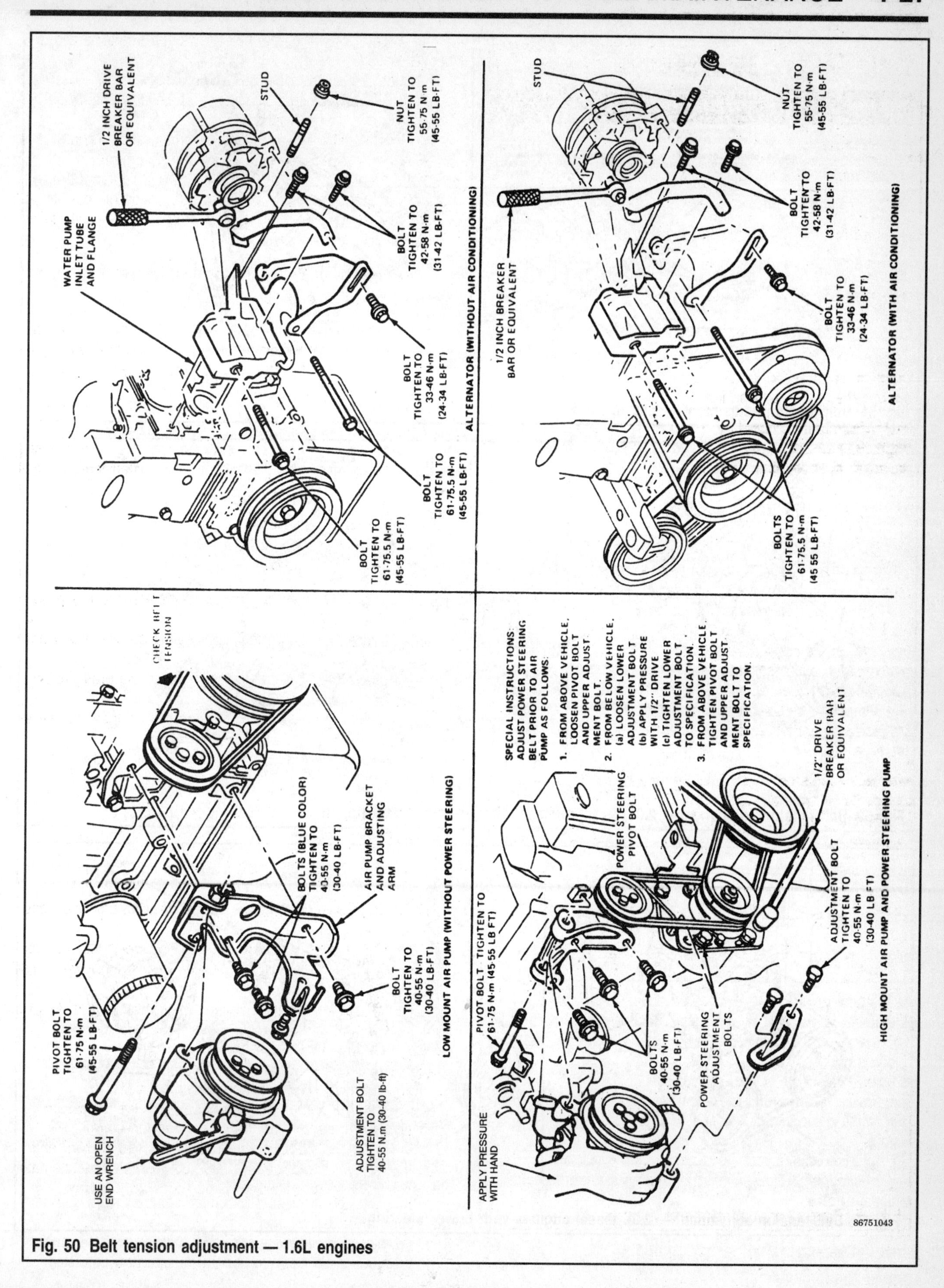

Fig. 50 Belt tension adjustment — 1.6L engines

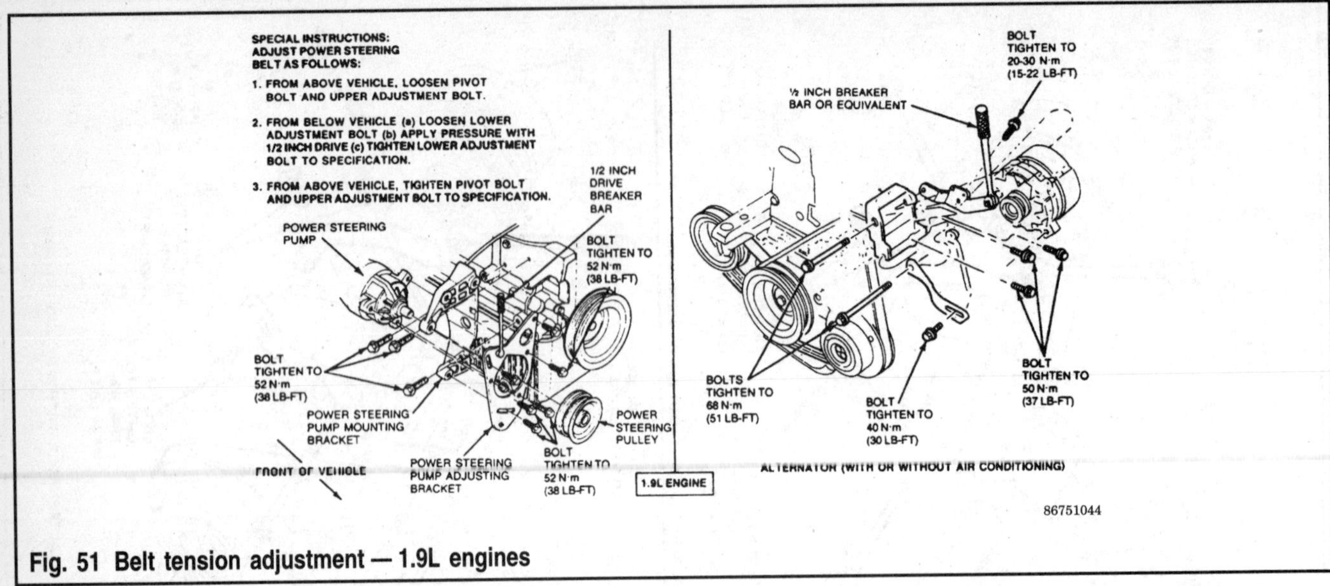

Fig. 51 Belt tension adjustment — 1.9L engines

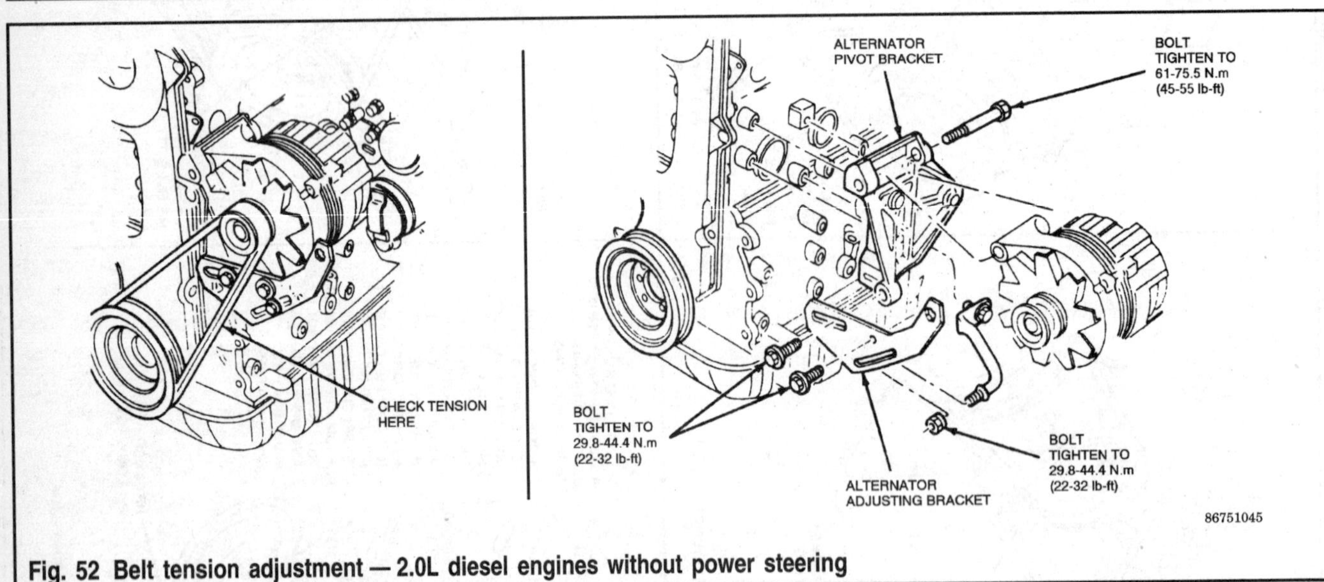

Fig. 52 Belt tension adjustment — 2.0L diesel engines without power steering

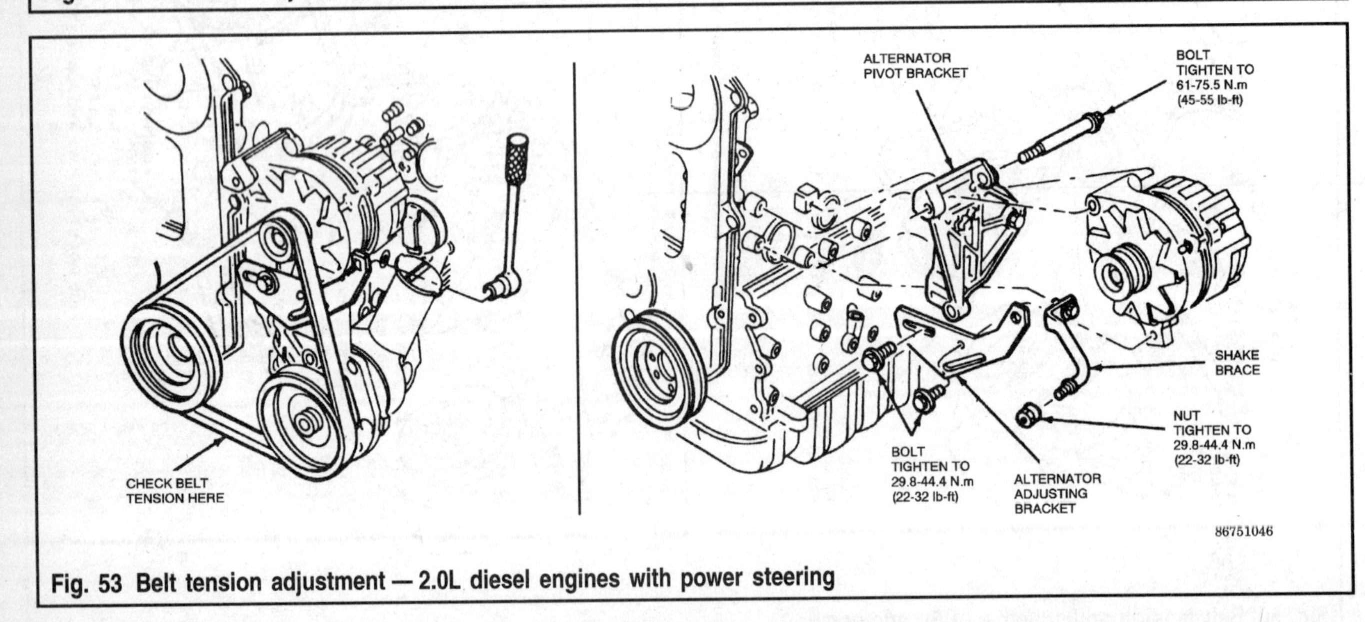

Fig. 53 Belt tension adjustment — 2.0L diesel engines with power steering

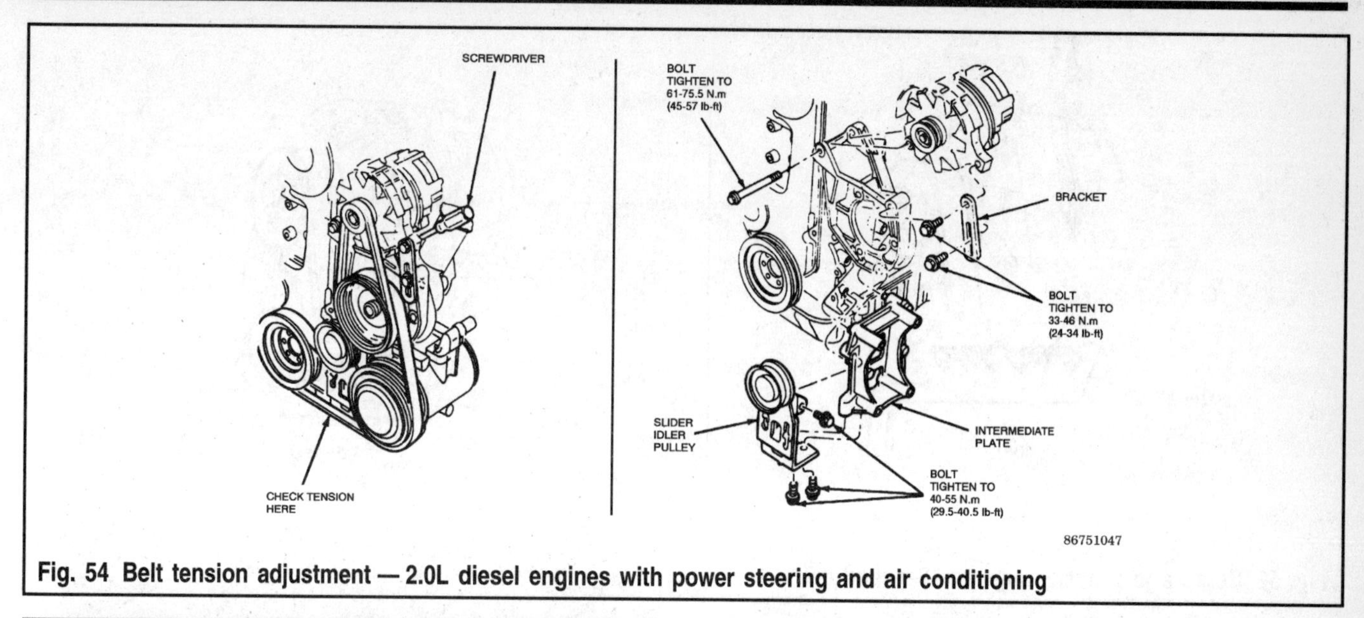

Fig. 54 Belt tension adjustment — 2.0L diesel engines with power steering and air conditioning

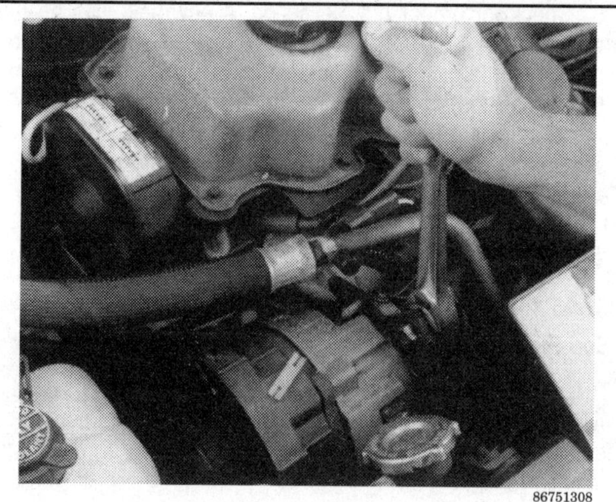

Fig. 55 Use a ½ in. ratchet to lever the alternator bracket to tension the belt — 1988 Escort

7. On 1989-90, as well as some 1988 models, adjust the alternator belt as follows:

a. Install a ½ in. breaker bar or equivalent to the support bracket behind the alternator.

b. Apply tension to the belt using the breaker bar. Using a suitable belt tension gauge, set the proper belt tension.

c. The tension should be 140-180 lbs (190-245 Nm) for a new belt and 120-140 lbs. (163-190 Nm) for a used belt.

d. Secure the alternator pivot bolt, leaving it loose enough to allow the alternator to move. While maintaining the proper belt tension, tighten the alternator adjustment bolt to 30 ft. lbs. (40 Nm).

e. Remove the belt tension gauge and breaker bar, then idle the engine for five minutes.

f. With the ignition switch in the **OFF** position, check the belt tension. If the tension is below 120 lbs. (55 kg), re-tension the belt with the tension gauge in place. Keep pressure on the breaker bar so that the existing tension on the belt is not lost. Slowly loosen the alternator adjustment bolt to allow belt tension to increase to used belt specification, then tighten the adjustment bolt.

g. Tighten the alternator pivot bolt to 50 ft. lbs. (68 Nm) and support bracket bolt to 35 ft. lbs. (47 Nm).

➡The power steering pump belt on the 1989-90 models is adjusted in the same manner as the alternator belt.

1.8L Engines

➧ See Figures 57 and 58

ALTERNATOR AND WATER PUMP

1. Loosen the alternator adjusting bolt.
2. Raise and safely support the vehicle.
3. Loosen the alternator mounting bolt.

➡Do not pry against the stator frame. Position the prybar against a stronger point, such as the area around a case bolt.

4. Position a suitable belt tension gauge on the longest accessible span of belt and tighten the belt. Adjust the tension to 86-103 lbs. (39-46 kg) for a new belt or 68-86 lbs. (31-39 kg) for a used belt.
5. If a belt tension gauge is not available, adjust the tension to 0.31-0.35 in. (8-9mm) deflection for a new belt or 0.35-0.39 in. (9-10mm) deflection for a used belt.
6. Tighten the alternator adjusting bolt to 14-19 ft. lbs. (19-25 Nm).
7. Tighten the alternator mounting bo lt to 27-38 ft. lbs. (37-52 Nm).
8. Lower the vehicle.

POWER STEERING PUMP AND AIR CONDITIONING COMPRESSOR

1. Raise and safely support the vehicle.
2. Loosen the power steering pump mounting bolt and nuts.
3. Adjust the power steering pump and air conditioning compressor belt tension by turning the pump adjusting bolt.
4. Tighten the power steering pump mounting nut near the pump adjusting bolt.

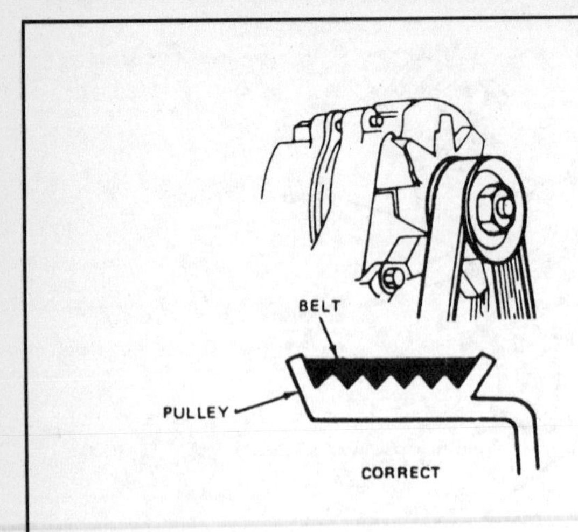

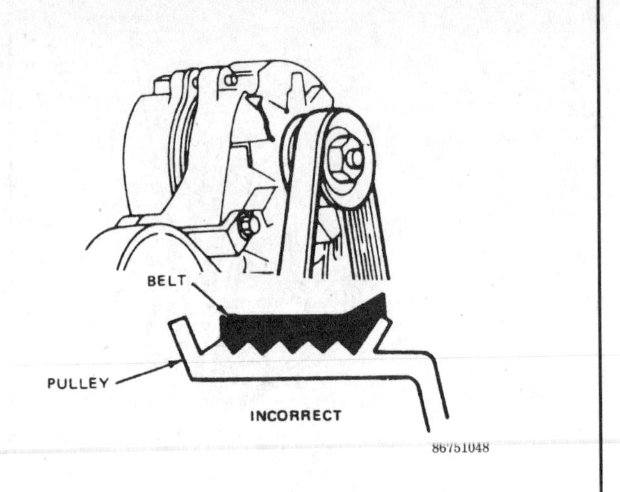

Fig. 56 Be sure to properly align the V-ribbed belt

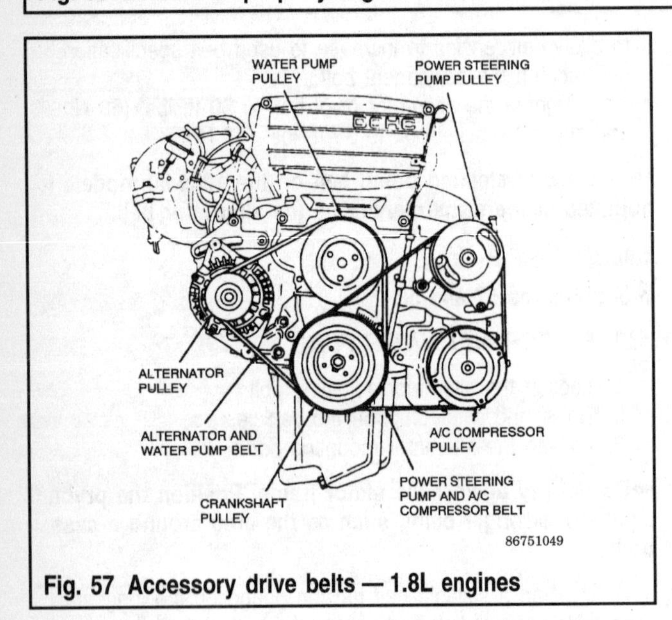

Fig. 57 Accessory drive belts — 1.8L engines

5. Check for proper belt deflection. A new belt, with no run time, should be 0.31-0.35 in. (8-9mm). A used belt, with more than 10 minutes of run time, should be 0.35-0.39 in. (9-10mm).
6. Tighten the power steering pump mounting nut, located near the adjusting bolt, to 27-38 ft. lbs. (37-52 Nm).
7. Tighten the pump mounting bolt behind the pulley to 27-40 ft. lbs. (36-54 Nm), and the remaining pump mounting nut to 23-34 ft. lbs. (31-46 Nm).
8. Lower the vehicle.

1991-95 1.9L Engines

See Figures 59 and 60

The accessory drive belt for 1991-95 1.9L engines, has no provision for manual belt adjustment. These engines use an automatic belt tensioner. Drive belt slack is taken up by the automatic tensioner.

Movement of the automatic tensioner assembly during engine operation is not a sign of a malfunctioning tensioner. This movement is the tensioner self-adjusting and is required to maintain constant belt tension.

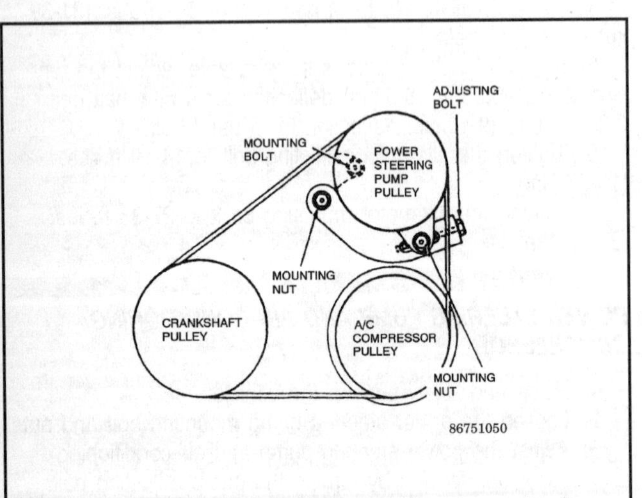

Fig. 58 Removal and installation of the power steering pump and air conditioning compressor belt — 1.8L engines

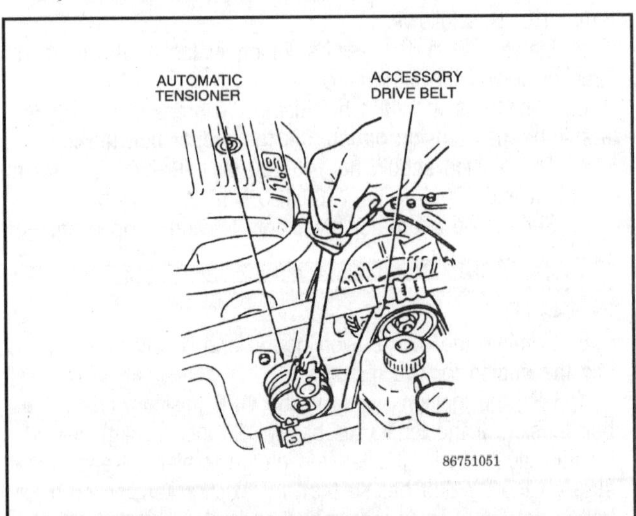

Fig. 59 Removal and installation of the accessory drive belt — 1.9L engines

Fig. 60 Drive belt routing — 1.9L engines

2.0L Engine With V-Ribbed Belts

1. Loosen the two idler pulley bracket bolts. Turn the adjusting bolt until the belt is adjusted to specifications.

➡**Turning the wrench to the right tightens the belt adjustment, and turning the wrench to the left loosens belt tension.**

2. Tighten the two idler pulley bracket bolts to specifications.
3. Check the belt tension and reset if not to specifications.

REMOVAL & INSTALLATION

Except 1991-90 1.9L Engines

1. Loosen the pivot bolt and/or the adjustment bolt on the accessories which need belts replaced.
2. Move the driven unit (power steering pump, air pump, etc.) toward or away from the engine to loosen the belt. Remove the belt.

To install:

3. Install the new bolt on the driven unit and either move toward or away from the engine to put tension on the belt.
4. Snug up the mounting and/or adjusting bolt to hold the driven unit, but do not completely tighten.
5. Use the procedure for the deflection method of belt adjustment.

1991-95 1.9L Engines

1. Insert a 3/8 in. drive ratchet or a breaker bar in the automatic tensioner, then pull the tool toward the front of the vehicle.
2. While releasing the belt tension, remove the drive belt from the tensioner pulley and slip it off the remaining accessory pulleys.

To install:

3. Position the drive belt over the accessory pulleys.
4. Insert the 3/8 in. drive ratchet or a breaker bar inserted in the automatic tensioner, then pull the tool toward the front of the vehicle.
5. While holding the tool in this position, slip the drive belt behind the tensioner pulley and release the tool.
6. Remove the tool from the automatic tensioner.
7. Check that all V-grooves make proper contact with the pulley.

Automatic Tensioner Assembly

1991-95 1.9L ENGINES

1. Remove the accessory drive belt, as outlined previously.
2. Remove the automatic tensioner mounting bolt.
3. Remove the automatic tensioner from the vehicle.

To install:

4. Place the automatic tensioner into position and install the mounting bolt.
5. Reinstall the accessory drive belt, as outlined previously.

CHILTON TIPS

1989 ESCORT

If your 1989 Escort is having problems with rattles, squeaks and squeals coming from the engine compartment, it may be caused by a loose accessory drive belt. New accessory drive belt specifications are now available.

Tighten the accessory drive belt to the new retightening specifications. Refer to the following procedure for service details.

Check to see if the accessory drive belt is loose. If it is loose, take the following action:

1. Check the accessory drive belt for cracking and/or glazing. Determine if it should be replaced.
2. Loosen the pivot bolt and/or the adjustment bolt.
3. Install a 1/2 in. breaker bar or equivalent to the support bracket behind the alternator.
4. Apply tension to the belt using the breaker bar. Use a suitable belt tension gauge to set the proper belt tension.
5. The tension should be 200-220 lbs. (90-99 kg) for a new belt with A/C and 170-190 lbs. (77-85 kg) for a new belt without A/C; 150-170 lbs. for a used belt with A/C and 120-140 lbs. (54-63 kg) for a used belt without A/C.

6. Secure the alternator pivot bolt, leaving it loose enough to allow the alternator to move. While maintaining the proper belt tension, tighten the alternator adjustment bolt to 30 ft. lbs. (40 Nm).

7. Remove the belt tension gauge and breaker bar and idle the engine for five minutes.

8. With the ignition switch in the **OFF** position, check the belt tension. If the tension is below 120 lbs. (54 kg), re-tension the belt with the tension gauge in place. Keep pressure on the breaker bar so that the existing tension on the belt is not lost, slowly loosen the alternator adjustment bolt to allow belt tension to increase to used belt specifications, then tighten the adjustment bolt.

9. Tighten the alternator pivot bolt to 51 ft. lbs. (72 Nm), alternator attaching bolt to 51 ft. lbs. (72 Nm) and alternator brace arm to alternator 18 ft. lbs. (25 Nm).

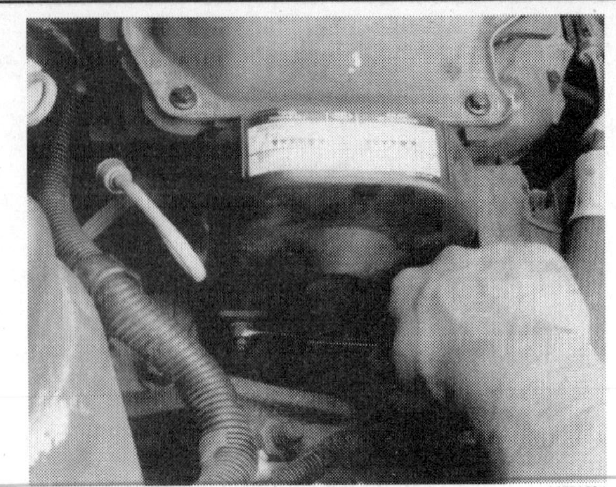

Fig. 61 Remove the timing belt cover to inspect the timing belt — 1988 Escort shown

Timing Belts

INSPECTION

See Figures 61 and 62

WARNING

Severe engine damage may occur if the timing belt breaks. The 1.6L and 2.0L diesel engines have an "interference" design in which a broken timing belt will allow the the valves to contact the pistons.

Ford advises that the timing belt should be replaced every 60,000 miles (96,000 km). Replacing the timing belt before its recommended interval is a wise choice. It is far less expensive to replace the belt than to repair the engine damage which results from the belt breaking.

Inspect the belt for cracks, missing teeth and wear on any of the surfaces. Inspect the sprockets for grease and other deposits. If any of these conditions exist, the belt should be replaced. Please refer to Section 3 for procedures on timing belt removal and installation.

Fig. 62 The timing belt should be inspected for wear, cracks, missing teeth, and the like

Hoses

CAUTION

When working on or around the cooling system, be aware that the cooling fan motor can come on automatically. The cooling fan motor is controlled by a temperature-sensitive switch and may activate while the engine is off. It will continue to run until the correct temperature is reached. Before working on or around the fan, disconnect the negative battery cable or the fan wiring connector.

REMOVAL AND INSTALLATION

See Figure 63

1. Open the hood and cover the fenders to protect them from scratches.

2. Disconnect the negative battery cable at the battery.

3. Place a suitable drain pan under the radiator and drain the cooling system. Place a small hose on the end of the radiator petcock, this will direct the coolant into the drain pan.

CAUTION

When draining the coolant, keep in mind that cats and dogs are attracted by ethylene glycol antifreeze, and are quite likely to drink any that is left in an uncovered container or in puddles on the ground. This will prove fatal in sufficient quantity. Always drain the coolant into a sealable container. Coolant may be reused unless it is contaminated or several years old.

4. After the radiator has drained, position the drain pan under the lower hose. Loosen the lower hose clamps, disconnect the hose from the water pump inlet pipe and allow to drain. Disconnect the other end of the hose from the radiator and remove the hose.

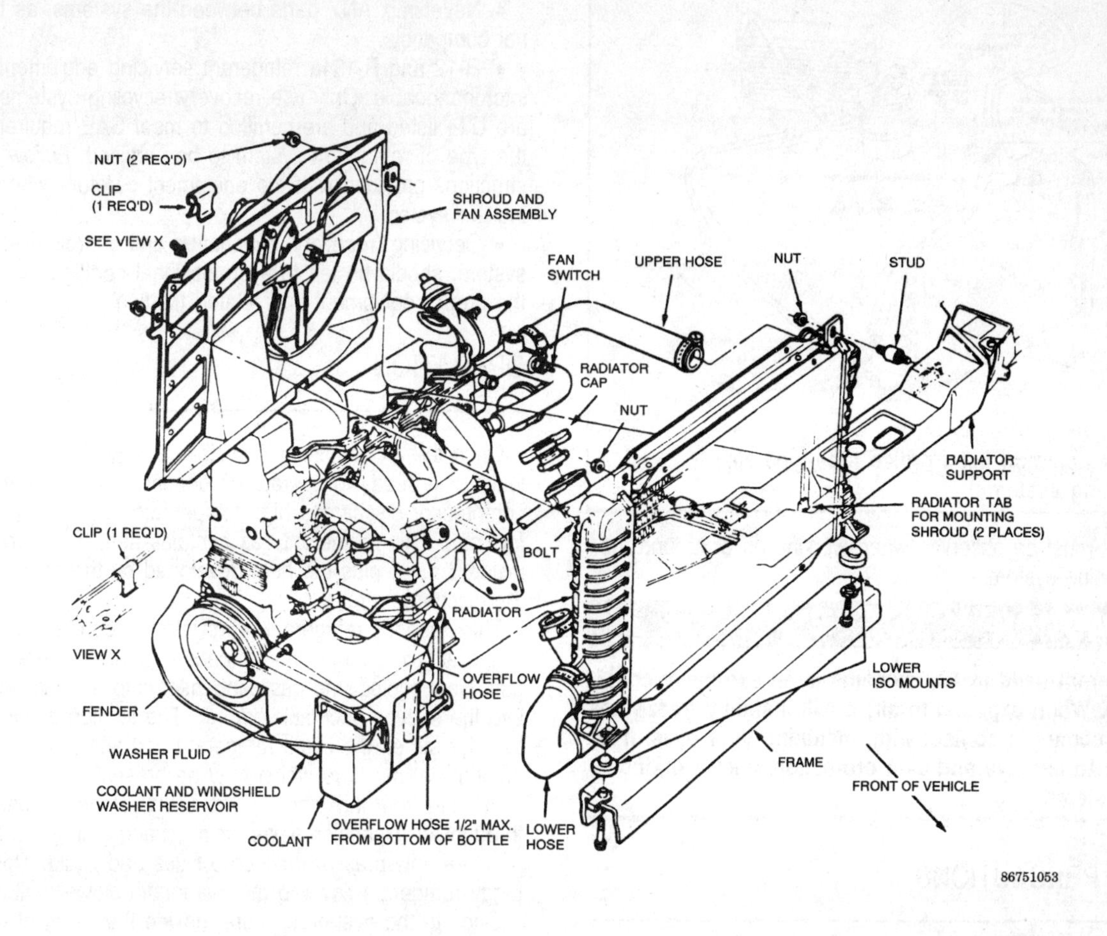

Fig. 63 A common cooling system

5. Loosen the clamps retaining the upper hose, disconnect and remove the hose.

➡If only the upper hose is to be replaced, drain off enough coolant so the level is below the hose.

6. If heater hoses need replacement, drain the coolant, loosen the clamps and remove the hose(s).

To install:

7. Installation the new hose(s) in the place of the old ones.
8. Be sure the petcock is closed. Fill the cooling system with the required protective mixture of water and coolant/antifreeze. Connect the negative battery cable.
9. Run the engine until normal operating temperature is reached. Shut off the engine and check to ensure there are no coolant leaks. When the engine cools, recheck the coolant level in the radiator, or reservoir container.

Air Conditioning System

➧ See Figure 64

The air conditioning system incorporated in your vehicle is of the fixed orifice tube-cycling clutch type. This system is designed to cycle the air conditioning compressor ON and OFF to maintain the desired cooling level and prevent evaporator freeze-up. The system components are the compressor, magnetic clutch, condenser, evaporator, suction accumulator/ drier and the connecting refrigerant lines. The system is controlled by the fixed orifice tube and a pressure cycling switch.

The refrigerant used on pre-1994 air conditioning systems is Refrigerant-12 (R-12). R-12 is a non-explosive, non-flammable, non-corrosive, has practically no odor and is heavier than air. The refrigerent used on cars produced 1994-later is R-134a, which is free of ozone-eating chlorofluorocarbons (CFC's). Although R-12 is classified as a safe refrigerant, however certain

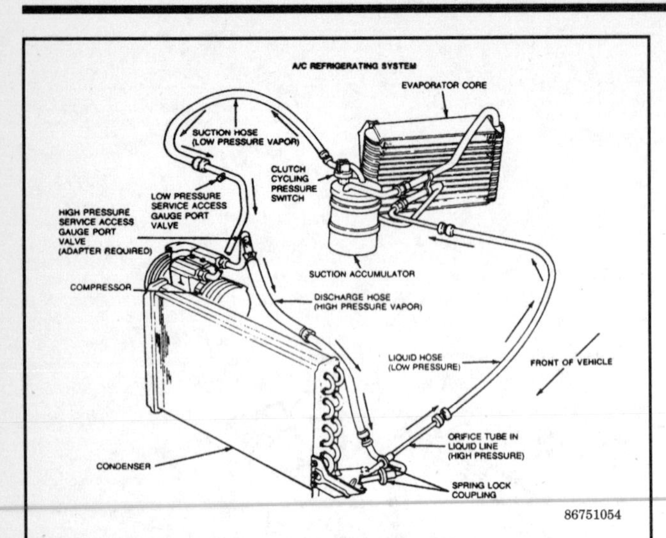

Fig. 64 A common fixed orifice tube-type air conditioning system

precautions must be observed when working on or around the air conditioning system.

CAUTION

The refrigerant used in A/C systems is an extremely cold substance. When exposed to air, it will instantly freeze any surface it comes in contact with, including your eyes. It is imperative to use eye and skin protection when working on A/C systems.

SAFETY PRECAUTIONS

➡R-12 refrigerant is a chlorofluorocarbon which, when released into the atmosphere, contributes to the depletion of the ozone layer. Ozone filters out harmful radiation from the sun. Consult the laws in your area before servicing the air conditioning system. In some states it is illegal to perform repairs involving refrigerant unless the work is done by a certified technician. It is also likely that you will not be able to purchase R-12 without proof that you are properly trained and certified to work on A/C systems.

- The refrigerant used in A/C systems is an extremely cold substance. When exposed to air, it will instantly freeze any surface it comes in contact with, including your eyes.
- Although normally non-toxic, refrigerant gas becomes highly poisonous in the presence of an open flame. One good whiff of the vapor formed by refrigerant can be fatal. Keep all forms of fire (including cigarettes) well clear of the air conditioning system.
- It has been established that the chemicals in R-12 (used on models up to and including 1993) contribute to the damage occurring in the upper atmosphere. On 1994-1995 models, R-134a refrigerant is used. Both of these refrigerant systems must be discharged using the proper recovery/recycling equipment.
- Do not mix refrigerants. They are NOT compatible.
- On R-134a systems, use only the recommended refrigerant oil designed for the R-134a compressor. Intermixing the recommended oil with any other type will result in compressor failure.
- Never mix ANY parts between the systems, as they are not compatible.
- R-12 and R-134a refrigerant servicing equipment is not interchangeable. Only use recovery/recycling systems which are U.L. listed and are certified to meet SAE requirements for the type of refrigerant system to be serviced. Follow the instructions provided with the equipment carefully when discharging the system.
- Servicing (recovery, evacuation and charging) of the A/C system, should be left to a professional certified mechanic with the proper equipment and related training.

OPERATION

Once the air conditioning system is fully charged and free of leaks, it is ready to operate on demand. When turned on, the compressor discharges high temperature and high pressure refrigerant. This refrigerant gas contains heat transferred from inside the car plus the heat developed by the compressor on the discharge stroke.

This gaseous refrigerant flows into the condenser. Because of the airflow through the condenser, heat is removed from the gas. Now cooled, the gas condenses into a liquid and flows into the suction accumulator/drier. The suction accumulator/drier stores the liquid refrigerant and filters out small amounts of moisture which may be present.

Flowing from the receiver, the liquid refrigerant passes through an expansion valve which changes it into a low temperature, low pressure mixture of gas and liquid. This cold and foggy refrigerant flows to the evaporator/blower unit.

Once in the evaporator core, (inside the cabin of the vehicle) the refrigerant is exposed to the warmer air being moved by the blower fan. The refrigerant changes to a gas within the evaporator and absorbs heat from the air being circulated by the fan. After being fully vaporized within the evaporator, the heated refrigerant gas is drawn out of the evaporator to the compressor where the cycle continues.

The efficiency of any air conditioning system is controlled not only by the system itself but by outside factors such as air temperature, humidity, forward speed of the car and amount of sunlight entering the car.

SYSTEM INSPECTION

A lot of A/C problems can be avoided by running the air conditioner at least once a week, regardless of the season. Simply let the system run for at least five minutes a week (even in the winter), and you will keep the internal parts lubricated as well as preventing the hoses from hardening.

Checking For A/C Oil Leaks

Refrigerant leaks show up only as oily areas on the various components because the compressor oil is transported around the entire system along with the refrigerant. Look for oily spots on all the hoses and lines (especially on the hose and tube connections). If there are oily deposits, the system may have a leak, and you should have it checked by a qualified mechanic.

Check the A/C Compressor Belt

The compressor drive belt should be checked frequently for tension and condition. Refer to the information earlier in this section.

Keep the A/C Condenser Clear

The condenser is mounted in front of the radiator (and is often mistaken for the radiator). It serves to remove heat from the air conditioning system and to cool the refrigerant. Proper air flow through the condenser is critical to the operation of the system.

Periodically inspect the front of the condenser for bent fins or foreign material (dirt, bugs, leaves, etc.). If any cooling fins are bent, straighten them carefully with needle nose pliers. You can remove any debris with a stiff bristle brush or hose.

REFRIGERANT LEVEL CHECKS

The easiest way to check the air conditioning is to turn it on; if cold air is supplied, the system is probably in good order. A properly charged system which is used frequently is not likely to need maintenance. It is not uncommon to find cars several years old running on the original charge in the system. If working properly, the system does not require periodic recharging.

If a problem is suspected, the first order of business when checking the refrigerant is to find the sight glass. It is usually located in the head of the suction accumulator/drier at the right side of the bulkhead. Due to the recessed locations of some receive/driers, the glass may be located in its own block, anywhere in the liquid line running to the evaporator. It should be visible by looking at the air conditioning lines running across the engine compartment near the radiator.

Once you've found it, wipe off the small glass window and proceed as follows:

1. With the engine running and the air conditioner switched on inside the vehicle, look for the flow of refrigerant through the sight glass. If the system is working properly, you'll see a continuous flow of clear refrigerant in the sight glass, with perhaps an occasional bubble if the system is operating at high temperatures.
2. Cycle the air conditioner on and off to make sure what you are seeing is refrigerant. Since the fluid is clear, it is possible to mistake a completely discharged system for one that is fully charged. Turn the system off and watch the sight glass; if there is refrigerant in the system, you'll see bubbles during the OFF cycle. If you see no bubbles when the system is running and cold air is flowing from the air vents inside, the system is OK.

➡The air conditioning system may turn itself off automatically to prevent the evaporator from freezing. If this happens while you're looking at the sight glass, don't mistake it for a failure. Wait a short while and the system will re-engage.

3. If you observe bubbles in the sight glass while the system is operating, the system is low on refrigerant. The only reason for this is a leak somewhere; have it checked by a professional. Running the air conditioning with an insufficient charge may damage the compressor.
4. Oil streaks in the sight glass are an indication of trouble. Most of the time, oil will appear as a series of streaks although it may also be a solid stream. In either case, it means reduced cooling and possibly compressor replacement.

GAUGE SETS

▶ See Figure 65

Generally described, this tool is a set of two gauges, a manifold and three hoses. By connecting the proper hoses to the car's system, the gauges can be used to "see" the air conditioning system at work. Do not use the gauge set as a means for discharging the system.

DISCHARGING, EVACUATING AND CHARGING

Discharging, evacuating and charging the air conditioning system must be performed by a properly trained and certified mechanic in a facility equipped with suitable recovery/recycling equipment meeting SAE standards.

Windshield Wiper Blades

▶ See Figure 66

At least twice a year, check the windshield washer spray and wiper operation. Check and replace worn wiper blades. If necessary, use a pin to clean out the spray nozzles.

REMOVAL & INSTALLATION

1981-90 Vehicles

▶ See Figure 67

1. Turn the ignition switch **ON**.
2. Turn the wiper control ON. Cycle the wiper arm and blade assembly; then turn the ignition switch **OFF** when the

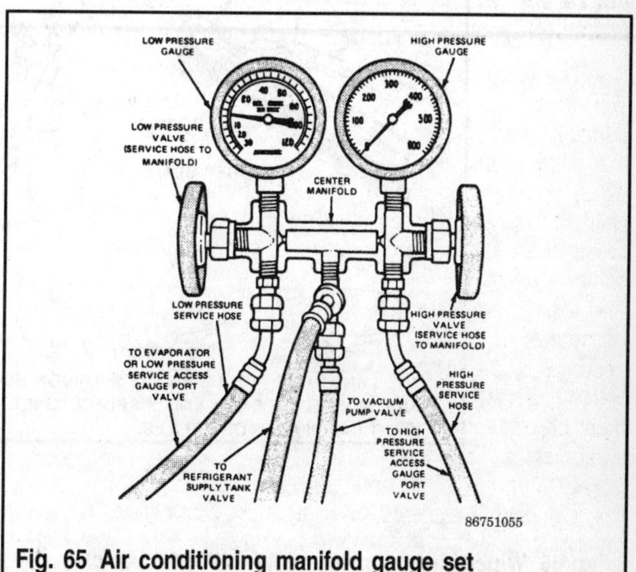

Fig. 65 Air conditioning manifold gauge set

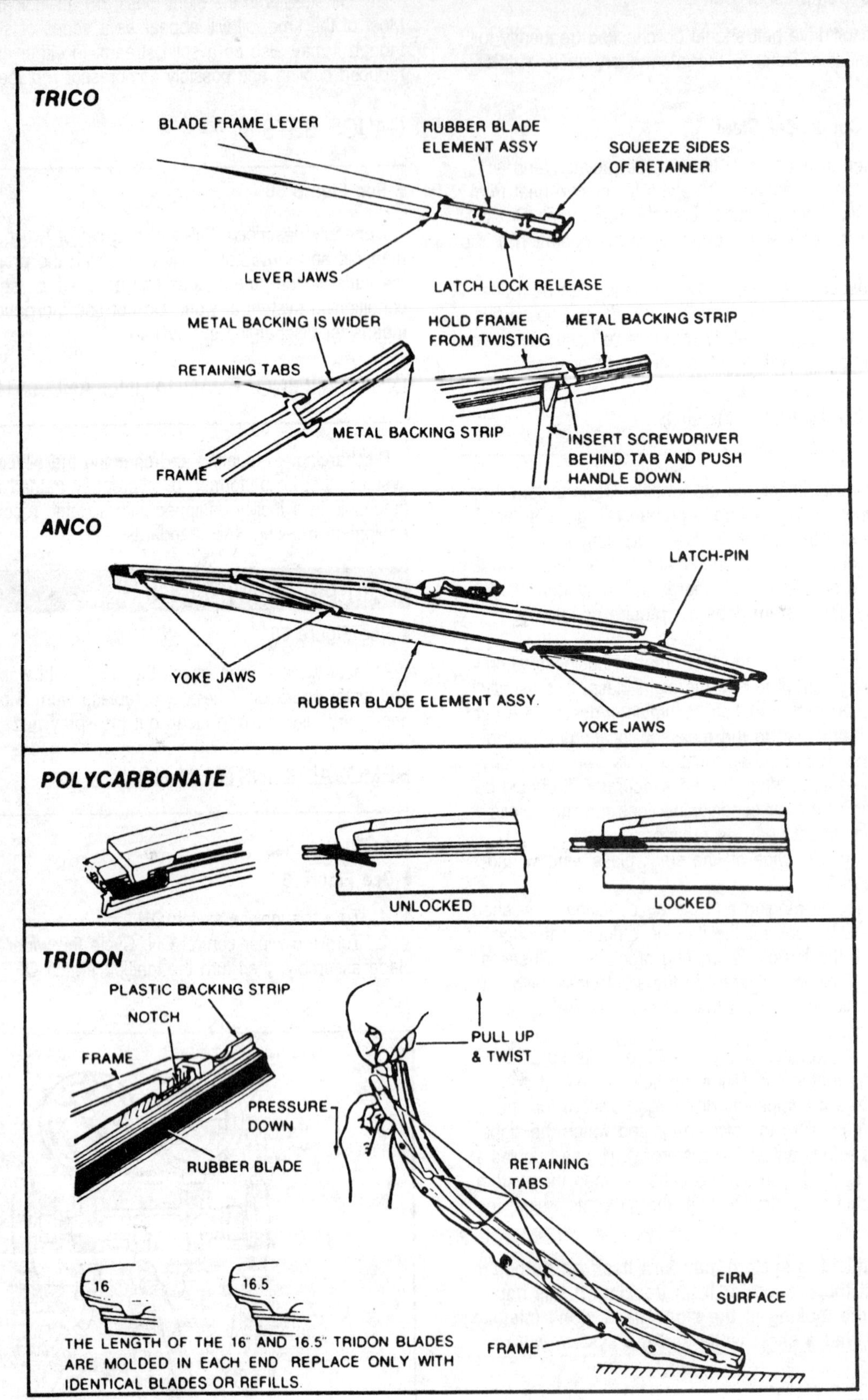

Fig. 66 Wiper insert replacement — 1981-90 vehicles

wiper arm and blade assembly is at a position on the windshield where removal can be accomplished without difficulty.

3. To remove the blades, pull the wiper arm out and away from the windshield.

- Trico® type — grasp the wiper blade assembly and pull away from the mounting pin of the wiper arm.
- Tridon® type — pull back on the spring lock, where the arm is connected to the blade, and pull the wiper blade assembly from the wiper arm.

4. Install the new wiper blade in place of the one removed.
5. Check the operation of the wipers.

1991-95 Models

See Figure 68

1. Turn the ignition switch **ON**.
2. Turn the wiper control ON. Cycle the wiper arm and blade assembly; then turn the ignition switch **OFF**when the wiper arm and blade assembly is at a position on the windshield where removal can be accomplished without difficulty.
3. Push down on the spring coil and move the wiper blade back and forth to remove it from the wiper.
4. To install, position the wiper blade and move the blade back and forth while pressing the wiper blade to the wiper arm.
5. Check the operation of the wipers.

Tires and Wheels

See Figures 69, 70 and 71

It is a good practice to perform regular wheel and tire inspection, as follow:

- Check your tires whenever you stop for fuel. Look for low or underinflated tires.
- At least once a month check all tire pressure. Check the tire pressure when cold, not after a long drive.
- At least twice a year, check for worn tires and loose wheel lug nuts. Also, check the pressure in the spare tire.

All tires are equipped with built-in tread wear indicator bars that show up as ½ in. (12.7mm) wide smooth bands across the tire when $^1/_{16}$ in. (1.5mm) of tread remains. The appear-

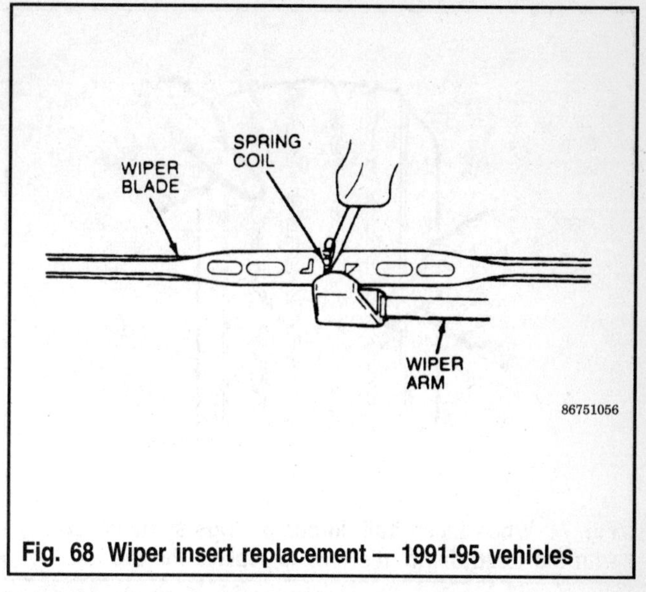

Fig. 68 Wiper insert replacement — 1991-95 vehicles

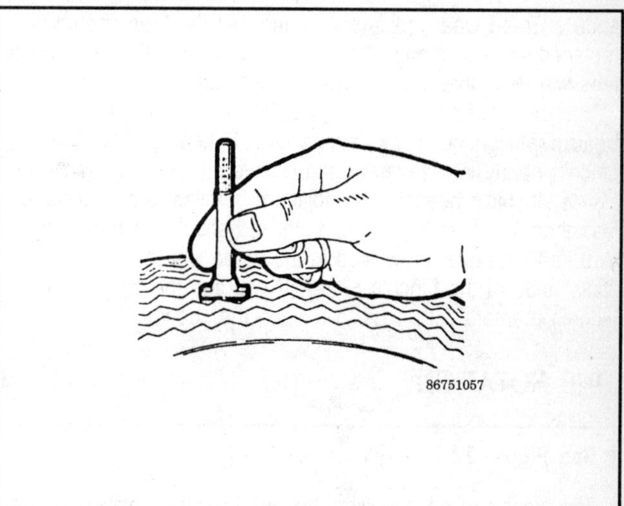

Fig. 69 Checking the remaining useful life of a tire with a tread depth gauge

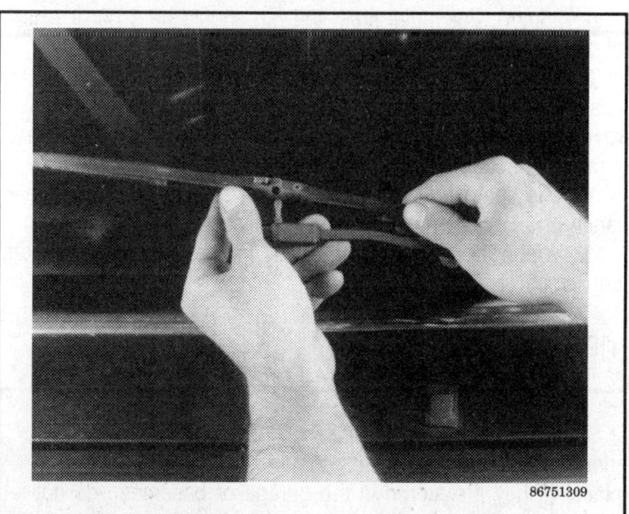

Fig. 67 Replacing the wiper inserts is a simple operation — 1988 Escort shown

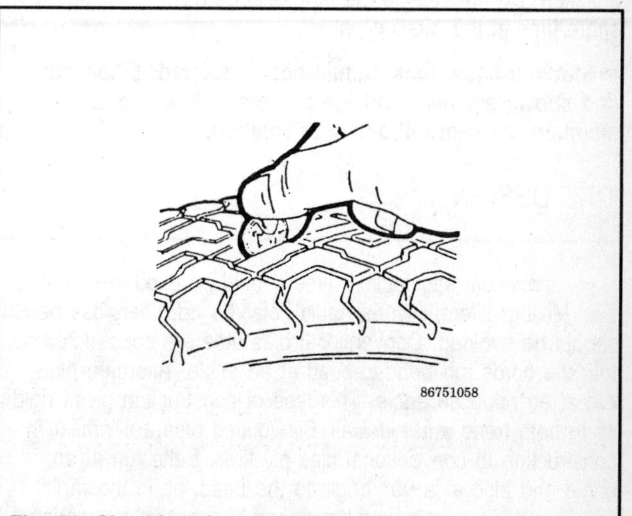

Fig. 70 Checking the remaining useful life of a tire with a Lincoln head penny

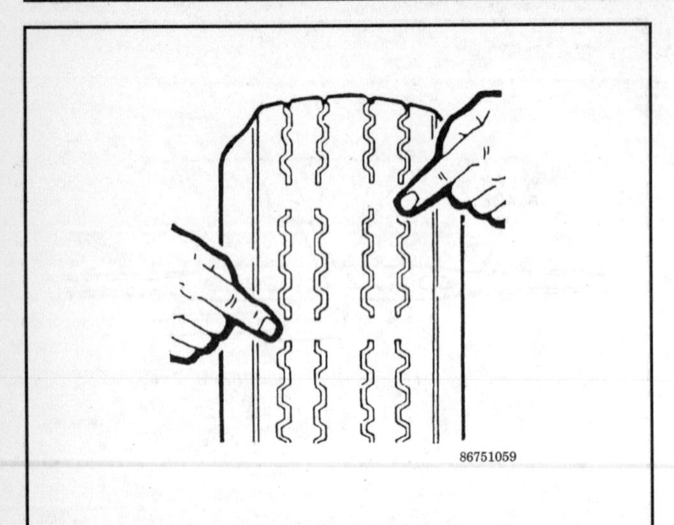

Fig. 71 When these built in bump strips show up even with the tread depth, it's time to replace the tire

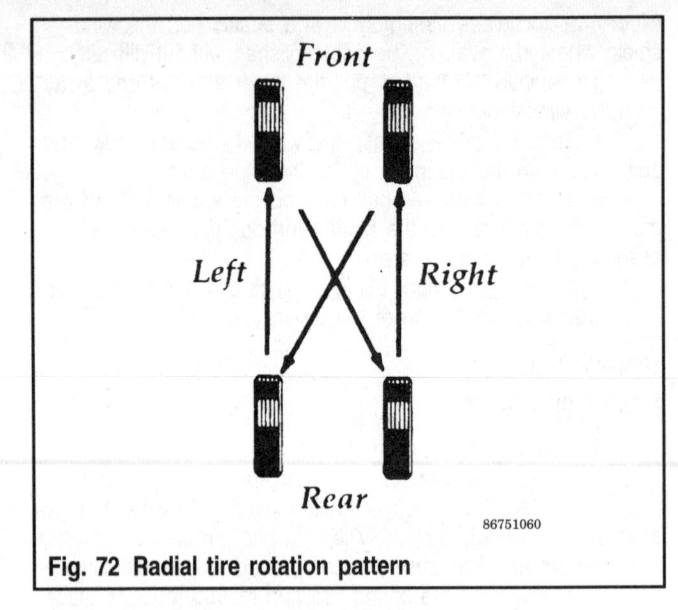

Fig. 72 Radial tire rotation pattern

ance of tread wear indicators means that the tires should be replaced. In fact, many states have laws prohibiting the use of tires with less than 1/16 in. (1.5mm) of tread.

You can check you own tread depth with an inexpensive tread depth gauge or by using a Lincoln head penny. Slip the Lincoln penny into several tread grooves. If you can see the top of Lincoln's head in two adjacent grooves, the tires have less than 1/16 in. (1.5mm) tread left and should be replaced. You can measure snow tires in the same way by using the "tails" side of the Lincoln penny. If you see the top of the Lincoln memorial, it's time to replace the snow tires.

TIRE ROTATION

See Figure 72

Tire wear can be equalized by switching the position of the tires about every 6000 miles (9600 km). Including a conventional spare in the rotation pattern can give up to 20% more tire life. If tires show uneven wear patterns, have them checked. Do not include the new SpaceSaver® or temporary spare tires in the rotation pattern.

Studded snow tires should not be rotated. When studded snows are taken off the car, mark them, so you can maintain the same direction of rotation.

TIRE DESIGN

For maximum satisfaction, tires should be used in sets of five. Mixing different types (radial, bias/belted, fiberglass belted) should be avoided. Conventional bias tires are constructed so that the cords run bead-to-bead at an angle. Alternate plies run at an opposite angle. This type of construction gives rigidity to both tread and sidewall. Bias/belted tires are similar in construction to conventional bias ply tires. Belts run at an angle and also at a 90° angle to the bead, as in the radial tire. Tread life is improved considerably over the conventional bias tire. The radial tire differs in construction, but instead of the carcass plies running at an angle of 90° to each other, they run at an angle of 90° to the bead. This gives the tread a great deal of rigidity and the sidewall a great deal of flexibility and accounts for the characteristic bulge associated with radial tires.

Remember that the tire sizes and wheel diameters should be selected to maintain ground clearance and tire load capacity equivalent to the minimum specified tire. Radial tires should always be used in sets of five, but in an emergency radial tires can be used with caution on the rear axle only. If this is done, both tires on the rear should be of radial design.

When buying new tires, give some thought to the following points, especially if you are considering a switch to larger tires or a different profile series;

1. All four tires must be of the same construction type. This rule should not be violated, radial, bias and bias belted tires should not be mixed.
2. The wheels should be the correct width for the tire. Tire dealers have charts of tire and rim compatibility. A mis-match will cause sloppy handling and rapid tire wear. The tread width should match the rim width (inside bead to inside bead) within 1 in. (25mm). For radial tires, the rim should be 80% or less of the tire (not tread) width.
3. The height (mounted diameter) of the new tires can change the speedometer accuracy, engine speed at a given road speed, fuel mileage, acceleration and ground clearance. Tire manufacturers furnish full measurement specifications.
4. The spare tire should be usable, at least for short distance and low speed operations, with new tires.
5. There should not be any body interference when loaded, on bumps or in turns.

TIRE STORAGE

Store the tires at proper inflation pressures if they are mounted on wheels. All tires should be kept in a cool, dry place. If they are stored in the garage or basement, do not let them stand on a concrete floor; set them on strips of wood.

Tire Size Comparison Chart

"Letter" sizes			Inch Sizes	Metric-inch Sizes		
"60 Series"	"70 Series"	"78 Series"	1965–77	"60 Series"	"70 Series"	"80 Series"
			5.50-12, 5.60-12	165/60-12	165/70-12	155-12
		Y78-12	6.00-12			
		W78-13	5.20-13	165/60-13	145/70-13	135-13
		Y78-13	5.60-13	175/60-13	155/70-13	145-13
			6.15-13	185/60-13	165/70-13	155-13, P155/80-13
A60-13	A70-13	A78-13	6.40-13	195/60-13	175/70-13	165-13
B60-13	B70-13	B78-13	6.70-13	205/60-13	185/70-13	175-13
			6.90-13			
C60-13	C70-13	C78-13	7.00-13	215/60-13	195/70-13	185-13
D60-13	D70-13	D78-13	7.25-13			
E60-13	E70-13	E78-13	7.75-13			195-13
			5.20-14	165/60-14	145/70-14	135-14
			5.60-14	175/60-14	155/70-14	145-14
			5.90-14			
A60-14	A70-14	A78-14	6.15-14	185/60-14	165/70-14	155-14
	B70-14	B78-14	6.45-14	195/60-14	175/70-14	165-14
	C70-14	C78-14	6.95-14	205/60-14	185/70-14	175-14
D60-14	D70-14	D78-14				
E60-14	E70-14	E78-14	7.35-14	215/60-14	195/70-14	185-14
F60-14	F70-14	F78-14, F83-14	7.75-14	225/60-14	200/70-14	195-14
G60-14	G70-14	G77-14, G78-14	8.25-14	235/60-14	205/70-14	205-14
H60-14	H70-14	H78-14	8.55-14	245/60-14	215/70-14	215-14
J60-14	J70-14	J78-14	8.85-14	255/60-14	225/70-14	225-14
L60-14	L70-14		9.15-14	265/60-14	235/70-14	
	A70-15	A78-15	5.60-15	185/60-15	165/70-15	155-15
B60-15	B70-15	B78-15	6.35-15	195/60-15	175/70-15	165-15
C60-15	C70-15	C78-15	6.85-15	205/60-15	185/70-15	175-15
	D70-15	D78-15				
E60-15	E70-15	E78-15	7.35-15	215/60-15	195/70-15	185-15
F60-15	F70-15	F78-15	7.75-15	225/60-15	205/70-15	195-15
G60-15	G70-15	G78-15	8.15-15/8.25-15	235/60-15	215/70-15	205-15
H60-15	H70-15	H78-15	8.45-15/8.55-15	245/60-15	225/70-15	215-15
J60-15	J70-15	J78-15	8.85-15/8.90-15	255/60-15	235/70-15	225-15
	K70-15		9.00-15	265/60-15	245/70-15	230-15
L60-15	L70-15	L78-15, L84-15	9.15-15			235-15
	M70-15	M78-15				255-15
		N78-15				

Note: Every size tire is not listed and many size comparisons are approximate, based on load ratings. Wider tires than those supplied new with the vehicle, should always be checked for clearance.

86751061

TIRE INFLATION

Tire inflation is generally the most ignored item of auto maintenance, a potentially costly and hazardous oversight. When underinflated, tires wear unevenly requiring early replacement, and the contact patch of a poorly inflated tire is less stable and therefore provides less grip. An underinflated tire is more prone to bottoming-out over bumps and potholes leading to bent wheels, flats, or both. Increased load (such as when carrying passengers, cargo or both) will exacerbate any of the above problems. Studies have shown gasoline mileage can drop as much as 0.8% for every 1 psi (6.9 kPa) of underinflation.

Two items should be a permanent fixture in every glove compartment: a tire pressure gauge and a tread depth gauge. Check the tire pressure, including the spare, regularly with a pocket type gauge or preferably, a dial gauge. (Avoid dropping a dial gauge or exposing it to sudden shocks, as this will cause it to go out of calibration.) Kicking the tires won't tell you a thing, and the gauge on a service station air hose is notoriously inaccurate.

A plate located on the left door will tell the proper pressure for the tires. Ideally, inflation pressure should be checked BEFORE driving when the tires are COLD. (When driven on, tires flex, create friction, and the air inside them expands increasing pressure.) Every 10°F (5.5°C) rise or drop in temperature means a difference of 1 psi (6.9 kPa), which explains why the tire seems to lose air on a cold night or into the Fall and Winter seasons. When it is impossible to check the tires COLD, allow for pressure build-up due to heat. If the **HOT** pressure exceeds the COLD pressure by more than 15 psi (103.5 kPa), reduce vehicle speed, load or both. This is a sure sign that excess internal heat is being created in the tire, and temperature could continue to rise. If the heat approaches the temperature at which the tire was cured during manufacture, the tread could separate from the body.

:*:*CAUTION

Never attempt to counteract excessive pressure build-up by bleeding off air pressure (letting some air out). This will produce the opposite of the desired effect by allowing more tire flex and friction, further raising the tire temperature.

➡Before starting a long trip with lots of luggage, you can add about 2-4 psi (14-28 kPa) to the tires to make them run cooler but never exceed the maximum inflation pressure on the side of the tire.

CARE OF SPECIAL WHEELS

To clean aluminum wheels, wheel covers and wheel ornamentation, use a mild soap and water solution and rinse thoroughly with clean water. Do not use steel wool, abrasive type cleaner or a strong detergents containing high alkaline or caustic agents to the protective coating and discoloration may be a result. Automatic car wash tire brushes may damage aluminum and styled road wheel protective coatings. Before using such a service, be sure abrasive type brushes are not being used.

FLUIDS AND LUBRICANTS

Fuel and Engine Oil Recommendations

➧ See Figures 73 and 74

GASOLINE ENGINES

It is important to use fuel of the proper octane rating in your vehicle. Octane rating is based on the quantity of anti-knock compounds added to the fuel and it determines the speed at which it burns. The fuel recommended for your vehicle is "unleaded gasoline" having a Research Octane Number (RON) of 91, or an Antiknock Index of 87. Leaded gasoline will quickly interfere with the operation of the catalytic converter and will render the converter useless. This condition will cause the emission levels (hydrocarbons and carbon monoxide) to exceed the manufacturer's specifications. It will also void your warranty and cost a considerable amount of money for catalytic converter replacement.

Using a high quality unleaded gasoline will help maintain the driveability, fuel economy and emissions performance of your vehicle. A properly formulated gasoline will be comprised of well refined hydrocarbons and chemical additives and will perform the following:

- Minimize varnish, lacquer and other induction system deposits.
- Prevent gum formation or other deterioration.
- Protect the fuel tank and other fuel system components from corrosion or degradation.
- Provide the correct seasonally and geographically adjusted volatility. This will provide easy starting in the winter, will avoid fuel system icing and it will avoid vapor lock in the summer.

In addition, the fuel will be free of water debris and other impurities. Some driveability deterioration on multi-port electronically fuel injected vehicles can be traced to continuous use of certain gasolines which may have insufficient amounts of detergent additives to provide adequate deposit control protection.

DIESEL ENGINES

Fuel makers produce two grades of diesel fuel — No. 1 and No. 2-for use in automotive diesel engines. Generally speaking, No. 2 fuel is recommended over No. 1 for driving in temperatures above 20°F (7°C). In fact, in many areas, No. 2 diesel is

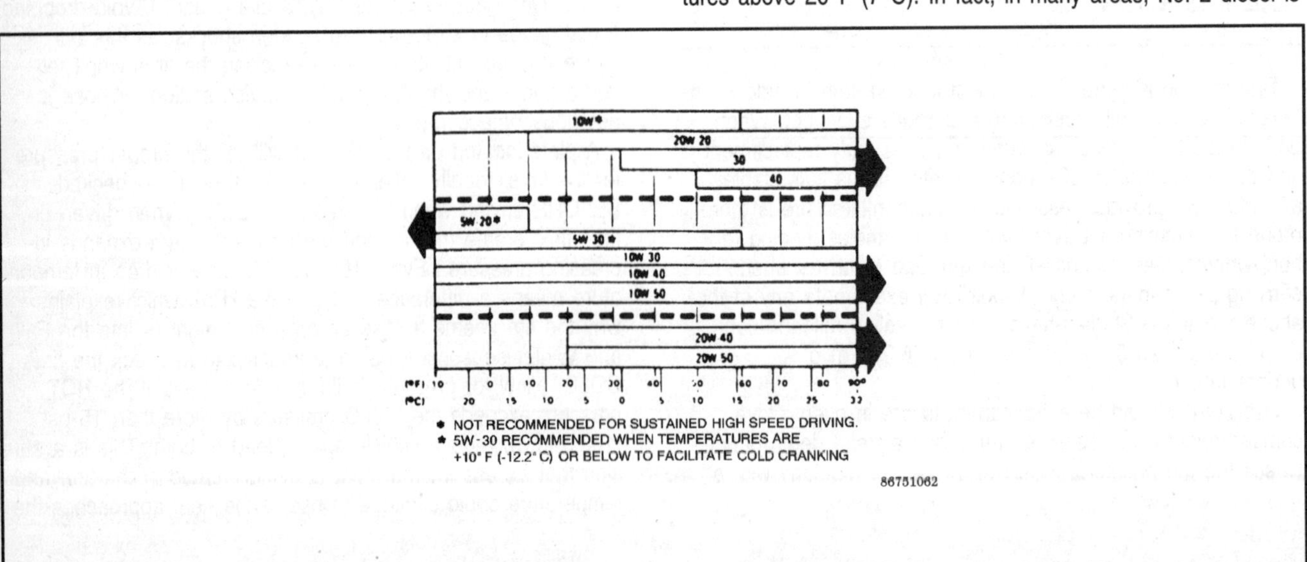

Fig. 73 Engine oil viscosity recommendation — 1981-83

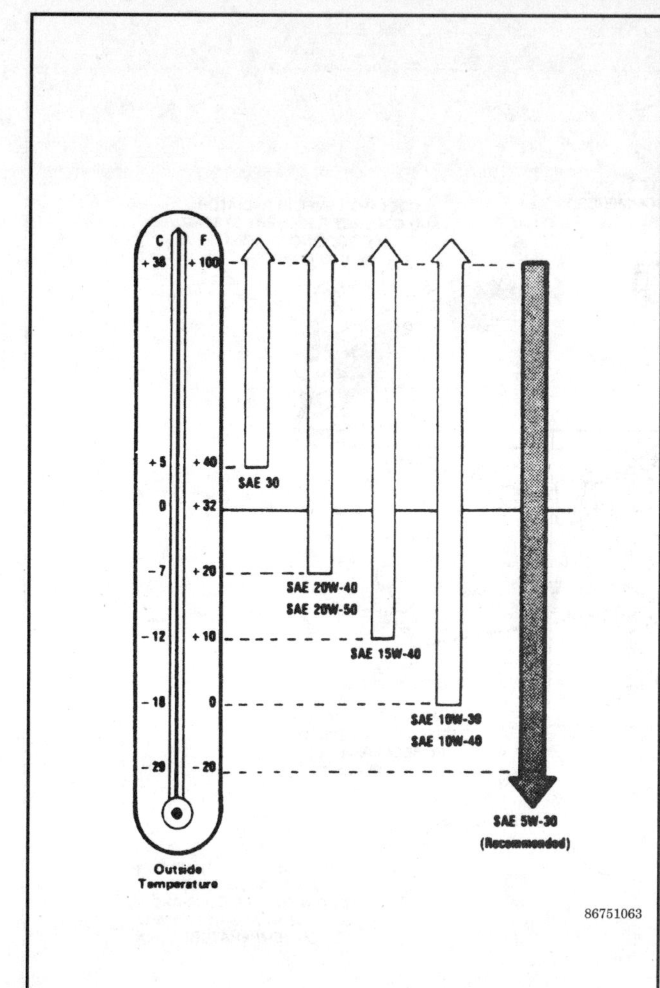

Fig. 74 Engine oil viscosity recommendation — 1984-95 models

the only fuel available. By comparison, No. 2 diesel fuel is less volatile than No. 1 fuel, and gives better fuel economy. No. 2 fuel is also a better injection pump lubricant.

Two important characteristics of diesel fuel are its cetane number and its viscosity.

The cetane number of a diesel fuel refers to the ease with which a diesel fuel ignites. High cetane numbers mean that the fuel will ignite with relative ease or that it ignites well at low temperatures. Naturally, the lower the cetane number, the higher the temperature must be to ignite the fuel. Most commercial fuels have cetane numbers that range from 35 to 65. No. 1 diesel fuel generally has a higher cetane rating than No. 2 fuel.

Viscosity is the ability of a liquid, in this case diesel fuel, to flow. Using straight No. 2 diesel fuel below 20°F (7°C) can cause problems, because this fuel tends to become cloudy, meaning wax crystals begin forming in the fuel. The temperature of 20°F (7°C) is often call the clouding point for No. 2 fuel. In extremely cold weather, No. 2 fuel can stop flowing altogether. In either case, fuel flow is restricted, which can result in a no start condition or poor engine performance. Fuel manufacturers often winterize No. 2 diesel fuel by using various fuel additives and blends (No. 1 diesel fuel, kerosene, etc.) to lower its wintertime viscosity. Generally speaking, though, No. 1 diesel fuel is more satisfactory in extremely cold weather.

Do not use number 1-D diesel fuel in temperatures above +20°F (7°C) as damage to the engine may result. Also fuel economy will be reduced with the use of number 1-D diesel fuel.

The 2.0L diesel engines are equipped with an electric fuel heater to prevent cold fuel problems. For best results in cold weather use winterized number 2-D diesel fuel which is blended to minimize cold weather operation problems.

****CAUTION**

DO NOT add gasoline, gasohol, alcohol or cetane improvers to the diesel fuel. Also, DO NOT use fluids such as ether (starting fluid) in the diesel air intake system. The use of these liquids or fluids will cause damage to the engine and/or fuel system.

Gasoline engines are required to use engine oil meeting API classification SG or SG/CC or SG/CD. Viscosity grades 10W-30 or 10W-40 are recommended on models before 1984 and 5W-30 or 10W-30 on models 1984 and later. See the viscosity to temperature chart in this section.

Diesel engines require different engine oil from those used in gasoline engines. Besides doing the things gasoline engine oil does, diesel oil must also deal with increased engine heat and the diesel blow-by gases, which create sulfuric acid, a high corrosive.

If your vehicle is equipped with a diesel engine, be sure to check your owner's manual for the recommended oil viscosity to be used. There should be a diesel engine supplement included with your owner's manual.

Engine

OIL LEVEL CHECK

See Figures 75, 76, 77, 78, 79, 80 and 81

It is a good idea to check the engine oil each time or at least every other time you fill your gas tank.

1. Be sure your vehicle is on a level surface. Shut off the engine and wait for a few minutes to allow the oil to drain back into the oil pan.
2. Remove the engine oil dipstick and wipe clean with a rag.
3. Reinsert the dipstick and push it down until it is fully seated in the tube.
4. Remove and check the oil level indicated on the dipstick. If the oil level is below the lower mark, add one quart (0.9L).
5. If you wish, you may carefully fill the oil pan to the upper mark on the dipstick with less than a full quart (0.9L). Do not, however, add a full quart (0.9L) when it would overfill the crankcase (level above the upper mark on the dipstick). The excess oil will generally be consumed at an excessive rate even if no damage to the engine seals occurs.

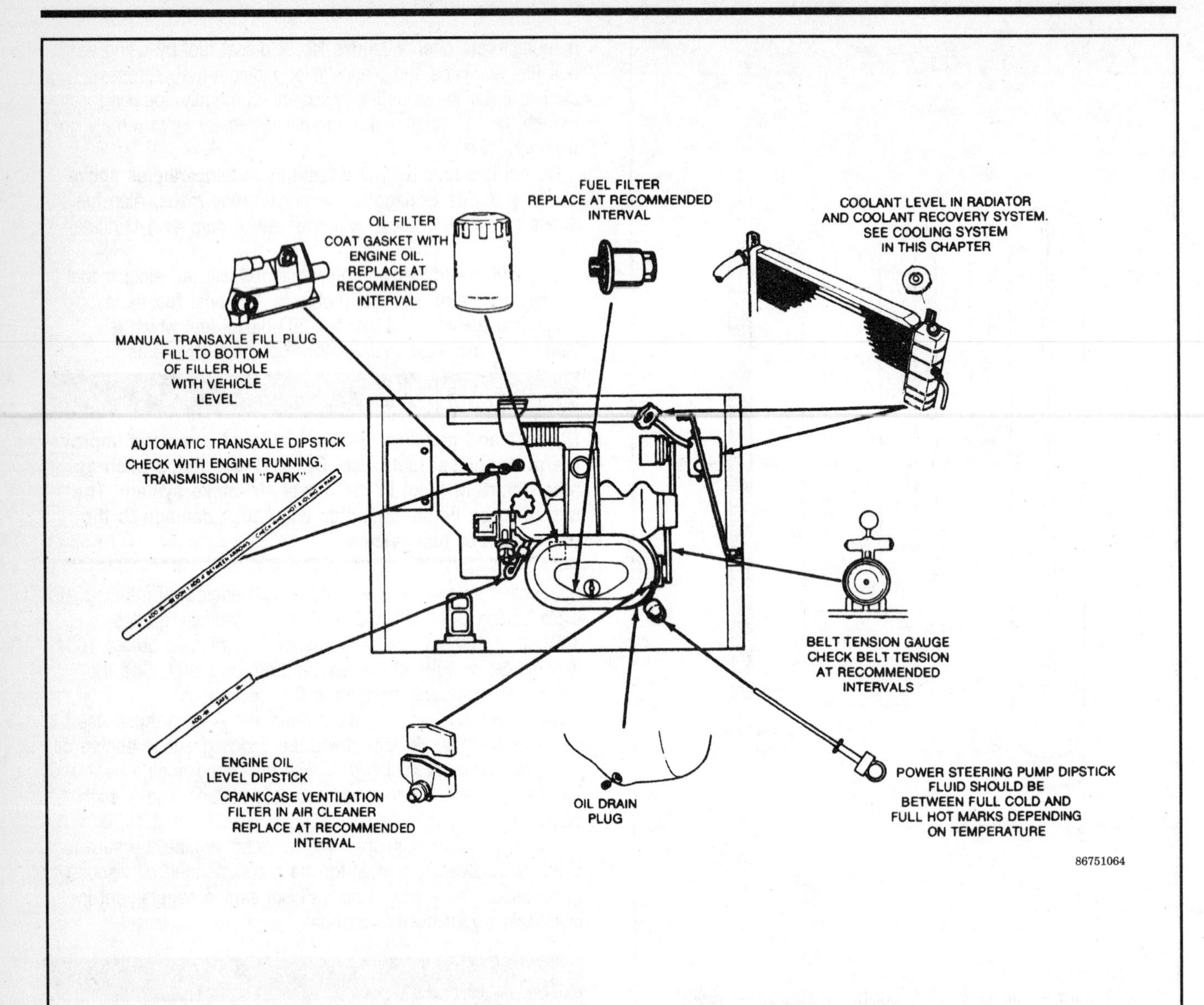

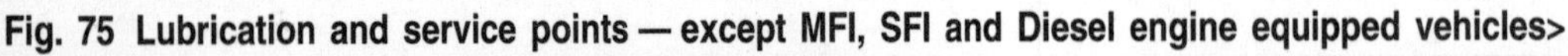

Fig. 75 Lubrication and service points — except MFI, SFI and Diesel engine equipped vehicles>

Fig. 76 Check the oil level on the dipstick at every gasoline stop

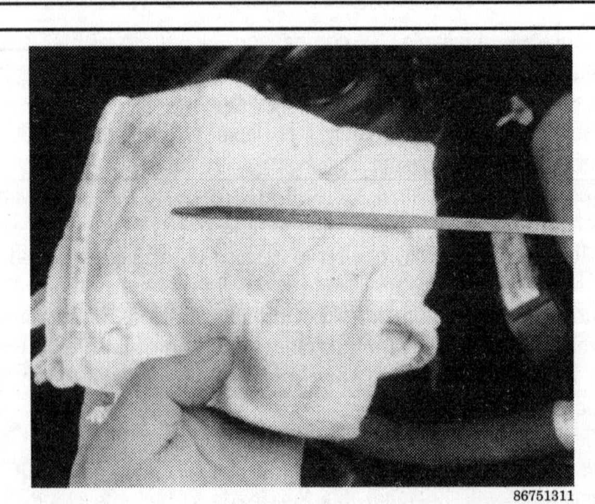

Fig. 77 After the engine has been turned off a few minutes, pull and wipe the dipstick with a clean rag and re-insert to measure the oil level

86751312

Fig. 78 Pour oil through the filler cap on the rocker arm cover

OIL AND FILTER CHANGE

➧ **See Figures 82, 83 and 84**

If your 1981-84 vehicle is operated under normal conditions, the manufacturer recommends changing the engine oil and oil filter every 12 months or 7,500 miles (12,000 km), whichever comes first. However, if this vehicle is operated under severe service, it is recommended that the engine oil and oil filter be changed every three months or 3,000 miles (4800 km), whichever comes first.

The recommended engine oil and filter service interval on 1985 and later vehicles is every three months or 3000 miles

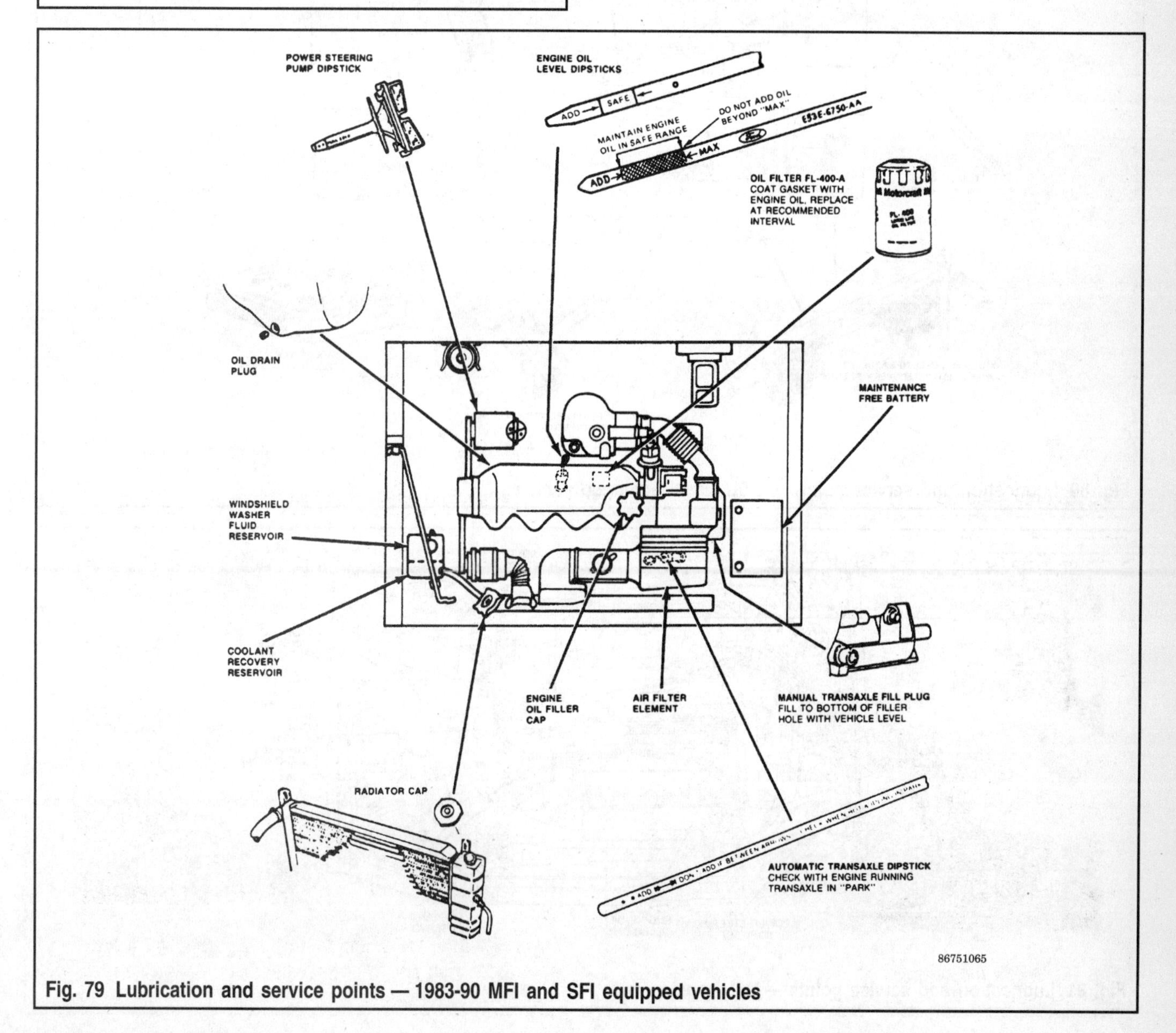

86751065

Fig. 79 Lubrication and service points — 1983-90 MFI and SFI equipped vehicles

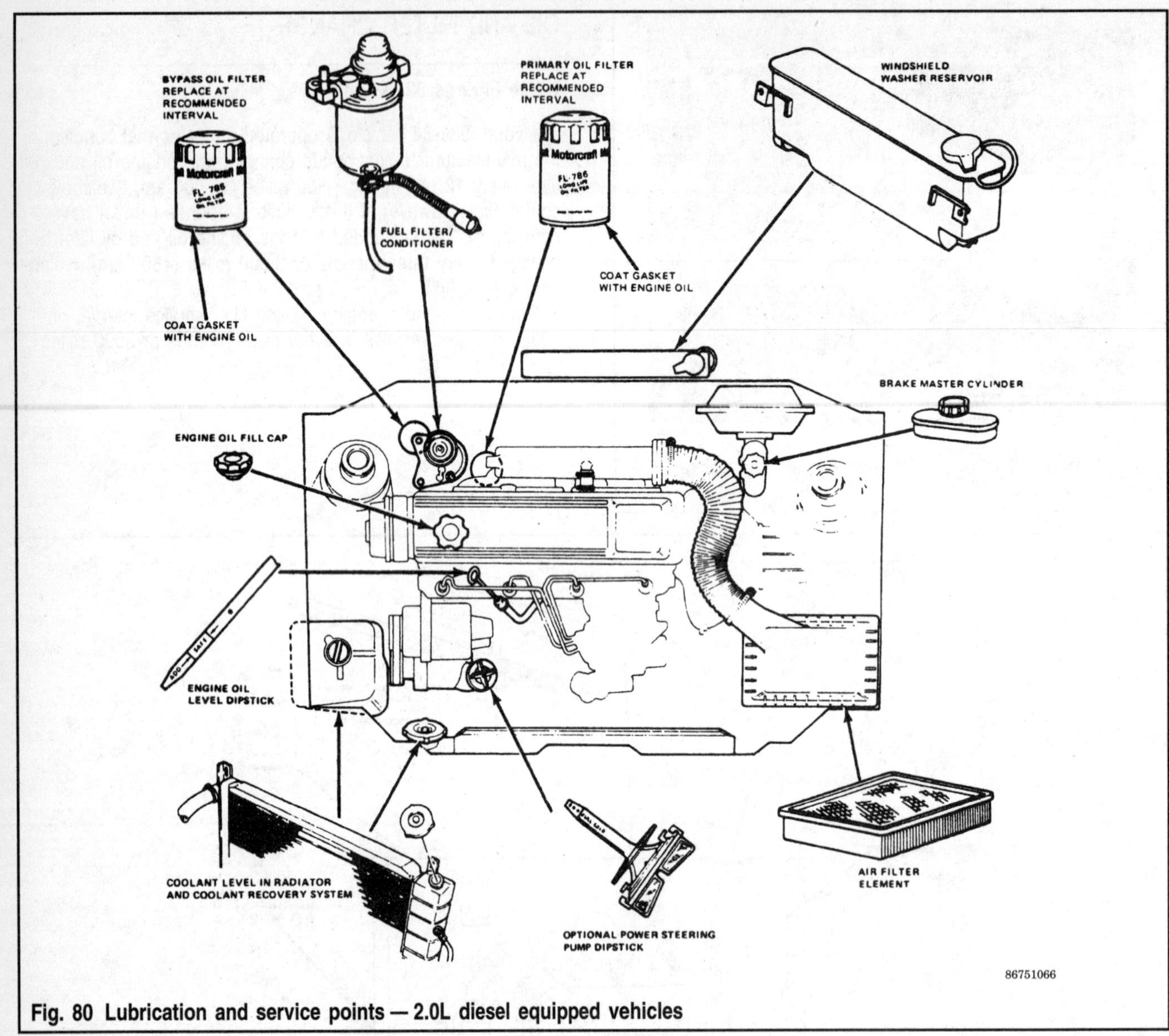

Fig. 80 Lubrication and service points — 2.0L diesel equipped vehicles

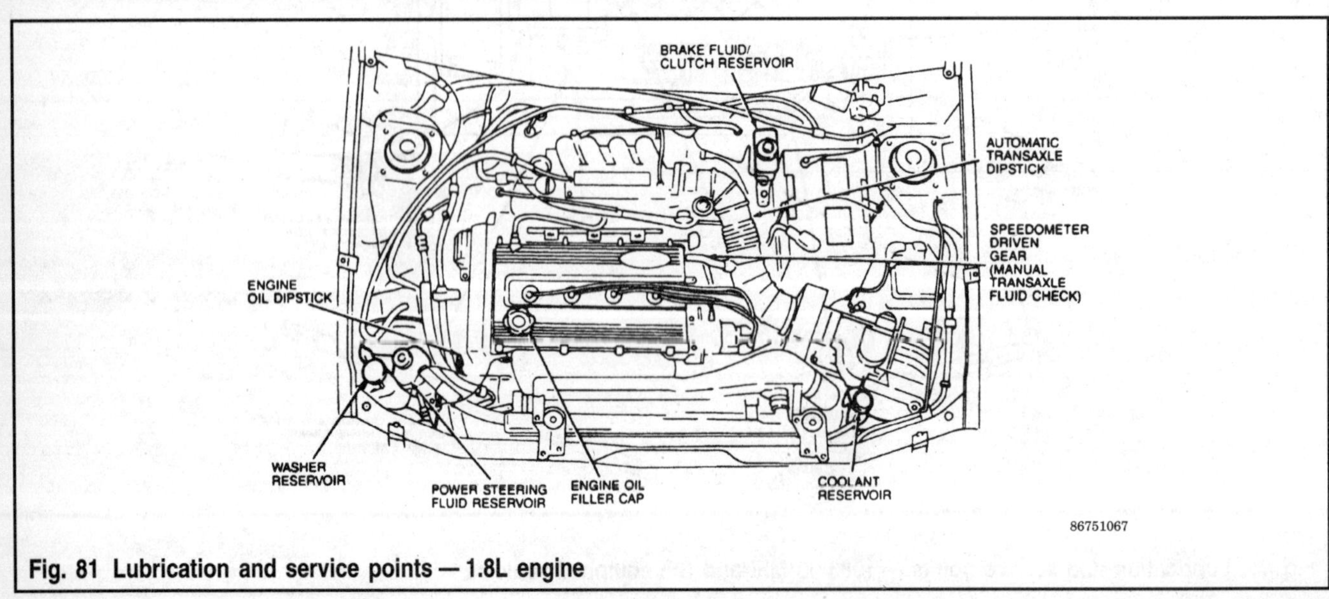

Fig. 81 Lubrication and service points — 1.8L engine

(4800 km), which ever comes first. If operated in severe dusty conditions, more frequent intervals may be required.

1. Make sure the engine is at normal operating temperature (this promotes complete draining of the old oil).

****CAUTION**

The EPA warns that prolonged contact with used engine oil may cause a number of skin disorders, including cancer. You should make every effort to minimize your exposure to used engine oil. Protective gloves should be worn when changing the oil. Wash your hands and any other exposed skin areas as soon as possible after exposure to used engine oil. Soap and water, or waterless hand cleaner should be used.

2. Apply the parking brake and block the wheels. Raise and support the vehicle safely.

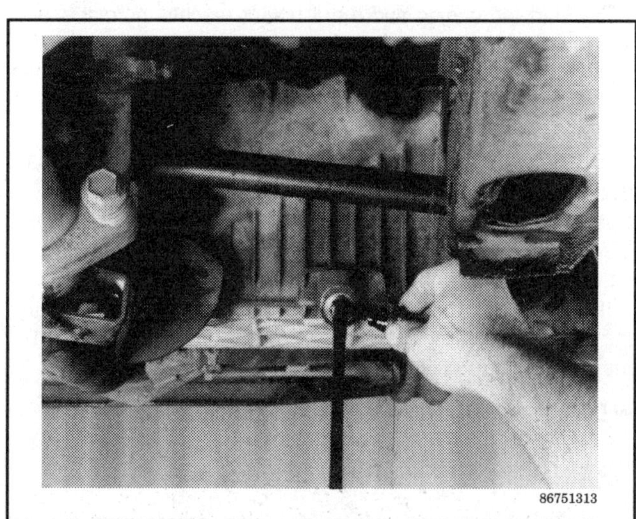

86751313

Fig. 82 With the vehicle level, drain the oil completely from the pan

86751314

Fig. 83 Remove the filter and let the oil drain from this location as well

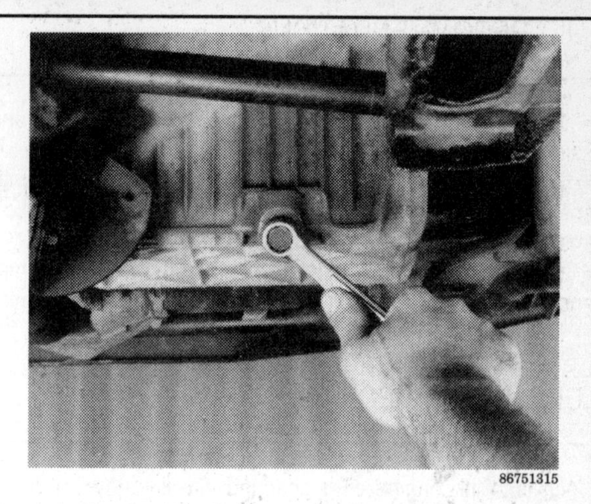

86751315

Fig. 84 Tighten the drain plug bolt but to not over-torque — be especially careful with aluminum oil pans as shown

3. Place a suitable drain pan (approximately a gallon and a half capacity) under the engine oil pan drain plug. Use the proper size wrench, loosen and remove the plug. Allow all the old oil to drain. Wipe the pan and the drain plug with a clean rag. Inspect the drain plug gasket, replace if necessary.

4. Reinstall and tighten the drain plug. DO NOT OVERTIGHTEN.

5. Move the drain pan under the engine oil filter. Use a strap wrench and loosen the oil filter (do not remove), allow the oil to drain. Unscrew the filter the rest of the way by hand. Use a rag, if necessary, to keep from burning your fingers. When the filter comes loose from the engine, turn the mounting base upward to avoid spilling the remaining oil.

6. Wipe the engine filter mount clean with a rag. Coat the rubber gasket on the new oil filter with clean engine oil, applying it with a finger. Carefully start the filter onto the threaded engine mount. Turn the filter until it touches the engine mounting surface. Tighten the filter, by hand, ½ turn more or as recommended by the filter manufacturer.

7. Lower the vehicle. Refill the crankcase with 4 quarts (3.79L) of engine oil. Replace the filler cap and start the engine. Allow the engine to idle and check for oil leaks. Shut off the engine, wait for several minutes, then check the oll level with the dipstick. Add oil if necessary.

➡Store the used oil in a suitable container, made for that purpose, until you can find a service station or garage that will accept the used oil for recycling.

Manual Transaxle

The manual transaxle (MTX) is a front wheel drive powertrain unit. The transmission and differential are housed in a two piece light weight aluminum alloy housing which is bolted to the back of the engine.

The transaxle is fully synchronized in all forward gears with reverse provided by a sliding gear. All gears, except reverse, are helical cut for quiet operation.

The MTX and engine assembly is mounted transversely in the vehicle.

FLUID RECOMMENDATIONS

- 1981-82 manual transaxles — Motorcraft Automatic Transmission Fluid (ATF) — Type F
- 1983-88 manual transaxles — Motorcraft Type F Automatic Transmission Fluid (ATF) or Motorcraft Dexron®II Automatic Transmission Fluid (ATF)
- 1989-95 manual transaxles — Motorcraft Type F Automatic Transmission Fluid (ATF) or MERCON® Automatic Transmission Fluid (ATF)

FLUID LEVEL CHECK

Each time the engine oil is changed, the fluid level of the transaxle should be checked. The vehicle must be evenly supported on jackstands (front and back) or on a lift, if available. To check the fluid, remove the filler plug, located on the upper front (driver's side) of the transaxle with a 9/16 in. wrench or a 3/8 inch. extension and rachet.

➡The filler plug has a hex-head or it has a flat surface with a cut-in 3/8 in. square box. Do not mistake any other bolts for the filler. Damage to the transaxle could occur if the wrong plug is removed.

The oil level should be even with the edge of the filler hole or within 1/4 in. (6mm) of the hole. If the oil level is not as specified, add the recommended lubricant until the proper level is reached.

➡A rubber bulb syringe, such as a turkey baster, will be helpful in adding the recommended lubricant.

DRAIN AND REFILL

Changing the fluid in a manual transaxle is not necessary under normal operating conditions. However, the fluid levels should be checked at normal intervals. The only two ways to drain the oil from the transaxle is by removing it and then turning the transaxle on its side to drain or by using a suction tool. When refilling the transaxle, the lubricant level should be even with the edge of the filler hole or within 1/4 inch. (6mm) of the hole.

Automatic Transaxle

The automatic transaxle (ATX) is a front wheel drive powertrain unit. The transmission and differential are housed in a compact, one-piece case and bolted to the back of the engine. The 1991-95 Escort/Tracer is equipped with an electronically controlled automatic transaxle (4EAT). An electronic and mechanical feature control all forward gear shifting speed and torque converter lockup, for quietness and economy.

The ATX and engine assembly is mounted transversely in the vehicle.

FLUID RECOMMENDATIONS

- 1981-85 automatic transaxles — Motorcraft Dexron®II Automatic Transmission Fluid (ATF)
- 1985½-87 automatic transaxles — Motorcraft Type H Automatic Transmission Fluid (ATF)
- 1988-95 automatic transaxles — Motorcraft MERCON® Automatic Transmission Fluid (ATF)

FLUID LEVEL CHECK

➧ See Figures 85, 86, 87, 88 and 89

A dipstick is provided in the engine compartment to check the level of the automatic transaxle.

1. Position the vehicle on level surface.
2. Apply the parking brake and place the transaxle selector lever in the **P** position.
3. Start the engine and run it until it reaches normal operating temperatures.
4. Move the selector lever through all detent positions, then return to the **P** position. DO NOT TURN OFF THE ENGINE DURING THE FLUID LEVEL CHECK.
5. Clean all dirt from the dipstick cap before removing the dipstick. Remove the dipstick and wipe clean. Reinsert the dipstick making sure it is fully seated. Pull the dipstick out of the tube and check the fluid level. The fluid level should be between the FULL and ADD marks.

If necessary, use a long funnel to add enough fluid through the dipstick tube/filler to bring the level to the FULL mark on the dipstick. Use only the specified lubricant.

➡Do not overfill. Make sure the dipstick is fully seated.

DRAIN AND REFILL/PAN AND FILTER SERVICE

➧ See Figures 90 and 91

If your vehicle is equipped with an automatic transaxle and the region in which you live has severe cold weather, a multi-viscosity automatic transaxle fluid should be used. Ask your auto parts retailer about the availability of MV Automatic Transaxle Fluid.

If you operate you vehicle under severe conditions, such as dusty conditions, tow a trailer, have extended idling or low speed operation, it may be necessary to change the ATX fluid at regular intervals (20 months, 20,000 miles or more often).

Use of fluid other than specified could result in transaxle malfunctions and/or failure.

1. Raise the vehicle and safely support it on jackstands or a lift, if available.
2. Place a suitable drain pan underneath the transaxle oil pan. Loosen the oil pan mounting bolts and allow the fluid to drain until it reaches the level of the pan flange. Remove the attaching bolts, leaving one end attached so that the pan will tip and the rest of the fluid will drain.
3. Remove the oil pan. Thoroughly clean the pan. Remove the old gasket. Make sure that the gasket mounting surfaces are clean.

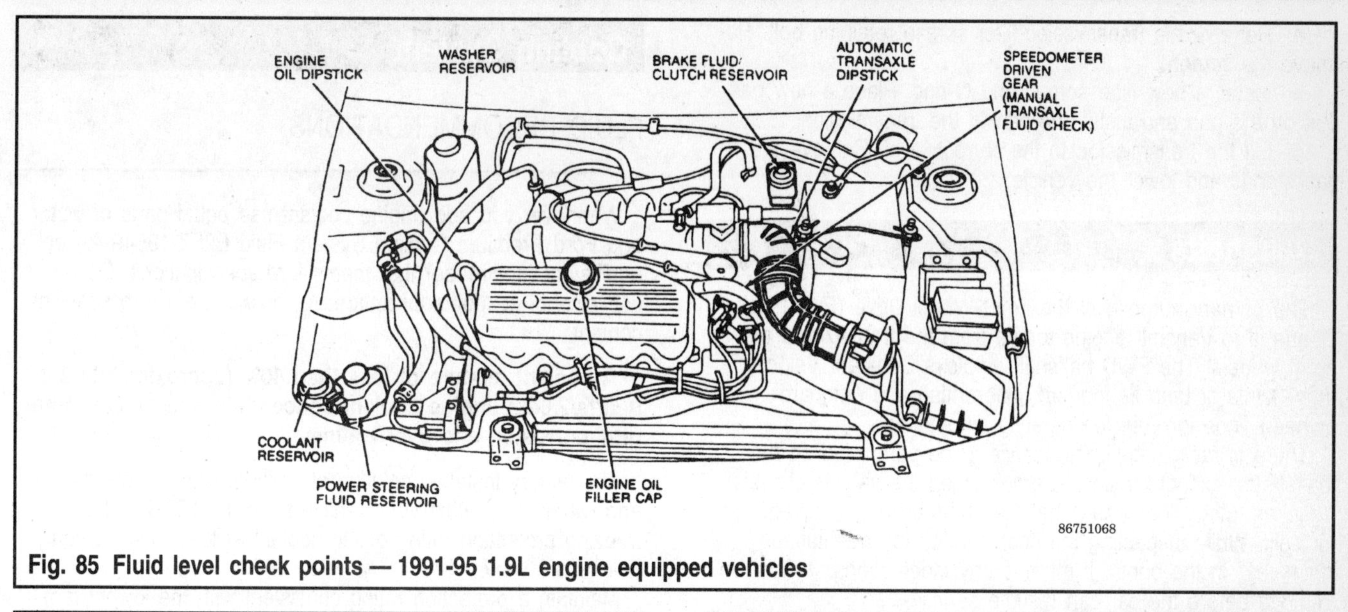

Fig. 85 Fluid level check points — 1991-95 1.9L engine equipped vehicles

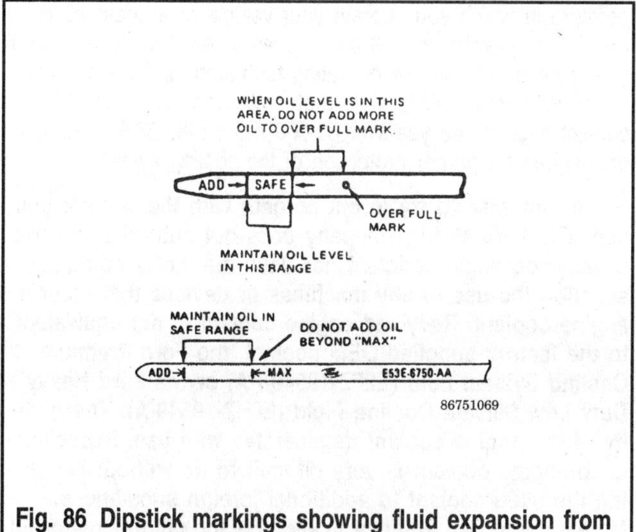

Fig. 86 Dipstick markings showing fluid expansion from "room" to normal operating temperature

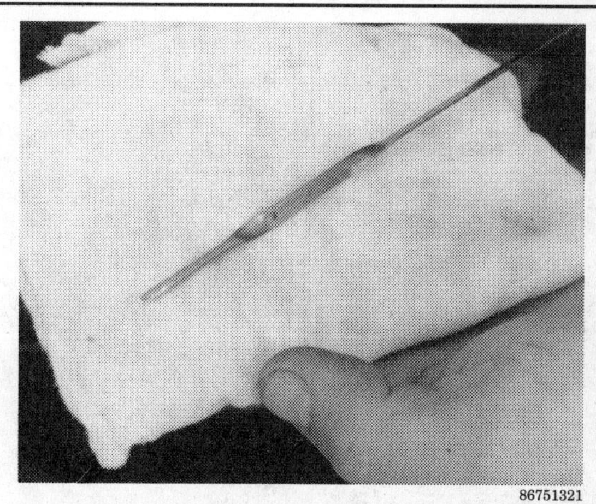

Fig. 88 The fluid level is checked by wiping the dipstick, re-inserting and reading the fluid level against the dipstick markings

Fig. 87 Check the dipstick for the automatic transmission fluid when the engine is running and warmed up

Fig. 89 Add ATF using a long funnel to reach the dipstick tube/filler

4. Remove the transmission filter screen retaining bolt. Remove the screen.
5. Install a new filter screen and O-ring. Place a new gasket on the pan and install the pan to the transmission.
6. Fill the transmission to the correct level. Remove the jackstands and lower the vehicle.

Halfshafts

The primary purpose of the Front Wheel Drive (FWD) halfshafts is to transmit engine torque from the transaxle to the front wheels. The FWD halfshaft employs Constant Velocity (CV) joints at both its inboard (differential) and outboard (wheel) ends for vehicle operating smoothness.

There is no maintenance service to be performed on the halfshafts; except for an inspection when the vehicle chassis requires lubrication. Verify that the boots are not cracked, torn or split. While inspecting the boots, watch for indentations "dimples" in the boots. If there is any indentations, it must be remove before the car can resume service.

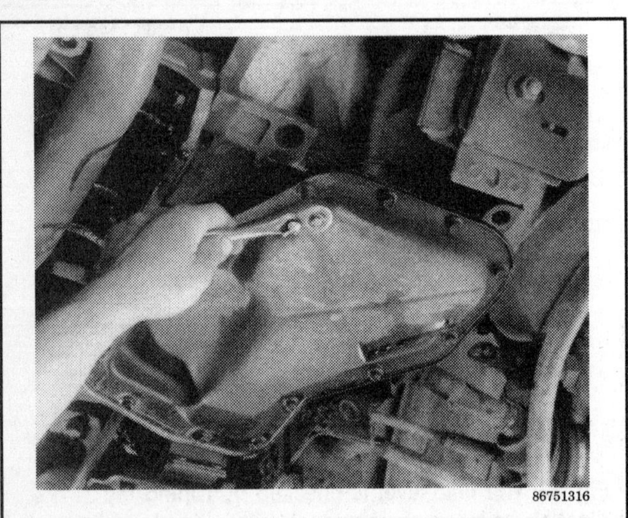

Fig. 90 Remove the bolts supporting the transaxle fluid pan (which in this case is damaged and leaking)

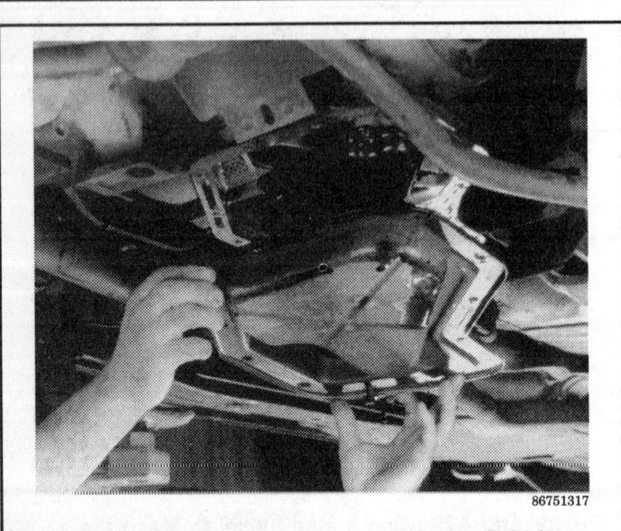

Fig. 91 Carefully lower the pan to drain the fluid into a suitable container

Cooling System

FLUID RECOMMENDATIONS

Whenever you add engine coolant use equal parts of water and Ford Premium Cooling System Fluid E2FZ-19549-AA or equivalent (antifreeze) that meets ford specifications. Do not use alcohol or methanol antifreeze, or mix them with specified coolant.

➡A coolant mixture of less than 40% (approximately 3.0 quarts/2.84L) engine coolant concentrate may result in engine corrosion and overheating.

The factory installed solution of Ford cooling system fluid and water will protect your vehicle to 35°F (1.7°C). Check the freezing protection rating of the coolant at least once a year, just before winter.

Maintain a protection rating consistent with the lowest temperature in which you operate your vehicle or at least 20°F (-6.7°C) to prevent engine damage as a result of freezing and to ensure proper engine operating temperature. Rust and corrosion inhibitors tend to deteriorate with time. Changing the coolant every three years or 30,000 miles (48,000 km) is recommended for proper protection of the cooling system.

➡It is not wise to try to cut corners with the coolant you use. The Ford Motor Company does not authorize the use of recycled engine coolant nor does the motor company sanction the use of any machines or devices that recycle engine coolant. Recycled engine coolant is not equivalent to the factory supplied OEM coolant, the Ford Premium Cooling System fluid (E2FZ-19549-AA) or the Ford Heavy Duty Low Silicate Cooling Fluid (E6HZ-19549-A). The quality of the engine coolant degenerates with use. Recycling used engine coolant is very difficult to do without exposing the used coolant to additional foreign substances. Merely adding an additive to the coolant will not restore it. Always use new engine coolant that meets the Ford coolant specifications for the engine being serviced.

⁂CAUTION

The disposal of all used engine coolant must always be done in accordance with all applicable Federal, State and Local laws and regulations.

FLUID LEVEL CHECK

➧ See Figures 92 and 93

The cooling system of your vehicle utilizes, among other components, a radiator and an expansion tank. When the engine is running, heat is generated. The rise in temperature causes the coolant to expand and this increases internal pressure. When a certain pressure is reached, a pressure relief valve in the radiator filler cap (pressure cap) is lifted from its seat and allows coolant to flow through the radiator filler neck, down a hose, and into the expansion reservoir.

When the system temperature and pressure are reduced in the radiator, the water in the expansion reservoir is siphoned back into the radiator.

Check the level in the coolant recovery reservoir at least one month. With the cold engine the level must be maintained at or above the ADD mark. At normal operating temperatures, the coolant level should be at the FULL HOT mark. If the level is below the recommended level a 50/50 mixture of coolant (antifreeze) and water should be added to the reservoir. If the reservoir is empty, add the coolant to the radiator and then fill the reservoir to the required level.

⁂CAUTION

The cooling fan motor is controlled by a temperature-sensitive switch. The fan may come on and run when the engine is off. It will continue to run until the correct temperature is reached. Avoid getting your fingers, loose clothing, etc. caught in the fan blades. Never remove the radiator cap under any circumstances when the engine is operating. Before removing the cap, switch the engine OFF and wait until it has cooled. Even then, use extreme care when removing the cap from a hot radiator. Wrap a thick cloth around the cap and turn it slowly to the first stop. Step back while the pressure is released from the cooling system. When you are sure all the pressure has been released, press down on the cap, still with a cloth, turn and remove it.

Check the coolant level in the radiator at least once a month, only when the engine is cool. Whenever coolant checks are made, check the condition of the radiator cap rubber seal. Make sure it is clean and free of any dirt particles. Rinse off with water if necessary. When replacing the radiator cap, also make sure that the radiator filler neck seat is clean. Check that the overflow hose in the reservoir is not kinked and is inserted to within ½ in. (13mm) of the bottom of the bottle.

Anytime you add coolant to the radiator, use a 50/50 mixture of coolant and water. If you have to add coolant more than once a month, or if you have to add more than 1 quart (0.9L) at a time, have the cooling system checked for leaks.

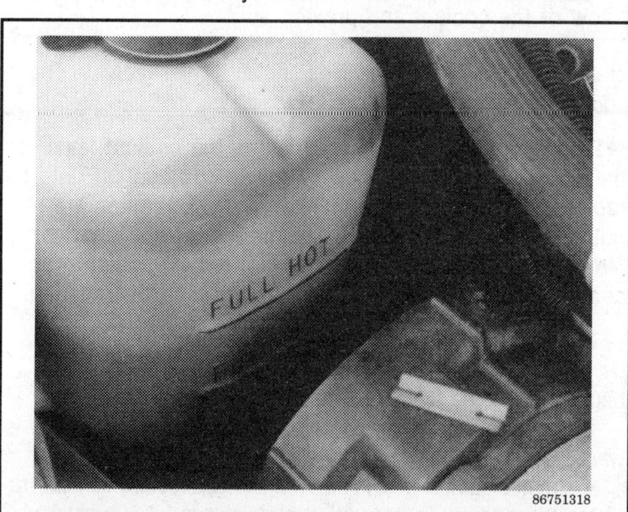

86751318

Fig. 92 Check the coolant overflow tank by reading the appropriate markings on the bottle

86751319

Fig. 93 Check the fluid level in the radiator by removing the cap once the engine is cold

DRAIN AND REFILL

➧ See Figures 94, 95, 96, 97 and 98

To drain the coolant, connect an 18 in. (457mm) long, ⅜ in. (9.5mm) inside diameter hose to the nipple on the drain valve located on the bottom of the radiator. With the engine cool, set the heater control to the maximum heat position, remove the radiator cap and open the drain valve or remove allen head plug $^{3}/_{16}$ (in.) allowing the coolant to drain into a container. When all of the coolant is drained, remove the ⅜ in. hose and close the drain valve. There may be some coolant left in the engine block cavities, to drain the block, located the engine block coolant drain plug on the side of the engine block and drain the coolant out. Prior to reinstalling any coolant plugs or drain valves be sure to coat the threads with a suitable thread sealer or Teflon® tape.

⁂CAUTION

When draining the coolant, keep in mind that cats and dogs are attracted by ethylene glycol antifreeze, and are quite likely to drink any that is left in an uncovered container or in puddles on the ground. This will prove fatal in sufficient quantity. Always drain the coolant into a sealable container. Coolant may be reused unless it is contaminated or several years old.

➡If there is any evidence of rust or scaling in the cooling system, the system should be flushed thoroughly before refilling.

Refill the coolant system as follows:

1. Install block drain plug, if removed and close the draincock. With the engine in the **OFF** position, add 50 percent

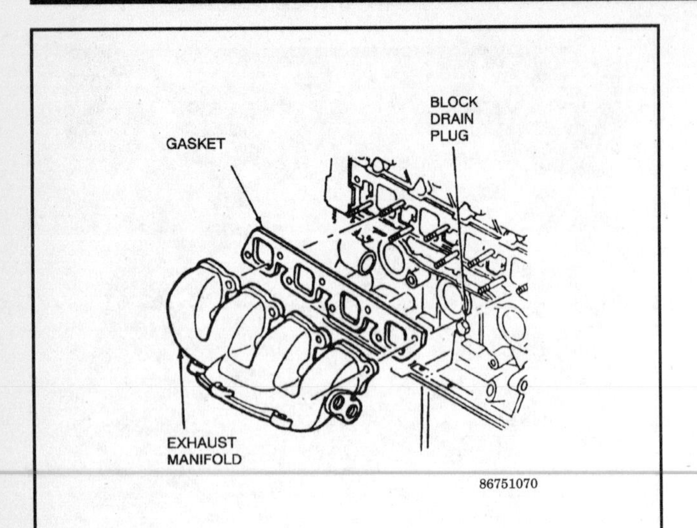

Fig. 94 Engine block drain plug — 1.6L engine

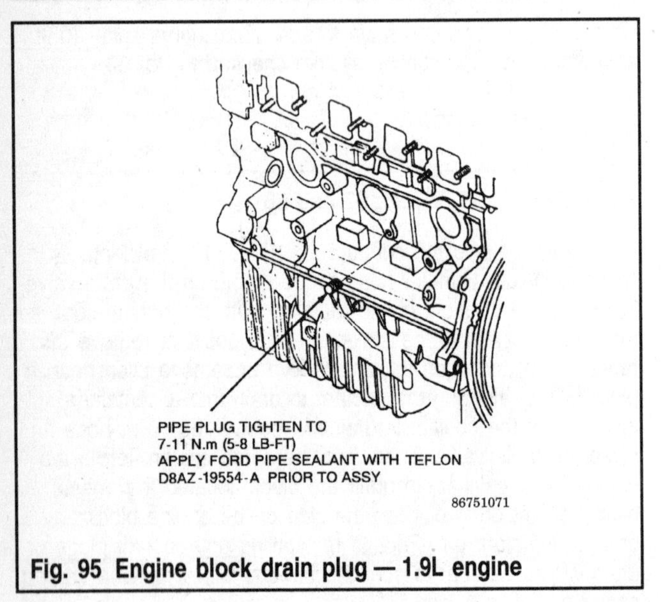

Fig. 95 Engine block drain plug — 1.9L engine

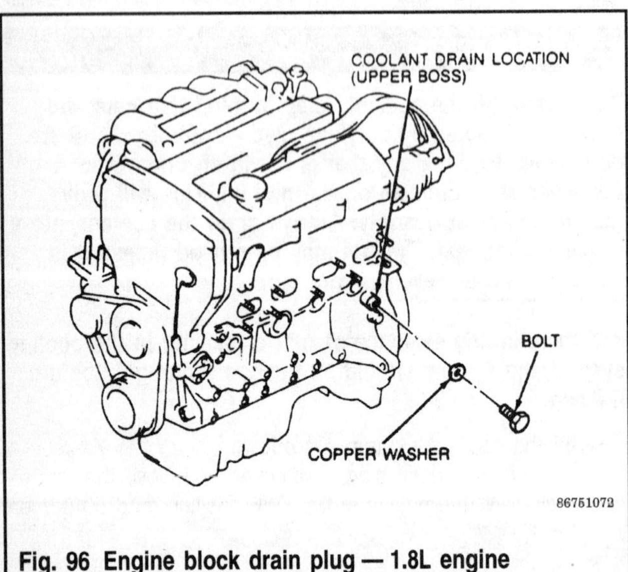

Fig. 96 Engine block drain plug — 1.8L engine

86751323

Fig. 97 Drain the coolant from the radiator using a 3/8 in. (9.5mm) inside diameter hose

Fig. 98 Refill the radiator using a funnel to direct the flow of the coolant and prevent spills

of system's capacity of specified coolant to the radiator. Then add water until the radiator is full.

➡Be sure to wait several minutes as the coolant level in the radiator drops, continue to slowly add coolant until the radiator remains full (approximately 10-15 minutes are required to fill the system). A coolant mixture of less than 30% — approximately 2.1 quarts (2L) engine coolant concentrate may result in engine corrosion and overheating.

2. Reinstall the radiator cap to the pressure relief position by installing the cap to the fully installed position and then backing off to the first stop.

3. Start and idle the engine until the upper radiator hose is warm.

4. Immediately shut **OFF** the engine. Cautiously remove radiator cap and add water until the radiator is full. Reinstall radiator cap securely.

5. Add coolant to the ADD mark on the reservoir, then fill to the **FULL HOT** mark with water.

6. Check system for leaks and return the heater temperature control to normal position.

FLUSHING AND CLEANING THE SYSTEM

1. Drain the cooling system as outlined in this section. Then add water until the radiator is full.
2. Reinstall the radiator cap to the pressure relief position by installing the cap to the fully installed position and then backing off to the first stop.
3. Start and idle the engine until the upper radiator hose is warm.
4. Immediately shut off the engine. Cautiously drain the water by opening the draincock.
5. Repeat Steps 1-4 as many times as necessary until nearly clear water comes out of the radiator. Allow remaining water to drain and then close the petcock.
6. Disconnect the overflow hose from the radiator filler neck nipple.
7. Remove the coolant recovery reservoir from the fender apron and empty the fluid. Flush the reservoir with clean water, drain and install the reservoir and overflow hose and clamp to the radiator filler neck.
8. Refill the coolant system as outlined in this section.
9. If the radiator has been removed, it is possible to back-flush the system as follows:
   a. Back-flush the radiator, ensuring the radiator cap is in position. Turn the radiator upside down. Position a high pressure water hose in the bottom hose location and back-flush. The radiator internal pressure must not exceed 20 psi.
   b. Remove the thermostat housing and thermostat. Back-flush the engine by positioning a high pressure hose into the engine through the thermostat location and back-flush the engine.

➡If the radiator is showing signs of rust and wear, it may be a good idea while the radiator is out of the vehicle, to thoroughly clean and get the cooling fins free from debris. Then using a suitable high temperature rustproof engine paint, paint the exterior of the radiator assembly.

Brake Master Cylinder

FLUID RECOMMENDATION

The brake fluid to be used in the vehicles covered by this manual should be only DOT 3 brake fluid. Ford recommends specifically Ford High Performance DOT 3 Brake Fluid C6AZ-19542-AA or equivalent.

FLUID LEVEL CHECK

See Figures 99 and 100

The brake master cylinder is located under the hood, on the left side firewall. Before removing the master cylinder reservoir cap, make sure the vehicle is positioned on a level surface. Wipe clean the cover and the area around the master cylinder, before opening it up. When satisfied nothing will contaminate the fluid, then open the master cylinder to inspect the fluid.

To open the master cylinder cover for earlier cars without translucent (see through) reservoirs: Pry the retaining clip off to the side and remove the master cylinder cover. If the level of the brake fluid is within 1/4 in. (6mm) of the top, the fluid level is OK. If the level is less than half the volume of the reservoir, check the brake system for leaks. Leaks in the brake system most commonly occur at the wheel cylinders or at the front calipers. Leaks at brake lines or the master cylinder can also be cause brake fluid loss.

There is a rubber diaphragm at the top of the master cylinder cap. As the fluid level lowers due to normal brake shoe wear or leakage, the diaphragm takes up the space. This is to prevent the loss of brake fluid from the vented cap and to help stop contamination by dirt. After filling the master cylinder to the proper level with brake fluid (Type DOT 3), but before replacing the cap, fold the rubber diaphragm up into the cap, then replace the cap on the reservoir and snap the retaining clip back in place.

On later vehicles with the translucent master cylinder reservoir, check the brake fluid by visually inspecting the fluid level against the level markings on its side. It should be between the MIN and the MAX level marks embossed on the side of the reservoir. If the level is low, remove the reservoir cap and fill to the MAX level with DOT 3 brake fluid.

The level will decrease with accumulated mileage. This is a normal condition associated with the wear of the disc brake linings. If the fluid is excessively low, have the brake system checked.

➡To avoid the possibility of brake failure that could result in property damage or personal injury, do not allow the master cylinder to run dry. Never reuse brake fluid that has been drained from the hydraulic system or fluid that has been allowed to stand in an open container for an extended period of time.

Clutch Master Cylinder

The 1991-95 Escort/Tracer is equipped with a hydraulic clutch control system. The system consists of a fluid reservoir, master cylinder, pressure line and a slave cylinder. The hydraulic clutch control system is tapped into the brake master cylinder reservoir and utilizes brake fluid for its operation.

FLUID RECOMMENDATIONS

Use a **DOT** 3 brake fluid meeting Ford specifications such as Ford Heavy Duty Brake Fluid.

FLUID LEVEL CHECK

Inspecting the brake master cylinder fluid level through the translucent master cylinder reservoir. It should be between the **MIN** and the **MAX** level marks embossed on the side of the

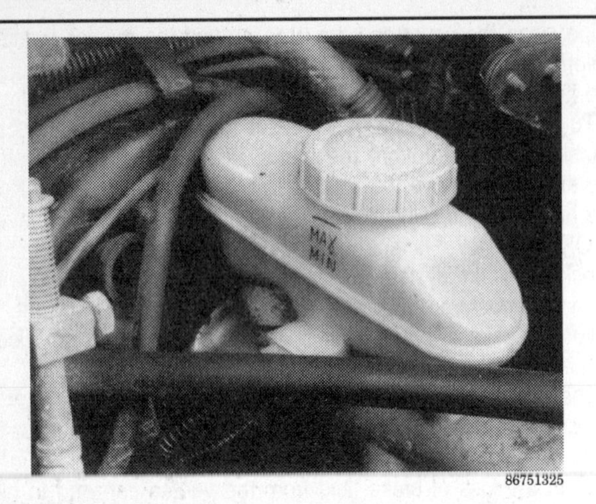

Fig. 99 The brake fluid level should be checked periodically by looking at it through the translucent reservoir (on cars so equipped) — 1988 Escort shown

Fig. 100 Add brake fluid through the reservoir filler after wiping possible contaminants away with a clean cloth

reservoir. If the level is found to be low, remove the reservoir cap and fill to the **MAX** level with DOT 3 brake fluid.

➡Never reuse brake fluid that has been drained from the hydraulic system or fluid that has been allowed to stand in an open container for an extended period of time.

Power Steering Pump Reservoir

FLUID RECOMMENDATION

Use only power steering fluid that meets Ford Specifications such as Motorcraft Type **F** Automatic Transmission and Power Steering Fluid or an equivalent type **F** fluid which displays a Ford registration number (2P followed by six numerals). Whenever the dipstick is inserted, always make sure it is properly seated and locked.

FLUID LEVEL CHECK

See Figures 101, 102 and 103

Run the engine until it reaches normal operating temperature. While the engine is idling, turn the steering wheel all the way to the right and then to the left, and repeat several times. Shut **OFF** the engine. Open the hood and remove the power steering pump dipstick. Wipe the dipstick clean and reinstall into the pump reservoir. Withdraw the dipstick and note the fluid level shown. The level must show between the cold full mark and the hot full mark. Add fluid if necessary, buy do not overfill. Remove any excess fluid with a suction bulb or suction gun.

Chassis Greasing

See Figures 104 and 105

Chassis greasing is considered essential to the life and performance of your vehicle. The chassis should be checked and greased, if required, at least twice a year, and more often if the vehicle is operating in dust areas or under heavy-duty conditions. When greasing the chassis, use Long Life Lubricant (Ford Part No. C1AZ-19590-B or equivalent). The following chart indicates the vehicle's chassis lubrication points.

Body Lubrication and Maintenance

Body lubrication and maintenance is considered essential to the life and performance of your vehicle. Lubricate the door hinges, hood latch and auxiliary catch, lock cylinders, pivots, etc. When greasing the body components, use a high quality Polyethylene Grease (Ford Part No. D7AZ-19584-A or equivalent). When lubricating door and window weatherstrips, use silicone lubricant. This service also help to reduce friction between the glass frame and the rubber weatherstrips.

Fig. 101 Checking the power steering fluid — 1988 Escort shown

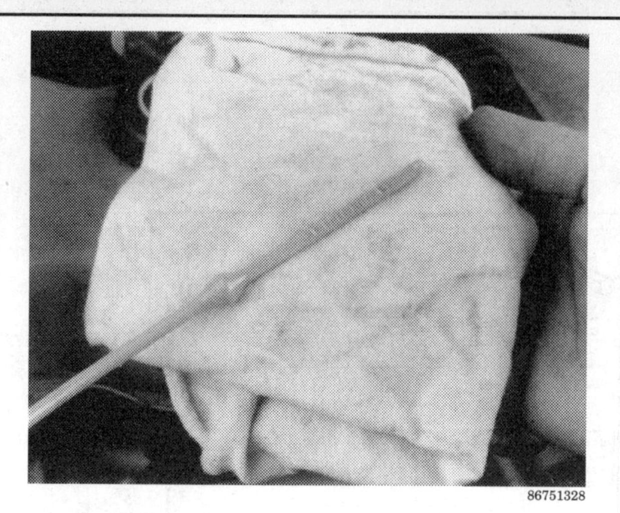

86751328

Fig. 102 Clean the power steering dipstick, then reinsert and withdraw to check the fluid level

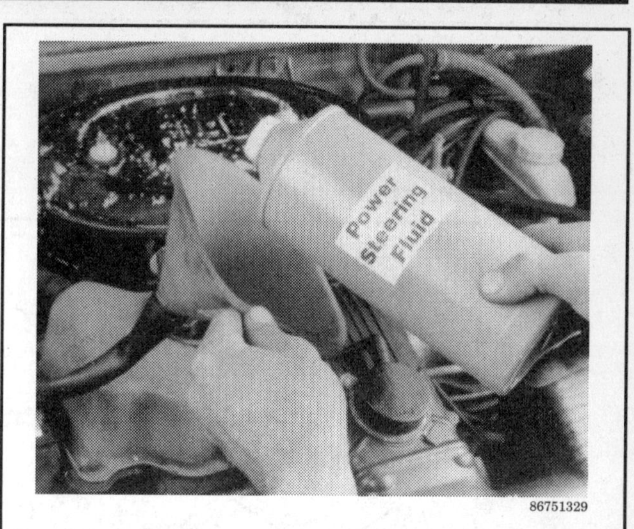

86751329

Fig. 103 Add power steering fluid through the dipstick tube using a long funnel

Item	Part Name	Ford Part No.	Ford Specification
*Hinges, Hinge Checks and Pivots	Polyethylene Grease	D7AZ-19584-A	ESB-M1C106-B
Hood Latch and Auxiliary Catch	Polyethylene Grease	D7AZ-19584-A	ESB-M1C106-B
Lock Cylinders	Lock Lubricant	D8AZ-19587-A	ESB-M2C20-A
Steering Gear Housing (Manual)	Steering Gear Grease	D8AZ-19578-A	ESA-M1C175-A
Steering Gear (Power)	Grease	C3AZ-19578-A	ESW-M1C87-A
Steering-Power (Pump Reservoir)	Motorcraft Auto. Trans. Fluid — Type F	XT-1-QF	ESW-M2C33-F
Speedometer Cable	Speedometer Cable Lube	D2AZ-19581-A	ESF-M1C160-A
Engine Coolant	Cooling System Fluid	E2FZ-19549-A	ESE-M97B44-A
Front Wheel Bearings and Hubs Front Wheel Bearing Seals Rear Wheel Bearings	Long Life Lubricant	C1AZ-19590-B	ESA-M1C75-B
Brake Master Cylinder	H.D. Brake Fluid	C6AZ-19542-A	ESA-M6C25-A
Brake Master Cylinder Push Rod and Bushing	Motorcraft SAE 10W-30 Engine Oil	XO-10W30-QP	ESE-M2C153-B
Drum Brake Shoe Ledges	Disc Brake Caliper Slide Grease	D7AZ-19590-A	ESA-M1C172-A
Parking Brake Cable	Polyethylene Grease	D0AZ-19584-A	ESB-M1C93-B
Brake Pedal Pivot Bushing	Motorcraft SAE 10W-30 Engine Oil	XO-10W30-QP	ESE-M2C153-B
Tire Mounting Bead (of Tire)	Tire Mounting Lube	D9AZ-19583-A	ESA-M1B6-A
Clutch Pedal Pivot Bushing	Motorcraft SAE 10W-30 Engine Oil	XO-10W30-QP	ESE-M2C153-B
Clutch Pedal Quadrant and Pawl Pivot Holes Clutch Cable Connection Transmission End Clutch Release Lever — At Fingers (Both Sides and Fulcrum) Clutch Release Bearing Retainer	Long Life Lubricant	C1AZ-19590-B	ESA-M1C75-B

*For door hinges, use Disc Brake Caliper slide grease D7AZ-19590-A.
DEXRON* is a registered trademark of General Motors Corporation.

86751080

Fig. 104 Chassis and body lubricant specifications

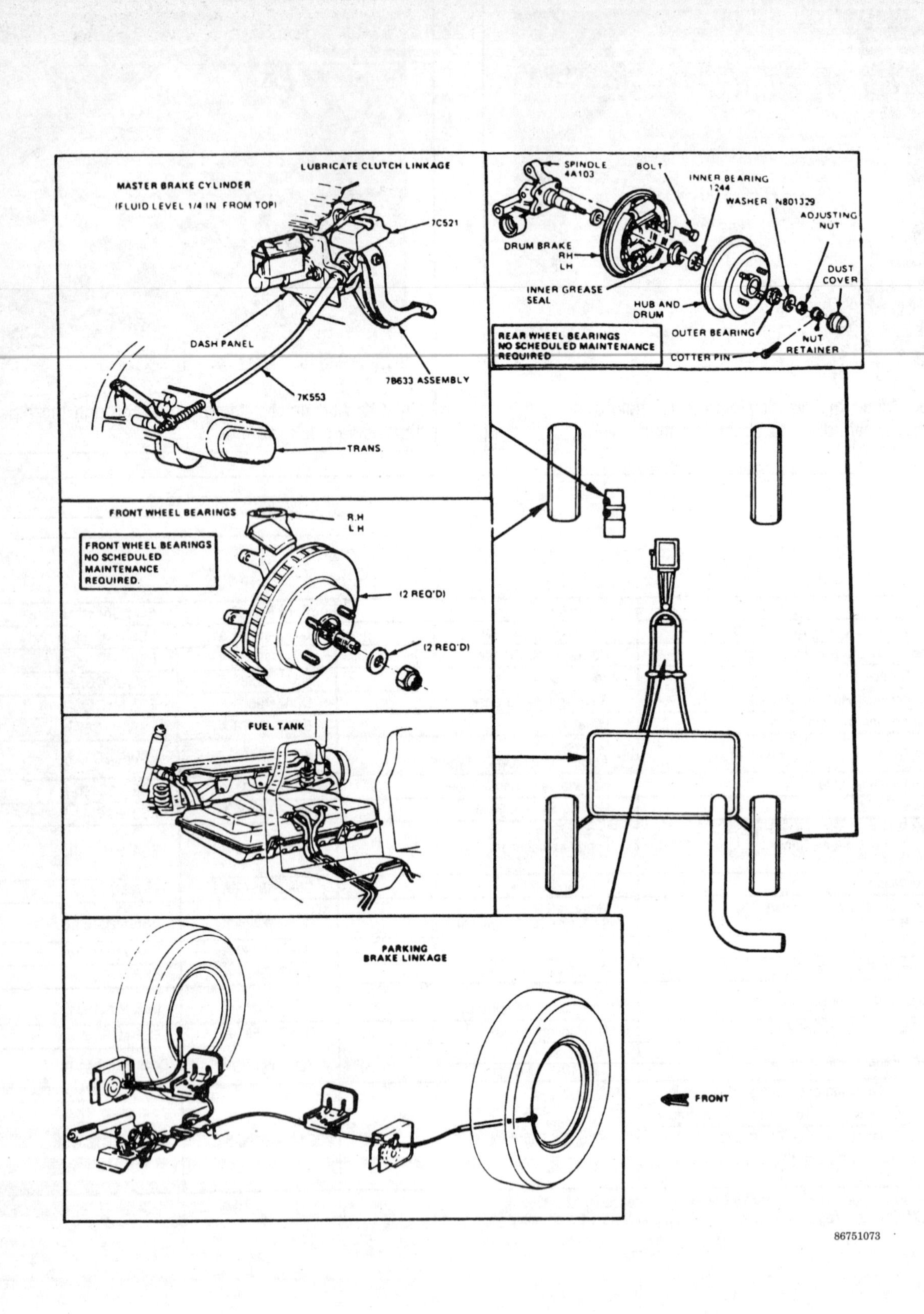

Fig. 105 Common chassis lubrication points

TOWING THE VEHICLE

Preparatory Steps

Release the parking brake, and place the transmission in NEUTRAL. As a general rule, a vehicle being towed, should be pulled with the driving wheels OFF the ground. If the driving wheels cannot be raised off the ground, place them on a dolly.

➡It is recommended that your vehicle be towed from the front, unless conditions do not allow it. Towing the vehicle backwards with the front wheels on the ground, may cause internal damage to the transaxle. Under no circumstances, should J-hooks be used to tow the vehicle. The manufacturer recommends that T-hooks be used when towing the vehicle, EXCEPT 1991-95 vehicles. When it is necessary to tow the 1991-95 Escort/Tracer, do not use the hook loops under the front and rear of the vehicle. These hook loops were designed for transport tie-down purposes ONLY and using them for towing could result in damage to the vehicle.

When the vehicle is being towed, the steering wheel must be clamped in the straight-ahead position with a steering wheel clamping device designed for towing service use, such as those provided by towing system manufacturers.

➡If conditions requires that the vehicle be pulled from the rear, do not use the vehicle's steering column to lock the wheels in A straight-ahead position.

If the ignition key is not available, place a dolly underneath the front wheels of the vehicle and tow with the rear wheels off the ground.

Attaching the Vehicle

TOWING SLINGS

➧ See Figures 106 and 107

The use of a special wide-belt sling should be used to lift and tow the vehicle, if metal-to-metal contact and possible damage to chrome or lower body panels is to be avoided.

FRONT T-HOOK PROCEDURE

ESCORT/LYNX AND EXP/LN7

1. Position the T-hooks in the shipping tie-down slots located on the frame rail ahead of the front wheels.
2. On Escort/Lynx, position a 4x4 wood block on the metal flange or just behind it.
3. On EXP/LN7, position a 4x4 wood block between the metal flange and the air dam.

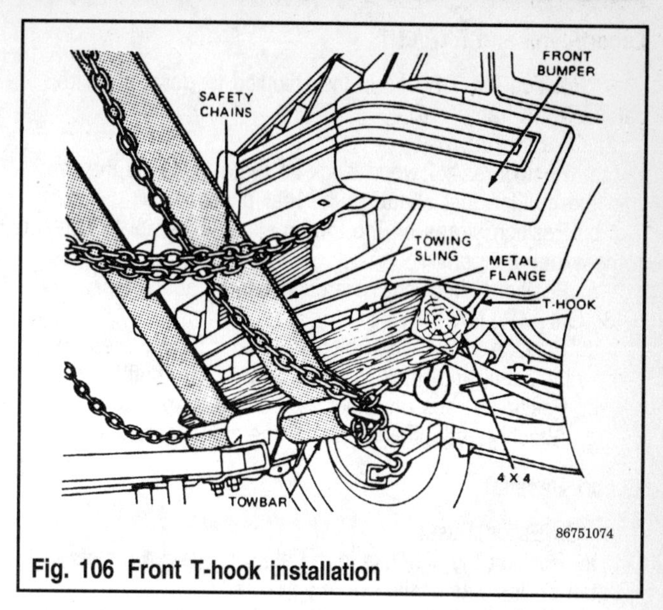

Fig. 106 Front T-hook installation

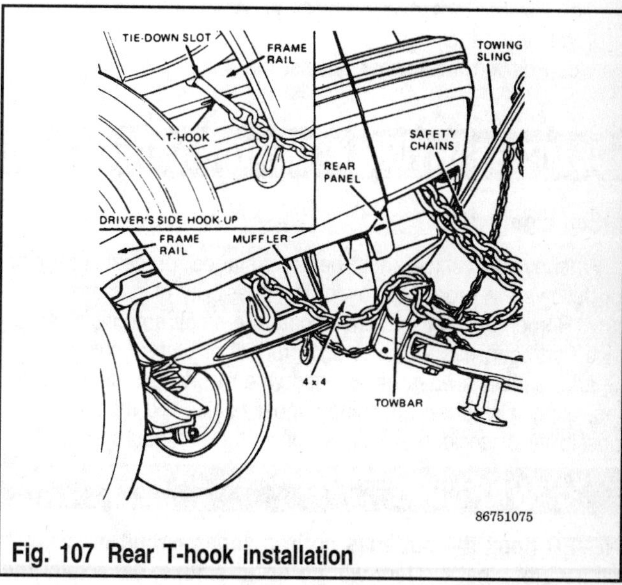

Fig. 107 Rear T-hook installation

4. Position straps on the towing sling around the license plate.
5. Attach safety chains around energy absorbers.

Escort Base/GT

1. Position the T-hooks in the shipping tie-down slots located on the frame rail ahead of the front wheels.
2. On Escort Base, position 4x4 under the radiator support.
3. On Escort GT, position 4x4 under fog lamp brackets and against towing tabs.
4. Position the towbar against the 4x4.
5. On Escort Base, attach safety chains around energy absorbers.
6. On Escort GT, attach safety chains around stablizer bar, outboard of brackets.

REAR T-HOOK PROCEDURE

Escort/Lynx and EXP/LN7

1. Position the T-hooks in the shipping tie-down slots located on the frame rail.
2. On Escort/Lynx:
   a. Position a 4x4 wood block so that it contacts the rear of the muffler, just ahead of the rear panel.
   b. Position straps on the towing sling so as not to contact the exhaust pipe.
   c. Position safety chains around energy absorbers.
3. On EXP/LN7:
   a. Position a 4x4 wood block so that it is just ahead of the rear panel and is close to the rear of the muffler.
   b. Position straps on either side of the license plate.
   c. Attach safety chains around energy absorbers.

Escort Base/GT

1. On Escort Base:
   a. Position the T-hooks in the shipping tie-down slots located on the frame rail.
   b. Position a 4x4 wood block under the tailpipe, forward of valance panel.
   c. Position the towbar against the 4x4.
   d. Attach safety chains around energy absorbers.
2. On Escort GT:
   a. Position the T-hooks in the shipping tie-down slots located on the frame rail, rear of rear wheels.
   b. Position a 4x4 wood block under the rear bumper bracket.
   c. Position the towbar against a 4x4 wood block directly under rear bumper.
   d. Attach safety chains around inner end of lower control arms.

1991-95 Models

If the vehicle requires towing, it is recommended that a wrecker equipped with a wheel lift be used. The weight of the vehicle should be supported by the lifting device placed under the wheels. Using this technique, the vehicle can be towed from the front or the rear. If the vehicle is to be towed from the rear, the front wheels MUST be placed on a dolly to prevent damage to the transaxle. Make certain the parking brake is released prior to towing the vehicle.

Towing Speed

When towing the vehicle, with driving wheels on the ground, do not exceed 35 mph (56 km/h). Also, do not tow the vehicle for a distance exceeding 50 miles (80 km), or transmission damage can occur.

JUMP STARTING A DEAD BATTERY

See Figure 108

Whenever a vehicle must be jump started, precautions must be followed in order to prevent the possibility of personal injury. Remember that batteries contain a small amount of explosive hydrogen gas which is a byproduct of battery charging. Sparks should always be avoided when working around batteries, especially when attaching jumper cables. To minimize the possibility of accidental sparks, follow the procedure carefully.

WARNING

NEVER hook the batteries up in a series circuit or the entire electrical system will go up in smoke, especially the starter!

Cars equipped with a diesel engine utilize two 12 volt batteries, one on either side of the engine compartment. The batteries are connected in a parallel circuit (positive terminal to positive terminal, negative terminal to negative terminal). Hooking the batteries up in parallel circuit increases battery cranking power without increasing total battery voltage output. Output remains at 12 volts. On the other hand, hooking two 12 volt batteries up in a series circuit (positive terminal to negative terminal, positive terminal to negative terminal) increases total battery output to 24 volts (12 volts plus 12 volts).

Jump Starting Precautions

1. Be sure that both batteries are of the same voltage. All vehicles covered by this manual and most vehicles on the road today utilize a 12 volt charging system.
2. Be sure that both batteries are of the same polarity (have the same grounded terminal; in most cases NEGATIVE).
3. Be sure that the vehicles are not touching or a short circuit could occur.
4. On serviceable batteries, be sure the vent cap holes are not obstructed.
5. Do not smoke or allow sparks anywhere near the batteries.
6. In cold weather, make sure the battery electrolyte is not frozen. This can occur more readily in a battery that has been in a state of discharge.
7. Do not allow electrolyte to contact your skin or clothing.

Jump Starting Procedure

1. Make sure that the voltages of the two batteries are the same. Most batteries and charging systems are of the 12 volt variety.
2. Pull the jumping vehicle (with the good battery) into a position so the jumper cables can reach the dead battery and that vehicle's engine. Make sure that the vehicles do NOT touch.
3. Place the transmissions of both vehicles in NEUTRAL or PARK, as applicable, then firmly set their parking brakes.

➡If necessary for safety reasons, both vehicle's hazard lights may be operated throughout the entire procedure without significantly increasing the difficulty of jump starting the dead battery.

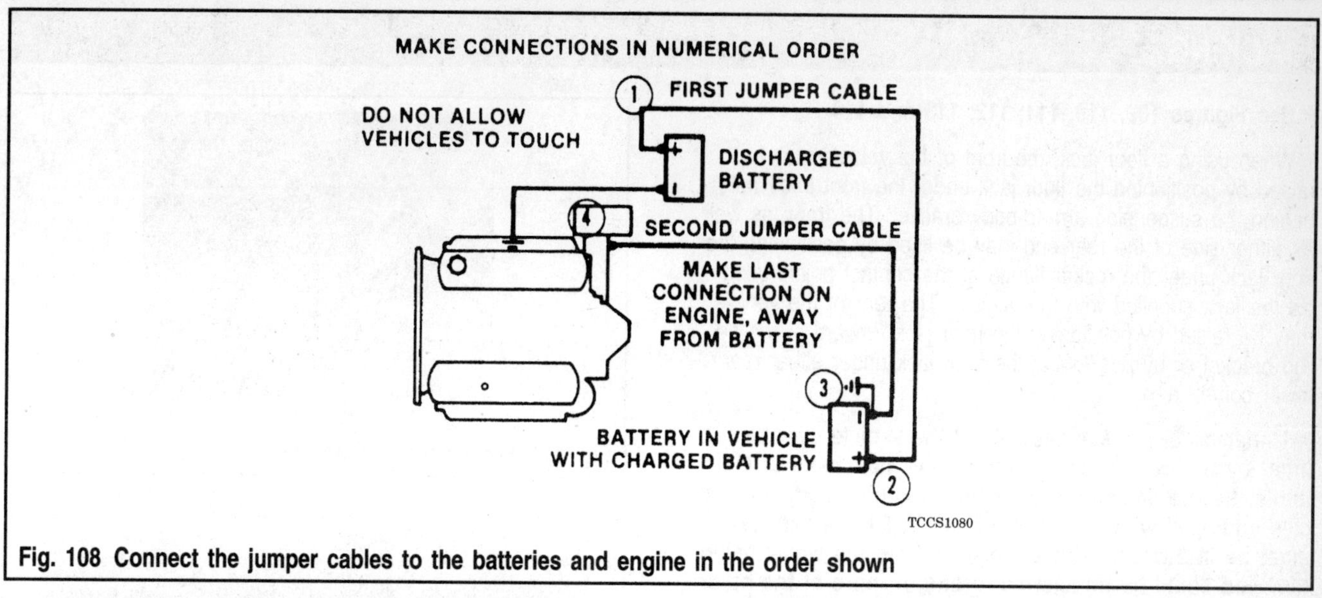

Fig. 108 Connect the jumper cables to the batteries and engine in the order shown

4. Turn all lights and accessories off on both vehicles. Make sure the ignition switches on both vehicles are turned to the **OFF** position.
5. Cover the battery cell caps with a rag, but do not cover the terminals.
6. Make sure the terminals on both batteries are clean and free of corrosion or proper electrical connection will be impeded. If necessary, clean the battery terminals before proceeding.
7. Identify the positive (+) and negative (-) terminals on both batteries.
8. Connect the first jumper cable to the positive (+) terminal of the dead battery, then connect the other end of that cable to the positive (+) terminal of the booster (good) battery.
9. Connect one end of the other jumper cable to the negative (-) terminal of the booster battery and the other cable clamp to an engine bolt head, alternator bracket or other solid, metallic point on the dead battery's engine. Try to pick a ground on the engine that is positioned away from the battery, in order to minimize the possibility of the two clamps touching should one loosen during the procedure. DO NOT connect this clamp to the negative (-) terminal of the bad battery.

⁂CAUTION

Be very careful to keep the jumper cables away from moving parts (cooling fan, belts, etc.) on both engines.

10. Check to make sure that the cables are routed away from any moving parts, then start the donor vehicle's engine. Run the engine at moderate speed for several minutes to allow the dead battery a chance to receive some initial charge.
11. With the donor vehicle's engine still running slightly above idle, try to start the vehicle with the dead battery. Crank the engine for no more than 10 seconds at a time and let the starter cool for at least 20 seconds between tries. If the vehicle does not start within three tries, it is likely that something else is also wrong.
12. Once the vehicle is started, allow it to run at idle for a few seconds to make sure that it is properly operating.
13. Turn on the headlights, heater blower and, if equipped, the rear defroster of both vehicles in order to reduce the severity of voltage spikes and subsequent risk of damage to the vehicles' electrical systems when the cables are disconnected.
14. Carefully disconnect the cables in the reverse order of connection. Start with the negative cable that is attached to the engine ground, then the negative cable on the donor battery. Disconnect the positive cable from the donor battery, then disconnect the positive cable from the formerly dead battery. Be careful when disconnecting the cables from the positive terminals not to allow the alligator clips to touch any metal on either vehicle or a short circuit and sparks will occur.

JACKING

➧ See Figures 109, 110, 111, 112, 113 and 114

When using a floor jack, the front of the vehicle may be raised by positioning the floor jack under the front body rail behind the suspension arm-to-body bracket. The front, as well as either side of the rear end may be lifted by positioning the floor jack under the rocker flange at the contact points used for the jack supplied with the vehicle. The rear of the vehicle may be raised by positioning the floor jack forward of the tie rod bracket or by positioning the floor jack under either rear lower control arm.

➡Under no circumstances should the vehicle ever be lifted by the front or rear control arms, halfshafts or CV-joints. Severe damage to the vehicle could result. On vehicles equipped with All Wheel Drive (AWD), the vehicle must be in 2-wheel drive or rotation from the wheel being removed could be transferred to one or more of the other wheels, causing the vehicle to move or fall off the jack. The service jack provided with the vehicle is only intended to be used during emergencies, such as changing a flat tire. Never use the service jack to hoist the vehicle for any other service. Refer to the owner's manual when using the jack supplied with the vehicle.

86751330

Fig. 109 Front rocker flange jacking point

86751331

Fig. 110 Front body rail jacking point

86751332

Fig. 111 A jack stand is necessary for any service in which the car must be raised

86751333

Fig. 112 Rear rocker flange jacking point

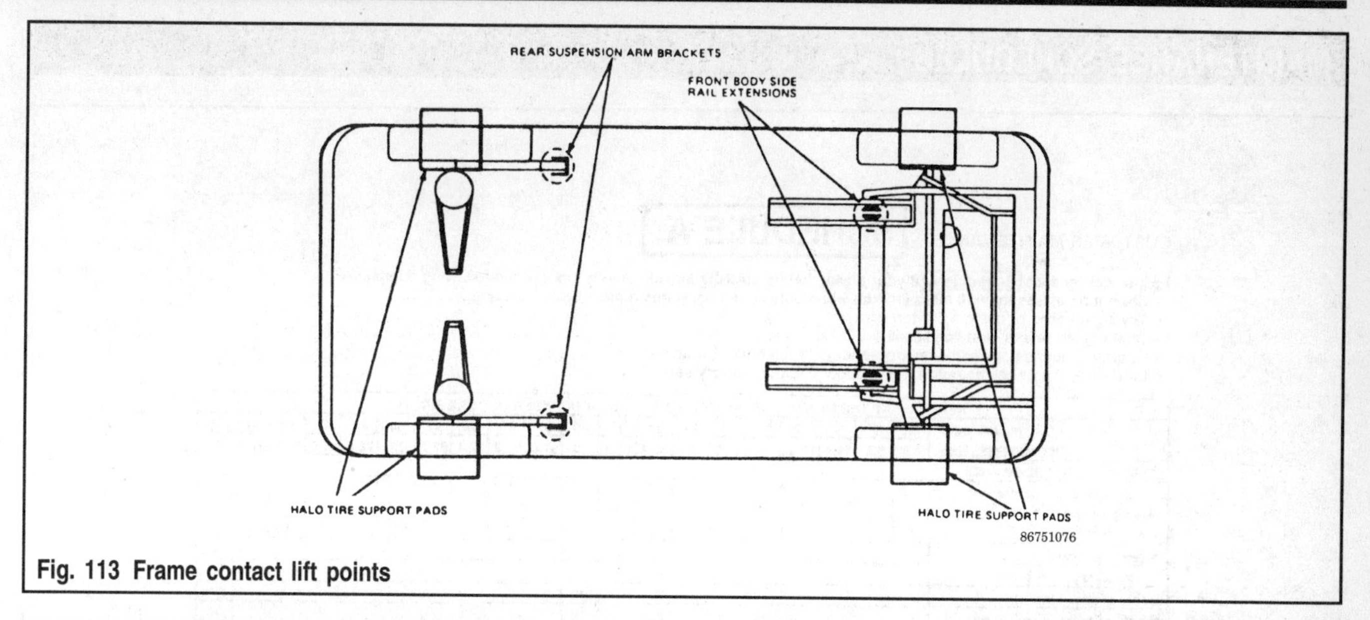

Fig. 113 Frame contact lift points

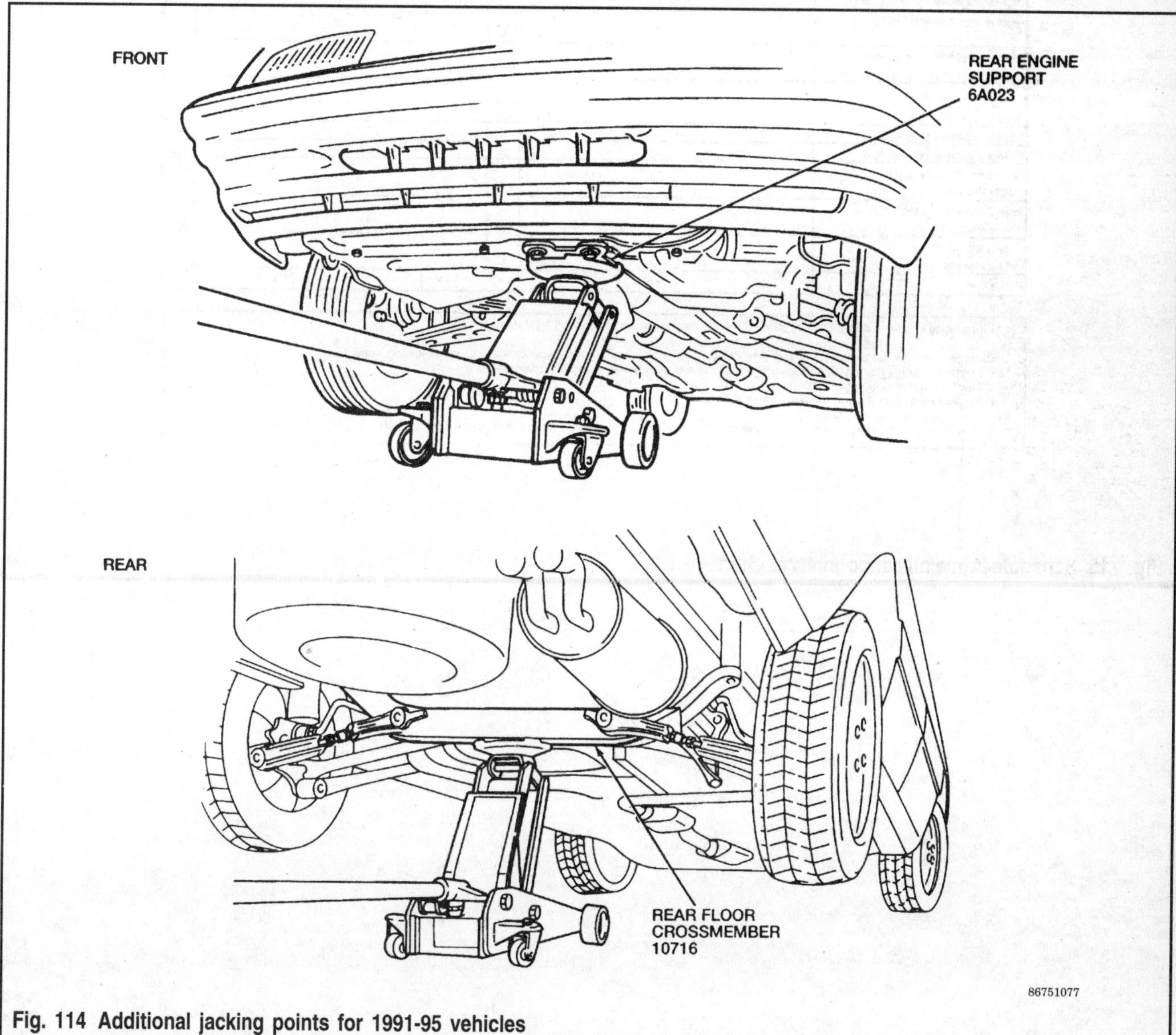

Fig. 114 Additional jacking points for 1991-95 vehicles

MAINTENANCE SCHEDULES

CUSTOMER MAINTENANCE **SCHEDULE A**

Follow maintenance **Schedule A** if your driving habits **MAINLY** include one or more of the following conditions:

- Short trips of less than 10 miles (16 km) when outside temperatures remain below freezing.
- Towing a trailer, or using a car-top carrier.
- Operating in severe dust conditions.
- Operating during hot weather in stop-and-go "rush hour" traffic.
- Extensive idling, such as police, taxi or door-to-door delivery service.

PERFORM AT THE MONTHS OR DISTANCES SHOWN, WHICHEVER OCCURS FIRST																				
MILES (000)	3	6	9	12	15	18	21	24	27	30	33	36	39	42	45	48	51	54	57	60
KILOMETERS (000)	4.8	9.6	14.4	19.2	24	28.8	33.6	38.4	43.2	48	52.8	57.6	62.4	67.2	72	76.8	81.6	86.4	91.2	96
EMISSION CONTROL SERVICE																				
Change engine oil and oil filter (every 3 months) OR 3,000 miles whichever occurs first	X	X	X	X	X	X	X	X	X	X	X	X	X	X	X	X	X	X	X	X
Replace spark plugs										X										X
Inspect accessory drive belt(s)										X										X
Replace air cleaner filter (1)										X(1)										X(1)
Replace crankcase emission filter (1)										X(1)										X(1)
Replace engine coolant EVERY 36 months OR										X										X
Check engine coolant protection, hoses and clamps	ANNUALLY																			
GENERAL MAINTENANCE																				
Inspect exhaust heat shields										X										X
Change automatic transaxle fluid										(2)										(2)
Inspect disc brake pads and rotors (front) (3)										X(3)										X(3)
Inspect brake linings and drums (rear) (3)										X(3)										X(3)
Inspect and repack rear wheel bearings										X										X
Rotate tires		X					X					X					X			

(1) If operating in severe dust, more frequent intervals may be required, consult your dealer.

(2) Change automatic transmission fluid if your driving habits frequently include one or more of the following conditions:
- Operation during hot weather (above 90°F, 32°C), carrying heavy loads and in hilly terrain.
- Towing a trailer or using a car-top carrier.
- Police, taxi or door-to-door delivery service.

(3) If your driving includes continuous stop-and-go driving or driving in mountainous areas, more frequent intervals may be required.

86751078

Fig. 115 Schedule A maintenance interval chart

CUSTOMER MAINTENANCE **SCHEDULE B**

Follow maintenance **Schedule B** if, generally, you drive your vehicle on a daily basis for more than 10 miles (16 km) and **NONE OF THE DRIVING CONDITIONS SHOWN IN SCHEDULE A APPLY TO YOUR DRIVING HABITS.**

PERFORM AT THE MONTHS OR DISTANCES SHOWN, WHICHEVER OCCURS FIRST								
MILES (000)	7.5	15	22.5	30	37.5	45	52.5	60
KILOMETERS (000)	12	24	36	48	60	72	84	96
EMISSION CONTROL SERVICE								
Change engine oil and oil filter — **every 6 months** or 7500 miles, whichever occurs first	X	X	X	X	X	X	X	X
Replace spark plugs				X				X
Change crankcase filter (1)				X(1)				X(1)
Inspect accessory drive belt(s)				X				X
Replace air cleaner filter (1)				X(1)				X(1)
Replace engine coolant (every 36 months) OR				X				X
Check engine coolant protection, hoses and clamps	ANNUALLY							
GENERAL MAINTENANCE								
Check exhaust heat shields				X				X
Inspect disc brake pads and rotors (front) (2)				X(2)				X(2)
Inspect brake linings and drums (rear) (2)				X(2)				X(2)
Inspect and repack rear wheel bearings.				X				X
Rotate tires	X		X		X		X	

86751079

Fig. 116 Schedule B maintenance interval chart

Item	Part Name	Ford Part No.	Ford Specification
*Hinges, Hinge Checks and Pivots	Polyethylene Grease	D7AZ-19584-A	ESB-M1C106-B
Hood Latch and Auxiliary Catch	Polyethylene Grease	D7AZ-19584-A	ESB-M1C106-B
Lock Cylinders	Lock Lubricant	D8AZ-19587-A	ESB-M2C20-A
Steering Gear Housing (Manual)	Steering Gear Grease	D8AZ-19578-A	ESA-M1C175-A
Steering Gear (Power)	Grease	C3AZ-19578-A	ESW-M1C87-A
Steering-Power (Pump Reservoir)	Motorcraft Auto Trans. Fluid — Type F	XT-1-QF	ESW-M2C33-F
Speedometer Cable	Speedometer Cable Lube	D2AZ-19581-A	ESF-M1C160-A
Engine Coolant	Cooling System Fluid	E2FZ-19549-A	ESE-M97B44-A
Front Wheel Bearings and Hubs Front Wheel Bearing Seals Rear Wheel Bearings	Long Life Lubricant	C1AZ-19590-B	ESA-M1C75-B
Brake Master Cylinder	H.D. Brake Fluid	C6AZ-19542-A	ESA-M6C25-A
Brake Master Cylinder Push Rod and Bushing	Motorcraft SAE 10W-30 Engine Oil	XO-10W30-QP	ESE-M2C153-B
Drum Brake Shoe Ledges	Disc Brake Caliper Slide Grease	D7AZ-19590-A	ESA-M1C172-A
Parking Brake Cable	Polyethylene Grease	D0AZ-19584-A	ESB-M1C93-B
Brake Pedal Pivot Bushing	Motorcraft SAE 10W-30 Engine Oil	XO-10W30-QP	ESE-M2C153-B
Tire Mounting Bead (of Tire)	Tire Mounting Lube	D9AZ-19583-A	ESA-M1B6-A
Clutch Pedal Pivot Bushing	Motorcraft SAE 10W-30 Engine Oil	XO-10W30-QP	ESE-M2C153-B
Clutch Pedal Quadrant and Pawl Pivot Holes Clutch Cable Connection Transmission End Clutch Release Lever — At Fingers (Both Sides and Fulcrum) Clutch Release Bearing Retainer	Long Life Lubricant	C1AZ-19590-B	ESA-M1C75-B

*For door hinges, use Disc Brake Caliper slide grease D7AZ-19590-A.
DEXRON® is a registered trademark of General Motors Corporation.

86751080

Fig. 117 Chassis and body lubricant specifications

CAPACITIES

Year	Model	Engine ID/VIN	Engine Displacement Liters (cc)	Engine Oil with Filter (qts.)	Transmission (pts.) 4-Spd	Transmission (pts.) 5-Spd	Transmission (pts.) Auto. (4)	Transfer Case (pts.)	Drive Axle Front (pts.)	Drive Axle Rear (pts.)	Fuel Tank (gal.)	Cooling System (qts.)
1981	Escort/Lynx	2	1.6 (1606)	4.0	5.0	-	16.6	-	(1)	-	(2)	(3)
1982	Escort/Lynx	2	1.6 (1606)	4.0	5.0	-	16.6	-	(1)	-	(2)	(3)
	EXP/LN7	2	1.6 (1606)	4.0	5.0	6.2	16.6	-	(1)	-	(2)	(3)
1983	Escort/Lynx	2	1.6 (1606)	4.0	5.0	6.2	16.6	-	(1)	-	(2)	(3)
	Escort/Lynx	4	1.6 (1606)	4.0	5.0	6.2	16.6	-	(1)	-	(2)	(3)
	Escort/Lynx	5	1.6 (1606)	4.0	5.0	6.2	16.6	-	(1)	-	(2)	(3)
	EXP/LN7	2	1.6 (1606)	4.0	5.0	6.2	16.6	-	(1)	-	(2)	(3)
	EXP/LN7	4	1.6 (1606)	4.0	5.0	6.2	16.6	-	(1)	-	(2)	(3)
	EXP/LN7	5	1.6 (1606)	4.0	5.0	6.2	16.6	-	(1)	-	(2)	(3)
1984	Escort/Lynx	2	1.6 (1606)	4.0	5.0	6.2	16.6	-	(1)	-	(2)	(3)
	Escort/Lynx	4	1.6 (1606)	4.0	5.0	6.2	16.6	-	(1)	-	(2)	(3)
	Escort/Lynx	5	1.6 (1606)	4.0	5.0	6.2	16.6	-	(1)	-	(2)	(3)
	Escort/Lynx	7	1.6 (1606)	4.0	5.0	6.2	16.6	-	(1)	-	(2)	(3)
	Escort/Lynx	8	1.6 (1606)	4.0	5.0	6.2	16.6	-	(1)	-	(2)	(3)
	Escort/Lynx	H	2.0 (2000)	7.2	5.0	6.2	16.6	-	(1)	-	(2)	(3)
	EXP	2	1.6 (1606)	4.0	5.0	6.2	16.6	-	(1)	-	(2)	(3)
	EXP	4	1.6 (1606)	4.0	5.0	6.2	16.6	-	(1)	-	(2)	(3)
	EXP	5	1.6 (1606)	4.0	5.0	6.2	16.6	-	(1)	-	(2)	(3)
	EXP	8	1.6 (1606)	4.0	5.0	6.2	16.6	-	(1)	-	(2)	(3)
1985	Escort/Lynx	2	1.6 (1606)	4.0	5.0	6.2	16.6	-	(1)	-	(2)	(3)
	Escort/Lynx	4	1.6 (1606)	4.0	5.0	6.2	16.6	-	(1)	-	(2)	(3)
	Escort/Lynx	5	1.6 (1606)	4.0	5.0	6.2	16.6	-	(1)	-	(2)	(3)
	Escort/Lynx	7	1.6 (1606)	4.0	5.0	6.2	16.6	-	(1)	-	(2)	(3)
	Escort/Lynx	8	1.6 (1606)	4.0	5.0	6.2	16.6	-	(1)	-	(2)	(3)
	Escort/Lynx	9	1.9 (1901)	4.0	5.0	6.2	16.6	-	(1)	-	(2)	(3)
	Escort/Lynx	H	2.0 (2000)	7.2	5.0	6.2	16.6	-	(1)	-	(2)	(3)
	EXP	2	1.6 (1606)	4.0	5.0	6.2	16.6	-	(1)	-	(2)	(3)
	EXP	4	1.6 (1606)	4.0	5.0	6.2	16.6	-	(1)	-	(2)	(3)
	EXP	5	1.6 (1606)	4.0	5.0	6.2	16.6	-	(1)	-	(2)	(3)
	EXP	8	1.6 (1606)	4.0	5.0	6.2	16.6	-	(1)	-	(2)	(3)
	EXP	9	1.9 (1901)	4.0	5.0	6.2	16.6	-	(1)	-	(2)	(3)
1986	Escort/Lynx	9	1.9 (1901)	4.0	5.0	6.2	16.6	-	(1)	-	(2)	(3)
	Escort/Lynx	J	1.9 (1901)	4.0	5.0	6.2	16.6	-	(1)	-	(2)	(3)
	Escort/Lynx	H	2.0 (2000)	7.2	5.0	6.2	16.6	-	(1)	-	(2)	(3)
	EXP	9	1.9 (1901)	4.0	5.0	6.2	16.6	-	(1)	-	(2)	(3)
	EXP	J	1.9 (1901)	4.0	5.0	6.2	16.6	-	(1)	-	(2)	(3)
1987	Escort/Lynx	9	1.9 (1901)	4.0	5.0	6.2	16.6	-	(1)	-	13.0	(3)
	Escort/Lynx	J	1.9 (1901)	4.0	5.0	6.2	16.6	-	(1)	-	13.0	(3)
	Escort/Lynx	H	2.0 (2000)	7.2	5.0	6.2	16.6	-	(1)	-	13.0	(3)
1988	Escort	9	1.9 (1901)	4.0	5.0	6.2	16.6	-	(1)	-	13.0	(3)
	Escort	J	1.9 (1901)	4.0	5.0	6.2	16.6	-	(1)	-	13.0	(3)
1989	Escort	9	1.9 (1901)	4.0	5.0	6.2	16.6	-	(1)	-	13.0	(3)
	Escort	J	1.9 (1901)	4.0	5.0	6.2	16.6	-	(1)	-	13.0	(3)
1990	Escort	9	1.9 (1901)	4.0	5.0	6.2	16.6	-	(1)	-	13.0	(3)
	Escort	J	1.9 (1901)	4.0	5.0	6.2	16.6	-	(1)	-	13.0	(3)
1991	Escort/Tracer	8	1.8 (1844)	4.0	-	7.2	13.4	-	(1)	-	13.2	7.5
	Escort/Tracer	J	1.9 (1901)	4.0	5.0	6.2	13.4	-	(1)	-	13.0	(3)

86751C12

CAPACITIES

Year	Model	Engine ID/VIN	Engine Displacement Liters (cc)	Engine Oil with Filter (qts.)	Transmission (pts.) 4-Spd	5-Spd	Auto. ④	Transfer Case (pts.)	Drive Axle Front (pts.)	Rear (pts.)	Fuel Tank (gal.)	Cooling System (qts.)
1992	Escort/Tracer	8	1.8 (1844)	4.0	-	7.2	13.4	-	①	-	13.2	7.5
	Escort/Tracer	J	1.9 (1901)	4.0	-	6.2	13.4	-	①	-	13.0	③
1993	Escort/Tracer	8	1.8 (1844)	4.0	-	7.2	13.4	-	①	-	13.2	7.5
	Escort/Tracer	J	1.9 (1901)	4.0	-	6.2	13.4	-	①	-	13.0	③
1994	Escort/Tracer	8	1.8 (1844)	4.0	-	7.2	13.4	-	①	-	13.2	7.5
	Escort/Tracer	J	1.9 (1901)	4.0	-	5.7	13.4	-	①	-	11.9	5.3
1995	Escort/Tracer	8	1.8 (1844)	4.0	-	7.2	13.4	-	①	-	13.2	⑤
	Escort/Tracer	J	1.9 (1901)	4.0	-	5.7	13.4	-	①	-	11.9	⑤

① Included in transaxle capacity

② Standard tank: 13 gals.
Base model: 10 gals.

③ Without A/C: 8.3 qts.
Manual trans. w/ A/C: 7.3 qts.
Auto trans. w/ A/C: 7.8 qts.

④ Includes torque converter

⑤ Manual transaxle: 5.3 qts.
Automatic transaxle: 6.3 qts.

86751C13

2 ENGINE PERFORMANCE AND TUNE-UP

TUNE-UP PROCEDURES

Spark Plugs

See Figures 1 and 2

Spark plugs are used to ignite the air and fuel mixture in the cylinders as the piston approaches Top Dead Center (TDC) on its compression stroke. The controlled explosion that results forces the piston down, turning the crankshaft and the rest of the drive train.

Ford recommends that spark plugs be changed every 30,000-60,000 miles (48,000-96,500 km). Under severe driving conditions, those intervals should be more frequent. Severe driving conditions are:

1. Extended periods of idling or low speed operation, such as off-road or door-to-door delivery.
2. Driving short distances — less than 10 miles (16 km) — when the average temperature is below 10°F (12°C) for 60 days or more.
3. Vehicle frequently operated in excessively dusty conditions.

In normal operation, plug gap increases about 0.001 in. (0.025mm) for every 1000-2500 miles (1600-4000 km). As the gap increases, the plug's voltage requirement also increases. It requires greater voltage to jump the wider gap. Take this into consideration when added to the fact that the voltage requirement increases and about two to three times as much voltage to fire a plug at higher speeds than at idle.

When you remove the spark plugs, check their condition. They are a good indicator of the engine's operating conditions. It's probably a good idea to remove and inspect the spark plugs at regular intervals, approximately every 12,000 miles (19,300 km), just so you can keep an eye on the mechanical state of the engine, as well as check plug wear and re-gap, if necessary.

A small deposit of light tan or gray material on a spark plug that has been used for any period of time is considered normal. Any other color, or abnormal amounts of deposit, indicate that there is something amiss in the engine.

The gap between the center electrode and the side or ground electrode can be expected to increase not more than 0.001 in. (0.025mm) every 1000 miles (1600 km) under normal conditions. When, and if, a plug fouls and begins to misfire, you will have to investigate, correct the cause of the fouling and either clean or replace the plug.

There are several reasons why a spark plug would foul and you can determine the fault just by observing the plug.

SPARK PLUG HEAT RANGE

Spark plug heat range is the ability of the plug to dissipate heat. The longer the insulator (or the farther it extends into the engine), the hotter the plug will operate; the shorter the insulator the cooler it will operate. A plug that absorbs little heat and remains too cool will quickly accumulate deposits of oil and carbon since it is not hot enough to burn them off. This leads to plug fouling and consequently to misfiring. A plug that absorbs too much heat will have no deposits, but, due to the excessive heat, the electrodes will burn away quickly and in some instances, preignition may result. Pre-ignition takes place when plug tips get so hot that they glow sufficiently to ignite the fuel/air mixture before the actual spark occurs. This early ignition will usually cause a pinging during low speeds and heavy loads.

The general rule of thumb of choosing the correct heat range when picking a spark plug is as follows:

- Cooler plug — if most of your driving is long distance, high speed travel
- Hotter plug — if most of your driving involves short distances or heavy stop and go traffic.

Original equipment plugs can be termed "Compromise Plugs", but most drivers never have the need for changing their plugs from the factory recommended heat range.

REMOVAL & INSTALLATION

See Figures 3, 4, 5 and 6

➡Removal and installation of the spark plugs requires a special deep socket. Specially designed spark plug wire removal pliers are also good to have. The special pliers have cupped jaws that grip the plug wire boot and make the job of twisting and pulling the wire from the plug easier and they do not put pulling force on the crimped-on connector.

1. Disconnect the negative battery cable.
2. Remove the air cleaner assembly and air intake tube, as required.
3. Remove the plug wire, using the spark plug wire removal tool.
4. The plug wire boot has a cover which shields the plug cavity (in the head) against dirt. After removing the wire, blow out the cavity with air or clean it out with a small brush so dirt will not fall into the engine when the spark plug is removed.
5. Remove the spark plug with a plug socket. Turn the socket counterclockwise to remove the plug. Be sure to hold the socket straight on the plug to avoid breaking the insulator (a deep socket designed for spark plugs has a rubber cushion built-in to help prevent plug breakage).
6. Once the plug is removed, compare it with the spark plug illustrations to determine the engine condition. This is very important because spark plug readings are vital signs of engine condition and pending problems.

To install:

➡Two different plug designs are used on early 1.6L engines: gasket-equipped and tapered seat (no gasket). DO NOT INTERCHANGE TYPES!

7. If the old plugs are to be reused, clean and re-gap them. If new spark plugs are to be installed, always check the gap. Use a round wire feeler gauge to check plug gap. The correct size gauge should pass through the electrode gap with a slight drag. If you are unsure whether you accurately set the gap, try the next smaller or the next size larger. The smaller gauge should go through easily and the larger should not go through at all. If adjustment is necessary use the bending tool on the end of the gauge. When adjusting the gap, always

Tracking Arc
High voltage arcs between a fouling deposit on the insulator tip and spark plug shell. This ignites the fuel/air mixture at some point along the insulator tip, retarding the ignition timing which causes a power and fuel loss.

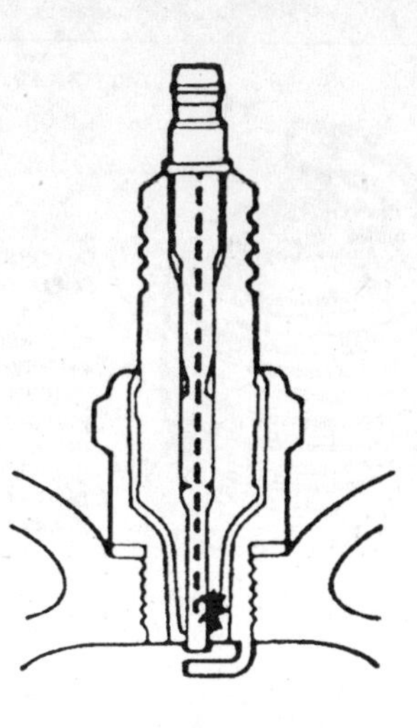

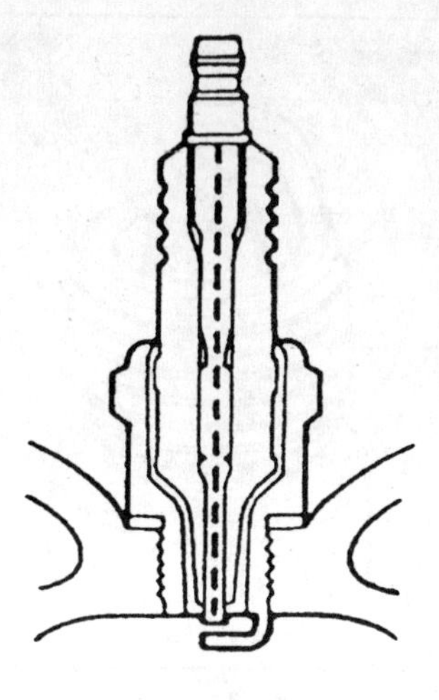

Wide Gap
Spark plug electrodes are worn so that the high voltage charge cannot arc across the electrodes. Improper gapping of electrodes on new or "cleaned" spark plugs could cause a similar condition. Fuel remains unburned and a power loss results.

Flashover
A damaged spark plug boot, along with dirt and moisture, could permit the high voltage charge to short over the insulator to the spark plug shell or the engine. A buttress insulator design helps prevent high voltage flashover.

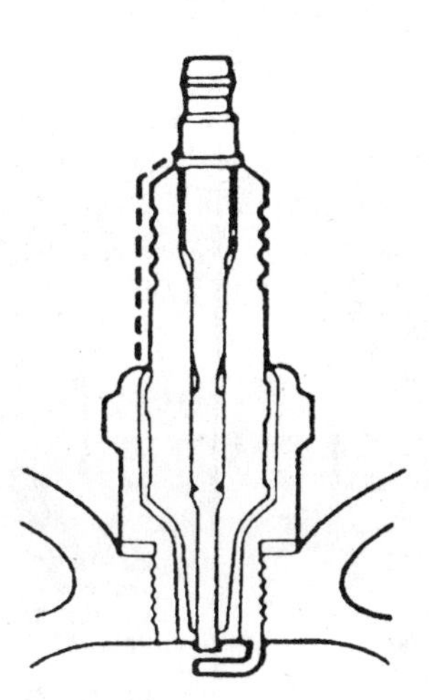

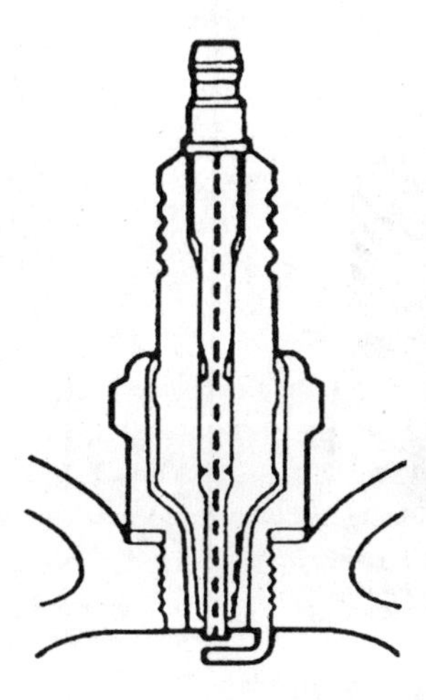

Fouled Spark Plug
Deposits that have formed on the insulator tip may become conductive and provide a "shunt" path to the shell. This prevents the high voltage from arcing between the electrodes. A power and fuel loss is the result.

Bridged Electrodes
Fouling deposits between the electrodes "ground out" the high voltage needed to fire the spark plug. The arc between the electrodes does not occur and the fuel air mixture is not ignited. This causes a power loss and exhausting of raw fuel.

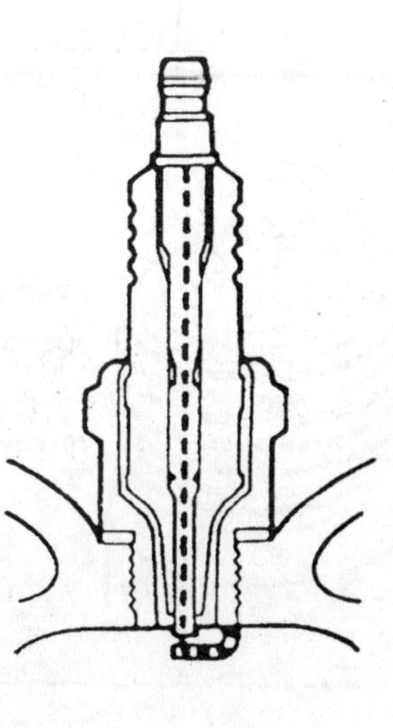

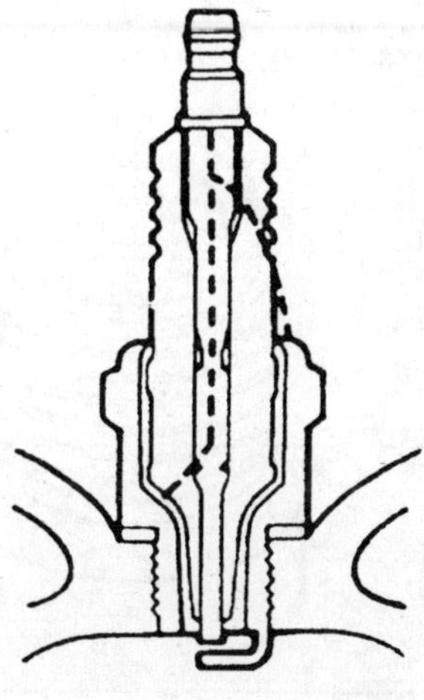

Cracked Insulator
A crack in the spark plug insulator could cause the high voltage charge to "ground out." Here, the spark does not jump the electrode gap and the fuel air mixture is not ignited. This causes a power loss and raw fuel is exhausted.

tccs201a

Fig. 1 Used spark plugs which show damage may indicate engine problems

GAP BRIDGED

IDENTIFIED BY DEPOSIT BUILD-UP CLOSING GAP BETWEEN ELECTRODES.

CAUSED BY OIL OR CARBON FOULING. REPLACE PLUG, OR, IF DEPOSITS ARE NOT EXCESSIVE THE PLUG CAN BE CLEANED.

OIL FOULED

IDENTIFIED BY WET BLACK DEPOSITS ON THE INSULATOR SHELL BORE ELECTRODES.

CAUSED BY EXCESSIVE OIL ENTERING COMBUSTION CHAMBER THROUGH WORN RINGS AND PISTONS, EXCESSIVE CLEARANCE BETWEEN VALVE GUIDES AND STEMS, OR WORN OR LOOSE BEARINGS. CORRECT OIL PROBLEM. REPLACE THE PLUG.

CARBON FOULED

IDENTIFIED BY BLACK, DRY FLUFFY CARBON DEPOSITS ON INSULATOR TIPS, EXPOSED SHELL SURFACES AND ELECTRODES.

CAUSED BY TOO COLD A PLUG, WEAK IGNITION, DIRTY AIR CLEANER, DEFECTIVE FUEL PUMP, TOO RICH A FUEL MIXTURE, IMPROPERLY OPERATING HEAT RISER OR EXCESSIVE IDLING. CAN BE CLEANED.

NORMAL

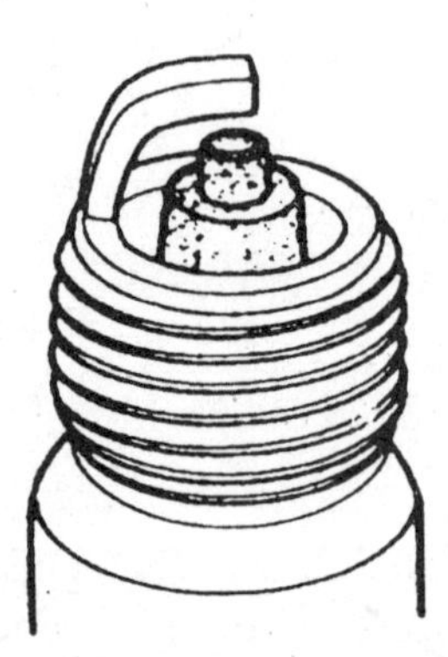

IDENTIFIED BY LIGHT TAN OR GRAY DEPOSITS ON THE FIRING TIP.

PRE-IGNITION

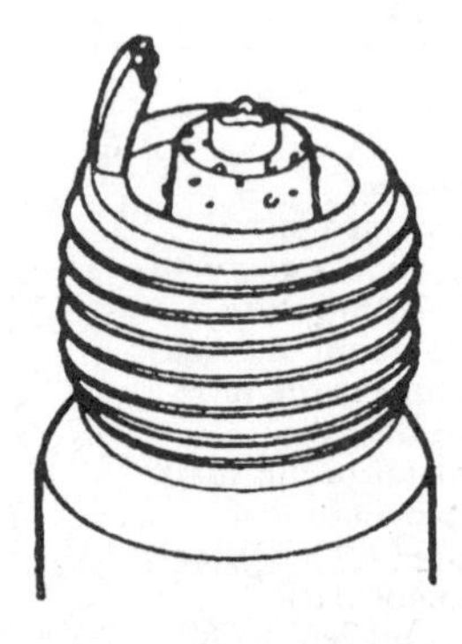

IDENTIFIED BY MELTED ELECTRODES AND POSSIBLY BLISTERED INSULATOR. METALIC DEPOSITS ON INSULATOR INDICATE ENGINE DAMAGE.

CAUSED BY WRONG TYPE OF FUEL, INCORRECT IGNITION TIMING OR ADVANCE, TOO HOT A PLUG, BURNT VALVES OR ENGINE OVERHEATING. REPLACE THE PLUG.

OVERHEATING

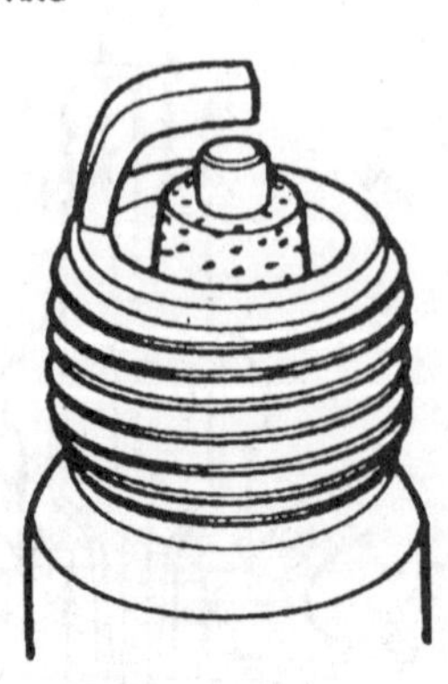

IDENTIFIED BY A WHITE OR LIGHT GRAY INSULATOR WITH SMALL BLACK OR GRAY BROWN SPOTS AND WITH BLUISH-BURNT APPEARANCE OF ELECTRODES.

CAUSED BY ENGINE OVER-HEATING, WRONG TYPE OF FUEL, LOOSE SPARK PLUGS, TOO HOT A PLUG, LOW FUEL PUMP PRESSURE OR INCORRECT IGNITION TIMING. REPLACE THE PLUG.

FUSED SPOT DEPOSIT

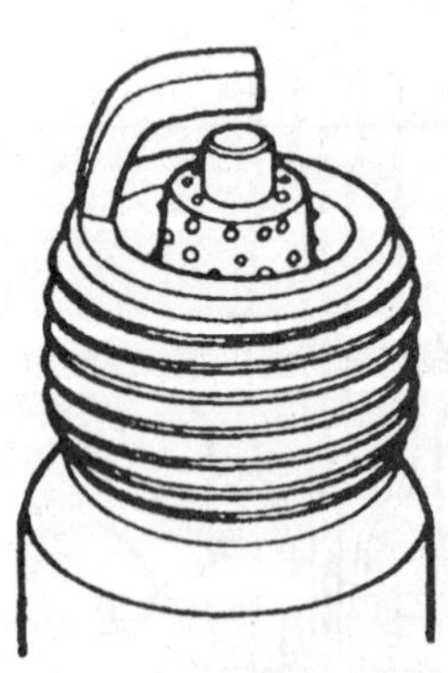

IDENTIFIED BY MELTED OR SPOTTY DEPOSITS RESEMBLING BUBBLES OR BLISTERS.

CAUSED BY SUDDEN ACCELERATION. CAN BE CLEANED IF NOT EXCESSIVE, OTHERWISE REPLACE PLUG.

tccs2002

Fig. 2 Inspect the spark plug to determine engine running conditions

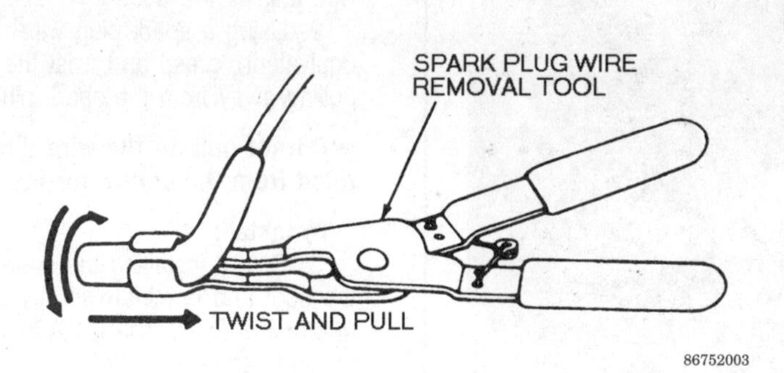

Fig. 3 This special tool does not stress the connectors at the spark plug boots while making removal easier

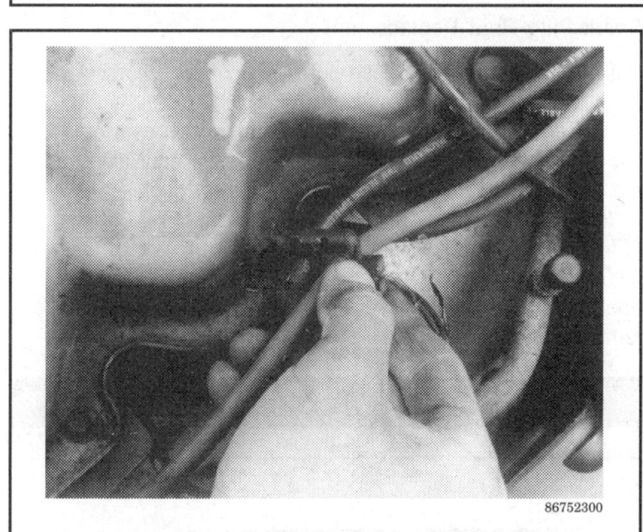

Fig. 4 Disconnect and reposition any plug wire separators that make it difficult to access the wire

Fig. 6 Carefully remove the spark plug for inspection and replacement

Fig. 5 After cleaning around the spark plugs, use a spark plug socket to loosen the plugs

bend the side electrode. The center electrode is fixed and is not adjustable.

8. Squirt a drop of penetrating oil on the threads of the spark plug and install it. Don't oil the threads heavily. Turn the plug in clockwise by hand until it is snug.
9. When the plug is finger-tight, use a torque wrench to tighten it to the specified value.
10. Install the plug wire and boot firmly over the spark plug after coating the inside of the boot and terminal with a thin coat of dielectric compound (Motorcraft D7AZ-19A331-A or the equivalent).
11. Proceed to the next spark plug.

Spark Plug Wires

➧ See Figure 7

Your vehicle is equipped with an electronic ignition system which utilizes 8mm wires to conduct the hotter spark produced. The boots on these wires are designed to cover the spark plug cavities in the cylinder head.

86752307

Fig. 7 Labeling the wires and the cap (if necessary) prevents confusion upon re-installation

REMOVAL & INSTALLATION

➡To avoid confusion, when replacing spark plug wires, remove and tag the wires, labeling each according to which cylinder it is connected to. Do each one at a time or mark the corresponding number on the cap to ensure proper connection.

1. Carefully inspect the wires before removing them from the spark plugs, coil or distributor cap. Look for visible damage such as cuts, pinches, cracks or torn boots. Replace any wires that show signs of damage. If the boot is damaged, it may be replaced by itself. It is not necessary to replace the complete wire just for the boot.
2. Using a spark plug wire removal tool (T74P-6666-A or equivalent), grasp and twist the boot back and forth while pulling away from the spark plug.

➡Do not pull on the wire directly, or it may become separated from the connector inside the boot.

To install:

3. Before installing the spark plug wire, coat the inside of the boot and terminal with a thin coat of dielectric compound (Motorcraft D7AZ-19A331-A or equivalent). Install the wires, making certain they fit firmly over the plug, coil or distributor cap.
4. Remove the wire retaining brackets from the old high-tension wire set and install them on the new set, in the same relative position. Install the wires in the brackets.

Spark Plug Boot Replacement

If it is necessary to replace only the boot on a particular wire, use the following procedure:

1. Carefully cut off the old boot. Apply a thin coat of dielectric grease (Motorcraft D7AZ-19A331-A or the equivalent) to the area of the wire that will contact the new boot.
2. Position the new boot onto the special tool (T74P-6666-A or equivalent).
3. Position the tool onto the wire terminal and slide the boot onto the wire. Remove the tool from the end of the wire terminal.

FIRING ORDERS

➧ See Figures 8, 9 and 10

➡To avoid confusion, when replacing spark plug wires, remove and tag the wires one at a time.

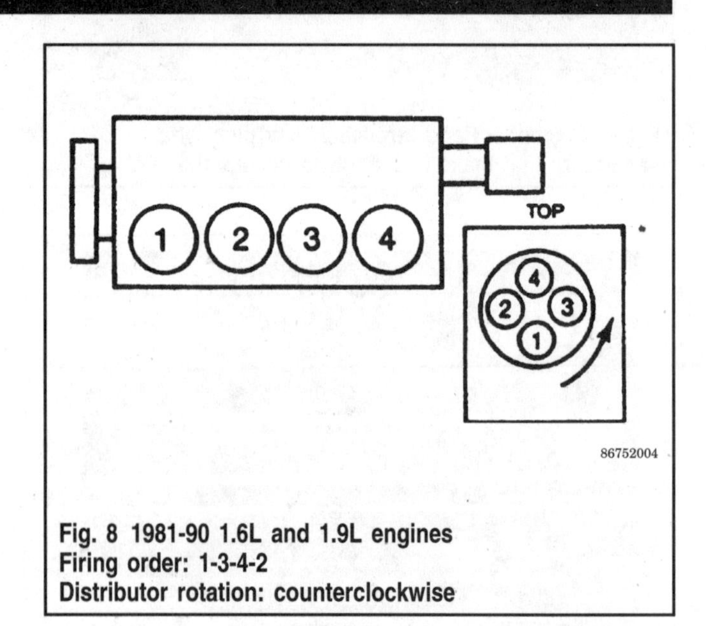

86752004

Fig. 8 1981-90 1.6L and 1.9L engines
Firing order: 1-3-4-2
Distributor rotation: counterclockwise

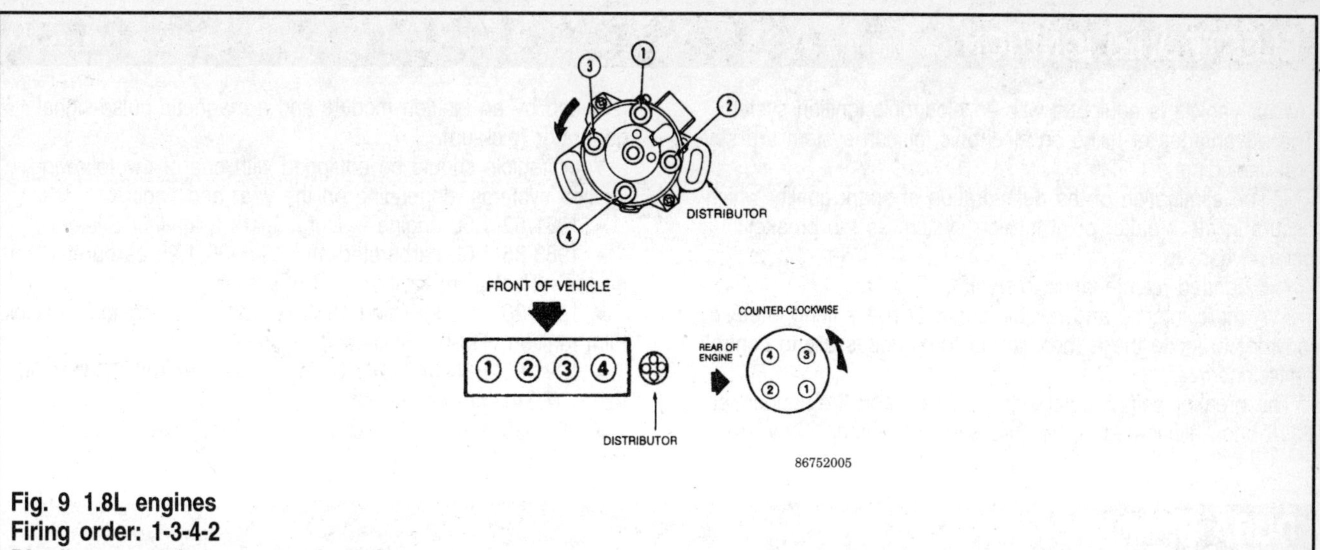

Fig. 9 1.8L engines
Firing order: 1-3-4-2
Distributor rotation: counterclockwise

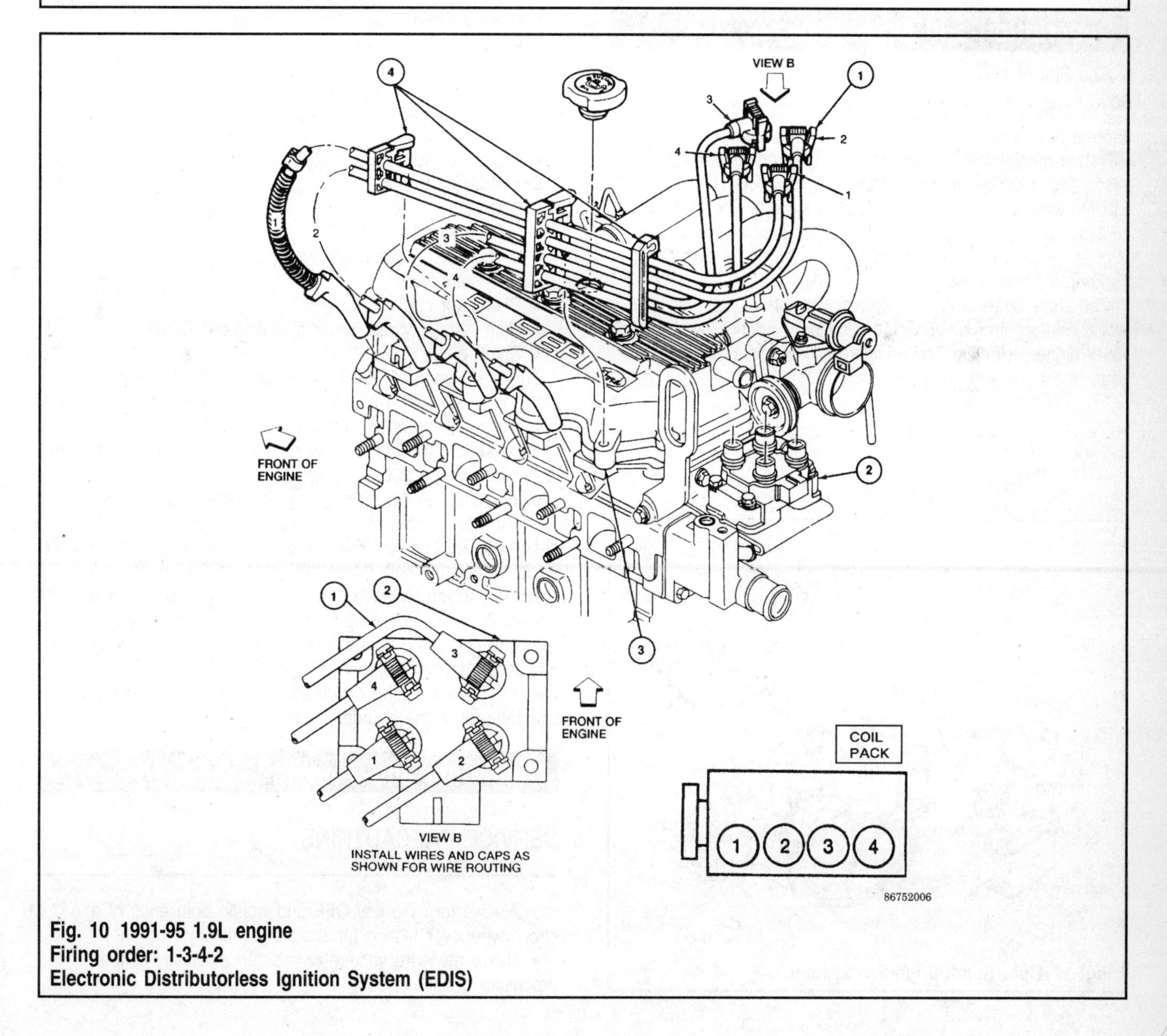

Fig. 10 1991-95 1.9L engine
Firing order: 1-3-4-2
Electronic Distributorless Ignition System (EDIS)

ELECTRONIC IGNITION

Your vehicle is equipped with an electronic ignition system. The advantages of using an electronic ignition system are several, including:

- The elimination of the deterioration of spark quality which occurs in the breaker point ignition system as the breaker points wear.
- Extended maintenance intervals.
- A more intense and reliable spark at every firing impulse in order to ignite the leaner gas mixtures necessary to control emissions.

The breaker points, point actuating cam and the condenser have been eliminated in the solid state distributor. They are replaced by an ignition module and a magnetic pulse-signal generator (pick-up).

Your vehicle should be equipped with one of the following ignition systems, depending on the year and engine:

- 1981-82 1.6L engine — Dura Spark II Ignition System
- 1983-85 1.6L carbureted and 1985-90 1.9L carbureted engines — Thick Film Ignition (TFI-I) System
- 1983-90 1.6L MFI and 1986-90 1.9L MFI engines — Thick Film Ignition (TFI-IV) System
- 1991-95 1.8L MFI DOHC engines — Electronic Spark Advance (ESA) Ignition System
- 1991-95 1.9L SFI — Electronic Distributorless Ignition System (EDIS)

DURA SPARK II IGNITION SYSTEM

Description and Operation

See Figure 11

The Dura Spark II ignition system of 1981-82 features a tang-driven distributor assembly with a top weight centrifugal advance mechanism, a concentric vacuum advance mechanism, and a concentric coil stator assembly. The Dura Spark II ignition system is a solid state ignition system. The system employs a 14mm spark plug, which uses a screw-on gasket. The spark plug boots include a seal for the spark plug cavity to keep it clean and dry.

The Dura Spark II ignition system consists of common electronic primary and conventional secondary circuits, designed to carry higher voltages. The primary and secondary circuits consists of the following components:

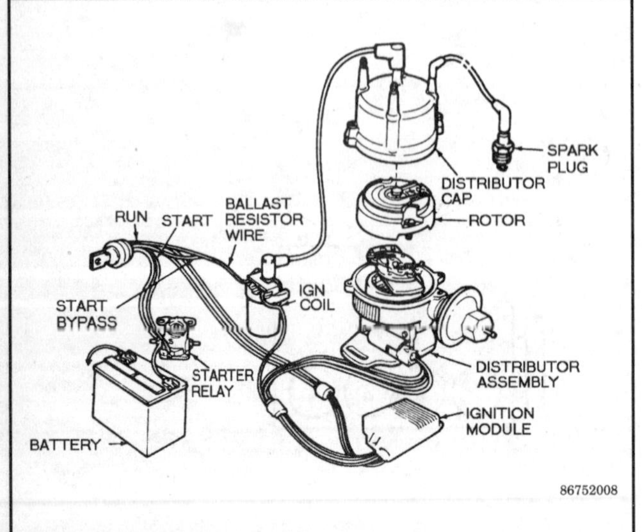

Fig. 11 Dura Spark II ignition system

Primary Circuit

- Battery
- Ignition switch
- Ballast resistor (start bypass wire)
- Ignition coil primary winding
- Ignition module
- Distributor stator assembly

Secondary Circuit

- Battery
- Ignition switch
- Ignition coil secondary winding
- Distributor rotor
- Distributor cap
- High voltage wires (spark plug and coil wires)
- Spark plugs

The basic operation of the distributor is the same as a solid state distributor. With the ignition switch in the **ON** position, the primary circuit current is directed from the battery, through the ignition switch, the ballast resistor, the ignition coil primary, the ignition module and back to the battery through the ignition system ground in the distributor. When the engine is being cranked, the rotating armature induces a signal in the stator assembly. This current flow causes a magnetic field to be built up in the ignition coil. When the poles on the armature and the stator assembly align, the ignition module turns the primary current flow off, collapsing the magnetic field in the ignition coil. The collapsing field induces a high voltage in the ignition coil secondary windings. The ignition coil wire then conducts the high voltage to the distributor where the cap and rotor distributes it to the appropriate spark plug.

Diagnosis and Testing

SERVICE PRECAUTIONS

- Always turn the key **OFF** and isolate both ends of a circuit whenever testing for short or continuity.
- Never measure voltage or resistance directly at the processor connector.

• Always disconnect solenoids and switches from the harness before measuring for continuity, resistance or energizing with a 12 volt source.

• When disconnecting connectors, inspect for damaged or pushed-out pins, corrosion, loose wires, etc. Repair or replace if necessary.

PRELIMINARY CHECKS

1. Visually inspect the engine compartment to ensure that all vacuum lines and spark plug wires are properly routed and securely connected.
2. Examine all wiring harnesses and connectors for insulation damage, burns, damage from overheating, loose or broken connections. Check that the TFI module is securely fastened to the side of the distributor.
3. Be certain that the battery is fully charged and that all accessories are **OFF** during the diagnosis.

CHECKING THE START CIRCUIT

See Figure 12

1. Connect a spark tester between the ignition coil wire and a good engine ground.
2. Crank the engine and check for spark at the tester.
3. If no spark occurs, check the following:
   a. Measure the resistance of the ignition coil secondary wire (high voltage wire). Resistance should not exceed 5000 ohms per foot.
   b. Inspect the ignition coil for damage or carbon tracking.
   c. Also, check that the distributor shaft is rotating, when the engine is being cranked.
   d. If the results in Steps a, b, and c are okay, go to "Supply Voltage Circuits" test in this section.
4. If a spark did occur, go to the "Run Circuit" test in this section.

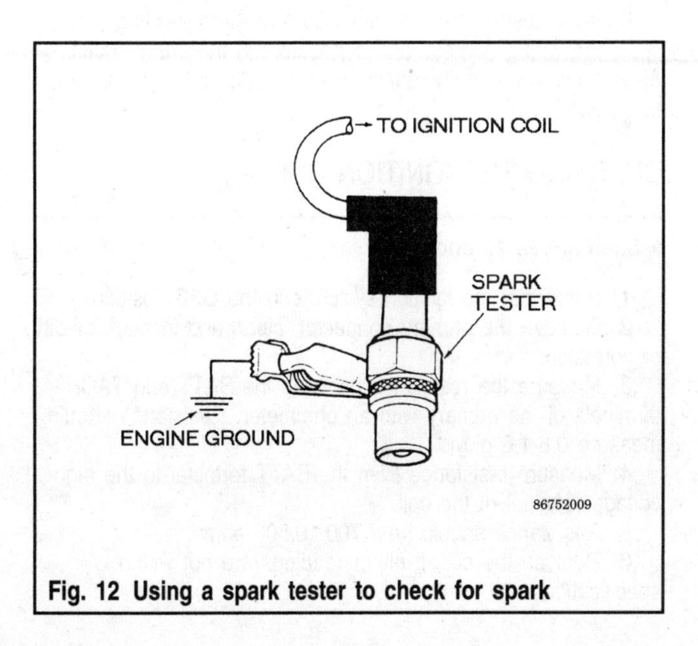

Fig. 12 Using a spark tester to check for spark

CHECKING THE RUN CIRCUIT

1. Turn the ignition switch from **OFF** to **ON** several times. A spark should occur each time the switch goes from the **OFF** to **ON** position.
2. Remove the spark tester and reconnect the coil wire to the distributor cap.
3. If a spark did occur, inspect the distributor cap, adapter, rotor for cracks, carbon tracking, or for a lack of silicone compound. Also, check that the roll pin is securing the armature to the sleeve in the distributor.
4. If no spark occurs, go to "Module Voltage" test in this section.

CHECKING THE MODULE VOLTAGE

See Figure 13

1. Turn the ignition switch from **OFF**.
2. Carefully insert a small straight pin in the RED module wire.

Do not allow the straight pin to contact electrical ground, while performing this test.

3. Attach the negative terminal of a volt meter to the distributor base.
4. Measure the battery voltage.
5. Measure the voltage at the straight pin, with ignition switch in **ON**.
6. Turn the ignition switch **OFF**. Remove the straight pin and seal the wire with liquid silicone.
7. If the results are within 90% of battery voltage, go to the "Ballast Resistor" test in this section.
8. If the results are not within 90% of battery voltage, inspect the wiring harness between the module and ignition switch. Also, check for a faulty ignition switch.

CHECKING THE BALLAST RESISTOR

See Figure 14

1. Disconnect and inspect the ignition module 2-wire connector (RED and WHITE).
2. Disconnect and inspect the ignition coil connector.
3. Measure the ballast resistor between the battery terminal of the ignition coil connector and the wiring harness connector mating with the RED module wire. The results should be 0.8-1.6 ohms.
4. If the results is less than 0.8 ohms or greater than 1.6 ohms, replace the ballast resistor.
5. If the results is okay, the problem is either intermittent or not in the ignition system.

CHECKING THE SUPPLY VOLTAGE CIRCUITS

See Figure 15

1. Remove the spark tester and reconnect the coil wire to the distributor cap.

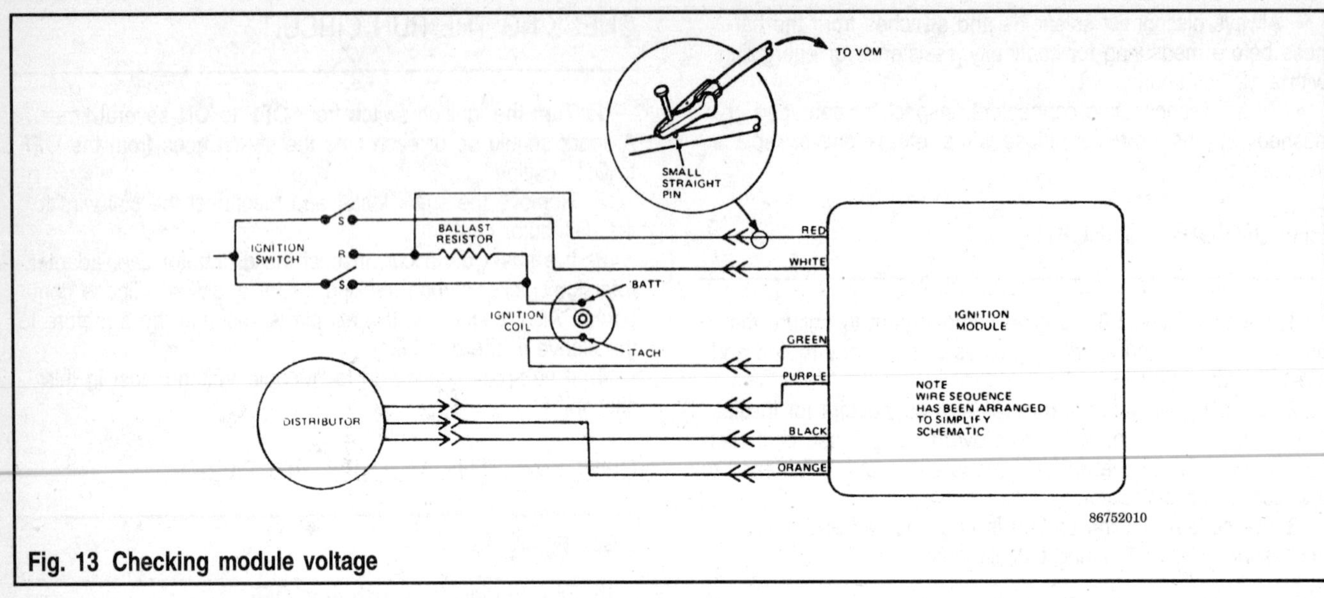

Fig. 13 Checking module voltage

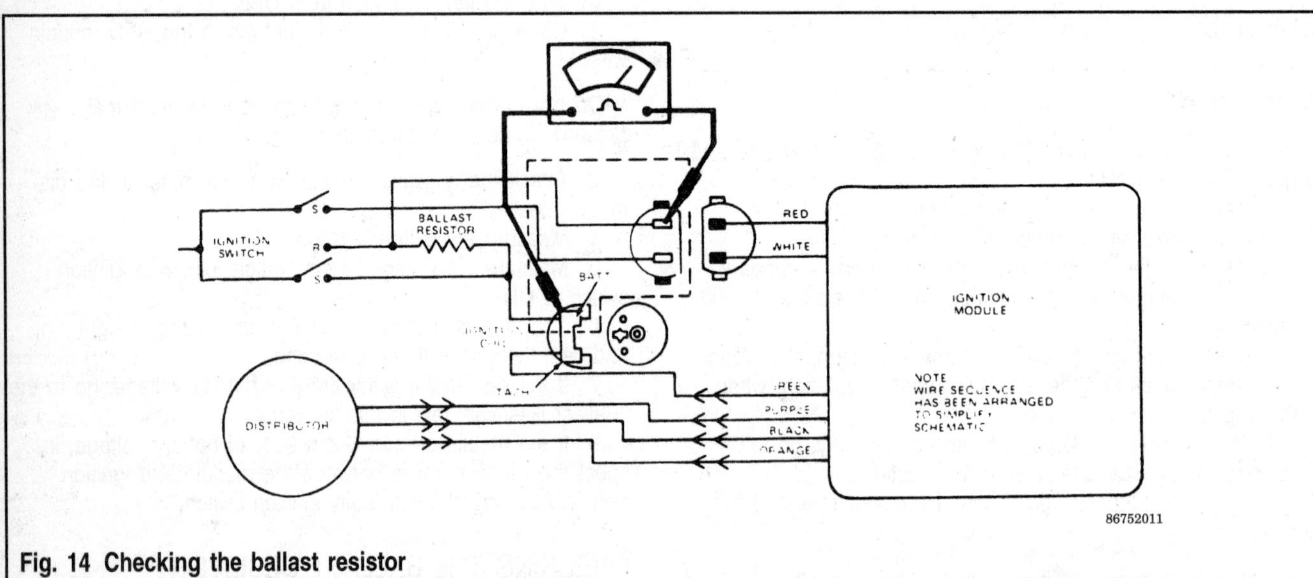

Fig. 14 Checking the ballast resistor

2. If the starter relay has an I terminal, disconnect the cable from the starter relay to the starter motor.
3. If the starter relay does not have an I terminal, disconnect the wire to the S terminal of the starter relay.
4. Carefully insert a small straight pin in the RED and WHITE module wire.

➡Do not allow the straight pin to contact electrical ground, while performing this test.

5. Measure the battery voltage.
6. Measure the voltage at the following points:
   a. RED wire (Run Circuit) — with ignition switch turned **ON**.
   b. WHITE wire (Start Circuit) — with ignition switch turned to **START**.
   c. Ignition Coil "Battery Terminal" (Ballast Resistor Bypass Circuit) — with ignition switch in **START**.
7. If the results are within 90% of battery voltage, go to the "Ignition Coil" test in this section.
8. If the results are not within 90% of battery voltage, inspect the wiring harness and connectors in the faulty circuit. Also, check for a faulty ignition switch, radio capacitor or ignition coil.

CHECKING THE IGNITION COIL

▶ See Figures 16 and 17

1. Verify that the ignition switch is in the **OFF** position.
2. Remove the primary connector, clean and inspect for dirt or corrosion.
3. Measure the resistance between the BATT and TACH terminals of the primary with an ohmmeter. Resistance should measure 0.8-1.6 ohms.
4. Measure resistance from the BATT terminal to the high voltage terminal of the coil.
5. Resistance should be 7,700-10,500 ohms.
6. Replace the coil, if either readings are not within specifications.

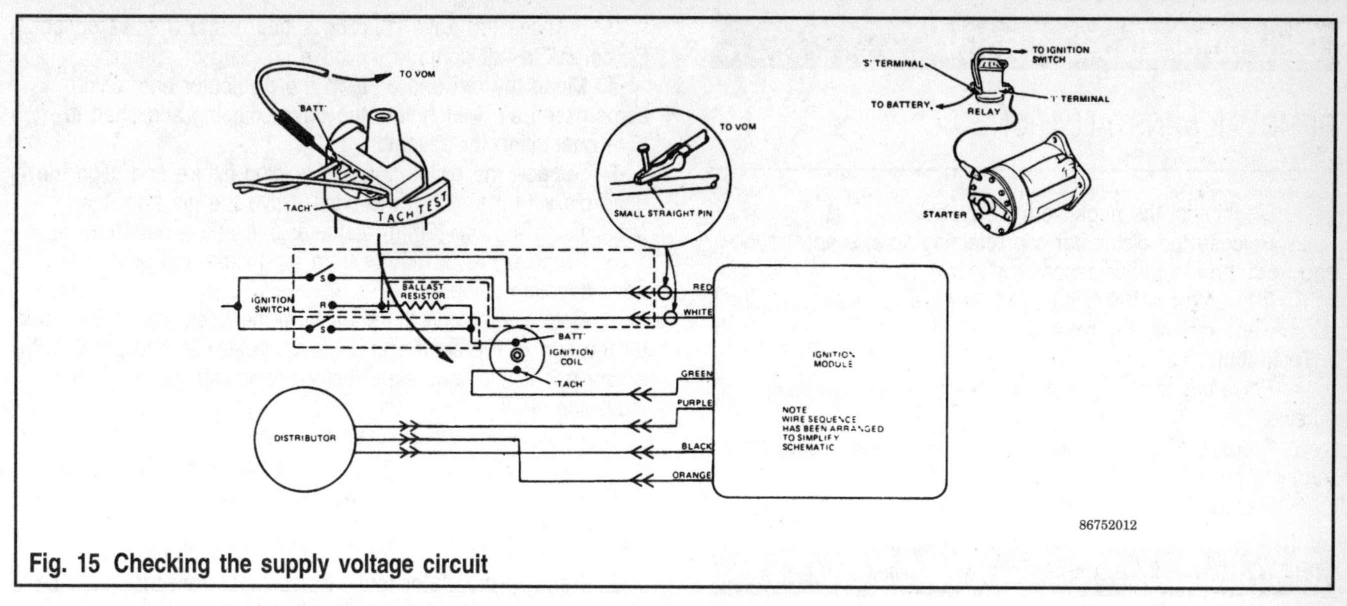

Fig. 15 Checking the supply voltage circuit

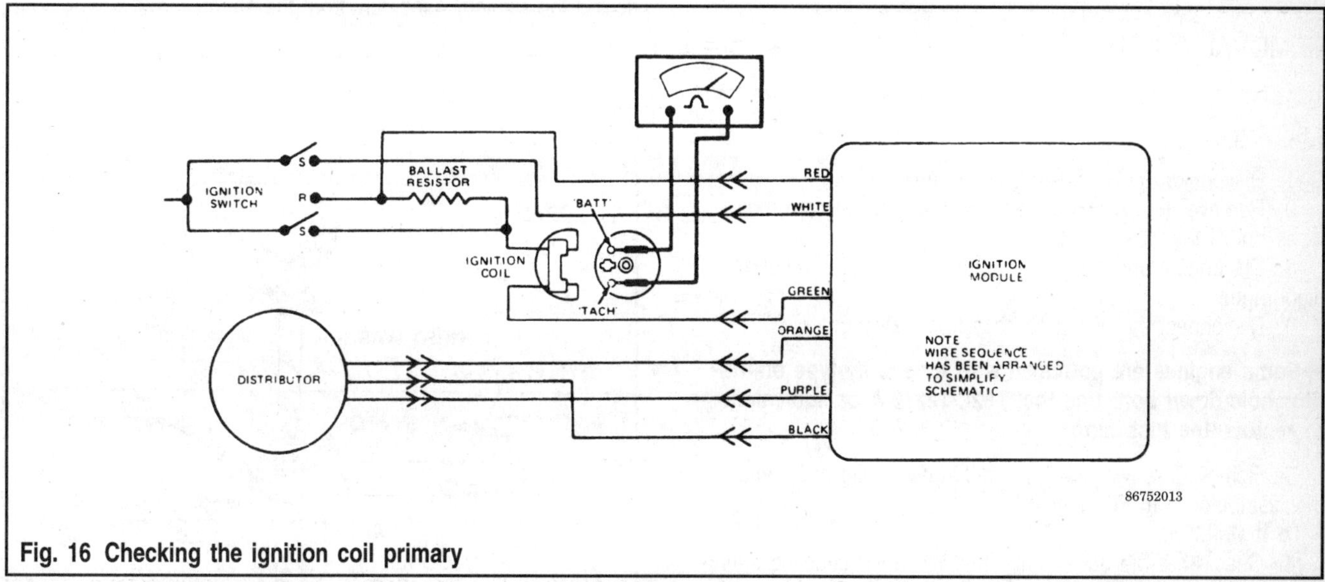

Fig. 16 Checking the ignition coil primary

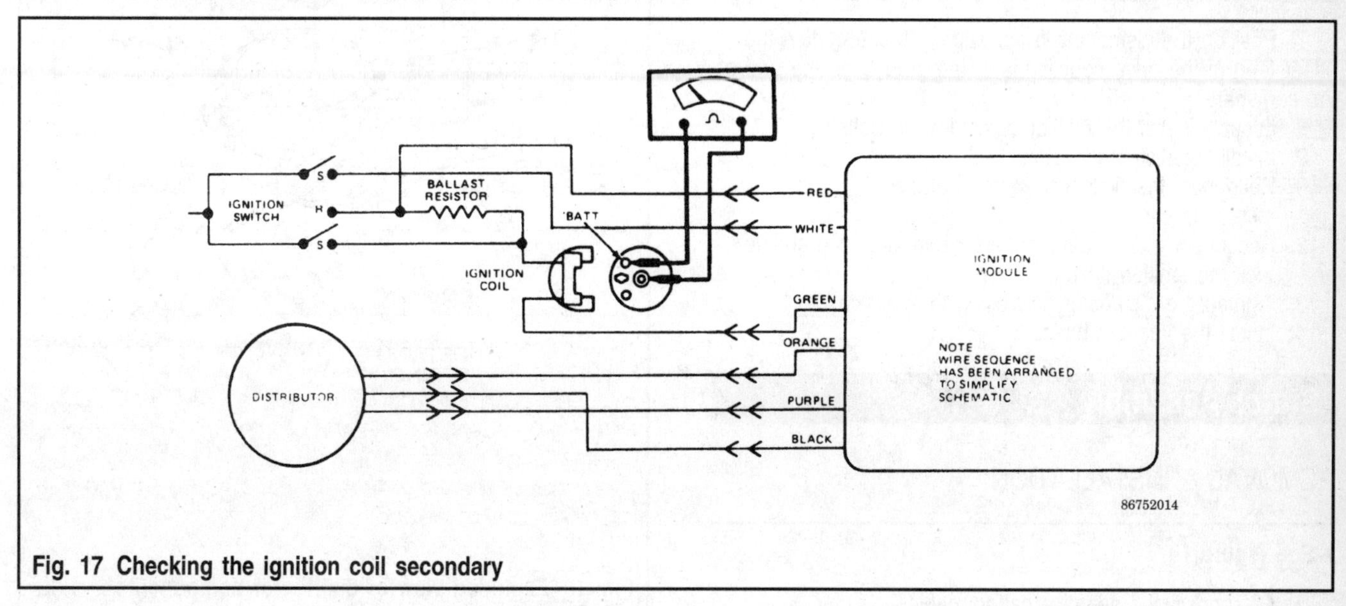

Fig. 17 Checking the ignition coil secondary

Distributor Cap and Rotor

REMOVAL & INSTALLATION

1. Disconnect the negative battery cable.
2. Release the distributor cap retaining screws and lift the cap from the distributor assembly.
3. If the rotor is being replaced, remove the rotor retaining screws and remove the rotor.

To install:

4. Place the rotor into position and install the retaining screws.
5. Properly fit the cap onto the distributor and secure the retaining screws.
6. Reconnect the negative battery cable.

Distributor

REMOVAL & INSTALLATION

1.6L Engine

1. Disconnect the negative battery cable.
2. Remove the distributor cap and position the cap and wires out of the way.
3. Disconnect and plug the vacuum hose at the vacuum diaphragm.
4. Disconnect the wiring harness to the distributor.

➡Some engines are equipped with a security-type distributor hold-down bolt. Use tool T82L-12270-A or equivalent to remove the distributor.

5. Remove the two distributor hold-down bolts and remove the distributor from the engine.

To install:

6. Check that the base O-ring and the drive coupling spring is in place.
7. Position the distributor in the engine. Make certain the offset tang of the drive coupling is in the groove on the end of the camshaft.
8. Loosely install the distributor hold-down bolts.
9. Install the distributor rotor.
10. Reconnect the distributor wiring harness.
11. Install the cap.
12. Reconnect the negative battery cable, start the engine and check the ignition timing.
13. Tighten the distributor hold-down to specification.
14. Install the vacuum hose.

Stator Assembly

REMOVAL & INSTALLATION

➧ See Figure 18

1. Disconnect the negative battery cable.
2. Remove the distributor from the engine.
3. Remove the drive coupling spring, using a small prytool. Be careful to not damage the drive coupling or spring.
4. Clean the dirt and oil from the distributor end, using compressed air. Matchmark the drive coupling and shaft to note orientation for assembly.
5. Support the distributor in a holding fixture and align the drive pin with the slot in the base. Drive the pin from the shaft, using a $^1/_8$ in. (3mm) diameter drift and a hammer.
6. Remove the distributor from the fixture and place the drive coupling aside.
7. Before removing the shaft from the base, check for burrs on the end of the shaft and drive pin hole. File and polish with emery paper and wipe clean before removing the shaft. Remove the shaft.
8. Remove the stator retaining screws.
9. Remove the connector from the top of the TFI module.
10. Remove the three screws that secure the stator retainer to the base.
11. Carefully lift the stator assembly out of the base.
12. Remove the stator retainer assembly from the stator by pulling the retainer assembly from the stator.

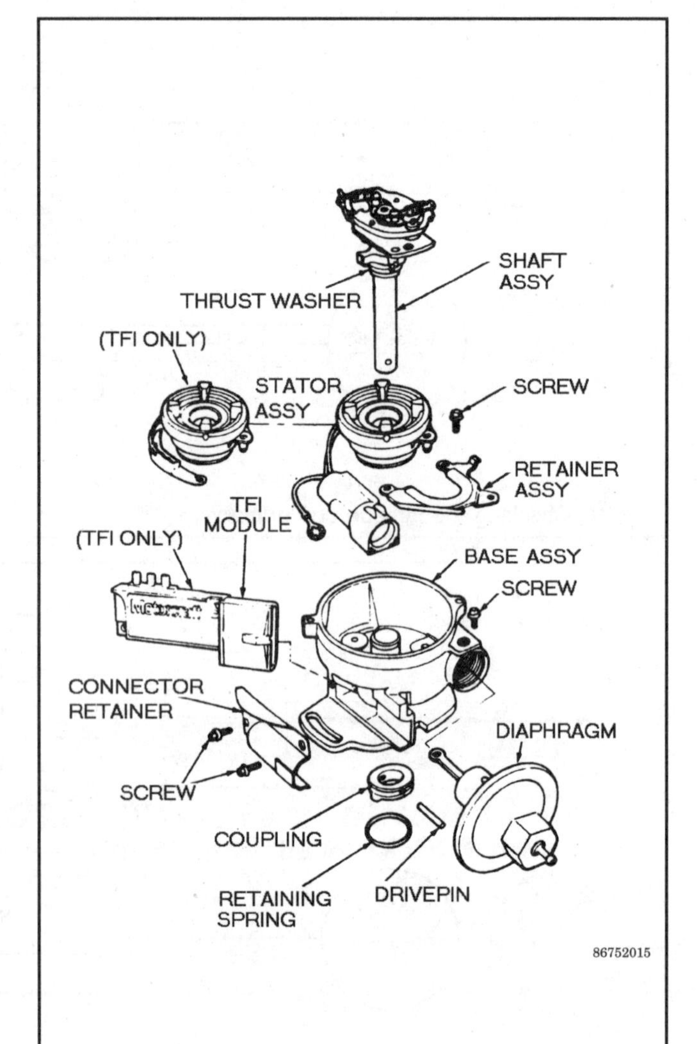

Fig. 18 Exploded view of distributor components — 1.6L carbureted engine

13. Check the stator bumper for excess wear. Check the diaphragm O-ring for cracks or tears. Check the bushing for signs of excessive heat concentration. Check the oil seal for tears or cuts. Check the spring retainer that holds the shaft oil seal against the shaft. It must have no kinks or breaks. Replace the component which shows any of these wear sings.

To install:

14. Attach the stator retainer to the stator assembly, by sliding the stator bumper into the groove in the bottom of the stator with the horseshoe opening at the diaphragm rod pivot pin.
15. Place the connector on the top of the TFI module with the three pins aligned and press down to seat the connector.
16. Place the stator assembly over the base bushing with the diaphragm pivot pin approximately in the front of the diaphragm mounting hole.
17. Line up the holes in the stator retainer plate with the holes in the base.
18. Install the three retaining screws.
19. Check the stator assembly for free rotation.
20. Install the connector-to-base retaining screws.
21. Place the two stator wires behind the wire guard that is part of the connector so that the wires are not twisted or tangled.
22. Install the diaphragm.
23. Apply a light coat of M2C162A or equivalent oil to the distributor shaft below the armature.
24. Install the shaft and place the drive coupling over the shaft. Line up the reference marks. Start the pin into the drive coupling and shaft. Drive the pin into the shaft until the pin is flush with the step in the drive coupling.
25. Check for free rotation.
26. Install the drive coupling spring in the groove on the drive coupling.
27. Install the distributor assembly in the engine.
28. Install the distributor cap and rotor.
29. Reconnect the negative battery cable.
30. Recheck the initial timing. Adjust, if necessary.

THICK FILM IGNITION (TFI) SYSTEM

Description and Operation

See Figures 19, 20, 21 and 22

The original Thick Film Integrated (TFI) ignition system was incorporated on 1.6L engines, in late 1982. In 1983, a second version of the TFI ignition system (TFI-IV) was added. The earlier TFI was carried over for 1.6L and 1.9L carbureted engines through 1986. The TFI-IV system, meanwhile, was used on 1.6L MFI and 1.9L CFI/MFI engines. Engines equipped with TFI-IV, employed a newly designed spark plug which has an extended reach 14mm tapered seat, a new design multipoint rotor and a distributor (universal distributor), which eliminate the conventional centrifugal and vacuum advance mechanisms, used on the earlier Dura Spark II Ignition System.

The distributor used on 1.6L carbureted and 1.9L non-MFI/SFI engines is a carry-over design distributor with a top weight centrifugal advance mechanism and concentric coil stator assembly. The distributor used on 1.6L MFI engines is a universal distributor design which has a tang-driven die-cast base. This distributor incorporates an integrally mounted TFI-IV module, a vane switch stator assembly which replaces the current coil stator. The distributor also contains a provision for fixing octane adjustment. The overall design of this distributor eliminates the conventional centrifugal and vacuum advance mechanisms.

The basic operation of the distributor (with concentric coil stator assembly) is the same as the Dura Spark II ignition system. The rotating armature induces a signal in the stator assembly causing the ignition module to turn the ignition coil current ON and OFF.

During model year 1985½-90, the operation of the universal distributor assembly used on the 1.9L MFI engine is accomplished through a Hall effect vane switch assembly, causing the ignition coil to be switched OFF and ON by the ECC-IV computer and TFI-IV modules. The vane switch is an encapsulated package consisting of a Hall sensor on one side and a permanent magnet on the other side. The distributor contains a

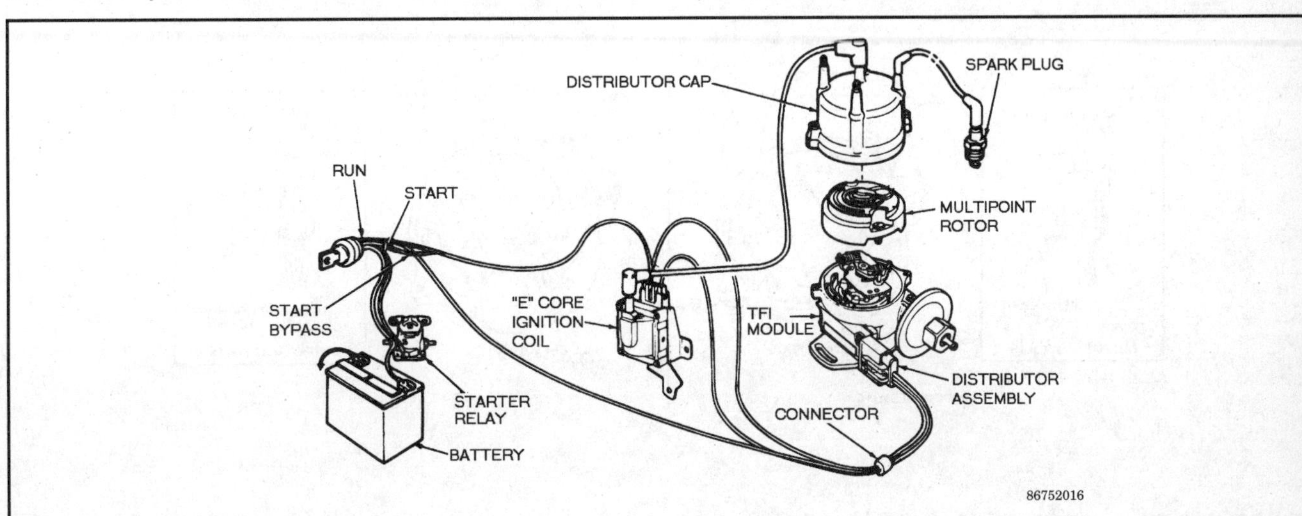

Fig. 19 Thick Film Integrated Ignition System (TFI-I) — 1982-85 1.6L carbureted engine and 1985-86 1.9L carbureted engine

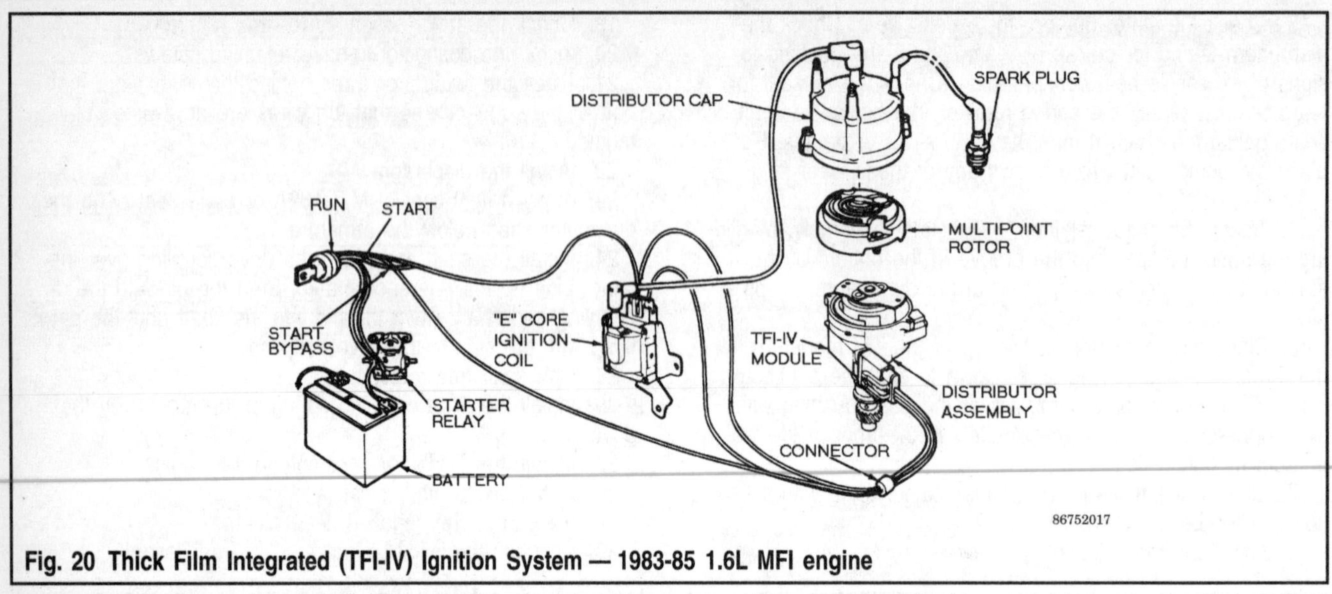

Fig. 20 Thick Film Integrated (TFI-IV) Ignition System — 1983-85 1.6L MFI engine

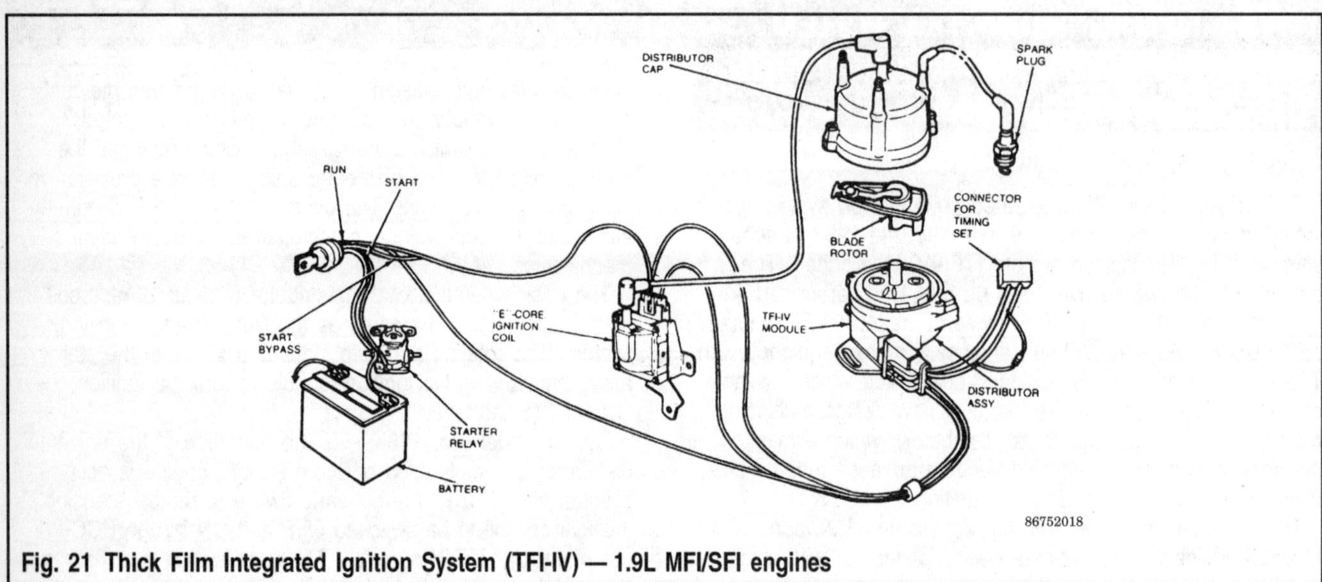

Fig. 21 Thick Film Integrated Ignition System (TFI-IV) — 1.9L MFI/SFI engines

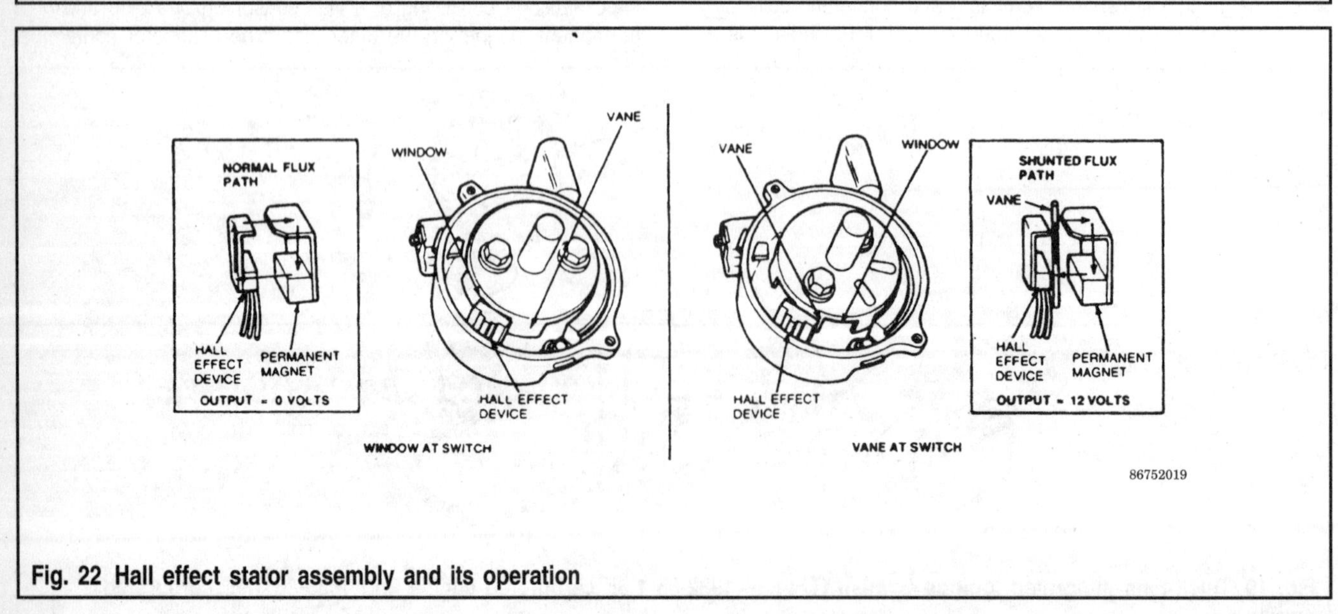

Fig. 22 Hall effect stator assembly and its operation

provision to change the basic distributor calibration with the use of a replaceable octane rod, from the standard of 0° to either 3° or 6° retard rods. No other calibration changes are possible. The TFI-IV system features a "push start" mode which allows manual transaxle vehicles to be push started. Automatic transaxle vehicles must not be push started.

A rotary armature, made of ferrous metal, is used to trigger the Hall effect switch. When the window of the armature is between the magnet and the Hall effect device, a magnetic flux field is completed from the magnet through the Hall effect device back to the magnet. As the vane passes through the opening, the flux lines are shunted through the vane and back to the magnet. A voltage is produced while the vane passes through the opening. When the vane clears the opening, the window causes the signal to go to 0 volts. The signal is then used by the EEC-IV system for crankshaft position sensing and the computation of the desired spark advance based on the engine demand and calibration. The voltage distribution is accomplished through a conventional rotor, cap and ignition wires.

Diagnosis and Testing

SERVICE PRECAUTIONS

- Always turn the key **OFF** and isolate both ends of a circuit whenever testing for short or continuity.
- Never measure voltage or resistance directly at the processor connector.
- Always disconnect solenoids and switches from the harness before measuring for continuity, resistance or energizing by means of a 12 volts source.
- When disconnecting connectors, inspect for damaged or pushed-out pins, corrosion, loose wires, etc. Service if required.

PRELIMINARY CHECKS

1. Visually inspect the engine compartment to ensure that all vacuum lines and spark plug wires are properly routed and securely connected.
2. Examine all wiring harnesses and connectors for insulation damage, burned, overheated, loose or broken conditions. Check that the TFI module is securely fastened to the side of the distributor.
3. Be certain that the battery is fully charged and that all accessories are **OFF** during the diagnosis.

TFI-IV IGNITION COIL SECONDARY VOLTAGE

1. Connect a spark tester between the ignition coil wire and a good engine ground.
2. Crank the engine and check for spark at the tester.
3. Turn the ignition switch **OFF**.
4. If no spark occurs, check the following:
   a. Inspect the ignition coil for damage or carbon tracking.
   b. Also, check that the distributor shaft is rotating, when the engine is being cranked.
   c. Measure the resistance of the ignition coil wire. If greater than 7000 ohms replace it.
   d. If the results in Steps a, b and c are okay, go to Ignition Coil Primary Circuit Switching test.
5. If a spark did occur, check the distributor cap and rotor for damage or carbon tracking. Go to Wiring Harness test.

TFI-IV IGNITION COIL PRIMARY CIRCUIT SWITCHING

▸ See Figure 23

1. Disconnect the wiring harness from the ignition coil. Check for dirt, corrosion or damage.
2. Attach a 12 volt DC test light between the coil TACH terminal and a good engine ground.
3. Crank the engine and observe the lamp.
4. If the light flashes or lights without flashing, go to Ignition Coil test.
5. If there is no light or a very dim light, disconnect the harness from the ignition module.
6. Disconnect the wire at the S terminal of the starter relay.
7. Measure the battery voltage.
8. Carefully insert a small straight pin in the appropriate terminal.

➡Do not allow the straight pin to contact the electrical ground, while performing this test.

9. Measure the voltage at the following points:
   a. Terminal No. 3 (Run Circuit) — with ignition switch turned to **ON** and **START**.
   b. Terminal No. 4 (Start Circuit) — with ignition switch turned to **START**.
   c. Terminal No. 2 (To ignition coil terminal) — with ignition switch turned **ON**.
10. Turn the ignition switch **OFF** and remove the straight pin.
11. Reconnect the S terminal wire at the starter relay.

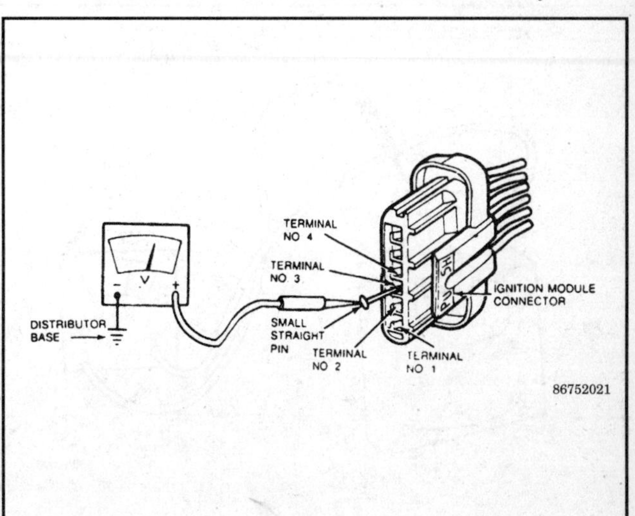

Fig. 23 Check the wiring harness at the ignition module connector

12. If the results are within 90% of battery voltage, check the stator assembly.
13. If the results are not within 90% of battery voltage, inspect the wiring harness and connectors in the faulty circuit. Also, check for a faulty ignition switch.

TFI-IV IGNITION COIL

See Figures 24 and 25

1. Verify that the ignition switch is in the OFF position.
2. Remove the primary connector, clean and inspect for dirt or corrosion.
3. Measure the resistance between the BATT and TACH terminals of the primary with an ohmmeter. Resistance should measure 0.3-1.0 ohms.
4. Measure resistance from the BATT terminal to the high voltage terminal of the coil.
5. Resistance should be 6500-11,000 ohms.

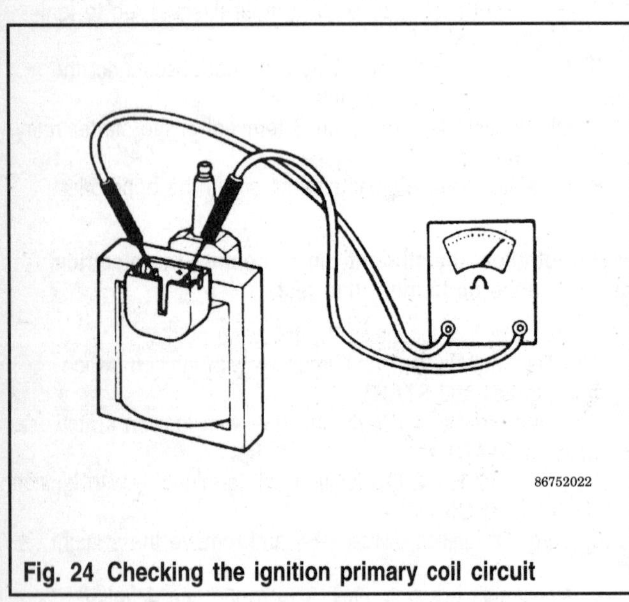

Fig. 24 Checking the ignition primary coil circuit

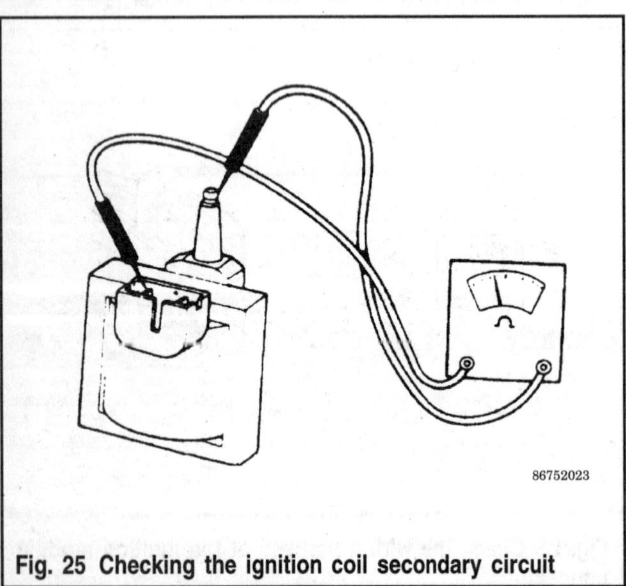

Fig. 25 Checking the ignition coil secondary circuit

6. Replace the coil, if either readings are not within specifications.

STATOR ASSEMBLY

1. Remove the distributor assembly from the engine.
2. Remove the ignition module from the distributor.
3. Check the stator assembly wires and terminals.
4. Measure the resistance of the stator. Readings should be 650-1,300 ohms.
5. If the readings are not within specifications, replace the stator assembly.

IGNITION COIL SECONDARY VOLTAGE CRANK MODE TFI-IV — EEC

See Figure 26

1. Connect a spark tester between the ignition coil wire and a good engine ground.
2. Crank the engine and check for spark at the tester.
3. Turn the ignition switch **OFF**.
4. If no spark occurs, check the following:
   a. Inspect the ignition coil for damage or carbon tracking.
   b. Also, check that the distributor shaft is rotating, when the engine is being cranked.
   c. If the results in Steps a, and b are okay, go to Stator — TFI test.
5. If a spark did occur, check the distributor cap and rotor for damage or carbon tracking. Go to "Ignition Coil Secondary Voltage (Run Mode)" test.

IGNITION COIL SECONDARY VOLTAGE (RUN MODE) TFI-IV — EEC

1. Fully apply the parking brake. Place the gear shift lever in P (automatic transaxle) or N (manual transaxle).

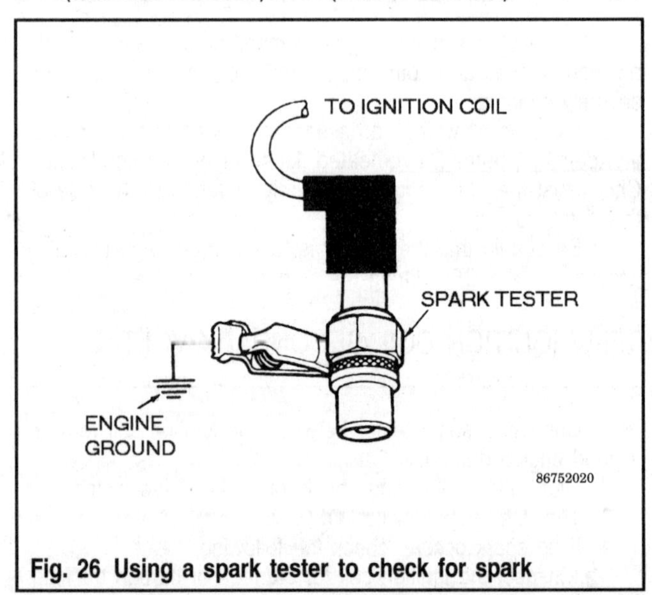

Fig. 26 Using a spark tester to check for spark

2. Disconnect the S terminal wire at the starter relay. Then, attach a remote starter switch.
3. Turn the ignition switch to the **ON** position.
4. Using the remote starter switch, crank the engine and check for spark.
5. Turn the ignition switch **OFF**.
6. If no spark occurs, go to the Wiring Harness test.
7. If a spark did occur, the problem is not in the ignition system.

WIRING HARNESS TFI-IV — EEC

1. Push the connector tabs and separate the wiring harness connector from the ignition module. Check for dirt, corrosion or damage.
2. Check that the S terminal wire at the starter relay is disconnected.
3. Measure the battery voltage.
4. Carefully insert a small straight pin in the appropriate terminal.

➡Do not allow the straight pins to contact electrical ground, while performing this test.

5. Measure the voltage at the following points:
   a. TFI Without CCD — Terminal No. 3 (Run Circuit) — with ignition switch turned to **ON** and **START**.
   b. TFI Without CCD — Terminal No. 4 (Start Circuit) — with ignition switch turned to **START**.
   c. TFI With CCD — Terminal No. 3 (Run Circuit) — with ignition switch turned to **ON** and **START**.
6. Turn the ignition switch **OFF** and remove the straight pin.
7. Reconnect the S terminal wire at the starter relay.
8. If the results are within 90% of battery voltage, replace the TFI module.
9. If the results are not within 90% of battery voltage, inspect the wiring harness and connectors in the faulty circuit. Also, check for a faulty ignition switch.

STATOR — TFI

➧ See Figure 27

1. Fully apply the parking brake. Place the gear shift lever in P (automatic transaxle) or N (manual transaxle).
2. Disconnect the harness connector at the TFI module and connect the TFI tester.
3. Disconnect the S terminal wire at the starter relay. Then, attach a remote starter switch.
4. Using the remote starter switch, crank the engine and check the status of the two LED lamps.
5. Remove the tester and remote switch.
6. Reconnect the wire at the starter relay and harness to the TFI module.
7. If the PIP light blinks, go to the TFI module test.
8. If the PIP light did not blink, remove the distributor cap, crank the engine and check that the distributor shaft rotates. If okay, go to the Stator TFI-IV test.

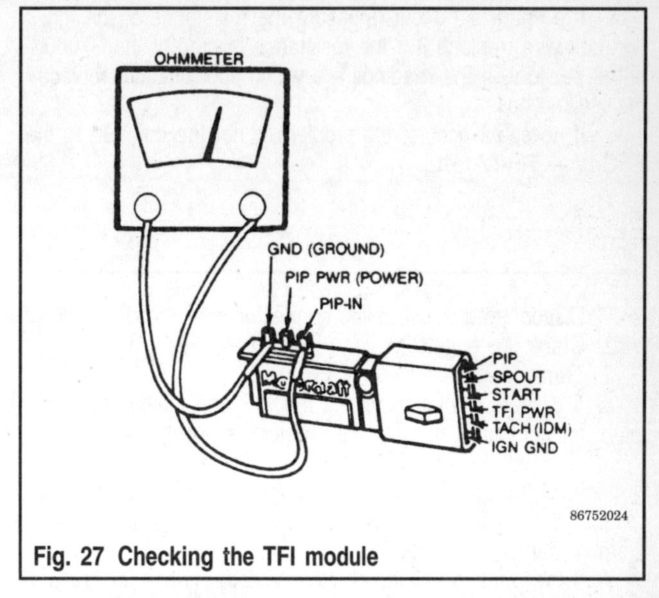

Fig. 27 Checking the TFI module

STATOR — TFI-IV

1. Remove the distributor from the engine. Remove the TFI module from the distributor.
2. Measure the resistance between the TFI module terminals, as follow:
   a. GND-PIP In — should be greater than 500 ohms.
   b. PIP PWR-PIP IN — should be less than 2000 ohms.
   c. PIP PWR-TFI PWR — should be less than 200 ohms.
   d. GND-IGN GND — should be less than 2 ohms.
   e. PIP In-PIP — should be less than 200 ohms.
3. If the readings are within the specified value, replace the stator.
4. If the readings are not as specified, replace the TFI.

TFI MODULE — EEC

1. Use the status of the tach light from the Stator — TFI test.
2. If the tach light blink, go to Ignition Coil Wire and Coil test.
3. If the tach light did not blink, replace the TFI module, then check for spark, as indicated in the Ignition Coil Secondary Voltage test. If the spark was not present, replace the coil also.

IGNITION COIL WIRE AND COIL TFI-IV — EEC

1. Disconnect the ignition coil connector and check for dirt, corrosion or damage.
2. Substitute a known good coil and check for spark using the spark tester.

➡The possibility of dangerously high voltage may be present when performing this test. Do not hold the coil while performing this test.

3. Crank the engine and check for spark.
4. Turn the ignition switch **OFF**.

5. If a spark did occur, measure the resistance of the ignition coil wire, replace it if the resistance is greater than 7000 ohms per foot. If the readings are within specification, replace the ignition coil.
6. If no spark occurs, the problem is not the coil. Go to the EEC-IV — TFI-IV test.

EEC-IV — TFI-IV

1. Disconnect the pin-in-line connector near the distributor.
2. Crank the engine.
3. Turn the ignition switch **OFF**.
4. If a spark did occur, check the PIP and ignition ground wires for continuity. If okay, the problem is not the ignition.
5. If no spark occurs, check the voltage at the positive terminal of the ignition coil, with the ignition switch turned **ON**.
6. If the reading is not within battery voltage, check for a worn or damaged ignition switch.
7. If the reading is within battery voltage, check for faults in the wiring between the coil and TFI module terminal No. 2 or any additional wiring or components connected to that circuit.

Distributor Cap & Rotor

REMOVAL & INSTALLATION

1. Disconnect the negative battery cable.
2. Mark the distributor cap towers with the cylinders to assist during spark plug wires installation.
3. Disconnect the coil and spark plug wires at the distributor.
4. Remove the distributor cap retaining screws.
5. Remove the cap and rotor.

To install:

6. If removed, install the inner and outer covers and rotor.
7. Place the distributor cap into position and install the retaining screws.
8. Connect the coil and the spark plug wires.
9. Connect the negative battery cable.

Distributor Assembly

➧ See Figures 28, 29, 30 and 31

REMOVAL & INSTALLATION

1. Disconnect the negative battery cable.
2. Remove the distributor cap and position the cap and wires out of the way. You may opt to mark the wires or the cap so as to avoid confusion when replacing the wires on the cap.
3. Disconnect and plug the vacuum hose at the vacuum diaphragm (carbureted only).
4. Disconnect the wiring harness to the distributor.

➡Some engines are equipped with a security-type distributor hold-down bolt. Use tool T82L-12270-A or equivalent to remove the distributor.

5. Matchmark the distributor base to the rocker arm cover to allow more accurate timing upon reinstallation.
6. Remove the two distributor hold-down bolts and remove the distributor from the engine.

To install:

7. Check that the base O-ring and the drive coupling spring is in place.
8. Position the distributor in the engine. Make certain the offset tang of the drive coupling is in the groove on the end of the camshaft.
9. Loosely install the distributor hold-down bolts.
10. Install the distributor rotor.
11. Reconnect the distributor wiring harness.
12. Install the cap.
13. Reconnect the negative battery cable, start the engine and check the ignition timing.
14. Tighten the distributor hold-down to specification.
15. Install the vacuum hose (carbureted only).

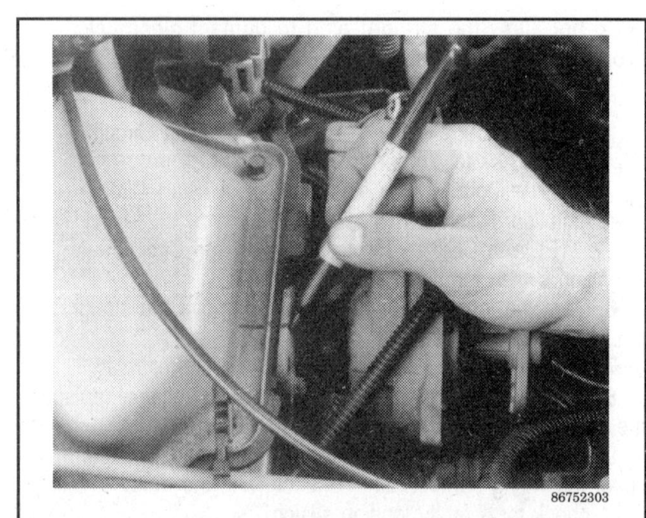

86752303

Fig. 28 Matchmark the distributor to the rocker cover in order to assure installation in the original position

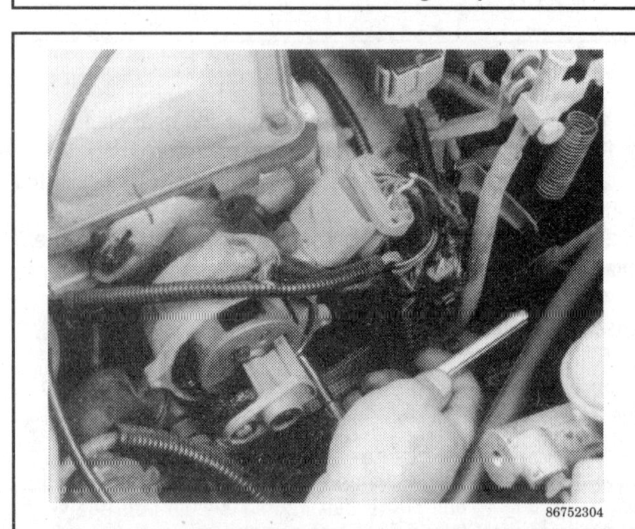

86752304

Fig. 29 After detaching the wiring, remove the hold-down bolts using a ratchet and socket

Fig. 30 The distributor assembly (with rotor still attached) is removed for inspection

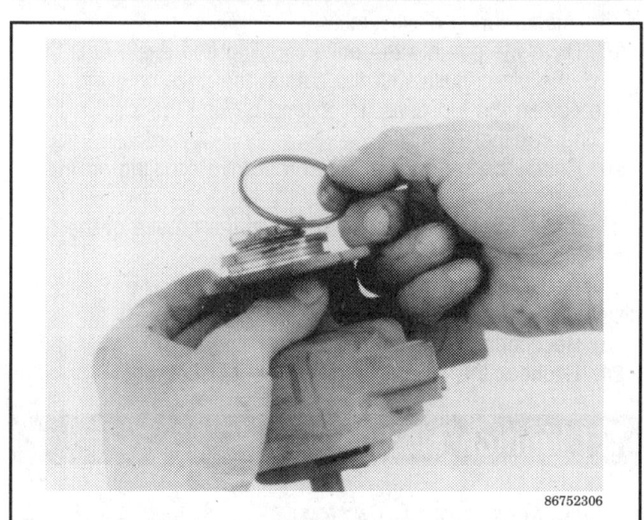

Fig. 31 Inspect the O-ring and replace if dry, cracked or compressed

Stator Assembly

REMOVAL & INSTALLATION

1.6L and 1.9L non-MFI/SFI Engines

See Figure 32

1. Disconnect the negative battery cable.
2. Remove the distributor from the engine.
3. Remove the drive coupling spring, using a small prytool. Be careful to not damage the drive coupling or the spring.
4. Clean the dirt and oil from the distributor end, using compressed air. Matchmark the drive coupling and shaft to note orientation for assembly.
5. Support the distributor in a holding fixture and align the drive pin with the slot in the base. Drive the pin from the shaft, using a 1/8 in. (3mm) diameter drift (1.6L engine) or a 3/32 in. (2.5mm) diameter drift (1.9L non-MFI/SFI engine) and a hammer.
6. Remove the distributor from the fixture and place the drive coupling aside.
7. Before removing the shaft from the base, check for burrs on the end of the shaft and the drive pin hole. File and polish with emery paper and wipe clean before removing the shaft. Then remove the shaft.
8. Remove the stator retaining screws.
9. Remove the connector from the top of the TFI module.
10. Remove the three screws that secure the stator retainer to the base.
11. Carefully lift the stator assembly out of the base.
12. Remove the stator retainer assembly from the stator by pulling the retainer assembly from the stator.
13. Check the stator bumper from excess wear. Check the diaphragm O-ring for cracks or tears. Check the bushing for signs of excessive heat concentration. Check the oil seal for tears or cuts. Check the spring retainer that holds the shaft oil seal against the shaft. It must have no kinks or breaks. Replace the component which shows any of these signs.

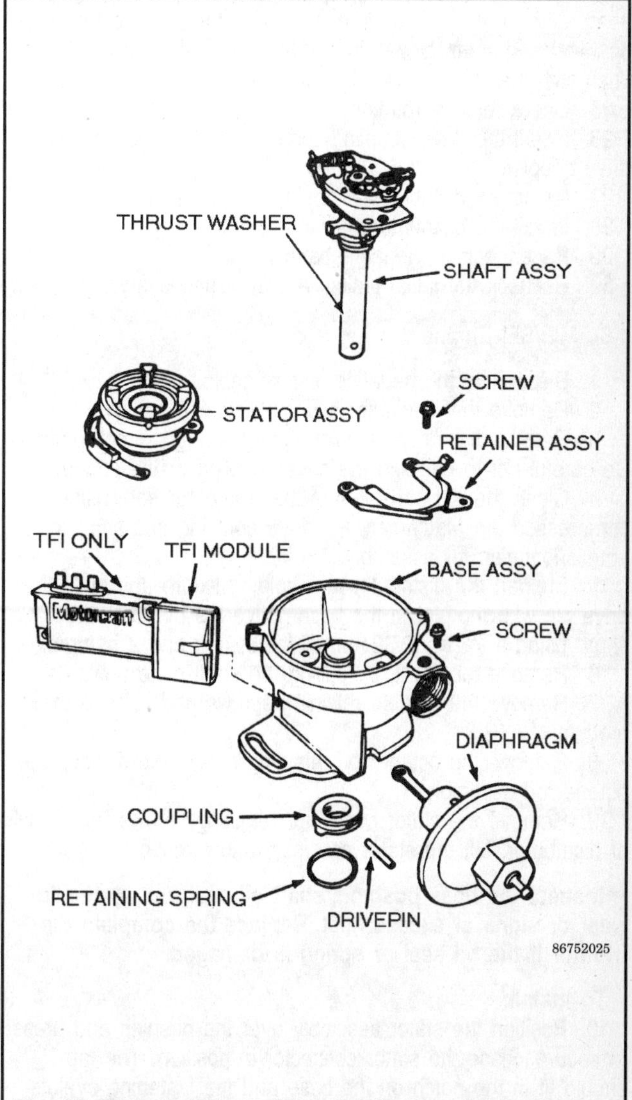

Fig. 32 Exploded view of the distributor components — 1.6L carbureted and 1.9L non-MFI/SFI engines

To install:

14. Attach the stator retainer to the stator assembly, by sliding the stator bumper into the groove in the bottom of the stator with the horseshoe opening at the diaphragm rod pivot pin.
15. Place the connector on the top of the TFI module with the three pins aligned and press down to seat the connector.
16. Place the stator assembly over the base bushing with the diaphragm pivot pin approximately in the front of the diaphragm mounting hole.
17. Line up the holes in the stator retainer plate with the holes in the base.
18. Install the three retaining screws.
19. Check the stator assembly for free rotation.
20. Install the connector-to-base retaining screws.
21. Place the two stator wires behind the wire guard that is part of the connector so that the wires are not twisted or tangled.
22. Install the diaphragm.
23. Apply a light coat of M2C162A or equivalent oil to the distributor shaft below the armature.
24. Install the shaft and place the drive coupling over the shaft. Line up the reference marks. Start the pin into the drive coupling and shaft. Drive the pin into the shaft until the pin is flush with the step in the drive coupling.
25. Check for free rotation.
26. Install the drive coupling spring in the groove on the drive coupling.
27. Install the distributor assembly in the engine.
28. Install the distributor cap and rotor.
29. Reconnect the negative battery cable.
30. Recheck the initial timing. Adjust, if necessary.

1.9L MFI/SFI Engine

1. Disconnect the negative battery cable.
2. Remove the distributor assembly from the engine.
3. Remove the drive coupling spring, using a small prytool. Be careful not to damage the drive coupling or the spring.
4. Clean the dirt and oil from the distributor end, using compressed air. Matchmark the drive coupling and shaft to note orientation for assembly.
5. Support the distributor in a holding fixture and align the drive pin with the slot in the base. Drive the pin from the shaft, using a 5/32 in. (2.38mm) diameter drift and a hammer.
6. Remove the shaft, by pulling the shaft plate upwards.
7. Remove the module retaining screws and remove the module.
8. Remove the octane rod retaining screw and remove the octane rod assembly.
9. Remove the stator connector retaining screws from bowl of distributor. Lift the stator assembly and remove.

➡Inspect the base bushing, shaft oil seal and spring for wear or signs of excess heat. Replace the complete distributor if the oil seal or spring is damaged.

To install:

10. Position the stator assembly over the bushing and press to secure. Place the stator connector in position. The tab should fit in the notch on the base and the fastening eyelets aligned with the screw holes. Be certain the wires are positioned away from moving parts.
11. Install the stator retaining screws. Tighten to 15-35 inch lbs. (1.7-4.0 Nm).
12. Place the seal on the octane rod and insert rod through the base octane rod hole.
13. Place the end of the octane rod onto the same post as the original stator. Only one post should easily fit in the octane rod hole. Install the retaining screw and tighten to 15-35 inch lbs. (1.7-4.0 Nm).
14. Wipe the back of the module and its mounting surface in the distributor clean. Coat the base of the TFI ignition module uniformly with a 1/32 in. (0.8mm) of silicone compound dielectric compound WA-10 or equivalent.
15. Invert the distributor base so the stator connector is in full view. Then, insert the module. Be certain the three module pins are inserted into the stator connector.
16. Install the module retaining screws and tighten to 15-35 inch lbs. (1.7-4.0 Nm).
17. Apply a light coat of engine oil to the distributor shaft, beneath the armature. Install the shaft.
18. Place the drive coupling over the shaft and align the marks made during disassembly.
19. Drive the pin into the drive coupling and shaft, until the end of the pin is flush with the step in the drive coupling. Make certain the pin does not extend beyond the step in the coupling in either direction.
20. Check for free movement of the drive coupling on the pin.
21. Install the drive coupling spring in the groove of the drive coupling.
22. Install the distributor assembly into the engine. Install the distributor cap and wires.
23. Reconnect the negative battery cable.
24. Recheck the initial timing. Adjust, if necessary.

TFI Ignition Module

REMOVAL & INSTALLATION

➧ See Figure 33

1. Disconnect the negative battery cable.
2. Remove the distributor from the engine.
3. Place the distributor assembly on a work bench.
4. Remove the two TFI module retaining screws. Pull the right side of the module down the distributor mounting flange and then back up to disengage the module terminals from the connector in the distributor base. The module may then be pulled toward the flange and away from the distributor.

➡Do not attempt to lift the module from the mounting surface, except as explained in Step 3, as pins will break at the distributor module connector.

To install:

5. Coat the baseplate of the TFI ignition module uniformly with a 1/32 in. (0.8mm) of silicone dielectric compound WA-10 or equivalent.
6. Position the module on the distributor base mounting flange. Carefully position the module toward the distributor bowl and engage the three connector pins securely.

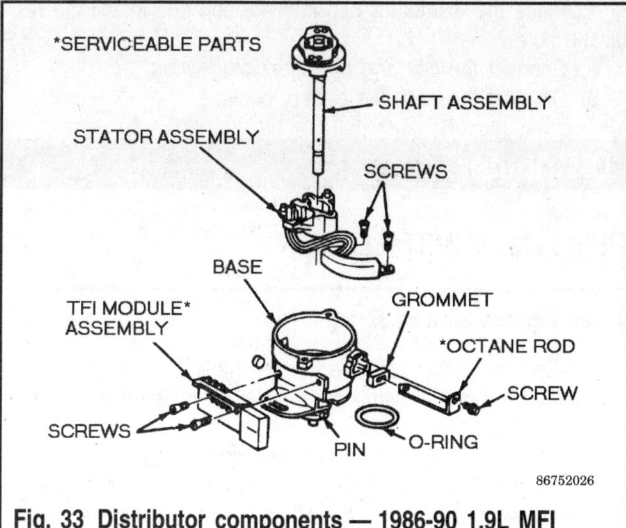

Fig. 33 Distributor components — 1986-90 1.9L MFI engines

7. Install the retaining screws. Tighten to 15-35 inch lbs. (1.7-4.0 Nm), starting with the upper right screw.
8. Install the distributor into the engine. Install the distributor cap and wires.
9. Reconnect the negative battery cable.
10. Recheck the initial timing. Adjust, if necessary.

ELECTRONIC SPARK ADVANCE (ESA) IGNITION SYSTEM

Description and Operation

See Figure 34

The 1991-95 Ford Escorts and Mercury Tracers equipped with the 1.8L engine use an ignition system similar to the transistorized systems used in other contemporary Ford Motor Company vehicles. The ignition system consists of an ignition coil, ignition module, distributor, spark plugs and spark plug wires. Ignition spark timing is accomplished by the Ignition Control Module (ICM), Electronic Control Assembly (ECA), Crankshaft Position (CKP) sensor and a cylinder identification sensor located in the distributor. Models from 1994 and 1995 are further equipped with a Camshaft Position Sensor (CMP) located in the distributor. This additional sensor informs the Powertrain Control Module (PCM) of the camshaft position and allows the more precise fuel metering provided for by the 1994 and 1995 models' Sequential (multi-port) Fuel Injection.

When the engine is in the starting mode, crankshaft position and engine rpm are sensed by the CKP sensor. Piston travel information is sensed by the Cylinder Identification (CID) sensor. The ECA then signals the ignition module, telling it when to fire the coil. The module controls the current through the ignition primary winding by turning the current ON between firing points to build up a magnetic field around the coil windings. It then turns the current OFF on a signal from the pulse generator and the pickup coil. Once the current is turned OFF, the field collapses and a high voltage pulse is transmitted to the central terminal in the distributor cap and through the rotor to the distributor cap terminal for the respective spark plug to fire. Ignition timing is controlled by the ECA.

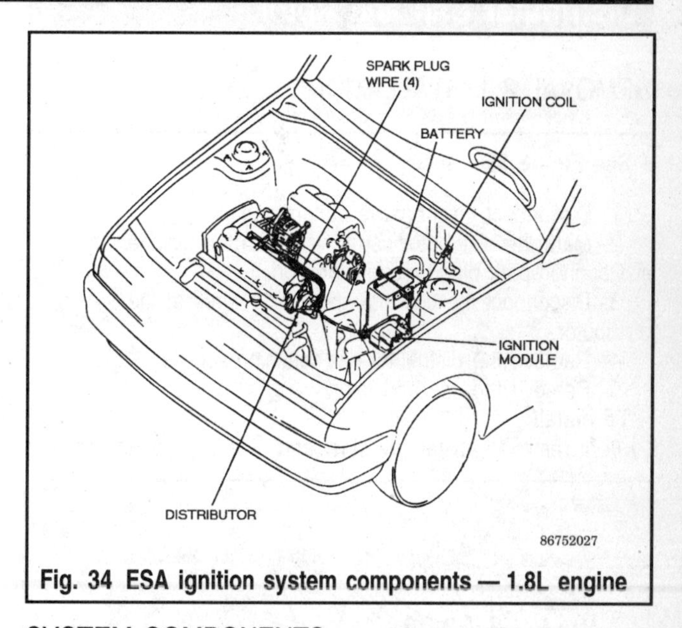

Fig. 34 ESA ignition system components — 1.8L engine

SYSTEM COMPONENTS

Ignition Coil

The ignition coil transforms the primary voltage (battery voltage) into approximately 28,000 volts on its secondary circuit each time it receives an Ignition Diagnostic Monitor (IDM) signal from the ignition module.

Ignition Module

The ignition module receives spark output signal from the ECA to turn the ignition coil ON and OFF.

Distributor

The distributor houses the crankshaft position sensor, camshaft position sensor (1994-95 only), cylinder identification sensor and the rotor. This unit, with the exception of cap and rotor replacement, is not serviceable. If it is found faulty, it must be replaced (along with its built-in sensors) as a unit.

Diagnosis and Testing

SERVICE PRECAUTIONS

- Always turn the key **OFF** and isolate both ends of a circuit whenever testing for short or continuity.
- Always disconnect solenoids and switches from the harness before measuring for continuity, resistance or energizing by way of a 12 volt source.
- When disconnecting connectors, inspect for damaged or pushed-out pins, corrosion, loose wires, etc. Service if required.
- Electronic modules are sensitive to static electrical charges. If the module is exposed to these charges, damage may result.

Distributor Cap and Rotor

REMOVAL & INSTALLATION

See Figure 35

1. Disconnect the negative battery cable.
2. Mark the distributor cap towers with the cylinders to assist during spark plug wires installation.
3. Disconnect the coil and spark plug wires at the distributor.
4. Remove the distributor cap retaining screws.
5. Remove the cap and rotor.

To install:

6. If removed, install the inner and outer covers and rotor.
7. Place the distributor cap into position and install the retaining screws.
8. Connect the coil and the spark plug wires.
9. Connect the negative battery cable.

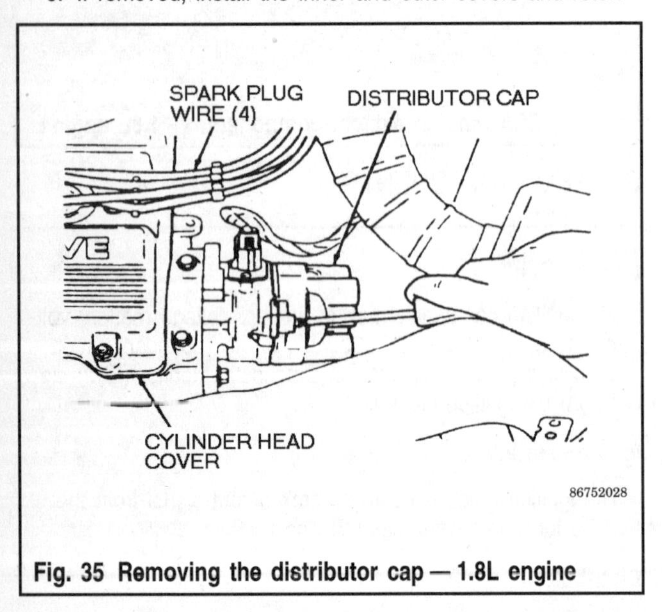

Fig. 35 Removing the distributor cap — 1.8L engine

Distributor

REMOVAL & INSTALLATION

See Figures 36 and 37

1. Disconnect the negative battery cable.
2. Disconnect the distributor electrical connector and coil wire at the cap.
3. Remove the distributor cap and position it to the side. If the distributor unit is not being replaced, scribe a reference mark across the distributor base flange and the cylinder head.
4. Remove the distributor mounting bolt and flange. Remove the distributor from the engine.

Do not rotate the engine while the distributor assembly is removed. Do not attempt to disassemble and service the distributor unit. The distributor unit should be replaced as an assembly.

5. Fit a new O-ring to the distributor unit, if required. Lubricate the seal with engine oil.
6. Install the distributor unit into the engine. Make certain the drive tangs engage with the camshaft slots.
7. Align the reference mark and install the mounting bolt finger-tight.
8. Install the distributor cap. Reconnect the distributor electrical connector and coil wire to the cap.
9. Reconnect the negative battery cable and recheck ignition timing.
10. Tighten the distributor mounting bolt to 14-19 ft. lbs. (19-25 Nm).

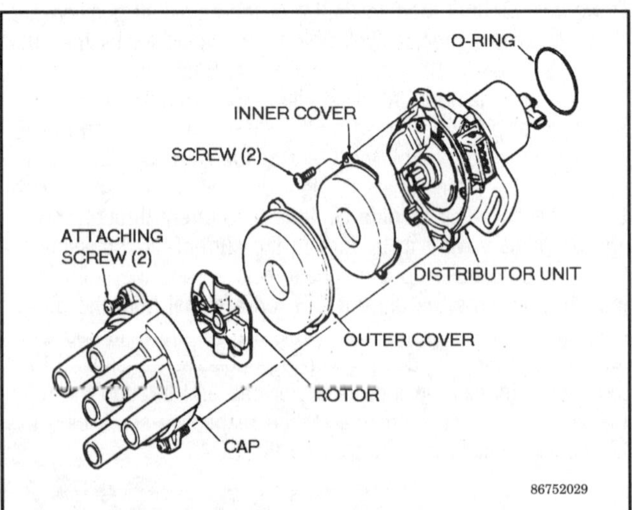

Fig. 36 Exploded view of the distributor assembly — 1.8L engine

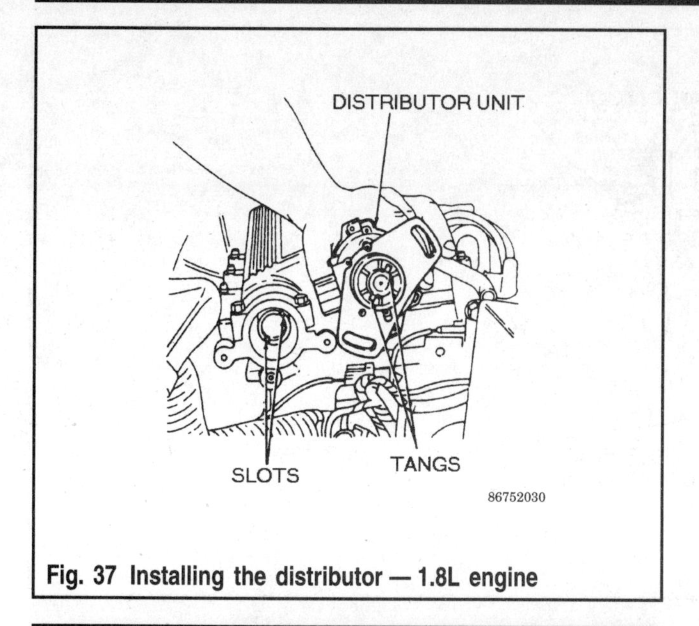

Fig. 37 Installing the distributor — 1.8L engine

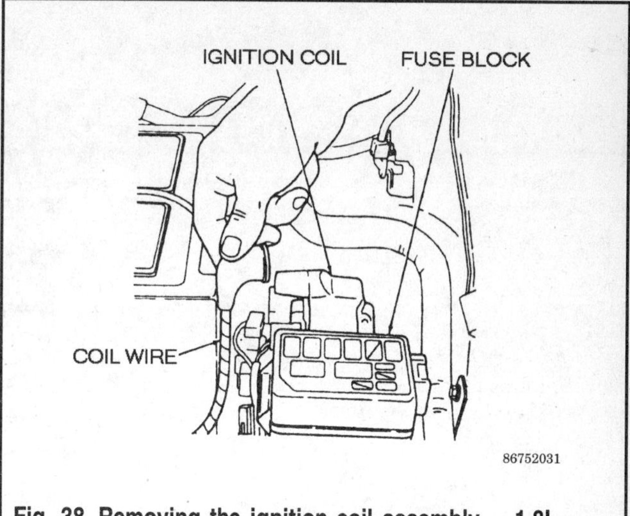

Fig. 38 Removing the ignition coil assembly — 1.8L engine

Ignition Coil

REMOVAL & INSTALLATION

➧ See Figure 38

1. Disconnect the negative battery cable.
2. Disconnect the ignition connector and coil wire from the coil.
3. Remove the ignition coil mounting nuts and remove the coil and bracket.

To install:

4. If removed, install the bracket to the ignition coil.
5. Place the ignition coil and bracket into its mounting position and install the mounting nuts.
6. Connect the ignition connector and coil wire to the coil.
7. Reconnect the negative battery cable.

Ignition Module

REMOVAL & INSTALLATION

➧ See Figure 39

1. Disconnect the negative battery cable.
2. Disconnect the ignition module electrical connector.
3. Remove the nuts and screws from the ignition module.
4. Remove the ignition module.
5. If replacing the suppression capacitor, remove the capacitor electrical connector and capacitor mounting nut. Remove the suppression capacitor.

To install:

6. Place the ignition module into its mounting position and install the nuts and screws.
7. Connect the ignition module electrical connector.
8. If removed, place the suppression capacitor into position and install the mounting nut. Reconnect the capacitor electrical connector.
9. Reconnect the negative battery cable.

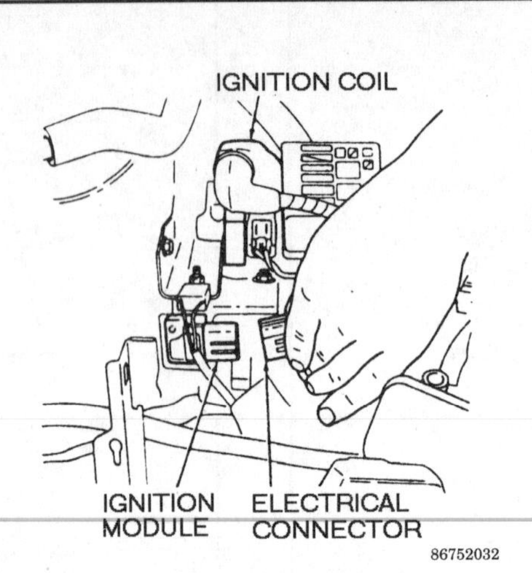

Fig. 39 Removing the ignition module — 1.8L engine

ELECTRONIC DISTRIBUTORLESS IGNITION SYSTEM (EDIS)

Description and Operation

➧ See Figure 40

The 1991-95 Ford Escort and Mercury Tracers, equipped with the 1.9L engine, use a high data rate EDIS system. This ignition system is controlled by an EDIS module and the EEC-IV module operating in union. The system is designed to deliver a full energy spark at a crank angle selected by the EEC-IV. This system is a modified version of the Distributorless Ignition System (DIS). The EDIS consists of a Variable Reluctance Sensor (VRS), an EDIS module, and EEC-IV processor and a coil pack.

Technically speaking, the EDIS functions similarly to the DIS. The most obvious difference has to do with the Profile Ignition Pickup (PIP) signal. In the DIS, the PIP is a signal generated by a Hall-effect device and passed through the DIS module to the EEC-IV. PIP provided the EEC-IV with base timing information. In the EDIS, the crankshaft position sensing and rpm is accomplished by the use of a trigger wheel and a Variable Reluctance Sensor (VRS). The position is determined by a missing tooth on the sensor wheel.

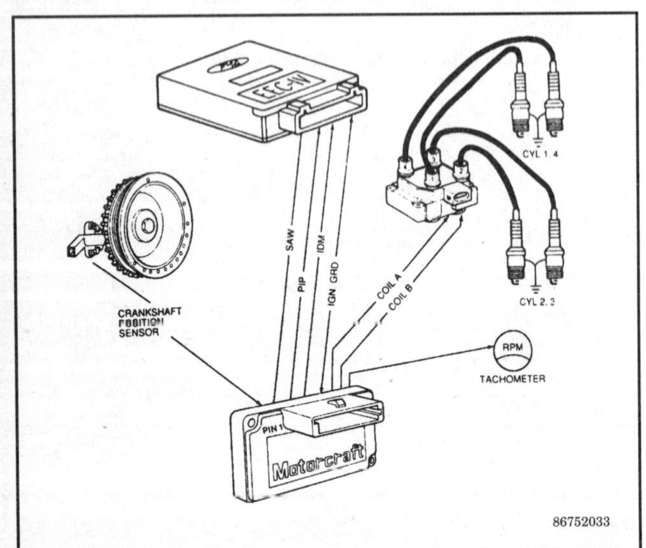

Fig. 40 EDIS system components — 1991-95 1.9L engine

The EDIS operates by sending crankshaft position information from the VRS to the EDIS module. The module generates a PIP signal and sends it to the EEC-IV processor. The processor responds with a Spark Angle Word (SAW) signal containing advance or retard timing information back to the EDIS module. The ignition coil pack, turned **ON** and then **OFF** by the EDIS module. This condition fires two spark plugs at once, one for the cylinder on its compression stroke and the other for the mating cylinder which is on its exhaust stroke. The next time the coil is fired, the situation is reversed.

The module generates an Ignition Diagnostic Monitor (IDM) signal to the processor which is used to indicate a failure mode and also provide a tach output signal. In addition, the IDM line indicates Key ON/Engine OFF (KOEO) status. By providing a pulse, the KOEO signal communicates module power on status.

The EDIS operates by sending crankshaft position information from the VRS to the EDIS module. The module generates a PIP signal and sends it to the EEC-IV processor. The processor responds with a Spark Angle Word (SAW) signal containing advance or retard timing information back to the EDIS module. The ignition coil pack, turned **ON** and then **OFF** by the EDIS module. This condition fires two spark plugs at once, one for the cylinder on its compression stroke and the other for the mating cylinder which is on its exhaust stroke. The next time the coil is fired, the situation is reversed.

The module generates an Ignition Diagnostic Monitor (IDM) signal to the processor which is used to indicate a failure mode and also provide a tach output signal. In addition, the IDM line indicates Key ON/Engine OFF (KOEO) status. By providing a pulse, the KOEO signal communicates module power on status.

SYSTEM COMPONENTS

Coil Pack

➧ See Figure 41

The coil pack is controlled by the EDIS module, firing 2 spark plugs at once. One is for the cylinder being fired, which is on its compression stroke and the other is for the cylinder on its exhaust stroke.

EDIS Module

➧ See Figure 42

The EDIS module is a microprocessor based device with coil drivers which make decisions about spark timing and coil firing. The module controls the coil, based on information from the VRS signal and a pulse width modulated signal (SAW) generated from the EEC-IV processor.

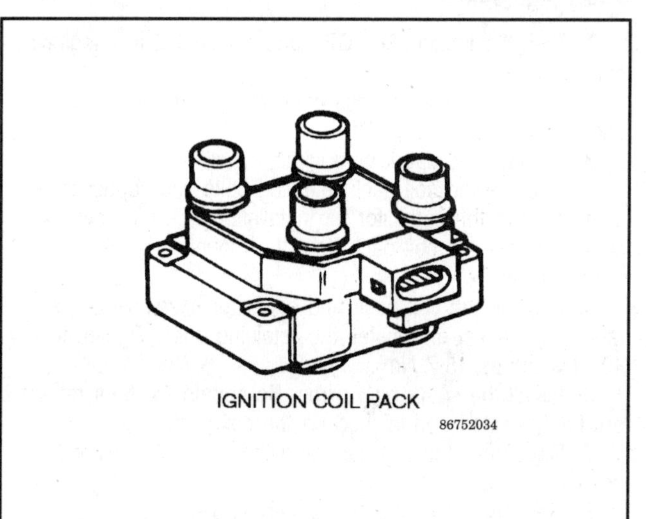

Fig. 41 Ignition coil pack assembly — 1991-95 1.9L SFI engine

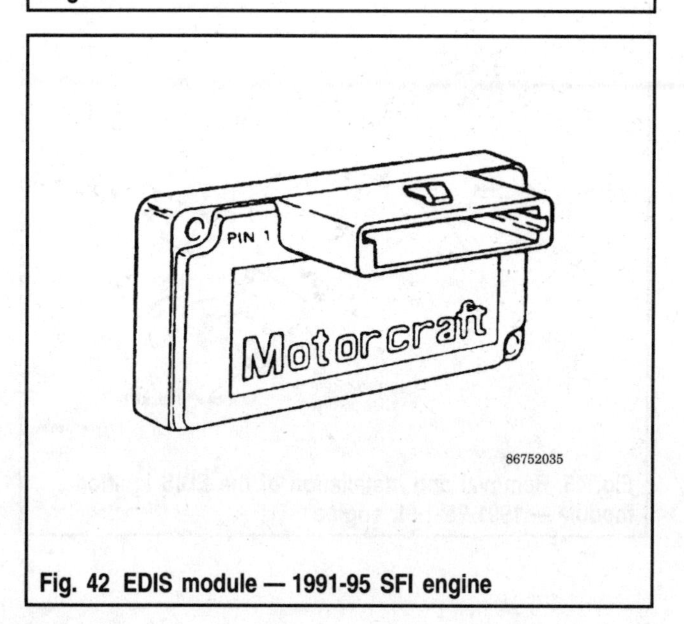

Fig. 42 EDIS module — 1991-95 SFI engine

Variable Reluctance Sensor (VRS)

➧ See Figure 43

The VRS is a passive electromagnetic device which senses movement of a 36 minus 1 tooth wheel located behind the crankshaft pulley. The sensor generates an A.C. voltage signal, which increases with engine rpm and provides engine speed and crankshaft position information to the EDIS module.

EEC-IV Processor

The EEC-IV processor is an electronic unit which receives Ignition, Ground and PIP signals from the EDIS module then generates a SAW output signal based upon engine speed, load, temperature and other sensor information.

Diagnoses and Testing

SERVICE PRECAUTIONS

- Always turn the key **OFF** and isolate both ends of a circuit whenever testing for short or continuity.
- Never measure voltage or resistance directly at the processor connector.
- Always disconnect solenoids and switches from the harness before measuring for continuity, resistance or energizing by way of a 12 volt source.
- When disconnecting connectors, inspect for damaged or pushed-out pins, corrosion, loose wires, etc. Service if required.

PRELIMINARY CHECKS

1. Visually inspect the engine compartment to ensure that all vacuum lines and spark plug wires are properly routed and securely connected.
2. Examine all wiring harnesses and connectors for insulation damage, burned, overheated, loose or broken conditions.

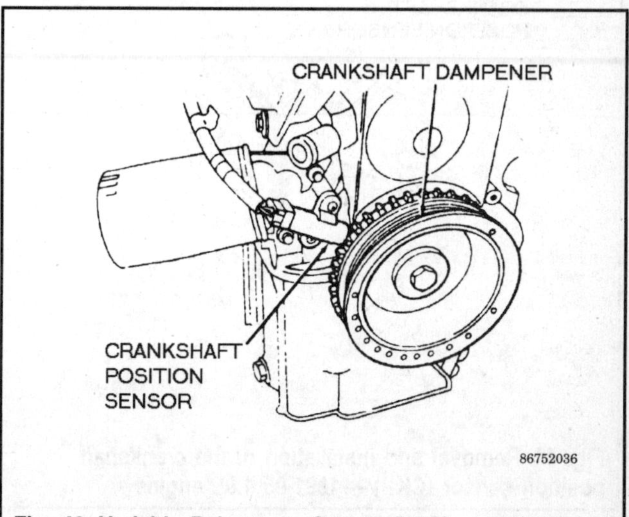

Fig. 43 Variable Reluctance Sensor (VRS) — 1991-95 1.9L SFI engine

3. Be certain that the battery is fully charged and that all accessories are **OFF** during the diagnosis.

Crankshaft Position Sensor

REMOVAL & INSTALLATION

1991-95 1.9L Engine

➧ See Figure 44

1. Turn the ignition key **OFF** and disconnect the negative battery cable.
2. Raise the vehicle and support it safely.
3. Remove the right side splash shield.
4. Disconnect the sensor electrical connector, remove the retaining screws and remove the sensor.

To install:

5. Position the sensor on the oil pump housing and install the retaining screws. Tighten to 40-61 inch lbs. (5-7 Nm).
6. Reconnect the sensor electrical connector.
7. Install the splash shield and lower the vehicle.
8. Reconnect the negative battery cable.

EDIS Ignition Module

REMOVAL & INSTALLATION

1991-95 1.9L Engine

➧ See Figure 45

1. Turn the ignition key **OFF** and disconnect the negative battery cable.
2. Remove the module bracket retaining bolts.
3. Carefully pull the bracket and module assembly straight upward and disconnect the module electrical connector.
4. Remove the module-to-bracket retaining screws and remove the module from the bracket.

To install:

5. Position the module on the bracket and install the retaining screws. Tighten to 24-35 inch lbs. (3-4 Nm).
6. Reconnect the module connector.
7. Fit the module and bracket assembly into position and install the retaining bolts. Tighten to 62-88 inch lbs. (7-10 Nm).
8. Reconnect the negative battery cable.

EDIS Coil Pack

REMOVAL & INSTALLATION

1991-95 1.9L Engine

➧ See Figure 46

1. Turn the ignition key **OFF** and disconnect the negative battery cable.
2. Disconnect the harness connectors from the coil pack and capacitor assembly.
3. Remove the spark plug wires.
4. Remove the coil pack retaining bolts and capacitor assembly. Save the capacitor for installation with the new coil pack. Remove the coil pack from the mounting bracket.

To install:

5. Position the coil pack and capacitor assembly on its mounting bracket and install the retaining bolts. Tighten to 40-61 inch. lbs. (5-7 Nm).
6. Install the spark plug wires. Be certain the boot retainers are firmly seated and latched on the coil pack.
7. Reconnect the coil pack and the capacitor electrical connectors.
8. Reconnect the negative battery cable.

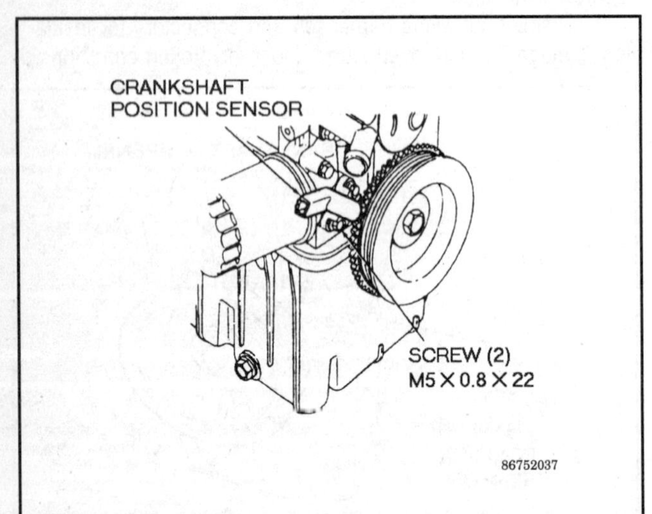

Fig. 44 Removal and installation of the crankshaft position sensor (CKP) — 1991-95 1.9L engine

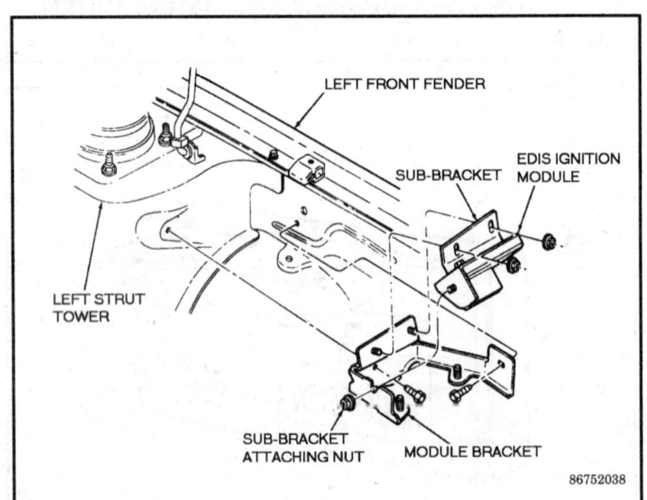

Fig. 45 Removal and installation of the EDIS ignition module — 1991-95 1.9L engine

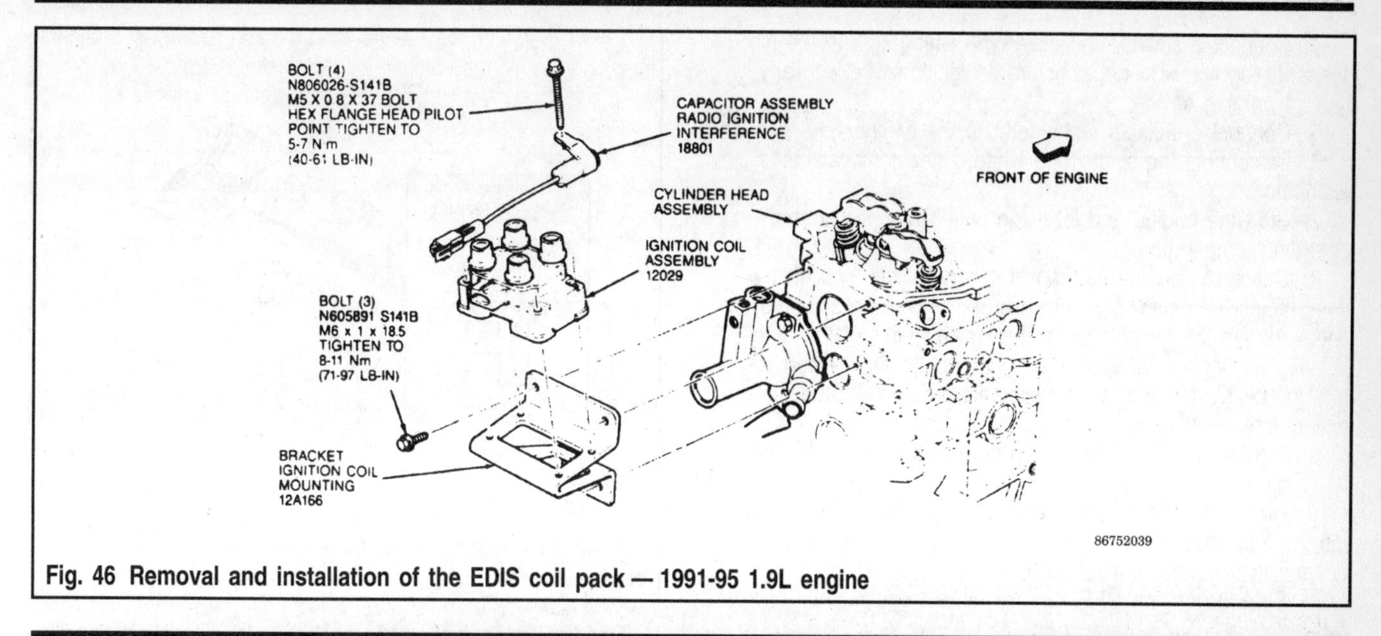

Fig. 46 Removal and installation of the EDIS coil pack — 1991-95 1.9L engine

IGNITION TIMING

Adjustment

The timing marks on 1.6L and 1985-90 1.9L engines consist of a notch on the crankshaft pulley and a graduated scale molded into the camshaft drive belt cover. The number of degrees before or after Top Dead Center (TDC) represented by each mark can be interpreted according to the decal affixed to the top of the belt cover (emissions decal).

1.6L AND 1.9L (CARBURETED) ENGINES

See Figure 47

1. Place the transaxle in the P or N position. Firmly apply the parking brake and block the wheels.
2. Turn OFF all accessories (A/C, heater, radio, etc.).
3. Once the timing marks are located, clean with a stiff brush or solvent, if necessary.
4. Remove the vacuum hoses from the distributor vacuum advance connection at the distributor and plug the hoses.
5. Connect a suitable inductive-type timing light to the No. 1 spark plug wire. Do not puncture an ignition wire with any type of probing device.
6. Connect a suitable tachometer to the engine.
7. If the vehicle is equipped with a barometric pressure switch, disconnect it from the ignition module and place a jumper wire across the pins at the ignition module connector (yellow and black wires).
8. Start the engine and let it run until it reaches normal operating temperature.
9. Check the engine idle rpm if it is not within specifications, adjust as necessary. After the rpm has been adjusted or checked, aim the timing light at the timing marks. If they are not aligned, loosen the distributor clamp bolts slightly and rotate the distributor body until the marks are aligned under timing light illumination.

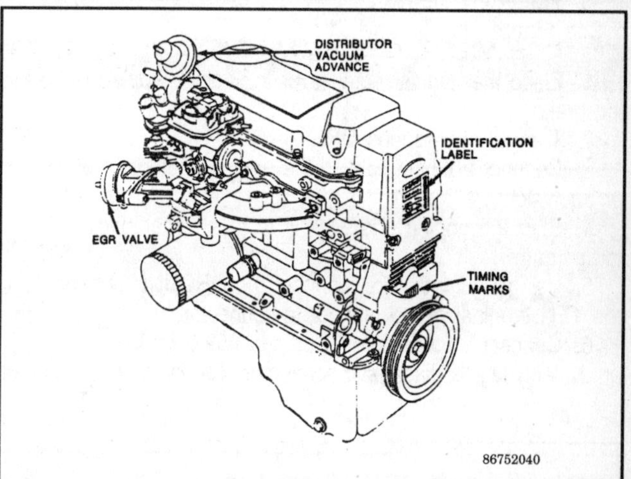

Fig. 47 Location of the ignition timing marks necessary to check and adjust timing — 1.6L and 1985-90 1.9L carbureted engines

10. Tighten the distributor clamp bolts and recheck the ignition timing. Turn the engine **OFF**, remove all test equipment.
11. Unplug and reconnect the vacuum hoses.
12. Remove the jumper from the ignition module connector and reconnect it.

1.6L MFI ENGINE AND 1986-90 1.9L CFI/MFI ENGINES

See Figure 48

1. Place the transaxle in the P or N position. Firmly apply the parking brake and block the wheels.
2. Turn OFF all accessories (A/C, heater, etc.).
3. If necessary, once locating the timing marks, clean with a stiff brush or solvent.

4. Connect a suitable inductive type timing light to the No. 1 spark plug wire. Do not puncture an ignition wire with any type of probing device.
5. Connect a suitable tachometer to the engine.
6. Disconnect the single wire white connector near the distributor.
7. Start the engine and let it run until it reaches normal operating temperature.
8. Check the engine idle rpm if it is not within specifications, adjust as necessary. After the rpm has been adjusted or checked, aim the timing light at the timing marks. If they are not aligned, loosen the distributor clamp bolts slightly and rotate the distributor body until the marks are aligned under timing light illumination.
9. Tighten the distributor clamp bolts and recheck the ignition timing.
10. Reconnect the single wire white connector near the distributor and check timing advance to verify the distributor is advancing beyond the initial setting.
11. Shut the engine **OFF**, remove all test equipment.

1.8L ENGINE

See Figures 49, 50 and 51

1. Place the gear selector lever in P or N. Apply the parking brake.
2. Turn all accessories **OFF**.
3. Connect a timing light to the engine (Rotunda 059-00005 or equivalent).
4. Start the engine and allow it to reach operating temperature.
5. Using a jumper wire, connect the GROUND terminal to the TEN terminal of the diagnostic connector.
6. Connect a tachometer (Rotunda 059-00010 or equivalent) to the diagnostic connector. Tachometer (+) positive lead to the IG terminal and the negative lead to the battery negative post.
7. Check the ignition timing. Timing should be 10° BTDC at 700-800 rpm. The mark on the pulley should be aligned with the corresponding mark on the timing belt cover.
8. If not, loosen the distributor mounting bolt and turn the distributor until the marks are aligned. Tighten the distributor mounting bolt to 14-19 ft. lbs. (19-25 Nm).
9. Remove the jumper wire, timing light and tachometer.

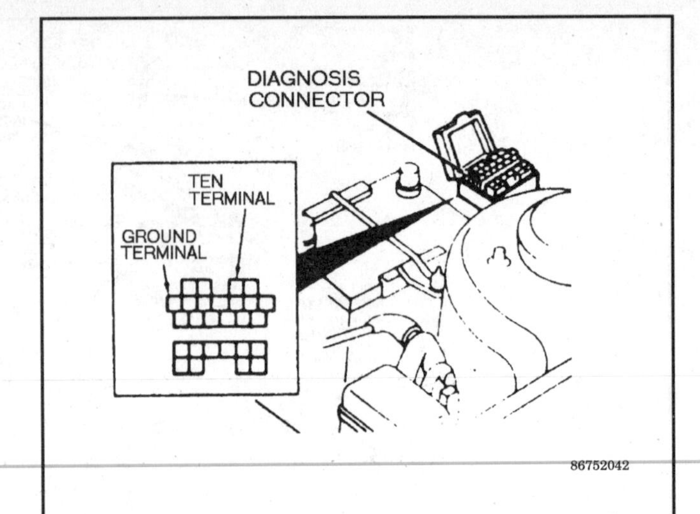

Fig. 49 Diagnostic connector identification — 1.8L engine

1991-95 1.9L ENGINE

The 1.9L engine, used during model year 1991-95, is equipped with an Electronic Distributorless Ignition System (EDIS). Ignition timing adjustment is not possible on the EDIS system.

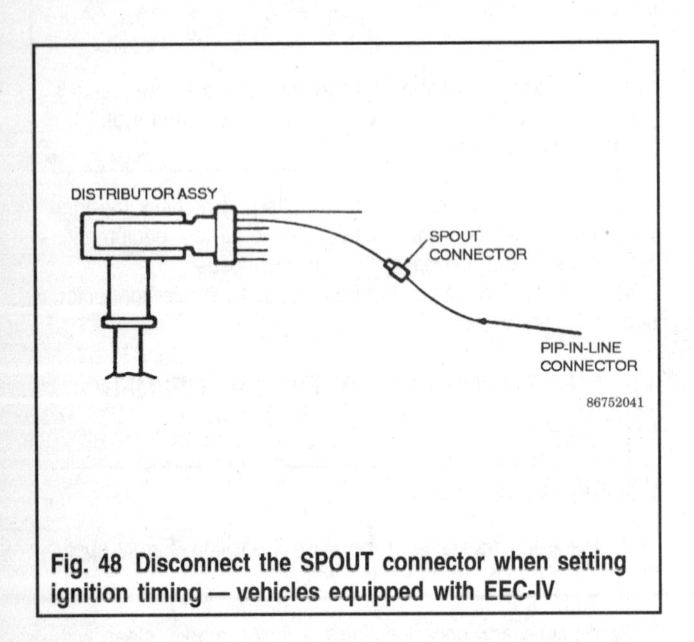

Fig. 48 Disconnect the SPOUT connector when setting ignition timing — vehicles equipped with EEC-IV

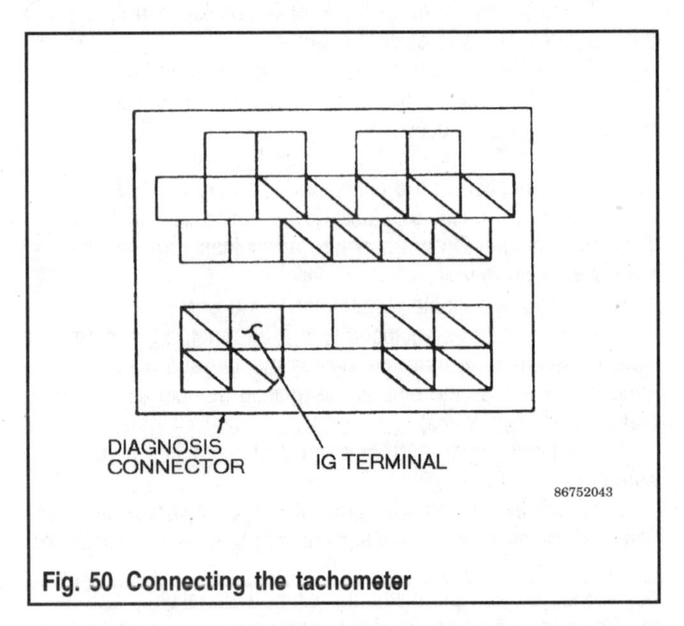

Fig. 50 Connecting the tachometer

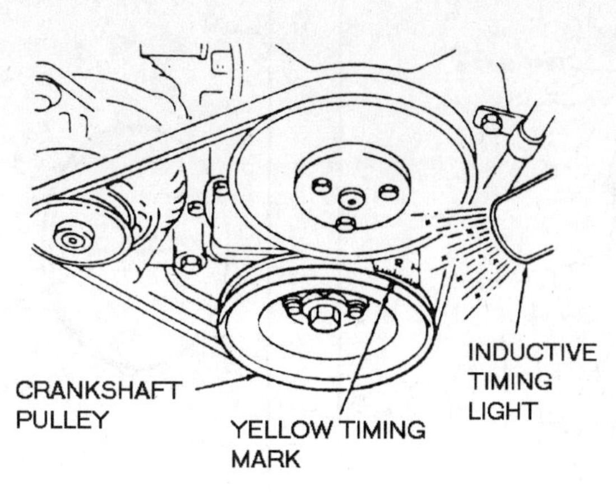

Fig. 51 Checking the ignition timing — 1.8L engine

VALVE LASH

Valve adjustment determines how far the valves enter the cylinder and how long they stay open and closed.

If the valve clearance is too large, part of the lift of the camshaft will be used in removing the excessive clearance. Consequently, the valve will not be opening as far as it should. This condition has two effects: the valve train components will emit a tapping sound as they take up the excessive clearance and the engine will perform poorly because the valves don't open fully and allow the proper amount of gases to flow into and out of the engine.

If the valve clearance is too small, the intake valve and the exhaust valves will open too far and they will not fully seat on the cylinder head when they close. When a valve seats itself on the cylinder head, it does two things: it seals the combustion chamber so that none of the gases in the cylinder escape and it cools itself by transferring some of the heat it has absorbed from the combustion in the cylinder to the cylinder head which then transfers the heat to the engine's cooling system. If the valve clearance is too small, the engine will run poorly because of the gases escaping from the combustion chamber. The valves will also become overheated and will warp, since they cannot transfer heat unless they are touching the valve seat in the cylinder head.

Adjustment

GASOLINE ENGINES

The intake and exhaust valves are driven by the camshaft, working through hydraulic lash adjusters and stamped steel rocker arms. The lash adjusters eliminate the need for periodic valve lash adjustments.

DIESEL ENGINE

➧ See Figures 52, 53, 54 and 55

1. Disconnect the breather hose from the intake manifold and remove the camshaft cover.
2. Rotate crankshaft until No. 1 piston is at TDC on the compression stroke.
3. Using a Go-No-Go feeler gauge, check the valve shim to cam lobe clearance for No. 1 and No. 2 intake valves, and No. 1 and No. 3 exhaust valves.

Valve adjustment specifications:

- Intake Valves: 0.20-0.30mm (0.008-0.011 in.).
- Exhaust Valves: 0.30-0.40mm (0.011-0.015 in.).

4. Rotate crankshaft one complete revolution. Measure valve clearance for No. 3 and No. 4 intake valves, and No. 2 and No. 4 exhaust valves.

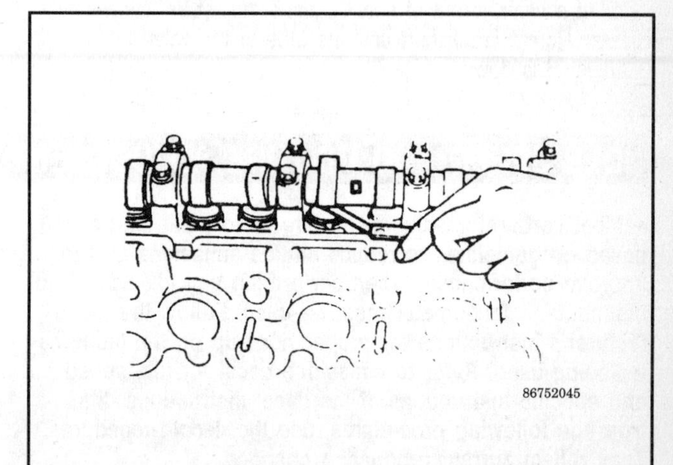

Fig. 52 Checking the valve clearance — 2.0L diesel engine

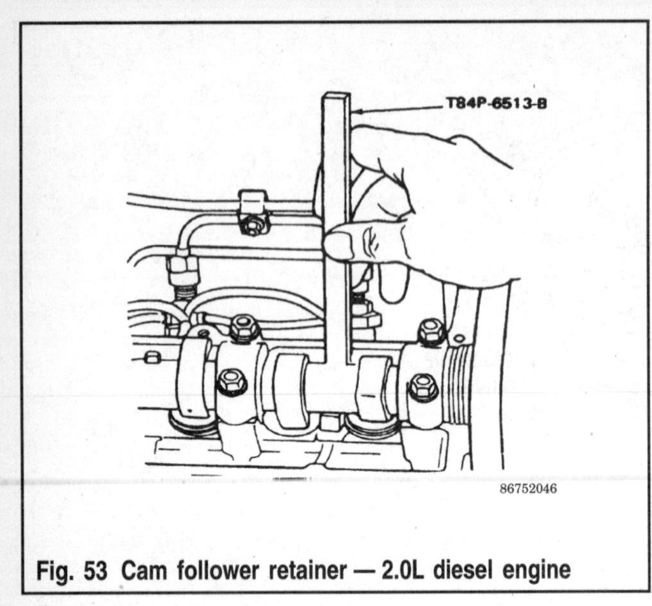

Fig. 53 Cam follower retainer — 2.0L diesel engine

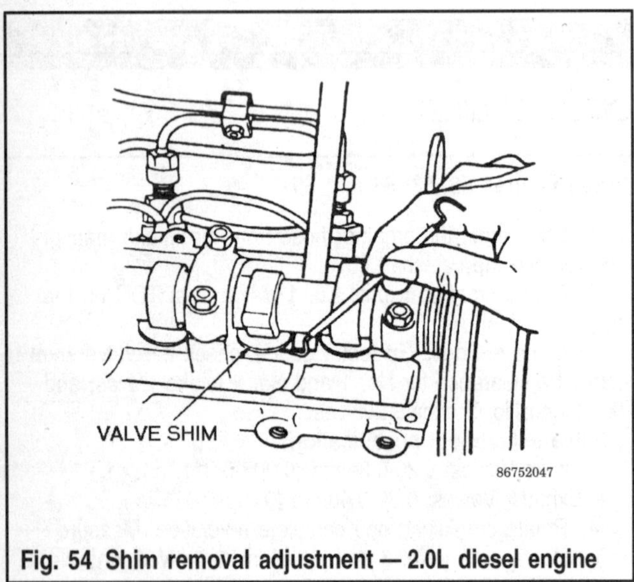

Fig. 54 Shim removal adjustment — 2.0L diesel engine

5. If a valve is out of specifications, adjust as follows:
a. Rotate crankshaft until the lobe of the valve to be adjusted is down.

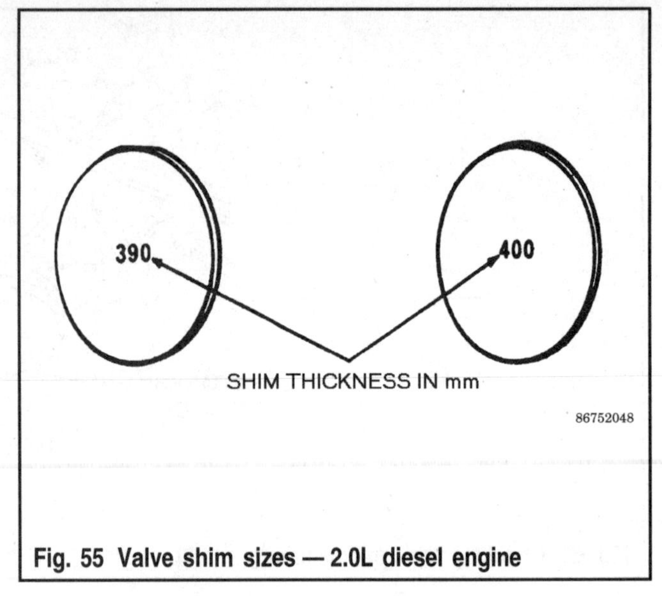

Fig. 55 Valve shim sizes — 2.0L diesel engine

b. Install cam follower retainer, T84P-6513-B.
c. Rotate crankshaft until the cam lobe is on the base circle.
d. Using O-ring pick tool T71P-19703-C or equivalent, pry the valve adjusting shim out of the cam follower.
e. Valve shims are available in thicknesses ranging from 0.13-0.18 in. (3.40mm to 4.60mm).
f. If the valve was too tight, install a new shim, of the appropriate size.
g. If the valve was too loose, install a new shim of the appropriate size.

➡Shim thickness is stamped on valve shim. Install new shim with numbers down, to avoid wearing the numbers off the shim. If numbers have been worn off, use a micrometer to measure shim thickness.

6. Rotate crankshaft until cam lobe is down and remove cam follower retainer.
7. Recheck valve clearance.
8. Repeat Steps 4, 5 and 6 for each valve to be adjusted.
9. Make sure the camshaft cover gasket is fully seated in the camshaft cover and install the valve cover. Tighten the bolts to 5-7 ft. lbs. (7-9 Nm).
10. Connect the breather hose.

IDLE SPEED AND MIXTURE ADJUSTMENT — GASOLINE ENGINES

➡Most carburetor adjustments are factory set, and are based on guidelines to reduce engine emissions and to improve performance. When performing any idle speed adjustments, a tachometer must be used. Follow the manufacturer's instructions for proper hook-up on the tachometer being used. Refer to emissions decal for idle speed and specific instructions. If the decal instructions differ from the following procedures, use the decal procedures. They reflect current production changes.

Curb Idle

CARBURETED VEHICLES

1.6L And 1.9L Engine

740 CARBURETOR WITHOUT IDLE SPEED CONTROL

See Figures 56 and 57

1. Place the transaxle in P or N. Set the parking brake and block the wheels. Connect a tachometer to the engine.
2. Bring the engine to normal operating temperature.

3. Disconnect and plug the vacuum hose at the Thermactor air control valve bypass sections.

4. Place the fast idle adjustment screw on the second highest step of the fast idle cam. Run the engine until the cooling fan comes on.

5. Slightly depress the throttle to allow the fast idle cam to rotate. Place the transaxle in the specified gear, and check and adjust, if necessary, the curb idle rpm to specification.

➡Engine cooling fan must be running when checking curb idle rpm. (Use of a jumper wire is necessary.)

6. Place the transaxle in P or N. Increase the engine rpm momentarily. Place the transaxle in the specified position and recheck curb idle rpm. Readjust if required.

7. If the vehicle is equipped with a dashpot, check/adjust clearance to specification.

8. Remove the plug from the hose at the Thermactor air control valve bypass sections and reconnect.

9. If the vehicle is equipped with an automatic transaxle and curb idle adjustment is more than 50 rpm, an automatic transaxle linkage adjustment may be necessary.

1.6L AND 1.9L ENGINES WITH 740 & 5740 CARBURETOR AND MECHANICAL VACUUM IDLE SPEED CONTROL (ISC)

➧ See Figure 58

1. Place the transaxle in P or N. Set the parking brake and block the wheels. Connect a tachometer to the engine.

2. Bring the engine to normal operating temperature.

3. Disconnect and plug the vacuum hose at the Thermactor air control valve bypass section.

4. Place the fast idle adjustment screw on the second highest step of the fast idle cam. Run the engine until the cooling fan comes on.

5. Slightly depress the throttle to allow the fast idle cam to rotate. Place the transaxle in D (fan on) and check curb idle rpm to specification.

➡Engine cooling fan must be running when checking curb idle rpm.

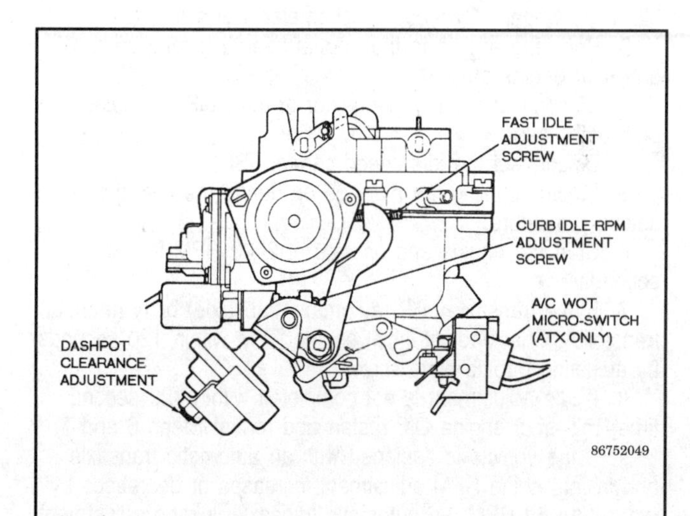

Fig. 56 Curb idle rpm and fast idle rpm — 1.6L with 740-2-bbl. carburetor

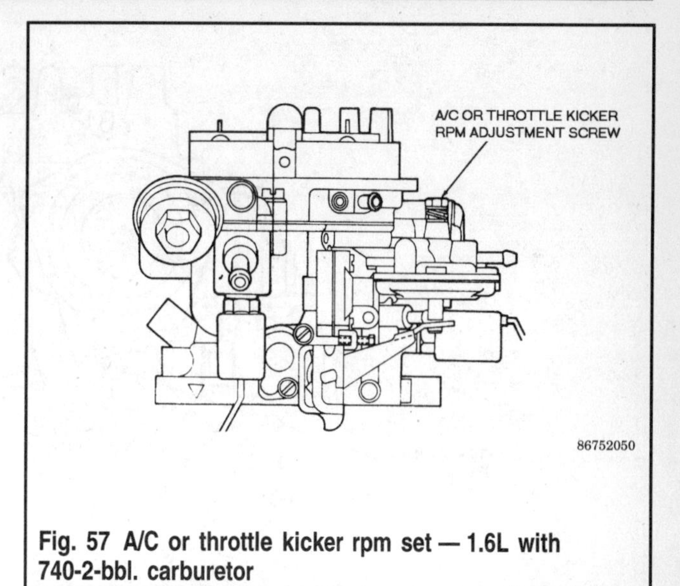

Fig. 57 A/C or throttle kicker rpm set — 1.6L with 740-2-bbl. carburetor

6. If adjustment is required:

a. Place the transaxle in P. Deactivate the ISC by removing the vacuum hose at the ISC and plugging the hose.

b. Turn ISC adjusting screw until ISC plunger is clear of the throttle lever.

c. Place the transaxle in the D position, if rpm is not at the ISC retracted speed (fan on), adjust rpm by turning the throttle stop adjusting screw.

d. Place the transaxle in P. Remove plug from the ISC vacuum line and reconnect the ISC.

e. Place transaxle in D. If rpm is not at the curb idle speed (fan on), adjust by turning the ISC adjustment screw.

7. Place transaxle in P or N. Increase the engine rpm momentarily. Place the transaxle in the specified position and recheck the curb idle rpm. Readjust if necessary.

8. Remove the plug from the Thermactor air control valve bypass section hose and reconnect.

9. If the vehicle is equipped with an automatic transaxle and curb idle adjustment is more than 50 rpm, an automatic transaxle linkage adjustment may be necessary.

1.6L AND 1.9L ENGINES WITH 740 & 5740 CARBURETOR AND VACUUM OPERATED THROTTLE MODULATOR (VOTM)

➧ See Figure 59

1. Place the transaxle in P or N. Set the parking brake and block the wheels. Connect a tachometer to the engine.

2. Bring the engine to normal operating temperature.

3. To check/adjust VOTM rpm:

a. Place air conditioning heat selector in Heat position, blower switch on High.

b. Disconnect the vacuum hose from VOTM and plug, install a slave vacuum hose from the intake manifold vacuum to the VOTM.

4. Disconnect and plug the vacuum hose at the Thermactor air control valve bypass section.

5. Run the engine until the engine cooling fan comes on.

6. Place the transaxle in specified gear, and check/adjust VOTM rpm to specification.

➡Engine cooling fan must be running when checking VOTM rpm. Adjust rpm by turning screw on VOTM.

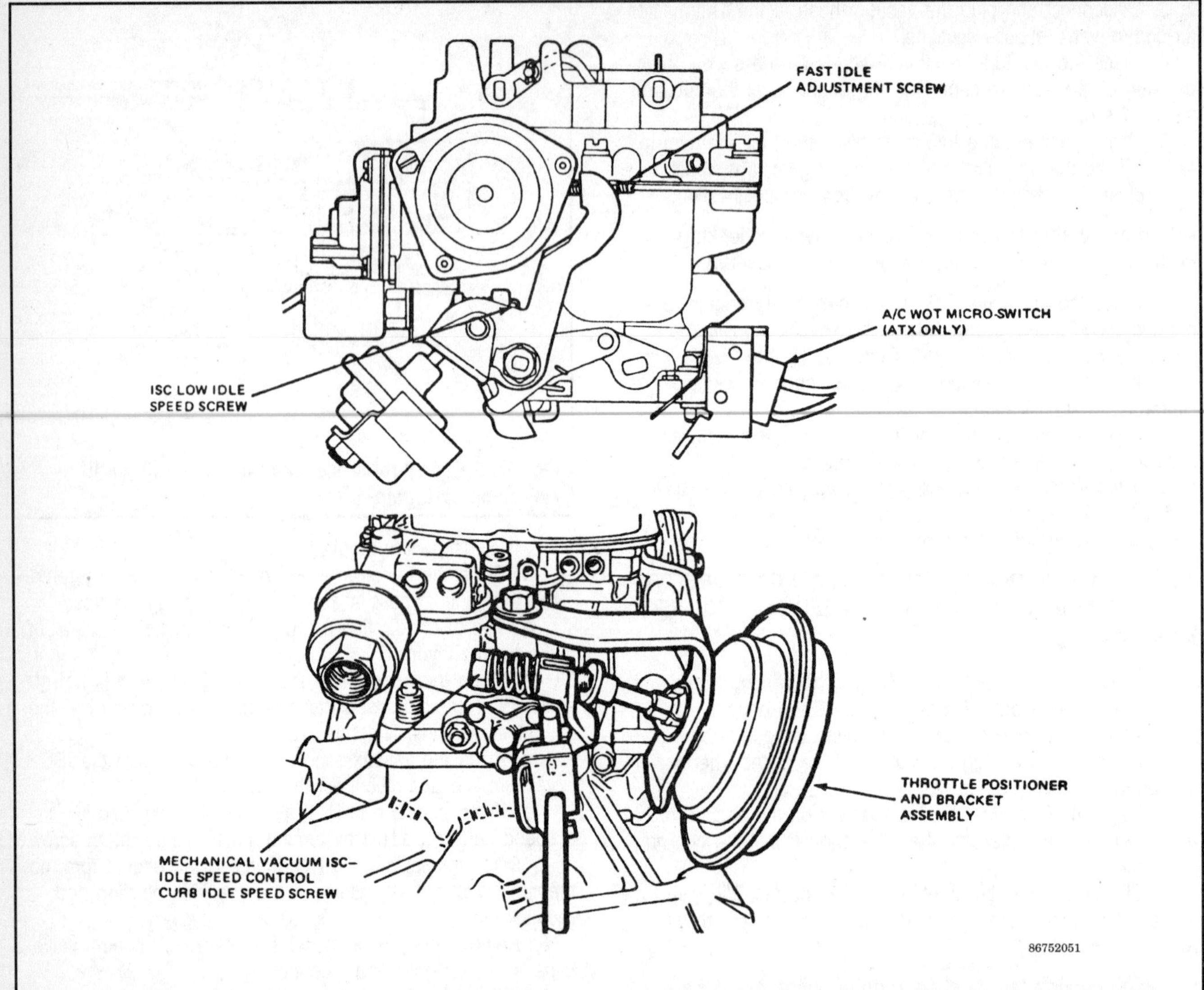

Fig. 58 Curb idle rpm and fast idle rpm — 1.9L with 740-2-bbl. carburetor and mechanical vacuum Idle Speed Control (ISC)

7. Remove the slave vacuum hose. Remove the plug from the VOTM vacuum hose and reconnect the hose to the VOTM.
8. Return the intake manifold vacuum supply source to original location.
9. Remove the plug from the vacuum hose at the Thermactor air control valve bypass section and reconnect.

FUEL INJECTED VEHICLES

Gasoline Engines

1983-85 1.6L AND 1986 1.9L MODELS

➡Curb idle RPM is controlled by the EEC-IV processor and the Idle Speed Control (ISC) device (part of the fuel charging assembly). The purpose of this procedure, is to provide a means of verifying the initial engine RPM setting with the ISC disconnected. If engine idle RPM is not within specification after performing this procedure, it will be necessary to have 1.6L or 1.9L MFI EEC-IV diagnostics performed.

1. Place the transaxle in P or N. Set the parking brake and block the wheels. Connect a tachometer to the engine.
2. Bring the engine to the normal operating temperature and shut engine off.
3. Disconnect vacuum connector at the EGR solenoids and plug both lines.
4. Disconnect the idle speed control (ISC) power lead.
5. Electric cooling fan must be on during the idle speed setting procedure.
6. Start the engine and operate at 2000 RPM for 60 seconds.
7. Place transaxle in P (automatic transaxle) or N (manual transaxle). Check/adjust initial engine RPM within 120 seconds by adjusting throttle plate screw.
8. If idle adjustment is not completed within 120 second time limit, shut engine Off, restart and repeat Steps 6 and 7.
9. If the vehicle is equipped with an automatic transaxle and initial engine RPM adjustment increases or decreases by more than 50 RPM, an automatic transaxle linkage adjustment may be necessary.

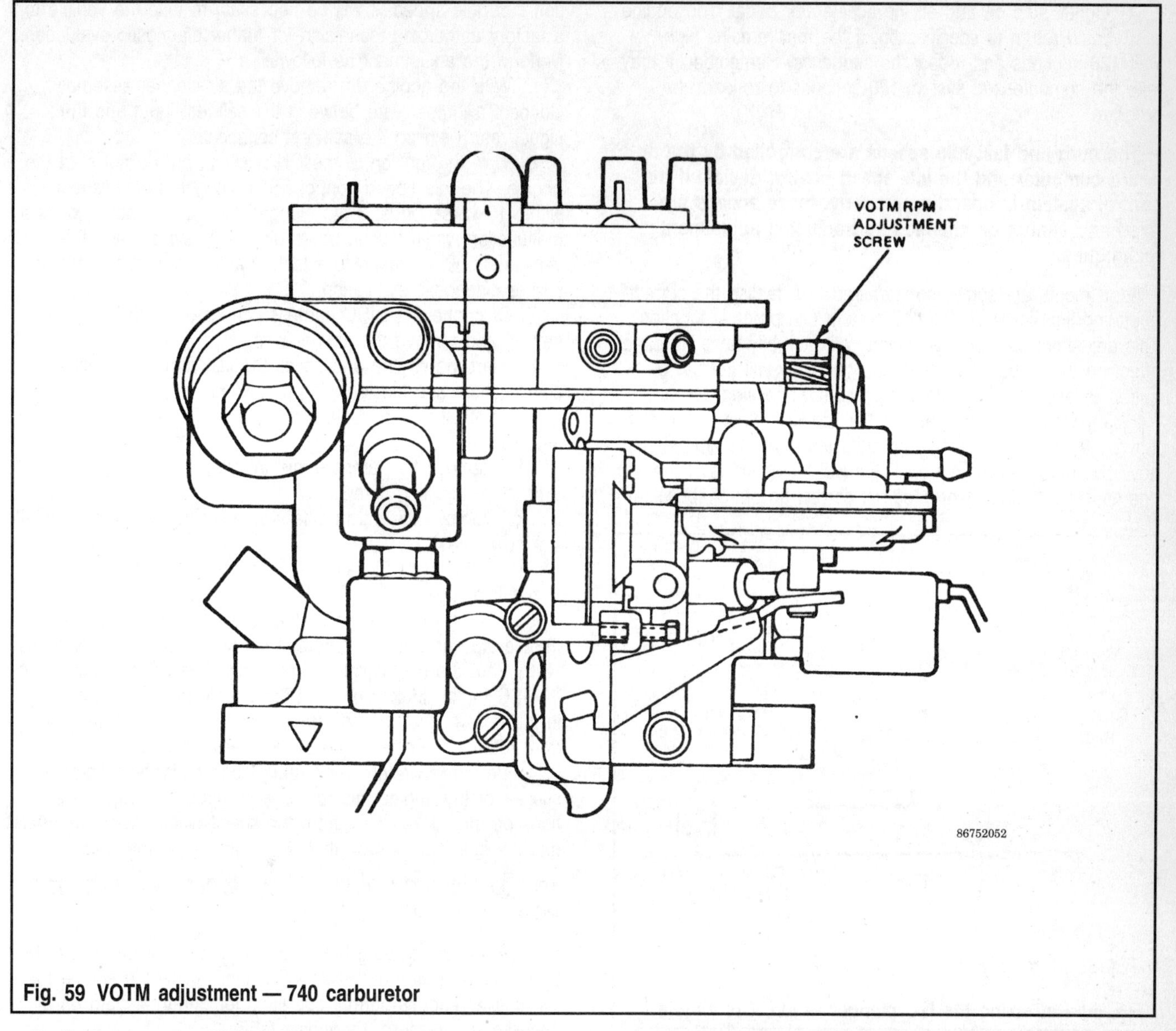

Fig. 59 VOTM adjustment — 740 carburetor

10. Turn the engine **OFF**. Remove the plugs from the EGR vacuum lines at the EGR solenoid and reconnect.

11. Reconnect the idle speed control (ISC) power lead.

1987-90 MODELS WITH CENTRAL FUEL INJECTION (CFI)

See Figures 60 and 61

The idle speed and the idle speed mixture adjustments are controlled by the on board vehicle computerized engine controls. Also in order to adjust the idle speed on this model, it is necessary to remove the CFI assembly from the vehicle, so as to gain access to, and remove the tamper resistant plug covering the throttle stop adjusting screw. This procedure should be performed by an authorized factory technician.

It is recommended that the idle speed control motor be checked to see if is is functioning correctly, before performing the curb idle adjustment. This can be done as follows:

1. Start the engine and run it for at least 30 seconds and turn the ignition switch to the **OFF** position. Visually inspect the ISC motor to see if it is retracting and repositioning.

If for any reason the battery has been disconnected or the vehicle has had to be jump started, this procedure may need to be performed.

2. Set the parking brake and block the wheels. Make all checks and or adjustments at normal operating temperature with all accessories off. Only a suitable tachometer is needed for this procedure. Before any adjustments are made, check for vacuum leaks and repair as necessary.

3. Place the transaxle in P (automatic transaxle) or N (manual transaxle). Idle the engine for approximately 120 seconds, and check to see that the idle speed is within specifications. The engine rpm should then increase by approximately 75 rpm, when the transaxle is put in Drive or Neutral.

4. Lightly step on and off the accelerator pedal. The engine rpm should return to specification. If the rpm remains high, wait 120 seconds and repeat the sequence. Remember, it may take the computerized system 120 seconds to re-learn the program.

➡The curb and fast idle speeds are controlled by the on-board computer and the idle speed control device. If the control system is operating properly, these speeds are fixed and cannot be changed by traditional adjustment techniques.

Adjustments are sometimes required to establish the correct operating limit in which the ISC system can properly function. This adjustment, as outlined below, will normally have no direct affect on the actual idle speed and generally will not be required unless, the curb idle is higher than specified.

Misadjustment of the operating limit could restrict the operating range of the ISC system, so adjustment of this limit should never be made unless a specific causal factor exists. If the operating limit adjustment does not correct an out-of-specification curb idle speed, it will be necessary to take the vehicle to a factory authorized technician for further diagnostic evaluation. Perform the adjustment as follows:

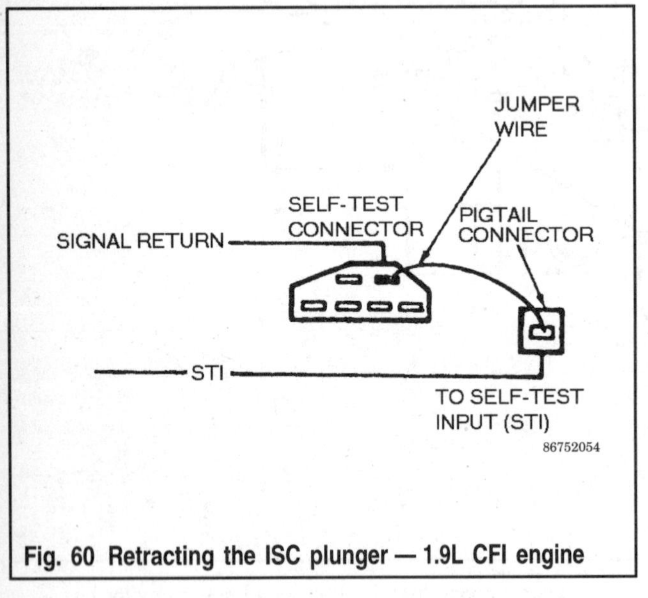

Fig. 60 Retracting the ISC plunger — 1.9L CFI engine

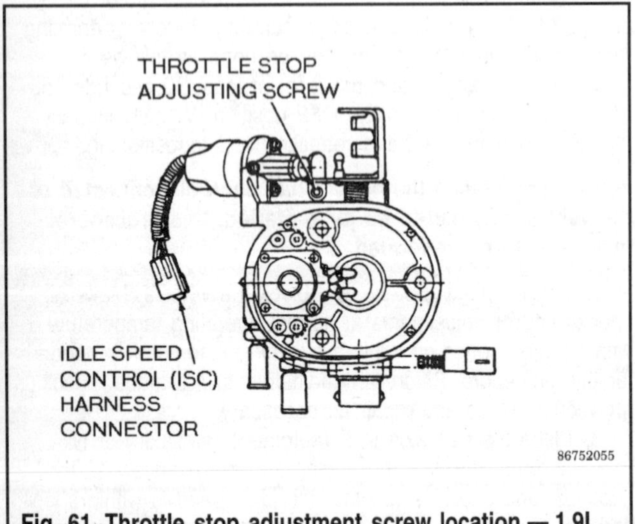

Fig. 61 Throttle stop adjustment screw location — 1.9L CFI engine

5. With the engine off, remove the air cleaner assembly. Connect a jumper wire between the self-test input and the signal return pin on the self test connector.

6. Turn the ignition to the **ON** position, but do not start the engine. The idle speed control (ISC) plunger should retract within 10-15 seconds. If the plunger does not retract there is a malfunction within the on board diagnostic system and the vehicle should be taken to a factory authorized technician for further diagnostic evaluation.

7. Disconnect the ISC harness connector. Turn the ignition key off and remove the jumper wire.

8. Start the engine and check the idle rpm, if not within specification, use the following procedure:

a. With the engine off, remove the CFI assembly from the vehicle.

b. Remove the tamper-resistant plug that covers the throttle stop adjusting screw.

c. Remove the old throttle stop adjusting screw and install a new screw.

d. Install the CFI assembly back on the intake manifold/engine.

9. Start the engine and let the idle stabilize. Adjust the throttle stop adjusting screw until the specified rpm is reached.

10. Shut the engine off and reconnect the vehicle harness to the ISC motor. Make sure that the throttle plate is not binding in the bore or that the linkage is preventing the throttle plate from returning. Reinstall the air cleaner assembly.

11. Be sure to refer to the under-hood emission/calibration sticker for the engine idle rpm specification. If the specifications on the sticker differ from the specifications from this manual, the specifications on the sticker should be followed.

1987-90 1.9L HIGH OUTPUT (HO) MODELS WITH MULTI-PORT FUEL INJECTION (MFI)

1. Apply the parking brake and block the wheels. Place the transaxle in neutral and start the engine. Allow the engine to run until it reaches normal operating temperature. Turn off all accessories and turn the engine **OFF**.

2. Disconnect the idle speed control motor harness connector. Start the engine and run it at 2000 rpm for approximately one minute and return it to idle.

3. Disconnect the EGR vacuum connection at the EGR solenoid and plug both lines (if so equipped). Disconnect the idle speed control bypass air solenoid power lead (if so equipped).

4. With the transaxle in D (automatic transaxle) or N (manual transaxle), check to see that the idle speed is 900-1000 rpm. If the idle speed is not within specifications, go on to the next Step.

5. Make sure that the cooling fan is OFF. Turn the throttle plate adjusting screw until the idle is within specifications. Adjustment must be made within 2 minutes after returning to idle.

6. If the idle speed adjustment was necessary, repeat Steps 2 through 5. Once the idle has been set to specifications, turn the ignition **OFF**. Reconnect the ISC connector. Make sure that the throttle plate is not binding in the bore or that the linkage is preventing the throttle plate from returning.

7. To make sure that the adjustment was good, run the engine at 2000 rpm for approximately one minute and return it

to idle, Be sure to refer to the under hood emission/calibration sticker for the engine idle rpm specification.

1991-95 1.8L MFI DOHC and 1.9L SFI

The curb idle and fast idle speeds are controlled by the EEC-IV processor and the Idle Speed Control Device. The idle speed control device is not adjustable. A large increase or decrease in closed plate airflow from the calibrated level will not allow this device to effectively control the speed. If this condition exists, it is recommended that the vehicle be taken to an authorized factory technician for further diagnostic evaluation.

2.0L Diesel Engine

See Figure 62

A special diesel engine tachometer is required for this procedure.

1. Place the transaxle in N.
2. Bring the engine up to normal operating temperature. Stop engine.
3. Remove the timing hole cover. Clean the flywheel surface and install reflective tape.
4. Idle speed is measured with manual transaxle in N.
5. Check curb idle speed, using Rotunda 99-0001 or equivalent. Curb idle speed is specified on the vehicle Emissions Control Information decal (VECI). Adjust to specification by loosening the locknut on the idle speed bolt. Turn the idle speed adjusting bolt clockwise to increase, or counterclockwise to decrease engine idle speed. Tighten the locknut.
6. Place transaxle in N. Increase the engine rpm momentarily and recheck the curb idle rpm. Readjust if necessary.
7. Turn air conditioning ON. Check the idle speed. Adjust to specification by loosening the nut on the air conditioning throttle kicker and rotating the screw.

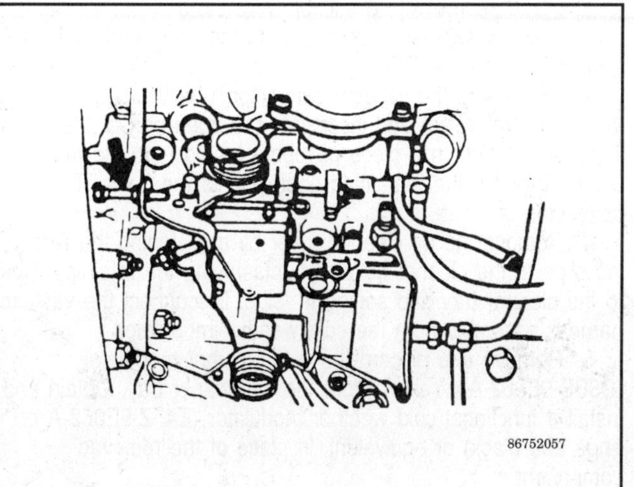

Fig. 62 Curb idle adjustment — 2.0L diesel engine

Fast Idle

ADJUSTMENT

1.6L and 1.9L Engines

1. Place the transaxle in P or N. Set the parking brake and block the wheels. Connect tachometer to the engine.
2. Bring the engine to normal operating temperature.
3. Disconnect the vacuum hose at the EGR and plug.
4. Place the fast idle adjustment screw on the second highest step of the fast idle cam. Run engine until the cooling fan comes on.
5. Check, and if necessary, adjust fast idle rpm to specification. If adjustment is required, loosen locknut, adjust and retighten.

Engine cooling fan must be running when checking fast idle rpm. (Use a jumper wire is necessary).

6. Remove the plug from the EGR hose and reconnect.

Dashpot Clearance

ADJUSTMENT

1.6L and 1.9L Carbureted Engines

If so equipped, dashpot must be adjusted when the curb idle speed is adjusted.

1. With the engine OFF, push the dashpot plunger in as far as possible and check the clearance between the plunger and the throttle lever pad.

Refer to the emissions decal for proper dashpot clearance. If not available, set the clearance to 0.118-0.158 in. in. (3.0-4.0mm).

2. Adjust the dashpot clearance by loosening the mounting locknut and rotating the dashpot.

If the locknut is very tight, remove the mounting bracket, hold it in a suitable device so that it will not bend, and loosen the locknut. Reinstall the bracket and dashpot.

3. After gaining the required clearance, tighten the locknut and recheck adjustment.

Air Conditioning Throttle Kicker

ADJUSTMENT

1.6L and 1.9L Engines

1. Place the transaxle in P or N.
2. Bring engine to normal operating temperature.
3. Identify vacuum source to air bypass section of air supply control valve. If vacuum hose is connected to carburetor,

disconnect and plug hose at air supply control valve. Install slave vacuum hose between intake manifold and air bypass connection on air supply control valve.

4. To check/adjust air conditioning or throttle kicker rpm:

a. If the vehicle is equipped with air conditioning, place selector to maximum cooling, blower switch on High and disconnect the air conditioning compressor clutch wire.

b. If the vehicle is equipped with kicker and no air conditioning, disconnect vacuum hose from kicker and plug. Install slave vacuum hose from intake manifold vacuum to kicker.

5. Run the engine until the engine cooling fan comes ON.

6. Place the transaxle in the specified gear and check/adjust air conditioning or throttle kicker rpm to specification.

➡Engine cooling fan must be running when checking air conditioning or throttle kicker rpm. Adjust rpm by turning screw on the kicker.

7. If slave vacuum hose was installed to check/adjust kicker rpm, remove slave vacuum hose. Remove the plug from the kicker vacuum hose and reconnect the hose to the kicker.

8. Remove the slave vacuum hose. Return the intake manifold supply source to original condition. Remove the plug from the carburetor vacuum hose and reconnect to the air bypass valve.

TROUBLESHOOTING TIPS

This following Chilton Troubleshooting Tips are for specific (known) problems and answers dealing only with certain models and years.

Escort/Lynx And EXP/LN7

1984 MODELS

Some models may exhibit signs of a rough idle or the engine stalling or both. This problem could be caused by the malfunctioning EGR valve position sensor that has been installed on the vehicle. The EGR valve position sensor (EVP) with date codes prior to October 12, 1984 may cause this rough idle and stalling problem in some models, particularly 1984 California vehicles equipped with the EEC-III system. These vehicles do not have the computer memory to track the intermittent component concerns making the diagnosis more difficult.

When servicing the 1984 EEC-III equipped vehicles with this problem, check the EVP sensor. Replace the EVP sensor if the part is E43F-9G428-A2A with a date code prior to October 12, 1984. The date code is listed below the part number on the sensor. Normal diagnostic procedures will usually detect the above conditions on all EEC-IV applications. Be sure that the replacement EVP sensor has a date code of October 12, 1984 or later. The EVP sensors with part number E43F-9G428-A1A/A1B are not effected and all date codes are acceptable for service.

When determining the date number on the EVP sensor, use the following example as a guide, date number 4C7B:

- The 4 indicates the year 1984.
- The C indicates the month, the months are lined up in the following manner:
- A = January, B= February, C = March, etc.
- The 7 indicates the day of the month.
- The B indicates the shift that produced the sensor. A = 1st, B = 2nd and C = 3rd shift.

1. So, by using the example, it states that sensor was built on March 7, 1984 by the second shift.

With 1.6L Engine and Automatic Transaxle

Some of these models may exhibit conditions of stalling and or no-start during cold engine operation, This can be corrected by installing a new purge control valve in the evaporative emission control system and removing the cold weather modulator.

1. Remove and discard the T connector (D9AE-9E645-AB) from the existing evaporative emission control harness (E4EE-9C987-BA).

2. Install purge control valve E3TZ-9B-963-A in the evaporative emission control harness where the T connector used to be located.

a. Position the new purge control valve in such a way that the round portion (top of the cap) is right side up with the 3/8 in. (9.5mm) and the 1/4 in. (6mm) nipple pointing towards the battery.

b. Route the 1/4 in. (6mm) hose under the 3/8 in. (9.5mm) hose from the carburetor Bowl Vent Valve and attach it to the 1/4 in. (6mm) nipple on the purge control valve. Attach a piece of 5/32 in. (4mm) bulk hose 13 in. (330mm) long to the end of the 3/16 in. (4.8mm) open port of the purge control valve and secure with a suitable wire strap.

c. Attach a 3-way T connector to the open end of the 13 in. (330mm) hose.

3. Disconnect the vacuum connector, (the vacuum line from the air control valve) and insert into the open port of the 3-way T connector. Attach a piece of rubber tubing from the air control valve to the remaining open port of the 3-way T connector.

4. Remove the air cleaner cover by unfastening the retaining clips to the cleaner cover by unfastening the retaining clips to the cleaner tray and setting it aside. Disconnect the vacuum harness assembly from the cold weather modulator.

5. Remove and discard the cold weather modulator (D8BE-9E862-AA Yellow) from the air cleaner tray. Obtain and install a functional cold weather modulator (E4FZ-9E862-A orange and black) or equivalent, in place of the removed component

6. Reconnect the vacuum harness that was removed in Step 4.

GASOLINE ENGINE TUNE-UP SPECIFICATIONS

Year	Engine ID/VIN	Engine Displacement Liters (cc)	Spark Plugs Gap (in.)	Ignition Timing (deg.) MT	Ignition Timing (deg.) AT	Fuel Pump (psi)	Idle Speed (rpm) MT	Idle Speed (rpm) AT	Valve Clearance In.	Valve Clearance Ex.
1981	2	1.6 (1606)	0.044	8B	8B	4-6	700	700	HYD	HYD
1982	2	1.6 (1606)	0.044	8B	8B	4-6	700	700	HYD	HYD
1983	2	1.6 (1606)	0.044	8B	8B	4-6	700	700	HYD	HYD
	4	1.6 (1606)	0.044	12B	12B	4-6	800	800	HYD	HYD
	5	1.6 (1606)	0.044	10B	10B	35-45	800	750	HYD	HYD
1984	2	1.6 (1606)	0.044	8B	8B	4-6	700	700	HYD	HYD
	4	1.6 (1606)	0.044	12B	12B	4-6	800	800	HYD	HYD
	5	1.6 (1606)	0.044	10B	10B	35-45	800	750	HYD	HYD
	7	1.6 (1606)	0.044	12B	14B	4-6	800	800	HYD	HYD
	8	1.6 (1606)	0.044	8B	8B	35-45	800	750	HYD	HYD
1985	2	1.6 (1606)	0.044	8B	8B	4-6	700	700	HYD	HYD
	4	1.6 (1606)	0.044	12B	12B	4-6	800	800	HYD	HYD
	5	1.6 (1606)	0.044	10B	10B	35-45	800	750	HYD	HYD
	7	1.6 (1606)	0.044	12B	14B	4-6	800	800	HYD	HYD
	8	1.6 (1606)	0.044	8B	8B	35-45	800	750	HYD	HYD
	9	1.9 (1901)	0.044	10B	10B	4-6	750	750	HYD	HYD
1986	9	1.9 (1901)	0.044	10B	10B	4-6	750	750	HYD	HYD
	J	1.9 (1901)	0.044	10B	10B	35-45	900	800	HYD	HYD
1987	9	1.9 (1901)	0.044	10B	10B	30-45	750	750	HYD	HYD
	J	1.9 (1901)	0.044	10B	10B	35-45	900	800	HYD	HYD
1988	9	1.9 (1901)	0.044	10B	10B	30-45	950	950	HYD	HYD
	J	1.9 (1901)	0.044	10B	10B	13-17	950	950	HYD	HYD
1989	9	1.9 (1901)	0.044	10B	10B	30-45	950	950	HYD	HYD
	J	1.9 (1901)	0.044	10B	10B	17-35	950	950	HYD	HYD
1990	9	1.9 (1901)	0.044	10B	10B	30-45	950	950	HYD	HYD
	J	1.9 (1901)	0.044	10B	10B	17-35	950	950	HYD	HYD
1991	8	1.8 (1844)	0.041	10B	10B	64-85	750	750	HYD	HYD
	J	1.9 (1901)	0.054	10B	10B	17-35	950	950	HYD	HYD
1992	8	1.8 (1844)	0.041	10B	10B	64-85	750	750	HYD	HYD
	J	1.9 (1901)	0.054	10B	10B	17-35	950	950	HYD	HYD
1993	8	1.8 (1844)	0.041	10B	10B	64-85	750	750	HYD	HYD
	J	1.9 (1901)	0.054	10B	10B	17-35	950	950	HYD	HYD
1994	8	1.8 (1844)	0.041	10B	10B	31-38	750	750	HYD	HYD
	J	1.9 (1901)	0.054	10B	10B	30-45	780	780	HYD	HYD
1995	8	1.8 (1844)	0.041	10B	10B	31-38 ①	750	750	HYD	HYD
	J	1.9 (1901)	0.054	10B	10B	30-34 ①	780	780	HYD	HYD

NOTE: The Vehicle Emission Control Information label often reflects specification changes made during production. The label figures must be used if they differ from those in this chart.

B - Before Top Dead Center

HYD - Hydraulic

① Fuel pressure with engine running, pressure regulator vacuum hose connected

86752C14

DIESEL ENGINE TUNE-UP SPECIFICATIONS

Year	Engine ID/VIN	Engine Displacement cu. in. (cc)	Valve Clearance Intake (in.)	Valve Clearance Exhaust (in.)	Intake Valve Opens (deg.)	Injection Pump Setting (deg.)	Injection Nozzle Pressure (psi) New	Injection Nozzle Pressure (psi) Used	Idle Speed (rpm)	Cranking Compression Pressure (psi)
1984	H	2.0 (1998)	0.010 ①	0.014	13	TDC ②	1990-2105	1849-1990	675-775	390-435@2000
1985	H	2.0 (1998)	0.010 ①	0.014	13	TDC ②	1990-2105	1849-1990	675-775	390-435@2000
1986	H	2.0 (1998)	0.010 ①	0.014	13	TDC ②	1990-2105	1849-2100	675-775	390-435@2000
1987	H	2.0 (1998)	0.010 ①	0.014	13	TDC ②	1990-2105	1849-2100	675-775	390-435@2000

NOTE: The Vehicle Emission Control Information label often reflects specification changes made during production. The label figures must be used if they differ from those in this chart.

TDC - Top Dead Center

① Valve clearance specifications are set cold

② With engine hot

86752C15

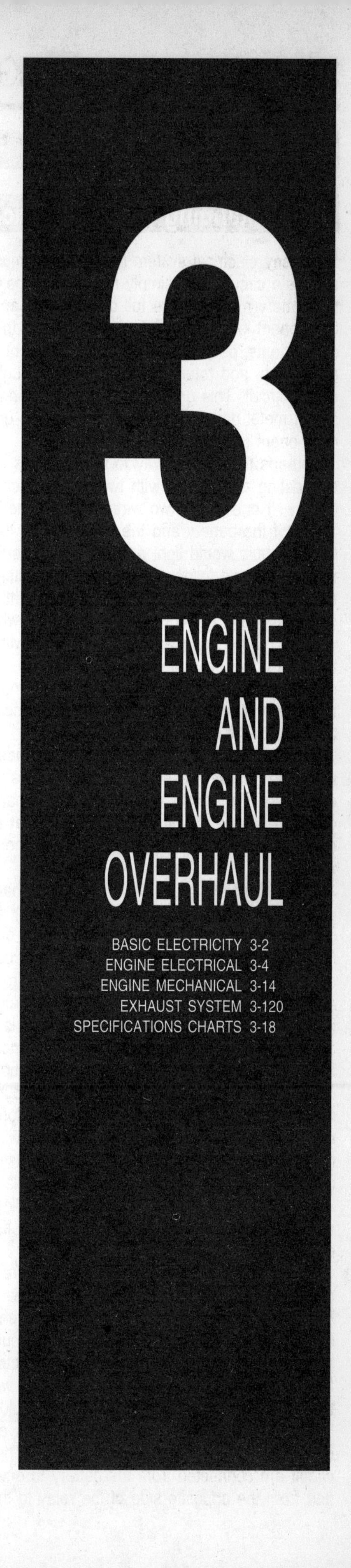
3
ENGINE AND ENGINE OVERHAUL
BASIC ELECTRICITY 3-2
ENGINE ELECTRICAL 3-4
ENGINE MECHANICAL 3-14
EXHAUST SYSTEM 3-120
SPECIFICATIONS CHARTS 3-18

BASIC ELECTRICITY

Understanding Basic Electricity

For any electrical system to operate, it must make a complete circuit. This simply means that the power flow from the battery must make a full circle. When an electrical component is operating, power flows from the battery to the components, passes through the component (load) causing it to function, and returns to the battery through the ground path of the circuit. This ground may be either another wire or the actual metal part of the vehicle depending upon how the component is designed.

Perhaps the easiest way to visualize this is to think of connecting a light bulb with two wires attached to it to the battery. If one of the two wires was attached to the negative (-) post of the battery and the other wire to the positive (+) post, the light bulb would light and the circuit would be complete. Electricity could follow a path from the battery to the bulb and back to the battery. It's not hard to see that with longer wires on our light bulb, it could be mounted anywhere on the vehicle. Further, one wire could be fitted with a switch so that the light could be turned on and off at will. Various other items could be added to our primitive circuit to make the light flash, become brighter or dimmer under certain conditions, or advise the user that it's burned out.

Some automotive components are grounded through their mounting points. The electrical current runs through the chassis of the vehicle and returns to the battery through the ground (-) cable; if you look, you'll see that the battery ground cable connects between the battery and the body of the vehicle.

Every complete circuit must include a "load" (something to use the electricity coming from the source). If you were to connect a wire between the two terminals of the battery (DON'T do this) without the light bulb, the battery would attempt to deliver its entire power supply from one pole to another almost instantly. This is a short circuit. The electricity is taking a short cut to get to ground and is not being used by any load in the circuit. This sudden and uncontrolled electrical flow can cause great damage to other components in the circuit and can develop a tremendous amount of heat. A short in an automotive wiring harness can develop sufficient heat to melt the insulation on all the surrounding wires and reduce a multiple wire cable to one sad lump of plastic and copper. Two common causes of shorts are broken insulation (thereby exposing the wire to contact with surrounding metal surfaces or other wires) or a failed switch (the pins inside the switch come out of place and touch each other).

Some electrical components which require a large amount of current to operate also have a relay in their circuit. Since these circuits carry a large amount of current (amperage or amps), the thickness of the wire in the circuit (wire gauge) is also greater. If this large wire were connected from the load to the control switch on the dash, the switch would have to carry the high amperage load and the dash would be twice as large to accommodate wiring harnesses as thick as your wrist. To prevent these problems, a relay is used. The large wires in the circuit are connected from the battery to one side of the relay and from the opposite side of the relay to the load. The relay is normally open, preventing current from passing through the circuit. An additional, smaller wire is connected from the relay to the control switch for the circuit. When the control switch is turned on, it grounds the smaller wire to the relay and completes its circuit. The main switch inside the relay closes, sending power to the component without routing the main power through the inside of the vehicle. Some common circuits which may use relays are the horn, headlights, starter and rear window defogger systems.

It is possible for larger surges of current to pass through the electrical system of your vehicle. If this surge of current were to reach the load in the circuit, it could burn it out or severely damage it. To prevent this, fuses, circuit breakers and/or fusible links are connected into the supply wires of the electrical system. These items are nothing more than a built-in weak spot in the system. It's much easier to go to a known location (the fusebox) to see why a circuit is inoperative than to dissect 15 feet of wiring under the dashboard, looking for what happened.

When an electrical current of excessive power passes through the fuse, the fuse blows and breaks the circuit, preventing the passage of current and protecting the components.

A circuit breaker is basically a self repairing fuse. It will open the circuit in the same fashion as a fuse, but when either the short is removed or the surge subsides, the circuit breaker resets itself and does not need replacement.

A fuse link (fusible link or main link) is a wire that acts as a fuse. One of these is normally connected between the starter relay and the main wiring harness under the hood. Since the starter is the highest electrical draw on the vehicle, an internal short during starting could direct about 130 amps into the wrong places. Consider the damage potential of introducing this current into a system whose wiring is rated at 15 amps and you'll understand the need for protection. Since this link is very early in the electrical path, it's the first place to look if nothing on the vehicle works, but the battery seems to be charged and is properly connected.

Electrical problems generally fall into one of three areas:

- The component that is not functioning is not receiving current.
- The component is receiving power but not using it or using it incorrectly (component failure).
- The component is improperly grounded.

The circuit can be can be checked with a test light and a jumper wire. The test light is a device that looks like a pointed screwdriver with a wire on one end and a bulb in its handle. A jumper wire is simply a piece of wire with alligator clips on each end. If a component is not working, you must follow a systematic plan to determine which of the three causes is the villain.

1. Turn on the switch that controls the item not working.

➡Some items only work when the ignition switch is turned ON.

2. Disconnect the power supply wire from the component.
3. Attach the ground wire on the test light to a good metal ground.

4. Touch the end probe of the test light to the power wire; if there is current in the wire, the light in the test light will come on. You have now established that current is getting to the component.

5. Turn the ignition or dash switch **OFF** and reconnect the wire to the component.

If the test light did not go on, then the problem is between the battery and the component. This includes all the switches, fuses, relays and the battery itself. The next place to look is the fusebox; check carefully either by eye or by using the test light across the fuse clips. The easiest way to check is to simply replace the fuse. If the fuse is blown, and upon replacement, immediately blows again, there is a short between the fuse and the component. This is generally (not always) a sign of an internal short in the component. Disconnect the power wire at the component again and replace the fuse; if the fuse holds, the component is the problem.

If all the fuses are good and the component is not receiving power, find the switch for the circuit. Bypass the switch with the jumper wire. This is done by connecting one end of the jumper to the power wire coming into the switch and the other end to the wire leaving the switch. If the component comes to life, the switch has failed.

*****WARNING**

Never substitute the jumper for the component. The circuit needs the electrical load of the component. If you bypass it, you will cause a short circuit.

Checking the ground for any circuit can mean tracing wires to the body, cleaning connections or tightening mounting bolts for the component itself. If the jumper wire can be connected to the case of the component or the ground connector, you can ground the other end to a piece of clean, solid metal on the vehicle. Again, if the component starts working, you've found the problem.

A systematic search through the fuse, connectors, switches and the component itself will almost always yield an answer. Loose and/or corroded connectors, particularly in ground circuits, are becoming a larger problem in modern vehicles. The computers and on-board electronic (solid state) systems are highly sensitive to improper grounds and will change their function drastically if one occurs.

Remember that for any electrical circuit to work, ALL the connections must be clean and tight.

Engine Electrical Systems

BASIC OPERATING PRINCIPLES

Battery

The battery is the first link in the chain of mechanisms which work together to provide cranking of the automobile engine. In most modern vehicles, the battery is a lead/acid electrochemical device consisting of six 2v subsections (cells) connected in series so the unit is capable of producing approximately 12v of electrical pressure. Each subsection consists of a series of positive and negative plates held a short distance apart in a solution of sulfuric acid and water.

The two types of plates are of dissimilar metals. This causes a chemical reaction to be set up, and it is this reaction which produces current flow from the battery when its positive and negative terminals are connected to an electrical appliance such as a lamp or motor. The continued transfer of electrons would eventually convert the sulfuric acid to water, and make the two plates identical in chemical composition. As electrical energy is removed from the battery, its voltage output tends to drop. Thus, measuring battery voltage and battery electrolyte composition are two ways of checking the ability of the unit to supply power. During the starting of the engine, electrical energy is removed from the battery. However, if the charging circuit is in good condition and the operating conditions are normal, the power removed from the battery will be replaced by the alternator which will force electrons back through the battery, reversing the normal flow, and restoring the battery to its original chemical state.

Starting System

The battery and starting motor are linked by very heavy electrical cables designed to minimize resistance to the flow of current. Generally, the major power supply cable that leaves the battery goes directly to the starter, while other electrical system needs are supplied by a smaller cable. During starter operation, power flows from the battery to the starter and is grounded through the vehicle's frame and the battery's negative ground strap.

The starting motor is a specially designed, direct current electric motor capable of producing a great amount of power for its size. One thing that allows the motor to produce a great deal of power is its tremendous rotating speed. It drives the engine through a tiny pinion gear (attached to the starter's armature), which drives the very large flywheel ring gear at a greatly reduced speed. Another factor allowing it to produce so much power is that only intermittent operation is required of it. Thus, little allowance for air circulation is required, and the windings can be built into a very small space.

The starter solenoid is a magnetic device which employs the small current supplied by the start circuit of the ignition switch. This magnetic action moves a plunger which mechanically engages the starter and closes the heavy switch connecting it to the battery. The starting switch circuit consists of the starting switch contained within the ignition switch, a transaxle neutral safety switch or clutch pedal switch, and the wiring necessary to connect these in series with the starter solenoid or relay.

The pinion, a small gear, is mounted to a one way drive clutch. This clutch is splined to the starter armature shaft. When the ignition switch is moved to the **START** position, the solenoid plunger slides the pinion toward the flywheel ring gear via a collar and spring. If the teeth on the pinion and flywheel match properly, the pinion will engage the flywheel immediately. If the gear teeth butt one another, the spring will be compressed and will force the gears to mesh as soon as the starter turns far enough to allow them to do so. As the solenoid plunger reaches the end of its travel, it closes the contacts that connect the battery and starter and then the engine is cranked.

As soon as the engine starts, the flywheel ring gear begins turning fast enough to drive the pinion at an extremely high rate of speed. At this point, the one-way clutch begins allowing the pinion to spin faster than the starter shaft so that the starter will not operate at excessive speed. When the ignition switch is released from the starter position, the solenoid is de-energized, and a spring pulls the gear out of mesh interrupting the current flow to the starter.

Some starters employ a separate relay, mounted away from the starter, to switch the motor and solenoid current on and off. The relay replaces the solenoid electrical switch, but does not eliminate the need for a solenoid mounted on the starter used to mechanically engage the starter drive gears. The relay is used to reduce the amount of current the starting switch must carry.

Charging System

The automobile charging system provides electrical power for operation of the vehicle's ignition system, starting system and all the electrical accessories. The battery serves as an electrical surge or storage tank, storing (in chemical form) the energy originally produced by the engine driven generator. The system also provides a means of regulating output to protect the battery from being overcharged and to avoid excessive voltage to the accessories.

The storage battery is a chemical device incorporating parallel lead plates in a tank containing a sulfuric acid/water solution. Adjacent plates are slightly dissimilar, and the chemical reaction of the two dissimilar plates produces electrical energy when the battery is connected to a load such as the starter motor. The chemical reaction is reversible, so that when the generator is producing a voltage (electrical pressure) greater than that produced by the battery, electricity is forced into the battery, and the battery is returned to its fully charged state.

Newer automobiles use alternating current generators or alternators, because they are more efficient, can be rotated at higher speeds, and have fewer brush problems. In an alternator, the field rotates while all the current produced passes only through the stator winding. The brushes bear against continuous slip rings. This causes the current produced to periodically reverse the direction of its flow. Diodes (electrical one way valves) block the flow of current from traveling in the wrong direction. A series of diodes is wired together to permit the alternating flow of the stator to be rectified back to 12 volts DC for use by the vehicles's electrical system.

The voltage regulating function is performed by a regulator. The regulator is often built in to the alternator; this system is termed an integrated or internal regulator.

ENGINE ELECTRICAL

Ignition Coil

TESTING

1.6L and 1.9L Non-MFI Engines

➧ See Figures 1 and 2

1. Verify that the ignition switch is in the **OFF** position.
2. Remove the primary connector, clean and inspect for dirt or corrosion.
3. Measure the resistance between the BATT and TACH terminals of the primary with an ohmmeter. Resistance should measure 0.8-1.6 ohms.
4. Measure resistance from the BATT terminal to the high voltage terminal of the coil.
5. The resistance should be 7,700-10,500 ohms.
6. If either readings are not within specification, replace the coil.

1.6L MFI and 1.9L MFI Engines Through 1990

➧ See Figures 3 and 4

1. Verify that the ignition switch is in the **OFF** position.
2. Remove the primary connector, clean and inspect for dirt or corrosion.
3. Measure the resistance between the BATT and TACH terminals of the primary with an ohmmeter. Resistance should measure 0.3-1.0 ohms.
4. Measure resistance from the BATT terminal to the high voltage terminal of the coil.
5. Resistance should be between 6,500-11,000 ohms.
6. Replace the coil, if either readings are not within specification.

1991-95 1.9L MFI/SFI Engines

➧ See Figure 5

1. Disconnect the coil pack from the vehicle harness.
2. Use a DVOM, set on the 2k ohms scale.
3. Measure the resistance between VBAT (+) and C2 pins of the coil.
4. If the resistance is less than 0.4 ohms, replace the ignition coil pack.

REMOVAL & INSTALLATION

Except 1991-95 1.8L and 1.9L Engines

1. Disconnect the negative battery cable.
2. Disconnect the ignition coil wiring harness, at the coil.
3. Remove the high voltage coil lead.
4. Remove the ignition coil retaining bolts and remove the coil assembly.

To install:

5. Place the ignition coil into position and install the retaining screws.
6. Reconnect the ignition coil high voltage wire and wiring harness.
7. Reconnect the negative battery cable.

1.8L (DIS) Engines

➧ See Figure 6

1. Disconnect the negative battery cable.

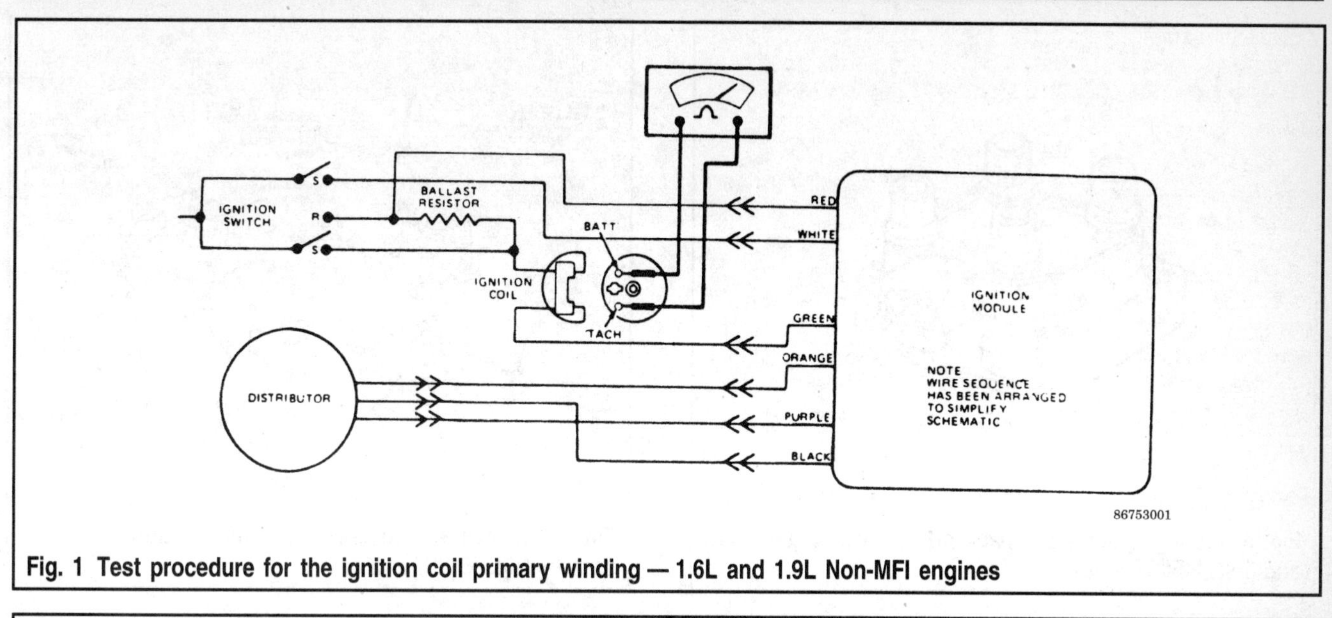

Fig. 1 Test procedure for the ignition coil primary winding — 1.6L and 1.9L Non-MFI engines

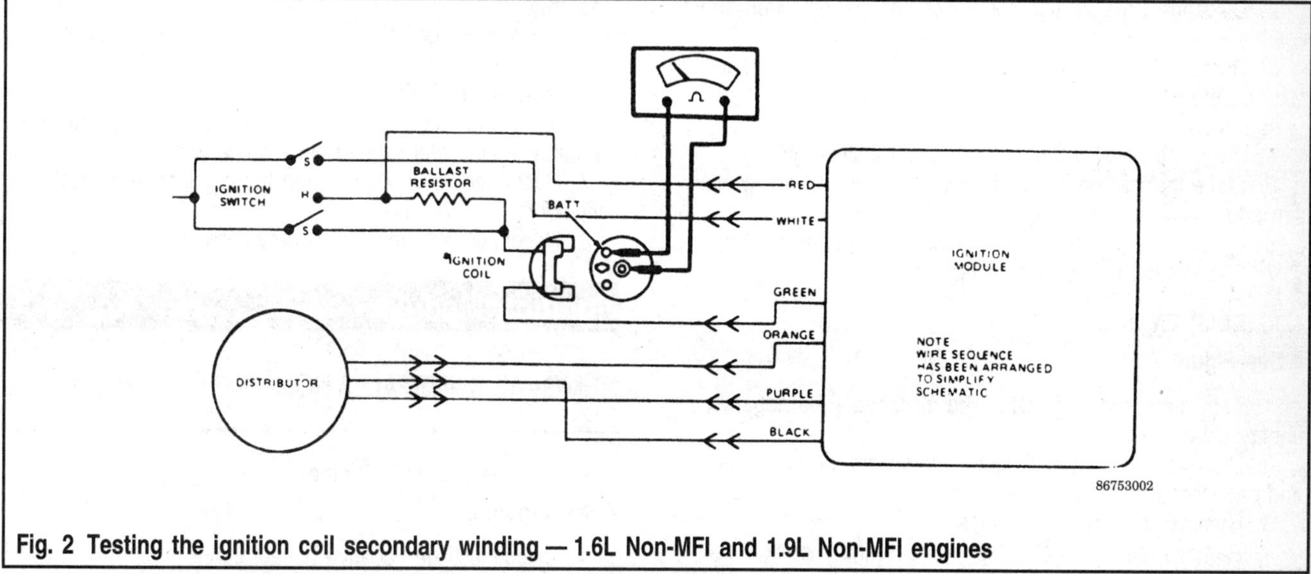

Fig. 2 Testing the ignition coil secondary winding — 1.6L Non-MFI and 1.9L Non-MFI engines

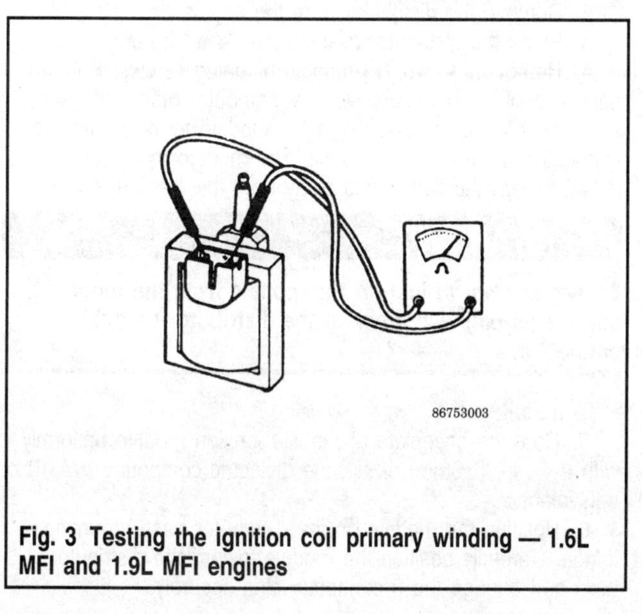

Fig. 3 Testing the ignition coil primary winding — 1.6L MFI and 1.9L MFI engines

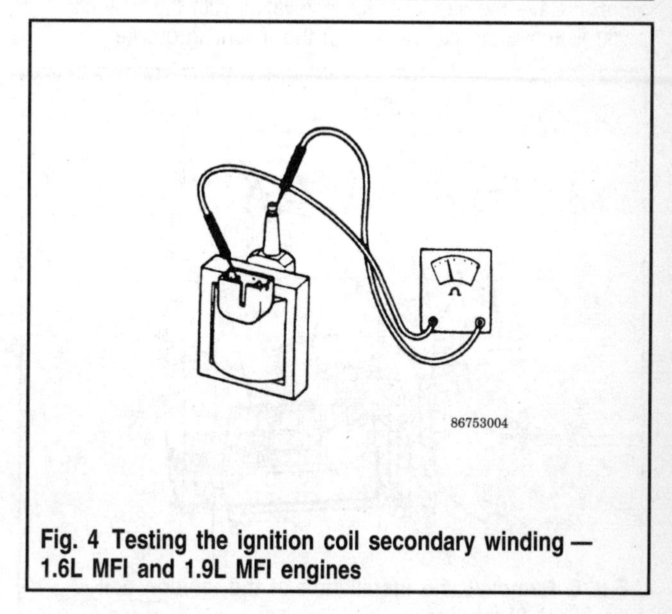

Fig. 4 Testing the ignition coil secondary winding — 1.6L MFI and 1.9L MFI engines

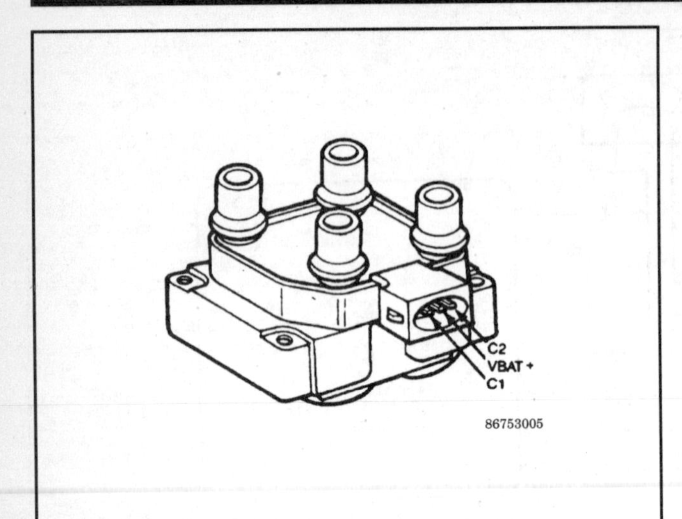

Fig. 5 Testing ignition coil pack primary winding — 1.8L and 1.9L MFI/SFI engine

2. Disconnect the ignition connector and coil wire from the coil.
3. Remove the ignition coil mounting nuts and remove the coil and bracket.

To install:

4. If removed, install the bracket to the ignition coil.
5. Place the ignition coil and bracket into its mounting position and install the mounting nuts.
6. Engage the ignition connector and coil wire to the coil.
7. Reconnect the negative battery cable.

1.9L (EDIS) Engines

➧ See Figure 7

1. Turn the ignition key **OFF** and disconnect the negative battery cable.
2. Disconnect the harness connectors from the coil pack and capacitor assembly.
3. Remove the spark plug wires.
4. Remove the coil pack retaining bolts and capacitor assembly. Save the capacitor for installation with the new coil pack. Remove the coil pack from the mounting bracket.

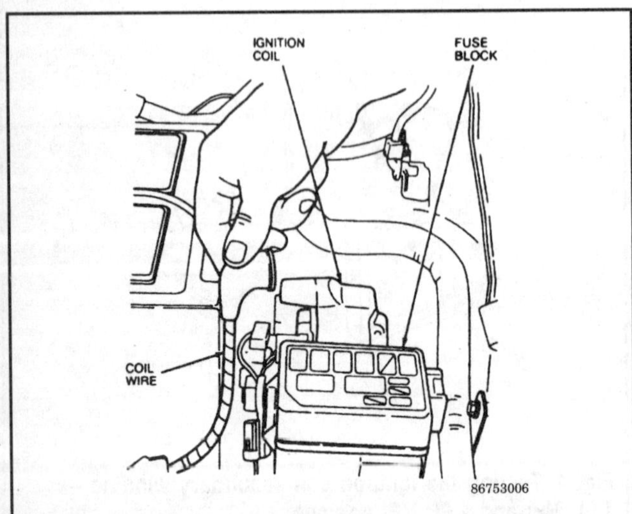

Fig. 6 Removal and installation of the ignition coil pack — 1.8L engine

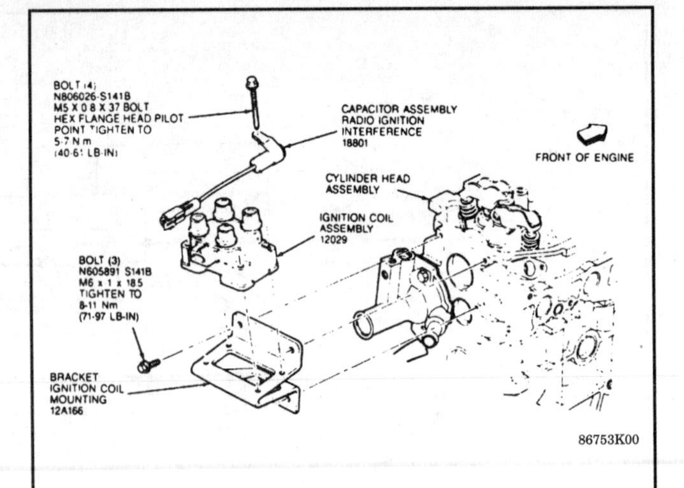

Fig. 7 Removal and installation of the ignition coil pack — 1.9L (EDIS) engine

To install:

5. Position the coil pack and capacitor assembly on its mounting bracket and install the retaining bolts. Tighten to 40-61 inch lbs. (5-7 Nm).
6. Install the spark plug wires. Be certain the boot retainers are firmly seated and latched onto the coil pack.
7. Reconnect the coil pack and the capacitor electrical connectors.
8. Reconnect the negative battery cable.

Ignition Module

REMOVAL & INSTALLATION

1.6L MFI and 1.9L MFI Engines

➧ See Figure 8

1. Disconnect the negative battery cable.
2. Remove the distributor from the engine.
3. Place the distributor assembly on a work bench.
4. Remove the two TFI module retaining screws. Pull the right side of the module down the distributor mounting flange and then back up to disengage the module terminals from the connector in the distributor base. The module may then be pulled toward the flange and away from the distributor.

****WARNING**

Do not attempt to just lift the module from the mounting surface as pins will break at the distributor module connector.

To install:

5. Coat the baseplate of the TFI ignition module uniformly with a 1/32 in. (0.8mm) of silicone dielectric compound WA-10 or equivalent.
6. Position the module on the distributor base mounting flange. Carefully position the module toward the distributor bowl and engage the 3 connector pins securely.

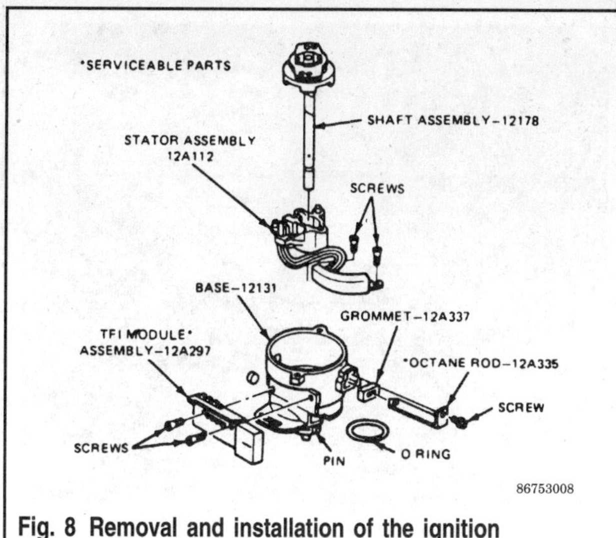

Fig. 8 Removal and installation of the ignition module — 1.6L MFI and 1.9L MFI engines

7. Install the retaining screws. Tighten to 15-35 inch lbs. (1.7-4.0 Nm), starting with the upper right screw.
8. Install the distributor into the engine. Install the cap and wires.
9. Reconnect the negative battery cable.
10. Start the engine and check the initial timing. Adjust, if necessary.

1.8L (ESA) Engine

➧ See Figure 9

1. Disconnect the negative battery cable.
2. Disconnect the ignition module electrical connector.
3. Remove the nuts and screws from the ignition module.
4. Remove the ignition module.
5. If replacing the suppression capacitor, remove the capacitor electrical connector and capacitor mounting nut. Remove the suppression capacitor.

To install:

6. Place the ignition module into its mounting position and install the nuts and screws.
7. Connect the ignition module electrical connector.

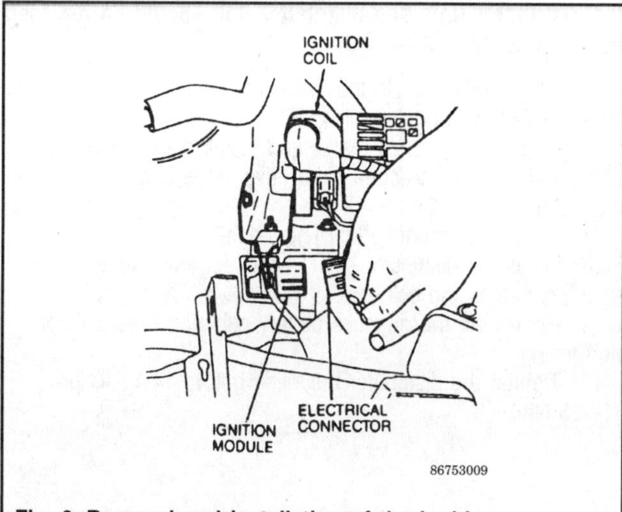

Fig. 9 Removal and installation of the ignition module — 1.8L engine

8. If removed, place the suppression capacitor into position and install the mounting nut. Reconnect the capacitor electrical connector.
9. Reconnect the negative battery cable.

1.9L (EDIS) Engine

➧ See Figure 10

1. Turn the ignition key **OFF** and disconnect the negative battery cable.
2. Remove the module bracket retaining bolts.
3. Carefully pull the bracket and module assembly straight upward and disconnect the module electrical connector.
4. Remove the module-to-bracket retaining screws and remove the module from the bracket.

To install:

5. Position the module on the bracket and install the retaining screws. Tighten to 24-35 inch lbs. (3-4 Nm).
6. Reconnect the module connector.
7. Fit the module and bracket assembly into position and install the retaining bolts. Tighten to 62-88 inch lbs. (7-10 Nm).
8. Reconnect the negative battery cable.

Distributor

REMOVAL & INSTALLATION

Except 1.8L Engines

➧ See Figures 11, 12 and 13

1. Disconnect the negative battery cable.
2. Remove the distributor cap with wires attached and position the cap and wires out of the way. Mark the position of the rotor tip to the distributor.
3. Disconnect and plug the vacuum hose at the vacuum diaphragm (2V only).
4. Disconnect the wiring harness to the distributor.

➡Some engines are equipped with a security type distributor hold-down bolt. Use tool T82L-12270-A or equivalent to remove the distributor.

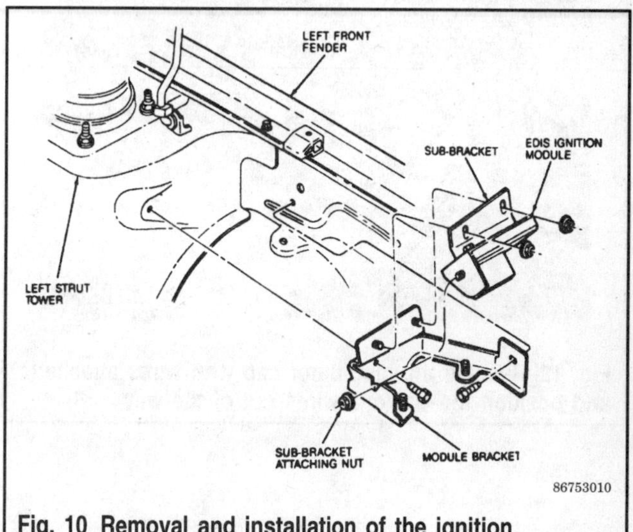

Fig. 10 Removal and installation of the ignition module — 1.9L (EDIS) engine

5. Mark the position of the distributor on the engine.
6. Remove the two distributor hold-down bolts and remove the distributor from the engine.

To install:

7. If the engine was turned while the distributor was removed from the engine, perform the following steps:
   a. Turn the number one piston to top dead center of the compression stroke.
   b. Turn the ignition rotor to align it with the number spark plug wire.
   c. Proceed to install the distributor as follows.
8. Check that the base O-ring and the drive coupling spring is in place. Position the rotor tip with the mark made earlier.
9. Position the distributor in the engine. Make certain the offset tang of the drive coupling is in the groove on the end of the camshaft.

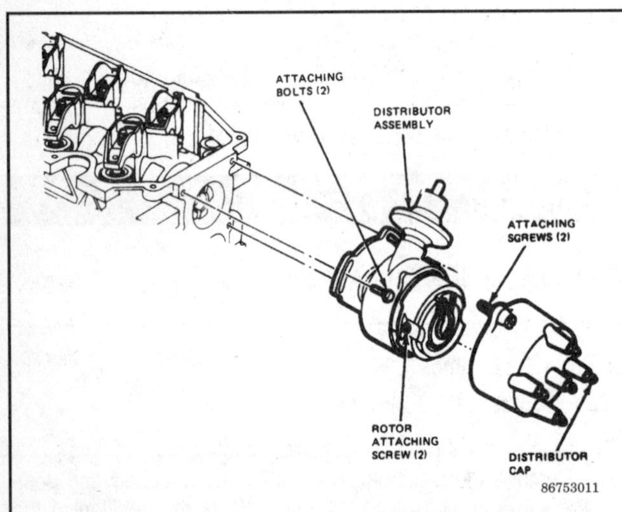

Fig. 11 Removal and installation of the distributor assembly

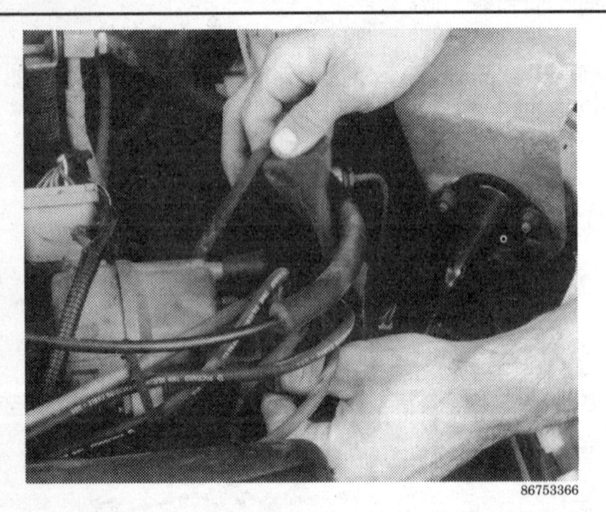

Fig. 12 Remove the distributor cap with wires attached and position the cap and wires out of the way

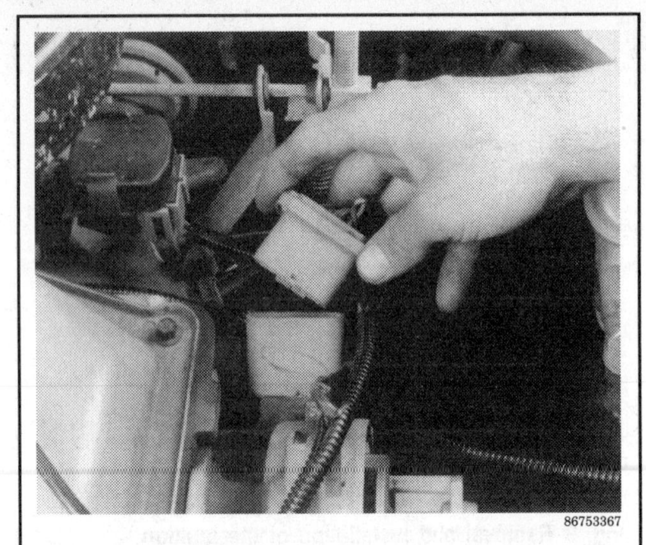

Fig. 13 Disconnect the wiring harness to the distributor

10. Loosely install the distributor hold-down bolts.
11. Reconnect the distributor wiring harness.
12. Install the cap.
13. Reconnect the negative battery cable, start the engine and check the ignition timing.
14. Tighten the distributor hold-down to specification.
15. Install the vacuum hose (2V only).

1.8L Engine

See Figures 14 and 15

1. Disconnect the negative battery cable.
2. Disconnect the distributor electrical connector and coil wire at the cap.
3. Remove the distributor cap and position it to the side. If the distributor unit is not being replaced, scribe a reference mark across the distributor base flange and the cylinder head. Also, mark the position of the rotor tip to the distributor.
4. Remove the distributor mounting bolt and flange. Remove the distributor from the engine.

Do not rotate the engine while the distributor assembly is removed. Do not attempt to disassemble and service the distributor unit. The distributor unit should be replaced as an assembly.

5. Fit a new O-ring to the distributor unit, if required. Lubricate the seal with engine oil.
6. Align the reference marks and install the distributor unit into the engine. Make certain the drive tangs engage with the camshaft slots.
7. Install the mounting bolt finger-tight.
8. Install the distributor cap. Reconnect the distributor electrical connector and coil wire to the cap.
9. Reconnect the negative battery cable and recheck ignition timing.
10. Tighten the distributor mounting bolt to 14-19 ft. lbs. (19-25 Nm).

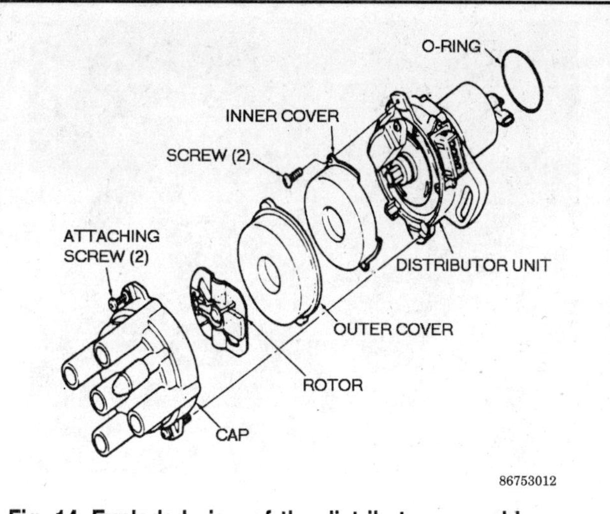

Fig. 14 Exploded view of the distributor assembly — 1.8L engine

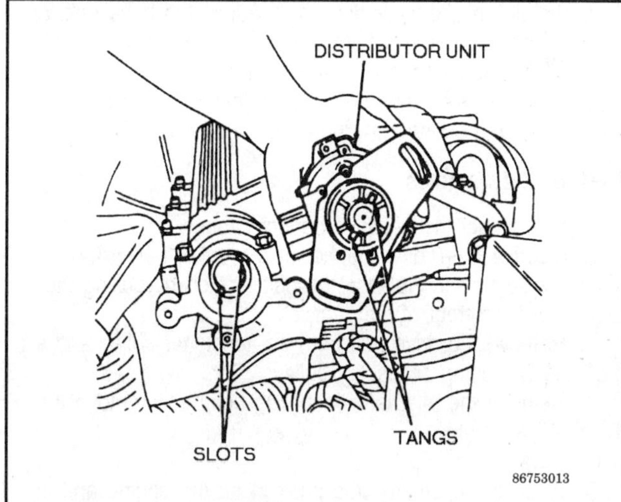

Fig. 15 Installation of the distributor assembly — 1.8L engine

Alternator

PRECAUTIONS

To prevent damage to the alternator and voltage regulator, the following precautionary measures must be taken when working with the electrical system:

- Never reverse battery connections. Always check the battery polarity visually. This is to be done before any connections are made to ensure that all of the connections correspond to the battery ground polarity of the car.
- Booster batteries must be connected properly. Make sure the positive cable of the booster battery is connected to the positive terminal of the battery which is getting the boost. Engines must be shut off before cables are connected.
- Disconnect the battery cables before using a fast charger; the charger has a tendency to force current through the diodes in the opposite direction for which they were designed.
- Never use a fast charger as a booster for starting the car.
- Never disconnect the voltage regulator while the engine is running unless, as noted, for testing purposes.
- Do not ground the alternator output terminal.
- Do not operate the alternator on an open circuit with the field energized.
- Do not attempt to polarize the alternator.
- Disconnect the battery cables and remove the alternator before using an electric arc welder on the car.
- Protect the alternator from excessive moisture. If the engine is to be steam cleaned, cover or remove the alternator.

REMOVAL & INSTALLATION

Except 1991-95 1.9L Engines

➧ See Figures 16, 17, 18, 19 and 20

1. Disconnect the negative battery cable.
2. If equipped with a pulley cover shield, remove the shield at this time.
3. Loosen the alternator pivot bolt. Remove the adjustment bracket to alternator bolt (and nut, if equipped). Pivot the alternator to gain slack in the drive belt and remove the belt.

➡To gain access to the alternator pivot bolt on 1.8L engines, it will be necessary to safely raise and support the vehicle.

4. Disconnect and label (for correct installation) the alternator wiring.

➡Some models use a push-on wiring connector on the field and stator connections. Pull or push straight when removing or installing, or damage to the connectors may occur.

5. Remove the pivot bolt and the alternator.

To install:

6. Position the alternator assembly onto the vehicle. Install the alternator pivot and adjuster arm bolts, but do not tighten them at this time.

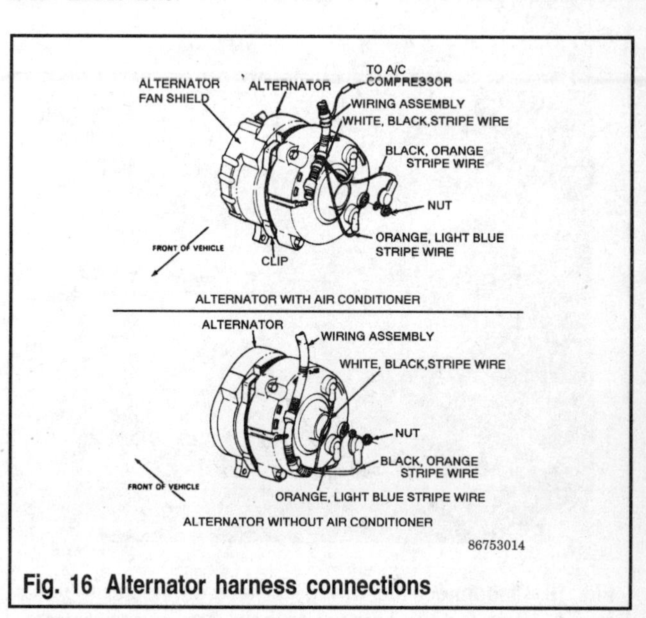

Fig. 16 Alternator harness connections

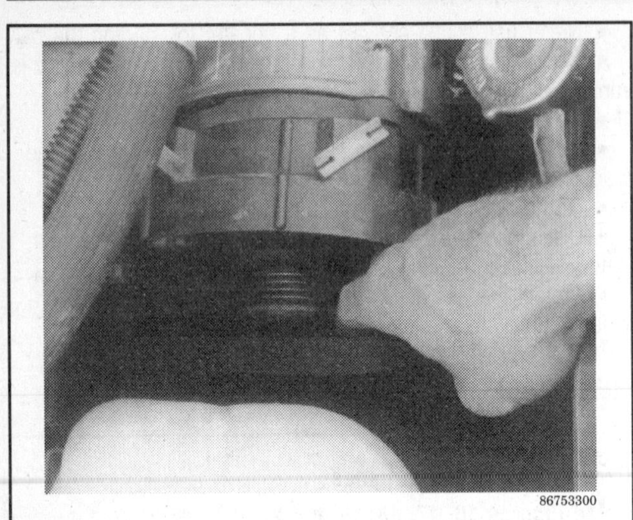
86753300

Fig. 17 Remove and set aside the alternator belt — 1988 1.9L models shown

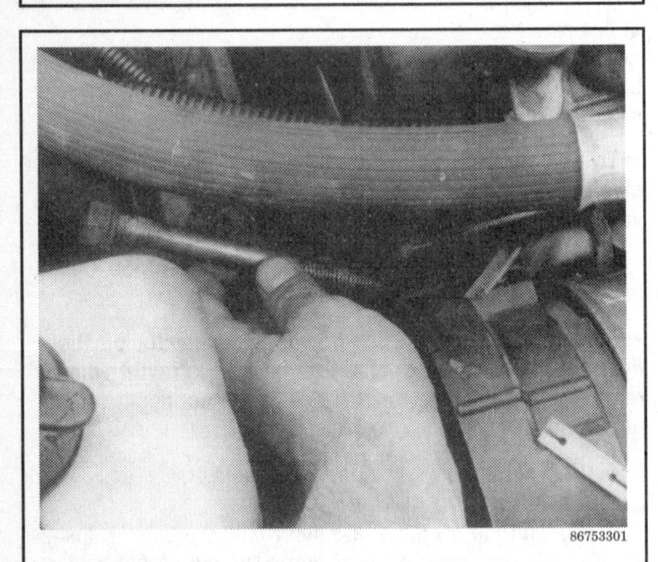
86753301

Fig. 18 Remove the alternator pivot bolt

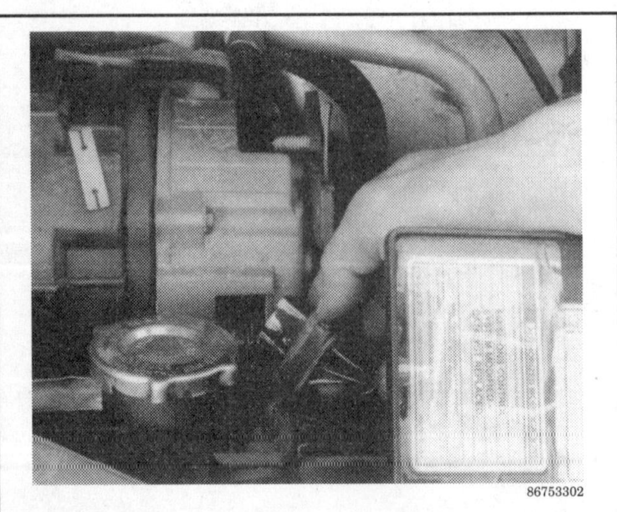
86753302

Fig. 19 Disconnect the wiring harness connector — you may want to tag the harness to help with re-connecting

86753303

Fig. 20 Remove the alternator when it is completely detached

7. Install the alternator drive belt. Adjust the drive belt tension so that there is approximately $^1/_4$-$^1/_2$ in. (6-13mm) deflection on the longest span between the pulleys.

8. Reconnect the alternator wiring. Install the pulley shield, if equipped and connect the negative battery cable.

1991-95 1.9L Engines

1. Disconnect the negative battery cable.
2. Insert a $^3/_8$ in. drive ratchet or a breaker bar in the automatic tensioner. Release the belt tension by pulling the tool toward the front of the vehicle.
3. Remove the drive belt from the tensioner pulley and slip it off the remaining accessory pulleys.
4. Remove the alternator mounting bolts and remove the alternator assembly.

To install:

5. Place the alternator into position on the engine and install the mounting bolts.
6. Position the drive belt over the accessory pulleys.
7. Insert the $^3/_8$ in. drive ratchet or a breaker bar in the automatic tensioner, and pull the tool toward the front of the vehicle.
8. While holding the tool in this position, slip the drive belt behind the tensioner pulley and release the tool. Remove the tool.
9. Check that all V-grooves are properly installed in pulleys.

BRUSH REPLACEMENT

➡If the alternator on the 1991-95 engines requires service, it must be replaced as an assembly.

External Fan Type

➧ See Figures 21 and 22

1. Disconnect the negative battery cable.
2. Remove the regulator assembly as described in this section.
3. Hold the regulator in one hand and break off the tab covering the screw head. Remove the two screws attaching the regulator to the brush holder.

4. Separate the regulator, retaining nuts, brushes and brush springs from the brush holder.

To install:

5. Install the replacement brush springs and brushes. Install the retaining nuts.
6. Install the regulator assembly to the alternator rear housing.
7. Reconnect the negative battery cable.

Internal Fan and Regulator Type

➧ **See Figures 23 and 24**

1. Disconnect the negative battery cable.
2. Remove the alternator assembly from the engine.
3. Remove the regulator assembly from the alternator, as described in this section.
4. Using a soldering iron, remove the solder from the brush pigtails and remove the brushes. Remove the brush springs.

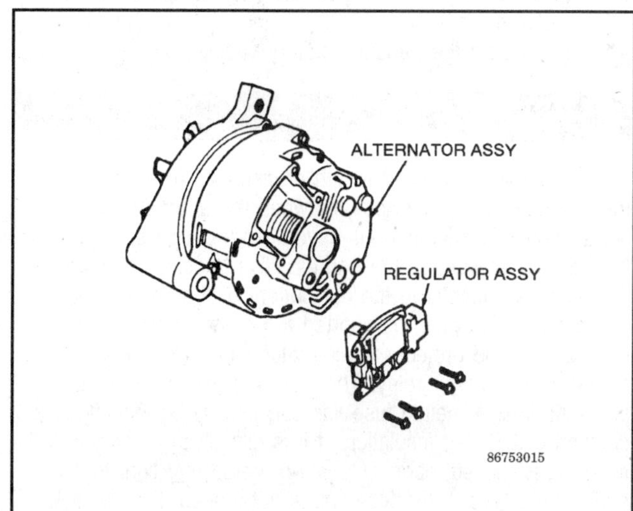

Fig. 21 Removal and replacement of the regulator assembly — external fan type

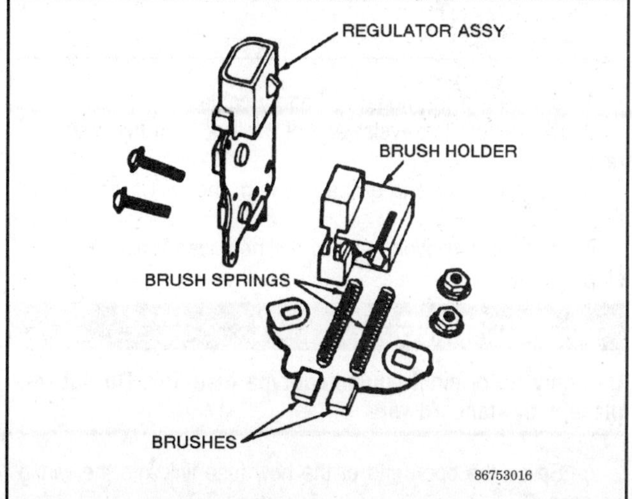

Fig. 22 Replacement position of the brushes — external fan type

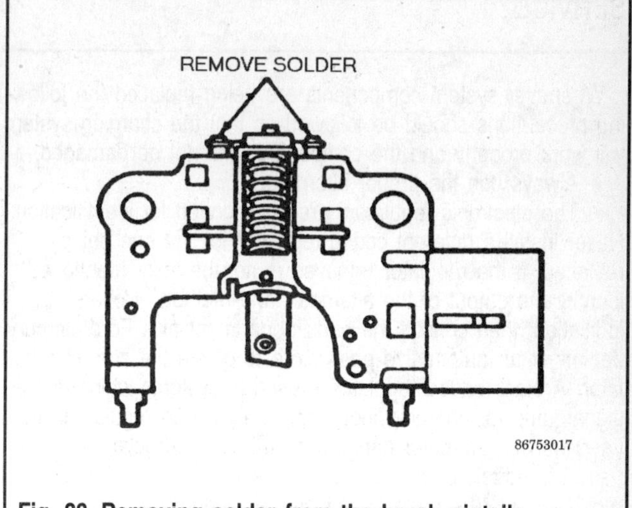

Fig. 23 Removing solder from the brush pigtails — internal fan and regulator type

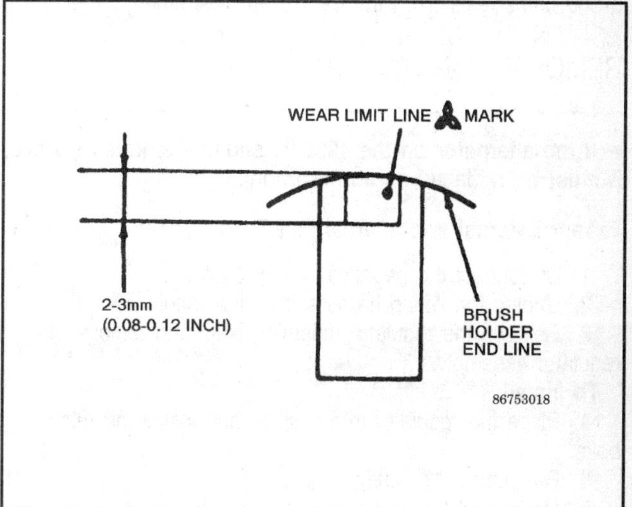

Fig. 24 Installing brushes — internal fan and regulator type

To install:

5. Install the new brush springs.
6. Solder the brushes to the pigtail so that the wear limit line of the brush projects 0.08-0.12 in. (2-3mm) out from the end of the brush holder.
7. Install the regulator assembly.
8. Install the alternator to the engine.
9. Reconnect the negative battery cable.

Regulator

➡Three different types of regulators are used, depending on model, engine, alternator output and type of dash mounted charging indicator used (light or ammeter). The regulators are 100 percent solid state and are calibrated and preset by the manufacturer. No readjustment is required or possible on these regulators.

SERVICE

Whenever system components are being replaced the following precautions should be followed so that the charging system will work properly and the components will not be damaged.

- Always use the proper alternator.
- The electronic regulators are color coded for identification. Never install a different coded regulator for the one being replaced. If the regulator removed is not the color mentioned, identify the output of the alternator and method of charging indication, then consult the parts department of a Ford/Mercury dealer, or an automotive parts store to obtain the correct regulator. A black coded regulator is used in systems which use a signal lamp for charging indication. Gray coded regulators are used with an ammeter gauge. Neutral coded regulators are used on models equipped with a diesel engine. The special regulator must be used on vehicles equipped with a diesel engine to prevent glow plug failure.
- Models using a charging lamp indicator are equipped with a 500 ohms resistor on the back of the instrument panel.

REMOVAL & INSTALLATION

➡If the alternator on the 1991-95 engines requires service, it must be replaced as an assembly.

Except External and Internal Fan Type

1. Disconnect the negative battery cable.
2. Unplug the wiring harness from the regulator.
3. Remove the regulator mounting bolts and remove the regulator assembly.

To install:

4. Place the regulator into position and install the retaining bolts.
5. Reconnect the wiring harness.
6. Reconnect the negative battery cable.

External Fan Type

1. Disconnect the negative battery cable.
2. Disconnect the wiring harness from the alternator/regulator assembly.
3. Remove the four screws attaching the regulator to the alternator rear housing.
4. Remove the regulator, with brush holder attached, from the alternator.

To install:

5. Fit the regulator assembly to the alternator rear housing and install the retaining screws.
6. Reconnect the alternator wiring harness.
7. Reconnect the negative battery cable.

Internal Fan Type

➡To replace the regulator and/or brushes it will be necessary to disassemble the alternator assembly.

1. Disconnect the negative battery cable.
2. Remove the alternator assembly from the engine.
3. Place a soldering iron (200 watt class) on the bearing box for approximately 3-4 minutes. If the bearing is not heated, the bearing may not pull out due to the rear bearing and rear bracket fit.
4. Scribe a reference mark across the alternator front housing and rear housing.
5. Remove the front housing-to-rear housing attaching bolts.
6. Insert a flat tip prytool between the front housing and rear housing and separate them. Do not force the tool in too far, because the stator may be scratched.
7. Using a soldering iron, remove the regulator from the rectifier.

To install:

8. Place the regulator into position and re-solder the assembly.
9. Assemble the front housing and rear housing, while aligning the reference marks made during disassemble.
10. Install the front housing-to-rear housing attaching bolts.
11. Install the alternator to the engine.
12. Reconnect the negative battery cable.

Fuse Link

The fuse link is a short length of insulated wire contained in the alternator wiring harness, between the alternator and the starter relay. The fuse link is several wire gauge sizes smaller than the other wires in the harness. If a booster battery is connected incorrectly to the car battery or if some component of the charging system is shorted to ground, the fuse link should melt and protect the alternator. The fuse link is attached to the starter relay. The insulation on the wire states it is a fuse link. A melted fuse link can usually be identified by cracked or bubbled insulation. If it is difficult to determine if the fuse link is melted, connect a self-powered test light to both ends of the wire. If the fuse link is not melted, the test light will light showing that an open circuit does not exist in the wire.

REPLACEMENT

1. Disconnect the negative battery cable.
2. Disconnect the eyelet end of the link from the starter relay.
3. Cut the other end of the link from the wiring harness at the splice.
4. Connect the eyelet end of the new fuse link to the starter relay.

⁂WARNING

Use only an original equipment-type fuse link. Do not replace with standard wire.

5. Splice the open end of the new fuse link into the wiring harness.
6. Solder the splice with rosin core solder and wrap the splice with electrical tape. This splice must be soldered.
7. Connect the negative battery cable.

Battery

REMOVAL & INSTALLATION

➡On vehicles equipped with diesel engines, the battery is located in the luggage compartment.

1. Loosen the battery cable bolts and spread the ends of the battery cable terminals.
2. Disconnect the negative battery cable first.
3. Disconnect the positive battery cable.
4. Remove the battery hold-down.
5. Wearing heavy gloves, clean the cable terminals and battery with an acid neutralizing solution and terminal cleaning brush. Remove the battery. Be careful not to tip the battery and spill acid on yourself or the car during removal.

To install:

6. Wearing heavy gloves, place the battery in its mount under the hood. Use care not to spill the acid.
7. Install the battery hold-down.
8. Install the positive battery cable first.
9. Install the negative battery cable.
10. Apply a light coating of grease to the cable ends.

Starter

REMOVAL & INSTALLATION

Gasoline Engines

➧ See Figures 25, 26 and 27

1. Disconnect the negative battery cable.
2. Raise and safely support the vehicle.
3. Disconnect the wiring harness from the starter motor.
4. On models that are equipped with a manual transaxle, remove the three nuts that attach the roll restrictor brace to the starter mounting studs at the transaxle. Remove the brace. On models that are equipped with an automatic transaxle, remove the nose bracket mounted on the starter studs.
5. Remove the two bolts attaching the rear starter support bracket, remove the retaining nut from the rear of the starter motor and remove the support bracket.
6. On models equipped with a manual transaxle, remove the three starter mounting studs and the starter motor. On models equipped with a automatic transaxle, remove the two starter mounting studs and the starter motor.

To install:

7. Position the starter to the transaxle housing. Install the attaching studs or bolts. Tighten the studs or bolts to 30-40 ft. lbs. (41-54 Nm).
8. On vehicles equipped with a roll restrictor brace, install the brace on the starter mounting studs at the transaxle housing.
9. Position the starter rear support bracket to the starter. Attach the two attaching bolts. Connect the starter cable to the starter terminal.
10. Lower the vehicle and connect the negative battery cable.

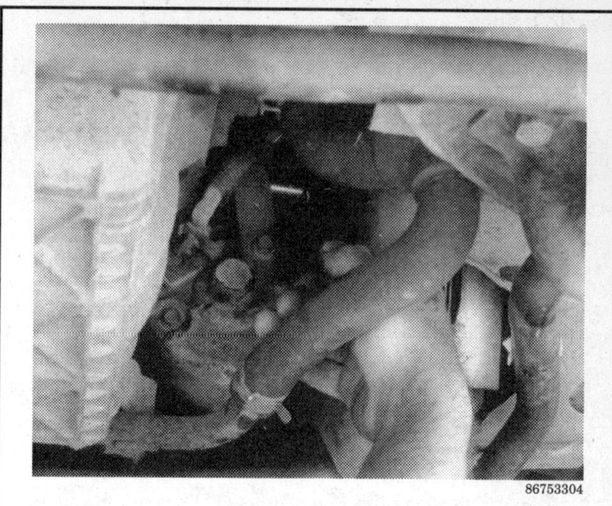

86753304

Fig. 25 Remove the two bolts attaching the rear starter bracket — 1988 1.9L CFI Escort

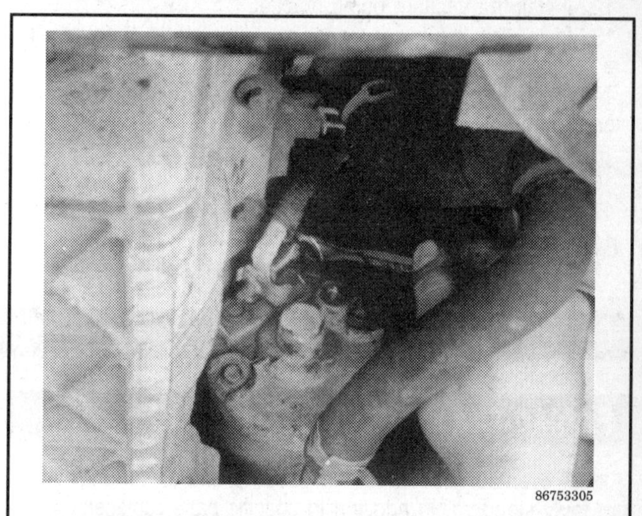

86753305

Fig. 26 Disconnect the wiring harness from the terminal on the starter motor

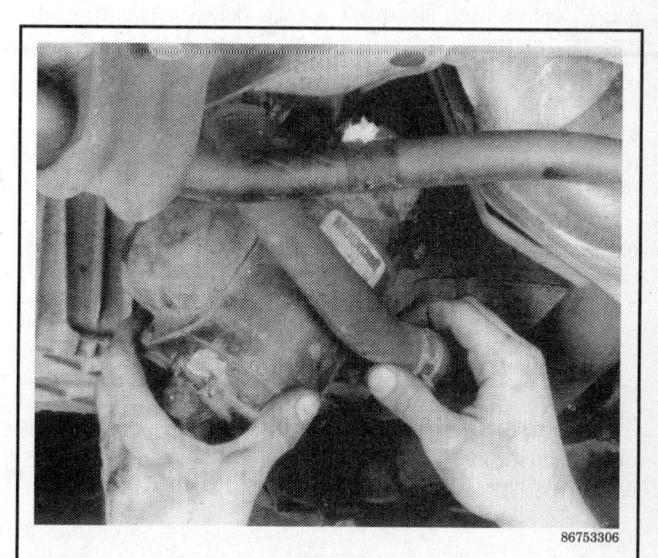

86753306

Fig. 27 Once disconnected, remove the starter

Diesel Engines

1. Remove the battery cover (in the luggage compartment) and disconnect the negative battery cable.
2. Unfasten the cable assembly at the fender apron relay and the starter solenoid.
3. Remove the upper starter mounting stud bolt.
4. Raise and safely support the front of the vehicle on jackstands.
5. Disconnect the vacuum hose from the vacuum pump.
6. Remove the three starter support bracket screws and the bracket.
7. Remove the power stering hose bracket.
8. Remove the ground wire assembly and cable support on the starter bolt studs.
9. Remove the two starter mounting studs and position out of the way of the starter.
10. Remove the vacuum pump bracket. Remove the starter.

To install:

11. Position the starter in place.
12. Install the vacuum pump bracket.
13. Install the two lower starter mounting studs, then install the starter support bracket.
14. Install the cable support bracket and ground cable to the starter stud bolts.
15. Install the power steering hose bracket.
16. Connect the vacuum hose to the pump.
17. Lower the vehicle to the ground.
18. Connect the cable assembly to the solenoid and relay.
19. Install the upper starter mounting stud bolt.
20. Connect the negative battery cable, then check the starter for proper operation.

SOLENOID/RELAY REPLACEMENT

➡On 1981-90 gasoline-engine models, a relay is used to control the starter engagement. Other models use a solenoid.

1981-90 Vehicles

1. Disconnect the negative battery cable.
2. Remove the nuts securing the battery-to-relay lead and relay-to-starter lead.
3. Remove the relay mounting bolts and remove the relay.
4. Install the new relay, bolt it in place and re-connect the leads.

1991-95 Vehicles

1. Disconnect the negative battery cable.
2. Remove the starter, as described in this section.
3. Remove the positive brush connector from the solenoid motor "M" terminal.
4. Remove the solenoid retaining screws and remove the solenoid.
5. Install the new solenoid, screw in place and re-connect the connectors.
6. Install the starter and re-connect the negative battery cable.

ENGINE MECHANICAL

Engine Overhaul

Most overhaul procedures for gasoline and diesel engines are fairly standard. In addition to specific parts replacement procedures and complete specifications for each individual engine, this section is also a guide to acceptable rebuilding procedures. Examples of standard rebuilding practice are shown and should be used along with specific details concerning your particular engine.

Competent and accurate machine shop services will insure maximum performance, reliability and engine life. In most instances, it is more profitable for the do-it-yourself mechanic to remove, clean and inspect the component, buy the necessary parts and deliver these to a shop for actual machine work.

On the other hand, much of the assembly work (crankshaft, block, bearings, piston rods, and other components) is well within the scope of the do-it-yourself mechanic.

TOOLS

The tools required for an engine overhaul or parts replacement will depend on the depth of your involvement. With few exceptions, they will be the tools found in any mechanic's tool kit (see Section 1). More in-depth work will require some or all of the following:

- a dial indicator (reading in thousandths) mounted on a universal base
- micrometers and telescope gauges
- jaw and screw-type pullers
- scraper
- valve spring compressor
- ring groove cleaner
- piston ring expander and compressor
- ridge reamer
- cylinder hone or glaze breaker
- Plastigage®
- engine stand

The use of most of these tools is illustrated in this section. Many can be rented for a one-time use from a local parts jobber or tool supply house specializing in automotive tools. Occasionally, the use of special tools is called for. See the information on Special Tools and Safety Notice in the front of this book before substituting another tool.

INSPECTION TECHNIQUES

Procedures and specifications are given in this section for inspecting, cleaning and assessing the wear limits of most major components. Other procedures such as Magnaflux® and Zyglo® can be used to locate material flaws and stress cracks. Magnaflux® is a magnetic process applicable only to ferrous (iron containing) materials. The Zyglo® process coats the material with a flourescent dye penetrate and can be used on any material Check for suspected surface cracks can be more readily made using spot check dye. The dye is sprayed onto the suspected area, wiped off and the area sprayed with a developer. Cracks will show up brightly.

OVERHAUL NOTES

Aluminum has become extremely popular for use in engines, due to its low weight. Observe the following precautions when handling aluminum parts:

- Never hot tank aluminum parts; the caustic hot-tank solution will eat the aluminum.
- Remove all aluminum parts (identification tag, etc.) from engine parts prior to the tanking.
- Always coat threads lightly with engine oil or anti-seize compounds before installation, to prevent seizure.
- Never over-torque bolts or spark plugs, especially in aluminum threads.

When assembling the engine, any parts that will be in frictional contact must be pre-lubed to provide lubrication at initial start-up. Any product specifically formulated for this purpose can be used, but engine oil is not recommended as a prelube.

When semi-permanent (locked, but removable) installation of bolts or nuts is desired, threads should be cleaned and coated with Loctite® or other similar, commercial non-hardening sealant.

REPAIRING DAMAGED THREADS

See Figures 28, 29, 30, 31 and 32

Several methods of repairing damaged threads are available. Heli-Coil® (shown here), Keenserts® and Microdot® are among the most widely used. All involve basically the same principle (drilling out stripped threads, tapping the hole and installing a pre-wound insert), making welding, plugging and oversize fasteners unnecessary.

Two types of thread repair inserts are usually supplied: a standard type for most Inch Coarse, Inch Fine, Metric Course and Metric Fine thread sizes and a spark lug type to fit most spark plug port sizes. Consult the individual manufacturer's catalog to determine exact applications. Typical thread repair kits will contain a selection of pre-wound threaded inserts, a tap (corresponding to the outside diameter threads of the insert) and an installation tool. Spark plug inserts usually differ because they require a tap equipped with pilot threads and a combined reamer/tap section. Most manufacturers also supply blister packed thread repair inserts separately in addition to a master kit containing a variety of taps and inserts plus installation tools.

Before effecting a repair to a threaded hole, remove any snapped, broken or damaged bolts or studs. Penetrating oil can be used to free frozen threads. The offending item can be removed with locking pliers or with a screw or stud extractor. After the hole is clear, the thread can be repaired.

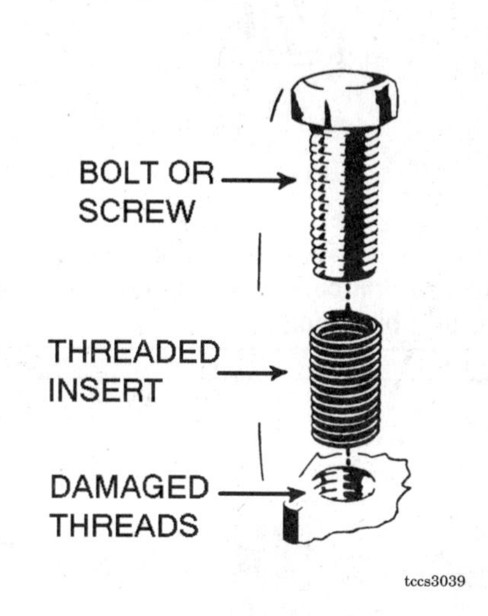

Fig. 28 Damaged bolt hole threads can be replaced with thread repair inserts

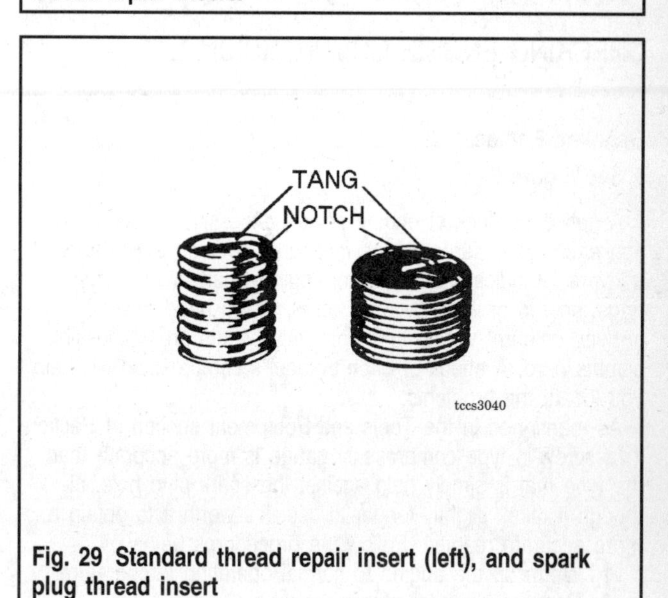

Fig. 29 Standard thread repair insert (left), and spark plug thread insert

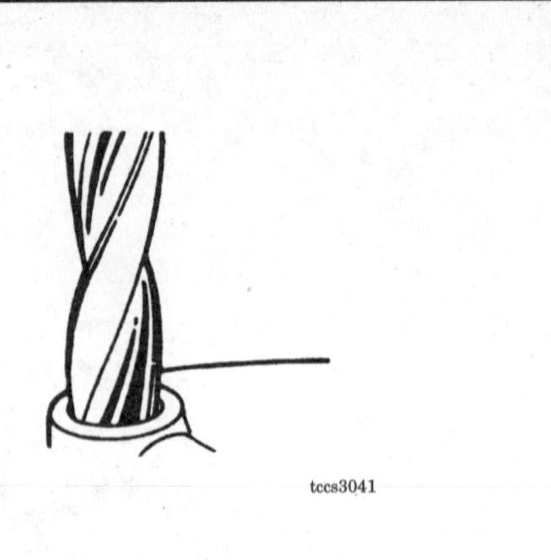

Fig. 30 Drill out the damaged threads with the specified drill. Be sure to drill completely through the hole or to the bottom of a blind hole

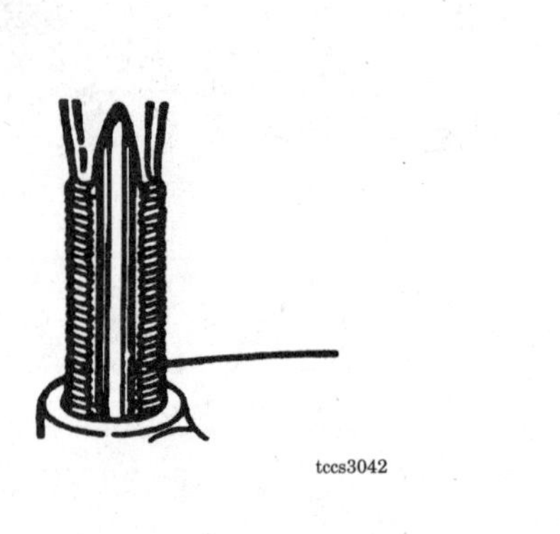

Fig. 31 Using the kit, tap the hole in order to receive the threaded insert. Keep the tap well-oiled and back it out frequently to avoid clogging the threads

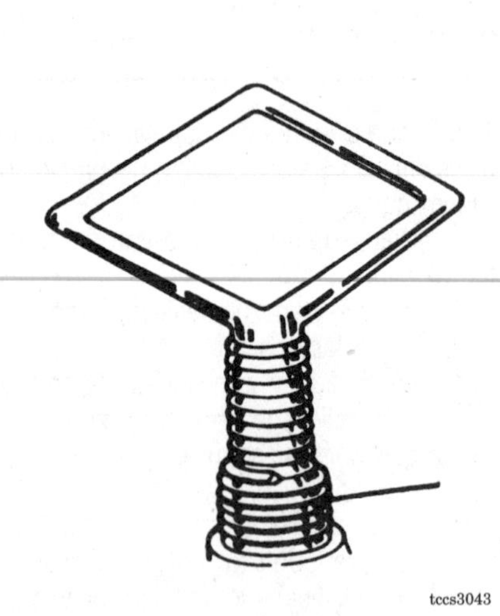

Fig. 32 Screw the threaded insert into the installer tool until the tang engages the slot. Thread the installer tool into the hole until it is 1/4 or 1/2 turn below the top surface, then remove the tool and break off the tang using a punch.

CHECKING ENGINE COMPRESSION

Gasoline Engines

➧ See Figure 33

A noticeable lack of engine power, excessive oil consumption and/or poor fuel mileage measured over an extended period are all indicators of internal engine wear. Worn piston rings, scored or worn cylinder bores, blown head gaskets, sticking or burnt valves and worn valve seats are all possible culprits here. A check of each cylinder's compression will help you locate the problems.

As mentioned in the Tools and Equipment section of Section 1, a screw-in type compression gauge is more accurate than the type that is simply held against the spark plug hole, although it takes slightly longer to use. It's worth it to obtain a more accurate reading. Follow the procedures below.

1. Warm up the engine to normal operating temperature.
2. Remove all spark plugs.

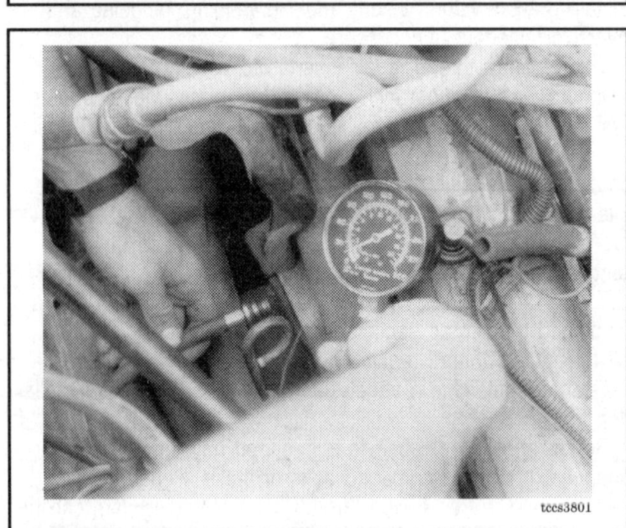

Fig. 33 A screw-in type compression gauge is more accurate and easier to use without an assistant

3. Disconnect the primary lead from the ignition coil/module.

4. Disconnect all fuel injector electrical connections, if applicable.

5. Screw the compression gauge into the No. 1 spark plug hole until the fitting is snug.

➡Be careful not to crossthread the plug hole. On aluminum cylinder heads use extra care, as the threads in these heads are easily ruined.

6. Have an assistant depress the accelerator pedal fully. Then, while you read the compression gauge, ask the assistant to crank the engine two or three times in short bursts using the ignition switch.

7. Read the compression gauge at the end of each series of cranks, and record the highest of these readings. Repeat this procedure for each of the engine's cylinders. Maximum compression should be 175-185 psi (1206-1275 kPa). A cylinder's compression pressure is usually acceptable if it is not less than 80% of maximum. The difference between each cylinder should be no more than 12-14 psi (83-96 kPa).

8. If a cylinder is unusually low, pour a tablespoon of clean engine oil into the cylinder through the spark plug hole and repeat the compression test. If the compression comes up after adding the oil, it is very likely that the cylinder's piston rings or bore are damaged or worn. If the pressure remains low, the valves may not be seating properly (a valve job is needed), or the head gasket may be blown near that cylinder. If compression in any two adjacent cylinders is low, and if the addition of oil doesn't help the compression, there is leakage past the head gasket. Oil and coolant water in the combustion chamber can result from this problem. There may be evidence of water droplets on the engine dipstick when a head gasket has blown.

Diesel Engines

➧ See Figure 34

Checking cylinder compression on diesel engines is basically the same procedure as on gasoline engines except for the following:

1. A special compression gauge adaptor suitable for diesel engines (because these engines have much greater compression pressures) must be used.

2. Remove the injector tubes and remove the injectors from each cylinder.

➡Don't forget to remove the washer underneath each injector. Otherwise, it may get lost when the engine is cranked.

3. When fitting the compression gauge adaptor to the cylinder head, make sure the bleeder of the gauge (if equipped) is closed.

4. When reinstalling the injector assemblies, install new washers underneath each injector.

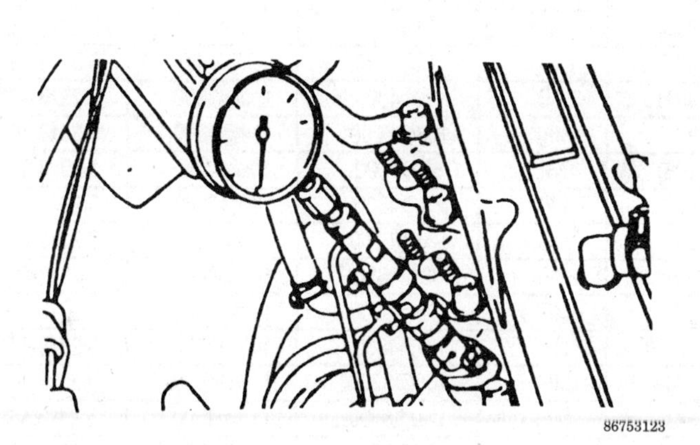

Fig. 34 For diesel engines, checking compression requires a special adapter and gauge

GENERAL ENGINE SPECIFICATIONS

Year	Engine ID/VIN	Engine Displacement Liters (cc)	Fuel System Type	Net Horsepower @ rpm	Net Torque @ rpm (ft. lbs.)	Bore x Stroke (in.)	Com-pression Ratio	Oil Pressure @ rpm
1981	2	1.6 (1606)	2 BBL	70@4600	89@2600	3.15x3.13	9.0:1	35-65@2000
1982	2	1.6 (1606)	2 BBL	70@4600	89@2600	3.15x3.13	9.0:1	35-65@2000
1983	2	1.6 (1606)	2 BBL	70@4600	89@2600	3.15x3.13	9.0:1	35-65@2000
	4	1.6 (1606)	2 BBL	80@5400	88@3000	3.15x3.13	9.0:1	35-65@2000
	5	1.6 (1606)	MFI	84@5200	90@2800	3.15x3.13	9.0:1	35-65@2000
1984	2	1.6 (1606)	2 BBL	70@4600	89@2600	3.15x3.13	9.0:1	35-65@2000
	4	1.6 (1606)	2 BBL	80@5400	88@3000	3.15x3.13	9.0:1	35-65@2000
	5	1.6 (1606)	MFI	84@5200	90@2800	3.15x3.13	9.0:1	35-65@2000
	8	1.6 (1606)	MFI	120@5200	120@3400	3.15x3.13	9.0:1	35-65@2000
	7	1.6 (1606)	2 BBL	80@5400	88@3000	3.15x3.13	9.0:1	35-65@2000
	H	2.0 (1998)	DSL	52@4000	82@2400	3.39x3.39	22.7:1	55-60@2000
1985	2	1.6 (1606)	2 BBL	70@4600	89@2600	3.15x3.13	9.0:1	35-65@2000
	4	1.6 (1606)	2 BBL	80@5400	88@3000	3.15x3.13	9.0:1	35-65@2000
	5	1.6 (1606)	MFI	84@5200	90@2800	3.15x3.13	9.0:1	35-65@2000
	8	1.6 (1606)	MFI	120@5200	120@3400	3.15x3.13	9.0:1	35-65@2000
	7	1.6 (1606)	2 BBL	80@5400	88@3000	3.15x3.13	9.0:1	35-65@2000
	H	2.0 (1998)	DSL	52@4000	82@2400	3.39x3.39	22.7:1	55-60@2000
	9	1.9 (1901)	2 BBL	86@4800	100@3000	3.23x3.46	9.0:1	35-65@2000
1986	9	1.9 (1901)	2 BBL	86@4800	100@3000	3.23x3.46	9.0:1	35-65@2000
	J	1.9 (1901)	MFI	108@5200	114@4000	3.23x3.46	9.0:1	35-65@2000
	H	2.0 (1998)	DSL	52@4000	82@2400	3.39x3.39	22.7:1	55-60@2000
1987	9	1.9 (1901)	2 BBL	86@4800	100@3000	3.23x3.46	9.0:1	35-65@2000
	J	1.9 (1901)	MFI	108@5200	114@4000	3.23x3.46	9.0:1	35-65@2000
	H	2.0 (1998)	DSL	52@4000	82@2400	3.39x3.39	22.7:1	55-60@2000
1988	9	1.9 (1901)	CFI	86@4800	100@3000	3.23x3.46	9.0:1	35-65@2000
	J	1.9 (1901)	MFI	108@5200	114@4000	3.23x34.6	9.0:1	35-65@2000
1989	9	1.9 (1901)	CFI	86@4800	100@3000	3.23x3.46	9.0:1	35-65@2000
	J	1.9 (1901)	MFI	108@5200	114@4000	3.23x34.6	9.0:1	35-65@2000
1990	9	1.9 (1901)	CFI	86@4800	100@3000	3.23x3.46	9.0:1	35-65@2000
	J	1.9 (1901)	MFI	108@5200	114@4000	3.23x3.46	9.0:1	35-65@2000
1991	8	1.8 (1844)	MFI	127@6500	114@4500	3.23x3.46	9.0:1	35-65@2000
	J	1.9 (1901)	MFI	108@5200	114@4000	3.23x3.46	9.0:1	35-65@2000
1992	8	1.8 (1844)	MFI	127@6500	114@4500	3.23x3.46	9.0:1	35-65@2000
	J	1.9 (1901)	MFI	88@4400	108@4000	3.23x3.46	9.0:1	35-65@2000
1993	8	1.8 (1844)	MFI	127@6500	114@4500	3.23x3.46	9.0:1	35-65@2000
	J	1.9 (1901)	MFI	88@4400	108@4000	3.23x3.46	9.0:1	35-65@2000
1994	8	1.8 (1844)	SFI	127@6500	114@4500	3.27x3.35	9.0:1	35-65@2000
	J	1.9 (1901)	SFI	88@4400	108@4000	3.23x3.346	9.0:1	35-65@2000
1995	8	1.8 (1844)	SFI	127@6500	114@4500	3.27x3.35	9.0:1	35-65@2000
	J	1.9 (1901)	SFI	88@4400	108@4000	3.23x3.346	9.0:1	35-65@2000

BBL - Barrel (carburetor)
CFI - Central Fuel Injection
DSL - Diesel
MFI - Multi-port Fuel Injection
VV - Variable Venturi carburetor

86753C21

VALVE SPECIFICATIONS

Year	Engine ID/VIN	Engine Displacement Liters (cc)	Seat Angle (deg.)	Face Angle (deg.)	Spring Test Pressure (lbs. @ in.)	Spring Installed Height (in.)	Stem-to-Guide Clearance (in.) Intake	Stem-to-Guide Clearance (in.) Exhaust	Stem Diameter (in.) Intake	Stem Diameter (in.) Exhaust
1981	2	1.6 (1606)	45	45.5	200@1.09	1.480	0.0008-0.0027	0.0018-0.0037	0.316	0.316
1982	2	1.6 (1606)	45	45.5	200@1.09	1.480	0.0008-0.0027	0.0018-0.0037	0.316	0.316
1983	2	1.6 (1606)	45	45.5	200@1.09	1.480	0.0008-0.0027	0.0018-0.0037	0.316	0.316
	4	1.6 (1601)	45	45.5	216@1.016	1.450-1.480	0.0008-0.0027	0.0018-0.0037	0.316	0.316
	5	1.6 (1601)	45	45.5	216@1.016	1.450-1.480	0.0008-0.0027	0.0018-0.0037	0.316	0.316
1984	2	1.6 (1606)	45	45.5	200@1.09	1.480	0.0008-0.0027	0.0018-0.0037	0.316	0.316
	4	1.6 (1601)	45	45.5	216@1.016	1.450-1.480	0.0008-0.0027	0.0018-0.0037	0.316	0.316
	5	1.6 (1601)	45	45.5	216@1.016	1.450-1.480	0.0008-0.0027	0.0018-0.0037	0.316	0.316
	7	1.6 (1606)	45	45.5	200@1.09	1.480	0.0008-0.0027	0.0018-0.0037	0.316	0.316
	8	1.6 (1601)	45	45.5	216@1.016	1.450-1.480	0.0008-0.0027	0.0018-0.0037	0.316	0.316
	H	2.0 (1998)	45	45.5	NA	1.776	0.0016-0.0029	0.0018-0.0031	0.3138	0.3138
1985	2	1.6 (1606)	45	45.5	200@1.09	1.480	0.0008-0.0027	0.0018-0.0037	0.316	0.316
	4	1.6 (1601)	45	45.5	216@1.016	1.450-1.480	0.0008-0.0027	0.0018-0.0037	0.316	0.316
	5	1.6 (1601)	45	45.5	216@1.016	1.450-1.480	0.0008-0.0027	0.0018-0.0037	0.316	0.316
	7	1.6 (1606)	45	45.5	200@1.09	1.480	0.0008-0.0027	0.0018-0.0037	0.316	0.316
	8	1.6 (1601)	45	45.5	216@1.016	1.450-1.480	0.0008-0.0027	0.0018-0.0037	0.316	0.316
	9	1.9 (1901)	45	45	200@1.09	1.440-1.480	0.0008-0.0027	0.0018-0.0037	0.316	0.315
	H	2.0 (1998)	45	45.5	NA	1.776	0.0016-0.0029	0.0018-0.0031	0.3138	0.3138
1986	9	1.9 (1901)	45	45	200@1.09	1.440-1.480	0.0008-0.0027	0.0018-0.0037	0.316	0.315
	J	1.9 (1901)	45	45	216@1.016	1.440-1.480	0.0008-0.0027	0.0018-0.0037	0.316	0.315
	H	2.0 (1998)	45	45.5	NA	1.776	0.0016-0.0029	0.0018-0.0031	0.3138	0.3138

86753C22

VALVE SPECIFICATIONS

Year	Engine ID/VIN	Engine Displacement Liters (cc)	Seat Angle (deg.)	Face Angle (deg.)	Spring Test Pressure (lbs. @ in.)	Spring Installed Height (in.)	Stem-to-Guide Clearance (in.)		Stem Diameter (in.)	
							Intake	Exhaust	Intake	Exhaust
1987	9	1.9 (1901)	45	45	200@1.09	1.440-1.480	0.0008-0.0027	0.0018-0.0037	0.316	0.315
	J	1.9 (1901)	45	45	216@1.016	1.440-1.480	0.0008-0.0027	0.0018-0.0037	0.316	0.315
	H	2.0 (1998)	45	45.5	NA	1.776	0.0016-0.0029	0.0018-0.0031	0.3138	0.3138
1988	9	1.9 (1901)	45	45	200@1.09	1.440-1.480	0.0008-0.0027	0.0018-0.0037	0.316	0.316
	J	1.9 (1901)	45	45	216@1.016	1.440-1.480	0.0008-0.0027	0.0018-0.0037	0.316	0.316
1989	9	1.9 (1901)	45	45	200@1.09	1.440-1.480	0.0008-0.0027	0.0018-0.0037	0.316	0.315
	J	1.9 (1901)	45	45	216@1.016	1.440-1.480	0.0008-0.0027	0.0018-0.0037	0.316	0.315
1990	9	1.9 (1901)	45	45	200@1.09	1.440-1.480	0.0008-0.0027	0.0018-0.0037	0.316	0.315
	J	1.9 (1901)	45	45	216@1.016	1.440-1.480	0.0008-0.0027	0.0018-0.0037	0.316	0.315
1991	8	1.8 (1844)	45	45	-	①	0.0010-0.0024	0.0012-0.0026	0.2350-0.2356	0.2348-0.2354
	J	1.9 (1901)	45	45	216@1.016	1.440-1.480	0.0008-0.0027	0.0018-0.0037	0.316	0.315
1992	8	1.8 (1844)	45	45	-	①	0.0010-0.0024	0.0012-0.0026	0.2350-0.2356	0.2348-0.2354
	J	1.9 (1901)	45	45	216@1.016	1.440-1.480	0.0008-0.0027	0.0018-0.0037	0.316	0.315
1993	8	1.8 (1844)	45	45	-	①	0.0010-0.0024	0.0012-0.0026	0.2350-0.2356	0.2348-0.2354
	J	1.9 (1901)	45	45	216@1.016	1.440-1.480	0.0008-0.0027	0.0018-0.0037	0.316	0.315
1994	8	1.8 (1844)	45	45	-	①	0.0010-0.0024	0.0012-0.0026	0.2350-0.2356	0.2348-0.2354
	J	1.9 (1901)	45	45.6	200@1.09	1.440-1.480	0.0008-0.0027	0.0018-0.0037	0.3159-0.3167	0.3149-0.3156
1995	8	1.8 (1844)	45	45	-	①	0.0010-0.0024	0.0012-0.0026	0.2350-0.2356	0.2348-0.2354
	J	1.9 (1901)	45	45.6	200@1.09	1.440-1.480	0.0008-0.0027	0.0018-0.0037	0.3159-0.3167	0.3149-0.3156

NA - Not Available

① Spring height measured unloaded. Standard free length: 1.821 in. (46.26mm).

86753C23

CAMSHAFT SPECIFICATIONS

All measurements given in inches.

Year	Engine ID/VIN	Engine Displacement Liters (cc)	Journal Diameter 1	2	3	4	5	Elevation In.	Ex.	Bearing Clearance	Camshaft End-Play
1981	2	1.6 (1606)	1.761-1.762	1.771-1.772	1.781-1.782	1.791-1.792	1.801-1.802	0.229	0.229	0.0008-0.0028	0.0018-0.0060
1982	2	1.6 (1606)	1.761-1.762	1.771-1.772	1.781-1.782	1.791-1.792	1.801-1.802	0.229	0.229	0.0008-0.0028	0.0018-0.0060
1983	2	1.6 (1606)	1.761-1.762	1.771-1.772	1.781-1.782	1.791-1.792	1.801-1.802	0.229	0.229	0.0008-0.0028	0.0018-0.0060
	4	1.6 (1606)	1.761-1.762	1.771-1.772	1.781-1.782	1.791-1.792	1.801-1.802	0.240	0.240	0.0008-0.0028	0.0018-0.0060
	5	1.6 (1606)	1.761-1.762	1.771-1.772	1.781-1.782	1.791-1.792	1.801-1.802	0.240	0.240	0.0008-0.0028	0.0018-0.0060
1984	2	1.6 (1606)	1.761-1.762	1.771-1.772	1.781-1.782	1.791-1.792	1.801-1.802	0.229	0.229	0.0008-0.0028	0.0018-0.0060
	4	1.6 (1606)	1.761-1.762	1.771-1.772	1.781-1.782	1.791-1.792	1.801-1.802	0.240	0.240	0.0008-0.0028	0.0018-0.0060
	5	1.6 (1606)	1.761-1.762	1.771-1.772	1.781-1.782	1.791-1.792	1.801-1.802	0.240	0.240	0.0008-0.0028	0.0018-0.0060
	7	1.6 (1606)	1.761-1.762	1.771-1.772	1.781-1.782	1.791-1.792	1.801-1.802	0.240	0.240	0.0008-0.0028	0.0018-0.0060
	8	1.6 (1606)	1.761-1.762	1.771-1.772	1.781-1.782	1.791-1.792	1.801-1.802	0.240	0.240	0.0008-0.0028	0.0018-0.0060
	H	2.0 (1998)	1.2582-1.2589	1.2582-1.2589	1.2582-1.2589	1.2582-1.2589	1.2582-1.2589	NA	NA	0.0010-0.0026	0.0008-0.0059
1985	2	1.6 (1606)	1.761-1.762	1.771-1.772	1.781-1.782	1.791-1.792	1.801-1.802	0.229	0.229	0.0008-0.0028	0.0018-0.0060
	4	1.6 (1606)	1.761-1.762	1.771-1.772	1.781-1.782	1.791-1.792	1.801-1.802	0.240	0.240	0.0008-0.0028	0.0018-0.0060
	5	1.6 (1606)	1.761-1.762	1.771-1.772	1.781-1.782	1.791-1.792	1.801-1.802	0.240	0.240	0.0008-0.0028	0.0018-0.0060
	7	1.6 (1606)	1.761-1.762	1.771-1.772	1.781-1.782	1.791-1.792	1.801-1.802	0.240	0.240	0.0008-0.0028	0.0018-0.0060
	8	1.6 (1606)	1.761-1.762	1.771-1.772	1.781-1.782	1.791-1.792	1.801-1.802	0.240	0.240	0.0008-0.0028	0.0018-0.0060
	9	1.9 (1901)	1.8007-1.8017	1.8007-1.8017	1.8007-1.8017	1.8007-1.8017	1.8007-1.8017	0.240	0.240	0.0013-0.0033	0.0018-0.0060
	H	2.0 (1998)	1.2582-1.2589	1.2582-1.2589	1.2582-1.2589	1.2582-1.2589	1.2582-1.2589	NA	NA	0.0010-0.0026	0.0008-0.0059
1986	9	1.9 (1901)	1.8007-1.8017	1.8007-1.8017	1.8007-1.8017	1.8007-1.8017	1.8007-1.8017	0.240	0.240	0.0013-0.0033	0.0018-0.0060
	J	1.9 (1901)	1.8007-1.8017	1.8007-1.8017	1.8007-1.8017	1.8007-1.8017	1.8007-1.8017	0.240	0.240	0.0013-0.0033	0.0018-0.0060
	H	2.0 (1998)	1.2582-1.2589	1.2582-1.2589	1.2582-1.2589	1.2582-1.2589	1.2582-1.2589	NA	NA	0.0010-0.0026	0.0008-0.0059

86753C04

CAMSHAFT SPECIFICATIONS

All measurements given in inches.

Year	Engine ID/VIN	Engine Displacement Liters (cc)	Journal Diameter					Elevation		Bearing Clearance	Camshaft End-Play
			1	2	3	4	5	In.	Ex.		
1987	9	1.9 (1901)	1.8007-1.8017	1.8007-1.8017	1.8007-1.8017	1.8007-1.8017	1.8007-1.8017	0.240	0.240	0.0013-0.0033	0.0018-0.0060
	J	1.9 (1901)	1.8007-1.8017	1.8007-1.8017	1.8007-1.8017	1.8007-1.8017	1.8007-1.8017	0.240	0.240	0.0013-0.0033	0.0018-0.0060
	H	2.0 (1998)	1.2582-1.2589	1.2582-1.2589	1.2582-1.2589	1.2582-1.2589	1.2582-1.2589	NA	NA	0.0010-0.0026	0.0008-0.0059
1988	9	1.9 (1901)	1.8007-1.8017	1.8007-1.8017	1.8007-1.8017	1.8007-1.8017	1.8007-1.8017	0.240	0.240	0.0013-0.0033	0.0018-0.0060
	J	1.9 (1901)	1.8007-1.8017	1.8007-1.8017	1.8007-1.8017	1.8007-1.8017	1.8007-1.8017	0.240	0.240	0.0013-0.0033	0.0018-0.0060
1989	9	1.9 (1901)	1.8007-1.8017	1.8007-1.8017	1.8007-1.8017	1.8007-1.8017	1.8007-1.8017	0.240	0.240	0.0013-0.0033	0.0018-0.0060
	J	1.9 (1901)	1.8007-1.8017	1.8007-1.8017	1.8007-1.8017	1.8007-1.8017	1.8007-1.8017	0.240	0.240	0.0013-0.0033	0.0018-0.0060
1990	9	1.9 (1901)	1.8007-1.8017	1.8007-1.8017	1.8007-1.8017	1.8007-1.8017	1.8007-1.8017	0.235-0.240	0.235-0.240	0.0013-0.0033	0.002-0.006
	J	1.9 (1901)	1.8007-1.8017	1.8007-1.8017	1.8007-1.8017	1.8007-1.8017	1.8007-1.8017	0.235-0.240	0.235-0.240	0.0013-0.0033	0.002-0.006
1991	8	1.8 (1844)	1.0213-1.0222	1.0213-1.0222	1.0213-1.0222	1.0213-1.0222	1.0213-1.0222	1.7281- (1) 1.7360	1.7280- (1) 1.7360	0.0014-0.0032	0.0028-0.0075
	J	1.9 (1901)	1.8007-1.8017	1.8007-1.8017	1.8007-1.8017	1.8007-1.8017	1.8007-1.8017	0.240-0.245	0.240-0.245	0.001-0.003	0.001-0.006
1992	8	1.8 (1844)	1.0213-1.0222	1.0213-1.0222	1.0213-1.0222	1.0213-1.0222	1.0213-1.0222	1.7281- (1) 1.7360	1.7280- (1) 1.7360	0.0014-0.0032	0.0028-0.0075
	J	1.9 (1901)	1.8007-1.8017	1.8007-1.8017	1.8007-1.8017	1.8007-1.8017	1.8007-1.8017	0.240-0.245	0.240-0.245	0.0013-0.0033	0.002-0.006
1993	8	1.8 (1844)	1.0213-1.0220	1.0213-1.0220	1.0213-1.0220	1.0213-1.0220	1.0213-1.0220	1.7281- (1) 1.7360	1.7280- (1) 1.7360	0.0014-0.0032	0.0028-0.0075
	J	1.9 (1901)	1.8007-1.8017	1.8007-1.8017	1.8007-1.8017	1.8007-1.8017	1.8007-1.8017	0.240-0.245	0.240-0.245	0.0013-0.0033	0.002-0.006
1994	8	1.8 (1844)	1.0213-1.0222	1.0213-1.0222	1.0213-1.0222	1.0213-1.0222	1.0213-1.0222	1.7281- (1) 1.7360	1.7480- (1) 1.7560	0.0014-0.0032	0.0028-0.0075
	J	1.9 (1901)	1.8007-1.8017	1.8007-1.8017	1.8007-1.8017	1.8007-1.8017	1.8007-1.8017	0.2400-0.2450	0.2400-0.2450	0.0013-0.0033	0.0018-0.0060
1995	8	1.8 (1844)	1.0213-1.0222	1.0213-1.0222	1.0213-1.0222	1.0213-1.0222	1.0213-1.0222	1.7281- (1) 1.7360	1.7480- (1) 1.7560	0.0014-0.0032	0.0028-0.0075
	J	1.9 (1901)	1.8007-1.8017	1.8007-1.8017	1.8007-1.8017	1.8007-1.8017	1.8007-1.8017	0.2400-0.2450	0.2400-0.2450	0.0013-0.0033	0.0020-0.0060

NA - Not Available

(1) Figure shown indicates total lobe height in inches

86753C05

CRANKSHAFT AND CONNECTING ROD SPECIFICATIONS

All measurements are given in inches.

Year	Engine ID/VIN	Engine Displacement Liters (cc)	Crankshaft Main Brg. Journal Dia.	Crankshaft Main Brg. Oil Clearance	Crankshaft Shaft End-play	Crankshaft Thrust on No.	Connecting Rod Journal Diameter	Connecting Rod Oil Clearance	Connecting Rod Side Clearance
1981	2	1.6 (1606)	2.2826-2.2834	0.0008-0.0015	0.004-0.008	3	1.885-1.886	0.0002-0.0003	0.004-0.011
1982	2	1.6 (1606)	2.2826-2.2834	0.0008-0.0015	0.004-0.008	3	1.885-1.886	0.0002-0.0003	0.004-0.011
1983	2	1.6 (1606)	2.2826-2.2834	0.0008-0.0015	0.004-0.008	3	1.885-1.886	0.0002-0.0003	0.004-0.011
	4	1.6 (1606)	2.2826-2.2834	0.0008-0.0015	0.004-0.008	3	1.885-1.886	0.0002-0.0003	0.004-0.011
	5	1.6 (1606)	2.2826-2.2834	0.0008-0.0015	0.004-0.008	3	1.885-1.886	0.0002-0.0003	0.004-0.011
1984	2	1.6 (1606)	2.2826-2.2834	0.0008-0.0015	0.004-0.008	3	1.885-1.886	0.0002-0.0003	0.004-0.011
	4	1.6 (1606)	2.2826-2.2834	0.0008-0.0015	0.004-0.008	3	1.885-1.886	0.0002-0.0003	0.004-0.011
	5	1.6 (1606)	2.2826-2.2834	0.0008-0.0015	0.004-0.008	3	1.885-1.886	0.0002-0.0003	0.004-0.011
	7	1.6 (1606)	2.2826-2.2834	0.0008-0.0015	0.004-0.008	3	1.885-1.886	0.0002-0.0003	0.004-0.011
	8	1.6 (1606)	2.2826-2.2834	0.0008-0.0015	0.004-0.008	3	1.885-1.886	0.0002-0.0003	0.004-0.011
	H	2.0 (1998)	2.3598-2.3605	0.0012-0.0020	0.0011-0.0016	3	2.0055-2.0061	0.0010-0.0020	0.0043-0.0103
1985	2	1.6 (1606)	2.2826-2.2834	0.0008-0.0015	0.004-0.008	3	1.885-1.886	0.0002-0.0003	0.004-0.011
	4	1.6 (1606)	2.2826-2.2834	0.0008-0.0015	0.004-0.008	3	1.885-1.886	0.0002-0.0003	0.004-0.011
	5	1.6 (1606)	2.2826-2.2834	0.0008-0.0015	0.004-0.008	3	1.885-1.886	0.0002-0.0003	0.004-0.011
	7	1.6 (1606)	2.2826-2.2834	0.0008-0.0015	0.004-0.008	3	1.885-1.886	0.0002-0.0003	0.004-0.011
	8	1.6 (1606)	2.2826-2.2834	0.0008-0.0015	0.004-0.008	3	1.885-1.886	0.0002-0.0003	0.004-0.011
	9	1.9 (1901)	2.2827-2.2835	0.0008-0.0015	0.004-0.008	3	1.8854-1.8862	0.0008-0.0015	0.004-0.011
	H	2.0 (1998)	2.3598-2.3605	0.0012-0.0020	0.0011-0.0016	3	2.0055-2.0061	0.0010-0.0020	0.0043-0.0103
1986	9	1.9 (1901)	2.2827-2.2835	0.0008-0.0015	0.004-0.008	3	1.8854-1.8862	0.0008-0.0015	0.004-0.011
	J	1.9 (1901)	2.2827-2.2835	0.0008-0.0015	0.004-0.008	3	1.8854-1.8862	0.0008-0.0015	0.004-0.011
	H	2.0 (1998)	2.3598-2.3605	0.0012-0.0020	0.0011-0.0016	3	2.0055-2.0061	0.0010-0.0020	0.0043-0.0103

86753C06

CRANKSHAFT AND CONNECTING ROD SPECIFICATIONS

All measurements are given in inches.

		Engine	Crankshaft				Connecting Rod		
Year	Engine ID/VIN	Displacement Liters (cc)	Main Brg. Journal Dia.	Main Brg. Oil Clearance	Shaft End-play	Thrust on No.	Journal Diameter	Oil Clearance	Side Clearance
1987	9	1.9 (1901)	2.2827-2.2835	0.0008-0.0015	0.004-0.008	3	1.8854-1.8862	0.0008-0.0015	0.004-0.011
	J	1.9 (1901)	2.2827-2.2835	0.0008-0.0015	0.004-0.008	3	1.8854-1.8862	0.0008-0.0015	0.004-0.011
	H	2.0 (1998)	2.3598-2.3605	0.0012-0.0020	0.0011-0.0016	3	2.0055-2.0061	0.0010-0.0020	0.0043-0.0103
1988	9	1.9 (1901)	2.2827-2.2835	0.0008-0.0015	0.004-0.008	3	1.8854-1.8862	0.0008-0.0015	0.004-0.011
	J	1.9 (1901)	2.2827-2.2835	0.0008-0.0015	0.004-0.008	3	1.8854-1.8862	0.0008-0.0015	0.004-0.011
1989	9	1.9 (1901)	2.2827-2.2835	0.0008-0.0015	0.004-0.008	3	1.8854-1.8862	0.0008-0.0015	0.004-0.011
	J	1.9 (1901)	2.2827-2.2835	0.0008-0.0015	0.004-0.008	3	1.8854-1.8862	0.0008-0.0015	0.004-0.011
1990	9	1.9 (1901)	2.2827-2.2835	0.0008-0.0015	0.004-0.008	3	1.8854-1.8862	0.0008-0.0015	0.004-0.011
	J	1.9 (1901)	2.2827-2.2835	0.0008-0.0015	0.004-0.008	3	1.8854-1.8862	0.0008-0.0015	0.004-0.011
1991	8	1.8 (1844)	1.9661-1.9668	0.0009-0.0017	0.0031-0.0120	4	1.7692-1.7699	0.0011-0.0027	0.0043-0.0120
	J	1.9 (1901)	2.2827-2.2835	0.0008-0.0015	0.004-0.008	3	1.8854-1.8862	0.0008-0.0015	0.004-0.011
1992	8	1.8 (1844)	1.9661-1.9668	0.0007-0.0014	0.0031-0.0120	4	1.7692-1.7699	0.0011-0.0027	0.0043-0.0120
	J	1.9 (1901)	2.2827-2.2835	0.0008-0.0015	0.004-0.008	3	1.8854-1.8862	0.0008-0.0015	0.004-0.011
1993	8	1.8 (1844)	1.9661-1.9668	0.0007-0.0014	0.0031-0.0120	4	1.7692-1.7699	0.0011-0.0027	0.0043-0.0120
	J	1.9 (1901)	2.2827-2.2835	0.0008-0.0015	0.004-0.008	3	1.8854-1.8862	0.0008-0.0015	0.004-0.011
1994	8	1.8 (1844)	1.9661-1.9668	0.0007-0.0014	0.0031-0.0120	4	1.7692-1.7699	0.0011-0.0030	0.0043-0.0120
	J	1.9 (1901)	2.2827-2.2835	0.0008-0.0015	0.004-0.008	3	1.7279-1.7287	0.0008-0.0015	0.004-0.011
1995	8	1.8 (1844)	1.9661-1.9668	0.0007-0.0014	0.0031-0.0120	4	1.7692-1.7699	0.0011-0.0030	0.0043-0.0120
	J	1.9 (1901)	2.2827-2.2835	0.0008-0.0015	0.0040-0.0080	3	1.7279-1.7287	0.0008-0.0015	0.0040-0.0110

86753C07

PISTON AND RING SPECIFICATIONS

All measurements are given in inches.

Year	Engine ID/VIN	Engine Displacement Liters (cc)	Piston Clearance	Ring Gap Top Compression	Ring Gap Bottom Compression	Ring Gap Oil Control	Ring Side Clearance Top Compression	Ring Side Clearance Bottom Compression	Ring Side Clearance Oil Control
1981	2	1.6 (1606)	0.0018-0.0026	0.012-0.020	0.012-0.020	0.016-0.055	0.001-0.003	0.002-0.003	SNUG
1982	2	1.6 (1606)	0.0018-0.0026	0.012-0.020	0.012-0.020	0.016-0.055	0.001-0.003	0.002-0.003	SNUG
1983	2	1.6 (1606)	0.0018-0.0026	0.012-0.020	0.012-0.020	0.016-0.055	0.001-0.003	0.002-0.003	SNUG
	4	1.6 (1606)	0.0018-0.0026	0.012-0.020	0.012-0.020	0.016-0.055	0.001-0.003	0.002-0.003	SNUG
	5	1.6 (1606)	0.0018-0.0026	0.012-0.020	0.012-0.020	0.016-0.055	0.001-0.003	0.002-0.003	SNUG
1984	2	1.6 (1606)	0.0018-0.0026	0.012-0.020	0.012-0.020	0.016-0.055	0.001-0.003	0.002-0.003	SNUG
	4	1.6 (1606)	0.0018-0.0026	0.012-0.020	0.012-0.020	0.016-0.055	0.001-0.003	0.002-0.003	SNUG
	5	1.6 (1606)	0.0018-0.0026	0.012-0.020	0.012-0.020	0.016-0.055	0.001-0.003	0.002-0.003	SNUG
	7	1.6 (1606)	0.0018-0.0026	0.012-0.020	0.012-0.020	0.016-0.055	0.001-0.003	0.002-0.003	SNUG
	8	1.6 (1606)	0.0018-0.0026	0.012-0.020	0.012-0.020	0.016-0.055	0.001-0.003	0.002-0.003	SNUG
	H	2.0 (1998)	0.0013-0.0020	0.0079-0.0157	0.0079-0.0157	0.0079-0.0157	0.0020-0.0035	0.0016-0.0031	SNUG
1985	2	1.6 (1606)	0.0018-0.0026	0.012-0.020	0.012-0.020	0.016-0.055	0.001-0.003	0.002-0.003	SNUG
	4	1.6 (1606)	0.0018-0.0026	0.012-0.020	0.012-0.020	0.016-0.055	0.001-0.003	0.002-0.003	SNUG
	5	1.6 (1606)	0.0018-0.0026	0.012-0.020	0.012-0.020	0.016-0.055	0.001-0.003	0.002-0.003	SNUG
	7	1.6 (1606)	0.0018-0.0026	0.012-0.020	0.012-0.020	0.016-0.055	0.001-0.003	0.002-0.003	SNUG
	8	1.6 (1606)	0.0018-0.0026	0.012-0.020	0.012-0.020	0.016-0.055	0.001-0.003	0.002-0.003	SNUG
	9	1.9 (1901)	0.0016-0.0024	0.010-0.020	0.010-0.020	0.016-0.055	0.0015-0.0032	0.0015-0.0035	SNUG
	H	2.0 (1998)	0.0013-0.0020	0.0079-0.0157	0.0079-0.0157	0.0079-0.0157	0.0020-0.0035	0.0016-0.0031	SNUG
1986	9	1.9 (1901)	0.0016-0.0024	0.010-0.020	0.010-0.020	0.016-0.055	0.0015-0.0032	0.0015-0.0035	SNUG
	J	1.9 (1901)	0.0016-0.0024	0.010-0.020	0.010-0.020	0.016-0.055	0.0015-0.0032	0.0015-0.0035	SNUG
	H	2.0 (1998)	0.0013-0.0020	0.0079-0.0157	0.0079-0.0157	0.0079-0.0157	0.0020-0.0035	0.0016-0.0031	SNUG

86753C08

PISTON AND RING SPECIFICATIONS

All measurements are given in inches.

		Engine		Ring Gap			Ring Side Clearance		
Year	Engine ID/VIN	Displacement Liters (cc)	Piston Clearance	Top Compression	Bottom Compression	Oil Control	Top Compression	Bottom Compression	Oil Control
1987	9	1.9 (1901)	0.0016-0.0024	0.010-0.020	0.010-0.020	0.016-0.055	0.0015-0.0032	0.0015-0.0035	SNUG
	J	1.9 (1901)	0.0016-0.0024	0.010-0.020	0.010-0.020	0.016-0.055	0.0015-0.0032	0.0015-0.0035	SNUG
	H	2.0 (1998)	0.0013-0.0020	0.0079-0.0157	0.0079-0.0157	0.0079-0.0157	0.0020-0.0035	0.0016-0.0031	SNUG
1988	9	1.9 (1901)	0.0016-0.0024	0.010-0.020	0.010-0.020	0.016-0.055	0.0015-0.0032	0.0015-0.0035	SNUG
	J	1.9 (1901)	0.0016-0.0024	0.010-0.020	0.010-0.020	0.016-0.055	0.0015-0.0032	0.0015-0.0035	SNUG
1989	9	1.9 (1901)	0.0016-0.0024	0.010-0.020	0.010-0.020	0.016-0.055	0.0015-0.0032	0.0015-0.0035	SNUG
	J	1.9 (1901)	0.0016-0.0024	0.010-0.020	0.010-0.020	0.016-0.055	0.0015-0.0032	0.0015-0.0035	SNUG
1990	9	1.9 (1901)	0.0016-0.0024	0.010-0.020	0.010-0.020	0.016-0.055	0.0015-0.0032	0.0015-0.0035	SNUG
	J	1.9 (1901)	0.0016-0.0024	0.010-0.020	0.010-0.020	0.016-0.055	0.0015-0.0032	0.0015-0.0035	SNUG
1991	8	1.8 (1844)	0.0015-0.0020	0.006-0.012	0.006-0.012	0.008-0.028	0.0012-0.0026	0.0012-0.0028	SNUG
	J	1.9 (1901)	0.0016-0.0024	0.010-0.020	0.010-0.020	0.016-0.055	0.0015-0.0032	0.0015-0.0035	SNUG
1992	8	1.8 (1844)	0.0015-0.0020	0.006-0.012	0.006-0.012	0.008-0.028	0.0012-0.0026	0.0012-0.0028	SNUG
	J	1.9 (1901)	0.0016-0.0024	0.010-0.020	0.010-0.020	0.016-0.055	0.0015-0.0032	0.0015-0.0035	SNUG
1993	8	1.8 (1844)	0.0015-0.0020	0.006-0.012	0.006-0.012	0.008-0.028	0.0012-0.0026	0.0012-0.0028	SNUG
	J	1.9 (1901)	0.0016-0.0024	0.010-0.020	0.010-0.020	0.016-0.055	0.0015-0.0032	0.0015-0.0035	SNUG
1994	8	1.8 (1844)	0.0015-0.0020	0.006-0.012	0.006-0.012	0.008-0.028	0.0012-0.0026	0.0012-0.0028	SNUG
	J	1.9 (1901)	0.0120-0.0280	0.010-0.030	0.010-0.030	0.016-0.066	0.0015-0.0032	0.0015-0.0035	SNUG
1995	8	1.8 (1844)	0.0015-0.0020	0.0060-0.0120	0.0060-0.0120	0.0080-0.0280	0.0012-0.0026	0.0012-0.0028	SNUG
	J	1.9 (1901)	0.0120-0.0280	0.0100-0.0300	0.0100-0.0300	0.0160-0.0660	0.0015-0.0032	0.0015-0.0035	SNUG

86753C09

Engine

REMOVAL & INSTALLATION

CAUTION

When draining the coolant, keep in mind that cats and dogs are attracted by ethylene glycol antifreeze, and are quite likely to drink any that is left in an uncovered container or in puddles on the ground. This will prove fatal in sufficient quantity. Always drain the coolant into a sealable container. Coolant should be reused unless it is contaminated or several years old. The EPA warns that prolonged contact with used engine oil may cause a number of skin disorders, including cancer! You should make every effort to minimize your exposure to used engine oil. Protective gloves should be worn when changing the oil. Wash your hands and any other exposed skin areas as soon as possible after exposure to used engine oil. Soap and water, or waterless hand cleaner should be used.

1981-85 1.6L and 1985-90 1.9L Engines

ENGINE AND TRANSAXLE ASSEMBLY

The following procedures are for engine and transaxle removal and installation as an assembly. The engine and transaxle assembly are removed together as a unit from underneath the vehicle. Provision must be made to safely raise and support the vehicle for powertrain removal and installation. When performing engine removal and installation procedures on the 1.9L engine, check and record the distance between the crankshaft damper and the frame rail, and the distance between the transaxle and frame rail. Check the manual transaxle at the transaxle case. Check the automatic transaxle at the oil pump housing. This check should be done before the engine is removed and after the engine is installed. If necessary, loosen the motor mount-to-engine bolts to shift the engine to obtain the proper engine/transaxle to frame rail clearance. Proper clearances are necessary to ensure the half shaft alignment. The crankshaft damper-to-frame rail clearance should be 0.47-0.77 in. (12.0-20mm). The transaxle to frame rail clearance should be 0.79-1.17 in. (20.0-30.0mm).

1. Disconnect the negative battery cable.
2. With a permanent pen, mark the location of the hinges and remove the hood.
3. Remove the air cleaner, hot air tube and alternator fresh air intake tube.
4. Drain the radiator, engine oil and transaxle fluid.
5. Remove the coil the mounting bracket and the coil wire harness.
6. If the vehicle is equipped with air conditioning, remove the compressor from the engine with the refrigerant hoses still attached. Position compressor to the side.
7. Disconnect the upper and lower radiator hose.
8. Disconnect the heater hoses from the engine.
9. If equipped with an automatic transaxle disconnect and plug the cooler lines at the rubber coupler.
10. Disconnect the electric fan.
11. Remove the fan motor and shroud assembly as a unit, and remove the radiator.
12. If equipped with power steering, remove the filler tube.
13. Disconnect the following electrical connections:
    a. Main wiring harness
    b. Neutral safety switch (automatic only)
    c. Choke cap wire
    d. Starter cable
    e. Alternator wiring
14. Disconnect the fuel supply and return lines. Relieve fuel pressure on fuel injected models before disconnecting fuel lines.
15. Disconnect the three altitude compensator lines if so equipped. Mark each line as you remove it, for easy installation.
16. Disconnect and label the vacuum lines from the "tree" on the firewall.
17. Disconnect the power brake booster vacuum line.
18. Disconnect the cruise control if so equipped.
19. Disconnect all carburetor linkage.
20. Disconnect all engine vacuum lines. Mark each line as you remove it, for easy installation.
21. Disconnect the clutch cable if so equipped.
22. Remove the thermactor pump bracket bolt.
23. Install engine support T81P-6000-A or equivalent. Using a short piece of chain, attach it to the engine using the 10 mm bolt holes at the transaxle, the exhaust manifold side of the head, and the thermactor bracket hole. Tighten the J-bolt. Place a piece of tape around the J-bolt threads where the bolt passes through the bottom of the support bar. This will act as a reference later.
24. Raise and safely support the vehicle with jackstands.
25. Remove the splash shields.
26. If equipped with a manual transaxle, remove the roll restrictor at the engine and body.
27. Remove the stabilizer bar.
28. Remove the lower control arm through-bolts at the body brackets.
29. Disconnect the left tie rod at the steering knuckle.
30. Disconnect the secondary air tube (catalyst) at the check valve.
31. Disconnect the exhaust system at the exhaust manifold and tail pipe.
32. Remove the right halfshaft from the transaxle. Some fluid will leak out when the shaft is removed.
33. Remove the left side halfshaft.
34. Remove the shipping plugs T81P-1177-B or equivalent in the differential seals.
35. Disconnect the speedometer cable.
36. If equipped with an automatic transaxle, disconnect the shift selector cable. On manual transaxles, disconnect the shift control rod.

➡Mark the position of the shift control before disconnecting it.

37. If equipped with power steering, disconnect the pump return line at the pump, and the pressure line at the intermediate fitting.
38. Remove the left front motor mount attaching bracket and remove the mount with its through-bolt. Remove the left rear motor mount stud nut. Carefully reach into the engine compartment and loosen the engine support bar J-bolt until the left

rear motor mount stud clears the mounting bracket. Remove the left rear mount to transaxle attaching bracket.

39. Lower the vehicle, then tighten the support bar J-bolt until the piece of tape installed earlier contacts the bottom of the support bar. Attach a lifting sling to the engine, disconnect the right engine/transaxle mount and lift the engine from the vehicle.

To Install:

40. Attach a lowering sling to the engine, reconnect the right engine mount and lower the engine into the vehicle.

41. Install the left front motor mount attaching bracket and install the mount with its through-bolt. Install the left rear motor mount stud nut. Reach into the engine compartment and tighten the engine support bar J-bolt until the left rear motor mount stud clears the mounting bracket. Install the left rear mount to transaxle attaching bracket.

42. If equipped with power steering, reconnect the pump return line at the pump, and the pressure line at the intermediate fitting.

43. If equipped with an automatic transaxle, reconnect the shift selector cable. On manual transaxles, reconnect the shift control rod.

44. Reconnect the speedometer cable.

45. Install shipping plugs T81P-1177-B or equivalent in the differential seals.

46. Install the left side halfshaft.

47. Install the right halfshaft to the transaxle.

48. Reconnect the exhaust system at the exhaust manifold and tail pipe.

49. Reconnect the secondary air tube (catalyst) at the check valve.

50. Reconnect the left tie rod at the steering knuckle.

51. Install the lower control arm through-bolts at the body brackets.

52. Install the stabilizer bar.

53. If equipped with a manual transaxle, install the roll restrictor at the engine and body.

54. Install the splash shields.

55. Raise and safely support the vehicle with jackstands.

56. Remove the engine support T81P-6000-A or equivalent.

57. Install the thermactor pump bracket bolt.

58. Reconnect the clutch cable if so equipped.

59. Reconnect all engine vacuum lines. Mark each line as you Install it, for easy installation.

60. Reconnect all carburetor linkages.

61. Reconnect the cruise control if so equipped.

62. Reconnect the power brake booster vacuum line.

63. Reconnect the vacuum lines to the "tree" on the firewall.

64. Reconnect the three altitude compensator lines if so equipped. Mark each line as you Install it for easy installation.

65. Reconnect the fuel supply and return lines.

66. Reconnect the following electrical connections:

a. Main wiring harness
b. Neutral safety switch (automatic only)
c. Choke cap wire
d. Starter cable
e. Alternator wiring

67. If equipped with power steering, install the filler tube.

68. Install the fan motor, shroud assembly and the radiator.

69. Reconnect the electric fan.

70. If equipped with an automatic transaxle reconnect and plug the cooler lines at the rubber coupler.

71. Reconnect the heater hoses to the engine.

72. Reconnect the upper and lower radiator hose.

73. If the vehicle is equipped with air conditioning, install the compressor to the engine.

74. Install the coil the mounting bracket and the coil wire harness.

75. Refill the radiator, engine oil and transaxle fluid.

76. Reconnect the battery cable.

77. Install the air cleaner, hot air tube and alternator fresh air intake tube.

78. Install the hood.

ENGINE ASSEMBLY ONLY

1. Disconnect the negative battery cable.

2. Mark the position of the hinges on the hood underside and remove the hood.

3. Remove the air cleaner assembly. Remove the air feed duct and the heat tube. Remove the air duct to the alternator.

4. If equipped with air conditioning, remove compressor with line still connected and position it out of the way.

5. Drain the cooling system. Remove the drive belts from the alternator and thermactor pump. Disconnect the thermactor air supply hose. Disconnect the wiring harness at the alternator. Remove alternator and thermactor.

6. Disconnect and remove the upper and lower radiator hoses. If equipped with an automatic transaxle, disconnect and plug the fluid cooler lines at the radiator.

7. Disconnect the heater hoses from the engine. Unplug the electric cooling fan wiring harness. Remove the fan and radiator shroud as an assembly.

8. Remove the radiator. Label and disconnect all vacuum lines, including the power brake booster, from the engine. Label and disconnect all linkages, including the kickdown linkage if the vehicle is equipped with an automatic transaxle. Remove the wiring harness connectors from the engine.

9. If equipped with fuel injection, discharge the system pressure. Remove supply and return fuel lines to the fuel pump. Plug the line from the gas tank.

10. Raise and safely support the car on jackstands. Remove the clamp from the heater supply and return tubes. Remove the tubes.

11. Disconnect the battery cable from the starter motor. Remove the brace or bracket from the back of the starter and remove the starter.

12. Disconnect the exhaust system from the exhaust manifold. Drain the engine oil.

13. Remove the brace in front of the bell housing (flywheel or converter) inspection cover. Remove the inspection cover.

14. Remove the crankshaft pulley. If equipped with a manual transaxle, remove the timing belt cover lower attaching bolts.

15. If equipped with an automatic transaxle, remove the torque converter to flywheel mounting nuts.

16. Remove the lower engine to transaxle attaching bolts.

17. Loosen the hose clamps on the bypass hose and remove the hose from the intake manifold.

18. Remove the bolt and nut attaching the right front mount insulator to the engine bracket.

19. Lower the car from the jackstands.

20. Attach an engine lifting sling to the engine. Connect a chain hoist to the lifting sling and remove all slack. Remove the through-bolt from the right front engine mount and remove the insulator.

21. If the car is equipped with a manual transaxle, remove the timing belt cover upper mounting bolts and remove the cover.

22. Remove the right front insulator attaching bracket from the engine.

23. Position a floor jack under the transaxle. Raise the jack just enough to take the weight of the transaxle.

24. Remove the upper bolts connecting the engine and transaxle.

25. Slowly raise the engine and separate from the transaxle. Be sure the torque converter stays on the transaxle. Remove the engine from the car. On models equipped with manual transaxles, the engine must be separated from the input shaft of the transaxle before raising.

To install:

26. Slowly lower the engine and connect it to the transaxle.

27. Install the upper bolts connecting the engine and transaxle.

28. Lower the jack under the transaxle.

29. Install the right front insulator attaching bracket to the engine.

30. If the car is equipped with a manual transaxle, install the timing belt cover upper mounting bolts and install the cover.

31. Remove the engine sling from the engine. Install the through-bolt to the right front engine mount and install the insulator.

32. Raise the car and support on jackstands.

33. Install the bolt and nut attaching the right front mount insulator to the engine bracket.

34. Install the bypass hose to the intake manifold and tighten the clamps.

35. Install the lower engine to transaxle attaching bolts.

36. If equipped with an automatic transaxle, install the torque converter to the flywheel.

37. Install the crankshaft pulley. If equipped with a manual transaxle, install the timing belt cover lower attaching bolts.

38. Install the brace in front of the bell housing (flywheel or converter) inspection cover. Install the inspection cover.

39. Reconnect the exhaust system to the exhaust manifold. Refill the engine oil.

40. Reconnect the battery cable to the starter motor. Install the brace or bracket to the back of the starter and install the starter.

41. Lower the car from the jackstands. Install the clamp to the heater supply and return tubes.

42. If equipped with fuel injection, install the supply and return fuel lines.

43. Install the radiator. Reconnect all vacuum lines, including power brake booster, to the engine. Reconnect all linkages, including the kickdown linkage if equipped with an automatic transaxle. Reconnect the wiring harness connectors to the engine.

44. Reconnect the heater hoses to the engine. Unplug the electric cooling fan wiring harness. Install the fan and radiator shroud as an assembly.

45. Reconnect the upper and lower radiator hoses. If equipped with an automatic transaxle, reconnect the fluid cooler lines at the radiator.

46. Refill the cooling system. Install alternator and thermactor. Install the drive belts to the alternator and thermactor pump. Reconnect the thermactor air supply hose. Reconnect the wiring harness at the alternator.

47. Reconnect the negative battery cable. If equipped with air conditioning, install the compressor.

48. Install the air cleaner assembly. Install the air feed duct and the heat tube. Install the air duct to the alternator.

49. Install the hood.

Diesel Engines

➡The following procedure covers removal and installation of the 2.0L diesel engine and transaxle as an assembly. The engine and transaxle assembly are removed together as a unit from underneath the vehicle. The vehicle must be safely raised and supported for powertrain removal and installation.

1. With a permanent marker or a metal scribe, mark the position of the hood hinges and remove the hood.

2. Remove the negative ground cable from the battery that is located in the luggage compartment.

3. Remove the air cleaner assembly.

4. Position a drain pan under the lower radiator hose. Remove the hose and drain the engine coolant.

5. Remove the upper radiator hose from the engine.

6. Disconnect the cooling fan at the electrical connector.

7. Remove the radiator shroud and cooling fan as an assembly, then remove the radiator.

8. Remove the starter cable from the starter.

9. Properly discharge the air conditioning system using a recovery/recycling machine. Remove the pressure and suction lines from the air conditioning compressor.

10. Identify and disconnect all vacuum lines as necessary.

11. Disconnect the engine harness connectors (two) at the dash panel. Disconnect the glow plug relay connectors at the dash panel.

➡Connectors are located under the plastic shield on the dash panel. Remove and save plastic retainer pins. Disconnect the alternator wiring connector on the right hand fender apron.

12. Detach the clutch cable from the shift lever on the transaxle.

13. Disengage the injection pump throttle linkage.

14. Disconnect the fuel supply and return hoses on the engine.

15. Detach the power steering pressure and return lines at the power steering pump, if so equipped. Remove the power steering lines bracket at the cylinder head.

16. Install engine support tool D79P-8000-A or equivalent to the existing engine lifting eye.

17. Raise vehicle and safely support on jackstands.

18. Remove the bolt attaching the exhaust pipe bracket to the oil pan.

19. Remove the two exhaust pipe to exhaust manifold attaching nuts.

20. Pull the exhaust system out of the rubber insulating grommets and set it aside.

21. Disconnect the speedometer cable from the transaxle.

22. Position an drain pan under the heater hoses. Remove one heater hose from the water pump inlet tube. Remove the other heater hose from the oil cooler.

23. Remove the bolts attaching the control arms to the body. Remove the stabilizer bar bracket retaining bolts, then remove the brackets.

24. Remove the halfshaft assemblies from the transaxle at this time.
25. On M/T models, remove the shift stabilizer bar-to-transaxle attaching bolts, then remove the shift mechanism to shift shaft attaching nut and bolt at the transaxle.
26. Remove the left hand rear insulator mount bracket from body bracket by removing the two nuts.
27. Remove the left hand front insulator to transaxle mounting bolts.
28. Lower vehicle. Install lifting equipment to the two existing lifting eyes on engine.

****CAUTION**

Do not allow the front wheels to touch the floor!

29. Remove the engine support tool D79L-8000-A, or equivalent.
30. Remove the right hand insulator intermediate bracket to engine bracket bolts, intermediate bracket to insulator attaching nuts and the nut on the bottom of the double-ended stud attaching the intermediate bracket to the engine bracket. Remove the bracket.
31. Carefully lower the engine and the transaxle assembly to the floor.

To install:

32. Raise the vehicle and safely support.
33. Position the engine and transaxle assembly directly below the engine compartment.
34. Slowly lower the vehicle over the engine and transaxle assembly.

****CAUTION**

Do not allow the front wheels to touch the floor!

35. Install the lifting equipment to both existing engine lifting eyes on engine.
36. Raise the engine and transaxle assembly up through engine compartment and position accordingly.
37. Install right hand insulator intermediate attaching nuts and intermediate bracket to engine bracket bolts. Install nut on bottom of double ended stud attaching intermediate bracket to engine bracket. Tighten to 75-100 ft. lbs. (102-135 Nm).
38. Install engine support tool D79L-8000-A or equivalent to the engine lifting eye.
39. Remove the lifting equipment.
40. Raise vehicle.
41. Position a suitable floor or transaxle jack under engine. Raise the engine and transaxle assembly into mounted position.
42. Install insulator to bracket nut and tighten to 75-100 ft. lbs. (102-135 Nm).
43. Tighten the left hand rear insulator bracket to body bracket nuts to 75-100 ft. lbs. (102-135 Nm).
44. Install the lower radiator hose and install retaining bracket and bolt.
45. Install the shift stabilizer bar to transaxle attaching bolt. Tighten to 23-35 ft. lbs. (31-47 Nm).
46. Install the shift mechanism to input shift shaft (on transaxle) bolt and nut. Tighten to 7-10 ft. lbs. (10-13 Nm).
47. Install the lower radiator hose to the radiator.
48. Install the speedometer cable to the transaxle.
49. Connect the heater hoses to the water pump and oil cooler.
50. Position the exhaust system up and into insulating rubber grommets located at the rear of the vehicle.
51. Install the exhaust pipe to exhaust manifold bolts.
52. Install the exhaust pipe bracket to the oil pan bolt.
53. Place the stabilizer bar and control arm assembly into position. Install control arm to body attaching bolts. Install the stabilizer bar brackets and tighten all fasteners.
54. Halfshaft assemblies must be installed at this time.
55. Lower the vehicle.
56. Remove the engine support tool D79L-6000-A or equivalent.
57. Connect the alternator wiring at right hand fender apron.
58. Connect the engine harness to main harness and glow plug relays at dash panel.
59. Install the plastic shield.
60. Connect the vacuum lines.
61. Install the air conditioning discharge and suction lines to air conditioning compressor, if so equipped. Do not charge system at this time.
62. Connect the fuel supply and return lines to the injection pump.
63. Connect the injection pump throttle cable.
64. Install the power steering pressure and return lines. Install bracket.
65. Connect the clutch cable to shift lever on transaxle.
66. Connect the battery cable to starter.
67. Install the radiator shroud and coolant fan assembly. Tighten attaching bolts.
68. Connect the coolant fan electrical connector.
69. Install the upper radiator hose to engine.
70. Fill and bleed the cooling system.
71. Install the negative ground battery cable to battery.
72. Install the air cleaner assembly.
73. Install the hood, aligning the marks previously made.
74. Charge air conditioning system, if so equipped. The system can be charged at a later time if outside source is used.
75. Check and refill all fluid levels, (power steering, engine and transaxle).
76. Start the vehicle. Check for leaks.

1.8L Engine

WITH AUTOMATIC TRANSAXLE

1. Disconnect the negative battery cable.
2. Mark the position of the hood hinges and remove the hood.
3. If equipped with air conditioning, properly discharge the system using a recovery/recycling machine.
4. Drain the cooling system.
5. Remove the air duct connecting the throttle body and resonance chamber.
6. Disconnect the power brake vacuum supply hose from the power booster.
7. If equipped with speed control, disconnect the necessary vacuum hoses from the intake plenum.
8. Disconnect the electrical connectors from the power steering pump, water thermoswitch, temperature sending unit,

oil pressure switch, fuel injector wiring harness, exhaust gas oxygen sensor, throttle position sensor and distributor.

➡Mark the position of the connectors prior to removal to ease reinstallation.

9. Disconnect all engine ground straps.
10. Disconnect the ignition coil high tension lead from the distributor.
11. Disconnect the accelerator and kickdown cables from the throttle cam.
12. Remove the accelerator and kickdown cable bracket from the intake plenum and set the assembly aside.
13. Disconnect the heater core inlet and outlet hoses at the bulkhead.
14. Relieve the fuel system pressure.
15. Remove the necessary fuel line clips and disconnect the fuel pressure and return lines.
16. Remove the upper radiator hose.
17. Disconnect the electrical connectors from the cooling fan and the radiator thermoswitch.
18. Remove the starter motor.
19. Raise and safely support the vehicle.
20. Remove the right upper and both left and right lower splash shields.
21. Remove the radiator lower hose.
22. Disconnect the two transaxle cooling lines from the radiator and plug the lines.
23. Remove the air conditioner line routing bracket from the radiator and position the line aside.
24. Remove the halfshaft bearing support.
25. Remove the inspection plate from the oil pan, place a wrench on the crankshaft pulley, and rotate the crankshaft to gain access to the torque converter nuts. Remove the nuts.
26. Remove the power steering and air conditioner drive belt.
27. Remove the crankshaft pulley.
28. Remove the exhaust flex-pipe and mounting flange assembly from the exhaust manifold.
29. If equipped with air conditioning, remove the compressor.
30. Remove the power steering pump and bracket assembly with the hoses still connected. Suspend the pump with wire, aside of the work area.
31. Remove all accessible transaxle-to-engine bolts from the engine block.
32. Lower the vehicle.
33. Remove the radiator mounting brackets and the resonance duct.
34. Remove the radiator, fan and shroud assembly from the vehicle.
35. Remove the vacuum chamber canister located next to the intake plenum.
36. Remove the pressure regulator and bracket assembly and set it aside.
37. Remove the shutter valve actuator and bracket assembly and set it aside.
38. Remove the alternator and water pump drive belt and remove the alternator.
39. Install a suitable engine removal sling onto the engine lifting brackets. Place a suitable engine hoist into position and support the engine.
40. Remove the oil pan-to-transaxle attaching bolts and the remaining transaxle-to-engine bolts from the engine block.
41. Remove the engine vibration dampener.
42. Remove the engine mount.
43. Carefully separate the engine from the transaxle, then remove the engine from the vehicle.
44. Install the engine onto a suitable engine stand.

To install:

45. Install a suitable engine removal sling onto the engine lifting brackets.
46. Place a suitable engine hoist into position and install the engine sling. Remove the engine from the engine stand and lower it into the engine compartment.
47. Install the transaxle-to-engine upper right bolt and tighten to 41-59 ft. lbs. (55-80 Nm).

➡Make sure the torque converter studs are properly seated in the flexplate mounting holes.

48. Install the engine mount. Tighten the bolt and nuts to 49-69 ft. lbs. (67-93 Nm).
49. Install the engine vibration dampener. Tighten the bolt and nuts to 41-50 ft. lbs. (55-80 Nm).
50. Remove the engine sling from the lifting brackets and remove the engine hoist.
51. Install the remaining transaxle-to-engine bolts and tighten to 41-59 ft. lbs. (55-80 Nm).
52. Install the alternator and the alternator and water pump drive belt.
53. Install the shutter valve actuator and bracket assembly.
54. Install the pressure regulator and bracket assembly.
55. Install the vacuum chamber canister located next to the intake plenum.
56. Place the power steering pump and bracket assembly into its mounting position.
57. Place the radiator, fan and shroud assembly into its mounting position.
58. Install the radiator mounting brackets along with the resonance duct. Tighten the mounting bolts to 69-95 inch lbs. (7.8-11.0 Nm).
59. Connect the cooling fan and radiator thermoswitch electrical connectors.
60. Raise and safely support the vehicle.
61. Install the oil pan-to-transaxle attaching bolts and tighten to 27-38 ft. lbs. (37-52 Nm).
62. Install the power steering pump and bracket assembly. Tighten the bolts to 27-38 ft. lbs. (37-52 Nm).
63. Install the lower radiator hose and clamps.
64. Connect the two transaxle cooling lines to the radiator.
65. If equipped, install the air conditioning compressor.
66. Install the air conditioning hose routing bracket to the radiator, if equipped. Tighten the bracket attaching nuts to 56-82 inch lbs. (6.4-9.3 Nm).
67. Install the crankshaft pulley and tighten the bolts to 109-152 inch lbs. (12-17 Nm).
68. Place a wrench on the crankshaft pulley and rotate the crankshaft to gain access to the torque converter studs. Install the torque converter nuts and tighten to 25-36 ft. lbs. (34-49 Nm). Install the transaxle inspection plate.
69. Install the power steering and air conditioning, if equipped, drive belt.
70. Install the halfshaft bearing support and tighten the bolts to 31-46 ft. lbs. (42-62 Nm).
71. Install the starter motor.

72. Connect the heater core inlet and outlet hoses at the bulkhead.
73. Install the exhaust flex-pipe, with a new gasket, to the exhaust manifold. Tighten the pipe-to-converter attaching nuts to 23-34 ft. lbs. (31-46 Nm).
74. Install the right and left lower splash shields and the right upper splash shield. Tighten the bolts to 69-95 inch lbs. (7.8-11.0 Nm).
75. Lower the vehicle.
76. Install the upper radiator hose and clamps.
77. Unplug the fuel pressure and return lines and connect them to the fuel rail. Install the necessary fuel line clips.
78. Install the accelerator and kickdown cable bracket onto the intake plenum. Tighten the bolts to 69-95 inch lbs. (7.8-11.0 Nm). Install the accelerator and kickdown cables onto the throttle cam.
79. Connect the power brake vacuum supply hose to the vacuum booster.
80. If equipped, connect the vehicle speed control vacuum hoses to the intake plenum.
81. Connect all engine ground straps.
82. Connect all remaining electrical connectors to their original locations, as marked during the removal procedure.
83. Connect the ignition coil high-tension lead into the distributor.
84. Install the air duct and resonance chamber assembly.
85. Fill the cooling system.
86. If equipped, evacuate and recharge the air conditioning system.
87. Install the hood, aligning the marks that were made during the removal procedure.
88. Connect the negative battery cable.
89. Start the engine and check for leaks. Stop the engine and check the fluid levels.

WITH MANUAL TRANSAXLE

➡The 1.8L engine equipped with a manual transaxle requires the engine and transaxle to be removed as an assembly.

1. Disconnect the negative battery cable.
2. Mark the position of the hood hinges and remove the hood.
3. If equipped with air conditioning, properly discharge the system using a recovery/recycling machine.
4. Drain the cooling system.
5. Remove the resonance duct and the air cleaner assembly.
6. Remove the battery and the battery tray.
7. Disconnect the accelerator cable from the throttle cam and remove the accelerator cable bracket from the intake plenum.
8. Remove the upper radiator hose and disconnect the radiator overflow hose from the radiator filler neck.
9. Disconnect the radiator thermoswitch and cooling fan electrical connectors.
10. Remove the attaching nuts to the radiator mounting brackets and remove the brackets.
11. Disconnect the alternator, oil pressure switch, throttle position sensor, idle speed control, manual lever position switch, fuel injector wiring harness, back-up light switch, water thermoswitch, oxygen sensor, power steering pump and distributor electrical connectors.

➡Mark the position of the connectors prior to removal to ease reinstallation.

12. Disconnect all engine ground straps.
13. Disconnect the ignition coil high-tension lead from the distributor.
14. Properly relieve the fuel system pressure.
15. Disconnect the fuel pressure and return lines.
16. Disconnect the heater core inlet and outlet, power brake vacuum supply, purge control vacuum and, if equipped, speed control vacuum hoses.

➡Mark the position of the hoses prior to removal to ease reinstallation.

17. Raise and safely support the vehicle on jackstands.
18. Remove the right upper and lower splash shields.
19. Remove the clutch slave cylinder pipe bracket from the transaxle with the hose still connected. Position the slave cylinder aside.

➡Be careful not to damage the pipe or the hose.

20. Disconnect the shift control rod and the extension bar from the transaxle.
21. Remove the battery duct.
22. Remove the radiator lower hose.
23. Remove the power steering and, if equipped, air conditioning compressor drive belt.
24. Remove the power steering pump and bracket assembly with the hoses still connected. Suspend the pump with wire aside of the work area.
25. Remove the air conditioning hose routing bracket, if equipped, from the transaxle crossmember and position the air conditioning hose aside.
26. If equipped, remove the air conditioning compressor with the hoses still connected. Suspend the compressor with wire aside of the work area.
27. Disconnect the speedometer cable from the transaxle.
28. Remove the exhaust pipe front mounting flange and support bracket from the exhaust manifold.
29. Mark the location and disconnect the wires from the starter motor.
30. Remove the stabilizer bar.
31. Remove the tie rod ends from the steering knuckles.
32. Remove the halfshafts from the transaxle.
33. Remove the transaxle front and rear mount attaching nuts from the crossmember.
34. Lower the vehicle.
35. Remove the radiator, fan and shroud assembly from the vehicle.
36. Install a suitable engine removal sling onto the engine lifting brackets.
37. Place a suitable engine hoist into position and support the engine.
38. Remove the engine vibration dampener.
39. Remove the engine mount, transaxle upper mount and the transaxle support bracket.
40. Remove the engine and transaxle assembly.
41. Remove the intake plenum support bracket.
42. Remove the starter motor.

43. Remove the transaxle front mount.
44. Remove all oil pan-to-transaxle bolts and transaxle-to-engine attaching bolts from the engine block and separate the transaxle from the engine.
45. Remove the clutch assembly from the engine.
46. Install the engine onto a suitable engine stand.

To install:

47. Install a suitable engine removal sling onto the engine lifting brackets. Place a suitable engine hoist into position and install the engine sling.
48. Remove the engine from the engine stand and lower the engine with the hoist still supporting it.
49. Install the clutch assembly.
50. Install the transaxle onto the engine.
51. Install the transaxle-to-engine bolts and tighten to 47-66 ft. lbs. (64-89 Nm).
52. Install the oil pan-to-transaxle attaching bolts and tighten to 27-38 ft. lbs. (37-52 Nm).
53. Position the transaxle front mount onto the transaxle and install the attaching bolts. Tighten the bolts to 27-38 ft. lbs. (37-52 Nm).
54. Position the starter motor into the transaxle housing and install the mounting bolts. Tighten the bolts to 27-38 ft. lbs. (37-52 Nm).
55. Install the intake plenum support bracket. Tighten the bolts to 27-38 ft. lbs. (37-52 Nm) and the nut to 14-19 ft. lbs. (19-25 Nm).
56. Using the engine hoist, position the engine and transaxle assembly into the engine compartment and align the engine mounting points with the engine mount and the mounting holes in the transaxle crossmember.
57. Install the attaching nuts to the transaxle front and rear mounts and the transaxle crossmember.
58. Position the engine mount into the vehicle.
59. Install the engine mount through-bolt and nut. Tighten them to 49-69 ft. lbs. (67-93 Nm).
60. Install the engine mount-to-engine attaching nuts. Tighten the nuts to 54-76 ft. lbs. (74-103 Nm).
61. Install the engine mount vibration dampener and attaching bolt and nut. Tighten the bolt and nut to 41-59 ft. lbs. (55-80 Nm).
62. Place the clutch slave cylinder and pipe assembly into its proper mounting position.
63. Install the engine support bracket and attaching bolts. Tighten the bolts to 41-59 ft. lbs. (55-80 Nm).
64. Install the transaxle upper mount and install the attaching bolts. Tighten the bolts to 32-45 ft. lbs. (43-61 Nm).
65. Install the transaxle upper mount attaching nuts. Tighten the nuts to 49-69 ft. lbs. (67-93 Nm).
66. Place the radiator, fan and shroud assembly into its mounting position.
67. Install the radiator mounting brackets and tighten the nuts to 69-95 inch lbs. (7.8-11.0 Nm).
68. Install the upper radiator hose and connect the expansion reservoir overflow tube to the radiator filler neck.
69. Connect the cooling fan and radiator thermoswitch electrical connectors.
70. Raise and safely support the vehicle.
71. Install the lower radiator hose.
72. Install the halfshafts.
73. Install the tie rod ends into the steering knuckle.
74. Install the stabilizer bar.
75. Connect the wires to the starter motor according to their positions as marked during the removal procedure.
76. Install the exhaust front mounting flange to the exhaust manifold while making sure to install a new gasket. Tighten the flange-to-manifold attaching nuts to 23-34 ft. lbs. (31-46 Nm).
77. Install the exhaust pipe support bracket. Tighten the bracket attaching bolts to 27-38 ft. lbs. (37-52 Nm).
78. Install the speedometer cable into the transaxle.
79. If equipped, install the air conditioning compressor. Tighten the mounting bolts to 15-22 ft. lbs. (20-30 Nm).
80. Install the air conditioning routing bracket, if equipped, to the transaxle crossmember. Tighten the bolt to 56-82 inch lbs. (6.4-9.3 Nm).
81. Install the power steering pump and bracket assembly. Tighten the pump mounting bolts to 27-38 ft. lbs. (37-52 Nm).
82. Install the power steering and air conditioning, if equipped, drive belt.
83. Install the battery duct and tighten the attaching bolts to 69-95 inch lbs. (7.8-11.0 Nm).
84. Install the extension bar to the transaxle and tighten the attaching nut to 23-34 ft. lbs. (31-46 Nm).
85. Connect the shift control rod to the transaxle and tighten the attaching nut to 12-17 ft. lbs. (16-23 Nm).
86. Install the clutch slave cylinder attaching bolts and tighten to 12-17 ft. lbs. (16-23 Nm).
87. Position the slave cylinder pipe and install the routing bracket and attaching bolt. Tighten the bolt to 12-17 ft. lbs. (16-23 Nm).
88. Install the right upper and lower splash shields. Tighten the bolts to 69-95 inch lbs. (7.8-11.0 Nm).
89. Lower the vehicle.
90. Connect the heater core and vacuum hoses according to their original positions as marked during the removal procedure.
91. Connect the fuel pressure and return lines.
92. Connect the ignition coil high tension lead into the distributor.
93. Connect all engine ground straps.
94. Connect all remaining electrical connectors according to the locations marked during the removal procedure.
95. Install the accelerator cable bracket to the intake plenum and connect the accelerator cable to the throttle cam.
96. Install the battery tray and the battery.
97. Install the air cleaner assembly and the resonance duct.
98. Fill the cooling system.
99. If equipped, evacuate and recharge the air conditioning system.
100. Install the hood, aligning the marks that were made during the removal procedure.
101. Connect the negative battery cable.
102. Start the engine and check for leaks. Stop the engine and check the fluid levels.

1991-95 1.9L Engine

WITH AUTOMATIC TRANSAXLE

➡On automatic transaxle vehicles, the engine is lifted from the engine compartment with the transaxle assembly remaining in the vehicle, attached to the mounts.

1. Mark the position of the hood hinges and remove the hood.

2. Disconnect the negative battery cable.
3. Drain the cooling system.
4. Remove the air intake duct.
5. Remove the crankcase ventilation hose from the rocker arm cover and the vacuum hose from the bottom side of the throttle body.
6. Disconnect the power brake booster supply hose.
7. Disconnect the following electrical connectors:
   a. Fuel charging harness, located at the right shock tower.
   b. Alternator harness, from the back side of the alternator.
   c. Oxygen sensor.
   d. Ignition coil.
   e. Radio suppressor, mounted on the coil bracket.
   f. Coolant temperature sensor, cooling fan sensor and temperature gauge sending unit, mounted on a common water tube near the thermostat housing.
   g. Radiator cooling fan.

➡Mark the position of the electrical connectors to aid reinstallation.

8. Remove the idle air bypass valve.
9. Remove the ground strap from the stud on the left side of the cylinder head near the ignition coil.
10. Disconnect the accelerator cable and the transaxle kickdown cable from the throttle lever. Remove the cable bracket from the intake manifold and position aside.
11. Disconnect both heater hoses at the engine compartment bulkhead.
12. Properly relieve the fuel system pressure and disconnect the fuel supply and return hoses at the fuel supply manifold.
13. Remove the upper radiator hose.
14. Raise and safely support the vehicle.
15. Remove the right side and the right and left front splash shields.
16. Remove the lower radiator hose from the radiator.
17. Position a drain pan under the radiator and remove the lower transaxle oil cooler line.
18. Remove the two oil cooler line retaining bracket bolts from the bottom of the radiator.
19. Remove the radiator fan shroud lower mounting bolts.
20. Lower the vehicle.
21. Remove the radiator fan shroud upper mounting bolts and remove the fan and shroud assembly from the vehicle.
22. Remove the upper transaxle oil cooler line from the radiator and remove the radiator from the vehicle.
23. If equipped with air conditioning, properly discharge the system using a recovery/recycling machine.
24. Disconnect the air conditioning suction line at the suction accumulator/drier. Plug or cap the openings to prevent the entrance of dirt and moisture.
25. Remove the accessory drive belt.
26. Remove the power steering return hose from the pump reservoir and the high-pressure hose from the power steering pump.
27. Remove the power steering and air conditioner line retainer bracket bolts from the alternator bracket. Position the hoses aside.
28. Remove the accessory drive belt automatic tensioner assembly.
29. Raise and safely support the vehicle.
30. Remove the drive belt idler pulley.
31. If equipped, remove the four air conditioning compressor mounting bolts. Remove the compressor assembly with the lines attached and position aside. Safety wire the compressor to the vehicle sub-frame.
32. Remove the catalytic converter inlet pipe.
33. Remove the transaxle kickdown cable support bracket from the back side of the engine block. Position the cable and the bracket aside.
34. Disconnect the oil pressure switch.
35. Disconnect the relay wire and the positive battery cable from the starter.
36. Remove the flywheel inspection shield.
37. Remove the four torque converter attaching nuts.
38. Remove the crankshaft dampener.
39. Remove the four engine-to-transaxle bolts.
40. Lower the vehicle.
41. Remove the four starter motor mounting bolts and remove the starter out of the top of the engine compartment.
42. Remove the four transaxle-to-engine mounting bolts.
43. Connect an engine removal sling to suitable engine lifting brackets. Position a suitable engine hoist and support the engine.
44. Remove the right engine mount dampener and mount assembly.
45. With the engine assembly supported by the engine hoist, carefully separate the assembly from the transaxle.
46. Lift the engine assembly out of the vehicle.
47. Install the engine onto a suitable engine stand.

To install:

48. Attach the engine removal sling to the engine lifting brackets and remove the engine from the stand with the engine hoist.
49. Carefully lower the engine into the vehicle and join the engine to the transaxle. Make sure the torque converter studs correctly engage the flywheel and the alignment dowels engage the transaxle housing.
50. Install the four transaxle-to-engine bolts, but do not fully tighten them at this time.
51. Install the right engine mount insulator and dampener.
52. Position the engine hoist aside and remove the sling from the engine lifting brackets.
53. Raise and safely support the vehicle.
54. Install the four engine-to-transaxle bolts, but do not fully tighten them at this time.
55. Install the crankshaft dampener and tighten the attaching bolt to 81-96 ft. lbs. (110-130 Nm).
56. Install the four torque converter attaching nuts and tighten to 25-36 ft. lbs. (34-49 Nm). Install the flywheel inspection plate.
57. Connect the oil pressure switch.
58. Install the kickdown cable support bracket.
59. If equipped, position the air conditioning compressor on the bracket and install the four mounting bolts. Tighten the bolts to 15-22 ft. lbs. (20-30 Nm).
60. Install the catalytic converter inlet pipe.
61. Lower the vehicle.
62. From above, position the starter motor and install the 3 mounting bolts. Connect the positive battery cable and the relay wire to the starter.
63. Tighten the two transaxle-to-engine bolts to 40-59 ft. lbs. (55-80 Nm).

64. Install the power steering high-pressure hose on the pump.

65. Install the accessory drive belt idler pulley and automatic tensioner.

66. Install the power steering return hose on the pump reservoir.

67. Install the power steering hose retainer bracket on the alternator bracket.

68. Install the accessory drive belt.

69. If equipped, connect the air conditioner suction line to the accumulator.

70. Install the radiator assembly.

71. Connect the upper transaxle oil cooler line at the radiator.

72. Position the cooling fan and shroud assembly and install the upper mounting bolts.

73. Raise and safely support the vehicle.

74. Install the lower shroud bolts and connect the lower transaxle oil cooler line.

75. Install the oil cooler line retaining bracket bolts.

76. Install the lower radiator hose.

77. Tighten the five engine-to-transaxle bolts to 27-38 ft. lbs. (37-52 Nm).

78. Install the left and right front splash shields and the right side splash shield.

79. Lower the vehicle.

80. Install the upper radiator hose.

81. Connect both heater hoses at the engine compartment bulkhead.

82. Install the accelerator cable bracket and attach the accelerator and kickdown cables to the throttle lever.

83. Install the idle air bypass valve.

84. Install the ground strap on the stud at the front left side of the cylinder head, near the ignition coil.

85. Connect the remaining electrical connectors according to the positions marked during the removal procedure.

86. Connect the fuel supply and return lines. Be sure to install the fuel line safety clips.

87. Connect the power brake supply hose, the vacuum hose on the bottom side of the throttle body, and the crankcase ventilation hose to the rocker arm cover.

88. Install the air intake duct.

89. Connect the negative battery cable.

90. Fill the cooling system.

91. Install the hood, aligning the marks that were made during the removal procedure.

92. Start the engine and check for leaks. Stop the engine and check the fluid levels.

93. If equipped, evacuate and recharge the air conditioning system.

WITH MANUAL TRANSAXLE

➡On manual transaxle vehicles, the 1.9L engine assembly is removed with the transaxle attached.

1. Mark the position of the hood hinges and remove the hood.

2. Disconnect the battery cables and remove the battery and the battery tray.

3. Drain the cooling system.

4. Remove the air cleaner.

5. Disconnect the crankcase ventilation hose from the rocker arm cover and the vacuum hose from the bottom side of the throttle body.

6. Remove the power brake supply hose.

7. Disconnect the following electrical connectors:

a. Fuel charging harness, located at the right shock tower.

b. Alternator harness, from the back side of the alternator.

c. Oxygen sensor.

d. Ignition coil.

e. Radio suppressor, mounted on the coil bracket.

f. Coolant temperature sensor, cooling fan sensor and temperature gauge sending unit, mounted on a common water tube near the thermostat housing.

g. Radiator cooling fan.

➡Mark the position of the electrical connectors to aid reinstallation.

8. Remove the idle air bypass valve.

9. Remove the ground strap from the stud on the left side of the cylinder head near the ignition coil.

10. Disconnect the accelerator cable from the throttle lever. Remove the cable bracket from the intake manifold and position aside.

11. Disconnect both heater hoses at the engine compartment bulkhead.

12. Properly relieve the fuel system pressure using a recovery/recycling machine. Disconnect the fuel supply and return hoses at the fuel supply manifold.

13. Remove the upper radiator hose.

14. If equipped, properly discharge the air conditioning system and disconnect the suction line at the accumulator.

15. Remove the accessory drive belt and the automatic tensioner and idler pulley.

16. Disconnect the power steering return hose from the pump reservoir and the high pressure hose from the pump.

17. Remove the power steering hose and air conditioning line retainer brackets from the alternator bracket.

18. Raise and safely support the vehicle.

19. Remove the right and left side and front splash shields.

20. Disconnect the lower radiator hose from the radiator and remove the radiator fan shroud lower mounting bolts.

21. If equipped, remove the four air conditioning compressor mounting bolts. Remove the compressor assembly with the lines attached and position aside. Secure the compressor to the vehicle sub-frame.

22. Remove the catalytic converter inlet pipe.

23. Disconnect the oil pressure switch.

24. Disconnect the relay wire and the positive battery cable at the starter.

25. Remove the transaxle extension bar and shift control rod.

26. Remove the crankshaft dampener.

27. Remove the front wheel and tire assemblies.

28. Remove both halfshaft assemblies.

29. Install suitable transaxle plugs into the differential side gears.

✲✲WARNING

Failure to install the transaxle plugs may allow the differential side gears to move out of position.

30. Disconnect the speedometer cable and the neutral switch on the transaxle.
31. Remove the clutch slave cylinder and line as an assembly from the transaxle and set it aside.
32. Remove the transaxle front and rear mount bolts.
33. Lower the vehicle.
34. Remove the radiator fan shroud upper mounting bolts and remove the fan shroud assembly from the vehicle.
35. Connect a suitable engine removal sling to the engine lifting brackets. Connect the sling to a suitable engine hoist, position the hoist and support the engine.
36. Remove the right engine mount dampener and mount assembly.
37. Remove the transaxle upper mount.
38. Lift the engine and transaxle assembly out of the vehicle and set it down on the floor.

To install:

39. Carefully lower the engine and transaxle assembly into the vehicle with the engine hoist.
40. Position the transaxle on its mounts and install the transaxle upper mount.
41. Install the right engine mount and mount dampener.
42. Remove the engine removal sling and the hoist.
43. Position the fan shroud assembly and install the upper mounting bolts.
44. Raise and safely support the vehicle.
45. Install the front and rear transaxle mount bolts.
46. Install the clutch slave cylinder and line assembly.
47. Connect the neutral switch and the speedometer cable.
48. Remove the transaxle plugs and install the halfshaft assemblies.
49. Install the crankshaft dampener and tighten the bolt to 81-96 ft. lbs. (110-130 Nm).
50. Install the transaxle extension bar and shift control rod.
51. Connect the relay wire and the positive battery cable to the starter.
52. Connect the oil pressure switch.
53. Install the catalytic converter inlet pipe.
54. If equipped, position the air conditioning compressor on its bracket and install the four mounting bolts.
55. Install the radiator fan shroud lower mounting bolts and install the lower radiator hose.
56. Install the left and right side and front splash shields.
57. Lower the vehicle.
58. Install the power steering hoses and install the power steering hose and air conditioner line retainer brackets.
59. Install the accessory drive belt idler pulley and automatic tensioner and install the accessory drive belt.
60. If equipped, connect the air conditioner suction line.
61. Install the upper radiator hose.
62. Connect the fuel supply and return hoses to the fuel supply manifold.
63. Connect both heater hoses.
64. Install the accelerator cable bracket on the intake manifold and connect the cable to the throttle lever.
65. Install the ground strap on the stud at the front left side of the cylinder head.
66. Install the idle air bypass valve.
67. Connect the remaining electrical connectors according to the positions marked during the removal procedure.
68. Connect the power brake supply hose, the crankcase ventilation hose and the vacuum line at the bottom of the throttle body.
69. Install the air cleaner assembly.
70. Install the battery tray and the battery. Connect the battery cables.
71. Fill the cooling system.
72. Install the hood, aligning the marks that were made during the removal procedure.
73. Start the engine and check for leaks. Stop the engine and check the fluid levels.
74. If equipped, evacuate and recharge the air conditioning system according to the proper procedure.

Engine Mounts

REMOVAL & INSTALLATION

Gasoline Engines

RIGHT ENGINE INSULATOR (No. 3A)

See Figure 35

1. Disconnect the negative battery cable. Place a floor jack and a block of wood under the engine oil pan. Raise the engine approximately ½ in. (13mm) or enough to take the load off of the insulator.
2. Remove the lower support bracket attaching nut, bottom of the double-ended stud. Remove the insulator-to-support bracket attaching nuts. Do not remove the nut on top of the double ended stud.
3. Remove the insulator support bracket from the vehicle. Remove the insulator attaching nuts through the right hand front wheel opening.
4. Remove the insulator attaching bolts through the engine compartment. Work the insulator out of the body and remove it from the vehicle.

To install:

5. Work the insulator into the body opening.
6. Position the insulator and install the attaching nuts and bolts. Tighten the nuts to 75-100 ft. lbs. (100-135 Nm) and tighten the bolts to 37-55 ft. lbs. (50-75 Nm).
7. Install insulator support casting on top of the insulator and engine support bracket. Make sure the double-edged stud is through the hole in the engine bracket.
8. Tighten the insulator support casting-to-insulator attaching nuts to 55-75 ft. lbs. (75-100 Nm). Install and tighten lower support bracket nut to 60-90 ft. lbs. (80-120 Nm).
9. Install the insulator casting-to-engine bracket bolt and tighten to 60-90 ft. lbs. (80-120 Nm).
10. Lower engine. Connect negative battery cable.

LEFT REAR ENGINE INSULATOR (No. 4)

See Figure 36

1. Disconnect the negative battery cable. Raise the vehicle and support safely. Place a transaxle jack and a block of wood under the transaxle.
2. Raise the transaxle approximately ½ in. (13mm) or enough to take the load off of the insulator.

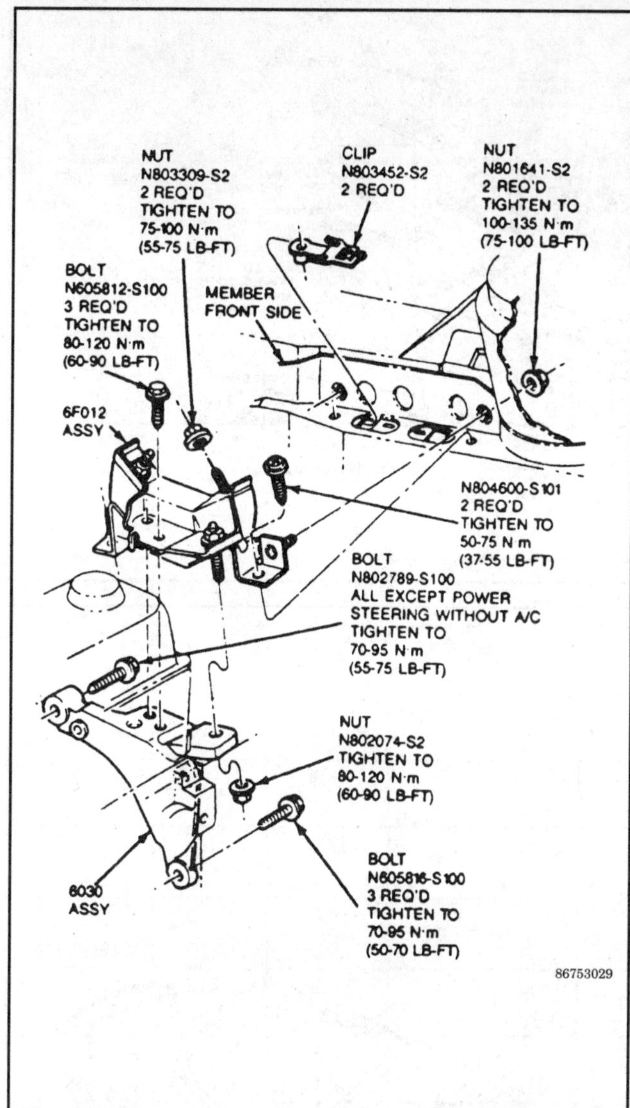

Fig. 35 Right hand No. 3A engine insulator (mount) — gasoline engines

3. Remove the insulator attaching nuts from the support bracket. Remove the two through-bolts and remove the insulator from the transaxle.

To install:

4. Install the insulator over the left rear transaxle housing and support bracket studs.
5. Install the two insulator through-bolts and tighten to 30-45 ft. lbs. (41-61 Nm).
6. Install two insulator-to-support bracket attaching nuts. Tighten to 80-100 ft. lbs. (108-136 Nm).
7. Lower vehicle and remove floor jack. Connect negative battery cable.

➡To remove the left rear support bracket, remove the left rear engine insulator No. 4. Then remove the support bracket attaching bolts. When installing the support bracket, tighten the attaching bolts to 45-65 ft. lbs. (61-88 Nm).

LEFT FRONT ENGINE INSULATOR (No. 1)

➧ See Figure 37

1. Disconnect the negative battery cable. Raise and the vehicle and support safely. Place a transaxle jack and a block of wood under the transaxle. Raise the transaxle approximately ½ in. (13mm) or enough to take the load off of the insulator.
2. Remove the insulator-to-support bracket attaching nut. Remove the insulators and transaxle attaching bolts and remove the insulator from the vehicle.
3. Complete the installation of the insulator by reversing the removal procedure. Tighten the insulator to transaxle attaching bolts to 25-37 ft. lbs. (35-50 Nm). Tighten the insulator-to-support bracket nut to 80-100 ft. lbs. (108-136 Nm).

Diesel Engines

➧ See Figure 38

FRONT ENGINE MOUNT

1. Disconnect the negative battery cable.
2. Support the engine and transaxle using a floor jack and a wood block. Raise the engine approximately ½ in. (13mm) to unload engine mount.
3. Remove the nut from the engine mount. It is removed from underneath the vehicle.
4. Remove the top bolts from the engine mount.
5. Lower the engine assembly 1-2 in. (25-50mm) for clearance.
6. From inside the right hand front wheel well, remove the two nuts attaching engine mount to fender apron.
7. Remove the two bolts attaching the engine mount to the right hand front rail.
8. Slide the engine mount toward the engine until the studs clear fender apron. Remove the mount.

To install:

9. Position the engine mount on the right hand front side members and loosely install the two attaching bolts.
10. From inside the right hand wheel well, install the two attaching nuts and tighten to 75-100 ft. lbs. (100-135 Nm). Tighten the two mount bolts on the right front rail to 37-55 ft. lbs. (50-75 Nm).
11. Raise the engine until the engine bracket contacts the engine mount.
12. Install nut B and the top bolts. Tighten to 60-90 ft. lbs. (80-120 Nm).
13. Remove the floor jack and wood block.
14. Connect the negative battery cable.

FRONT TRANSAXLE MOUNT

1. Disconnect the negative battery cable.
2. Support the transaxle with a floor jack and wood block.
3. Remove the three bolts attaching the mount to transaxle. Raise the engine approximately ½ in. (13mm) to unload the mount.
4. Remove nut attaching mount to left hand stabilizer bar bracket and remove mount.

To install:

5. Position the mount on the stabilizer bar bracket and install the three bolts attaching the mount to the transaxle and tighten to 25-37 ft. lbs. (35-50 Nm).
6. Install attaching nut to the stabilizer bar bracket and tighten to 80-100 ft. lbs. (108-136 Nm).

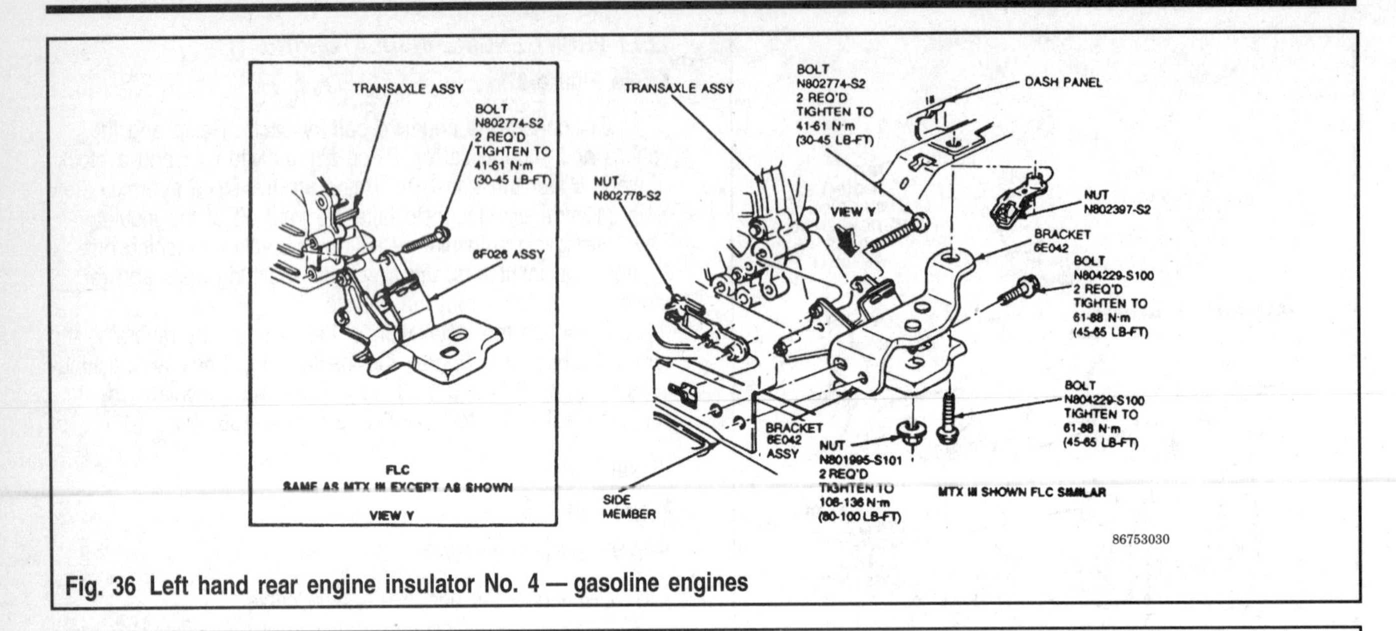

Fig. 36 Left hand rear engine insulator No. 4 — gasoline engines

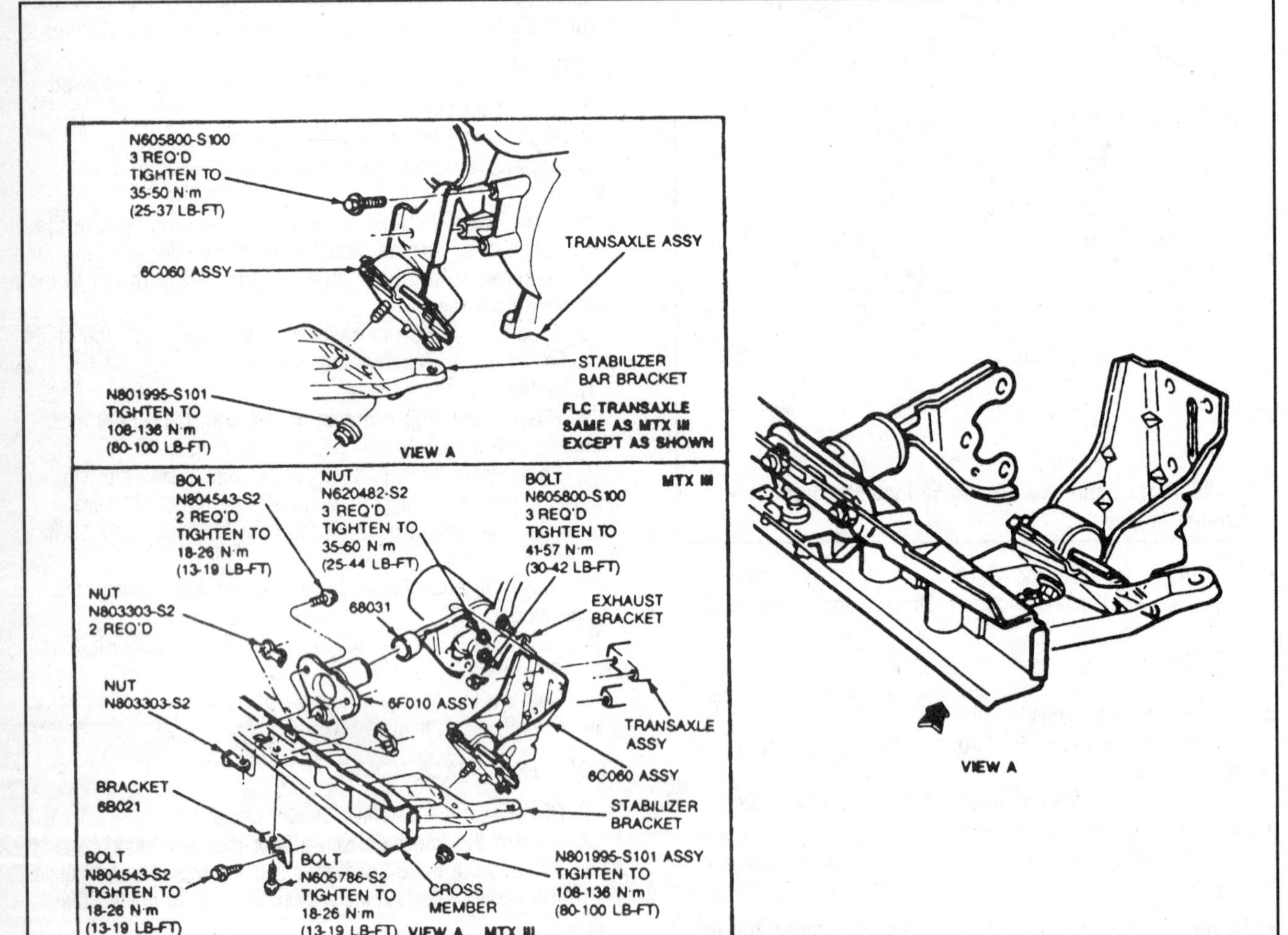

Fig. 37 Left hand rear engine insulator No. 1 — gasoline engines

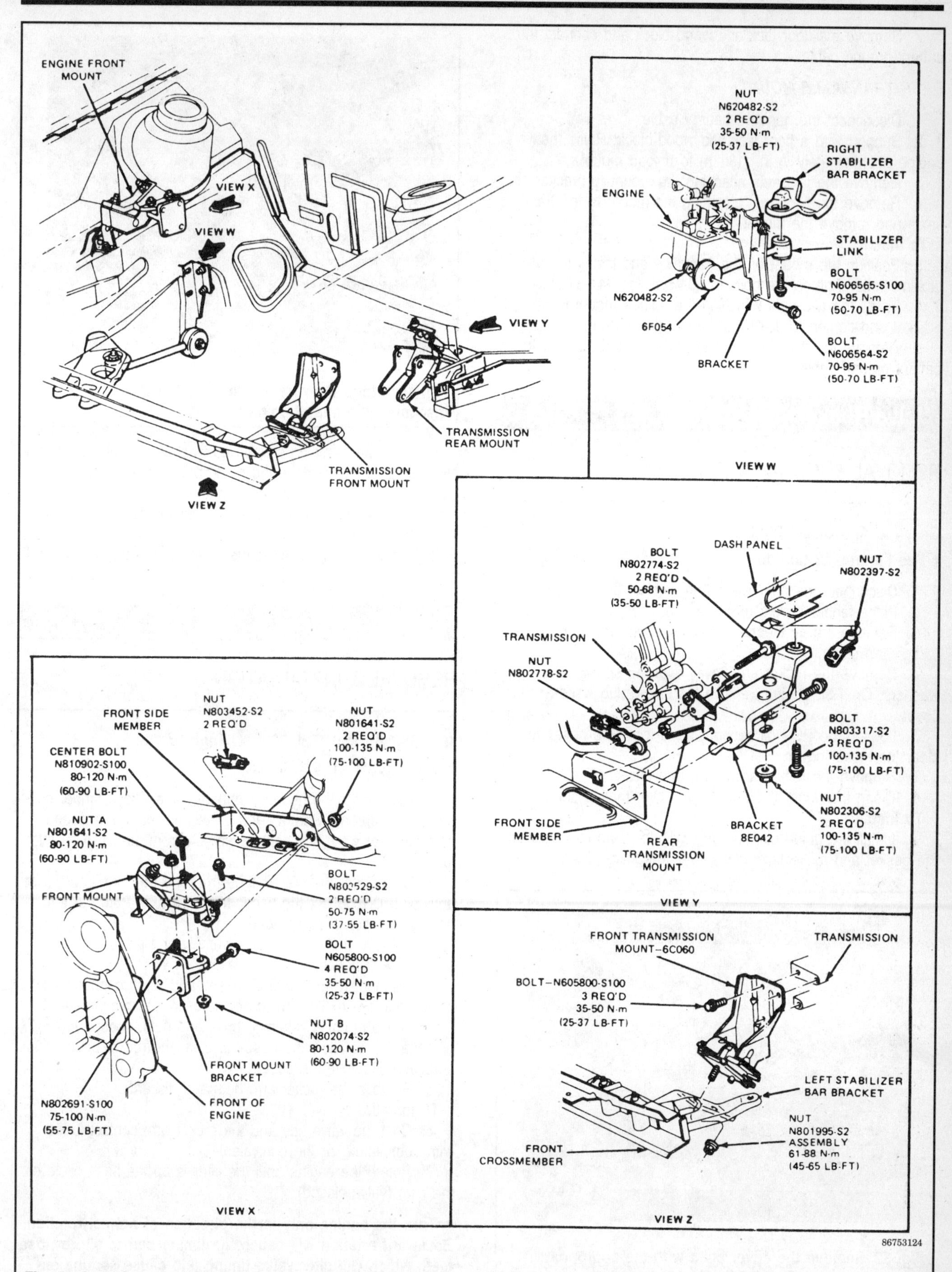

Fig. 38 Location of engine mounts, their required fasteners and torque specifications — 1984-87 diesel engines

7. Remove the floor jack and wood block and connect the battery ground cable.

REAR TRANSAXLE MOUNT

1. Disconnect the negative battery cable.
2. Support with a floor jack and wood block. Raise the engine approximately ½ in. (13mm) to unload mount.
3. Remove the two nuts attaching the mount to bracket.
4. Remove the two bolts attaching the mount to the transaxle and remove the mount.

To install:

5. Position the mount on the transaxle and install the attaching bolts. Tighten the bolts to 30-45 ft. lbs. (41-61 Nm).
6. Install the two nuts attaching the engine mount to the bracket and tighten to 80-100 ft. lbs. (108-136 Nm).
7. Remove the floor jack and wood block and connect the battery ground cable.

Valve/Rocker Arm Cover

REMOVAL & INSTALLATION

Gasoline And Diesel Engines

➧ See Figures 39 and 40

1. Disconnect the negative battery cable.
2. Place fender covers on the aprons.
3. Remove the air cleaner and all vacuum hoses from the rocker arm cover.
4. Remove the rocker arm cover retaining screws and washers. On 1.8L engine, remove the spark plug wires at the cover.
5. Loosen the PCV oil separator and allow the hoses to clear the rocker cover.
6. Remove the rocker arm cover and gasket.
7. Clean the head and rocker arm cover mating surfaces.

To install:

8. Install the guide pins into the cylinder head and position the gasket and rocker arm cover over the guide pins.

86753307

Fig. 39 Remove the cover bolts with the appropriate ratchet and socket — 1988 1.9L CFI Escort shown

86753308

Fig. 40 Lifting the rocker arm cover off after disconnecting and unbolting

9. Start two retaining screw and washer assemblies into the cylinder head and remove the guide pins. Install all retaining screw and washer assemblies and tighten to specification.
10. Connect all vacuum hoses and install the air cleaner assembly. On 1.8L engine reconnect the spark plug wires.
11. Connect the negative battery cable, start the engine and check for leaks.

Rocker Arms

REMOVAL & INSTALLATION

1981-85 1.6L and 1986-90 1.9L Engines

➧ See Figures 41, 42 and 43

1. Disconnect the negative battery cable. Place fender covers on the aprons. Remove the air cleaner nuts and disconnect the duct work and valve assembly from the fresh air inlet tube.
2. Disconnect the hot air tube from the hot air shroud, if so equipped. Disconnect the vacuum source tube from the temperature sensor, if so equipped.
3. Remove the air cleaner assembly and place it on a suitable work bench.
4. Disconnect and label all hoses and wires connected to or crossing the rocker arm cover. Loosen and remove all of the rocker arm cover retaining bolts and nuts. Loosen the PCV oil separator to allow the hoses to clear the rocker cover, if so equipped. Remove the cover.
5. Remove the rocker arm nuts and discard.

To install:

6. Coat the valve tips and the rocker arm contact areas with Lubriplate® or the equivalent.
7. Rotate the engine until the lifter is on the base circle of the cam (valve closed).

➡Turn the engine only in the direction of normal rotation. Backward rotation will cause the timing belt to slip or lose teeth which will alter valve timing and cause serious engine damage.

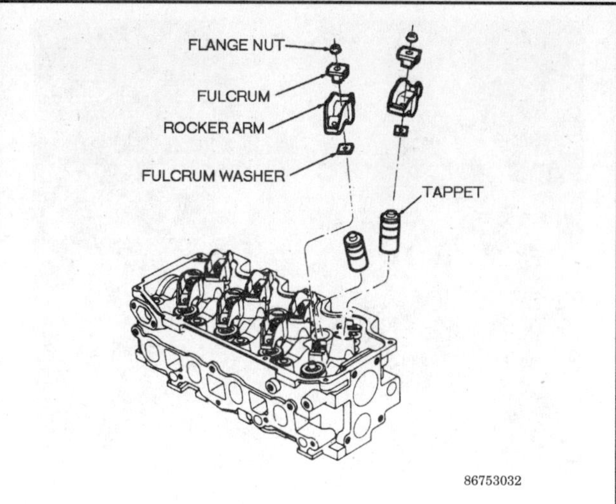

Fig. 41 Exploded view of the upper valve train — 1.6L and 1985-87 1.9L engines

Fig. 42 A single bolt holds this rocker arm to its mounting — 1988 1.9L CFI engine

Fig. 43 When installing the rocker arms, use a torque wrench and tighten to the proper specification

8. Install the rocker arm and new hex flange nuts or fulcrum and bolt. Be sure the lifter is on the base circle of the cam for each rocker arm as it is installed. Be sure that each fulcrum is seated in the rocker arm pedestal slot. Install the attaching nuts and tighten them to 15-22 ft. lbs. (19-30 Nm).
9. Clean the rocker arm cover mating surfaces. Install a new gasket, then install the cover. Connect all hoses and wires.

1991-95 1.9L Engine

➧ See Figure 44

1. Disconnect the negative battery cable.
2. Place fender covers on the aprons.
3. Remove the rocker arm (valve) cover.
4. Remove the rocker arm nuts, fulcrums, rocker arms and fulcrum washers. Keep all parts in order so they can be reinstalled in their original position.

To install:

5. Before installation, coat the valve tips, rocker arm and fulcrum contact areas with Lubriplate® or equivalent.
6. Rotate the engine until the lifter is on the base circle of the cam (valve closed).

➡Be sure to turn the engine only in the normal direction of rotation. Backward rotation will cause the timing belt to slip or lose teeth, altering the valve timing and causing serious engine damage.

7. Install the rocker arm and components and tighten the rocker arm bolts to 17-22 ft. lbs. (23-30 Nm). Be sure the lifter is on the base circle of the cam for each rocker arm as it is installed.
8. Install a new gasket and the rocker arm cover. Install the three retaining bolts and tighten to 4-9 ft. lbs. (5-12 Nm).

➡Do not use any type of sealer with the rocker arm cover silicone gasket.

9. Connect all vacuum hoses and install the spark plug wire retainers, if equipped.
10. Connect the negative battery cable.

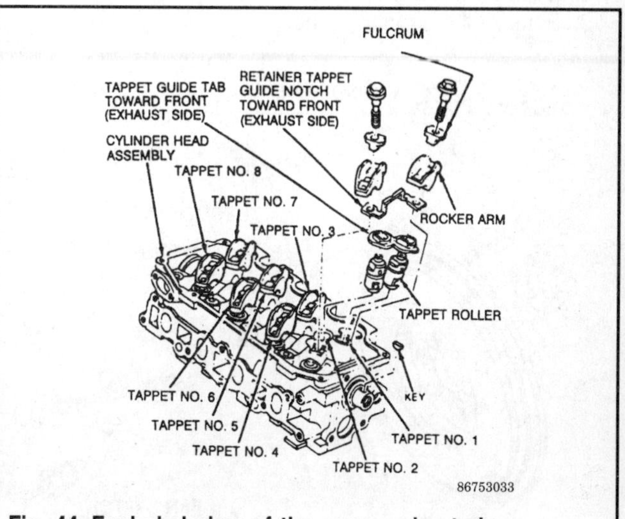

Fig. 44 Exploded view of the upper valve train — 1988-95 1.9L engines

Thermostat

REMOVAL & INSTALLATION

CAUTION

When draining the coolant, keep in mind that cats and dogs are attracted by ethylene glycol antifreeze, and are quite likely to drink any that is left in an uncovered container. Always drain the coolant into a sealable container.

1981-85 1.6L and 1985-90 1.9L Engines

See Figures 45, 46, 47, 48 and 49

1. Disconnect the negative battery cable.
2. Place fender covers on the aprons.
3. Drain the cooling system.
4. Disconnect the wire connector at the thermostat housing thermoswitch.
5. Loosen the top radiator hose clamp. Remove the thermostat housing mounting bolts and lift up the housing.
6. Remove the thermostat by turning counterclockwise.
7. Clean the thermostat housing and engine gasket mounting surfaces.

To install:

8. Install new mounting gasket and fully insert the thermostat to compress the mounting gasket. Turn the thermostat clockwise to secure in housing.
9. Position the housing onto the engine. Install the mounting bolts and tighten to specification.
10. Refill the cooling system.
11. Connect the negative battery cable, start the engine and check for leaks.

1.8L Engine

1. Disconnect the negative battery cable.
2. Drain the cooling system.
3. Remove the air intake tube.

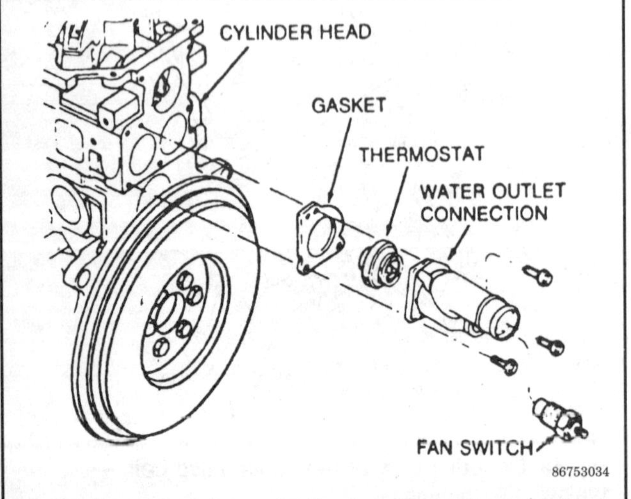

Fig. 45 Exploded view of thermostat location — 1985-90 1.9L engines

Fig. 46 For thermostat removal, unplug the wiring from the thermal switch in the housing

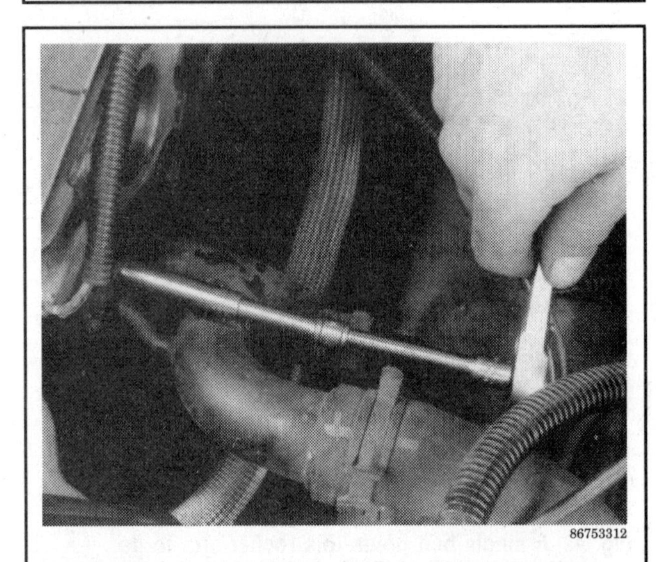

Fig. 47 Remove the water outlet retaining bolts

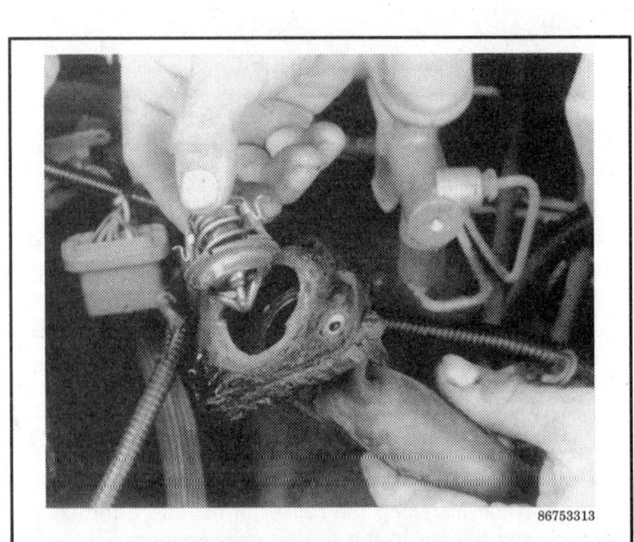

Fig. 48 Once the outlet is removed, rotate the thermostat counterclockwise and remove

Fig. 49 To install, first scrape the old gasket with a scraper — make sure not to gouge the mating surface

4. Disconnect the water thermoswitch connector, the engine wiring harness ground strap from the connector above the housing, and the exhaust gas oxygen sensor electrical connector.
5. Remove the upper radiator hose from the housing.
6. Remove the thermostat housing attaching bolt and nut and remove the housing. Remove the gasket and the thermostat.

To install:

7. Clean the thermostat housing and cylinder head gasket surfaces.
8. Position the thermostat, gasket and housing on the cylinder head.
9. Install the attaching bolt and nut and tighten to 14-19 ft. lbs. (19-26 Nm).
10. Install the upper radiator hose.
11. Connect the oxygen sensor electrical connector, the engine wiring harness ground strap, and the thermoswitch electrical connector.
12. Install the air intake tube.
13. Connect the negative battery cable.
14. Start the engine and bring to normal operating temperature. Check for coolant leaks. Check the coolant level and add as necessary.

1991-95 1.9L Engine

See Figures 50 and 51

1. Disconnect the negative battery cable.
2. Drain the cooling system.
3. Remove the air intake tube, crankcase breather and PCV hose.
4. Remove the ignition coil pack and bracket.
5. Remove the upper radiator hose.
6. Remove the heater hose inlet tube bracket bolt and remove the heater hose inlet tube from the thermostat housing.
7. Remove the three thermostat housing attaching bolts and remove the thermostat housing and gasket.

Do not pry off the housing.

8. Remove the thermostat and the rubber seal from the housing.

To install:

9. Clean the thermostat housing pocket and cylinder head mating surfaces.
10. Place the thermostat into position, fully inserted to compress the rubber seal inside the housing.

Make sure the thermostat tabs engage properly into the housing slots.

11. Position the thermostat housing and gasket on the cylinder head.
12. Install the three attaching bolts and tighten to 8.0-11.5 ft. lbs. (11-15 Nm).
13. Install the heater hose inlet pipe and the heater hose inlet pipe bracket bolt.
14. Install the upper radiator hose.
15. Install the ignition coil and bracket.
16. Install the crankcase breather, PCV hoses and the air intake tube.
17. Connect the negative battery cable.
18. Refill the cooling system.
19. Start the engine and bring to normal operating temperature. Check for coolant leaks. Check the coolant level and add as necessary.

Cooling System Bleeding

When the entire cooling system is drained, the following procedure should be used to ensure complete filling of the system.

1. Install the block drain plug, if removed, and close the draincock. With the engine off, add antifreeze to the radiator to a level of 50 percent of the total cooling system capacity. Then add water until it reaches the radiator filler neck seat.
2. Install the radiator cap to the first notch to keep spillage to a minimum.
3. Start the engine and let it idle until the upper radiator hose is warm. This indicates that the thermostat is open and coolant is flowing through the entire system.
4. Carefully remove the radiator cap and top off the radiator with water. Install the cap on the radiator securely.
5. Fill the coolant recovery reservoir to the FULL COLD mark with antifreeze, then add water to the FULL HOT mark. This will ensure that a proper mixture is in the coolant recovery bottle.
6. Check for leaks at the draincock and the block drain plug.

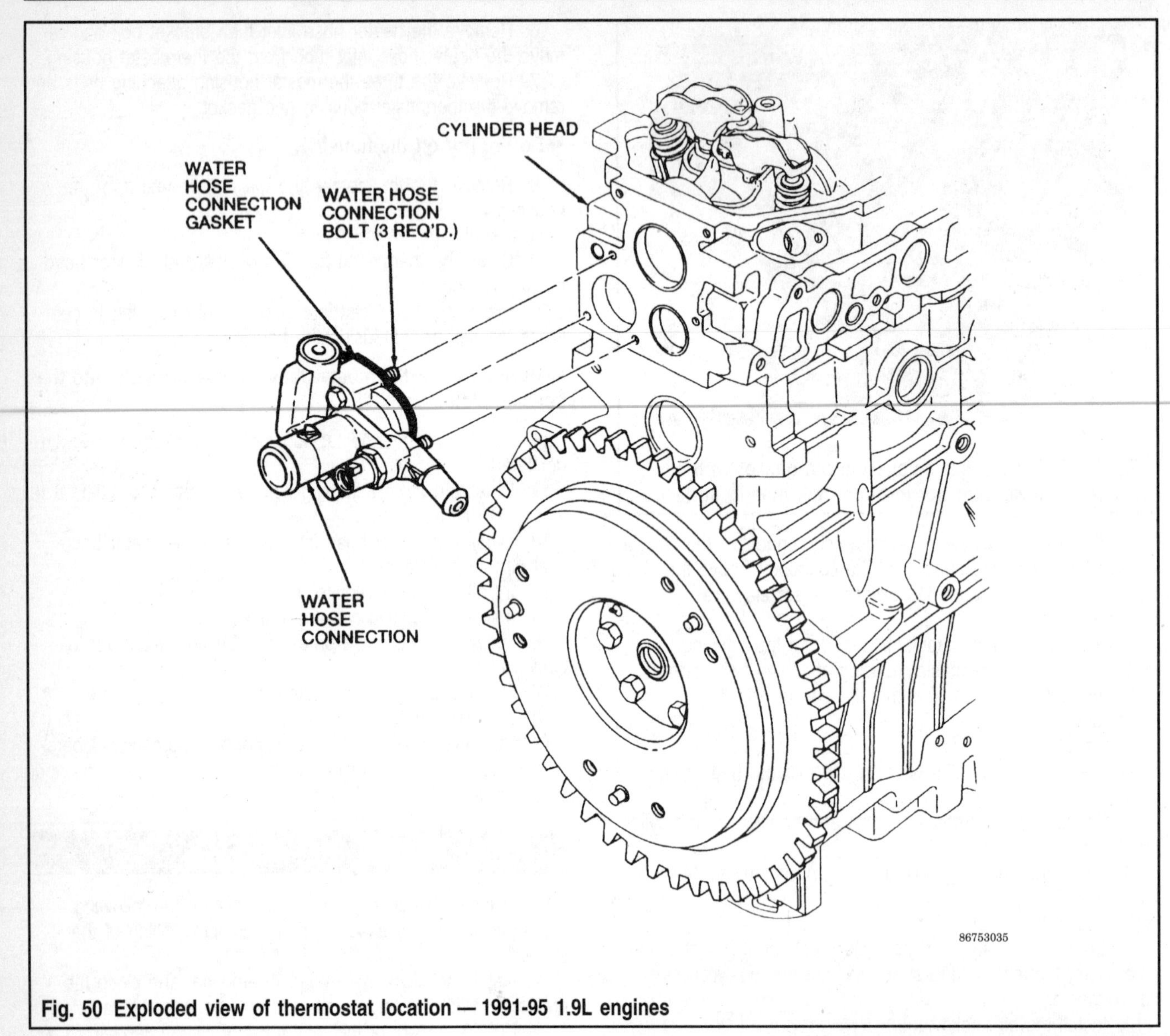

Fig. 50 Exploded view of thermostat location — 1991-95 1.9L engines

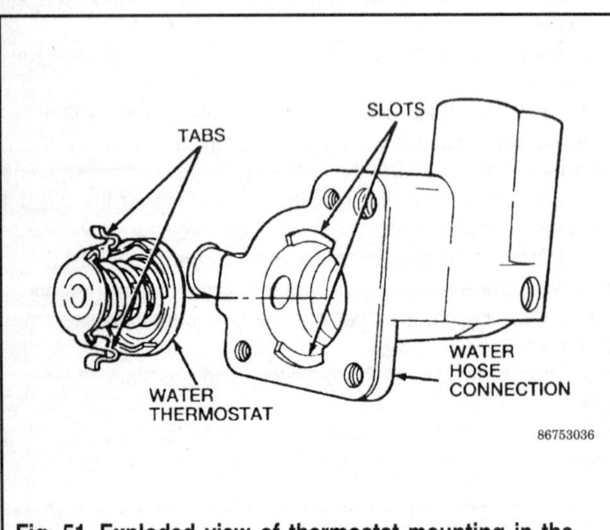

Fig. 51 Exploded view of thermostat mounting in the water hose connection — 1991-95 1.9L engines

Intake Manifold

REMOVAL & INSTALLATION

CAUTION

When draining the coolant, keep in mind that cats and dogs are attracted by ethylene glycol antifreeze, and are quite likely to drink any that is left in an uncovered container or in puddles on the ground. This will prove fatal in sufficient quantity. Always drain the coolant into a sealable container. Coolant should be reused unless it is contaminated or several years old.

1.6L and 1.9L Non-MFI Engines

See Figure 52

1. Disconnect the negative battery terminal.
2. Remove the air cleaner housing.

3. Partially drain the cooling system and disconnect the heater hose from under the intake manifold.
4. Disconnect and label all vacuum and electrical connections.
5. Disconnect the fuel line and carburetor linkages.
6. Disconnect the EGR vacuum hose and supply tube.
7. Raise the vehicle and support it safely.
8. Remove the three bottom intake manifold nuts.
9. Lower the vehicle.
10. If equipped with automatic transaxle disconnect the throttle valve linkage at the carburetor and remove the cable bracket attaching bolts.
11. If equipped with power steering, remove the thermactor pump drive belt, the pump, the mounting bracket, and the by-pass hose.
12. Remove the fuel pump, if required.
13. Remove the intake bolts, the manifold, and gasket.

➡Do not lay the intake manifold flat as the gasket surfaces may become damaged.

To install:

14. Install the intake manifold, and gasket.
15. Install the fuel pump, if removed.
16. Install the thermactor pump drive belt, the pump, the mounting bracket, and the by-pass hose, as required.
17. If equipped with automatic transaxle reconnect the throttle valve linkage at the carburetor and install the cable bracket attaching bolts.
18. Raise the vehicle and support it safely.
19. Install the three bottom intake manifold nuts.
20. Lower the vehicle.
21. Reconnect the EGR vacuum hose and supply tube.
22. Reconnect the fuel line and carburetor linkages.
23. Reconnect all vacuum and electrical connections.
24. Reconnect the heater hose to under the intake manifold and refill the cooling system.
25. Install the air cleaner housing.
26. Reconnect the negative battery terminal.

Diesel Engines

➧ See Figure 53

1. Disconnect the negative battery cable.
2. Place fender covers on the aprons.
3. Drain the cooling system.

➡When draining the coolant, keep in mind that cats and dogs are attracted by the ethylene glycol antifreeze, and are quite likely to drink any that is left in an uncovered container. Always drain the coolant into a sealable container.

4. Disconnect the air inlet duct from the intake manifold and install the protective cap in the intake manifold (part or Protective Cap Set T84P-9395-A or equivalent).
5. Disconnect the glow plug resistor electrical connector.
6. Disconnect the breather hose.
7. Disconnect the upper radiator hose at the thermostat housing.
8. Disconnect the tow coolant hoses at the thermostat housing.
9. Unplug the connectors to the temperature sensors in the thermostat housing.
10. Remove the bolts attaching the intake manifold to the cylinder head and remove the intake manifold.
11. Clean the intake manifold and cylinder head gasket mating surfaces.

To install:

12. Install the intake manifold, using a new gasket, and tighten the bolts to 12-16 ft. lbs.
13. Attach the temperature sensor connectors.
14. Connect the lower coolant hose to the thermostat housing and tighten the hose clamp.
15. Connect the upper coolant tube, using a new gasket and tighten bolts to 5-7 ft. lbs.
16. Install the upper radiator hose to the thermostat housing.
17. Install the breather hose.
18. Plug in the glow plug resistor electrical connector.
19. Remove the protective cap and install the air inlet duct.
20. Fill and bleed the cooling system.
21. Start the engine and check for intake air leaks and coolant leaks.

1.8L Engine

➧ See Figures 54 and 55

1. Properly relieve the fuel system pressure.
2. Disconnect the negative battery cable.
3. Tag and disconnect the necessary vacuum hoses from the intake manifold and plenum.
4. Remove the vacuum chamber canister from the intake plenum.
5. Disconnect the idle speed control and bypass air hoses from the intake plenum.
6. Disconnect the accelerator cable and, if equipped with automatic transaxle, the kickdown cable from the throttle cam. Remove the cable bracket from the intake plenum.
7. Tag and disconnect the throttle body electrical connectors.
8. Disconnect the fuel pressure and return line spring lock couplings.
9. Disconnect the PCV hose from the intake plenum and the cylinder head cover.
10. Disconnect the fuel pressure regulator vacuum hose and the fuel injector wiring harness electrical connectors.
11. Remove the fuel rail mounting bolts and remove the fuel rail.
12. Remove the two bolts from the transaxle vent tube and remove the vent tube from the intake plenum.
13. Remove the intake manifold upper mounting nuts.
14. Raise and safely support the vehicle.
15. Remove the intake plenum support bracket and the intake manifold lower mounting nuts.
16. Lower the vehicle.
17. Remove the intake manifold, intake plenum and throttle body as an assembly from the vehicle.
18. Remove the intake manifold gasket.
19. If necessary, separate the intake plenum and throttle body from the intake manifold.
20. Clean all gasket mating surfaces.

To install:

21. If necessary, install the throttle body and intake plenum onto the intake manifold.
22. Install the intake manifold gasket.

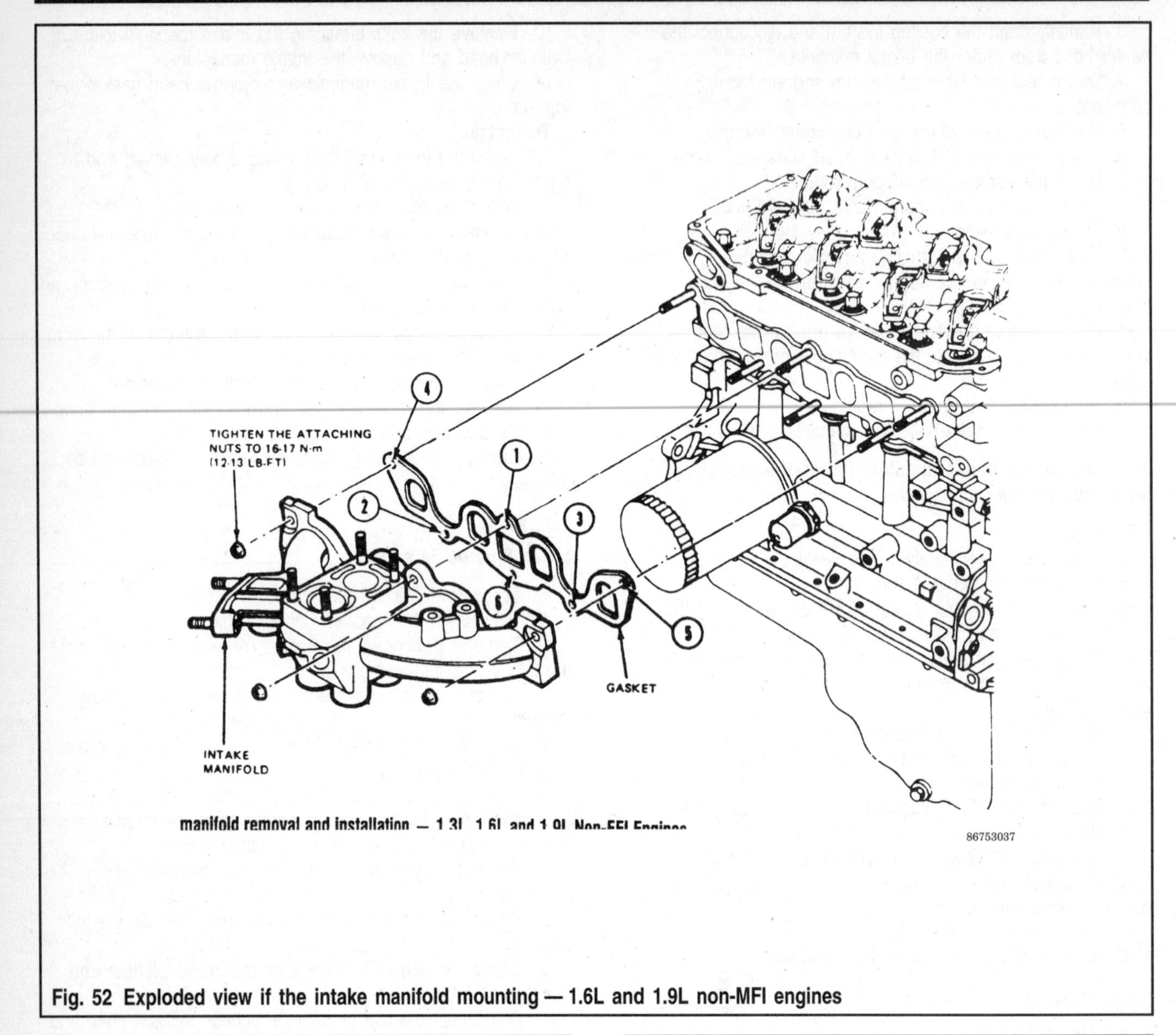

Fig. 52 Exploded view if the intake manifold mounting — 1.6L and 1.9L non-MFI engines

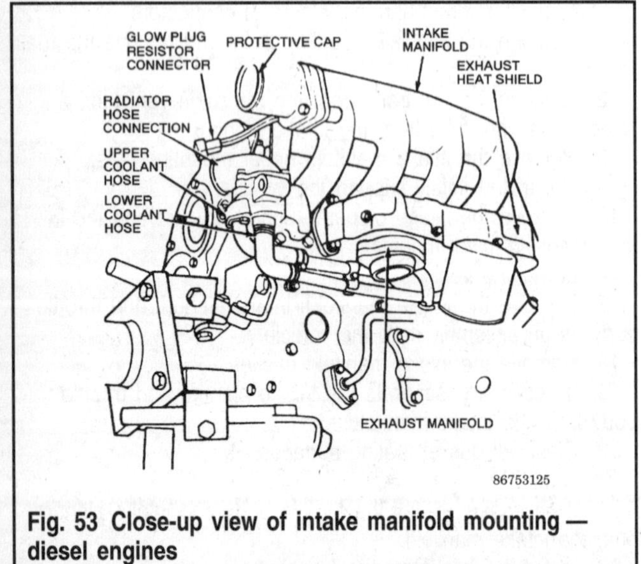

Fig. 53 Close-up view of intake manifold mounting — diesel engines

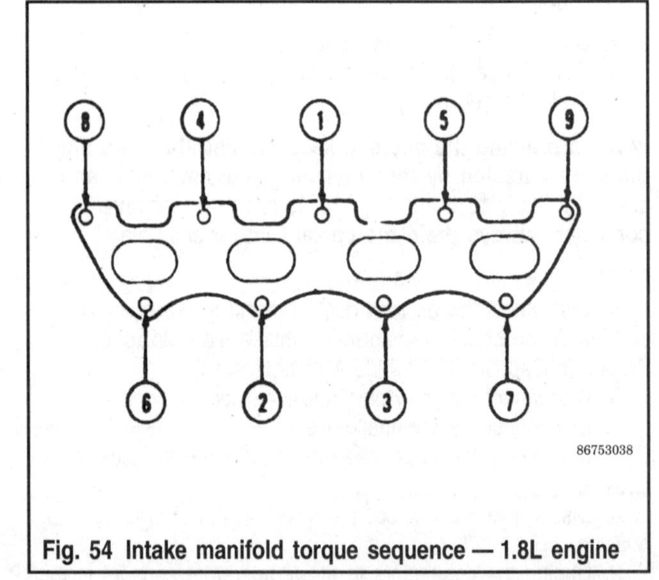

Fig. 54 Intake manifold torque sequence — 1.8L engine

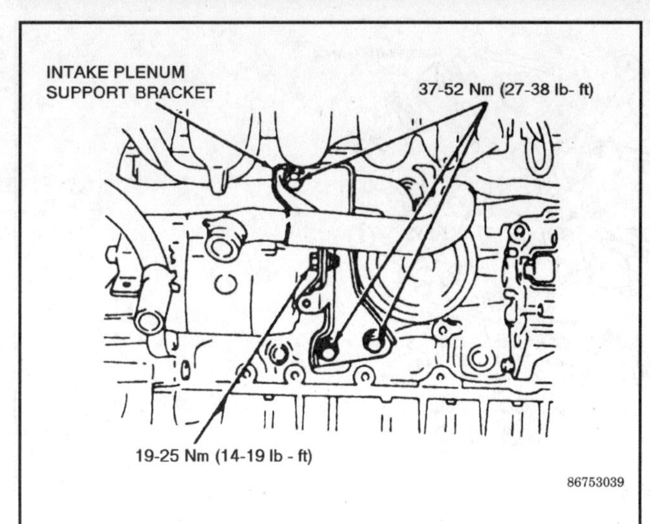

Fig. 55 Intake plenum support bracket torque specifications — 1.8L engine

23. Install the intake manifold, intake plenum and throttle body assembly onto the intake manifold mounting studs.
24. Install the mounting nuts and tighten to 14-19 ft. lbs. (19-25 Nm) in the proper sequence.
25. Raise and safely support the vehicle.
26. Install the intake plenum support bracket and tighten the bolts to specification.
27. Lower the vehicle.
28. Place the fuel rail into position and install the mounting bolts. Tighten the bolts to 14-19 ft. lbs. (19-25 Nm).
29. Connect the fuel injector wiring harness electrical connectors and connect the vacuum hose to the pressure regulator.
30. Connect the PCV hose to the intake plenum and cylinder head cover.
31. Connect the fuel pressure and return line spring lock couplings.
32. Install the transaxle vent tube that bolts onto the intake plenum.
33. Connect the electrical connectors to the throttle body and the necessary vacuum hoses to the intake plenum and throttle body.
34. Connect the idle speed control and bypass air hoses to the intake plenum.
35. Install the cable bracket onto the intake plenum and connect the accelerator and, if equipped, kickdown cables to the throttle cam.
36. Install the inlet air duct that connects to the throttle body and the resonance chamber.
37. Connect the negative battery cable.

1983-90 CFI and MFI Engines

See Figures 56, 57, 58, 59, 60 and 61

1. Raise and secure the hood in the open position.
2. Install protective fender covers.
3. Properly relieve the fuel system pressure. Disconnect the negative battery cable.
4. Partially drain the cooling system and disconnect the heater hose at the fitting located on the side of the intake manifold.

➡If equipped with an automatic transaxle, removing the ATF dipstick and its housing may provide a little extra room to work.

5. Remove air cleaner assembly.
6. Identify, tag and disconnect the vacuum hoses.
7. Identify, tag and disconnect wiring connectors at the following points:
   a. Coolant temperature sensor
   b. Air charge temperature sensor
8. Remove the Exhaust Gas Recirculation (EGR) supply tube.
9. Raise and safely support the vehicle.
10. Remove the Ported Vacuum Switch (PVS) hose connectors. Label the connectors and set aside.
11. Remove the bottom four intake manifold retaining nuts (locations 2, 3, 6 and 7).
12. Lower the vehicle.
13. Disconnect the fuel lines at the the throttle body.
14. Disconnect the accelerator and, if equipped, the speed control cable.
15. Disconnect the throttle valve linkage at the throttle body and remove the cable bracket attaching bolts on vehicles equipped with an automatic transaxle.
16. Remove the remaining three intake manifold attaching nuts, intake manifold and gasket.

➡Do not lay the intake manifold flat as the gasket surfaces may be damaged.

To install:

17. Make sure the mating surfaces on the intake manifold and the cylinder head are clean and free of gasket material.
18. Install a new intake manifold gasket.
19. Position the intake manifold on the engine and install the attaching nuts. Tighten the nuts, in sequence (refer to the appropriate drawing), to 12-15 ft. lbs. (16-20 Nm).
20. Connect the throttle valve linkage and install the cable bracket attaching bolts, if removed, on vehicles with automatic transaxle.
21. Connect the accelerator cable and, if equipped, the speed control cable.
22. Connect fuel lines at the fuel charging assembly.
23. Raise and safely support the vehicle.
24. Connect the heater hose to the fitting located on side of the intake manifold.
25. Lower the vehicle.
26. Connect the EGR supply tube.
27. Connect the wiring connectors at the following points:
   a. Coolant the temperature sensor
   b. Air charge temperature sensor
28. Connect all vacuum hoses.
29. Install the air cleaner assembly.
30. Fill the cooling system to specified level.
31. Connect the negative battery cable.
32. Start the engine and check for fuel and coolant leaks. Bring the engine to normal operating temperature and check again for coolant leaks.

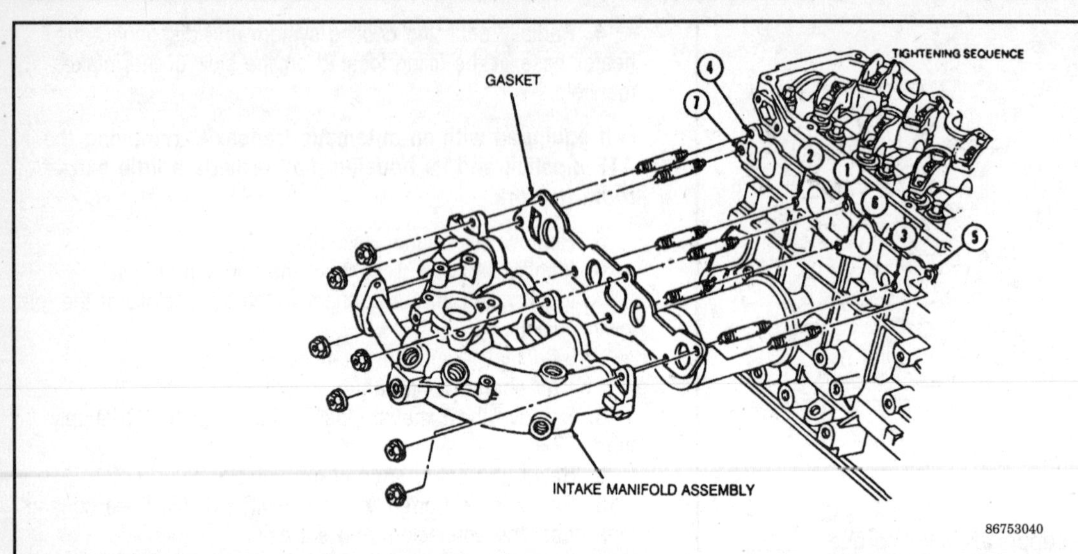

Fig. 56 Exploded view of intake manifold mounting and torque sequence — 1988-90 1.9L CFI engine

Fig. 57 Remove the cable bracket attaching bolts on vehicles equipped with an automatic transaxle

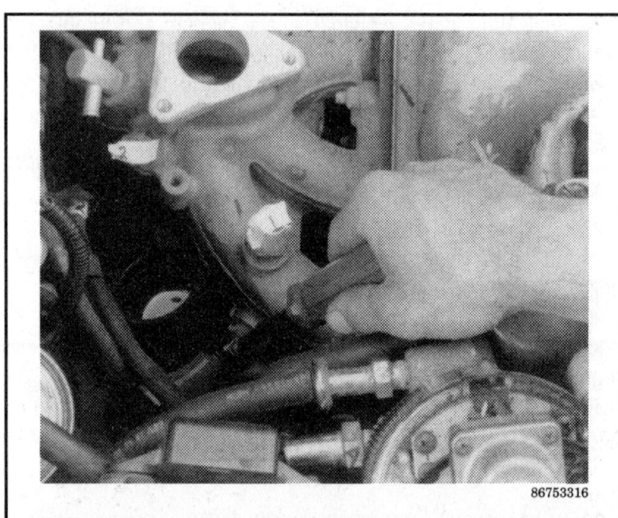

Fig. 59 Disconnect the heater hose at the fitting located on the side of the intake manifold

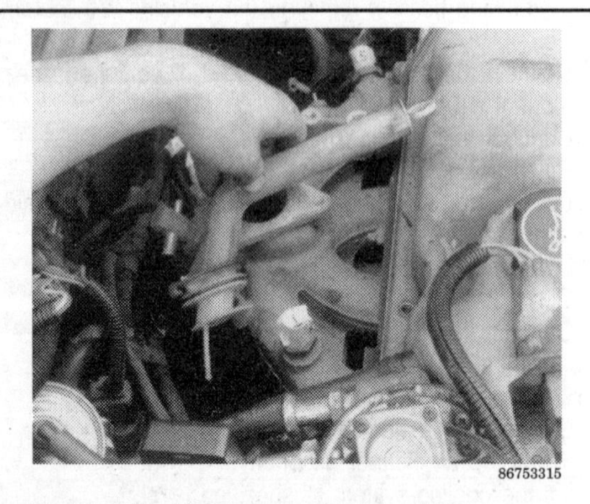

Fig. 58 On AT vehicles, removing the ATF dipstick/housing may provide extra clearance — but you don't have to remove the throttle body for intake removal

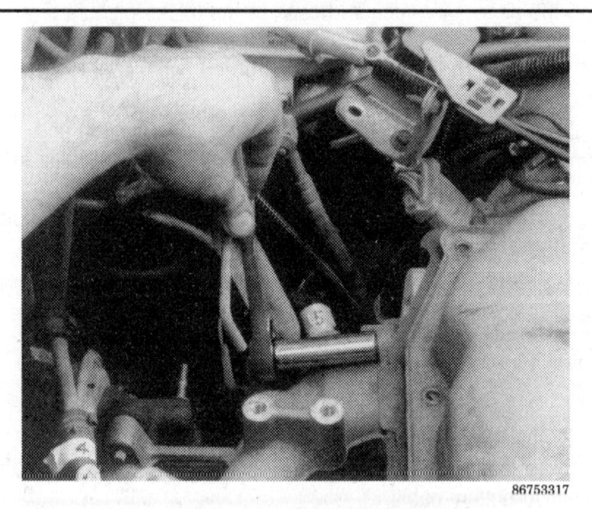

Fig. 60 With everything disconnected, remove the intake manifold mounting nuts — 1988 CFI engine

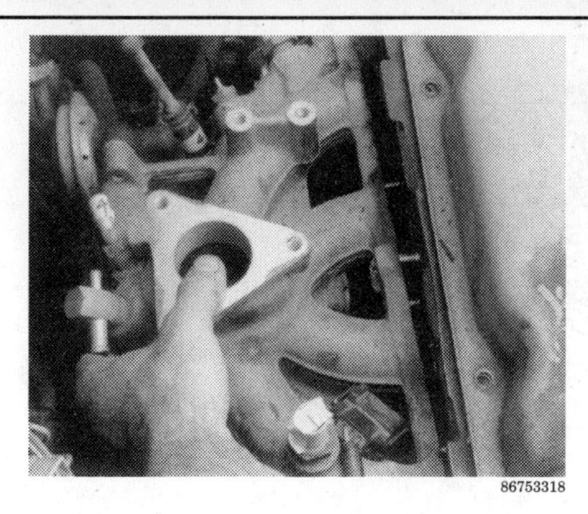

Fig. 61 After removing the fasteners, carefully pull the manifold and gasket from the cylinder head — although this shows no throttle body, the manifold can be removed with it intact

1988-90 1.9L MFI/HO Engines

See Figure 62

1. Disconnect the negative battery cable.
2. Properly relieve the fuel system pressure.
3. Remove the engine air cleaner outlet tube between the vane air meter and the air throttle body by loosening the two clamps.
4. Disconnect and remove the accelerator and speed control cables, if equipped, from the accelerator mounting bracket and throttle lever.
5. Disconnect the top manifold vacuum fitting connections by disconnecting the rear vacuum line to the dash panel vacuum tree and the vacuum line at the intake manifold tee.
6. Disconnect the PCV system by disconnecting the hoses from the PCV valve at the intake manifold connection.
7. Disconnect the EGR vacuum line at the EGR valve. Disconnect the EGR tube from the upper intake manifold by supporting the connector while loosening the compression nut.
8. Disconnect the upper support manifold bracket by removing the top bolt only. Leave the bottom bolts attached.
9. Disconnect the electrical connectors at the main engine harness, near the No. 1 runner, and at the ECT sensor located in the heater supply tube.
10. Remove the fuel supply and return lines.
11. Remove the six manifold mounting nuts.
12. Disconnect the lower support manifold bracket by removing the top bolt only. Leave the bottom bolts attached.
13. Remove the manifold with the wiring harness and gasket.
14. If necessary, at this time remove subassemblies from the intake manifold such as the throttle body, fuel rail, fuel injectors, etc.
15. Clean and inspect the mounting faces of the manifold assembly and cylinder head. Both surfaces must be clean, dry and flat.

To install:

16. Clean the manifold stud threads with a wire brush. If excessively corroded, replace them with new studs. Coat the threads with a suitable anti-sieze compound, or clean oil.
17. Install a new gasket.
18. Install the manifold assembly to the cylinder head and secure with the top middle nut. Tighten the nut finger-tight only at this time.
19. Install the fuel return line to the fitting in the fuel supply manifold. Install the two manifold mounting nuts, finger-tight.
20. Install the remaining three manifold mounting nuts. Tighten all six nuts to 12-15 ft. lbs. (16-20 Nm) in the proper sequence.
21. Connect the upper and lower manifold support brackets and tighten the bolts to 15-22 ft. lbs. (20-30 Nm).
22. Install the EGR tube with oil-coated compression nut tightened to 30-40 ft. lbs. (40-55 Nm).
23. Connect the vacuum line to the throttle body port and connect the large PCV vacuum line to the upper manifold fitting.
24. Connect the rear manifold vacuum connections at the dash panel vacuum tree and connect the vacuum line(s) to the upper manifold.
25. Connect the accelerator and, if equipped, speed control cables.
26. Install the air supply tube. Tighten the clamps to 12-20 inch lbs. (1.4-2.3 Nm).
27. Connect the wiring harness at the coolant temperature sensor in the heater supply tube and the main engine harness, near the No. 1 runner.
28. Connect the fuel supply hose from the fuel filter to the fuel rail and connect the fuel return line.
29. Reconnect the spring-lock coupling retaining clips on the fuel inlet and return fittings.
30. Fill the cooling system.
31. Connect the negative battery cable.
32. Start the engine and bring to normal operating temperature. Check for leaks. Stop the engine and check the coolant level.

1991-95 1.9L Engine

1. Properly relieve the fuel system pressure.
2. Disconnect the negative battery cable.
3. Partially drain the cooling system.
4. Remove the air intake tube.
5. Disconnect the fuel injector harness from the engine control harness at the right shock tower.
6. Disconnect the crankshaft position sensor.
7. Disconnect the fuel supply and return lines.
8. Remove the accelerator cable and, if equipped with automatic transaxle, kickdown cable from the throttle lever. Remove the cable bracket from the intake manifold and position the cables aside.
9. Remove the power brake supply hose, PCV line and the vacuum line from the bottom of the throttle body.
10. Remove the seven attaching nuts from the intake manifold studs, slide the manifold assembly off of the studs and remove it from the cylinder head. Remove and discard the intake manifold gasket.

To install:

11. Clean and inspect the mounting faces of the intake manifold and cylinder head. Both surfaces must be clean and flat.
12. Clean and oil the manifold studs and position a new gasket over them.
13. Install the intake manifold and the attaching nuts. Tighten the nuts to 12-15 ft. lbs. (16-20 Nm).

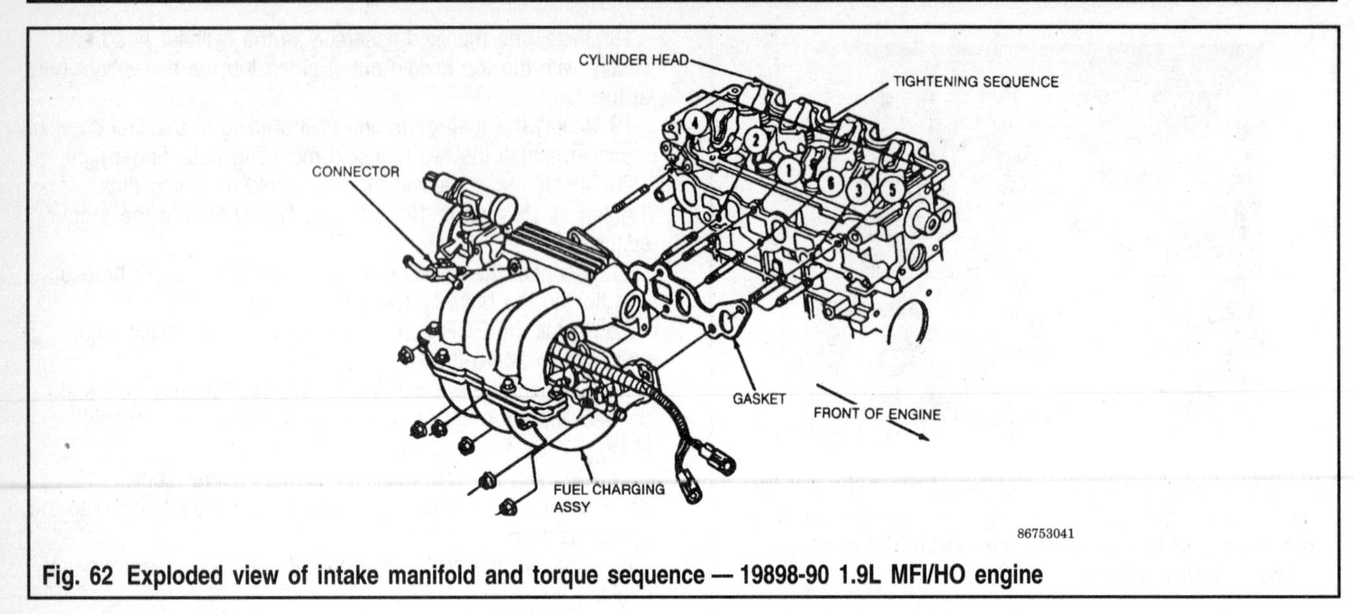

Fig. 62 Exploded view of intake manifold and torque sequence — 19898-90 1.9L MFI/HO engine

14. Install the vacuum line on the bottom of the throttle body, the power brake supply hose and the PCV line.
15. Install the accelerator cable bracket and connect the accelerator cable and, if equipped, kickdown cable on the throttle lever.
16. Connect the crankshaft position sensor electrical connector.
17. Connect the fuel supply and return lines. Install the fuel line retaining clips.
18. Connect the two fuel injector harness connectors to the engine control harness at the right shock tower.
19. Install the air intake tube.
20. Refill the cooling system.
21. Connect the negative battery cable.
22. Start the engine and bring to normal operating temperature. Check for leaks. Stop the engine and check the coolant level.

Exhaust Manifold

REMOVAL & INSTALLATION

CAUTION

When draining the coolant, keep in mind that cats and dogs are attracted by ethylene glycol antifreeze, and are quite likely to drink any that is left in an uncovered container or in puddles on the ground. This will prove fatal in sufficient quantity. Always drain the coolant into a sealable container. Coolant may be reused unless it is contaminated or several years old.

1.6L Turbocharged Engine

See Figure 63

1. Disconnect the negative battery cable. Remove the cooling fan finger shield from the radiator support.
2. Loosen the compressor outlet hose clamp at the throttle housing.
3. Remove the hose from the turbocharger compressor outlet and rotate the hose up out of the way.
4. Disconnect the compressor inlet hose from the turbocharger.
5. Remove the alternator bracket along with the alternator.
6. Disconnect the oxygen sensor electrical connector.
7. Raise and safely support the vehicle.
8. Disconnect the oil supply line at the coolant outlet and at the turbocharger.
9. Disconnect the oil return line from the bottom of the turbocharger center housing and the cylinder block.
10. Lower the vehicle. Remove the exhaust pipe-to-turbocharger attaching nuts and move the exhaust pipe away from the studs.
11. Remove the bolt attaching the exhaust shield to the water outlet connector.
12. Remove the nuts attaching the exhaust manifold to the cylinder head. Slide the exhaust manifold and turbocharger away from the cylinder head enough to remove the exhaust shield.
13. Remove the turbocharger and exhaust manifolds as an assembly.
14. If the exhaust manifold is being replaced, remove the exhaust oxygen sensor.

To install:

15. Ensure the mating surfaces on the exhaust manifold and the cylinder head are clean and free of gasket material. The exhaust manifold gasket has a top and a bottom to it, be sure to install it correctly.
16. Position the exhaust manifold and turbocharger assembly onto the cylinder head studs. The exhaust manifold studs for the turbocharged engine are different than the studs for a non-turbocharger engine.
17. Raise and safely support the vehicle. Reconnect the oil supply line at the coolant outlet and at the turbocharger.
18. Reconnect the oil return line to the bottom of the turbocharger center housing and the cylinder block.
19. Install the exhaust manifold nuts and tighten them to 16-19 ft. lbs.
20. Lower the vehicle. Install the bolt attaching the exhaust shield to the water outlet connector.

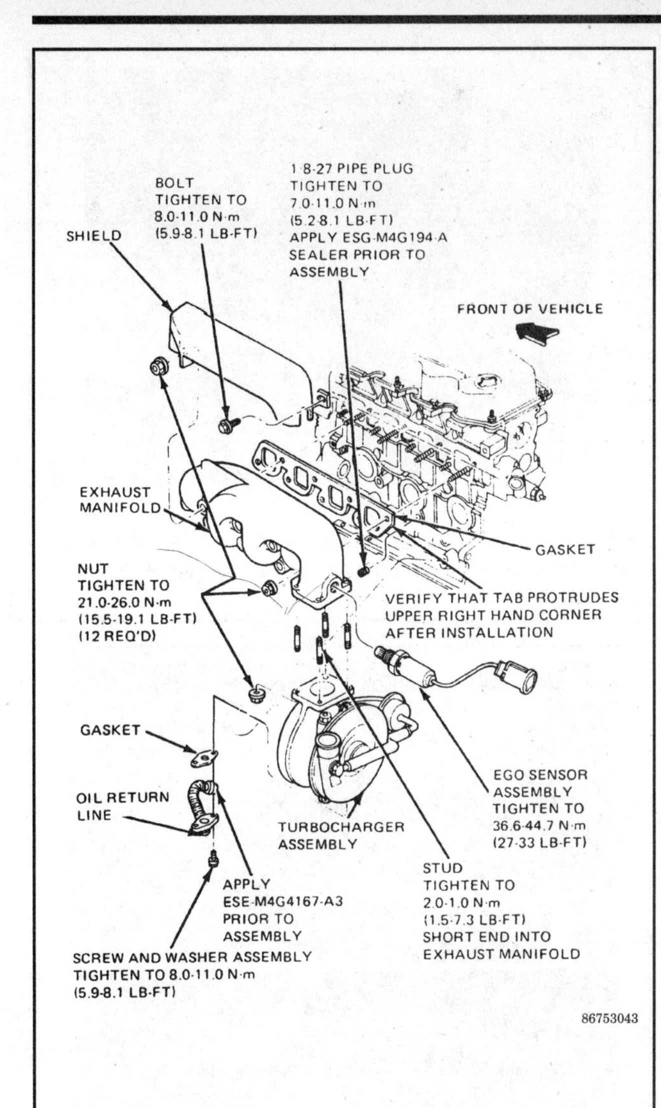

Fig. 63 Exploded view of exhaust manifold gasket mounting and torque figures — 1984-85 1.6L turbocharged engines

21. Install the exhaust pipe-to-turbocharger attaching nuts.
22. Reconnect the oxygen sensor electrical connector.
23. Install the alternator bracket along with the alternator.
24. Reconnect the compressor inlet hose from the turbocharger.
25. Install the hose to the turbocharger compressor outlet.
26. Tighten the compressor outlet hose clamp at the throttle housing.

➡After installing the turbocharger, or after an oil and filter change, disconnect the coil wire to the distributor and crank the engine with the starter motor until the oil pressure light on the dash goes out. Oil pressure must be up before starting the engine. Also always make sure that you use Turbo-approved motor oil when changing the oil in your turbocharged vehicle. Failure to use such an oil can cause premature bearing failure in your turbocharger assembly.

27. Install the cooling fan finger shield to the radiator support. Reconnect the negative battery cable.

Diesel Engines

1. Disconnect the negative battery cable.
2. Place fender covers on the aprons.
3. Remove the nuts attaching the muffler inlet pipe to the exhaust manifold.
4. Remove the bolts attaching the heat shield to the exhaust manifold.
5. Remove the nuts attaching the exhaust manifold to cylinder head and remove the exhaust manifold.

To install:

6. Install the exhaust manifold, using new gaskets, and tighten nuts to 16-20 ft. lbs. (21-27 Nm).
7. Install the exhaust shield and tighten bolts to 12-16 ft. lbs. (21-27 Nm).
8. Connect the muffler inlet pipe to the exhaust manifold and tighten the nuts to 25-35 ft. lbs. (34-47 Nm).
9. Start the engine and check for exhaust leaks.

1.8L Engine

1. Disconnect the negative battery cable.
2. Remove the resonance duct.
3. Partially drain the cooling system and disconnect the upper radiator hose.
4. Remove the cooling fan.
5. Raise and safely support the vehicle.
6. Remove the exhaust pipe from the exhaust manifold and remove the gasket.
7. Remove the two bolts from the exhaust pipe support bracket.
8. Remove the left lower splash shield.
9. Lower the vehicle.
10. Disconnect the oxygen sensor electrical connector.
11. Remove the exhaust manifold heat shield mounting bolts and remove the shield.
12. Remove the exhaust manifold mounting nuts and remove the assembly.
13. Remove all gasket material from the cylinder head and exhaust manifold.

To install:

14. Install a new gasket onto the exhaust manifold mounting studs.
15. Place the exhaust manifold onto the mounting studs and install the manifold mounting nuts. Tighten the nuts to 28-34 ft. lbs. (38-46 Nm).
16. Place the heat shield into its mounting position and install the shield mounting bolts. Tighten the bolts to 69-95 inch lbs. (7.8-11.0 Nm).
17. Connect the oxygen sensor electrical connector.
18. Install the cooling fan.
19. Connect the upper radiator hose.
20. Install the resonance duct.
21. Raise and safely support the vehicle.
22. Install the exhaust pipe support bracket.
23. Install a new gasket and install the exhaust pipe to the exhaust manifold. Tighten the attaching nuts to 23-34 ft. lbs. (31-46 Nm).
24. Install the left lower splash shield and tighten the bolts to 69-95 inch lbs. (7.8-11.0 Nm).
25. Lower the vehicle.
26. Refill the cooling system.
27. Connect the negative battery cable.

1981-85 1.6L (Except Turbo) and 1985-90 1.9L Engine

See Figures 64, 65, 66, 67, 68, 69, 70, 71 and 72

1. Disconnect the negative battery cable.
2. Remove the air cleaner assembly.
3. Disconnect the electric fan wire.
4. Remove the radiator shroud bolts and radiator shroud.
5. Remove the air conditioning hose bracket.
6. Remove the oxygen sensor from the exhaust manifold.
7. Remove the exhaust manifold heat shield.
8. Disconnect the EGR tube at the exhaust manifold.
9. Remove the exhaust manifold retaining nuts.
10. Raise and safely support the vehicle.
11. Remove the anti-roll brace.
12. Disconnect the water tube brackets.
13. Disconnect the exhaust pipe at the catalytic converter.

➡The exhaust pipe may also be unbolted from the manifold instead of the catalytic converter.

14. Remove the exhaust manifold and gasket. Discard the gasket and replace with new.

To install:

15. Clean the exhaust manifold gasket contact areas.
16. Position the gasket and exhaust manifold.
17. Install the exhaust pipe to the catalyst.
18. Install the anti-roll brace. Install the water tube brackets.
19. Lower the vehicle.
20. Install the exhaust manifold retaining nuts. Tighten to 16-20 ft. lbs. (21-26 Nm).
21. Install the exhaust manifold heat shield.
22. Install the oxygen sensor in exhaust manifold. Tighten to 30-40 ft. lbs. (40-50 Nm).
23. Connect the EGR tube.
24. Install the air conditioning hose brackets.
25. Position the shroud and fan assembly on radiator and install bolts.
26. Connect the electric fan wire.
27. Connect the battery cable.
28. Install the air cleaner assembly.

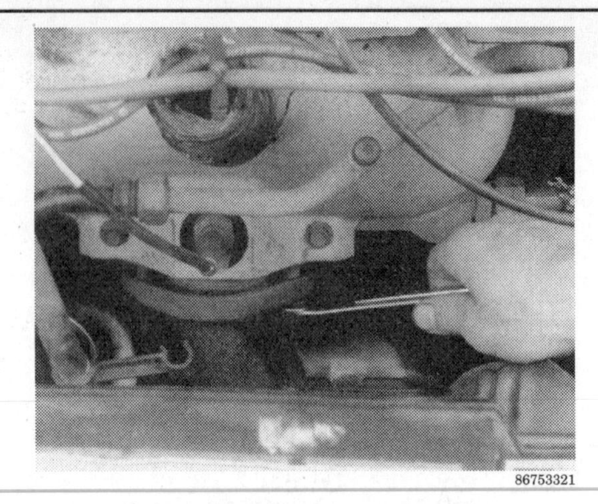

Fig. 65 Instead of detaching the exhaust pipe at the catalytic converter, you may remove the header at the manifold

Fig. 66 Remove the ground strap and detach the head pipe at the catalytic converter

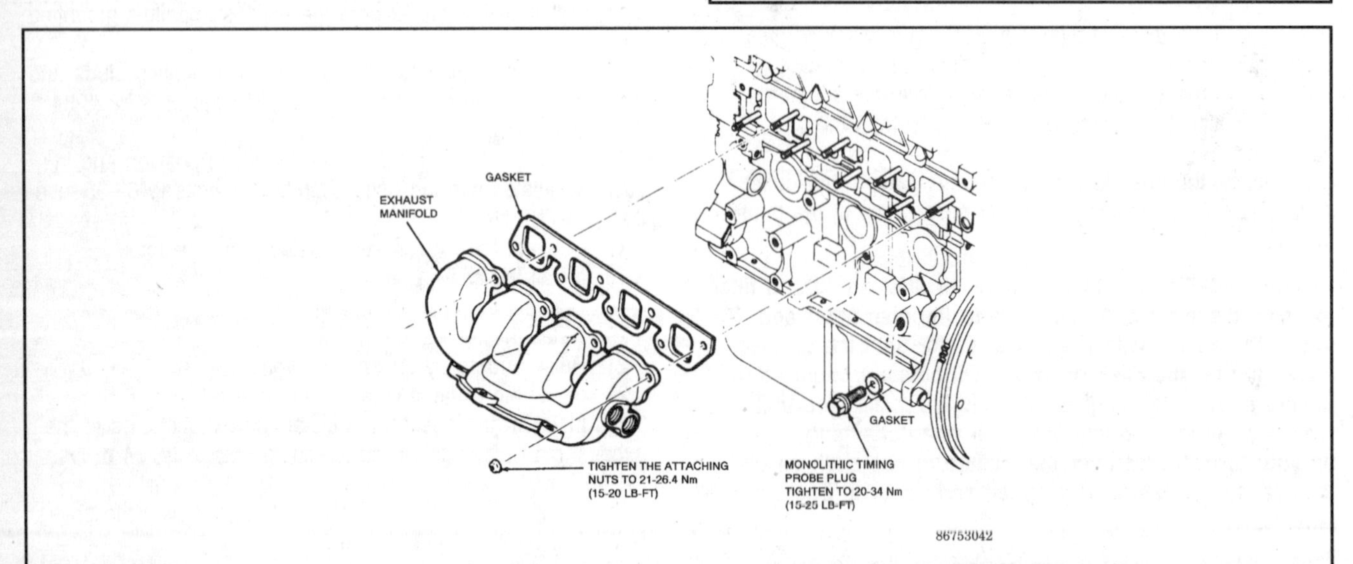

Fig. 64 Exploded view of intake manifold mounting and torque sequence — 1.6L and 1985-88 1.9L engine

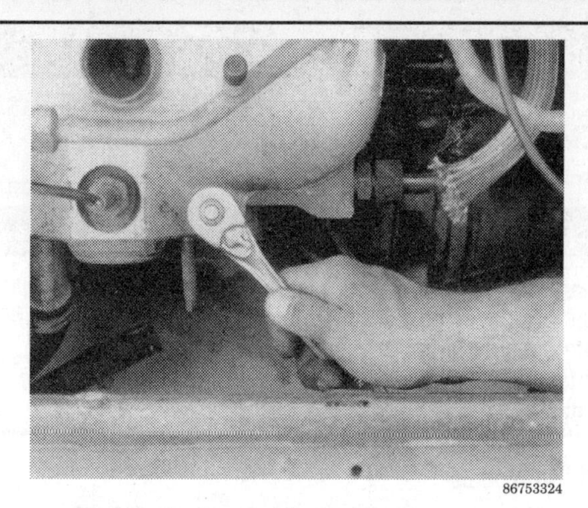
86753324

Fig. 67 Remove the A/C hose bracket to make room for heat shield removal — also shown is a ground strap removed in the same operation

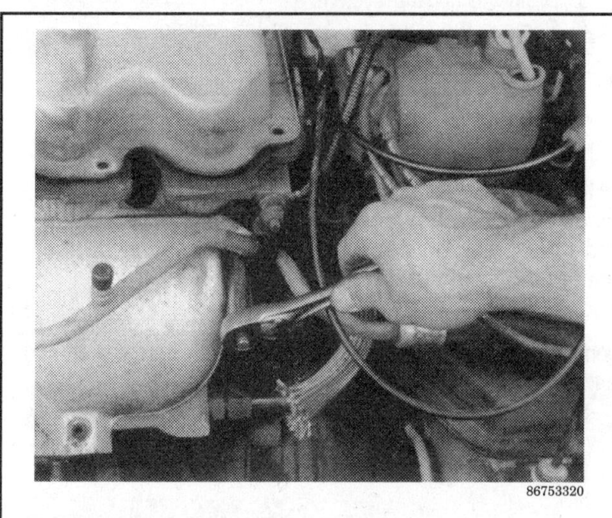
86753320

Fig. 68 Unbolt the exhaust manifold heat shield using the correct (metric) socket — 1988 CFI engine

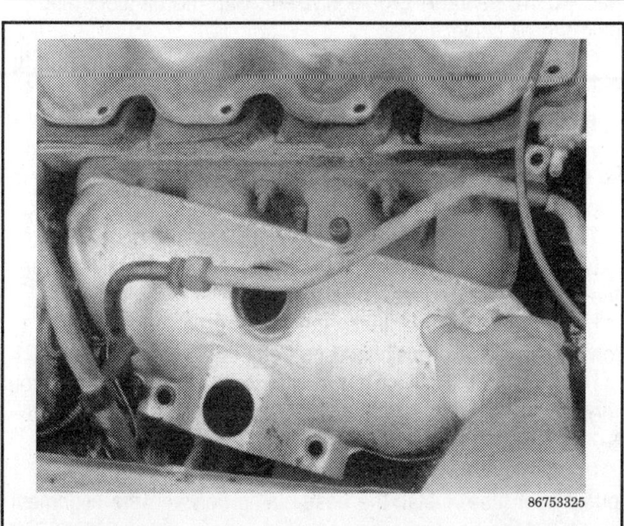
86753325

Fig. 69 After the oxygen sensor has been removed, the unbolted heat shield is clear for removal

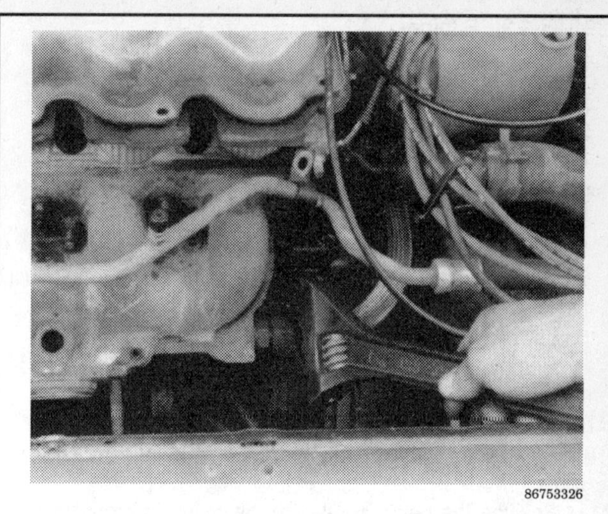
86753326

Fig. 70 Disconnect the EGR tube at the exhaust manifold

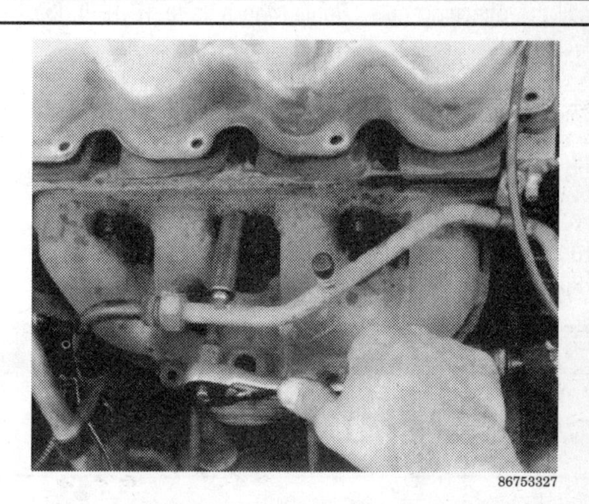
86753327

Fig. 71 Unbolt the manifold using a socket and extension — take care with heavily corroded fasteners. A shot of penetrating lube is a good idea

86753328

Fig. 72 Remove the exhaust manifold — if (unlike in the photo) the header pipe is still attached, pull the assembly out by carefully contorting the angled pipe

1991-95 1.9L Engine

1. Disconnect the negative battery cable.
2. Remove the accessory drive belt.
3. Remove the alternator.
4. Remove the radiator cooling fan and the shroud assembly.
5. Remove the exhaust manifold heat shield.
6. Raise and safely support the vehicle.
7. Remove the two catalytic converter inlet pipe-to-exhaust manifold attaching nuts.
8. Lower the vehicle.
9. Remove the eight exhaust manifold attaching nuts and remove the exhaust manifold and gasket.

To install:

10. Clean the cylinder head and exhaust manifold gasket surfaces.
11. Position the new gasket onto the manifold mounting studs.
12. Position the exhaust manifold on the cylinder head and install the attaching nuts. Tighten the nuts to 16-19 ft. lbs. (21-26 Nm).
13. Raise and safely support the vehicle.
14. Install the catalytic converter inlet pipe-to-exhaust manifold attaching nuts.
15. Lower the vehicle.
16. Install the exhaust manifold heat shield.
17. Install the radiator cooling fan and shroud assembly.
18. Install the alternator and the accessory drive belt.
19. Connect the negative battery cable.

Turbocharger

REMOVAL & INSTALLATION

1. Remove the turbocharger and exhaust manifold as an assembly.
2. Remove the four turbocharger retaining bolts and remove the turbocharger assembly. If the exhaust manifold is being replaced, remove the oxygen sensor.
3. Install the four turbocharger retaining bolts and tighten them to 16-19 ft. lbs. Ensure the mating surfaces on the exhaust manifold and the cylinder head are clean and free of gasket material. The exhaust manifold gasket has a top and a bottom to it, be sure to install it correctly.

To install:

4. Install the exhaust manifold and turbocharger assembly onto the cylinder head studs.

Radiator

REMOVAL & INSTALLATION

CAUTION

When draining the coolant, keep in mind that cats and dogs are attracted by ethylene glycol antifreeze, and are quite likely to drink any that is left in an uncovered container. Always drain the coolant into a sealable container.

1981-90 Models

See Figures 73, 74, 75, 76, 77, 78, 79, 80, 81, 82 and 83

1. Disconnect the negative battery cable.
2. Place fender covers on the aprons.
3. Drain the cooling system.
4. Remove the upper hose from the radiator.
5. Remove the cover (with printed instruction sheet) from the top of the radiator support, if equipped.
6. Remove the two fasteners retaining the upper end of the fan shroud to the radiator and sight shield.

If equipped with air conditioning, remove the nut and screw retaining the upper end of the fan shroud to the radiator at the cross support and nut and screw at the inlet end of the tank.

7. Disconnect the electric cooling fan motor wires and air conditioning discharge line (if A/C equipped) from the shroud and remove the fan shroud from the vehicle.
8. Loosen the hose clamp and disconnect the radiator lower hose from the radiator.
9. Disconnect the overflow hose from the radiator filler neck.
10. If equipped with an automatic transaxle, disconnect the oil cooler hoses at the transaxle using a line disconnect tool, part No. T82-9500-AH, or equivalent. Cap the oil tubes and plug the oil cooler hoses.
11. Remove the two nuts retaining the top of the radiator to the radiator support. If the stud loosens, make sure it is tightened before the radiator is installed. Tilt the top of the radiator rearward to allow clearance with the upper mounting stud and lift the radiator from the vehicle. Make sure the mounts do not stick to the radiator lower mounting brackets.

To install:

12. Make sure the lower radiator mounts are installed over the bolts on the radiator support.
13. Position the radiator to the support making sure the lower brackets are positioned properly on the lower mounts.
14. Position the top of the radiator to the mounting studs on the radiator support and install two retaining nuts. Tighten to 5-7 ft. lbs. (7-9 Nm).
15. Connect the radiator lower hose to the engine water pump inlet tube. Install the hose clamp between the alignment marks on the hose.
16. Check to make sure the lower radiator hose is properly positioned on the outlet tank and install the hose clamp. The

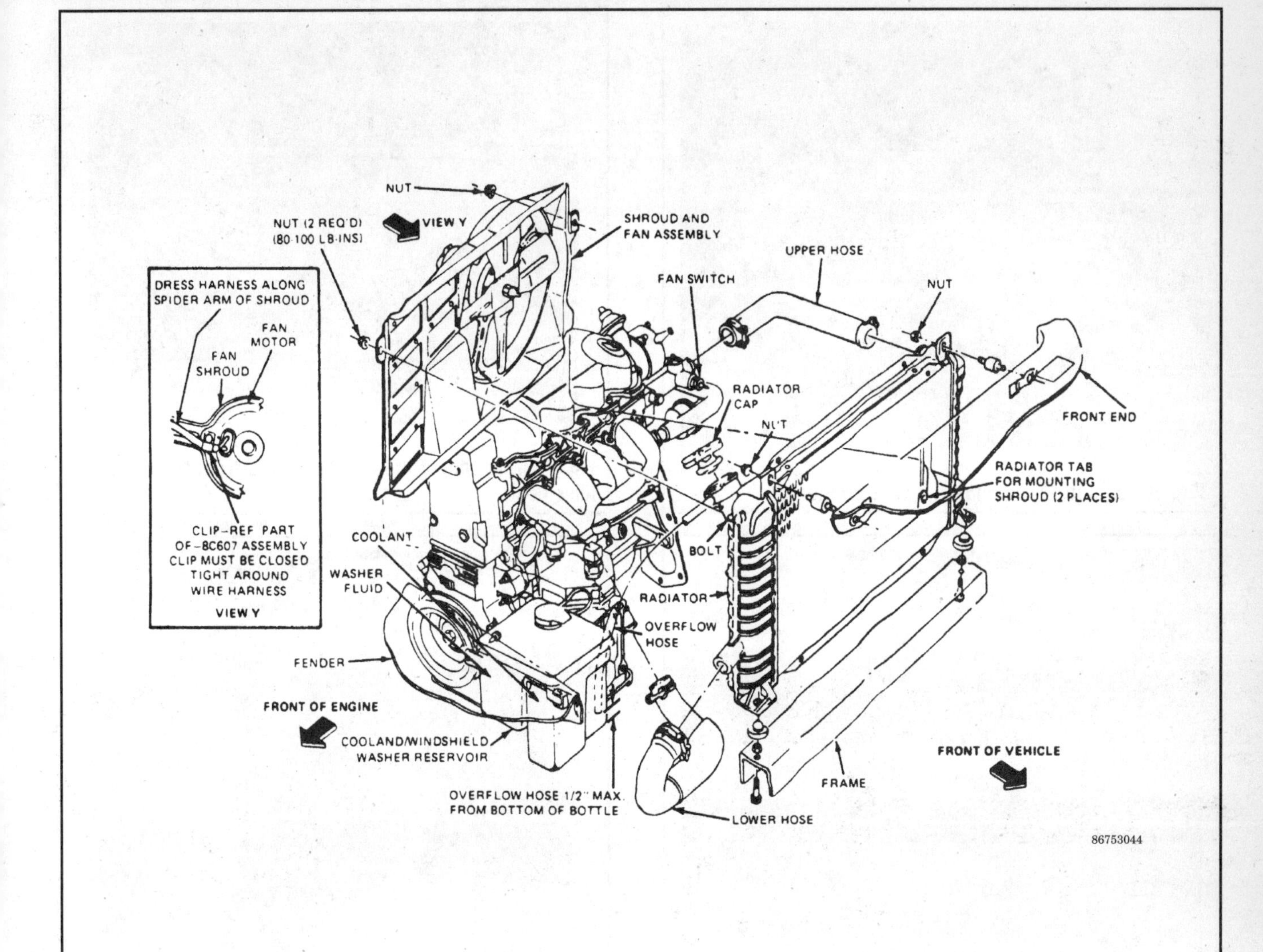

Fig. 73 Common cooling system components

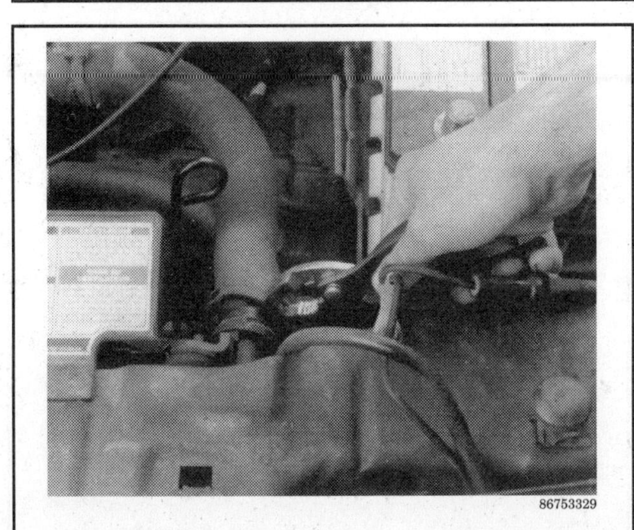

Fig. 74 Remove the clamp and then the upper hose from the radiator

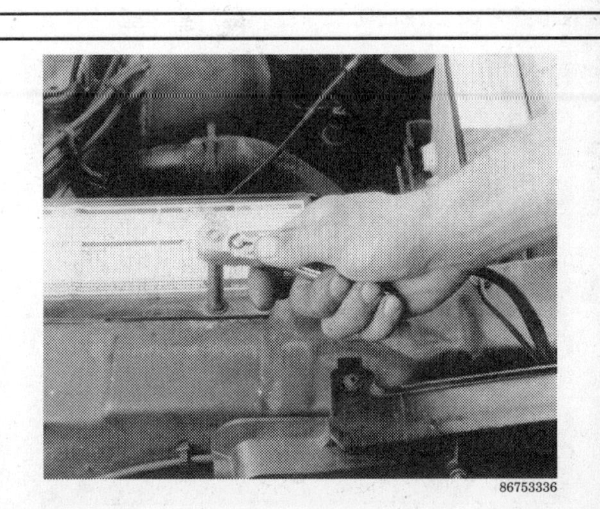

Fig. 75 Remove the cover from the radiator support to provide access to the cooling system components beneath

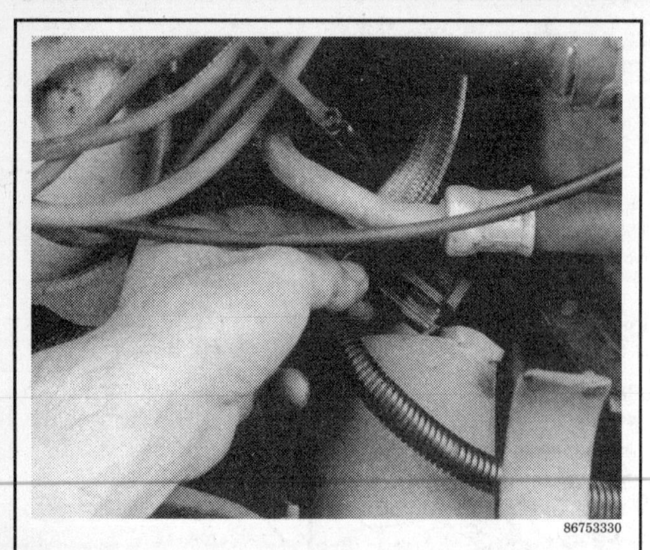
86753330

Fig. 76 Unplug the cooling fan wire connector

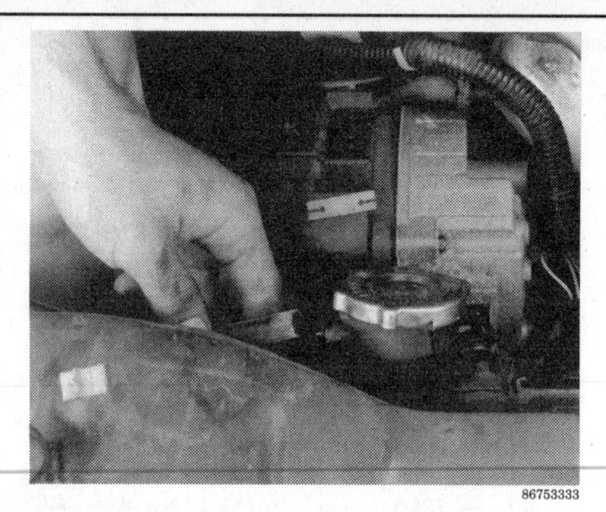
86753333

Fig. 79 Disconnect the overflow hose from the radiator filler neck

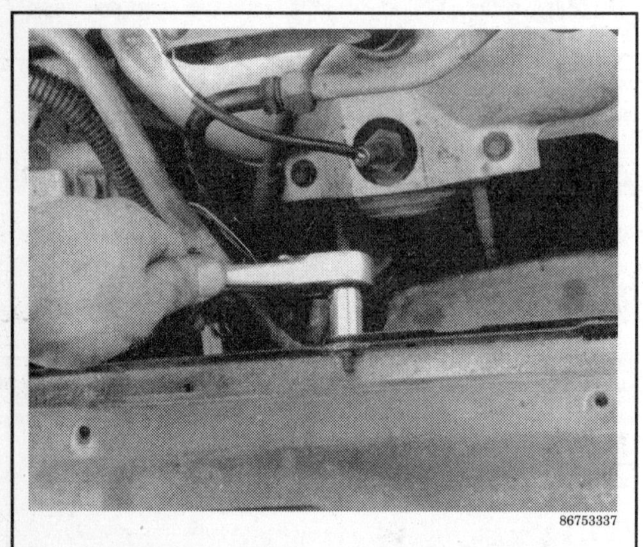
86753337

Fig. 77 Unbolt the radiator shroud from the radiator

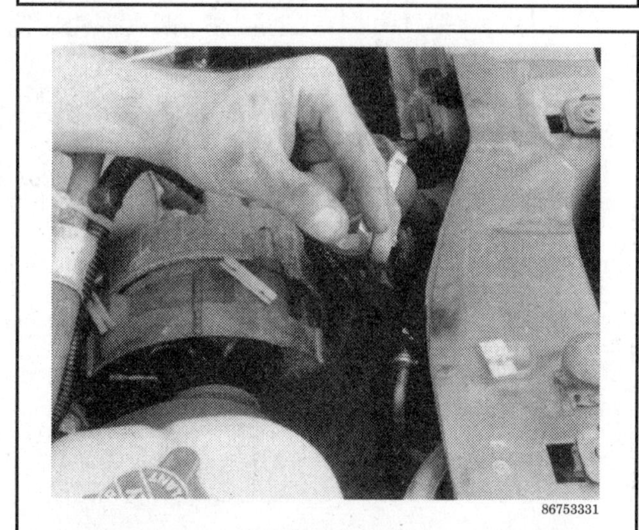
86753331

Fig. 80 If equipped with air conditioning, unscrew the coupling to the oil cooler line

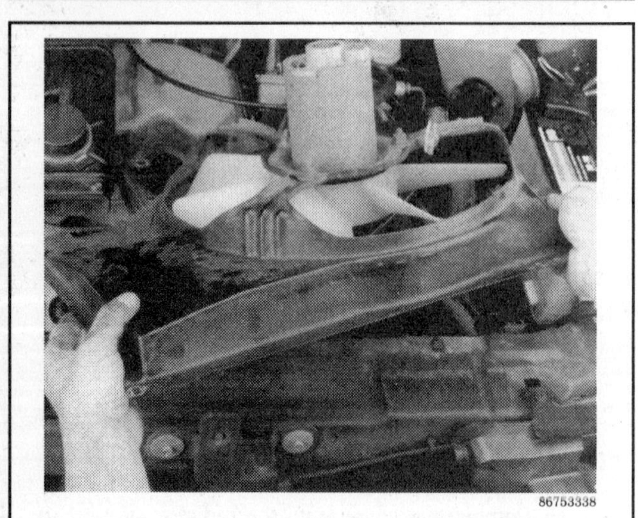
86753338

Fig. 78 Once free, remove the radiator shroud and cooling fan as an assembly, then position aside

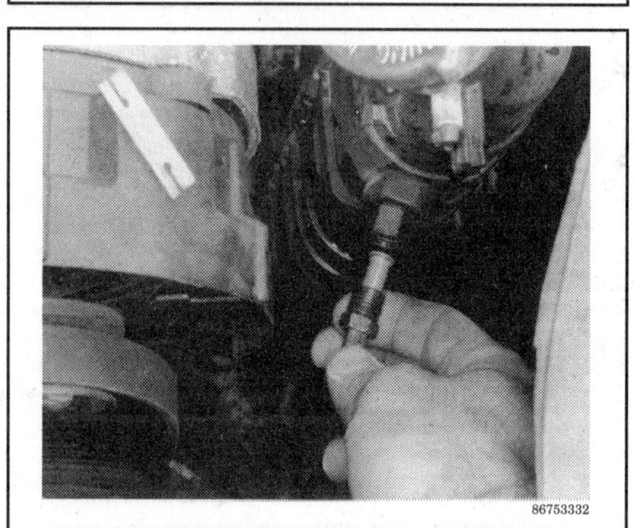
86753332

Fig. 81 When disconnected, pull the oil cooler line away from the radiator

Fig. 82 Remove the two nuts retaining the top of the radiator to the radiator support

Fig. 83 When completely free, carefully angle the radiator out from its mounting position

stripe on the lower hose should be indexed with the rib on the tank outlet.

17. Connect the oil cooler hoses to the automatic transaxle oil cooler lines, if equipped. Use an appropriate oil resistant sealer.

18. Position the fan shroud to the radiator lower mounting bosses. On vehicles with air conditioning, insert the lower edge of the shroud into the clip at the lower center of the radiator. Install the two nuts and bolts that retain the upper end of the fan shroud to the radiator. Tighten the nuts to 35-41 inch lbs. (4-5 Nm). Do not overtighten.

19. Connect the electric cooling fan motor wires to the wire harness.

20. Connect the upper hose to the radiator inlet tank fitting and install the constant tension hose clamp.

21. Connect the overflow hose to the nipple just below the radiator filler neck.

22. Install the air intake tube or sight shield.

23. Connect the negative battery cable.

24. Refill the cooling system. Start the engine and allow to come to normal operating temperature. Check for leaks. Confirm the operation of the electric cooling fan.

1991-95 models

See Figure 84

1. Disconnect the negative battery cable.
2. Place fender covers on the aprons.
3. Raise and safely support the vehicle. Drain the cooling system.
4. Remove the right side and front splash shields and remove the lower radiator hose.
5. If equipped with an automatic transaxle, remove the lower oil cooler line from the radiator. Remove the oil cooler line brackets from the bottom of the radiator.
6. Lower the vehicle.
7. If equipped with an automatic transaxle and air conditioning, remove the seal located between the radiator and the fan shroud.
8. If equipped with an automatic transaxle, remove the upper oil cooler line from the radiator.
9. If equipped with the 1.8L engine, remove the resonance duct from the radiator mounts.
10. Unplug the cooling fan motor electrical connector and the cooling fan thermoswitch electrical connector.
11. Remove the three fan shroud attaching bolts and remove the shroud assembly by pulling it straight up.
12. Remove the upper radiator hose and the two upper radiator mounts. Remove the radiator by lifting it straight up.

To install:

13. Make sure the radiator lower mounts are installed over the bolts on the radiator support.
14. Position the radiator to the support, making sure the lower brackets are positioned properly on the lower mounts.
15. Install the radiator upper mounts, making sure the locating pegs are positioned correctly. Install the upper radiator hose.
16. Lower the cooling fan shroud assembly into place and install the three shroud attaching bolts.
17. Connect the cooling fan motor electrical connector and thermoswitch electrical connector.

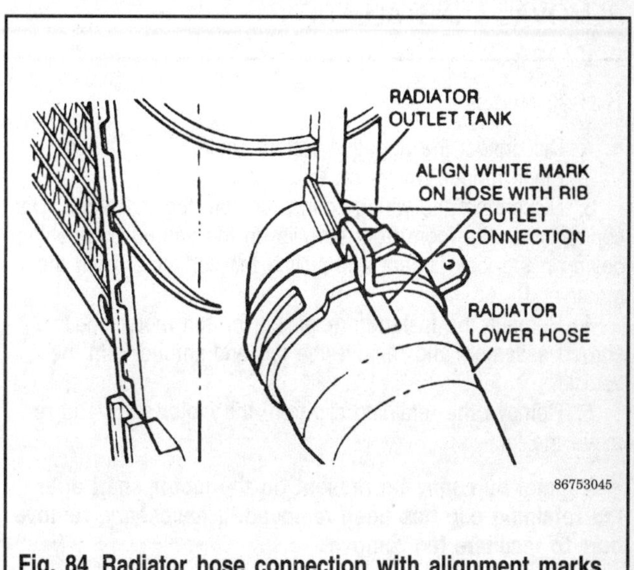

Fig. 84 Radiator hose connection with alignment marks

18. If equipped with the 1.8L engine, install the resonance duct on the radiator mounts.
19. Install the upper oil cooler line on the radiator.
20. If equipped with an automatic transaxle and air conditioning, install the seal between the radiator and fan shroud.
21. Raise and safely support the vehicle. Install the lower oil cooler line on the radiator.
22. Install the lower radiator hose and install the right side and front splash shields.
23. Lower the vehicle and fill the cooling system.
24. Connect the negative battery cable, start the engine and check for coolant leaks.

Electrical Cooling Fan

The electro-drive cooling fan system consists of a fan and electric motor attached to a fan shroud located behind the radiator. The system utilizes a coolant temperature switch which is usually mounted in the thermostat housing. Vehicles that are equipped with air conditioning, have a cooling fan controller and a cooling fan relay for the system. On vehicles with a standard heater, the engine cooling fan is powered through the cooling fan relay.

The electro-drive cooling fan is wired to operate only when the ignition switch is in the **RUN** position. A thermal switch mounted in the thermostat housing activates the fan when the coolant reaches a specified temperature. When the temperature is approximately 210°F (85°C), the thermal switch closes thus starting the fan.

The electric fan also operates when the air conditioner (if equipped) is turned on. When the temperature drops to between 185-193°F (85-90°C) the thermal switch opens and the fan shuts off.

CAUTION

Since the fan is governed by temperature the engine does not have to be ON for the fan to operate, disconnect the wiring harness to the fan when performing any under-hood operations on or near the cooling fan assembly.

REMOVAL & INSTALLATION

1981-90 Models

1. Disconnect the negative battery cable.
2. Place fender covers on the aprons.
3. Disconnect the wiring connector from the fan motor. Disconnect the wire loom from the clip on the shroud by pushing down on the lock fingers and pulling the connector from the motor end.
4. Remove the fasteners retaining the fan motor and shroud assembly and remove the fan and shroud from the vehicle.
5. Remove the retaining clip from the motor shaft and remove the fan.

➡A metal burr may be present on the motor shaft after the retaining clip has been removed. If necessary, remove burr to facilitate fan removal.

6. Unbolt and withdraw the fan motor from the shroud.

To install:

7. Install the fan motor in position in the fan shroud. Install the retaining nuts and washers or screws and tighten to 44-66 inch lbs. (5-8 Nm).
8. Position the fan assembly on the motor shaft and install the retaining clip.
9. Position the fan, motor and shroud as an assembly in the vehicle. Install the retaining nuts or screws and tighten nuts to 35-41 inch lbs. (4-5 Nm) and screws to 23-33 inch lbs. (3-4 Nm).
10. Install the fan motor wire loom in the clip provided on the fan shroud. Connect the wiring connector to the fan motor. Be sure the lock fingers on the connector snap firmly into place.
11. Reconnect the battery cable.
12. Check the fan for proper operation.

1991-95 Models

1. Disconnect the negative battery cable.
2. Place fender covers on the aprons.
3. On 1.8L engine equipped vehicles, remove the resonance duct from the radiator mounts.
4. Disconnect the cooling fan motor electrical connector.
5. Remove the three shroud attaching bolts and remove the cooling fan shroud assembly by pulling it straight up.
6. Working on a bench, remove the cooling fan retainer clip. Remove the cooling fan from the motor shaft.
7. Unclip the cooling fan motor electrical harness retainers and remove the harness from the retainers.
8. Remove the cooling fan motor attaching screws and remove the cooling fan motor from the shroud assembly.

To install:

9. Place the cooling fan motor in the shroud assembly and install the attaching screws.
10. Position the cooling fan motor electrical harness in the harness retainers and clip the retainers shut.
11. Install the cooling fan on the cooling motor shaft and install the retainer clip.
12. Carefully lower the cooling fan shroud assembly into place and install the attaching bolts. Connect the cooling fan motor electrical connector.
13. If equipped with 1.8L engine, install the resonance duct on the radiator mounts.
14. Connect the negative battery cable.
15. Check the fan for proper operation.

TESTING

1981-90 Models

1. Check the fuse or circuit breaker for power to the cooling fan motor.
2. Remove the connector(s) at the cooling fan motor(s). Connect a jumper wire and apply battery voltage to the positive terminal of the cooling fan motor.

3. Using an ohmmeter, check for continuity in the cooling fan motor.

➡**Remove the cooling fan connector at the fan motor before performing continuity checks. Check continuity of the motor windings only. The cooling fan control circuit is connected electrically to the ECM through the cooling fan relay center. Ohmmeter battery voltage must not be applied to the ECM.**

4. Ensure proper continuity of the cooling fan motor ground circuit at the chassis ground connector.

1991-95 Models

1. Make sure the ignition key is **OFF**.
2. Apply 12 volts to the yellow wire at the cooling fan motor on all except 1.8L vehicles equipped with 4EAT automatic transaxle and 1.9L vehicles equipped with air conditioning. Replace the motor if it does not run.
3. On 1.8L vehicles equipped with 4EAT automatic transaxle or 1.9L vehicles equipped with air conditioning, apply 12 volts to the blue wire on the 1.8L engine or the light green/yellow wire on the 1.9L engine at the cooling fan motor. Replace the motor if it does not run.

RELAY LOCATIONS

Air Conditioning Fan Controller — located on the right side of the dash, forward of the evaporator mounting bracket, behind the glove box.

Cooling Fan Relay — located on the left hand side of the instrument panel or could be incorporated in the air conditioning fan controller unit.

Water Pump

REMOVAL & INSTALLATION

✱✱CAUTION

When draining the coolant, keep in mind that cats and dogs are attracted by ethylene glycol antifreeze, and are quite likely to drink any that is left in an uncovered container or in puddles on the ground. This will prove fatal in sufficient quantity. Always drain the coolant into a sealable container.

1981-85 1.6L and 1985-90 1.9L Engines

➧ See Figures 86, 85 and 87

1. Disconnect the negative battery cable. Place fender covers on the aprons. Drain the cooling system.
2. Remove the alternator drive belt. If equipped with air conditioning or power steering, remove the drive belts.
3. Use a wrench on the crankshaft pulley to rotate the engine so No. 1 piston is on TDC of the compression stroke.

➡**Turn the engine only in the direction of normal rotation. Backward rotation will cause the timing belt to slip or lose teeth.**

4. Remove the timing belt cover.
5. Loosen the belt tensioner attaching bolts, then secure the tensioner over as far as possible.
6. Pull the belt from the camshaft, tensioner, and water pump sprocket. Do not remove it from, or allow it to change its position on, the crankshaft sprocket.

✱✱WARNING

Do not rotate the engine with the timing belt removed or serious engine damage could occur. The 1.6L engines and diesel engines are of the "interference type," meaning it is possible for the valves to contact the pistons if their reciprocation is not carefully timed and controlled. An engine allowed to spin freely without the timing belt could bend valves and scuff pistons almost instantly.

7. Remove the camshaft sprocket.
8. Remove the rear timing cover stud. Remove the heater return tube hose connection at the water pump inlet tube.
9. Remove the water pump inlet tube fasteners and the inlet tube and gasket.
10. Remove the water pump to the cylinder block bolts and remove the water pump and its gasket.

To install:

11. To install, make sure the mating surfaces on the pump and the block are clean.
12. Using a new gasket and sealer, install the water pump and tighten the bolts on 1981-87 models, tighten to 30-40 ft. lbs. (40-55 Nm). Make sure the pump impeller is able to turn freely.
13. Install the water pump inlet tube and the inlet tube gasket and fasteners.
14. Install the rear timing cover stud. Install the heater return tube hose connection at the water pump inlet tube.
15. Install the camshaft sprocket.
16. Install the belt from the camshaft, timing belt tensioner, and water pump sprocket.

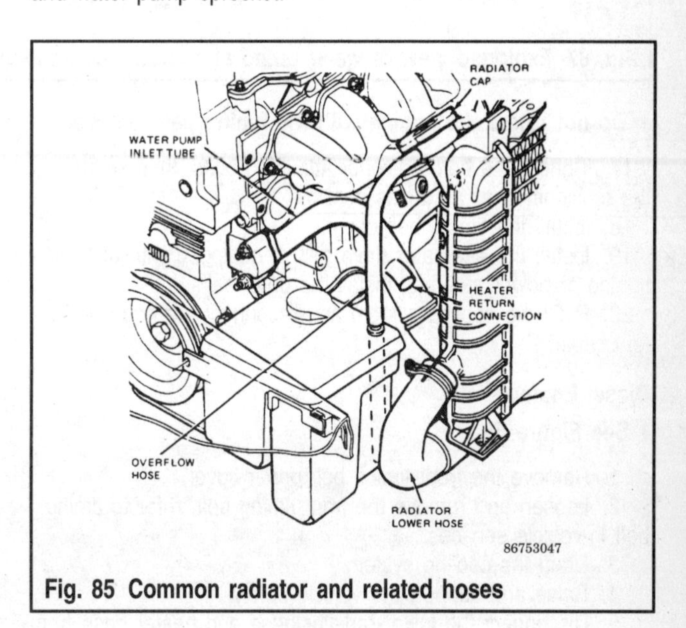

Fig. 85 Common radiator and related hoses

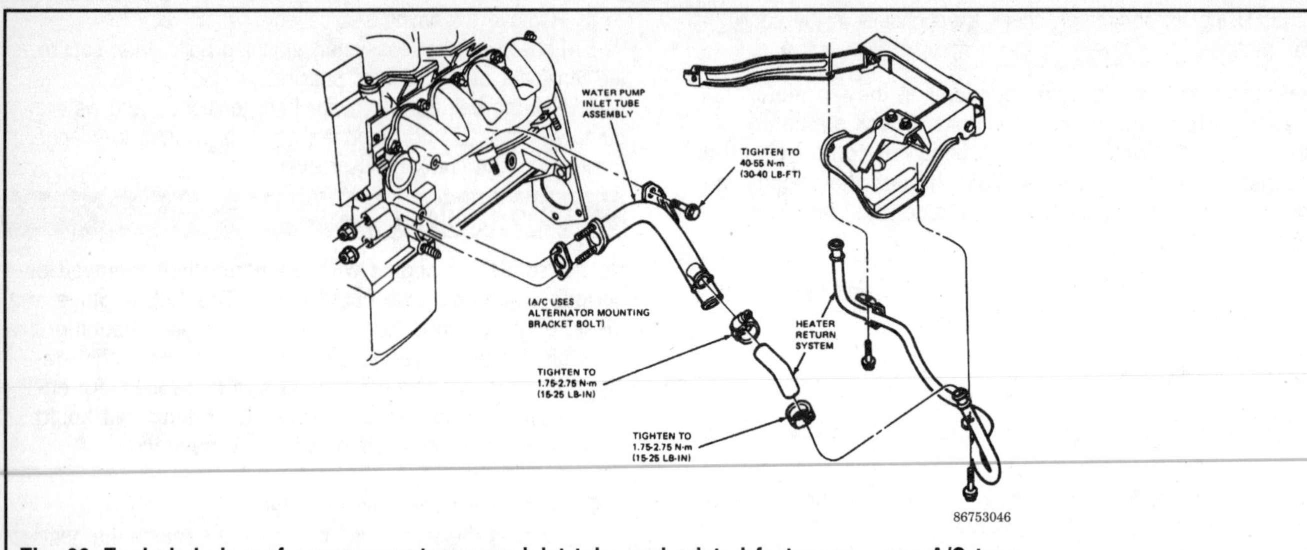

Fig. 86 Exploded view of common water pump inlet tube and related fasteners — non-A/C type

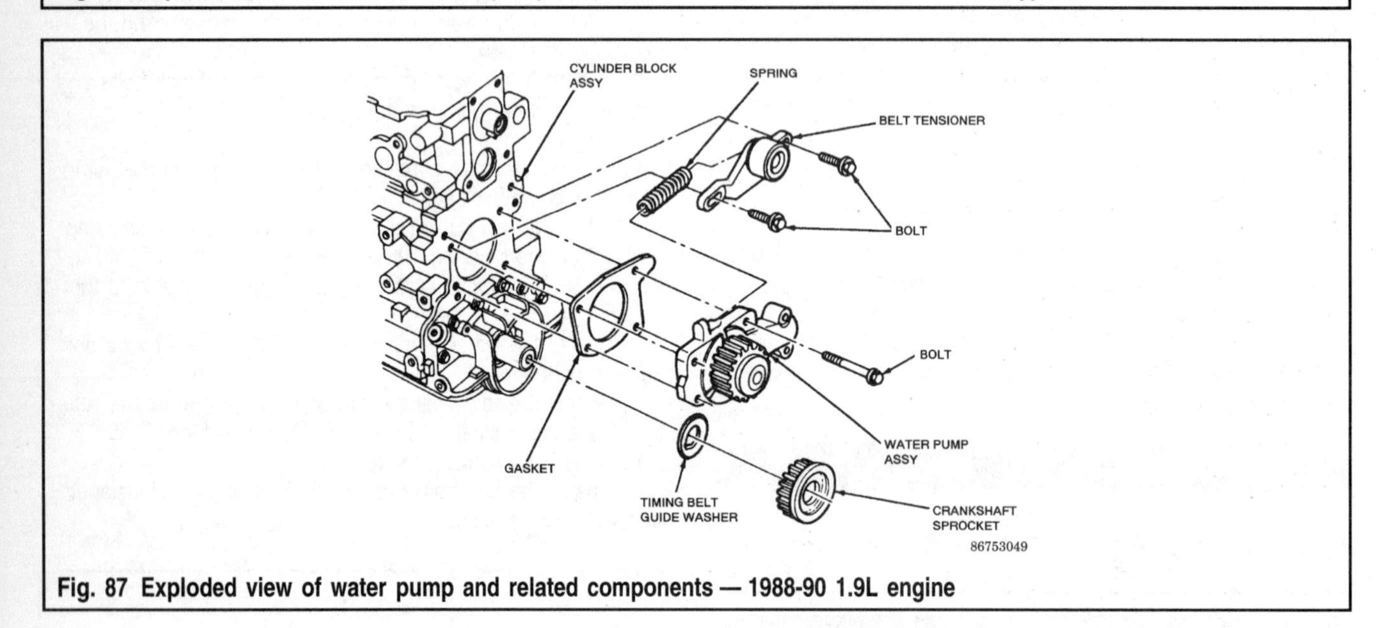

Fig. 87 Exploded view of water pump and related components — 1988-90 1.9L engine

➡Do not rotate the engine with the timing belt removed.

17. Tighten the belt tensioner attaching bolts, then secure the tensioner over as far as possible.
18. Install the timing belt cover.
19. Install the alternator drive belt. If equipped with air conditioning or power steering, install the drive belts.
20. Refill the cooling system and reconnect the negative battery cable.

Diesel Engine

➧ See Figure 88

1. Remove the front timing belt upper cover.
2. Loosen and remove the front timing belt, refer to timing belt in-vehicle services.
3. Drain the cooling system.
4. Raise and support the vehicle safely.
5. Disconnect the lower radiator hose and heater hose from the water pump.
6. Disconnect the coolant tube from the thermostat housing and discard gasket.
7. Remove the three bolts attaching the water pump to the crankcase. Remove the water pump. Discard gasket.

To install:

8. Clean the water pump and crankshaft gasket mating surfaces.
9. Install the water pump, using a new gasket. Tighten bolts to 23-34 ft. lbs. (31-46 Nm).
10. Connect the coolant tube from the thermostat housing to the water pump using a new gasket. Tighten bolts to 5-7 ft. lbs. (7-10 Nm).
11. Connect the heater hose and lower radiator hose to the water pump.
12. Lower the vehicle.
13. Fill and bleed the cooling system.
14. Adjust the front timing belt.
15. Run the engine and check for coolant leaks.
16. Install the front timing belt upper cover.

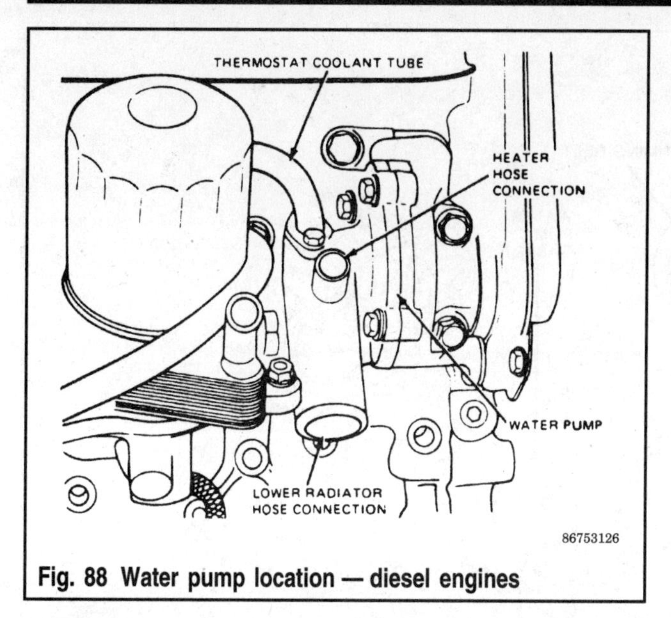

Fig. 88 Water pump location — diesel engines

1.8L Engine

➧ See Figure 89

1. Disconnect the negative battery cable.
2. Drain the cooling system.
3. Remove the timing belt.
4. Raise and safely support the vehicle.
5. Remove the engine oil dipstick tube bracket bolt(s) from the water pump.
6. Remove the two bolts and the gasket from the water inlet pipe.
7. Remove all but the uppermost water pump mounting bolt.
8. Lower the vehicle.
9. Remove the remaining bolts and the water pump assembly.
10. If the water pump is being reused, remove all gasket material from the water pump. Remove all gasket material from the engine block.

To install:

11. Install a new gasket onto the water pump.
12. Place the water pump into its mounting position, then install the uppermost bolt.
13. Raise and safely support the vehicle.
14. Install the remaining water pump mounting bolts and tighten all bolts to 14-19 ft. lbs. (19-25 Nm).
15. Install a new gasket onto the water inlet pipe.
16. Install the two bolts from the water inlet pipe to the water pump and tighten to 14-19 ft. lbs. (19-25 Nm).
17. Install the bolt to the engine oil dipstick tube bracket.
18. Lower the vehicle.
19. Install the timing belt.
20. Fill the cooling system.
21. Connect the negative battery cable.
22. Start the engine and allow it to reach operating temperature. Check for coolant leaks. Check the coolant level and add coolant, as necessary.

1991-95 1.9L Engine

➧ See Figure 90

1. Disconnect the negative battery cable.
2. Drain the cooling system.
3. Remove the accessory drive belt and its automatic tensioner.
4. Remove the timing belt cover and the timing belt.
5. Raise and safely support the vehicle.
6. Remove the lower radiator hose and remove the heater hose from the water pump.
7. Lower the vehicle.
8. Support the engine with a suitable floor jack.
9. Remove the right engine mount attaching bolts and roll the engine mount aside.
10. Remove the water pump attaching bolts.
11. Using the floor jack, raise the engine enough to provide clearance for removing the water pump.
12. Remove the water pump and the gasket from the engine through the top of the engine compartment.

To install:

13. Make sure the mating surfaces of the cylinder block and water pump are clean and free of gasket material.
14. If the water pump is to be replaced, transfer the timing belt tensioner components to the new water pump.
15. With the engine supported and raised with a suitable floor jack, place the water pump and the gasket on the cylinder block and install the four attaching bolts. Tighten the bolts to 15-22 ft. lbs. (20-30 Nm).
16. Install the timing belt and cover.
17. Roll the engine mount into position and install the mount bolts. Remove the floor jack.
18. Raise and safely support the vehicle.
19. Install the lower radiator hose and install the heater hose on the pump.
20. Install the crankshaft dampener and the splash shield.
21. Lower the vehicle.
22. Install the drive belt automatic tensioner and the accessory drive belt.
23. Connect the negative battery cable.
24. Refill the cooling system.
25. Start the engine and allow to reach normal operating temperature. Check for coolant leaks. Check the coolant level and add as necessary.

Cylinder Head

REMOVAL & INSTALLATION

✻✻WARNING

To reduce the possibility of cylinder head warpage and/or distortion, do not remove the cylinder head while the engine is warm. Always, allow the engine to cool entirely before disassembly.

1981-90 Engines

➧ See Figures 91, 92, 93, 94, 95, 96 and 97

1. Disconnect the negative battery cable.
2. Drain the cooling system, disconnect the heater hose under the intake manifold, and disconnect the upper radiator hose at the cylinder head.

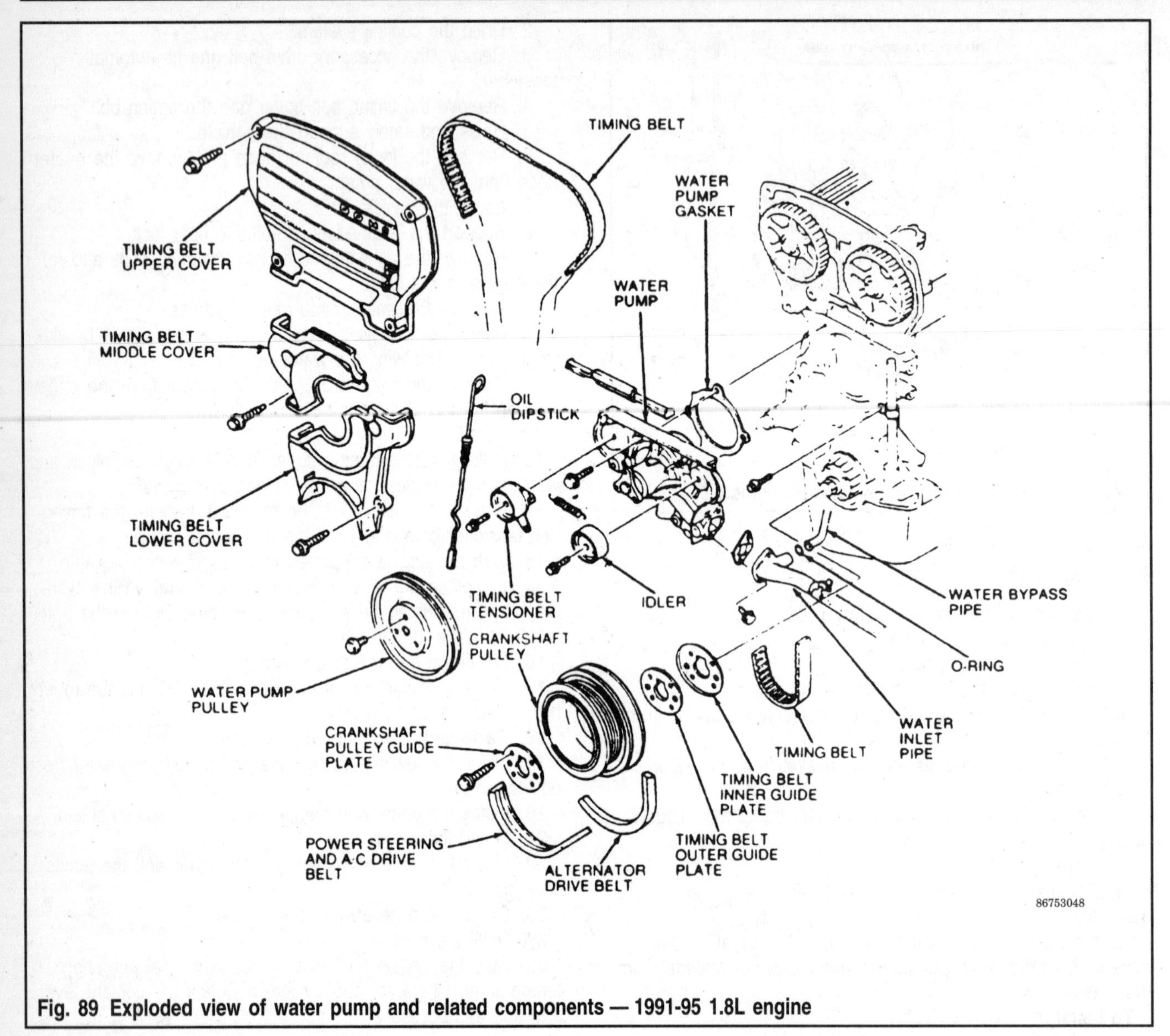

Fig. 89 Exploded view of water pump and related components — 1991-95 1.8L engine

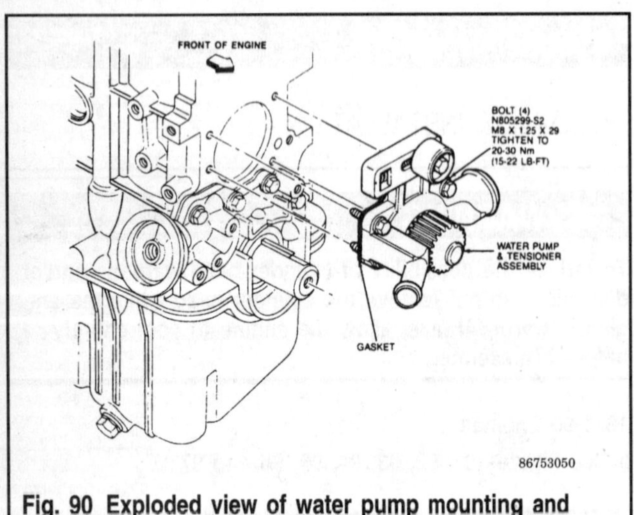

Fig. 90 Exploded view of water pump mounting and torque figures for attaching hardware — 1991-95 1.9L engine

3. Disconnect the wiring from the cooling fan switch, remove the air cleaner assembly, remove the PCV hose, and disconnect all interfering vacuum hoses after marking them for reassembly.

4. Remove the rocker arm cover and disconnect all accessory drive belts. Remove the crankshaft pulley. Remove the timing belt cover.

5. Set the No.1 cylinder to the top dead center compression stroke. (See distributor removal and installation procedure for details.)

6. Remove the distributor cap and spark plug wires as an assembly.

7. Loosen both belt tensioner attaching bolts using special Ford tool T81P-6254-A or the equivalent. Secure the belt tensioner as far left as possible. Remove the timing belt and discard.

➡Once the tension on the timing belt has been released, the belt cannot be used again.

8. For 1.6L engines: disconnect the tube at the EGR valve, then remove the PVS hose connectors using tool T81P-8564-A or equivalent. Label the connectors and set aside.

9. Disconnect the choke wire, the fuel supply and return lines, the accelerator cable and speed control cable (if equipped). Disconnect the altitude compensator, if equipped, from the dash panel and place on the heater/air conditioner air intake.

WARNING

Exercise care not to damage the compensator.

10. Remove the alternator and its bracket.

11. If equipped with power steering, remove the thermactor pump drive belt, the pump and its bracket. If equipped with a turbocharger, refer to the previous section for removal procedure. Refer to Section 5 for pressure relieving and removal instructions.

12. Raise the vehicle and disconnect the exhaust pipe from the manifold.

13. Lower the vehicle and remove the cylinder head bolts and washers. Discard the bolts, they cannot be used again.

14. Remove the cylinder head with the manifolds attached. Remove and discard the head gasket. Do not place the cylinder head with combustion chambers down or damage to the spark plugs or gasket surfaces may result.

To install:

15. Clean all gasket material from the mating surfaces of the block and cylinder head, then rotate the crankshaft so that the No.1 piston is 90° BTDC. In this position, the crankshaft pulley keyway will be at 9 o'clock.

16. Turn the camshaft so its keyway is at 6 o'clock. When installing the timing belt, turn the crankshaft keyway back to 12 o'clock but do not turn the camshaft from its 6 o'clock position. The crankshaft is turned 90° BTDC to prevent the valves from hitting the pistons when the cylinder head is installed.

➡To ensure proper squish height upon reassembly, no cylinder block deck machining or use of a replacement crankshaft, piston or connecting rod that causes the squish height to be over or under specification, is permitted. If only the head gasket is replaced, the squish height should be within specification. If parts other than the head gasket are replaced, check the squish height. If the squish height is out of specification, replace the parts again and recheck the squish height.

17. Position the cylinder head gasket on the block and install the cylinder head using new bolts and washers. Tighten the bolts to 44 ft. lbs. in the sequence shown, then back off two turns and retighten to 44 ft. lbs. After tightening, turn the bolts an additional 90° in the same sequence. Complete the bolt tightening by turning an additional 90° in the same sequence. Always use new head bolts when reinstalling the cylinder head.

WARNING

The camshaft and crankshaft must not be turned until the timing gears and belt are installed. If the camshaft or crankshaft rotate before the timing belt is in place, severe piston and valve damage could occur.

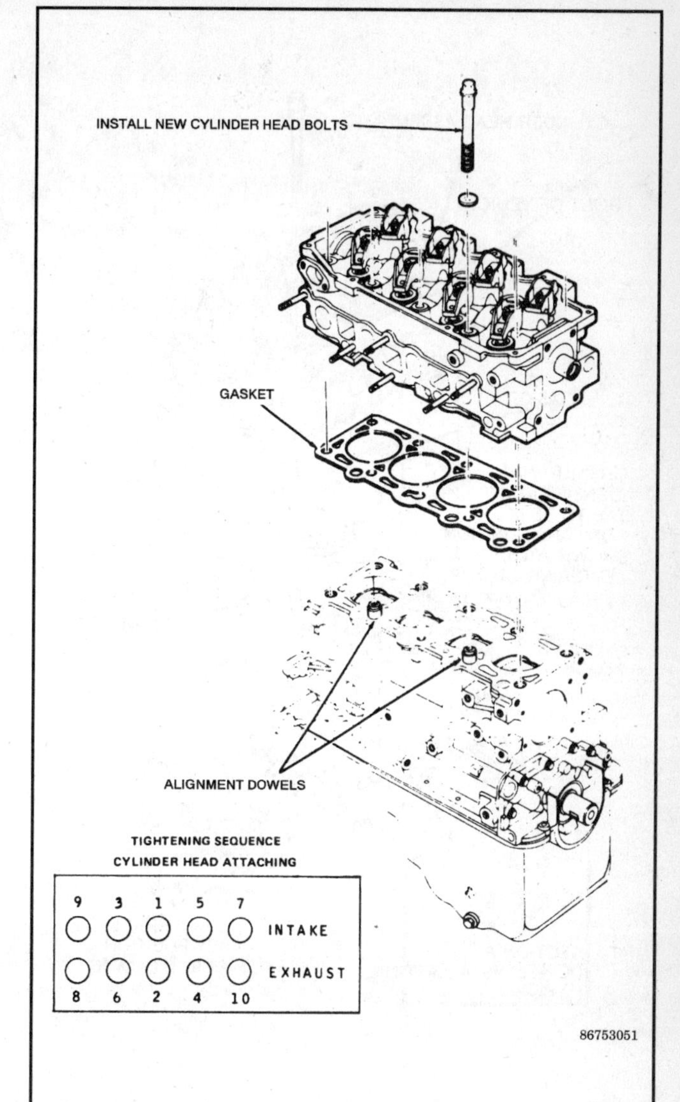

Fig. 91 Exploded view of cylinder head mounting and torque sequence — 1.6L engines

18. Raise the vehicle and safely support it on jackstands.

19. Connect the exhaust system at the exhaust pipe.

20. Install the thermacter pump mounting bracket, pump and drive belt (if removed). Apply Loctite® or equivalent to the attaching bolts.

21. Install the alternator bracket, the alternator and connect the wiring harness and alternator air intake tube.

22. Connect the altitude compensator (if equipped).

23. Connect the accelerator cable and, if equipped, the speed control cable.

24. Connect the fuel supply and return lines at the metal connector, located on the right side of the engine.

25. Connect the choke cap.

26. Connect the EGR tube to the EGR valve.

27. Install the timing belt and timing belt cover.

28. Install the crankshaft pulley.

29. Replace the distributor cap and spark plug wires.

30. Make sure the mating surfaces of the cylinder head and rocker arm cover are clean and free of material. Apply a $^{3}/_{16}$ (4.75mm) bead of sealer D6AZ-19562-B or equivalent to the rocker arm cover flange.

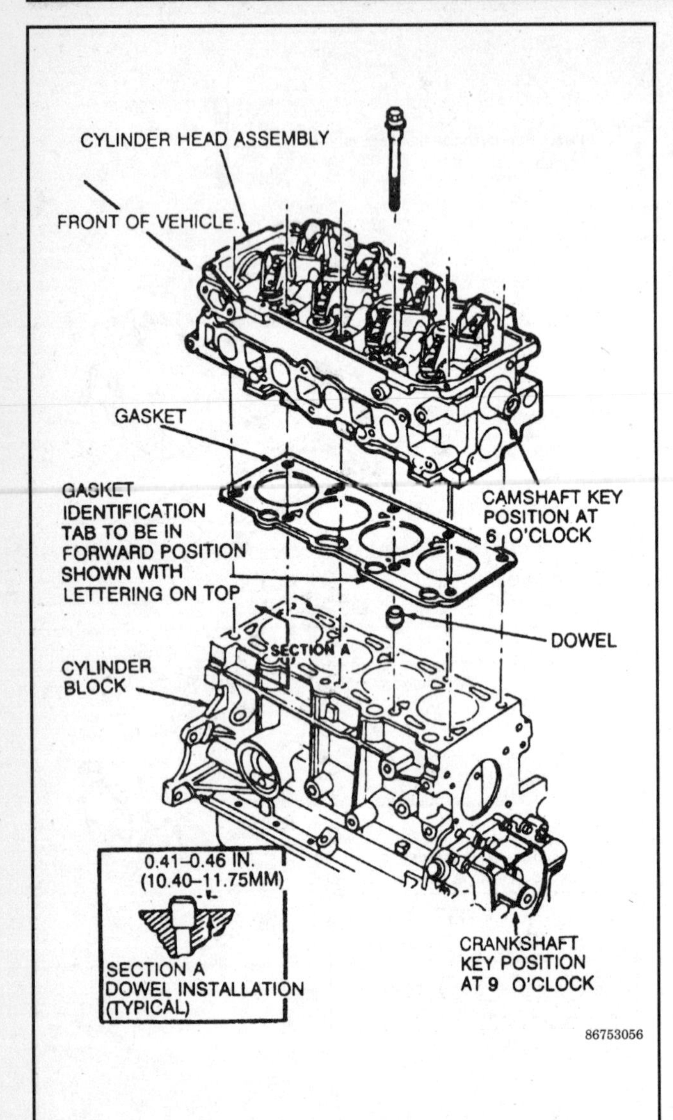

Fig. 92 Exploded view of cylinder head mounting and related components — 1985-87 1.9L engines

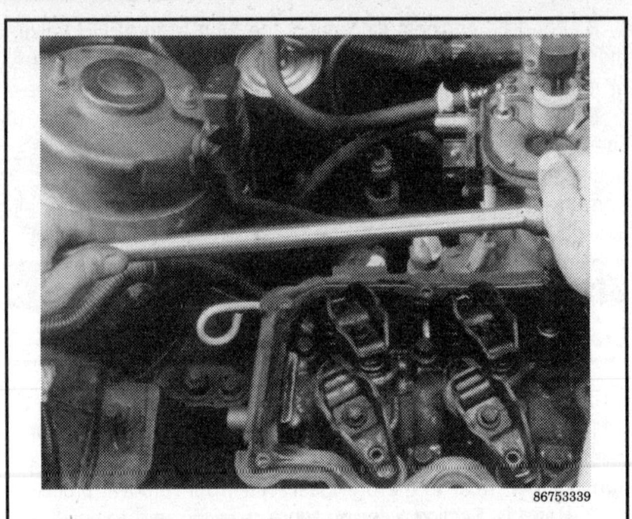

Fig. 94 Remove the cylinder head bolts and washers — 1988 1.9L engine shown

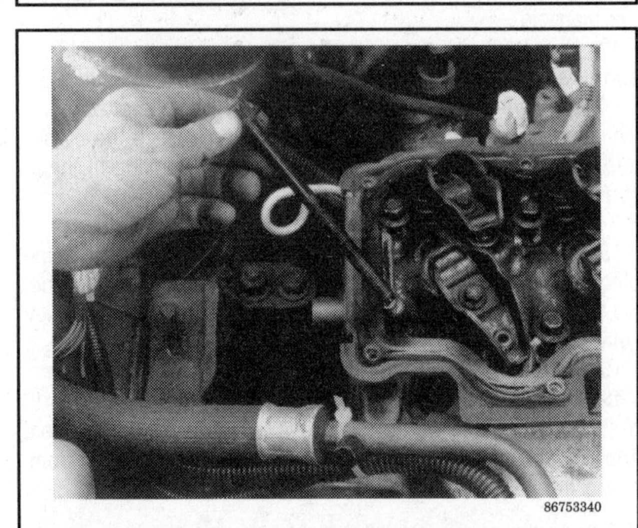

Fig. 95 As you untighten them, pull out the long cylinder head bolts and discard them

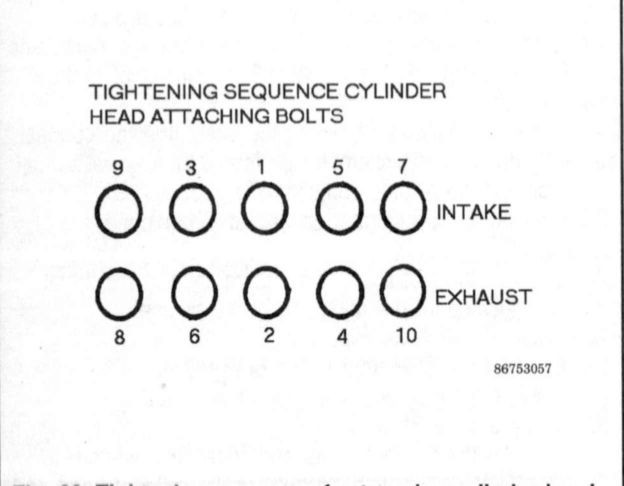

Fig. 93 Tightening sequence for torquing cylinder head bolts — 1985-87 1.9L engines

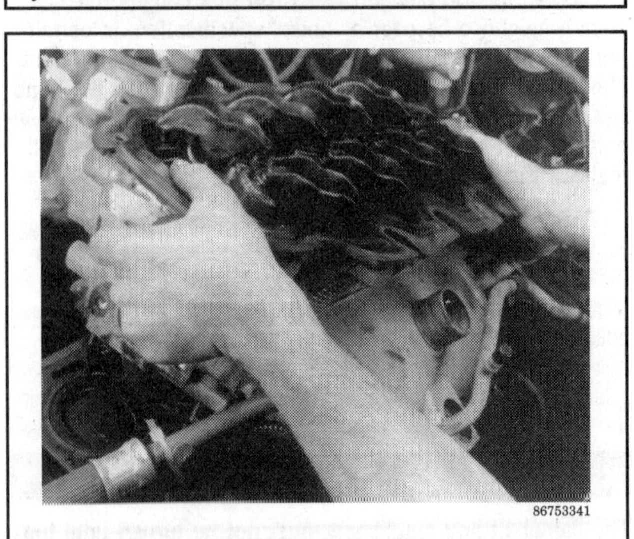

Fig. 96 Remove the cylinder head and attached manifolds — 1988 1.9L engine shown

Fig. 97 A torque wrench is essential to properly tightening the cylinder head bolts

31. Position the rocker arm cover on the cylinder head and install the attaching bolts. Tighten the attaching bolts to 6-8 ft. lbs. (8-11 Nm).
32. Attach all vacuum hoses that were removed. Plug in the wiring terminal to the cooling fan switch.
33. Connect the upper radiator hose at the cylinder head.
34. Connect the heater hose to the fitting located below the intake manifold.
35. Fill the cooling system with an approved coolant.
36. Connect the negative ground cable.
37. Start the engine and check for vacuum, coolant and oil leaks. After the engine has reached operating temperature, carefully check the coolant level and add coolant, if necessary.
38. Adjust the ignition timing and connect the distributor line.
39. Install the PCV hose. Install the air cleaner assembly. Remove the protective aprons. Close the hood.

Diesel Engines

See Figures 98, 99, 100, 101 and 102

1. Disconnect the negative battery cable.
2. Place fender covers on the aprons.
3. Drain the cooling system.
4. Remove the rocker arm cover, front and rear timing belt covers. Loosen the front and rear timing belts.
5. Raise the vehicle and support it safely.
6. Disconnect the muffler inlet pipe at the exhaust manifold. Lower the vehicle.
7. Disconnect the air inlet duct at the air cleaner and intake manifold. Plug the opening.
8. Unplug the electrical connectors and vacuum hoses to the temperature sensors located in the thermostat housing.
9. Disconnect the upper and lower coolant hoses, and the upper radiator hose at the thermostat housing.
10. Disconnect and remove the injection lines at the injection pump and nozzles. Cap all lines and fittings.
11. Disconnect the glow plug harness from the main engine harness.
12. Remove the cylinder head bolts in the reverse of the tightening sequence shown. Remove the cylinder head.
13. Remove the glow plugs. Then, remove the pre-chamber cups from the cylinder head using a brass drift.

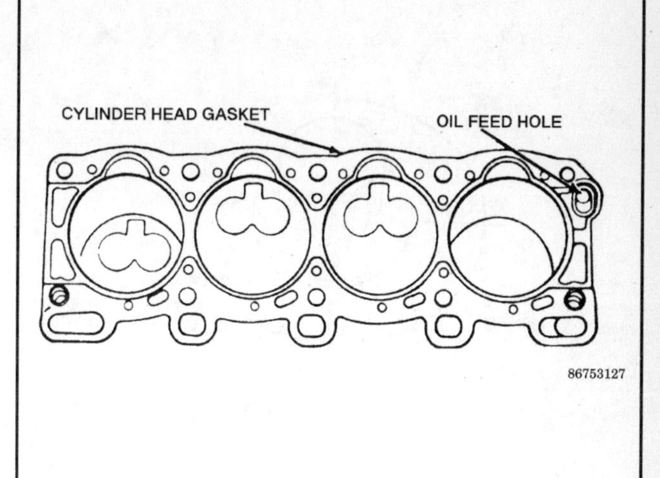

Fig. 98 Install the cylinder head gasket as shown — diesel engines

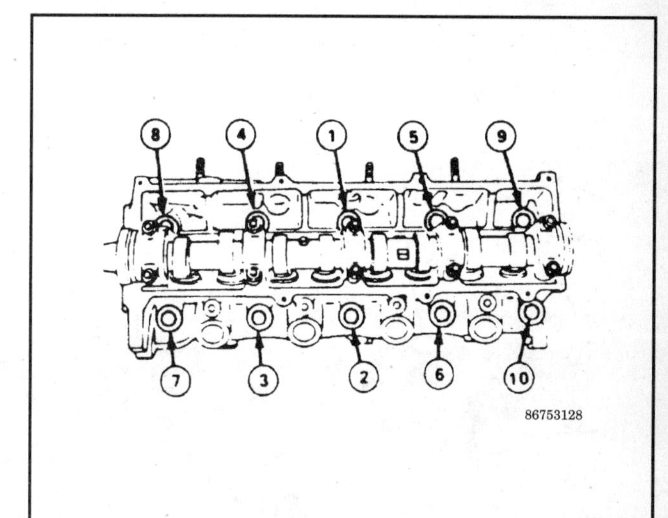

Fig. 99 Tighten the cylinder head bolts in the sequence shown — diesel engines

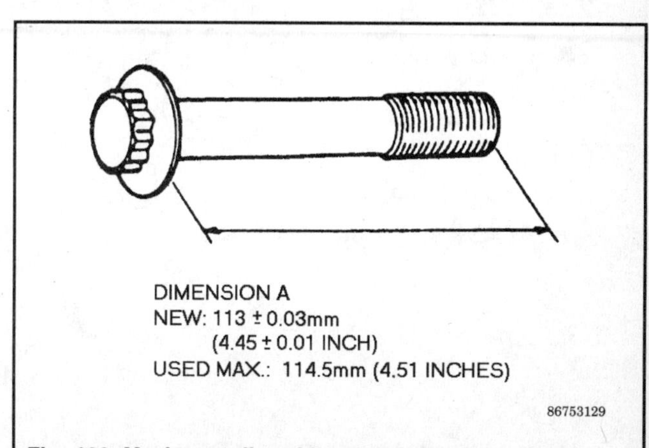

Fig. 100 Maximum allowable stretch for the cylinder head bolts (shown above) determines whether a bolt is reusable or not — do not compromise the tight seal required for these high-compression engines — diesel engines

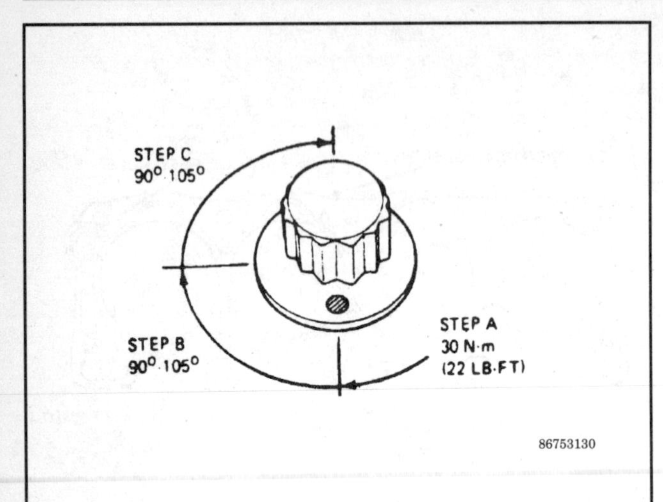

Fig. 101 Tighten the cylinder head bolts in three steps as shown — diesel engines

To install:

14. Clean the pre-chambers and cup in the cylinder head and the gasket mating surfaces.
15. Install the pre-chambers in the cylinder heads, making sure the locating pins are aligned with the slots provided.
16. Install the glow plugs and tighten to 11-15 ft. lbs. (15-20 Nm). Connect glow plug harness to the glow plugs. Tighten the nuts to 5-7 ft. lbs. (7-9 Nm).

WARNING

Carefully blow out the head bolt threads in the crankcase with compressed air. Failure to thoroughly clean the thread bores can result in incorrect cylinder head torque or possible cracking of the crankcase.

17. Position a new cylinder head gasket on the crankcase making sure the cylinder head oil feed hold is not blocked.

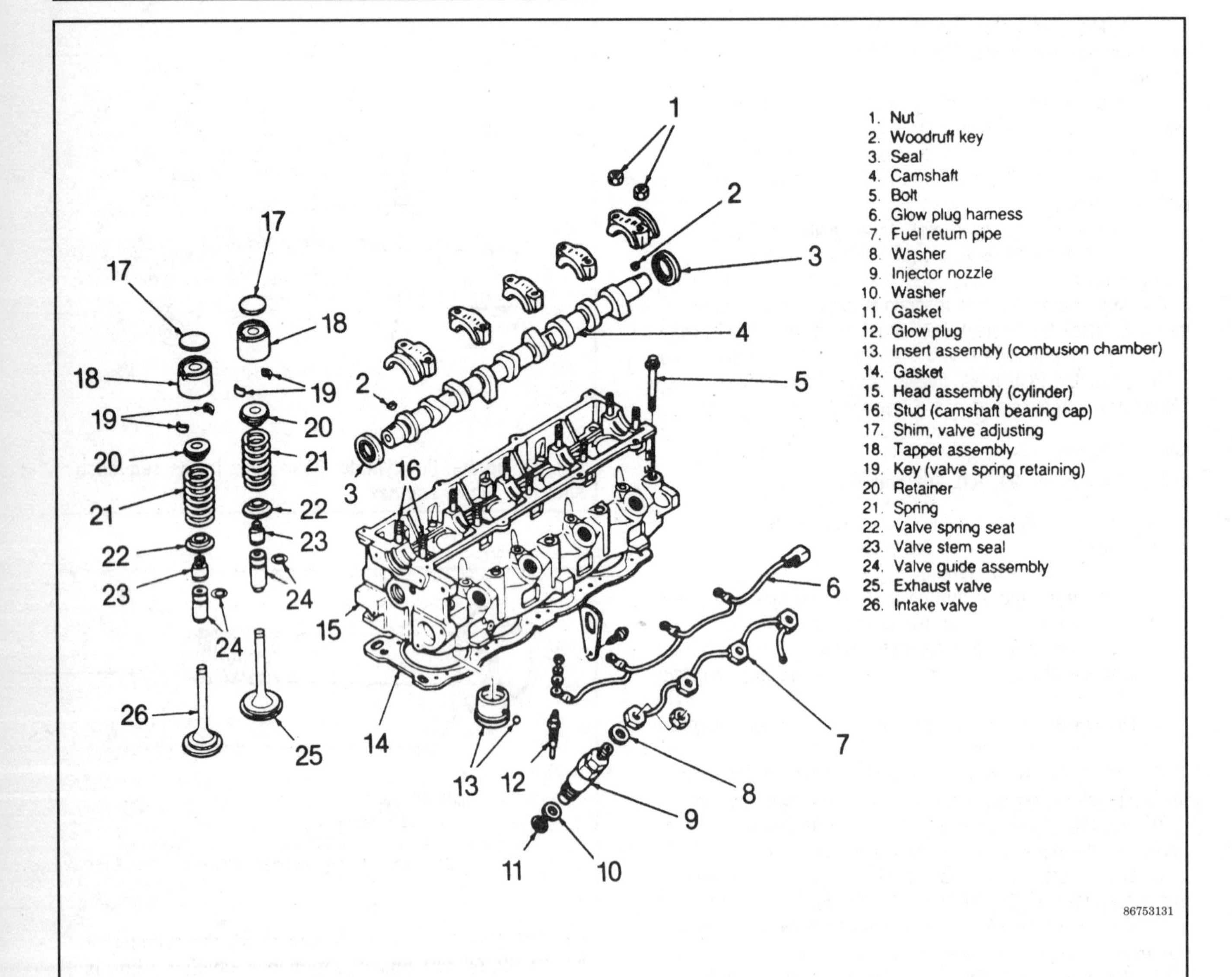

Fig. 102 Exploded view and legend for cylinder head components — diesel engines

18. Measure each cylinder head bolt dimension **A**. If the bolt has stretched to measure more than 4.51 in., (114.5mm) replace the head bolt.

➡Rotate the camshaft in the cylinder head until the cam lobes for No. 1 cylinder are at the base circle (both valves closed). Then, rotate the crankshaft clockwise until No. 1 piston is halfway up in the cylinder bore toward TDC. This is to prevent contact between the pistons and valves.

19. Install the cylinder head on the crankcase.

➡Before installing the cylinder head bolts, paint a white reference dot on each one, and apply a light coat of engine oil on the bolt threads.

20. Tighten cylinder head bolts as follows:
    a. Tighten bolts to 22 ft. lbs. (30 Nm) in the sequence shown.
    b. Using the painted reference marks, tighten each bolt in sequence, another 90°-105°.
    c. Repeat Step B turning the bolts another 90°-105°.
21. Connect the glow plug harness to main engine harness.
22. Remove the protective caps and install injection lines to the injection pump and nozzles. Tighten capnuts to 18-22 ft. lbs.
23. Bleed the air from the fuel system.
24. Connect the upper (with a new gasket) and lower coolant hoses, and the upper radiator hose to the thermostat housing. Tighten upper coolant hose bolts to 5-7 ft. lbs. (7-9 Nm)
25. Connect the electrical connectors and the vacuum hoses to the temperature sensors in the thermostat housing.
26. Remove the protective cover and install the air inlet duct to the intake manifold and air cleaner.
27. Raise the vehicle and support it safely. Connect the muffler inlet pipe to the exhaust manifold. Tighten the nuts to 25-35 ft. lbs. (34-47 Nm).
28. Lower the vehicle.
29. Install and adjust the front and rear timing belt.
30. Install the front upper timing belt cover and rear timing belt cover. Tighten the bolts to 5-7 ft. lbs. (7-9 Nm)
31. Check and adjust the valves as outlined. Install the rocker arm cover and tighten the bolts to 5-7 ft. lbs. (7-9 Nm)
32. Fill and bleed the cooling system.
33. Check and adjust the injection pump timing.
34. Connect the battery ground cable to battery. Run the engine and check for oil, fuel and coolant leaks.

1.8L Engine

➧ See Figures 103, 104, 105 and 106

1. Properly relieve the fuel system pressure.
2. Disconnect the negative battery cable.
3. Drain the cooling system.
4. Remove the bolts from the timing belt upper and middle covers. Remove the covers and gaskets.
5. Manually rotate the crankshaft in the direction of normal engine rotation and align the timing marks located on the camshaft pulleys and seal plate.
6. Loosen the timing belt tensioner lockbolt and temporarily secure the tensioner spring in the fully extended position.
7. Remove the timing belt from the camshaft pulleys and secure it aside to prevent damage during the removal and installation of the cylinder head.

➡Do not allow the timing belt to become contaminated by oil or grease.

8. Tag and remove the vacuum hoses from the valve head cover.
9. Tag and remove the spark plug wires from the spark plugs and position the wires aside.
10. Remove the cylinder head cover and gasket.
11. Remove the air duct from the resonance chamber and throttle body.
12. Disconnect the accelerator cable and, if equipped with automatic transaxle, the kickdown cable from the throttle cam. Remove the cable bracket from the intake plenum.
13. Tag and remove all vacuum lines from the intake plenum.
14. Tag and remove all necessary electrical connectors from the cylinder head, exhaust manifold, intake plenum, and throttle body. Disconnect the ground straps.
15. Remove the upper radiator hose.
16. Remove the transaxle-to-engine block upper-right bolt.
17. Disconnect the fuel pressure and return lines and plug the lines.
18. Disconnect the ignition coil high-tension lead from the distributor.
19. Tag and disconnect the necessary hoses connected to the cylinder head and intake plenum.
20. Remove the two bolts from the transaxle vent tube routing brackets.
21. Raise and safely support the vehicle.
22. Remove the bolt from the water pump-to-cylinder head hose bracket.
23. Remove the front exhaust mounting flange and exhaust pipe support bracket from the exhaust manifold.
24. Remove the intake plenum support bracket.
25. Lower the vehicle.
26. Remove the cylinder head bolts in the proper sequence.
27. Remove the cylinder head assembly, with the intake plenum and exhaust manifold attached, from the vehicle.
28. Remove the intake plenum and exhaust manifold.

To install:

29. Remove all dirt, oil and old gasket material from all gasket contact surfaces.
30. Install the intake plenum and exhaust manifold.
31. Install a new head gasket onto the top of the engine block, using the dowel pins for reference.
32. Place the cylinder head into its mounting position on top of the engine block.
33. Lubricate the cylinder head bolts with engine oil and install them finger-tight. Tighten the bolts in the proper sequence (see drawing) to 56-60 ft. lbs. (76-81 Nm).
34. Install the two bolts to the transaxle vent tube routing brackets.
35. Connect the heater hoses to the cylinder head and install the clamps.
36. Connect the ignition coil high-tension lead to the distributor.
37. Connect the fuel pressure and return lines to the fuel supply manifold and install the safety clips.

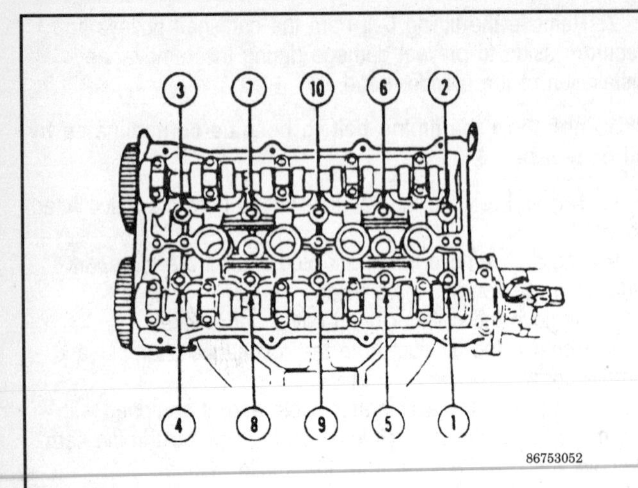

Fig. 103 Removal sequence for cylinder head bolts — 1.8L engines

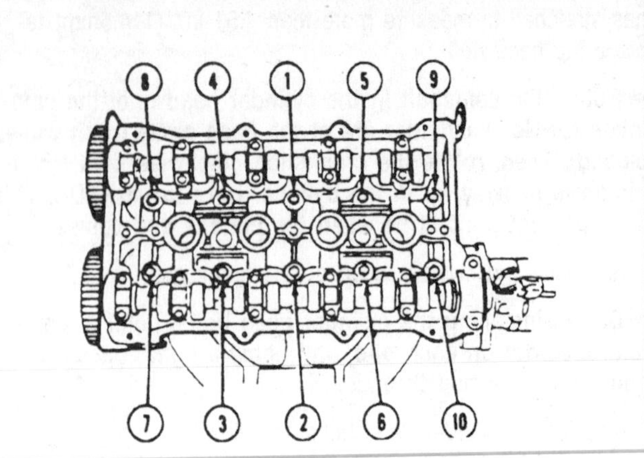

Fig. 106 Torque sequence for cylinder head bolts

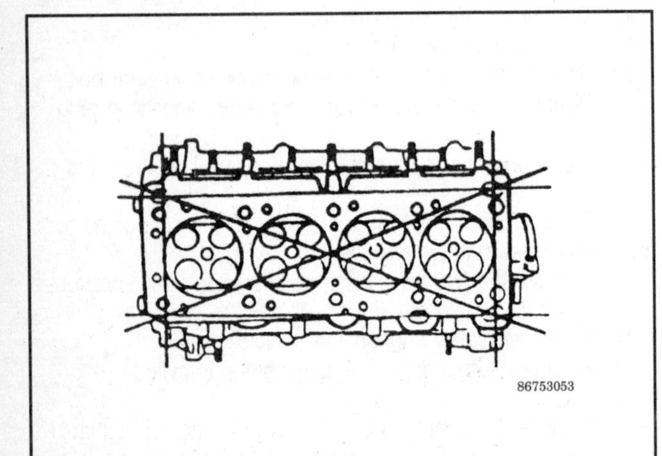

Fig. 104 Measurement locations for checking cylinder head warpage — 1.8L engines

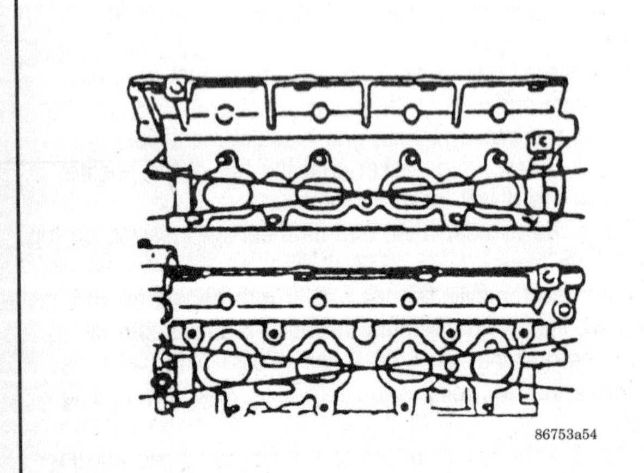

Fig. 105 Measurement locations for checking manifold contact surface warpage — 1.8L engines

38. Install the transaxle-to-engine block upper-right bolt. If equipped with a manual transaxle, tighten the bolt to 47-66 ft. lbs. (64-89 Nm). If equipped with an automatic transaxle, tighten the bolt to 41-59 ft. lbs. (55-80 Nm).
39. Install the upper radiator hose and clamps.
40. Connect the ground straps and connect the electrical connectors that were disconnected at the cylinder head, exhaust manifold, intake plenum, and throttle body.
41. Connect the vacuum lines to the intake plenum.
42. Install the accelerator and kickdown cable bracket onto the intake plenum and tighten the bolts to 69-95 inch lbs. (7.8-11.0 Nm). Connect the cable(s) to the throttle cam.
43. Install the cylinder head cover and gasket, then connect the hose running from the plenum to the cylinder head cover. Tighten the cover bolts to 43-78 inch lbs. (4.9-8.8 Nm).
44. Install the air duct to the resonance chamber and throttle body and tighten the clamps. Connect the hose going from the air duct to the cylinder head cover.
45. Install and connect the spark plug wires.
46. Raise and safely support the vehicle.
47. Install the intake plenum support bracket. Tighten the bolts to 27-38 ft. lbs. (37-52 Nm) and the nut to 14-19 ft. lbs. (19-25 Nm).
48. Install the bolt to the water pump-to-cylinder head hose bracket.
49. Install the exhaust front mounting flange with a new gasket to the exhaust manifold. Tighten the flange-to-manifold attaching nuts to 23-34 ft. lbs. (31-46 Nm).
50. Install the exhaust pipe support bracket. Tighten the bracket attaching bolts to 27-38 ft. lbs. (37-52 Nm).
51. Make sure the yellow ignition timing mark on the crankshaft pulley is aligned with the TDC mark on the timing belt cover.
52. Lower the vehicle.
53. Make sure the timing marks on the camshaft pulleys and seal plate are aligned. Install the timing belt so there is no looseness at the idler pulley side or between the two camshaft pulleys.

➡Do not turn the crankshaft counterclockwise.

54. Turn the crankshaft two turns clockwise by hand and verify that the yellow ignition timing mark on the crankshaft pulley is aligned with the timing mark on the timing belt cover. Verify that the timing marks on the camshaft pulley and seal plate are aligned.

➡If the timing marks are not aligned, remove the timing belt and repeat the procedure.

55. Turn the crankshaft 1⅚ turns clockwise by hand and align the 4th tooth to the right of the I and E timing marks on the camshaft pulleys with the seal plate alignment marks.
56. Loosen the timing belt tensioner lockbolt and apply tension to the timing belt. Tighten the tensioner lockbolt to 27-38 ft. lbs. (37-52 Nm).
57. Turn the crankshaft 2⅙ turns clockwise and verify that the timing marks on the camshaft pulleys and the seal plate are aligned.
58. Install new gaskets onto the timing belt upper and middle covers and install the covers. Tighten the mounting bolts to 69-95 inch lbs. (8-11 Nm).
59. Fill the cooling system.
60. Connect the negative battery cable.
61. Start the engine and check for leaks.

1991-95 1.9L Engine

1. Properly relieve the fuel system pressure.
2. Disconnect the negative battery cable.
3. Drain the cooling system.
4. Remove the air intake duct.
5. Remove the crankcase breather hose from the rocker arm cover and the vacuum hose from the bottom of the throttle body.
6. Remove the power brake supply hose.
7. Disconnect the electrical connectors at the following:
   a. Fuel charging harness.
   b. Alternator harness.
   c. Crank angle sensor.
   d. Oxygen sensor.
   e. Ignition coil.
   f. Radio suppressor.
   g. Coolant temperature sensor, cooling fan sensor and temperature sending unit.

➡Tag the connectors prior to removal to aid reinstallation.

8. Remove the ground strap from the stud on the left side of the cylinder head.
9. Disconnect the accelerator and the transaxle kickdown cables from the throttle lever and remove the cable bracket from the intake manifold.
10. Disconnect the heater hose containing the coolant temperature switches at the bulkhead.
11. Remove the upper radiator hose.
12. Disconnect the fuel supply and return lines.
13. Remove the oil level indicator tube mounting nut from the cylinder head stud.
14. Remove the power steering hose and the air conditioner line retainer bracket bolts from the alternator bracket.
15. Remove the accessory drive belt, alternator, and the drive belt automatic tensioner.
16. Raise and safely support the vehicle.
17. Remove the right side splash shield and remove the crankshaft dampener.
18. Remove the catalytic converter inlet pipe.
19. Remove the starter wiring harness from the retaining clip below the intake manifold.
20. Set the engine No. 1 cylinder on TDC.
21. Lower the vehicle.
22. Support the engine with a suitable floor jack.
23. Remove the right engine mount dampener and the right engine mount retaining bolts from the mount bracket on the engine. Loosen the right engine mount through-bolt and roll the mount back aside.
24. Remove the timing belt cover.
25. Loosen the belt tensioner attaching bolt and pry the tensioner as far toward the rear of the engine as possible. Tighten the attaching bolt while in this position.
26. Remove the timing belt.
27. Roll the right engine mount back into position and install the mounting bolts. Lower the floor jack.
28. Remove the heater hose support bracket retaining bolt and the alternator bracket-to-cylinder head mounting bolt.
29. Remove the rocker arm cover.
30. Remove and discard the cylinder head bolts.
31. Remove the cylinder head with the exhaust and intake manifolds attached. Discard the cylinder head gasket.

➡Do not lay the cylinder head flat. Damage to the spark plugs, valves or gasket surfaces may result.

To install:

32. Clean all gasket material from the mating surfaces on the cylinder head and block and clean out the head bolt holes in the block. Check the cylinder head squish height.

➡No cylinder block deck machining or use of replacement crankshaft, piston or connecting rod causing the assembled squish height to be over or under tolerance specification, is permitted. If no parts other than the head gasket are replaced, the squish height should be within specification. If parts other than the head gasket are replaced, check the squish height. If the squish height is out of specification, replace the parts again and recheck the squish height.

33. Install the dowels in the cylinder block, if removed. Check the dowel height, it should be 0.41-0.46 in. (10.40-11.75mm) above the surface of the block. A dowel that is too long will not allow the cylinder head to sit properly.
34. Position the cylinder head gasket on the cylinder block.

➡The cylinder head attaching bolts cannot be tightened to the specified torque more than once and must therefore be replaced when installing a cylinder head.

35. Install the cylinder head and install new bolts and washers in the following order:
   a. Apply a light coat of engine oil to the threads of the new cylinder head bolts and install the new bolts into the head.
   b. Tighten the cylinder head bolts in sequence to 44 ft. lbs. (60 Nm).
   c. Loosen the cylinder head bolts approximately two turns and then torque again to 44 ft. lbs. (60 Nm) using the same torque sequence.

d. After setting the torque again, turn the head bolts 90° in sequence and to complete the head bolt installation, turn the head bolts an additional 90° in the same torque sequence.

36. Install the rocker arm cover and the alternator bracket-to-cylinder head bolt.

37. Support the engine with a suitable floor jack.

38. Remove the right engine mount-to-mount bracket bolts. Roll the mount aside.

39. Make sure cylinder No. 1 is at TDC.

40. Install the timing belt and the timing belt cover.

41. Roll the right engine mount into place and install the two mounting bolts and the mount dampener. Remove the floor jack.

42. Raise and safely support the vehicle.

43. Install the crankshaft dampener.

44. Install the starter wiring harness on the retaining clip below the intake manifold.

45. Install the catalytic converter inlet pipe and the right side splash shield.

46. Lower the vehicle.

47. Install the alternator and the accessory drive belt automatic tensioner. Install the accessory drive belt.

48. Install both the power steering hose and air conditioner line retainer bracket bolts. Install the oil level indicator tube retainer bolt.

49. Connect the fuel supply and return lines.

50. Install the upper radiator hose and connect the heater hose at the engine compartment bulkhead. Install the heater hose support bracket retaining bolt.

51. Install the accelerator cable bracket on the intake manifold and connect the accelerator and kickdown cables to the throttle lever.

52. Install the ground strap at the left side of the cylinder head.

53. Connect all remaining electrical connectors according to their positions marked during the removal procedure.

54. Connect the power brake supply hose, crankcase breather hose and the vacuum line at the bottom of the throttle body.

55. Install the air intake duct.

56. Connect the negative battery cable.

57. Fill and bleed the cooling system.

58. Start the engine and check for leaks. Stop the engine and check the coolant level. Add fluid as necessary.

PISTON SQUISH HEIGHT

See Figures 107, 108, 109 and 110

Before final installation of the cylinder head to the engine, piston "squish height" must be checked. Squish height is the clearance of the piston dome to the cylinder head dome at piston TDC. No rework of the head gasket surfaces (slabbing) or use of replacement parts (crankshaft, piston and connecting rod) that causes the assembled squish height to be over or under the tolerance specification is permitted.

➡If no parts other than the head gasket are replaced, the piston squish height should be within specification. If parts other than the head gasket are replaced, check the squish height. If out of specification, replace the parts again and recheck the squish height.

1. Clean all gasket material from the mating surfaces on the cylinder head and engine block.

2. Place a small amount of soft lead solder or lead shot of an appropriate thickness on the piston spherical areas.

3. Rotate the crankshaft to lower the piston in the bore and install the head gasket and cylinder head.

➡A compressed (used) head gasket is preferred for checking squish height.

4. Install used head bolts and tighten the head bolts to 30-44 ft. lbs. (40-60 Nm) following proper sequence.

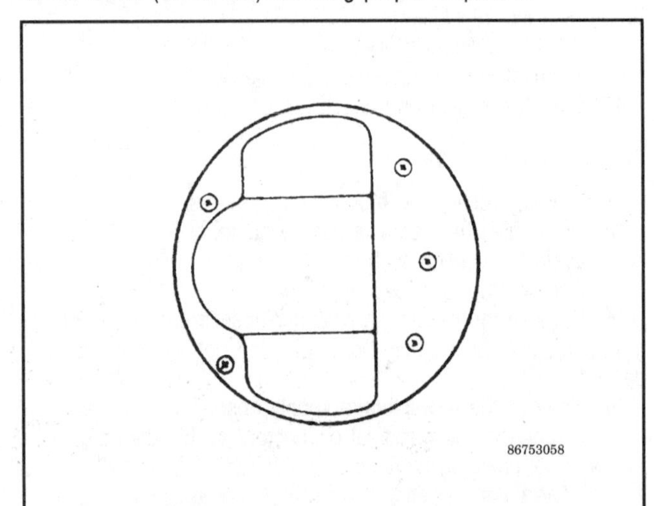

86753058

Fig. 107 Locations to place lead shot or solder to measure piston squish height — 1985-87 1.9L engines

Piston Squish Height

CAUTION: Before final installation of the cylinder head to the engine, piston "squish height" must be checked. Squish height is the clearance of the piston dome to the cylinder head dome at piston TDC. No rework of the head gasket surfaces (stabbing), or use of replacement parts (crankshaft, piston and connecting rod) causing the assembled squish height to be over or under the tolerance specification is permitted.

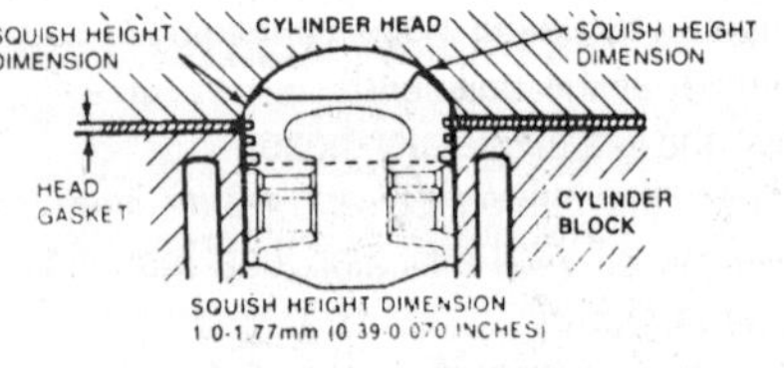

86753a58

Fig. 108 Cross-sectional view of squish height measurements — 1985-87 1.9L engines

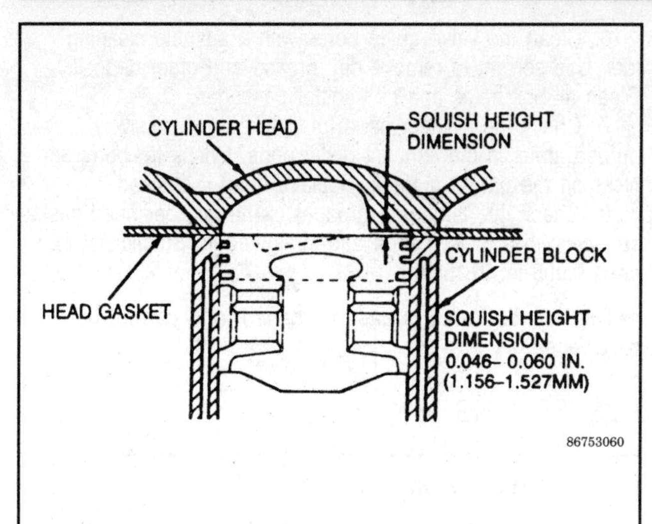

Fig. 109 Cross-sectional view of squish height measurements — 1988-90 1.9L MFI engines

Fig. 110 Cross-sectional view of squish height measurements — 1988-90 MFI HO and all 1991-95 engines

5. Rotate the crankshaft to move the piston through its TDC position.

6. Remove the cylinder head and measure the thickness of the compressed solder to determine squish height at TDC. For the 1981-90 MFI HO engine, all 1981-90 non-MFI, and 1991-95 1.9L models, the compressed lead piece should be 0.039-0.070 in. (1.0-1.77mm). For 1983-90 MFI engines, the compressed lead piece should be: 0.046-0.060 in. (1.156-1.527mm) for MFI engine.

CLEANING AND INSPECTION

Gasoline Engines

➧ See Figures 111 and 112

1. Place the head on a workbench and remove any manifolds that are still connected. Remove all rocker arm retaining parts and the rocker arms, if still installed, or the camshaft (see Camshaft Removal).

2. Turn the cylinder head over so that the mounting surface is facing up and supported evenly on wooden blocks.

➡Exercise extra care when cleaning aluminum cylinder heads.

3. Use a scraper and remove all of the gasket material stuck to the head mounting surface. Mount a wire carbon removal brush in an electric drill. With the valves installed to protect the valve seats, clean away the carbon on the valves and head combustion chambers. After the valves are removed, clean the valve guides bores. Use cleaning solvent to remove dirt, grease and other deposits from the valves.

➡When scraping or decarbonizing the cylinder head, take care not to scuff, nick or otherwise damage the gasket mounting surface.

4. Number the valve heads with a permanent felt-tip marker for cylinder location.

Fig. 111 Use a scraper to remove old gasket material before installing the cylinder head and new gasket

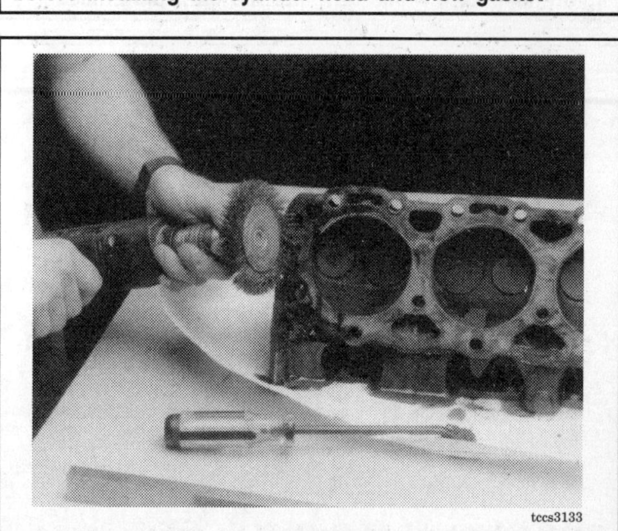

Fig. 112 An electric drill equipped with a wire wheel will expedite complete gasket removal

Diesel Engines

See Figures 113 and 114

1. Install the cylinder head in a suitable holding fixture.
2. With the valves installed to protect the valve seats, remove deposits from the combustion chambers and valve heads with a scraper and wire brush.

➡The cylinder head is aluminum and should be handled carefully to prevent damage.

3. Using a suitable valve spring compressor, remove the valve spring retainer locks, retainer, spring and damper assemblies, intake valve oil seals and valves.

➡Keep each individual valve assembly together so that they may be returned to their original positions.

4. Remove the glow plugs and injection nozzles.
5. Remove the pre-combustion chambers by inserting a 5/16 in. x 8 in. (8mm x 203mm) brass drift into the glow plug hole, and lightly tap with a hammer.

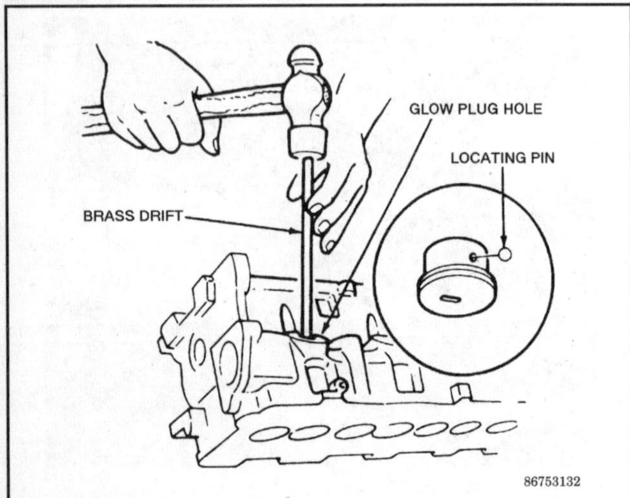

Fig. 113 Remove the pre-combustion chambers by lightly tapping a brass drift into the glow plug holes

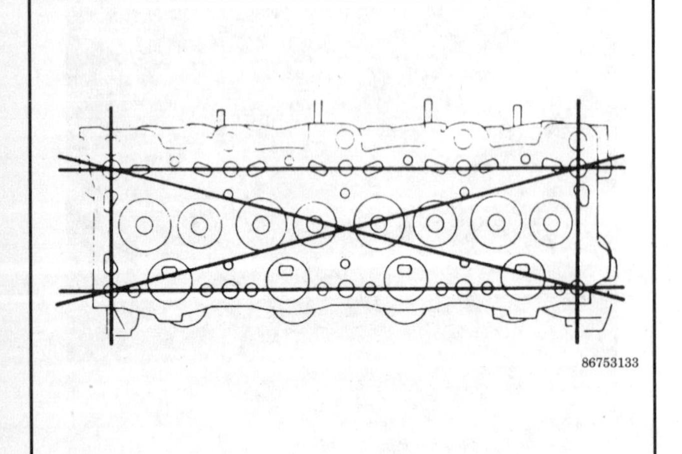

Fig. 114 Check the cylinder head for warpage using a straightedge and feeler gauge across the dimensions shown

6. Clean the valve guide bores with a suitable cleaning tool. Use solvent to remove dirt, grease and other deposits. Clean all bolt holes and oil transfer passages.
7. Check the cylinder head for cracks or excessively burned areas in the exhaust outlet ports. Check for burrs and nicks on the gasket surface. Replace head if cracked.
8. Check the flatness (warpage) of the cylinder head gasket surface with a feeler gauge and straightedge. Should not exceed 0.006 in. (0.15mm).

➡The cylinder head is case hardened, and cannot be resurfaced.

RESURFACING

See Figures 115 and 116

➡If the cylinder head of your gasoline engine is found to be warped, it will be necessary to have it resurfaced by a machine shop.

Except 1.8L Engines

Place a straightedge across the gasket surface of the head. Using a feeler gauge, determine the clearance at the center and along the length between the head and straightedge. Measure clearance at the center and along the lengths of both diagonals. If warpage exceeds 0.003 in. (0.076mm) in a 6 in. (152mm) span, or 0.006 in. (0.15mm) over the total length, the cylinder head must be resurfaced. Replace the head if it is cracked.

1.8L Engines

1. Inspect the cylinder head for damage, cracks, and leakage of water and oil. Using a straightedge and a feeler gauge, measure the cylinder head for warpage by laying the straightedge across the the cylinder head end-to-end. Measure any gap with the feeler gauge in six directions (see drawing) The maximum distortion allowable is 0.004 in. (0.10mm).
2. If the cylinder head distortion exceeds 0.004 in. (0.10mm), machine the cylinder head surface. The cylinder

Fig. 115 Check the cylinder head for warpage along the center using a straightedge and a feeler gauge

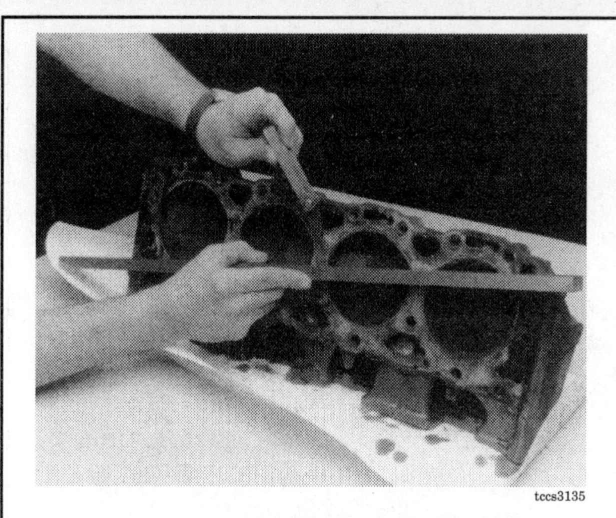

Fig. 116 Be sure to check for warpage across the cylinder head at both diagonals

Fig. 117 Use a spring compressor to dismantle the assembly. Note: the air hose threaded into the spark plug hole permits the procedure without head removal

head must be replaced if the cylinder head height is not within 5.268-5.276 in. (133.8-134.0mm).

3. Inspect the manifold contact surface distortion in four directions. The maximum distortion allowable is 0.006 in. (0.15mm). If the distortion exceeds specification, machine the manifold contact surface or replace the cylinder head, as necessary.

Valves, Springs and Seals

REMOVAL & INSTALLATION

Gasoline Engines

See Figures 117, 118, 119, 120, 121, 122, 123, 124, 125 and 126

A valve spring compressor is needed to remove each valve assembly. Valve spring compressors are available at most auto parts and auto tool shops. A small magnet is very helpful for removing the keepers (keys) and spring seats.

1. Disconnect the negative battery cable.
2. Place fender covers on the aprons.
3. Remove the cylinder head from the engine and place it on a clean work bench.

It is possible to perform this procedure without removing the cylinder head. To do so, compressed air must be used to pressurize the cylinder and keep the valve in place. If the valve is not held as described, it will fall into the cylinder when the retaining hardware is removed. The valve's cylinder must be at the TDC of the compression stroke.

4. With the cylinder head removed, install the spring compressor so that the fixed side of the tool is flat against the valve head in the combustion chamber, and the opposite end toward the spring retainer.
5. If performing this procedure without removing the cylinder head, use a suitable overhead valve spring compressor.

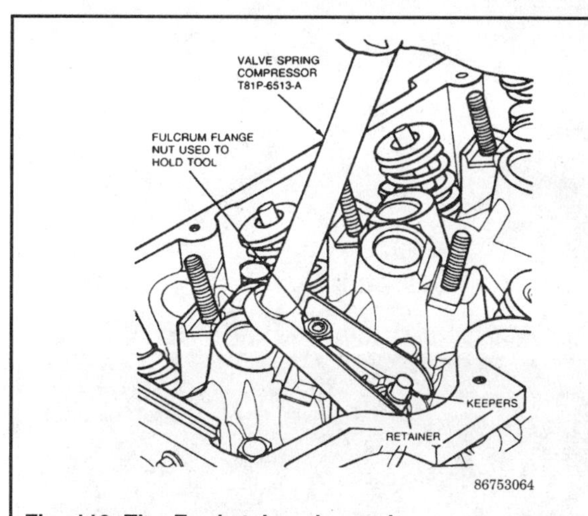

Fig. 118 The Ford-style valve spring compressor operates as shown to remove the tension from the valve spring retainer

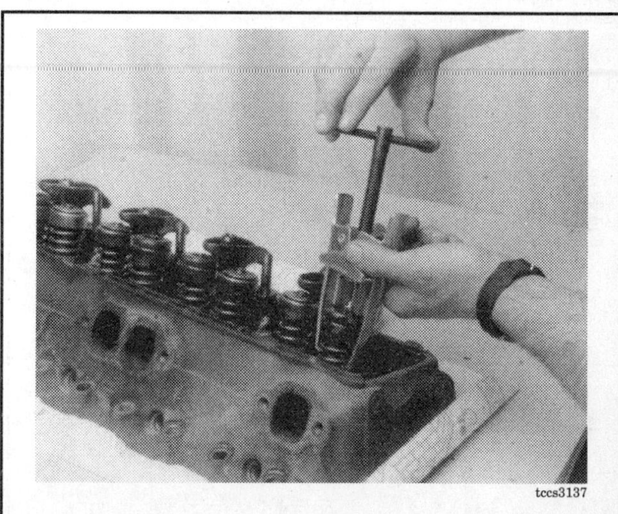

Fig. 119 Use a valve spring compressor tool to relieve spring tension from the valve caps

tccs3138

Fig. 120 A small magnet will help removal of the valve keys

tccs3139

Fig. 121 Be careful not to lose the valve keys

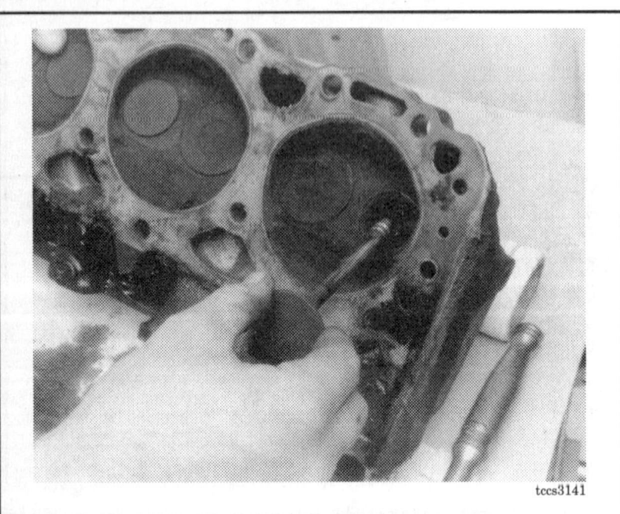
tccs3141

Fig. 123 Invert the cylinder head and withdraw the valve from the cylinder head bore

tccs3810

Fig. 122 Remove the spring from the valve stem in order to access the seal

tccs3802

Fig. 124 With the valves removed, a wire wheel may be used to clean the combustion chambers of carbon deposits — take care not to damage the aluminum

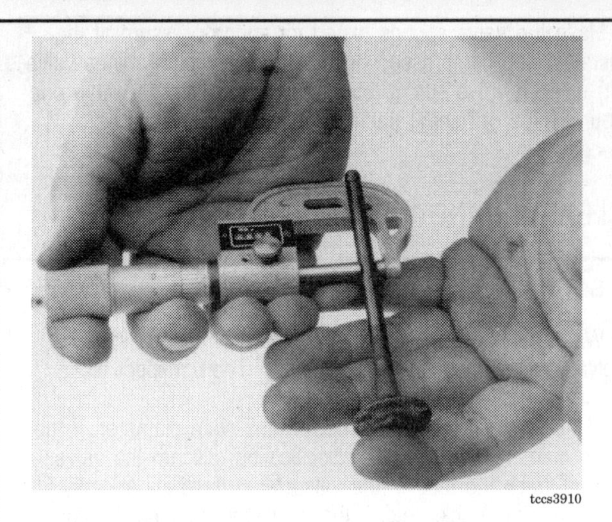

tccs3910

Fig. 125 A dial gauge may be used to check valve stem-to-guide clearance

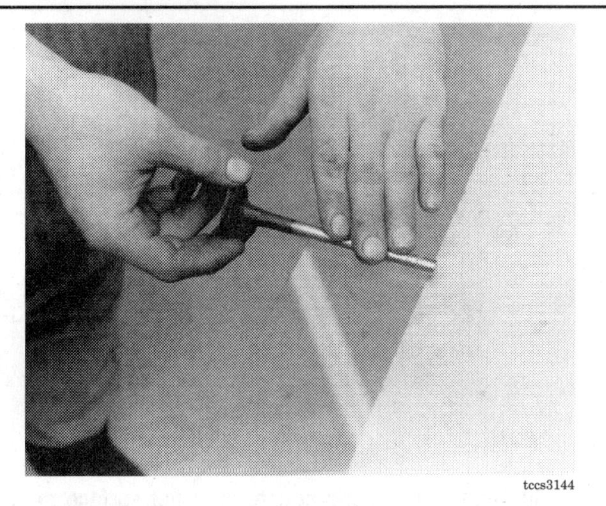

tccs3144

Fig. 126 Valve stems may be rolled on a flat surface to check for bends

6. Compress the spring assembly.

➡As the spring is compressed, the keepers (keys) will be revealed. Remove them from the valve stem with the magnet as they are easily fumbled and lost.

7. Remove the keys, spring retainer, spring, seal from the cylinder head. Invert the head and withdraw the valves from the cylinder bore. Keep the assemblies intact so they will be re-installed in their original positions.
8. Remove the remaining valves from the cylinder head, keeping all parts together.
9. Clean and inspect the valve components, as outlined in this section.

To install:

10. Install the valve into the cylinder head. Assemble the seal, spring and spring retainer.

➡Always use new valve seals.

11. Install the spring compressor, and compress the spring retainer until the keeper (key) groove on the valve stem is fully revealed. Then, install the the keepers

➡It may be necessary to apply a little grease to the grooves on the valve stem to hold the keepers until the spring compressor is released.

12. Slowly release the spring compressor until the spring retainer covers the keepers. Remove the spring compressor tool.

➡Lightly tap the end of each valve stem with a rubber mallet to ensure proper fit of the retainers and keepers.

13. Install the remaining valve assemblies in the cylinder head.
14. After installing the valve spring, measure the distance between the spring mounting pad and the lower edge of the spring retainer. Compare the measurement to specifications. If the installed height is incorrect, add shims (special washers) between the spring mounting pad and the spring. Use only shims designed for valve springs, available at at most parts stores.

Diesel Engines

See Figures 127, 128 and 129

➡With No. 1 piston at TDC, the valve springs and seals for No. 1 and No. 4 cylinders can be removed. To remove the springs and seal for No. 2 and No. 3 cylinders, rotate the crankshaft one complete revolution, until the timing mark on the flywheel is at TDC.

1. Remove the camshaft and followers.
2. Using valve spring compressor tool T84P-6513-A or equivalent and a magnet, depress the valve spring and remove the valve keepers.
3. Remove the valve spring retainer, valve spring and valve spring seat.
4. Remove the valve stem seal, using tool T72J-6571 or equivalent.

To install:

5. Install a new valve stem seal, using tool T84P-6571-A or equivalent.
6. Install the valve spring seat, valve spring and valve spring retainer. Compress the spring and install the valve keepers.
7. Install the camshaft and followers.

CHECKING VALVE SPRINGS

See Figures 130 and 131

Place the valve spring on a flat surface next to a carpenter's square. Measure the height of the spring, and rotate the spring against the edge of the square to measure distortion. If the spring height varies (by comparison) by more than $1/16$ in. (1.6mm), or if the distortion exceeds $1/16$ in. (1.6mm), replace the spring.

➡Spring height may be measured with a caliper gauge, if available.

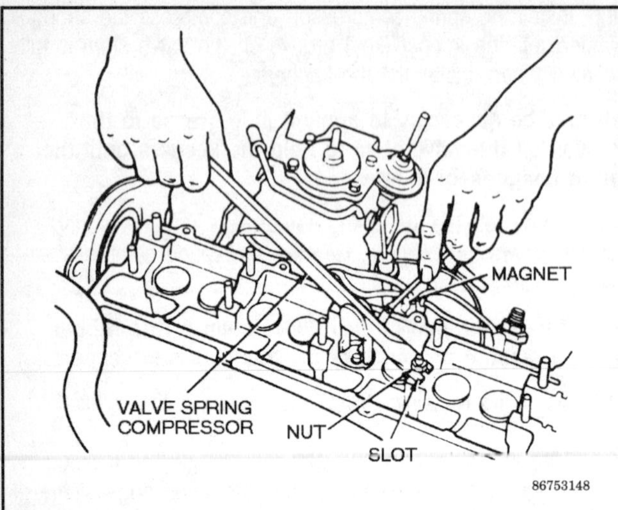

Fig. 127 A a valve spring compressor is shown in use disassembling valve assembly

Have the valve springs tested for spring pressure at the installed and compressed height (installed height minus valve lift) using a valve spring tester. Springs should be within one pound (plus or minus) each other. Replace springs as necessary.

CLEANING AND INSPECTION

See Figure 132

Wash each valve assembly, one at a time, in a suitable solvent. Allow the components to dry. Then, inspect all components.

1. Using a micrometer, check valve stem diameter. If the stem diameter is not within specification, discard the valve.
2. Check the face of the valve for surface imperfections such as pits, cracks, etc. If the face runout cannot be corrected by refinishing, discard the valve.

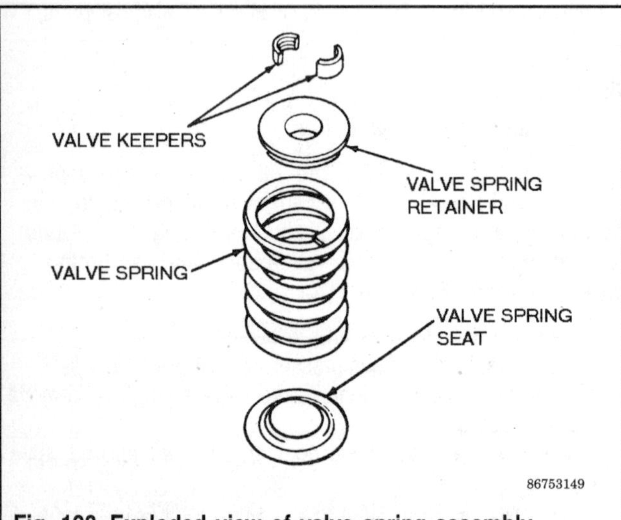

Fig. 128 Exploded view of valve spring assembly — diesel engines

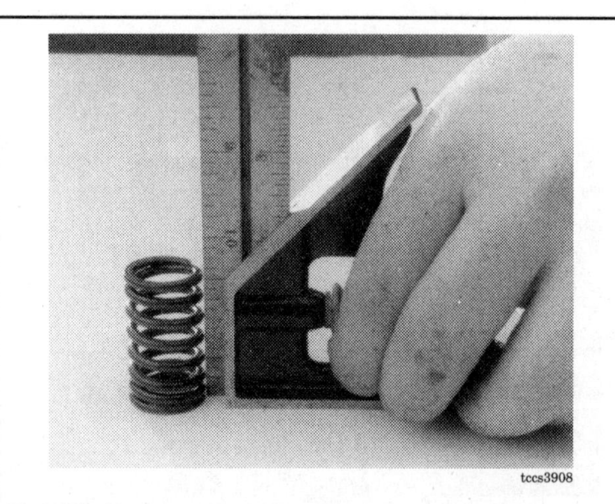

Fig. 130 Use a carpenter's square on a flat surface to check valve spring squareness — revolve the spring slowly to see any variance

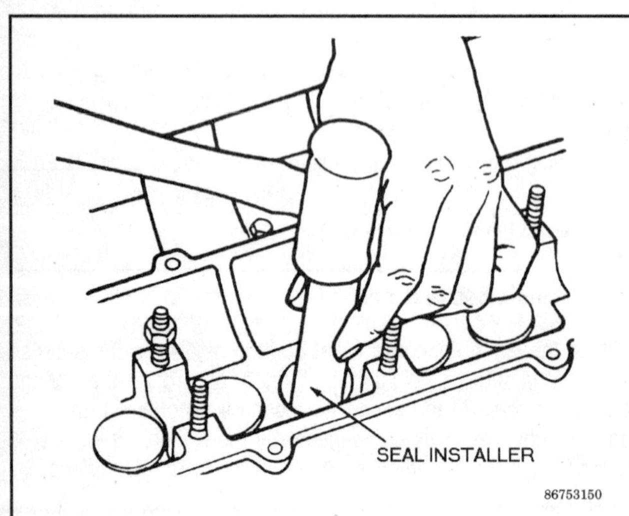

Fig. 129 Press-fit the valve stem seal with care and the proper tools

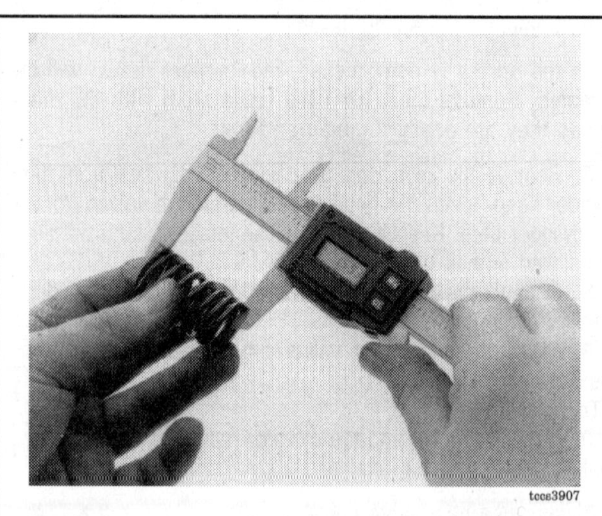

Fig. 131 Use a caliper gauge to check the valve spring free-length

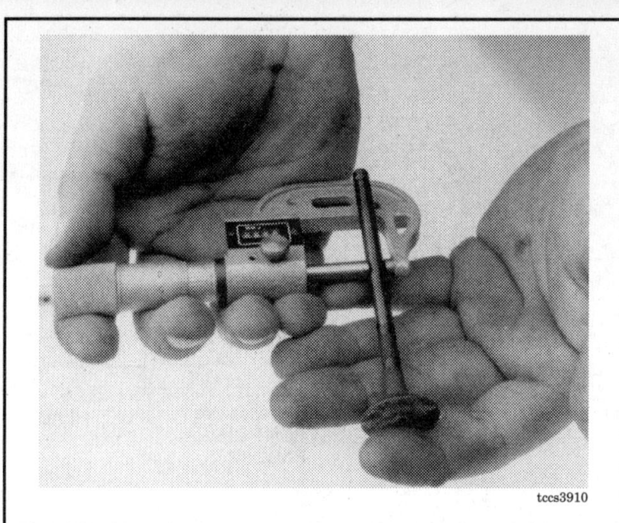

Fig. 132 Use a micrometer to check the valve stem diameter

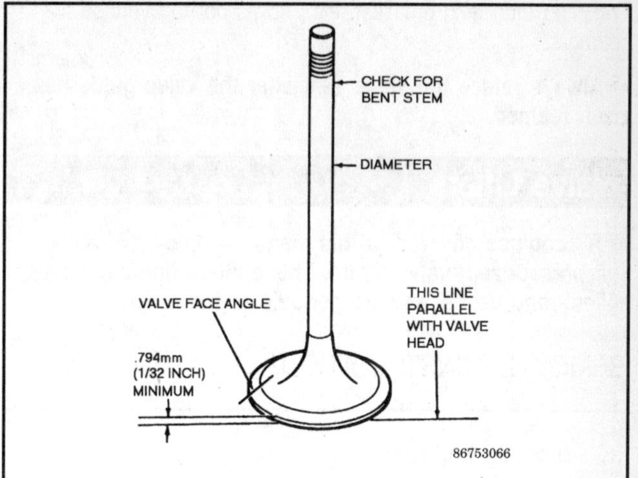

Fig. 133 Critical dimensions for valve refacing — sample valve shown, refer to the specifications for your particular application

VALVE AND SEAT REFACING

See Figures 133, 134 and 135

The valve refacing operation should be closely coordinated with the valve seat refacing operations so that the finished angles of the valve face and valve seat will be to specification and provide a compression-tight fit.

Be sure that the grinding surface of the refacer is properly dressed.

Grind the valve seat to specified degree angle. Remove only enough stock to clean up pits and grooves or to correct the valve seat runout. After the seat has been refaced, use a seat width scale or a machinist scale to measure the seat width. Narrow the seat, if necessary, to bring it within specification. If the valve seat width exceeds the maximum limit, remove enough stock from the top edge and/or bottom edge of the seat to reduce the width to specification.

Reface the valve, if the valve face runout is excessive and/or pits or grooves are evident. Remove only enough stock to clean up pits and grooves or to correct the runout.

If the edge of the valve head is less than 1/32 in. (0.794mm) thick after grinding, replace the valve as it will run too hot in the engine.

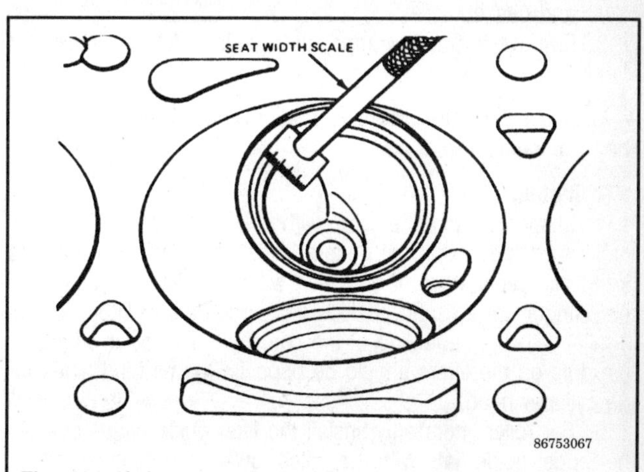

Fig. 134 If the valve seat width exceeds the maximum limit, remove enough stock from the top edge and/or bottom edge of the seat to reduce the width to specification

VALVE GUIDES REAMING

See Figure 136

If the valve stem-to-guide clearance exceeds the service clearance, it will be necessary to ream a valve guide. Ream the valve guide to accept the next oversize valve stem. A hand reaming kit can be purchased at most auto parts and auto tool shops.

When replacing a standard size valve with an oversize valve, always use the reamer in sequence (smallest oversize

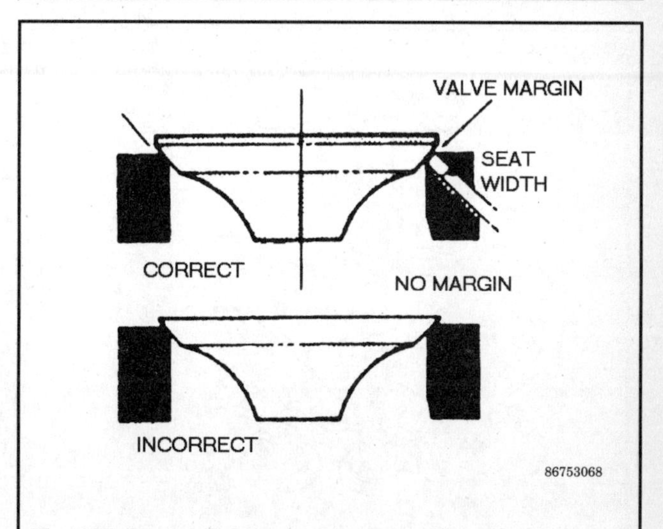

Fig. 135 Proper fit between the valve face and its seat is critical to a compression-tight seal

first, and then next smallest, etc.) so as not to overload the reamers.

➡Always reface the valve seat after the valve guide has been reamed.

Valve Lifters

➡All engines covered in this manual employ hydrauilic (oil pressurized) valve lifters. These lifters operate more quietly and do not require periodic adjustments.

REMOVAL & INSTALLATION

1.6L and 1.9L Engines

See Figures 137 and 138

1. Disconnect the negative battery cable.
2. Remove the air cleaner assembly. Remove rocker arm cover and gasket.
3. Remove the rocker arms, lifter guides, lifter retainers and lifters.

➡Always return the lifters to their original bores unless they are being replaced.

To install:

4. Lubricate each lifter bore with clean engine oil.
5. If equipped with flat bottom lifters, install with the oil hole in the plunger upward. If equipped with roller lifters, install with the plunger upward and position the guide flats of lifters to be parallel with the centerline of the camshaft. The color orientation dots on the lifters should be opposite the oil feed holes in the cylinder head.
6. For roller lifters only, install the lifter guide plates over the tappet guide flats with the notch toward the exhaust side. For flat lifters, no guide plate is required.
7. Lubricate the lifter plunger cap and valve tip with engine oil.

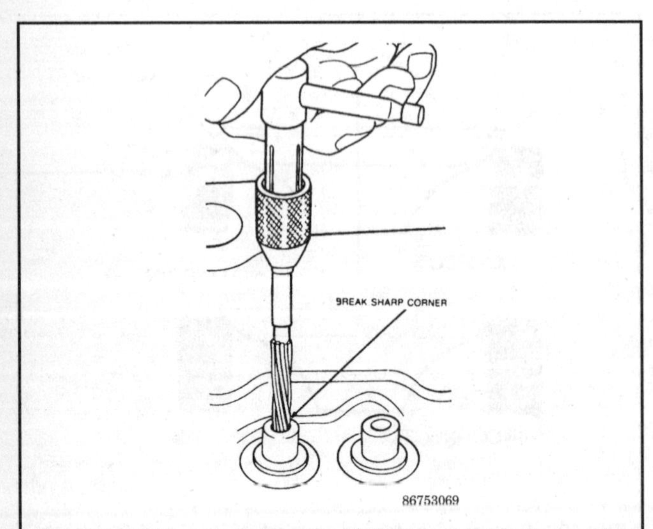

Fig. 136 Use a reamer to carefully ream the valve guide for the next oversize valve

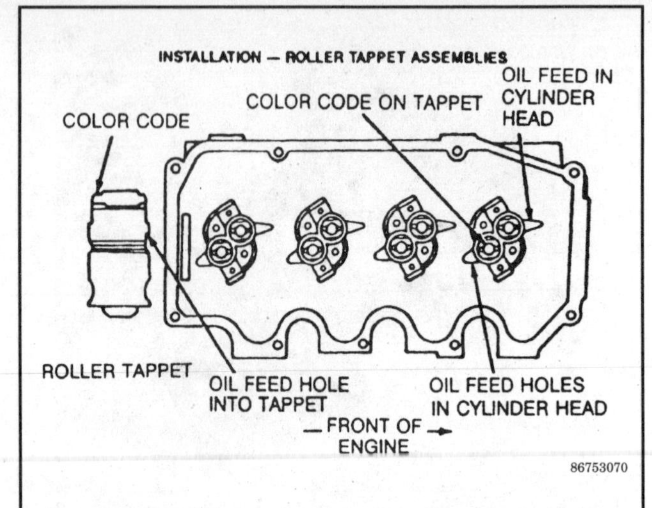

Fig. 137 Installation guide for roller tappets — 1.6L and 1.9L engines

Fig. 138 Once the way is clear, pull the lifter from its bore — ALWAYS return lifters to their original bores

8. Install the lifter guide plate retainers into rocker arm fulcrum slots, in both the intake and exhaust side. Align the notch to be with the exhaust valve lifter.
9. Install four rocker arms in lifter position No's 3, 6, 7 and 8.
10. Lubricate the rocker arm surface that will contact the fulcrum surface with engine oil.
11. Install four fulcrums. The fulcrums must be fully seated in the slots of cylinder head.
12. Install four bolts. Tighten to 17-22 ft. lbs. (23-30 Nm).
13. Rotate the engine until the camshaft sprocket keyway is in the 6 o'clock position.
14. Repeat steps 9-12 in lifter position No's 1, 2, 4 and 5.
15. Install the rocker arm cover and gasket. Install the air cleaner assembly.
16. Connect the negative battery cable.

1.8L Engine

1. Disconnect the negative battery cable.
2. Remove the camshafts.

3. Mark the hydraulic lash adjusters and the cylinder head with alignment marks so the hydraulic lash adjusters can be installed in their original positions.

4. Remove the hydraulic lash adjusters from the cylinder head.

To install:

5. Apply clean engine oil to the hydraulic lash adjuster friction surfaces.

6. If the hydraulic lash adjusters are being reused, install them in the positions from which they were removed.

7. Make sure the hydraulic lash adjusters move smoothly in their bores.

8. Install the camshafts.

9. Connect the negative battery cable.

OVERHAUL

➡The lifter assemblies should be keep in proper sequence so that they can be installed in their original position. If any part of the lifter assembly needs to be replaced, replace the entire assembly.

1. Remove the plunger cap retainer from the lifter assembly.

2. Remove the plunger cap, plunger assembly and return spring from the lifter body assembly.

➡Disassemble each lifter separately so as not to intermix the parts.

3. Thoroughly clean all the parts in clean solvent and wipe them with a clean, lint-free cloth.

4. Inspect the lifter assembly and discard the entire lifter if any part shows pitting, scoring, galling excessive wear or evidence of non-rotation.

Oil Pan

REMOVAL & INSTALLATION

CAUTION

The EPA warns that prolonged contact with used engine oil may cause a number of skin disorders, including cancer! You should make every effort to minimize your exposure to used engine oil. Protective gloves should be worn when handling used engine oil. Clean hands and other exposed skin area as soon as possible. Waterless hand cleaner or soap and water should be used.

All 1.6L and 1.9L Gasoline Engines

See Figures 139, 140, 141, 142, 143, 144, 145, 146, 147, 148 and 149

1. Disconnect the negative cable at the battery.

2. Raise the vehicle and support safely.

3. Remove the drain plug and drain the engine oil into a suitable container.

➡It may be necessary to disconnect coolant lines to allow clearance for the oil pan.

4. Disconnect the starter cable at its terminal on the starter.

5. Remove the knee-brace located at the front of the starter.

6. Remove the starter attaching bolts and starter.

7. Remove the knee-braces at the transaxle.

8. Disconnect the exhaust inlet pipe at the manifold and catalytic converter. Remove pipe.

9. Remove the oil pan retaining bolts and oil pan.

10. Remove the oil pan gasket and discard.

To install:

11. Clean the oil pan gasket surface and the mating surface on the cylinder block. Wipe the oil pan rail with a solvent-soaked, lint-free cloth to remove all traces of oil.

12. Remove to clean the oil pump pick up tube and screen assembly. Install tube and screen assembly using a new gasket.

13. Apply a bead of suitable silicone rubber sealer at the corner of the oil pan front and rear seals and at the seating point of the oil pump to the block retainer joint.

14. Install the oil pan gasket in the pan ensuring the press fit tabs are fully engaged in the gasket channel.

15. Install the oil pan attaching bolts. Tighten the bolts lightly until the two oil pan-to-transaxle bolts can be installed.

➡If the oil pan is installed on the engine outside of the vehicle, a transaxle case or equivalent, fixture must be bolted to the block to line-up the oil pan flush with the rear face of the block.

16. Tighten the two pan-to-transaxle bolts to 30-40 ft. lbs. (40-54 Nm).

17. Tighten the oil pan flange-to-cylinder block bolts to 15-22 ft. lbs. (20-30 Nm) in the proper sequence.

18. Install the transaxle inspection plate.

19. Install the starter, knee brace at the starter and connect the starter cable.

20. Install the exhaust inlet pipe. Lower the vehicle and fill the crankcase.

21. Connect negative battery cable.

22. Start the engine and check for oil leaks.

Diesel Engines

See Figure 150

1. Disconnect the negative battery cable.

2. Raise and safely support the vehicle.

3. Drain the engine oil.

4. Remove bolts attaching oil pan to crankcase, and remove pan.

5. Clean oil pan and crankcase gasket mating surfaces.

To install:

6. Apply a 1/8 in. (3mm) bead of silicone sealer or equivalent, to oil pan-to-crankcase mating surface.

7. Install the oil pan. Tighten the bolts to 5-7 ft. lbs. (7-10 Nm).

8. Lower the vehicle.

9. Fill crankcase with specified quantity and quality of engine oil.

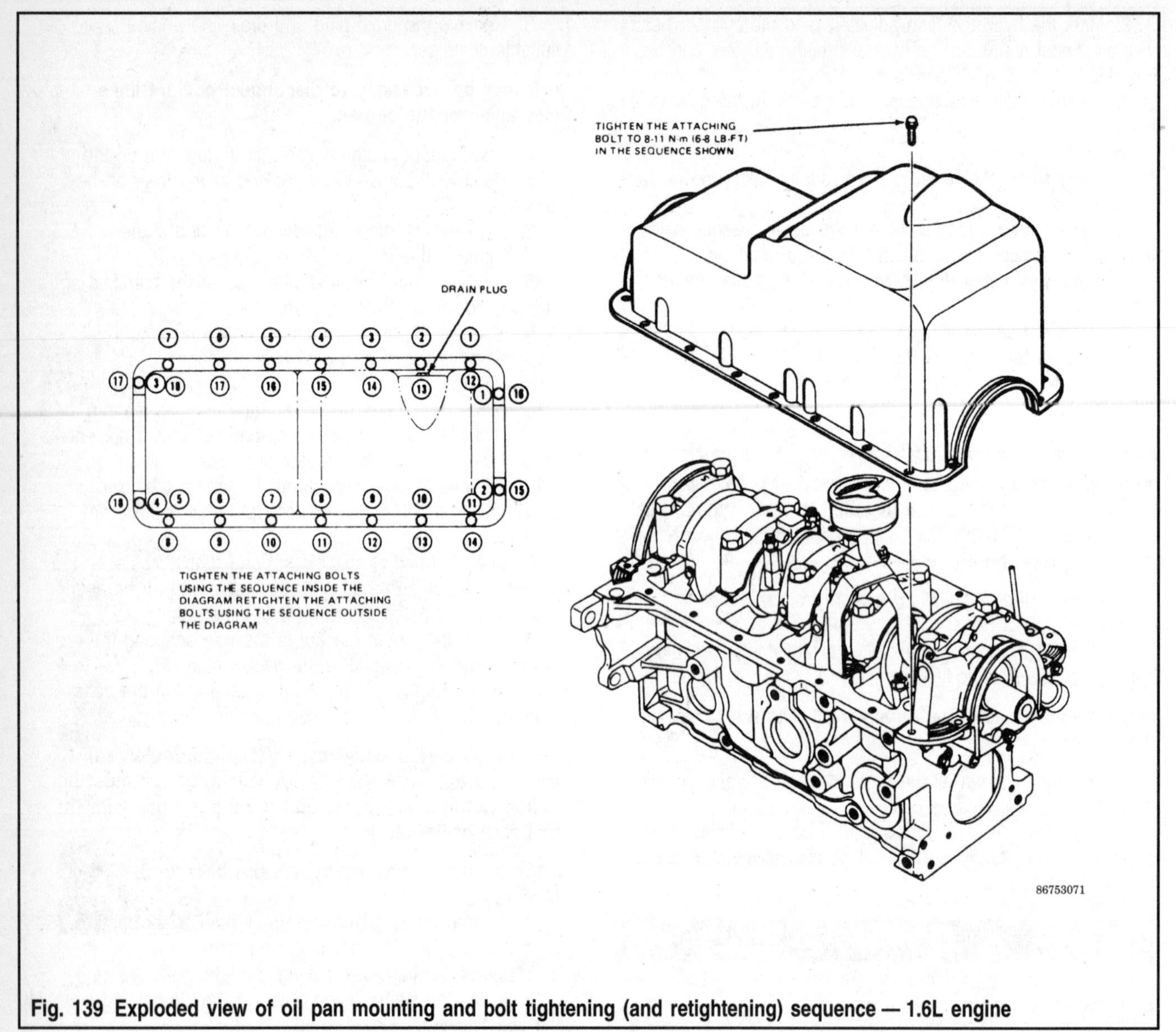

Fig. 139 Exploded view of oil pan mounting and bolt tightening (and retightening) sequence — 1.6L engine

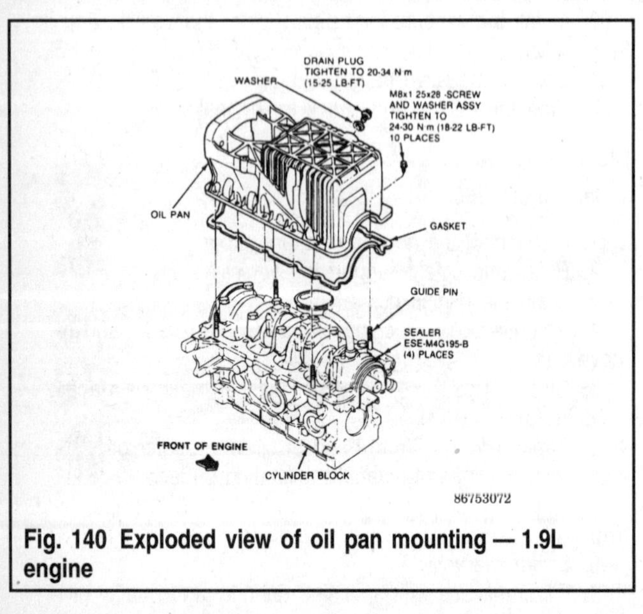

Fig. 140 Exploded view of oil pan mounting — 1.9L engine

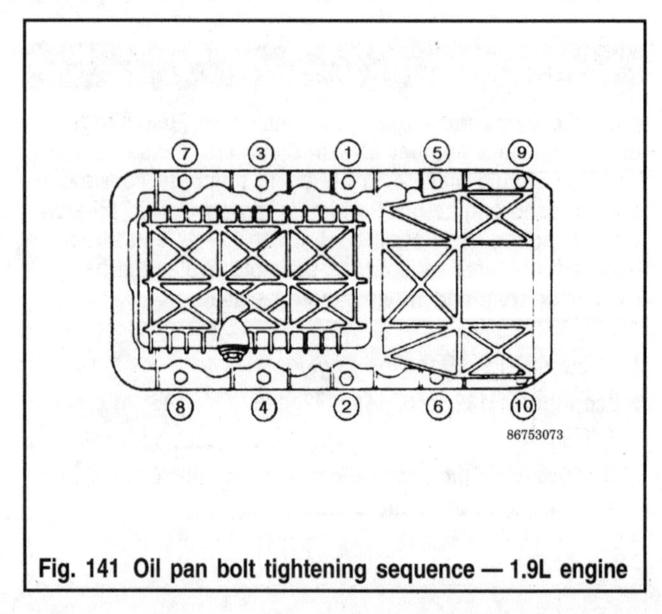

Fig. 141 Oil pan bolt tightening sequence — 1.9L engine

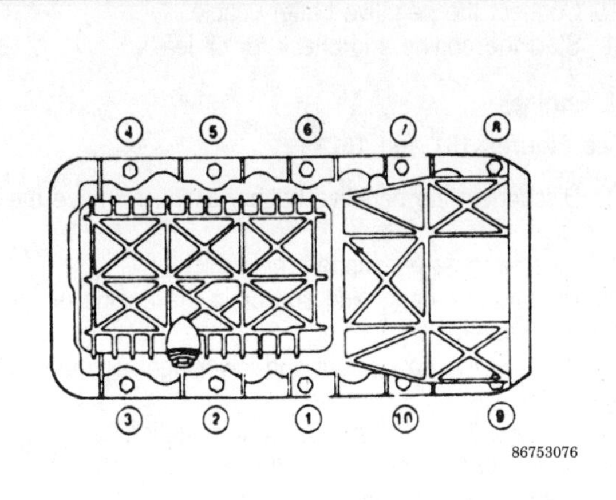

Fig. 142 Oil pan tightening sequence — 1988-90 1.9L engines

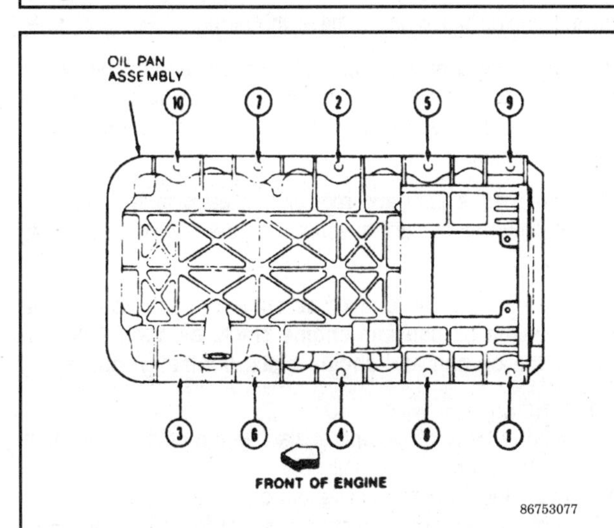

Fig. 143 Oil pan tightening sequence — 1990-95 1.9L engines

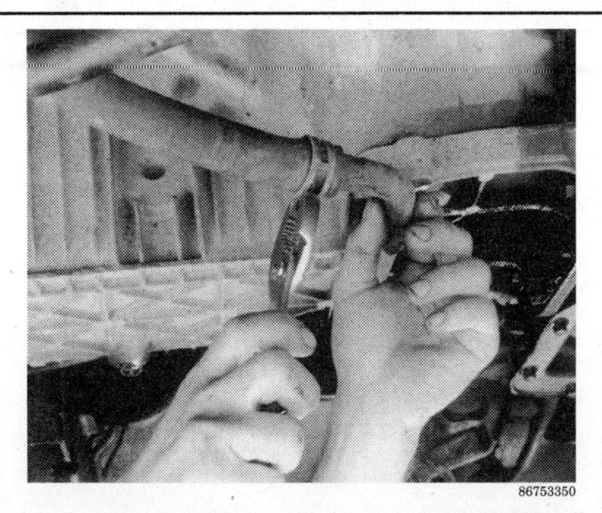

Fig. 144 Disconnect the coolant line to make way for lowering the oil pan — 1988 1.9L Escort

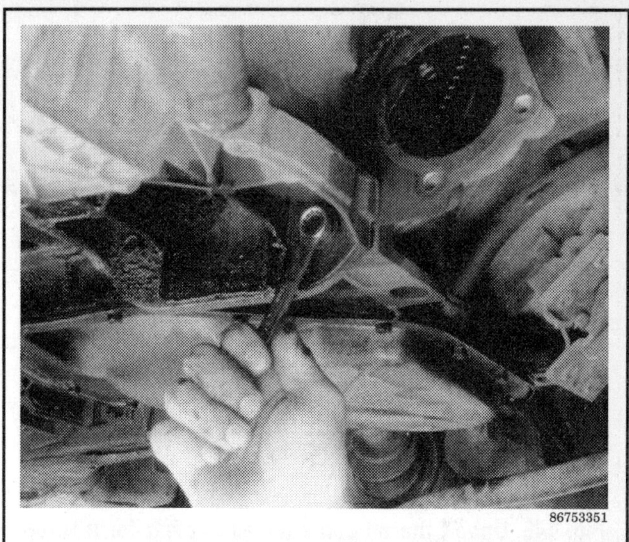

Fig. 145 Unbolt the oil-pan-to-transaxle fasteners

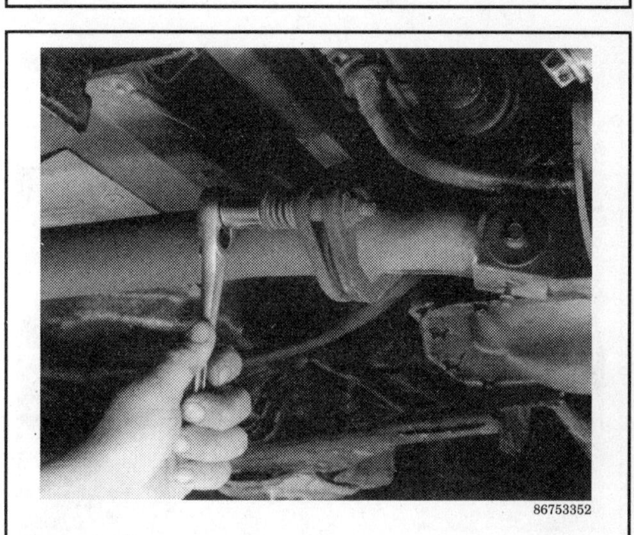

Fig. 146 Disconnect the exhaust pipe at the manifold and the rear flange (shown)

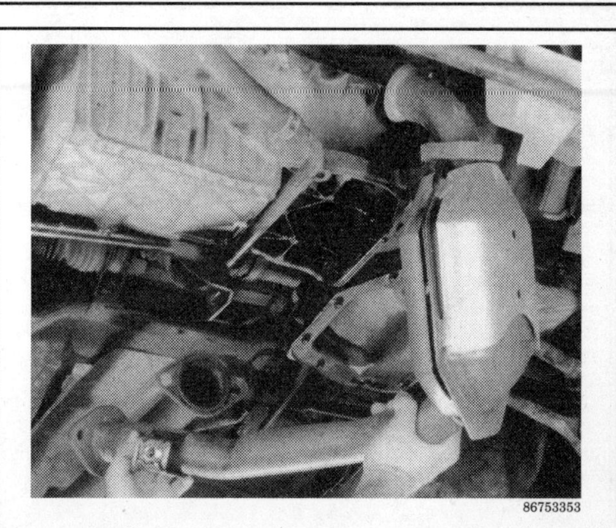

Fig. 147 Remove the exhaust pipe to make way for the oil pan removal

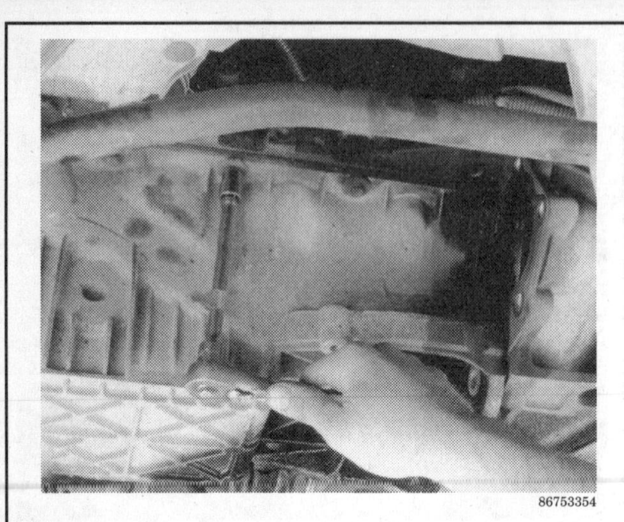

Fig. 148 Unbolt the oil pan after all is clear for it to be removed

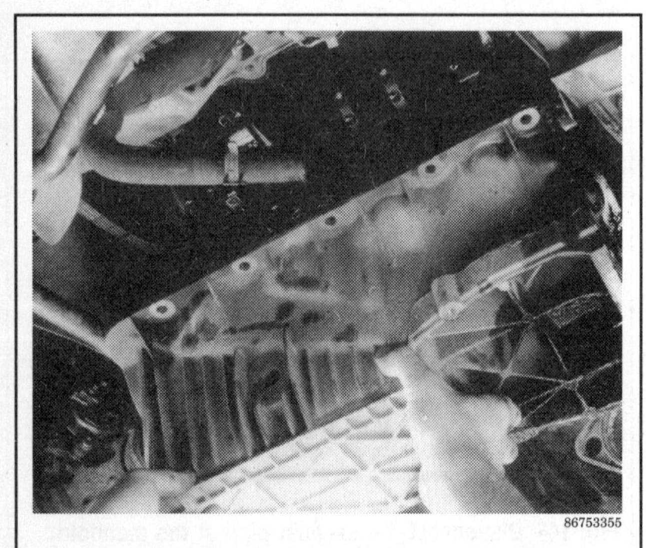

Fig. 149 Lower the oil pan carefully from the engine

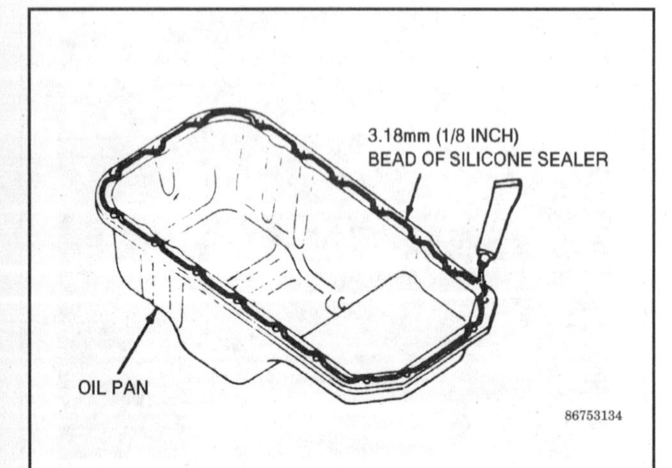

Fig. 150 The oil pan should be sealed with an appropriate heat resistant silicone — diesel engines

10. Connect the negative battery cable.
11. Start the engine and check for oil leaks.

1.8L Engine

➧ See Figures 151 and 152

1. Disconnect the negative battery cable. Remove the oil filler cap.
2. Raise and safely support the vehicle.
3. Remove the drain plug and drain the engine oil into a suitable container.
4. Remove the upper right and lower right and left splash shields.
5. Remove the exhaust pipe front mounting flange and exhaust pipe support bracket from the exhaust manifold.
6. Remove the oil pan-to-transaxle attaching bolts.
7. Support the oil pan with a suitable jackstand.
8. Remove the oil pan-to-engine block attaching bolts.
9. At the most rearward points of the oil pan (next to the transaxle) use a suitable tool to carefully pry the oil pan away from the engine block and remove the oil pan.

➡Do not force a prying tool between the engine block and the oil pan contact surface when trying to remove the oil pan. This may damage the oil pan contact surface and cause oil leakage.

10. Remove the front and rear oil pan gaskets and end seals. Remove all sealant material from the engine block and oil pan.

➡When removing the crankcase stiffeners and sealant material from the oil pan and engine block, be careful not to damage the oil pan and engine block contact surfaces.

To install:

11. Apply a bead of silicone sealant to the crankcase stiffeners along the inside of the bolt holes.
12. Install the crankcase stiffeners onto the oil pan.
13. Apply sealant to the proper areas of the end seals. Be sure to install the end seals with the projections in the notches.
14. Install the front and rear end seals onto the oil pan.

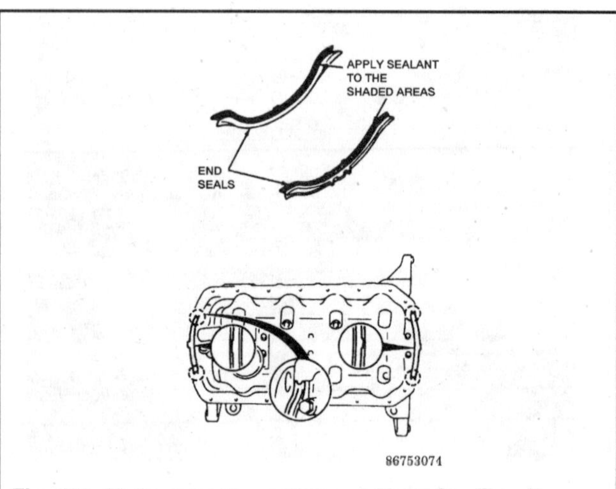

Fig. 151 Make sure the mating surfaces for the oil pan end seals are clean and dry — then apply sealant as shown-1.8L engines

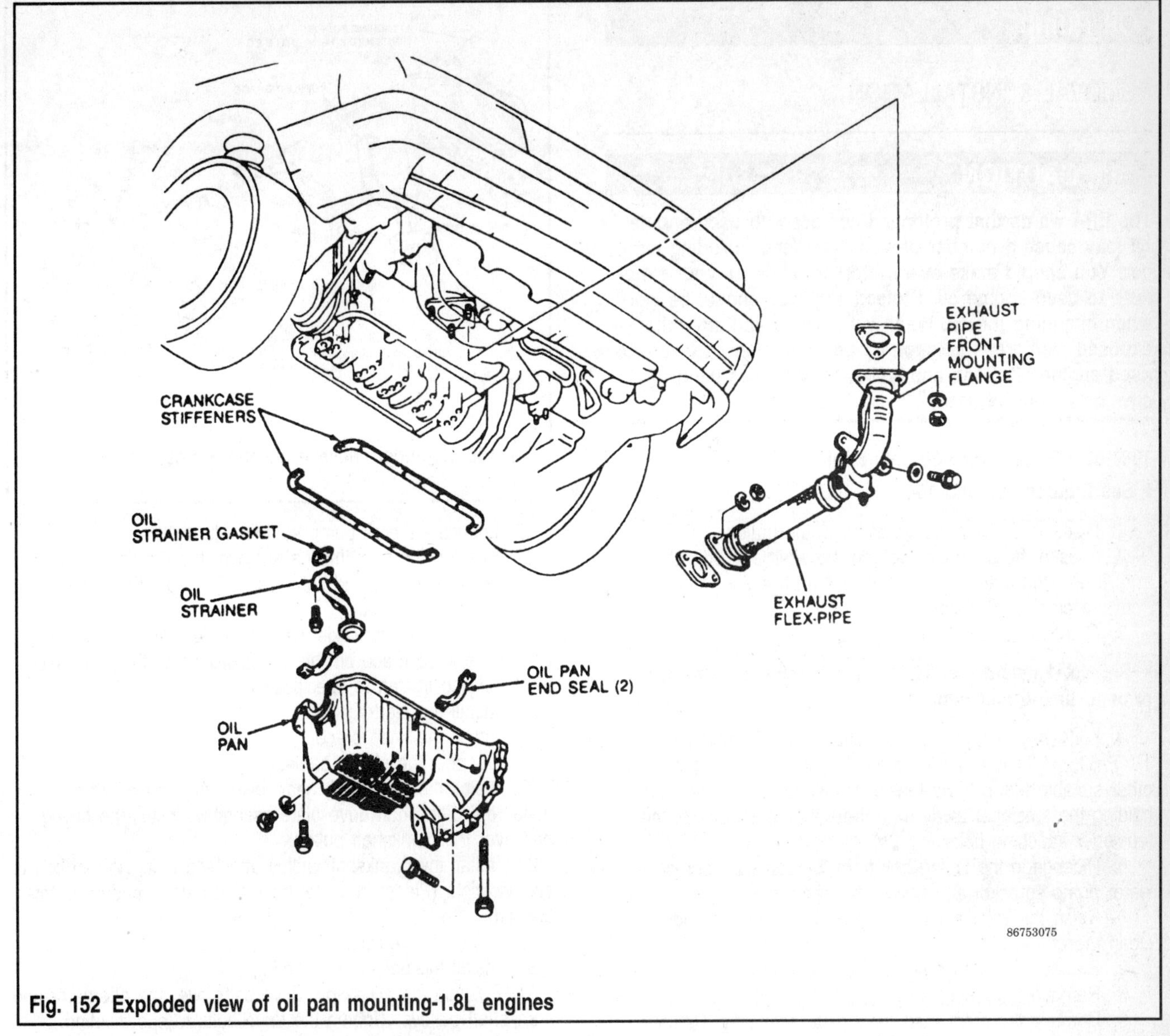

Fig. 152 Exploded view of oil pan mounting-1.8L engines

15. Apply a continuous bead of silicone sealant to the oil pan along the inside of the bolt holes. Overlap the sealant ends.

16. Place the oil pan into its mounting position and install the oil pan-to-engine block attaching bolts. Tighten the bolts to 69-95 inch lbs. (7.8-11.0 Nm).

➡If the oil pan attaching bolts are to be reused, the old sealant must be removed from the bolt threads. Tightening the old attaching bolts with old sealant still on them may cause cracking inside the bolt holes.

17. Install the oil pan-to-transaxle attaching bolts and tighten them to 27-38 ft. lbs. (37-52 Nm).

18. Install the oil drain plug and tighten it to 22-30 ft. lbs. (29-41 Nm).

19. Install the front exhaust mounting flange to the exhaust manifold, then install a new gasket. Tighten the mounting flange-to-exhaust manifold attaching nuts to 23-34 ft. lbs. (31-46 Nm).

20. Install the exhaust pipe support bracket, then tighten the bolts to 27-38 ft. lbs. (37-52 Nm).

21. Install the splash shields. Tighten the bolts to 69-95 inch lbs. (7.8-11.0 Nm).

22. Lower the vehicle.

23. Fill the crankcase with the proper type and quantity of engine oil. Install the filler cap.

24. Connect the negative battery cable.

Oil Pump

REMOVAL & INSTALLATION

CAUTION

The EPA warns that prolonged contact with used engine oil may cause a number of skin disorders, including cancer! You should make every effort to minimize your exposure to used engine oil. Protective gloves should be worn when changing the oil. Wash your hands and any other exposed skin areas as soon as possible after exposure to used engine oil. Soap and water, or waterless hand cleaner should be used.

1981-85 1.6L and 1985-90 1.9L Engines

See Figures 153 and 154

1. Disconnect the negative cable at the battery.
2. Loosen the alternator bolt on the alternator adjusting arm. Lower the alternator to remove the accessory drive belt from the crankshaft pulley.
3. Remove the timing belt cover.

Set No. 1 cylinder at TDC of the compression stroke prior to timing belt removal.

4. Loosen both belt tensioner attaching bolts using Tool T8AP-6254-A or equivalent on the left bolt. Using a prybar or other suitable tool pry the tensioner away from the belt. While holding the tensioner away from the belt, tighten one of the tensioner attaching bolts.
5. Disengage the timing belt from the camshaft sprocket, water pump sprocket and crankshaft sprocket.
6. Raise the vehicle and safely support on jackstands. Drain the crankcase.
7. Remove the crankshaft pulley attaching bolt.
8. Remove the timing belt.
9. Remove the crankshaft drive plate assembly. Remove the crankshaft pulley. Remove the crankshaft sprocket.
10. Disconnect the starter cable at the starter.
11. Remove the knee brace from the engine.
12. Remove the starter.
13. Remove the rear section of the knee brace and inspection plate at the transaxle.
14. Remove the oil pan retaining bolts and oil pan. Remove the front and rear oil pan seals. Remove the oil pan side gaskets. Remove the oil pump attaching bolts, oil pump and gasket. Remove the oil pump seal.
15. Make sure the mating surfaces on the cylinder block and the oil pump are clean and free of gasket material.
16. Remove the oil pick-up tube and screen assembly from the pump for cleaning.

To install:

17. Lubricate the outside diameter of the oil pump seal with engine oil.
18. Install the oil pump seal using seal installer T81P-6700-A or equivalent.
19. Install the pick-up tube and screen assembly on the oil pump. Tighten attaching bolts to 6-9 ft. lbs. (8-12 Nm).

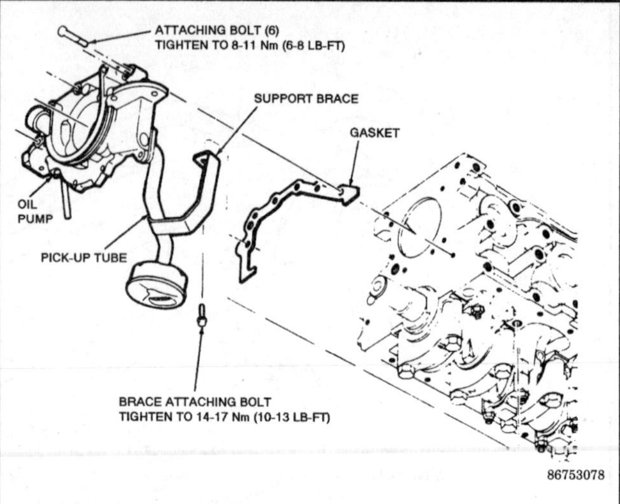

Fig. 153 Exploded view of oil pump mounting — 1.6L engines

20. Lubricate the oil pump seal lip with light engine oil.
21. Position the oil pump gasket over the locating dowels. Install attaching bolts and tighten to 5-7 ft. lbs. (7-9 Nm).
22. Install the oil pan.
23. Position the transaxle inspection plate and the rear section of the knee brace on the transaxle. Install the two attaching bolts and tighten to specification.
24. Install the starter.
25. Install the knee brace.
26. Connect the starter cable.
27. Install the crankshaft gear. Install the crankshaft pulley. Install the crankshaft drive plate assembly. Install the timing belt over the crankshaft pulley.
28. Install the crankshaft pulley attaching bolt. Tighten bolt to specification. (Please refer to the timing belt procedure in this section).
29. Lower the vehicle.
30. Install the engine front timing cover.
31. Position the accessory drive belts over the alternator and crankshaft pulleys. Tighten the drive belts to specification.
32. Connect the negative cable at the battery. Fill the crankcase to the proper level with the specified oil.
33. Start the engine and check for oil leaks. Make sure the oil pressure indicator lamp has gone out after a second or two. If the lamp remains on after several seconds, immediately shut off the engine. Determine the cause and correct the condition.

Diesel Engines

See Figure 155

1. Disconnect the negative battery cable.
2. Drain the engine oil.
3. Remove the oil pan.
4. Loosen the front timing belt.
5. Remove the bolts attaching the oil pump to the crankcase, then remove pump.
6. Remove crankshaft front oil seal.

To install:

7. Clean the oil pump and crankcase gasket mating surfaces.
8. Apply a 1/8 in. (3mm) bead of silicone sealer or equivalent, on oil pump-to-crankcase mating surface.

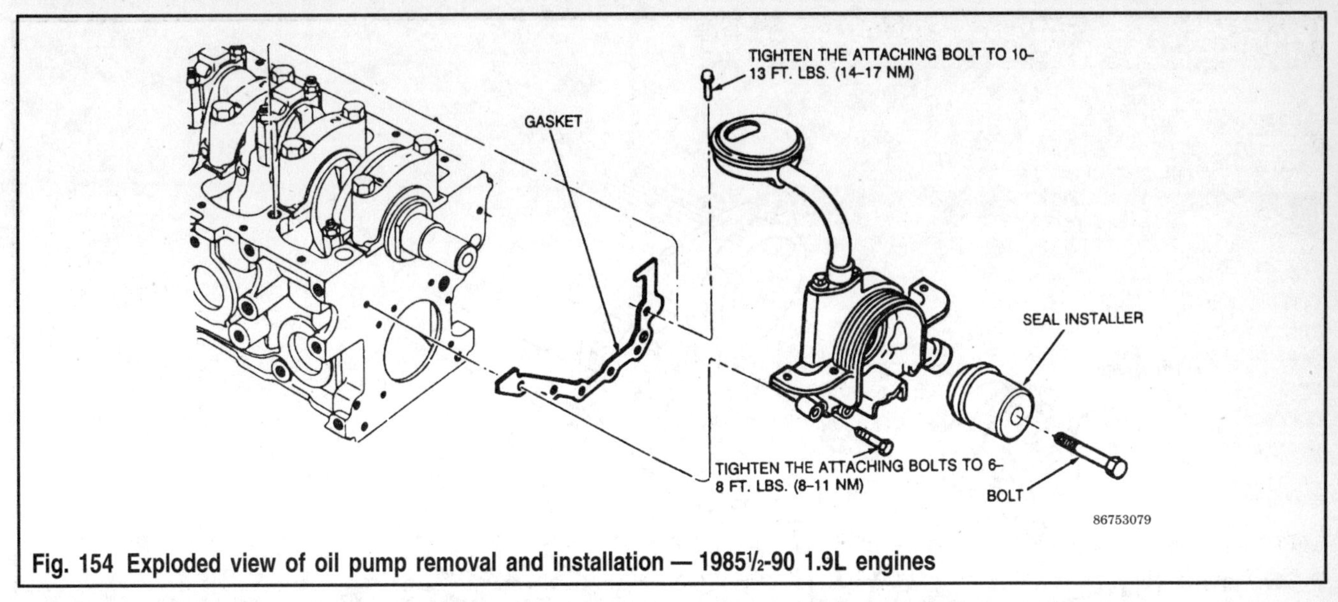

Fig. 154 Exploded view of oil pump removal and installation — 1985½-90 1.9L engines

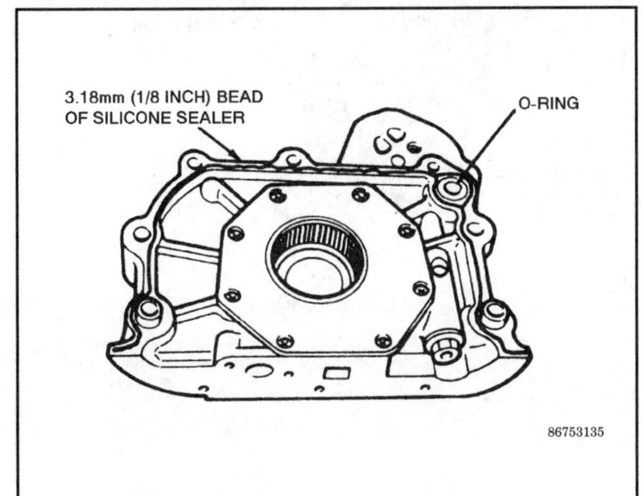

Fig. 155 The oil pump (shown) should be mounted using an approved silicone sealant

9. Install a new O-ring.
10. Install the oil pump, ensuring the oil pump inner gear engages with the splines on crankshaft. Tighten the 10mm bolts to 23-34 ft. lbs. (32-47 Nm) and 8mm bolts to 12-16 ft. lbs. (16-23 Nm).
11. Install a new crankshaft front oil seal.
12. Clean the oil pan-to-crankcase mating surfaces.
13. Apply a ⅛ in. (3mm) bead of silicone sealer or equivalent to the oil pan-to-crankcase mating surface.
14. Install the oil pan. Tighten bolts to 5-7 ft. lbs. (7-10 Nm).
15. Adjust the front timing belt.
16. Fill the crankcase with the recommended motor oil.
17. Connect the negative battery cable.
18. Start the engine and check for oil, fuel and coolant leaks.

1.8L Engine

➧ See Figure 156

1. Disconnect the negative battery cable.
2. Remove the timing belt and crankshaft pulley.
3. Unbolt and remove the oil pan.
4. Unbolt the oil strainer mounting bolts and remove the oil strainer and gasket.
5. If equipped, remove the air conditioning compressor mounting bolts and position the compressor so it is free from the work area.
6. Remove the air conditioning compressor mounting bracket.
7. Remove the mounting bolt from the engine oil dipstick tube bracket and remove the alternator lower mounting bolt.
8. Remove all oil pump mounting bolts and remove the oil pump. Remove all gasket material from the oil pump.

To install:

9. Install a new gasket onto the oil pump.
10. Place the oil pump into its mounting position and install the pump mounting bolts. Tighten the bolts to 14-19 ft. lbs. (19-25 Nm).
11. Place the dipstick tube bracket bolt into its mounting position and install the mounting bolt.
12. Install the alternator lower mounting bolt and tighten to 27-38 ft. lbs. (37-52 Nm).
13. Install a new gasket onto the oil strainer, place the strainer into its mounting position and install the mounting bolts. Tighten to 69-95 inch lbs. (7.8-11.0 Nm).
14. Install the oil pan.
15. If equipped, place the air conditioning compressor bracket into its mounting position and install the mounting bolts. Tighten the bolts to 15-22 ft. lbs. (20-30 Nm).
16. Install the crankshaft pulley and timing belt.
17. Connect the negative battery cable.
18. Start the engine and check for oil leaks. Make sure the oil pressure indicator lamp has gone out after a second or two. If the lamp remains on after several seconds, immediately shut off the engine. Determine the cause and correct the condition.

1991-95 1.9L Engine

➧ See Figure 157

1. Disconnect the negative battery cable.
2. Remove the accessory drive belt and the automatic tensioner.
3. Support the engine with a suitable floor jack.

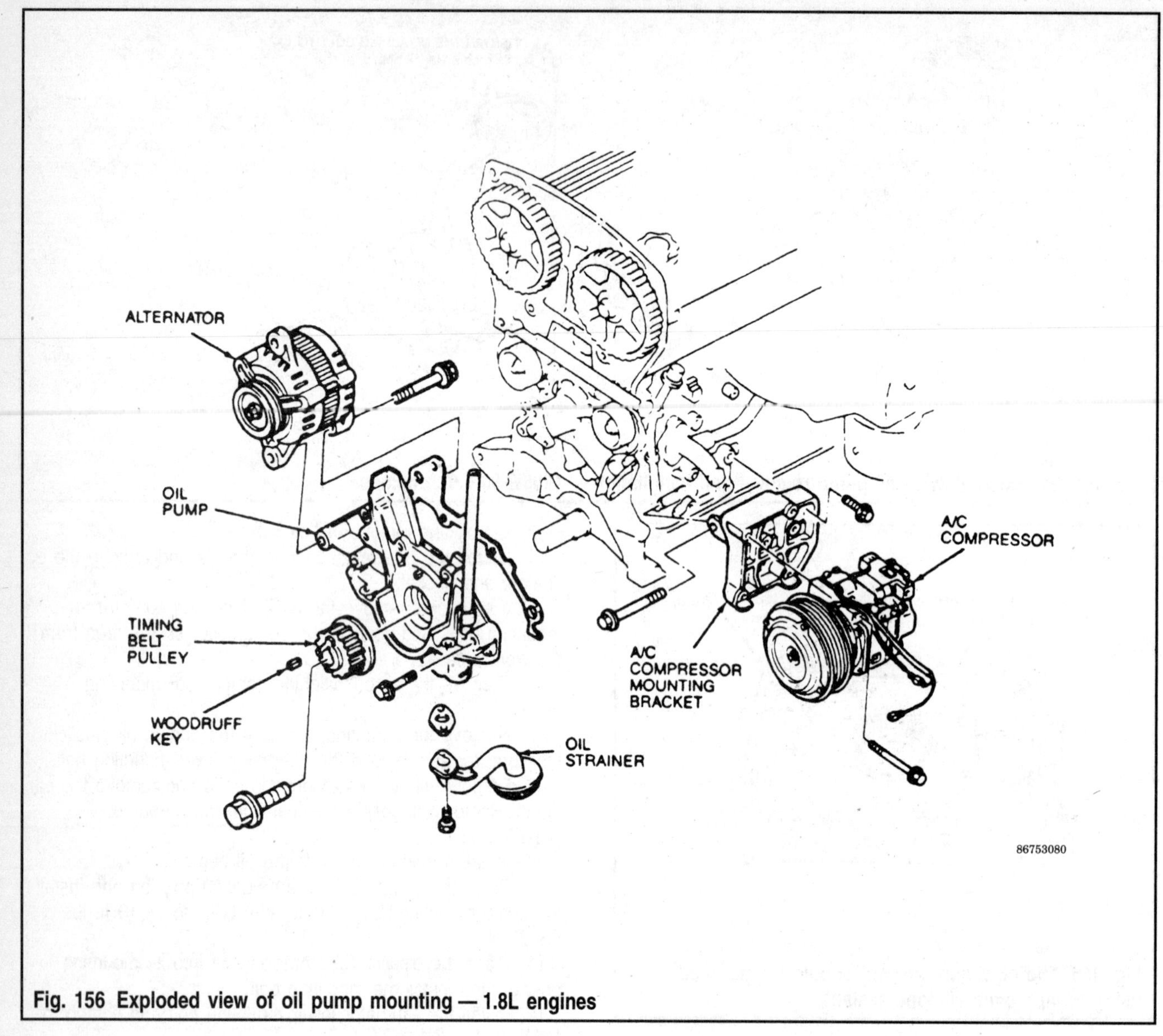

Fig. 156 Exploded view of oil pump mounting — 1.8L engines

4. Remove the right engine mount dampener and remove the right engine mount bolts from the mount bracket.
5. Loosen the mount through-bolt and roll the mount aside.
6. Remove the timing belt cover.
7. Make sure the No. 1 cylinder is at TDC.
8. Roll the engine mount back into place and install the two mount bolts. Remove the floor jack.
9. Loosen the belt tensioner attaching bolt and pry the tensioner to the rear of the engine. Tighten the attaching bolt.
10. Raise and safely support the vehicle.
11. Remove the right side splash shield.
12. Remove the catalytic converter inlet pipe.
13. Drain and remove the oil pan. Remove the oil filter.
14. Remove the crankshaft dampener and the timing belt.
15. Remove the crankshaft sprocket and the timing belt guide from the crankshaft.
16. Disconnect the crank angle sensor.
17. Remove the 6 oil pump-to-engine bolts and remove the oil pump assembly from the engine. Remove and discard the gasket.
18. Remove the crankshaft seal from the pump and discard.

To install:

19. Make sure the pump mating surfaces on the cylinder block and oil pump are clean and free of gasket material.
20. Remove the oil pickup tube and screen assembly from the pump for cleaning.
21. Lubricate the outside diameter of the crankshaft seal with engine oil and install the seal with a suitable installation tool. Lubricate the seal lip with clean engine oil.
22. Position the oil pump gasket on the cylinder block.
23. Using a suitable tool, position the pump drive gear to allow the pump to pilot over the crankshaft and seat firmly on the cylinder block.

➡The pump drive gear can be accessed through the oil pickup hole in the body of the pump. Do not install the oil pump pickup tube and screen until the pump has been correctly installed on the cylinder block.

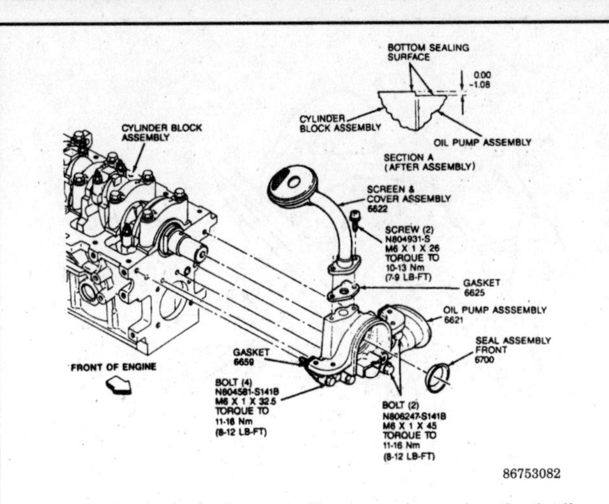

Fig. 157 Exploded view of oil pump mounting including related components and torque specifications — 1991-95 1.9L engines

24. Install the six oil pump bolts and tighten to 8-12 ft. lbs. (11-16 Nm).

➡When the oil pump bolts are tightened, the gasket must not be below the cylinder block sealing surface.

25. Install the pickup tube and screen assembly on the oil pump using a new gasket. Tighten the attaching screws to 7-9 ft. lbs. (10-13 Nm).
26. Install the timing belt guide over the end of the crankshaft and install the crankshaft sprocket.
27. Make sure the No. 1 cylinder is at TDC.
28. Position the timing belt over the sprockets.
29. Connect the crank angle sensor.
30. Install the oil pan and the crankshaft dampener.
31. Install the catalytic converter inlet pipe.
32. Install the splash shield and lower the vehicle.
33. Install the timing belt. Tighten the tensioner attaching bolt to 17-22 ft. lbs. (23-30 Nm).
34. Support the engine with a suitable floor jack.
35. Remove the right engine mount bolts and roll the mount back.
36. Install the timing belt cover.
37. Roll the engine mount back into place and install the attaching bolts. Tighten the mount through-bolt and install the mount dampener.
38. Remove the floor jack.
39. Install the accessory drive belt automatic tensioner and the accessory drive belt.
40. Fill the crankcase with the proper type and amount of engine oil.
41. Connect the negative battery cable, start the engine and check for leaks.

INSPECTION AND OVERHAUL

Except 1.8L Engine

➧ See Figures 158 and 159

➡The oil pump internal components are not serviceable. If any component is out of specification, the pump must be replaced.

1. Remove the oil pump from the vehicle.
2. Inspect the inside of the pump housing for damage or excessive wear.
3. Check the mating surface for wear. Minor scuff marks are normal, but if the cover, gears or housing are excessively worn, scored or grooved, replace the pump.
4. Inspect the rotor for nicks, burrs or score marks. Remove minor imperfections with an oil stone.
5. Measure the inner-to-outer rotor tip clearance. This clearance should be 0.002-0.007 in. (0.05-0.18mm).

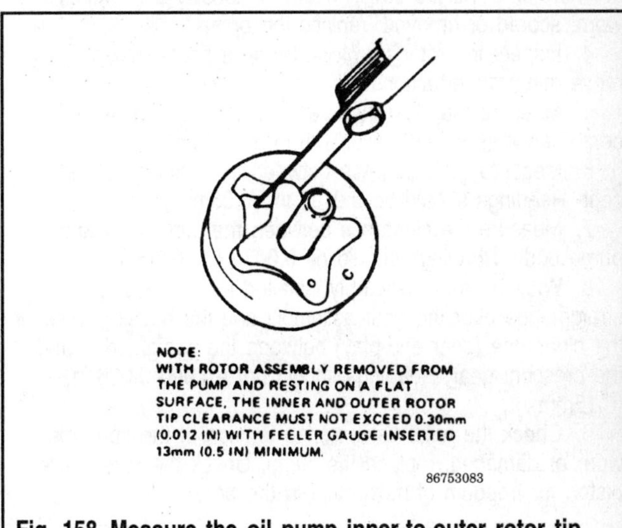

Fig. 158 Measure the oil pump inner-to-outer rotor tip clearance in this manner — gasoline engines

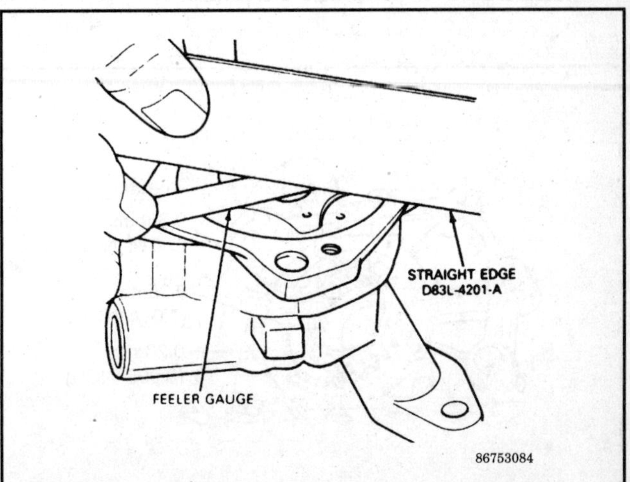

Fig. 159 Measure the oil pump rotor end-play using a straightedge and feeler gauge as shown — gasoline engines

6. With the rotor assembly installed in the housing, place a straightedge across the rotor assembly and housing. Measure the rotor end-play or clearance, between the the inner and outer rotors. This clearance should be 0.0005-0.0035 in. (0.013-0.0089mm).

7. Check the relief valve spring tension. If the spring is worn or damaged, replace the pump. Check the relief valve piston for freedom of movement in the bore.

Diesel Engine

➧ See Figures 160 and 161

➡The oil pump internal components are not serviceable. If any components are out of specification, the pump assembly must be replaced.

1. Remove the oil pump from the vehicle.
2. Inspect the inside of the pump housing for damage or excessive wear.
3. Check the mating surface for wear. Minor scuff marks are normal, but if the cover, gears or housing are excessively worn, scored or grooved, replace the pump.
4. Inspect the rotor for nicks, burrs or score marks. Remove minor imperfections with an oil stone.
5. Measure the clearance between the outer gear and crescent. Readings should be 0.0138 in. (0.35mm).
6. Measure the clearance between the inner gear and crescent. Readings should be 0.0138 in. (0.35mm).
7. Measure the clearance between the outer gear and pump body. Readings should be 0.0079 in. (0.20mm).
8. With the rotor assembly installed in the housing, place a straightedge over the gear assembly and the housing. Measure the clearance (gear end-play) between the straightedge and the crescent gear. Readings should not exceed 0.006 in. (0.15mm).
9. Check the relief valve spring tension. If the spring is worn or damaged, replace the pump. Check the relief valve piston for freedom of movement in the bore.

1.8L Engine

1. Remove the oil pump from the vehicle.

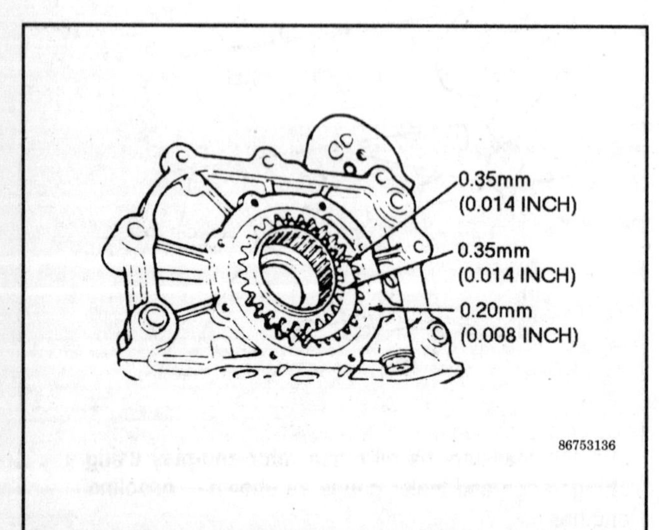

Fig. 160 Measure the oil pump gear clearance as indicated — diesel engines

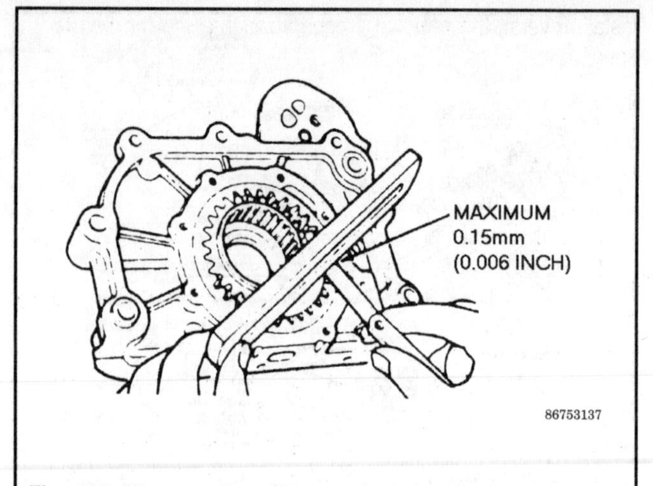

Fig. 161 Measure the oil pump housing to the crescent gear clearance with a straightedge and feeler gauge — diesel engines

2. Use a suitable feeler gauge to check the outer rotor tooth tip clearance. The maximum allowable clearance is 0.0079 in. (0.20mm).
3. Use a suitable feeler gauge to inspect the outer rotor-to-pump body clearance. The maximum allowable clearance is 0.0087 in. (0.22mm).
4. Use a straightedge and a feeler gauge to inspect the oil pump side clearance. The maximum allowable side clearance is 0.0055 in. (0.14mm).
5. Inspect the pressure spring for breakage or weak retraction. Inspect the pressure spring free length; it should be 1.791 in. (45.5mm).

Crankshaft Damper

REMOVAL & INSTALLATION

1981-90 1.9L Engines

1. Disconnect the negative battery cable.
2. Remove the accessory drive belts.
3. Connect an engine support tool, part No. D79P-6000-B, or equivalent to the engine.
4. With the engine supported, remove the right hand side engine bolt mount.
5. Remove the drive plate assembly.
6. Remove the crankshaft damper (pulley).

To install:

7. Position the crankshaft damper (pulley) on the crankshaft.
8. Install the drive plate and crankshaft pulley retaining bolt. Tighten to specification.
9. Install the accessory drive belt(s).
10. Connect the negative battery cable.

1.8L Engine

The 1.8L engine does not use a crankshaft damper, but it does employ a conventional pulley. The remove the pulley, remove any belts that interfere with and/or are attached to the pulley, and remove using a suitable puller, if necessary. To install, reverse the removal procedure, tightening the bolt to specification.

1991-95 1.9L Engine

1. Disconnect the negative battery cable.
2. Remove the accessory drive belt.
3. Raise and safely support the vehicle.
4. Remove the right side splash shield.
5. Remove the flywheel inspection shield.
6. Using a suitable tool to hold the flywheel, remove the crankshaft damper (pulley) bolt and washer.

To install:

7. Position the dampener on the crankshaft and install the retaining bolt and washer. Tighten to 81-96 ft. lbs. (110-130 Nm).
8. Install the splash shield and flywheel inspection shield.
9. Lower the vehicle.
10. Install the accessory drive belt.
11. Connect the negative battery cable.

Timing Belt Cover

REMOVAL & INSTALLATION

1981-85 1.6L and 1985-90 1.9L Engines

➧ See Figures 162 and 163

1. Disconnect the negative battery cable.
2. Remove the accessory drive belt(s).
3. Remove the crankshaft pulley and drive plate.
4. Remove the two upper and lower timing belt cover attaching bolts.
5. Remove the timing belt cover.

To install:

6. Place the timing belt cover into position and install the attaching bolts.
7. Install the crankshaft pulley and drive plate.
8. Install the accessory drive belt(s).
9. Connect the negative battery cable.

1.8L Engine

➧ See Figure 164

1. Disconnect the negative battery cable.
2. Remove the timing belt upper cover and gasket.
3. Loosen the water pump pulley bolts.
4. Remove the alternator and water pump accessory drive belt.
5. Remove the water pump pulley bolts and remove the pulley.
6. Raise and safely support the vehicle.
7. Remove the right wheel and tire assembly.
8. Remove the right upper and lower splash shields.
9. Remove the air conditioning belt, if equipped, and power steering accessory drive belt.
10. Remove the crankshaft pulley, crankshaft pulley guide plate and timing belt outer and inner guide plates.
11. Remove the timing belt middle and lower covers along with the gaskets.

To install:

12. Install the timing belt middle and lower covers along with the gaskets.
13. Install the timing belt inner and outer guide plates, the crankshaft pulley and the crankshaft pulley guide plate. Tighten the bolts to 109-152 inch lbs. (12-17 Nm).
14. Install the air conditioning belt, if equipped, and power steering accessory drive belt.
15. Install the splash shields and tighten the bolts to 69-95 inch lbs. (7.8-11.0 Nm).
16. Install the water pump pulley and tighten the bolts to 69-95 inch lbs. (7.8-11.0 Nm).
17. Install the alternator and water pump accessory drive belt.
18. Install the right wheel and tire assembly and lower the vehicle.
19. Install the timing belt upper cover and gasket. Tighten the bolts to 69-95 inch lbs. (7.8-11.0 Nm).
20. Connect the negative battery cable.

1991-95 1.9L Engine

➧ See Figure 165

1. Disconnect the negative battery cable.
2. Remove the accessory drive belt(s).
3. Remove the drive belt automatic tensioner.
4. Remove the two timing belt cover attaching nuts and remove the timing belt cover from the mounting studs.

To install:

5. Position the timing belt cover on the mounting studs.
6. Install the attaching nuts and tighten to 3-5 ft. lbs. (5-7 Nm).
7. Install the drive belt automatic tensioner and drive belt.
8. Connect the negative battery cable.

Gasoline Engine Timing Belt

REMOVAL & INSTALLATION

1981-85 1.6L and 1985-90 1.9L Engines

➧ See Figures 166, 167, 168 and 169

1. Disconnect the negative battery cable.
2. Remove the timing belt cover.

➡Align the timing mark on the camshaft sprocket with the timing mark on the cylinder head.

3. Install the timing belt cover and confirm that the timing mark on the crankshaft pulley aligns with the TDC on the front cover.
4. Remove the timing belt cover.
5. Loosen both timing belt tensioner attaching bolts using a torque wrench adapter (T81P-6254-A or equivalent).
6. Pry the belt tensioner away from the belt as far as possible and tighten one of the tensioner attaching bolts.
7. Remove the crankshaft pulley and remove the timing belt.

➡With the timing belt removed and the No. 1 piston at TDC, do not rotate the camshaft.

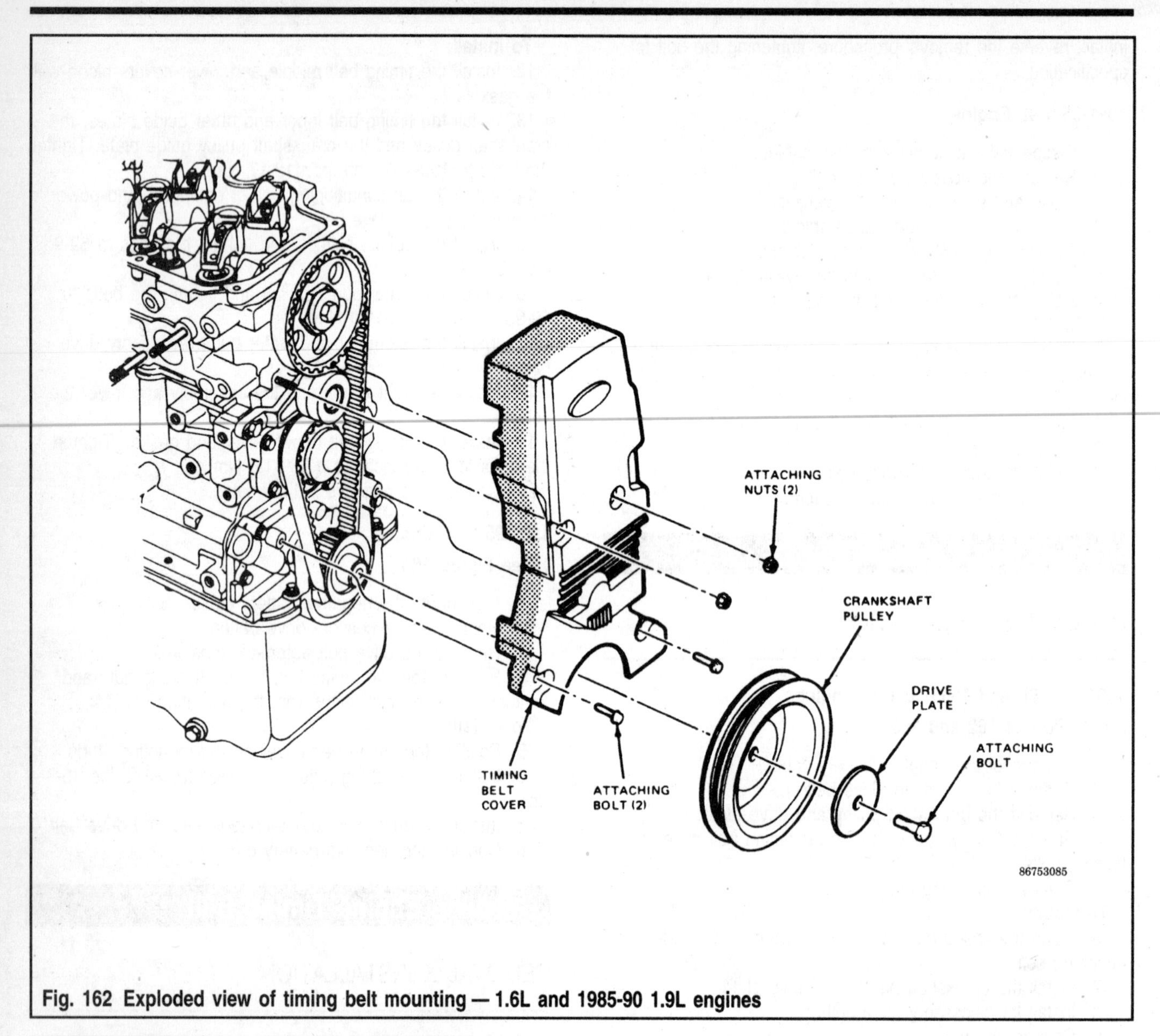

Fig. 162 Exploded view of timing belt mounting — 1.6L and 1985-90 1.9L engines

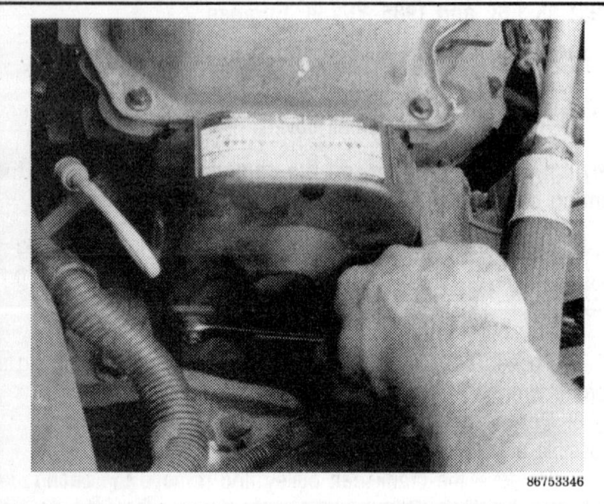

Fig. 163 Remove the timing belt cover attaching bolts — 1988 1.9L engine shown

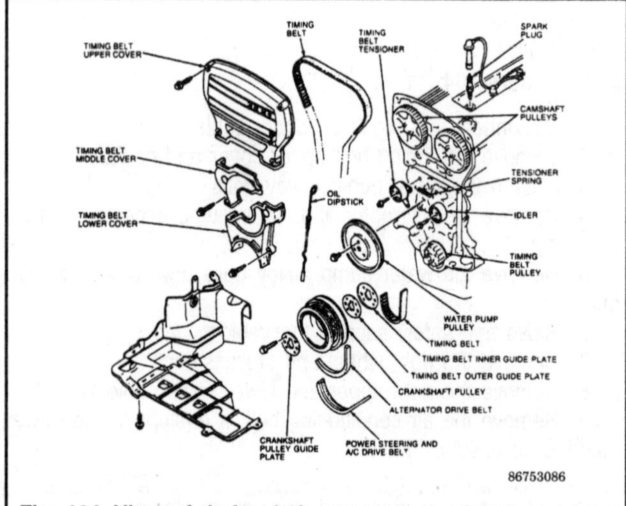

Fig. 164 View of timing belt covers and related components — 1.8L engines

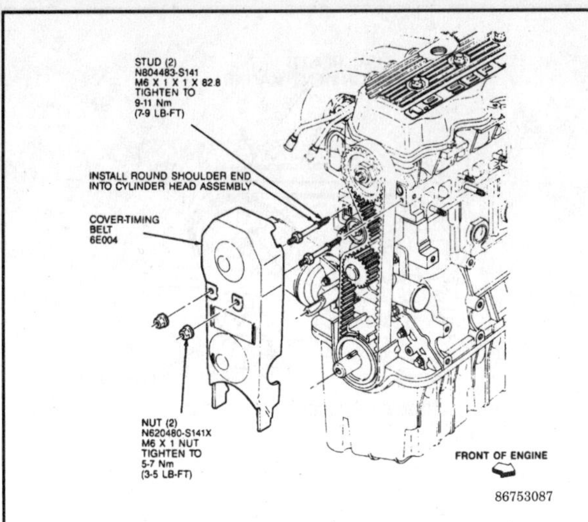

Fig. 165 Mounting position of the timing belt cover and torque figures — 1991-95 1.9L engines

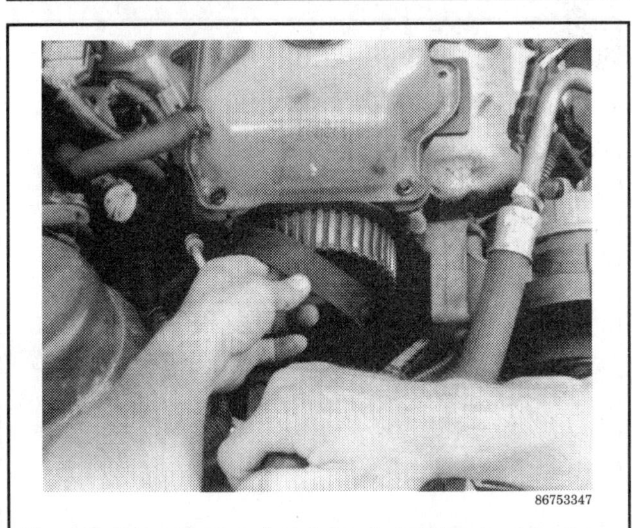

Fig. 166 Once tension is released and the crank pulley is removed, slide the timing belt from the cam pulley

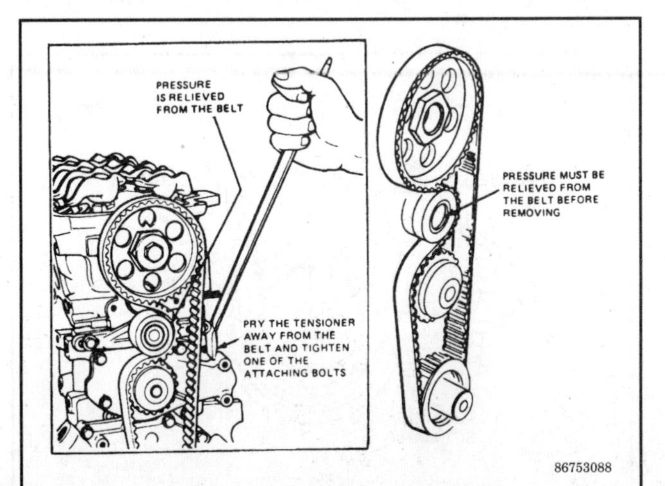

Fig. 167 For timing belt removal, relieve the tensioner pressure from the belt as demonstrated — 1.6L, 1985-90 1.9L engines

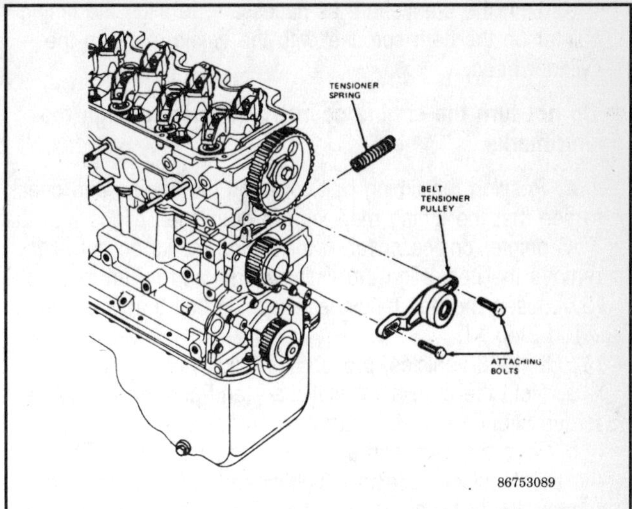

Fig. 168 Exploded view of the timing belt tensioner mounting position — 1.6L and 1985-90 1.9L engines

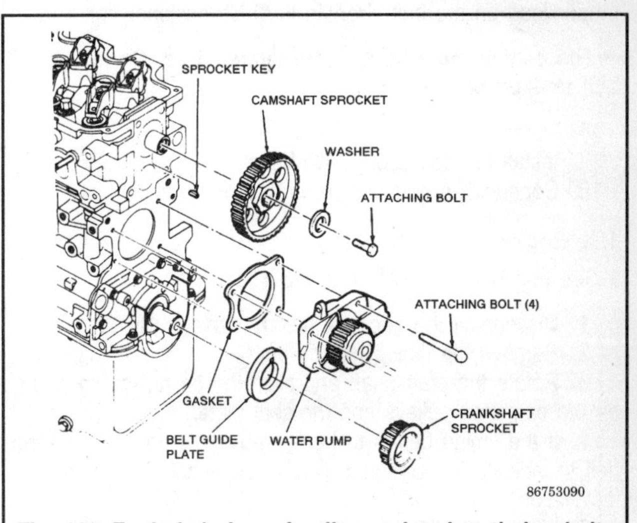

Fig. 169 Exploded view of pulleys related to timing belt mounting — 1.6L and 1985-90 1.9L engines

To install:

8. Install the timing belt over the sprockets in the counterclockwise direction, starting at the crankshaft. Keep the belt span from the crankshaft to the camshaft tight as the belt is installed over the remaining sprockets.
9. Loosen the belt tensioner attaching bolts and allow the tensioner to snap against the belt.
10. Tighten one of the tensioner attaching bolts.
11. Install the crankshaft pulley, driveplate and pulley attaching bolt. Hold the crankshaft pulley stationary and tighten the pulley attaching bolt to 74-90 ft. lbs. (100-121 Nm).
12. To seat the belt on the sprocket teeth, complete the following:
    a. Connect the negative battery terminal.
    b. Crank the engine several revolutions.
    c. Disconnect the negative battery terminal.

d. Turn the crankshaft, as necessary, to align the timing pointer on the cam sprocket with the timing mark on the cylinder head.

➡Do not turn the engine counterclockwise to align the timing marks.

e. Position the timing belt cover on the engine and check to see that the timing mark on the crankshaft aligns with the TDC pointer on the cover. If the timing marks do not align, remove the belt, align the timing marks and return to Step 9.

13. Loosen the belt tensioner attaching bolt that was tightened in Step 11.

14. On 1988 vehicles, proceed as follows:

a. Hold the crankshaft stationary and position a suitable torque wrench onto the camshaft sprocket bolt.

b. Turn the camshaft sprocket counterclockwise. Tighten the belt tensioner attaching bolt when the torque wrench reads: 27-32 ft. lbs. (36-43 Nm). For a used belt (in service for 30 days or more), tighten the 10 ft. lbs. (13 Nm).

15. On 1989-90 vehicles, the tensioner spring will apply the proper load on the belt. Tighten the belt tensioner bolt.

➡The engine must be at room temperature. Do not set belt tension on a hot engine.

16. Install the timing belt cover.

17. Install the accessory drive belts.

18. Connect the negative battery cable.

1.8L Engine

▶ See Figures 170, 171, 172 and 173

1. Disconnect the negative battery cable.
2. Remove the timing belt covers.
3. Rotate the crankshaft and align the timing marks located on the camshaft pulleys and the seal plate.
4. If the timing belt is to be reused, mark an arrow on the belt to indicate its rotational direction to enable correct reinstallation.
5. Loosen the timing belt tensioner lockbolt and remove the timing belt.

To install:

6. Temporarily secure the timing belt tensioner in the far left position with the spring fully extended, then tighten the lockbolt.
7. Make sure the timing marks on the timing belt pulley and the engine block are aligned.
8. Make sure the timing marks on the camshaft pulleys and the seal plate are aligned.
9. Install the timing belt.
10. Loosen the tensioner lockbolt. Using a suitable prying tool, position the timing belt tensioner so the timing belt is taut, then tighten the tensioner lockbolt.
11. Turn the crankshaft two turns clockwise and align the timing belt pulley mark with the mark on the engine block.
12. Make sure the camshaft pulley marks are aligned with the seal plate marks.

➡If the timing marks are not aligned, remove the belt and repeat the procedure.

13. Turn the crankshaft 1⅚ turns clockwise and align the timing belt pulley mark with the tension set mark, at approximately the 10 o'clock position.

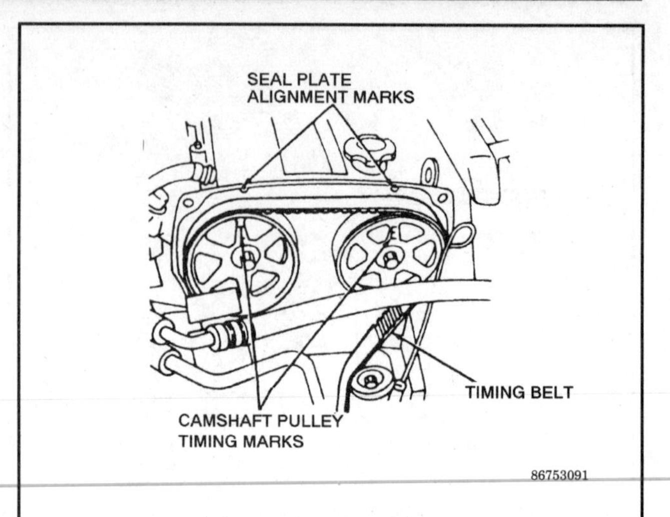

Fig. 170 Timing marks are located on the camshaft pulleys as shown — 1.8L engines

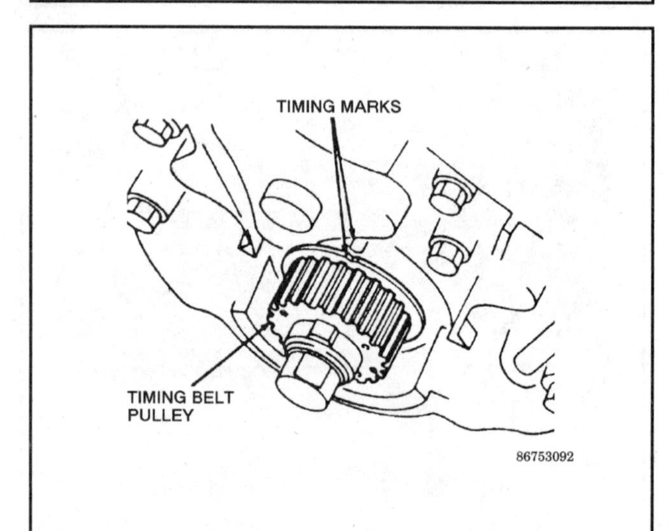

Fig. 171 Timing belt pulley and engine block timing marks — 1.8L engines

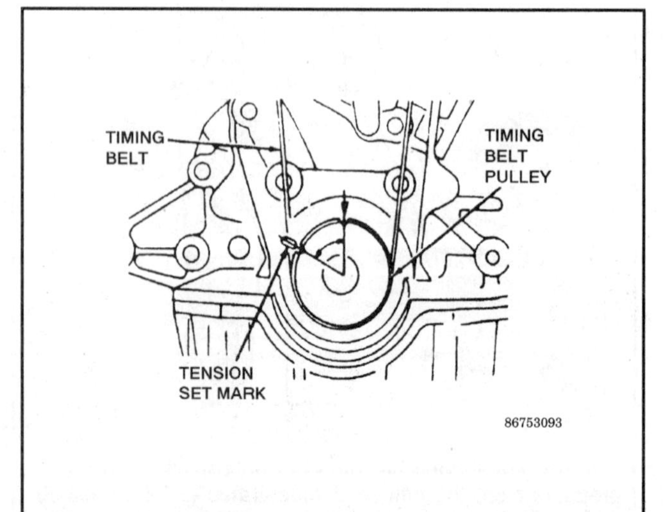

Fig. 172 Set mark for tensioning the timing belt — 1.8L engines

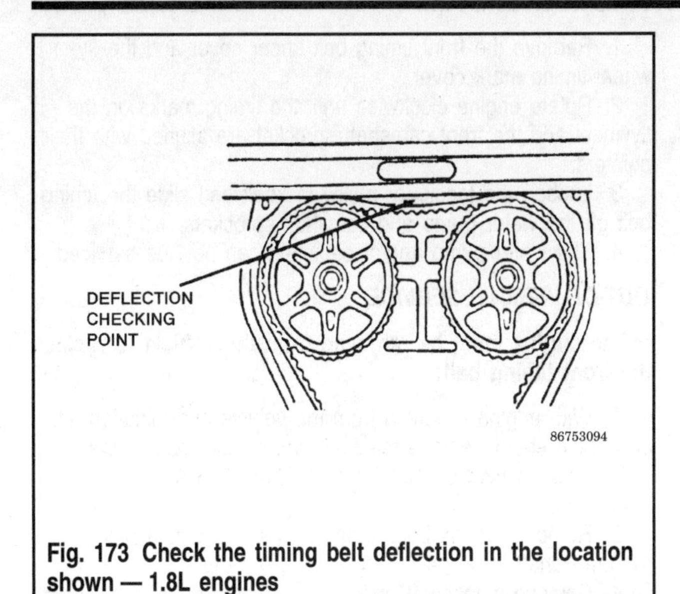

Fig. 173 Check the timing belt deflection in the location shown — 1.8L engines

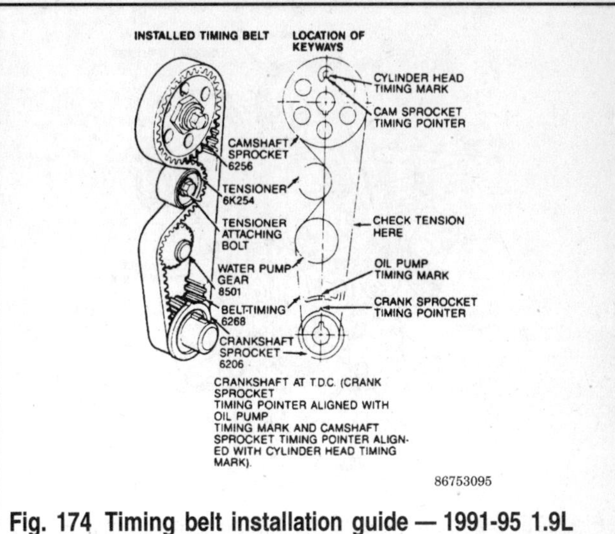

Fig. 174 Timing belt installation guide — 1991-95 1.9L engines

14. Apply tension to the timing belt tensioner and install the tensioner lockbolt. Tighten the bolt to 27-38 ft. lbs. (37-52 Nm).
15. Turn the crankshaft 2¹⁄₆ turns clockwise and make sure the timing marks are aligned.
16. Measure the timing belt deflection by applying 22 lbs. (10 kg) of pressure on the belt between the camshaft pulleys. The timing belt deflection should be 0.35-0.45 in. (9.0-11.5mm). If necessary, adjust the timing belt deflection.
17. Turn the crankshaft two turns clockwise and make sure the timing marks are aligned.

➡If the timing marks are not aligned, repeat the procedure beginning at Step 9.

18. Install the timing belt covers and the remaining components according to the proper procedure.
19. Connect the negative battery cable.

1991-95 1.9L Engine

See Figure 174

1. Disconnect the negative battery cable.
2. Remove the accessory drive belt automatic tensioner and the accessory drive bolt.
3. Remove the timing belt cover.
4. Align the timing mark on the camshaft sprocket with the timing mark on the cylinder head.
5. Confirm that the timing mark on the crankshaft sprocket is aligned with the timing mark on the oil pump housing.
6. Loosen the belt tensioner attaching bolt, pry the tensioner away from the timing belt and retighten the bolt.
7. Remove the spark plugs.
8. Raise and safely support the vehicle.
9. Remove the right side splash shield.
10. Remove the flywheel inspection shield.
11. Use a suitable tool to hold the flywheel in place.
12. Remove the crankshaft dampener bolt and washer and remove the dampener.
13. Remove the timing belt.

➡With the timing belt removed and the No. 1 piston at TDC, do not rotate the camshaft.

To install:

14. Install the timing belt over the sprockets in a counterclockwise direction starting at the crankshaft. Keep the belt span from the crankshaft to the camshaft tight while positioning the belt over the remaining sprockets.
15. Loosen the belt tensioner attaching bolt, then allow the tensioner to snap against the belt.
16. Rotate the crankshaft clockwise two complete revolutions. This will allow the tensioner spring to properly load the timing belt.

➡Do not turn the engine counterclockwise to align the timing marks.

17. Tighten the tensioner attaching bolt to 17-22 ft. lbs. (23-30 Nm).
18. Install the crankshaft dampener and the bolt and washer. Tighten the bolt to 81-96 ft. lbs. (110-130 Nm).
19. Install the flywheel inspection shield.
20. Install the splash shield and lower the vehicle.
21. Install the spark plugs.
22. Install the timing belt cover.
23. Install the accessory drive belt automatic tensioner and the accessory drive belt.
24. Connect the negative battery cable.

Diesel Engine Timing Belt

FRONT TIMING BELT

See Figures 175 and 176

Removal & Installation

IN-VEHICLE SERVICE

➡This procedure is for loosening the front timing belt for in-vehicle service of the water pump, camshaft, or cylinder head. The timing belt cannot be replaced with the engine installed in the vehicle.

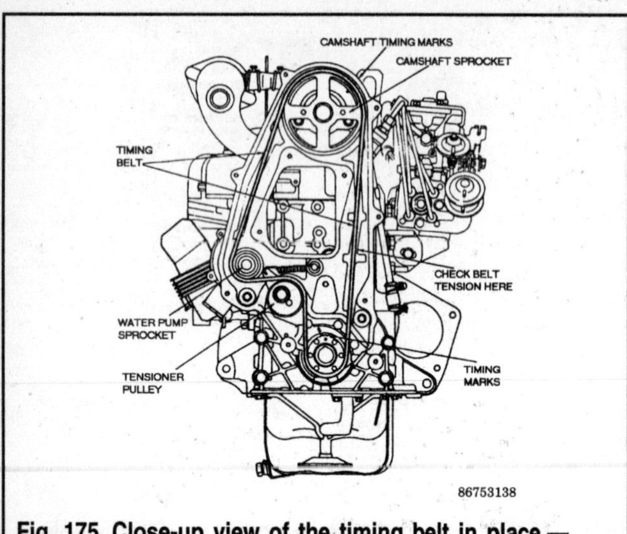

Fig. 175 Close-up view of the timing belt in place — diesel engines

1. Remove the front timing belt upper cover and the flywheel timing mark cover.
2. Rotate engine clockwise until the timing marks on the flywheel and the front camshaft sprocket are aligned with their pointers.
3. Loosen the tensioner pulley lockbolt and slide the timing belt off the water pump and camshaft sprockets.
4. The water pump and/or camshaft can now be serviced.

OUT-OF-VEHICLE SERVICE

➡The engine must be removed from the vehicle to replace the front timing belt.

1. With engine removed from the vehicle and installed on an engine stand, remove the front timing belt upper cover.
2. Install a flywheel holding tool T84P-6375-A, or equivalent.
3. Remove the six bolts attaching the crankshaft pulley to the crankshaft sprocket.
4. Remove crankshaft pulley.
5. Remove the front timing belt lower cover.

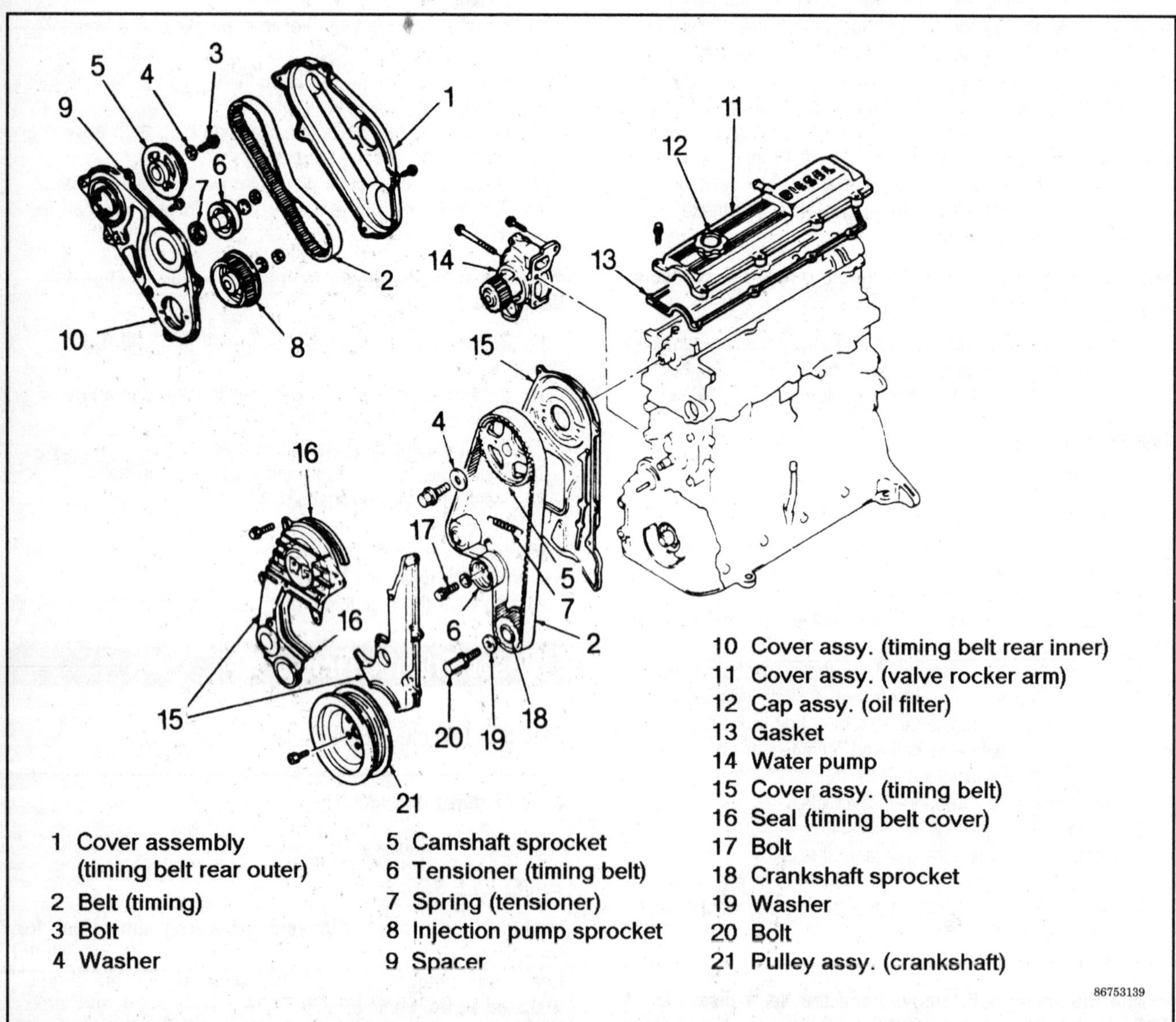

Fig. 176 Exploded view and legend describing the front and rear timing gear — diesel engines

6. Loosen the tensioning pulley and remove the timing belt.
7. Align the camshaft sprocket with the timing mark.

➡Check the crankshaft sprocket to see that the timing marks are aligned.

8. Remove the tensioner spring from the pocket in the front timing belt upper cover and install it in the slot in the tensioner lever and over the stud in the crankcase.
9. Push the tensioner lever toward the water pump as far as it will travel and tighten the lockbolt snug.
10. Install the timing belt.
11. Adjust the timing belt tension.
12. Install the front timing belt lower cover and tighten the bolts to 5-7 ft. lbs. (7-9 Nm).
13. Install the crankshaft pulley and tighten the bolts to 17-24 ft. lbs. (23-32 Nm).
14. Install the front timing belt upper cover and tighten the bolts to 5-7 ft. lbs. (7-9 Nm).

Adjustment

➧ See Figures 177, 178, 179, 180 and 181

1. Remove the flywheel timing mark cover.
2. Remove the front timing belt upper cover.
3. Remove the belt tension spring from the storage pocket in the front cover.
4. Install the tensioner spring in the belt tensioner lever and over the stud mounted on the front of the crankcase.
5. Loosen the tensioner pulley lockbolt.
6. Rotate the crankshaft pulley two revolutions clockwise until the flywheel TDC timing mark aligns with the pointer on the rear cover plate.
7. Check the front camshaft sprocket to see that it is aligned with its timing mark.
8. Tighten the tensioner lockbolt to 23-34 ft. lbs. (32-46 Nm).
9. Check the belt tension using the Rotunda Belt Tension Gauge model 21-0028 or equivalent. Belt tension should be 33-44 lbs. (15-20 kg).
10. Remove the tensioner spring and install it in the storage pocket in the front cover.

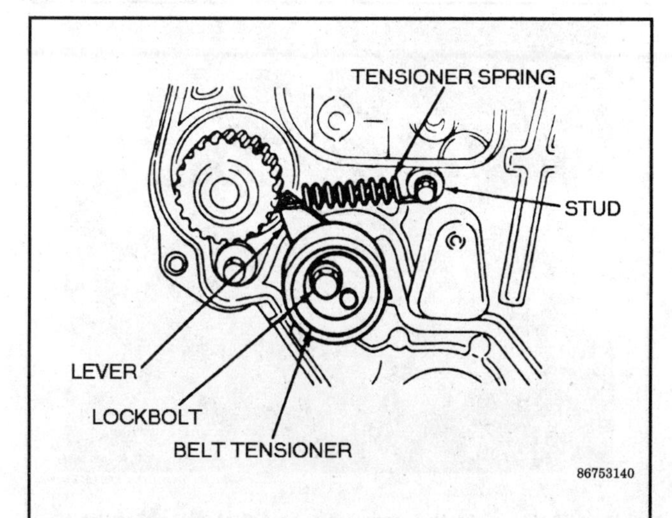

Fig. 177 Close-up view of the tensioner system for the front timing belt — diesel engines

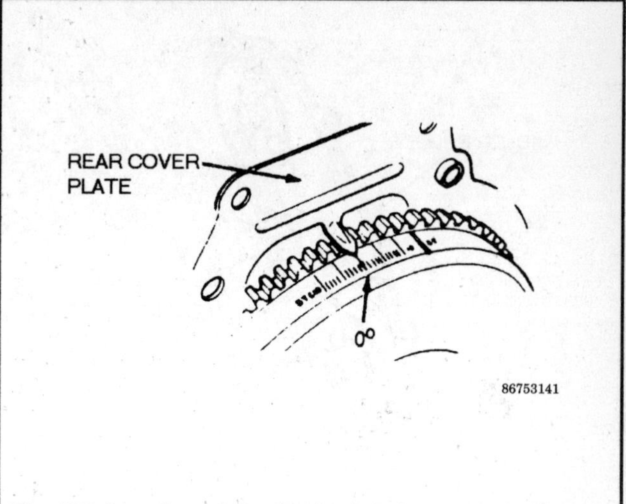

Fig. 178 Location of the flywheel timing mark — diesel engines

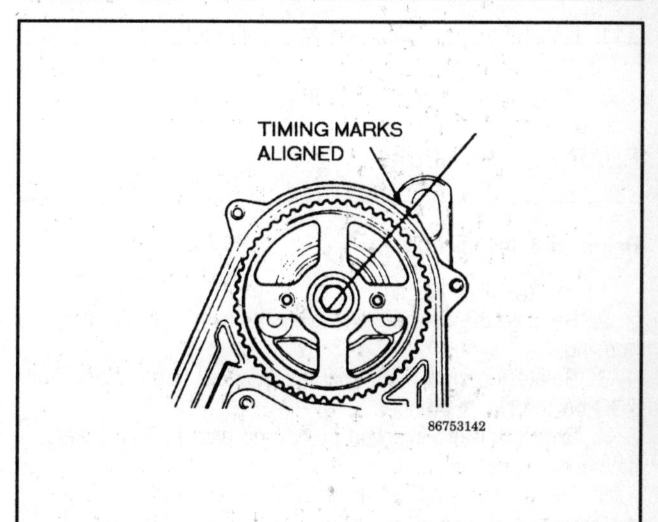

Fig. 179 Location of the camshaft timing mark — diesel engines

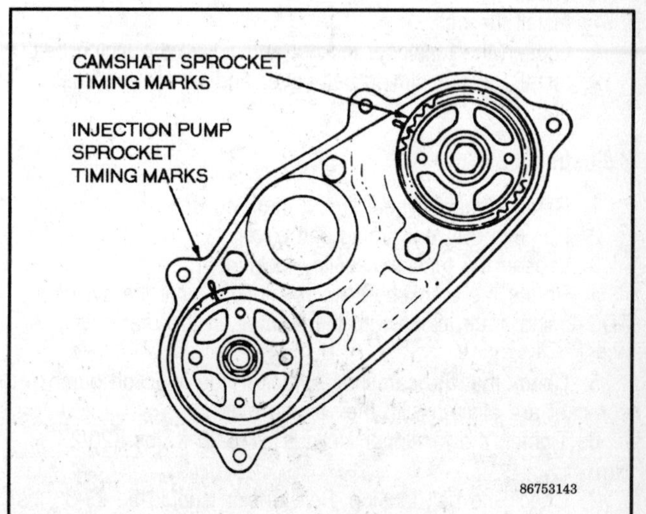

Fig. 180 Location of timing marks for the camshaft and injection pump sprocket — diesel engines

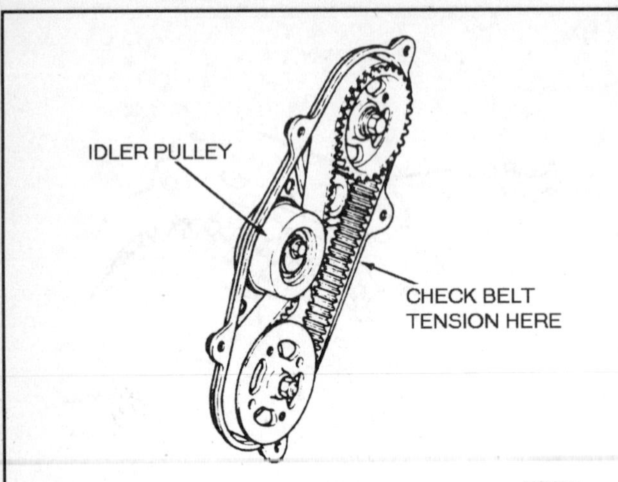

Fig. 181 Close-up of the rear timing belt tensioner — diesel engines

11. Install the front cover and tighten the attaching bolts to 5-7 ft. lbs. (7-9.5 Nm).
12. Install the flywheel timing mark cover.

REAR TIMING BELT

Removal & Installation

1. Remove the rear timing belt cover.
2. Remove the flywheel timing mark cover from the clutch housing.
3. Rotate the crankshaft until the flywheel timing mark is at TDC on the No. 1 cylinder.
4. Check that the injection pump and camshaft sprocket timing marks are aligned.
5. Loosen the tensioner locknut. With a suitable prytool inserted in the slot provided, rotate the tensioner clockwise to relieve the belt tension. Tighten locknut snug.
6. Remove the timing belt.

To install:

7. Install the belt.
8. Loosen the tensioner locknut and adjust the timing belt.
9. Install the rear timing belt cover and tighten the bolts to 5-7 ft. lbs. (7-9.5 Nm).

Adjustment

1. Remove the flywheel timing mark cover.
2. Remove the rear timing belt cover.
3. Loosen the tensioner pulley locknut.
4. Rotate the crankshaft two revolutions until the flywheel TDC timing mark aligns with the pointer on the rear cover plate.
5. Check that the camshaft sprocket and injection pump sprocket are aligned with their timing marks.
6. Tighten the tensioner locknut to 15-20 ft. lbs. (20-27 Nm).
7. Check the belt tension. Belt tension should be 22-33 lbs. (10-15 kg).

8. Install the rear timing belt cover. Tighten the 6mm bolts to 5-7 ft. lbs. (7-9 Nm) and the 8mm bolt to 12-16 ft. lbs. (16-22 Nm).
9. Install the flywheel timing mark cover.

Timing Sprockets

REMOVAL & INSTALLATION

1981-90 Gasoline Engines

➧ See Figures 182 and 183

1. Disconnect the negative battery cable.
2. Remove the timing belt cover and timing belt.

➡With the timing belt removed and pistons at TDC, do not rotate the engine.

3. Remove the camshaft sprocket attaching bolt and washer and the camshaft sprocket.
4. Remove the crankshaft sprocket.

To install:

5. Install the camshaft sprocket and attaching bolt and washer. Tighten to 37-46 ft. lbs. (50-62 Nm) on 1988 vehicles or 71-84 ft. lbs. (95-115 Nm) on 1989-95 vehicles.
6. Install the crankshaft sprocket.
7. Install the timing belt and cover.
8. Connect the negative battery cable.

Diesel Engines

➧ See Figures 184 and 185

➡This procedure includes front oil seal removal.

1. Disconnect the negative battery cable.
2. Place fender covers on the aprons.
3. Remove the crankshaft pulley and front timing belt.
4. Remove the crankshaft sprocket retaining bolt. Remove the crankshaft timing sprocket, using tool T47P-6700-B or equivalent.

Fig. 182 Remove the camshaft sprocket attaching bolt and washer

Fig. 183 Once unbolted, slide off the camshaft sprocket from the shaft

5. Remove the crankshaft front oil seal, using tool T77L-9533-B or equivalent. Discard the old seal.

To install:

6. Coat the sealing surface of the new seal with engine oil. Install the seal using tool T84P-6019-A or equivalent.
7. Install the crankshaft timing sprocket.
8. Install and adjust the timing belt.
9. Install the crankshaft pulley.
10. Connect the negative battery cable.

1.8L Engine

1. Disconnect the negative battery cable.
2. Remove the timing belt.
3. Remove the valve cover mounting bolts and remove the cover and gasket.
4. While holding the camshaft with a wrench, remove the camshaft pulley lockbolt. Remove the camshaft pulley.
5. Remove the crankshaft (timing belt) pulley locking bolt.
6. Remove the timing belt pulley. If necessary, use a suitable puller.
7. Remove the Woodruff® key from the crankshaft.

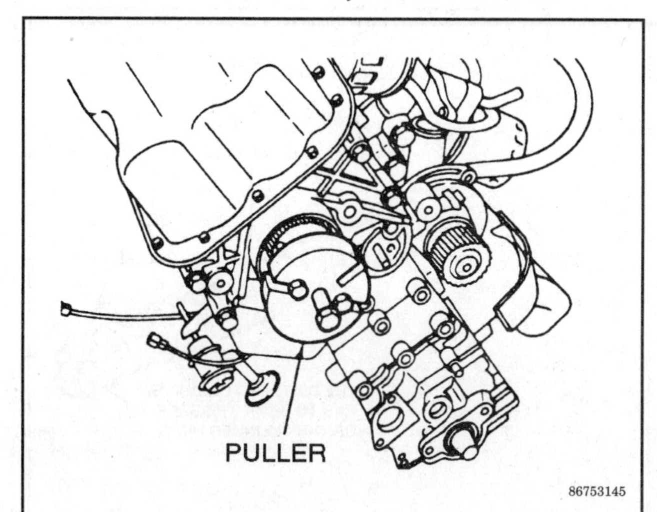

Fig. 184 Here a special tool is in place to remove the front oil seal — diesel engines

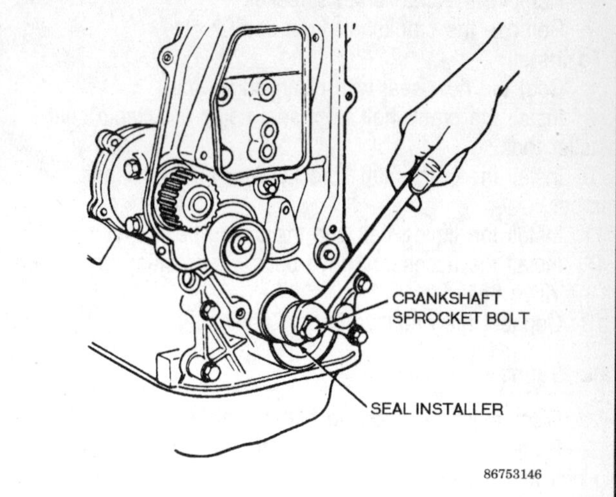

Fig. 185 A seal installation tool is here used to press in the new front oil seal

To install:

8. Install the timing belt pulley onto the shaft while making sure to match the alignment grooves.
9. Install the Woodruff® key with the tapered end facing the oil pump.
10. Install the timing belt pulley locking bolt and tighten to 80-87 ft. lbs. (108-118 Nm).
11. Install the camshaft pulley with the timing mark aligned to the timing mark on the seal plate.
12. While holding the camshaft with a wrench, install the camshaft pulley lockbolt. Tighten the bolt to 36-45 ft. lbs. (49-61 Nm).
13. Install a new cylinder head cover gasket onto the cylinder head.
14. Place the cylinder head cover into its mounting position and install the mounting bolts. Tighten the cylinder head cover bolts to 43-78 inch lbs. (4.9-8.8 Nm).
15. Connect the spark plug wires to the spark plugs and connect the vacuum hoses to the cylinder head cover.
16. Install the timing belt and timing belt covers according to the proper procedure.

Front Oil Seal

REMOVAL & INSTALLATION

➡The procedure for diesel engines is found under "Timing Sprockets."

1981-85 1.6L and 1985-90 1.9L Engine

1. Disconnect the negative battery cable.
2. Remove the accessory drive belts.
3. Remove the timing belt cover.
4. Remove the timing belt.

➡With the timing belt removed and pistons at TDC, do not rotate the engine. If the camshaft must be rotated, align the crankshaft pulley to 90° BTDC.

5. Remove the crankshaft damper.

6. Remove the crankshaft sprocket.
7. Remove the crankshaft front seal.

To install:

8. Coat the new seal with clean engine oil.
9. Install the crankshaft front seal using a suitable seal installer tool.
10. Install the crankshaft sprocket and the crankshaft damper.
11. Install the timing belt and the timing belt cover.
12. Install the accessory drive belts, then adjust the tension of the drive belts.
13. Connect the negative battery cable.

1.8L Engine

1. Disconnect the negative battery cable.
2. Remove the timing belt, then the timing belt pulley locking bolt and the pulley itself. If necessary, use a suitable puller.
3. Remove the Woodruff® key.
4. If necessary, cut the lip of the front oil seal to ease removal.
5. Use a suitable pry tool to remove the oil seal.

To install:

6. Lubricate the lip of the new oil seal with clean engine oil.
7. Using a suitable installation tool, install the seal evenly until it is flush with the edge of the oil pump body.
8. Install the timing belt pulley onto the shaft while making sure to match the alignment grooves.
9. Install the Woodruff® key with the tapered end facing the oil pump.
10. Install the timing belt pulley locking bolt. Tighten the locking bolt to 80-87 ft. lbs. (108-118 Nm).
11. Install the timing belt.
12. Connect the negative battery cable.

1991-95 1.9L Engine

1. Disconnect the negative battery cable.
2. Remove the accessory drive belt.
3. Raise and safely support the vehicle.
4. Remove the right side splash shield.
5. Remove the flywheel inspection shield.
6. Use a suitable tool to hold the flywheel in place.
7. Remove the crankshaft bolt and washer, then remove the crankshaft dampener.
8. Remove the timing belt.
9. Remove the crankshaft sprocket and belt guide.
10. Using a suitable seal remover, remove the crankshaft seal from the oil pump body.

To install:

11. Lubricate the lip of the new seal with clean engine oil.
12. Install the new seal using a suitable installation tool.
13. Install the belt guide and crankshaft sprocket.
14. Install the timing belt.
15. Position the crankshaft dampener on the crankshaft. Install the attaching bolt and washer and tighten to 81-96 ft. lbs. (110-130 Nm).
16. Remove the flywheel holding tool and install the inspection shield.
17. Install the right splash shield and lower the vehicle.
18. Install the accessory drive belt.
19. Connect the negative battery cable.
20. Start the engine and check for leaks.

Camshaft

REMOVAL & INSTALLATION

1.6L Engines

➧ See Figures 186, 187 and 188

➡The camshaft can be removed with the engine in the vehicle.

1. Remove the fuel pump and plunger. Set the engine to TDC on the compression stroke of No. 1 cylinder. Remove the negative battery cable.
2. Remove the alternator drive belt. Remove the power steering and air conditioning compressor drive belts, if equipped.
3. Remove the timing belt cover.
4. Remove the distributor.
5. Remove the rocker arms.
6. Remove the hydraulic valve lash adjusters. Keep the parts in order, as they must be returned to their original positions.
7. Remove and discard the timing belt.
8. Remove the camshaft sprocket and key.
9. Remove the camshaft thrust plate.
10. Remove the ignition coil and coil bracket.
11. Remove the camshaft through the back of the head towards the transaxle.

To install:

12. Before installing the camshaft, coat the bearing journals, cam lobe surfaces, the seal and thrust plate groove with engine oil. Install the camshaft through the rear of the cylinder head. Rotate the camshaft during installation.
13. Install the camshaft thrust plate and tighten the two attaching bolts to 7-11 ft. lbs.
14. Install the cam sprocket and key.
15. Install a new timing belt. and the the timing belt cover.

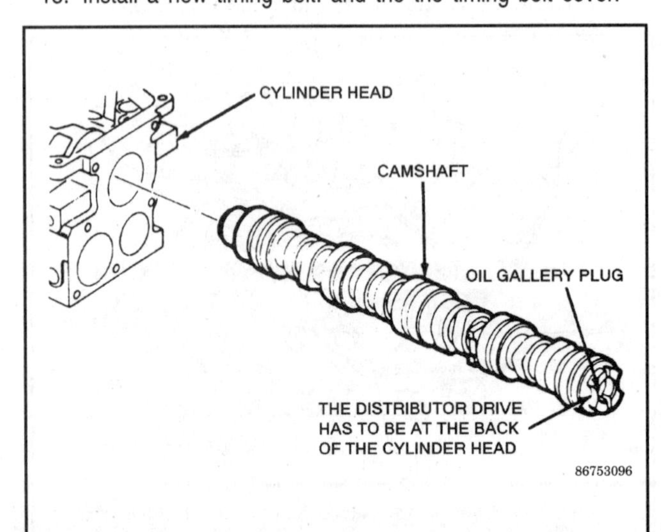

Fig. 186 Install the camshaft in the cylinder head as shown — 1.6L and 1.9L engines

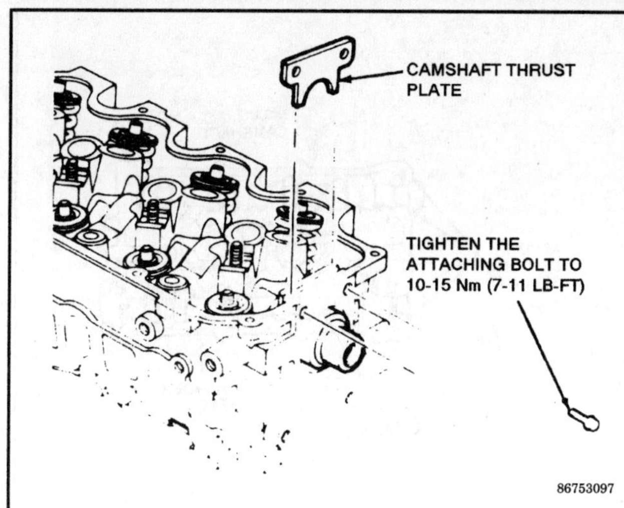

Fig. 187 Exploded view of the camshaft thrust plate mounting and torque figures — 1.6L and 1.9L engines

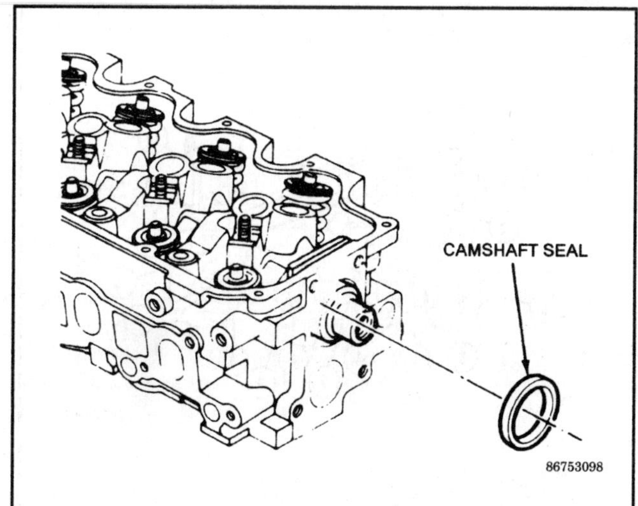

Fig. 188 The camshaft seal mounts in the end of the cylinder head as shown — 1.6L and 1.9L engines

16. Install the fuel pump.
17. Install the rocker arm assembly.
18. Install the distributor assembly, then the rocker arm cover.
19. Install the PCV hose and air cleaner assembly.
20. Connect the negative battery cable.
21. Start the engine and check the ignition timing.

Diesel Engines

See Figure 189

1. Disconnect the negative battery cable.
2. Place fender covers on the aprons.
3. Remove the rocker arm cover.
4. Remove the flywheel timing mark cover from the clutch housing.
5. Rotate the crankshaft until No. 1 cylinder is at TDC.
6. Remove the front and rear timing belt covers.
7. Loosen the front timing belt tensioner, and remove the belt from the camshaft sprocket.
8. Hold the camshaft on the boss provided on the camshaft and loosen the bolt attaching the front and rear camshaft sprockets to the camshaft.
9. Using puller tool T77F-4220-B1 or equivalent, remove the camshaft sprockets.

Be careful not to drop the woodruff keys when removing the camshaft sprockets. Follow Step 10 and 11 exactly as described to avoid damage to the cylinder head and/or camshaft.

10. Remove No. 1, No. 3 and No. 5 camshaft bearing caps first.
11. For camshaft bearing caps No. 2 and No. 4, loosen as follows:
    a. Loosen one of the nuts 2-3 turns.
    b. Then, loosen the remaining nuts, one at a time, 2-3 turns.
    c. Repeat this sequence, turning each nut 2-3 turns at a time, until all nuts are loose.
12. Remove the camshaft and discard the camshaft seal.
13. Remove the cam followers and note their location so they can be returned to their original positions.

To install:

14. Install the cam followers in their original positions.

Follow Step 20 and 21 exactly as described to avoid damage to the cylinder head and/or camshaft. The camshaft bearings are to be installed with the arrows pointing toward the front of the engine. No. 2, No. 3 and No. 4 bearing caps have their numbers cast in the top surface. No. 1 and No. 5 bearings are not marked. However, No. 1 bearing cap has a slot to fit over the camshaft thrust flange.

15. Position the camshaft in the cylinder head and install the No. 2 and No. 4 bearing caps as follows:
    a. Tighten one of the nuts 2-3 turns.
    b. Then tighten the remaining nuts, one at a time, 2-3 turns.
    c. Repeat this sequence, turning each nut 2-3 turns at a time, until the bearing caps are seated.

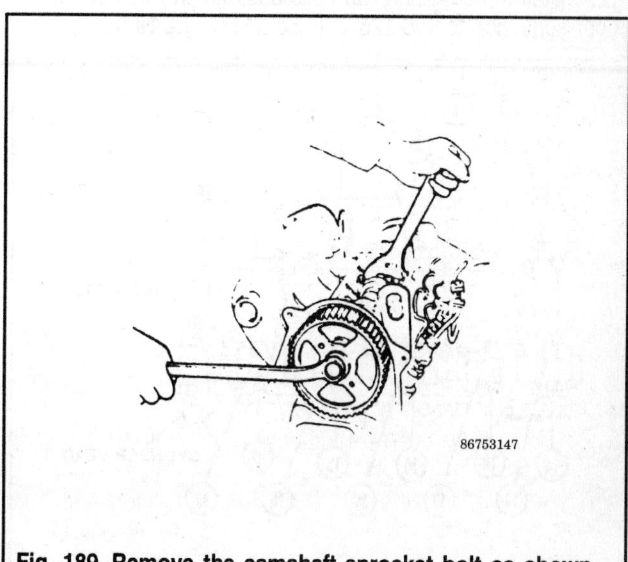

Fig. 189 Remove the camshaft sprocket bolt as shown

16. Install No. 1, No. 3 and No. 5 bearing caps. Tighten nuts for all five bearing caps to 15-19 ft. lbs. (20-27 Nm).
17. Install a new rear camshaft oil seal using a 1 7/16 in. socket and a hammer.
18. Install a new front camshaft oil seal.
19. Install the front and rear camshaft sprockets. While holding the camshaft with an adjustable wrench. Tighten the sprocket bolts to 41-59 ft. lbs. (56-82 Nm).
20. Install and adjust the front and rear timing belts.
21. Check and adjust the valves.
22. Install the rocker arm cover and breather hose.
23. Connect the negative battery cable.

1.8L Engine

➧ **See Figures 190, 191 and 192**

1. Disconnect the negative battery cable.
2. Remove the distributor assembly.
3. Remove the camshaft pulleys.
4. Remove the seal plate mounting bolts and remove the seal plate.
5. Loosen the camshaft cap bolts in the correct sequence (see accompanying drawing).
6. Remove the camshaft caps and note their mounting locations for installation reference.

➡The camshaft caps are numbered and have arrow marks for installation and direction reference.

7. Remove the camshaft and camshaft oil seal.

To install:

8. Apply clean engine oil to the camshaft journals and bearings.
9. Place the camshaft into its mounting position.

➡The exhaust camshaft has a groove which must be installed into the distributor drive gear.

10. Apply silicone sealant to the required areas (see accompanying drawing).
11. Install the camshaft caps according to the cap numbers and arrow marks.
12. Install the camshaft cap bolts and tighten them in the proper sequence to 100-126 inch lbs. (11.3-14.2 Nm).

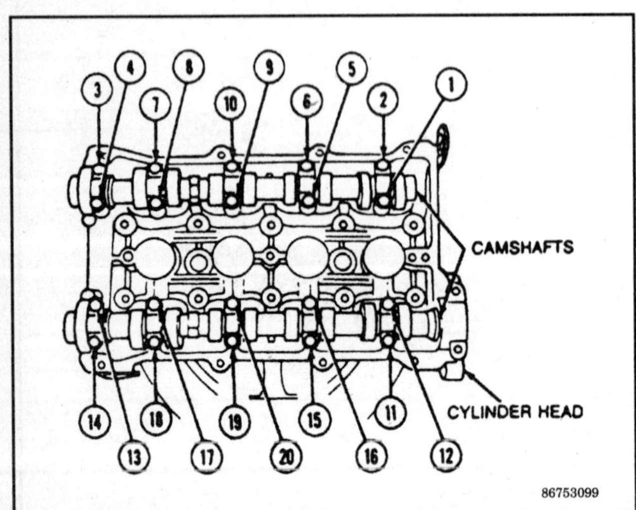

Fig. 190 Camshaft cap bolt loosening sequence — 1.8L engines

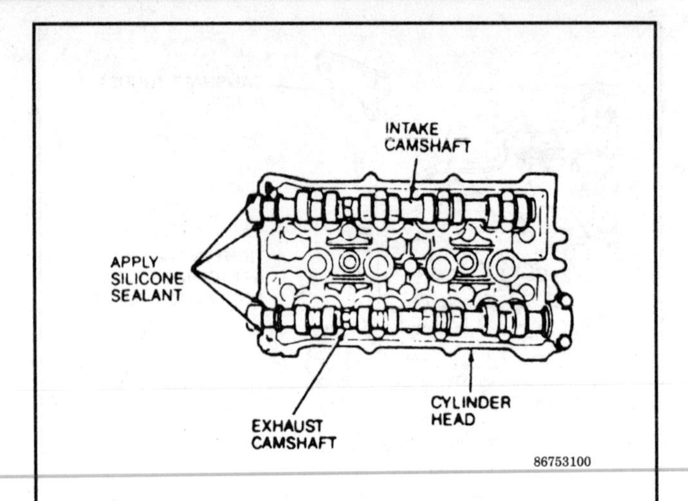

Fig. 191 Apply silicone sealer as shown — 1.8L engines

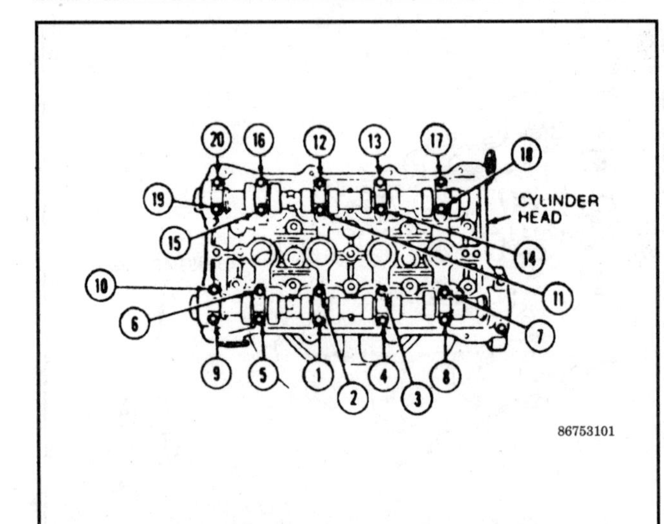

Fig. 192 Tighten the cap bolts in the sequence shown — 1.8L engines

13. Apply a small amount of clean engine oil to the lip of a new camshaft oil seal. Using a suitable installation tool, install the new seal.
14. Place the seal plate into its mounting position and install the mounting bolts. Tighten the bolts to 69-95 inch lbs. (7.8-11.0 Nm).
15. Install the camshaft pulleys and the distributor assembly.
16. Connect the negative battery cable.

1985-95 1.9L Engine

1. Disconnect the negative battery cable.
2. Remove the air cleaner or air intake duct.
3. Remove the accessory drive belts and the crankshaft pulley.
4. Remove the timing belt cover and the rocker arm cover.
5. Set the engine No. 1 cylinder at TDC prior to removing the timing belt.

➡Make sure the crankshaft is positioned at TDC. Do not turn the crankshaft until the timing belt is installed.

6. Remove the rocker arms and lifters.
7. Remove the distributor assembly on 1985-90 vehicles. On 1991-95 vehicles, remove the ignition coil assembly.
8. Remove the timing belt.
9. Remove the camshaft sprocket and key.
10. Remove the camshaft thrust plate.
11. Remove the ignition coil and coil bracket on 1985-90 vehicles. On 1991-95 vehicles, remove the cup plug from the back of the cylinder head.
12. Remove the camshaft through the back of the head toward the transaxle.
13. Remove and discard the camshaft seal.

To install:

14. Thoroughly coat the camshaft bearing journals, cam lobe surfaces and thrust plate groove with a suitable lubricant.

➡Before installing the camshaft, apply a thin film of lubricant to the lip of the camshaft seal.

15. Install a new camshaft seal and install the camshaft through the rear of the cylinder head. Rotate the camshaft during installation.
16. Install the camshaft thrust plate. Tighten attaching bolts to 6-9 ft. lbs. (8-13 Nm).
17. Align and install the cam sprocket over the cam key. Install the attaching washer and bolt. While holding the camshaft stationary, tighten the bolt to 37-46 ft. lbs. (50-62 Nm) on 1988 vehicles or 71-84 ft. lbs. (95-115 Nm) on 1989-95 vehicles.
18. On 1988-90 vehicles, install the ignition coil and coil bracket. On 1991-95 vehicles, install the cup plug using a suitable sealer. Use the sealer sparingly, as excess sealer may clog the oil holes in the camshaft.
19. Install the timing belt.
20. Install the timing belt cover.
21. Install the distributor assembly on 1985-90 vehicles. On 1991-95 vehicles, install the ignition coil assembly.
22. Install a new rocker arm cover gasket, if required.

➡Make sure the surfaces on the cylinder head and rocker arm cover are clean and free of sealant material.

23. Install the valve cover.
24. Install the air intake duct or the air cleaner assembly.
25. Connect the negative battery cable.

INSPECTION

➧ See Figures 193, 194 and 195

Degrease the camshaft using safe solvent, clean all oil grooves. Visually inspect the cam lobes and bearing journals for excessive wear. If a lobe is questionable, check all lobes and journals with a micrometer.

Measure the lobes from nose to base and again at 90°. The lift is determined by subtracting the second measurement from the first. If all exhaust lobes and all intake lobes are not identical, the camshaft must be reground or replaced. Measure the bearing journals and compare to the specifications. If a journal is worn there is a good chance that the cam bearings are worn too, requiring replacement.

If the lobes and journals appear intact, place the front and rear cam journals in V-blocks and rest a dial indicator on the

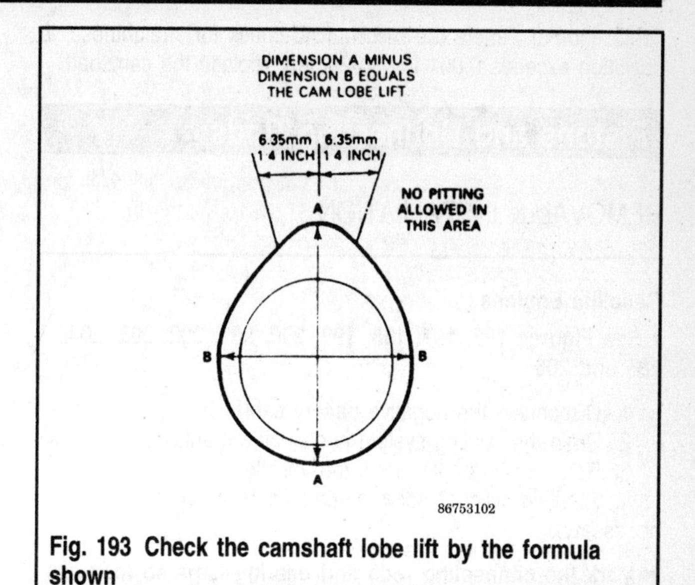

Fig. 193 Check the camshaft lobe lift by the formula shown

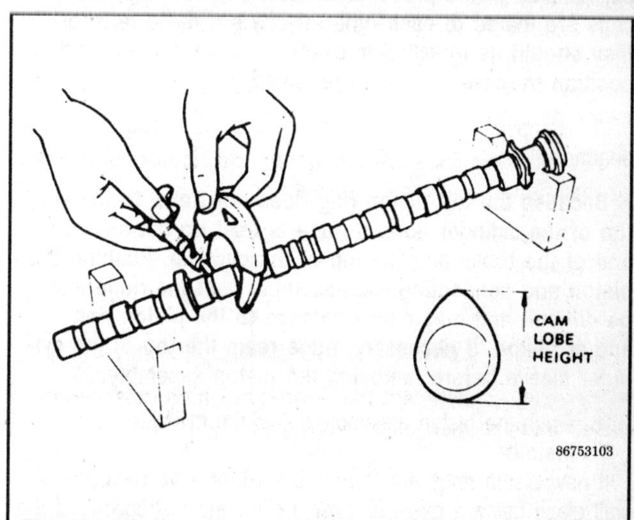

Fig. 194 Measure the camshaft lobe height using a precision micrometer

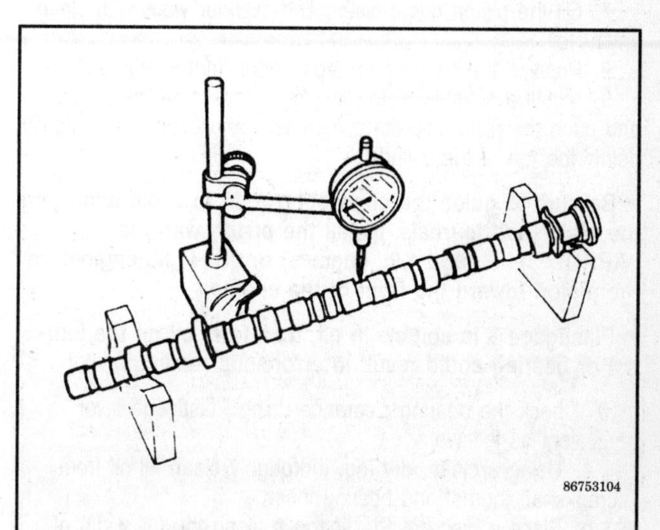

Fig. 195 To measure camshaft runout, revolve the shaft and measure with a dial indicator

center journal. Rotate the camshaft to check for straightness, if deviation exceeds 0.001 in. (0.025mm), replace the camshaft.

Pistons and Connecting Rods

REMOVAL & INSTALLATION

Gasoline Engines

See Figures 196, 197, 198, 199, 200, 201, 202, 203, 204, 205 and 206

1. Disconnect the negative battery cable.
2. Drain the cooling system and engine crankcase.
3. Remove the engine from the vehicle.
4. Remove cylinder head, oil pan and front cover (if necessary).

Mark the connecting rods and bearing caps so they can be installed in the proper cylinders. The bearings and caps are mated to each other. If any are to be reused, they should be installed in exactly the same place and position they were in when removed.

5. Remove the connecting rod bearing caps and the bearings.

Because the top piston ring does not travel to the very top of the cylinder bore, a ridge is built up between the end of the travel and the top of the cylinder. Pushing the piston and connecting rod assembly past the ridge may be difficult and may cause damage to the piston ring and/or piston. If necessary, ridge ream the top of the cylinder sleeve before removing the piston assembly.

6. Push the piston assembly out of the cylinder.

To install:

If new piston rings are to be installed, remove the cylinder wall glaze using a glaze breaker. Follow the instructions of the tool manufacturer. Clean the cylinder bores with soap and water solution after deglazing or honing. Properly dry and oil the cylinder walls immediately after cleaning.

7. Oil the piston rings, piston and cylinder walls with clean engine oil.
8. Position the piston ring gaps approximately 90° apart.
9. Install a suitable piston ring compressor on the piston and push the piston in with a hammer handle, until it is slightly below the top of the cylinder.

Be sure to guide the connecting rods to avoid damaging the crankshaft journals. Install the piston with the "ARROW" (1.6L and 1.9L engines) or "F" (1.8L engine) on the piston toward the front of the engine.

Plastigage® is soluble in oil, therefore, oil on the journal or bearing could result in erroneous readings.

10. Check the bearing clearance using Plastigage®, or equivalent as follows:
    a. Using a clean, dry rag, thoroughly clean all oil from crankshaft journal and bearing insert.
    b. Place a piece of Plastigage® along the full width of the bearing insert, reinstall cap, and tighten to specifications.

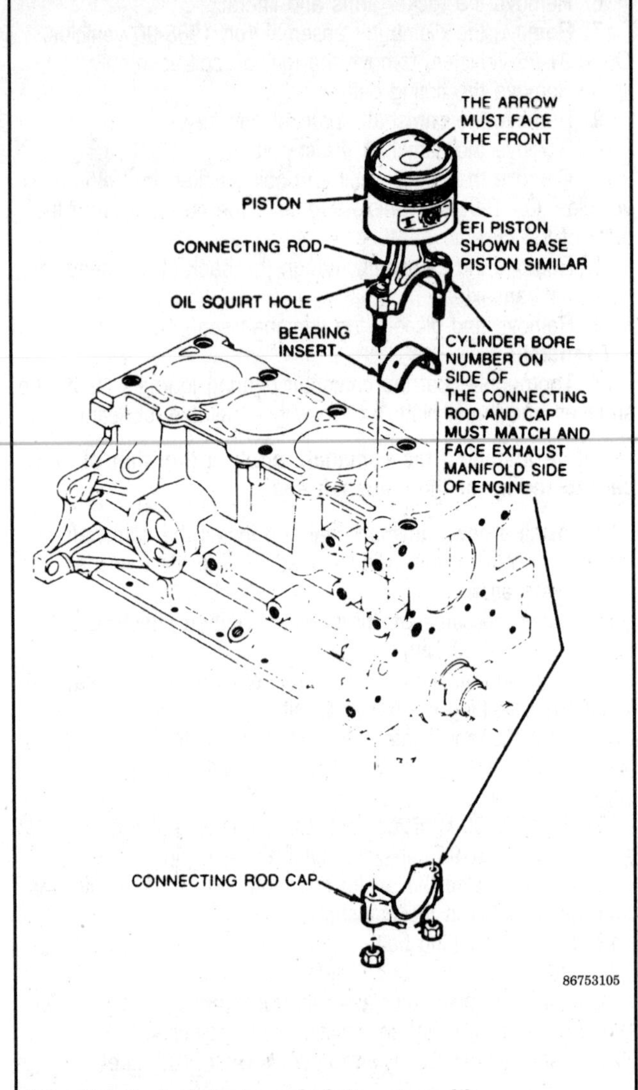

Fig. 196 Exploded view of piston assembly installation — 1.6L and 1.9L engines

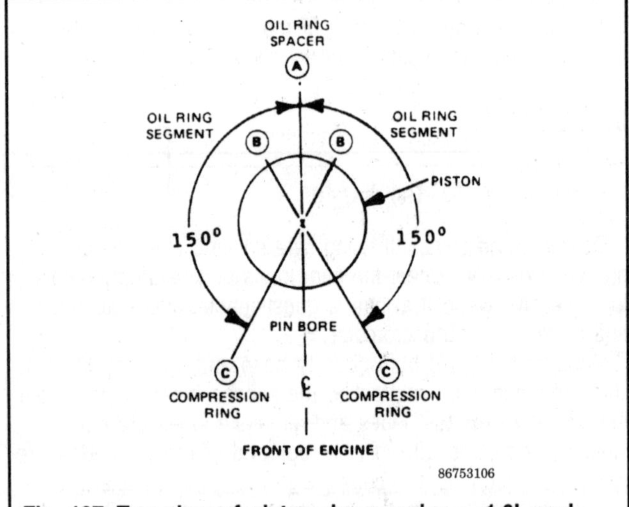

Fig. 197 Top view of piston ring spacing — 1.6L and 1.9L engines

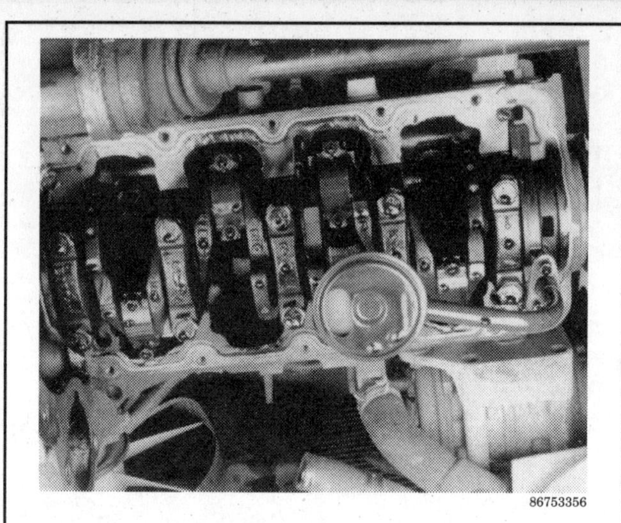

86753356

Fig. 198 Once the oil pan is removed, unbolt the connecting rod bearings and caps — 1988 1.9L engine

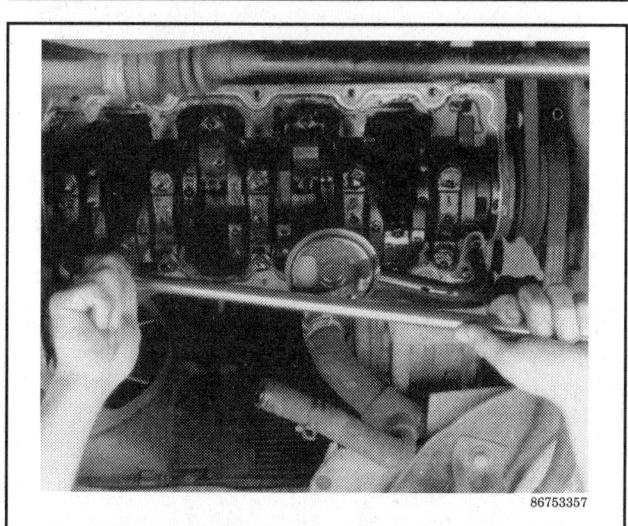

86753357

Fig. 199 A long-handled breaker bar provides good control when loosening the retaining nuts

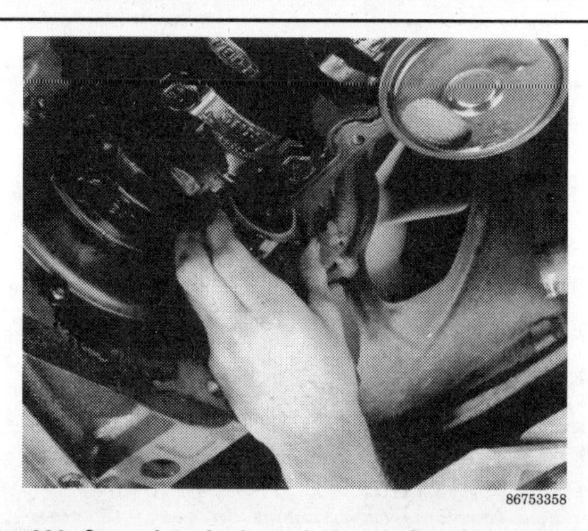

86753358

Fig. 200 Once detached, mark the cap/bearing assembly for installation — if you reuse the caps and bearings, they MUST go back as originally removed

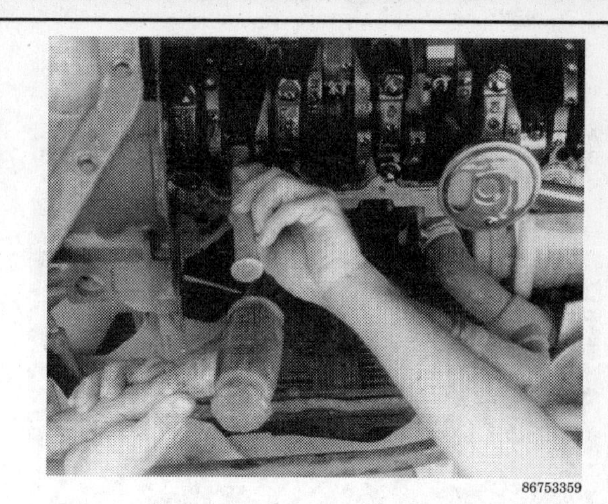

86753359

Fig. 201 If the piston is snug, a slight tap with a soft drift may be helpful — but DON'T forget to ream the ridge at the bore's top

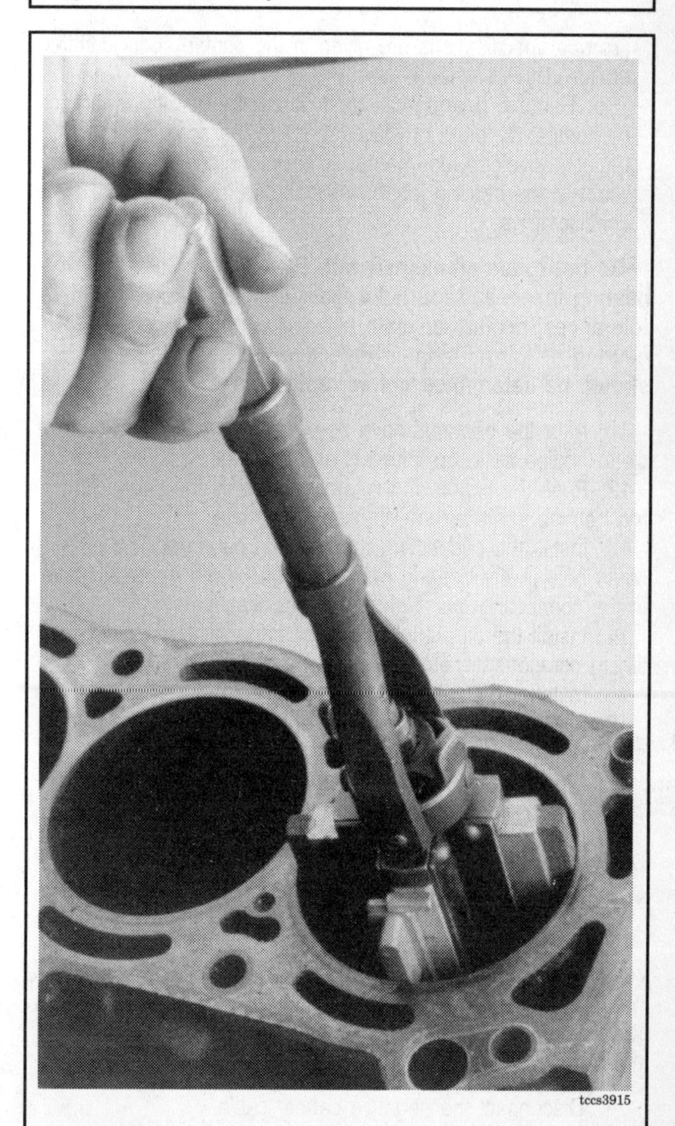

tccs3915

Fig. 202 Remove the ridge from the cylinder bore using a ridge cutter

tccs3803

Fig. 203 Protect the crankshaft and cylinders from damage with lengths of hose over the rod studs

86753360

Fig. 204 An accurate torque wrench is essential in tightening the nuts to the proper torque specification

(Torque specifications are given in the engine specifications earlier in this section.)

c. Remove bearing cap, and determine bearing clearance by comparing width of Plastigage® to the scale on Plastigage® envelope. Journal taper is determined by comparing width of the bearing insert, reinstall cap, and tighten to specifications.

➡Do not rotate crankshaft with Plastigage® installed. If bearing insert and journal appear intact, and are within tolerances, no further main bearing service is required. If bearing or journal appear defective, cause of failure should be determined before replacement.

11. After the bearings have been fitted, apply a light coat of clean engine oil to the journals and bearings.
12. Push the piston all the way down until the connecting rod bearing seats on the crankshaft journals.
13. Install the connecting rod cap and bearings. The oil squirt hole in the bearing must be aligned with the squirt hole in the connecting rod. Tighten to specification.
14. Install the oil pump pickup, oil pan, cylinder head and timing components, as necessary.
15. Install the engine in the vehicle.
16. Fill the crankcase with the recommended engine oil. Fill and bleed the cooling system.
17. Connect the negative battery cable.
18. Run the engine and check for leaks.

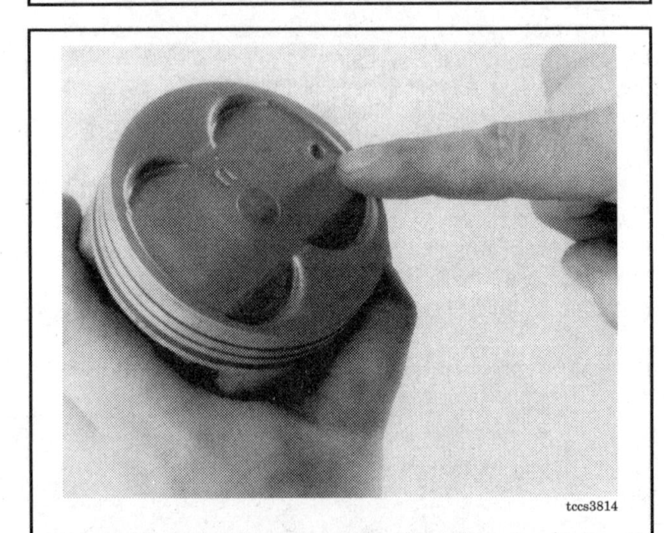

tccs3814

Fig. 205 Most pistons are marked to indicate positioning (usually a mark means the side facing front)

tccs3914

Fig. 206 Installing the piston into the block using a ring compressor and the handle of a hammer

Diesel Engines

➧ See Figures 207, 208, 209 and 210

➡Although, in most cases, the pistons and connecting rods can be removed from the engine (after the cylinder head and oil pan are removed) while the engine is still in the vehicle, it is much easier to remove the engine from the vehicle.

1. Disconnect the negative battery cable.
2. Drain the cooling system and engine crankcase.
3. Remove the engine from the vehicle.

4. Remove cylinder head(s), oil pan and front cover (if necessary).

➡**Mark the connecting rods and bearing caps so they can be installed in original order as when found.**

5. Remove the connecting rod bearing caps and the bearings.

➡**Because the top piston ring does not travel to the very top of the cylinder bore, a ridge is built up between the end of the travel and the top of the cylinder. Pushing the piston and connecting rod assembly past the ridge may be difficult and may cause damage to the piston. If necessary, ridge ream the top of the cylinder sleeve before removing the piston assembly.**

6. Place lengths of rubber hose over the connecting rod studs to protect the crankshaft and cylinders from damage and push the piston assembly out of the cylinder.

To install:

➡**If new piston rings are to be installed, remove the cylinder wall glaze. Follow the instructions of the tool manufacturer. Clean the cylinder bores with soap and water solution after deglazing or honing. Properly dry and oil the cylinder walls immediately after cleaning.**

7. Coat the piston rings, piston and cylinder walls with clean engine oil.
8. Position the piston ring gaps approximately 90° apart. Place the top and second rings in the opposite direction of the pre-combustion chamber.
9. Install a suitable piston ring compressor on the piston and push the piston in with a hammer handle, until it is slightly below the top of the cylinder.

➡**Be sure to guide the connecting rods to avoid damaging the crankshaft journals. Install the piston with the "F" mark on the piston toward the front of the engine.**

10. Check the bearing clearance. After the bearings have been fitted, apply a light coat of clean engine oil to the journals and bearings.

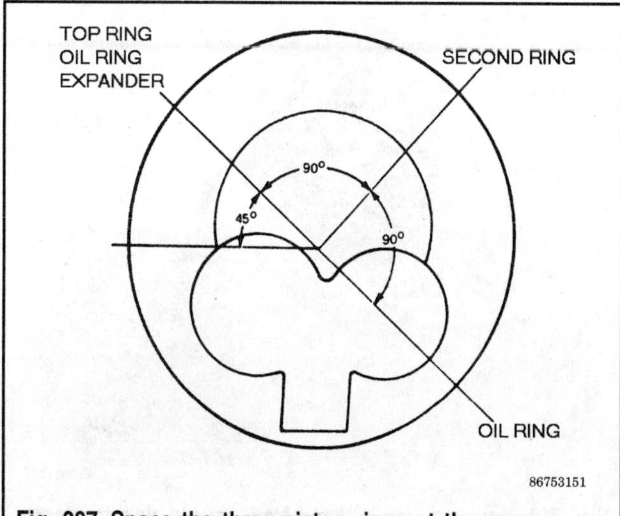

Fig. 207 Space the three piston rings at the proper intervals — diesel engines

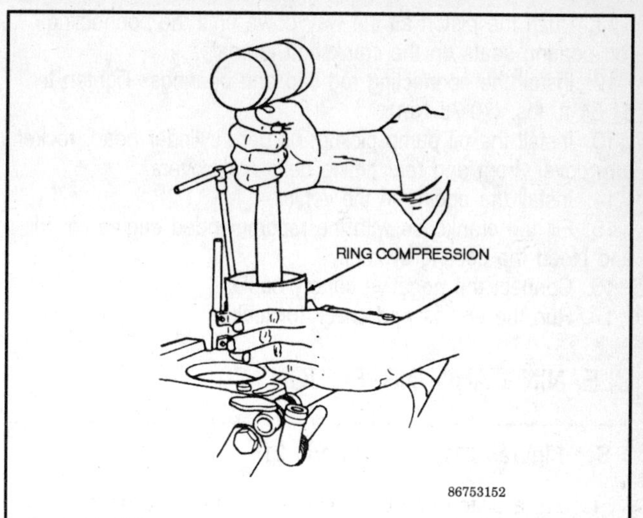

Fig. 208 With the rings compressed, carefully push the piston into the cylinder bore — diesel engines

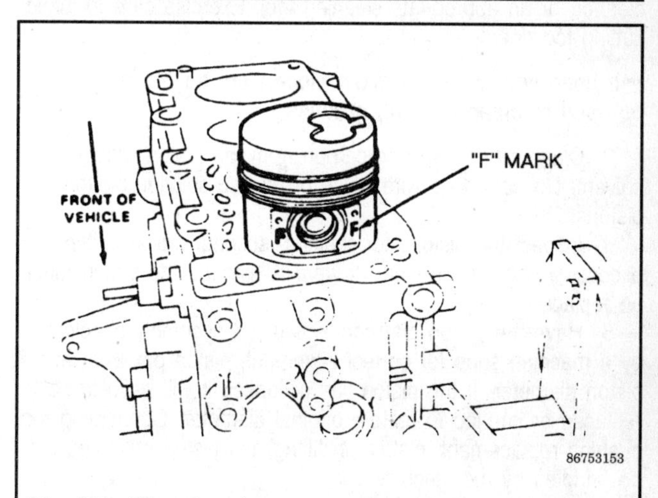

Fig. 209 Align the piston correctly with the "F" mark facing the front of the engine when installing — diesel engines

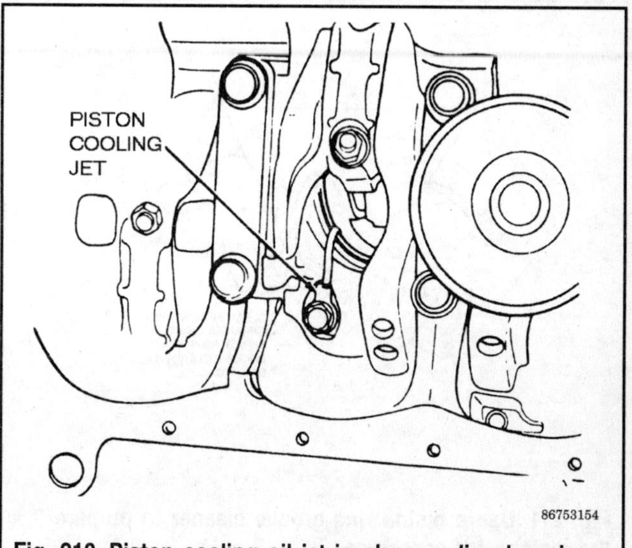

Fig. 210 Piston cooling oil jet in place — diesel engines

11. Push the piston all the way down until the connecting rod bearing seats on the crankshaft journals.
12. Install the connecting rod cap and bearings. Tighten to 51-54 ft. lbs. (70-75 Nm).
13. Install the oil pump pickup, oil pan, cylinder head, rocker arm cover, front and rear timing belts and covers.
14. Install the engine in the vehicle.
15. Fill the crankcase with the recommended engine oil. Fill and bleed the cooling system.
16. Connect the negative battery cable.
17. Run the engine and check for leaks.

CLEANING AND INSPECTION

See Figures 211, 212, 213 and 214

1. Use a piston ring expander and remove the rings from the piston.
2. Clean the ring grooves using a piston ring groove cleaner, or an appropriate cleaning tool. Exercise care to avoid cutting too deeply.

➡If used with care, a broken piece from an old ring may be used to clean the ring grooves.

3. Clean all varnish and carbon from the piston with a safe solvent. Do not use a wire brush or caustic solution on the pistons.
4. Inspect the pistons for scuffing, scoring, cracks, pitting or excessive ring groove wear. If wear is evident, the piston must be replaced.
5. Have the piston and connecting rod assembly checked by a machine shop for correct alignment, piston pin wear and piston diameter. If the piston has collapsed it will have to be replaced or knurled to restore original diameter. Connecting rod bushing replacement, piston pin fitting and piston changing can be handled by the machine shop.

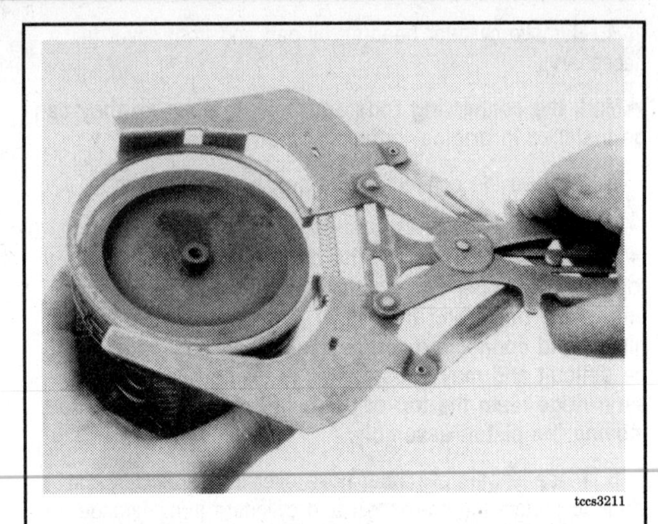

tccs3211

Fig. 212 Use a ring expander to remove the piston rings

tccs3208

Fig. 213 Clean the piston grooves using a ring groove cleaner

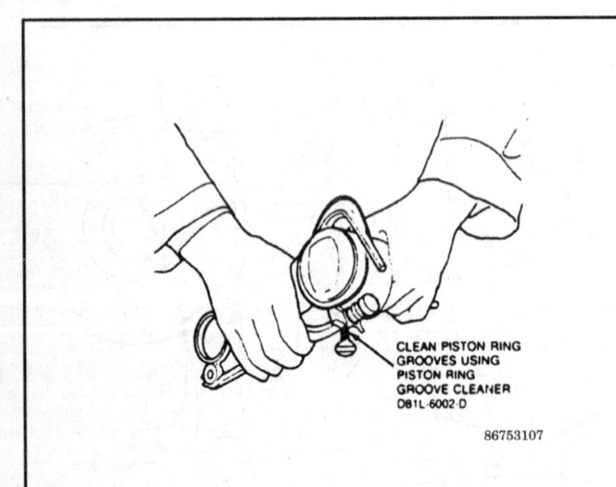

Fig. 211 Use a piston ring groove cleaner to prepare the pistons for new rings

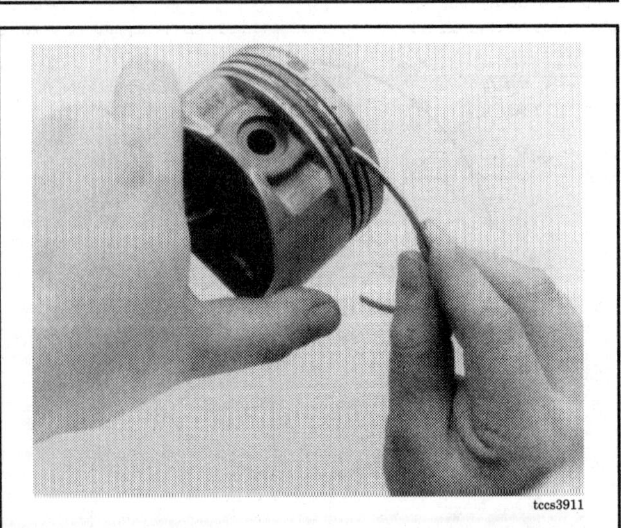

tccs3911

Fig. 214 You can use a piece from an old ring to clean the ring grooves, but BE CAREFUL, the ring is sharp

CYLINDER BORE

➧ See Figures 215, 216, 217 and 218

Inspect the cylinder walls for scoring, roughness or other signs of wear. Check the bore for out-of-round and taper. Measure the bore with an accurate telescope gauge and a micrometer; measure the cylinder bore diameter following the directions of the manufacturer. Measure the diameter of each cylinder bore at the top, middle and bottom with the gauge placed at right angles and parallel to the centerline of the engine.

Calculate piston-to-cylinder bore clearance by subtracting the piston diameter from the cylinder bore measurement(s). If the clearance is within specification, a finish honing or glaze breaking is all that will be required. If the clearance is excessive, the engine will have to be bored and oversized pistons will have to be installed.

PISTON RING REPLACEMENT

➧ See Figures 219 and 220

1. Take the new piston rings and compress them, one at a time into each cylinder in which they will be used. Press the ring about 1 in. (25mm) below the top of the cylinder block using an inverted piston.
2. Use a feeler gauge and measure the distance between the ends of the ring. This is called measuring the ring end-gap. Compare the reading to the one called for in the specifications table. If the measurement is too small, when the engine heats up the ring ends will butt together and cause damage. File the ends of the ring with a fine file to obtain necessary clearance.
3. Inspect the ring grooves on the piston for excessive wear or taper. If necessary, have the grooves recut for use with a standard ring and spacer. A competent machine shop can handle the job for you.
4. Check the ring grooves by rolling the new piston ring around the groove to check for burrs or carbon deposits. If any are found, remove with a fine file. Hold the ring in the groove

tccs3210

Fig. 216 Measure the piston's outer diameter using a micrometer

tccs3913

Fig. 217 Using a ball type cylinder hone is an easy way to hone the cylinder bore

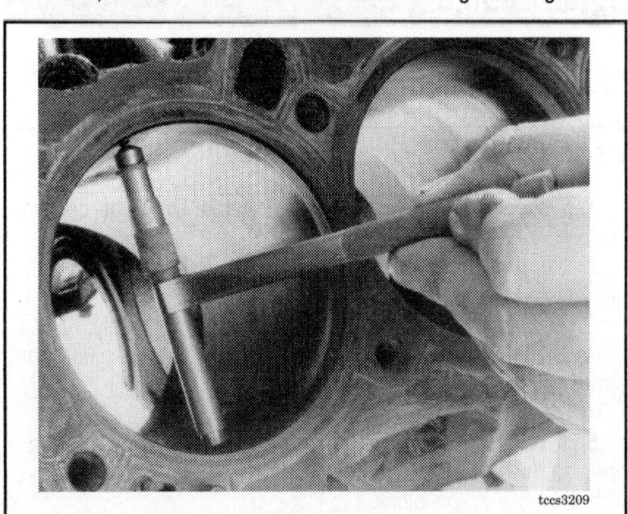
tccs3209

Fig. 215 A telescoping gauge may be used to measure the cylinder bore diameter

tccs3216

Fig. 218 A properly cross-hatched cylinder bore

and measure side clearance with a feeler gauge. If the clearance is excessive, spacer(s) will have to be added.

➡**Always add spacers above the piston ring.**

5. Install the ring on the piston, lower oil ring first. Use a ring installing tool (piston ring expander) on the compression rings. Consult the instruction sheet that comes with the rings to be sure they are installed with the correct side up. A mark on the ring usually faces upward.

6. When installing oil rings, first, install the expanding ring in the groove. Hold the ends of the ring butted together (they must not overlap) and install the bottom rail (scraper) with the end about 1 in. (25mm) away from the butted end of the control ring. Install the top rail about 1 in. (25mm) away from the butted end of the control but on the opposite side from the lower rail. Be careful not to scrape the piston when installing oil control rings.

7. Install the two compression rings. The lower ring first.

8. Consult the illustration for ring positioning. Arrange the rings as shown.

PISTON PIN REPLACEMENT

1. Matchmark the piston head and the connecting rod for reassembly.
2. Position the piston assembly in a piston pin removal tool.
3. Following the tool manufacturer's instructions, press the pin from the piston.
4. Check the piston pin bore for damage and replace defective components as required. Check the piston pin for damage. Replace as required.
5. Installation is the reverse of the removal procedure.

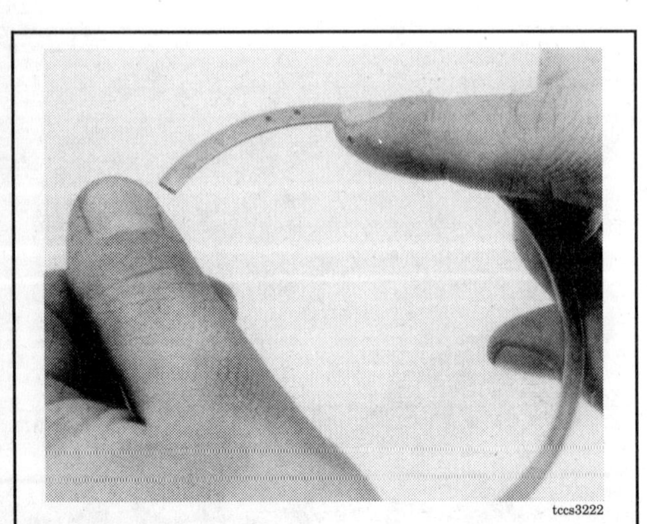

Fig. 219 Most piston rings are marked to show which side should face upward

Fig. 220 Checking the ring-to-ring groove clearance

Freeze Plugs

REMOVAL & INSTALLATION

➧ **See Figures 221 and 222**

1. Disconnect the negative battery cable. Drain the cooling system.
2. Remove the necessary components to gain access to the freeze plug that requires service.
3. As required, raise and support the vehicle safely.
4. Using a hammer and punch to loosen the old plug, then remove it.

To install:

5. If using a new metal freeze plug, position it over the opening in the block. Lightly tap it in place until it sits flush with the bore in the block.
6. If using the rubber type freeze plug, position it over the opening in the block and, using the proper tool, lock it in place.

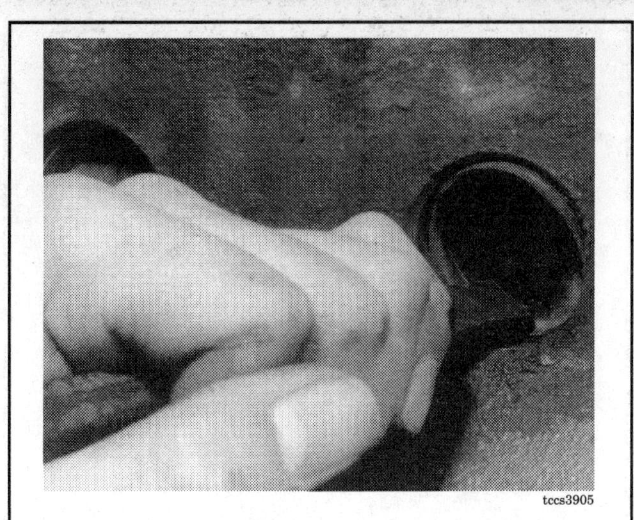

Fig. 221 Using a hammer and punch, the freeze plug can be loosened in the block

Fig. 222 Once the freeze plug has been loosened, it can be removed from the block

7. Install all the removed components. Lower the vehicle, as required.
8. Fill the cooling system and check for leaks.

Rear Main Seal

REMOVAL & INSTALLATION

Gasoline Engines

See Figures 223, 224, 225, 226 and 227

1. Disconnect the negative battery cable.
2. Remove the transaxle assembly.
3. Install a suitable flywheel holding tool and remove the flywheel retaining bolts. Remove the flywheel

WARNING

Be careful not to damage the seal surface. Gouging it could make an oil-tight seal impossible and could make necessary the replacement of the crankshaft.

4. On 1.6L and 1.9L engines, remove the rear cover plate. With a sharp awl, punch a hole into the seal metal surface between the lip and the block. Screw in the threaded end of the removal tool, part No. T77L-9533-B, or equivalent, and remove the seal.
5. On 1.8L engines, remove the rear cover mounting bolts, if necessary, and remove the rear cover. Using a suitable prytool protected with a rag, remove the crankshaft rear oil seal.

To install:

6. Inspect the crankshaft seal area for any damage which may cause the seal to leak. If there is damage evident, you will have to service or replace the crankshaft as necessary.
7. If servicing a 1.8L engine, and the rear cover was removed, install the rear cover and tighten the bolts to 69-95 inch lbs. (7.8-11 Nm).
8. Clean the seal mounting surfaces. Coat the crankshaft seal area and seal lip with engine oil.
9. Using a suitable seal installer, install the new rear seal cover. Install the cover plate.
10. Install the flywheel and using a suitable flywheel holding tool, tighten the flywheel retaining bolts to 131-137 ft. lbs. (180-190 Nm).
11. Install the clutch and transaxle assemblies. Connect the negative battery. Start the engine and check for oil leaks.

Diesel Engines

1. Disconnect the negative battery cable.
2. Remove the transaxle and clutch assemblies.
3. Install a suitable flywheel holding tool and remove the flywheel retaining bolts. Remove the flywheel
4. Remove the rear main seal.

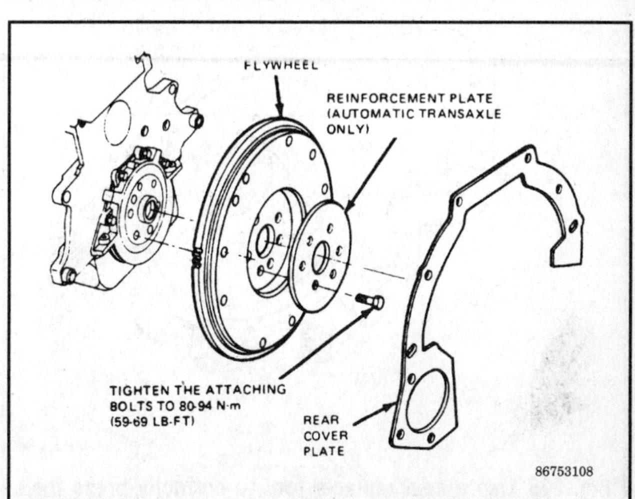

Fig. 223 Exploded view of the rear crankshaft seal location and proximal components — 1.6L and 1.9L engine

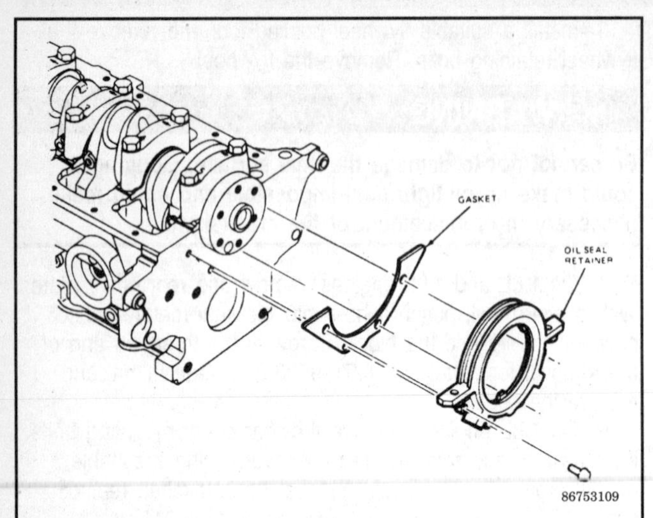

Fig. 224 Exploded view of the rear crankshaft oil seal retainer — 1.6L and 1.9L engine

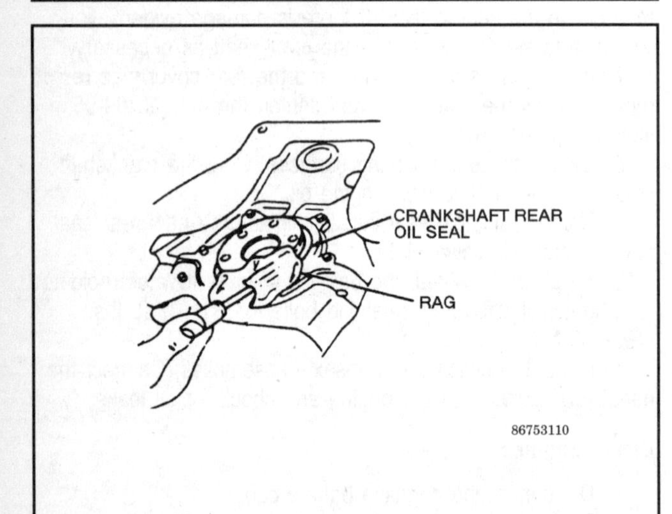

Fig. 225 Use a suitable prytool and a rag (as shown) to remove the rear crankshaft oil seal — 1.8L engines

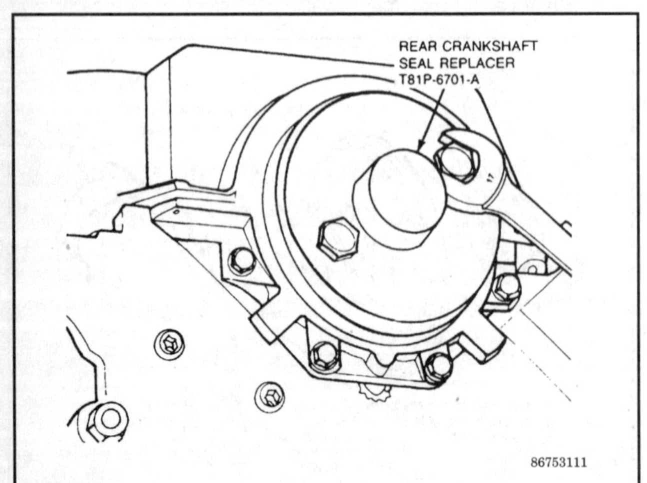

Fig. 226 Use a seal replacer tool to correctly press the rear crankshaft oil seal in place — 1.6L and 1.9L engines

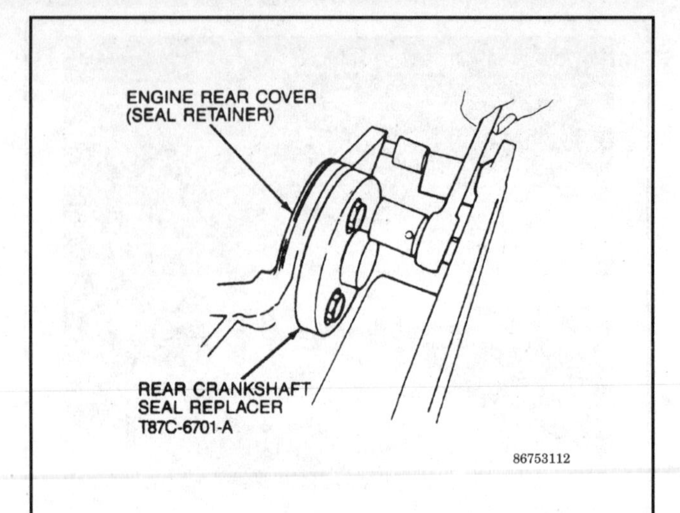

Fig. 227 This purpose-made seal replacer tool greatly aids rear oil seal replacement — 1.8L engine shown

To install:

5. Inspect the crankshaft seal area for any damage which may cause the seal to leak. If there is damage evident, service or replace the crankshaft as necessary.
6. Clean the seal mounting surfaces. Coat the crankshaft and seal with engine oil.
7. Using a suitable seal installer, install the new rear main seal.

➡The flat edge of the seal installer must be parallel to the oil pan or damage to the seal retainer and/or oil pan may result.

8. Install the flywheel and using a suitable flywheel holding tool, tighten the flywheel retaining bolts to 131-137 ft. lbs. (180-190 Nm).
9. Install the clutch and transaxle assemblies. Connect the negative battery. Start the engine and check for oil leaks.

Crankshaft and Main Bearings

REMOVAL & INSTALLATION

Gasoline Engines

➧ See Figures 228, 229, 230, 231, 232, 233, 234, 235 and 236

※※CAUTION

When draining the coolant, keep in mind that cats and dogs are attracted by ethylene glycol antifreeze, and are quite likely to drink any that is left in an uncovered container or in puddles on the ground. This will prove fatal in sufficient quantity. Always drain the coolant into a sealable container. Coolant should be reused unless it is contaminated or several years old. The EPA warns that prolonged contact with used engine oil may cause a number of skin disorders, including cancer! You should make every effort to minimize your exposure to used engine oil. Protective gloves should be worn when changing the oil. Wash your hands and any other exposed skin areas as soon as possible after exposure to used engine oil. Soap and water, or waterless hand cleaner should be used.

1. Disconnect the negative battery cable.
2. Drain the cooling system and engine crankcase.
3. Remove the engine from the vehicle.
4. Remove the crankshaft front pulley, front cover, timing belt and sprockets, water pump, cylinder head, oil pan and oil pump assembly.
5. Remove the rear oil seal cover or retainer bolts and remove the cover or retainer, as required.
6. Remove the connecting rod caps and pistons.

➡Mark the connecting rods and bearing caps so they can be installed in the proper cylinders. The bearings and caps are mated to each other. If any are to be reused, they should be installed in exactly the same place and position they were in when removed.

7. Remove the lower bearing caps and bearing inserts. Keep them in order.

➡On 1.8L engine, remove the main bearing caps in the specified sequence.

8. Carefully lift the crankshaft out of the crankcase.
9. Remove the main bearing inserts and thrust bearing from the engine block and bearing caps.
10. On 1.8L engine, remove the oil jet mounting bolt and remove the oil jet and gaskets. Discard the gaskets.

➡For cleaning purposes, the oil gallery and coolant drain plugs can be removed.

To install:

11. Wash the cylinder block thoroughly to remove all foreign material and dry before assembling other components. Check to ensure all oil holes are fully open and clean. Check to ensure the bearing inserts and bearing bores are clean. Clean

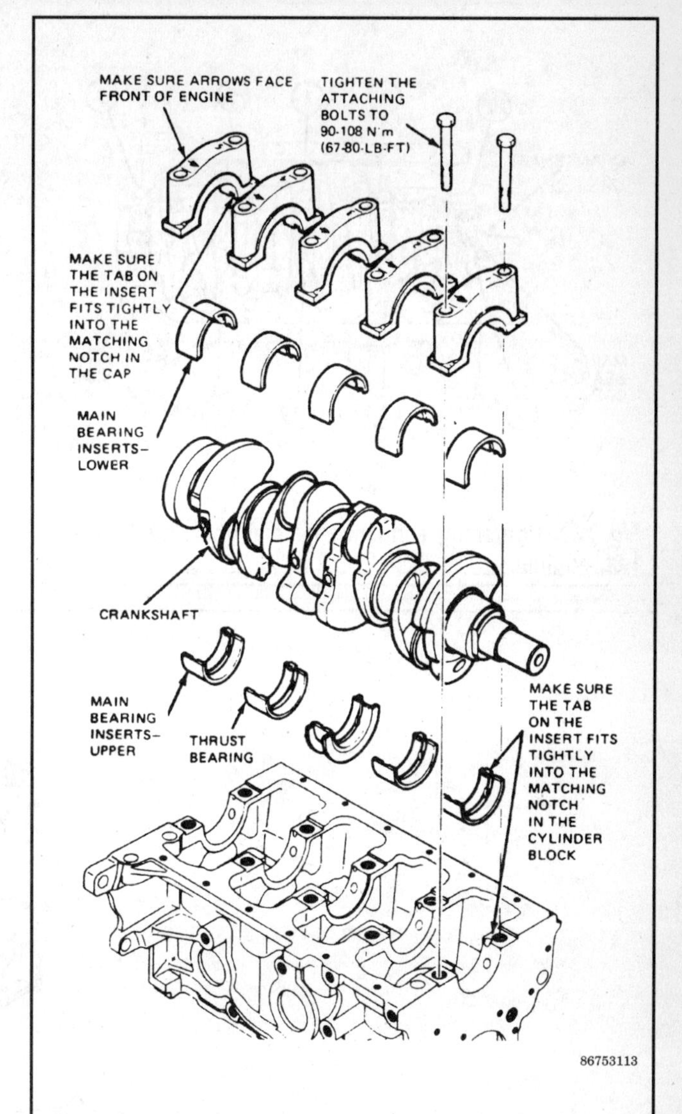

Fig. 228 Exploded view of crankshaft assembly and torque figures — 1.6L and 1.9L engines

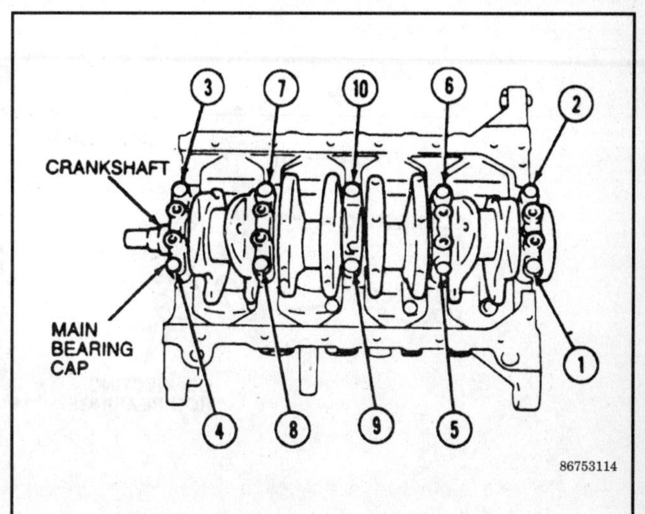

Fig. 229 Removal sequence for main bearing caps — 1.8L engines

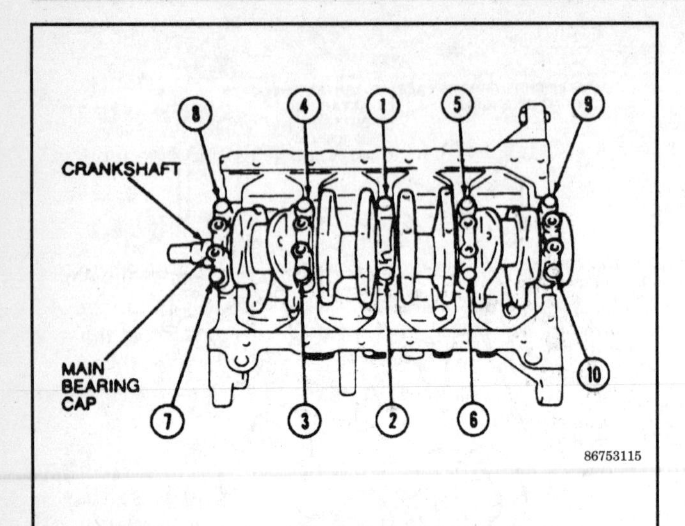

Fig. 230 Tightening sequence for main bearing caps — 1.8L engines

Fig. 232 Remove the oil pan and the five main bearings are in clear view, ready for removal — 1988 1.9L engine

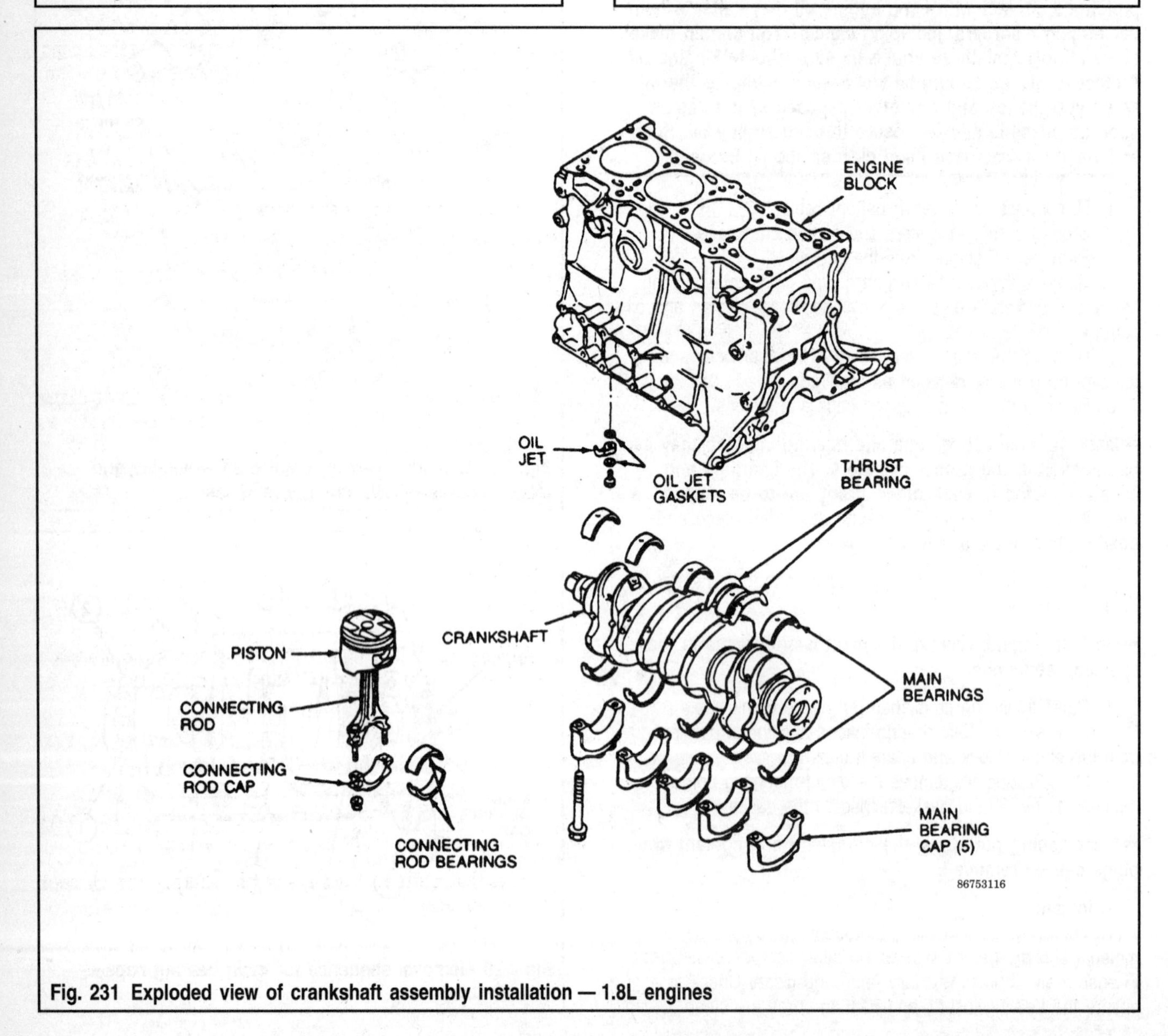

Fig. 231 Exploded view of crankshaft assembly installation — 1.8L engines

Fig. 233 A long breaker bar provides sufficient leverage and control in unbolting the main bearing caps

Fig. 234 Lower the bearing/cap and place where they won't be disturbed — if any are reused, you MUST install in the exact original placement

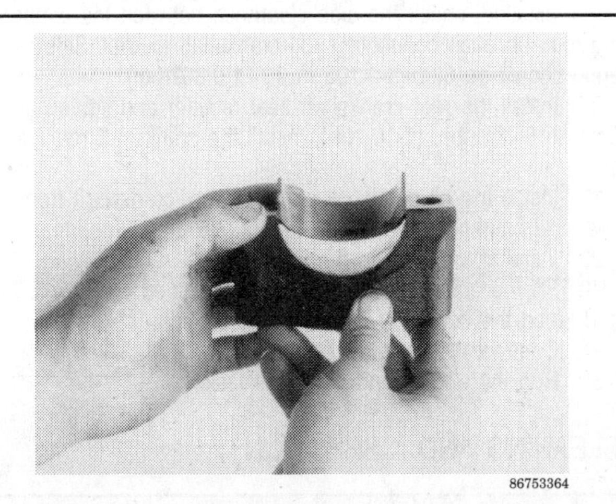

Fig. 235 The main bearings let the crankshaft ride on a micro-fine sheet of oil (their precision tolerances must be kept in specification)

the mating surfaces of the crankcase and each main bearing cap. Check the bearing clearances.

12. On 1.8L engine, install the oil jet with new gaskets. Tighten the mounting bolt to 104-156 inch lbs. (12-18 Nm).

➡During assembly, all bearing surfaces must be lubricated before assembly or installation.

13. Install the main bearing inserts in the cylinder block.

➡The main bearing caps are numbered 1-5 with the No. 1 at the front of the engine. If the main bearing caps are equipped with arrows, the arrows face the front of the engine. On 1.8L engine, the No. 4 bearing is the thrust bearing. On 1.6L and 1.9L engines, the center upper insert is the thrust bearing.

14. Lubricate the crankshaft journals and carefully lower the crankshaft into place. Be careful not to damage the bearing surfaces.

15. Install the main bearing inserts in the main caps and install the caps.

16. After the bearing has been fitted, apply a light coat of engine oil to the journal and bearings. Install the bearing caps in their original locations (Refer to the numbers on caps). The caps must be installed with the arrows pointing toward the front of the engine. Oil the bolts and tighten to specification. Repeat the procedure for the remaining bearings.

➡Turn the crankshaft to check for turning torque. The turning torque should not exceed 4.5 ft. lbs. (6 Nm).

17. Check the crankshaft end-play.

18. Install the pistons and connecting rod caps. Check the clearance of each bearing, as follows:

   a. Using a clean, dry rag, thoroughly clean all oil from crankshaft journal and bearing insert.

   b. Place a piece of Plastigage® along the full width of the bearing insert, reinstall cap, and tighten to specifications. (Torque specifications are given in the engine specifications earlier in this section.)

   c. Remove bearing cap, and determine bearing clearance by comparing width of Plastigage® to the scale on Plastigage® envelope. Journal taper is determined by comparing width of the bearing insert, reinstall cap, and tighten to specifications.

➡Do not rotate crankshaft with Plastigage® installed. If bearing insert and journal appear intact, and are within tolerances, no further main bearing service is required. If bearing or journal appear defective, cause of failure should be determined before replacement.

19. After the connecting rod bearings have been fitted, apply a light coat of engine oil to the journal and bearings.

20. Turn the crankshaft throw to the bottom of its stroke. Pull the piston all the way down until the rod bearing seats on the crankshaft journal. Check the crankshaft end-play.

➡Guide the rod to prevent crankshaft journal and oil cooling jet damage.

21. Install the connecting rod cap. Align the marks on the rods with the marks on the caps. Tighten to specification.

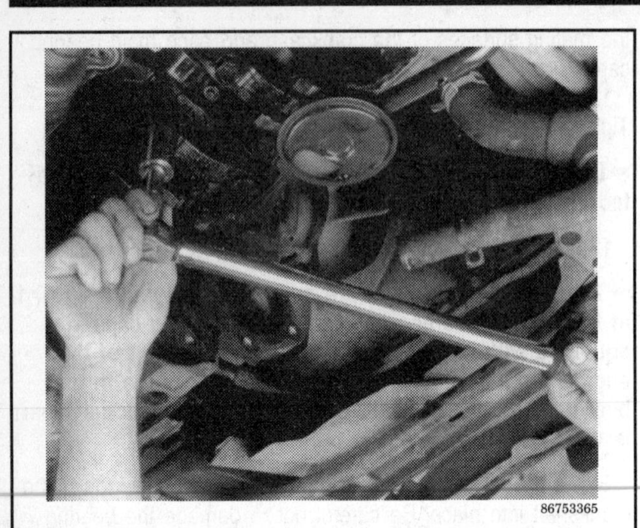
86753365

Fig. 236 Use a reliable torque wrench when installing the main bearing caps

22. After the piston and connecting rod assemblies have been installed, check the side clearance between the connecting rods on each connecting rod crankshaft journal.
23. Install the rear crankshaft seal and cover. Tighten to specification.
24. Install the oil pump assembly, oil pan, cylinder head, water pump, timing belt and sprockets, front cover and crankshaft pulley.
25. Install the engine in the vehicle.
26. Fill the crankcase with the recommended engine oil. Fill and bleed the cooling system.
27. Connect the negative battery cable.
28. Run the engine and check for leaks.

Diesel Engines

See Figure 237

1. Disconnect the negative battery cable.
2. Drain the cooling system and engine crankcase.
3. Remove the engine from the vehicle.
4. Remove the crankshaft front pulley, front timing belt, crankshaft sprocket, cylinder head, oil pan, oil pump pickup and oil pump.
5. Remove the rear oil seal retainer bolts and remove the rear oil seal retainer.
6. Remove the piston assemblies.

Mark the connecting rods and bearing caps so they can be installed in the proper cylinders.

7. Remove the main bearing caps and bearings.

The main bearing caps are numbered 1-5 and must be installed in their original positions.

8. Carefully lift the crankshaft out of the crankcase so that the No. 3 thrust bearing surfaces are not damaged.
9. Remove the main bearing inserts from the engine block and bearing caps.

To install:

10. Check to ensure the bearing inserts and bearing bores are clean. Clean the mating surfaces of the crankcase and each main bearing cap.
11. Place the upper main bearing inserts in their bores with the tang in the slot.

The oil holes in the bearing inserts must be aligned with the holes in the crankcase.

12. Install the lower main bearing inserts in the bearing caps.
13. Carefully lower the crankshaft into place. Be careful not to damage the bearing surfaces.
14. Check the clearance of each main bearing as outlined in this section.
15. After the bearing has been fitted, apply a light coat of engine oil to the journal and bearings. Install the bearing cap in their original locations. Tighten to specification. Repeat the procedure for the remaining bearings.
16. Install the thrust bearing cap with bolts finger-tight.
17. Pry the crankshaft forward against the thrust surface of the upper half of the bearing.
18. Hold the crankshaft forward and pry the thrust bearing cap to the rear. This aligns the thrust surfaces of both halves of the bearing.
19. Retain forward pressure of the crankshaft. Tighten No. 3 cap bolts to 61-65 ft. lbs. (84-90 Nm).
20. Force the crankshaft toward the rear of the engine.
21. Check the crankshaft end-play, as outlined in this section.
22. Install the new bearing inserts in the connecting rods and caps. Check the clearance of each bearing, as outlined in this section.
23. After the connecting rod bearings have been fitted, apply a light coat of engine oil to the journal and bearings.
24. Turn the crankshaft throw to the bottom of its stroke. Pull the piston all the way down until the rod bearing seats on the crankshaft journal.

Guide the rod to prevent crankshaft journal and oil cooling jet damage.

25. Install the connecting rod cap. Align the marks on the rods with the marks on the caps. Tighten to specification.
26. After the piston and connecting rod assemblies have been installed, check the side clearance between the connecting rods on each connecting rod crankshaft journal. Side clearance should be 0.0043-0.103 in. (0.11-0.262mm).
27. Install the rear crankshaft seal retainer and tighten the bolts to 5-7 ft. lbs. (7-10 Nm). Install the crankshaft rear oil seal.
28. Install the oil pump, oil pump pickup, crankshaft front oil seal and crankshaft pulley.
29. Install the engine in the vehicle.
30. Fill the crankcase with the recommended engine oil. Fill and bleed the cooling system.
31. Connect the negative battery cable.
32. Run the engine and check for leaks.

CLEANING AND INSPECTION

See Figures 238, 239 and 240

1. Handle the crankshaft with care to avoid possible fractures or damage to the finish surface.

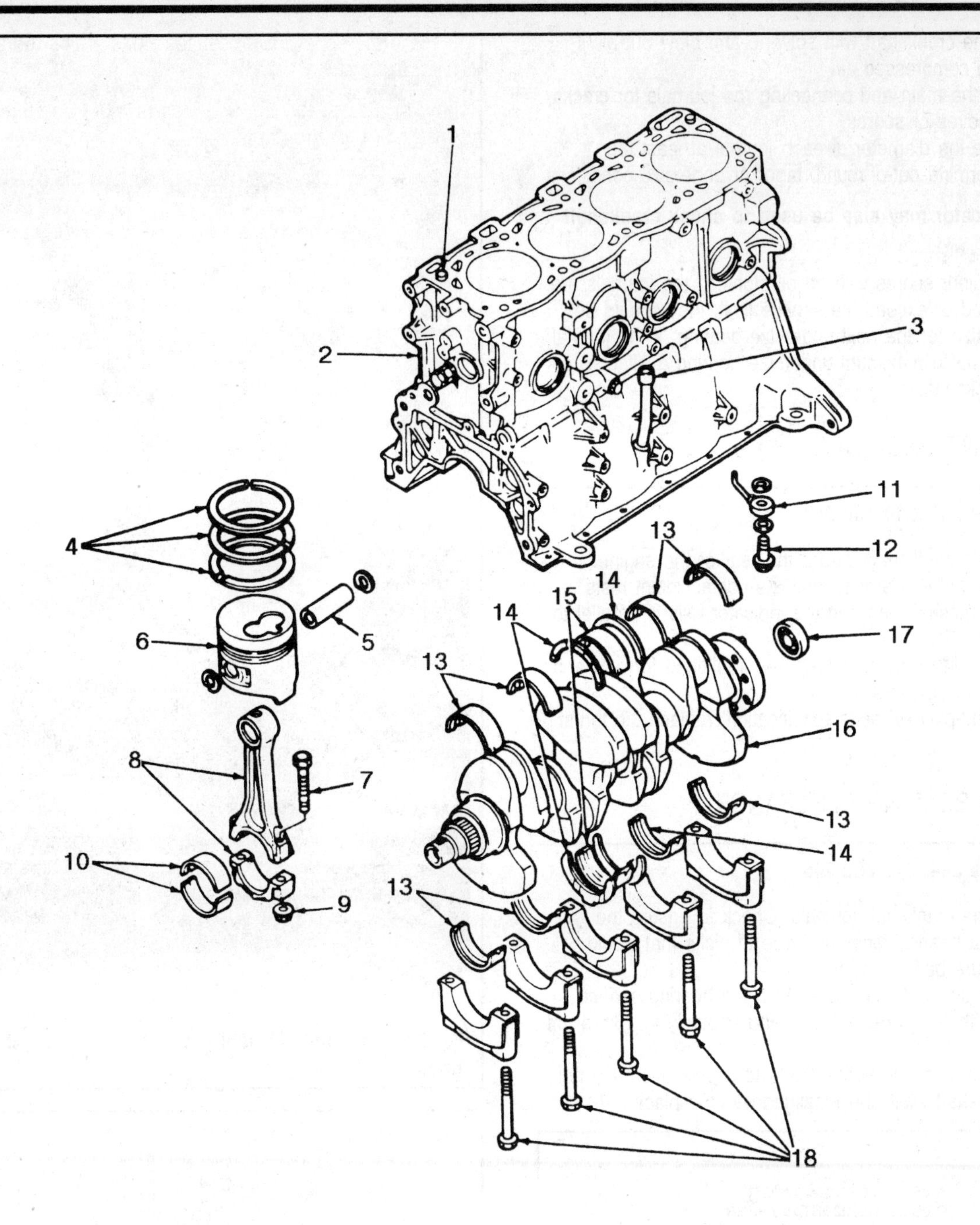

1 Dowel pin (cylinder head to cylinder block)
2 Block assembly (cylinder)
3 Tube assembly (oil level indicator)
4 Piston rings
5 Piston pin
6 Piston
7 Bolt
8 Rod assembly
9 Nut
10 Rod bearing
11 Oil jet assembly (piston cooling)
12 Bolt
13 Main bearing
14 Thrust bearing
15 Main bearing
16 Crankshaft
17 Seal (crankshaft rear oil)
18 Bolt

86753156

Fig. 237 Exploded view of internal crankcase components — diesel engines

2. Clean the crankshaft with solvent, and blow out all passages with compressed air.
3. Inspect the main and connecting rod journals for cracks, scratches, grooves or scores.
4. Measure the diameter of each journal at least four places to determine out-of-round, taper or undersize conditions.

➡A dial indicator may also be used to check crankshaft runout.

5. Dress minor scores with an oil stone. If the journals are severely marred or exceed the service limit, they should be refinished to size for the next undersize bearing. If the journal will not clean up to maximum undersize bearing available, replace the crankshaft.

CRANKSHAFT END-PLAY

See Figures 241, 242 and 243

1. Force the crankshaft toward the rear of the engine.
2. Install a dial indicator so that the contact point rests against the crankshaft end and the indicator axis is parallel to the crankshaft axis.
3. Zero the dial indicator. Push the crankshaft forward and note the reading on the dial.
4. If the end-play exceeds specification, replace the thrust bearing.

CHECKING BEARING CLEARANCE

See Figures 244, 245 and 246

1. Clean the crankshaft journals. Check to ensure the journals and thrust bearing faces and free of nicks that would cause premature bearing wear.
2. Place a piece of Plastigage® on the bearing surface across full width of the bearing cap and about ¼ in. (6mm) off center.
3. Install the cap and tighten bolts to specification. Do not turn the crankshaft while the Plastigage® is in place.

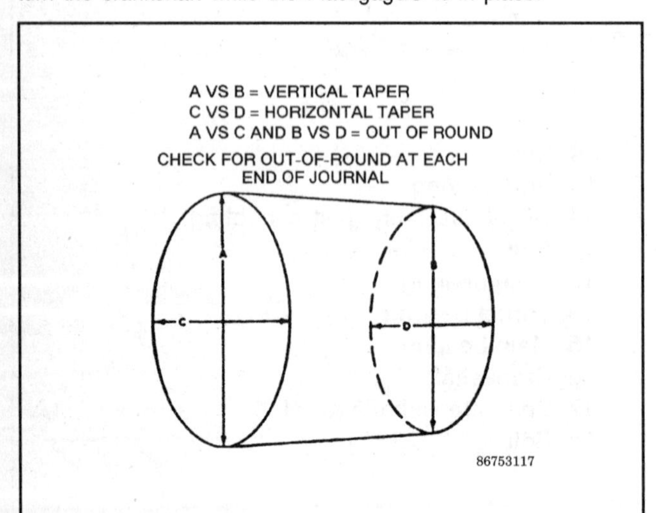

Fig. 238 Measure the condition of the crankshaft journals as shown

Fig. 239 A mounted a dial gauge to read crankshaft runout

Fig. 240 Turn the crankshaft slowly by hand while checking the gauge

Fig. 241 A dial gauge may be used to check crankshaft end-play

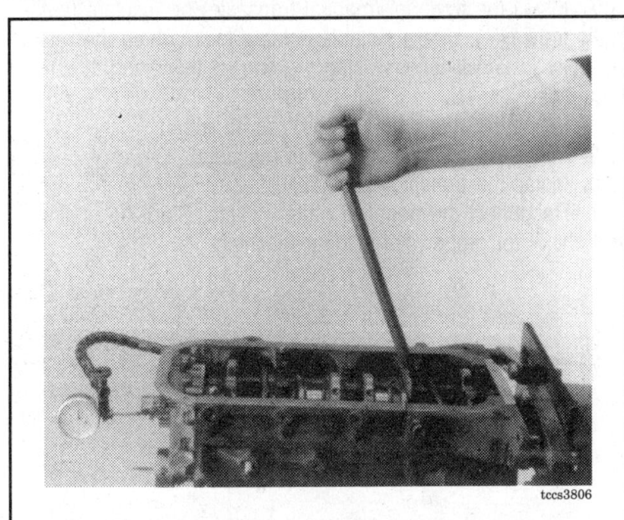

Fig. 242 Carefully pry the shaft back and forth while reading the dial gauge for play

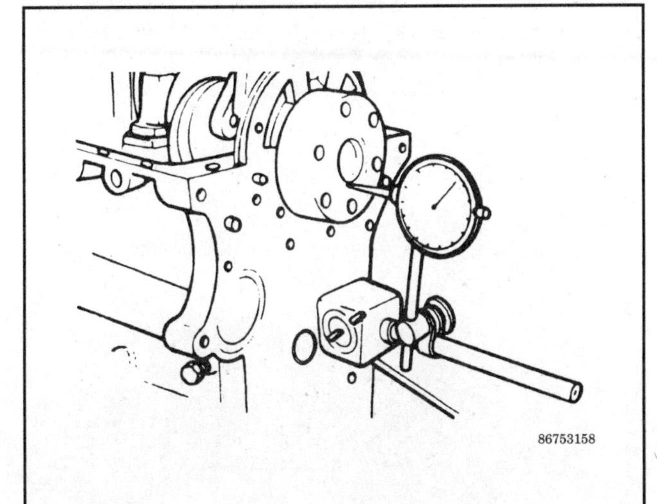

Fig. 243 A dial indicator is needed to measure crankshaft end-play — diesel engines

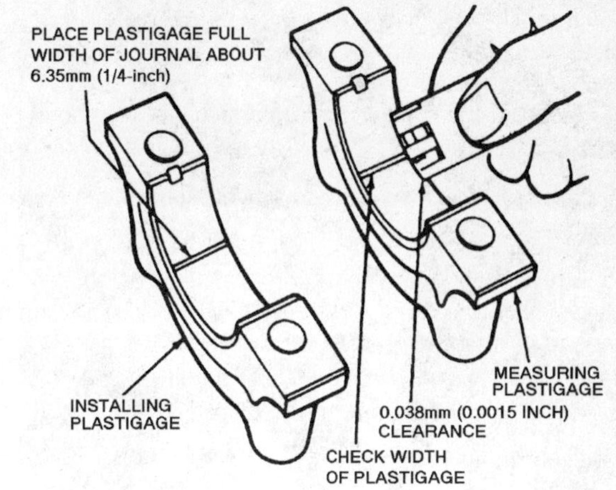

Fig. 244 Use Plastigage® (as shown) to measure bearing clearance

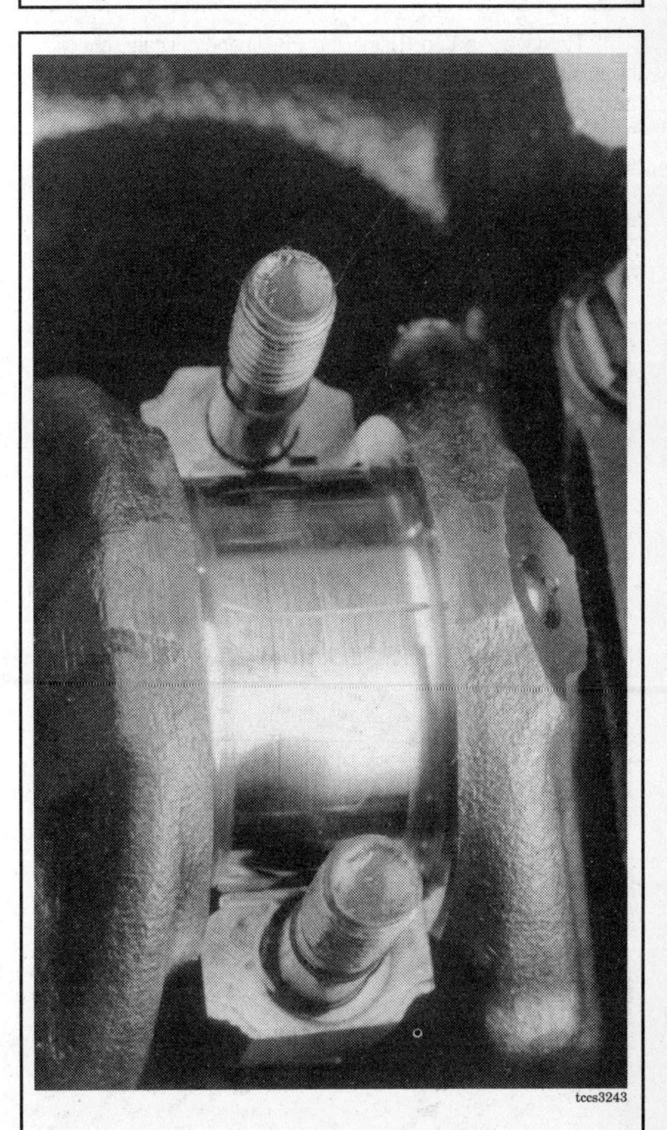

Fig. 245 Apply a strip of gauging material to the bearing journal, then install and torque the cap

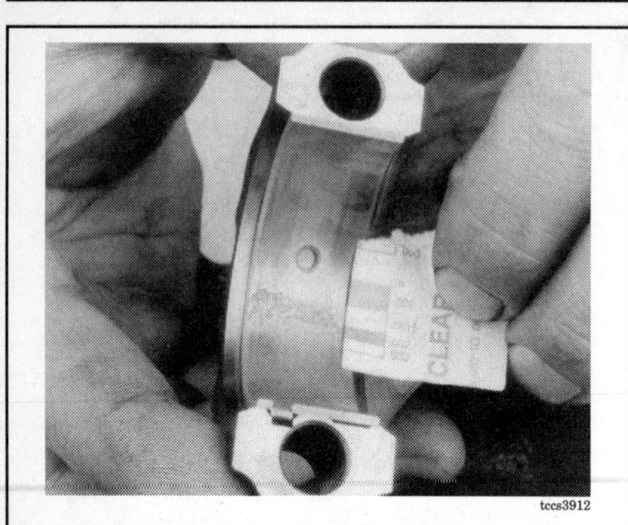

tccs3912

Fig. 246 After the bearing cap is removed, use the supplied gauge to check bearing clearances

4. Remove the cap. Using the Plastigage® scale, check the width of the Plastigage® at its widest point to determine the minimum clearance. Check the narrowest point to determine the maximum clearance. The difference between the readings is the taper of the journal.

5. After each bearing has been fitted, apply a light coat of engine oil to the journal and bearings. Install the bearing cap. Tighten to specification. Repeat the procedure for the remaining bearings.

Flywheel/Flexplate

REMOVAL & INSTALLATION

See Figures 247 and 248

1. Disconnect the negative battery cable.
2. Remove the transaxle assembly.
3. Remove the clutch assembly, if equipped.
4. Remove the rear cover plate, if so equipped.
5. Install a suitable holding tool and remove the flywheel (manual transaxle) or flexplate (automatic transaxle) retaining bolts. Remove the flywheel/flexplate.

To install:

6. Inspect the flywheel (manual transaxle) or flexplate (automatic transaxle) for cracks, heat checks or other damage that would make it unfit for further service. Replace with a new one, if required.
7. Install the flywheel (manual transaxle) or flexplate (automatic transaxle). Use a suitable holding tool, tighten the retaining bolts to specifications using the correct tightening sequence.
8. Install the rear cover plate, if so equipped.
9. Install the clutch assembly, if equipped.
10. Install the transaxle assembly.
11. Reconnect the negative battery cable. Start the engine and check for proper starter gear meshing.

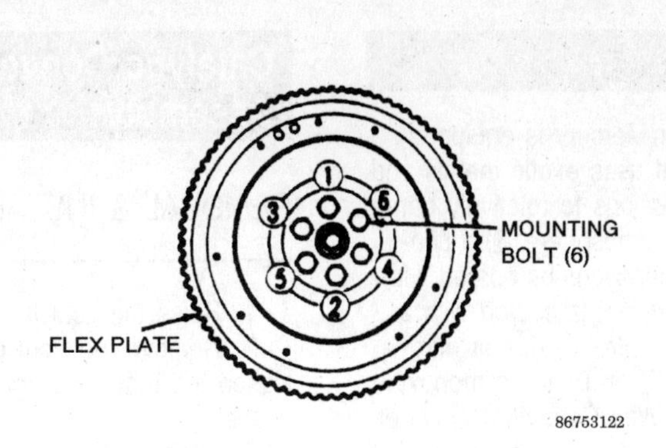

Fig. 247 The flywheel/flexplate bolts should be correctly tightened using a crisscross sequence

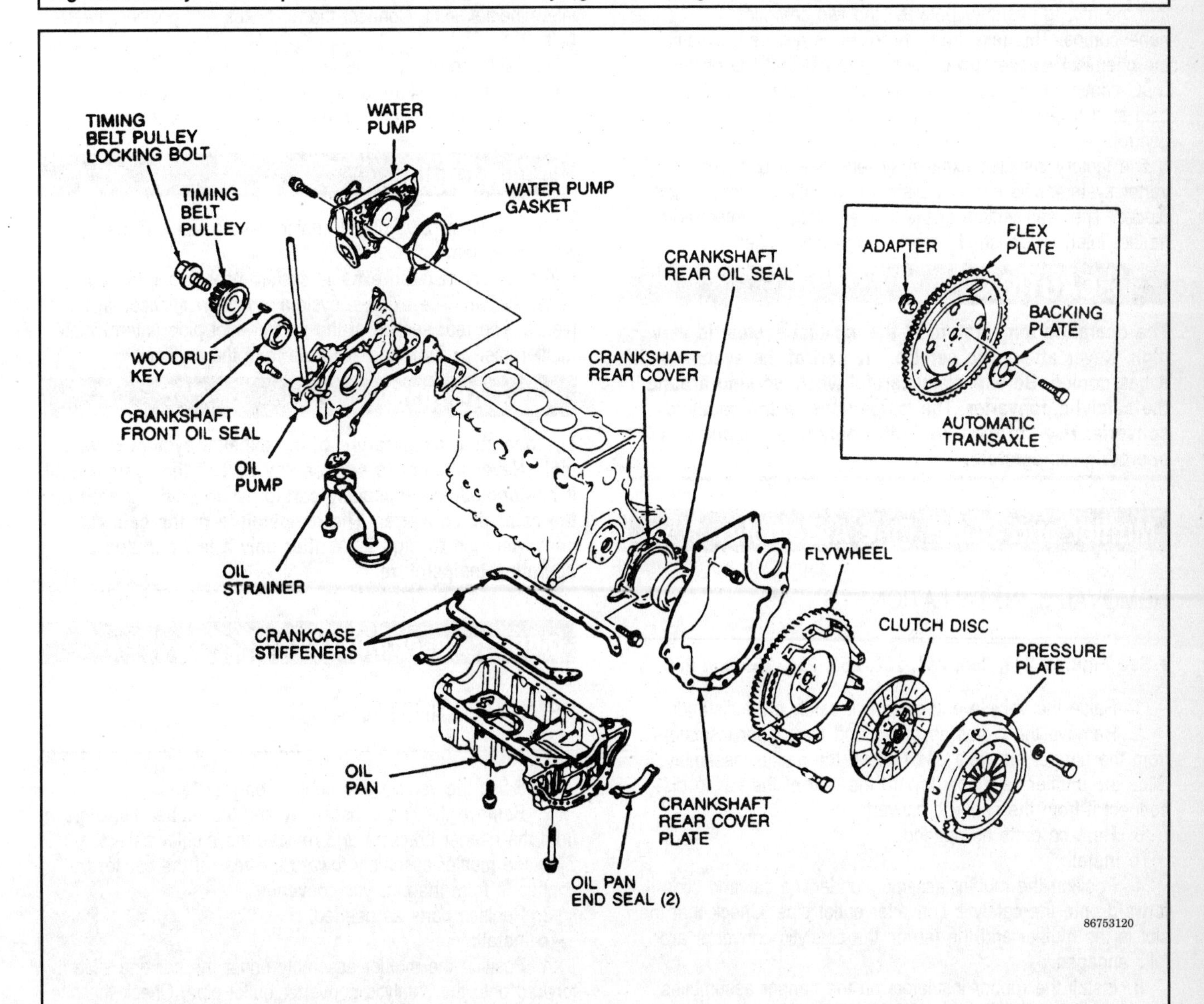

Fig. 248 Exploded view flywheel and other lower engine components in relation to the cylinder block — 1.8L engines

EXHAUST SYSTEM

Gasoline Engines

The exhaust system on your Ford or Mercury is equipped with a catalytic converter, a device that uses exotic metals and the exhaust's own heat to convert emissions to relatively harmless byproducts before they reach the atmosphere. The converter contains two separate ceramic honeycombs coated with different catalytic material. The front catalyst is coated with a rhodium/platinum catalyst designed to control oxides of nitrogen (NOx), unburned hydrocarbons (HC) and carbon monoxide (CO). This is therefore called a Three Way Catalytic Converter (TWC). The rear catalyst is coated with platinum/palladium and is called a conventional oxidation catalyst (COC).

The TWC operates on the exhaust gases as they arrive from the engine. As the gases flow from the TWC to the COC converter, they mix with the air in the secondary air system into the mixing chamber between the two ceramic honeycombs. This (oxygen carrying) air is required to optimize the chemical reaction (oxidation) of the HC and CO on the COC converter. Air is diverted upstream of the TWC during cold start to provide faster catalyst light off and better HC/CO control.

The factory installed exhaust system uses a one-piece converter system. The exhaust system is usually serviced in four pieces. The rear section of the muffler inlet pipe (intermediate muffler inlet) is furnished separate from the muffler.

CAUTION

The operating temperature of the exhaust system is very high. Never attempt to service any part of the system until it has cooled. Be especially careful when working around the catalytic converter. The temperature of the catalytic converter rises to high level after only a few minutes of operating temperature.

Muffler and Outlet Pipe Assembly

REMOVAL & INSTALLATION

See Figures 249, 250, 251, 252, 253, 254, 255 and 256

1. Raise the vehicle and support it safely on jackstands.
2. Remove the U-bolt assembly and the rubber insulators from the hanger brackets and remove the muffler assembly. Slide the muffler assembly toward the rear of the car to disconnect it from the catalytic converter.
3. Replace parts as needed.

To install:

4. Position the muffler assembly under the car and slide it forward onto the catalytic converter outlet pipe. Check that the slot in the muffler and the tab on the catalytic converter are fully engaged.
5. Install the rubber insulators on the hanger assemblies. Install the U-bolt and tighten
6. Check the system for leaks. Lower the vehicle.

Catalytic Converter and/or Pipe Assembly

REMOVAL & INSTALLATION

1. Raise the vehicle and support it safely on jackstands.
2. Remove the front catalytic converter flange fasteners, loosen the rear U-bolt connection and disconnect the air hoses.
3. Separate the catalytic converter inlet and outlet connections. Remove the catalytic converter.

To install:

4. Install the catalytic converter onto the muffler.
5. Install the catalytic converter and muffler assembly to the inlet pipe/flex joint. Connect the air hoses and position the U-bolt.
6. Align the exhaust system into position and, starting at the front of the system, tighten all the nuts and bolts.
7. Check the system for leaks. Lower the vehicle.

Diesel Engine

The 4-cylinder 2.0L diesel engine uses a single-piece type exhaust system.

The factory installed exhaust system uses a one-piece converter system. The exhaust system is usually serviced in four pieces. The rear section of the muffler inlet pipe (intermediate muffler inlet) is furnished separate from the muffler.

CAUTION

The operating temperature of the exhaust system is very high. Never attempt to service any part of the system until it has cooled. Be especially careful when working around the catalytic converter. The temperature of the catalytic converter rise to high level after only a few minutes of operating temperature.

Muffler Assembly

REMOVAL & INSTALLATION

1. Raise the vehicle and support on jackstands.
2. Remove the U-bolt assembly and the rubber insulators from the hanger brackets and remove the muffler assembly. Slide the muffler assembly toward the rear of the car to disconnect it from the catalytic converter.
3. Replace parts as needed.

To install:

4. Position the muffler assembly under the car and slide it forward onto the catalytic converter outlet pipe. Check that the slot in the muffler and the tab on the catalytic converter are fully engaged.

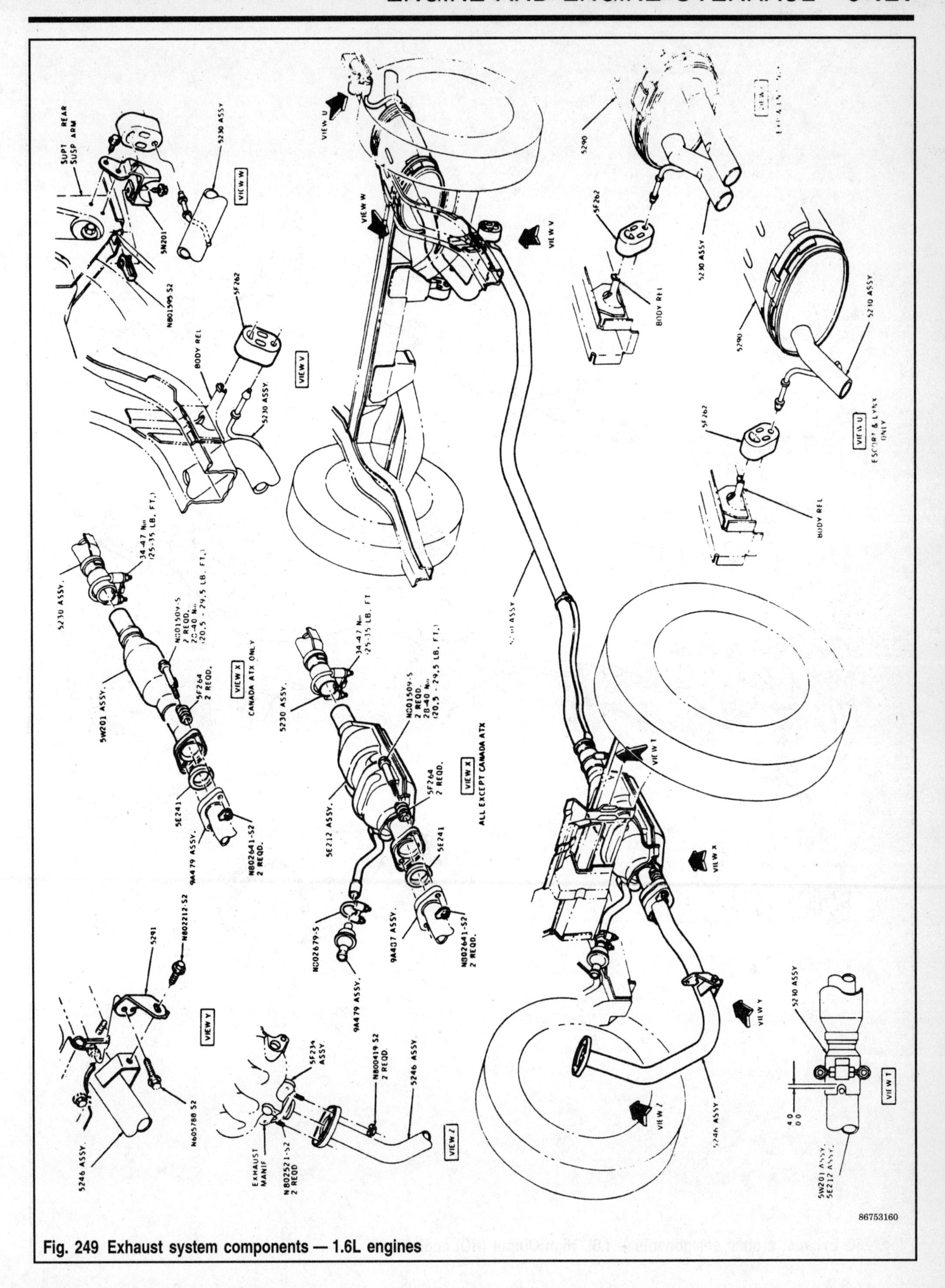

Fig. 249 Exhaust system components — 1.6L engines

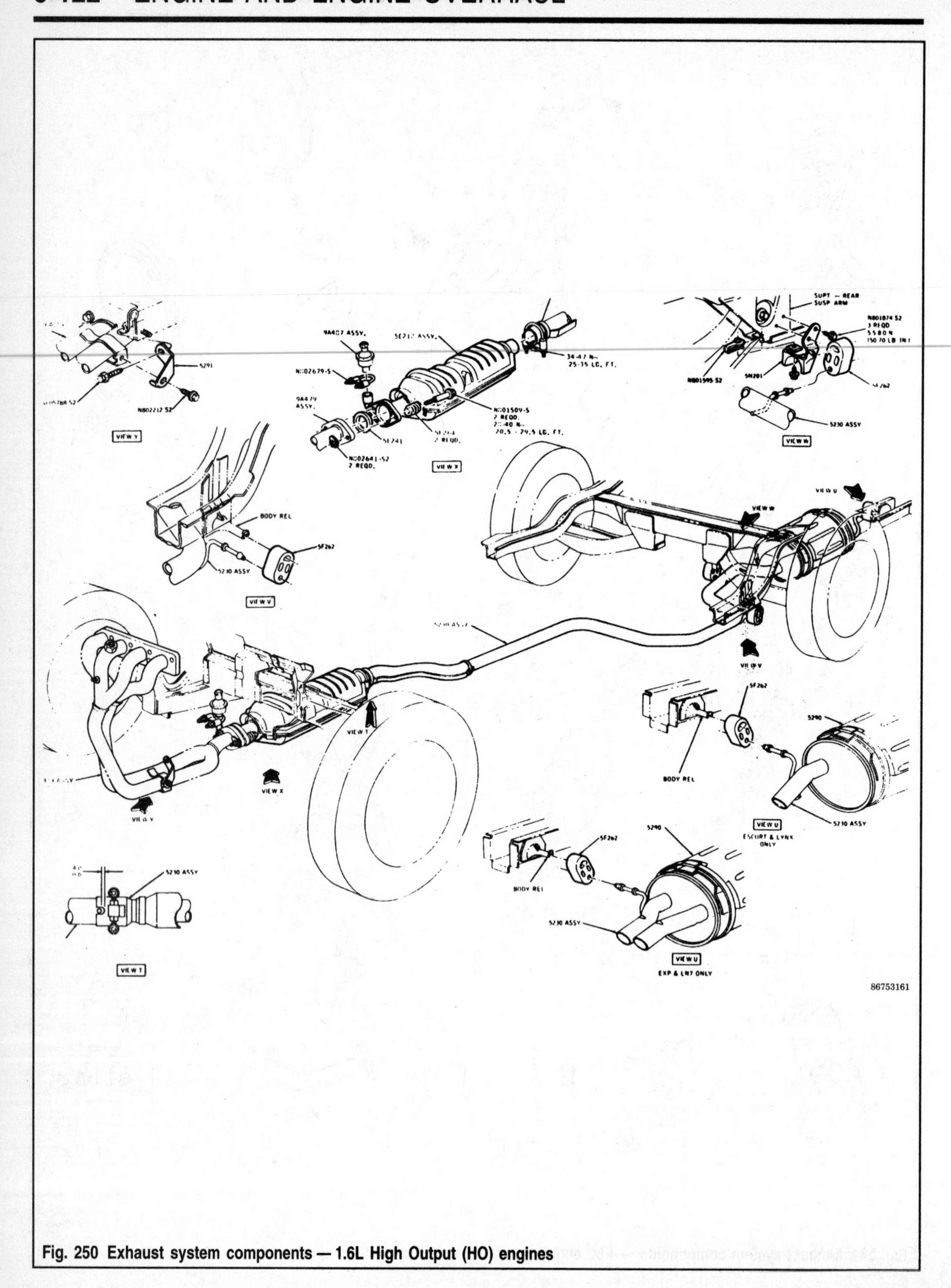

Fig. 250 Exhaust system components — 1.6L High Output (HO) engines

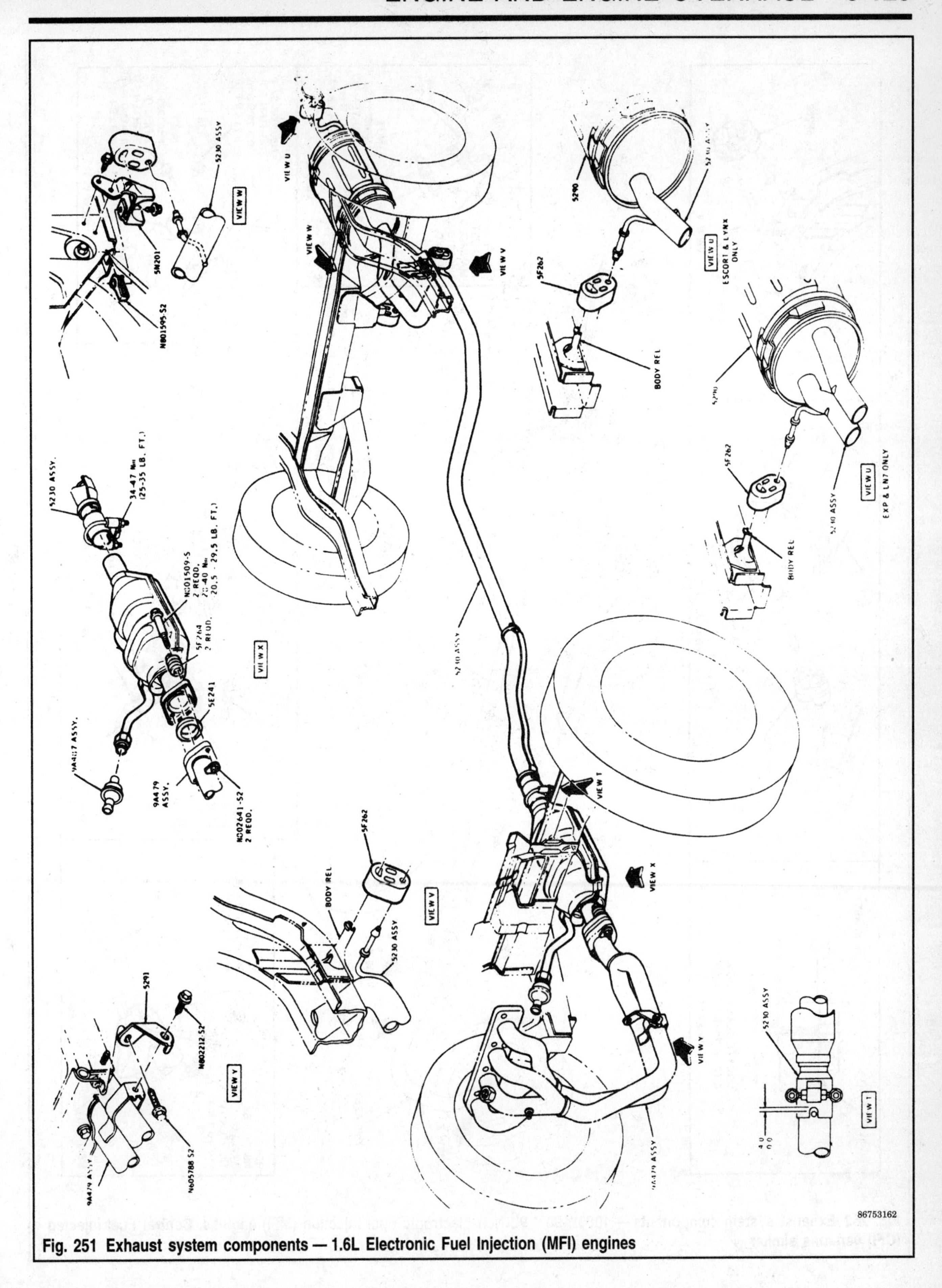

86753162

Fig. 251 Exhaust system components — 1.6L Electronic Fuel Injection (MFI) engines

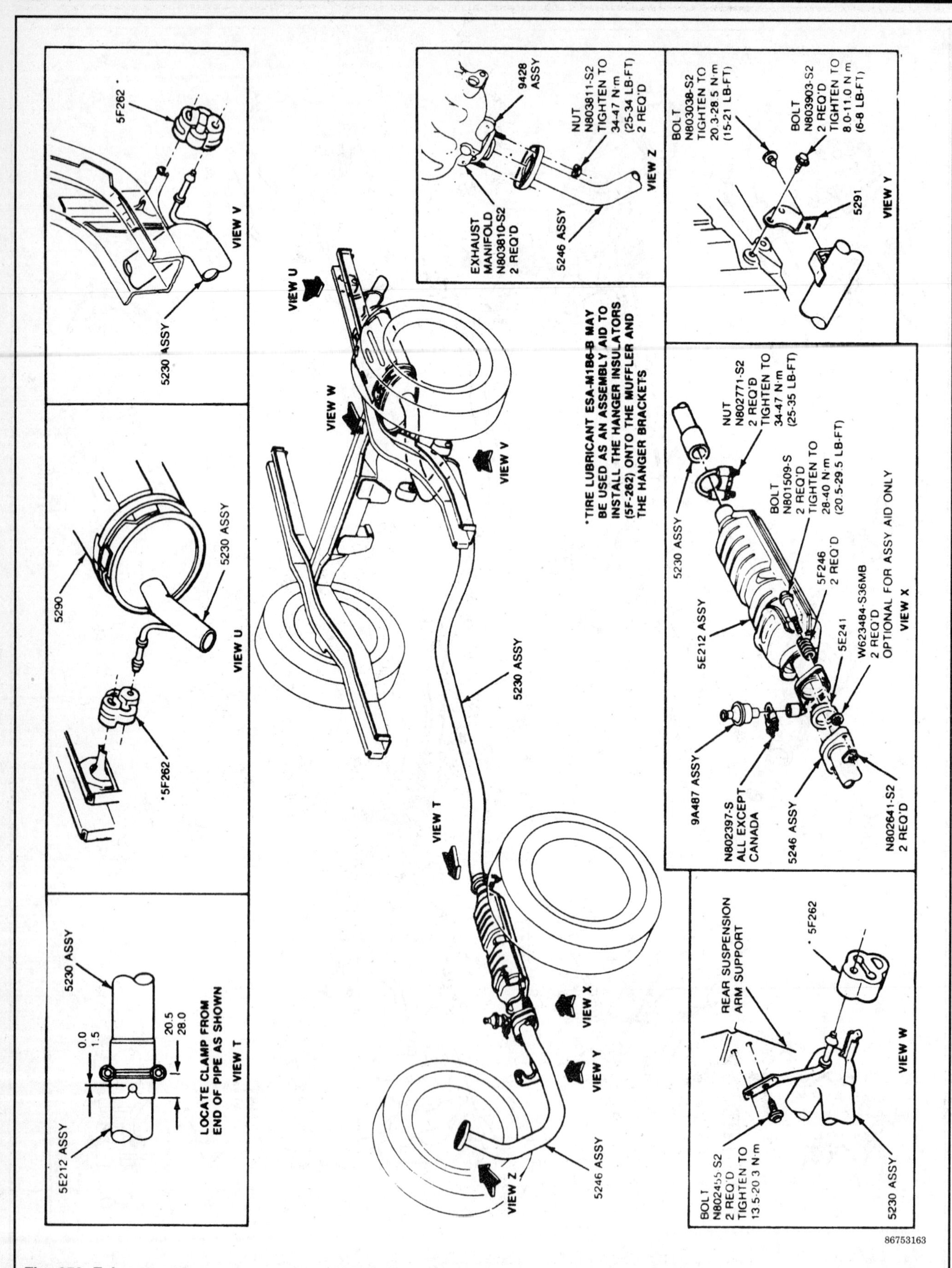

Fig. 252 Exhaust system components — 1985½-90 1.9L Non-Electronic Fuel Injection (MFI) engines. Central Fuel Injected (CFI) versions similar

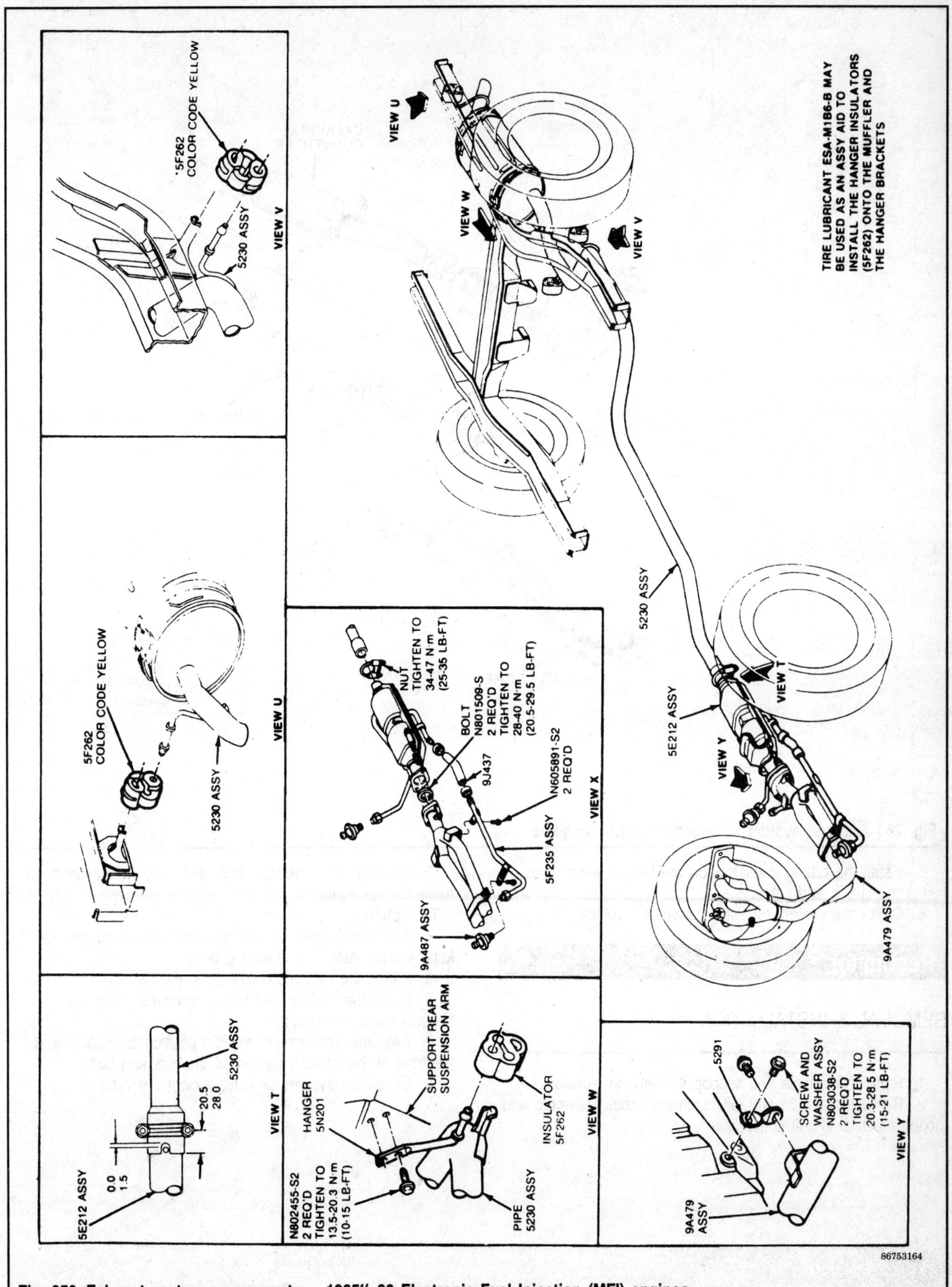

Fig. 253 Exhaust system components — 1985½-90 Electronic Fuel Injection (MFI) engines

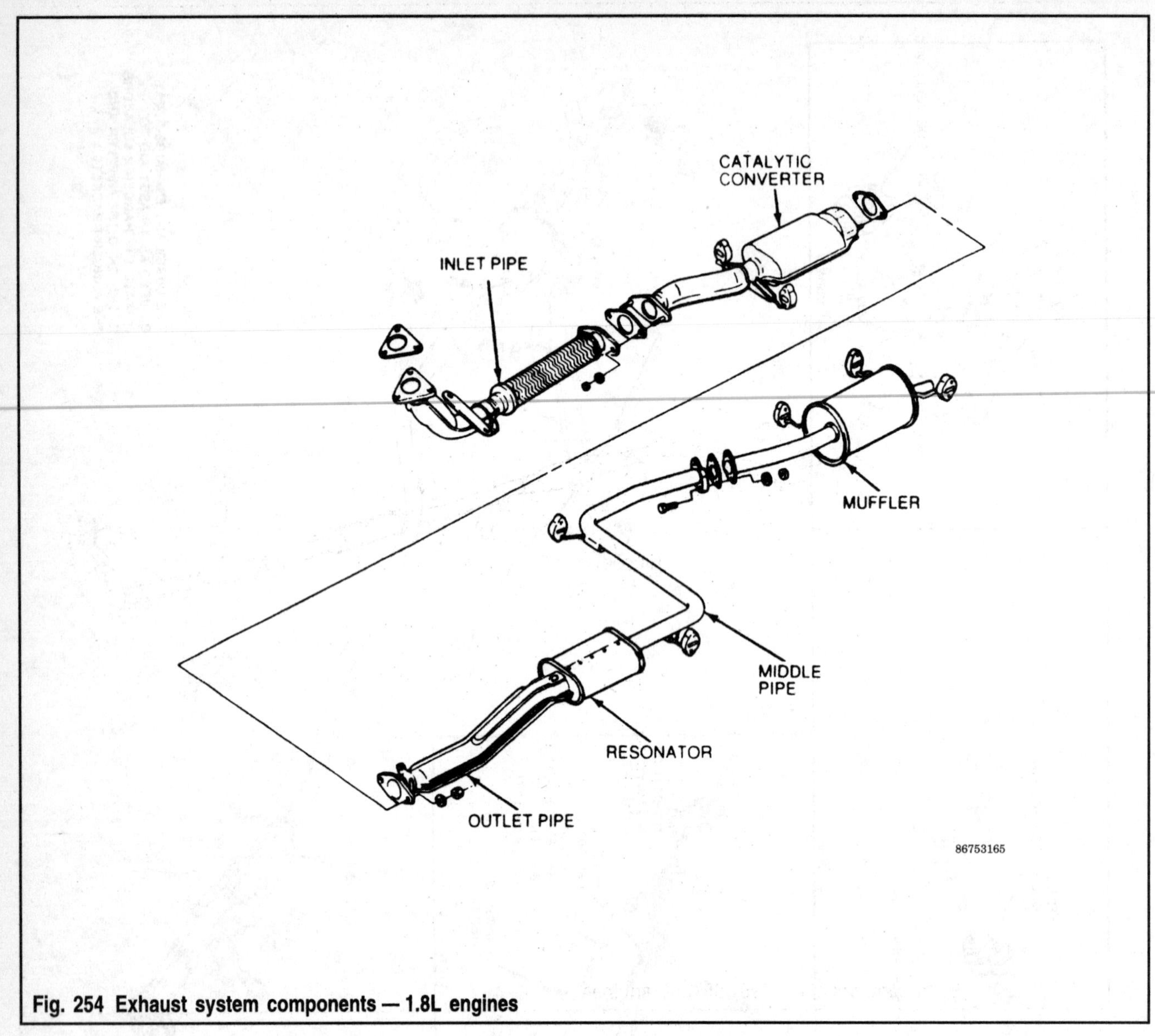

Fig. 254 Exhaust system components — 1.8L engines

5. Install the rubber insulators on the hanger assemblies. Install the U-bolt and tighten
6. Check the system for leaks. Lower the vehicle.

Resonator

REMOVAL & INSTALLATION

1. Raise the vehicle and support it safely on jackstands.
2. Remove the right and left resonator flange fasteners and loosen the rear U-bolt connection.
3. Separate the resonator inlet and outlet connections. Remove the resonator.

To install:

4. Align the flanges on the resonator and using new gaskets, loosely install the attaching bolts.
5. Attach the catalytic converter to the muffler.
6. Install the muffler inlet to the resonator outlet pipe. Loosely install the U-bolts.
7. Align the exhaust system into position and, starting at the front of the system, tighten all the nuts and bolts.
8. Check the system for leaks. Lower the vehicle.

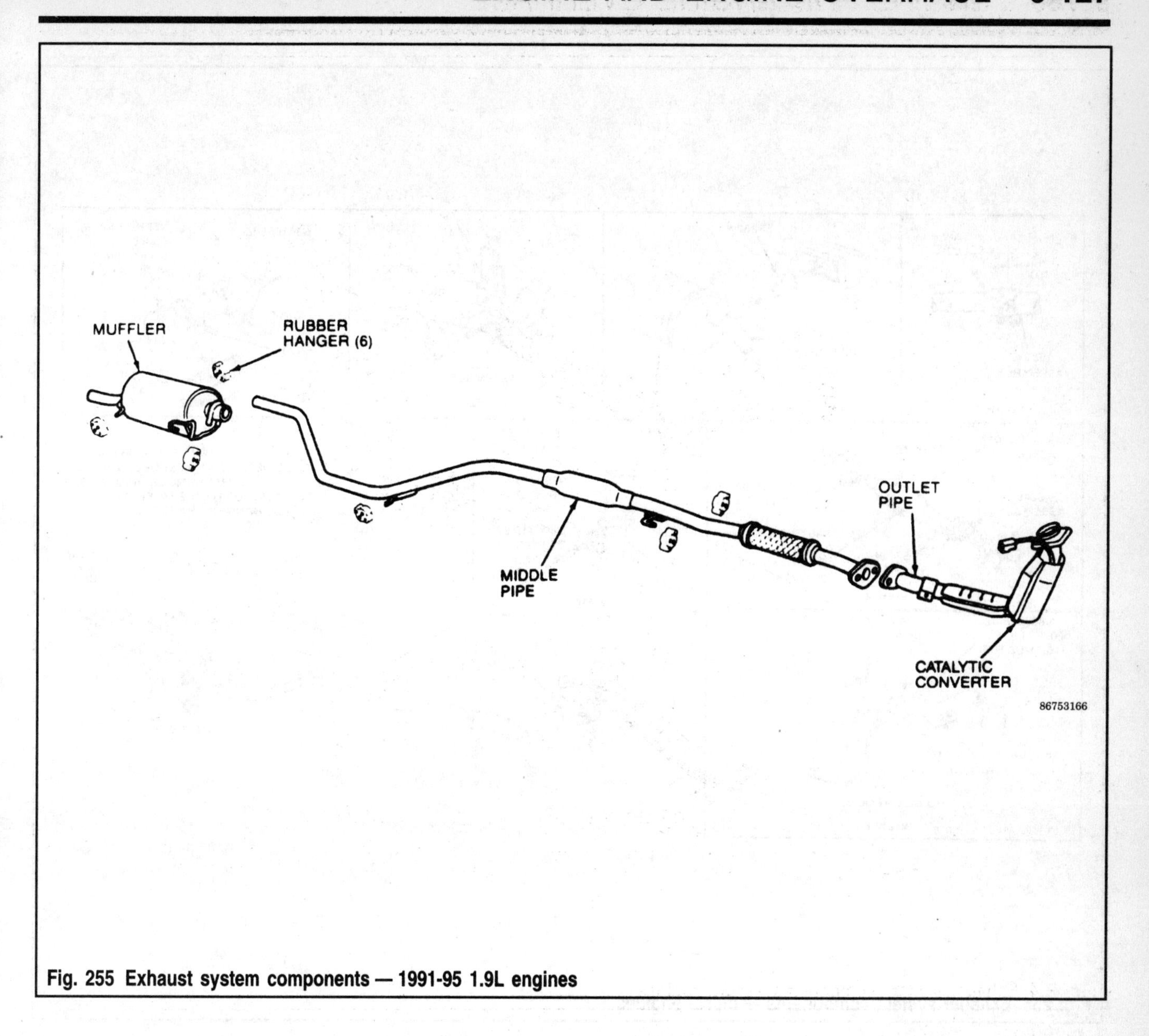

Fig. 255 Exhaust system components — 1991-95 1.9L engines

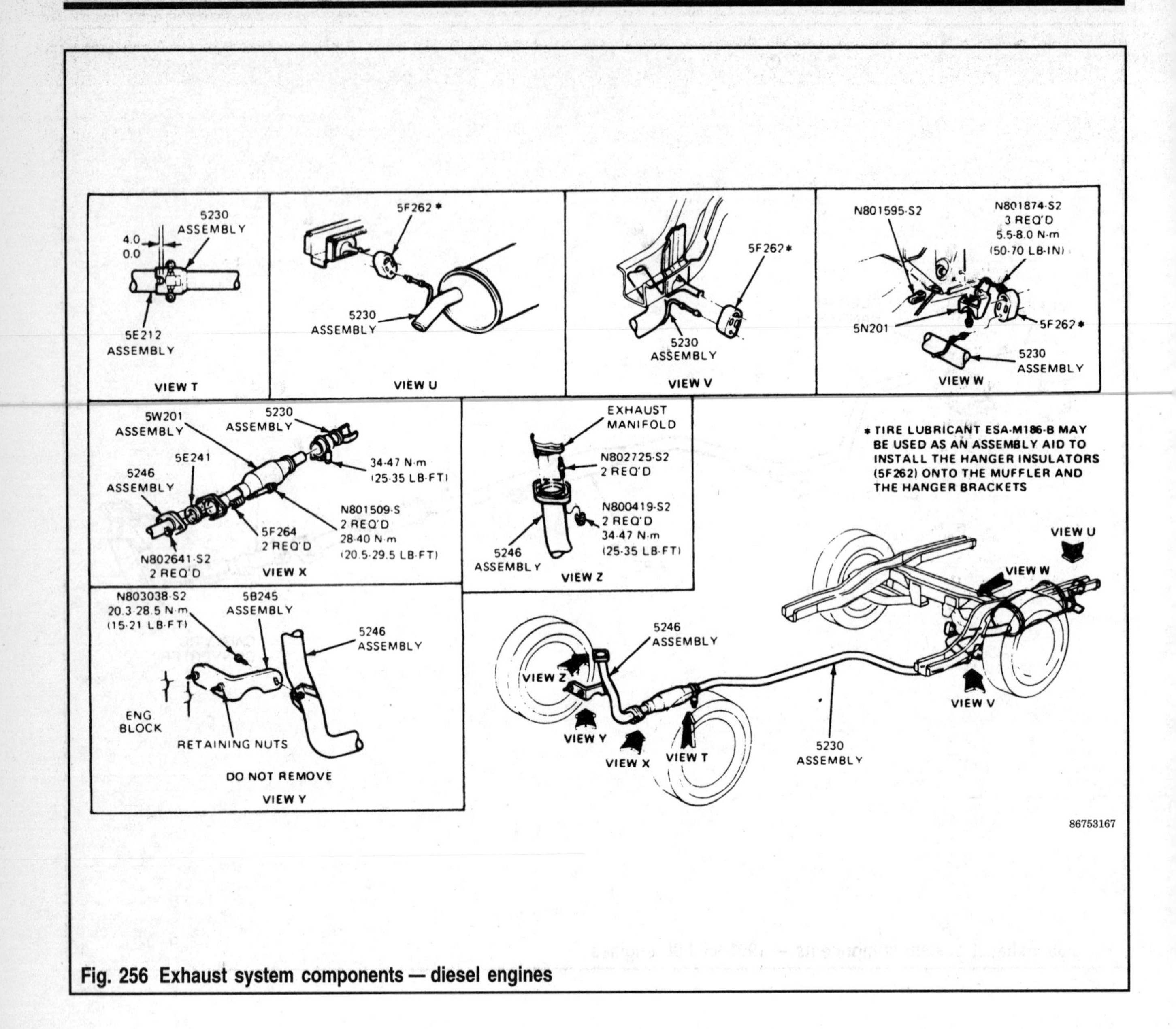

Fig. 256 Exhaust system components — diesel engines

GASOLINE ENGINE TORQUE SPECIFICATIONS

Component	U.S.	Metric
Spark Plugs		
1981–82 1.3L and 1.6L engines:	17–22 ft. lbs.	23–30 Nm
1983–85 1.6L engines:	10–15 ft. lbs.	7–20 Nm
1991–95 1.8L engines:	11–17 ft. lbs.	14–23 Nm
1986–90 1.9L engines:	7–15 ft. lbs.	9–20 Nm
1991–95 1.9L engines:	88–176 inch lbs.	10–20 Nm
Distributor Hold-down Bolts		
1981–82 1.3L and 1.6L engines:	3.7–5.2 ft. lbs.	5.0–7.0 Nm
1983–85 1.6L engines:	3.7–5.2 ft. lbs.	5.0–7.0 Nm
1991–95 1.8L engines:	14–19 ft. lbs.	19–25 Nm
1986–90 1.9L engines:	3.7–5.2 ft. lbs.	5.0–7.0 Nm
Distributor Diaphragm Retaining Screws		
1981–82 1.3L and 1.6L engines:	1.8–3.0 ft. lbs.	2.5–4.0 Nm
1983–85 1.6L engines:	1.8–3.0 ft. lbs.	2.5–4.0 Nm
1986–87 1.9L engines:	1.8–3.0 ft. lbs.	2.5–4.0 Nm
Stator Assembly Retainer Plate Screws		
1981–82 1.3L and 1.6L engines:	1.8–3.0 ft. lbs.	2.5–4.0 Nm
1983–85 1.6L engines:	1.8–3.0 ft. lbs.	2.5–4.0 Nm
1986–87 1.9L engines:	1.8–3.0 ft. lbs.	2.5–4.0 Nm
1988–90 1.9L engines:	15–35 inch lbs.	1.7–4.0 Nm
Connector Hold-down Plate Screws		
1981–82 1.3L and 1.6L engines:	1.8–3.0 ft. lbs.	2.5–4.0 Nm
1983–85 1.6L engines:	1.8–3.0 ft. lbs.	2.5–4.0 Nm
1986–87 1.9L engines:	1.8–3.0 ft. lbs.	2.5–4.0 Nm
1988–90 1.9L engines:	15–35 inch lbs.	1.7–4.0 Nm
Distributor Cap Hold-down Screws		
1981–82 1.3L and 1.6L engines:	33–43 inch lbs.	2.0–2.6 Nm
1983–85 1.6L engines:	33–43 inch lbs.	2.0–2.6 Nm
1986–90 1.9L engines:	18–23 inch lbs.	2.0–2.6 Nm
Distributor Rotor Hold-down Screws		
1981–82 1.3L and 1.6L engines:	2.1–2.9 ft. lbs.	2.8–3.9 Nm
1983–85 1.6L engines:	2.1–2.9 ft. lbs.	2.8–3.9 Nm
1986–87 1.9L engines:	25–35 inch lbs.	2.8–3.9 Nm
TFI Ignition Module Mounting Screws		
1981–82 1.3L and 1.6L engines:	9–16 inch lbs.	1.1–1.8 Nm
1983–85 1.6L engines:	9–16 inch lbs.	1.1–1.8 Nm
1986–87 1.9L engines:	25–35 inch lbs.	2.8–3.9 Nm
1988–90 1.9L engines:	15–35 inch lbs.	1.7–4.0 Nm
EDIS Ignition Module Mounting Screws		
1991–95 1.9L engines:	24–35 inch lbs.	3–4 Nm
EDIS Ignition Module Bracket-to-Body Bracket		
1991–95 1.9L engines:	62–88 inch lbs.	7–10 Nm
Crankshaft Position Sensor Mounting Screws		
1991–95 1.9L engines:	40–61 inch lbs.	5–7 Nm
Ignition Coil Pack Mounting Bolts		
1991–95 1.9L engines:	40–61 inch lbs.	5–7 Nm
Ignition Coil Pack Bracket-to-Cylinder Head		
1991–95 1.9L engines:	71–97 inch lbs.	8–11 Nm

Do Not Over-Tighten spark plugs.
Excessive tightening can result in striped threads in the cylinder head.

Do Not Under-Tighten spark plugs.
Insufficient tightness can permit the plug to loosen; subsequent overheating due to preignition will result in engine damage.

86753C01

DIESEL ENGINE TORQUE SPECIFICATIONS

Component	English	Metric
Alternator		
Pulley Nut:	60–100 ft. lbs.	81–135 Nm
Through Bolt:	35–60 inch lbs.	4–6.7 Nm
Rectifier Assembly Mounting Screw:	25–35 inch lbs.	3–4 Nm
Brush Holder Mounting Screw:	20–30 inch lbs.	2–4 Nm
Regulator Mounting Screw:	25–35 inch lbs.	3–4 Nm
Bearing Retainer Screw:	24–42 inch lbs.	3–4.5 Nm
Starter		
Through Bolt:	5–7 ft. lbs.	7–9 Nm
Mounting Bolt:	- ft. lbs.	39–56 Nm
Solenoid Mounting Screws:	5–7 ft. lbs.	7–9 Nm
Camshaft Pulley		
Front:	41–48 ft. lbs.	56–66 Nm
Raar:	41–48 ft. lbs.	56–66 Nm
Camshaft Caps:	14.5–19.5 ft. lbs.	20–27 Nm
Connecting Rod Caps:	48–51 ft. lbs.	66–75 Nm
Crankshaft Pulley:	115.7–123 ft. lbs.	160–170 Nm
Cylinder Head Cover:	5.1–7.2 ft. lbs.	7–10 Nm
Exhaust Manifold:	15.9–19.5 ft. lbs.	22–27 Nm
Flywheel:	130.2–137.4 ft. lbs.	180–190 Nm
Glow Plugs:	10.8–14.5 ft. lbs.	15–20 Nm
Injection Nozzles:	43.4–50.6 ft. lbs.	60–70 Nm
Injection Pump Pulley:	43.4–50.6 ft. lbs.	60–70 Nm
Injection Pump Bracket		
Bolt:	23.1–34.0 ft. lbs.	32–47 Nm
Nut:	11.6–16.6 ft. lbs.	16–23 Nm
Injection Pump Body		
Bolt:	23.1–34.0 ft. lbs.	32–47 Nm
Nut:	11.6–16.6 ft. lbs.	16–23 Nm
Intake Manifold:	11.6–16.6 ft. lbs.	16–23 Nm
Main Bearing Caps:	60.8–65.1 ft. lbs.	84–90 Nm
Oil Jets:	23.1–34.0 ft. lbs.	32–47 Nm
Oil Pan:	5.1–7.2 ft. lbs.	7–10 Nm
Oil Pump Body:	9.–13 ft. lbs.	12–18 Nm
Oil Pump Gear Cover (Screw):	5.1–7.2 ft. lbs.	7–10 Nm
Oil Strainer:	5.1–7.2 ft. lbs.	7–10 Nm
Thermostat Casing (Bolt):	11.6–16.6 ft. lbs.	16–23 Nm
Thermostat Cover (Bolt):	5.1–7.2 ft. lbs.	7–10 Nm
Water Pump:	23.1–34.0 ft. lbs.	32–47 Nm

86753C02

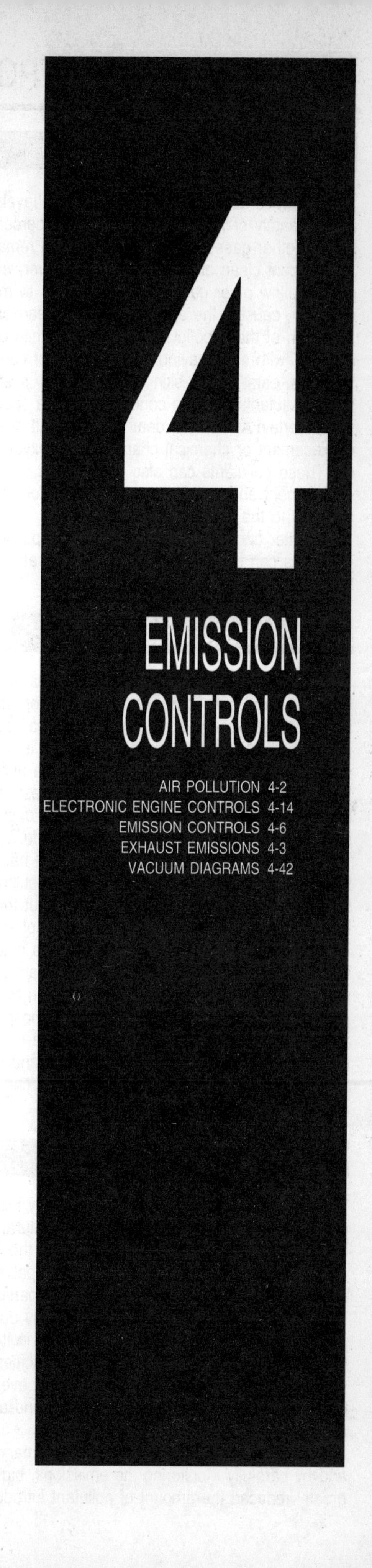

4 EMISSION CONTROLS

AIR POLLUTION

The earth's atmosphere, at or near sea level, consists approximately of 78 percent nitrogen, 21 percent oxygen and 1 percent other gases. If it were possible to remain in this state, 100 percent clean air would result. However, many varied causes allow other gases and particulates to mix with the clean air, causing the air to become unclean or polluted.

Certain of these pollutants are visible while others are invisible, with each having the capability of causing distress to the eyes, ears, throat, skin and respiratory system. Should these pollutants become concentrated in a specific area and under certain conditions, death could result due to the displacement or chemical change of the oxygen content in the air. These pollutants can also cause great damage to the environment and to the many man made objects that are exposed to the elements.

To better understand the causes of air pollution, the pollutants can be categorized into 3 separate types, natural, industrial and automotive.

Natural Pollutants

Natural pollution has been present on earth since before man appeared and continues to be a factor when discussing air pollution, although it causes only a small percentage of the overall pollution problem existing today. It is the direct result of decaying organic matter, wind born smoke and particulates from such natural events as plain and forest fires (ignited by heat or lightning), volcanic ash, sand and dust which can spread over a large area of the countryside.

Such a phenomenon of natural pollution has been seen in the form of volcanic eruptions, with the resulting plume of smoke, steam and volcanic ash blotting out the sun's rays as it spreads and rises higher into the atmosphere. As it travels into the atmosphere the upper air currents catch and carry the smoke and ash, while condensing the steam back into water vapor. As the water vapor, smoke and ash traveled on their journey, the smoke dissipates into the atmosphere while the ash and moisture settle back to earth in a trail hundreds of miles long. In some cases, lives are lost and millions of dollars of property damage result. Ironically, man can only stand by and watch it happen.

Industrial Pollutants

Industrial pollution is caused primarily by industrial processes, the burning of coal, oil and natural gas, which in turn produce smoke and fumes. Because the burning fuels contain large amounts of sulfur, the principal ingredients of smoke and fumes are sulfur dioxide and particulate matter. This type of pollutant occurs most severely during still, damp and cool weather, such as at night. Even in its less severe form, this pollutant is not confined to just cities. Because of air movements, the pollutants move for miles over the surrounding countryside, leaving in its path a barren and unhealthy environment for all living things.

Working with Federal, State and Local mandated regulations and by carefully monitoring the emissions, big business has greatly reduced the amount of pollutant introduced from its industrial sources, striving to obtain an acceptable level. Because of the mandated industrial emission clean up, many land areas and streams in and around the cities that were formerly barren of vegetation and life, have now begun to move back in the direction of nature's intended balance.

Automotive Pollutants

The third major source of air pollution is automotive emissions. The emissions from the internal combustion engine were not an appreciable problem years ago because of the small number of registered vehicles and the nation's small highway system. However, during the early 1950's, the trend of the American people was to move from the cities to the surrounding suburbs. This caused an immediate problem in transportation because the majority of suburbs were not afforded mass transit conveniences. This lack of transportation created an attractive market for the automobile manufacturers, which resulted in a dramatic increase in the number of vehicles produced and sold, along with a marked increase in highway construction between cities and the suburbs. Multi-vehicle families emerged with a growing emphasis placed on an individual vehicle per family member. As the increase in vehicle ownership and usage occurred, so did pollutant levels in and around the cities, as suburbanites drove daily to their businesses and employment, returning at the end of the day to their homes in the suburbs.

It was noted that a fog and smoke type haze was being formed and at times, remained in suspension over the cities, taking time to dissipate. At first this "smog", derived from the words "smoke" and "fog", was thought to result from industrial pollution but it was determined that automobile emissions shared the blame. It was discovered that when normal automobile emissions were exposed to sunlight for a period of time, complex chemical reactions would take place.

It is now known that smog is a photo chemical layer which develops when certain oxides of nitrogen (NOx) and unburned hydrocarbons (HC) from automobile emissions are exposed to sunlight. Pollution was more severe when smog would become stagnant over an area in which a warm layer of air settled over the top of the cooler air mass, trapping and holding the cooler mass at ground level. The trapped cooler air would keep the emissions from being dispersed and diluted through normal air flows. This type of air stagnation was given the name "Temperature Inversion".

Temperature Inversion

In normal weather situations, the surface air is warmed by heat radiating from the earth's surface and the sun's rays and will rise upward, into the atmosphere. Upon rising it will cool through a convection type heat exchange with the cooler upper air. As warm air rises, the surface pollutants are carried upward and dissipated into the atmosphere.

When a temperature inversion occurs, we find the higher air is no longer cooler, but is warmer than the surface air, causing the cooler surface air to become trapped. This warm air blanket can extend from above ground level to a few hundred or even a few thousand feet into the air. As the surface air is trapped, so are the pollutants, causing a severe smog condition. Should this stagnant air mass extend to a few thousand feet high, enough air movement with the inversion takes place to allow the smog layer to rise above ground level but the pollutants still cannot dissipate. This inversion can remain for days over an area, with the smog level only rising or lowering from ground level to a few hundred feet high. Meanwhile, the pollutant levels increase, causing eye irritation, respiratory problems, reduced visibility, plant damage and in some cases, even disease.

This inversion phenomenon was first noted in the Los Angeles, California area. The city lies in terrain resembling a basin and with certain weather conditions, a cold air mass is held in the basin while a warmer air mass covers it like a lid.

Because this type of condition was first documented as prevalent in the Los Angeles area, this type of trapped pollution was named Los Angeles Smog, although it occurs in other areas where a large concentration of automobiles are used and the air remains stagnant for any length of time.

Internal Combustion Engine Pollutants

Consider the internal combustion engine as a machine in which raw materials must be placed so a finished product comes out. As in any machine operation, a certain amount of wasted material is formed. When we relate this to the internal combustion engine, we find that through the input of air and fuel, we obtain power during the combustion process to drive the vehicle. The by-product or waste of this power is, in part, heat and exhaust gases with which we must dispose.

Heat Transfer

The heat from the combustion process can rise to over 4,000°F (2,204°C). The dissipation of this heat is controlled by a ram air effect, the use of cooling fans to cause air flow and a liquid coolant solution surrounding the combustion area to transfer the heat of combustion through the cylinder walls and into the coolant. The coolant is then directed to a thin-finned, multi-tubed radiator, from which the excess heat is transferred to the atmosphere by 1 of the 3 heat transfer methods, conduction, convection or radiation.

The cooling of the combustion area is an important part in the control of exhaust emissions. To understand the behavior of the combustion and transfer of its heat, consider the air/fuel charge. It is ignited and the flame front burns progressively across the combustion chamber until the burning charge reaches the cylinder walls. Some of the fuel in contact with the walls is not hot enough to burn, thereby snuffing out or quenching the combustion process. This leaves unburned fuel in the combustion chamber. This unburned fuel is then forced out of the cylinder and into the exhaust system, along with the exhaust gases.

Many attempts have been made to minimize the amount of unburned fuel in the combustion chambers due to the quenching, by increasing the coolant temperature and lessening the contact area of the coolant around the combustion area. However, design limitations within the combustion chambers prevent the complete burning of the air/fuel charge, so a certain amount of the unburned fuel is still expelled into the exhaust system, regardless of modifications to the engine.

EXHAUST EMISSIONS

Composition Of The Exhaust Gases

The exhaust gases emitted into the atmosphere are a combination of burned and unburned fuel. To understand the exhaust emission and its composition, we must review some basic chemistry.

When the air/fuel mixture is introduced into the engine, we are mixing air, composed of nitrogen (78 percent), oxygen (21 percent) and other gases (1 percent) with the fuel, which is 100 percent hydrocarbons (HC), in a semi-controlled ratio. As the combustion process is accomplished, power is produced to move the vehicle while the heat of combustion is transferred to the cooling system. The exhaust gases are then composed of nitrogen, a diatomic gas (N_2), the same as was introduced in the engine, carbon dioxide (CO_2), the same gas that is used in beverage carbonation, and water vapor (H_2O). The nitrogen (N_2), for the most part, passes through the engine unchanged, while the oxygen (O_2) reacts (burns) with the hydrocarbons (HC) and produces the carbon dioxide (CO_2) and the water vapors (H_2O). If this chemical process would be the only process to take place, the exhaust emissions would be harmless. However, during the combustion process, other compounds are formed which are considered dangerous. These pollutants are carbon monoxide (CO), hydrocarbons (HC), oxides of nitrogen (NOx) oxides of sulfur (SOx) and engine particulates.

HYDROCARBONS

Hydrocarbons (HC) are essentially fuel which was not burned during the combustion process or which has escaped into the atmosphere through fuel evaporation. The main sources of incomplete combustion are rich air/fuel mixtures, low engine temperatures and improper spark timing. The main sources of hydrocarbon emission through fuel evaporation on most cars used to be the vehicle's fuel tank and carburetor bowl.

To reduce combustion hydrocarbon emission, engine modifications were made to minimize dead space and surface area in the combustion chamber. In addition, the air/fuel mixture was made more lean through the improved control which feedback carburetion and fuel injection offers and by the addition of external controls to aid in further combustion of the hydrocarbons outside the engine. Two such methods were the addition of an air injection system, to inject fresh air into the exhaust manifolds and the installation of a catalytic converter, a unit that is able to burn traces of hydrocarbons without affecting the internal combustion process or fuel economy. The vehicles covered in this manual may utilize either, both or none of these methods, depending on the year and model.

To control hydrocarbon emissions through fuel evaporation, modifications were made to the fuel tank to allow storage of the fuel vapors during periods of engine shut-down.

Modifications were also made to the air intake system so that at specific times during engine operation, these vapors may be purged and burned by blending them with the air/fuel mixture.

CARBON MONOXIDE

Carbon monoxide is formed when not enough oxygen is present during the combustion process to convert carbon (C) to carbon dioxide (CO_2). An increase in the carbon monoxide (CO) emission is normally accompanied by an increase in the hydrocarbon (HC) emission because of the lack of oxygen to completely burn all of the fuel mixture.

Carbon monoxide (CO) also increases the rate at which the photo chemical smog is formed by speeding up the conversion of nitric oxide (NO) to nitrogen dioxide (NO_2). To accomplish this, carbon monoxide (CO) combines with oxygen (O_2) and nitric oxide (NO) to produce carbon dioxide (CO_2) and nitrogen dioxide (NO_2). ($CO + O_2 + NO = CO_2 + NO_2$).

The dangers of carbon monoxide, which is an odorless and colorless toxic gas are many. When carbon monoxide is inhaled into the lungs and passed into the blood stream, oxygen is replaced by the carbon monoxide in the red blood cells, causing a reduction in the amount of oxygen being supplied to the many parts of the body. This lack of oxygen causes headaches, lack of coordination, reduced mental alertness and should the carbon monoxide concentration be high enough, death could result.

NITROGEN

Normally, nitrogen is an inert gas. When heated to approximately 2,500°F (1,371°C) through the combustion process, this gas becomes active and causes an increase in the nitric oxide (NOx) emission.

Oxides of nitrogen (NOx) are composed of approximately 97-98 percent nitric oxide (NO). Nitric oxide is a colorless gas but when it is passed into the atmosphere, it combines with oxygen and forms nitrogen dioxide (NO_2). The nitrogen dioxide then combines with chemically active hydrocarbons (HC) and when in the presence of sunlight, causes the formation of photo chemical smog.

OZONE

To further complicate matters, some of the nitrogen dioxide (NO_2) is broken apart by the sunlight to form nitric oxide and oxygen. (NO_2 + sunlight = NO + O). This single atom of oxygen then combines with diatomic (meaning 2 atoms) oxygen (O_2) to form ozone (O_3). Ozone is one of the smells associated with smog. It has a pungent and offensive odor, irritates the eyes and lung tissues, affects the growth of plant life and causes rapid deterioration of rubber products. Ozone can be formed by sunlight as well as electrical discharge into the air.

The most common discharge area on the automobile engine is the secondary ignition electrical system, especially when inferior quality spark plug cables are used. As the surge of high voltage is routed through the secondary cable, the circuit builds up an electrical field around the wire, acting upon the oxygen in the surrounding air to form the ozone. The faint glow along the cable with the engine running that may be visible on a dark night, is called the "corona discharge." It is the result of the electrical field passing from a high along the cable, to a low in the surrounding air, which forms the ozone gas. The combination of corona and ozone has been a major cause of cable deterioration. Recently, different and better quality insulating materials have lengthened the life of the electrical cables.

Although ozone at ground level can be harmful, ozone is beneficial to the earth's inhabitants. By having a concentrated ozone layer called the "ozonosphere", between 10 and 20 miles (16-32km) up in the atmosphere, much of the ultra violet radiation from the sun's rays are absorbed and screened. If this ozone layer were not present, much of the earth's surface would be burned, dried and unfit for human life.

OXIDES OF SULFUR

Oxides of sulfur (SOx) were initially ignored in the exhaust system emissions, since the sulfur content of gasoline as a fuel is less than $^1/_{10}$ of 1 percent. Because of this small amount, it was felt that it contributed very little to the overall pollution problem. However, because of the difficulty in solving the sulfur emissions in industrial pollutions and the introduction of catalytic converter to the automobile exhaust systems, a change was mandated. The automobile exhaust system, when equipped with a catalytic converter, changes the sulfur dioxide (SO_2) into the sulfur trioxide (SO_3).

When this combines with water vapors (H_2O), a sulfuric acid mist (H_2SO_4) is formed and is a very difficult pollutant to handle since it is extremely corrosive. This sulfuric acid mist that is formed, is the same mist that rises from the vents of an automobile battery when an active chemical reaction takes place within the battery cells.

When a large concentration of vehicles equipped with catalytic converters are operating in an area, this acid mist may rise and be distributed over a large ground area causing land, plant, crop, paints and building damage.

PARTICULATE MATTER

A certain amount of particulate matter is present in the burning of any fuel, with carbon constituting the largest percentage of the particulates. In gasoline, the remaining particulates are the burned remains of the various other compounds used in its manufacture. When a gasoline engine is in good internal condition, the particulate emissions are low but as the engine wears internally, the particulate emissions increase. By visually inspecting the tail pipe emissions, a determination can be made as to where an engine defect may exist. An engine with light gray or blue smoke emitting from the tail pipe normally indicates an increase in the oil consumption through burning due to internal engine wear. Black smoke would indicate a defective fuel delivery system, causing the engine to operate in a rich mode. Regardless of the color of the smoke, the internal part of the engine or the fuel delivery system should be repaired to prevent excess particulate emissions.

Diesel and turbine engines emit a darkened plume of smoke from the exhaust system because of the type of fuel used. Emission control regulations are mandated for this type of emission and more stringent measures are being used to prevent excess emission of the particulate matter. Electronic components are being introduced to control the injection of the fuel at precisely the proper time of piston travel, to achieve the optimum in fuel ignition and fuel usage. Other particulate after-burning components are being tested to achieve a cleaner emission.

Good grades of engine lubricating oils should be used, which meet the manufacturers specification. Cut-rate oils can contribute to the particulate emission problem because of their low flash or ignition temperature point. Such oils burn prematurely during the combustion process causing emission of particulate matter.

The cooling system is an important factor in the reduction of particulate matter. With the cooling system operating at a temperature specified by the manufacturer, the optimum of combustion will occur. The cooling system must be maintained in the same manner as the engine oiling system, as each system is required to perform properly in order for the engine to operate efficiently for a long time.

Other Automobile Emission Sources

Before emission controls were mandated on internal combustion engines, other sources of engine pollutants were discovered, along with the exhaust emission. It was determined the engine combustion exhaust produced 60 percent of the total emission pollutants, fuel evaporation from the fuel tank and carburetor vents produced 20 percent, with the another 20 percent being produced through the crankcase as a by-product of the combustion process.

CRANKCASE EMISSIONS

Crankcase emissions are made up of water, acids, unburned fuel, oil fumes and particulates. The emissions are classified as hydrocarbons (HC) and are formed by the small amount of unburned, compressed air/fuel mixture entering the crankcase from the combustion area during the compression and power strokes, between the cylinder walls and piston rings. The head of the compression and combustion help to form the remaining crankcase emissions.

Since the first engines, crankcase emissions were allowed into the atmosphere through a road draft tube, mounted on the lower side of the engine block. Fresh air came in through an open oil filler cap or breather. The air passed through the crankcase mixing with blow-by gases. The motion of the vehicle and the air blowing past the open end of the road draft tube caused a low pressure area at the end of the tube. Crankcase emissions were simply drawn out of the road draft tube into the air.

To control the crankcase emission, the road draft tube was deleted. A hose and/or tubing was routed from the crankcase to the intake manifold so the blow-by emission could be burned with the air/fuel mixture. However, it was found that intake manifold vacuum, used to draw the crankcase emissions into the manifold, would vary in strength at the wrong time and not allow the proper emission flow. A regulating type valve was needed to control the flow of air through the crankcase.

Testing, showed the removal of the blow-by gases from the crankcase as quickly as possible, was most important to the longevity of the engine. Should large accumulations of blow-by gases remain and condense, dilution of the engine oil would occur to form water, soots, resins, acids and lead salts, resulting in the formation of sludge and varnishes. This condensation of the blow-by gases occurs more frequently on vehicles used in numerous starting and stopping conditions, excessive idling and when the engine is not allowed to attain normal operating temperature through short runs.

FUEL EVAPORATIVE EMISSIONS

Gasoline fuel is a major source of pollution, before and after it is burned in the automobile engine. From the time the fuel is refined, stored, pumped and transported, again stored until it is pumped into the fuel tank of the vehicle, the gasoline gives off unburned hydrocarbons (HC) into the atmosphere. Through the redesign of storage areas and venting systems, the pollution factor was diminished, but not eliminated, from the refinery standpoint. However, the automobile still remained the primary source of vaporized, unburned hydrocarbon (HC) emissions.

Fuel pumped from an underground storage tank is cool but when exposed to a warmer ambient temperature, will expand. Before controls were mandated, an owner would fill the fuel tank with fuel from an underground storage tank and park the vehicle for some time in warm area, such as a parking lot. As the fuel would warm, it would expand and should no provisions or area be provided for the expansion, the fuel would spill out of the filler neck and onto the ground, causing hydrocarbon (HC) pollution and creating a severe fire hazard. To correct this condition, the vehicle manufacturers added overflow plumbing and/or gasoline tanks with built in expansion areas or domes.

However, this did not control the fuel vapor emission from the fuel tank. It was determined that most of the fuel evaporation occurred when the vehicle was stationary and the engine not operating. Most vehicles carry 5-25 gallons (19-95 liters) of gasoline. Should a large concentration of vehicles be parked in one area, such as a large parking lot, excessive fuel vapor emissions would take place, increasing as the temperature increases.

To prevent the vapor emission from escaping into the atmosphere, the fuel system is designed to trap the vapors while the vehicle is stationary, by sealing the system from the atmosphere. A storage system is used to collect and hold the fuel vapors from the carburetor (if equipped) and the fuel tank when the engine is not operating. When the engine is started, the storage system is then purged of the fuel vapors, which are drawn into the engine and burned with the air/fuel mixture.

EMISSION CONTROLS

There are three basic sources of automotive pollution in the modern internal combustion engine. They are the crankcase with its accompanying blow-by vapors, the fuel system with its evaporation of unburned gasoline and the combustion chambers with their resulting exhaust emissions. Pollution arising from the incomplete combustion of fuel generally falls into three categories: hydrocarbons (HC), carbon monoxide (CO) and oxides of nitrogen (NOx).

Engines are equipped with an air pump system, Positive Crankcase Ventilation (PVC), Exhaust Gas Recirculation (EGR), electronic ignition, catalytic converter, thermostatically controlled air cleaner, and an evaporative emissions system. Electronic engine controls are used on various engines, depending on model and year.

The belt driven air pump injects clean air either into the exhaust manifold, or downstream into the catalytic converter, depending on engine conditions. The oxygen contained in the injected air supports continued combustion of the hot carbon monoxide (CO) and hydrocarbon (HC) gases, reducing their release into the atmosphere.

No external PCV valve is used on the Escort and Lynx PCV system through 1990. Instead, an internal baffle and an orifice control flow of crankcase gases. On 1991 and later models, a conventional PCV valve is used.

The backpressure modulated EGR valve is mounted next to the carburetor on the intake manifold. Vacuum applied to the EGR diaphragm raises the pintle valve from its seat, allowing hot exhaust gases to be drawn into the intake manifold with the intake charge. The exhaust gases reduce peak combustion temperature; lower temperatures reduce the formation of oxides of nitrogen (NOx).

The dual brick catalytic converter is mounted in the exhaust system, ahead of the muffler. Catalytic converters use noble metals (platinum and palladium) and great heat 1,200°F (650°C) to catalytically oxidize HC and CO gases into H_2O and CO_2. The Thermactor system is used as a fresh air (and therefore, oxygen) supply.

The thermostatically controlled air cleaner housing is able to draw fresh air from two sources: cool air from outside the car (behind the grille), or warm air obtained from a heat stove encircling the exhaust manifold. A warm air supply is desirable during cold engine operation because it promotes better atomization of the air/fuel mixture, while cool air promotes better combustion in a hot engine.

Instead of venting gasoline vapors into the atmosphere, an evaporative emission system captures the vapors and stores them in a charcoal filled canister, located ahead of the left front wheel arch. When the engine is running, a purge control solenoid allows fresh air to be drawn through the canister. The fresh air and vapors are then routed to the carburetor/throttle body, to be mixed with the intake charge.

Crankcase Ventilation System

OPERATION

See Figures 1, 2 and 3

The Positive Crankcase Ventilation (PCV) system cycles crankcase gases back through the engine where they are burned.

The PCV valve (used on 1991-95 models) regulates the amount of ventilating air and blow-by gas to the intake manifold and also prevents backfire from traveling into the crankcase.

The vent system for 1.6L and 1.9L engines does not depend on a flow of scavenging air, as do most other engines. On the 1.6L engine, the vent system evacuates the crankcase vapors drawn into the intake manifold in metered amounts according to the manifold depression and the fixed orifice as they become available. If availability is low, air may be drawn in along with the vapors. If the availability is high, some vapors will be delivered to the intake manifold and any amount over that will go into the air cleaner. The fixed orifice is the critical point of this system. On 1.9L engines, the vent system evacuates the crankcase vapors drawn into the intake manifold in metered amounts through a dual orifice valve assembly.

COMPONENT TESTING

1981-90 Models

1.6L ENGINES

1. Start the engine and allow it to idle.
2. Locate the PCV hose leading from the air cleaner to the intake manifold. Pinch it closed with a pair of pliers.
3. If the idle speed decreases, the system is ok.

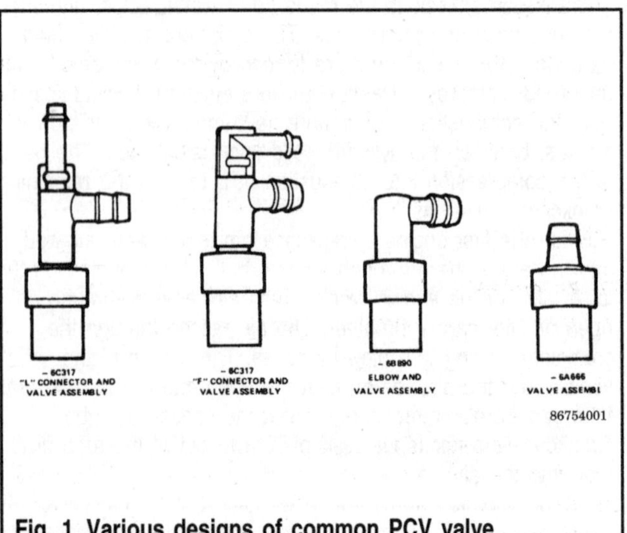

Fig. 1 Various designs of common PCV valve assemblies

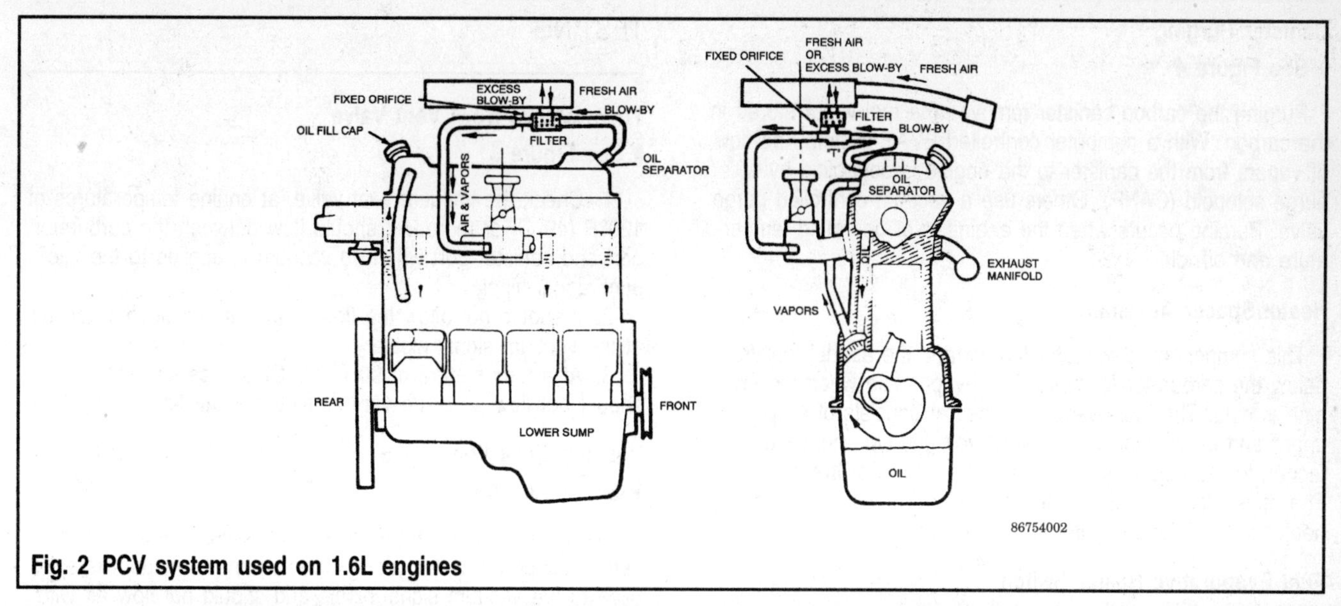

Fig. 2 PCV system used on 1.6L engines

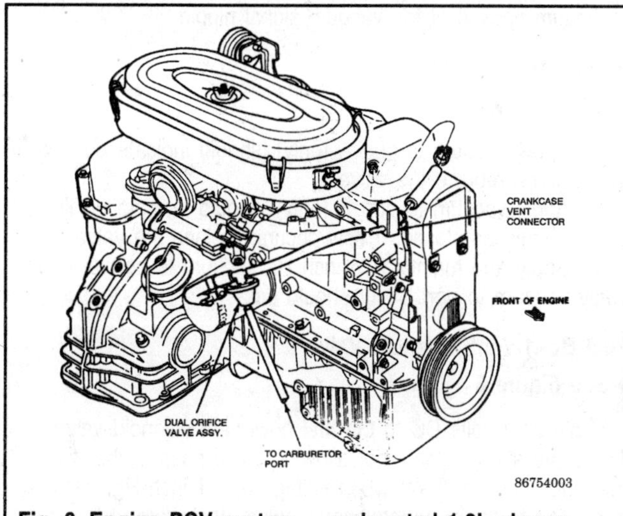

Fig. 3 Engine PCV system — carbureted 1.9L shown, CFI models similar)

1.9L ENGINES

1. Remove the vacuum control hose at the dual orifice valve assembly. This leads to the carburetor/throttle body.
2. Apply manifold vacuum to the port.
3. If no significant change in engine rpm is noticed, replace the dual orifice valve assembly.
4. If there is a significant change in engine rpm, the system is ok.

1991-95 Models

1. With the engine **OFF**, remove the PCV valve from the grommet.
2. Shake the PCV valve.
   a. If the valve rattles when shaken, re-connect it.
   b. If it does not rattle, replace it.
3. Start the engine and allow it to idle. Disconnect the hose from the air cleaner and check for vacuum at the hose. If vacuum exists, the system is functioning normally.
4. If vacuum does not exist, the system is plugged or the evaporative valve is leaking.
   a. Disconnect the evaporative hose, cap the tee and recheck the system. If vacuum exists, the PCV system is functioning. Check the evaporative emission system.
   b. If vacuum still does not exist at the PCV, check for vacuum back through the system (filler cap, PCV valve, hoses and the rocker cover bolt torque). Service the defective components as required.

REMOVAL & INSTALLATION

To remove the PCV valve, simply pull it out of the valve cover and/or hose. On models not equipped with these valves, remove the PCV hoses by pulling and twisting them from their ports. Always check the hoses for clogging, breaks and deterioration.

Evaporative Emission Controls (EVAP)

OPERATION

Fuel Tank Venting

Trapped fuel vapors inside the fuel tank are vented through an orifice to the vapor valve assembly on top of the tank. These vapors leave the valve assembly through a single vapor line and continue to the canister, for storage, until they are purged to the engine for burning.

Carburetor Venting

The vapors from the fuel bowl are are vented to the carbon canister when the engine is stopped. When the engine is started and a specified engine temperature is reached, the vapors will be drawn into the engine for burning. These vapors are controlled by the canister purge solenoid, the canister purge valve, the carburetor fuel bowl solenoid vent valve and the carburetor fuel bowl thermal vent valve (if used).

Canister Purging

➧ See Figure 4

Purging the carbon canister removes the fuel vapor stored in the carbon. With a computer controlled EVAP system, the flow of vapors from the canister to the engine is controlled by a purge solenoid (CANP). Others use a vacuum controlled purge valve. Purging occurs when the engine is at operating temperature and off idle.

Heater/Spacer Assembly

This component is a heater that warms the air/fuel mixture below the carburetor for better fuel evaporation when the engine is cold. The fuel evaporation heater consists of a spacer, upper and lower gaskets and a 12 volt grid-type heater attached to the bottom side of the primary bore of the spacer. The offset design of the heater mounting bracket positions the heater in the intake manifold inlet opening.

Fuel Evaporative Heater Switch

The evaporative heater switch is mounted at the rear of the engine, on the bottom of the intake manifold. It controls the relay and the heater element in the early fuel evaporative emission system, based on engine temperature. The normally closed switch will activate the relay and the heater at low engine temperature and will open at the specified calibration of the temperature switch. This will open the control relay, which in turn will shut off the early fuel evaporation heater after the engine has warmed up.

Fuel/Vacuum Separator

The fuel/vacuum separator is used in carbureted systems in order to prevent fuel travel to a vacuum operated device. This component requires positive orientation to insure that any fuel collected will drain back to the carburetor. If the separator becomes clogged or cracked, it must be replaced.

TESTING

Thermostatic Bowl Vent Valve

➧ See Figure 5

1. Check the vacuum vent valve, at engine temperatures of 120°F (49°C) or more. Air should flow between the carburetor port and canister port when no vacuum is applied to the vacuum signal nipple.
2. It should not allow the flow of air with a vacuum applied at the vacuum signal nipple.
3. At a temperature of 90°F (32°C) or less, the valve should not flow air or be very restrictive to air flow.

Vacuum Bowl Vent Valve

➧ See Figure 6

The vacuum bowl vent valve should flow air between the carburetor port and the canister port when no vacuum is applied to the vacuum signal nipple and should not flow air with a vacuum applied at the vacuum signal nipple.

Purge Control Valve

➧ See Figure 7

1. Apply vacuum to port A (only), should indicate no flow. If flow occurs, replace the valve.
2. Apply vacuum to port B (only), should indicate no flow. Valve should be closed. If flow occurs, replace the valve.
3. Apply and maintain 16 inch Hg vacuum to port A, and apply vacuum to port B. Air should pass.

Fuel Bowl Vent Solenoid Valve

➧ See Figure 8

Apply 9-14 volts DC to the fuel bowl vent solenoid valve. The valve should close, not allowing air to pass. If the valve does not close or leaks when voltage and 1 inch Hg. vacuum is applied to the carburetor port, replace the valve.

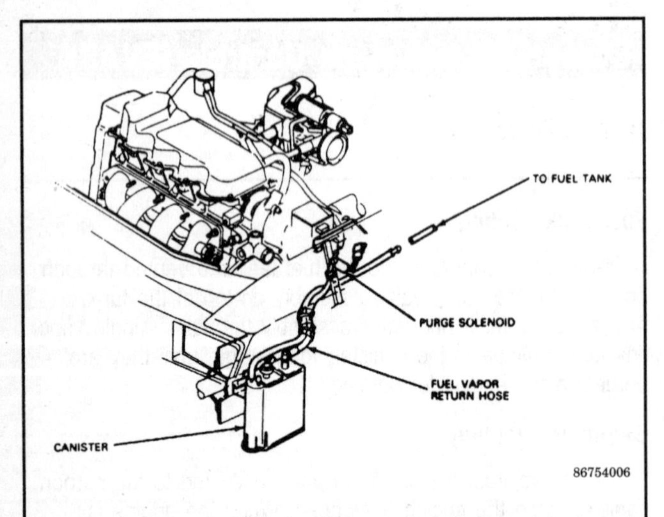

Fig. 4 Canister purging system — 1.9L EFI shown, others similar

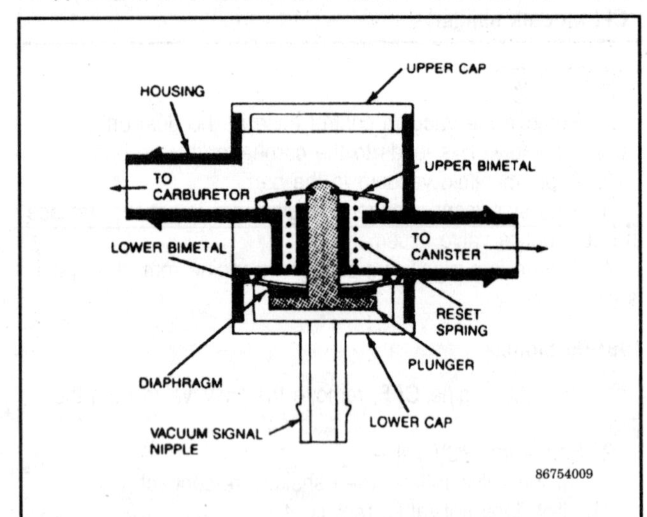

Fig. 5 Cross-sectional view of the thermostatic bowl vent valve

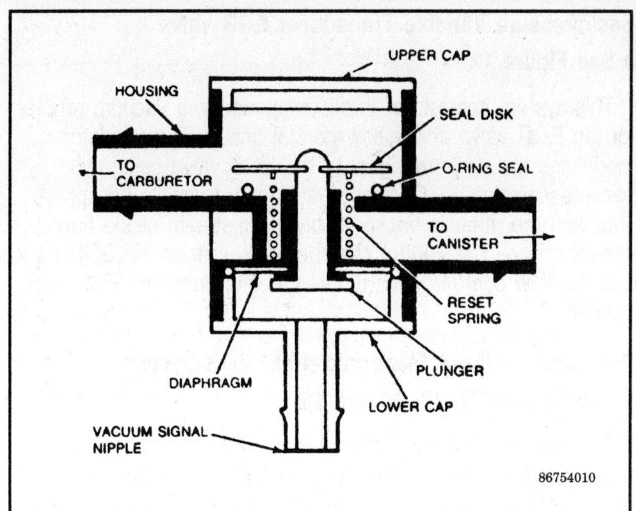

Fig. 6 Cross-sectional view of the vacuum bowl vent valve

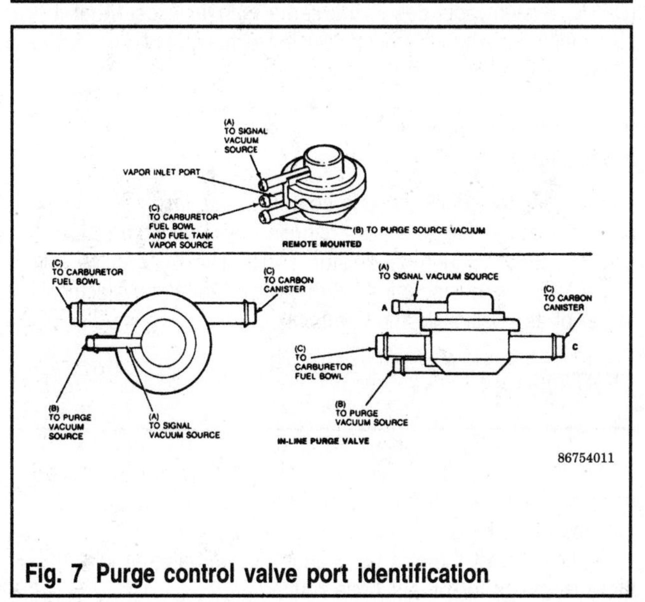

Fig. 7 Purge control valve port identification

Heater/Spacer Assembly

1. When the engine coolant temperature is below 128°F (53°C), the switch is closed.
2. When the heater relay is energized, the relay contacts close allowing current to flow through the relay and to the heater.
3. The heater operates for approximately the first three minutes of cold engine operation which aids in a leaner choke calibration for improved emissions without cold drive-away problems.
4. At ambient temperatures of less than 40°F (4°C), the leaner choke calibrations reduce loading and spark plug fouling.
5. The heater grid is functioning if radiant heat can be detected when the heater grid is energized.

➡Do not probe the heater grid while the grid is in the heat mode, as it is possible to cause a direct short in the circuit. The heater is designed to operate at a constant temperature of approximately 320-383°F (160-195°C), and could result in burns if touched.

REMOVAL & INSTALLATION

Removal and installation of the evaporative emission control system components consists of labeling and disconnecting hoses, loosening retaining screws and removing the part which is to be replaced from its mounting point.

➡When replacing any EVAP system hose, always use hoses that are fuel-resistant or marked EVAP. Use of hoses which are not fuel-resistant will lead to premature hose failure.

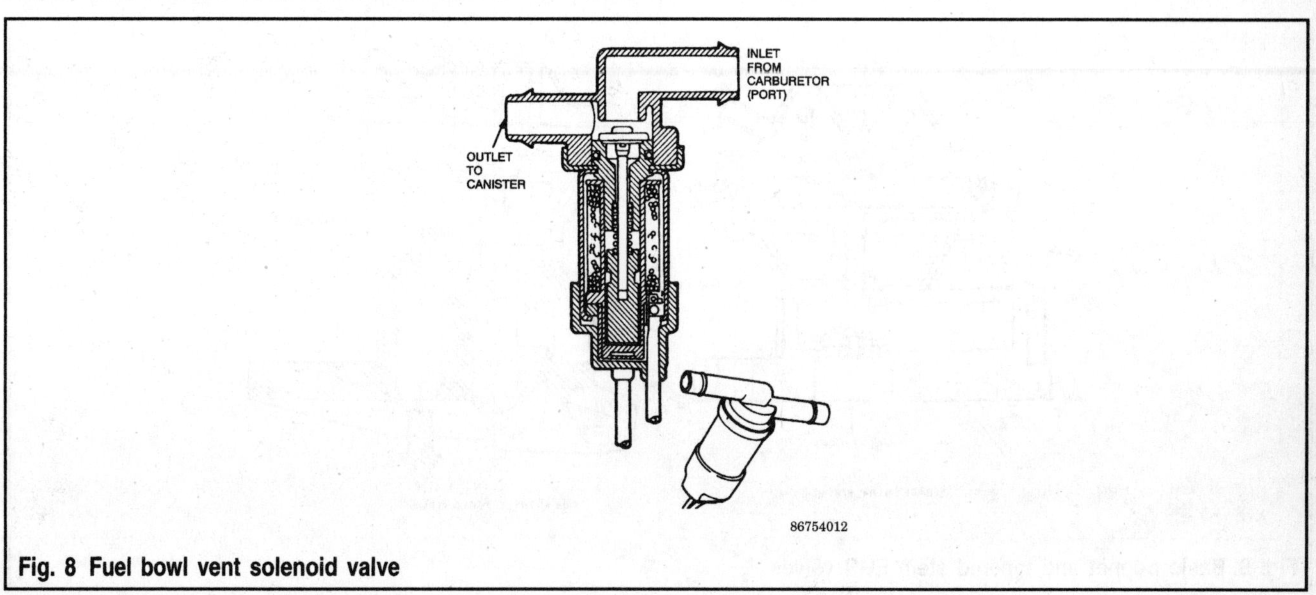

Fig. 8 Fuel bowl vent solenoid valve

Exhaust Gas Recirculation System

OPERATION

The Exhaust Gas Recirculation (EGR) system is designed to reintroduce small amounts of exhaust gas into the combustion cycle, thus reducing the generation of Nitrous Oxides (NOx). The amount of exhaust gas reintroduced and the timing of the cycle varies by calibration and is controlled by various factors such as engine speed, altitude, engine vacuum, exhaust system backpressure, coolant temperature and throttle angle.

➡A malfunctioning EGR valve can cause one or more of the following:

- Detonation
- Rough idle or stalling on deceleration
- Hesitation or surge
- Abnormally low power at wide-open throttle

Basic Poppet or Tapered Stem Design

See Figure 9

The basic EGR valve has two passages in the base connecting the exhaust system to the intake manifold. These passages are blocked by a valve that is opened by vacuum and closed by spring pressure. Both the poppet or the tapered stem design function in the same manner.

Integral Backpressure Transducer EGR Valve

See Figure 10

This poppet-type or tapered (pintle) valve cannot be opened by vacuum until the bleed hole is closed by exhaust backpressure. Once the valve opens, it seeks a level dependent upon exhaust backpressure flowing through the orifice and in so doing, oscillates at that level. The higher the signal vacuum and exhaust backpressure, the more the valve opens.

Backpressure Variable Transducer EGR Valve

See Figure 11

This system consists of three components: a vacuum regulator, an EGR valve and a flow control orifice. The regulator modulates the vacuum signal to the EGR valve using two backpressure inputs. One input is standard vehicle backpressure and the other is backpressure downstream of the flow control orifice. The control chamber pick-up is in the EGR tube and the flow control orifice is integral with upstream EGR tube connector.

Pressure Feedback Electronic (PFE) EGR System

See Figures 12, 13, 14 and 15

The PFE is a subsonic closed loop EGR system that controls EGR flow rate by monitoring the pressure drop across a remotely located sharp-edge orifice. With a PFE system, the EGR valve only serves as a pressure regulator rather than a flow metering device. The Differential Pressure Feedback EGR (DPFE) System operates in the same manner except that it also monitors exhaust pressure in the exhaust system. This allows for a more accurate control.

Electronic EGR System

See Figure 16

The electronic EGR valve is controlled according to computer demands. The valve is controlled by a vacuum signal from the EGR Vacuum Regulator (EVR). The EGR Valve Position (EVP) sensor, mounted on the valve, sends an electrical signal of its position to the computer.

TESTING

1. Check that all vacuum lines are properly routed, all connections are secured and vacuum hoses are not cracked, crimped or broken.
2. Check that there is no vacuum to the valve at idle. If there is, check for proper hose routing.

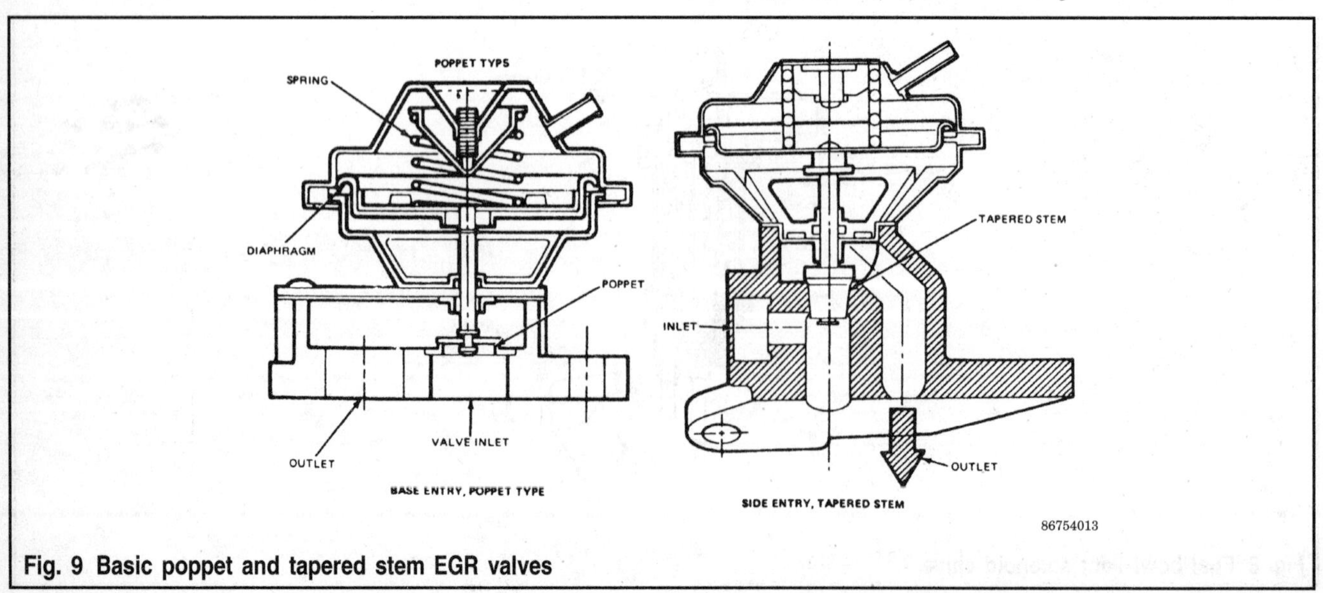

Fig. 9 Basic poppet and tapered stem EGR valves

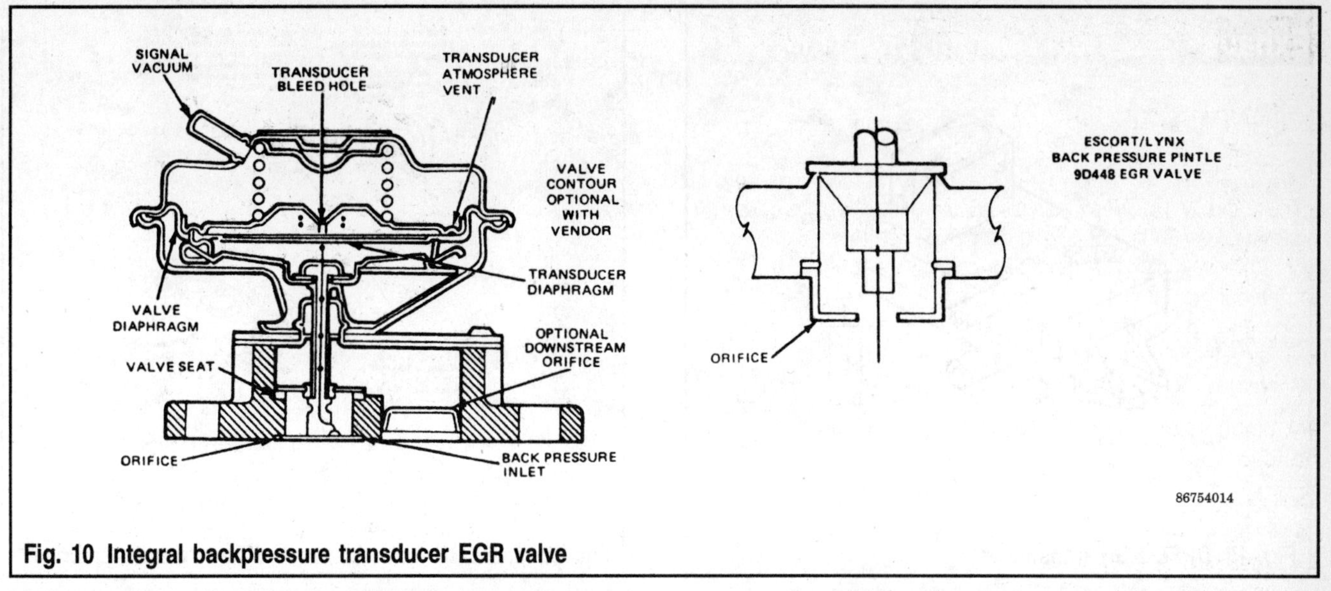

Fig. 10 Integral backpressure transducer EGR valve

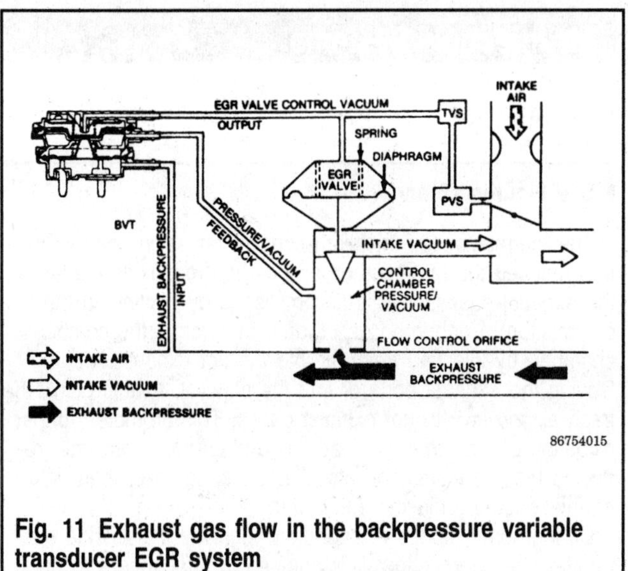

Fig. 11 Exhaust gas flow in the backpressure variable transducer EGR system

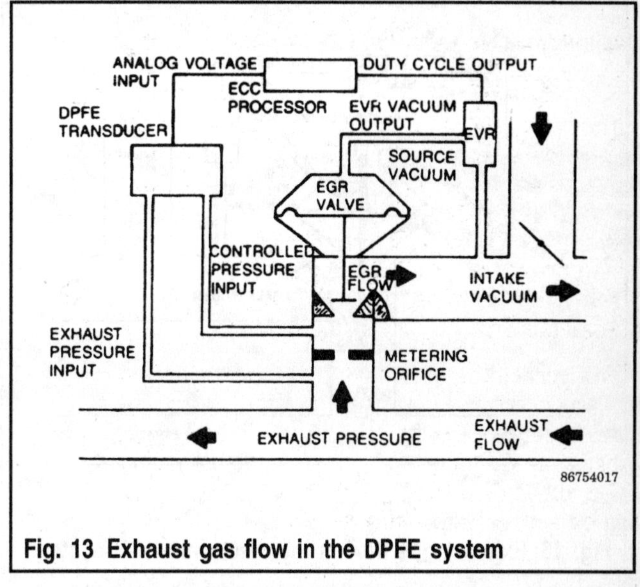

Fig. 13 Exhaust gas flow in the DPFE system

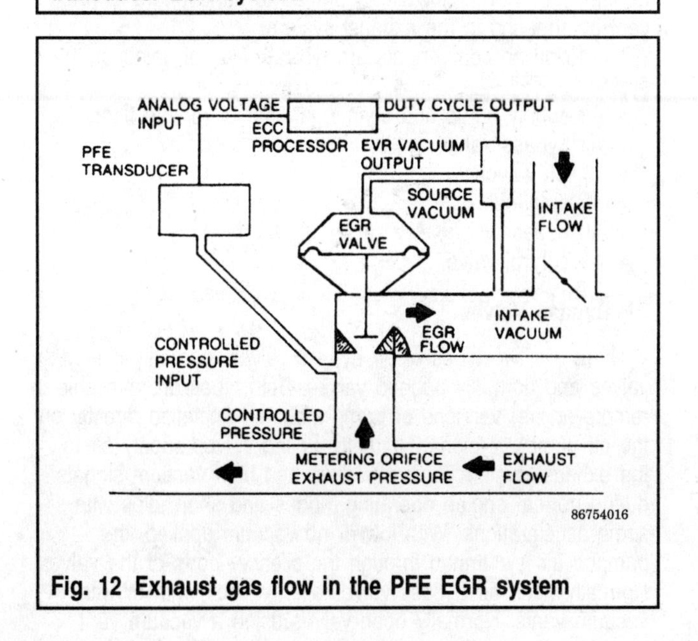

Fig. 12 Exhaust gas flow in the PFE EGR system

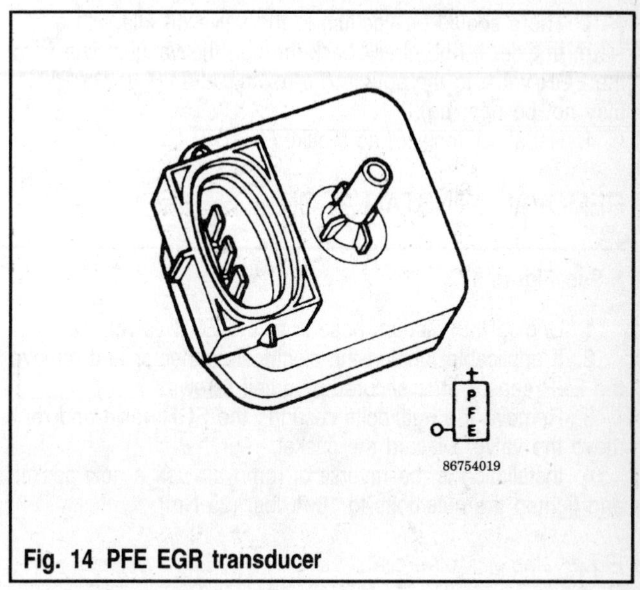

Fig. 14 PFE EGR transducer

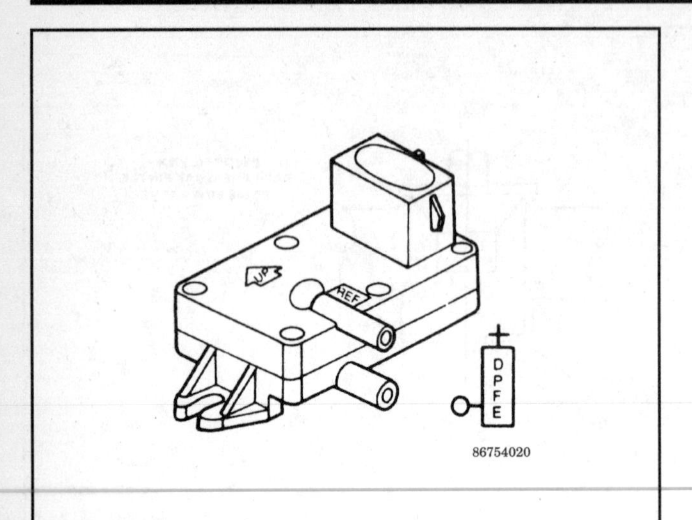

Fig. 15 DPFE EGR transducer

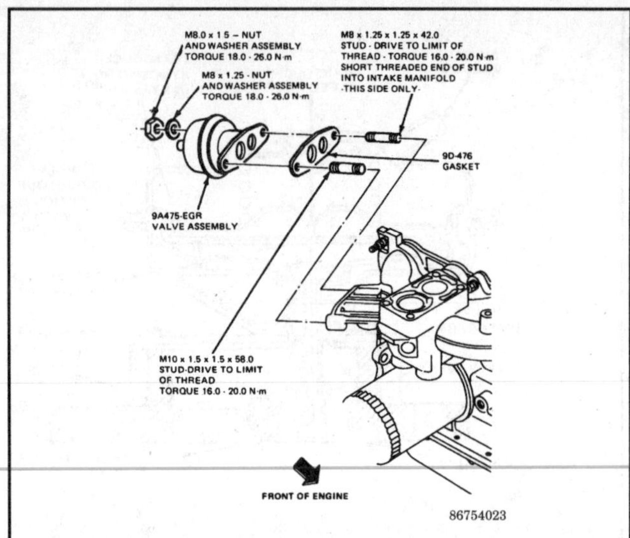

Fig. 17 The EGR valve is secured by two nuts or bolts

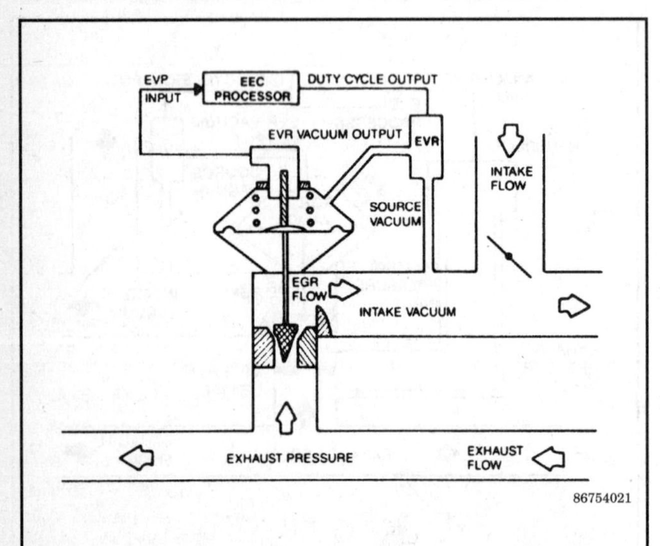

Fig. 16 Exhaust gas flow in the electronic EGR system

3. There should be vacuum to the valve off idle with a warm engine. If not, check back through the vacuum line from the EGR valve to the source (For example: TVS and/or PVS may not be opening).
4. Repair or replace, as required.

REMOVAL & INSTALLATION

➧ See Figure 17

1. Unplug the vacuum hose from the EGR valve.
2. If applicable, unplug the electrical connector and remove the EVP sensor. It is secured by small screws.
3. Remove the nuts/bolts securing the EGR valve and remove the valve. Discard the gasket.
4. Installation is the reverse of removal. Use a new gasket and tighten the nuts/bolts to 18 ft. lbs. (25 Nm).

Air Injection Systems

OPERATION

➧ See Figures 18 and 19

The thermactor (air injection) exhaust emission control system reduces the hydrocarbon and carbon monoxide content of the exhaust gases. This is accomplished by continuing the combustion of unburned gases after they leave the combustion chamber, by injecting fresh air into the hot exhaust stream leaving the exhaust ports or into the catalyst. At this point, the fresh air mixes with hot exhaust gases. This promotes further oxidation of both the hydrocarbons and carbon monoxide, reducing their concentration and converting some of them into harmless carbon dioxide and water.

During some modes of operation (highway cruise/wide open throttle), the thermactor air is dumped to atmosphere to prevent overheating in the exhaust system.

The following components are typical of an air injection system:

- Air supply pump and centrifugal filter or remote filter
- Air bypass valve
- Check valves
- Air manifold
- Air hoses
- Air control valve

Air Bypass Valves

There are two types of air bypass valves: normally closed valves and normally opened valves. Both types are available in remote (inline) versions or pump mounted (installed directly on the air pump) versions. Normally closed valves supply air to the exhaust system during medium and high vacuum signals during normal engine operating modes and short idles with some accelerations. With low or no vacuum applied, the pumped air is dumped through the silencer ports of the valve. Normally open air bypass valves are available with or without vacuum vents. Normally open valves using a vacuum vent provide a timed air dump during decelerations and also dump

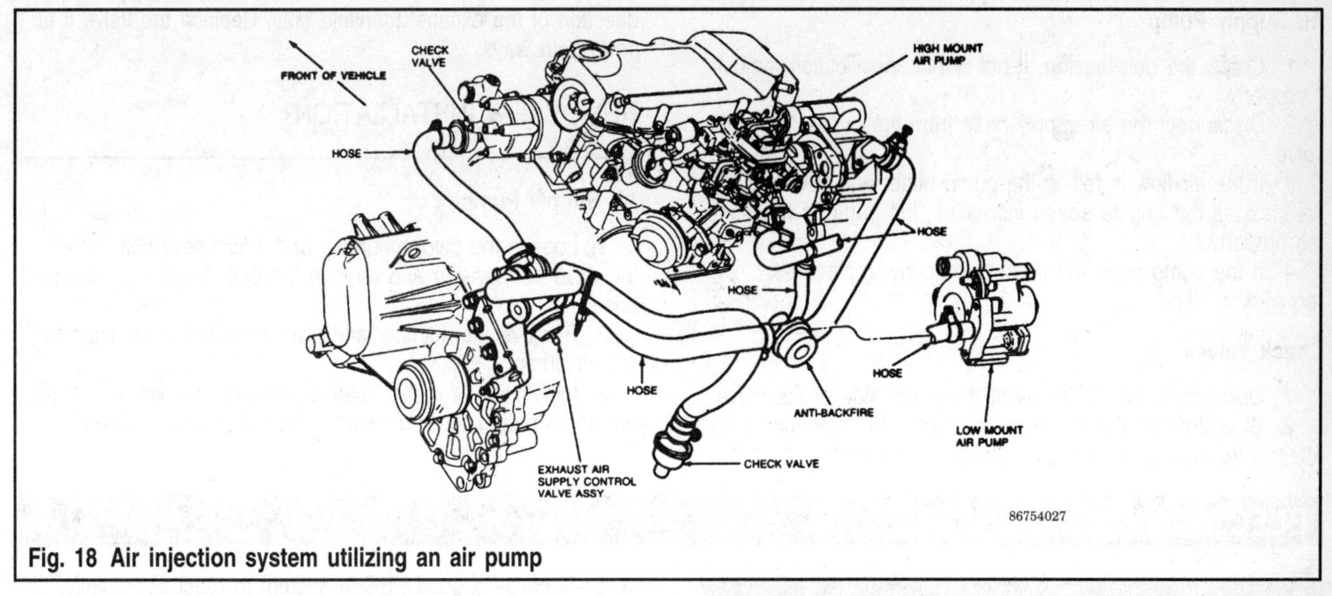

Fig. 18 Air injection system utilizing an air pump

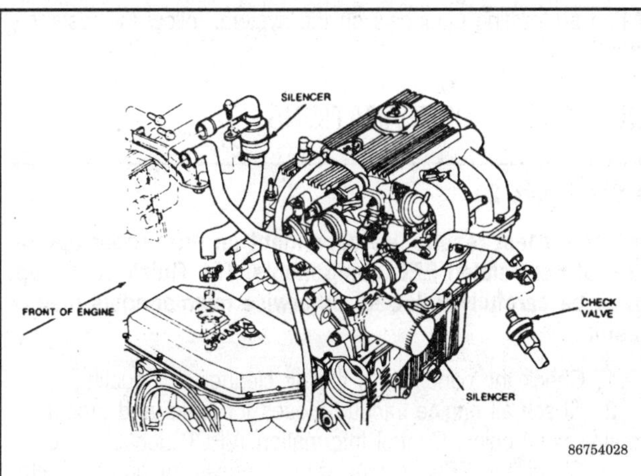

Fig. 19 Pulse air injection systems do not use an air pump

when a vacuum pressure difference is maintained between the signal port and the vent port. The signal port must have 3 in. Hg (10 kPa) or more vacuum than the vent port to hold the dump. This mode is required in order to protect the catalyst from overheating. Normally open air bypass valves without a vacuum vent provide a timed dump of air for 1.0 or 2.8 seconds when a sudden high vacuum of about 20 in. Hg (67.5 kPa) is applied to the signal port. This prevents backfire during deceleration.

Air Check Valve/Pulse Air Valve

The air check valve is a one-way valve that allows the thermactor air to pass into the exhaust system while preventing exhaust gases from passing in the opposite direction. The pulse air valve replaces the air pump in some thermactor systems. It draws air into the exhaust system on vacuum exhaust pulses and blocks the backflow of high pressure exhaust pulses. The fresh air completes the oxidation of exhaust gas components.

Anti-Backfire (Gulp) Valve

The anti-backfire (gulp) valve is located downstream from the air bypass valve. Its function is to divert a portion of the thermactor air to the intake manifold when it is triggered by intake manifold vacuum signals on deceleration. This helps prevent an overly rich mixture from entering the catalytic converter.

Air Supply Pump

➡This pump is only utilized by air injection systems, not pulse air systems.

The air supply is a belt driven, positive engagement vane-type pump, that supplies air for the thermactor system. The pump is available in two sizes: 11 cubic inch (180cc) and 19 cubic inch (311cc), depending on the particular vehicle application. The 11 cubic inch (180cc) pump receives air through a remote filter that is attached to the air inlet nipple or through an impeller-type centrifugal air filter fan. The 19 cubic inch (311cc) pump uses an impeller-type centrifugal air filter fan which separates dirt, dust and other contaminants from the intake air, using centrifugal force. The air supply pump does not have a built in pressure relief valve, but the system does use a bypass valve.

TESTING

Anti-Backfire (Gulp) Valve

1. Disconnect the air supply hose from the air pump side of the anti-backfire valve.
2. Look inside the valve through the disconnect port and observe the valve pintle.
3. Accelerate the engine to about 3000 rpm. Release the throttle, the pintle should open and then close.
4. If it does not perform as indicated, replace the defective valve.

Air Supply Pump

1. Check the belt tension. If not within specification, adjust it properly.
2. Disconnect the air supply hose from the bypass control valve.
3. If the air flow is felt at the pump outlet and flow increases, as the engine speed increases, the pump is functioning properly.
4. If the pump does not perform properly, replace as required.

Check Valves

1. Disconnect the air supply at the pump side of the valve.
2. Blow through the check valve, toward the manifold, then attempt to suck back through the valve. Air should pass in the direction of the exhaust manifold only. Replace the valve if air flows both ways.

REMOVAL & INSTALLATION

Air Supply Pump

1. Loosen the pivot mounting and adjustment bolt. Relax the drive belt tension and remove the belt. Disconnect the air hoses.
2. Remove the adjuster and pivot nuts and bolts. Remove the air pump.
3. Installation is in the reverse order of removal. Adjust the belt to its proper tension (refer to Section 1 under "Belts."

ELECTRONIC ENGINE CONTROLS

Description

Ford's fourth generation engine control system is centered around a microprocessor called the Electronic Engine Control (EEC-IV) processor. The processor receives and sends electronic signals relaying pertinent engine management information (data) to and from a number of sensors and other electronic components. The processor contains a specific calibration for maintaining optimum emissions, fuel economy and driveability. By comparing the input signals to its own calibrated program, the processor generates output signals to the various relays, solenoids and actuators.

The EEC-IV processor, located under the instrument panel left of the steering column, communicates service information to the outside world by way of service codes. The service codes are two or three digit numbers representing the result of the self-test.

The service codes are transmitted through the Self-Test Output (STO) terminal, found in the self-test connector.

The processor stores the self-test program in its permanent memory. When activated, it checks the EEC-IV system by testing its memory and processing capability. The self-test also verifies if the various sensors and actuators are connected and operating properly.

The self-test is divided into three specialized tests:

- Key On, Engine Off (KOEO) is a static check of the processor inputs and outputs with the power **ON** but the engine **OFF**
- Engine Running is Self-Test is a dynamic check with the engine in operation and the vehicle at rest
- Continuous Self Test is a check of the sensor inputs for opens and shorts while the vehicle is in operation.

The KOEO and Engine Running tests are functional tests which only detect faults present at the time of the self-test. Continuous testing is an ongoing test that stores fault information for retrieval at a later time, during the self-test.

Testing

A working knowledge of the EEC-IV system is critical to efficient troubleshooting of the symptoms. Often a mechanical fault will cause a good EEC-IV system to react abnormally. When performing diagnosis on the system, follow the tests in order.

QUICK TEST PREPARATIONS

See Figure 20

➡Correct test results are dependent on the proper operation of non-related EEC components. The Quick Test Steps must be carefully followed, otherwise misdiagnosis may result.

1. Check the condition of the air cleaner and ducting.
2. Check all engine vacuum hoses for leaks and proper routing per Vehicle Control Information (VECI) decal.
3. Check the EEC system wiring harness for proper electrical connections, routing or corrosion.
4. Check the processor, sensors and actuators for physical damage.
5. Apply the parking brake. Place the shift lever in P for automatic transaxle, or N for manual transaxle.

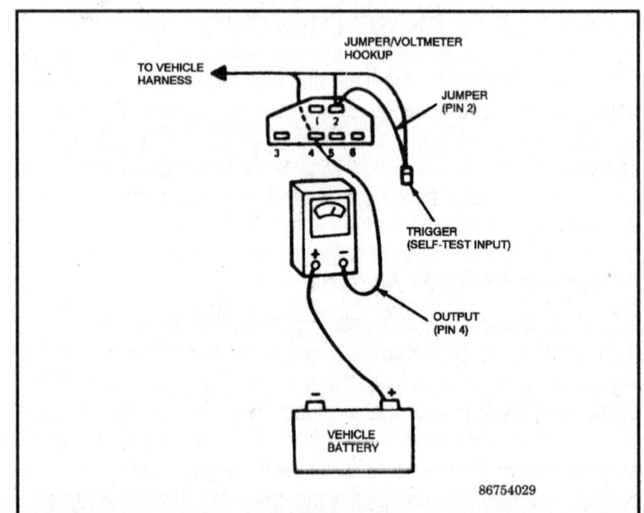

Fig. 20 An analog VOM can be used to check the EEC-IV system for service codes

6. Turn off all electrical loads (radio, lamps, A/C, etc.). Be sure the doors are closed whenever readings are made.

7. Ensure that the engine coolant is at its specified level.

8. Operate the engine until normal operating temperature is reached.

➡**While the engine is operating, check for leaks around the exhaust manifold, EGO sensor and vacuum hose connections.**

9. Turn the ignition switch **OFF**.

10. Service any items, if required.

11. Set an analog VOM to read 0-15 volts DC.

12. Connect a jumper wire from the Self-Test Input (STI) to pin 2 (signal return) on the self-test connector.

13. Connect the VOM from battery positive (+) to pin 4 of the Self-Test Output (STO) in the self-test connector.

KEY ON, ENGINE OFF SELF TEST

1. Check that the vehicle being tested has been properly prepared, according to the Quick Test preparations.

2. Activate the self-test by placing the key in the **RUN** position.

➡**Do not depress the throttle during the self-test.**

3. Observe and record all service codes indicated.

4. If no codes are displayed, continue with the Engine Running (ER) test. If codes are displayed, check the system's ability to set the ignition timing as follows:

a. Connect a timing light to the engine.

b. Perform the ER test. Wait until the last code is displayed (they can be ignored at this time).

c. Check the ignition timing. It should be equal to base timing plus 17-23 degrees.

➡**The timing must be checked within two minutes of the last code being displayed. Also, do not disconnect the ignition timing check (SPOUT) connector.**

d. If the timing is not as specified, the system should be diagnosed by your dealer or a reputable service facility. If the timing is ok, perform the ER test.

ENGINE RUNNING SELF-TEST

1. Disconnect the wire from the STI lead.

2. Start the engine. Run it at 2000 RPM for two minutes.

3. Turn the engine off, and wait 10 seconds.

4. Connect the wire to the STI lead.

5. Start the engine. The engine running test will progress as follows:

- Engine ID code. This code is equal to half the number of cylinders. A 4-cylinder engine will indicate a code 2.
- Dynamic response. The dynamic response code is a single pulse which appears 6-20 seconds after the engine ID code. It is not used on all models.
- Service codes.

6. After the engine ID code is displayed:

a. Turn the steering wheel (on power steering models) at least ½ turn, then release.

b. On M/T models, depress the clutch pedal, then release.

c. If equipped with the electronic overdrive transaxle, toggle the overdrive cancel switch.

7. If applicable, briefly depress the accelerator to wide open throttle when the dynamic response code occurs.

8. Observe and record all service codes indicated. When more than one service code is received, always start with the first code received.

9. Turn the ignition **OFF**.

10. After repairs are made, repeat the Quick Test.

CONTINUOUS MONITOR MODE (WIGGLE TEST)

1. Disconnect the wire from the STI lead.

2. Turn the ignition key **ON**, then connect the wire to the STI lead. Allow the KOEO and continuous memory codes to be displayed. You are now in the continuous monitor "wiggle test" mode.

3. Check all sensors by tapping them (to simulate road shock) and wiggle the connectors and wiring harnesses. The STO will be activated whenever a fault is detected. The fault will be indicated on the VOM by a deflection of 10.5 volts or greater.

INTERPRETING CODES

When service codes are reported on the analog voltmeter, it will be represented by sweeping movements of the voltmeter's needle across the dial face. All service codes are represented by 2 or 3 digit numbers. For example, 23 will be represented by two needle pulses (sweeps), then after a two-second pause, the needle will pulse three times.

CLEARING CODES

Perform the Key On, Engine Off (KOEO) quick test. When the service codes begin, exit the self-test program by removing the jumper from the STI to signal return. Exiting the quick test during code output will clear all codes stored in the continuous memory.

Year—1983
Model—Escort/Lynx, EXP/LN7
Engine—1.6L EFI (98 cid)
Engine Code—5

ECA SERVICE CODES

Code	Explanation
11	System pass
12	Idle Speed Control (ISC)—failed at elevated rpm
13	Idle Speed Control (ISC)—failed at idle rpm
21	Enginc coolant
23	Throttle Position (TP) sensor
24	Vane Air Temperature (VAT) sensor
26	Vane Air Flow (VAF) meter
41	Fuel always lean
42	Fuel always rich

Year—1984
Model—Escort, Lynx and EXP
Engine—1.6L EFI
Engine Code—5

ECA SERVICE CODES

Code		Explanation
11	O/R/C	System pass
12	R	Idle speed control, bypass air
13	R	Idle speed control, bypass air
14	C	Erratic ignition
15	O	Replace processor, repeat quick test
18	C	Ignition Diagnostic Monitor (IDM)
21	O/R/C	Engine Coolant Temperature (ECT) sensor
22	O/R/C	Barometric Pressure (BP) sensor
23	O/R	Throttle Position (TP) sensor
24	O/R	Vane Air Temperature (VAT) sensor
25	R	Knock sensor
26	O/R	Vane Air Flow (VAF) sensor
34	R	EGR on/off control
41	R/C	Fuel control, EFI
42	R/C	Fuel control, EFI
51	O/C	Engine Coolant Temperature (ECT) sensor
53	O/C	Throttle Position (TP) sensor
54	O/C	Vane Air Temperature (VAT) sensor

86754212

ECA SERVICE CODES

Code		Explanation
56	O/C	Vane Air Flow (VAF) sensor
61	O/C	Engine Coolant Temperature (ECT) sensor
63	O/C	Throttle Position (TP) sensor
64	O/C	Vane Air Temperature (VAT) sensor
66	O/C	Vane Air Flow (VAF) sensor
73	R	Throttle Position (TP) sensor
76	R	Vane Air Flow (VAF) sensor
77	R	Dynamic response test

Year—1984
Model—Escort, Lynx and EXP
Engine—1.6L EFI TC
Engine Code—8

ECA SERVICE CODES

Code		Explanation
11	O/R/C	System pass
12	R	Idle speed control, bypass air
13	R	Idle speed control, bypass air
14	C	Erratic ignition
15	O	Replace processor, repeat quick test
18	C	Ignition Diagnostic Monitor (IDM)
21	O/R/C	Engine Coolant Temperature (ECT) sensor
22	O/R/C	Barometric Pressure (BP) sensor
23	O/R	Throttle Position (TP) sensor
24	O/R	Vane Air Temperature (VAT) sensor
25	R	Knock sensor
26	O/R	Vane Air Flow (VAF) sensor
34	R	EGR on/off control
41	R/C	Fuel control, EFI
42	R/C	Fuel control, EFI
51	O/C	Engine Coolant Temperature (ECT) sensor
53	O/C	Throttle Position (TP) sensor
54	O/C	Vane Air Temperature (VAT) sensor
56	O/C	Vane Air Flow (VAF) sensor
61	O/C	Engine Coolant Temperature (ECT) sensor
63	O/C	Throttle Position (TP) sensor
64	O/C	Vane Air Temperature (VAT) sensor
66	O/C	Vane Air Flow (VAF) sensor
73	R	Throttle Position (TP) sensor
76	R	Vane Air Flow (VAF) sensor
77	R	Dynamic response test

86754213

Year—1985
Model—Escort, Lynx and EXP
Engine—1.6L EFI
Engine Code—5

ECA SERVICE CODES

Code		Explanation
11	O/R/C	System pass
12	R	Idle speed control, bypass air
13	R	Idle speed control, bypass air
14	C	Erratic ignition
18	C	Ignition Diagnostic Monitor (IDM)
21	O/R/C	Engine Coolant Temperature (ECT) sensor
22	O/R/C	Manifold Absolute Pressure/Barometric Pressure (MAP/BP)
23	O/R	Throttle Position Sensor (TPS)
24	O/R	Air Charge Temperature (ACT) sensor, VAT in meter
25	R	Knock sensor
26	O/R	Vane Air Flow (VAF) sensor
34	R	EGR on-off check
41	R/C	Fuel control, EFI
42	R/C	Fuel control, EFI
51	O/C	Engine Coolant Temperature (ECT) sensor
53	O/C	Throttle Position Sensor (TPS)
54	O/C	Air Charge Temperature (ACT) sensor, VAT in meter
56	O/C	Vane Air Flow (VAF) sensor
61	O/C	Engine Coolant Temperature (ECT) sensor
63	O/C	Throttle Position Sensor (TPS)
64	O/C	Air Charge Temperature (ACT) sensor, VAT in meter
66	O/C	Vane Air Flow (VAF) sensor
67	O	A/C and/or neutral drive switch
73	R	Throttle Position Sensor (TPS)
76	R	Vane Air Flow (VAF) sensor
77	R	Dynamic response test

86754214

Year—1985
Model—Escort, Lynx and EXP
Engine—1.6L EFI TC
Engine Code—8

ECA SERVICE CODES

Code		Explanation
11	O/R/C	System pass
12	R	Idle speed control, bypass air
13	R	Idle speed control, bypass air
14	C	Erratic ignition
18	C	Ignition Diagnostic Monitor (IDM)
21	O/R/C	Engine Coolant Temperature (ECT) sensor
22	O/R/C	Manifold Absolute Pressure/Barometric Pressure (MAP/BP)
23	O/R	Throttle Position Sensor (TPS)
24	O/R	Air Charge Temperature (ACT) sensor, VAT in meter
25	R	Knock sensor
26	O/R	Vane Air Flow (VAF) sensor
34	R	EGR on-off check
41	R/C	Fuel control, EFI
42	R/C	Fuel control, EFI
51	O/C	Engine Coolant Temperature (ECT) sensor
53	O/C	Throttle Position Sensor (TPS)
54	O/C	Air Charge Temperature (ACT) sensor, VAT in meter
56	O/C	Vane Air Flow (VAF) sensor
61	O/C	Engine Coolant Temperature (ECT) sensor
63	O/C	Throttle Position Sensor (TPS)
64	O/C	Air Charge Temperature (ACT) sensor, VAT in meter
66	O/C	Vane Air Flow (VAF) sensor
67	O	A/C and/or neutral drive switch
73	R	Throttle Position Sensor (TPS)
76	R	Vane Air Flow (VAF) sensor
77	R	Dynamic response test

86754215

Year—1986
Model—Escort and Lynx
Engine—1.9L EFI
Engine Code—9

ECA SERVICE CODES

Code		Explanation
11	O/R/C	System pass
12	R	Cannot control rpm during high rpm check
13	R	Cannot control rpm during low rpm check
14	C	PIP circuit failure
15	O	ECA read only memory (ROM) test failed
17	R	Rpm below self-test limit, set too low
18	C	Loss of tach input to ECU
21	O/R/C	ECT out of range
22	O/R/C	Barometric Pressure (BP) sensor out of test range
23	O/R	TP sensor out of self-test range
24	O/R	VAT sensor input out of test range
26	O/R	VAF sensor input out of self-test range
34	R	Insufficient EGR flow
41	R	Fuel system at adaptive limits, no HEGO switch system shows lean
41	C	Lack of EGO/HEGO switching detected system indicates lean
42	R	Lack of EGO/HEGO switches, indicates rich
42	C	No EGO/HEGO switches, indicates rich
51	O/C	ECT sensor indicated test maximum or open circuit
53	O/C	TP sensor circuit above maximum voltage
54	O/C	VAT sensor input exceeds test maximum
56	O/C	VAF circuit above maximum voltage
61	O/C	ECT sensor input below test minimum
63	O/C	TP sensor circuit below minimum voltage
64	O/C	VAT sensor input below test minimum
66	O/C	VAF below test minimum
67	O	Neutral switch open or A/C input high
73	R	Insufficient TP change, dynamic response test
76	R	Insufficient VAF output change, dynamic response test
77	R	Operator error, WOT not sensed during test

86754216

Year—1987
Model—Escort/Lynx
Body VIN—1 and 2
Engine—1.9L **Cylinder**—4
Fuel System—Multi-Point Injection (EFI)
Engine VIN—J

ECA SERVICE CODES

Code		Explanation
11	O/R/C	System pass
12	R	Rpm unable to reach upper test limit
13	R	Rpm unable to reach lower test limit
14	C	PIP circuit failure
15	O/C	Power interrupted to keep alive memory
16	R	Rpm unable to reach lower test limit
17	R	Curb idle—Idle Speed Control (Bypass air)
18	C	Loss of ignition signal to ECU—ignition grounded, spout, PIP, IDM
21	O/R	ECT sensor input out of test range
22	O/R/C	MAP sensor out of test range
23	O/R	TP sensor out of test range
26	O/R	VAF sensor out of self-test range
28	O/R	VAT sensor out of self-test range
41	R	Fuel Control—always lean
41	C	HEGO shows fuel system lean
42	R	HEGO shows system rich
42	C	HEGO shows fuel system lean
43	C	HEGO shows fuel system lean
47	R	Airflow at base idle
48	R	Airflow high at base idle
51	O/C	ECT sensor input exceeds test maximum
53	O/C	TP sensor input exceeds test maximum
56	O/C	VAF sensor input exceeds test maximum
58	O/C	VAT sensor input exceeds test maximum
61	O/C	ECT test sensor input below test minimum
63	O/C	TP sensor below test minimum
66	O/C	VAF sensor input below test minimum
67	O/C	Neutral drive switch open. A/C input high
68	O/C	VAT sensor input below test minimum
71	C	Re-initialization check—check EEC IV wiring position to secondary wiring
72	C	Power interrupt detected
73	R	Insufficient TP output change during test
76	R	Insufficient VAF output change during test
77	R	Wide open throttle not sensed during test
No Code		Unable to run self-test or output codes [1]
Code not listed		Does not apply to vehicle being tested [1]

O—Key On, Engine Off
R—Engine running
C—Continuous Memory
1 Refer to system diagnostics

86754217

Year–1987
Model–Escort/Lynx
Body VIN–1 and 2
Engine–1.9L CFI **Cylinder**–4
Fuel System–Central Fuel Injection (CFI)
Engine VIN–9

ECA SERVICE CODES

Code		Explanation
11	O/R/C	System pass
12	R	Rpm unable to reach upper test limit
13	R	Rpm unable to reach lower test limit
14	C	PIP circuit failure
15	O/C	Power interrupted to keep alive memory
16	R	Rpm unable to reach lower test limit
18	C	Loss of ignition signal to ECU–ignition grounded, spout, PIP, IDM
21	O/R	ECT sensor input out of test range
22	O/R/C	MAP sensor out of test range
23	O/R	TP sensor out of test range
24	O/R	ACT sensor out of self-test range
31	O/R/C	PFE sensor out of self-test range
32	R/C	PFE sensor sense a lack of pressure in exhaust system
33	R/C	PFE valve not opening
34	0	PFE sensor out of range
34	R/C	Defective PFE sensor
35	O/R/C	PFE circuit above maximum voltage
38	C	Idle track switch circuit open
41	R	EGO/HEGO circuit shows system lean
41	C	No EGO/HEGO switching detected, system lean
42	R	EGO/HEGO shows system rich
51	O/C	ECT sensor input exceeds test maximum
53	O/C	TP sensor input exceeds test maximum
54	O/C	ACT sensor input exceeds test maximum
55	R	Key power input to processor is open
58	R	Idle tracking switch circuit closed
58	0	Idle tracking switch circuit open
61	O/C	ECT test sensor input below test minimum
63	O/C	TP sensor below test minimum
64	O/C	ACT sensor input below test minimum
67	O/R	Neutral drive switch open. A/C input high
68	R	Idle tracking switch circuit open
68	0	Idle tracking switch closed
71	C	Idle tracking switch closed on pre-position
73	0	Insufficient TP change
84	O/R	EGR VAC regulator circuit failure
85	O/R	Canister purge circuit failure

86754218

ECA SERVICE CODES

Code		Explanation
87	O/R/C	Fuel pump primary circuit failure
93	O	TP sensor input low at max DC motor extension
98	R	Hard fault is present
99	R	EEC system has not learned to control idle
No Code		Unable to run self-test or output codes [1]
Code not listed		Does not apply to vehicle being tested [1]

O—Key On, Engine Off
R—Engine running
C—Continuous Memory
1 Refer to system diagnostics

Year—1988
Model—Escort
Body VIN—1 and 2
Engine—1.9L **Cylinder**—4
Fuel System—Multi-Point Injection (EFI)
Engine VIN—J

ECA SERVICE CODES

Code		Explanation
11	O/R/C	System pass
12	R	Rpm unable to reach upper test limit
13	R	Rpm unable to reach lower test limit
14	C	PIP circuit failure
15	O	ROM test failure
15	C	Power interrupted to keep alive memory
16	R	Rpm above self test limit, set too high (ISC off)
17	R	Rpm below self-test limit, set too low (ISC off)
18	C	Loss of tach input to ECU, spout grounded
18	R	Spout circuit open
19	R	Erratic rpm during test or rpm too low (ISC off)
21	O/R	ECT sensor input out of test range
22	O/R/C	MAP sensor input out of test range
23	O/R	TP sensor input out of test range
26	O/R	VAF sensor input out of self-test range
28	O/R	VAT sensor input out of self-test range
41	R	EGO/HEGO circuit shows system lean
41	C	No EGO/HEGO switching detected, system lean
42	R	EGO/HEGO shows system rich
42	C	No EGO/HEGO switching detected, system rich
43	C	EGO/HEGO lean at wide open throttle
47	R	Airflow at base idle

86754219

ECA SERVICE CODES

Code		Explanation
48	R	Airflow high at base idle
51	O/C	ECT sensor input exceeds test maximum
53	O/C	TP sensor input exceeds test maximum
56	O/C	VAF sensor input exceeds test maximum
58	O/C	VAT sensor input exceeds test maximum
61	O/C	ECT test sensor input below test minimum
63	O/C	TP sensor below test minimum
65	C	Failed to enter self-test mode
66	O/C	VAF sensor input below test minimum
67	O	Neutral drive switch open. A/C input high
67	C	Clutch switch circuit failure
68	O/C	VAT sensor input below test minimum
72	C	Power interrupt detected
73	R	Insufficient TP output change during test
76	R	Insufficient VAF output change during test
77	R	Wide open throttle not sensed during test
85	C	Adaptive lean limit reached
86	C	Adaptive rich limit reached
95	O/C	Fuel pump secondary circuit failure
96	O/C	Fuel pump secondary circuit failure
No Code		Unable to run self-test or output codes [1]
Code not listed		Does not apply to vehicle being tested [1]

O – Key On, Engine Off
R – Engine running
C – Continuous Memory
1 Refer to system diagnostics

Year – 1988
Model – Escort
Body VIN – 1 and 2
Engine – 1.9L **Cylinder** – 4
Fuel System – Central Fuel Injection (CFI)
Engine VIN – 9

ECA SERVICE CODES

Code		Explanation
11	O/R/C	System pass
12	R	Rpm unable to reach upper test limit
13	R	Rpm unable to reach lower test limit
13	O	DC motor did not follow dashpot
14	C	PIP circuit failure
15	O	ROM test failure
15	C	Power interrupted to keep alive memory

86754220

ECA SERVICE CODES

Code		Explanation
17	R	Rpm below self-test limit, set too low
18	C	Loss of tach input to ECU, spout grounded
18	R	Spout circuit open
19	R	Erratic rpm during test or rpm too low
21	O/R	ECT sensor input out of test range
22	O/R/C	MAP sensor input out of test range
23	O/R/C	TP sensor input out of test range
24	O/R	ACT sensor input out of test range
31	O/R/C	EVP circuit below minimum voltage
32	R/C	EGR valve not seated
33	R/C	EGR valve not opening
34	O	Defective PFE sensor
34	R/C	Excess exhaust back pressure
35	O/R/C	PFE circuit above maximum voltage
38	C	Idle track switch circuit open
41	R	EGO/HEGO circuit shows system lean
41	C	No EGO/HEGO switching detected, system lean
42	R	EGO/HEGO shows system rich
51	O/C	ECT sensor input exceeds test maximum
53	O/C	TP sensor input exceeds test maximum
54	O/C	ACT sensor input exceeds test maximum
55	R	Key power input to processor is open
58	R	Idle tracking switch circuit closed
58	O	Idle tracking switch circuit open
61	O/C	ECT test sensor input below test minimum
63	O/C	TP sensor below test minimum
64	O/C	ACT sensor input below test minimum
67	O/R	Neutral drive switch open. A/C input high
68	R	Idle tracking switch circuit open
68	O	Idle tracking switch closed
71	C	Idle tracking switch closed on pre-position
73	O	Insufficient TP change
84	O/R	EGR VAC regulator circuit failure
85	O/R	Canister purge circuit failure
87	O/R/C	Fuel pump primary circuit failure
93	O	TP sensor input low at max DC motor extension
95	O/C	Fuel pump secondary circuit failure
96	O/C	Fuel pump secondary circuit failure
98	R	Hard fault is present
99	R	EEC system has not learned to control idle
No Code		Unable to run self-test or output codes [1]
Code not listed		Does not apply to vehicle being tested [1]

O—Key On, Engine Off
R—Engine running
C—Continuous Memory
1 Refer to system diagnostics

86754221

Year—1989
Model—Escort
Body VIN—1 and 2
Engine—1.9L HO **Cylinder**—4
Fuel System—Multi-Point Injection (EFI)
Engine VIN—J

ECA SERVICE CODES

Code		Explanation
11	O/R/C	System pass
12	R	Rpm unable to reach upper test limit
13	R	Rpm unable to reach lower test limit
14	C	PIP circuit failure
15	O	ROM test failure
15	C	Power interrupted to keep alive memory
16	R	Rpm above self test limit, set too high (ISC off)
17	R	Rpm below self-test limit, set too low (ISC off)
18	C	Loss of tach input to ECU, spout grounded
18	R	Spout circuit open
19	R	Erratic rpm during test or rpm too low (ISC off)
21	O/R	ECT sensor input out of test range
22	O/R/C	MAP sensor input out of test range
23	O/R	TP sensor input out of test range
26	O/R	VAF sensor input out of self-test range
28	O/R	VAT sensor input out of self-test range
41	R	EGO/HEGO circuit shows system lean
41	C	No EGO/HEGO switching detected, system lean
42	R	EGO/HEGO shows system rich
42	C	No EGO/HEGO switching detected, system rich
43	C	EGO/HEGO lean at wide open throttle
47	R	Airflow at base idle
48	R	Airflow high at base idle
51	O/C	ECT sensor input exceeds test maximum
53	O/C	TP sensor input exceeds test maximum
56	O/C	VAF sensor input exceeds test maximum
58	O/C	VAT sensor input exceeds test maximum
61	O/C	ECT test sensor input below test minimum
63	O/C	TP sensor below test minimum
65	C	Failed to enter self-test mode
66	O/C	VAF sensor input below test minimum
67	O	Neutral drive switch open. A/C input high
67	C	Clutch switch circuit failure
68	O/C	VAT sensor input below test minimum
71	C	Software re-initialization detected
72	C	Power interrupt detected
73	R	Insufficient TP output change during test

86754222

ECA SERVICE CODES

Code		Explanation
76	R	Insufficient VAF output change during test
77	R	Wide open throttle not sensed during test
85	C	Adaptive lean limit reached
86	C	Adaptive rich limit reached
95	O/C	Fuel pump secondary circuit failure
96	O/C	Fuel pump secondary circuit failure
No Code		Unable to run self-test or output codes [1]
Code not listed		Does not apply to vehicle being tested [1]

O – Key On, Engine Off
R – Engine running
C – Continuous Memory
1 Refer to system diagnostics

Year – 1989
Model – Escort
Body VIN – 1 and 2
Engine – 1.9L **Cylinder** – 4
Fuel System – Central Fuel Injection (CFI)
Engine VIN – 9

ECA SERVICE CODES

Code		Explanation
11	O/R/C	System pass
12	R	Rpm unable to reach upper test limit
13	R	Rpm unable to reach lower test limit
13	0	DC motor did not follow dashpot
14	C	PIP circuit failure
15	0	ROM test failure
15	C	Power interrupted to keep alive memory
17	R	Rpm below self-test limit, set too low
18	C	Loss of tach input to ECU, spout grounded
18	R	Spout circuit open
19	R	Erratic rpm during test or rpm too low
21	O/R	ECT sensor input out of test range
22	O/R/C	MAP sensor input out of test range
23	O/R/C	TP sensor input out of test range
24	O/R	ACT sensor input out of test range
31	O/R/C	EVP circuit below minimum voltage
32	R/C	EGR valve not seated
33	R/C	EGR valve not opening
34	0	Defective PFE sensor
34	R/C	Excess exhaust back pressure
35	O/R/C	PFE circuit above maximum voltage

86754223

ECA SERVICE CODES

Code		Explanation
38	C	Idle track switch circuit open
41	R	EGO/HEGO circuit shows system lean
41	C	No EGO/HEGO switching detected, system lean
42	R	EGO/HEGO shows system rich
51	O/C	ECT sensor input exceeds test maximum
53	O/C	TP sensor input exceeds test maximum
54	O/C	ACT sensor input exceeds test maximum
55	R	Key power input to processor is open
58	R	Idle tracking switch circuit closed
58	0	Idle tracking switch circuit open
61	O/C	ECT test sensor input below test minimum
63	O/C	TP sensor below test minimum
64	O/C	ACT sensor input below test minimum
67	O/R	Neutral drive switch open. A/C input high
68	R	Idle tracking switch circuit open
68	0	Idle tracking switch closed
71	C	Idle tracking switch closed on pre-position
73	0	Insufficient TP change
84	O/R	EGR VAC regulator circuit failure
85	O/R	Canister purge circuit failure
87	O/R/C	Fuel pump primary circuit failure
93	0	TP sensor input low at max DC motor extension
95	O/C	Fuel pump secondary circuit failure
96	O/C	Fuel pump secondary circuit failure
98	R	Hard fault is present
99	R	EEC system has not learned to control idle
No Code		Unable to run self-test or output codes [1]
Code not listed		Does not apply to vehicle being tested [1]

0—Key On, Engine Off
R—Engine running
C—Continuous Memory
1 Refer to system diagnostics

86754224

Year—1990
Model—Escort
Body VIN—1 and 2
Engine—1.9L **Cylinder**—4
Fuel System—Central Fuel Injection (CFI)
Engine VIN—9

ECA SERVICE CODES

Code		Explanation
11	O/R/C	System pass
12	R	Cannot control rpm during self-test high rpm check
13	R	Cannot control rpm during self-test low rpm check
13	O	DC motor movement not detected
13	C	DC motor did not follow dashpot
14	C	PIP circuit failure
15	O	ECA ROM test failure
15	C	ECA KAM test failure
16	R	Idle rpm high with ISC off
17	R	Idle rpm low with ISC off
18	R	SPOUT circuit open
18	C	IDM circuit failure/SPOUT circuit grounded
19	R	Rpm for EGR test not achieved
21	O/R	ECT sensor input out of test range
22	O/R/C	MAP sensor input out of test range
23	O/R/C	TP sensor input out of test range
24	O/R	ACT sensor input out of test range
31	O/R/C	PFE circuit is below minimum voltage
32	R/C	EPT circuit voltage low (PFE)
33	R/C	EGR valve opening (PFE) not detected
34	O	Defective PFE sensor
34	R/C	EPT sensor voltage high (PFE)
35	O/R/C	PFE circuit above maximum voltage
38	C	Idle track switch circuit open
41	R	HEGO circuit shows system lean
41	C	No HEGO switching detected, system lean
42	R	HEGO shows system rich
51	O/C	ECT sensor circuit open
53	O/C	TP sensor input exceeds test maximum
54	O/C	ACT sensor circuit open
55	R	Keypower circuit open
58	R	Idle tracking switch circuit closed
58	O	Idle tracking switch circuit open
61	O/C	ECT test sensor input below test minimum
63	O/C	TP sensor below test minimum
64	O/C	ACT sensor input below test minimum
67	O/R	Neutral drive switch open. A/C input high

86754225

ECA SERVICE CODES

Code		Explanation
68	R	Idle tracking switch circuit open
68	0	Idle tracking switch closed
71	C	Idle tracking switch closed on pre-position
73	0	Insufficient TP change
84	0	EGR VAC regulator circuit failure
85	O/R	Canister purge circuit failure
87	O/R/C	Fuel pump primary circuit failure
93	0	TP sensor input low at max DC motor extension
95	O/C	Fuel pump circuit open—ECA to motor ground
96	O/C	Fuel pump circuit open—battery to ECA
98	R	Hard fault is present
99	R	EEC system has not learned to control idle
No Code		unable to run self-test or output codes[1]
Code not listed		does not apply to vehicle being tested[1]

O—Key On, Engine Off
R—Engine running
C—Continuous Memory

Year—1990
Model—Escort
Body VIN—4
Engine—1.9L MA **Cylinder**—4
Fuel System—Sequential Electronic Fuel (SEFI)
Engine VIN—9

ECA SERVICE CODES

Code		Explanation
11	O/R/C	System pass
12	R	Cannot control rpm during self-test high rpm check
13	R	Cannot control rpm during self-test low rpm check
14	C	PIP circuit failure
15	0	ECA ROM test failure
15	C	ECA KAM test failure
18	R	SAW circuit failure
18	C	IDM circuit failure/SPOUT circuit grounded
19	0	Failure in ECA internal voltage
19	C	CID circuit failure
21	O/R	ECT sensor input out of test range
23	O/R	TP sensor input out of test range
24	O/R	ACT sensor input out of test range
26	O/R	MAF sensor out of self-test range
29	C	Insufficient input from VSS

86754226

ECA SERVICE CODES

Code		Explanation
31	O/R/C	PFE circuit is below minimum voltage
32	R/C	PFE circuit voltage low
33	R/C	EGR valve opening not detected
34	O	PFE sensor voltage out of range
34	R/C	EPT sensor voltage high (PFE)
35	O/R/C	PFE circuit above maximum voltage
41	R	HEGO circuit shows system lean
41	C	No HEGO switching detected, system lean
42	R	HEGO shows system rich
45	C	Coil 1 primary circuit failure
46	C	Coil 2 primary circuit failure
51	O/C	ECT sensor circuit open
53	O/C	TP sensor input exceeds test maximum
54	O/C	ACT sensor circuit open
56	O/R/C	MAF circuit above maximum voltage
61	O/C	ECT indicates circuit grounded
63	O/C	TP sensor below test minimum
64	O/C	ACT indicates circuit grounded
66	R/C	MAF circuit below minimum voltage
67	O/R	Neutral drive switch open
67	C	Clutch switch circuit failure
72	R	Insufficient MAF change during dynamic response test
73	O	Insufficient TP change
74	R	Brake ON/OFF circuit failure/not actuated during self-test
77	R	Brief WOT not sensed during self-test/operator error
79	O	A/C ON/defrost on during self-test
83	O	High speed electro drive fan circuit failure
84	O/R	EGR VAC regulator circuit failure
87	O/C	Fuel pump primary circuit failure
88	O	Electro drive fan circuit failure
95	O/C	Fuel pump secondary circuit failure
96	O/C	Fuel pump secondary circuit failure
98	R	Hard fault is present—FMEM mode
No Code		unable to run self-test or output codes[1]
Code not listed		does not apply to vehicle being tested[1]

O—Key On, Engine Off
R—Engine running
C—Continuous Memory

86754227

Year—1991
Model—Escort
Body VIN—1
Engine—1.9L MA **Cylinder**—4
Fuel System—Sequential Electronic Fuel (SEFI)
Engine VIN—J

ECA SERVICE CODES

Code		Explanation
11 O/R/C		System pass
12	R	Cannot control rpm during self-test high rpm check
13	R	Cannot control rpm during self-test low rpm check
14	C	PIP circuit failure
15 0		EEC rOM test failure
15	C	EEC KAM test failure
18	R	SAW circuit failure
18	C	IDM circuit failure/SPOUT circuit grounded
19	0	Failure in EEC internal voltage
19	C	CID circuit failure
21 O/R		ECT sensoR out of test range
23 O/R		TP sensoR out of test range
24	O/R	ACT sensor input out of test range
26	O/R	MAF sensor out of self-test range
29	C	Insufficient input from VSS
31	O/R/C	PFE circuit is below minimum voltage
32	R/C	PFE circuit voltage low
33	R/C	EGR valve opening not detected
34	0	PFE sensor voltage out of range
35	O/R/C	PFE circuit above maximum voltage
41	R	HEGO circuit shows system lean
41	C	No HEGO switching detected
42	R	HEGO shows system rich
45	C	Coil 1 primary circuit failure
46	C	Coil 2 primary circuit failure
51	O/C	ECT sensor circuit open
53	O/C	TP sensor input exceeds test maximum
54	O/C	ACT sensor circuit open
56	O/R/C	MAF circuit above maximum voltage
61	O/C	ECT indicates circuit grounded
63	O/C	TP sensor below test minimum
64	O/C	ACT indicates circuit grounded
66	R/C	MAF circuit below minimum voltage
67	O/R	Neutral drive switch open
67	C	Clutch switch circuit failure
72	R	Insufficient MAF change during dynamic response test
73	0	Insufficient TP change

86754228

ECA SERVICE CODES

Code		Explanation
74	R	Brake ON/OFF circuit failure/not actuated during self-test
77	R	Brief WOT not sensed during self-test/operator error
79	0	A/C ON/defrost on during self-test
83	0	High speed electro drive fan circuit failure
84	O/R	EGR VAC regulator circuit failure
87	O/C	Fuel pump primary circuit failure
88	0	Electro drive fan circuit failure
95	O/C	Fuel pump secondary circuit failure
96	O/C	Fuel pump secondary circuit failure
98	R	Hard fault is present—FMEM mode
No Code		unable to run self-test or output codes[1]
Code not listed		does not apply to vehicle being tested[1]

O—Key On, Engine Off
R—Engine running
C—Continuous Memory

86754229

SERVICE CODE	SERVICE CODE DEFINITION
111 orc	System PASS
112 oc	Air Charge Temperature (ACT) indicates 123°C (254°F) / circuit grounded
113 oc	Air Charge Temperature (ACT) indicates -40°C (-40°F) / circuit grounded
114 or	Air Charge Temperature (ACT) out of Self-Test range
116 or	Engine Coolant Temperature (ECT) out of Self-Test range
117 oc	Engine Coolant Temperature (ECT) indicates 123°C (254°F) / circuit grounded
118 oc	Engine Coolant Temperature (ECT) indicates -40°C (-40°F) / circuit grounded
121 orc	Throttle Position voltage higher or lower than expected
122 oc	Throttle Position (TP) circuit below minimum voltage
123 oc	Throttle Position (TP) circuit above maximum voltage
124 c	Throttle Position (TP) sensor voltage higher than expected
125 c	Throttle Position (TP) sensor voltage lower than expected
129 r	Insufficient Mass Air Flow (MAF) change during Dynamic Response Test
157 c	Mass Air Flow (MAF) sensor below minimum voltage
158 oc	Mass Air Flow (MAF) sensor above maximum voltage
159 or	Mass Air Flow (MAF) sensor higher or lower than expected during KOEO, KOER
167 r	Insufficient Throttle Position (TP) change during Dynamic Response Test
171 c	Fuel system at adaptive limits, Oxygen Sensor (HEGO) unable to switch
172 rc	Lack of Oxygen Sensor (HEGO) switches, indicates lean
173 rc	Lack of Oxygen Sensor (HEGO) switches, indicates rich
179 c	Fuel system at lean adaptive limit at part throttle, system rich
181 c	Fuel system at rich adaptive limit at part throttle, system lean
182 c	Fuel system at lean adaptive limit at idle, system rich
183 c	Fuel system at rich adaptive limit at idle, system lean
184 c	Mass Air Flow (MAF) higher than expected
185 c	Mass Air Flow (MAF) lower than expected
186 c	Injector pulse width higher than expected
187 c	Injector pulse width lower than expected
211 c	Profile Ignition Pickup (PIP) circuit fault
212 c	Loss of Ignition Diagnostic Monitor (IDM) input to EEC processor / SPOUT circuit grounded
213 r	SPOUT circuit open
214 c	Cylinder Indentification (CID) circuit failure
215 c	Coil 1 primary circuit failure
216 c	Coil 2 primary circuit failure
226 o	Ignition Diagnostic Monitor (IDM) signal not received
326 rc	Pressure Feedback EGR (PFE) circuit voltage low
327 orc	Pressure Feedback EGR (PFE) circuit below minimum voltage
332 rc	Exhaust Gas Recirculation (EGR) valve opening not detected
335 o	Pressure Feedback EGR (PFE) sensor voltage out of range
336 rc	Exhaust pressure high / Pressure Feedback EGR (PFE) circuit voltage high
337 orc	Pressure Feedback EGR (PFE) circuit above maximum voltage
338 c	Engine coolant temperature lower than normal
339 c	Engine coolant temperature higher than normal
341 o	Octane Adjust (OCT ADJ) circuit open
411 r	Cannot control rpm during Self-Test low rpm check
412 r	Cannot control rpm during Self-Test high rpm check
452 c	Insufficient input from Vehicle Speed Sensor (VSS)
511 o	EEC processor Read Only Memory (ROM) test failed

86754230

Fig. 21 1992 Escort/Tracer service code definitions

SERVICE CODE		SERVICE CODE DEFINITION
512 c	▶	EEC processor Keep Alive Memory (KAM) test failed
513 o	▶	Failure in EEC processor internal voltage
522 o	▶	Vehicle not in park or neutral during KOEO / Neutral Drive Switch (NDS) circuit open
528 c	▶	Clutch Engage Switch (CES) circuit failure
536 rc	▶	Brake On / Off (BOO) circuit failure / not actuated during Self-Test
538 r	▶	Brief Wide Open Throttle (WOT) not sensed during Self-Test / operator error
539 o	▶	Air Conditioning On / Defrost ON during Self-Test
542 oc	▶	Fuel Pump secondary circuit failure
543 oc	▶	Fuel Pump secondary circuit failure
556 oc	▶	Fuel Pump relay primary circuit failure
558 o	▶	EGR Vacuum Regulator (EVR) circuit failure
563 o	▶	High Electro-Drive (HEDF) circuit failure
564 o	▶	Electro-Drive Fan (EDF) circuit failure
565 o	▶	Canister Purge (CANP) circuit failure
621 oc	▶	Shift Solenoid 1 (SS1) circuit failure
622 oc	▶	Shift Solenoid 2 (SS2) circuit failure
634 c	▶	Error in Transmission Select Switch (TSS) circuits
636 or	▶	Transmission Oil Temperature (TOT) sensor out of Self-Test range
637 oc	▶	Transmission Oil Temperature (TOT) sensor above maximum voltage
638 oc	▶	Transmission Oil Temperature (TOT) sensor below minimum voltage
639 rc	▶	Insufficient input from Transmission Speed Sensor (TSS)
641 oc	▶	Shift Solenoid 3 (SS3) circuit failure
643 oc	▶	Converter Clutch Control (CCC) circuit failure
998 r	▶	Hard fault is present—FMEM mode
NO CODES		Unable to initiate Self-Test or unable to output Self-Test codes
CODES NOT LISTED		Service codes displayed are not applicable to the vehicle being tested

KEY: o = Key On Engine Off (KOEO), r = Engine Running (ER), c = Continuous Memory

86754231

Fig. 22 1992 Escort/Tracer service code definitions (continued)

DIAGNOSTIC TROUBLE CODES	DEFINITIONS
111	System Pass
112	Intake Air Temp (IAT) sensor circuit below minimum voltage / 254°F indicated
113	Intake Air Temp (IAT) sensor circuit above maximum voltage / -40°F indicated
114	Intake Air Temp (IAT) higher or lower than expected
116	Engine Coolant Temp (ECT) higher or lower than expected
117	Engine Coolant Temp (ECT) sensor circuit below minimum voltage / 254°F indicated
118	Engine Coolant Temp (ECT) sensor circuit above maximum voltage / -40°F indicated
121	Closed throttle voltage higher or lower than expected
121	Indicates throttle position voltage inconsistent with the MAF sensor
122	Throttle Position (TP) sensor circuit below minimum voltage
123	Throttle Position (TP) sensor circuit above maximum voltage
124	Throttle Position (TP) sensor voltage higher than expected
125	Throttle Position (TP) sensor voltage lower than expected
126	MAP / BARO sensor higher or lower than expected
128	MAP sensor vacuum hose damaged / disconnected
129	Insufficient MAP / Mass Air Flow (MAF) change during dynamic response test KOER
136	Lack of Heated Oxygen Sensor (HO2S-2) switch during KOER, indicates lean (Bank #2)
137	Lack of Heated Oxygen Sensor (HO2S-2) switch during KOER, indicates rich (Bank #2)
139	No Heated Oxygen Sensor (HO2S-2) switches detected (Bank #2)
141	Fuel system indicates lean
144	No Heated Oxygen Sensor (HO2S-1) switches detected (Bank # 1)
157	Mass Air Flow (MAF) sensor circuit below minimum voltage.
158	Mass Air Flow (MAF) sensor circuit above maximum voltage
159	Mass Air Flow (MAF) higher or lower than expected
167	Insufficient throttle position change during dynamic response test KOER
171	Fuel system at adaptive limits, Heated Oxygen Sensor (HO2S-1) unable to switch (Bank # 1)
172	Lack of Heated Oxygen Sensor (HO2S-1) switches, indicates lean (Bank # 1)
173	Lack of Heated Oxygen Sensor (HO2S-1) switches, indicates rich (Bank # 1)
175	Fuel system at adaptive limits, Heated Oxygen Sensor (HO2S-2) unable to switch (Bank #2)
176	Lack of Heated Oxygen Sensor (HO2S-2) switches, indicates lean (Bank #2)
177	Lack of Heated Oxygen Sensor (HO2S-2) switches, indicates rich (Bank #2)
179	Fuel system at lean adaptive limit at part throttle, system rich (Bank # 1)
181	Fuel system at rich adaptive limit at part throttle, system lean (Bank # 1)
184	Mass Air Flow (MAF) higher than expected
185	Mass Air Flow (MAF) lower than expected
186	Injector pulsewidth higher than expected (with BARO sensor)
186	Injector pulsewidth higher or MAF lower than expected (without BARO sensor)
187	Injector pulsewidth lower than expected (with BARO sensor)
187	Injector pulsewidth lower or MAF higher than expected (without BARO sensor)
188	Fuel system at lean adaptive limit at part throttle, system rich (Bank #2)
189	Fuel system at rich adaptive limit at part throttle, system lean (Bank #2)
193	Flexible Fuel (FF) sensor circuit failure

86754232

Fig. 23 1993-95 Escort/Tracer service code definitions

DIAGNOSTIC TROUBLE CODES	DEFINITIONS
211	Profile Ignition Pickup (PIP) circuit failure
212	Loss of Ignition Diagnostic Monitor (IDM) input to PCM / SPOUT circuit grounded
213	SPOUT circuit open
214	Cylinder Identification (CID) circuit failure
215	PCM detected coil 1 primary circuit failure (EI)
216	PCM detected coil 2 primary circuit failure (EI)
217	PCM detected coil 3 primary circuit failure (EI)
218	Loss of Ignition Diagnostic Monitor (IDM) signal-left side (dual plug EI)
219	Spark timing defaulted to 10 degrees-SPOUT circuit open (EI)
221	Spark timing error (EI)
222	Loss of Ignition Diagnostic Monitor (IDM) signal-right side (dual plug EI)
223	Loss of Dual Plug Inhibit (DPI) control (dual plug EI)
224	PCM detected coil 1, 2, 3 or 4 primary circuit failure (dual plug EI)
225	Knock not sensed during dynamic response test KOER
226	Ignition Diagnostic Module (IDM) signal not received (EI)
232	PCM detected coil 1, 2, 3 or 4 primary circuit failure (EI)
238	PCM detected coil 4 primary circuit failure (EI)
241	ICM to PCM IDM pulsewidth transmission error (EI)
244	CID circuit fault present when cylinder balance test requested
311	AIR system inoperative during KOER (Bank # 1 w / dual HO2S)
312	AIR misdirected during KOER
313	AIR not bypassed during KOER
314	AIR system inoperative during KOER (Bank # 2 w / dual HO2S)
326	EGR (PFE / DPFE) circuit voltage lower than expected
327	EGR (EGRP / EVP / PFE / DPFE) circuit below minimum voltage
328	EGR (EVP) closed valve voltage lower than expected
332	Insufficient EGR flow detected (EGRP / EVP / PFE / DPFE)
334	EGR (EVP) closed valve voltage higher than expected
335	EGR (PFE / DPFE) sensor voltage higher or lower than expected during KOEO
336	Exhaust pressure high / EGR (PFE / DPFE) circuit voltage higher than expected
337	EGR (EGRP / EVP / PFE / DPFE) circuit above maximum voltage
338	Engine Coolant Temperature (ECT) lower than expected (thermostat test)
339	Engine Coolant Temperature (ECT) higher than expected (thermostat test)
341	Octane adjust service pin open
381	Frequent A / C clutch cycling
411	Cannot control RPM during KOER low RPM check
412	Cannot control RPM during KOER high RPM check
415	Idle Air Control (IAC) system at maximum adaptive lower limit
416	Idle Air Control (IAC) system at upper adaptive learning limit
452	Insufficient input from Vehicle Speed Sensor (VSS) to PCM
453	Servo leaking down (KOER IVSC test)
454	Servo leaking up (KOER IVSC test)
455	Insufficient RPM increase (KOER IVSC test)
456	Insufficient RPM decrease (KOER IVSC test)

86754233

Fig. 24 1993-95 Escort/Tracer service code definitions (continued)

DIAGNOSTIC TROUBLE CODES	DEFINITIONS
457	Speed control command switch(s) circuit not functioning (KOEO IVSC test)
458	Speed control command switch(s) stuck / circuit grounded (KOEO IVSC test)
459	Speed control ground circuit open (KOEO IVSC test)
511	PCM Read Only Memory (ROM) test failure KOEO
512	PCM Keep Alive Memory (KAM) test failure
513	PCM internal voltage failure (KOEO)
519	Power Steering Pressure (PSP) switch circuit open KOEO
521	Power Steering Pressure (PSP) switch circuit did not change states KOER
522	Vehicle not in PARK or NEUTRAL during KOEO / PNP switch circuit open
524	Low speed fuel pump circuit open—battery to PCM
525	Indicates vehicle in gear / A / C on
527	Park / Neutral Position (PNP) switch circuit open—A / C on KOEO
528	Clutch Pedal Position (CPP) switch circuit failure
529	Data Communication Link (DCL) or PCM circuit failure
532	Cluster Control Assembly (CCA) circuit failure
533	Data Communication Link (DCL) or Electronic Instrument Cluster (EIC) circuit failure
536	Brake On / Off (BOO) circuit failure / not actuated during KOER
538	Insufficient RPM change during KOER dynamic response test
538	Invalid cylinder balance test due to throttle movement during test (SFI only)
538	Invalid cylinder balance test due to CID circuit failure
539	A / C on / Defrost on during Self-Test
542	Fuel pump secondary circuit failure
543	Fuel pump secondary circuit failure
551	Idle Air Control (IAC) circuit failure KOEO
552	Secondary Air Injection Bypass (AIRB) circuit failure KOEO
553	Secondary Air Injection Diverter (AIRD) circuit failure KOEO
554	Fuel Pressure Regulator Control (FPRC) circuit failure
556	Fuel pump relay primary circuit failure
557	Low speed fuel pump primary circuit failure
558	EGR Vacuum Regulator (EVR) circuit failure KOEO
559	Air Conditioning On (ACON) relay circuit failure KOEO
563	High Fan Control (HFC) circuit failure KOEO
564	Fan Control (FC) circuit failure KOEO
565	Canister Purge (CANP) circuit failure KOEO
566	3-4 shift solenoid circuit failure KOEO (A4LD)
567	Speed Control Vent (SCVNT) circuit failure (KOEO IVSC test)
568	Speed Control Vacuum (SCVAC) circuit failure (KOEO IVSC test)
569	Auxiliary Canister Purge (CANP2) circuit failure KOEO
571	EGRA solenoid circuit failure KOEO
572	EGRV solenoid circuit failure KOEO
578	A / C pressure sensor circuit shorted
579	Insufficient A / C pressure change
581	Power to Fan circuit over current

86754234

Fig. 25 1993-95 Escort/Tracer service code definitions (continued)

DIAGNOSTIC TROUBLE CODES	DEFINITIONS
582	Fan circuit open
583	Power to Fuel pump over current
584	VCRM Power ground circuit open (VCRM Pin 1)
585	Power to A/C clutch over current
586	A/C clutch circuit open
587	Variable Control Relay Module (VCRM) communication failure
617	1-2 shift error
618	2-3 shift error
619	3-4 shift error
621	Shift Solenoid 1 (SS1) circuit failure KOEO
622	Shift Solenoid 2 (SS2) circuit failure KOEO
623	Transmission Control Indicator Light (TCIL) circuit failure
624	Electronic Pressure Control (EPC) circuit failure
625	Electronic Pressure Control (EPC) driver open in PCM
626	Coast Clutch Solenoid (CCS) circuit failure KOEO
627	Torque Converter Clutch (TCC) solenoid circuit failure
628	Excessive converter clutch slippage
629	Torque Converter Clutch (TCC) solenoid circuit failure
631	Transmission Control Indicator Lamp (TCIL) circuit failure KOEO
632	Transmission Control Switch (TCS) circuit did not change states during KOER
633	4x4L switch closed during KOEO
634	Transmission Range (TR) voltage higher or lower than expected
636	Transmission Fluid Temp (TFT) higher or lower than expected
637	Transmission Fluid Temp (TFT) sensor circuit above maximum voltage / -40°F (-40°C) indicated / circuit open
638	Transmission Fluid Temp (TFT) sensor circuit below minimum voltage / 290°F (143°C) indicated / circuit shorted
639	Insufficient input from Transmission Speed Sensor (TSS)
641	Shift Solenoid 3 (SS3) circuit failure
643	Torque Converter Clutch (TCC) circuit failure
645	Incorrect gear ratio obtained for first gear
646	Incorrect gear ratio obtained for second gear
647	Incorrect gear ratio obtained for third gear
648	Incorrect gear ratio obtained for fourth gear
649	Electronic Pressure Control (EPC) higher or lower than expected
651	Electronic Pressure Control (EPC) circuit failure
652	Torque Converter Clutch (TCC) solenoid circuit failure
653	Transmission Control Switch (TCS) did not change states during KOER
654	Transmission Range (TR) sensor not indicating PARK during KOEO
656	Torque Converter Clutch continuous slip error
657	Transmission over temperature condition occurred
659	High vehicle speed in park indicated

86754235

Fig. 26 1993-95 Escort/Tracer service code definitions (continued)

EEC-IV Symptoms And Possible Causes

For each symptom below, visual and mechanical checks and EEC-IV checks are listed in a suggested order. When the results indicate service/repairs be performed on either fuel or ignition system, the appropriate section in this manual should be referred to.

➡**Refer to Section 2 for Ignition system diagnosis and Section 5 for Fuel System diagnosis.**

STARTING/IDLE

No Start (Cranks)

FUEL SYSTEM

- Check the fuel pump inertia switch
- Check for fuel contamination/quality
- Check fuel filter

IGNITION SYSTEM

- Check distributor cap, adapter and rotor
- Inspect spark plug and plug wires
- Check ignition switch
- Check ignition coil for voltage
- Inspect the TFI, DIS or EDIS module for damage

POWER AND GROUNDS

- Check for low battery voltage
- Check the starter and starter circuit for voltage
- Inspect electrical connections, wires and harnesses

AIR/VACUUM

- Check vacuum lines for leaks or wear

OTHER

- Check engine coolant level
- Check thermostat for proper operation
- Check EGR valve stuck open
- Check for moisture entry into the EEC-IV module
- Check camshaft timing and cylinder compression

Stalls At Idle/Engine Will Not Stay Running

IGNITION SYSTEM

- Check distributor cap, adapter and rotor
- Inspect spark plug and plug wires
- Check ignition switch
- Check ignition coil for voltage
- Inspect the TFI, DIS or EDIS module for damage

FUEL SYSTEM

- Check the fuel pump inertia switch
- Check for fuel contamination/quality
- Check fuel filter

POWER AND GROUNDS

- Check for low battery voltage
- Check the starter and starter circuit for voltage
- Inspect electrical connections, wires and harnesses

AIR/VACUUM

- Check vacuum lines for leaks or wear

OTHER

- Check engine coolant level
- Check thermostat for proper operation
- Check EGR valve stuck open
- Check for moisture entry into the EEC-IV module
- Check camshaft timing and cylinder compression

Fast Idle/Slow Idle

AIR VACUUM

- Check vacuum lines for leaks or wear
- Check air filter

FUEL SYSTEM

- Check for correct fuel pressure
- Check for fuel contamination/quality
- Check fuel filter

IGNITION SYSTEM

- Check for correct base timing
- Check distributor cap, adapter and rotor
- Inspect spark plug and plug wires
- Inspect the TFI, DIS or EDIS module for damage

POWER AND GROUNDS

- Check for low battery voltage
- Inspect electrical connections, wires and harnesses

OTHER

- Check engine coolant and engine oil level
- Check thermostat for proper operation
- Check EGR valve sticking
- Check PCV valve or correct operation
- Check for exhaust blockage

Rough Idle

AIR/VACUUM

- Check vacuum lines for leaks or wear
- Check air filter

FUEL SYSTEM

- Check for correct fuel pressure
- Check for fuel contamination/quality
- Check fuel filter

IGNITION SYSTEM

- Check for correct base timing
- Check distributor cap, adapter and rotor
- Inspect spark plug and plug wires
- Inspect the TFI, DIS or EDIS module for damage

POWER AND GROUNDS

- Check for low battery voltage
- Inspect electrical connections, wires and harnesses

OTHER

- Check engine coolant level
- Check thermostat for proper operation
- Check EGR valve sticking
- Check PCV valve or correct operation
- Check for exhaust blockage

ENGINE RUNNING: STEADY SPEED/ACCELERATION/DECELERATION

Surges

AIR VACUUM

- Check vacuum lines for leaks or wear

FUEL SYSTEM

- Check for correct fuel pressure
- Check for fuel contamination/quality
- Check fuel line for restrictions

IGNITION SYSTEM

- Check for correct base timing
- Inspect the TFI, DIS or EDIS module for damage

OTHER

- Check EGR valve sticking
- Check PCV valve or correct operation
- Check for exhaust blockage
- Inspect electrical connections, wires and harnesses

Poor Power Or Sluggish

AIR VACUUM

- Check vacuum lines for leaks or wear

FUEL SYSTEM

- Check for correct fuel pressure
- Check for fuel contamination/quality
- Check for clogged fuel filter

IGNITION SYSTEM

- Check for correct base timing
- Check for wear or corrosion in distributor
- Inspect the TFI, DIS or EDIS module for damage

OTHER

- Check EGR valve sticking
- Check PCV valve or correct operation
- Check for exhaust blockage
- Inspect electrical connections, wires and harnesses
- Check for partially binding brakes

Spark Knock

AIR/VACUUM

- Check vacuum lines for leaks or wear

IGNITION SYSTEM

- Check for correct base timing
- Check for wear or corrosion in distributor
- Inspect the TFI, DIS or EDIS module for damage

FUEL SYSTEM

- Check for correct fuel pressure
- Check for fuel contamination/quality
- Check fuel lines for restrictions

OTHER

- Check EGR valve sticking
- Check PCV valve or correct operation
- Check for exhaust blockage
- Check engine coolant level
- Check thermostat for proper operation
- Inspect electrical connections, wires and harnesses

Stalls During Deceleration/Quick Stop

AIR/VACUUM

- Check vacuum lines for leaks or wear

IGNITION SYSTEM

- Check distributor cap, adapter and rotor
- Inspect spark plug and plug wires
- Check ignition switch
- Check ignition coil for voltage
- Inspect the TFI, DIS or EDIS module for damage

FUEL SYSTEM

- Check for correct fuel pressure
- Check the fuel pump inertia switch
- Check for fuel contamination/quality
- Check fuel filter

POWER AND GROUNDS

- Check for low battery voltage
- Inspect electrical connections, wires and harnesses

OTHER

- Check engine coolant level
- Check thermostat for proper operation
- Check EGR valve stuck open
- Check for moisture entry into the EEC-IV module
- Check camshaft timing and cylinder compression

Runs Rough

AIR/VACUUM

- Check vacuum lines for leaks or wear

FUEL SYSTEM

- Check for correct fuel pressure
- Check for fuel contamination/quality
- Check fuel filter

IGNITION SYSTEM

- Check for correct base timing
- Check distributor cap, adapter and rotor
- Inspect spark plug and plug wires
- Inspect the TFI, DIS or EDIS module for damage

POWER AND GROUNDS

- Check for alternator/regulator noise interference
- Inspect electrical connections, wires and harnesses

OTHER

- Check engine coolant level
- Check thermostat for proper operation
- Check EGR valve sticking
- Check PCV valve or correct operation
- Check for exhaust blockage
- Check camshaft timing and cylinder compression
- Check for broken or weak valve springs

VACUUM DIAGRAMS

Following is a listing of vacuum diagrams for most of the engine and emissions package combinations covered by this manual. Because vacuum circuits will vary based on various engine and vehicle options, always refer first to the vehicle emission control information label, if present. Should the label be missing, or should vehicle be equipped with a different engine from the car's original equipment, refer to the diagrams below for the same or similar configuration.

If you wish to obtain a replacement emissions label, most manufacturers make the labels available for purchase. The labels can usually be ordered from a local dealer.

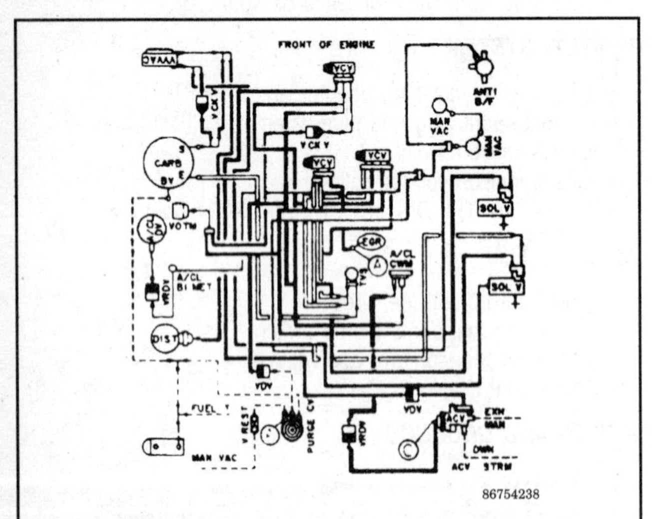

Fig. 27 1982 1.6L models (A/C-equipped), calibration code: 1-3S-R0

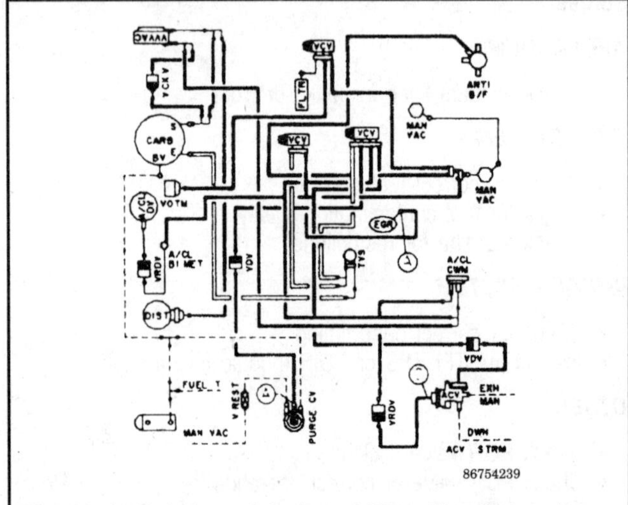

Fig. 28 1982 1.6L models (non-A/C), calibration code: 1-3S-R0

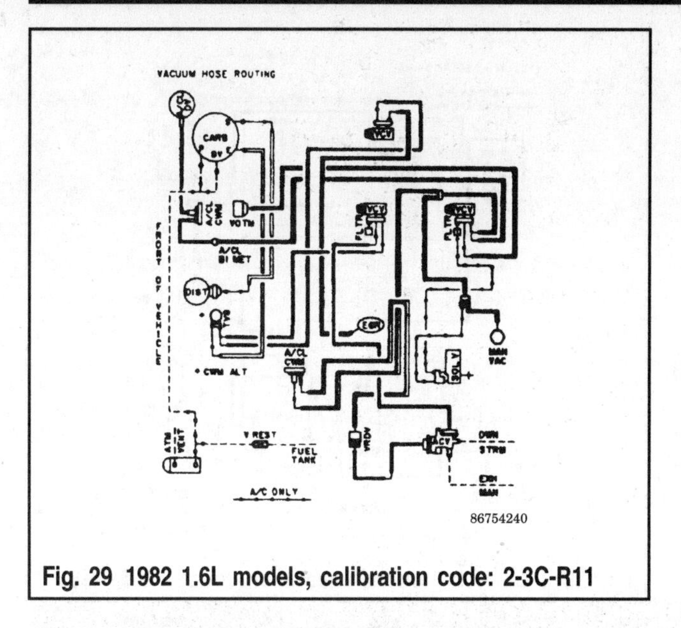

Fig. 29 1982 1.6L models, calibration code: 2-3C-R11

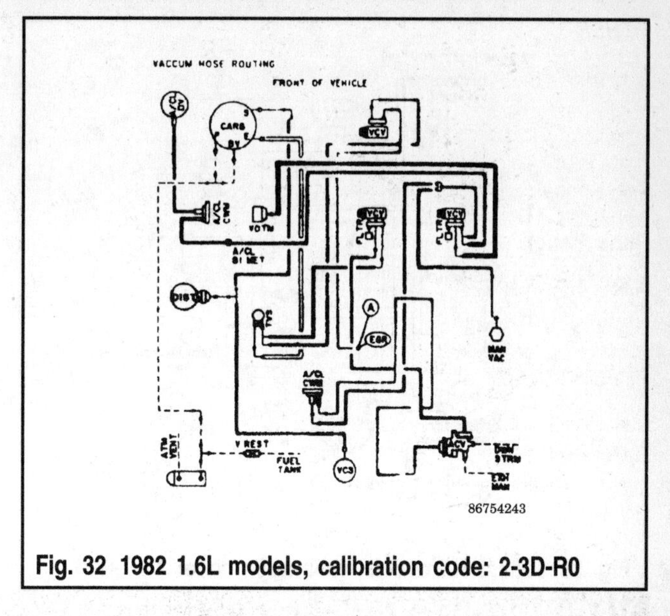

Fig. 32 1982 1.6L models, calibration code: 2-3D-R0

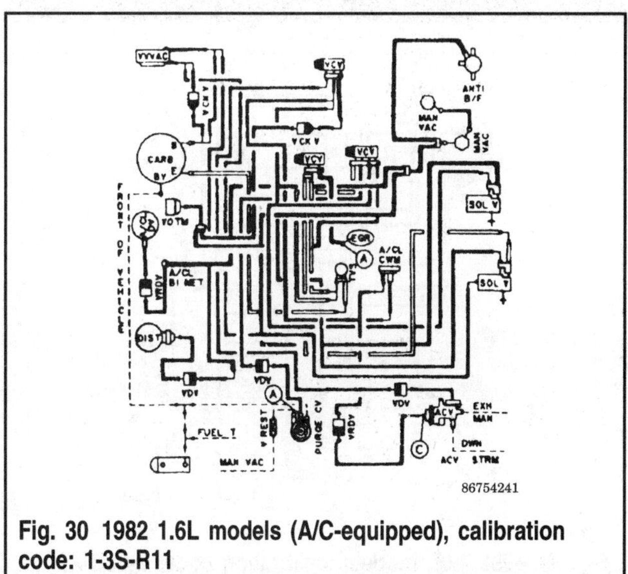

Fig. 30 1982 1.6L models (A/C-equipped), calibration code: 1-3S-R11

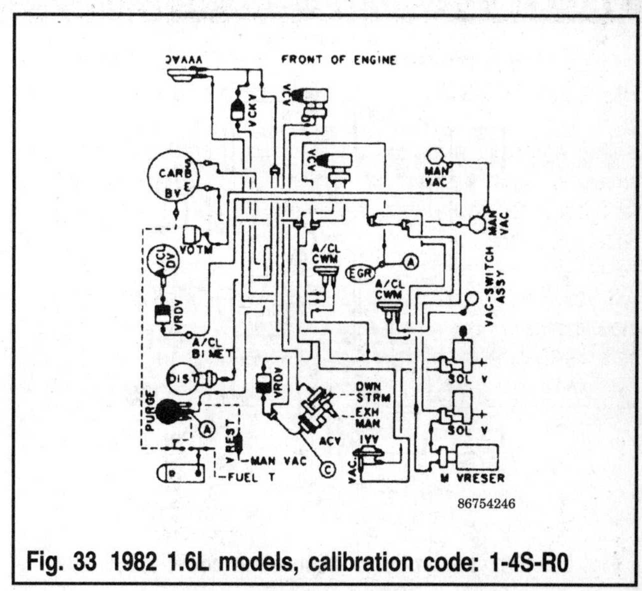

Fig. 33 1982 1.6L models, calibration code: 1-4S-R0

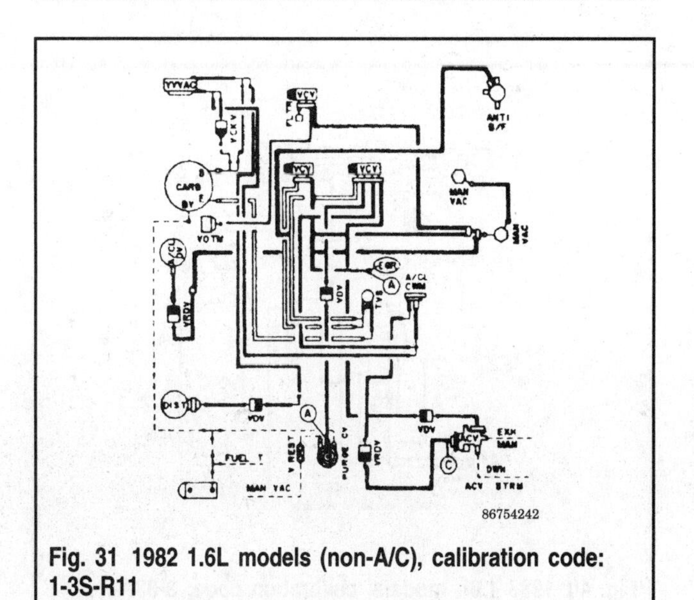

Fig. 31 1982 1.6L models (non-A/C), calibration code: 1-3S-R11

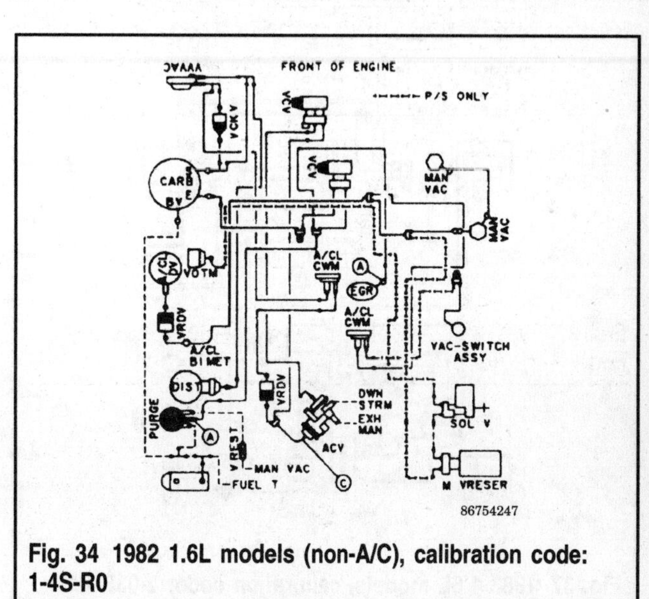

Fig. 34 1982 1.6L models (non-A/C), calibration code: 1-4S-R0

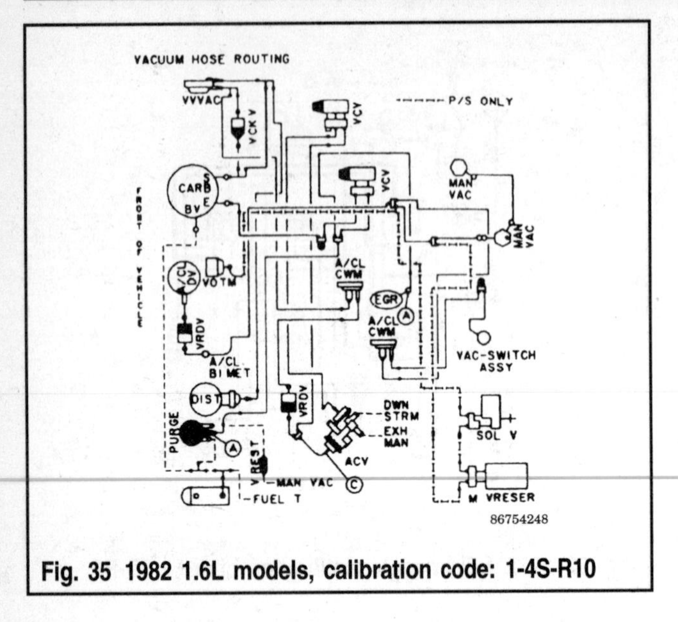

Fig. 35 1982 1.6L models, calibration code: 1-4S-R10

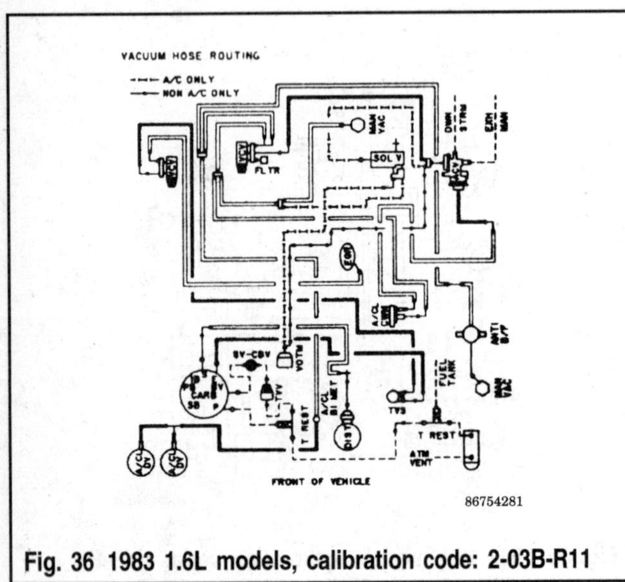

Fig. 36 1983 1.6L models, calibration code: 2-03B-R11

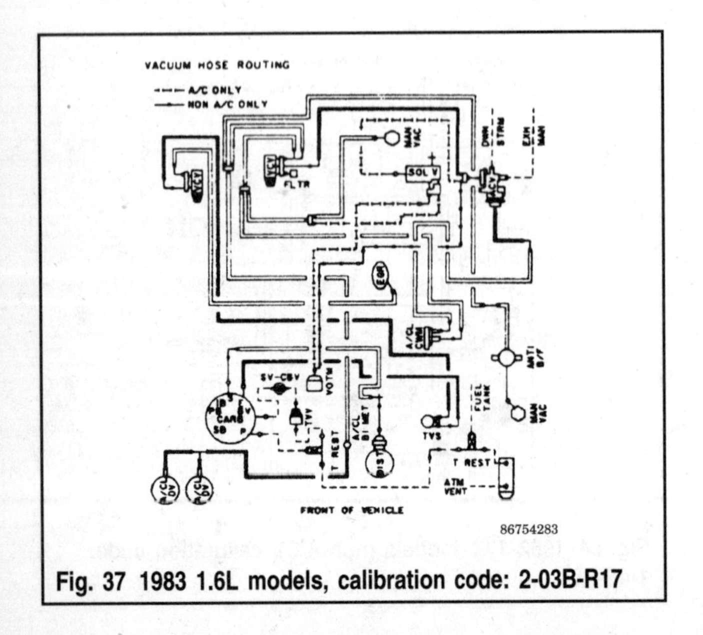

Fig. 37 1983 1.6L models, calibration code: 2-03B-R17

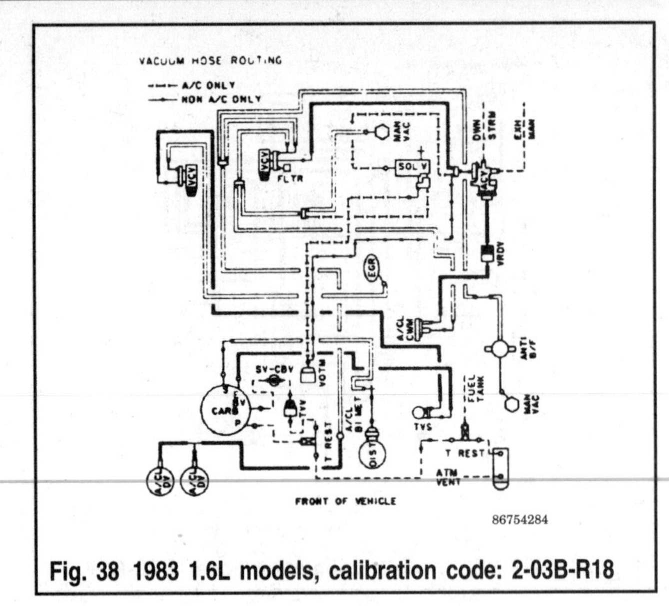

Fig. 38 1983 1.6L models, calibration code: 2-03B-R18

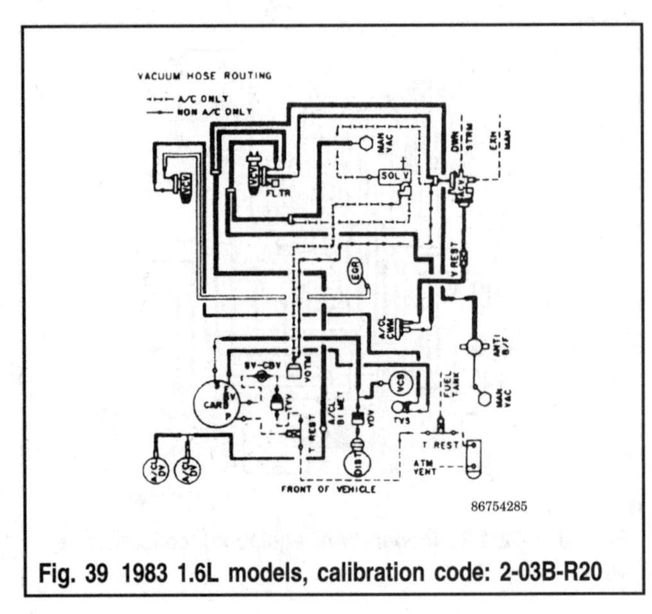

Fig. 39 1983 1.6L models, calibration code: 2-03B-R20

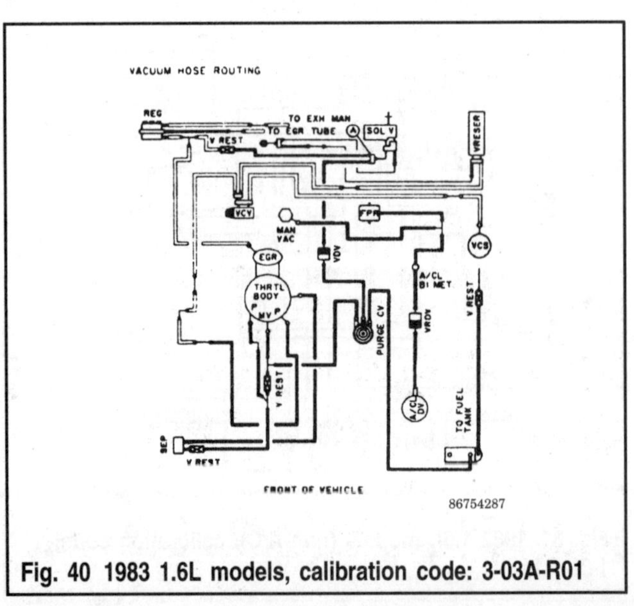

Fig. 40 1983 1.6L models, calibration code: 3-03A-R01

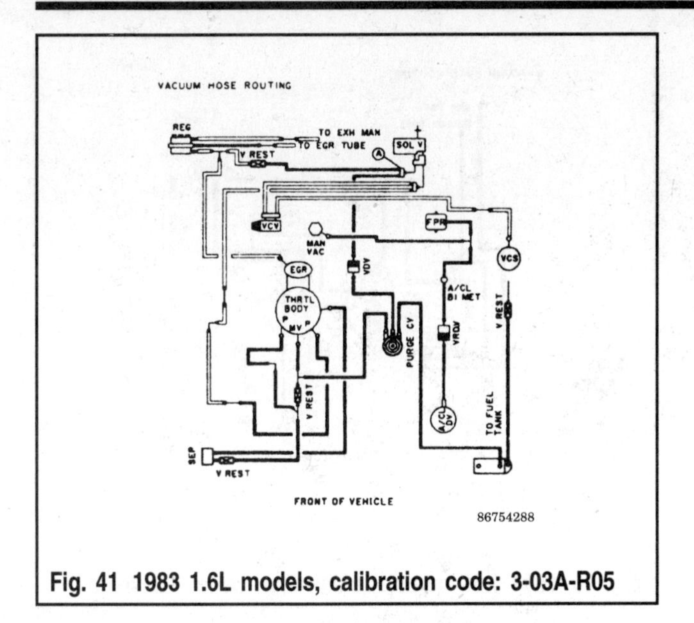

Fig. 41 1983 1.6L models, calibration code: 3-03A-R05

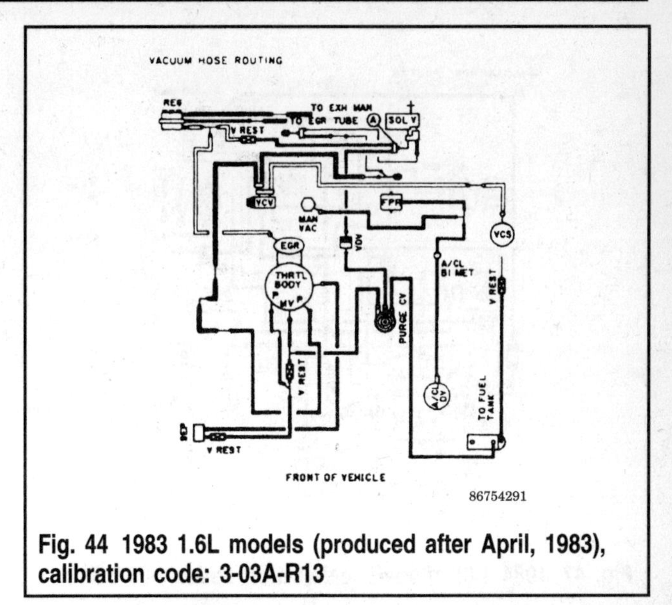

Fig. 44 1983 1.6L models (produced after April, 1983), calibration code: 3-03A-R13

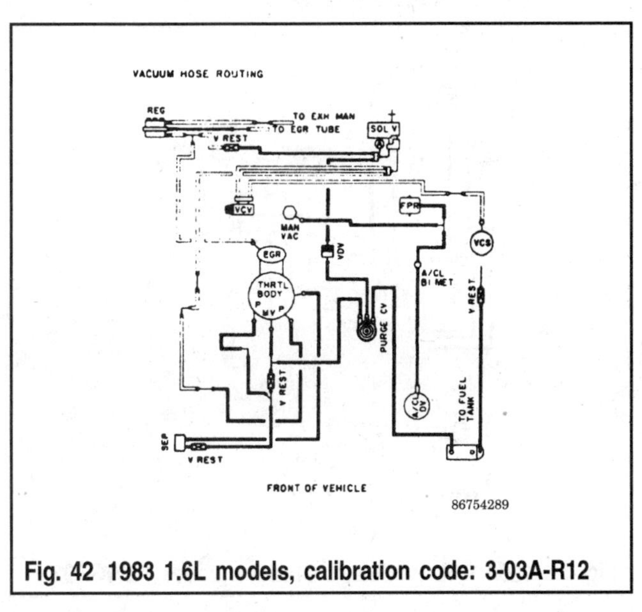

Fig. 42 1983 1.6L models, calibration code: 3-03A-R12

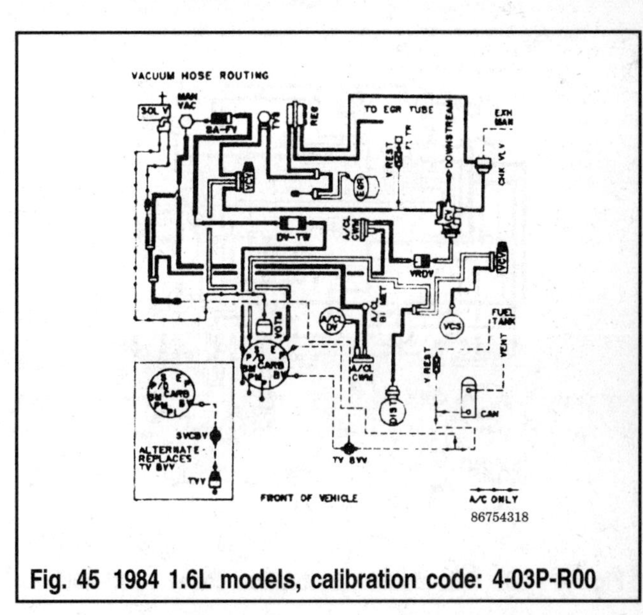

Fig. 45 1984 1.6L models, calibration code: 4-03P-R00

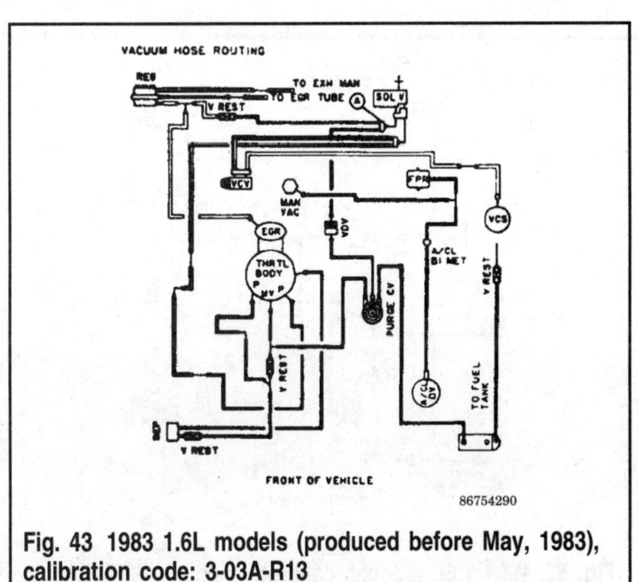

Fig. 43 1983 1.6L models (produced before May, 1983), calibration code: 3-03A-R13

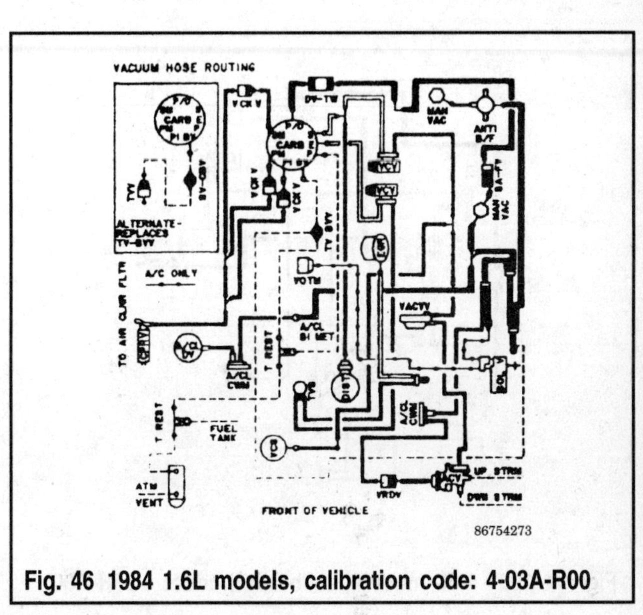

Fig. 46 1984 1.6L models, calibration code: 4-03A-R00

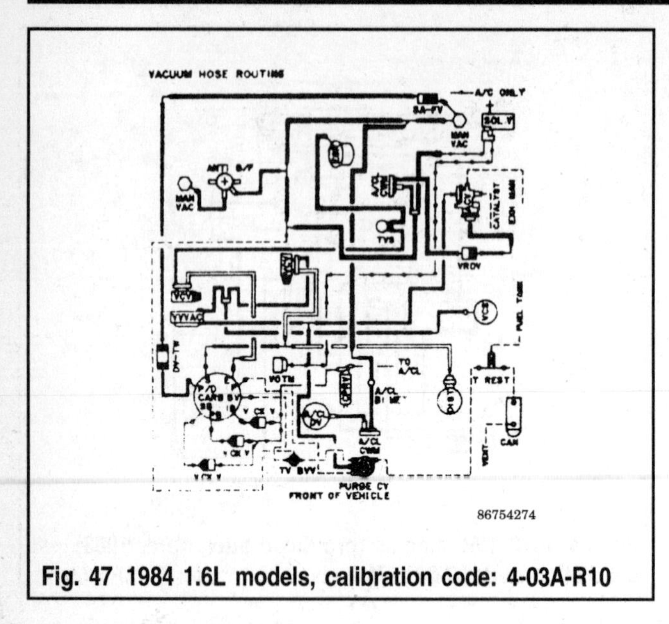

Fig. 47 1984 1.6L models, calibration code: 4-03A-R10

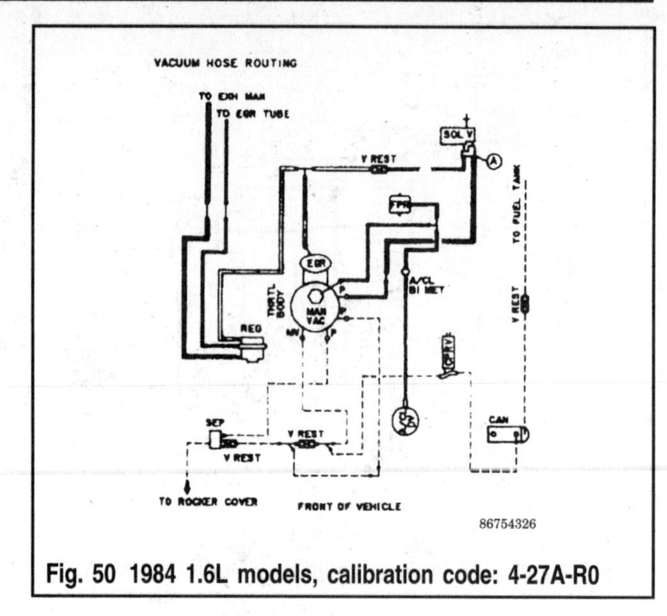

Fig. 50 1984 1.6L models, calibration code: 4-27A-R0

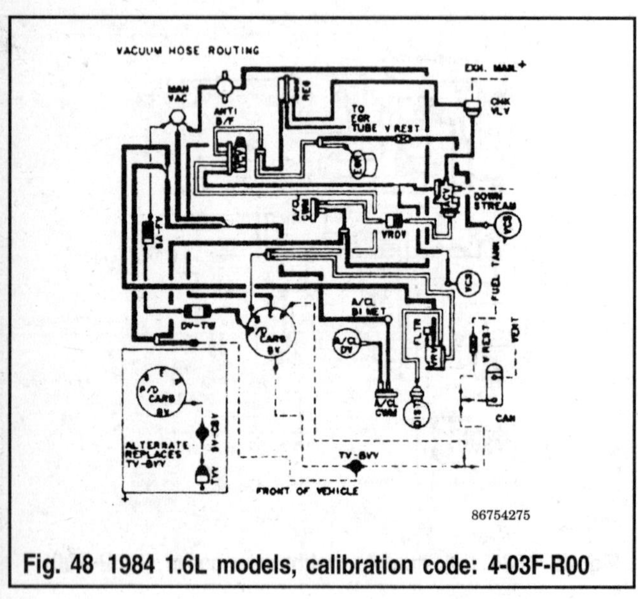

Fig. 48 1984 1.6L models, calibration code: 4-03F-R00

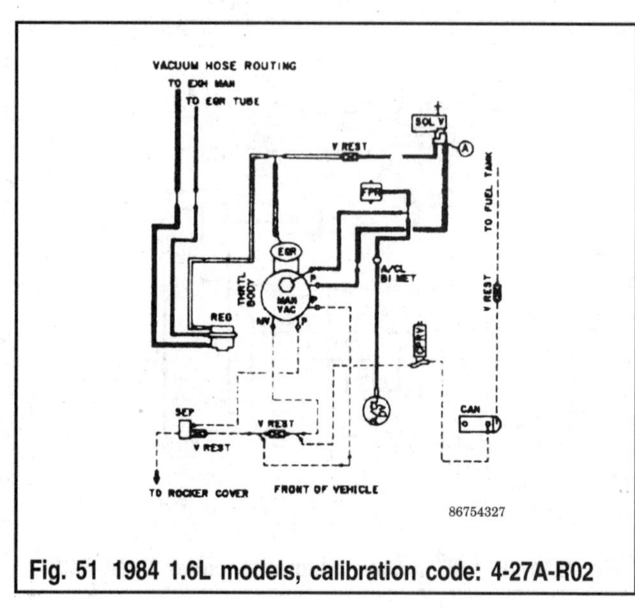

Fig. 51 1984 1.6L models, calibration code: 4-27A-R02

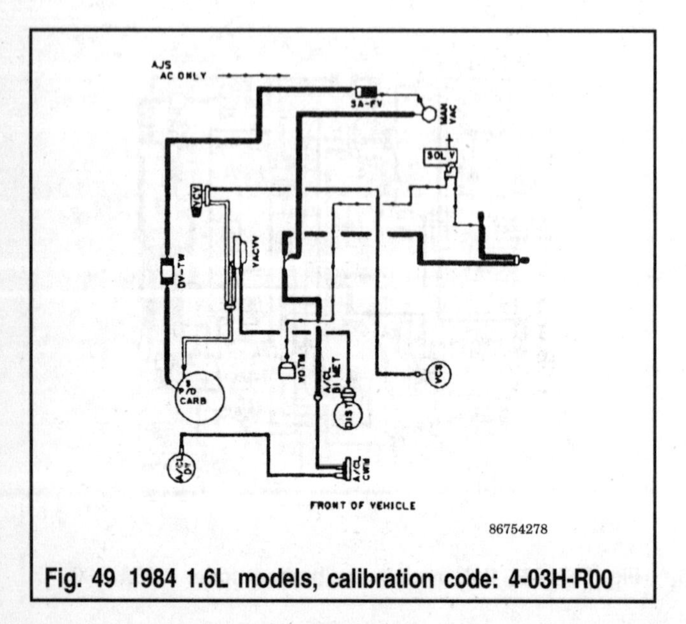

Fig. 49 1984 1.6L models, calibration code: 4-03H-R00

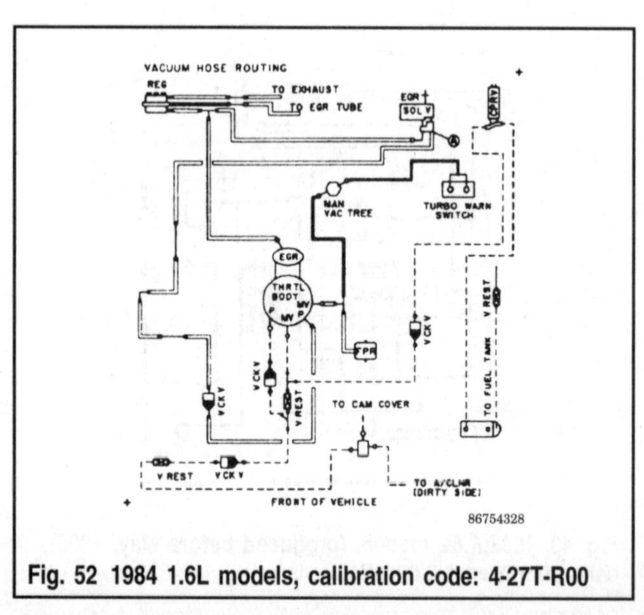

Fig. 52 1984 1.6L models, calibration code: 4-27T-R00

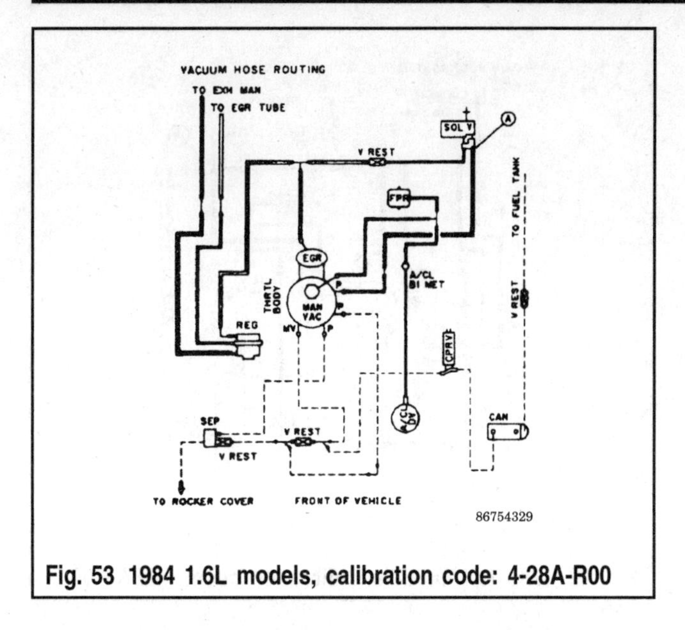

Fig. 53 1984 1.6L models, calibration code: 4-28A-R00

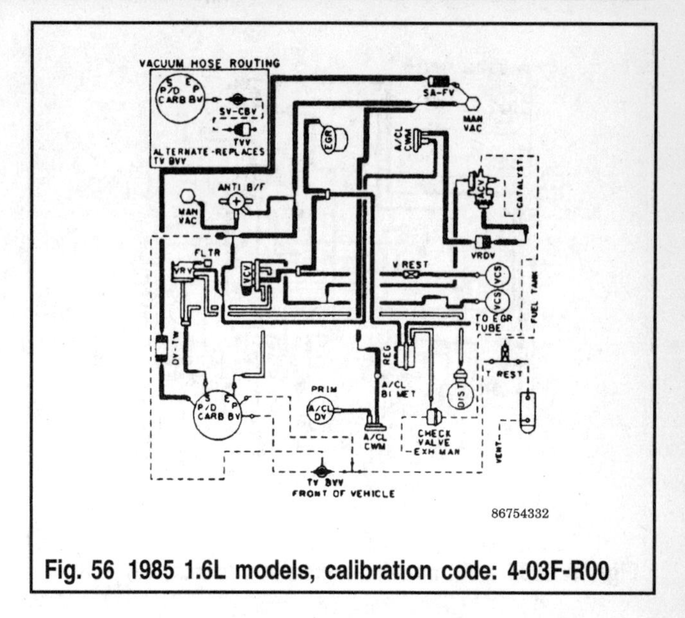

Fig. 56 1985 1.6L models, calibration code: 4-03F-R00

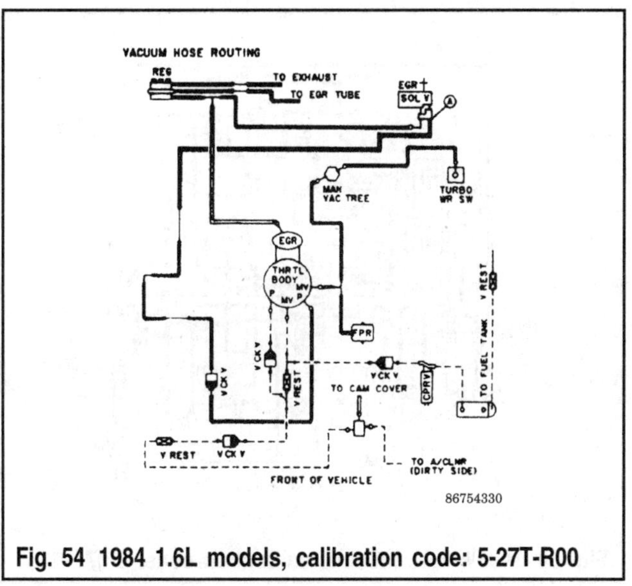

Fig. 54 1984 1.6L models, calibration code: 5-27T-R00

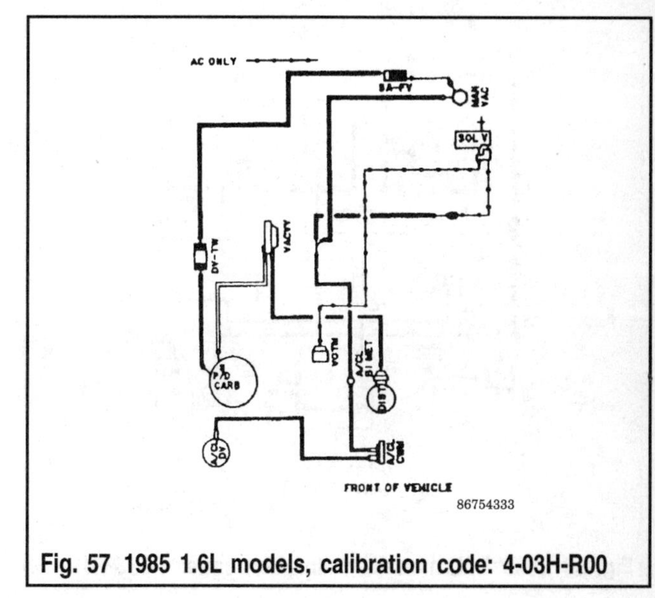

Fig. 57 1985 1.6L models, calibration code: 4-03H-R00

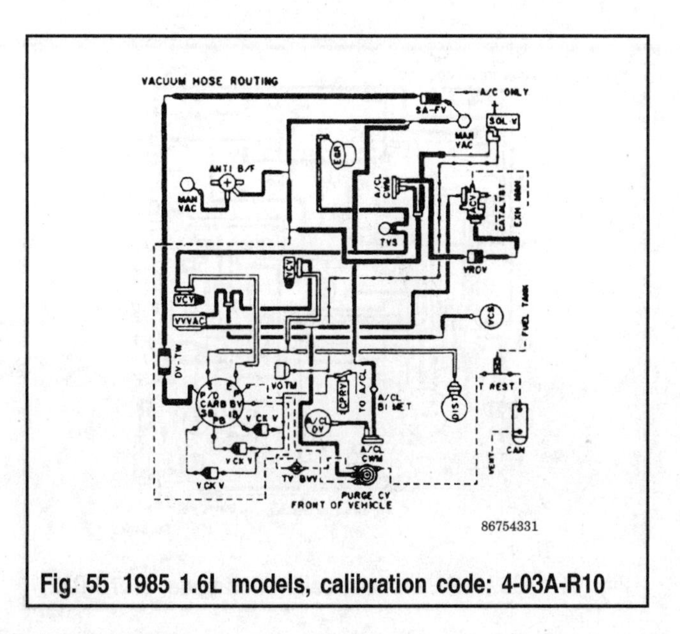

Fig. 55 1985 1.6L models, calibration code: 4-03A-R10

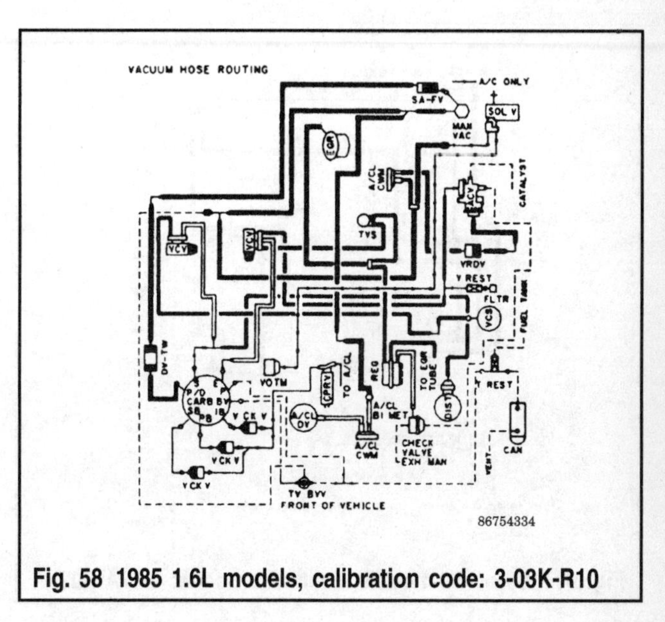

Fig. 58 1985 1.6L models, calibration code: 3-03K-R10

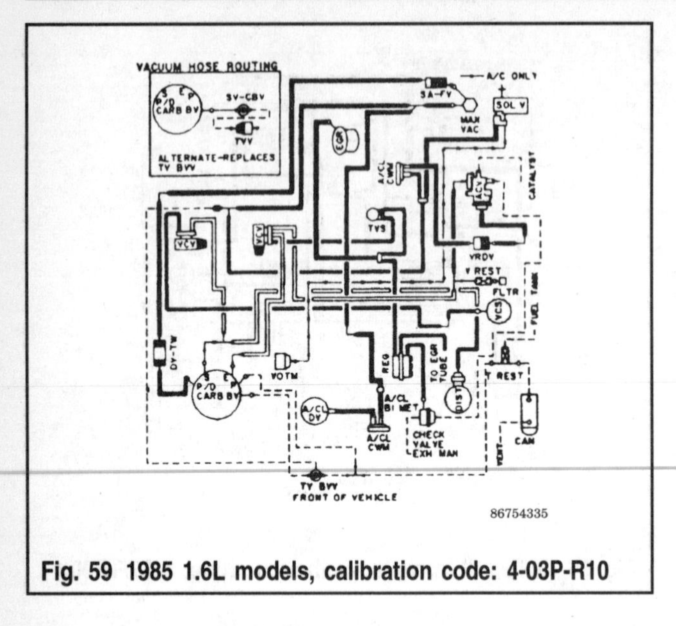

Fig. 59 1985 1.6L models, calibration code: 4-03P-R10

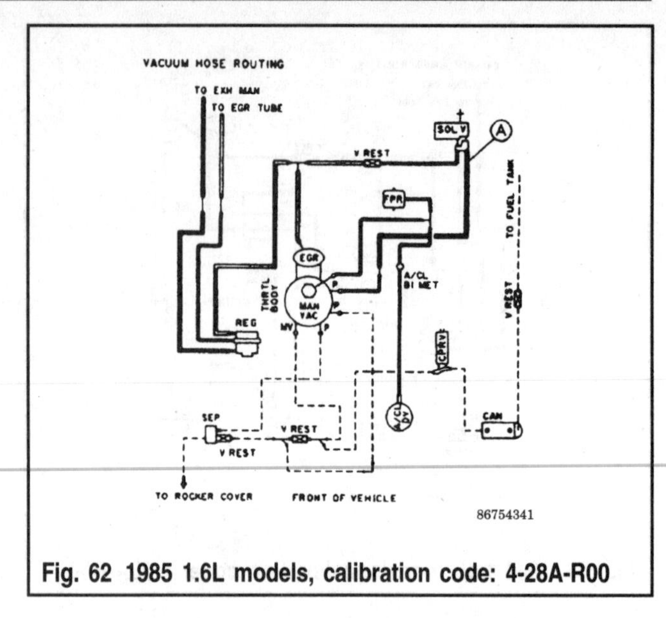

Fig. 62 1985 1.6L models, calibration code: 4-28A-R00

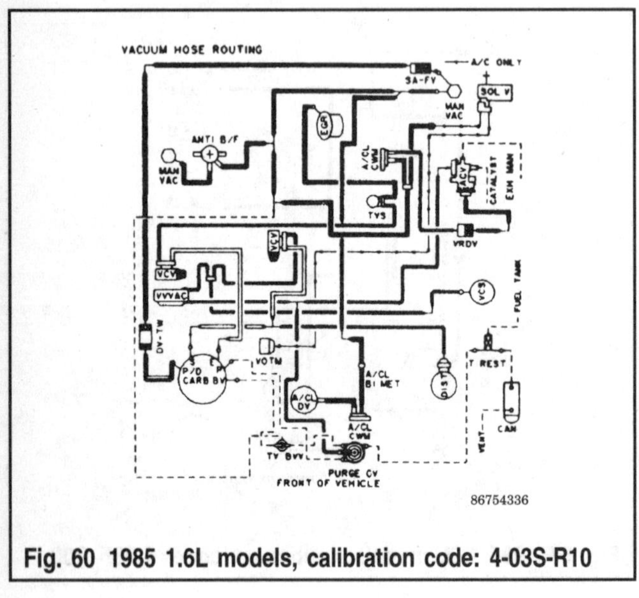

Fig. 60 1985 1.6L models, calibration code: 4-03S-R10

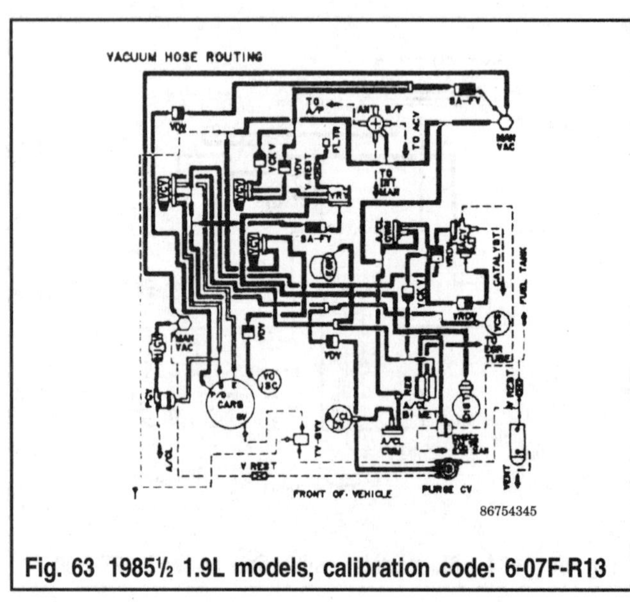

Fig. 63 1985½ 1.9L models, calibration code: 6-07F-R13

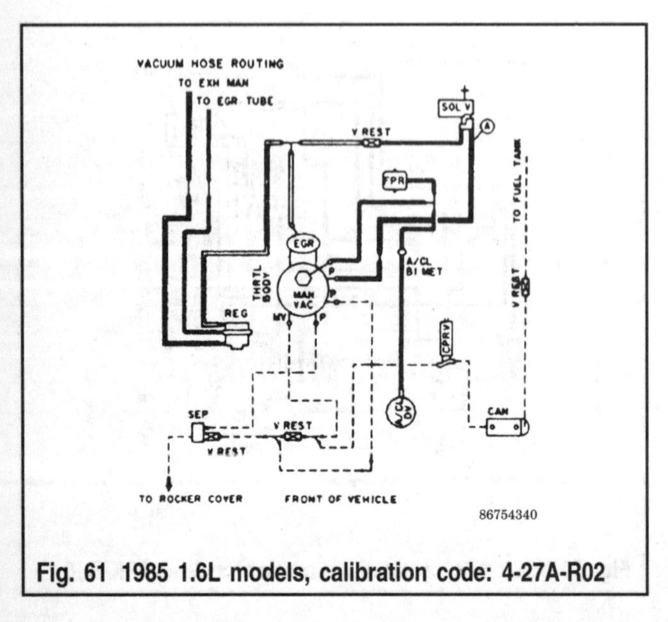

Fig. 61 1985 1.6L models, calibration code: 4-27A-R02

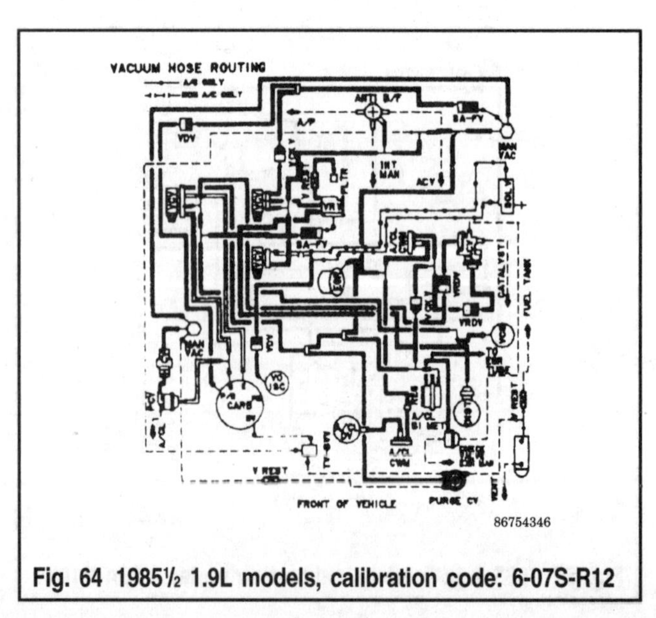

Fig. 64 1985½ 1.9L models, calibration code: 6-07S-R12

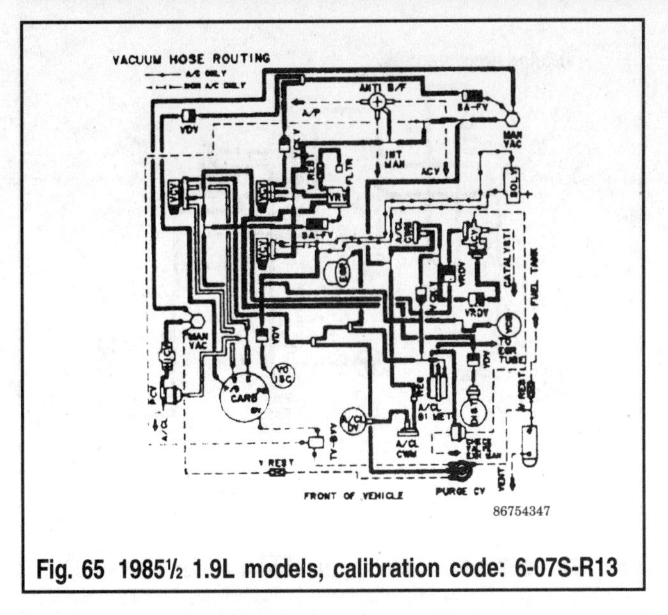

Fig. 65 1985½ 1.9L models, calibration code: 6-07S-R13

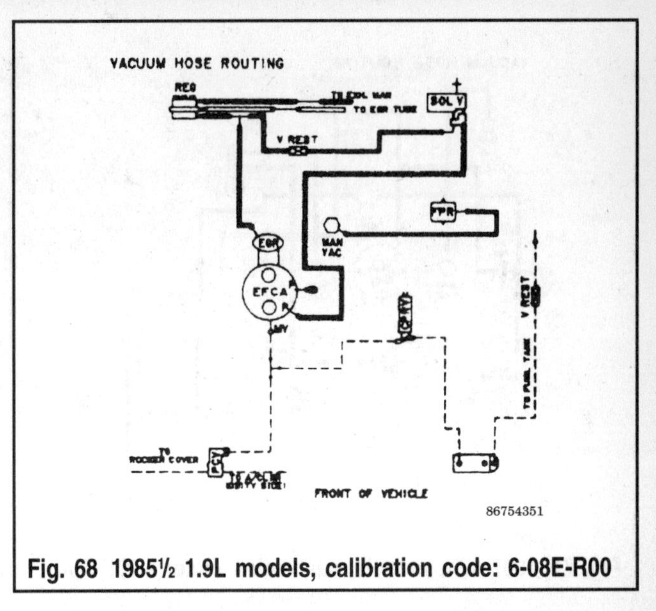

Fig. 68 1985½ 1.9L models, calibration code: 6-08E-R00

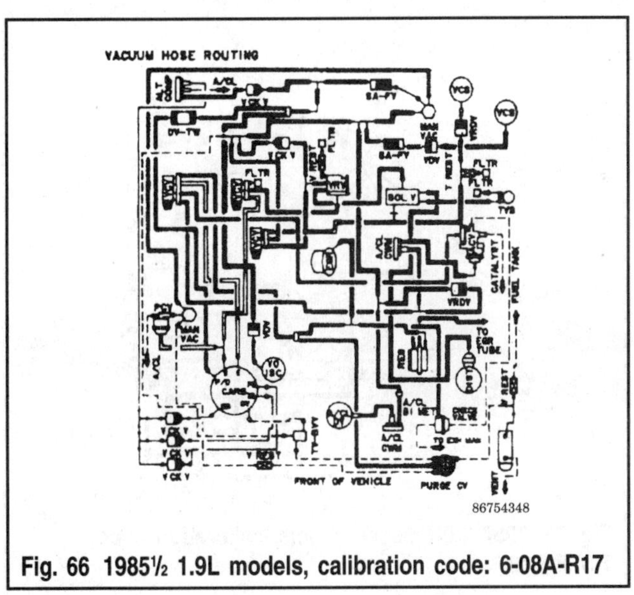

Fig. 66 1985½ 1.9L models, calibration code: 6-08A-R17

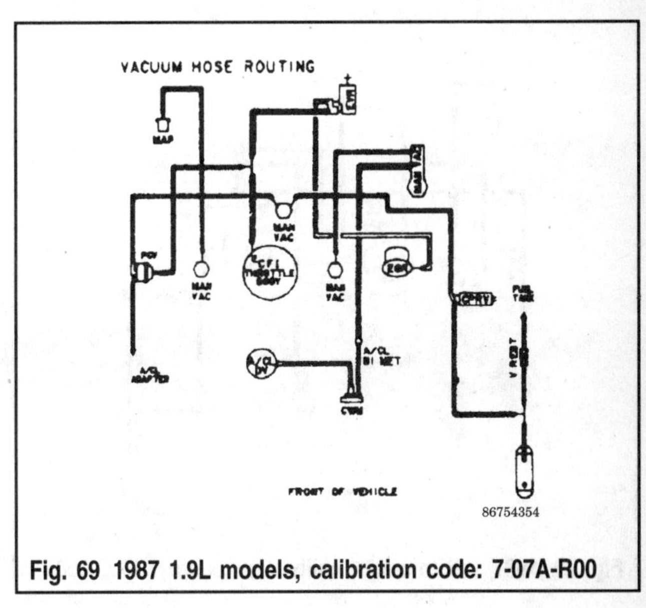

Fig. 69 1987 1.9L models, calibration code: 7-07A-R00

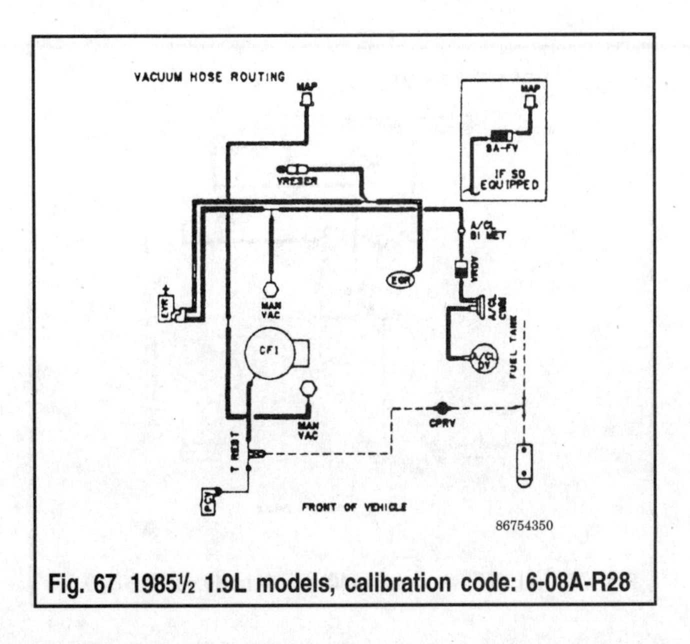

Fig. 67 1985½ 1.9L models, calibration code: 6-08A-R28

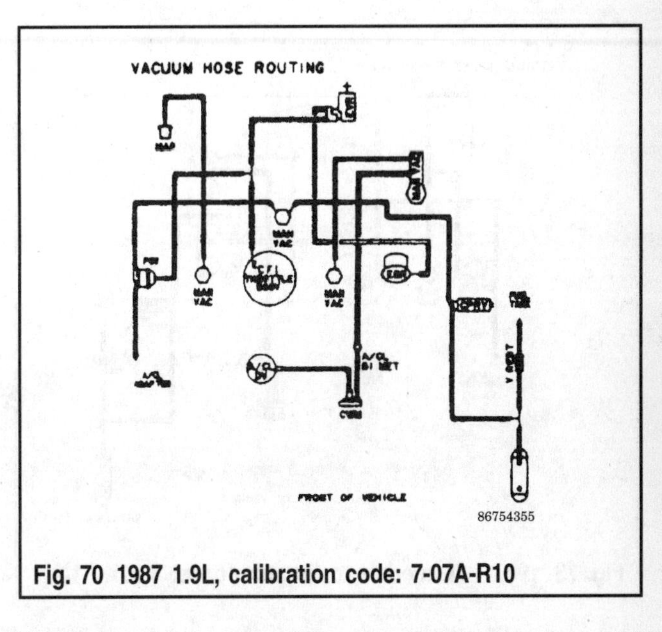

Fig. 70 1987 1.9L, calibration code: 7-07A-R10

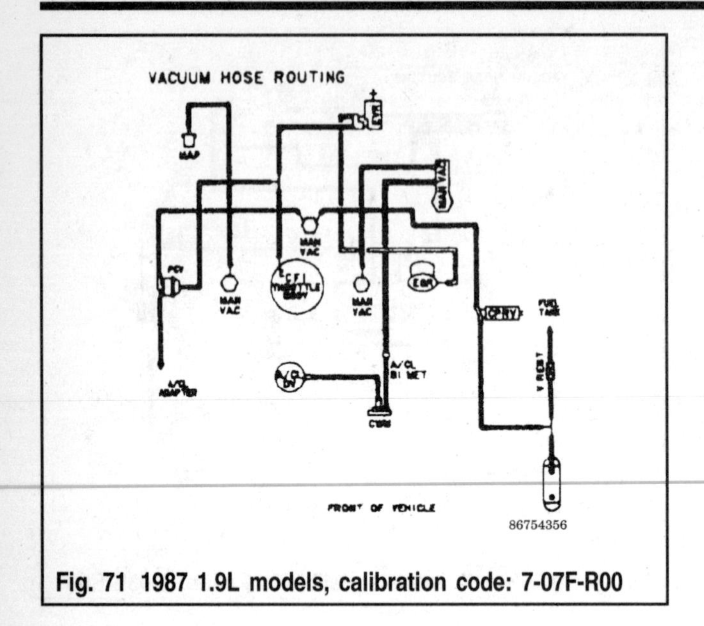

Fig. 71 1987 1.9L models, calibration code: 7-07F-R00

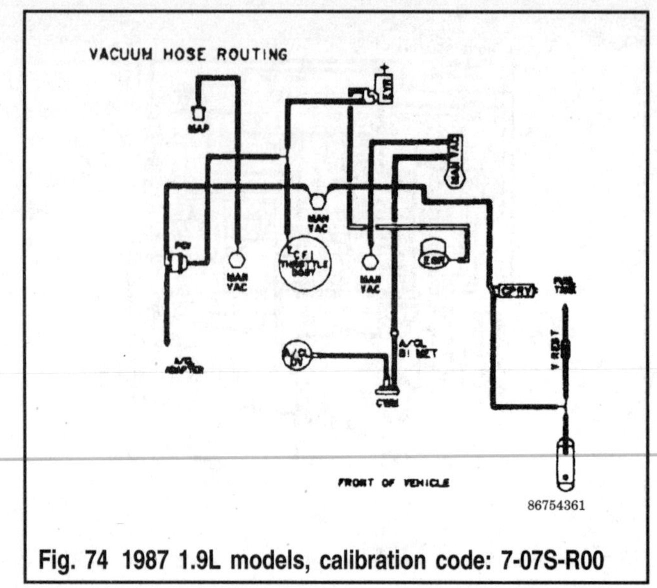

Fig. 74 1987 1.9L models, calibration code: 7-07S-R00

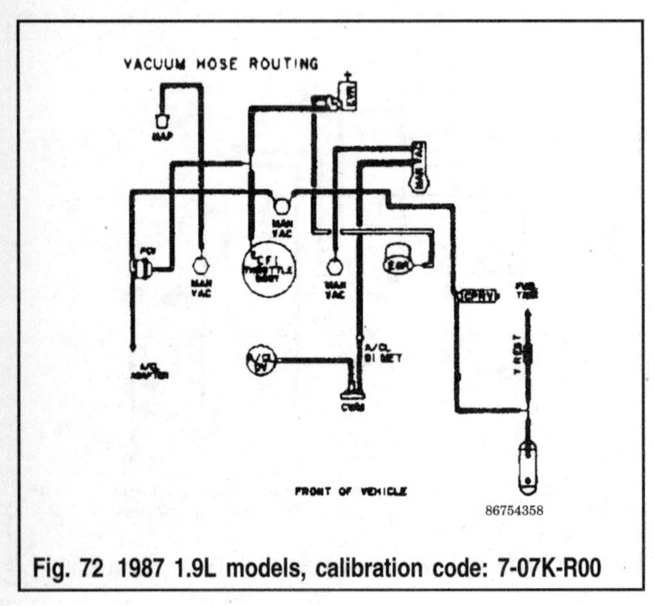

Fig. 72 1987 1.9L models, calibration code: 7-07K-R00

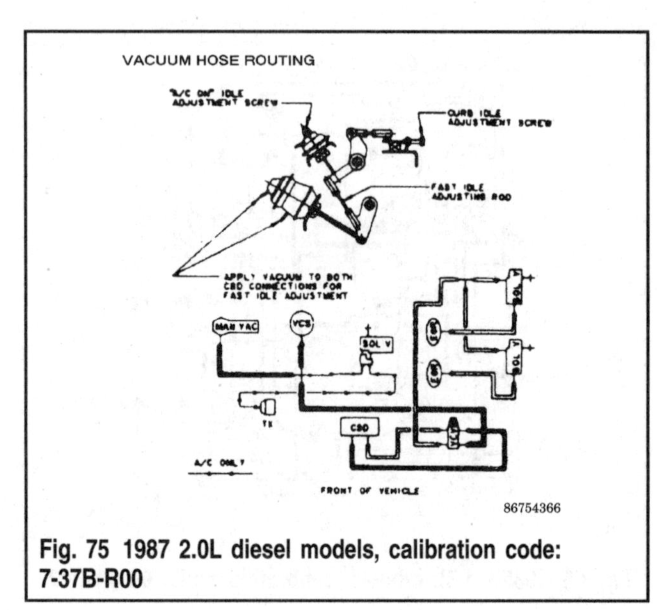

Fig. 75 1987 2.0L diesel models, calibration code: 7-37B-R00

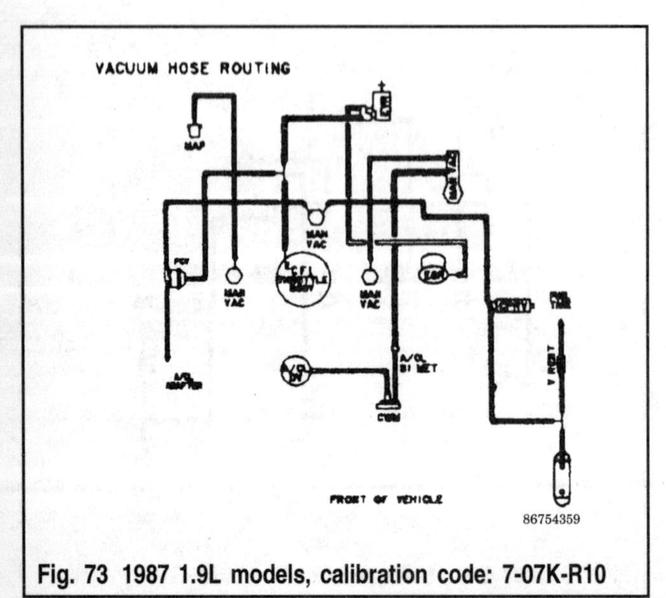

Fig. 73 1987 1.9L models, calibration code: 7-07K-R10

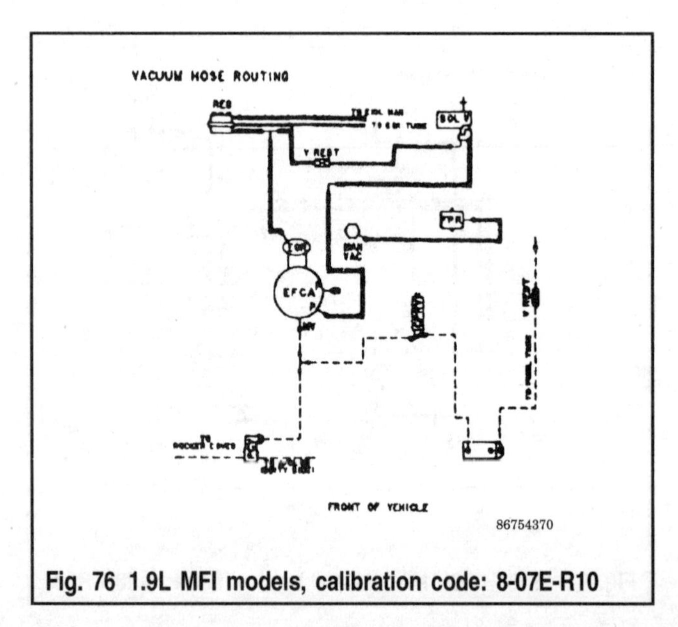

Fig. 76 1.9L MFI models, calibration code: 8-07E-R10

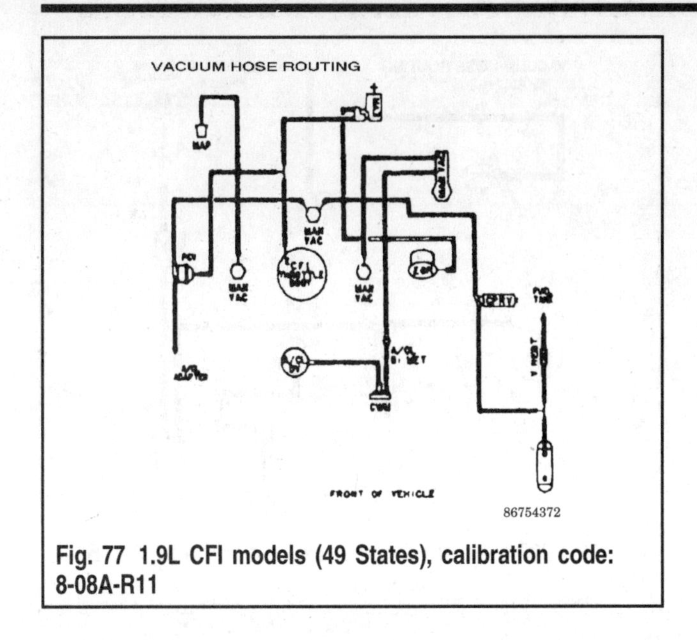

Fig. 77 1.9L CFI models (49 States), calibration code: 8-08A-R11

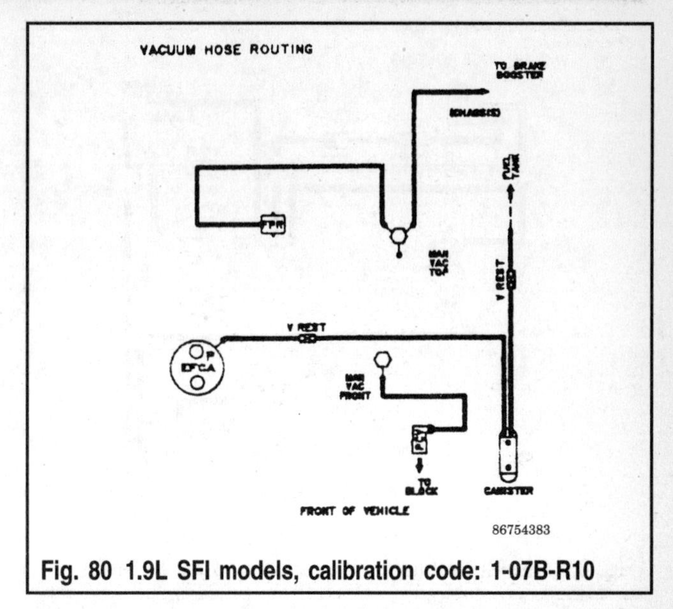

Fig. 80 1.9L SFI models, calibration code: 1-07B-R10

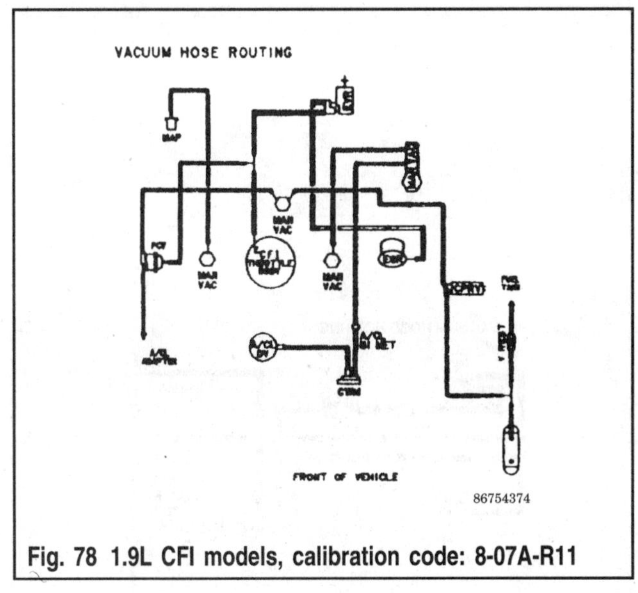

Fig. 78 1.9L CFI models, calibration code: 8-07A-R11

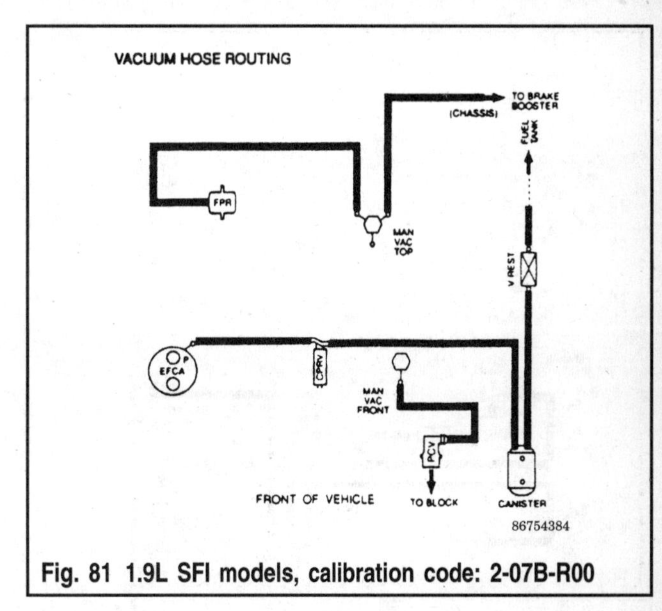

Fig. 81 1.9L SFI models, calibration code: 2-07B-R00

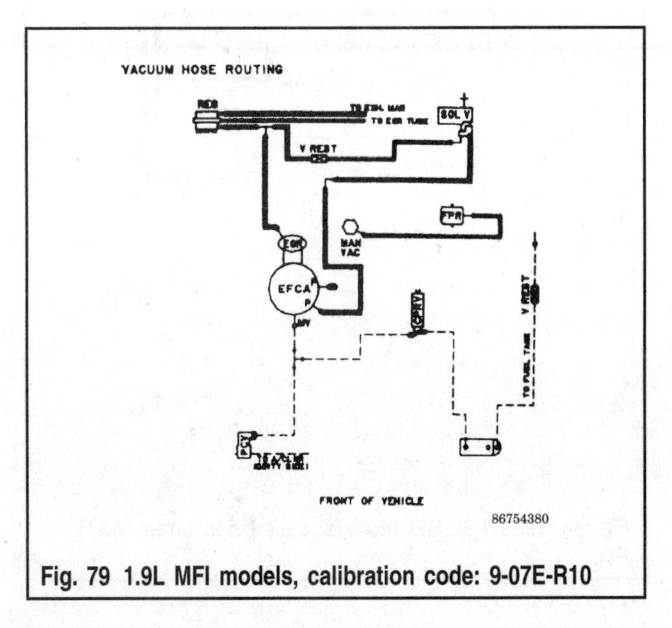

Fig. 79 1.9L MFI models, calibration code: 9-07E-R10

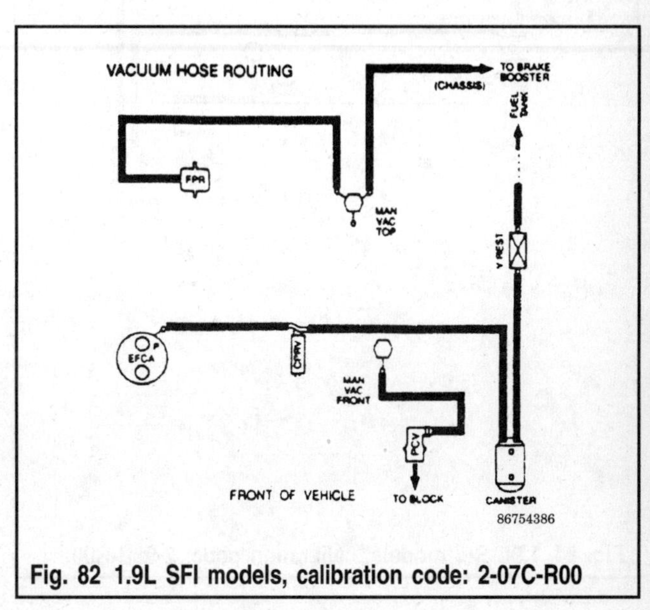

Fig. 82 1.9L SFI models, calibration code: 2-07C-R00

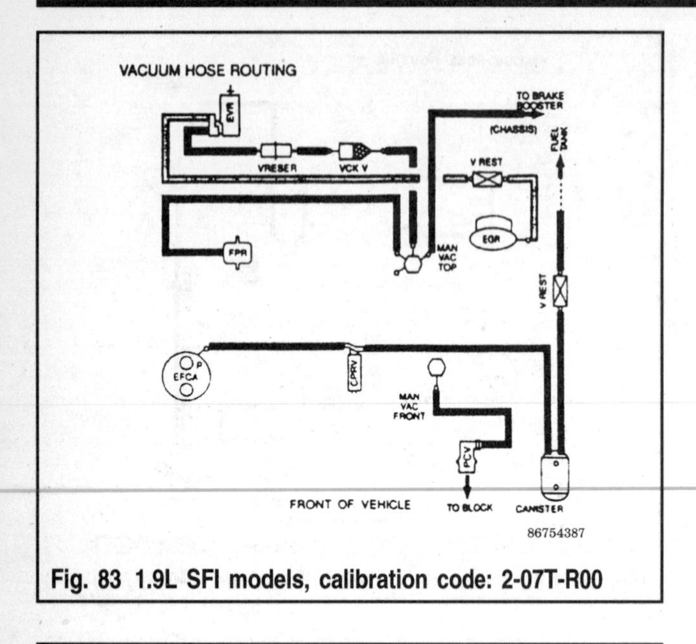

Fig. 83 1.9L SFI models, calibration code: 2-07T-R00

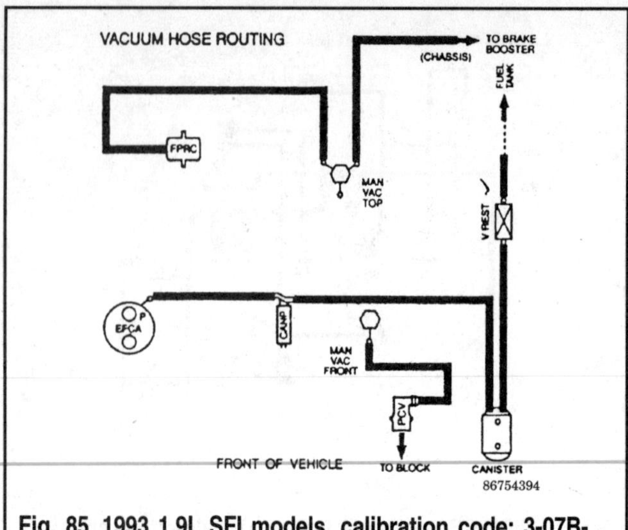

Fig. 85 1993 1.9L SFI models, calibration code: 3-07B-R00

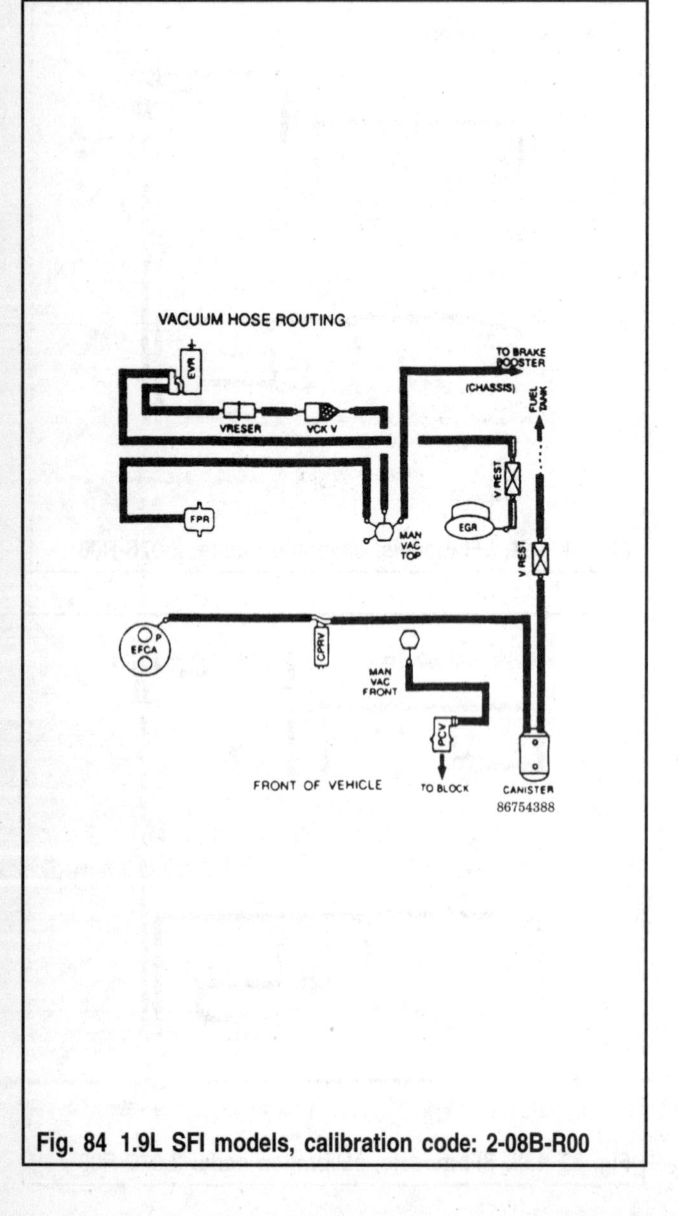

Fig. 84 1.9L SFI models, calibration code: 2-08B-R00

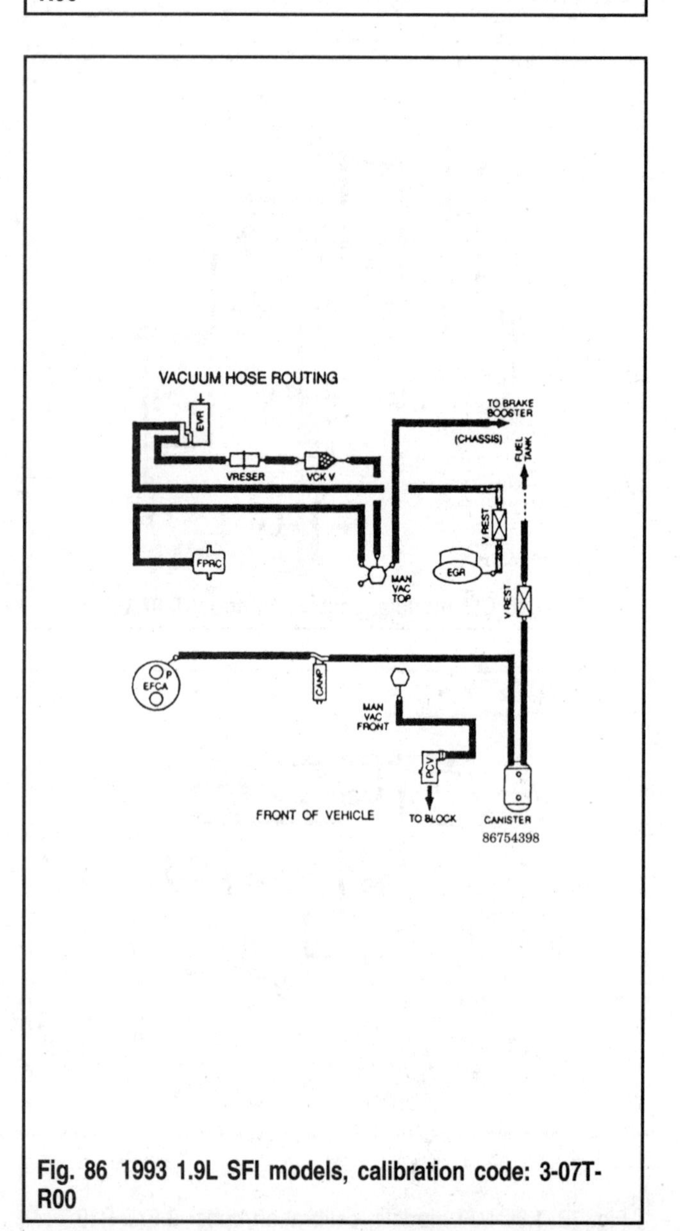

Fig. 86 1993 1.9L SFI models, calibration code: 3-07T-R00

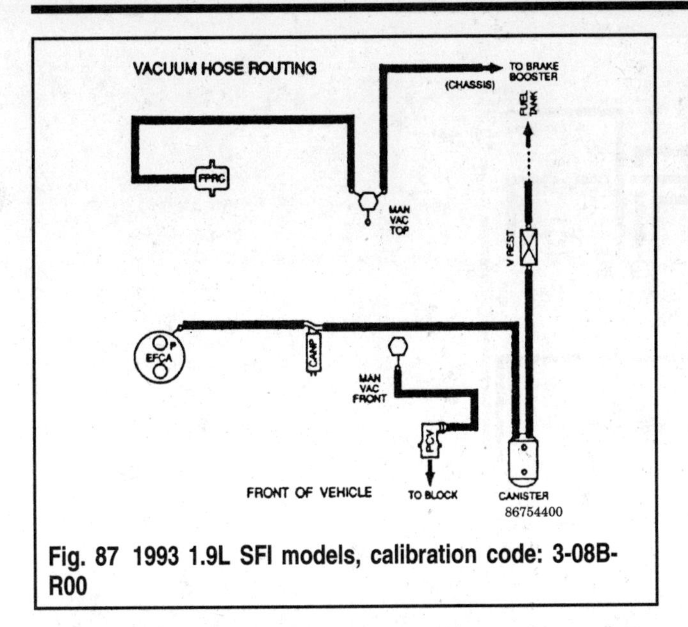

Fig. 87 1993 1.9L SFI models, calibration code: 3-08B-R00

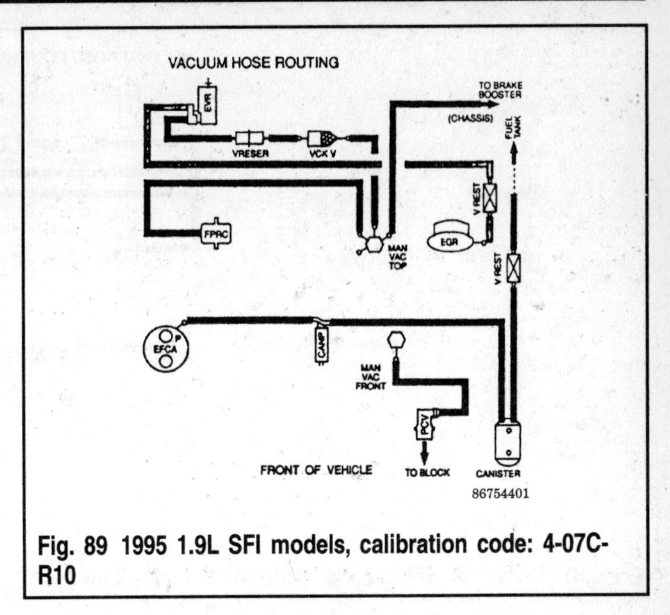

Fig. 89 1995 1.9L SFI models, calibration code: 4-07C-R10

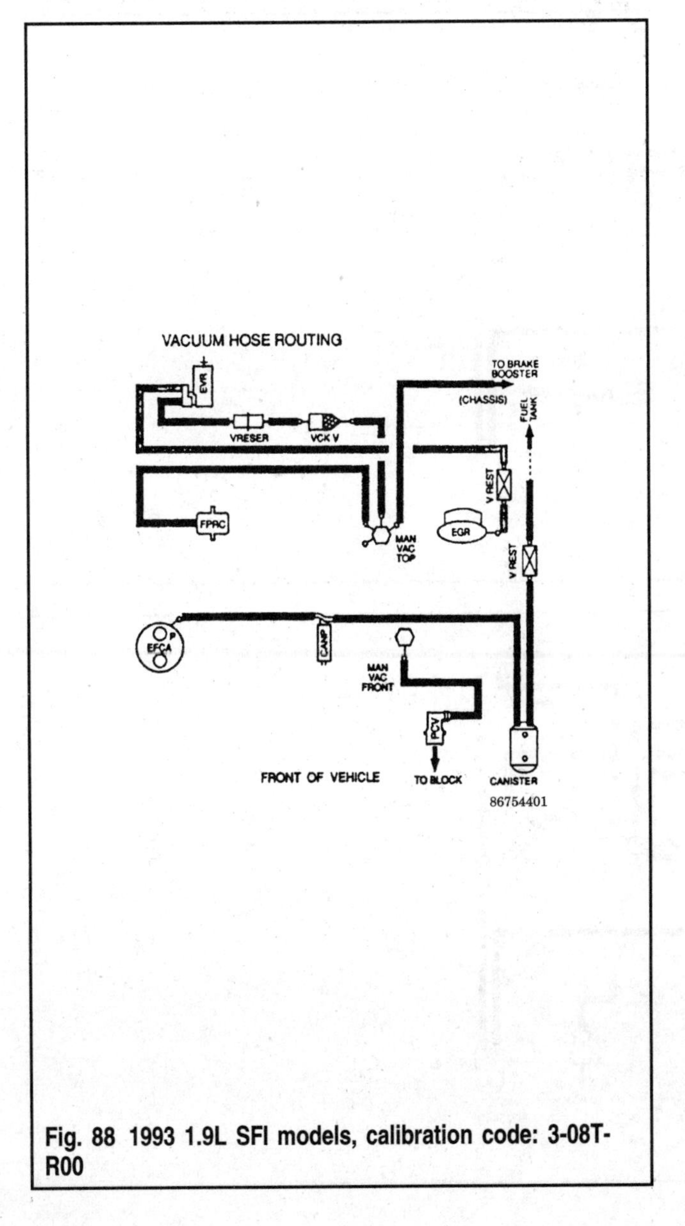

Fig. 88 1993 1.9L SFI models, calibration code: 3-08T-R00

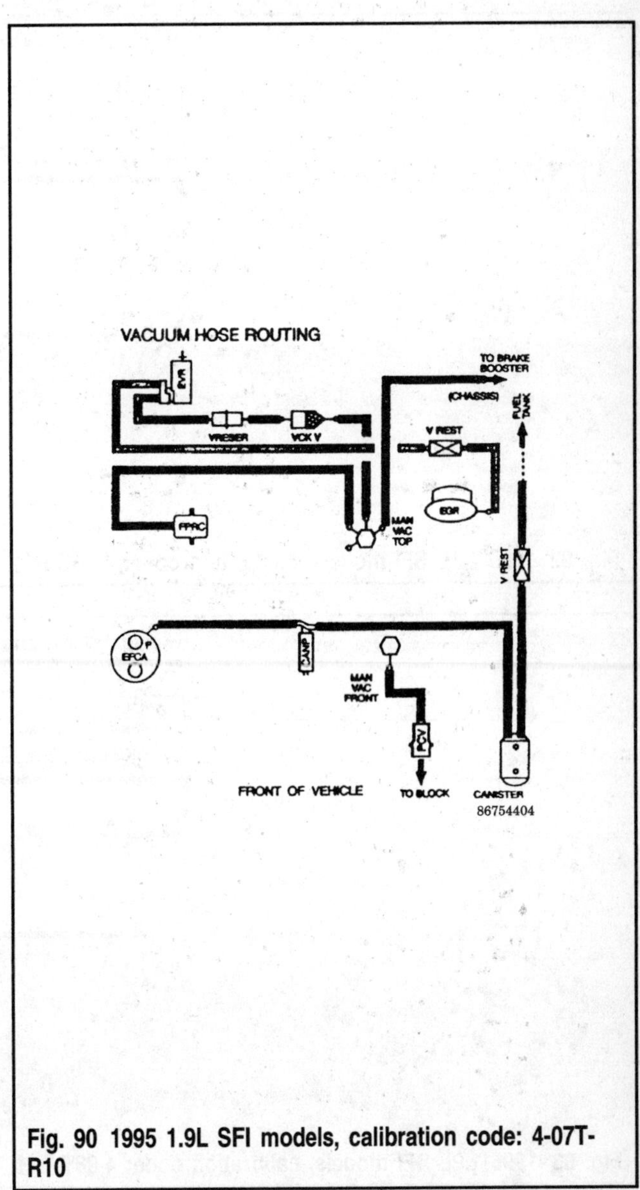

Fig. 90 1995 1.9L SFI models, calibration code: 4-07T-R10

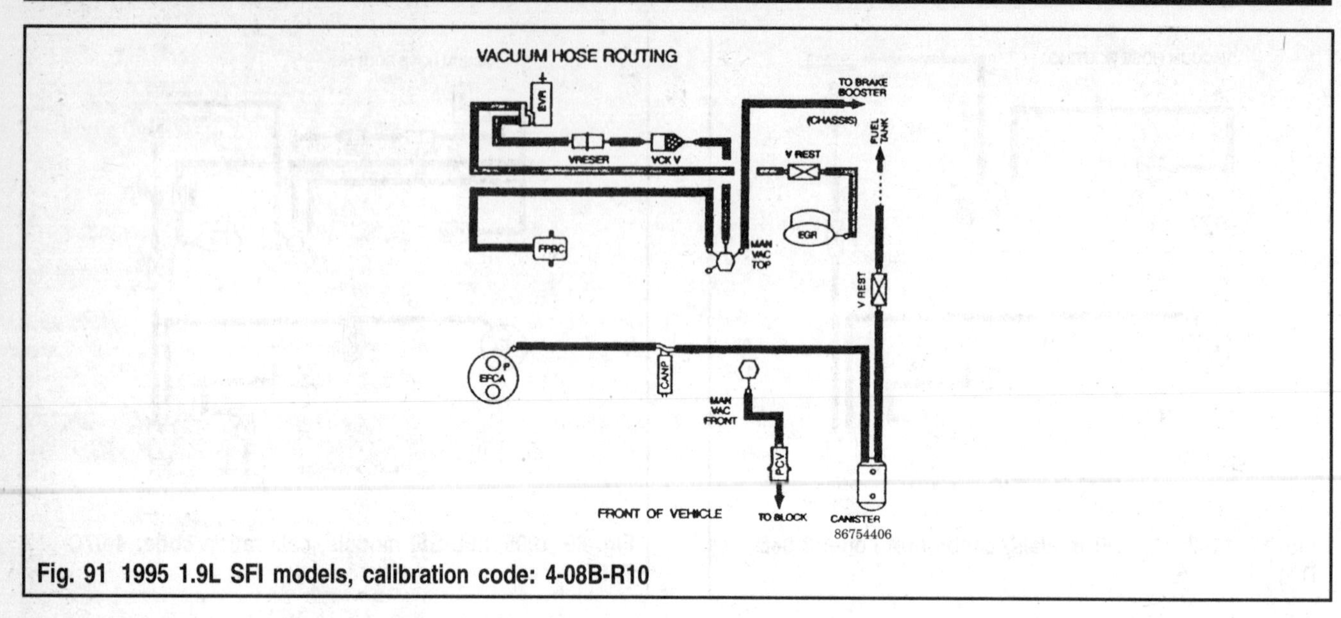

Fig. 91 1995 1.9L SFI models, calibration code: 4-08B-R10

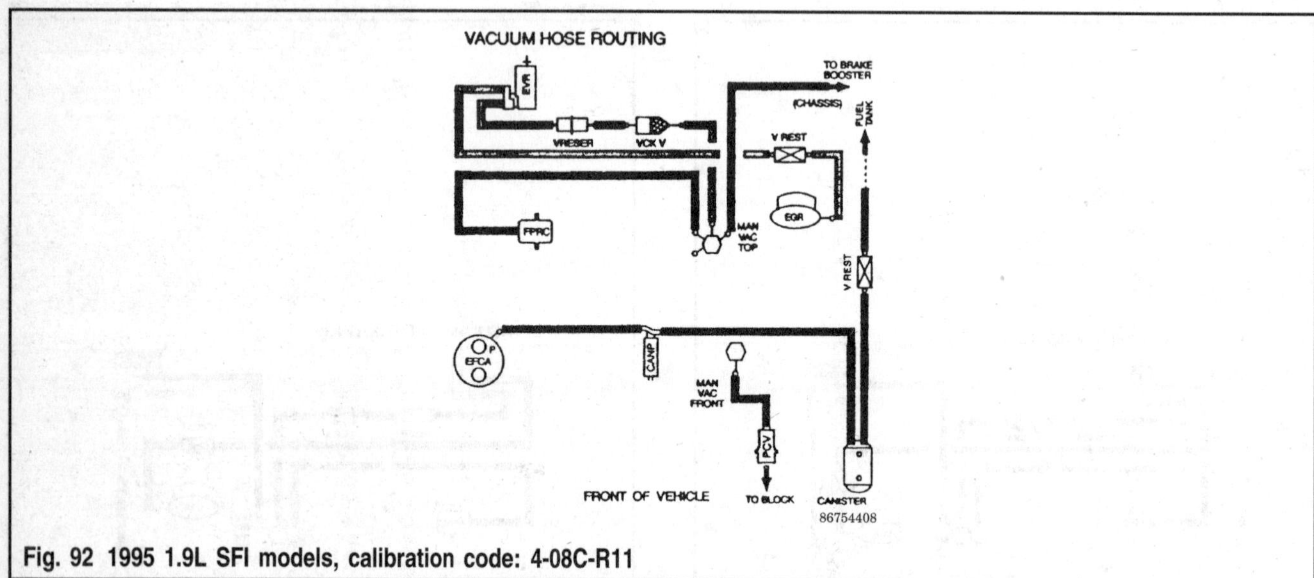

Fig. 92 1995 1.9L SFI models, calibration code: 4-08C-R11

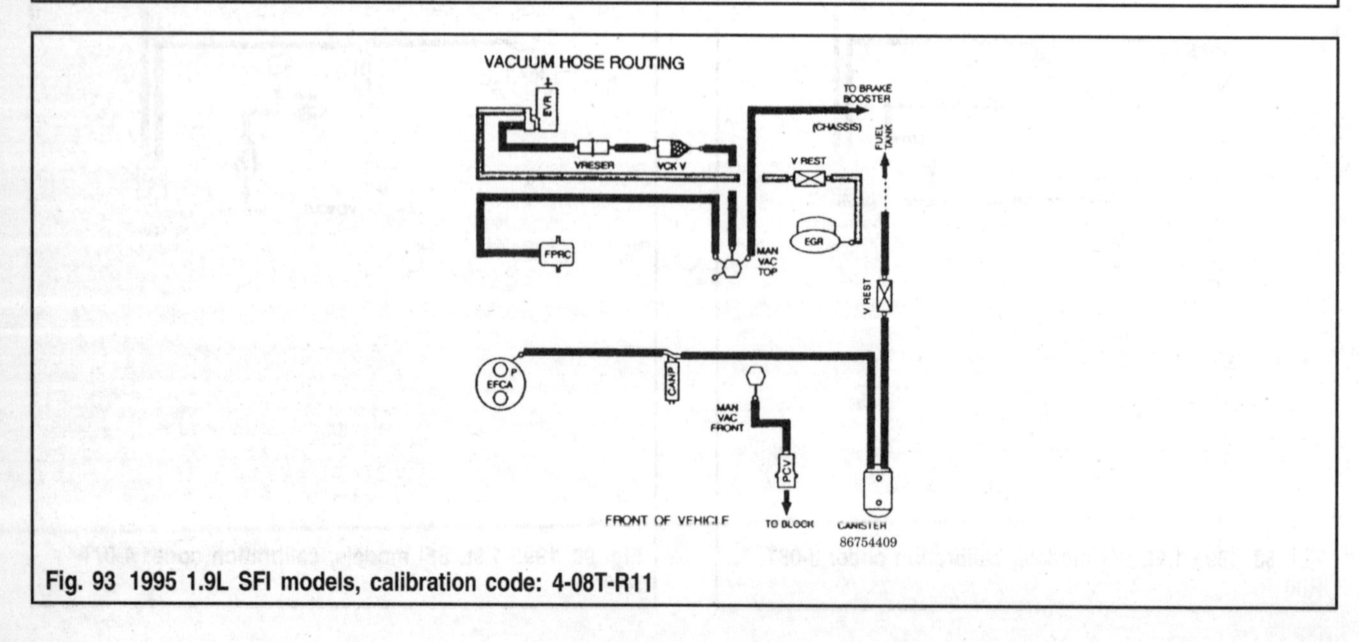

Fig. 93 1995 1.9L SFI models, calibration code: 4-08T-R11

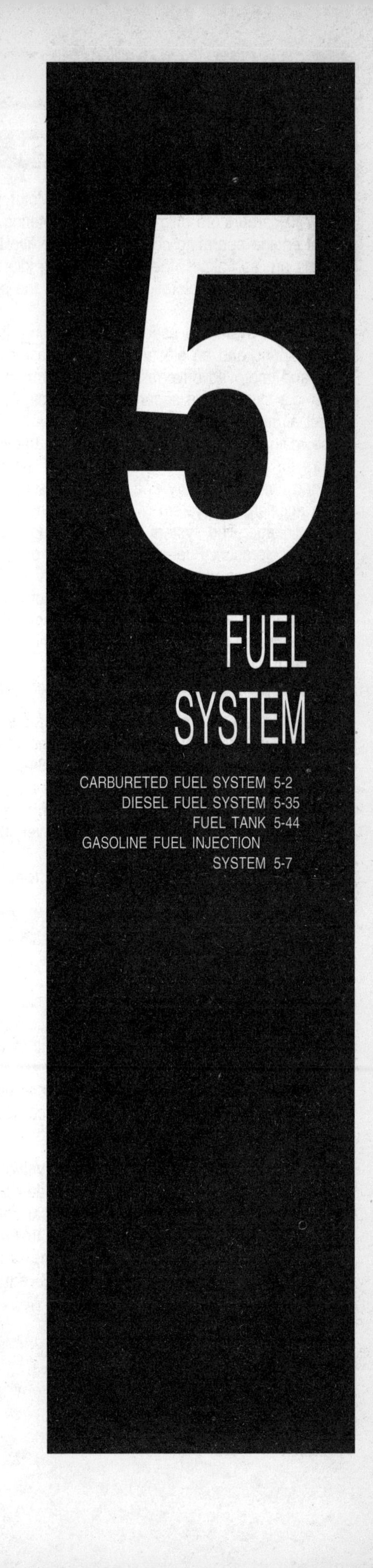

5 FUEL SYSTEM

CARBURETED FUEL SYSTEM

Carbureted vehicles which employ the Motorcraft model 740 and 5740 carburetors utilize five basic metering systems to control engine operating conditions. These five basic metering systems are as follows: the choke system, idle system, main metering system, acceleration system and the power enrichment system.

The choke system is used for cold starting. It incorporates a bimetal spring and an electric heater for faster cold weather starts and improved driveability during warm-up.

The idle system is a separate and adjustable system for the correct air/fuel mixture at both idle and low speed operation.

The main metering system provides the necessary air/fuel mixture for normal driving speeds. A main metering system is provided for both primary and secondary stages of operation.

The accelerating system is operated from the primary stage throttle linkage. The system provides fuel to the primary stage during acceleration. Fuel is provided by a diaphragm pump located on the carburetor.

The power enrichment system consists of a vacuum operated power valve and airflow regulated pullover system for the secondary carburetor barrel. The system is used in conjunction with the main metering system to provide acceptable performance during mid and heavy acceleration.

➡Besides the more common gasoline fueled 1.6L base and High Output (HO) engines, Ford also offered a methanol fueled 1.6L HO engine for 1984-85. With the exception of different carburetor jetting and alcohol-resistant seals, the methanol fueled vehicles utilize a comparable fuel delivery system. However, their fuel system service specifications may vary. Consult your local Ford/Mercury dealer for further information.

Mechanical Fuel Pump

▶ See Figure 1

The fuel pump is bolted to the left rear side of the cylinder head. It is mechanically operated by an eccentric lobe on the camshaft. A pushrod between the eccentric lobe and the rocker arm drives the pump.

The pump cannot be disassembled for any type of service. If testing indicates it is not within performance specifications, the pump assembly must be replaced.

➡The fuel pump has a rollover check valve in accordance with Federal Motor Vehicle Safety Standards (FMVSS). In the event of an accident in which the car rolls upside down, the valve is intended to prevent unwanted fuel spillage. When replacement of the fuel pump is necessary, the new pump must meet the same FMVSS requirement.

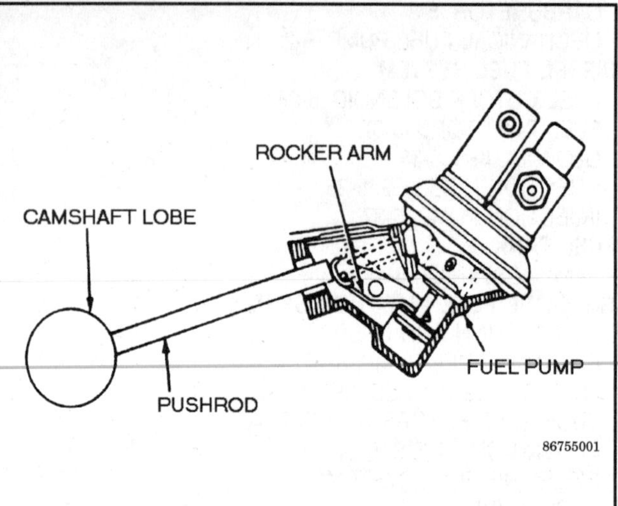

Fig. 1 A common mechanical fuel pump — 1.6L and 1.9L carbureted engines

REMOVAL & INSTALLATION

▶ See Figure 2

****CAUTION**

When working near the fuel system, do not smoke or have an open flame of any type nearby.

1. Disconnect the negative battery cable.
2. Loosen the threaded fuel line connection(s) a small amount. Do not remove lines at this time.
3. Loosen the mounting bolts approximately two turns. Apply force manually to loosen the fuel pump if gasket is stuck. Rotate the engine until the fuel pump camshaft lobe is near its low position. The tension on the fuel pump will be greatly reduced at the low camshaft position.
4. Disconnect the fuel pump inlet and outlet lines.
5. Remove the fuel pump attaching bolts and remove the pump and gasket. Discard the old gasket and replace with a new one.
6. Measure the fuel pump pushrod length. It should be at least 2.36 in. (60mm) in length. Replace if it is out of specification.

To install:

7. Remove all fuel pump gasket material from the engine and the fuel pump if installing the original pump.
8. Install the attaching bolts into the fuel pump and install a new gasket. Position the fuel pump on the mounting pad. Tighten the attaching bolts alternately and evenly and tighten to 11-19 ft. lbs. (15-25 Nm).
9. Install fuel lines to fuel pump. Start the threaded fitting by hand to avoid cross-threading. Tighten outlet nut to 15-18 ft. lbs. (20-24 Nm).
10. Start the engine and inspect for fuel leaks.
11. Stop the engine and check all fuel pump fuel line connections for fuel leaks by running a finger under the connections. Check for oil leaks at the fuel pump mounting gasket.

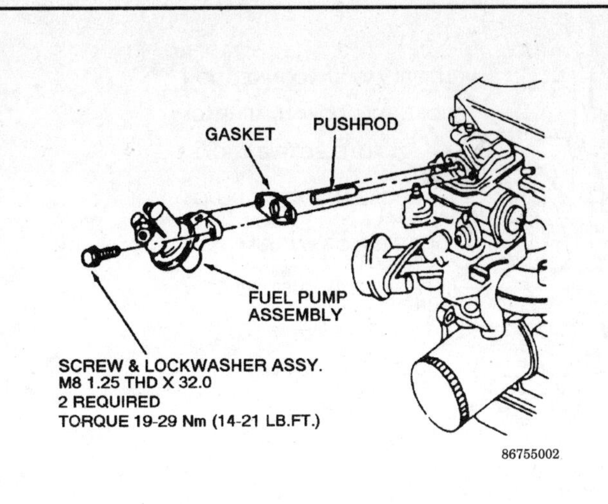

Fig. 2 Exploded view of mechanical fuel pump mounting

TESTING

The fuel pump can fail in two ways: it can fail to provide a sufficient volume of gasoline under the proper pressure to the carburetor, or it can develop an internal or external leak. An external leak will be evident; not so with an internal leak. A quick check for an internal leak is to remove the oil dipstick and examine the oil on it. A fuel pump with an internal leak will leak fuel into the oil pan. If the oil on the dipstick is very thin and smells of gas, a defective fuel pump could be the cause.

➡If the engine is excessively hot, allow it to cool for approximately 20-30 minutes.

Capacity (Volume) Test

1. Remove the carburetor air cleaner.
2. Wrap a shop rag around the fuel line and slowly disconnect the fuel line. Use an 11/16 in. backup wrench on the hex of the filter to prevent damage.
3. Connect a suitable rubber hose and clamp it to the fuel line.
4. Place a non-breakable 1 pint (473ml) minimum container at the end of the rubber hose.
5. Crank the engine 10 revolutions. If little or no fuel flows from the hose during the 10th revolution, the fuel pump is inoperative. Replace the fuel pump.
6. If the fuel flow is adequate, proceed to the following pressure test.

Pressure Test

1. Connect a suitable pressure gauge, 0-15 psi (0-103 kPa), to fuel filter end of fuel line. No tee is required.
2. Start engine and read pressure after 10 seconds. Pressure should read 4.5-6.5 psi (31-45 kPa) with fuel return line closed at fuel filter. Replace fuel pump if pressure is above or below specification.
3. Disconnect fuel pump and connect fuel line to fuel filter. Use a backup wrench on the filter and tighten fuel line to 15-18 ft. lbs. (20-24 Nm).

Carburetor

➧ See Figures 3, 4 and 5

ADJUSTMENTS

Most carburetor adjustments are factory-set to reduce engine emissions and improve performance.

Motorcraft 740 and 5740

FAST IDLE

1. Place the transaxle in P or N.
2. Bring the engine to normal operating temperature.
3. Disconnect and plug the vacuum hose at the EGR and purge valves.
4. Identify the vacuum source to the air bypass section of the air supply control valve. If a vacuum hose is connected to the carburetor, disconnect the hose and plug the hose at the air supply control valve.
5. Place the fast idle adjustment on the second step of the fast idle cam. Run the engine until the cooling fan comes on.
6. While the cooling fan is on, check the fast idle rpm. If adjustment is necessary, loosen the locknut and adjust to specification on under-hood decal.
7. Remove all plugs and reconnect hoses to their original position.

FAST IDLE CAM

1. Set the fast idle screw on the kickdown step of the cam against the shoulder of the top step.
2. Manually close the primary choke plate, and measure the distance between the downstream side of the choke plate and the air horn wall.
3. Adjust the right fork of the choke bimetal shaft, which engages the fast idle cam, by bending the fork up and down to obtain the required clearance.

DASHPOT

1. Set the throttle to curb idle position.
2. Fully depress the dashpot stem.
3. Measure the distance between the stem and the throttle lever.
4. Adjust by loosening the locknut and turning the dashpot.

FLOAT LEVEL

➧ See Figure 6

1. Unfasten the screws which fasten the air horn to the main body of the carburetor.
2. Remove the air horn from the carburetor.
3. Hold the air horn upside down, at about a 45° angle with the air horn gasket in position.
4. Use the gauge supplied with the rebuilding kit to measure the clearance between the float toe and air horn casting.
5. Adjust, if necessary, by removing the float and bending the adjusting tang. Use care when handling the float.

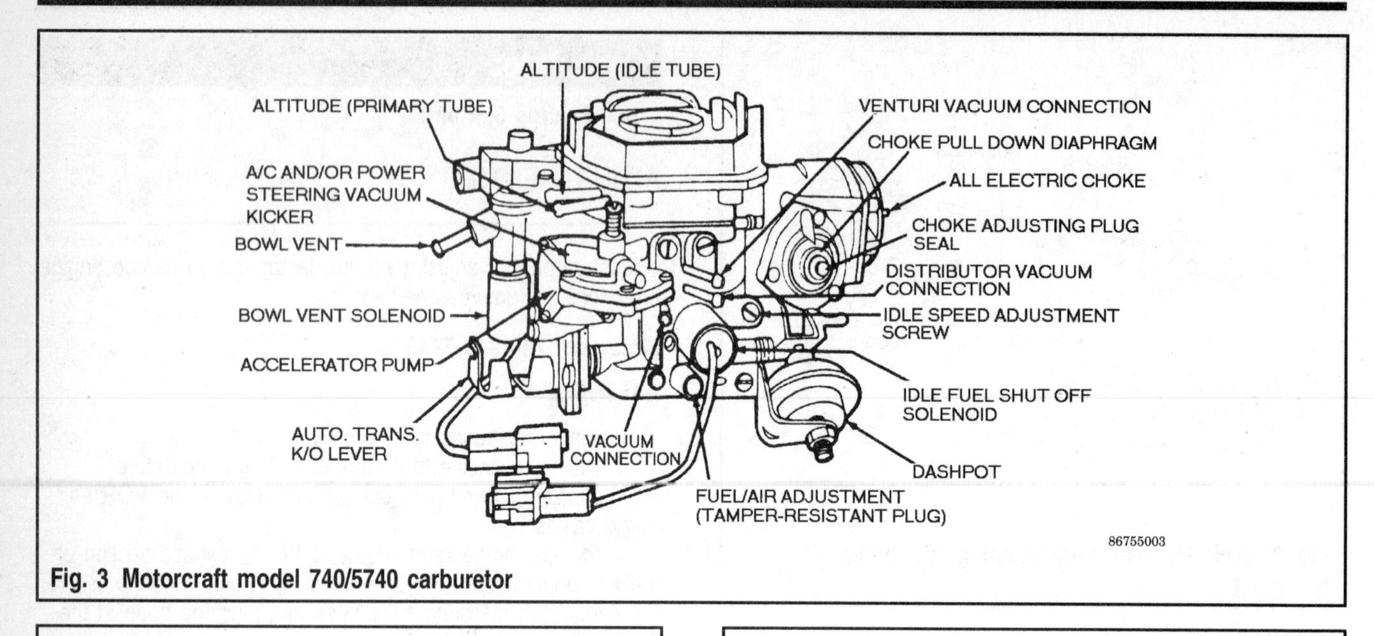

Fig. 3 Motorcraft model 740/5740 carburetor

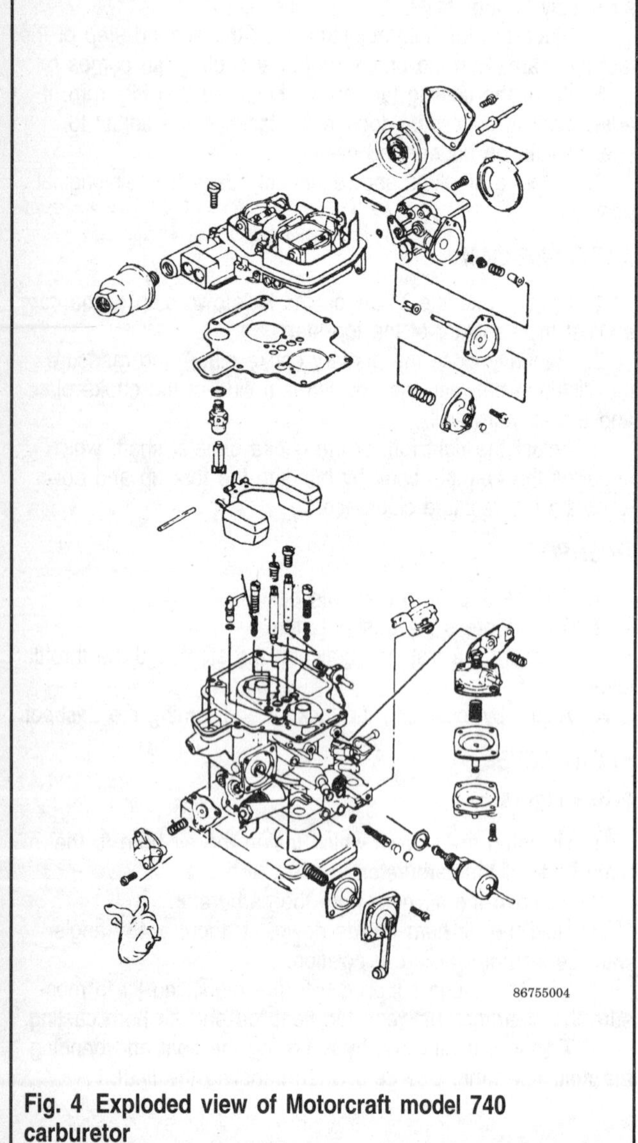

Fig. 4 Exploded view of Motorcraft model 740 carburetor

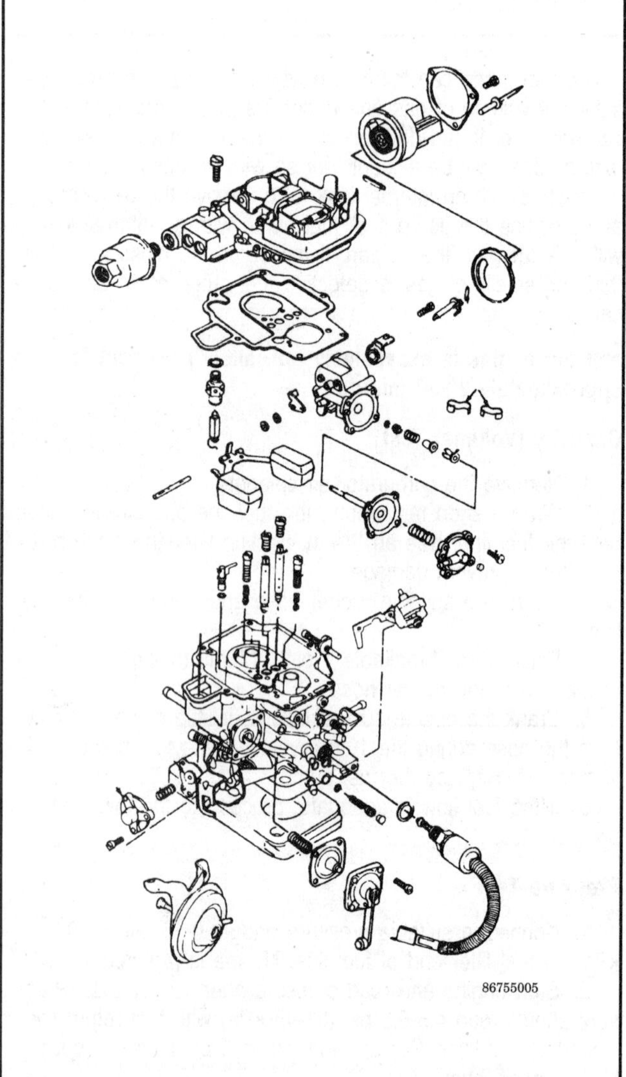

Fig. 5 Exploded view of Motorcraft model 5740 carburetor

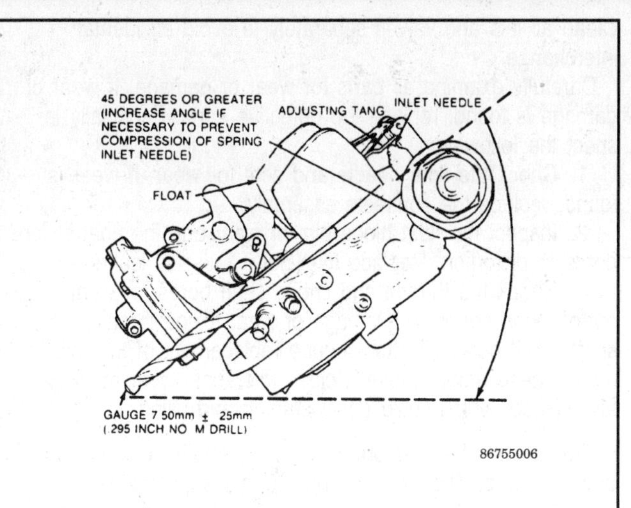

Fig. 6 Adjust the float level as shown — model 740/5740 carburetors

FLOAT DROP

➧ **See Figure 7**

1. Unfasten the screws which fasten the air horn to the main body of the carburetor.
2. Remove the air horn from the carburetor.
3. Hold the air horn in its normal installed position.
4. Measure the clearance from the gasket to the bottom of the float. This distance should be 1.38-2.00 in. (35-51mm).
5. Adjust, if necessary, by removing the float and bending the float drop adjusting tab.

REMOVAL & INSTALLATION

CAUTION

When working near the fuel system, do not smoke or have any open flame of any type nearby.

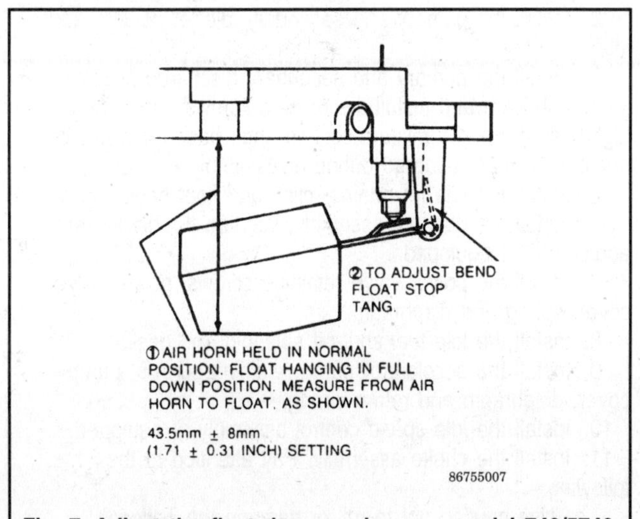

Fig. 7 Adjust the float drop as shown — model 740/5740 carburetors

Motorcraft 740 and 5740

1. Disconnect the negative battery cable.
2. Remove the air cleaner assembly.
3. Disconnect the throttle cable and speed control cable, if equipped.
4. Tag, then disconnect the bowl vent tube, altitude compensator tubes (idle, primary and secondary, if so equipped), air conditioning and/or power steering vacuum kicker (if so equipped).
5. Tag, then disconnect the EGR vacuum tube, venturi vacuum tube, distributor vacuum vacuum tube, ISC vacuum tube (if so equipped), choke pulldown motor vacuum tube, and fuel inlet line at filter.
6. Disconnect the idle solenoid wire and choke cap terminal connectors.
7. Remove the automatic transaxle throttle valve (TV) linkage, if so equipped.
8. Remove the four carburetor flange mounting nuts, using Tool T74P-95-10-A or equivalent. Remove the Wide Open Throttle (WOT) A/C cut-out switch, if so equipped.
9. Remove the carburetor assembly from the manifold.

To install:

10. Clean all gasket surfaces. Replace any gasket(s) as necessary.
11. Position the carburetor on the spacer and install the WOT A/C cut-out switch and attaching nuts, if so equipped.

➡To prevent leakage, distortion or damage to the carburetor body flange, alternately tighten each nut to specifications.

12. Install the automatic transaxle throttle valve (TV) linkage, if so equipped. Perform the TV adjustment.
13. Connect the choke cap and the idle solenoid terminal connectors.
14. Connect the fuel inlet line at the filter.
15. Reconnect: EGR vacuum tube, venturi vacuum tube, distributor vacuum vacuum tube, ISC vacuum tube (if so equipped), choke pulldown motor vacuum tube, and fuel inlet line at filter.
16. Reconnect: bowl vent tube, altitude compensator tubes (idle, primary and secondary if so equipped), air conditioning and/or power steering vacuum kicker (if so equipped).
17. Reconnect the throttle cable and speed control cable.
18. Start the engine and check for leaks. If any leaks are detected, shut off the engine immediately and correct the problem.
19. Install the air cleaner assembly.
20. Reconnect the negative battery cable.
21. Check and/or adjust the curb idle and fast idle speed as necessary.

OVERHAUL

Overhaul the carburetor in a clean, dust free area. Carefully disassembly the carburetor, referring often to the exploded views. Keep all similar and look-alike parts segregated during disassembly and cleaning to avoid accidental interchange during assembly. Make a note of all jet sizes.

➡To avoid damage to the carburetor or throttle plates, install carburetor legs on the base before disassembling or use an EGR spacer as a holding fixture. If legs are not available, install four bolts approximately 2¼ inch (57mm) long to the correct diameter, and eight nuts on the carburetor base.

Disassembly

1. Remove the fuel filter.
2. Remove the six air horn screws and washers.
3. Carefully remove the air horn and invert it.
4. Remove the float hinge pin, float and needle, needle seat and gasket.
5. Remove the choke cap and housing shield. Remove the choke housing retaining screws and remove the housing, disengaging the primary choke link.
6. Remove the choke pulldown cover retaining screws and remove the cover and spring.
7. Remove the choke housing shaft nut and lockwasher. Pull the lever assembly outward. Carefully slide the diaphragm assembly out.
8. Remove the idle speed control assembly, if equipped.
9. Remove the accelerator pump retaining screws, pump cover, diaphragm and return spring. Remove the pump nozzle with a pair of needle nose pliers.
10. Using Tool T81P-9510-A or equivalent, remove the idle fuel shut-off solenoid and gasket.
11. Remove the power valve retaining screws, power valve cover, spring and diaphragm.
12. Remove the dashpot assembly, vacuum throttle kicker and/or ISC, if equipped.
13. Remove the idle jet retainer clips and float bowl gasket.
14. Drill and remove the idle mixture plugs. Count and note the number of turns required to lightly seat the idle mixture screws. Remove the mixture screws and O-ring.
15. Note and remove the primary and secondary discharge nozzles.
16. Note and remove the primary and secondary idle jet holders and jets.
17. Remove the high speed air bleeds, main well tubes and main jets. This assembly is press fitted, but can usually be removed by hand.
18. Refer to the following cleaning and inspection procedure.

Cleaning and Inspection

When the carburetor is disassembled, wash all parts (except diaphragms, electric choke units. pump plunger, and any other plastic, leather, fiber, or rubber parts) in clean carburetor solvent. Do not leave parts in the solvent any longer than is necessary to sufficiently loosen the deposits. Excessive cleaning may remove the special finish from the float bowl and choke valve bodies, leaving these parts unfit for service. Rinse all parts in clean solvent and blow them dry with compressed air or allow them to air dry. Wipe clean all cork, plastic, leather, and fiber parts with a clean, lint free cloth.

Blow out all passages and jets with compressed air and be sure that there are no restrictions or blockages. Never use wire or similar tools to clean jets, fuel passages, or air bleeds. Clean all jets and valves separately to avoid accidental interchange.

Carefully examine all parts for wear or damage. If wear or damage is found, replace the defective parts. Especially inspect the following:

1. Check the float needle and seat for wear. If wear is found, replace the complete assembly.
2. Inspect the float hinge pin for wear and the float(s) for dents or distortion. Replace the float if fuel has leaked into it.
3. Check the throttle and choke shaft bores for wear or an out-of-round condition. Damage or wear to the throttle arm, shaft, shaft bore will often require replacement of the throttle body. These parts require a close tolerance; wear may allow air leakage, which could affect starting and idling.

➡Throttle shafts and bushings are usually not included in overhaul kits. They can be purchased separately.

4. Inspect the idle mixture adjusting needles for burrs or grooves. Any such condition requires replacement of the needle, since you will not be able to obtain a satisfactory idle.
5. Test the accelerator pump check valves. They should pass air in one direction but not the other. Test for proper seating by blowing and sucking on the valve. Replace the valve if necessary. If the valve is satisfactory, wash the valve again to remove breath moisture.
6. Check the bowl cover for warped surfaces with a straightedge.
7. Closely inspect the valves and seats for wear and damage, replacing as necessary.

After cleaning and checking all components, re-assemble the carburetor, using new parts. When re-assembling, make sure that all screw and jets are tight in their seats, but do not overtighten, as the tips will be distorted. Tighten all screws gradually, in rotation. Do not tighten needle valves into their seat; uneven jetting will result. Always use new gaskets. Be sure to adjust the float level when re-assembling.

Assembly

1. Install the high speed air bleeds, main well tubes and main jets.
2. Install the primary and secondary idle jet holders and jets.
3. Install the primary and secondary discharge nozzles.
4. Lubricate and install the mixture screws and O-ring. Lightly seat the idle mixture screws, then back them out the number of turns recorded during disassembly.
5. Install the idle jet retainer clips and float bowl gasket.
6. Install the dashpot assembly, vacuum throttle kicker and/or ISC, if equipped.
7. Install the power valve retaining screws, power valve cover, spring and diaphragm.
8. Install the idle fuel shut-off solenoid and gasket.
9. Install the accelerator pump retaining screws, pump cover, diaphragm and return spring.
10. Install the idle speed control assembly, if equipped.
11. Install the choke assembly. Pay attention to the following:
    a. Use caution not to roll or damage the Teflon® bushing.
    b. Both shaft arms must be to the left of the fast idle cam molded plastic steps.

c. The cam spring tab must be located to the left of the fast idle cam lever.

d. Check for freedom of movement of the choke mechanism.

12. Install a new air horn gasket.
13. Install the needle seat and gasket.
14. Install the inlet needle float and float hinge pin. Perform the float level and float drop adjustments.
15. Install the air horn assembly to the main body.
16. Install a new fuel filter.
17. Install the carburetor and perform the adjustments described earlier in this section.
18. After all adjustments are completed, install the idle mixture concealment plugs.

GASOLINE FUEL INJECTION SYSTEM

Description and Operation

There are three types of fuel injection systems used on the Ford Escort and Mercury Lynx:

- Central Fuel Injection (CFI)
- Multi-port Fuel Injection (MFI)
- Sequential Fuel Injection (SFI)

CENTRAL FUEL INJECTION (CFI) SYSTEM

See Figures 8 and 9

The Central Fuel Injection (CFI) system, used on 1987-90 1.9L CFI fuel injected engines, is classified as a single-point, pulse time, modulated injection system. Fuel is metered into the intake air stream according to engine demand by a single solenoid injection valve, mounted in a throttle body on the intake manifold.

The fuel charging assembly is comprised of five individual components which perform the air/fuel metering function to the engine. The throttle body assembly mounts to the conventional carburetor pad of the intake manifold and provides for packaging of:

- Air control is through a single butterfly vane mounted to the throttle body.
- Fuel injector nozzles an electro-mechanical device which meters and atomizes the fuel delivered to the engine.
- Fuel pressure regulator maintains the fuel supply pressure upon engine and fuel pump shut down.
- Fuel pressure diagnostic valve
- Cold engine speed control
- Throttle position sensor used by the computer (EEC) to determine the operating modes (closed throttle, part throttle and wide open throttle).

The system is supplied with fuel, by an in-tank mounted low pressure electric fuel pump. After being filtered, the fuel is sent to the fuel charging assembly injector fuel cavity and then to the regulator where the fuel delivery pressure is maintained at a nominal value of 14.5 psi (100 kPa). Excess fuel is returned to the fuel tank by a steel fuel return line.

The electrical system also incorporates an inertia switch. In the event of a collision, the electrical contacts in the inertia switch will open and the fuel pump will automatically shut OFF (even if the engine continues to operate).

****CAUTION**

If the inertia switch is tripped, never reset the switch without first inspecting the fuel system for leaks.

MULTI-PORT FUEL INJECTION (MFI)

Ford Motor Co. also refers to this system as Electronic Fuel Injection (EFI).

The Multi-port Fuel Injection (MFI) system is classified as a multi-point, pulse time, mass airflow fuel injection system. Fuel is metered into the intake air stream in accordance with engine demand through four injectors mounted on a tuned intake manifold.

The MFI system can be sub-divided into four distinct categories:

- Fuel Delivery
- Air Induction
- Sensors
- Electronic Control Unit

1.6L MFI Engine

See Figure 10

The Multi-port Fuel Injection (MFI) system, used on the 1.6L MFI engine, utilizes a new design fuel tank, fuel sender mounted pick-up tube, and an externally mounted high pressure electrical fuel pump. The fuel sender and pick-up tube rest in an internal pump cavity inside the fuel tank, allowing satisfactory pump operation during extreme vehicle maneuvers.

The electrical system has a fuel pump control relay controlled by the Electronic Engine Control (EEC) module. This provides power to the fuel pump under various operating conditions. The system pressure is controlled by a pressure regulator on the engine.

The electrical system also incorporates an inertia switch. In the event of a collision, the electrical contacts in the inertia switch will open and the fuel pump will automatically shut off (even if the engine continues to operate).

****CAUTION**

If the inertia switch is tripped, never reset the switch without first inspecting the fuel system for leaks.

1.8L MFI Engine

See Figure 11

The Multi-port Fuel Injection (MFI) system, used on the 1.8L MFI engine, supplies the engine with its air/fuel mixture. An air induction system and a fuel injection system work in conjunction with an Electronic Control Assembly (ECA). Sensors and switches (electronic input signals) send the ECA data concerning engine operating conditions. The ECA interprets this data

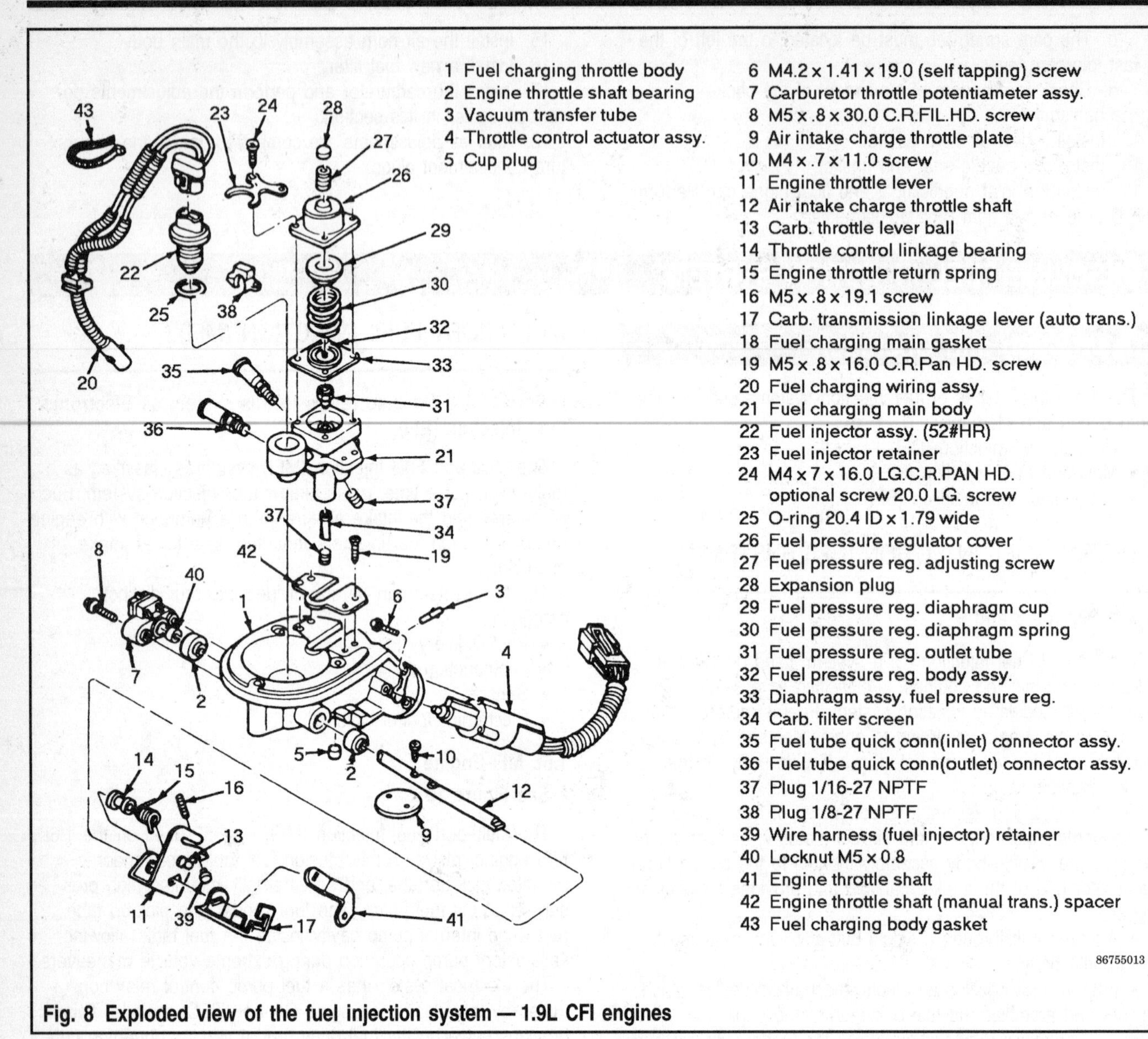

1 Fuel charging throttle body
2 Engine throttle shaft bearing
3 Vacuum transfer tube
4 Throttle control actuator assy.
5 Cup plug
6 M4.2 x 1.41 x 19.0 (self tapping) screw
7 Carburetor throttle potentiameter assy.
8 M5 x .8 x 30.0 C.R.FIL.HD. screw
9 Air intake charge throttle plate
10 M4 x .7 x 11.0 screw
11 Engine throttle lever
12 Air intake charge throttle shaft
13 Carb. throttle lever ball
14 Throttle control linkage bearing
15 Engine throttle return spring
16 M5 x .8 x 19.1 screw
17 Carb. transmission linkage lever (auto trans.)
18 Fuel charging main gasket
19 M5 x .8 x 16.0 C.R.Pan HD. screw
20 Fuel charging wiring assy.
21 Fuel charging main body
22 Fuel injector assy. (52#HR)
23 Fuel injector retainer
24 M4 x 7 x 16.0 LG.C.R.PAN HD. optional screw 20.0 LG. screw
25 O-ring 20.4 ID x 1.79 wide
26 Fuel pressure regulator cover
27 Fuel pressure reg. adjusting screw
28 Expansion plug
29 Fuel pressure reg. diaphragm cup
30 Fuel pressure reg. diaphragm spring
31 Fuel pressure reg. outlet tube
32 Fuel pressure reg. body assy.
33 Diaphragm assy. fuel pressure reg.
34 Carb. filter screen
35 Fuel tube quick conn(inlet) connector assy.
36 Fuel tube quick conn(outlet) connector assy.
37 Plug 1/16-27 NPTF
38 Plug 1/8-27 NPTF
39 Wire harness (fuel injector) retainer
40 Locknut M5 x 0.8
41 Engine throttle shaft
42 Engine throttle shaft (manual trans.) spacer
43 Fuel charging body gasket
86755013

Fig. 8 Exploded view of the fuel injection system — 1.9L CFI engines

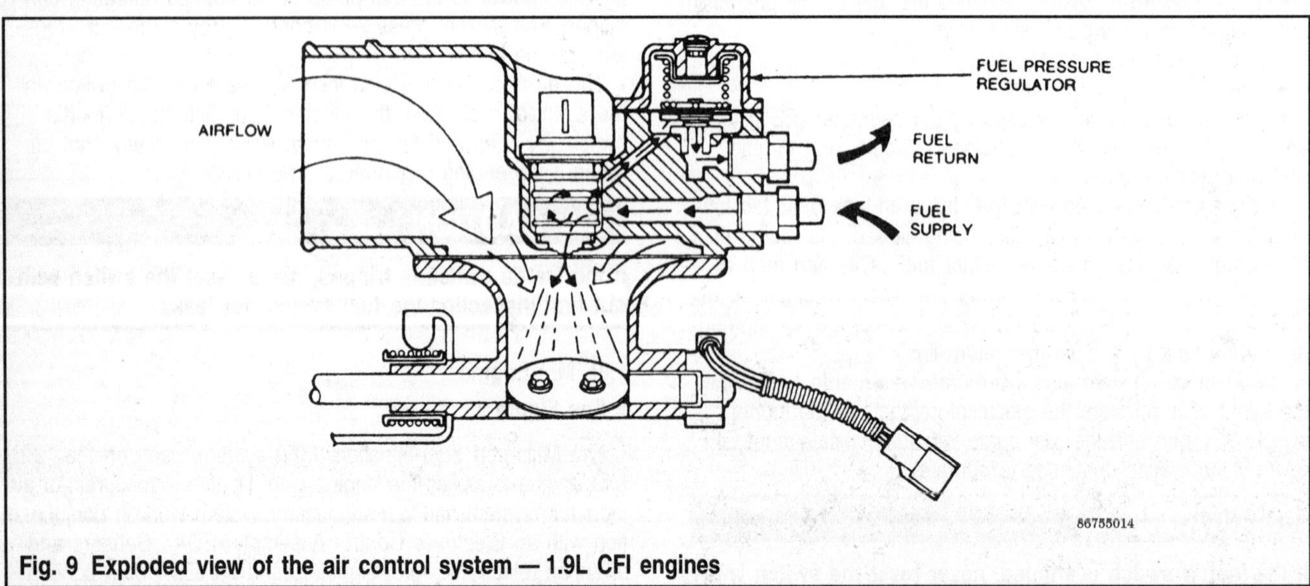

FUEL PRESSURE REGULATOR
AIRFLOW
FUEL RETURN
FUEL SUPPLY
86755014

Fig. 9 Exploded view of the air control system — 1.9L CFI engines

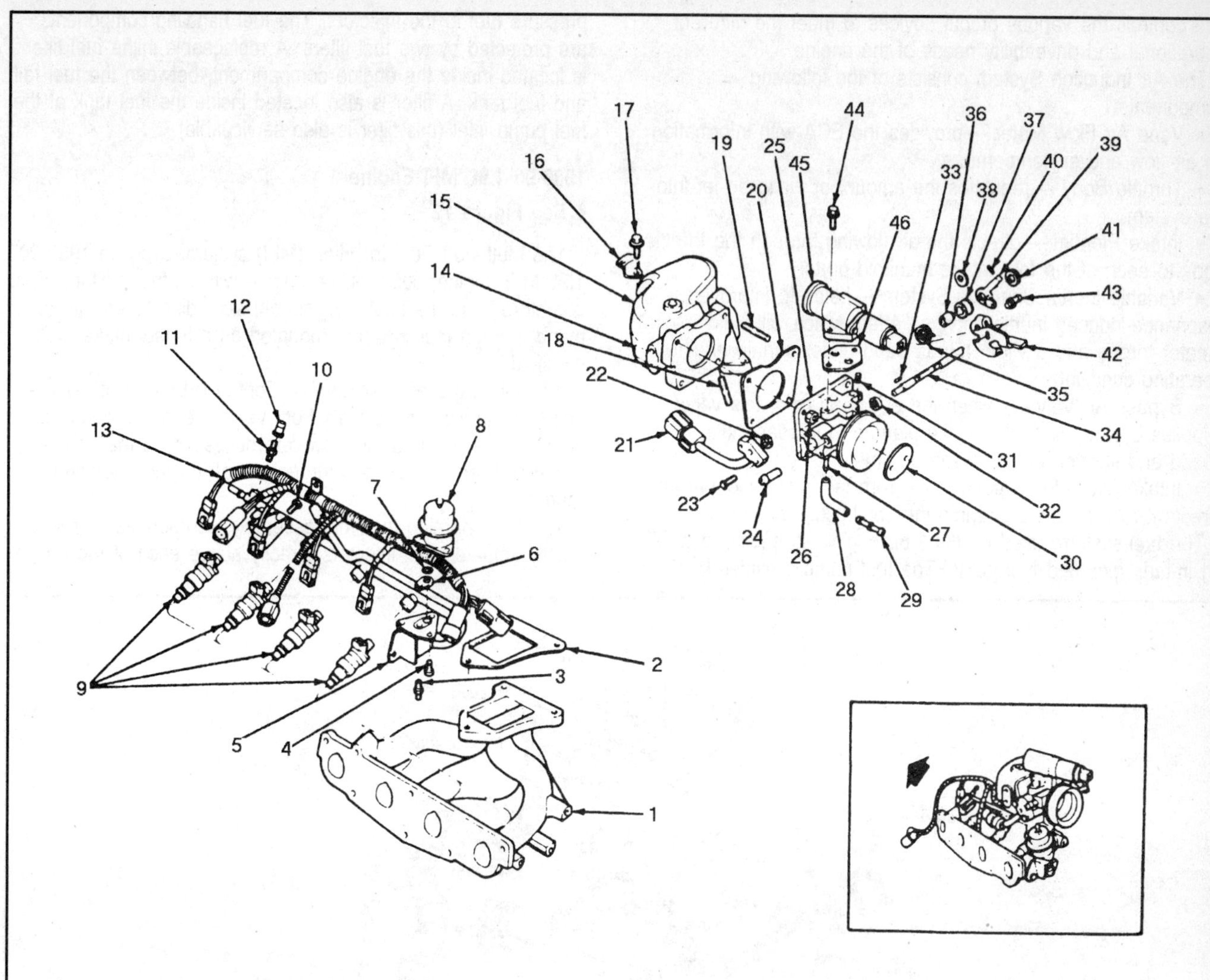

1 Intake lower manifold
2 Intake manifold upper gasket
3 1/4 flareless x 1/8 external pipe connector
4 M5 x .8 x 10 socket head screw
5 Fuel injection fuel supply manifold assembly
6 Fuel pressure regulator gasket
7 5/16 x .070 "O"ring seal
8 Fuel pressure regulator assembly
9 Fuel injector assembly
10 M8 x 1.25 x 20 HEX flange head bolt
11 Fuel pressure relief valve assembly
12 Fuel pressure relief cap
13 Fuel charging wiring harness
14 Carburetor identification decal
15 Intake upper manifold
16 Wiring harness retainer
17 M8 x 1.25 x 30 HEX flange head bolt
18 M6 x 1.0 x 1.0 x 40 stud
19 M8 x 1.25 x 1.25 x 47.5 stud
20 Air intake charge to intake manifold gasket
21 Throttle position potentiometer
22 Carburetor throttle shaft bushing
23 Screw and washer assembly M4 x 22
24 Emission inlet tube
25 Air intake charge throttle body
26 M8 x 1.25 nut
27 Tube
28 Vacuum hose
29 Connector
30 Air intake charge throttle plate
31 M4 x .7 x 8 screw
32 Throttle control shaft seal
33 Spring coiled 1/16 x .42 pin
34 Shaft
35 Throttle return spring
36 Accelerator pump over travel spring bushing
37 Throttle control linkage bearing
38 Throttle control torsion spring (MTX only) spacer
39 Carburetor transmission linkage lever
40 M5 x .8 x 16.25 slot head screw
41 Carburetor throttle shaft spacer
42 Carburetor throttle lever
43 Carburetor throttle lever ball
44 M6 x 1.0 x 20 HEX flange head bolt
45 Throttle air bypass valve assembly
46 Air bypass valve gasket

86755010

Fig. 10 Exploded view of the fuel injection system — 1.6L MFI engines

and controls the various output devices to meet the different operational and driveability needs of the engine.

The Air Induction System consists of the following components:

- Vane Air Flow Meter — provides the ECA with information on air flow and air temperature.
- Throttle Body — regulates the amount of air to be let into the system.
- Intake Plenum — directs the air flowing through the throttle body to each of the four intake manifold ports.
- Variable Inertia Charging System — helps to improve the resonance-induced inertia charging effect which will yield greater torque and a wider torque band under certain engine operating conditions.
- Bypass Air Valve — when the engine is cold, this valve supplies bypass air to the intake plenum to increase idle speed and shorten engine warm-up time.
- Intake Manifold — receives air from the intake plenum and directs it to the valves and into the combustion chambers.

The fuel system, used on the 1.8L engine, is equipped with an in-tank mounted fuel pump. The fuel pump provides high-pressure fuel to the injectors. The fuel handling components are protected by two fuel filters. A replaceable inline fuel filter is located inside the engine compartment, between the fuel rail and fuel tank. A filter is also located inside the fuel tank at the fuel pump inlet (this filter is also serviceable).

1986-90 1.9L MFI Engine

➧ See Figure 12

The Multi-port Fuel Injection (MFI) system, used on 1986-90 1.9L MFI engine, supplies the engine with air/fuel mixture. Fuel is metered into the intake air stream according to engine demand through four injectors mounted on a tuned intake manifold.

An on-board Electronic Engine Control (EEC) computer accepts electronic input signals from various engine sensors to compute the required fuel flow rate necessary to maintain a predetermined air/fuel ratio throughout all engine operating ranges.

The fuel charging manifold assembly incorporates four electrically actuated fuel injectors directly above each of the en-

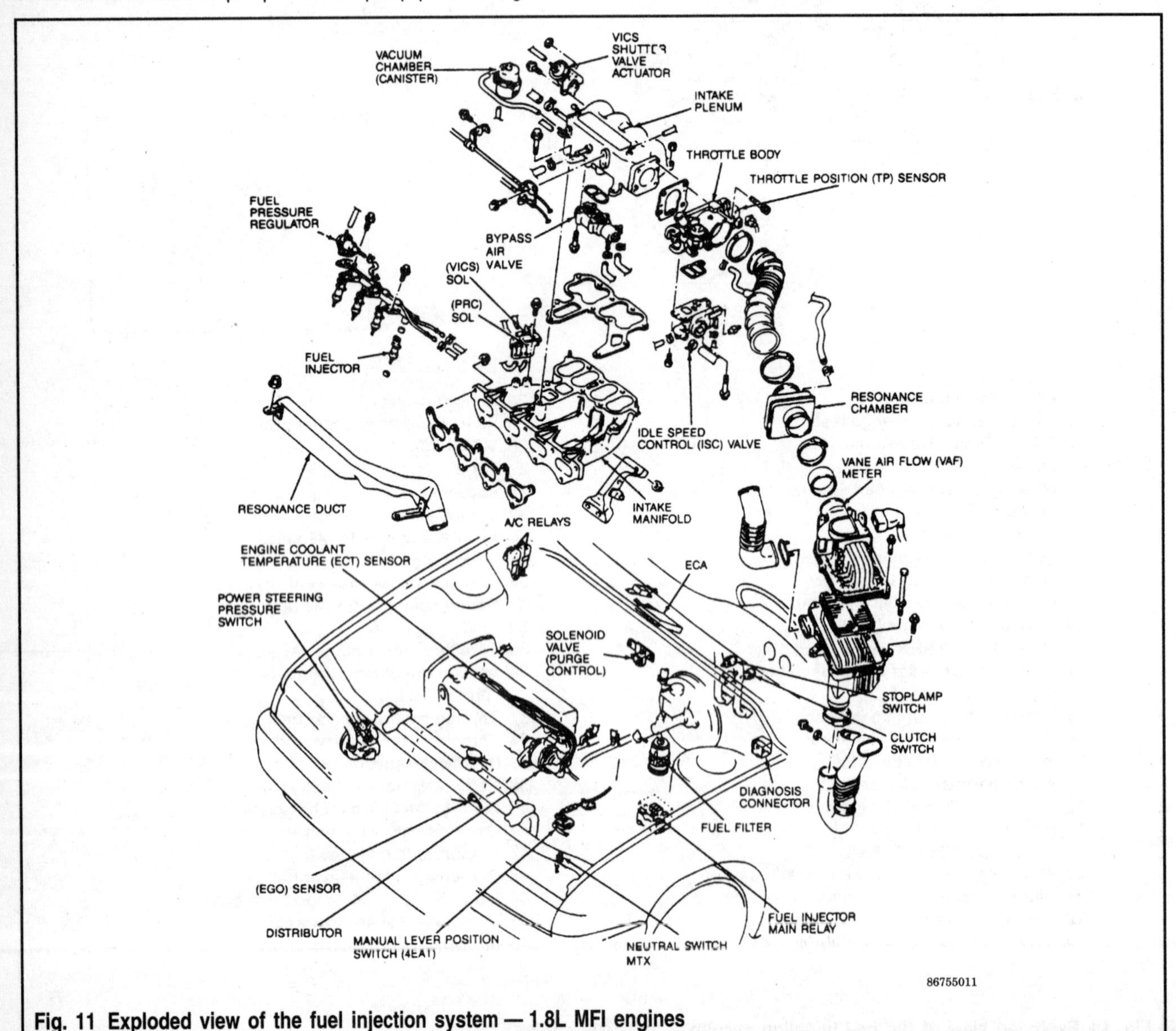

Fig. 11 Exploded view of the fuel injection system — 1.8L MFI engines

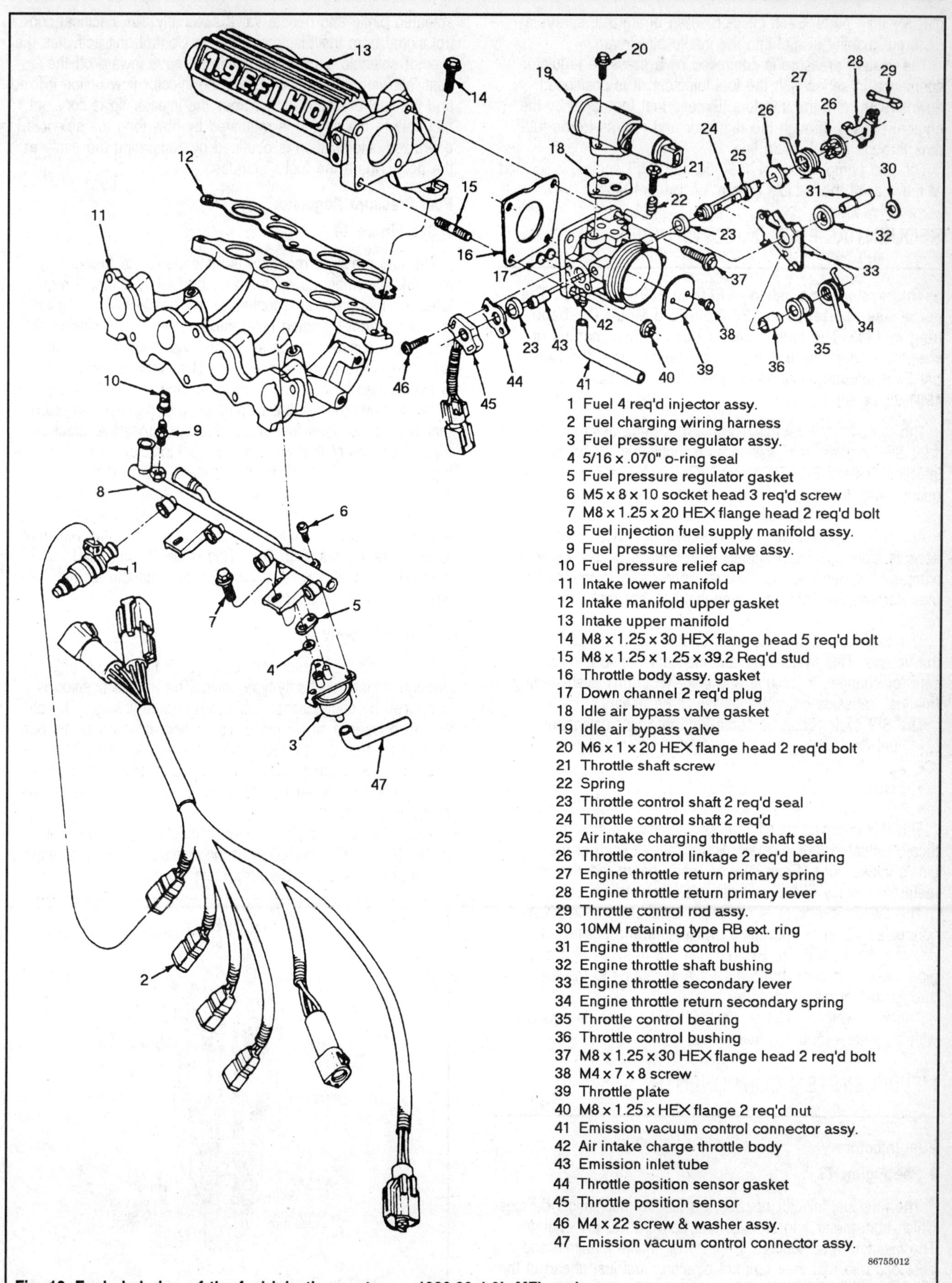
1.9 EFI HO
1 Fuel 4 req'd injector assy.
2 Fuel charging wiring harness
3 Fuel pressure regulator assy.
4 5/16 x .070" o-ring seal
5 Fuel pressure regulator gasket
6 M5 x 8 x 10 socket head 3 req'd screw
7 M8 x 1.25 x 20 HEX flange head 2 req'd bolt
8 Fuel injection fuel supply manifold assy.
9 Fuel pressure relief valve assy.
10 Fuel pressure relief cap
11 Intake lower manifold
12 Intake manifold upper gasket
13 Intake upper manifold
14 M8 x 1.25 x 30 HEX flange head 5 req'd bolt
15 M8 x 1.25 x 1.25 x 39.2 Req'd stud
16 Throttle body assy. gasket
17 Down channel 2 req'd plug
18 Idle air bypass valve gasket
19 Idle air bypass valve
20 M6 x 1 x 20 HEX flange head 2 req'd bolt
21 Throttle shaft screw
22 Spring
23 Throttle control shaft 2 req'd seal
24 Throttle control shaft 2 req'd
25 Air intake charging throttle shaft seal
26 Throttle control linkage 2 req'd bearing
27 Engine throttle return primary spring
28 Engine throttle return primary lever
29 Throttle control rod assy.
30 10MM retaining type RB ext. ring
31 Engine throttle control hub
32 Engine throttle shaft bushing
33 Engine throttle secondary lever
34 Engine throttle return secondary spring
35 Throttle control bearing
36 Throttle control bushing
37 M8 x 1.25 x 30 HEX flange head 2 req'd bolt
38 M4 x 7 x 8 screw
39 Throttle plate
40 M8 x 1.25 x HEX flange 2 req'd nut
41 Emission vacuum control connector assy.
42 Air intake charge throttle body
43 Emission inlet tube
44 Throttle position sensor gasket
45 Throttle position sensor
46 M4 x 22 screw & washer assy.
47 Emission vacuum control connector assy.
86755012

Fig. 12 Exploded view of the fuel injection system — 1986-90 1.9L MFI engines

gine's intake ports. Each injector, when energized, sprays a metered quantity of fuel into the intake air stream.

The system pressure is controlled by a pressure regulator connected in series with the fuel injectors. It is positioned downstream from the injectors. Excess fuel (not used by the engine) passes through the regulator and returns to the fuel tank through a fuel return line.

The fuel pump, used on 1986-90 1.9L MFI engine, is located at the rear of the vehicle in front of the fuel tank.

SEQUENTIAL FUEL INJECTION (SFI)

➡This system was called "SEFI" in 1991 and 1992. The name was shortened to "SFI" by Ford Motor Co. beginning in 1993. The later name is used in this manual to simplify understanding. By either designation, the Sequential Fuel Injection system is essentially the same for 1991-95 vehicles.

The Sequential Fuel Injection (SFI) system, used on 1991-95 1.9L SFI engines, is classified as a multi-point, pulse time fuel injection system. Fuel is metered into each intake port in sequence with the engine firing order through four injectors mounted on a tuned intake manifold.

An on-board Electronic Control Assembly (ECA) computer accepts electronic input signals from various engine sensors to compute the required fuel flow rate necessary to maintain a predetermined air/fuel ratio throughout all engine operating ranges.

The ECA also determines and compensates for the age of the vehicle. This system will automatically sense and compensate for changes in altitude and also will permit push-starting (manual transaxle only) the vehicle, if necessary.

The SFI system can be subdivided into four categories:

- Fuel Delivery
- Air Induction
- Sensors
- ECA

The fuel charging manifold assembly incorporates four electrically actuated fuel injectors directly above each of the engine's intake ports. Each injector, when energized, sprays a metered quantity of fuel into the intake air stream.

The system pressure is controlled by a pressure regulator connected in series with the fuel injectors and positioned downstream from them. Excess fuel, not required by the engine, passes through the regulator and returns to the fuel tank through a fuel return line.

The fuel system, used on the 1.9L SFI engine, is equipped with an in-tank mounted fuel pump.

MFI/SFI SYSTEM COMPONENTS

Fuel Injectors

➧ See Figure 13

The four fuel injector nozzles are electro-mechanical devices which both meter and atomize fuel delivered to the engine. The injectors are mounted in the lower intake manifold and are positioned so that their tips are directing fuel just ahead of the engine intake valves. The injector bodies consist of a solenoid actuated pintle and needle valve assembly. An electrical control signal from the Electronic Engine Control unit activates the injector solenoid causing the pintle to move inward off the seat, allowing fuel to flow. Since the injector flow orifice if fixed and the fuel pressure drop across the injector tip is constant, fuel flow to the engine is regulated by how long the solenoid is energized. Atomization is obtained by contouring the pintle at the point where the fuel separates.

Fuel Pressure Regulator

➧ See Figure 14

The fuel pressure regulator is attached to the fuel supply manifold assembly downstream of the fuel injectors. It regulates the fuel pressure supplied to the injectors. The regulator is a diaphragm operated relief valve in which one side of the diaphragm senses fuel pressure and the other side is subjected to intake manifold pressure. The nominal fuel pressure is established by a spring preload applied to the diaphragm. Balancing one side of the diaphragm with manifold pressure maintains a constant fuel pressure drop across the injectors. Fuel in excess of that used by the fuel injector varies depending on the volume of air flowing through the sensor. The temperature sensor in the air vane meter measures the incoming air temperature. These two electronic input signals, air volume and temperature, are used by the Electronic Control Assembly to compute the mass air flow. This value is then used to compute the fuel flow necessary for the optimum air/fuel ratio which is fed to the injectors.

Air Throttle Body Assembly

The throttle body assembly controls air flow to the engine through a single butterfly-type valve. The throttle position is controlled by conventional cable/cam throttle linkage. The aluminum body is a single piece die casting. It has a single bore with an air bypass channel around the throttle plate. This bypass channel controls both cold and warm engine idle airflow as regulated by an air bypass valve assembly mounted directly to the throttle body.

The valve assembly is an electro-mechanical device controlled by the EEC computer. It incorporates a linear actuator which positions a variable area metering valve.

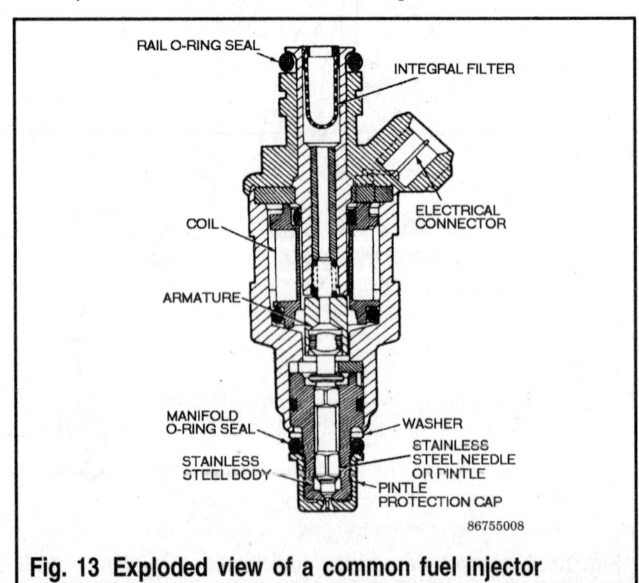

Fig. 13 Exploded view of a common fuel injector

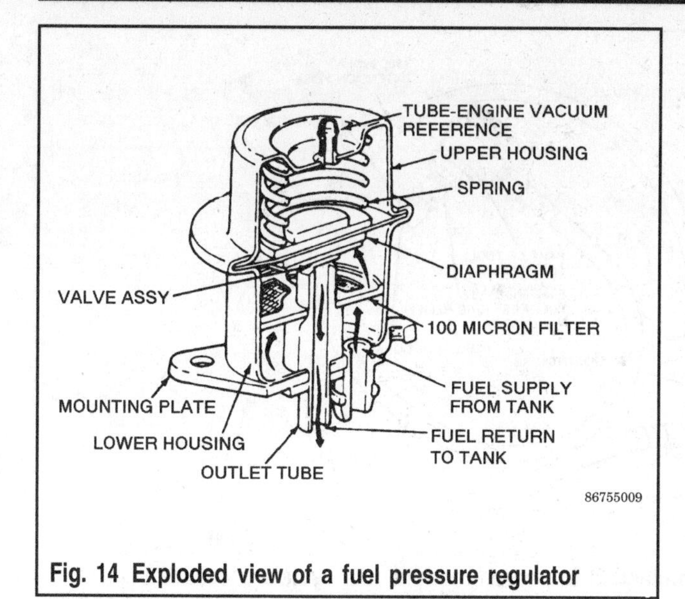

Fig. 14 Exploded view of a fuel pressure regulator

Other features of the air throttle body assembly include:

- An adjustment screw to set the throttle plate a a minimum idle airflow position
- A preset stop to locate the Wide Open Throttle (WOT) position
- A throttle body mounted throttle position sensor
- A PCV fresh air source located upstream of the throttle plate
- Individual ported vacuum taps (as required) for PCV and EVAP control signals

Fuel Supply Manifold Assembly

The fuel supply manifold assembly is the component that delivers high pressure fuel from the vehicle fuel supply line to the four fuel injectors. The assembly consists of a single preformed tube or stamping with four injector connectors, a mounting flange for the fuel pressure regulator, a pressure relief valve for diagnostic testing or field service fuel system pressure bleed down and mounting attachments which locate the fuel manifold assembly and provide fuel injector retention.

Air Intake Manifold

The air intake manifold is a two piece (upper and lower segment) aluminum casting. The length and diameter of the intake runners are tuned to optimize engine torque and power output. The manifold provides mounting flanges for the air throttle body assembly, fuel supply manifold and accelerator control bracket and the EGR valve and supply tube. Vacuum taps are provided to support various engine accessories. Pockets for the fuel injectors are machined to prevent both air and fuel leakage. The pockets, in which the injectors are mounted, are placed to direct the injector fuel spray immediately in front of each engine intake valve.

Service Precautions

Safety is the most important factor when performing not only fuel system maintenance but any type of maintenance. Failure to conduct maintenance and repairs in a safe manner may result in serious personal injury or death. Maintenance and testing of the vehicle's fuel system components can be accomplished safely and effectively by adhering to the following rules and guidelines.

- To avoid the possibility of fire and personal injury, always disconnect the negative battery cable unless the repair or test procedure requires that battery voltage be applied.
- Always relieve the fuel system pressure prior to disconnecting any fitting, fuel line connection or fuel system component (fuel injector, fuel rail, pressure regulator, etc.). Exercise extreme caution whenever relieving fuel system pressure to avoid exposing skin, face and eyes to fuel spray. Please be advised that fuel under pressure may penetrate the skin or any part of the body that it contacts.
- Always place a shop towel or cloth around the fitting or connection prior to loosening to absorb any excess fuel due to spillage. Ensure that all fuel spillage (should it occur) is quickly removed from engine surfaces. Ensure that all fuel soaked cloths or towels are deposited into a suitable waste container.
- Always keep a dry chemical (Class B) fire extinguisher near the work area.
- Do not allow fuel spray or fuel vapors to come into contact with a spark or open flame.
- Always use a backup wrench when loosing and tightening fuel line connection fittings. This will prevent unnecessary stress and torsion to fuel line piping. Always follow the proper torque specifications.
- Always replace worn fuel fitting O-rings with new. Do not substitute fuel hose or equivalent, where fuel pipe is installed.

Relieving Fuel System Pressure

1983-90 MFI AND CFI ENGINES

➧ See Figure 15

✲✲WARNING

The fuel system will remain pressurized for long periods of time after the engine is shut off. This pressure must be relieved before servicing the fuel system. A fuel diagnostic valve is provided for this purpose.

1. Locate the fuel diagnostic valve (pressure relief valve) on the fuel rail assembly.
2. Remove the air cleaner assembly.

➡Always place a shop towel or cloth around the fitting or connection prior to loosening, in order to absorb any excess fuel due to spillage.

3. Attach the pressure gauge tool (T80L-9974-A or equivalent) to the fuel diagnostic valve.
4. Operate the tool according to the manufacturer's instructions to relieve the fuel system pressure.

Alternate Method

1. Locate the inertia switch in the luggage compartment, then disconnect its electrical lead.
2. Crank the engine for a minimum of 15 seconds to reduce the pressure in the fuel system.

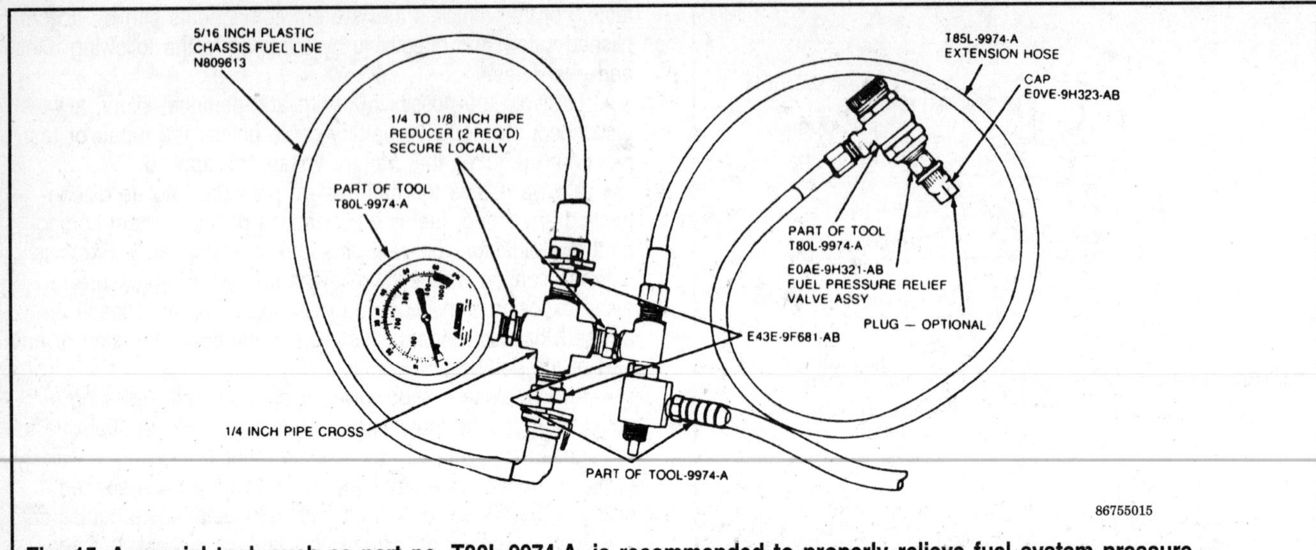

Fig. 15 A special tool, such as part no. T80L-9974-A, is recommended to properly relieve fuel system pressure

1991-95 ENGINES

1. Start the engine.
2. Remove the rear seat cushion.
3. Disconnect the fuel pump electrical connectors.
4. Wait for the engine to stall, then turn the ignition switch **OFF**. Disconnect the negative battery cable.
5. Connect the fuel pump electrical connectors.
6. Install the rear seat cushion.

Electric Fuel Pump

The fuel pump used on 1.6L MFI engines is an externally mounted high pressure electrical fuel pump. The fuel tank has an internal pump cavity in which the fuel sender and pick-up tube rest.

The fuel pump used on 1986-90 vehicles equipped with 1.9L MFI engines is externally mounted; it is located at the rear of the vehicle in front of the fuel tank.

On 1987-90 vehicles equipped with the 1.9L CFI engine, as well as all 1991-95 vehicles, the fuel pump is located inside the fuel tank.

REMOVAL & INSTALLATION

1983-90 1.9L MFI Engines

➧ **See Figure 16**

1. Relieve the fuel system pressure.
2. Disconnect the negative battery cable.
3. Raise and support the vehicle safely.
4. Remove the pump assembly from the vehicle, by loosening the mounting bolt A, until the assembly can be removed from the mounting bracket. Remove the parking brake cable from the clip on the pump.
5. Disconnect the electrical connector and disconnect the fuel pump outlet fitting at point C.
6. Disconnect the fuel pump inlet line from the pump at point B.

➡Either drain the fuel tank or raise the end of the line above the fuel level in the tank to prevent siphoning.

To install:

7. Install the fuel pump assembly on the fuel tank support bracket. Tighten the mounting bolt to 19.5-30 inch lbs. (2-3 Nm). Place the parking brake cable in the clip on the bracket.
8. Install the fuel inlet hose on the pump at point B.
9. Install the fuel outlet hose on the fuel line at point C.
10. Lower the vehicle.
11. Install the pressure gauge tool (T80L-9974-A or equivalent) on the fuel rail pressure fitting. Turn the ignition **ON** for two seconds and repeat turning the key **OFF** and **ON** for two seconds intervals, until the gauge shows at least 35 psi (241 kPa).
12. Check the connections for leaks. If any leaks are detected, shut off the engine immediately and correct the problem.

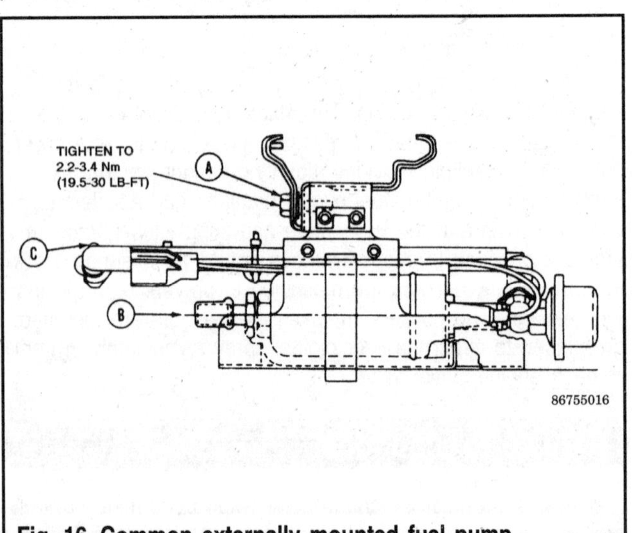

Fig. 16 Common externally mounted fuel pump assembly

13. Remove the pressure gauge tool, start the engine and recheck for leaks.

1991-95 Engines

➧ See Figure 17

****WARNING**

Extreme caution should be taken when removing the fuel tank from the vehicle! Ensure that all removal procedures are conducted in a well ventilated area! Have a sufficient amount of absorbent material in the vicinity of the work area to quickly contain any fuel spillage. Never store waste fuel in an open container, as it presents a serious fire hazard!

This procedure will require a new fuel pump gasket for pump installation, so be sure to have one before starting.

1. Relieve the fuel system pressure.
2. Disconnect the negative battery cable.
3. Remove the fuel from the fuel tank by pumping out through filler. Use care to prevent combustion from fuel spillage.
4. Raise and support the vehicle safely.
5. Disconnect and remove the fuel filler tube.
6. Support the fuel tank and remove the fuel tank support straps. Lower the fuel tank partially and remove the fuel lines, electrical connectors, and vent lines from the tank. Remove the fuel tank.
7. Clean any dirt from around the fuel pump attaching flange so that it will not enter the fuel tank during removal and installation.
8. Turn the fuel pump locking ring counterclockwise, and remove the locking ring.
9. Remove the fuel pump and bracket assembly.
10. Remove the seal gasket and discard.

To install:

11. Clean the fuel pump mounting flange and fuel tank mounting surface and the sealing ring groove.
12. Lightly coat the new seal ring gasket with a suitable lubricant compound part No. C1AZ-19590-B or equivalent, to hold the gasket in place during installation.
13. Install the fuel pump and sender. Ensure that the nylon filter is not damaged and the locating keys are in keyways and seal ring remains in place.
14. Hold assembly in place and install the locking ring finger-tight. Ensure that all locking tabs are under the tank lock ring tabs.
15. Secure the unit with the locking ring by rotating the ring clockwise using the fuel sender wrench tool D84P-9275-A or equivalent. Turn until the ring makes contact against the stop.
16. Remove the tank from the bench to vehicle and support the tank while connecting the fuel lines, vent line and electrical connectors to appropriate places.
17. Install the tank in the vehicle and secure with the retaining straps.
18. Lower the vehicle and pour a sufficient quantity of fuel in the tank to check for leaks. If any leaks are detected, correct the problem before operating the vehicle.
19. Connect negative battery cable.

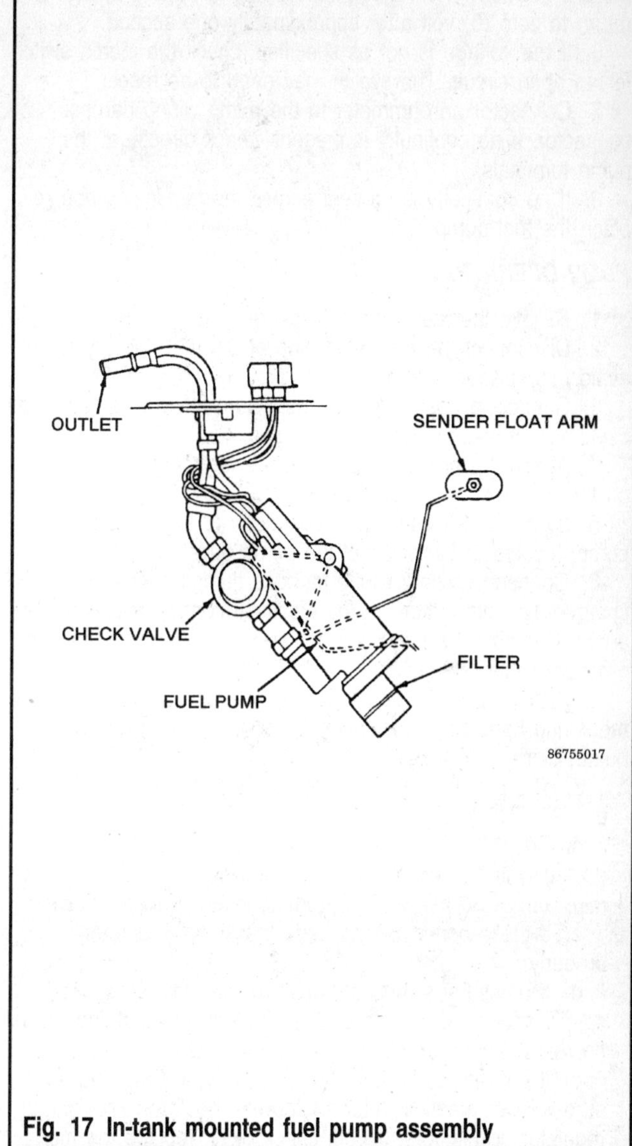

Fig. 17 In-tank mounted fuel pump assembly

20. Check fuel pressure.

➡If there are any leaks, correct them immediately. Do not put the vehicle back into use until all leaks are corrected.

21. Remove the pressure gauge, start the engine and check again for fuel leaks.

TESTING

1.6L MFI Engine

ELECTRICAL CIRCUIT

1. Ensure that the fuel tank contains a supply of fuel adequate for this procedure.
2. Make certain the ignition switch is **OFF**.
3. Check for signs of fuel leakage at all fittings and lines.
4. Disconnect the electrical connector just forward of the fuel pump inlet.
5. Attach a voltmeter to the wiring harness connector. Observe the voltmeter reading, when the ignition key is turned to

the **ON** position. The voltage should rise to battery voltage and return to zero (0) volt after approximately one second.

6. If the voltage is not as specified, check the inertia switch for an open circuit. The switch may need to be reset.

7. Connector an ohmmeter to the pump wiring harness connector. If no continuity is present, check directly at the pump terminals.

8. If no continuity is present across the terminals, then replace the fuel pump.

PUMP OPERATION

1. Relieve the fuel system pressure.
2. Disconnect the fuel return line at the fuel rail. Try to avoid fuel spillage.
3. Connect a hose from the fuel return fitting to a calibrated container, at least 1 quart (0.95 L) minimum.
4. Attach the pressure gauge to the fuel diagnostic valve on the fuel rail.
5. Disconnect the electrical connector to the electric fuel pump, located just forward of the pump outlet.
6. Connect auxiliary wiring harness (jumpers) from a fully charged 12 volts battery to the electrical connector to the fuel pump. Energize the fuel pump for 10 seconds. Check the fuel pressure while energized.
7. If there is no pressure, check for proper polarity made at the wiring harness. Also, check the connections to the fuel pump. Correct, if necessary.
   a. The gauge should indicate a reading between 35-45 psi (241-310 kPa).
   b. Check that the fuel flow is a minimum of 7.5 ounces (221 ml.) in 10 seconds and fuel pressure remains at a minimum of 30 psi (207 kPa) immediately after shutdown.
   c. If these conditions are met, the pump is operating properly.
   d. If pressure is met, but fuel flow quantity is not within specification, check for a blocked fuel filter or fuel line. If fuel flow is still not correct, replace the fuel pump.
   e. If both pressure and flow conditions are met, but pressure will not maintain after shutdown, check for a leaking regulator or injectors. If both check okay, replace the fuel pump.

1986-87 1.9L MFI Engine

ELECTRICAL CIRCUIT

➧ See Figure 18

1. Ensure that the fuel tank contains a supply of fuel adequate for this procedure.
2. Make certain the ignition switch is **OFF**.
3. Check for signs of fuel leakage at all fittings and lines.
4. Locate the inertia switch in the luggage compartment.
5. Disconnect the electrical connector from the inertia switch and connect an ohmmeter to one of the leads at the wiring harness. Check for continuity between either of the wires and ground.
6. If continuity is not present at either wire, the fuel tank must be removed from the vehicle and continuity must be checked between the wiring harness and the switch leads.
7. If the leads check okay, check for continuity across the pump terminals.
8. If no continuity is present across terminals, then replace the fuel pump and sender assembly.
9. If continuity is present across the pump terminals, check the ground circuit or the connections to the pump form the body connector.
10. Reconnect the inertia switch. Attach a voltmeter to the wiring harness on the pump side of the switch. (This would be the side which did indicate continuity).
11. Observe the voltmeter reading, when the ignition key is turn to the **ON** position. The voltmeter should read over 10 volts for one second and then return to zero (0).
12. If the voltage is not as specified, check the inertia switch for an open circuit. The switch may need to be reset. If okay, check the electrical circuit to find fault.

PUMP OPERATION

➧ See Figure 19

This test requires the use of a pressure gauge tool (T80L-9974-A or equivalent), which is attached to the diagnostic pressure tap fitting (fuel diagnostic valve). It also requires that the fuel system relay be modified, using one of the following relays: E3EB-9345-BA, CA, DA or E3TF-9345-AA.

1. Relieve the fuel system pressure.
2. Disconnect the fuel return line at the fuel rail. Try to avoid fuel spillage.
3. Connect a hose from the fuel return fitting to a calibrated container, at least 1 quart (0.95 L) minimum.
4. Attach the pressure gauge to the fuel diagnostic valve on the fuel rail.
5. Locate the fuel pump relay (left side of instrument panel, near the EEC-IV module) and remove it. The ground lead should be brought outside the vehicle and located nearby.
   a. Using the appropriate relay indicated above, modify the relay case by drilling a 1/8 in. (3mm) hole and cutting the skirt as indicated.
   b. Add 16-18 gauge jumper wire between pins 2 and 4 (please refer to the accompanying drawing).
   c. Add 8 ft. (2.4m) of flexible wire through the hole in the case to point B, as shown. Add a ground to the end of the added wire.

➡The leads should be soldered in place and as close to the base as possible, to permit insertion of the relay into socket with minimum interference.

6. Energize the fuel pump for 10 seconds by attaching a jumper to close the ground lead from the relay. Check the fuel pressure while energized. If there is no pressure, check that there is voltage pass the inertia switch. Correct, if necessary.
   a. The gauge should indicate a reading of 35-45 psi (241-310 kPa).
   b. Check that the fuel flow is a minimum of 7.5 ounces (221 ml) in 10 seconds and fuel pressure remains at a minimum of 30 psi (207 kPa) immediately after shutdown.
   c. If these conditions are met, the pump is operating properly.
   d. If both pressure and flow conditions are met, but pressure will not maintain after shutdown, check for a leaking regulator or injectors. If both check okay, replace the fuel pump.
7. After testing, replace the modified fuel pump relay with the original relay.

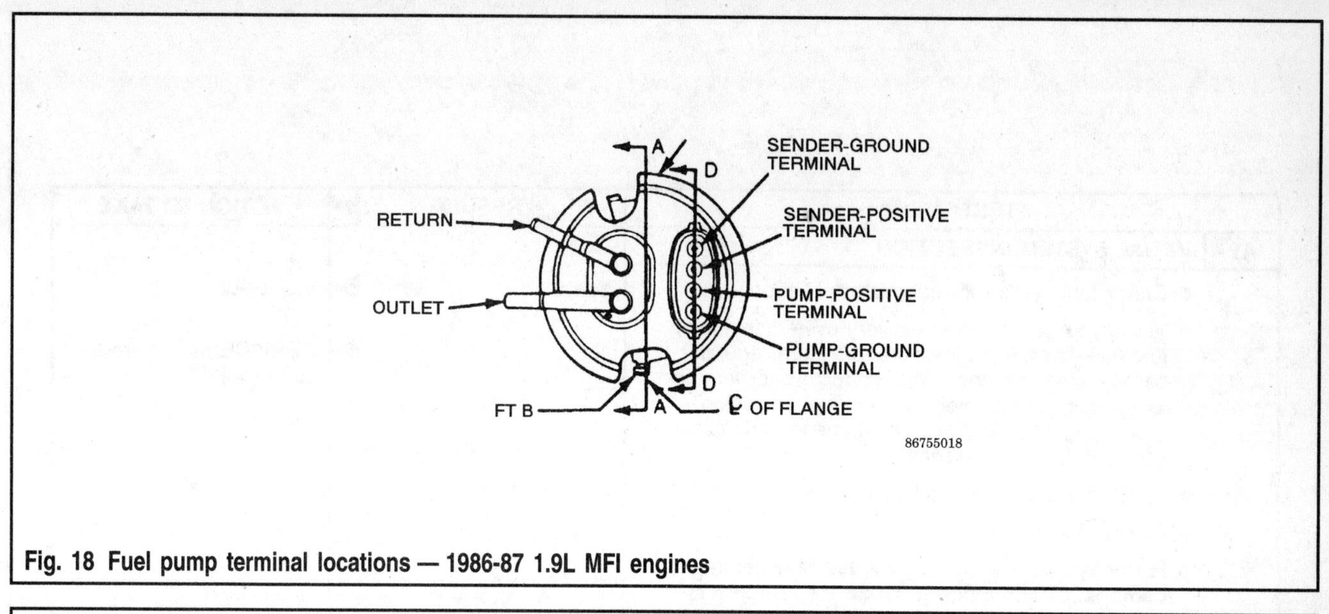

Fig. 18 Fuel pump terminal locations — 1986-87 1.9L MFI engines

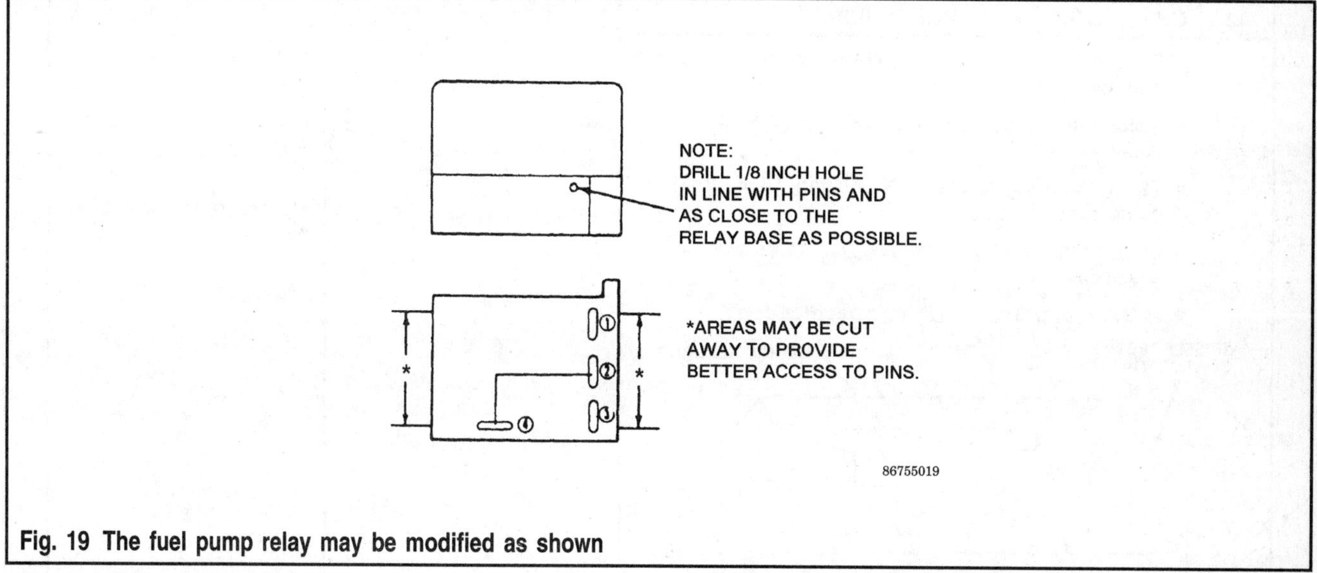

Fig. 19 The fuel pump relay may be modified as shown

1988-90 MFI and CFI Engines

➧ See Figures 20, 21, 22 and 23

Generally, any faults related to the electric fuel pump will result in a loss or reduction of fuel flow volume and/or pressure. The following diagnostic procedures will help determine if the electric fuel pump is functioning properly.

➡Exercise care when disconnecting fuel lines or when installing gauges, to avoid fuel spillage.

Unless otherwise stated, turn the fuel pump off at the conclusion of each step, by disconnecting the jumper or by turning the ignition switch **OFF**.

Normal fuel pressure specifications are as follows:

- 1987-90 1.9L CFI engines: 13-17 psi (90-117 kPa)
- 1988-90 1.9L MFI engines: 35-45 psi (241-310 kPa)

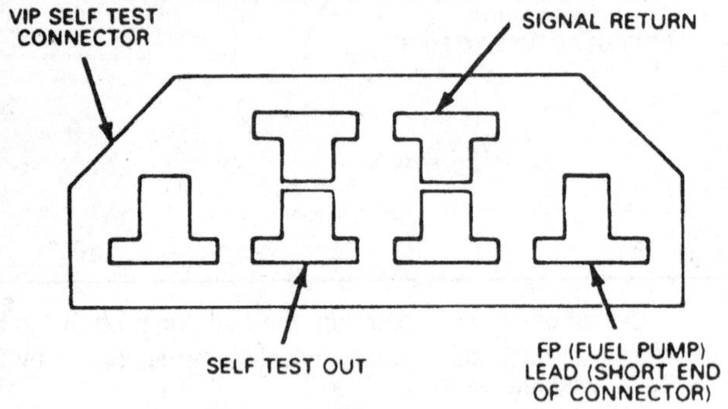

TEST STEP	RESULT	ACTION TO TAKE
A1 INITIAL SYSTEM INSPECTION		
• Check fuel system for adequate fuel supply. • Visually inspect the fuel delivery system including fuel tank lines, filter, injectors, pressure regulator, battery, electrical lines and connectors for leakage, looseness, cracks, pinching, kinking, corrosion, grounding, abrasion, or other damage caused by accident, collision, assembly or usage. • Verify that the battery is fully charged. • Check fuse integrity. • **Is the system free of any evidence of leakage, damage, or any evident cause for concern?**	Yes ▶ No ▶	GO to **A2**. SERVICE as required. GO to **A2**.
A2 CHECK STATIC FUEL PRESSURE		
• Ground fuel pump lead of self-test connector using a jumper at the FP lead. • Install Fuel Pressure Gauge T80L-9974-B or equivalent. • Turn ignition key to the RUN position. Verify fuel pump runs. • Observe fuel pressure reading. Compare with specifications. • **Is the fuel pressure within specification?** VIP SELF TEST CONNECTOR SIGNAL RETURN SELF TEST OUT FP (FUEL PUMP) LEAD (SHORT END OF CONNECTOR)	Yes ▶ No ▶	GO to **A3**. If pressure High, GO to **A5**. If pressure is low, GO to **A6**.
A3 CHECK STATIC LEAKDOWN		
• Run fuel pump for 10 seconds and note pressure (Ground FP lead of self test connector and turn ignition switch to the RUN position). • Turn off pump and monitor pressure for 60 seconds. (Disconnect ground or turn ignition switch to the OFF position). • **Does fuel line pressure remain within 34 kPa (5 psi) of shut off pressure for 60 seconds?**	Yes ▶ No ▶	GO to **A4**. GO to **A10**.

86755100

Fig. 20 Fuel pump diagnostic flow chart — 1988-90 1.9L MFI and CFI engines

	TEST STEP	RESULT ▶	ACTION TO TAKE
A4	CHECK VEHICLE UNDER LOAD CONDITIONS		
	• Remove and block vacuum line to pressure regulator. • Run vehicle at idle and then increase engine speed to 2000 RPM or more in short bursts. • **Does fuel system pressure remain within chart limits?** **NOTE: Operating vehicle under load (road test) should give same results.**	Yes ▶ No ▶	Fuel system is OK. DISCONNECT all test connections, RECONNECT vacuum line to regulator. GO to **A12**.
A5	CHECK FUEL PRESSURE		
	• Disconnect return line at fuel pressure regulator. Connect outlet of regulator to appropriate receptacle to catch return fuel. • Turn on fuel pump (ground FP lead and turn ignition to the ON position) and monitor pressure. • **Is fuel pressure within chart limits?**	Yes ▶ No ▶	CHECK return fuel line for restrictions. SERVICE as required. REPEAT **A2**. GO to **A3**. SERVICE or REPLACE fuel regulator as required. REPEAT **A2**. GO to **A3**.
A6	CHECK FUEL PUMP OPERATION		
	• Turn on fuel pump (ground FP lead and turn ignition to the RUN position). • Raise vehicle on hoist and use stethoscope to listen at fuel tank to monitor fuel pump noise, or listen at filler neck for fuel pump sound. • Is fuel pump running?	Yes ▶ No ▶	GO to **A9**. GO to **A7**.
A7	CHECK INERTIA SWITCH AND FUEL PUMP GROUND CONNECTOR		
	• Check if inertia switch is tripped. • Check fuel pump ground connection in vehicle. • **Is inertia switch and ground connection OK?**	Yes ▶ No ▶	GO to **A8**. SERVICE switch or ground connection as required. REPEAT **A2** and GO to **A3**.

86755101

Fig. 21 Fuel pump diagnostic flow chart (continued) — 1988-90 1.9L MFI and CFI engines

TEST STEP	RESULT ▶	ACTION TO TAKE
A8 CHECK VOLTAGE AT FUEL PUMP		
• Check for continuity through fuel pump to ground by connecting meter to pump power wire lead as close to pump as possible. • Check voltage as close to fuel pump as possible (turn on pump as outlined in A6). • Is voltage within 0.5 Volts of battery voltage and is there continuity through pump?	Yes ▶	REPLACE fuel pump. REPEAT **A2**. If pressure OK GO to **A3**. If presure not OK CHECK fuel pump connector for oversize connectors or other sources of open electrical circuit. SERVICE as required. REPEAT **A3**.
	No ▶	If voltage not present, CHECK fuel pump relay, EEC relay, and wiring for problem. If no ground, CHECK connection at fuel tank, etc. SERVICE as required. REPEAT **A2** and **A3**.
A9 CHECK FUEL PRESSURE REGULATOR		
• Replace fuel filter (if not replaced previously) and recheck pressure as in A2. If pressure not OK, continue. If pressure OK, go to A3. • Open return line at pressure regulator. Attach return fitting from regulator to suitable container to catch gasoline. • Turn on fuel pump as in A2. • **Is fuel being returned from regulator with low pressure in system?**	Yes ▶	SERVICE or REPLACE regulator as required. REPEAT **A2** and **A3**.
	No ▶	RECHECK systems for pressure restrictions. SERVICE as required. If no problem found, REPLACE fuel pump. GO to **A2** and **A3**.
A10 CHECK FUEL PRESSURE FOR LEAKS		
• Open return line at pressure regulator and attach suitable container to catch return fuel. Line should be clear to observe fuel flow. • Run fuel pump as in A2. • Turn off fuel pump by removing ground from self test connector or turning ignition to the OFF position. • Observe fuel return flow from regulator and system pressure when pump is off. • **Is there return flow when pump is turned off and system pressure is dropping?**	Yes ▶	REPLACE regulator. REPEAT **A2** and **A3**. If OK, GO to **A4**. If not OK, REPEAT **A2** and follow procedure.
	No ▶	GO to **A11**.

86755102

Fig. 22 Fuel pump diagnostic flow chart (continued) — 1988-90 1.9L MFI and CFI engines

TEST STEP		RESULT ▶	ACTION TO TAKE
A11	CHECK FUEL PUMP CHECK VALVE		
	• Open pressure line from fuel pump and attach pressure gauge to line and block line to allow pressure build up. • Operate pump momentarily as in A2 and bring pressure to about system pressure. • Observe fuel pressure for one minute. • **Does pressure remain within 34 kPa (5 psi) of starting pressure over one minute period?**	Yes ▶	CHECK injectors for leakage or regulator for internal leakage. SERVICE as required. Fuel pump check valve is OK. GO to **A4**.
		No ▶	CHECK lines and fittings from pump to rail for leakage, if none found REPLACE pump assembly. REPEAT **A2**. When OK GO to **A4**.
A12	CHECK FUEL FILTER FOR RESTRICTIONS		
	• Replace fuel line filter (if not previously replaced during this procedure) and repeat test A5. • **Does system pressure remain within chart limits?**	Yes ▶	System is OK. DISCONNECT all test connections and RECONNECT all loosened or removed parts and lines.
		No ▶	CHECK pressure lines for kinks or restrictions. CHECK at fuel pump for low voltage. CHECK for wrong size injectors (too large). If no problem found, REPLACE pump and REPEAT **A4**. If problem found, SERVICE as required. REPEAT **A4**.

86755103

Fig. 23 Fuel pump diagnostic flow chart (continued) — 1988-90 1.9L MFI and CFI engines

1991-95 Engines

➧ See Figures 24, 25, 26, 27 and 28

The fuel pump used on 1991-95 vehicles equipped with either 1.8L MFI or 1.9L SFI engines, is part of the in-tank fuel gauge sending unit. The fuel indication system consists of a fuel gauge, anti-slosh module, and a fuel gauge sending unit. The fuel gauge is connected to the fuel gauge sender through a slosh module. When the fuel level is low, resistance is high.

Push Connectors and Spring Lock Couplings

REMOVAL & INSTALLATION

➧ See Figure 29

The fuel system, depending on model year of the vehicle, may be equipped with push type connectors or spring lock couplings. When removing the fuel lines on these vehicles, it will be necessary to use Fuel Line Coupling Disconnect Tool D87L-9280-A or-B, or equivalent.

If the fuel system is equipped with spring lock couplings, remove the retaining clip from the spring lock coupling by hand only. Do not use any sharp tool or screwdriver as it may damage the spring lock coupling.

1. Twist the fitting to free it from any adhesion at the O-ring seals.
2. Fit Spring Lock Coupling Tool D87L-9280-A/B or equivalent to the coupling.
3. Close the tool and push it into the open side of the cage to expand garter spring and release the female fitting.
4. After the garter spring is expanded, pull the fittings apart.
5. Remove the tool from the disconnected coupling.

➡All vehicles require the large black clip to be installed on the supply side fuel line and the small gray clip to be installed on the return side fuel line (1989-95 vehicles).

Visual Inspection

1. Verify condition and location of all components in the indication system.
2. Visually inspect instrument cluster.

TEST STEP		RESULT	▶	ACTION TO TAKE
A1	VERIFY COMPLAINT			
	• Observe the gauge performance.	Gauge pointer does NOT move	▶	GO to A2.
		Gauge pointer does move	▶	GO to D1.
A2	VERIFY CLUSTER PERFORMANCE			
	• With the ignition ON, observe the other gauges and warning lights for proper operation.	Other gauges and warning lights operate correctly	▶	GO to C1.
		Other gauges and warning lights do NOT operate correctly	▶	GO to B1.

TEST STEP		RESULT	▶	ACTION TO TAKE
B1	VERIFY POWER AT FUSE PANEL			
	• Use a voltmeter to verify system voltage at the load side of warning indicators fuse.	System voltage is present at the load side of fuse	▶	GO to C1.
		System voltage is NOT present at the load side of fuse	▶	GO to B2.
B2	VERIFY POWER AT FUSE PANEL			
	• Use a voltmeter to verify system voltage at the feed side of warning indicator fuse.	System voltage is present at the feed side of fuse	▶	REPLACE the fuse; RETURN to A1.
		System voltage is NOT present at the feed side of fuse	▶	REPAIR the wiring to the fuse panel; RETURN to A1.

86755104

Fig. 24 Fuel pump diagnostic flow chart — 1991-95 1.8L and 1.9L engines

TEST STEP		RESULT	▶	ACTION TO TAKE
C1	VERIFY POWER AT CLUSTER			
	• Have cluster connector(s) remain intact. • Partially remove the cluster from the instrument panel. Use a voltmeter to verify system voltage at the cluster connector and / or gauge terminal.	Voltage is present at the cluster connector and gauge terminal	▶	GO to C2.
		System voltage is NOT present at the cluster connector and / or gauge terminal	▶	REPAIR the circuitry; RETURN to A1.
C2	VERIFY GROUND CIRCUITRY AT CLUSTER			
	• Use an ohmmeter to check the continuity of the cluster and gauge ground circuitry.	The ground circuitry is good	▶	GO to D1.
		Excessive resistance is in the ground circuitry	▶	REPAIR the circuitry; RETURN to A1.

TEST STEP		RESULT	▶	ACTION TO TAKE
D1	TEST BOX CHECK (LOW)			
	• Place the ignition switch in the OFF position. • Insert Gauge System Tester, Rotunda 021-00055 in the sender circuit. Disconnect circuit 14405 connector under the instrument panel and connect the tester to the cluster side of the connector. Set the tester to 22 ohms. • Place the ignition in the ON position. • Wait 60 seconds. • Read the fuel gauge.	Gauge reads E	▶	GO to D4.
		Gauge does NOT read E	▶	GO to D2.
D2	TEST BOX CHECK (RE-CHECK)			
	• Place the ignition switch in the OFF position. Then return to the ON position. Tap on the instrument panel. • Wait 60 seconds. • Read the fuel gauge.	Gauge reads E	▶	GO to D4.
		Gauge still does NOT read E	▶	GO to D3.

86755105

Fig. 25 Fuel pump diagnostic flow chart (continued) — 1991-95 1.8L and 1.9L engines

TEST STEP		RESULT	►	ACTION TO TAKE
D3	SLOSH MODULE BYPASS TEST			
	• Turn the ignition to the OFF position. Remove instrument cluster. Inspect the flex circuit. Remove the slosh module. Connect the jumper wire from the Gauge Tester directly to the fuel gauge "S" terminal. Install the instrument cluster. • Turn the ignition switch to the ON position. • Read the fuel gauge.	Gauge reads E	►	REPLACE the slosh module; RETURN to D1.
		Gauge does NOT read E	►	REPLACE the gauge. Install the slosh module and RETURN to D1.
D4	TEST BOX CHECK (HIGH)			
	• Place the ignition in the OFF position. With the Gauge System Tester in sender circuit, set the tester to 145 ohms. • Place the ignition switch in the ON position. • Wait 60 seconds. • Read the fuel gauge.	Gauge reads F	►	GO to D6.
		Gauge does NOT read F	►	GO to D5.
D5	SLOSH MODULE BYPASS TEST			
	• Turn the ignition to the OFF position. Remove the instrument cluster. Inspect the flex circuit. Remove the slosh module. Connect the jumper wire from the Gauge Tester directly to the fuel gauge "S" terminal. Install the instrument cluster. • Turn the ignition switch to the ON position. • Read the fuel gauge.	Gauge reads F	►	REPLACE the slosh module; RETURN to D1.
		Guage does NOT read F	►	REPLACE the fuel gauge; RETURN to D1.
D6	FUEL SENDER DIAGNOSIS			
	• Inspect fuel tank for distortion or damage.	Damaged	►	REPLACE fuel tank.
		Not damaged	►	GO to F1.

TEST STEP		RESULT	►	ACTION TO TAKE
F1	TEST BOX CHECK — EMPTY STOP			
	• Connect one lead of Digital Volt Ohmmeter 007-00001 or equivalent, to the fuel sender signal lead and the other lead to ground. **NOTE: Float rod is against empty stop (closest to filter).**	Ohmmeter reads 14-18 ohms	►	GO to F2.
		Ohmmeter reads less than 14 ohms or greater than 18 ohms	►	REPLACE fuel sender.
F2	TEST BOX CHECK — FULL STOP			
	• Connect one lead of Digital Volt Ohmmeter 007-00001 or equivalent, to the fuel sender signal lead and the other lead to sender ground. **NOTE: Float rod is against full stop.**	Ohmmeter reads 155-165 ohms	►	GO to F3.
		Ohmmeter reads less than 155 ohms or greater than 165 ohms	►	REPLACE the fuel sender.

86755106

Fig. 26 Fuel pump diagnostic flow chart (continued) — 1991-95 1.8L and 1.9L engines

	TEST STEP	RESULT	▶	ACTION TO TAKE
F3	TEST BOX CHECK — FLOAT ROD TRAVEL			
	• Connect one lead of Digital Volt Ohmmeter 007-00001 or equivalent, to the fuel sender signal lead and the other lead to sender ground. • Slowly move float rod from full stop to empty stop.	Ohmmeter reading jumps to open condition while decreasing	▶	REPLACE fuel sender.
		Ohmmeter reading decreases slowly	▶	GO to F4.
F4	FUEL SENDER INSPECTION			
	• Inspect fuel sender. • Inspect float and float rod.	Float rod is distorted	▶	REPLACE sender.
		Float is badly distorted / damaged hitting the filter. Loose on float rod	▶	REPLACE sender.
		If not distorted / damaged	▶	GO to F5.
F5	HARNESS CONNECTOR CHECK — EMPTY STOP			
	• Attach all fuel indication connectors. • Move float rod to empty position. • Turn ignition to the ON position. • Wait 60 seconds. • Read fuel gauge.	Gauge reads empty	▶	GO to F6.
		Gauge reads greater than empty	▶	GO to A1.
F6	HARNESS CONNECTOR CHECK — FULL STOP			
	• Attach all fuel indication connectors. • Move float rod to full stop position. • Turn ignition to the ON position. • Wait 60 seconds. • Read fuel gauge.	Gauge reads full	▶	Fuel sender checks OK.
		Gauge reads less than full	▶	GO to A1.

Low Fuel Warning Lamp Stays On Continually — More than 1/4 Tank Fuel Indication

	TEST STEP	RESULT	▶	ACTION TO TAKE
G1	VERIFY CONDITION			
	• Verify the condition.	Indicator lamp stays on with more than 1/4 tank fuel gauge indication	▶	GO to G2.

86755107

Fig. 27 Fuel pump diagnostic flow chart (continued) — 1991-95 1.8L and 1.9L engines

TEST STEP		RESULT	▶	ACTION TO TAKE
G2	CHECK ELFW MODULE			
	• Turn the ignition to the OFF position. • Disconnect Circuit 14405 connector under the instrument panel and connect a 56 ohm resistor between the fuel sender feed to the gauge and ground. • Turn the ignition to the ON position. • Wait 2 minutes.	Indicator lamp is OFF. Gauge pointer should indicate approximately 1/4 tank	▶	GO to G3.
		Indicator lamp is ON	▶	REPLACE the module at the instrument cluster.
G3	CHECK GAUGE AND LAMP			
	• Turn the ignition to the OFF position. • Replace the resistor from Test G2 with a 33 ohm resistor. • Turn the ignition to the ON position. • Wait 2 minutes.	Indicator lamp is OFF	▶	GO to H3.
		Lamp is ON, gauge is at 1/4 or above	▶	GO to A1.
		Indicator lamp is ON. Gauge pointer should indicate approximately 1/8 to 1/16 tank	▶	Low Fuel Warning operates properly.

Low Fuel Warning Lamp Stays Off Continually

TEST STEP		RESULT	▶	ACTION TO TAKE
H1	VERIFY CONDITION			
	• Verify the condition.	Indicator lamp stays OFF	▶	GO to H2.
H2	CHECK ELFW MODULE			
	• Turn the ignition to the OFF position. • Disconnect Circuit 14405 connector under the instrument panel and connect a 33 ohm resistor between the fuel sender feed to the gauge and ground. • Turn the ignition to the ON position. • Wait 2 minutes.	Indicator lamp is OFF	▶	GO to H3.
		Lamp is ON, gauge is at 1/4 or above	▶	GO to A1.
		Indicator lamp is ON. Gauge pointer should indicate approximately 1/8 to 1/16 tank	▶	Low Fuel Warning operates properly.
H3	CHECK INDICATOR LAMP			
	• With the Ignition switch in the ON position, ground the lamp circuit between the lamp and module.	Indicator lamp is ON	▶	REPLACE the module on the instrument cluster.
		Indicator lamp is OFF	▶	CHECK the power circuit to the lamp. REPLACE the lamp.

86755108

Fig. 28 Fuel pump diagnostic flow chart (continued) — 1991-95 1.8L and 1.9L engines

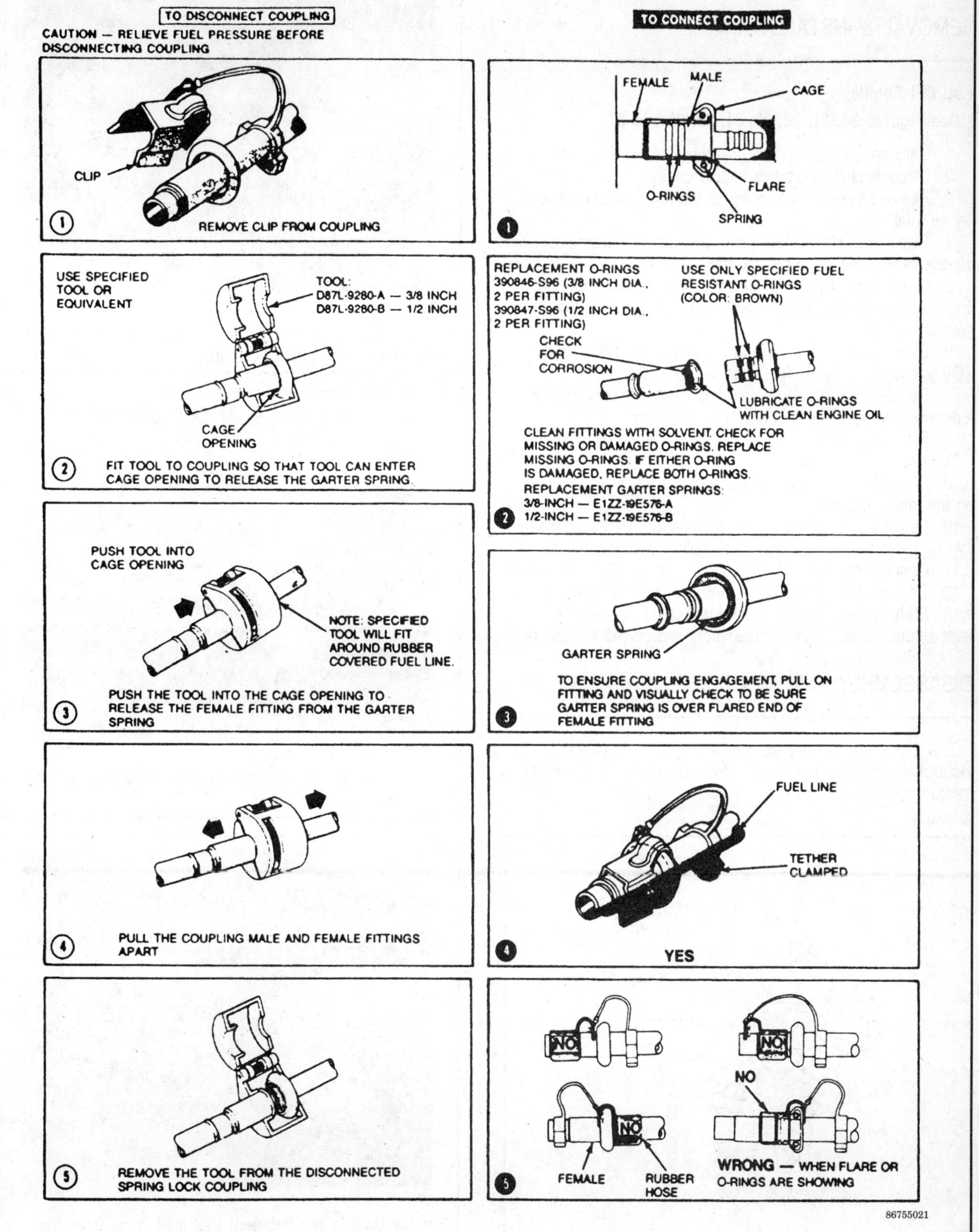

TO DISCONNECT COUPLING

CAUTION — RELIEVE FUEL PRESSURE BEFORE DISCONNECTING COUPLING

CLIP

① REMOVE CLIP FROM COUPLING

USE SPECIFIED TOOL OR EQUIVALENT

TOOL:
D87L-9280-A — 3/8 INCH
D87L-9280-B — 1/2 INCH

CAGE OPENING

② FIT TOOL TO COUPLING SO THAT TOOL CAN ENTER CAGE OPENING TO RELEASE THE GARTER SPRING.

PUSH TOOL INTO CAGE OPENING

NOTE: SPECIFIED TOOL WILL FIT AROUND RUBBER COVERED FUEL LINE.

③ PUSH THE TOOL INTO THE CAGE OPENING TO RELEASE THE FEMALE FITTING FROM THE GARTER SPRING

④ PULL THE COUPLING MALE AND FEMALE FITTINGS APART

⑤ REMOVE THE TOOL FROM THE DISCONNECTED SPRING LOCK COUPLING

TO CONNECT COUPLING

FEMALE
MALE
CAGE
FLARE
O-RINGS
SPRING

❶

REPLACEMENT O-RINGS
390846-S96 (3/8 INCH DIA., 2 PER FITTING)
390847-S96 (1/2 INCH DIA., 2 PER FITTING)

USE ONLY SPECIFIED FUEL RESISTANT O-RINGS (COLOR: BROWN)

CHECK FOR CORROSION

LUBRICATE O-RINGS WITH CLEAN ENGINE OIL

CLEAN FITTINGS WITH SOLVENT. CHECK FOR MISSING OR DAMAGED O-RINGS. REPLACE MISSING O-RINGS. IF EITHER O-RING IS DAMAGED, REPLACE BOTH O-RINGS.

REPLACEMENT GARTER SPRINGS:
3/8-INCH — E1ZZ-19E576-A
❷ 1/2-INCH — E1ZZ-19E576-B

GARTER SPRING

❸ TO ENSURE COUPLING ENGAGEMENT, PULL ON FITTING AND VISUALLY CHECK TO BE SURE GARTER SPRING IS OVER FLARED END OF FEMALE FITTING

FUEL LINE

TETHER CLAMPED

❹ YES

NO
NO
NO
NO
NO

❺ FEMALE

RUBBER HOSE

WRONG — WHEN FLARE OR O-RINGS ARE SHOWING

86755021

Fig. 29 Connect and disconnect spring lock couplings as shown

Fuel Charging Assembly

REMOVAL & INSTALLATION

1.9L CFI Engine

See Figures 30, 31, 32, 33, 34, 35, 36 and 37

1. Release the fuel system pressure.
2. Disconnect the negative battery cable.
3. Remove the air tube clamp at the fuel charging assembly air inlet.
4. Disconnect the throttle cable, and also the transaxle throttle valve lever on automatic transaxle vehicles.
5. Label, then unplug the electrical connector at the idle speed control (ISC), throttle position (TP) sensor and fuel injector.
6. Disconnect the fuel inlet and outlet connections, and PCV vacuum line at the fuel charging assembly.
7. Remove the three fuel charging assembly retaining fasteners and remove the fuel charging assembly.
8. Remove the mounting gasket form the intake manifold.

To install:

9. Clean the mounting surface and position a new gasket on the intake manifold.
10. Position the fuel charging assembly on the intake manifold and install the retaining nuts. Tighten to specifications.
11. Connect all electrical connectors, fuel and vacuum lines.
12. Connect the throttle cable, and TV cable, if equipped.
13. Start the engine and check for leaks. If any are detected, turn off the engine immediately and correct the leak(s).

DISASSEMBLY AND ASSEMBLY

This procedure will require a new throttle body gasket for its installation and four new O-rings for each of the injectors, so be sure to have the necessary parts on hand before starting

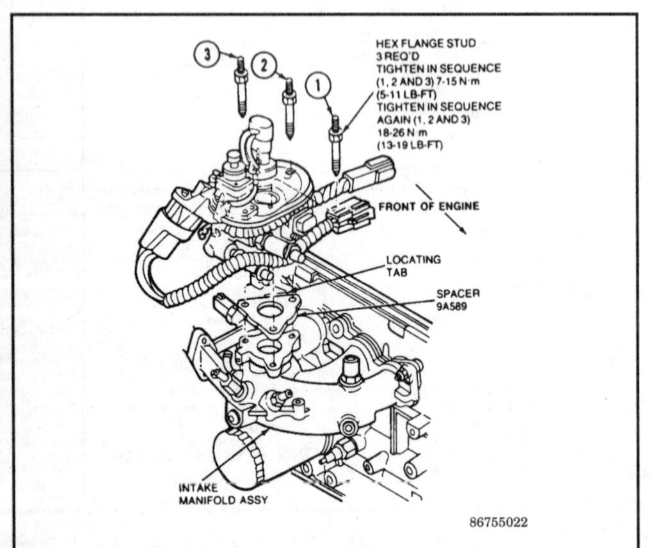

Fig. 30 Exploded view of the fuel charging assembly

Fig. 31 Unplug all electrical connectors for the throttle body removal — 1.9L CFI engines

Fig. 32 Remove the fuel inlet coupling retainer to allow disconnection of the line

Fig. 33 Unplug the (labeled) fuel inlet hose from the throttle body

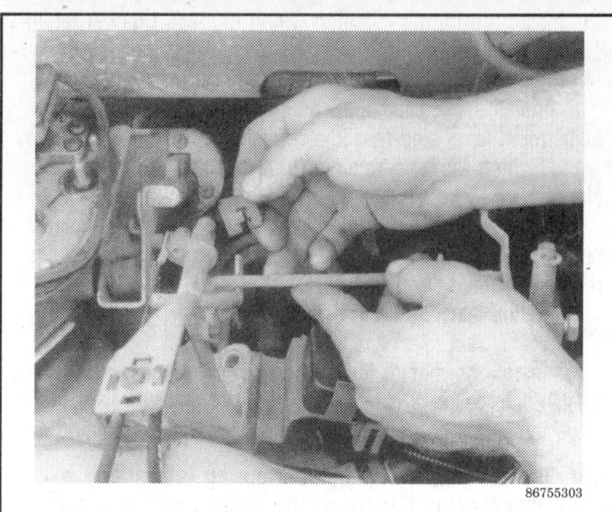
86755303
Fig. 34 Remove all retaining clips and disengage the throttle linkage

86755304
Fig. 35 Remove the three mounting bolts from the throttle body

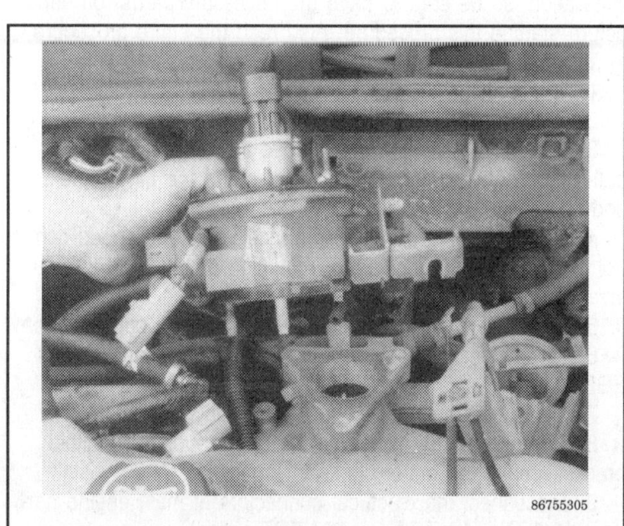
86755305
Fig. 36 Remove the throttle body assembly and set it in a clean location

86755306
Fig. 37 Ensure that the mounting surface is clean prior to mounting the throttle body

this procedure. Also read the entire procedure to anticipate any other items you may require.

➡To prevent damage to the throttle plates, the fuel charging assembly should be placed on a work stand during disassembly and assembly procedures. If a proper stand is not available, use four bolts, 2½ in. (64mm) long, as legs.

Install nuts on the bolts above and below the throttle body. The following is a step-by-step sequence of operations for completely overhauling the fuel charging assembly. Most components may be serviced without a complete disassembly of the fuel charging assembly. To replace individual components follow only the applicable steps. Use a separate container for the component parts of each sub-assembly to insure proper assembly. The automatic transaxle throttle valve lever must be adjusted whenever the fuel charging assembly is removed for service or replacement.

1. Remove the air cleaner stud. The air cleaner stud must be removed to separate the upper body from the throttle body.
2. Turn the fuel charging assembly over and remove four screws from the bottom of the throttle body.
3. Separate throttle body from main body. Set throttle body aside.
4. Carefully remove and discard gasket. Note if scraping is necessary, be careful not to damage gasket surfaces of main and throttle screws.
5. Remove the three pressure regulator retaining screws.
6. Remove the pressure regulator. Inspect the condition of the gasket and O-ring.
7. Disconnect electrical connectors at each injector. Pull the connectors outward.

➡Pull the connector and the wire. Tape to identify the connectors. They must be installed on same injector as removed.

8. Loosen but DO NOT REMOVE the wiring harness retaining screw (at multi-pin connector). Loosen the retaining screws at the single 10-pin connector.
9. Push in on the harness tabs to remove from the upper body.

10. Remove the fuel injector retainer screw.
11. Remove the injector retainer.
12. One at a time, pull injectors out of upper body. Identify each injector as "choke" or "throttle" side.

➡**Each injector has a small O-ring at its top. If the O-ring does not come out with the injector, carefully pick the O-ring out of the cavity in the throttle body.**

13. Remove fuel diagnostic valve assembly.
14. Note the position of index mark on choke cap housing.
15. Remove the three retaining ring screws.
16. If so equipped, perform the following:
  a. Remove the choke cap retaining ring, choke cap, and gasket.
  b. Remove the thermostat lever screw, and lever.
  c. Remove the fast idle cam assembly.
  d. Remove the fast idle control rod positioner.
  e. Hold the control diaphragm cover tightly in position, while removing the two retaining screws.
  f. Carefully, remove the cover, spring, and pull-down control diaphragm.
  g. Remove the fast idle retaining nut.
  h. Remove the fast idle cam adjuster lever, fast idle lever, spring and E-clip.
  i. Remove the throttle position sensor connector bracket retaining screw.
17. Remove the throttle position sensor retaining screws and slide the throttle position sensor off the throttle shaft.
18. If the CFI assembly is equipped with a throttle positioner, remove the throttle positioner retaining screw, and remove the throttle positioner. If the CFI assembly is equipped with an ISC DC Motor, remove the motor.

To assemble:

19. Install fuel pressure diagnostic valve and cap. Tighten valve to 48-84 inch lbs. (5-9 Nm). Tighten cap to 5-10 inch lbs. (0.6-2 Nm).
20. Lubricate new O-rings and install on each injector (use a light grade oil).
21. Identify the injectors and install them in their appropriate locations (choke or throttle side). Use a light twisting, pushing motion to install the injectors.
22. With the injectors installed, install the injector retainer into position.
23. Install the injector retainer screw, and tighten to 36-60 inch lbs. (4-7 Nm).
24. Install the injector wiring harness in upper body. Snap harness into position.
25. Tighten the injector wiring harness retaining screws, (if equipped with a single 10-pin connector), to 8-10 inch lbs. (1 Nm).
26. Snap the electrical connectors into position on injectors.
27. Lubricate the new fuel pressure regulator O-ring with light oil. Install O-ring and new gasket on regulator.
28. Install the pressure regulator in upper body. Tighten the retaining screws to 27-40 inch lbs. (3-4 Nm).
29. Depending upon the CFI assembly, install either the throttle positioner, or the ISC DC Motor.
30. Hold the throttle position sensor so the wire faces up.
31. Slide the throttle position sensor on the throttle shaft.
32. Rotate the throttle position sensor clockwise until aligned with the screw holes on throttle body. Install the retaining screws and tighten to 11-16 inch lbs. (1-2 Nm).
33. Install the throttle position wiring harness bracket retaining screw. Tighten the screw to 18-22 inch lbs. (2-3 Nm).
34. If so equipped, perform the following:
  a. Install the E-clip, fast idle lever and spring, fast idle adjustment lever and fast idle retaining nut.
  b. Tighten fast idle retaining nut to 16-20 inch lbs. (1-2 Nm).
  c. Install pull down control diaphragm, control modulator spring and cover. Hold cover in position and install the two retaining screws, and tighten to 13-19 inch lbs. (1-2 Nm).
  d. Install fast idle control rod positions
  e. Install fast idle cam.
  f. Install thermostat lever and retaining screws. Tighten to 13-19 inch lbs. (1-2 Nm).
  g. Install choke cap gasket, choke cap, and retaining ring.

➡**Be sure the choke cap bimetal spring is properly inserted between the fingers of the thermostat lever and choke cap index mark is properly aligned.**

35. Install the choke cap retaining screws. Tighten to 13-18 inch lbs. (1-2 Nm).
36. Install the fuel charging gasket on the upper body. Be sure the gasket is positioned over the bosses. Place the throttle body in position on the upper body.
37. Install the four upper body to throttle body retaining screws. Tighten to specification.
38. Install air cleaner stud. Tighten stud to 70-95 inch lbs. (8-11 Nm).

TESTING

➡**Testing the EEC-IV system requires special equipment and an expert knowledge of the system. Troubleshooting and servicing should be performed by qualified personnel only.**

1.9L MFI Engine

➧ **See Figure 38**

This procedure will require a new manifold gasket for its installation, so be sure to have the necessary part(s) on hand before starting this procedure. Also read the entire procedure to anticipate any other items you may require.

1. Disconnect the negative battery cable.
2. Drain the engine cooling system.
3. Loosen the clamps and remove the engine air cleaner outlet tube between the vane air meter and the air throttle body.
4. Disconnect and remove the accelerator and speed control cables from the accelerator mounting bracket and throttle lever, if equipped.
5. Disconnect the top manifold vacuum fitting connections.
6. Disconnect the PCV system hoses and vacuum line at EGR valve.
7. Disconnect the EGR tube form the intake manifold.
8. Remove the top bolt from the upper support manifold bracket. Leave the bottom bolts attached.
9. Disconnect the electrical connectors at main engine harness (near No. 1 runner) and at ECT sensor.
10. Remove the fuel supply and return lines.
11. Remove the manifold mounting nuts.

12. Remove the top bolt from the lower support manifold bracket. Leave the bottom bolts attached.
13. Remove the manifold with wiring harness and gasket.

To install:

14. Clean and inspect the mounting faces of the fuel charging manifold assembly and cylinder head. Clean and oil the manifold stud threads. Surfaces should be clean and flat.
15. Install a new gasket.
16. Install the manifold assembly to the head and secure with top middle nut. Tighten nut finger-tight only.
17. Install the fuel return line to fitting in fuel supply manifold. Install two manifold nuts finger-tight.
18. Install the remaining mounting nuts and tighten all to their specifications.
19. Connect the upper and lower manifold support brackets.
20. Install the EGR tube and PCV system.
21. Connect the accelerator, and if equipped, the speed control cables.
22. Reconnect the fuel lines and wiring harness.
23. Reconnect the negative battery cable and service the cooling system.

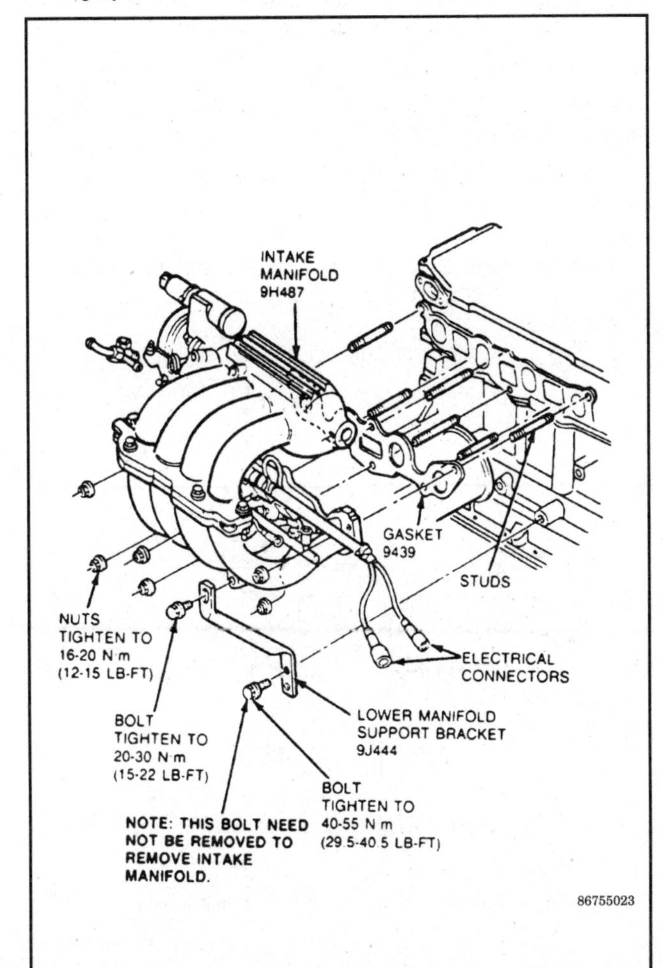

Fig. 38 Exploded view of the fuel charging assembly — 1.9L MFI engines

24. Use the EEC Self-Test connector to check for proper EEC sensor function.
25. Operate the engine until normal operating temperature is reached. As it warms up, check closely for leaks. If any leaks occur, turn off the engine immediately and correct the problem.
26. Check the idle speed and adjust if necessary.

REMOVAL & INSTALLATION

1.6L and 1.9L MFI Engine Sub-Assemblies

➡To prevent damage to the fuel charging assembly, the unit should be placed on a workbench during the disassembly and assembly procedures. The following is a step-by-step sequence of operations for servicing the assemblies of the fuel charging manifold. Some components may be serviced without a complete disassembly of the fuel charging manifold. To replace individual components, follow only the applicable steps.

These procedures are based on the fuel charging manifold having been removed from the vehicle.

UPPER INTAKE MANIFOLD

➧ See Figures 39 and 40

This procedure will require new gaskets for installation, so be sure to have the necessary parts prior to starting this procedure. Also read the entire procedure to anticipate any other items you may require.

1. Disconnect the engine air cleaner outlet tube from the air intake throttle body.
2. Unplug the throttle position sensor from the wiring harness.
3. Unplug the air bypass valve connector.
4. Remove the three upper manifold retaining bolts.
5. Remove upper manifold assembly and set it aside.
6. Remove and discard the gasket from the lower manifold assembly.

➡If scraping is necessary, be careful not to damage the gasket surfaces of the upper and lower manifold assemblies, or allow material to drop into the lower manifold.

7. Ensure that the gasket surfaces of the upper and lower intake manifolds are clean.

To install:

8. Place a new service gasket on the lower manifold assembly and mount the upper intake manifold to the lower, then install the three retaining bolts. Tighten to specifications.
9. Ensure the wiring harness is properly installed.
10. Attach the electrical connectors to the air bypass valve and throttle position sensor, and connect the vacuum hose to the fuel pressure regulator.
11. Connect the engine air cleaner outlet tube to the throttle body intake securing it with a hose clamp. Tighten to specification.

AIR INTAKE THROTTLE BODY

This procedure will require new gaskets for installation, so be sure to have the necessary parts prior to starting this pro-

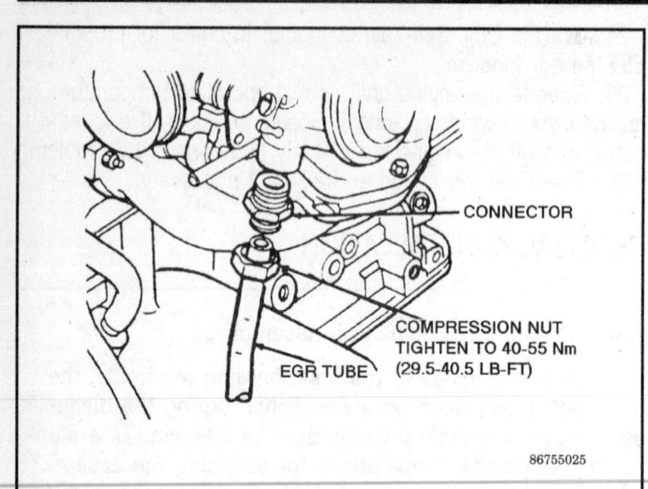

Fig. 39 Disconnect the EGR tube from the manifold as shown. Note the compression nut torque value upon installation

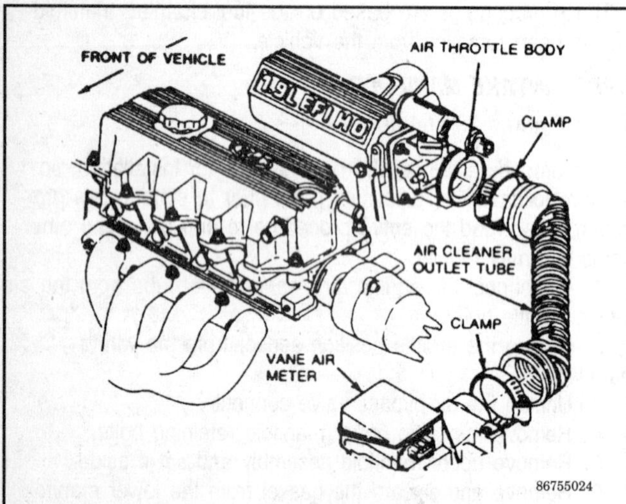

Fig. 40 Remove the upper intake manifold as an assembly — 1.6L and 1.9L MFI engines

cedure. Also read the entire procedure to anticipate any other items you may require.

1. Remove the four throttle body bolts. Ensure that the throttle position sensor connector and air bypass valve connector have been disconnected from the harness. Disconnect air cleaner outlet tube.
2. Identify and disconnect the vacuum hoses.
3. Remove the throttle bracket.
4. Carefully separate the throttle body from the upper intake manifold.
5. Remove and discard the gasket between the throttle body and the upper intake manifold.

➡If scraping of the gasket surface is necessary, be careful not to damage the surfaces of the throttle body and upper manifold assemblies, or allow material to drop into manifold.

6. Ensure that both throttle body and upper intake manifold gasket surfaces are clean.

To install:

7. Install the upper/throttle body gasket with the four bolts to the upper intake manifold. Tighten to 15-22 ft. lbs. (20-30 Nm).
8. Secure the throttle bracket and secure with retaining nuts. Tighten to 12-15 ft. lbs. (16-20 Nm).
9. Install the throttle bracket and secure with retaining nuts.
10. Connect the air bypass valve and throttle position sensor electrical connectors and the appropriate vacuum lines.
11. If the fuel charging assembly is still mounted to the engine, connect the engine air cleaner outlet tube to the throttle body intake securing it with a hose clamp. Tighten the hose clamp to 12-22 inch lbs. (1.4-2.3 Nm).

AIR BYPASS VALVE ASSEMBLY

➧ See Figures 41 and 42

1. Disconnect the air bypass valve assembly connector from the wiring harness.
2. Remove the two air bypass valve retaining screws.
3. Remove the air bypass valve and gasket.

➡If scraping is necessary, be careful not to damage the air bypass valve or throttle body gasket surfaces, or drop material into throttle body.

4. Ensure that both the throttle body and air bypass valve gasket surfaces are clean.

To install:

5. Install gasket on throttle body surface and mount the air bypass valve assembly securing it with retaining screws. Tighten to specifications.
6. Plug in the electrical connector to the air bypass valve.

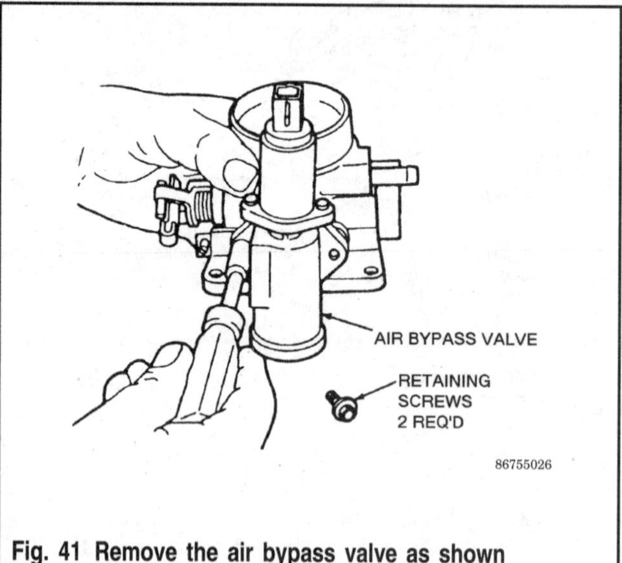

Fig. 41 Remove the air bypass valve as shown

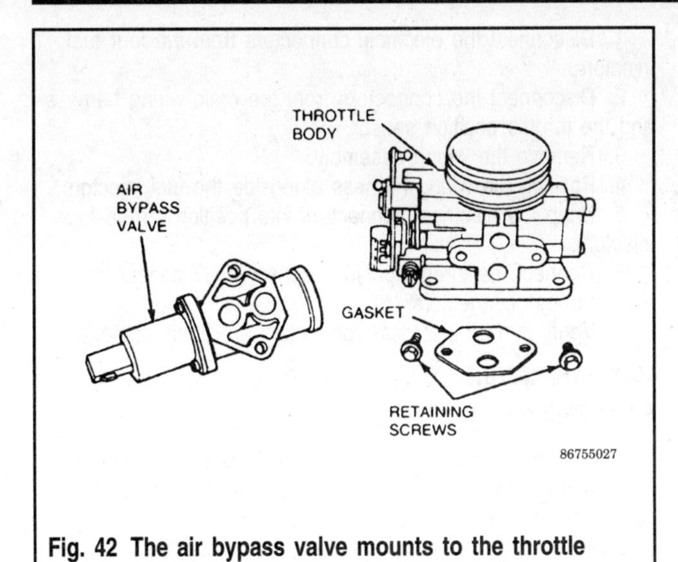

Fig. 42 The air bypass valve mounts to the throttle body as shown

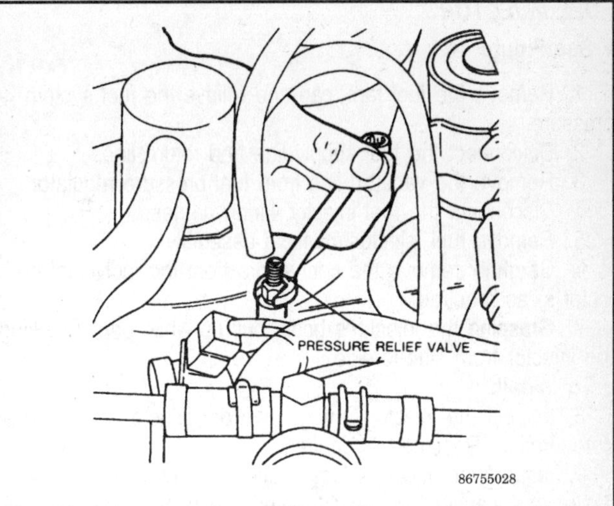

Fig. 43 An open-end wrench can be used to remove the pressure relief valve

THROTTLE POSITION SENSOR (TPS)

1. Disconnect the throttle position sensor from the wiring harness.

➡The TPS mounting screws have Pozidriv® heads. These heads look much like Phillips heads; however, attempting to use a Phillips screwdriver will probably damage them. To properly remove the TPS screws, use a Pozidriv® driver. Also, beginning in 1988, an adhesive thread locker was used to secure the TPS screws. In this case, a hammer and impact driver, if available, used with a Pozidriv® bit is strongly recommended.

2. Remove the throttle position sensor retaining screws.
3. Remove the throttle position sensor.
4. Install the throttle position sensor. Make sure that the rotary tangs on the sensor are in the proper alignment and the wires are pointing down.
5. Secure the sensor to the throttle body assembly with retaining screws. Tighten to specifications.

➡The throttle position sensor is not adjustable.

6. Connect the electrical connector to the harness.

PRESSURE RELIEF VALVE

➧ See Figure 43

1. If the fuel charging assembly is mounted to the engine, remove the fuel tank cap, then release fuel system pressure at the pressure relief valve on the fuel injection manifold using tool T80L-9974-A or equivalent. Note that the cap on the relief valve must be removed.
2. Using an open-end wrench or suitable deep-well socket, remove the pressure relief valve from the fuel injection manifold.
3. Install the pressure relief valve and cap. Tighten the valve to 48-84 inch lbs. (5.4-9.5 Nm) and the cap to 4-6 inch lbs. (0.45-0.68 Nm).

FUEL INJECTOR MANIFOLD ASSEMBLY

1. Remove the fuel tank cap and release the fuel system pressure.
2. Disconnect the fuel supply and fuel return lines.
3. Disconnect the wiring harness from the injectors.
4. Disconnect the vacuum line from the fuel pressure regulator valve.
5. Remove the two fuel injector manifolds retaining bolts.
6. Carefully disengage the manifold from the fuel injectors and remove the manifold.
7. Make sure the injector caps are clean and free of contamination.

To install:

8. Place the fuel injector manifold over the four injectors making sure the injectors are well seated in the fuel manifold assembly.
9. Secure the fuel manifold assembly to the charging assembly with the two retaining bolts.
10. Connect the fuel supply and fuel return lines.
11. Connect the fuel injector wiring harness.
12. Connect the vacuum line to fuel pressure regulator.

FUEL PRESSURE REGULATOR

1. Be sure that the assembly is de-pressurized by removing the fuel tank cap and releasing pressure from the fuel system.
2. Remove the vacuum line at the pressure regulator.
3. Remove the three Allen retaining screws from regulator housing.
4. Remove pressure regulator assembly, gasket and O-ring. Discard the gasket and inspect O-ring for signs of cracks or deterioration.

➡If scraping is necessary, be careful not to damage the fuel pressure regulator or fuel supply line gasket surfaces.

5. Lubricate the fuel pressure regulator O-ring with light oil ESF-M6C2-A or equivalent.
6. Make sure the gasket surfaces of fuel pressure regulator and fuel injection manifold are clean.
7. Install the O-ring and new gasket on regulator.
8. Install the fuel pressure regulator on the injector manifold. Tighten the three retaining screws to specifications.

FUEL INJECTOR

See Figure 44

1. Remove the fuel tank cap and relieve the fuel system pressure.
2. Disconnect the fuel supply line and return line.
3. Remove the vacuum line from fuel pressure regulator.
4. Disconnect the fuel injector wiring harness.
5. Remove fuel injector manifold assembly.
6. Carefully remove the connectors from the individual injector(s) as required.
7. Grasping the injector's body, pull up while gently rocking the injector from side-to-side.

To install:

8. Inspect the injector O-rings (two per injector) for signs of deterioration. Replace as required.
9. Inspect the injector plastic cover (covering the injector pintle) and washer for signs of deterioration. Replace as required.

➡ If the injector's "plastic hat" is missing, look for it in the intake manifold.

10. Lubricate new O-rings and install two on each injector (use a light grade oil ESF-M6C2-A or equivalent).
11. Install the injector(s). Use a light, twisting, pushing motion to install the injector(s).
12. Carefully seat the fuel injector manifold assembly on the four injectors and secure the manifold with attaching bolts. Tighten to specifications.
13. Connect the vacuum line to the fuel pressure regulator.
14. Connect fuel injector wiring harness.
15. Connect fuel supply and fuel return lines. Tighten fuel return line to specifications.
16. Check entire assembly for proper alignment and seating.

FUEL INJECTOR WIRING HARNESS

➡Be sure that the ignition is OFF and the fuel system is depressurized.

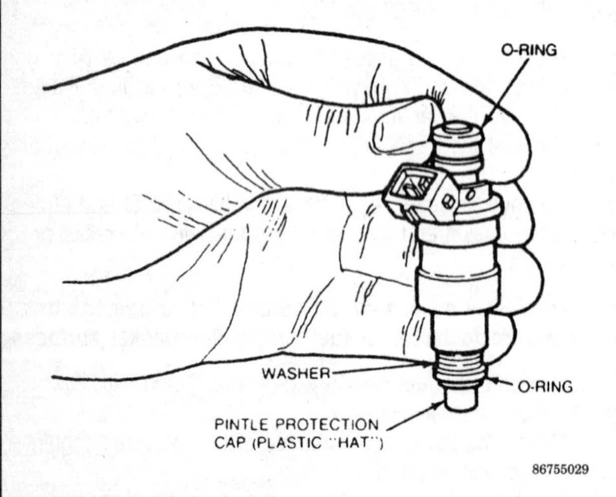

Fig. 44 Grasp and gently rock the injector back-and-forth, then pull up and remove

1. Disconnect the electrical connectors from the four fuel injectors.
2. Disconnect the connectors from the main wiring harness and the throttle position sensor.
3. Remove the wiring assembly.
4. Position the wiring harness alongside the fuel injectors.
5. Snap the electrical connectors into position on the four injectors.
6. Connect the throttle position sensor, ECT sensor and main harness connectors.
7. Verify that all electrical connectors are firmly seated.

VANE AIR METER

See Figure 45

1. Loosen the hose clamp which secures the air cleaner outlet hose to the vane air meter assembly and position the outlet hose out of the way.
2. Remove air intake and air outlet tube from the air cleaner.
3. Disengage the four spring clamps and remove the air cleaner front cover and air cleaner filter panel.
4. Remove the four screws and washers from the flange of the air cleaner where it is attached to the vane air meter assembly. Pull the air cleaner base away from the vane air meter and remove the air cleaner gasket. If the gasket shoes signs of deterioration, replace it.

➡If scraping is necessary, be careful not to damage the air cleaner outlet and vane air meter gasket surfaces.

5. Remove the electrical connector from the vane air meter assembly.
6. Remove the two screws and washers assemblies which secure the vane air meter assembly to the vane air meter bracket and remove the vane air meter assembly.

To install:

7. Clean the mounting surfaces of the air cleaner outlet flange and the vane air meter housing.
8. Place the four retaining screws through the four holes in the air cleaner outlet flange and place a new gasket over the screws.
9. Mount the vane air meter assembly to the vane air meter bracket using two screws and washers. Note that these screws are not the physical size and care must be taken to ensure that the proper screw is in the proper hole. Tighten screws to 6-9 ft. lbs. (8-12 Nm).
10. Secure the air cleaner outlet to the vane air meter with the four screws mentioned in Step 2. Tighten to 6-9 ft. lbs. (8-12 Nm). Make sure the gasket is properly sealed and aligned.
11. Secure the engine air cleaner outlet tube to the vane air meter assembly with the hose clamp. Tighten to 15-25 inch lbs. (2-3 Nm).
12. Install the engine air cleaner cover and snap spring clips into position.
13. Secure the air intake duct to air cleaner.
14. Connect all hoses to the air cleaner.

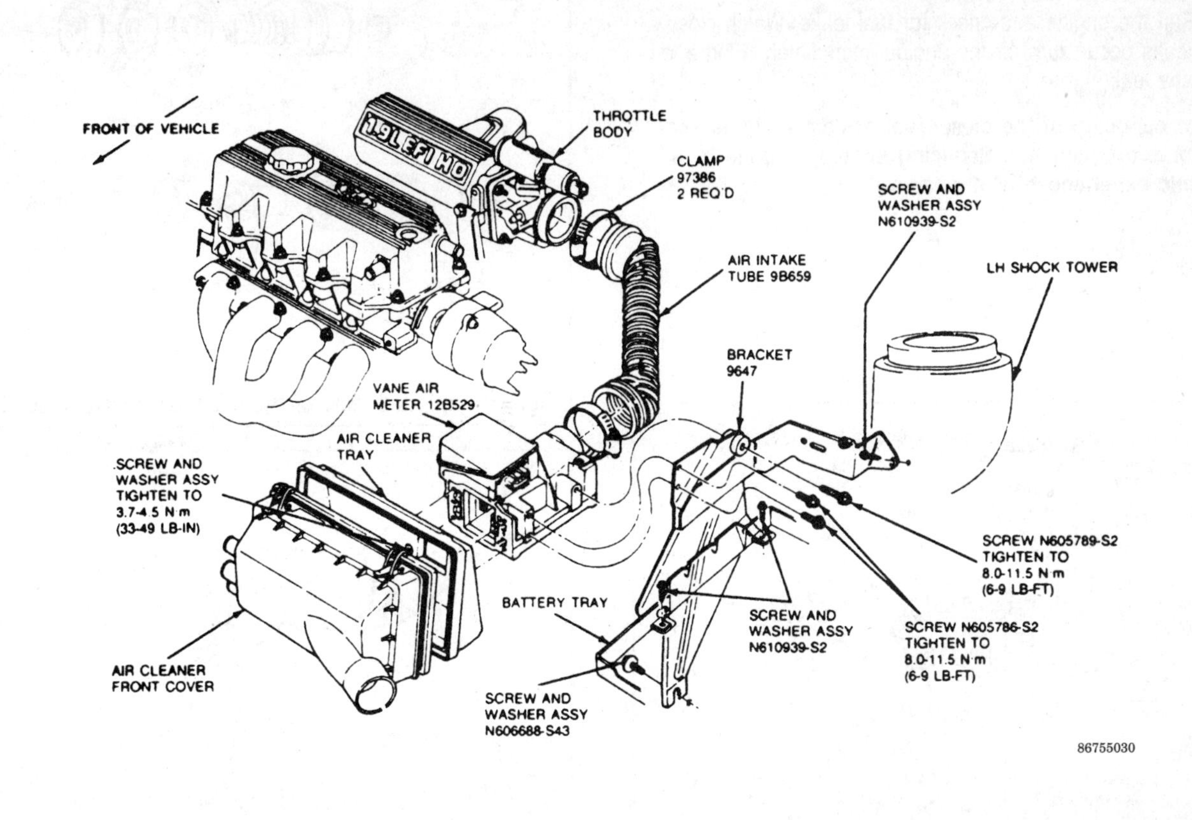

Fig. 45 Exploded view of the vane air meter mounting

DIESEL FUEL SYSTEM

See Figure 46

In the following procedures, special tools and/or parts may be required. Carefully read the applicable procedure(s) before beginning, to make sure you have all tools and parts necessary to complete the repair.

Injection Nozzles

REMOVAL & INSTALLATION

See Figures 47, 48 and 49

1. Disconnect and remove injection lines from the injection pump and nozzles. Cap all lines and fittings using Protective Cap Set T84P-9395-A or equivalent.
2. Remove nuts attaching the fuel return line to the nozzles, and remove return line and seals.
3. Remove nozzles using a 27mm deep-well socket.
4. Remove nozzles gaskets and washers from nozzle seat, using O-ring Pick Tool T71P-19703-C or equivalent.
5. Clean the outside of the nozzle assemblies using Nozzle Cleaning Kit, Rotunda model 14-0301 or equivalent, and a suitable solvent. Dry all parts thoroughly.

To install:

6. Position new sealing gaskets in the nozzle seats.

➡Install the gasket with the red painted surface facing up.

7. Position new copper washers in the nozzles bores.
8. Install the nozzles and tighten to 44-51 ft. lbs. (60-70 Nm).
9. Position the fuel return line on the nozzles, using new seals.

10. Install the fuel return line retaining nuts and tighten to 10 ft. lbs. (14 Nm).
11. Install the fuel lines on the injection pump and nozzles. Tighten the capnuts to 18-22 ft. lbs. (24-30 Nm).
12. Air bleed the fuel system.
13. Run the engine and check for fuel leaks. Watch closely. If any leaks occur, turn off the engine immediately. Find and repair any leak(s).

➡Other servicing of the diesel fuel system requires special tool and equipment. Servicing should be done by a mechanic experienced with diesels.

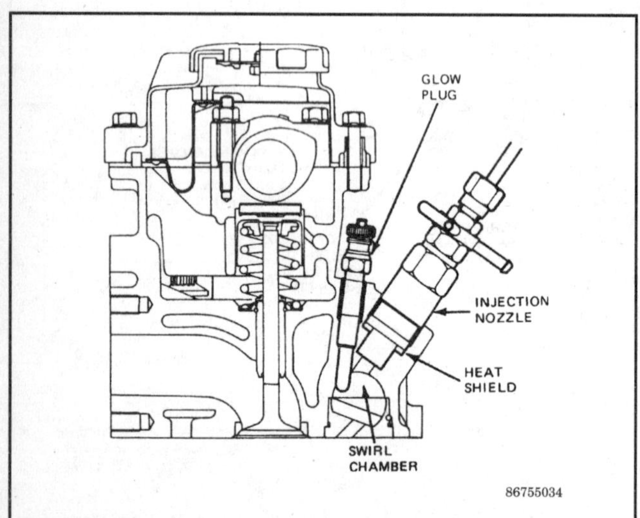

Fig. 46 Cross-sectional view of the diesel cylinder head and fuel supply components

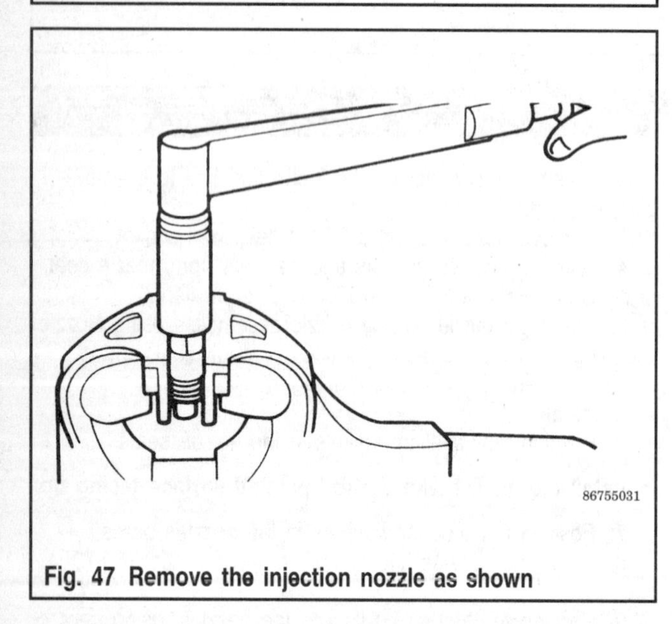

Fig. 47 Remove the injection nozzle as shown

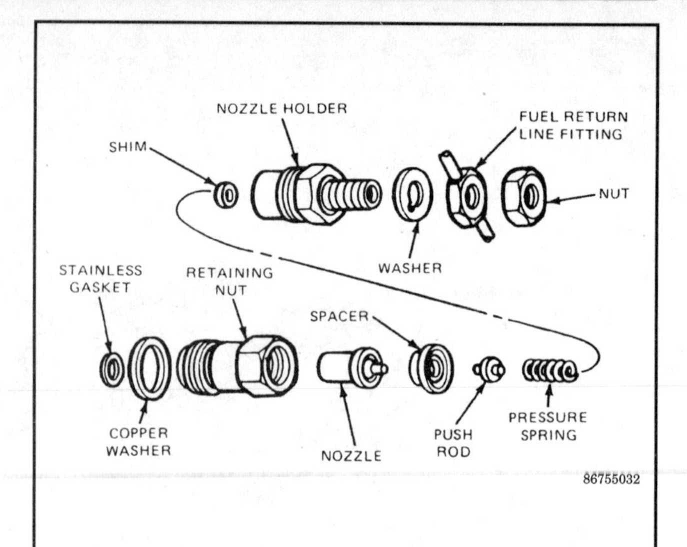

Fig. 48 Exploded view of the injection nozzle assembly

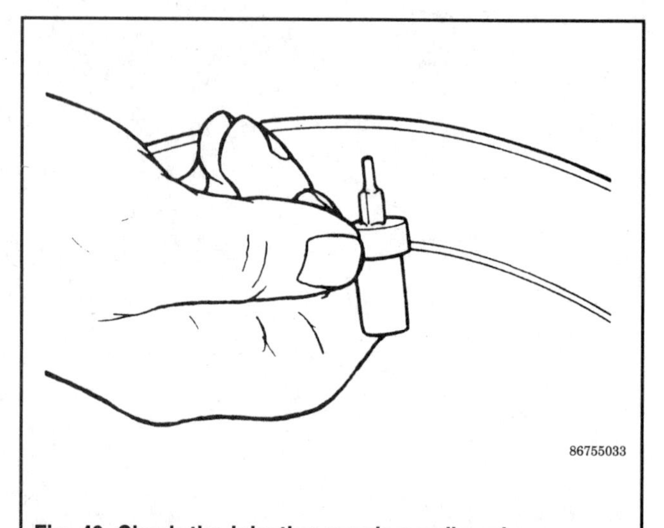

Fig. 49 Check the injection nozzle needle valve as shown

Fuel Cutoff Solenoid

REMOVAL & INSTALLATION

1. Disconnect the battery ground cable from the battery, located in the luggage compartment.
2. Remove the connector from the fuel cutoff solenoid.
3. Remove the fuel cutoff solenoid and discard the O-ring.

To install:

4. Install fuel cutoff solenoid using a new O-ring. Tighten to 30-33 ft. lbs. (40-45 Nm).
5. fasten the electrical connector.
6. Connect battery ground cable.
7. Run engine and check for fuel leaks. Watch closely. If any leaks occur, turn off the engine immediately. Find and repair any leak(s) detected.

Fuel Injectors

REMOVAL & INSTALLATION

1. Disconnect the negative battery cable.
2. Disconnect and remove the injection lines from the injection pump and nozzles. Cap all lines and fitting to prevent dirt contamination.
3. Remove the nuts attaching the fuel return line to the nozzles and remove the return line and seals.
4. Remove the injector nozzles using a 27mm socket. Remove the nozzle gaskets and washers from the nozzle seats using an O-ring pick tool.

To install:

5. Clean the outside of the nozzles with safety solvent and dry them thoroughly.
6. Position new sealing gaskets and heat shields in nozzle seats with the blue painted gasket surface facing up.
7. Position new copper gaskets in the nozzles bores. Install the nozzles and tighten to 44-51 ft. lbs. (60-70 Nm).
8. Position the fuel return line on the nozzles using new seals. Install the retaining nuts and tighten to 10 ft. lbs. (14 Nm).
9. Install the fuel lines on the injection pump and nozzles. Tighten to 18-22 ft. lbs. (25-29 Nm).
10. Air bleed the fuel system. Run the engine and check for fuel leaks. Watch closely. If any leaks occur, turn off the engine immediately. Find and repair any leak(s) detected.

Injection Pump

REMOVAL & INSTALLATION

1. Disconnect battery ground cable from the battery, located in the luggage compartment.
2. Disconnect air inlet duct from the air cleaner and intake manifold. Install protective cap in intake manifold.

➡Cap is part of Protective Cap Set, T84P-9395-A.

3. Remove rear timing belt cover and flywheel timing mark cover.
4. Remove rear timing belt.
5. Disconnect throttle cable and speed control cable, if so equipped.
6. Disconnect vacuum hoses at the altitude compensator and cold start diaphragm.
7. Disconnect fuel cutoff solenoid connector.
8. Disconnect fuel supply and fuel return hoses at injection pump.
9. Remove injection lines at the injection pump and nozzles. Cap all lines and fittings using Protective Cap Set T84P-9395-A or equivalent.
10. Rotate injection pump sprocket until timing marks are aligned. Install the two M8 x 1.25 bolts in holes to hold the injection pump sprocket. Remove sprocket retaining nut.
11. Remove injection pump sprocket using Gear Puller T77F-4220-B1 and Adapter D80L-625-4 or equivalent, using two M8 x 1.25 bolts installed in the threaded holes in the sprocket.
12. Remove bolt attaching the injection pump to the pump front bracket.
13. Remove the nuts attaching the injection pump to the pump rear bracket and remove the pump.

To install:

14. Install the injection pump in position on the pump bracket.
15. Install two nuts attaching the pump to the rear bracket and tighten to 23-34 ft. lbs. (32-47 Nm).
16. Install bolt attaching the pump to the front bracket and tighten to 12-16 ft. lbs. (16-23 Nm).
17. Install injection pump sprocket. Hold the sprocket in place using the procedure described in Step 10. Install the sprocket retaining nut and tighten to 51-58 ft. lbs. (70-80 Nm).
18. Remove the protective caps and install the fuel lines at the injection pump and nozzles. Tighten the fuel line capnuts to 18-22 ft. lbs. (25-29 Nm).
19. Connect the fuel supply and fuel return hoses at the injection pump.
20. Plug in the fuel cutoff solenoid connector.
21. Connect the vacuum lines to the cold start diaphragm and altitude compensator.
22. Connect the throttle cable and speed control cable, if so equipped.
23. Install and adjust the rear timing belt.
24. Remove protective cap and install the air inlet duct to the intake manifold and air cleaner.
25. Connect battery ground cable to battery.
26. Air bleed fuel system as outlined.
27. Check and adjust the injection pump timing.
28. Run engine and check for fuel leaks. Watch closely. If any leaks occur, turn off the engine immediately. Find and repair any leak(s) detected.
29. Check and adjust engine idle.

INJECTION TIMING

➡The engine coolant temperature must be above 176°F (80°C) before the injection timing can be checked and/or adjusted.

1. Disconnect the battery ground cable from the battery, located in the luggage compartment.
2. Remove the injection pump distributor head plug bolt and sealing washer.
3. Install a Static Timing Gauge Adapter, Rotunda part No. 14-0303 or equivalent with a metric dial indicator, so that the indicator pointer is in contact with the injection pump plunger.
4. Remove the timing mark cover from the transaxle housing. Align the timing mark (TDC) with the pointer on the rear engine cover plate.
5. Rotate the crankshaft pulley slowly, counterclockwise until the dial indicator pointer stops moving (approximately 30-50° BTDC).
6. Adjust the dial indicator to zero (0).

➡Confirm that the dial indicator pointer does not move from zero by slightly rotating the crankshaft left and right.

7. Turn the crankshaft clockwise until the crankshaft timing mark aligns with the indicator pin. The dial indicator should read 0.0392-0.0408 in. (0.98-1.02mm). If the reading is not within specification, adjust as follows:
   a. Loosen the injection pump attaching bolt and nuts.
   b. Rotate the injection pump toward the engine to advance timing and away from the engine to retard timing.
   c. Rotate the injection pump until the dial indicator reads 0.0392-0.0408 in. (0.98-1.02mm).
   d. Tighten the injection pump attaching nuts and bolt to 13-20 ft. lbs. (17.5-27 Nm).
   e. Repeat Steps 5-7 to check that the timing is adjusted correctly.
8. Remove the dial indicator and adapter and install the injection pump distributor head plug and tighten to 10-14 ft. lbs. (14-19 Nm).
9. Connect the battery ground cable to the battery.
10. Start the engine, then check and adjust idle rpm, if necessary. Check for fuel leaks. Watch closely. If any leaks occur, turn off the engine immediately. Find and repair any leak(s) detected.

Glow Plugs

The diesel start/glow plug control circuit applies power to the glow plugs which heat the combustion chambers, so that the cold diesel engine can be started.

DIESEL STARTING

Power is applied through heavy gauge wires to the starter relay located on the left-hand front fender apron, then to the starter solenoid. When the wait-to-start indicator light goes out, the ignition switch can be turned to the **START** position. Power is applied to the starter relay. The relay applies power to the solenoid coil, which in turn closes the contacts to apply battery power to the starter motor.

Even after the wait-to-start indicator goes out, the glow plugs must be kept hot because the combustion chambers may not be hot enough to keep the engine running smoothly. To compensate for this, the after-glow relay continues to provide power to the glow plugs until one of the following conditions occurs:

- The vehicle moves
- The coolant temperature rises above 86°F (30°C)
- The glow plug voltage goes above 5.7 volts

Vehicle movement is defined as a clutch switch closed (not depressed) and the neutral switch closed (transaxle in any position except Neutral). This means pin 10 of the diesel control module is grounded.

The coolant temperature is measured by the thermoswitch. Whenever the coolant temperature is above 86°F (30°C), the thermoswitch is opened and there is no voltage on pin No. 8. This will prevent the entire glow plug circuit from operating, because the engine is hot enough to start and run without the glow plugs working.

If the voltage on the glow plugs is over 5.7 volts, they may overheat and burn out. Therefore, if more than 5.7 volts is detected at pin 11 (with the pre-glow relay off), then the after-glow relay is shut off.

When the ignition is in the **START** position, 12 volts is put on pin No. 7 of the module. This causes the pre-glow relay to cycle on and off to keep the glow plugs hot. The pre-glow relay will cycle only during cranking.

Power from fusible link B (which is connected to the starter relay) is applied to the fuel solenoid with the ignition switch in the **START** or **RUN** position. The fuel solenoid opens the fuel line to permit the engine to run. When the ignition switch is in the **OFF** position, the solenoid cuts off fuel flow and stops the engine.

GLOW PLUG CONTROL

The solid state diesel control module is mounted under the left-hand side of the instrument panel. It controls glow plug pre-glow time, after-glow time and the operation of the wait-to-start indicator light.

When the ignition switch is placed in the **RUN** position, the wait indicator lamp lights and the pre-glow No. 1 relay and the after-glow No. 2 relay go into operation. Voltage from the ignition switch is applied through pin 6 of the control module and then to the relays through pins 2 and 3. The contacts of the pre-glow relay close and the power is applied from fusible link S (located at the left-hand side of the engine above the starter) to operate the glow plugs. The plugs then start to heat up.

With power applied to the glow plugs, voltage is returned through circuit 472 yellow wire with a black tracer to the control module at pin No. 11. After three seconds, the wait-to-start indicator goes out and stays out. The glow plugs are now warm enough for the engine to be started. After three more seconds the pre-glow relay opens. Power is now applied through the after-glow relay and the dropping resistor (located in the air intake at the engine manifold) to keep the glow plugs operating at a reduced voltage.

➡The after-glow and the pre-glow relays are located at the top center area of the dash panel, which could be either underneath the instrument panel or near the center of the firewall.

DIAGNOSIS AND TESTING

See Figures 50, 51, 52, 53 and 54

Follow the steps described in the accompanying charts.

REMOVAL & INSTALLATION

1. Disconnect the battery ground cable from the battery, located in the luggage compartment.
2. Disconnect the glow plug harness from the glow plugs.
3. Using a 12mm deep-well socket, remove the glow plugs.

To install:

4. Install the glow plugs, using a 12mm deep well socket. Tighten the glow plugs to 11-15 ft. lbs. (15-20 Nm).
5. Connect the glow plug harness to the glow plugs. Tighten the nuts to 5-7 ft. lbs. (7-9 Nm).

Wait-To-Start Lamp (Refer to Quick Start Control System Schematic)

TEST STEP	RESULT ▶	ACTION TO TAKE
E0 WAIT LAMP		
• Turn ignition to RUN. Wait lamp should stay on for 3 seconds, then go out.	OK ▶	GO to Glow Plug Control System in this Section.
	Lamp does not light ▶	GO to E1.
	Lamp lights, but does not go out ▶	REPLACE glow plug control module and REPEAT test Step E0.
E1 WAIT LAMP BULB		
• Connect a jumper wire between glow plug control module connector terminal No. 1 and ground. **NOTE: Located under LH side of instrument panel.** • Turn ignition to RUN. 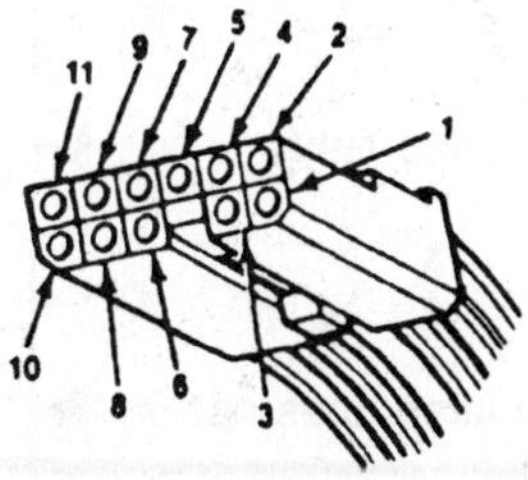	Wait lamp lights ▶	GO to E2.
	Wait lamp does not light ▶	REPLACE wait lamp bulb or SERVICE or REPLACE wait lamp wiring as necessary. REPEAT Test Step E0.
E2 TERMINAL 6 (POWER CIRCUIT)		
• Connect a 12V test lamp to connector terminal No. 6 and ground. • Turn ignition to RUN.	Test lamp lights ▶	REPLACE glow plug control module. REPEAT Test Step E0.
	Test lamp does not light ▶	SERVICE and/or REPLACE ignition switch and/or wiring as necessary. REPEAT Test Step E0.

86755109

Fig. 50 Glow plug system diagnosis

Glow Plug Control System (Refer to Quick Start Control System Schematic)

TEST STEP	RESULT ▶	ACTION TO TAKE
F0 CHECK VOLTAGE TO EACH GLOW PLUG		
• Place transmission gear selector in NEUTRAL. **NOTE: If engine coolant temperature is above 30°C (86°F), jumper connections at coolant thermoswitch.** • Turn ignition switch to RUN. • Using a voltmeter, check voltage at each glow plug lead. Minimum of 11 volts at each lead for 6 seconds, then drops to 4.2 to 5.3 volts.	Voltage OK ▶	REMOVE jumper from coolant thermoswitch. GO to F13.
	No voltage ▶	GO to F1.
	No voltage at 3 or less glow plugs ▶	REPLACE glow plug harness. REPEAT Test Step F0.
	Voltage is OK for 6 seconds, then drops to zero ▶	GO to F6.
	Voltage is OK for 6 seconds, then remains at a minimum of 11V ▶	REPLACE glow plug control module.
F1 ENGINE HARNESS TO GLOW PLUG HARNESS		
• Disconnect glow plug harness from engine harness and glow plugs. • Connect a self-powered test lamp between glow plug harness connector and each glow plug terminal.	Test lamp lights ▶	RECONNECT glow plug harness. GO to F2.
	Test lamp does not light ▶	SERVICE or REPLACE glow plug harness. REPEAT Test Step F0.
F2 TERMINAL 6 (POWER CIRCUIT)		
• Connect a 12 volt test lamp between glow plug control module terminal No. 6 and ground. • Turn ignition switch to RUN.	Test lamp lights ▶	GO to F3.
	Test lamp does not light ▶	SERVICE and/or REPLACE ignition switch and/or wiring as necessary. REPEAT Test Step F0.

86755110

Fig. 51 Glow plug system diagnosis (continued)

Glow Plug Control System

TEST STEP	RESULT ▶	ACTION TO TAKE
F3 TERMINAL 2 (NO. 1 GLOW PLUG RELAY SIGNAL)		
• Connect a 12 volt test lamp between glow plug control module terminal No. 2 (signal) and ground. • Turn ignition switch to RUN.	Test lamp lights for 6 seconds ▶	GO to **F4**.
	Test lamp does not light ▶	REPLACE quick start control unit. REPEAT Test Step **F3**.
F4 NO. 1 GLOW PLUG RELAY WIRING		
• Connect a 12 volt test lamp between No. 1 glow plug relay signal terminal and ground. • Turn ignition to RUN.	Test lamp lights for 6 seconds ▶	GO to **F5**.
	Test lamp does not light ▶	SERVICE or REPLACE wiring between quick start control unit terminal 2 and No. 1 glow plug relay. REPEAT Test Step **F4**.
F5 NO. 1 GLOW PLUG RELAY		
• Connect a voltmeter between No. 1 glow plug relay output terminal (to glow plugs) and ground. • Turn ignition switch to RUN.	11 volts or more for 6 seconds ▶	GO to **F12**.
	Less than 11 volts ▶	REPLACE No. 1 glow plug relay. REPEAT Test Step **F5**.
F6 TERMINAL NO. 3 (NO. 2 GLOW PLUG RELAY SIGNAL)		
• Connect a 12 volt test lamp between glow plug control module terminal No. 3 (signal) and ground. • Turn ignition switch to RUN.	Test lamp lights ▶	GO to **F8**.
	Test lamp does not light ▶	GO to **F7**.

86755111

Fig. 52 Glow plug system diagnosis (continued)

Glow Plug Control System

TEST STEP	RESULT	ACTION TO TAKE
F7 CLUTCH SWITCH/NEUTRAL SWITCH		
• Using a self-powered test lamp, check the functioning of clutch and neutral switch in both open and closed positions. • With transmission in gear and clutch pedal released, both switches should be open. • With transmission in Neutral and clutch pedal depressed, both switches should be closed.	OK ▶	GO to F8.
	NOT OK ▶	REPLACE malfunctioning clutch or neutral switch. REPEAT Test Step F7.
F8 NO. 2 GLOW PLUG RELAY WIRING		
• Connect a 12 volt test lamp between No. 2 glow plug relay signal terminal and ground. • Place transmission gear selector in Neutral. • Turn ignition switch to RUN.	Test lamp lights ▶	GO to F9.
	Test lamp does not light ▶	SERVICE or REPLACE wiring between glow plug control module terminal No. 3 and No. 2 glow plug relay. REPEAT Test Step F8.
F9 NO. 2 GLOW PLUG RELAY		
• Connect a 12 volt test lamp between No. 2 glow plug relay output terminal (to glow plugs) and ground. • Turn ignition to RUN.	Test lamp lights ▶	GO to F10.
	Test lamp does not light ▶	REPLACE No. 2 glow plug relay. REPEAT Test Step F9.
F10 DROPPING RESISTOR WIRING		
• Disconnect dropping resistor from wiring harness. • Connect a 12 volt test lamp between the dropping resistor input terminal on wiring harness and ground. • Turn ignition to RUN.	Test lamp lights ▶	GO to F11.
	Test lamp does not light ▶	SERVICE or REPLACE wiring between No. 2 glow plug relay and dropping resistor. REPEAT Test Step F10.

86755112

Fig. 53 Glow plug system diagnosis (continued)

Glow Plug Control System

TEST STEP	RESULT ▶	ACTION TO TAKE
F11 DROPPING RESISTOR		
• Connect an ohmmeter to the connector terminals on the resistor. • Set multiply by knob to X1. • Ohmmeter should indicate less than 1 ohm.	OK ▶	RECONNECT dropping resistor to wiring harness. GO to F12.
	NOT OK ▶	REPLACE dropping resistor. REPEAT Test Step F11.
F12 GLOW PLUG HARNESS		
• Connect a 12 volt test lamp between any glow plug terminal and ground. • Turn ignition to RUN.	Test lamp lights ▶	GO to F0.
	Test lamp does not light ▶	SERVICE or REPLACE wiring from No. 1 glow plug relay to glow plug harness. REPEAT Test Step F12.
F13 GLOW PLUGS		
• Disconnect leads from each glow plug. • Connect one lead of ohmmeter to glow plug terminal and one lead to a good ground. • Set ohmmeter multiply by knob to X1. • Test each glow plug.	Meter indicates less than one ohm ▶	Problem is not in glow plug system.
	Meter indicates one ohm or more ▶	REPLACE glow plug. REPEAT Test Step F13.

86755113

Fig. 54 Glow plug system diagnosis (continued)

6. Connect the battery ground cable to the battery in the luggage compartment.

7. Check to ensure proper glow plug system operation.

FUEL TANK

Tank Assembly

REMOVAL & INSTALLATION

This procedure will require a new flange gasket for installation. Be sure to have the necessary part(s) prior to starting this procedure. Also read the entire procedure prior to beginning to anticipate the need of any chemicals, tools or other items.

⁂CAUTION

Extreme caution should be taken when removing the fuel tank from the vehicle. Do not smoke and keep any open flame away from the work area. Ensure that all removal procedures are conducted in a well-ventilated area. Have a sufficient amount of absorbent material in the vicinity of the work area to quickly contain any fuel spillage. Never store waste fuel in an open container, as it presents a serious fire hazard.

1. Relieve the fuel system pressure, then disconnect the negative battery cable.
2. Remove the fuel from the fuel tank by pumping it out through the filler neck. Clean up any fuel spillage immediately.
3. Raise and safely support the rear of the vehicle, then remove the fuel filler tube (neck).
4. Support the fuel tank and remove the fuel tank straps, then lower the fuel tank enough to remove the fuel lines, electrical connectors and vent lines from the tank.
5. Remove the fuel tank from under the vehicle and place it on a suitable workbench. Remove any dirt around the fuel pump attaching flange.
6. Turn the fuel pump locking ring counterclockwise and remove the lock ring.
7. Remove the fuel pump from the fuel tank and discard the flange gasket.

To install:

8. Clean the fuel pump mounting flange and fuel tank mounting surface and seal ring groove.
9. Lightly coat the new seal ring gasket with a lubricant compound (part No. C1AZ-19590-B or equivalent), to hold the gasket in place during installation.
10. Install the fuel pump and sender. Ensure that the nylon filter is not damaged, that the locating keys are in the keyways, and that the seal ring remains in place.
11. Hold the assembly in place and install the locking ring finger-tight. Ensure that all locking tabs are under tank lock ring tabs.
12. Secure the unit with the locking ring by rotating the ring clockwise with fuel sender wrench tool D84P-9275-A or equivalent, until the ring is positioned against the stops.
13. Move the tank from the bench to the vehicle and support the tank, then properly connect the fuel lines, vent line and electrical connectors.
14. Install the tank in the vehicle and secure with its retaining straps.
15. Lower the vehicle and pour fresh fuel into the tank. Check for leaks and, if any are found, repair before proceeding.
16. Connect the negative battery cable.
17. Using a pressure gauge, check the fuel system pressure.
18. Remove the pressure gauge, then start the engine and recheck for fuel leaks. Correct any fuel leaks immediately.

SENDING UNIT REPLACEMENT

➡Before removing the fuel tank sending unit, make sure the tank is less than half full.

1. Remove the rear seat cushion.
2. Remove the screws securing the fuel pump cover and ground strap to the floor pan.
3. Unplug the electrical connector.
4. Remove the rubber grommet and wiring from the fuel pump cover.
5. For fuel injected models: relieve the fuel system pressure.
6. Disconnect the fuel lines from the fuel pump.
7. Remove the pump spanner nut using a spanner removal tool, or equivalent.
8. Remove the fuel pump and gasket from the fuel tank.
9. Unplug the fuel gauge sending unit electrical connector from the flange terminal.
10. Remove the bolts securing the fuel gauge sending unit to the fuel pump.
11. Remove the fuel gauge sending unit.

To install:

12. Position the fuel gauge sending unit and bolt to the fuel pump.
13. Plug in the sending unit electrical connector to the flange terminal.
14. Install a new gasket and install the fuel pump in the tank.

➡Prior to completely sealing the replacement sending unit, perform a quick test for proper operation by turning the ignition key ON to see whether the gauge on the dash registers correctly.

15. Connect the fuel lines.
16. Plug in the electrical connector.
17. Install the pump cover and ground strap to the floor pan.
18. Install the rear seat cushion.

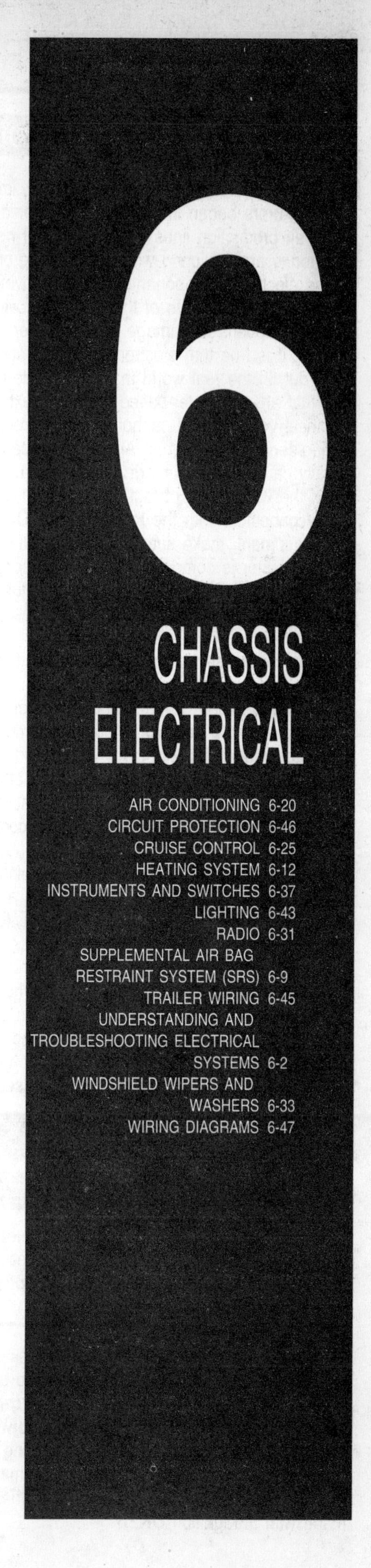

6 CHASSIS ELECTRICAL

UNDERSTANDING AND TROUBLESHOOTING ELECTRICAL SYSTEMS

Over the years covered by this manual, import and domestic manufacturers began incorporating electronic control systems into their production lines. In fact, most (if not all) new vehicles sold today are equipped with one or more on-board computer. These electronic components (with no moving parts) should theoretically last the life of the vehicle, provided nothing external happens to damage the circuits or memory chips.

While it is true that electronic components should never wear out, in the real world malfunctions do occur. It is also true that any computer-based system is extremely sensitive to electrical voltages and cannot tolerate careless or haphazard testing/service procedures. An inexperienced individual can literally cause major damage looking for a minor problem by using the wrong kind of test equipment or connecting test leads/connectors with the ignition switch **ON**. When selecting test equipment, make sure the manufacturer's instructions state that the tester is compatible with whatever type of system is being serviced. Read all instructions carefully and double check all test points before installing probes or making any test connections.

The following section outlines basic diagnosis techniques for dealing with automotive electrical systems. Along with a general explanation of the various types of test equipment available to aid in servicing modern automotive systems, basic repair techniques for wiring harnesses and connectors are also given. Read the basic information before attempting any repairs or testing. This will provide the background of information necessary to avoid the most common and obvious mistakes that can cost both time and money. Although the replacement and testing procedures are simple in themselves, the systems are not, and unless one has a thorough understanding of all components and their function within a particular system, the logical test sequence these systems demand cannot be followed. Minor malfunctions can make a big difference, so it is important to know how each component affects the operation of the overall system to find the ultimate cause of a problem without replacing good components unnecessarily. It is not enough to use the correct test equipment; the test equipment must be used correctly.

Safety Precautions

✲✲✲CAUTION

Whenever working on or around any electrical or electronic systems, always observe these general precautions to prevent the possibility of personal injury or damage to electronic components.

- Never install or remove battery cables with the key **ON** or the engine running. Jumper cables should be connected with the key **OFF** to avoid power surges that can damage electronic control units. Engines equipped with computer controlled systems should avoid both giving and getting jump starts due to the possibility of serious damage to components from arcing in the engine compartment when connections are made with the ignition **ON**.
- Always remove the battery cables before charging the battery. Never use a high output charger on an installed battery or attempt to use any type of "hot shot" (24 volt) starting aid.
- Exercise care when inserting test probes into connectors to insure good contact without damaging the connector or spreading the pins. Always probe connectors from the rear (wire) side, NOT the pin side, to avoid accidental shorting of terminals during test procedures.
- Never remove or attach wiring harness connectors with the ignition switch **ON**, especially to an electronic control unit.
- Do not drop any components during service procedures and never apply 12 volts directly to any component (like a solenoid or relay) unless instructed specifically to do so. Some component electrical windings are designed to safely handle only 4 or 5 volts and can be destroyed in seconds if 12 volts are applied directly to the connector.
- Remove the electronic control unit if the vehicle is to be placed in an environment where temperatures exceed approximately 176°F (80°C), such as a paint spray booth or when arc/gas welding near the control unit location.

Add-On Electrical Equipment

The electrical system in your car is designed to perform under reasonable operating conditions without interference between components. Before any additional electrical equipment is installed, it is recommended that you consult your dealer or a reputable repair facility familiar with the vehicle and its systems.

If the vehicle is equipped with mobile radio equipment and/or mobile telephone, it may have an effect upon the operation of the ECM. Radio Frequency Interference (RFI) from the communications system can be picked up by the car's wiring harnesses and conducted into the ECM, giving it the wrong messages at the wrong time. Although well shielded against RFI, the ECM should be further protected by taking the following measures:

- Install the antenna as far as possible from the ECM. Since the ECM is located behind the center console area, the antenna should be mounted at the rear of the car.
- Keep the antenna wiring a minimum of eight inches away from any wiring running to the ECM and from the ECM itself. NEVER wind the antenna wire around any other wiring.
- Mount the equipment as far from the ECM as possible. Be very careful during installation not to drill through any wires or short a wire harness with a mounting screw.
- Insure that the electrical feed wire(s) to the equipment are properly and tightly connected. Loose connectors can cause interference.
- Make certain that the equipment is properly grounded to the car. Poor grounding can damage expensive equipment.

Organized Troubleshooting

When diagnosing a specific problem, organized troubleshooting is a must. The complexity of a modern automobile demands that you approach any problem in a logical, organized manner. There are certain troubleshooting techniques that are standard:

1. Establish when the problem occurs. Does the problem appear only under certain conditions? Were there any noises, odors, or other unusual symptoms?

2. Isolate the problem area. To do this, make some simple tests and observations; then eliminate the systems that are working properly. Check for obvious problems such as broken wires, dirty connections or split/disconnected vacuum hoses. Always check the obvious before assuming something complicated is the cause.

3. Test for problems systematically to determine the cause once the problem area is isolated. Are all the components functioning properly? Is there power going to electrical switches and motors? Is there vacuum at vacuum switches and/or actuators? Is there a mechanical problem such as bent linkage or loose mounting screws? Performing careful, systematic checks will often turn up most causes on the first inspection without wasting time checking components that have little or no relationship to the problem.

4. Test all repairs after the work is done to make sure that the problem is fixed. Some causes can be traced to more than one component, so a careful verification of repair work is important to pick up additional malfunctions that may cause a problem to reappear or a different problem to arise. A blown fuse, for example, is a simple problem that may require more than another fuse to repair. If you don't look for a problem that caused a fuse to blow, a shorted wire for example, may go undetected.

Experience has shown that most problems tend to be the result of a fairly simple and obvious cause, such as loose or corroded connectors or air leaks in the intake system. This makes careful inspection of components during testing essential to quick and accurate troubleshooting.

TEST EQUIPMENT

➡Pinpointing the exact cause of trouble in an electrical system can sometimes only be accomplished by the use of special test equipment. The following describes commonly used test equipment and explains how to put it to best use in diagnosis. In addition to the information covered below, the manufacturer's instructions booklet provided with the tester should be read and clearly understood before attempting any test procedures.

Jumper Wires

Jumper wires are simple, yet extremely valuable, pieces of test equipment. They are basically test wires which are used to bypass sections of a circuit. The simplest type of jumper wire is a length of multi-strand wire with an alligator clip at each end. Jumper wires are usually fabricated from lengths of standard automotive wire and whatever type of connector (alligator clip, spade connector or pin connector) that is required for the particular vehicle being tested. The well equipped tool box will have several different styles of jumper wires in several different lengths. Some jumper wires are made with three or more terminals coming from a common splice for special purpose testing. In cramped, hard-to-reach areas it is advisable to have insulated boots over the jumper wire terminals in order to prevent accidental grounding, sparks, and possible fire, especially when testing fuel system components.

Jumper wires are used primarily to locate open electrical circuits, on either the ground (-) side of the circuit or on the hot (+) side. If an electrical component fails to operate, connect the jumper wire between the component and a good ground. If the component operates only with the jumper installed, the ground circuit is open. If the ground circuit is good, but the component does not operate, the circuit between the power feed and component may be open. By moving the jumper wire successively back from the lamp toward the power source, you can isolate the area of the circuit where the open is located. When the component stops functioning, or the power is cut off, the open is in the segment of wire between the jumper and the point previously tested.

You can sometimes connect the jumper wire directly from the battery to the hot terminal of the component, but first make sure the component uses 12 volts in operation. Some electrical components, such as fuel injectors, are designed to operate on about 4 volts and running 12 volts directly to the injector terminals can burn out the wiring.

By inserting an in-line fuse holder between a set of test leads, a fused jumper wire can be used for bypassing open circuits. Use a 5 amp fuse to provide protection against voltage spikes. When in doubt, use a voltmeter to check the voltage input to the component and measure how much voltage is normally being applied.

⁂CAUTION

Never use jumpers made from wire that is of lighter gauge than used in the circuit under test. If the jumper wire is of too small gauge, it may overheat and possibly melt. Never use jumpers to bypass high resistance loads in a circuit. Bypassing resistances, in effect, creates a short circuit. This may, in turn, cause damage and fire. Jumper wires should only be used to bypass lengths of wire.

Unpowered Test Lights

The 12 volt test light is used to check circuits and components while electrical current is flowing through them. It is used for voltage and ground tests. Twelve volt test lights come in different styles but all have three main parts; a ground clip, a probe, and a light. The most commonly used 12 volt test lights have pick-type probes. To use a 12 volt test light, connect the ground clip to a good ground and probe wherever necessary with the pick. The pick should be sharp so that it can be probed into tight spaces.

⁂CAUTION

Do not use a test light to probe electronic ignition spark plug or coil wires. Never use a pick-type test light to probe wiring on computer controlled systems unless specifically instructed to do so. Any wire insulation that is pierced by the test light probe should be taped and sealed with silicone after testing.

Like the jumper wire, the 12 volt test light is used to isolate opens in circuits. But, whereas the jumper wire is used to bypass the open to operate the load, the 12 volt test light is used to locate the presence of voltage in a circuit. If the test light glows, you know that there is power up to that point; if the 12 volt test light does not glow when its probe is inserted into the wire or connector, you know that there is an open circuit (no power). Move the test light in successive steps back toward the power source until the light in the handle does glow. When it glows, the open is between the probe and point which was probed previously.

➡The test light does not detect that 12 volts (or any particular amount of voltage) is present; it only detects that some voltage is present. It is advisable before using the test light to touch its terminals across the battery posts to make sure the light is operating properly.

Self-Powered Test Lights

The self-powered test light usually contains a 1.5 volt penlight battery. One type of self-powered test light is similar in design to the 12 volt unit. This type has both the battery and the light in the handle, along with a pick-type probe tip. The second type has the light toward the open tip, so that the light illuminates the contact point. The self-powered test light is a dual purpose piece of test equipment. It can be used to test for either open or short circuits when power is isolated from the circuit (continuity test). A powered test light should not be used on any computer controlled system or component unless specifically instructed to do so. Many engine sensors can be destroyed by even this small amount of voltage applied directly to the terminals.

Voltmeters

A voltmeter is used to measure voltage at any point in a circuit, or to measure the voltage drop across any part of a circuit. It can also be used to check continuity in a wire or circuit by indicating current flow from one end to the other. Voltmeters usually have various scales on the meter dial and a selector switch to allow the selection of different voltages. The voltmeter has a positive and a negative lead. To avoid damage to the meter, always connect the negative lead to the negative (-) side of circuit (to ground or nearest the ground side of the circuit) and connect the positive lead to the positive (+) side of the circuit (to the power source or the nearest power source). Note that the negative voltmeter lead will always be black and that the positive voltmeter will always be some color other than black (usually red). Depending on how the voltmeter is connected into the circuit, it has several uses.

A voltmeter can be connected either in parallel or in series with a circuit and it has a very high resistance to current flow. When connected in parallel, only a small amount of current will flow through the voltmeter current path; the rest will flow through the normal circuit current path and the circuit will work normally. When the voltmeter is connected in series with a circuit, only a small amount of current can flow through the circuit. The circuit will not work properly, but the voltmeter reading will show if the circuit is complete or not.

Ohmmeters

The ohmmeter is designed to read resistance (Ω) in a circuit or component. Although there are several different styles of ohmmeters, all will usually have a selector switch which permits the measurement of different ranges of resistance (usually the selector switch allows the multiplication of the meter reading by 10, 100, 1,000, and 10,000). A calibration knob allows the meter to be set at zero for accurate measurement. Since all ohmmeters are powered by an internal battery (usually 9 volts), the ohmmeter can be used as a self-powered test light. When the ohmmeter is connected, current from the ohmmeter flows through the circuit or component being tested. Since the ohmmeter's internal resistance and voltage are known values, the amount of current flow through the meter depends on the resistance of the circuit or component being tested.

The ohmmeter can be used to perform a continuity test for opens or shorts (either by observation of the meter needle or as a self-powered test light), and to read actual resistance in a circuit. It should be noted that the ohmmeter is used to check the resistance of a component or wire while there is no voltage applied to the circuit. Current flow from an outside voltage source (such as the vehicle battery) can damage the ohmmeter, so the circuit or component should be isolated from the vehicle electrical system before any testing is done. Since the ohmmeter uses its own voltage source, either lead can be connected to any test point.

➡When checking diodes or other solid state components, the ohmmeter leads can only be connected one way in order to measure current flow in a single direction. Make sure the positive (+) and negative (-) terminal connections are as described in the test procedures to verify the one-way diode operation.

In using the meter for making continuity checks, do not be concerned with the actual resistance readings. Zero resistance, or any reading, indicates continuity in the circuit. Infinite resistance indicates an open in the circuit. A high resistance reading where there should be none indicates a problem in the circuit. Checks for short circuits are made in the same manner as checks for open circuits except that the circuit must be isolated from both power and normal ground. Infinite resistance indicates no continuity to ground, while zero resistance indicates a dead short to ground.

Ammeters

An ammeter measures the amount of current flowing through a circuit in units called amperes or amps. Amperes are units of electron flow which indicate how fast the electrons are flowing through the circuit. Since Ohms Law dictates that current flow in a circuit is equal to the circuit voltage divided by the total circuit resistance, increasing voltage also increases the current level (amps). Likewise, any decrease in resistance will increase the amount of amps in a circuit. At normal operating voltage, most circuits have a characteristic amount of amperes, called "current draw" which can be measured using an ammeter. By referring to a specified current draw rating, measuring the amperes, and comparing the two values, one can determine what is happening within the circuit to aid in diagnosis. An open circuit, for example, will not allow any current to flow so the ammeter reading will be zero. More current flows through a heavily loaded circuit or when the charging system is operating.

An ammeter is always connected in series with the circuit being tested. All of the current that normally flows through the circuit must also flow through the ammeter; if there is any other path for the current to follow, the ammeter reading will not be accurate. The ammeter itself has very little resistance to current flow and therefore will not affect the circuit, but it will measure current draw only when the circuit is closed and electricity is flowing. Excessive current draw can blow fuses and drain the battery, while a reduced current draw can cause motors to run slowly, lights to dim and other components to not operate properly. The ammeter can help diagnose these conditions by locating the cause of the high or low reading.

Multimeters

Different combinations of test meters can be built into a single unit designed for specific tests. Some of the more common combination test devices are known as Volt/Amp testers, Tach/Dwell meters, or Digital Multimeters. The Volt/Amp tester is used for charging system, starting system or battery tests and consists of a voltmeter, an ammeter and a variable resistance carbon pile. The voltmeter will usually have at least two ranges for use with 6, 12 and/or 24 volt systems. The ammeter also has more than one range for testing various levels of battery loads and starter current draw. The carbon pile can be adjusted to offer different amounts of resistance. The Volt/Amp tester has heavy leads to carry large amounts of current and many later models have an inductive ammeter pickup that clamps around the wire to simplify test connections. On some models, the ammeter also has a zero-center scale to allow testing of charging and starting systems without switching leads or polarity. A digital multimeter is a voltmeter, ammeter and ohmmeter combined in an instrument which gives a digital readout. These are often used when testing solid state circuits because of their high input impedance (usually 10 megohms or more).

The tach/dwell meter that combines a tachometer and a dwell (cam angle) meter is a specialized kind of voltmeter. The tachometer scale is marked to show engine speed in rpm and the dwell scale is marked to show degrees of distributor shaft rotation. In most electronic ignition systems, dwell is determined by the control unit, but the dwell meter can also be used to check the duty cycle (operation) of some electronic engine control systems. Some tach/dwell meters are powered by an internal battery, while others take their power from the car battery in use. The battery powered testers usually require calibration much like an ohmmeter before testing.

TESTING

Open Circuits

To use the self-powered test light to check for open circuits, first isolate the circuit from the vehicle's 12 volt power source by disconnecting the battery or wiring harness connector. Connect the test light ground clip to a good ground and probe sections of the circuit sequentially with the test light. (start from either end of the circuit). If the light is out, the open is between the probe and the circuit ground. If the light is on, the open is between the probe and end of the circuit toward the power source.

Short Circuits

By isolating the circuit both from power and from ground, and using a self-powered test light, you can check for shorts to ground in the circuit. Isolate the circuit from power and ground. Connect the test light ground clip to a good ground and probe any easy-to-reach test point in the circuit. If the light comes on, there is a short somewhere in the circuit. To isolate the short, probe a test point at either end of the isolated circuit (the light should be on). Leave the test light probe engaged and open connectors, switches, remove parts, etc., sequentially, until the light goes out. When the light goes out, the short is between the last circuit component opened and the previous circuit opened.

➡The 1.5 volt battery in the test light does not provide much current. A weak battery may not provide enough power to illuminate the test light even when a complete circuit is made (especially if there are high resistances in the circuit). Always make sure that the test battery is strong. To check the battery, briefly touch the ground clip to the probe; if the light glows brightly the battery is strong enough for testing. Never use a self-powered test light to perform checks for opens or shorts when power is applied to the electrical system under test. The 12 volt vehicle power will quickly burn out the 1.5 volt light bulb in the test light.

Available Voltage Measurement

Set the voltmeter selector switch to the 20V position and connect the meter negative lead to the negative post of the battery. Connect the positive meter lead to the positive post of the battery and turn the ignition switch **ON** to provide a load. Read the voltage on the meter or digital display. A well charged battery should register over 12 volts. If the meter reads below 11.5 volts, the battery power may be insufficient to operate the electrical system properly. This test determines voltage available from the battery and should be the first step in any electrical trouble diagnosis procedure. Many electrical problems, especially on computer controlled systems, can be caused by a low state of charge in the battery. Excessive corrosion at the battery cable terminals can cause a poor contact that will prevent proper charging and full battery current flow.

Normal battery voltage is 12 volts when fully charged. When the battery is supplying current to one or more circuits it is said to be "under load". When everything is off the electrical system is under a "no-load" condition. A fully charged battery may show about 12.5 volts at no load; will drop to 12 volts under medium load; and will drop even lower under heavy load. If the battery is partially discharged the voltage decrease under heavy load may be excessive, even though the battery shows 12 volts or more at no load. When allowed to discharge further, the battery's available voltage under load will decrease more severely. For this reason, it is important that the battery be fully charged during all testing procedures to avoid errors in diagnosis and incorrect test results.

Voltage Drop

When current flows through a resistance, the voltage beyond the resistance is reduced (the larger the current, the greater the reduction in voltage). When no current is flowing, there is no voltage drop because there is no current flow. All points in the circuit which are connected to the power source are at the same voltage as the power source. The total voltage drop always equals the total source voltage. In a long circuit with many connectors, a series of small, unwanted voltage drops due to corrosion at the connectors can add up to a total loss of voltage which impairs the operation of the normal loads in the circuit.

INDIRECT COMPUTATION OF VOLTAGE DROPS

1. Set the voltmeter selector switch to the 20 volt position.
2. Connect the meter negative lead to a good ground.
3. While operating the circuit, probe all resistances loads in the circuit with the positive meter lead and observe the voltage readings. There should be little or no voltage drop before the first load.

DIRECT MEASUREMENT OF VOLTAGE DROPS

1. Set the voltmeter switch to the 20 volt position.
2. Connect the voltmeter negative lead to the ground side of the resistance load to be measured.
3. Connect the positive lead to the positive side of the resistance or load to be measured.
4. Read the voltage drop directly on the 20 volt scale.

Too high a voltage indicates too high a resistance. If, for example, a blower motor runs too slowly, you can determine if there is too high a resistance in the resistor pack. By taking voltage drop readings in all parts of the circuit, you can isolate the problem. Too low a voltage drop indicates too low a resistance. Take the blower motor for example again. If a blower motor runs too fast in the MED and/or LOW position, the problem can be isolated in the resistor pack by taking voltage drop readings in all parts of the circuit to locate a possibly shorted resistor. The maximum allowable voltage drop under load is critical, especially if there is more than one high resistance problem in a circuit because all voltage drops are cumulative. A small drop is normal due to the resistance of the conductors.

HIGH RESISTANCE TESTING

1. Set the voltmeter selector switch to the 4 volt position.
2. Connect the voltmeter positive lead to the positive post of the battery.
3. Turn on the headlights and heater blower to provide a load.
4. Probe various points in the circuit with the negative voltmeter lead.
5. Read the voltage drop on the 4 volt scale. Some average maximum allowable voltage drops are:
   - FUSE PANEL: 0.7 volts
   - IGNITION SWITCH: 0.5 volts
   - HEADLIGHT SWITCH: 0.7 volts
   - IGNITION COIL (+): 0.5 volts
   - ANY OTHER LOAD: 1.3 volts

➡Voltage drops are all measured while a load is operating; without current flow, there will be no voltage drop.

Resistance Measurement

The batteries in an ohmmeter will weaken with age and temperature, so the ohmmeter must be calibrated or "zeroed" before taking measurements. To zero the meter, place the selector switch in its lowest range and touch the two ohmmeter leads together. Turn the calibration knob until the meter needle is exactly on zero.

➡All analog (needle) type ohmmeters must be zeroed before use, but some digital ohmmeter models are automatically calibrated when the switch is turned on. Self-calibrating digital ohmmeters do not have an adjusting knob, but its a good idea to check for a zero readout before use by touching the leads together. All computer controlled systems require the use of a digital ohmmeter with at least 10 megohms impedance for testing. Before any test procedures are attempted, make sure the ohmmeter used is compatible with the electrical system or damage to the on-board computer could result.

To measure resistance, first isolate the circuit from the vehicle power source by disconnecting the battery cables or the harness connector. Make sure the key is **OFF** when disconnecting any components or the battery. Where necessary, also isolate at least one side of the circuit to be checked in order to avoid reading parallel resistances. Parallel circuit resistances will always give a lower reading than the actual resistance of either of the branches. When measuring the resistance of parallel circuits, the total resistance will always be lower than the smallest resistance in the circuit. Connect the meter leads to both sides of the circuit (wire or component) and read the actual measured ohms on the meter scale. Make sure the selector switch is set to the proper ohm scale for the circuit being tested to avoid misreading the ohmmeter test value.

✱✱WARNING

Never use an ohmmeter with power applied to the circuit. Like the self-powered test light, the ohmmeter is designed to operate on its own power supply. The normal 12 volt automotive electrical system current could damage the meter!

Wiring Harnesses

The average automobile contains about ½ mile of wiring, with hundreds of individual connections. To protect the many wires from damage and to keep them from becoming a confusing tangle, they are organized into bundles, enclosed in plastic or taped together and called wiring harnesses. Different harnesses serve different parts of the vehicle. Individual wires are color coded to help trace them through a harness where sections are hidden from view.

Automotive wiring or circuit conductors can be in any one of three forms:

1. Single strand wire
2. Multi-strand wire
3. Printed circuitry

Single strand wire has a solid metal core and is usually used inside such components as alternators, motors, relays and other devices. Multi-strand wire has a core made of many small strands of wire twisted together into a single conductor. Most of the wiring in an automotive electrical system is made up of multi-strand wire, either as a single conductor or grouped together in a harness. All wiring is color coded on the insulator, either as a solid color or as a colored wire with an identification stripe. A printed circuit is a thin film of copper or other conductor that is printed on an insulator backing. Occasionally, a printed circuit is sandwiched between two sheets of plastic for more protection and flexibility. A complete printed circuit, consisting of conductors, insulating material and connectors for lamps or other components is called a printed circuit board. Printed circuitry is used in place of individual wires or harnesses in places where space is limited, such as behind instrument panels.

Since automotive electrical systems are very sensitive to changes in resistance, the selection of properly sized wires is critical when systems are repaired. A loose or corroded connection or a replacement wire that is too small for the circuit will add extra resistance and an additional voltage drop to the circuit. A ten percent voltage drop can result in slow or erratic motor operation, for example, even though the circuit is complete. The wire gauge number is an expression of the cross-section area of the conductor. The most common system for expressing wire size is the American Wire Gauge (AWG) system.

Gauge numbers are assigned to conductors of various cross-section areas. As gauge number increases, area decreases and the conductor becomes smaller. A 5 gauge conductor is smaller than a 1 gauge conductor and a 10 gauge is smaller than a 5 gauge. As the cross-section area of a conductor decreases, resistance increases and so does the gauge number. A conductor with a higher gauge number will carry less current than a conductor with a lower gauge number.

➡Gauge wire size refers to the size of the conductor, not the size of the complete wire. It is possible to have two wires of the same gauge with different diameters because one may have thicker insulation than the other.

12 volt automotive electrical systems generally use 10, 12, 14, 16 and 18 gauge wire. Main power distribution circuits and larger accessories usually use 10 and 12 gauge wire. Battery cables are usually 4 or 6 gauge, although 1 and 2 gauge wires are occasionally used. Wire length must also be considered when making repairs to a circuit. As conductor length increases, so does resistance. An 18 gauge wire, for example, can carry a 10 amp load for 10 feet without excessive voltage drop; however if a 15 foot wire is required for the same 10 amp load, it must be a 16 gauge wire.

An electrical schematic shows the electrical current paths when a circuit is operating properly. It is essential to understand how a circuit works before trying to figure out why it doesn't. Schematics break the entire electrical system down into individual circuits and show only one particular circuit. In a schematic, no attempt is made to represent wiring and components as they physically appear on the vehicle; switches and other components are shown as simply as possible. Face views of harness connectors show the cavity or terminal locations in all multi-pin connectors to help locate test points.

If you need to backprobe a connector while it is on the component, the order of the terminals must be mentally reversed. The wire color code can help in this situation, as well as a keyway, lock tab or other reference mark.

WIRING REPAIR

Soldering is a quick, efficient method of joining metals permanently. Everyone who has the occasion to make wiring repairs should know how to solder. Electrical connections that are soldered are far less likely to come apart and will conduct electricity much better than connections that are only "pig-tailed" together. The most popular (and preferred) method of soldering is with an electrical soldering gun. Soldering irons are available in many sizes and wattage ratings. Irons with higher wattage ratings deliver higher temperatures and recover lost heat faster. A small soldering iron rated for no more than 50 watts is recommended, especially on electrical systems where excess heat can damage the components being soldered.

There are three ingredients necessary for successful soldering; proper flux, good solder and sufficient heat. A soldering flux is necessary to clean the metal of tarnish, prepare it for soldering and to enable the solder to spread into tiny crevices. When soldering, always use a rosin core solder which is non-corrosive and will not attract moisture once the job is finished. Other types of flux (acid core) will leave a residue that will attract moisture and cause the wires to corrode. Tin is a unique metal with a low melting point. In a molten state, it dissolves and alloys easily with many metals. Solder is made by mixing tin with lead. The most common proportions are 40/60, 50/50 and 60/40, with the percentage of tin listed first. Low priced solders usually contain less tin, making them very difficult for a beginner to use because more heat is required to melt the solder. A common solder is 40/60 which is well suited for all-around general use, but 60/40 melts easier and is preferred for electrical work.

Soldering Techniques

Successful soldering requires that the metals to be joined be heated to a temperature that will melt the solder, usually 360-460°F (182-238°C). Contrary to popular belief, the purpose of the soldering iron is not to melt the solder itself, but to heat the parts being soldered to a temperature high enough to melt the solder when it is touched to the work. Melting flux-cored solder on the soldering iron will usually destroy the effectiveness of the flux.

➡Soldering tips are made of copper for good heat conductivity, but must be "tinned" regularly for quick transference of heat to the project and to prevent the solder from sticking to the iron. To "tin" the iron, simply heat it and touch the flux-cored solder to the tip; the solder will flow over the hot tip. Wipe the excess off with a clean rag, but be careful as the iron will be hot.

After some use, the tip may become pitted. If so, simply dress the tip smooth with a smooth file and "tin" the tip again. Flux-cored solder will remove oxides but rust, bits of insulation and oil or grease must be removed with a wire brush or emery cloth. For maximum strength in soldered parts, the joint must start off clean and tight. Weak joints will result in gaps too wide for the solder to bridge.

If a separate soldering flux is used, it should be brushed or swabbed on only those areas that are to be soldered. Most solders contain a core of flux and separate fluxing is unnecessary. Hold the work to be soldered firmly. It is best to solder on a wooden board, because a metal vise will only rob the piece to be soldered of heat and make it difficult to melt the solder. Hold the soldering tip with the broadest face against the work to be soldered. Apply solder under the tip close to the work, using enough solder to give a heavy film between the iron and the piece being soldered, while moving slowly and making sure the solder melts properly. Keep the work level or the solder will run to the lowest part and favor the thicker parts, because these require more heat to melt the solder. If the soldering tip overheats (the solder coating on the face of the tip burns up), it should be retinned. Once the soldering is completed, let the soldered joint stand until cool. Tape and seal all soldered wire splices after the repair has cooled.

Wire Harness Connectors

Most connectors in the engine compartment or otherwise exposed to the elements are protected against moisture and dirt which could create oxidation and deposits on the terminals.

These special connectors are weather-proof. All repairs require the use of a special terminal and the tool required to service it. This tool is used to remove the pin and sleeve terminals. If removal is attempted with an ordinary pick, there is a good chance that the terminal will be bent or deformed. Unlike standard blade type terminals, these weather-proof terminals cannot be straightened once they are bent. Make certain that the connectors are properly seated and all of the sealing rings are in place when connecting leads. On some models, a hinge-type flap provides a backup or secondary locking feature for the terminals. Most secondary locks are used to improve connector reliability by retaining the terminals if the small terminal lock tangs are not positioned properly.

Molded-on connectors require complete replacement of the connection. This means splicing a new connector assembly into the harness. All splices should be soldered to insure proper contact. Use care when probing the connections or replacing terminals in them as it is possible to short between opposite terminals. If this happens to the wrong terminal pair, it is possible to damage certain components. Always use jumper wires between connectors for circuit checking and never probe through weatherproof seals.

Open circuits are often difficult to locate by sight because corrosion or terminal misalignment are hidden by the connectors. Merely wiggling a connector on a sensor or in the wiring harness may correct the open circuit condition. This should always be considered when an open circuit or a failed sensor is indicated. Intermittent problems may also be caused by oxidized or loose connections. When using a circuit tester for diagnosis, always probe connections from the wire side. Be careful not to damage sealed connectors with test probes.

All wiring harnesses should be replaced with identical parts, using the same gauge wire and connectors. When signal wires are spliced into a harness, use wire with high temperature insulation only. It is seldom necessary to replace a complete harness. If replacement is necessary, pay close attention to insure proper harness routing. Secure the harness with suitable plastic wire clamps to prevent vibrations from causing the harness to wear in spots or contact any hot components.

➡Weatherproof connectors cannot be replaced with standard connectors. Instructions are provided with replacement connector and terminal packages. Some wire harnesses have mounting indicators (usually pieces of colored tape) to mark where the harness is to be secured.

In making wiring repairs, its important that you always replace damaged wires with wires that are the same gauge as the wire being replaced. The heavier the wire, the smaller the gauge number. Wires are color-coded to aid in identification and whenever possible the same color coded wire should be used for replacement. A wire stripping and crimping tool is necessary to install solderless terminal connectors. Test all crimps by pulling on the wires; it should not be possible to pull the wires out of a good crimp.

Wires which are open, exposed or otherwise damaged are repaired by simple splicing. Where possible, if the wiring harness is accessible and the damaged place in the wire can be located, it is best to open the harness and check for all possible damage. In an inaccessible harness, the wire must be bypassed with a new insert, usually taped to the outside of the old harness.

When replacing fusible links, be sure to use fusible link wire, NOT ordinary automotive wire. Make sure the fusible segment is of the same gauge and construction as the one being replaced and double the stripped end when crimping the terminal connector for a good contact. The melted (open) fusible link segment of the wiring harness should be cut off as close to the harness as possible, then a new segment spliced in as described. In the case of a damaged fusible link that feeds two harness wires, the harness connections should be replaced with two fusible link wires so that each circuit will have its own separate protection.

➡Most of the problems caused in the wiring harness are due to bad ground connections. Always check all vehicle ground connections for corrosion or looseness before performing any power feed checks to eliminate the chance of a bad ground affecting the circuit.

Hard Shell Connectors

Unlike molded connectors, the terminal contacts in hard shell connectors can be replaced. Weatherproof hard-shell connectors with the leads molded into the shell have non-replaceable terminal ends. Replacement usually involves the use of a special terminal removal tool that depresses the locking tangs (barbs) on the connector terminal and allows the connector to be removed from the rear of the shell. The connector shell should be replaced if it shows any evidence of burning, melting, cracks, or breaks. Replace individual terminals that are burnt, corroded, distorted or loose.

The wire crimp must be made with all wire strands inside the crimp. The terminal must be fully compressed on the wire strands with the ends of the crimp tabs turned in to make a firm grip on the wire.

SUPPLEMENTAL AIR BAG RESTRAINT SYSTEM (SRS)

General Information

See Figure 1

In 1994, Ford Motor Co. began equipping Ford Escorts and Mercury Tracers with a driver's side Supplemental Air Bag Restraint System (SRS). In 1995, all models came standard with both driver's and passenger's side SRS (air bags).

The air bag is an additional safety device designed to work in conjunction with the three-point safety belt system. Safety belt use is necessary to obtain the best occupant protection and to receive the full advantages of the supplemental air bag.

Special attention should be given when working on a vehicle equipped with an air bag. If for any reason the indicator light on the dashboard should come on, consult an authorized dealer immediately for a thorough diagnostic examination.

SYSTEM OPERATION

The SRS is intended to increase protection in a certain types of collisions (primarily a frontal impact) by providing a soft buffer between the occupant(s) and the part of the car immediately in front of them (steering wheel, dashboard, windshield, etc.).

In the event of a crash, electronic impulses relayed by sensors deploy the gas-filled bag(s) within milliseconds. The driver's side air bag is in the steering wheel, and is deployed through a seam in the wheel. Once the signal is received, it reaches full inflation in approximately 40 milliseconds. The passenger's side air bag, if equipped, operates similarly from its location above the glove compartment.

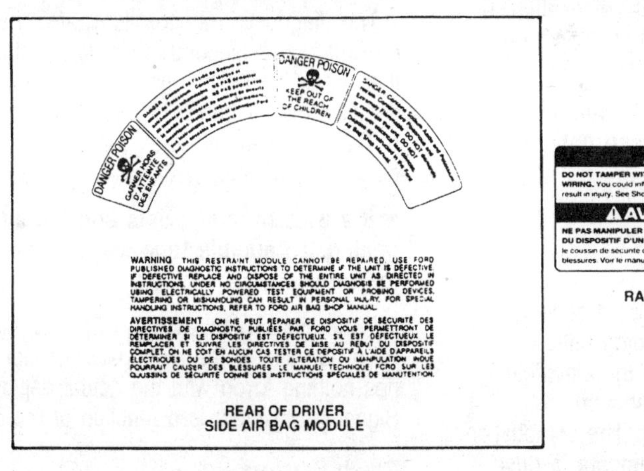

2002560A	WARNING	AVISO	AVERTISSEMENT
	• NEVER TRY TO REPAIR OR TEST THIS MODULE • USE VEHICLE SHOP MANUAL TO DIAGNOSE PROBLEMS • SEE AIR BAG SHOP MANUAL FOR HANDLING INSTRUCTIONS • TAMPERING OR MISHANDLING CAN RESULT IN PERSONAL INJURY	• NUNCA TRATE DE REPARAR O PROBAR ESTE MODULO • HAGA USO DEL MANUAL DE FABRICA DEL VEHICULO PARA EL DIAGNOSTICO DE FALLAS • REFIERASE AL MANUAL DE FABRICA DE LA BOLSA DE AIRE PARA INSTRUCCIONES DE MANEJO • ALTERACION O MAL MANEJO PUEDEN OCASIONAR DANOS PERSONALES	• NE JAMAIS TENTER DE REPARER NI DE TESTER CE MODULE • UTILISER LE MANUEL DE REPARATION POUR DIAGNOSTIQUER LES PROBLEMES • CONSULTER LE MANUEL TECHNIQUE DES SACS GONFLABLES POUR LES PROCEDURES A EMPLOUER • TOUTE ALTERATION OU MANIPULATION ERRONEE RISQUE D'ENTRAINER DES BLESSURES

PASSENGER SIDE AIR BAG MODULE

86756001

Fig. 1 Common air bag warning labels

SYSTEM COMPONENTS

The SRS consists of:

- The driver's side air bag module
- Passenger's side air bag module (beginning in 1995)
- Air bag diagnostic monitor
- RH radiator primary crash front air bag sensor and bracket
- LH radiator primary crash front air bag sensor and bracket
- Safing rear air bag sensor and bracket (LH kick panel)
- Electrical harness
- Air bag warning indicator
- Tone generator (internal to the air bag diagnostic monitor)

Air Bag Module

The air bag module, whether, driver's or passenger's, consists of an inflator, the air bag itself and the trim cover either on the steering wheel or above the glove box. The driver's side airbag is held in place by a mounting plate and retaining ring. The passenger's side air bag is mounted in a steel reaction housing and is held in place by brackets.

➡The individual air bag module components cannot be serviced. The air bag module may be serviced only as a complete assembly.

The module components are as follows:

INFLATOR

Inside the inflator is an igniter. When the impact sensors detect a crash the sensor contacts close, sending battery power to the igniter. The igniter then converts the electrical energy to thermal (heat) energy by firing the sodium azide/copper oxide generant inside the inflator. The combustion process produces nitrogen gas (and a small amount of dust) which expands and is channeled into the air bag. The nitrogen gas and dust are filtered and cooled during inflation of the air bag. The entire process takes several thousandths of a second to complete.

AIR BAG

The driver's air bag is constructed of neoprene coated nylon. The air bag for 1994 models inflates to a 28 in. (711mm) diameter and has a volume of 2.3 cubic feet. For 1995 models, the air bag inflates to a 26.5 in. (673mm) diameter, and its volume is 2.2 cubic feet. The passenger's side air bag is made of rip-stop nylon. The passenger's side air bag (1995 models only) is larger than the driver's and requires a different inflator with more gas generant to fill the air bag.

MOUNTING PLATE AND RETAINER RING

A mounting plate and retainer ring attach and seal the driver's air bag to the inflator. The mounting plate is used to attach the trim cover and to mount the entire module to the steering wheel.

REACTION HOUSING

Made of steel, the reaction housing contains the passenger's side air bag module. It supports the inflator and provides a reaction surface and support for the air bag. The air bag module is mounted on brackets and is connected by rods to the instrument panel.

TRIM COVER

➧ See Figure 2

The trim cover is the name given to the molded plastic cover(s) that conceal the airbags(s). The driver's side trim cover is in the center of the steering wheel, and is embossed with the letters "SRS." The passenger's side trim cover (1995 models only) is visible above the glove box. When the air bag is activated, tear seams molded into the trim cover separate to allow inflation.

Diagnostic Monitor

➧ See Figures 3 and 4

The diagnostic monitor continually monitors all air bag system components and wiring connections for possible faults. If a fault is detected, the air bag warning light (located on the instrument cluster) will illuminate.

The diagnostic monitor illuminates the air bag light for approximately six seconds when the ignition switch is turned **ON**, then turns it off. This indicates that the air bag light is operational. If the air bag light does not illuminate, or if it stays on or flashes at any time, a fault has been detected by the diagnostic monitor.

➡If a system fault exists and the air bag light is malfunctioning, an audible tone will be heard indicating the need for service.

Performing system diagnostics (overseeing the system) is the main purpose of the diagnostic monitor. The diagnostic monitor has nothing to do with the actual deployment of the air bag(s). Signal deployment is a function of the crash sensors.

Crash Sensors

➧ See Figures 5, 6 and 7

The crash sensors are electrical switches that react to decelerational force (in the forward direction). Each is designed to discriminate between impacts that do or do not require air bag deployment. When an impact occurs that requires air bag

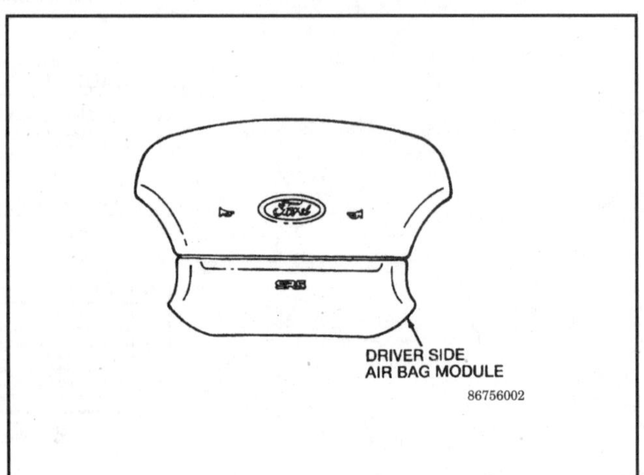

Fig. 2 The driver's side air bag module, when inflated, comes through the tear seam in the trim cover mounted on the steering wheel

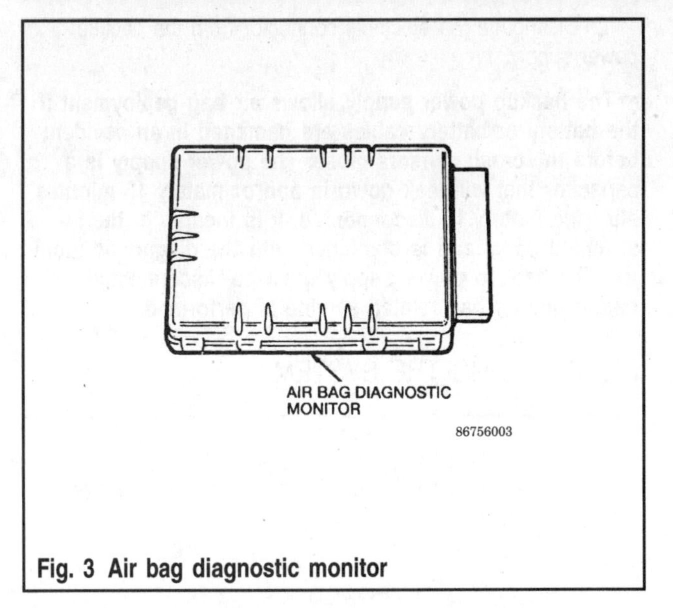

Fig. 3 Air bag diagnostic monitor

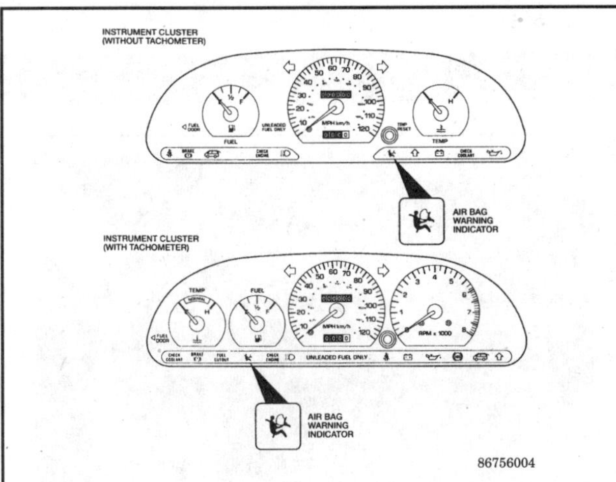

Fig. 4 The air bag warning indicator is the communication link between the SRS diagnostic monitor and the vehicle operator

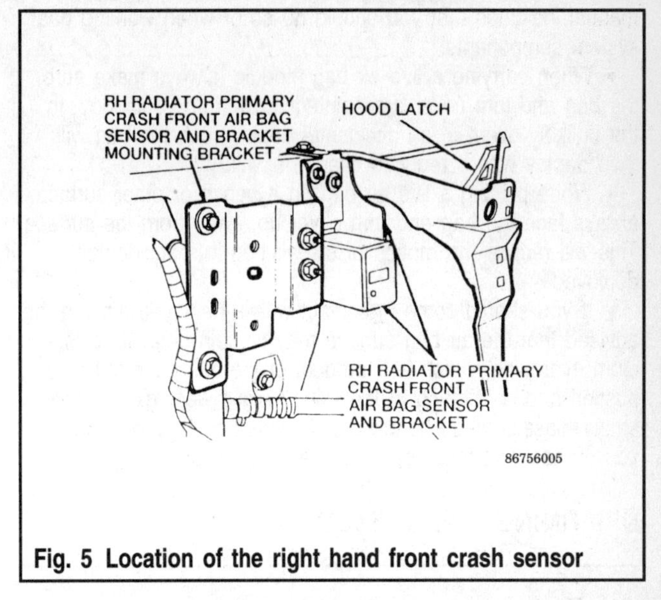

Fig. 5 Location of the right hand front crash sensor

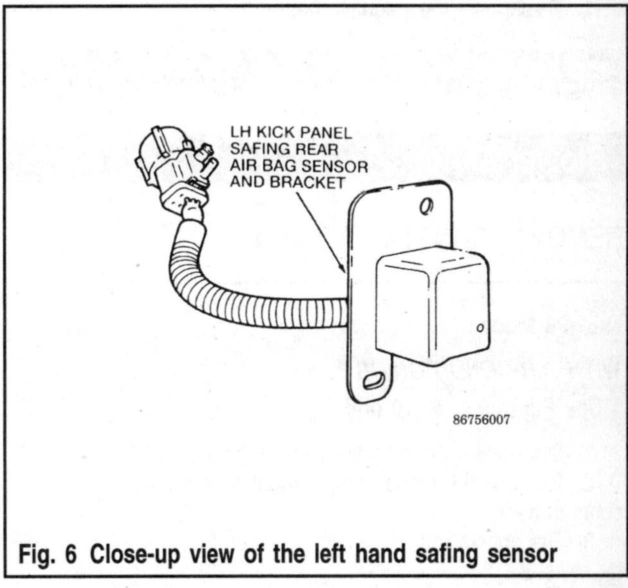

Fig. 6 Close-up view of the left hand safing sensor

deployment, the sensor contacts close and complete the electrical circuit necessary for system operation.

Three crash sensors are used on air bag equipped vehicles: a right hand radiator primary crash front air bag sensor, a left hand radiator primary crash front air bag sensor, and a left hand kick panel safing sensor.

Before the signal is given to deploy the air bag, at least two crash sensors, the safing and one of the two front sensors, must be activated (see drawing: "side view of the front crash sensor").

SERVICE PRECAUTIONS

- Always wear safety glasses when servicing an air bag vehicle, and when handling an air bag.
- Never attempt to service the steering wheel or steering column on an air bag equipped vehicle without first properly disarming the air bag system. The air bag system should be properly disarmed whenever ANY service procedure in this

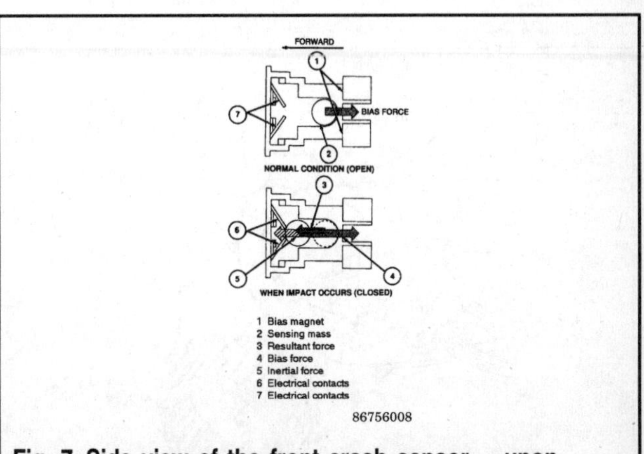

Fig. 7 Side view of the front crash sensor — upon impact a sensing mass pulls away from the bias magnet, rolls down the cylinder, makes electrical contact, completes the circuit and sends the signal to deploy

manual indicates that you should do so or when working near system components.

- When carrying a live air bag module, always make sure the bag and trim cover are pointed away from your body. In the unlikely event of an accidental deployment, the bag will then deploy with a reduced chance of injury.
- When placing a live air bag on a bench or other surface, always face the bag and trim cover up, away from the surface. This will reduce the motion of the air bag if is accidentally deployed.
- If you should come in contact with a deployed air bag, be advised that the air bag surface may contain deposits of sodium hydroxide, which is a product of the gas generant combustion and is irritating to the skin. Always wear gloves and safety glasses when handling a deployed air bag, and wash your hands with mild soap and water afterwards.

DISARMING THE SYSTEM

1. Disconnect the negative battery cable.
2. Disengage the electrical connector from the backup power supply.

➡The backup power supply allows air bag deployment if the battery or battery cables are damaged in an accident before the crash sensors close. The power supply is a capacitor that will leak down in approximately 15 minutes after the battery is disconnected. It is located in the instrument panel and is combined with the diagnostic monitor. The backup power supply must be disconnected before any air bag related service is performed.

REACTIVATING THE SYSTEM

1. Connect the backup power supply
2. Connect the negative battery cable. Verify proper operation of the air bag light.

HEATING SYSTEM

Blower Motor

REMOVAL & INSTALLATION

1981-90 Models

WITH AIR CONDITIONING

➧ See Figures 8, 9, 10 and 11

1. Disconnect the negative battery cable.
2. Remove the glove compartment door and glove compartment.
3. Disconnect the blower motor wires from the blower motor resistor.

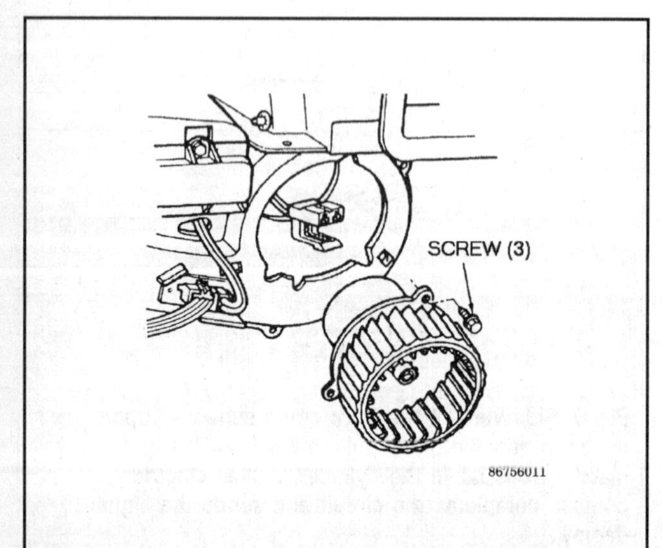

Fig. 8 The blower motor is secured by three screws

Fig. 9 Disconnect the blower motor wires from the blower motor resistor — 1988 Escort

4. Loosen the instrument panel at the lower right hand side prior to removing the motor through the glove compartment opening.
5. Remove the blower motor and mounting plate from the evaporator case.
6. Rotate the motor until the mounting plate flat clears the edge of the glove compartment opening and remove the motor.
7. Remove the hub clamp spring from the blower wheel hub. Then remove the blower wheel from the motor shaft.

To install:

8. If removed, assemble the blower wheel to the motor shaft and install the hub clamp.
9. Install the motor and blower wheel assembly.
10. Secure the instrument panel at the lower right hand side.
11. Connect the blower motor wires at the blower motor resistor.

86756701

Fig. 10 Unbolt the mounting plate from the case

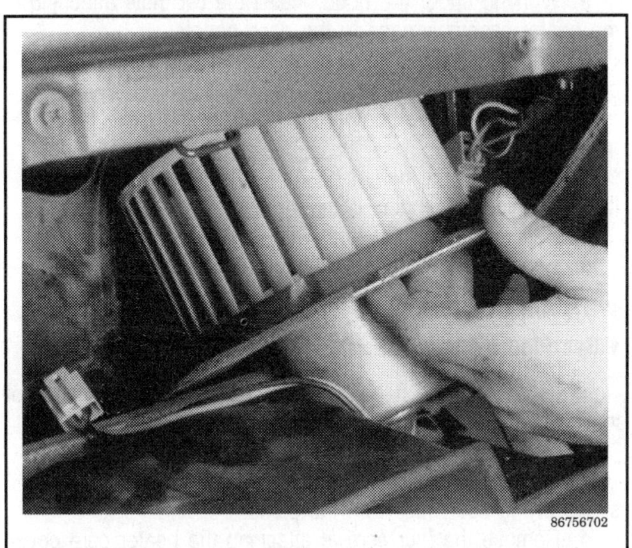
86756702

Fig. 11 The motor can now be removed from the case

12. Install the glove compartment door and the glove compartment.
13. Connect the negative battery cable.
14. Check the system for proper operation.

WITHOUT AIR CONDITIONING

1. Disconnect the negative battery cable.
2. Remove the air inlet duct assembly.
3. Remove the hub clamp spring from the blower wheel hub. Pull the blower wheel from the blower motor shaft.
4. Remove the blower motor flange attaching screws located inside the blower housing.
5. Pull the blower motor out from the blower housing (heater case) and disconnect the blower motor wires from the motor.

To install:

6. Connect the wires to the blower motor and position the motor in the blower housing.
7. Install the blower motor attaching screws.
8. Position the blower wheel on the motor shaft and install the hub clamp spring.
9. Install the air inlet duct assembly and the right ventilator assembly.
10. Connect negative battery cable.
11. Check the system for proper operation.

1991-95 Models

WITH AIR CONDITIONING

➧ See Figures 12 and 13

1. Disconnect the negative battery cable. If equipped, disable the SRS system.
2. Remove the trim panel below the glove compartment.
3. Remove the wiring bracket and bolt.
4. Disconnect the blower motor electrical connector.
5. Remove the three blower motor mounting bolts and remove the blower motor.
6. Remove the blower wheel retaining clip and remove the blower wheel from the blower motor.

To install:

7. If removed, attach the blower wheel to the motor shaft and install the retaining clip.
8. Install the motor and wheel assembly.
9. Plug in the blower motor electrical connector.
10. Install the wiring bracket and bolt.
11. Install the trim panel below the glove compartment.
12. Connect the negative battery cable.

WITHOUT AIR CONDITIONING

1. Disconnect the negative battery cable. If equipped, disable the SRS system.
2. Remove the trim panel below the glove compartment.
3. Remove the wiring bracket and bolt.
4. Disconnect the blower motor electrical connector.
5. Remove the three blower motor mounting bolts and remove the blower motor.
6. Remove the blower wheel retaining clip and remove the blower wheel from the blower motor.
7. Installation is the reverse of the removal procedure.

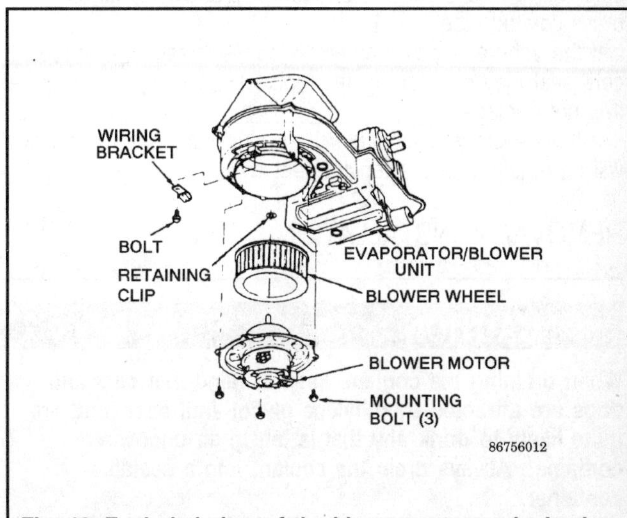

Fig. 12 Exploded view of the blower motor and wheel assembly

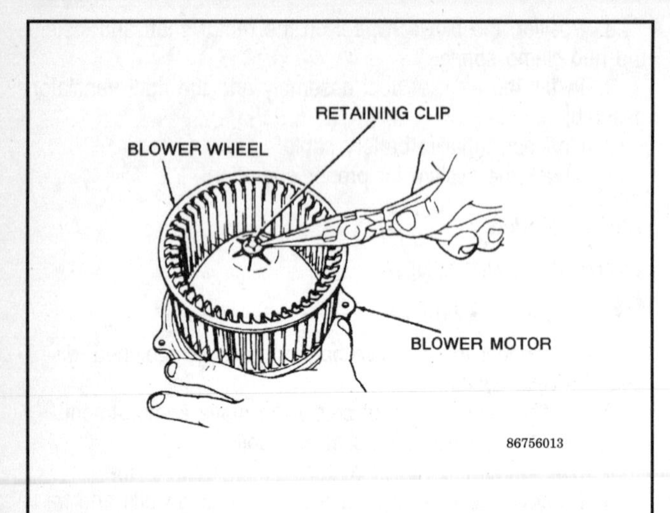

Fig. 13 Remove the blower wheel retaining clip with pliers

To install:

8. If removed, attach the blower wheel to the motor shaft and install the retaining clip.
9. Install the motor and wheel assembly.
10. Plug in the blower motor electrical connector.
11. Install the wiring bracket and bolt.
12. Install the trim panel below the glove compartment.
13. Connect the negative battery cable.

Heater Core

Vehicles may be equipped with either a brass or an aluminum heater core. It is important to positively identify the type of core being used because aluminum cores use different heater core-to-heater case seals than the copper/brass cores. Having the proper seal is necessary for proper sealing and heating system performance.

Identification can be made by looking at one of the core tubes after one of the hoses is disconnected. An aluminum core will have a silver colored tube. A brass core will have a brass colored tube.

If the vehicle is equipped with a copper/brass core, the old core seal may be used for the replacement core, providing that it is not damaged.

If the vehicle is equipped with an aluminum core, a new seal will be required for the replacement core.

REMOVAL & INSTALLATION

CAUTION

When draining the coolant, keep in mind that cats and dogs are attracted by ethylene glycol antifreeze, and are quite likely to drink any that is left in an uncovered container. Always drain the coolant into a sealable container.

1981-90 Models

See Figure 14

WITHOUT AIR CONDITIONING

1. Disconnect the negative battery cable.
2. Drain the coolant.
3. Disconnect the heater hoses from the core tubes at the firewall, inside the engine compartment. Plug the core tubes to prevent coolant spillage when the core is removed.
4. Open the glove compartment. Remove the glove compartment and the glove compartment liner.
5. Remove the core access plate screws and remove the access plate.
6. Working under the hood, remove the two nuts attaching the heater assembly case to the dash panel.
7. Remove the core through the glove compartment opening.

To install:

8. Install the core through the glove compartment opening.
9. Working under the hood, install the two nuts attaching the heater assembly case to the dash panel.
10. Install the core access plate screws and install the access plate.
11. Install the glove compartment. Install the glove compartment liner.
12. Reconnect the heater hoses to the core tubes at the firewall, inside the engine compartment.
13. Refill the cooling system with coolant.
14. Reconnect the negative battery cable.

WITH AIR CONDITIONING

See Figure 15

1. Disconnect the negative battery cable and drain the cooling system.
2. Disconnect the heater hoses from the heater core.
3. Working inside the vehicle, remove the two screws and separate the floor duct from the plenum.
4. Remove the four screws attaching the heater core cover to the plenum, remove the cover and remove the heater core.

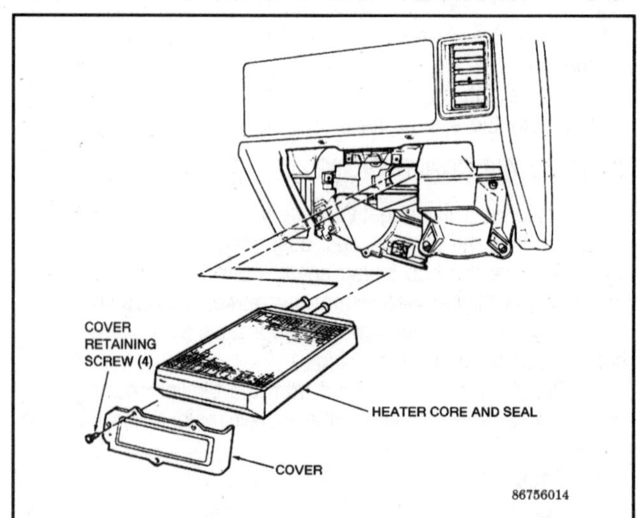

Fig. 14 It is necessary to remove the glove box to access the heater core

Fig. 15 Remove the heater core and cover from the plenum

To install:

5. Install the heater core and install the cover. Install the four screws attaching the heater core cover to the plenum.
6. Working inside the vehicle, Install the floor duct to the plenum with the two screws.
7. Reconnect the heater hoses to the heater core.
8. Reconnect the negative battery cable and refill the cooling system.

1991-95 Models

➧ See Figure 16

1. Disconnect the negative battery cable. If equipped, disable the SRS system.
2. Drain the cooling system.
3. Disconnect the heater hoses at the bulkhead.
4. Remove the instrument panel.
5. Disconnect the mode selector and temperature control cables from the cams and retaining clips.
6. Remove the necessary defroster duct screws and loosen the capscrew that secures the heater-to-blower clamp.

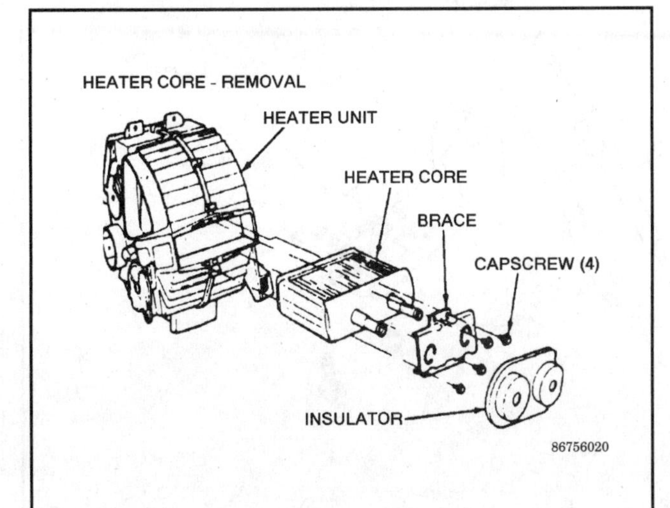

Fig. 16 Exploded view of the heater core mounting — 1991-95 models

7. Remove the three heater unit mounting nuts and disconnect the antenna lead from the retaining clip. Remove the heater unit.
8. Remove the insulator and the four brace capscrews. Remove the brace.
9. Remove the heater core from the heater unit.

To install:

10. Install the heater core into the heater unit and install the brace.
11. Install the brace capscrews and the insulator.
12. Position the heater unit and attach the defroster and floor ducting. Install the heater unit mounting nuts.
13. Tighten the heater-to-blower clamp capscrew and install the defroster duct screws. Connect the antenna lead to the retaining clip.
14. Install the instrument panel.
15. Connect and adjust the mode selector and temperature control cables. Connect the heater hoses at the bulkhead.
16. Fill the cooling system and connect the negative battery cable. Start the engine and check for leaks. Check the coolant level and fill as necessary.

Control Assembly

REMOVAL & INSTALLATION

➧ See Figures 17, 18 and 19

1. Move the selector lever to the MAX A/C position.
2. Disconnect the air inlet cable housing and retainer from the air conditioning case bracket. Disconnect the cable from the inlet door cam.
3. Move the temperature control lever to the COOL position and disconnect the temperature control cable housing and retainer from the air conditioning case bracket. Disconnect the cable self-adjusting clip from the crank arm.
4. Move the function selector lever to the PANEL position and disconnect the function cable housing and retainer from the air conditioning case bracket. Disconnect the cable self-adjusting clip from the cam pin.
5. Remove the instrument panel finish center.
6. Remove the four screws attaching the control assembly to the instrument panel.
7. Pull the control assembly out from the instrument panel. Move the control levers to the following: COOL, PANEL and RECIRC.
8. Disconnect the temperature cable housing from the control mounting bracket.
9. Disconnect the temperature cable wire from the control lever.
10. Disconnect the outside/recirc cable.
11. Disconnect the control assembly electrical connectors and remove the control assembly.

To install:

12. Position the control assembly near the instrument panel opening and connect the electrical connectors.
13. Move the control levers to the following: COOL, PANEL and RECIRC.
14. Connect the function cable wire and then the cable housing to the control assembly.

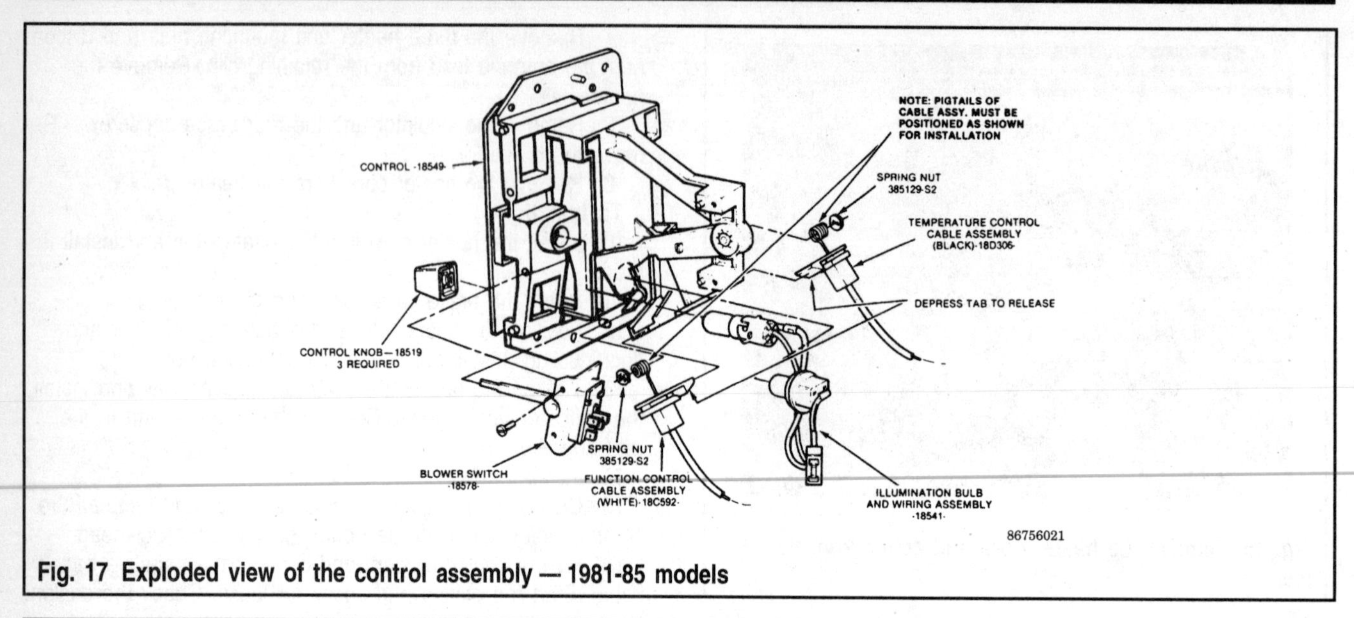

Fig. 17 Exploded view of the control assembly — 1981-85 models

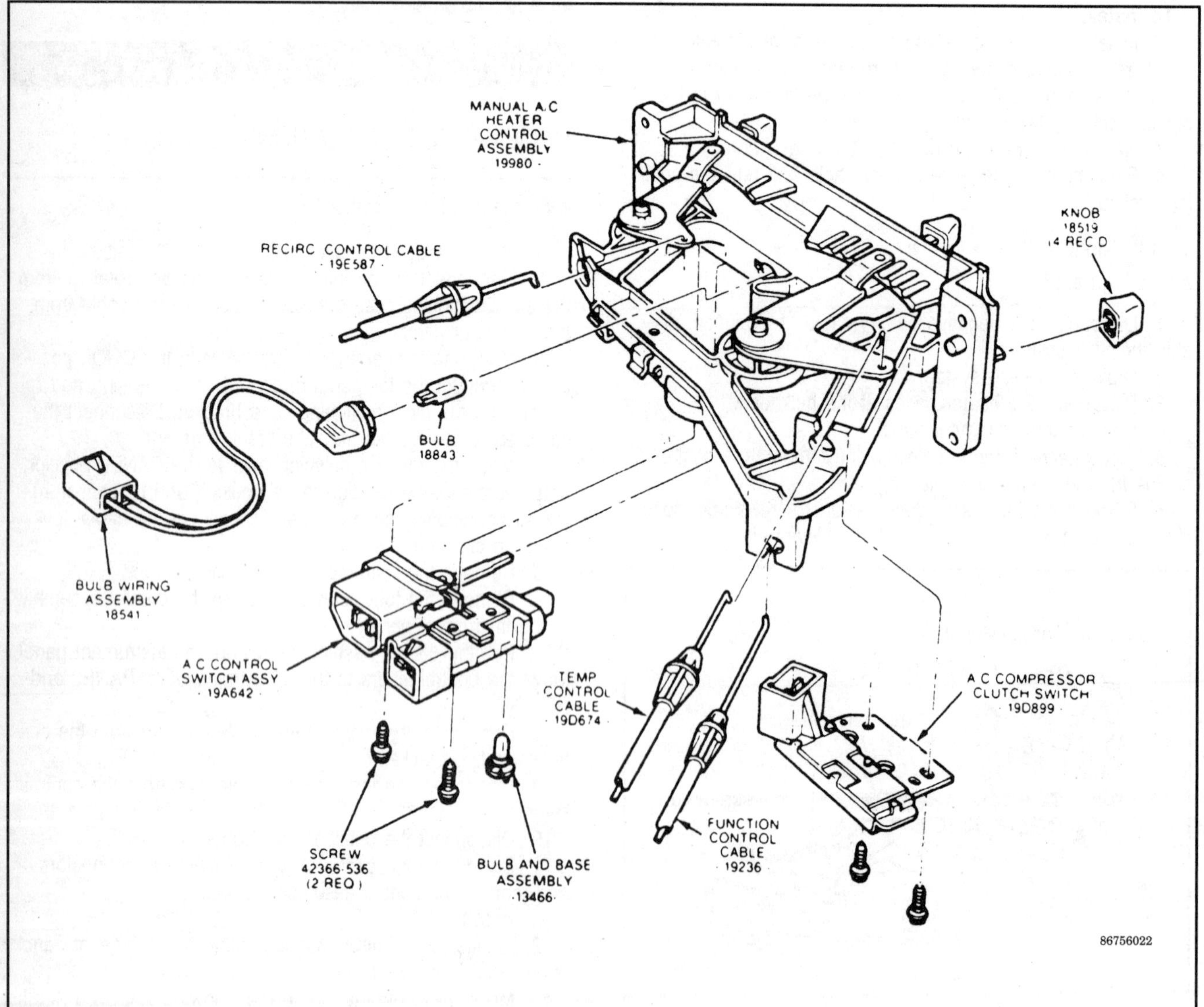

Fig. 18 Exploded view of the manual A/C and heater control assembly — 1985½-90 models

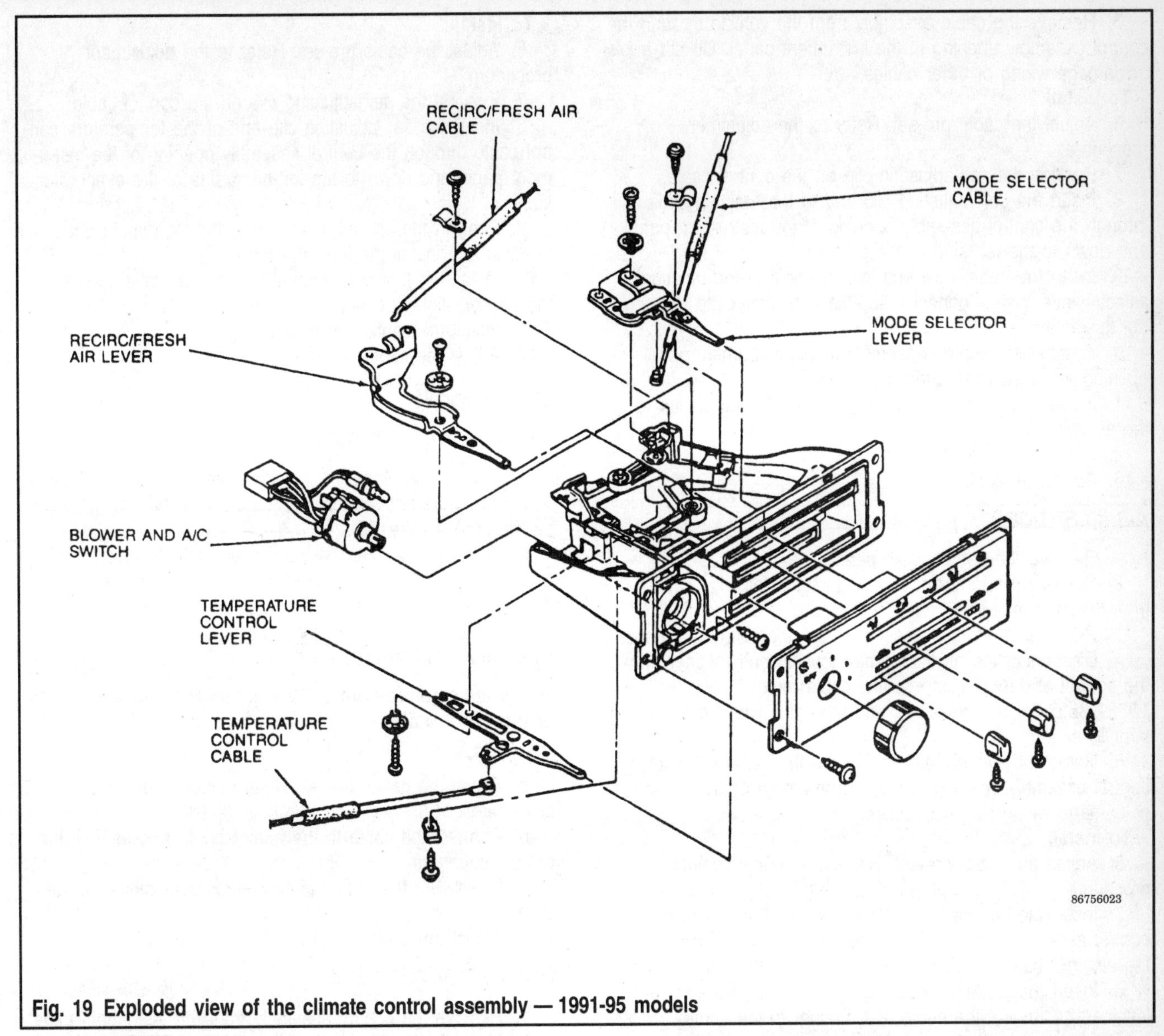

Fig. 19 Exploded view of the climate control assembly — 1991-95 models

15. Connect the outside recirc and then the temperature cable to the control assembly.
16. Position the control assembly onto the instrument panel and install the attaching screws.
17. Install the instrument panel finish center.
18. Move the selector lever to the MAX A/C position.
19. Place the cable end loop over the pin on the air door cam and position the wire under the tab on the cam. Slide the cable housing end retainer into the plenum cable bracket to secure the cable to the evaporator.
20. Move the temperature selector lever to the COOL position.
21. Connect the temperature control cable self-adjusting clip to the temperature door crank arm. Slide the cable housing end retainer into the evaporator end case bracket and engage the tabs.
22. Move the function selector lever to the PANEL position.
23. Connect the function cable self-adjusting clip to the cam pin on the side of the plenum.
24. Slide the cable housing end retainer into the plenum cable bracket and engage the tabs.
25. Move the function selector lever to the DEFROST (full right) position to adjust the cable.
26. Check the operation of all the control function levers.

Manual Control Cables

REMOVAL & INSTALLATION

1981-90 Models

FUNCTION SELECTOR

1. Remove the center finish panel.
2. Remove the function, temperature and air inlet cables from the air conditioning case.
3. Remove the control assembly from the instrument panel.
4. Disconnect the cable housing end retainer from the control assembly, using control cable removal tool T83P-18532-AH or equivalent, and the cable wire from the function selector lever arm.

5. Remove the cable assembly from the vehicle through the control assembly opening in the instrument panel. Do not hook or damage wiring or other cables.

To install:

6. Adjust the cable pre-set. Refer to the adjustment procedure.
7. Position the self-adjusting clip on the control cable.
8. Insert the self-adjusting clip end of the function cable through the control assembly opening of the instrument panel and down to the left side of the plenum.
9. Insert the cable wire end into the hole in the function selector lever arm. Connect the cable end retainer to the control assembly.
10. Position the control assembly to the instrument panel opening and install the attaching screws.
11. Install the function, temperature and air inlet cables to the air conditioning case.
12. Install the center finish panel.
13. Adjust the cable.

AIR INLET DOOR

1. Remove the center finish panel.
2. Remove the function, temperature and air inlet cables from the air conditioning case.
3. Remove the control assembly from the instrument panel.
4. Disconnect the air inlet cable housing end retainer from the control assembly using control cable removal tool T83P-18532-AH or equivalent, and the cable wire from the air door lever arm.
5. Remove the cable assembly from the vehicle through the control assembly opening in the instrument panel. Do not hook or damage wiring or other cables.

To install:

6. Adjust the cable pre-set. Refer to the adjustment procedure.
7. Insert the air inlet door cable, loop end first, through the control assembly opening of the instrument panel and over to the air door cam.
8. Insert the cable wire end into the hole in the air door lever arm. Connect the cable and retainer to the control assembly.
9. Position the control assembly to the instrument panel opening and install the attaching screws.
10. Install the function, temperature and air inlet cables to the air conditioning case.
11. Install the center finish panel.
12. Adjust the cable.

TEMPERATURE CONTROL

1. Remove the center finish panel.
2. Remove the function, temperature and air inlet cables from the air conditioning case.
3. Remove the control assembly from the instrument panel.
4. Move the temperature control lever to the COOL position and remove the temperature cable housing/end retainer from the control assembly with control cable removal tool T83P-18532-AH or equivalent. Disconnect the cable wire from the temperature control lever.
5. Remove the cable assembly from the vehicle through the control assembly opening in the instrument panel. Do not hook or damage wiring or other cables.

To install:

6. Adjust the cable pre-set. Refer to the adjustment procedure.
7. Position the self-adjusting clip on the control cable.
8. Insert the self-adjusting clip end of the temperature control cable through the control assembly opening of the instrument panel and down to the left-hand side of the evaporator case.
9. Position the control assembly to the instrument panel opening and install the four attaching screws.
10. Install the function, temperature and air inlet cables on the air conditioning case.
11. Install the center finish panel.
12. Adjust the cable.

1991-95 Models

TEMPERATURE CONTROL

1. Remove the control assembly from the instrument panel.
2. Move the temperature control lever to the COLD position on the control assembly.
3. To secure the cam in the proper position, insert cable locating key PNE7GH-18C408-A or equivalent, through the cam key slot to the heater case key boss opening.
4. Disconnect the cable from the retaining clip next to the temperature control cam.

➡The temperature control cam is located on the left side of the heater unit.

To install:

5. Adjust the cable pre-set. Refer to the adjustment procedure.
6. Connect the cable to the retaining clip and remove the cable locating key.
7. Make sure the temperature control lever moves its full stroke.
8. Adjust the cable.

MODE SELECTOR

1. Remove the control assembly from the instrument panel.
2. Move the mode selector lever to the DEFROST position on the control assembly.
3. Insert cable locating key PNE7GH-18C408-A or equivalent, through the mode cam key slot and heater case key boss opening, to secure the cam in the proper position.
4. Remove the trim panel below the glove compartment, if equipped.
5. Disconnect the cable from the retaining clip next to the mode selector cam.

➡The mode selector cam is located on the right side of the heater unit.

To install:

6. Adjust the cable pre-set. Refer to the adjustment procedure.
7. Make sure the mode selector lever is in the DEFROST position.
8. Connect the cable straight to the retaining clip.

➡Do not exert any force on the cam during cable installation.

9. Remove the cable locating key.

10. Install the trim panel, if equipped.
11. Make sure the mode selector lever moves its full stroke.
12. Adjust the cable.

RECIRC/FRESH AIR SELECTOR

1. Remove the control assembly from the instrument panel.
2. Move the recirc/fresh air lever to the FRESH position on the control assembly.
3. Remove the glove compartment.
4. Insert cable locating key PNE7GH-18C408-A or equivalent, through the fresh air door cam key slot and recirc door key boss opening to secure the cam in the proper position.
5. Disconnect the cable from the retaining clip next to the recirc/fresh air cam.

To install:

6. Adjust the cable pre-set. Refer to the adjustment procedure.
7. Connect the cable to the retaining clip and remove the cable locating key.
8. Install the glove compartment.
9. Make sure the recirc/fresh air lever moves its full stroke.
10. Adjust the cable.

ADJUSTMENT

See Figure 20

1. Insert the blade of a thin, small pry tool into the wire and loop (crank arm end) of the function or temperature control cable.
2. Hold the self-adjusting cable attaching clip with a suitable tool and slide it down the shaft (away from the end loop) approximately 1 in. (25mm).
3. Install the cable.
4. Move the control lever temperature to the COOL position and function to the OFF position.
5. Force the temperature cable to the WARM position and function lever to DEFROST. This positions the self-adjusting clip. Check for proper control operation.

Blower Switch

REMOVAL & INSTALLATION

1. Pull the blower switch knob from the blower switch shaft.
2. Remove the instrument cluster opening finish panel.
3. Remove the control assembly from the instrument panel.
4. Pull the control assembly from the instrument panel.
5. Unplug the connectors from the blower switch.
6. Remove the attaching screw and remove the blower switch.

To install:

7. Position the blower and install the attaching screw.
8. Engage the switch connectors.
9. Install the control assembly onto the instrument panel.
10. Push the knob onto the switch and check for proper operation.

Blower Resistor

REMOVAL & INSTALLATION

1. Empty the contents from the glove compartment.
2. Push the side of the glove box liner inward and pull the liner from the opening.
3. Unplug the wire connector from the resistor assembly.
4. Remove the attaching screws and remove the resistor through the glove box opening.

To install:

5. Install the resistor with the two attaching screws.
6. Engage the wire harness connectors.
7. Check the operation of the blower at all speeds.

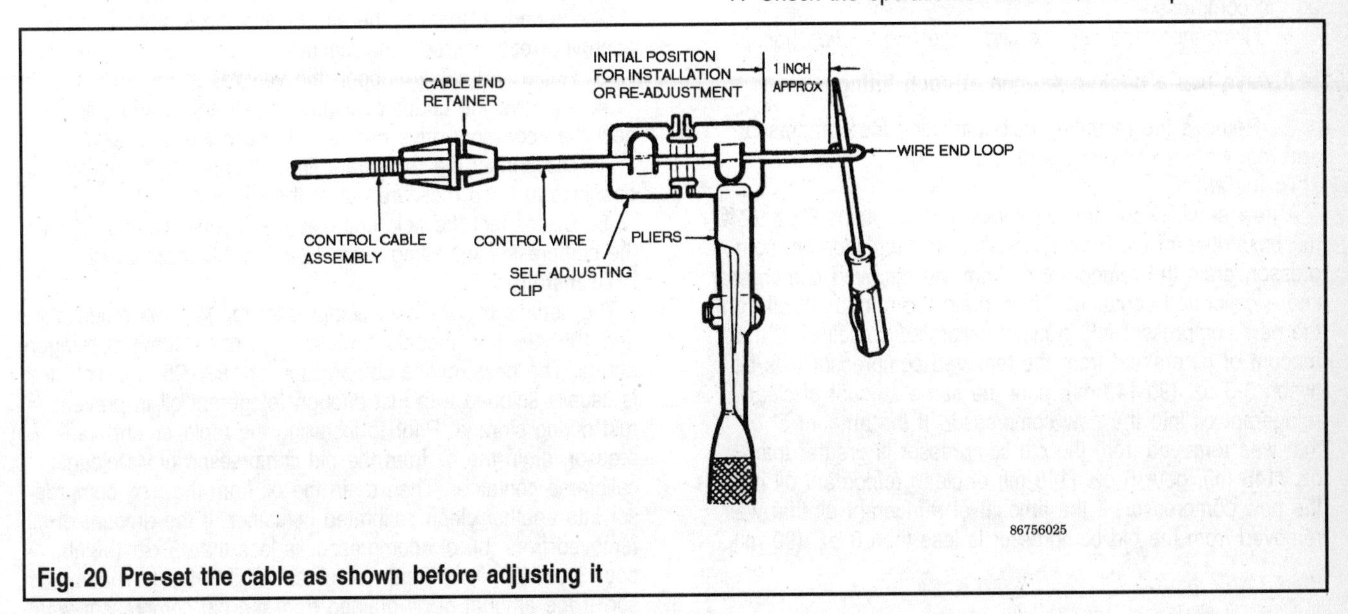

Fig. 20 Pre-set the cable as shown before adjusting it

AIR CONDITIONING

The air conditioning system used in the vehicles covered by this manual use either R-12 or R-134a type refrigerant. Before preforming any service to your A/C system, determine which type of refrigerant is needed.

Check the tags found on different parts of the A/C system in the engine compartment. Systems that use R-12 refrigerant have silver or white identification tags, while systems which use R-134a have yellow or gold identification tags.

➡The refrigerant R-12 is a chlorofluorocarbon which, when released into the atmosphere, can contribute to the depletion of the ozone layer. Ozone filters out harmful radiation from the sun. An approved R-12 recovery/recycling machine that meets SAE J1990 and J2210 standards must be employed when discharging the system. Follow the operating instructions provided with the approved equipment. Keep in mind that in some states/provinces, it may be illegal to service the A/C system without a license.

Compressor

REMOVAL & INSTALLATION

See Figure 21

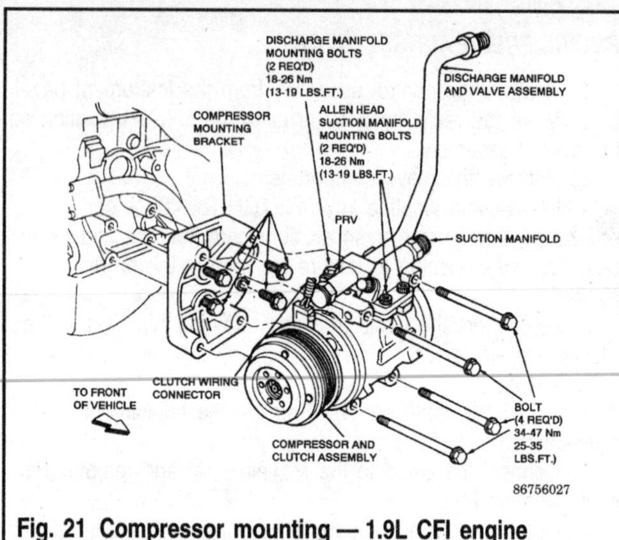

Fig. 21 Compressor mounting — 1.9L CFI engine shown, others are similar

1981-90 Models

➡Whenever the compressor is replaced, the suction accumulator/drier and the fixed orifice tube must also be replaced.

1. Disconnect the negative battery cable.
2. Properly discharge the air conditioning system using an approved recovery/recycling machine.
3. Remove the drive belt(s). For additional access, remove the alternator from the engine.
4. Disconnect the compressor clutch wires at the field coil on the compressor.
5. Disconnect and cap the discharge and suction hoses.

➡Always use a backup wrench at each fitting.

6. Remove the mounting bolts attaching the compressor and remove the compressor from the engine.

To install:

A new service replacement compressor contains 8 oz. (240 ml) of refrigerant oil. Prior to installing the replacement compressor, drain the refrigerant oil from the removed compressor into a calibrated container. Then, drain the refrigerant oil from the new compressor into a clean calibrated container. If the amount of oil drained from the removed compressor was between 3-5 oz. (90-148 ml), pour the same amount of clean refrigerant oil into the new compressor. If the amount of oil that was removed from the old compressor is greater than 5 oz. (148 ml), pour 5 oz. (148 ml) of clean refrigerant oil into the new compressor. If the amount of refrigerant oil that was removed from the old compressor is less than 3 oz. (90 ml), pour 3 oz. (90 ml) of clean refrigerant oil into the new compressor.

7. Place the compressor into position and install the mounting bolts. Tighten them to 25-35 ft. lbs. (34-47 Nm).
8. Connect the discharge and suction lines with new O-rings. Lightly lubricate the fittings with refrigerant oil first.
9. Connect the clutch wire to the field coil.
10. If removed, install the alternator to the engine.
11. Install the drive belt(s).
12. Evacuate, charge and leak test the system. Check the system for proper operation.

1991-95 Models

➡The suction accumulator/drier must be replaced whenever the A/C compressor is replaced.

1. Disconnect the negative battery cable.
2. Properly discharge the air conditioning system using an approved recovery/recycling machine.
3. Raise and safely support the vehicle.
4. Remove the undercover and splash shield and disconnect the accessory drive belt from the compressor pulley.
5. Disconnect the refrigerant lines. Immediately plug all openings to keep moisture out of the system.
6. Disconnect the field coil electrical connector and remove the compressor mounting bolts. Remove the compressor.

To install:

The service replacement compressor for 1991-92 models, and 1993-95 1.8L models contains 7.75 oz. (230ml) of refrigerant oil. The new service compressor for 1993-95 1.9L vehicles is usually shipped with just enough refrigerant oil to prevent rust during storage. Prior to installing the replacement compressor, drain the oil from the old compressor into a clean calibrated container. Then drain the oil from the new compressor into another clean calibrated container. If the amount of oil removed from the old compressor is less than 3 oz. (90ml), pour 3 oz. (90ml) of clean refrigerant oil into the new compressor. If the amount of oil drained from the old compressor was between 3-5 oz. (90-150ml), pour the same amount of clean refrigerant oil into the new compressor. If the amount of oil removed from the old compressor is greater than 5 oz. (150ml), pour 5 oz. (150ml) of clean oil into the new compressor. This will maintain the total system oil charge requirements.

7. Position the compressor and install the mounting bolts. Tighten the bolts for model 10P13 compressors to 15-22 ft. lbs. (20-30 Nm). Tighten the bolts for model FX-15 and FS-10 compressors to 31-44 ft. lbs. (41-61 Nm).
8. Install new O-rings lubricated with clean refrigerant oil on the lines. Position the lines and install the attaching bolts. Tighten the bolts for model 10P13 compressors to 13-17 ft. lbs. (18-23 Nm). Tighten the bolts for model FX-15 and FS-10 compressors to 12-19 ft. lbs. (16-26 Nm).
9. Connect the field coil electrical connector.
10. Attach the accessory drive belt to the compressor pulley and install the splash shield and undercover.
11. Lower the vehicle. Check the accessory drive belt for proper tension.
12. Connect the negative battery cable. Evacuate, charge and leak test the system. Observe all safety precautions.

Condenser

The A/C condenser core is a finned heat exchanger, essentially a separate radiator dedicated to the A/C system. It is usually made of aluminum and located in front of the cooling system radiator. The A/C condenser core cools the compressed refrigerant gas by making use of cool air between its fins and tubes to conduct the heat away from the refrigerant. As the refrigerant sheds its heat, it condenses into a liquid state.

REMOVAL & INSTALLATION

See Figures 22 and 23

Whenever the condenser is replaced, the suction accumulator/drier and the fixed orifice tube must also be replaced.

1. Disconnect the negative battery cable.
2. Drain the cooling system into a sealable container.
3. Properly discharge the air conditioning system using an approved recovery/recycling machine.
4. Remove the fan shroud retaining screws and remove the fan shroud. Disconnect the fan motor electrical connector.
5. Disconnect the upper and lower radiator hoses.
6. Disconnect and cap the transmission cooler lines.
7. Remove the radiator-to-support attaching nuts and remove the radiator from the vehicle.
8. Disconnect the liquid line and compressor discharge line from the condenser.
9. Remove the condenser-to-bracket retaining screws and remove the condenser from the vehicle.

To install:

10. Add 1 oz. (30ml) of clean refrigerant oil to a new replacement condenser. Place the condenser into position and install the condenser-to-bracket retaining screws.
11. Connect the refrigerant lines using new O-rings lubricated with clean refrigerant oil.
12. Place the radiator into position and install the radiator-to-support attaching nuts.

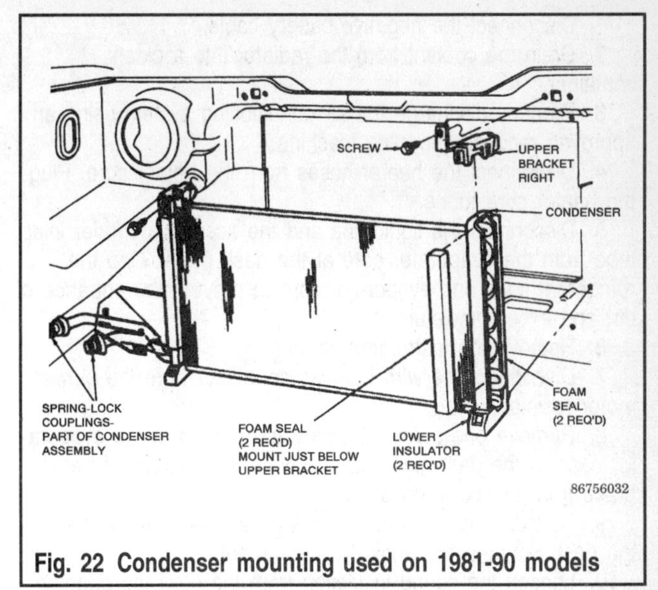

Fig. 22 Condenser mounting used on 1981-90 models

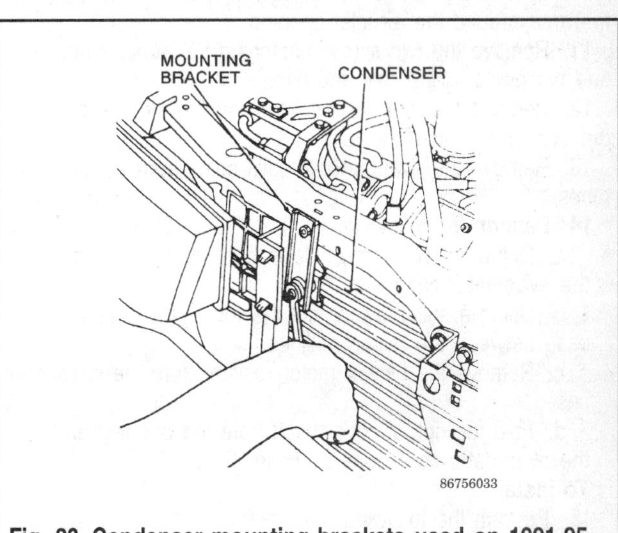

Fig. 23 Condenser mounting brackets used on 1991-95 models

13. Connect and cap the transmission cooler lines and upper and lower radiator hoses.
14. Install the fan shroud. Connect the fan motor electrical connector.
15. Fill the cooling system.
16. Evacuate, charge and leak test the system. Check the system for proper operation.

Evaporator Core

REMOVAL & INSTALLATION

1981-90 Models

See Figures 24 and 25

Whenever the evaporator core is removed, the suction accumulator/drier and the fixed orifice tube must also be replaced.

1. Disconnect the negative battery cable.
2. Drain the coolant from the radiator into a clean container.
3. Properly discharge the air conditioning system using an approved recovery/recycling machine.
4. Disconnect the heater hoses from the heater core. Plug the heater core tubes.
5. Disconnect the liquid line and the accumulator/drier inlet tube from the evaporator core at the dash panel. Cap the refrigerant lines and evaporator core to prevent the entrance of dirt and excess moisture.
6. Remove the instrument panel.
7. Disconnect the wire harness connector from the blower motor resistor.
8. Remove one screw attaching the bottom of the evaporator case to the dash panel and remove the instrument panel brace from the cowl top panel.
9. Remove the two nuts attaching the evaporator case to the dash panel in the engine compartment.
10. Loosen the sound insulation from the cowl top panel in the area around the air inlet opening.
11. Remove the two screws attaching the support bracket and the brace to the cowl top panel.
12. Remove the four screws attaching the air inlet duct to the evaporator case and remove the air inlet duct.
13. Remove the evaporator-to-cowl seals from the evaporator tubes.
14. Perform the following:
   a. Drill a $^3/_{16}$ in. (5mm) hole in both upright tabs on top of the evaporator case.
   b. Using a suitable tool, cut the top of the evaporator case between the raised outlines.
   c. Remove the blower motor resistor from the evaporator case.
   d. Fold the cutout cover back from the opening and lift the evaporator core from the case.

To install:

15. Perform the following procedure:
   a. Transfer the foam core seals to the new evaporator core.

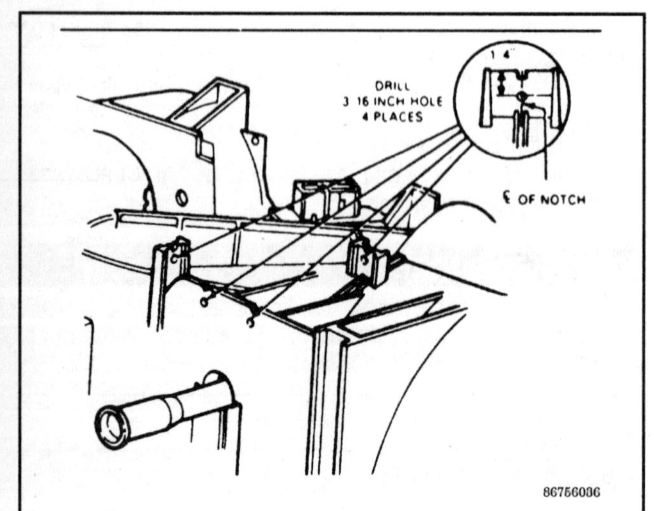

Fig. 24 Drill the evaporator case with a $^3/_{16}$ in. (5mm)drill bit in both upright tabs as shown

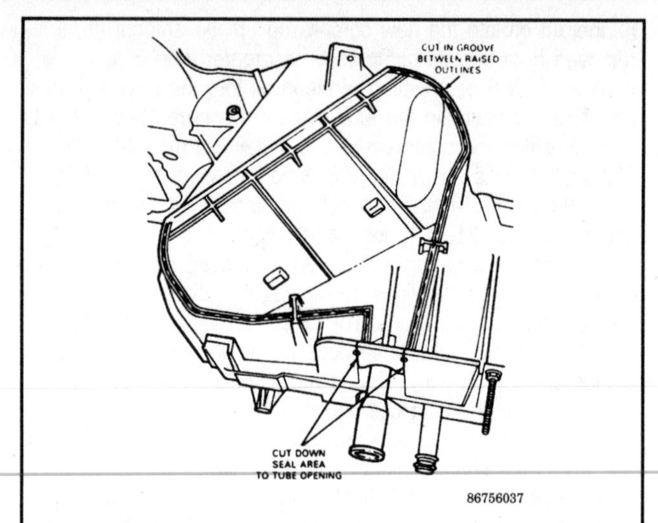

Fig. 25 Cut the top of the evaporator case along the line shown

   b. Position the evaporator core in the case and close the cutout cover.
   c. Install a spring nut on each of the two upright tabs and with the two holes drilled in the front flange. Make sure the holes in the spring nuts are aligned with the $^3/_{16}$ holes drilled in the tab and flange. Install and tighten the screw in each spring nut to secure the cutout cover in the closed position.
   d. Install caulking cord to seal the evaporator case against leakage along the cut line.
   e. Using new caulking cord, assemble the air inlet duct to the evaporator case.
   f. Install the blower motor resistor and install the foam seal over the evaporator core and heater core tubes.
16. Add 3 oz. (90 ml) of clean refrigerant oil to a new replacement evaporator core to maintain total system refrigerant oil requirements.
17. Position the evaporator case assembly to the dash panel and the cowl top panel at the air inlet opening. Install the two screws to attach the support bracket and brace to the cowl top panel.
18. Install the two nuts in the engine compartment to attach the evaporator case to the dash panel. Inspect the evaporator drain tube for a good seal and that the drain tube is through the opening and not obstructed.
19. Position the sound insulation around the air inlet duct on the cowl top panel.
20. Install the instrument panel.
21. Install 1 screw to attach the bottom of the evaporator assembly to the dash panel.
22. Connect the heater hoses to the heater core.
23. Using new O-rings lubricated with clean refrigerant oil, connect the liquid line and the accumulator/drier inlet tube to the evaporator core. Tighten each connection using a backup wrench to prevent component damage.
24. Fill the radiator with coolant and connect the negative battery cable.
25. Evacuate, charge and leak test the air conditioning system according to the proper procedure. Check the system for proper operation.

1991-95 Models

➧ See Figure 26

➡If the evaporator core requires replacement, the entire evaporator/blower unit must be replaced as an assembly. If the evaporator/blower unit is replaced, it will also be necessary to replace the accumulator/drier.

1. Disconnect the negative battery cable. If equipped, disable the SRS system.
2. Properly discharge the air conditioning system using an approved recovery/recycling machine.
3. Disconnect the high pressure line and the accumulator/drier inlet tube from the evaporator core at the bulkhead. Plug all ports to prevent the entrance of dirt and moisture.
4. Remove the glove compartment. If necessary for additional access, remove the trim panel below the glove compartment.
5. Disconnect the two electrical connectors from the resistor assembly and the electrical connector from the blower motor.
6. Remove the right dash side panel and the right lower dash trim panel and capscrews.
7. Remove the support bar and the support plate.
8. Disconnect the cable from the recirc/fresh air cam and retaining clip. Loosen the capscrew that secures the evaporator-to-heater clamp.
9. Remove the four mounting nuts from the evaporator/blower unit and remove the unit.

To install:

➡Make sure 3 oz. (90ml) of clean refrigerant oil is contained in the evaporator core of the replacement evaporator/blower unit.

10. Position the evaporator/blower unit and install the mounting nuts.
11. Tighten the capscrew that secures the evaporator-to-heater clamp. Connect the cable to the recirc/fresh air cam and adjust the cable.
12. Install the support plate and the support bar.
13. Install the right lower dash trim panel and the three capscrews. Install the right dash side panel.

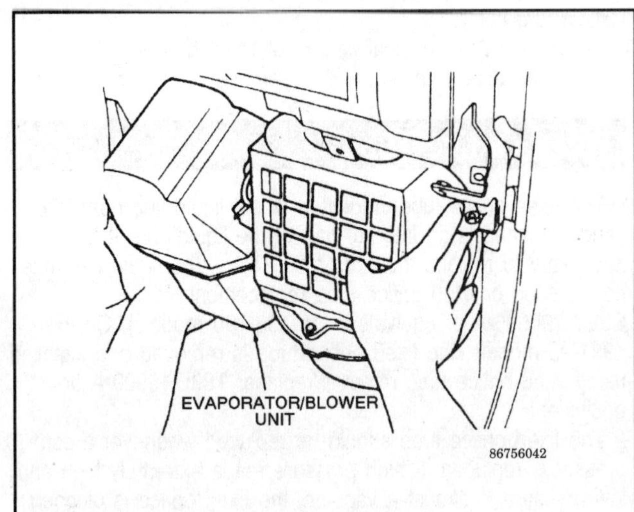

Fig. 26 When fully detached, remove the evaporator/blower unit

14. Connect the blower motor electrical connector and the two resistor assembly electrical connectors.
15. If necessary, install the trim panel below the glove compartment. Install the glove compartment.
16. Using new O-rings lubricated with clean refrigerant oil, connect the high pressure line and the accumulator/drier inlet tube to the evaporator core at the bulkhead.
17. Connect the negative battery cable. Evacuate, charge and leak test the system according to the proper procedure. Observe all safety precautions.

Accumulator/Drier

REMOVAL & INSTALLATION

1981-90 Models

EXCEPT 1990 ESCORT GT

1. Disconnect the negative battery cable. Properly discharge the refrigerant from the air conditioning system. Observe all safety precautions.
2. If equipped, remove the air pump from the engine.
3. Disconnect the suction hose the accumulator/drier inlet tube. Cap the openings.
4. Disconnect the wire harness connector from the pressure switch on top of the accumulator/drier.
5. Remove the two screws attaching the two strap clamps to the accumulator bracket and remove the accumulator/drier.

To install:

6. Drill a 1/2 in. (13mm) hole in the body of the removed accumulator/drier and drain the oil through the hole. Add the same amount of oil removed, plus 2 oz. (60 ml) of clean refrigerant oil to the new accumulator.
7. Using new O-rings lubricated with clean refrigerant oil, connect the refrigerant lines. Tighten the connection using a backup wrench, if applicable.
8. Position the two accumulator/drier mounting straps to the mounting bracket and install the two attaching screws.
9. Install the air pump, if equipped.
10. Evacuate, charge and leak test the system according to the proper procedure. Observe all safety precautions.
11. Check the system for proper operation.

1990 ESCORT GT

1. Disconnect the negative battery cable.
2. Properly discharge the air conditioning system using an approved recovery/recycling machine.
3. Remove the fuel filter bracket and move the fuel filter aside. Do not disconnect the fuel lines.
4. Disconnect the refrigerant hoses. Cap the lines to prevent the entry of dirt and moisture.
5. Remove the accumulator/drier top retaining nut.
6. Raise and safely support the vehicle.
7. Disconnect the catalytic converter and hose. Position it aside.
8. Drain the engine coolant and disconnect the lower heater hose.
9. Loosen the steel heater tube bracket.
10. Remove the accumulator/drier mounting bracket lower retaining screw and remove the bracket.

11. Remove the accumulator/drier and hose assembly from the vehicle.

To install:

12. Drill a 1/2 in. (13mm) hole in the body of the removed accumulator/drier and drain the oil through the hole. Add the same amount of oil removed, plus 2 oz. (60 ml) of clean refrigerant oil to the new accumulator.
13. Position the accumulator/drier and mounting bracket in the vehicle and install the mounting bracket lower retaining screw.
14. Tighten the steel heater tube bracket.
15. Connect the lower heater hose.
16. Connect the catalytic converter and hose.
17. Lower the vehicle.
18. Install the accumulator/drier retaining nut.
19. Connect the refrigerant lines. Use new O-rings and lubricate the fittings with clean refrigerant oil.
20. Move the fuel filter into position and install the fuel filter bracket.
21. Fill the radiator with coolant.
22. Evacuate, charge and leak test the system according to the proper procedure. Observe all safety precautions.
23. Check the system for proper operation.

1991-95 Models

1. Disconnect the negative battery cable.
2. Properly discharge the air conditioning system using an approved recovery/recycling machine.
3. If equipped with a 1.9L engine, remove the washer reservoir.
4. Disconnect the electrical connector from the clutch cycling pressure switch.
5. Disconnect the suction line from the accumulator/drier. Cap the opening.
6. If equipped with a 1.8L engine, loosen the mounting strap bolt. If equipped with a 1.9L engine, remove the two bolts and the mounting strap.
7. Disconnect the accumulator/drier from the evaporator outlet tube. Cap the opening.
8. Remove the accumulator/drier.

To install:

9. Drill a 1/2 in. (13mm) hole in the old accumulator body and drain the oil from the accumulator into a clean calibrated container. Add the same amount of oil as removed, plus 2 oz. (60ml) of clean refrigerant oil to a new accumulator/drier.
10. Position the accumulator on the vehicle.
11. Using new O-rings lubricated with clean refrigerant oil, connect the suction accumulator/drier to the evaporator outlet tube.
12. If equipped with a 1.8L engine, tighten the mounting strap bolt. If equipped with a 1.9L engine, position the mounting strap and install the two mounting bolts.
13. Using new O-rings lubricated with clean refrigerant oil, connect the suction line to the accumulator/drier.
14. Connect the electrical connector to the clutch cycling pressure switch.
15. If equipped with a 1.9L engine, install the washer reservoir.
16. Connect the negative battery cable. Evacuate, charge and leak test the system according to the proper procedure. Observe all safety precautions.

Cycling Clutch Switch

REMOVAL & INSTALLATION

➡It is not necessary to discharged the air conditioning system to replace the cycling clutch switch.

1. Unplug the wire harness connector from the pressure switch.
2. Unscrew the pressure switch from the suction accumulator/drier.

To install:

3. Lubricate the accumulator nipple O-ring with clean refrigerant oil.
4. Screw the pressure switch onto the accumulator nipple.

➡If the pressure threaded fitting is plastic, tighten the switch finger-tight only.

5. Engage the switch wire connector.
6. Operate the system and check for leaks and proper operation.

Cooling Fan Controller

REMOVAL & INSTALLATION

The cooling fan controller is attached to the top cowl panel behind the glove box opening with a screw. The controller can be serviced through the glove box opening.

1. Empty the contents from the glove compartment.
2. Push the side of the glove box liner inward and pull the liner from the opening. Allow the glove compartment and door to hang on its hinges.
3. Through the glove compartment opening, remove the controller attaching screw located on the cowl top panel and remove the controller.
4. Unplug the electrical connector from the controller.
5. Installation is the reverse of removal.

Fixed Orifice Tube

The fixed orifice tube is located in the liquid line near the condenser and is an integral part of the liquid line. If it is necessary to replace the fixed orifice tube, the liquid line must be replaced or fixed orifice tube replacement kit E5VY-190695-A or equivalent (on 1981-90 models). On the 1991-95 models, the fixed orifice tube is removed and installed using fixed orifice tube remover/replacer T83L-19990-A or equivalent.

The fixed orifice tube should be replaced whenever a compressor is replaced. If high pressure reads extremely high and low pressure is almost a vacuum, the fixed orifice is plugged and must be replaced.

REMOVAL & INSTALLATION

1981-90 Models

1. Disconnect the negative battery cable.
2. Discharge the refrigerant from the air conditioning system into an approved recovery/recycling machine.
3. Remove the liquid line from the vehicle.
4. Locate the orifice tube by three indented notches or a circular depression in the metal portion of the liquid line. Note the angular position of the ends of the liquid line so that it can be reassembled in the correct position.
5. Cut a 2½ in. (63.5mm) section from the tube at the orifice tube location. Do not cut closer than 1 in. (25mm) from the start of the bend in the tube.
6. Remove the fixed orifice tube from the housing.

To install:

7. Flush the two pieces of liquid line to remove any contaminants.
8. Lubricate the O-rings with clean refrigerant oil and assemble the orifice tube kit. Make sure the flow direction arrow is pointing toward the evaporator end of the liquid line and the taper of each compression ring is toward the compression nut.

➡The inlet tube will be positioned against the orifice tube tabs when correctly assembled.

9. While holding the hex of the tube in a vise, tighten each compression nut to 65-70 ft. lbs. (88-94 Nm) with a crow foot attachment on a torque wrench.
10. Assemble the liquid line to the vehicle using new O-rings lubricated with clean refrigerant oil.
11. Evacuate, charge and leak test the system according to the proper procedure. Observe all safety precautions.
12. Check the system for proper operation.

1991-95 Models

1. Disconnect the negative battery cable.
2. Discharge the refrigerant from the air conditioning system into an approved recovery/recycling machine.
3. Remove the refrigerant line with the orifice tube.
4. Using fixed orifice tube remover/replacer T83L-19990-A or equivalent, remove the fixed orifice tube from the refrigerant line.

To install:

5. Install the fixed orifice tube using the orifice tube remover/replacer.
6. Install the refrigerant line with new O-rings lubricated with clean refrigerant oil.
7. Connect the negative battery cable. Evacuate, charge and leak test the system according to the proper procedure. Observe all safety precautions.

Refrigerant Lines

REMOVAL & INSTALLATION

➡Whenever a refrigerant line is replaced, it will be necessary to replace the accumulator/drier.

1. Disconnect the negative battery cable.
2. Discharge the refrigerant from the air conditioning system into an approved recovery/recycling machine.
3. Disconnect and remove the refrigerant line using a wrench on each side of the tube O-fittings. If the refrigerant line has a spring-lock coupling, disconnect the fitting using a spring-lock coupling tool. This tool is available at most auto parts stores.

To install:

4. Route the new refrigerant line with the protective caps installed.
5. Connect the new refrigerant line into the system with new O-rings lubricated with clean refrigerant oil. Use two wrenches when tightening the tube O-fittings or engage the spring-lock coupling.
6. Connect the negative battery cable. Evacuate, charge and leak test the refrigerant system according to the proper procedure.

CRUISE CONTROL

When activated by the driver, the cruise control system is designed to maintain vehicle road speed without requiring further input from the accelerator pedal. To activate the cruise control system, the engine must be running and the vehicle speed must be greater than 30 mph (48 km/h).

The cruise control systems for 1981-90 models and 1991-95 models are very similar in design and operation, although there are some minor changes in service procedures.

The cruise control system consists of operator controls, a servo (throttle actuator) assembly, a speed sensor, a clutch switch, a Brake On/Off (BOO) switch, a vacuum dump valve, an amplifier assembly and the necessary wires and vacuum hoses.

System Diagnosis

To diagnose any malfunction with the cruise control system, first perform a thorough visual inspection. Begin by checking all items for abnormal conditions such as bare, broken or disconnected wires, and check for damaged or disconnected vacuum hoses as well. All vacuum hoses should be securely attached and routed with no kinks in them. The cruise control servo (throttle actuator) should operate freely and smoothly, and its cable should be adjusted as tightly as possible without opening the throttle plate or causing an increase in idle speed. Refer to the appropriate portions of this section for information pertaining to servo operation and cable adjustment. Check for a sticking brake and clutch switch (if equipped) as this could keep the system from engaging.

Once it has been determined the system is not operating properly, and all obvious trouble sources have been ruled out, refer troubleshooting to a reputable repair facility.

Control Switch

REMOVAL & INSTALLATION

1981-90 Models

➧ See Figure 27

1. Remove the retaining screws to the steering wheel pad cover and remove the cover. Remove the foam insert, if equipped.
2. Detach the wire connector from the steering wheel. Disconnect the horn wires from the pad cover.
3. Remove the cruise control switches by removing the two screws from each side. Refer to the illustration.

To install:

4. Position the control switches into the steering wheel pad cover and secure with the two screws.
5. Plug the horn wire connectors into place on the steering wheel pad cover.
6. Connect the wire to the steering wheel terminals.
7. Install the foam pad into the steering wheel. Be sure to not pinch the wiring on top of the pad.
8. Install the pad cover and screw in place.

1991-93 Models

ESCORT

1. Remove the steering wheel nuts from the back of the steering wheel.
2. Lift the cover and unplug the horn connector and the cruise control connectors.
3. Remove the two screws from the switch retaining bracket and the switch.

To install:

4. Position the switch and retaining bracket and install the screws.
5. Plug in the speed switch and the horn connectors.
6. Replace the steering wheel cover and secure with the two nuts.

TRACER

➡Two-spoke steering wheels have two wheel cover screws and four spoke steering wheels have four cover retaining screws.

1. Remove the steering wheel cover screws from the back of the steering wheel.
2. Lift the cover and disconnect the horn and the cruise control switch.
3. Remove the four screws from the switch retaining bracket and remove the bracket from the switch.

To install:

4. Position the switch and retaining bracket. Install the four screws.
5. Connect the cruise control and the horn terminals.
6. Position the steering wheel cover and the screws.

1994-95 Models

➧ See Figures 28 and 29

✲✲CAUTION

These models are equipped with a Supplemental Restraint System (SRS). Always disable the SRS system before working on or near its components. Refer to the disarming procedure in this section.

1. Make sure the wheels are straight ahead (to ensure alignment of the air bag sliding contact).
2. Disconnect the negative battery cable and wait one minute before proceeding. Disable the SRS system.
3. Remove the steering wheel.
4. Tape the air bag sliding contact to prevent disturbing it as you proceed.
5. Remove the four horn contact plate screws from the steering wheel.
6. Move to one side the horn contact plates to access the two rear steering wheel trim cover screws. Remove the screws and the steering wheel rear trim cover and set it aside.
7. Remove the four cruise control actuator switch screws holding the two cruise control actuator switches to the steering wheel. Remove the cruise control actuator switches.

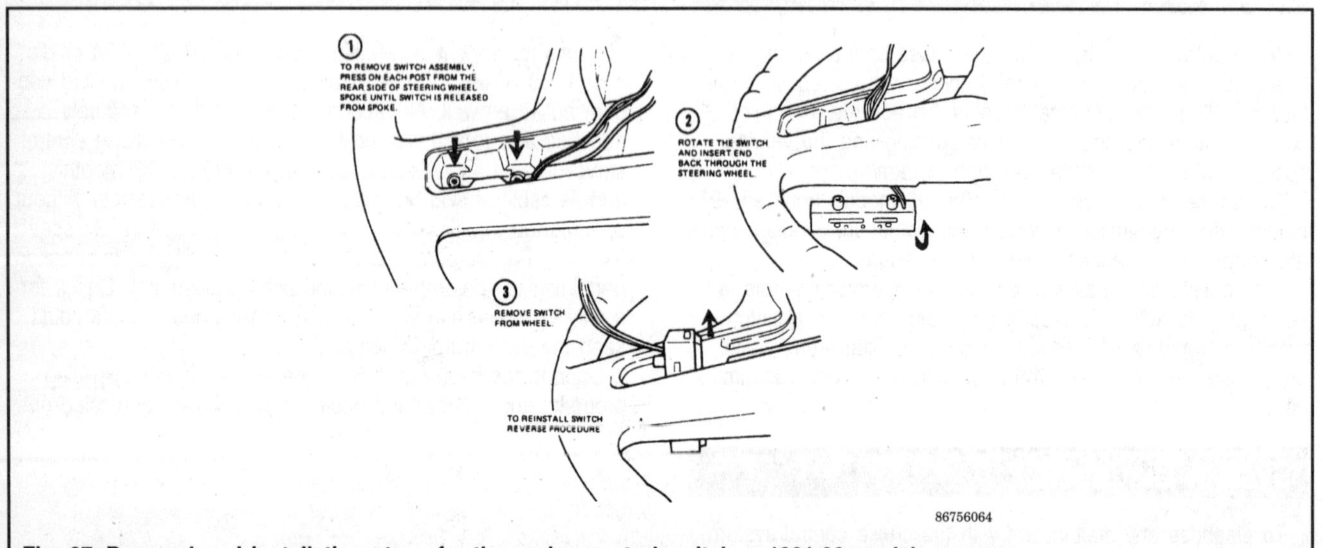

Fig. 27 Removal and installation steps for the cruise control switch — 1981-90 models

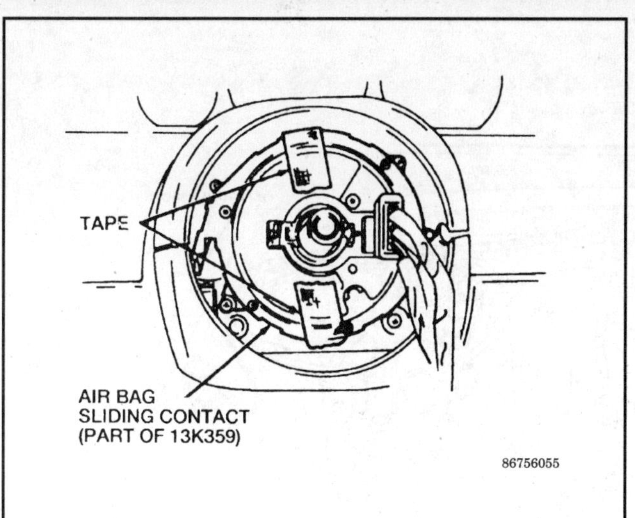

Fig. 28 Use tape as shown to prevent disturbing the air bag sliding contact

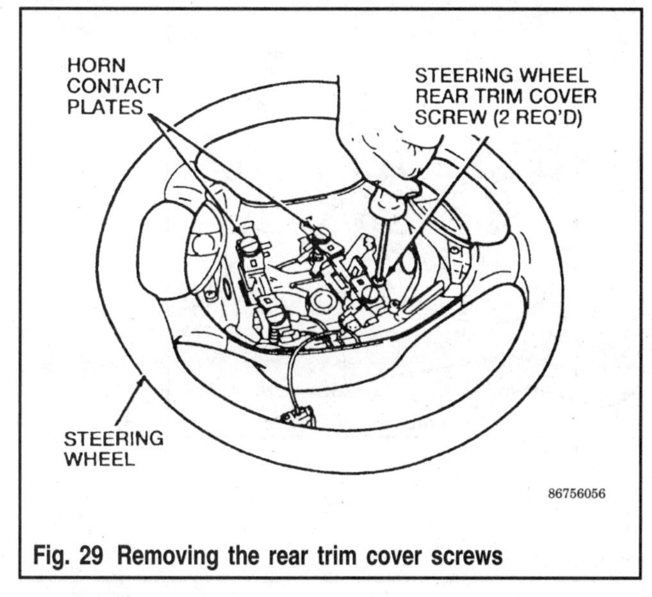

Fig. 29 Removing the rear trim cover screws

To install:

8. Position the cruise control actuator switches and install the screws.
9. Install the horn contact plates.
10. Install the steering wheel.

➡If you misalign the steering wheel upon installation, you will have to remove, re-position and install it again until it is in the correct position.

11. Connect the negative battery cable.

Cruise Control Servo (Throttle Actuator)

REMOVAL & INSTALLATION

1981-90 Models

See Figures 30 and 31

1. Disconnect the negative battery cable.
2. Remove the air cleaner and position it aside.
3. Remove the push pin and disconnect the cruise control actuator cable from the accelerator cable bracket.
4. Remove and label the vacuum hoses and electrical connector from the servo assembly.
5. Remove the servo-to-mounting bracket mounting nuts and carefully remove the servo and cable assembly.
6. Remove the two nuts holding the cable cover to the servo and pull off the cover. Remove the cable assembly.

To install:

7. Attach the cable to the servo. Then, install the servo to the mounting bracket.
8. Feed the actuator cable under the air cleaner air duct, if equipped, and snap the cable with adjuster onto the accelerator cable. Adjust the actuator cable as follows:
   a. Remove the cable retaining fastener.
   b. Disengage the throttle positioner.
   c. Set the carburetor at hot idle, if applicable.
   d. Pull on the actuator cable end tube to take up any slack.
   e. While holding the cable, insert the cable retaining clip and snap securely.
9. Connect the actuator cable to the accelerator cable bucket and install the push pin.
10. Connect the vacuum hoses and electrical connector.
11. Connect the negative battery cable.

1991-95 Models

See Figure 32

1. Remove the two cruise control servo rear bracket nuts.
2. Remove the cruise control servo bracket bolt that secures it to the body.
3. Label and remove the two vacuum lines from the servo.
4. Unplug the electrical connector from the servo.
5. Remove the retainer clip from the cruise control actuator housing.
6. Remove the two cruise control servo bracket nuts and the cruise control servo bracket from the cable side of the cruise control servo.
7. Slide the actuator away from the servo. Disconnect the actuator and remove the servo.

To install:

8. Position the servo and actuator in place and adjust the cruise control actuator in the following manner:
   a. With the cruise control retainer clip removed from the actuator housing, pull tightly on the cruise control actuator until all slack is taken out.

➡The accelerator cable will tighten around the throttle body pulley when slack is taken out of the actuator. It is important that the accelerator cable is adjusted properly before the cruise control actuator is adjusted.

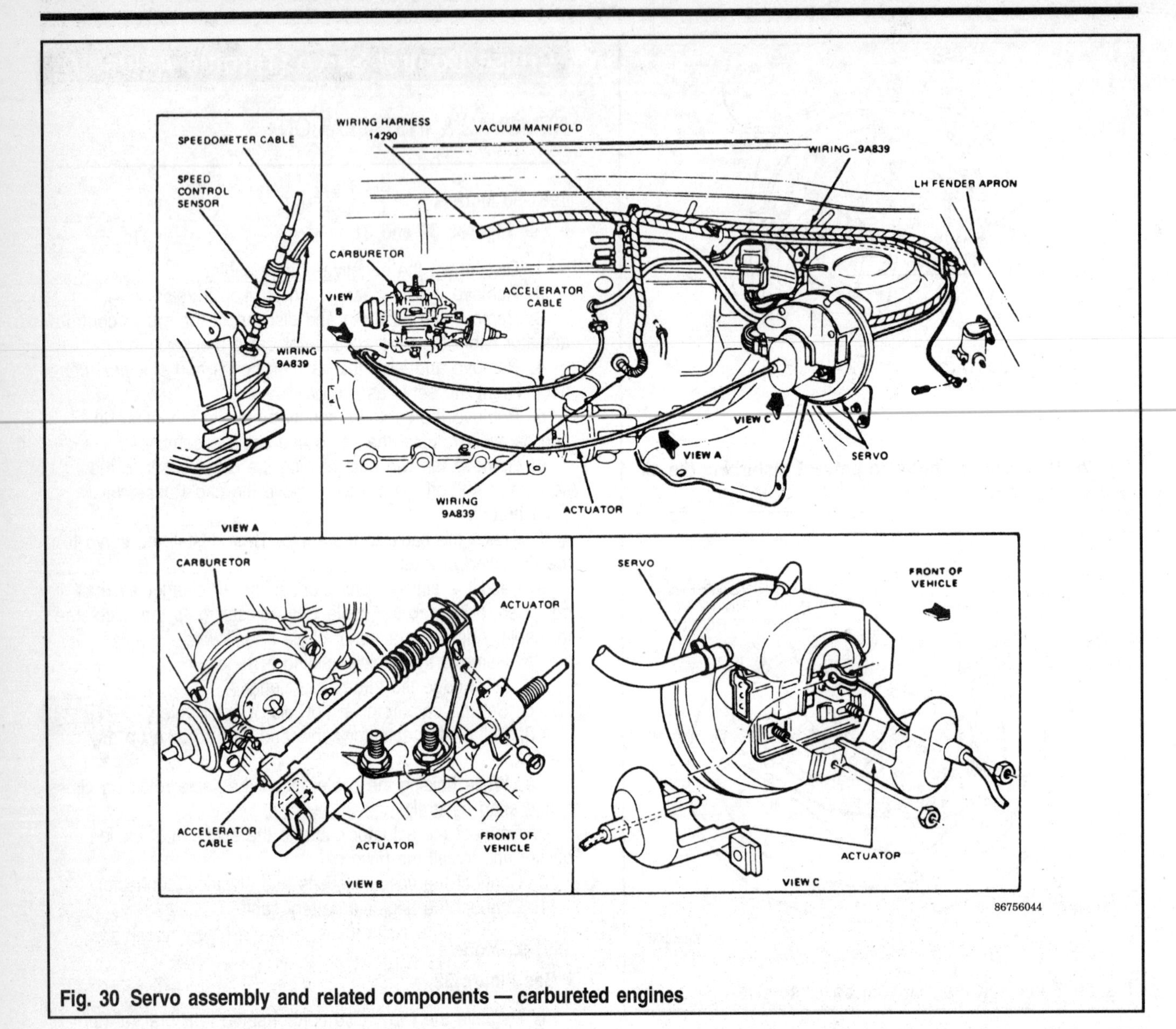

Fig. 30 Servo assembly and related components — carbureted engines

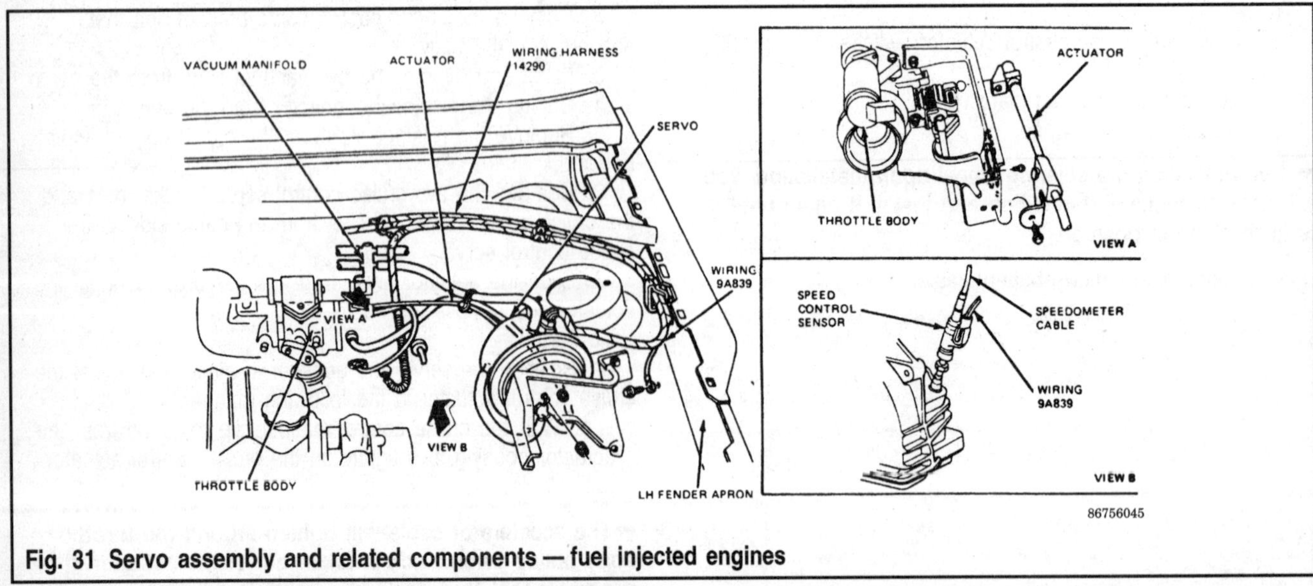

Fig. 31 Servo assembly and related components — fuel injected engines

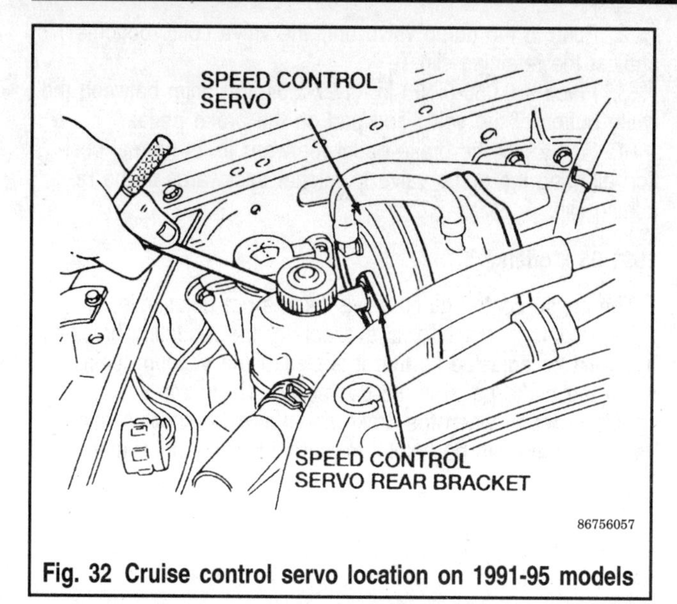

Fig. 32 Cruise control servo location on 1991-95 models

b. Install the cruise control retainer clip.

9. Install the remaining components in the reverse order of the removal procedure.

Speed Sensor

➧ See Figure 33

REMOVAL & INSTALLATION

1. Disconnect the negative battery cable.
2. Separate the electrical connector to the speed sensor.
3. Disconnect the speedometer cable at the sensor.
4. Remove the retaining bolt and the sensor.

To install:

5. Install the speed sensor. Install a new O-ring seal on the sensor.
6. Connect the speedometer cable.
7. Engage the electrical connector to the speed sensor.
8. Connect the negative battery cable.

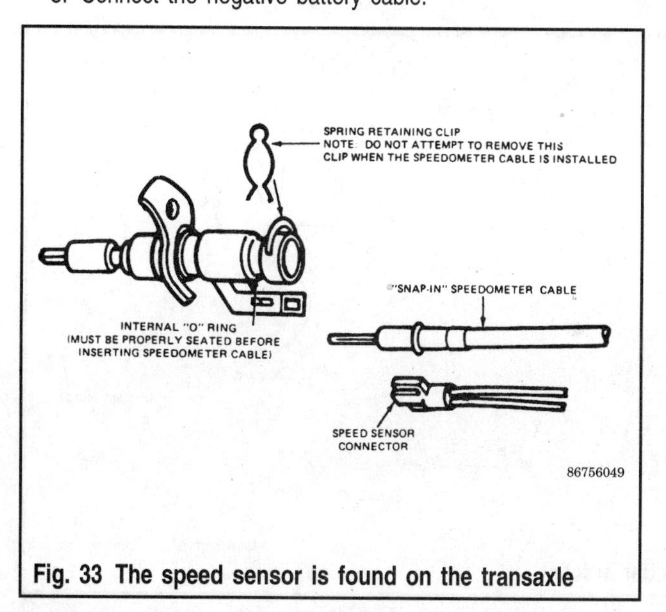

Fig. 33 The speed sensor is found on the transaxle

Clutch Switch

REMOVAL & INSTALLATION

1. Remove the bracket mounting screw.
2. Unplug the electrical connector.
3. For 1991-95 models, remove the retaining locknut.
4. Remove the switch and bracket assembly.
5. Remove the switch from the bracket.

To install:

6. Install the switch on the bracket.
7. Engage the electrical connector.
8. For 1991-95 models, install the locknut and tighten to 10-13 ft. lbs. (14-18 Nm).
9. Install the bracket mounting screw and adjust the clutch switch, as applicable.

ADJUSTMENT

The clutch switch is not adjustable. Tolerances are taken up by proper adjustment of the clutch pedal. Refer to Section 7 for clutch pedal adjustment procedures.

Brake On/Off (BOO) Switch

REMOVAL & INSTALLATION

➧ See Figure 34

1. Unplug the electrical connector.
2. Loosen the switch locknut.
3. Remove the switch from the brake pedal assembly.

To install:

4. Install the switch on the brake pedal bracket assembly.
5. Turn the switch until it contacts the brake pedal, then turn it an extra half of one turn.

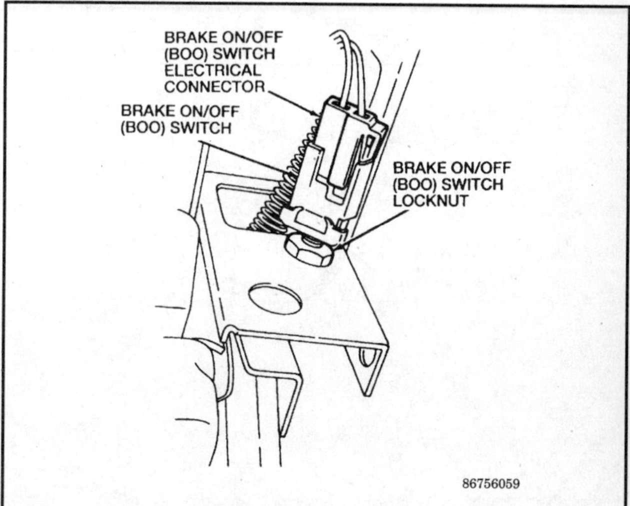

Fig. 34 The BOO switch is mounted on the brake pedal bracket

6. Tighten the locknut to 10-13 ft. lbs. (14-17 Nm). Plug the electrical connector into the switch.

Vacuum Dump Valve

REMOVAL & INSTALLATION

➧ See Figure 35

1. Remove the vacuum hose from the valve.
2. Remove the valve from the bracket.
3. Installation is reverse of removal. Adjust the valve.

ADJUSTMENT

1981-90 Models

➧ See Figure 36

1. Firmly depress the brake pedal and hold in position.
2. Push in the dump valve until the valve collar bottoms against the retaining clip.
3. Place a 0.050-0.100 in. (1.27-2.54mm) shim between the white button of the valve and pad on the brake pedal.
4. Firmly pull the brake pedal rearward to its normal position allowing the dump valve to ratchet backwards in the retaining clip.

1991-95 Models

The cruise control dump valve itself is not adjustable, although some adjustability is available at the mounting bracket. It should be adjusted so that it is closed (no vacuum leak) when the brake pedal is not depressed. The dump valve should be open when the brake pedal is depressed. A hand vacuum pump can be helpful in performing this adjustment.

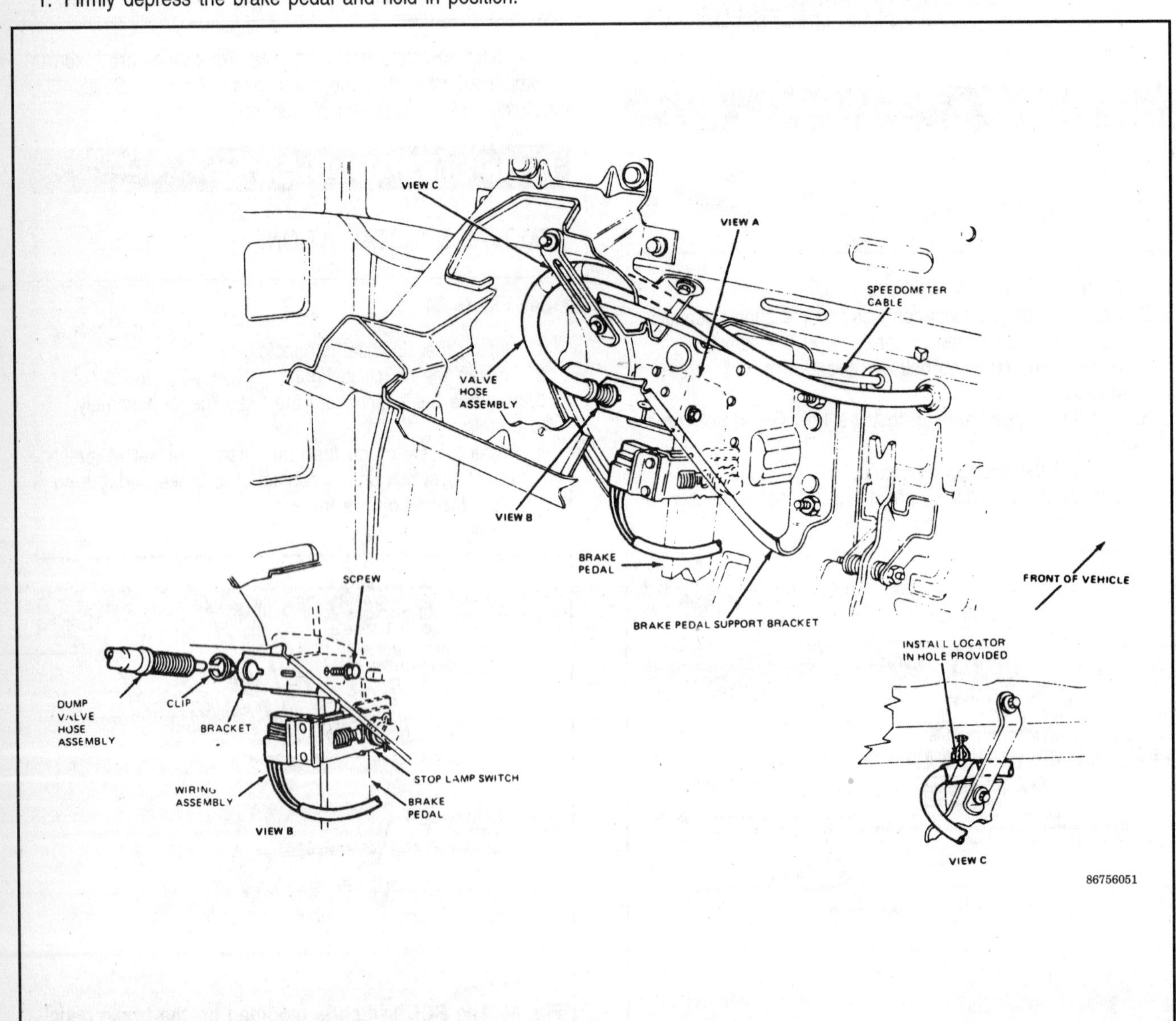

Fig. 35 The vacuum dump valve is positioned on the brake pedal bracket

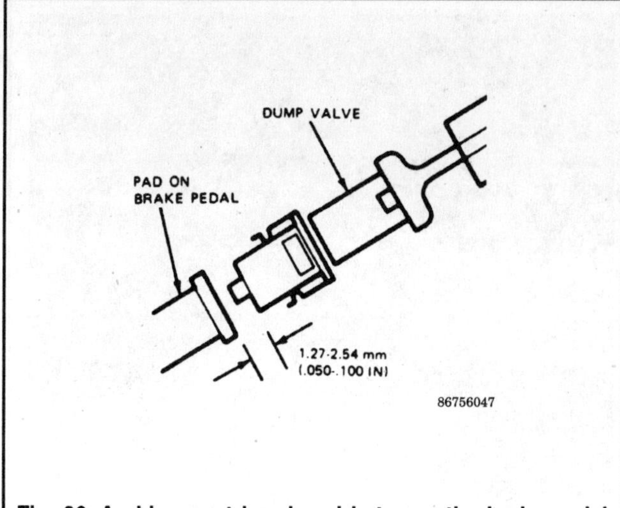

Fig. 36 A shim must be placed between the brake pedal pad and dump valve when adjusting

Amplifier Assembly

REMOVAL & INSTALLATION

➧ **See Figures 37 and 38**

The amplifier is located below the steering column on the instrument panel reinforcement on 1981-90 models. It is behind the right side kick panel on 1991-95 models.

1. For 1981-90 models, remove the two screws that secure the amplifier bracket to the instrument panel reinforcement. Remove the two bolts and nuts securing the amplifier assembly to the mounting bracket.
2. For 1991-95 models, remove the kick panel and unbolt the amplifier.
3. Unplug the electrical connectors at the amplifier.

To install:

4. Engage the electrical connectors to the amplifier.
5. Install the bolts and nuts which secure the amplifier to the bracket.
6. Install the amplifier and bracket assembly.

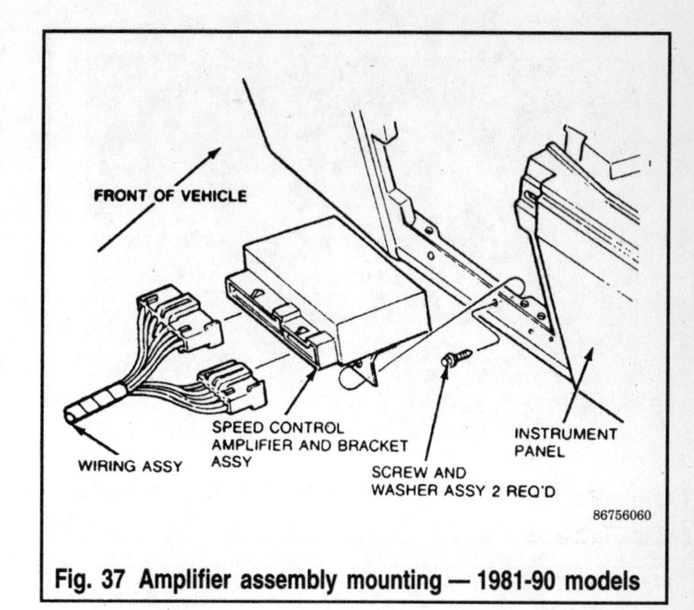

Fig. 37 Amplifier assembly mounting — 1981-90 models

Fig. 38 Amplifier assembly mounting — 1991-95 models

RADIO

Radio Receiver/Tape Player

REMOVAL & INSTALLATION

1981-85 Models

1. Disconnect the negative battery cable.

➡Remove the air conditioning floor duct, if so equipped.

2. Remove the ash tray and bracket.
3. Pull the knobs from the shafts.
4. Working under the instrument panel, remove the support bracket nut from the radio chassis.
5. Remove the shaft nuts and washers.
6. Carefully lower the radio down from behind the instrument panel. Disconnect the power lead, antenna, and speaker wires. Remove the radio.
7. Installation is the reverse of the removal procedure.

1986-90 Models

➧ **See Figures 39, 40, 41 and 42**

1. Disconnect the negative battery cable.
2. Remove the center instrument trim panel.
3. Remove the four bolts retaining the radio and mounting bracket to the instrument panel.
4. Pull the radio to the front and raise the back end of the radio slightly so the rear support bracket clears the clip in the

Fig. 39 The center instrument trim panel is secured by screws

Fig. 40 After the trim panel is removed, unscrew the four bolts retaining the radio and mounting bracket

Fig. 41 Pull the radio out and unplug the wiring connectors

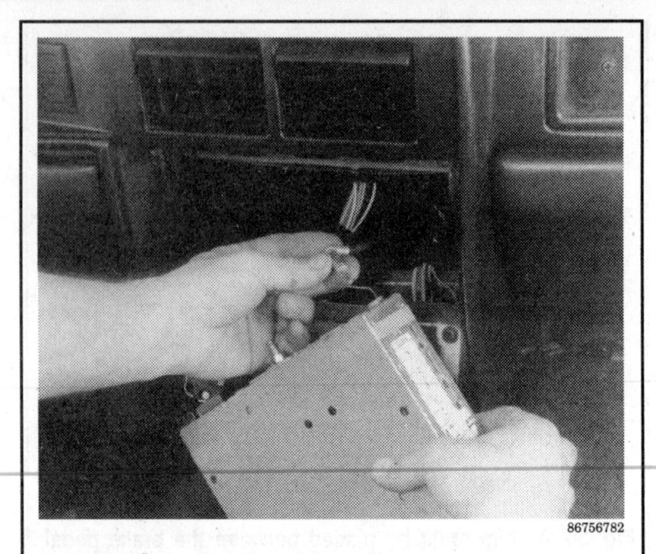

Fig. 42 Don't forget to unplug the antenna wire

instrument panel. Pull the radio out of the instrument panel slowly.

5. Unplug the wiring connectors and antenna cable.
6. Transfer the mounting brackets to the new radio, if necessary.
7. Installation is the reverse of the removal procedure. Tighten the retaining screws to 14-16 inch lbs. (1.5-1.9 Nm).

1991-95 Models

See Figure 43

1. Disconnect the negative battery cable.
2. Using radio removal tool T87P-19061-A or equivalent, pull the radio out from its mounting position so the antenna and the electrical connectors are accessible.
3. Unplug the antenna lead and the radio electrical connectors from the radio.
4. Remove the radio.
5. Installation is the reverse of the removal procedure.

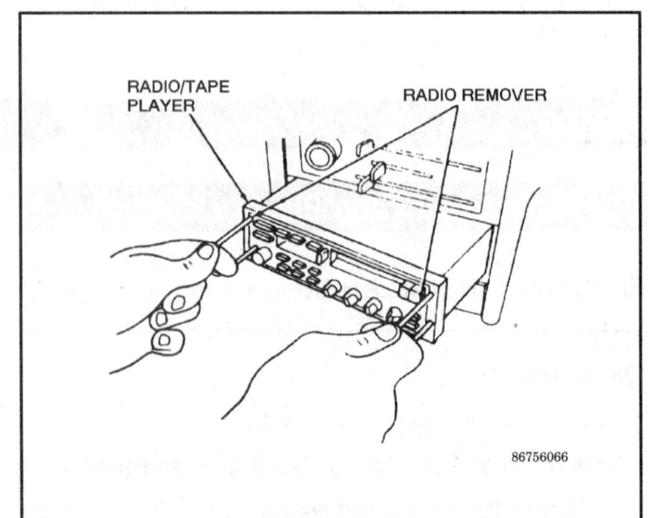

Fig. 43 Remove the radio as shown with the special removal tool — 1991-95 models

Speakers

REMOVAL & INSTALLATION

Front

The front door panel must be removed to gain access to the speaker. Remove the speaker retaining screws and remove the speaker; disconnect the speaker wiring. Most of the front speakers are set into a plastic sleeve or protector in the door. This protects the speaker from water and moisture in the door. Make sure the shield is in place when reinstalling the speakers.

Rear

On hatchbacks and wagons, remove the speaker grille or cover. Some are press-fit in place, others are held by plastic retaining pins. Look carefully before prying. Once the speaker is exposed, remove the retaining screws and remove the speaker. On sedans, the speakers are usually accessed through the trunk. Remove the speaker covers, then unplug the connectors and remove the retainers to remove the speaker. If the speakers are not accessible through the trunk, remove the speaker grilles from the rear shelf. Remove the retainers, then pull the speaker upwards slightly. Unplug the electrical connector and remove the speaker.

All the rear speakers sit in some type of support or frame. This provides both a firm mount and isolates the speaker from its surroundings, preventing distortion. Make sure the frame is present when reinstalling the speaker.

WINDSHIELD WIPERS AND WASHERS

Wiper Blade

REPLACEMENT

See Figures 44 and 45

Two types of wiper blades are used. One pivots on a pin on the arm and is secured by a spring tab on the blade. The other is secured by two small screws on the arm. On pivot pin types, pull up on the spring lock and pull the blade assembly from the pin. On screw types, simply remove the screws, then the blade. Installation is the reverse of removal.

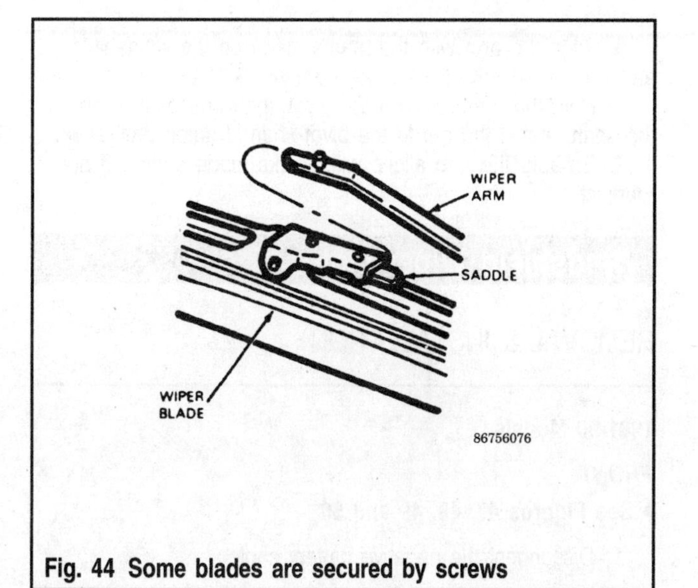

Fig. 44 Some blades are secured by screws

Wiper Arm

REMOVAL & INSTALLATION

1981-90 Models

See Figure 45

1. Mark the position of the arm on the windshield with a grease pencil or tape.
2. Raise the blade end of the arm off the windshield and move the slide latch away from the pivot shaft.
3. The wiper arm can now be pulled off of the pivot shaft.

To install:

4. With the arm and blade assemblies removed from the pivot shafts, turn on the wiper switch and allow the motor to move the pivot shaft three or four cycles, then turn off the wiper switch. This will place the pivot shafts in the park position.
5. Align the arm with the marks made on the windshield earlier.
6. Hold the arm head on the pivot shaft and push it onto the shaft. Hold the blade, then slide the latch into the groove under the pivot shaft. Lower the blade to the windshield.

If the blade does not touch the windshield, the slide latch is not completely in place.

7. Be sure the arm aligns with marks made earlier. If not, readjust.

1991-95 Models

See Figure 46

1. Mark the position of the arm on the windshield with a grease pencil or tape.
2. Open the hood.
3. Remove the nut securing the arm to the pivot shaft.

To install:

4. With the arm and blade assemblies removed from the pivot shafts, turn on the wiper switch and allow the motor to move the pivot shaft three or four cycles, then turn off the

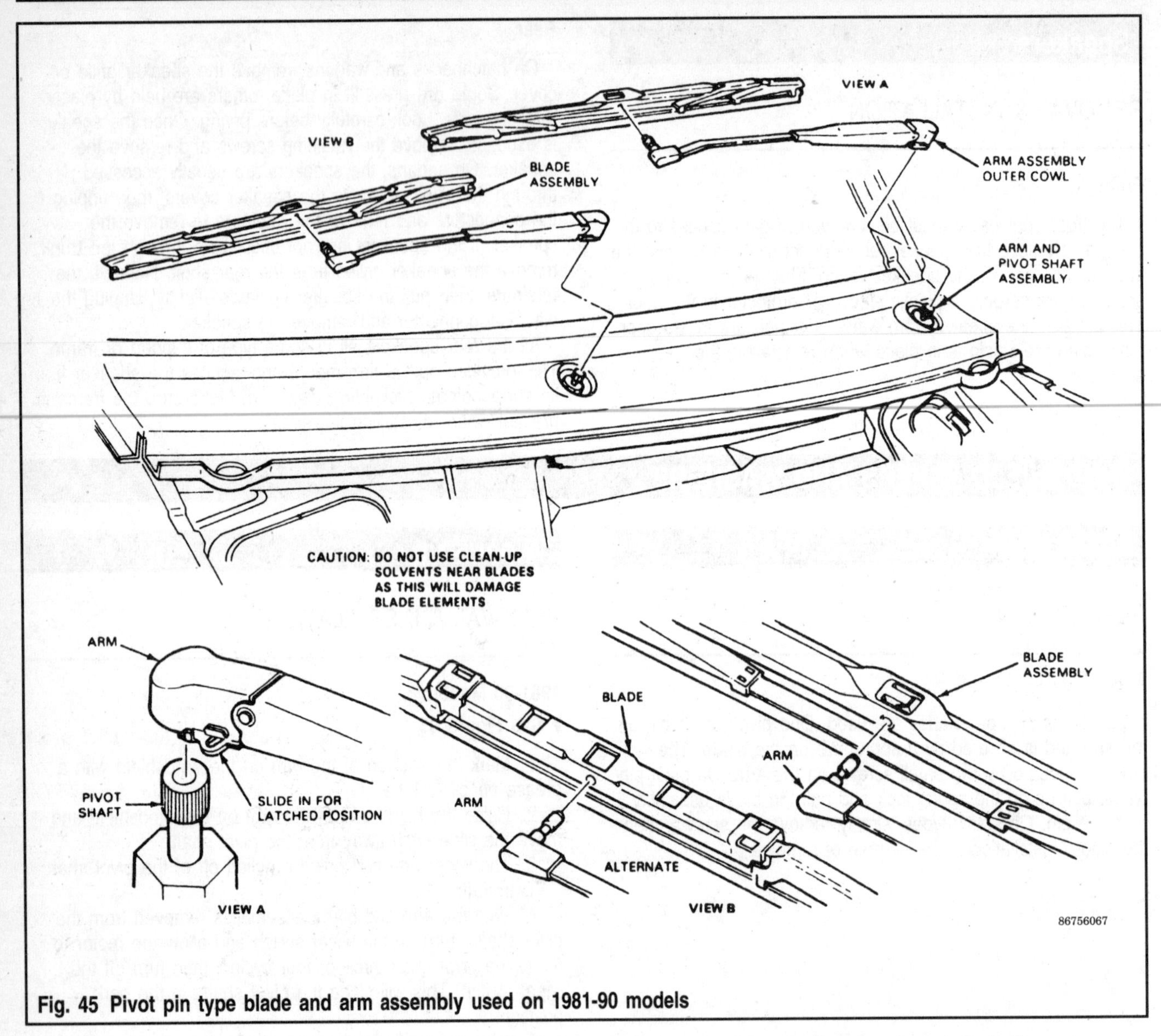

Fig. 45 Pivot pin type blade and arm assembly used on 1981-90 models

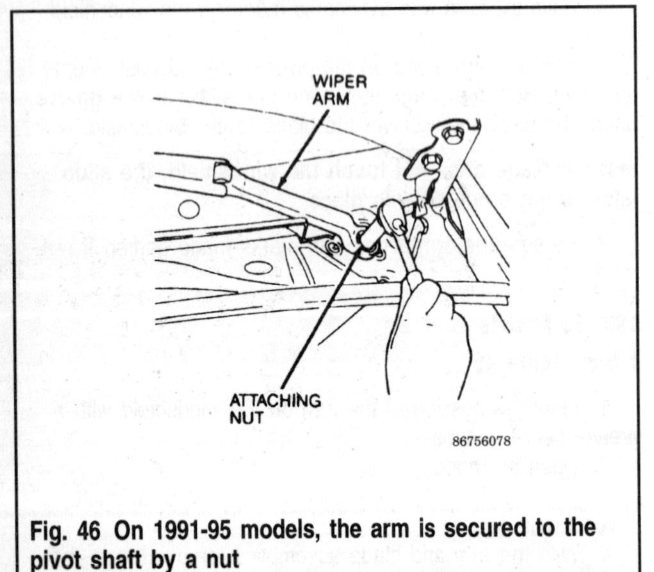

Fig. 46 On 1991-95 models, the arm is secured to the pivot shaft by a nut

wiper switch. This will place the pivot shafts in the park position.

5. Align the arm with the marks made on the windshield earlier.
6. Hold the arm head on the pivot shaft and push it onto the shaft. Install the nut to the pivot shaft. Tighten until snug.
7. Be sure the arm aligns with marks made earlier. If not, readjust.

Windshield Wiper Motor

REMOVAL & INSTALLATION

1981-90 Models

FRONT

See Figures 47, 48, 49 and 50

1. Disconnect the negative battery cable.

2. Unclip and lift the water shield cover from the cowl on the passenger's side.
3. Disconnect the power lead from the motor.
4. Remove the linkage retaining clip from the operating arm on the motor by lifting locking tab up and pulling clip away from pin.
5. Remove the attaching bolts from the motor and bracket assembly and remove.

To install:

6. Position the motor on the mounting bracket and install the retaining bolts.
7. Install the operating arm to the motor. Install the linkage retaining clip to the operating arm.
8. Engage the electrical lead to the motor.
9. Install the water shield cover to the cowl.
10. Connect the negative battery cable.

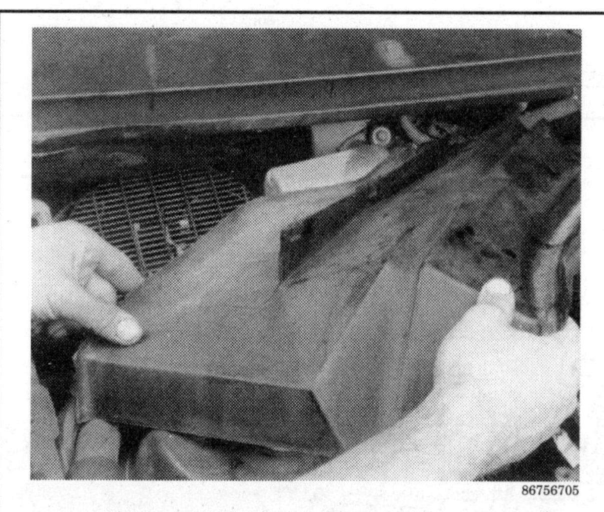
86756705

Fig. 47 Remove the water shield cover to access the wiper motor

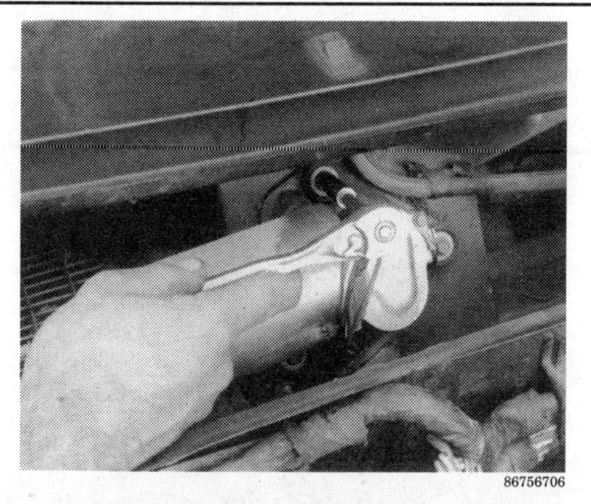
86756706

Fig. 48 After the linkage is disengaged and the motor is unplugged, remove the bolts that retain the wiper motor

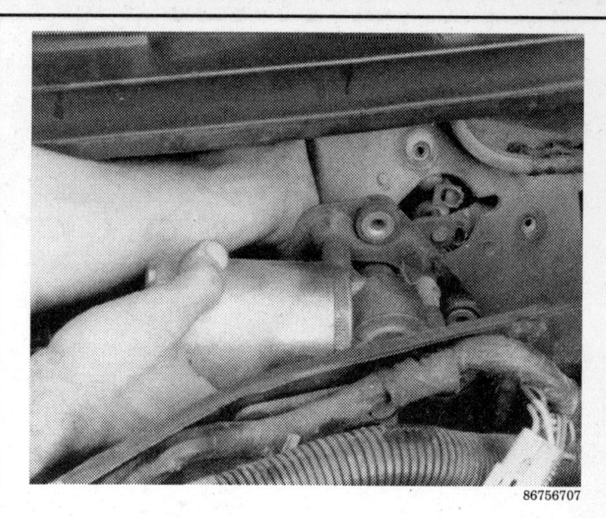
86756707

Fig. 49 Remove the motor while guiding the crank arm through the hole

REAR

➧ See Figure 51

1. Disconnect the negative battery cable.
2. Remove wiper arm.
3. Remove pivot shaft attaching nut and spacers.
4. On hatchback vehicles, remove liftgate inner trim panel. On station wagons, remove the screws attaching the license plate housing. Disconnect license plate light wiring and remove housing.
5. Unplug the electrical connector to wiper motor.
6. On hatchback vehicles, remove the three screws retaining the bracket to the door inner skin and remove complete motor, bracket and linkage assembly. On the station wagon, remove the motor and bracket assembly retaining screws and remove the motor and bracket assembly.
7. Installation is the reverse of the removal procedure.

1991-95 Models

FRONT

➧ See Figure 52

1. Disconnect the negative battery cable.
2. Remove the windshield wiper arms.
3. With the hood closed, remove the seven screw covers.
4. Remove the seven cowl grille retaining screws and remove the cowl grille.
5. Pry up the four baffle retaining clips and remove the baffle trim piece.

➡Make sure the motor is in the park position before disconnecting the linkage.

6. Remove the wiper linkage retaining clip and disconnect the wiper linkage from the motor.
7. Unplug the electrical connectors.
8. Remove the three motor mounting bolts until they are loose from the sheet metal mounting surface. Remove the motor.
9. Installation is the reverse of the removal procedure. Tighten the three motor mounting bolts to 61-87 inch lbs. (7-9 Nm).

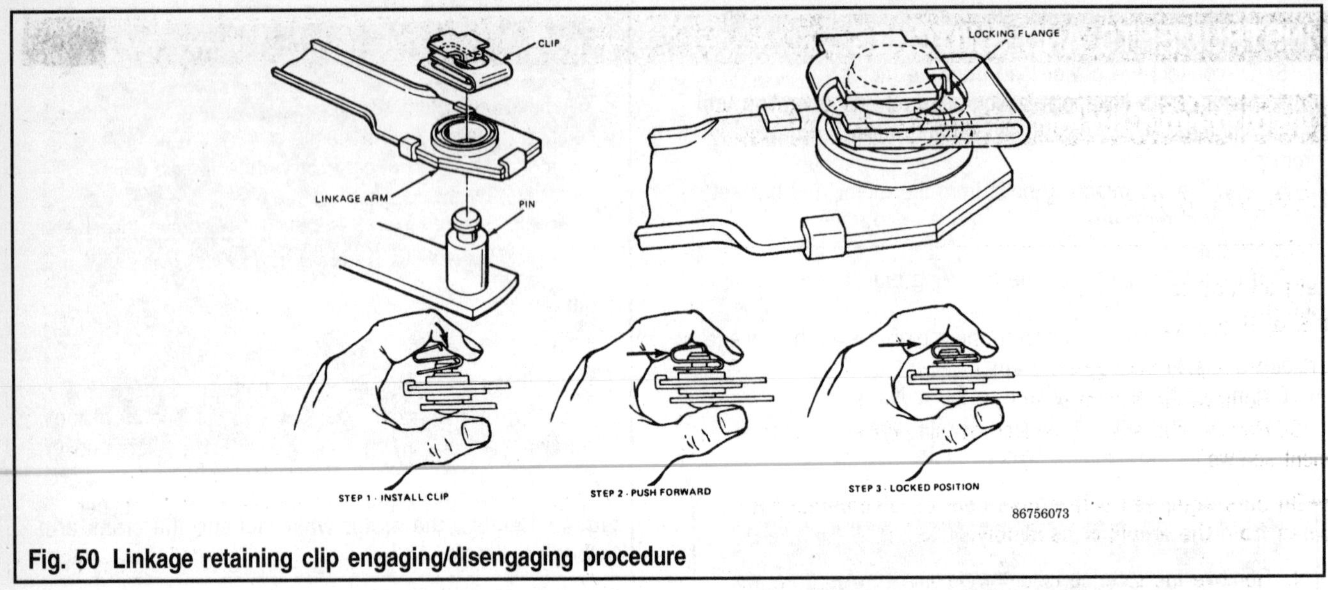

Fig. 50 Linkage retaining clip engaging/disengaging procedure

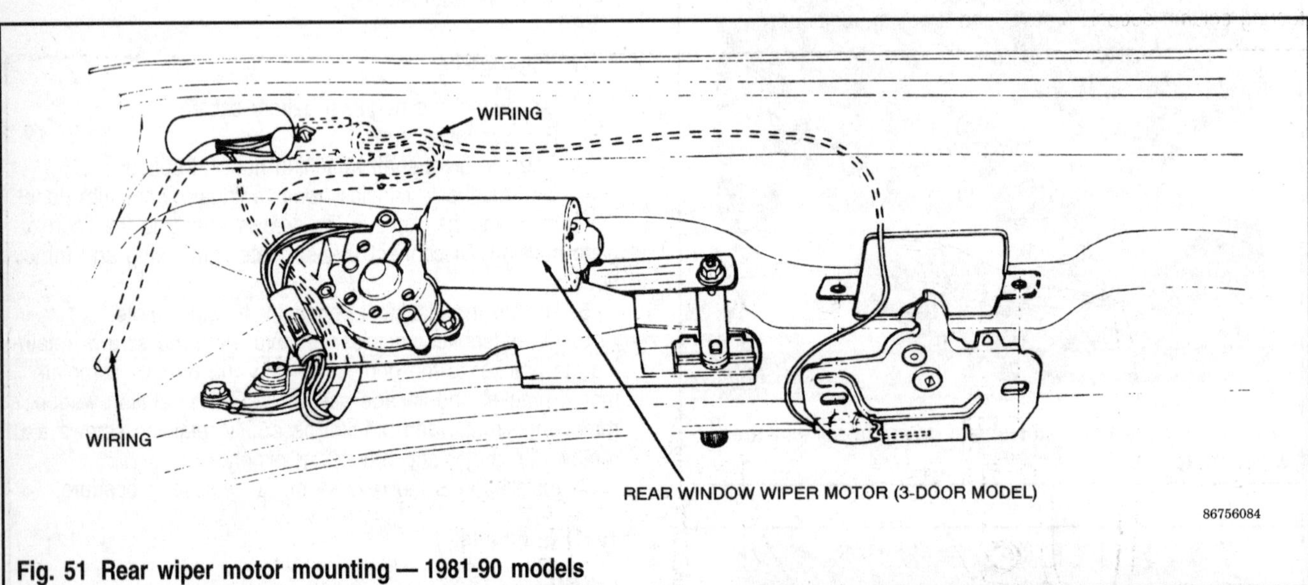

Fig. 51 Rear wiper motor mounting — 1981-90 models

REAR

1. Disconnect the negative battery cable.
2. Remove the wiper arm.
3. Remove the shaft seal from the outer bushing attaching nut.
4. Remove the outer bushing attaching nut and remove the outer bushing.
5. Remove the liftgate trim panel.
6. Unplug the wiper motor electrical connector.
7. Remove the three wiper motor mounting bolts and washers and remove the wiper motor.
8. Installation is the reverse of the removal procedure. Tighten the mounting bolts to 61-87 inch lbs. (7-9 Nm) and the outer bushing attaching nut to 35-52 inch lbs. (4-6 Nm).

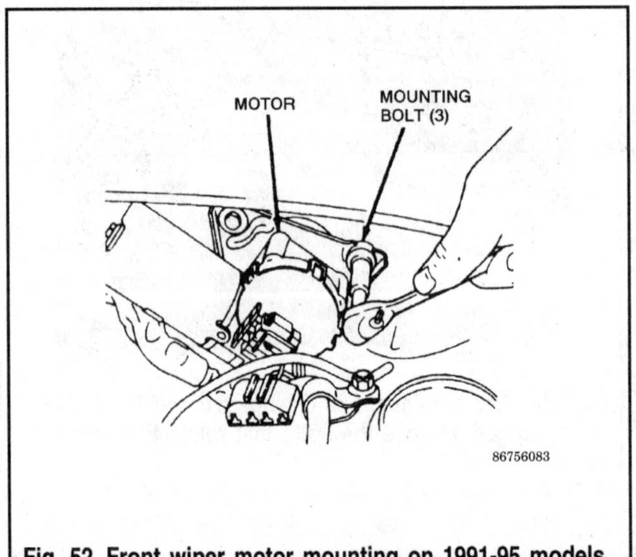

Fig. 52 Front wiper motor mounting on 1991-95 models

INSTRUMENTS AND SWITCHES

Instrument Cluster

REMOVAL & INSTALLATION

1981-85 Models

See Figure 53

1. Disconnect the negative battery terminal.
2. Remove the bottom steering column cover.
3. Remove the steering column opening cover reinforcement screws.

On cars equipped with cruise control, disconnect the wires from the amplifier assembly.

4. Remove the steering column retaining screws from the steering column support bracket and lower the column.
5. Remove the column trim shrouds.
6. Unplug all electrical connections from the column.
7. Remove the finish panel screws and the panel.
8. Remove the speedometer cable.
9. Remove the four cluster screws and remove the cluster.
10. Installation is the reverse of the removal procedure.

1986-90 Models

See Figure 54

1. Disconnect the negative battery cable.
2. Remove the two retaining screws at the bottom of the steering column opening and snap the steering column cover out.
3. Remove the 10 cluster opening finish panel retainer screws and remove the finish panel.
4. Remove the two upper and lower screws retaining the cluster to the instrument panel.

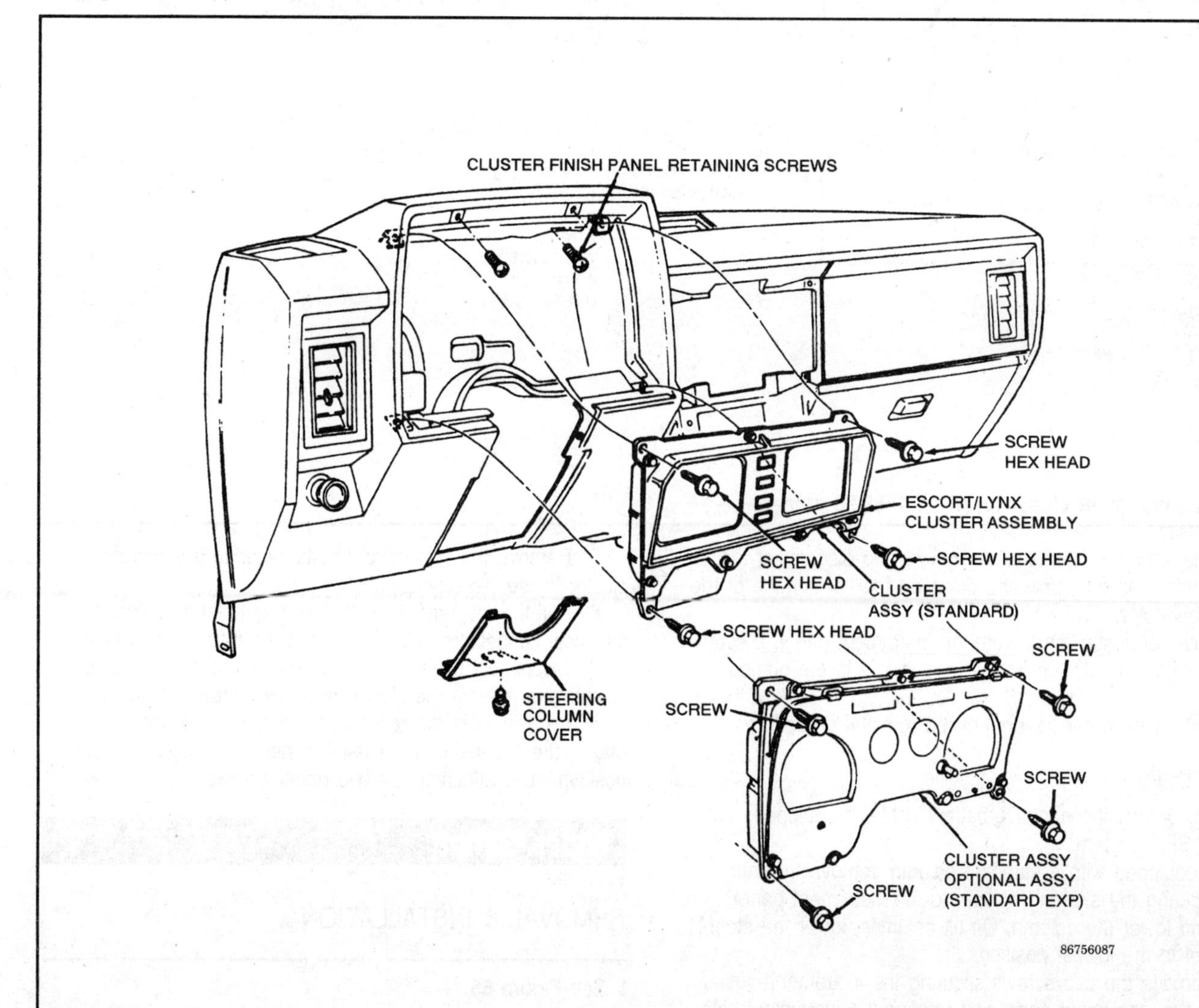

Fig. 53 Instrument cluster used on 1981-85 models

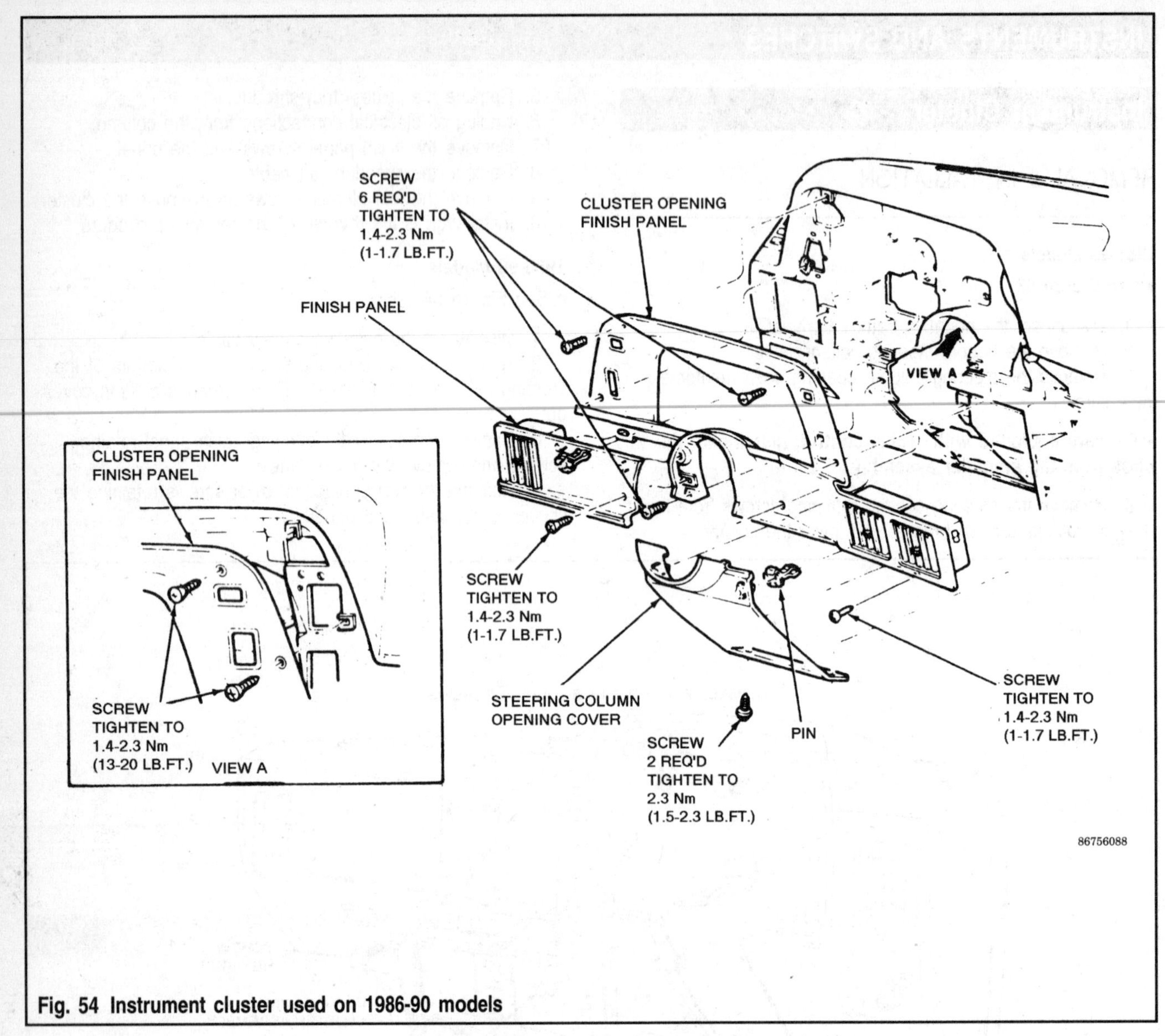

Fig. 54 Instrument cluster used on 1986-90 models

5. Reach under the instrument panel and disconnect the speedometer cable by pressing down on the flat surface of the plastic connector.
6. Pull the cluster away from the instrument panel. Disconnect the cluster feed plug from its receptacle in the printed circuit.
7. Installation is the reverse of the removal procedure.

1991-95 Models

1. Disconnect the negative battery cable. If equipped, disable the SRS system.
2. If equipped with a standard column, remove the four bolts securing the steering column to the instrument panel frame and lower the column. On tilt columns, lower the steering wheel to the lowest position.
3. Remove the cap screws securing the instrument cluster bezel to the instrument panel and remove the instrument cluster bezel.
4. Disconnect the speedometer cable at the transaxle by pulling the cable out of the vehicle speed sensor.
5. Remove the screws and bolts securing the instrument cluster to the instrument panel.
6. Pull the instrument cluster out slightly and unplug the electrical connectors from the rear of the instrument cluster.
7. Disconnect the speedometer cable from the instrument cluster and remove the cluster from the instrument panel.
8. Installation is the reverse of the removal procedure. Make sure the instrument cluster is held in its forward most position while attaching the two upper screws.

Wiper Switch

REMOVAL & INSTALLATION

➧ **See Figure 55**

This procedure applies to 1981-90 models. On later models, the wiper switch is part of the combination switch assembly.

1. Disconnect the negative battery cable.

2. Loosen the steering column attaching nuts enough to remove the upper trim shroud.
3. Remove the trim shrouds.
4. Unplug the electrical connector.
5. Peel back the foam sight shield. Remove the two hex head screws holding the switch and remove the wash/wipe switch.

To install:

6. Position the switch on the column and install the two hex head screws. Reposition the foam sight shield over the switch.
7. Engage the electrical connector.
8. Install the upper and lower trim shrouds.
9. Tighten the steering column attaching nuts.
10. Connect the negative battery cable to the battery terminal.
11. Check the switch for proper operation.

Rear Wiper Switch

REMOVAL & INSTALLATION

1. Remove the cluster finish panel.
2. Unplug the wiring connector from the rear washer switch.
3. Remove the washer switch from the instrument panel.

To install:

4. Install the cluster opening finish panel.
5. Engage the wiring connector.
6. Push the rear washer switch into the cluster finish panel until it snaps into place.

Headlight Switch

REMOVAL & INSTALLATION

See Figure 56

This procedure applies to 1981-90 models. On later models, the headlight switch is part of the combination switch assembly.

1. Disconnect the negative battery cable.
2. On vehicles without air conditioning, remove the left side air vent control cable retaining screws and let the cable hang.
3. Remove the fuse panel bracket retaining screws. Move the fuse panel assembly aside to gain access to the headlight switch.
4. Pull the headlight knob out to the ON position. Depress the headlight knob and shaft retainer button and remove the knob and shaft assembly from the switch.
5. Remove the headlight switch retaining bezel. Unplug the multiple connector plug and remove the switch from the instrument panel.

To install:

6. Install the headlight switch into the instrument panel. Connect the multiple connector and install the headlight switch retaining bezel.
7. Install the knob and shaft assembly by inserting the shaft into the switch and gently pushing until the shaft locks in position.
8. Move the fuse panel back into position and install the fuse panel bracket with the two retaining screws.
9. On vehicles without air conditioning, install the left side air vent control cable and bracket.
10. Connect the negative battery cable.

Combination Switch

On 1991-95 Models, the combination switch assembly is a multi-function switch that controls the headlights, parking lights

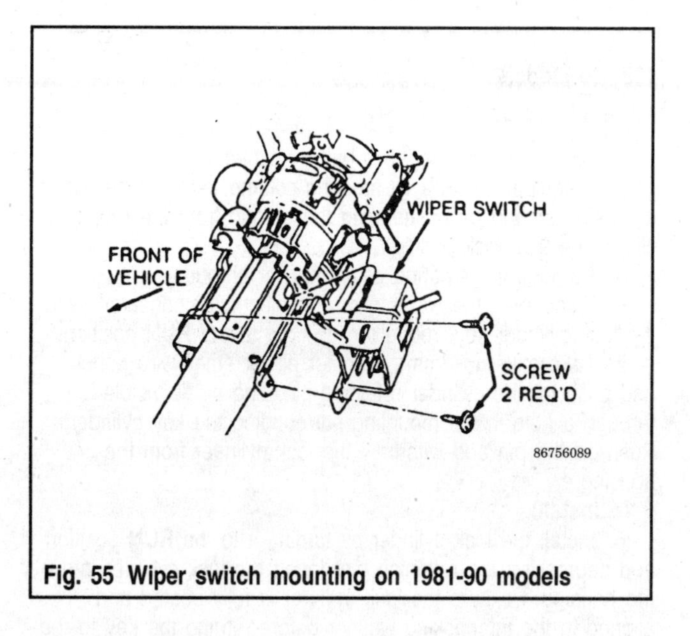

Fig. 55 Wiper switch mounting on 1981-90 models

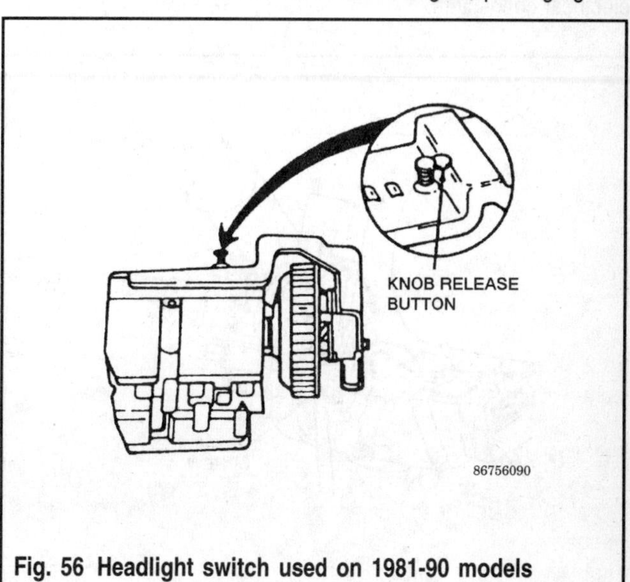

Fig. 56 Headlight switch used on 1981-90 models

and tail lights, the turn signals, headlight dimmer and window wipers.

REMOVAL & INSTALLATION

1991-95 Models

➧ See Figure 57

1. Disconnect the negative battery cable. For 1994-95 models, disarm the SRS.
2. Remove the steering wheel cover retaining screws from the back side of the steering wheel and remove the cover.
3. Unplug the horn electrical connector and the cruise control electrical connectors, if equipped.
4. Remove the steering wheel using a suitable puller.
5. Remove the four retaining screws from the steering column lower cover and remove the cover. Remove the upper cover.
6. Disconnect the three multi-function switch electrical connectors.
7. Remove the multi-function switch retaining screw, pull the electrical connectors from the retaining brackets and remove the switch.
8. Installation is the reverse of the removal procedure.

Clock

REMOVAL & INSTALLATION

1981-83 Vehicles

1. Disconnect the negative battery cable.
2. Remove the two center radio speaker grill retaining screws and remove the grille.
3. Remove the three retaining screws attaching the clock to the instrument panel.
4. Remove the clock from the opening and disconnect the electrical connectors.

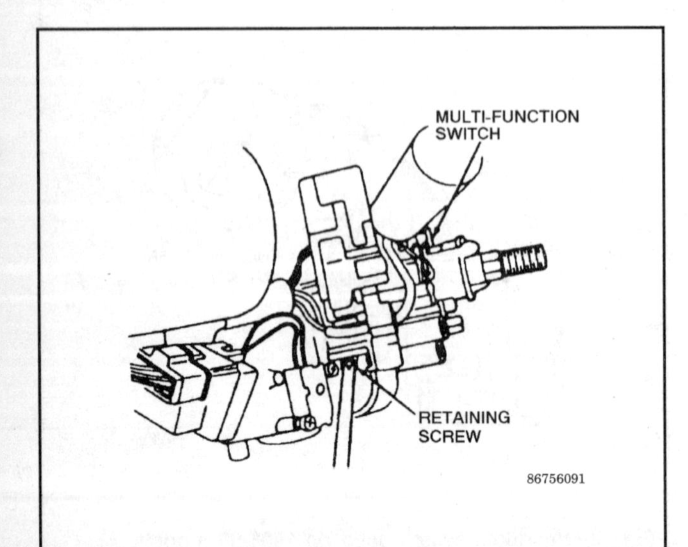

Fig. 57 Combination switch mounting — 1991-95 models

5. Installation is the reverse order of the removal procedure.

1984-85 Vehicles

1. Disconnect the negative battery cable.
2. Remove the eight cluster opening finish panel screws. Remove the finish panel by rocking upper edge toward the driver.
3. Remove the three retaining screws attaching the clock to the instrument panel.
4. Remove the clock from the opening and disconnect the electrical connections.
5. Installation is the reverse order of the removal procedure.

1986-95 Vehicles

1. Disconnect the negative battery cable.
2. Remove the roof console lenses by inserting a suitable tool in one of the notches on the side of the lenses.
3. Remove the two screws one on the inside of each lens opening.
4. Remove the front screw while supporting the console.
5. Remove the console from roof. Slide the connector shield off of the electrical connector.

➡The shield is moulded to fit securely over the connector. It may be necessary to lift a portion of the shield over the connector ribs before the shield will slide freely.

6. Disconnect the electrical halves. Remove the four retaining screws attaching the clock to the console panel.
7. Remove the locators and remove the clock from the opening.
8. Installation is the reverse order of the removal procedure.

Ignition Lock Cylinder

REMOVAL & INSTALLATION

1981-90 Models

➧ See Figure 58

1. Disconnect the negative battery cable.
2. If equipped with a tilt steering column, remove the upper extension shroud by unsnapping the shroud from the retaining clip at the 9 o'clock position.
3. Remove the steering column lower shroud.
4. Disconnect the warning buzzer electrical connector. With the lock cylinder key, rotate the cylinder to the **RUN** position.
5. Take a 1/8 in. (3mm) diameter pin or small wire punch and push on the cylinder retaining pin. The pin is visible through a hole in the mounting surrounding the key cylinder. Push on the pin and withdraw the lock cylinder from the housing.

To Install:

6. Install the lock cylinder by turning it to the **RUN** position and depressing the retaining pin. Insert the lock cylinder into the housing. Be sure the lock cylinder is fully seated and aligned in the interlocking washer before turning the key to the

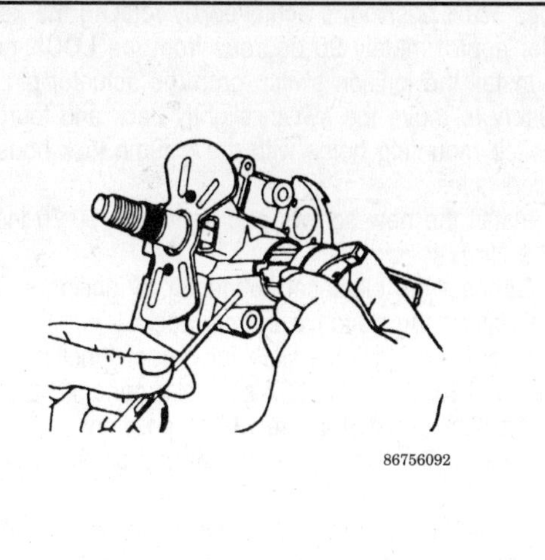

Fig. 58 Remove the lock cylinder as shown — 1981-90 models

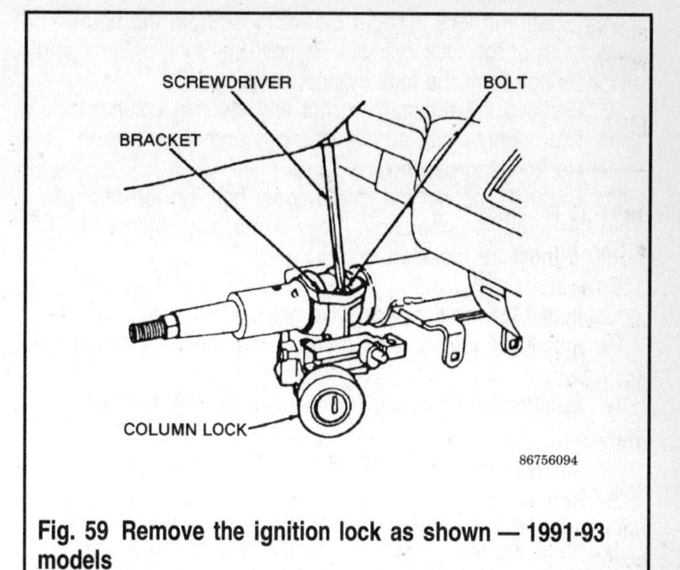

Fig. 59 Remove the ignition lock as shown — 1991-93 models

OFF position. This action will permit the cylinder retaining pin to extend into the cylinder housing hole.

7. Rotate the lock cylinder, using the lock cylinder key, to ensure correct mechanical operation in all positions.
8. Install the electrical connector for the key warning buzzer.
9. Install the lower steering column shroud or trim shroud halves.
10. Connect the negative battery cable.
11. Check for proper start in P or N. Also, make certain the start circuit cannot be actuated in the D and R positions and that the column is locked in the **LOCK** position.

1991-93 Models

➧ See Figure 59

1. Disconnect the negative battery cable.
2. Remove the steering wheel cover retaining screws from the back side of the steering wheel and remove the cover.
3. Disconnect the horn electrical connector and the cruise control electrical connectors, if equipped.
4. Remove the steering wheel using a suitable puller.
5. Remove the combination switch.
6. Disconnect the ignition switch electrical connector.
7. Remove the shift-lock cable mounting bracket bolt and position the bracket and cable aside.
8. Remove the four steering column upper mounting bracket bolts and lower the column.
9. Using a suitable hammer and chisel, make a groove in the head of each of the two column lock mounting bracket bolts.
10. Remove the bolts with a suitable screwdriver and discard the bolts.
11. Remove the steering column lock and mounting bracket.

To install:

12. Position the steering column lock and mounting bracket and install two new bolts, tightening them only enough to hold the column lock in position.
13. With the key in the ignition, verify the operation of the column lock. If necessary, reposition the column lock until it operates properly.
14. Tighten the mounting bracket bolts until the bolt heads break off.
15. Position the steering column and install the four upper mounting bracket bolts. Tighten the bolts to 80-123 inch lbs. (9-14 Nm).
16. If equipped with a tilt steering wheel, remove the upper mounting bracket retaining pin.
17. Position the shift-lock cable mounting bracket and install the bolt. Tighten to 37-55 inch lbs. (4-6 Nm).
18. Connect the ignition switch electrical connector.
19. Install the combination switch.
20. Install the steering wheel
21. Connect the horn electrical connector and the cruise control electrical connectors, if equipped.
22. Position the steering wheel cover and install the retaining screws.
23. Connect the negative battery cable.

1994-95 Models

1. Disconnect the negative battery cable. Disable the SRS system, if equipped.
2. Remove the steering wheel.
3. Remove the upper and lower shrouds.
4. If applicable, disconnect the air bag clockspring connector from the column harness.

➡Before removing the air bag clockspring from the steering shaft, secure the clockspring with tape to prevent the clockspring rotor from being turned accidentally and damaging the clockspring.

5. If applicable, remove the two screws that secure the clockspring to the retainer plate and remove the clockspring.
6. Remove the electrical connector from the key warning switch.
7. Using a 1/8 in. (3mm) diameter drill bit, drill out the retaining pin. Be careful not to drill deeper than 1/2 in. (13mm).
8. Place a chisel at the base of the ignition lock cylinder cap and, using a hammer, strike the chisel with sharp blows to break the cap away from the lock cylinder.
9. Using a 3/8 in. (10mm) diameter drill bit, drill down the middle of the ignition lock key slot approximately 1 3/4 in.

(44mm) until the lock cylinder breaks loose from the break-away base of the lock cylinder. Remove the lock cylinder and drill shavings from the lock cylinder housing.

10. Remove the retainer, washer and steering column lock gear. Thoroughly clean all drill shavings and other foreign materials from the casting.

11. Carefully inspect the lock cylinder housing for damage from the foregoing operation. If any damage is evident, the housing must be replaced.

To install:

12. Install the ignition lock drive gear, washer and retainer.

13. Install the ignition lock cylinder and check for smooth operation.

14. Engage the electrical connector to the key warning switch.

15. If equipped with an air bag, install the clockspring as follows:

a. Place the clockspring onto the steering shaft. Install the two retaining screws that secure the clockspring to the retainer plate. Make sure the ground wire is secured with the lower retaining screw. Remove the tape that was installed during the removal procedure.

b. Connect the clockspring wire to the column harness.

16. Install the steering wheel on the steering column.

17. Connect the negative battery cable and enable the SRS system (if equipped).

Ignition Switch

REMOVAL & INSTALLATION

1981-90 Models

1. Disconnect the negative battery cable.

2. Remove the steering column upper and lower trim shrouds by removing the self-tapping screws. The steering column attaching nuts may have to be loosened enough to allow removal of the upper shroud.

3. Remove the two bolts and nuts holding the steering column assembly to the steering column bracket assembly and lower the steering column to the seat.

4. Remove the steering column shrouds.

5. Disconnect the electrical connector from the ignition switch.

6. Rotate ignition lock cylinder to the **RUN** position.

7. Remove the screws attaching the switch to the lock cylinder housing.

8. Disengage the ignition switch from the actuator pin.

To install:

9. Check to see that the actuator pin slot in the ignition switch is in the **RUN** position.

➡A new switch assembly will be pre-set in the RUN position.

10. Make certain the ignition key lock cylinder is in approximately the **RUN** position to properly locate the lock actuator pin. The **RUN** position is achieved by rotating the key lock cylinder approximately 90 degrees from the **LOCK** position.

11. Install the ignition switch onto the actuator pin. It may be necessary to move the switch slightly back and fourth to align the switch mounting holes with the column lock housing threaded holes.

12. Install the new screws and tighten to 50-70 inch lbs. (5.6-7.9 Nm).

13. Connect the electrical connector to ignition switch.

14. Connect the negative battery cable.

15. Check the ignition switch for proper function including **START** and **ACC** positions. Also make certain the steering column is locked when in the **LOCK** position.

16. Position the top half of the shroud on the steering column.

17. Install the two bolts and nuts attaching the steering column assembly to the steering column bracket assembly. Tighten to 15-25 ft. lbs. (20-34 Nm).

18. Position lower shroud to upper shroud and install five self-tapping screws.

1991-95 Models

1. Disconnect the negative battery cable and disable the SRS system (if equipped).

2. Remove the combination switch.

3. Disconnect the ignition switch electrical connector.

4. Remove the three ignition switch mounting screws and remove the ignition switch.

5. Installation is the reverse of the removal procedure. Check the switch for proper operation.

Speedometer Cable

REMOVAL & INSTALLATION

1. Remove the instrument cluster.

2. Pull the speedometer cable from the casing. If the cable is broken, disconnect the casing from the transaxle and remove the broken piece from the transaxle end.

3. Lubricate the new cable with graphite lubricant. Feed the cable into the casing from the instrument panel end.

4. Attach the cable to the speedometer. Install the cluster.

Speedometer, Tachometer and Gauges

REMOVAL & INSTALLATION

Once the instrument cluster has been removed, the speedometer, tachometer and gauges can usually be replaced using the same basic procedure. In most cases, removal of the gauges involves disassembling the printed circuit board and front lens from the cluster. The gauges are normally secured by a series of small screws or bolts. Be careful not to damage the indicator needles and gauge faces when disassembling.

Printed Circuit Board

REMOVAL & INSTALLATION

The printed circuit board is attached to the back of the instrument cluster. It is usually secured by a series of screws/nuts and by the bulb sockets. These sockets are normally removed by first twisting, then pulling them from the cluster. Do not force any components as they are easily damaged.

LIGHTING

Headlights

REMOVAL & INSTALLATION

Sealed Beam Type

➧ See Figure 60

1. Remove the headlamp bezel by removing the retaining screws. After the screws are removed, pull the bezel slightly forward. Certain models have upper locking tabs which disengage by lifting out on the lower edge and pulling downward. Disconnect the parking light and remove the headlight bezel.
2. Remove the lamp retaining ring screws. Pull the headlamp out slightly and unplug the connector.
3. Installation is in the reverse order of removal. Turn the headlights on and check for proper operation.

Aerodynamic Type

➧ See Figures 61 and 62

➡The replaceable halogen headlamp bulb contains gas under pressure. The bulb may shatter if the glass envelope is scratched or the bulb is dropped. Handle the bulb carefully. Grasp the bulb ONLY by its plastic base. Do not touch the glass as deposits left by your fingers will cause hot spots when the bulb is illumined which may cause it to prematurely fail. Keep the bulb out of the reach of children.

1. Check to see that the headlight switch is in the OFF position.
2. Raise the hood and locate the bulb installed in the rear of the headlight body.
3. Remove the electrical connector by depressing the locktab and pulling the connector rearward.
4. Remove the bulb retaining ring by rotating it counterclockwise (when viewed from the rear) about 1/8 of a turn, then slide the ring off the plastic base.

➡Keep the bulb retaining ring, it will be reused with the new bulb.

5. Carefully remove the headlight bulb from its socket in the reflector by gently pulling it straight backward out of the socket.

To install:

6. With the flat side of the plastic base of the bulb facing upward, insert the glass envelope of the bulb into the socket. Turn the base slightly to the left or right, if necessary, to align the grooves in the forward part of the plastic base with the corresponding locating tabs inside the socket. When the grooves are aligned, push the bulb firmly into the socket until the mounting flange on the base contacts the rear face of the socket.
7. Slip the bulb retaining ring over the rear of the plastic base against the mounting flange. Lock the ring into the socket by rotating the ring counterclockwise. A stop will be felt when the retaining ring is fully engaged.

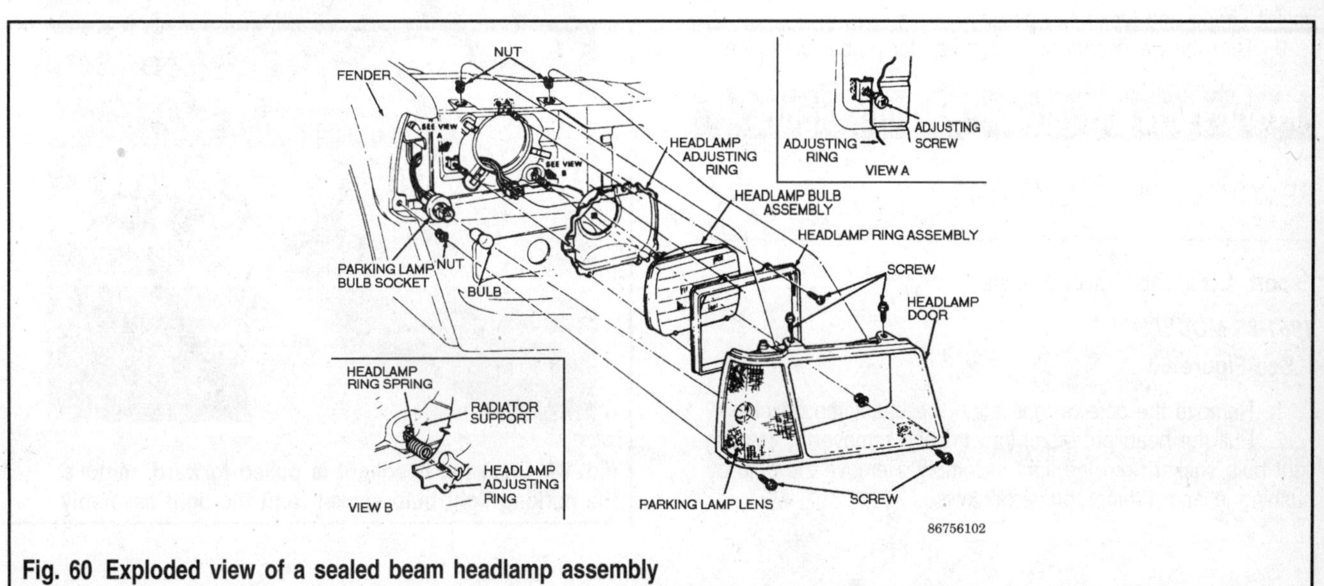

Fig. 60 Exploded view of a sealed beam headlamp assembly

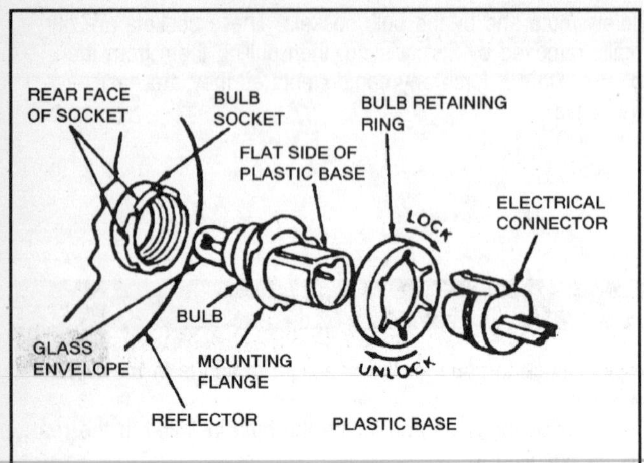

Fig. 61 The bulb is secured by a retaining ring

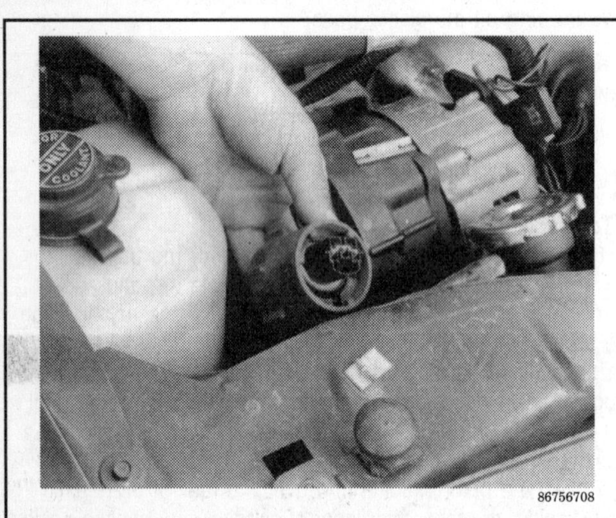

Fig. 62 Do not touch the glass portion of the bulb when removing or installing it

8. Push the electrical connector into the rear of the plastic until it snaps and locks into position.
9. Turn the headlights on and check for proper operation.

Front Turn Signal and Parking Lights

REMOVAL & INSTALLATION

Escort, Lynx and Tracer Models

1981-85 MODELS

See Figure 60

1. Remove the screws that retain the headlamp bezel.
2. Pull the headlight bezel forward and remove the parking light bulb socket from the light assembly. Remove the bulb by pushing in and turning counterclockwise.
3. To install, reverse the procedure.

1986-95 MODELS

See Figures 63 and 64

1. Remove the three screws attaching the parking light to the headlight housing.
2. Pull the parking light forward.
3. From the side, remove the bulb socket and replace the bulb.
4. To install, reverse the removal procedure.

EXP and LN7 Models

See Figure 65

1. Remove the two parking light retaining screws and pull the light assembly forward.
2. Remove the bulb socket by twisting and remove the bulb.
3. To install, reverse the removal procedure.

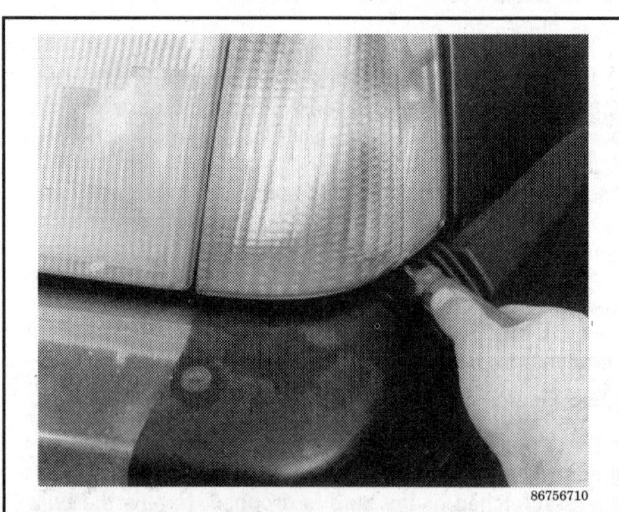

Fig. 63 Remove the screws that retain the parking light to the headlight housing

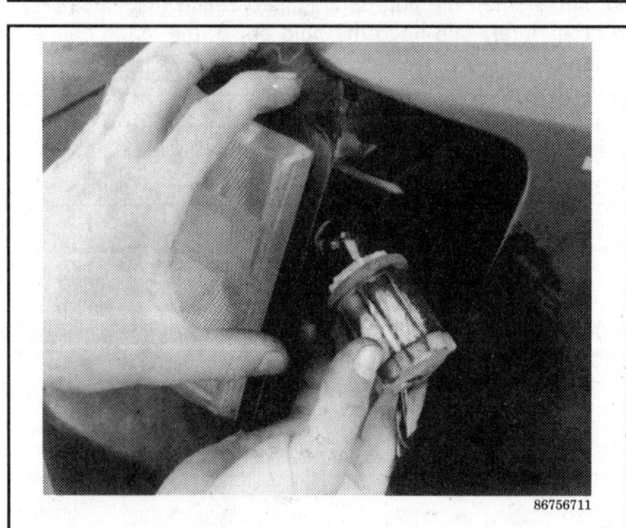

Fig. 64 Once the headlight is pulled forward, remove the parking light bulb socket from the light assembly

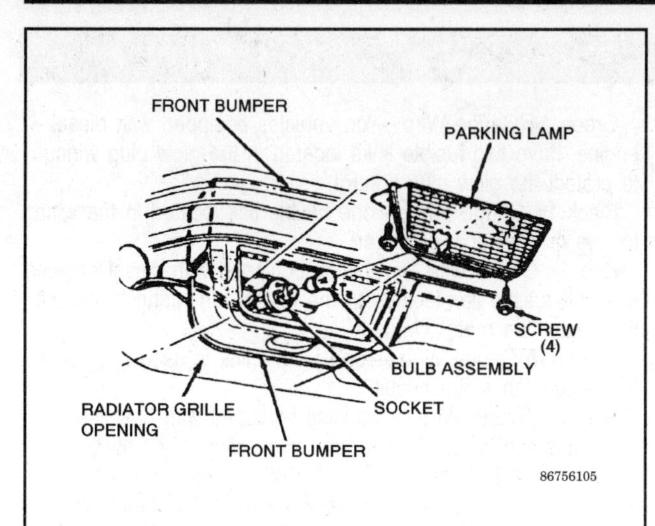

Fig. 65 Exploded view of the front turn signal and parking light mounting — EXP/LN7

Rear Turn Signal, Brake and Parking Lights

REMOVAL & INSTALLATION

Except Wagons

1. Remove the luggage compartment rear trim panel.
2. Remove the socket(s) from the lamp body and replace the bulb(s).
3. Installation is the reverse of removal.

Wagons

1. Remove the screws retaining the light assembly to the rear quarter opening.
2. Pull the light assembly out of the opening and remove the light socket to replace the bulb.
3. To install, reverse the procedure.

High Mount Stop Lamp

REMOVAL & INSTALLATION

1. Remove the two screws from the lens face.
2. Remove the socket and replace the bulb.
3. Installation is the reverse order of the removal procedure.

TRAILER WIRING

Wiring the car for towing is fairly easy. There are a number of good wiring kits available and these should be used, rather than trying to design your own. All trailers will need brake lights and turn signals as well as tail lights and side marker lights. Most states require extra marker lights for overly wide trailers. Also, most states have recently required back-up lights for trailers, and most trailer manufacturers have been building trailers with back-up lights for several years.

Additionally, some Class I, most Class II and just about all Class III trailers will have electric brakes.

Add to this number an accessories wire, to operate trailer internal equipment or to charge the trailer's battery, and you can have as many as seven wires in the harness.

Determine the equipment on your trailer and buy the wiring kit necessary. The kit will contain all the wires needed, plus a plug adapter set which included the female plug, mounted on the bumper or hitch, and the male plug, wired into, or plugged into the trailer harness.

When installing the kit, follow the manufacturer's instructions. The color coding of the wires is standard throughout the industry.

One point to note: some domestic vehicles, and most imported vehicles, have separate turn signals. On most domestic vehicles, the brake lights and rear turn signals operate with the same bulb. For those vehicles with separate turn signals, you can purchase an isolation unit so that the brake lights won't blink whenever the turn signals are operated, or, you can go to your local electronics supply house and buy four diodes to wire in series with the brake and turn signal bulbs. Diodes will isolate the brake and turn signals. The choice is yours. The isolation units are simple and quick to install, but far more expensive than the diodes. The diodes, however, require more work to install properly, since they require the cutting of each bulb's wire and soldering in place of the diode.

One final point, the best kits are those with a spring loaded cover on the vehicle mounted socket. This cover prevents dirt and moisture from corroding the terminals. Never let the vehicle socket hang loosely; always mount it securely to the bumper or hitch.

CIRCUIT PROTECTION

Circuit Breakers

Circuit breakers operate when an electrical circuit overloads, or exceeds its rated amperage. Once activated, they may be reset.

There are two kinds of circuit breakers. One type will automatically reset itself after a given length of time, the second will not reset itself until the problem in the circuit has been repaired.

Circuit breakers are used to protect the various components of the electrical system, such as headlights and windshield wipers. The circuit breakers for the vehicles this manual covers are located either in the control swltch or mounted on or near the fuse panel.

Turn Signal and Hazard Flasher

The turn signal flasher is located on the front side of the fuse panel.

The hazard warning flasher is located on the rear side of the fuse panel.

Fuses and the Fuse Panel

Fuses are a one-time circuit protection. If a circuit is overloaded or shorts, the thin metal fuse acts like a weak (and expendable) link in a chain by burning. This cuts off electrical flow before the circuit is damaged. Fuses inserted to replace blown fuses will continue to blow unless the circuit is first repaired.

The fuse panel is located below and to the left of the steering column.

Fuse Link

The fuse link is a short length of special, Hypalon (high temperature) insulated wire, integral with the engine compartment wiring harness and should not be confused with standard wire. It is several wire gauges smaller than the circuit which it protects. Under no circumstances should a fuse link replacement repair be made using a length of standard wire cut from bulk stock or from another wiring harness.

Fusible links are used to prevent major wire harness damage in the event of a short circuit or an overload condition in the wiring circuits that are normally not fused, due to carrying high amperage loads or because of their locations within the wiring harness. Each fusible link is of a fixed value for a specific electrical load and should a fusible link fail, the cause of the failure must be determine and repaired prior to installing a new fusible link of the same value. The following is a listing of fusible links wire gauges and their locations:

➡The color coding of replacement fusible links may vary from the production color coding that is outlined in the text that follows.

Green 14 Gauge Wire — on vehicles equipped with diesel engine, have two fusible links located in the glow plug wiring to protect the glow plug control.

Black 16 Gauge Wire — one fusible link located in the wiring for the rear window defogger.

Red 18 Gauge wire — vehicles equipped with diesel engines use one fusible link located in the heater fan wiring to protect the heater fan motor circuit.

Brown 18 Gauge Wire — one fusible link is used to protect the heater fan motor circuit.

Blue 20 Gauge Wire — vehicles equipped with gasoline engines use two fusible links in the wire between the starter relay and the EFE heater. On 1988-95 vehicles, a fusible link is installed in the engine compartment near the starter relay and protects the passive restraint module circuit. Vehicles equipped with diesel engine, uses one fusible link to protect the vacuum pump circuit.

➡Always disconnect the negative battery cable before servicing the vehicle's electrical system.

FUSIBLE LINK REPAIR

1. Determine which circuit is damaged, its location and the cause of the open fuse link. If the damaged fuse link is one of three fed by a common No. 10 or 12 gauge feed wire, determine the specific affected circuit.
2. Disconnect the negative battery cable.
3. Cut the damaged fuse link from the wiring harness and discard it. If the fuse link is one of three circuits fed by a single feed wire, cut it out of the harness at each splice end and discard it.
4. To repair any fuse link in a 3-link group with one feed:
   a. After cutting the open link out of the harness, cut each of the remaining undamaged fuse links close to the feed wire weld.
   b. Strip approximately ½ in. (13mm) of insulation from the detached ends of the two good fuse links. Insert two wire ends into one end of a butt connector and carefully push one stripped end of the replacement fuse link into the same end of the butt connector and crimp all three firmly together.

➡Care must be taken when fitting the three fuse links into the butt connector as the internal diameter is a snug fit for three wires. Make sure to use a proper crimping tool. Pliers, side cutter, etc. will not apply the proper crimp to retain the wires and withstand a pull test.

   c. After crimping the butt connector to the three fuse links, cut the weld portion from the feed wire and strip approximately ½ in. (13mm) of insulation from the cut end. Insert the stripped end into the open end of the butt connector and crimp very firmly.
   d. To attach the remaining end of the replacement fuse link, strip approximately ½ in. (13mm) of insulation from the wire end of the circuit from which the blown fuse link was removed, and firmly crimp a butt connector or equivalent to the stripped wire. Then, insert the end of the replacement link into the other end of the butt connector and crimp firmly.

e. Using rosin core solder with a consistency of 60 percent tin and 40 percent lead, solder the connectors and the wires at the repairs and insulate with electrical tape.

5. To replace any fuse link on a single circuit in a harness, cut out the damaged portion, strip approximately ½ in. (13mm) of insulation from the two wire ends and attach the appropriate replacement fuse link to the stripped wire ends with two proper size butt connectors. Solder the connectors and wires and insulate with tape.

6. To repair any fuse link which has an eyelet terminal on one end such as the charging circuit, cut off the open fuse link behind the weld, strip approximately ½ in. (13mm) of insulation from the cut end. Attach the appropriate new eyelet fuse link to the cut stripped wire with an appropriate size butt connector. Solder the connectors and wires at the repair and insulate with tape.

7. Connect the negative battery cable to the battery and test the system for proper operation.

➡Do not mistake a resistor wire for a fuse link. The resistor wire is generally longer and has print stating, "Resistor-don't cut or splice".

When attaching a single No. 16, 17, 18 or 20 gauge fuse link to a heavy gauge wire, always double the stripped wire end of the fuse link before inserting and crimping it into the butt connector for positive wire retention.

WIRING DIAGRAMS

➡Unless specifically stated otherwise, each chart for a given model year covers ALL the vehicles of that year that are covered by this manual. Charts that cover a range of years or are for only a limited series of vehicles within a model year (for example, "EFI-equipped," or "diesel," etc.) will be noted accordingly. Make sure you consult the correct chart for the vehicle you are working on.

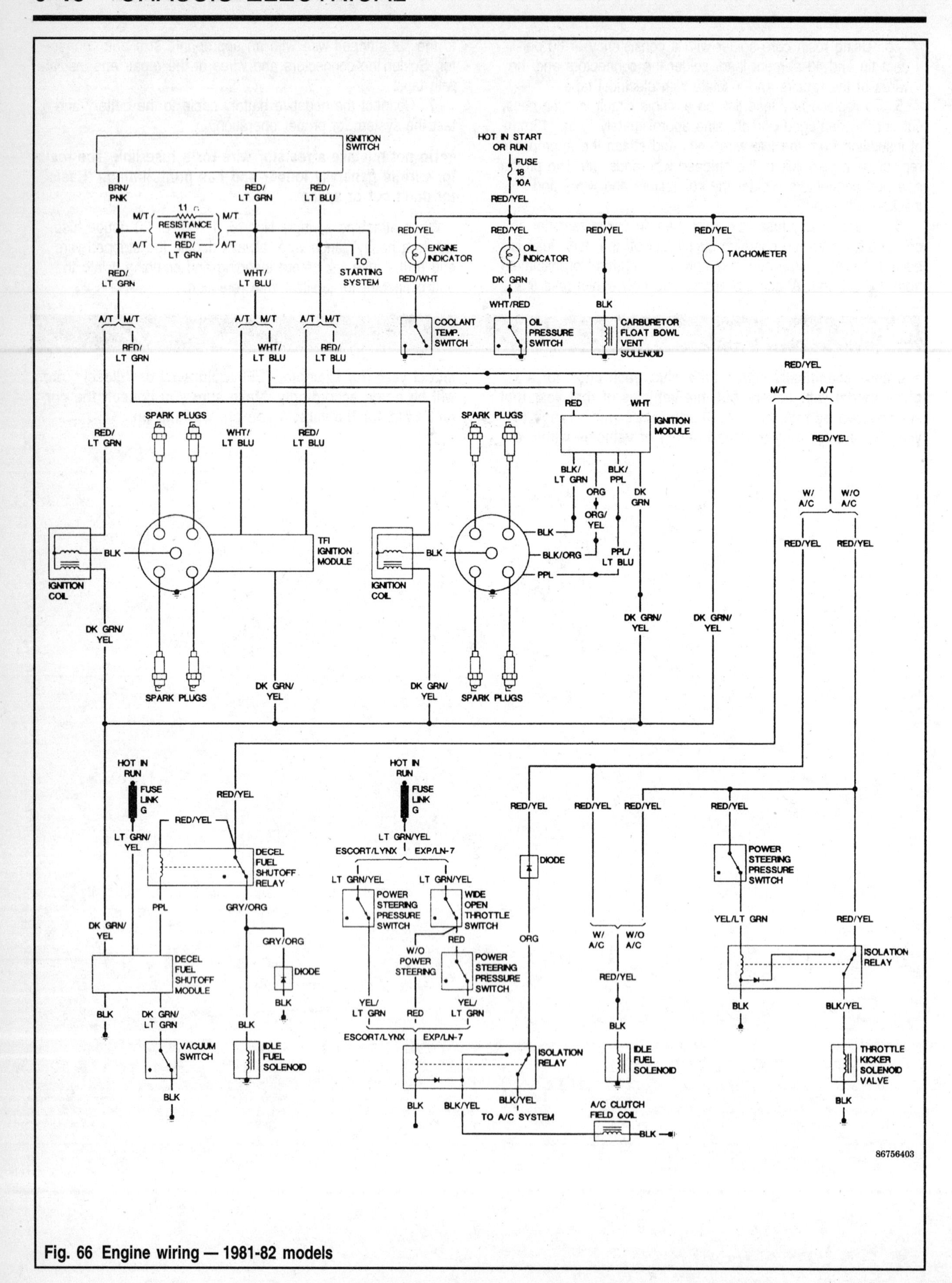

Fig. 66 Engine wiring — 1981-82 models

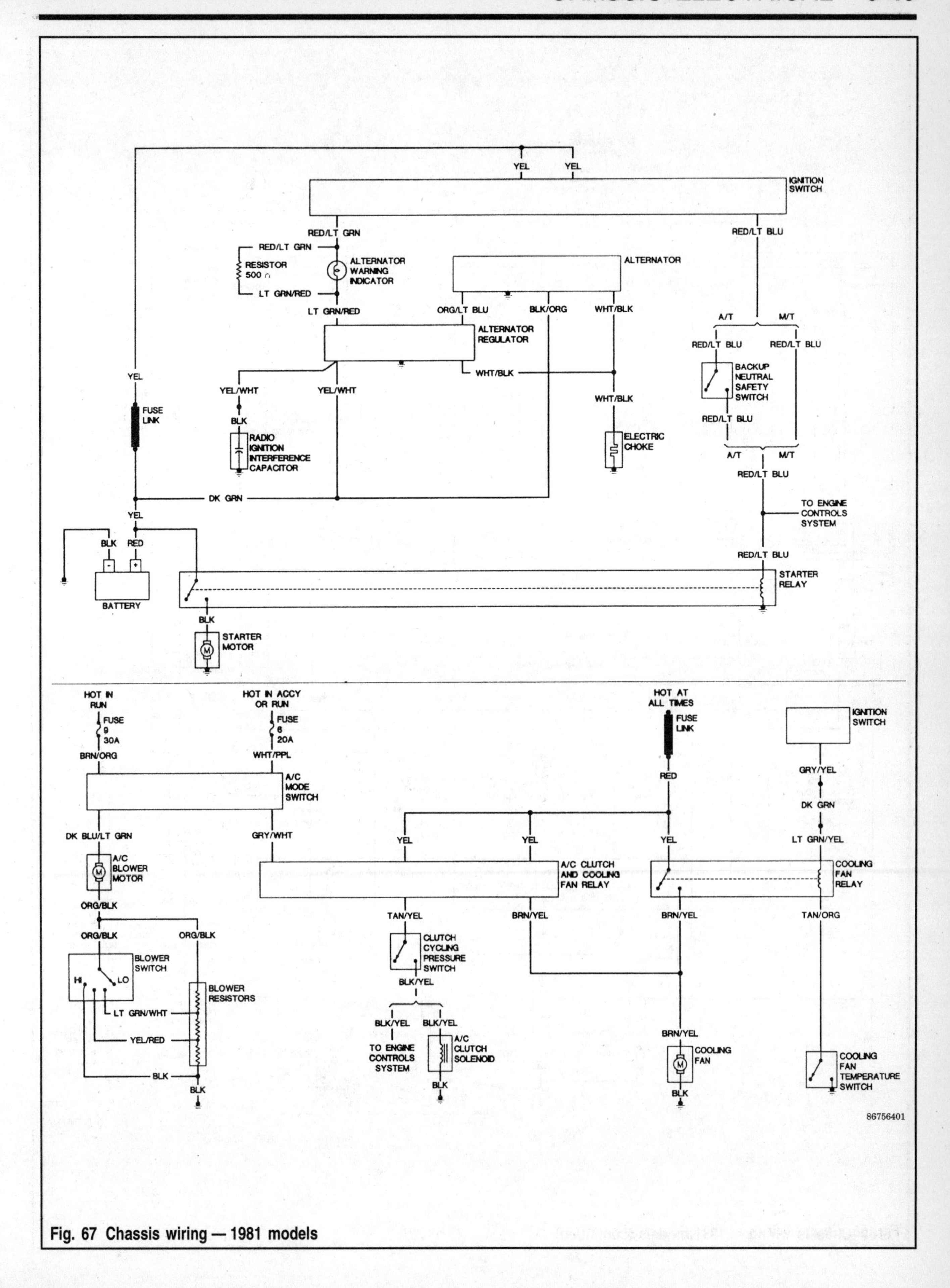

Fig. 67 Chassis wiring — 1981 models

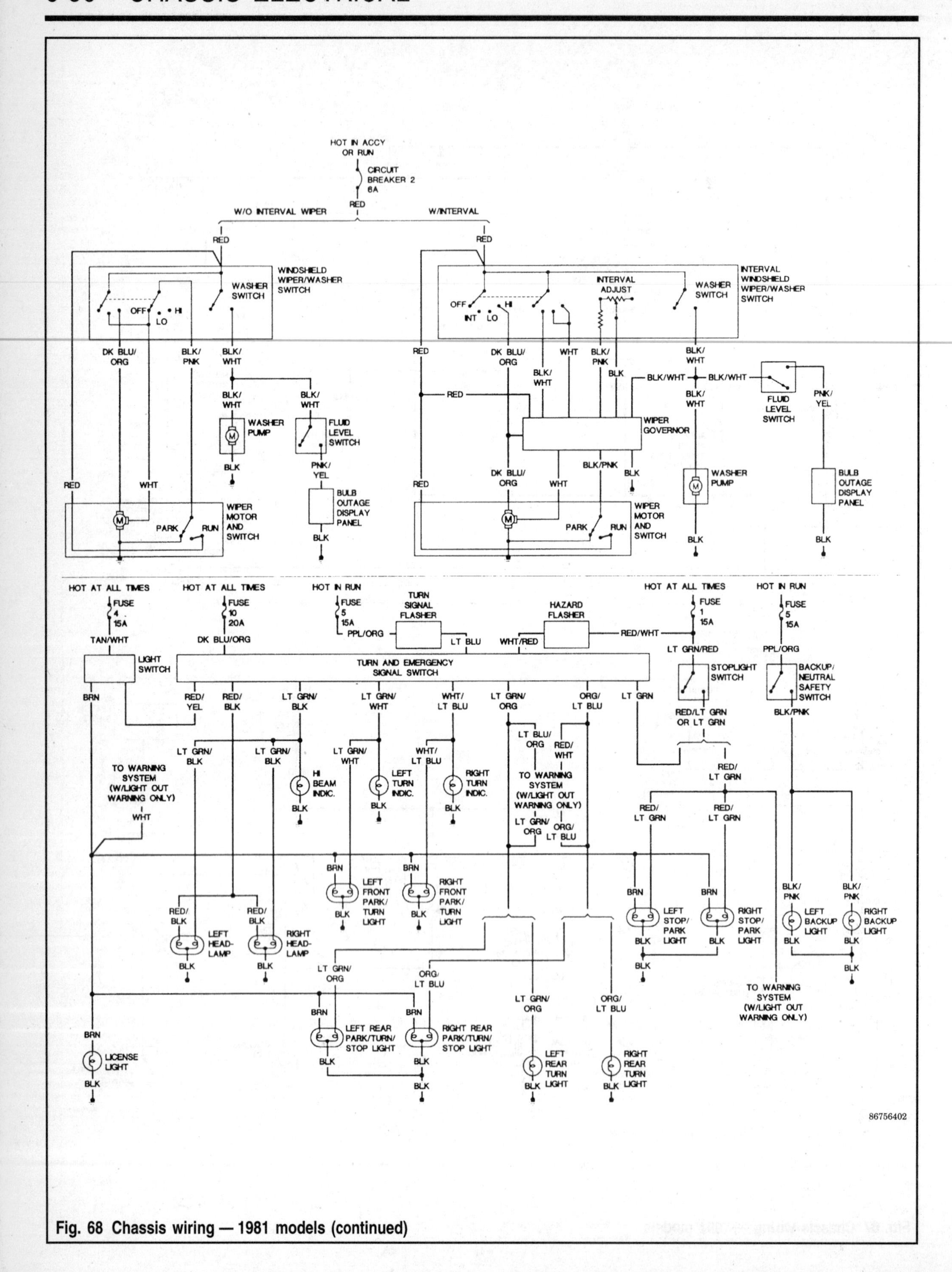

86756402

Fig. 68 Chassis wiring — 1981 models (continued)

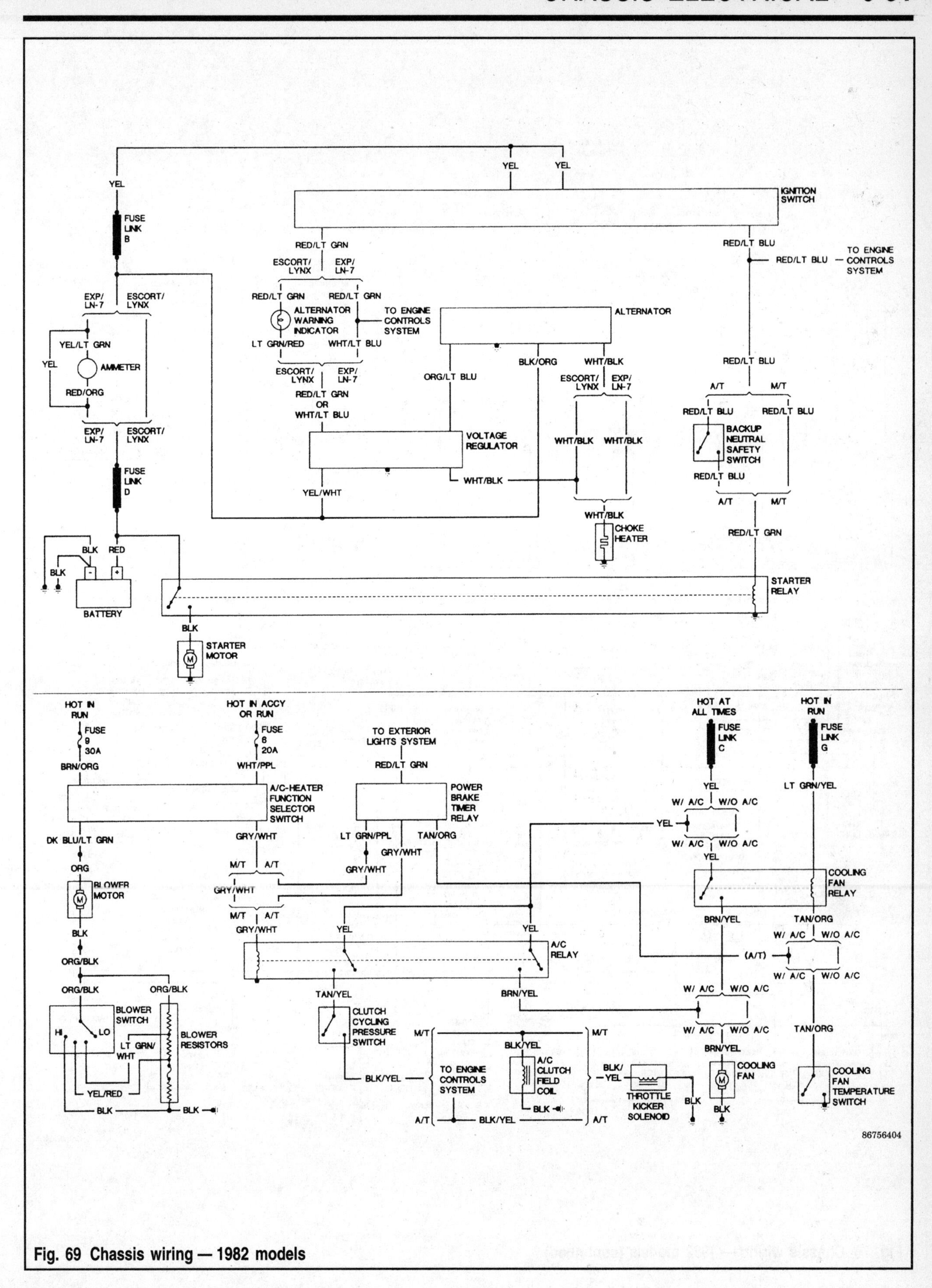

Fig. 69 Chassis wiring — 1982 models

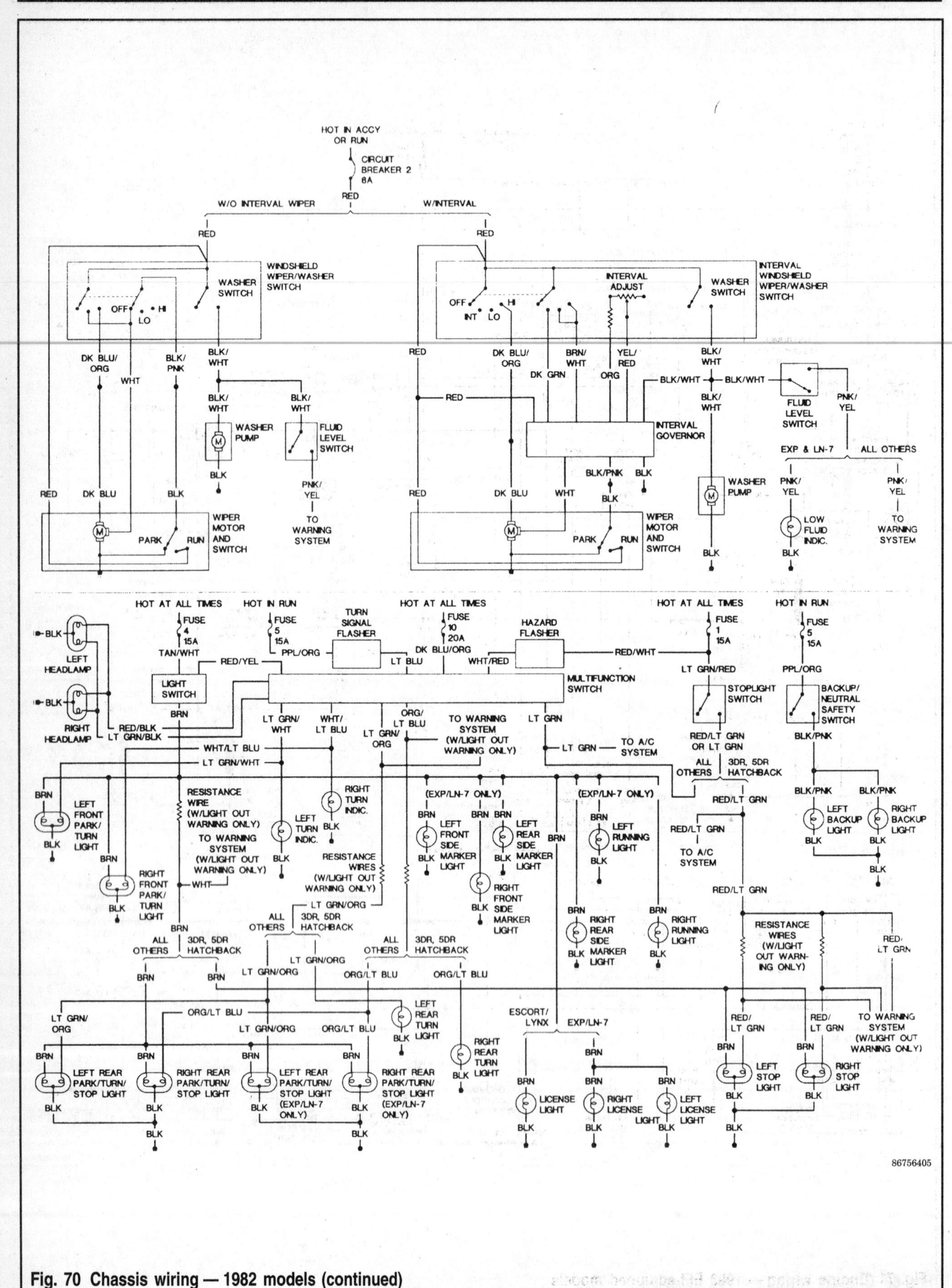

Fig. 70 Chassis wiring — 1982 models (continued)

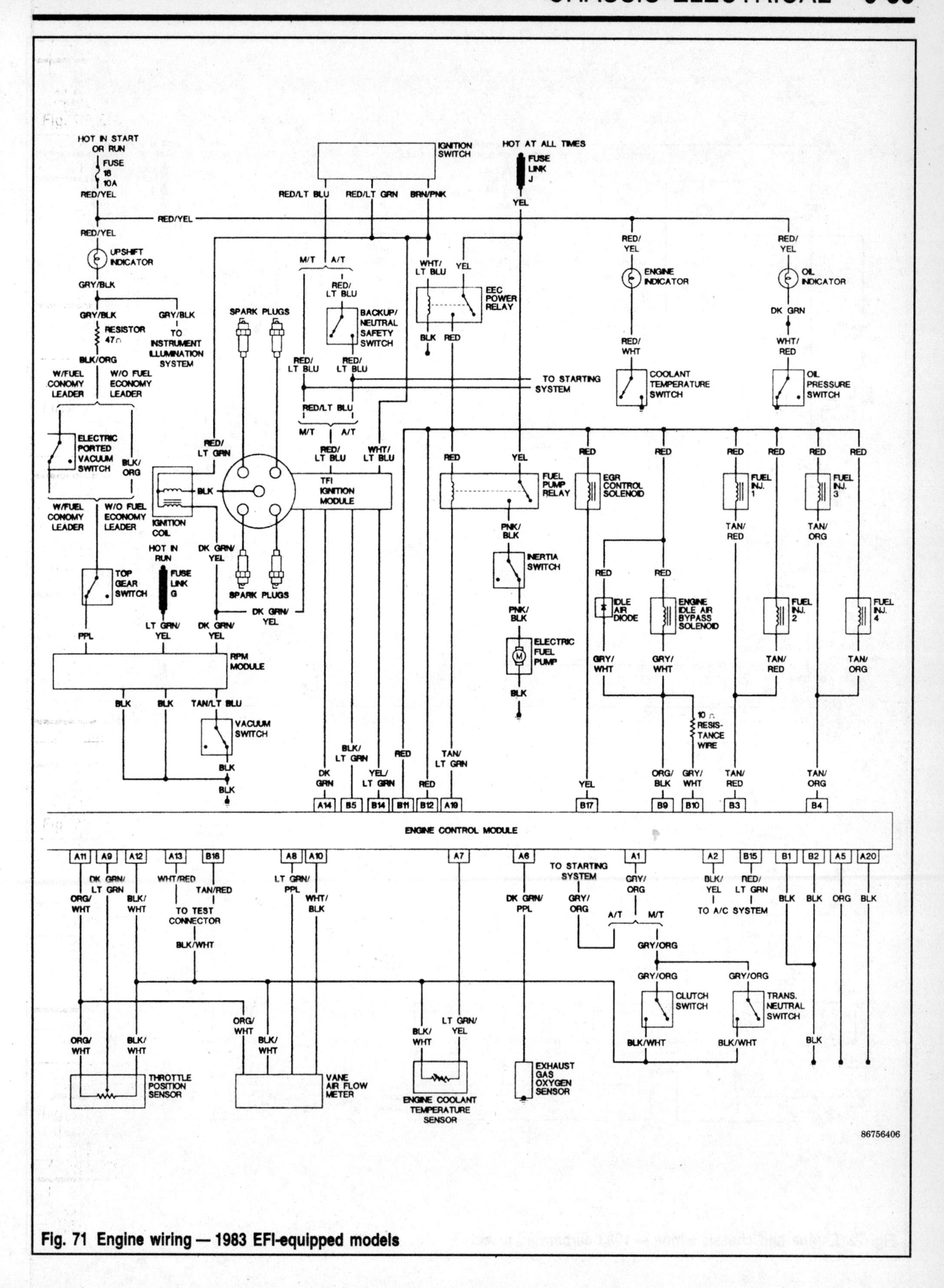

Fig. 71 Engine wiring — 1983 EFI-equipped models

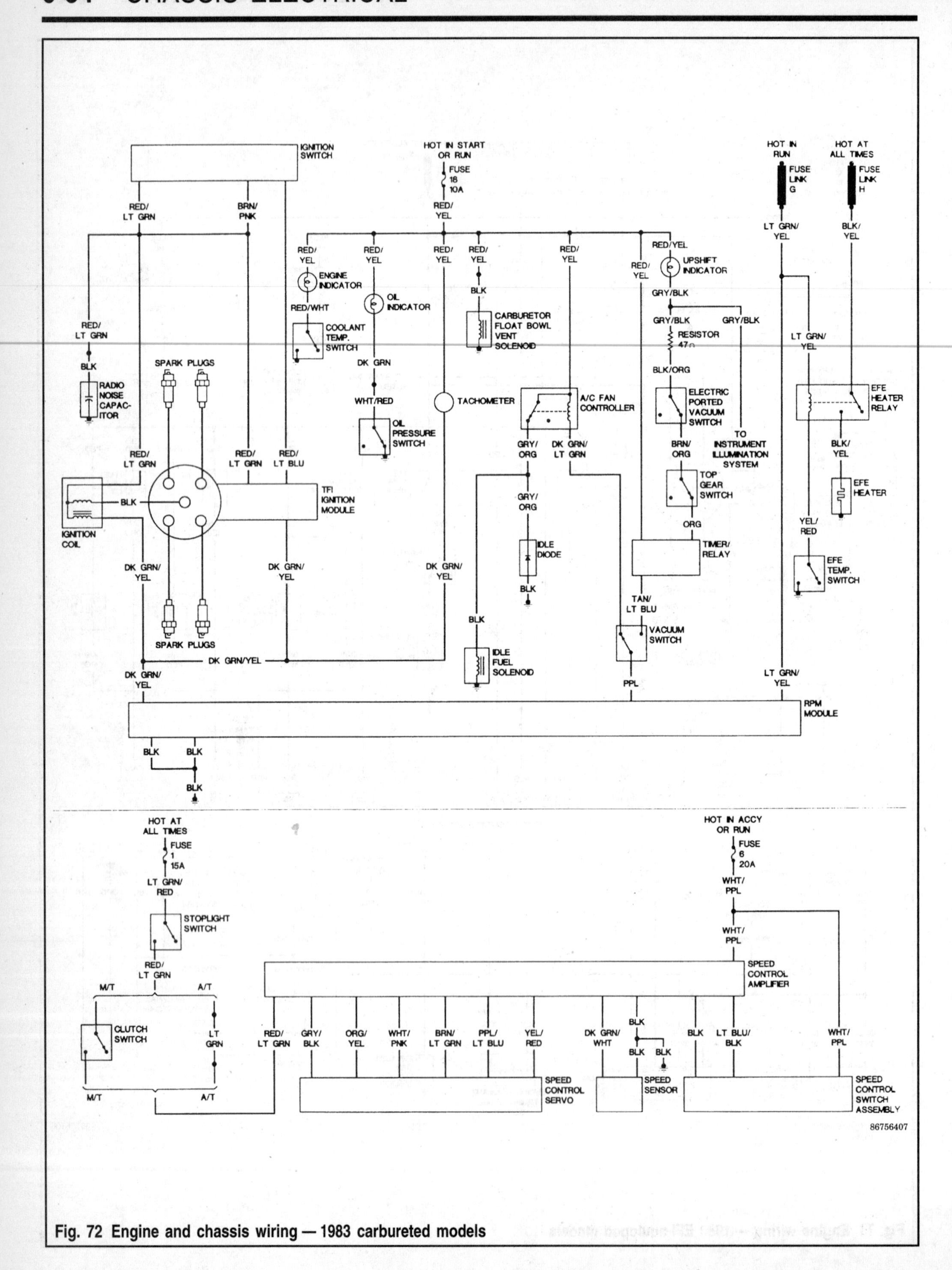

Fig. 72 Engine and chassis wiring — 1983 carbureted models

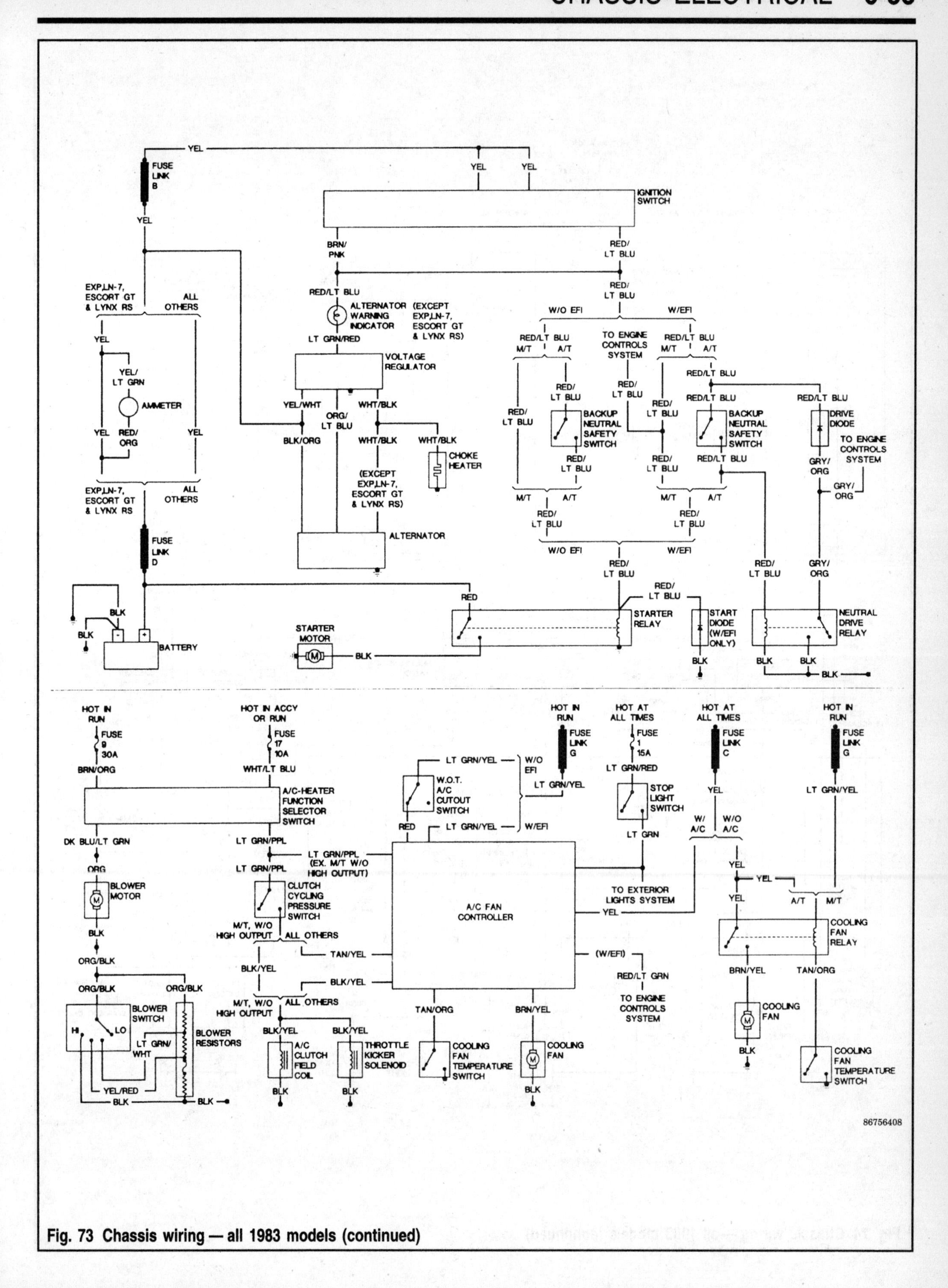

Fig. 73 Chassis wiring — all 1983 models (continued)

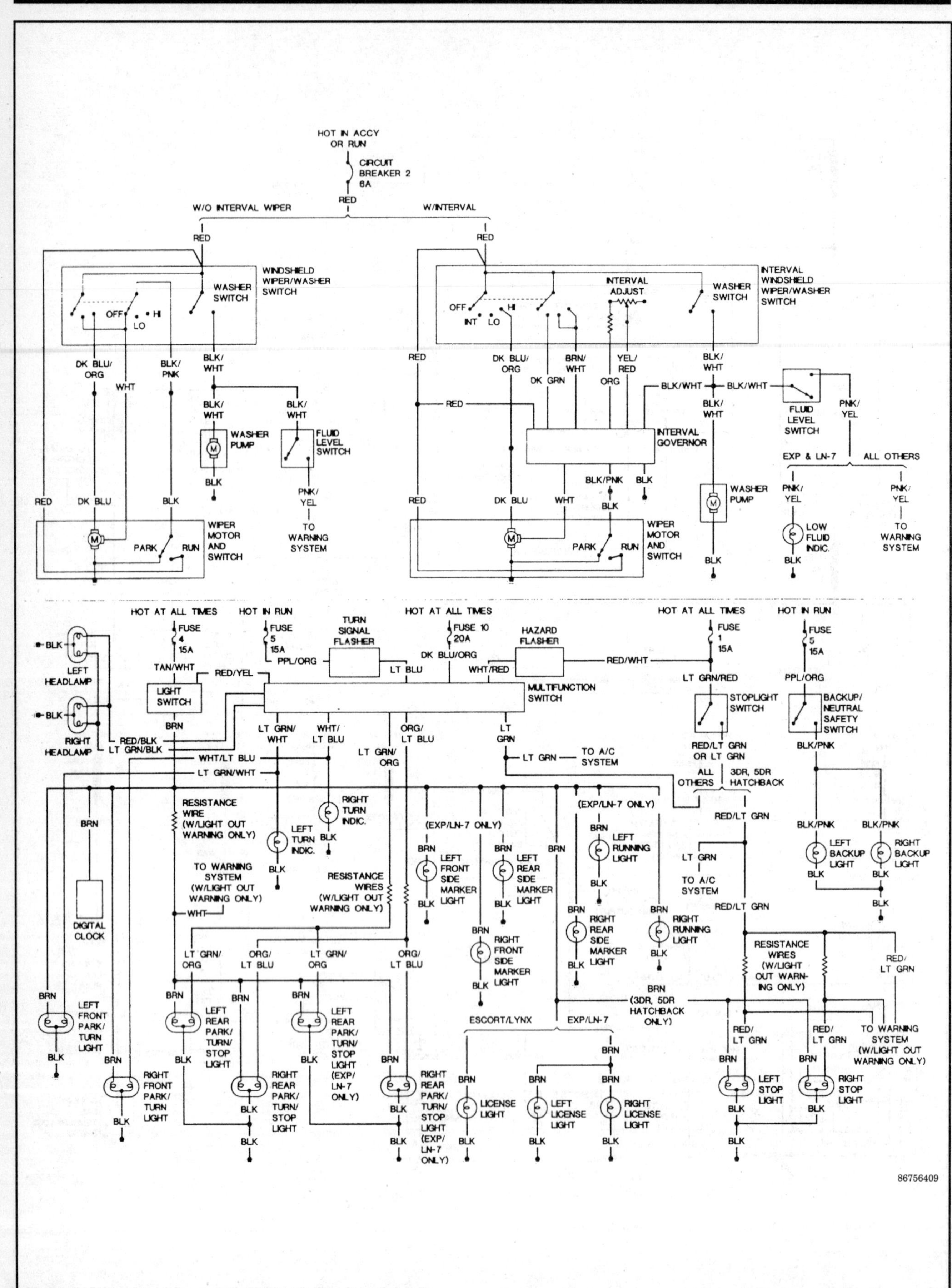

Fig. 74 Chassis wiring — all 1983 models (continued)

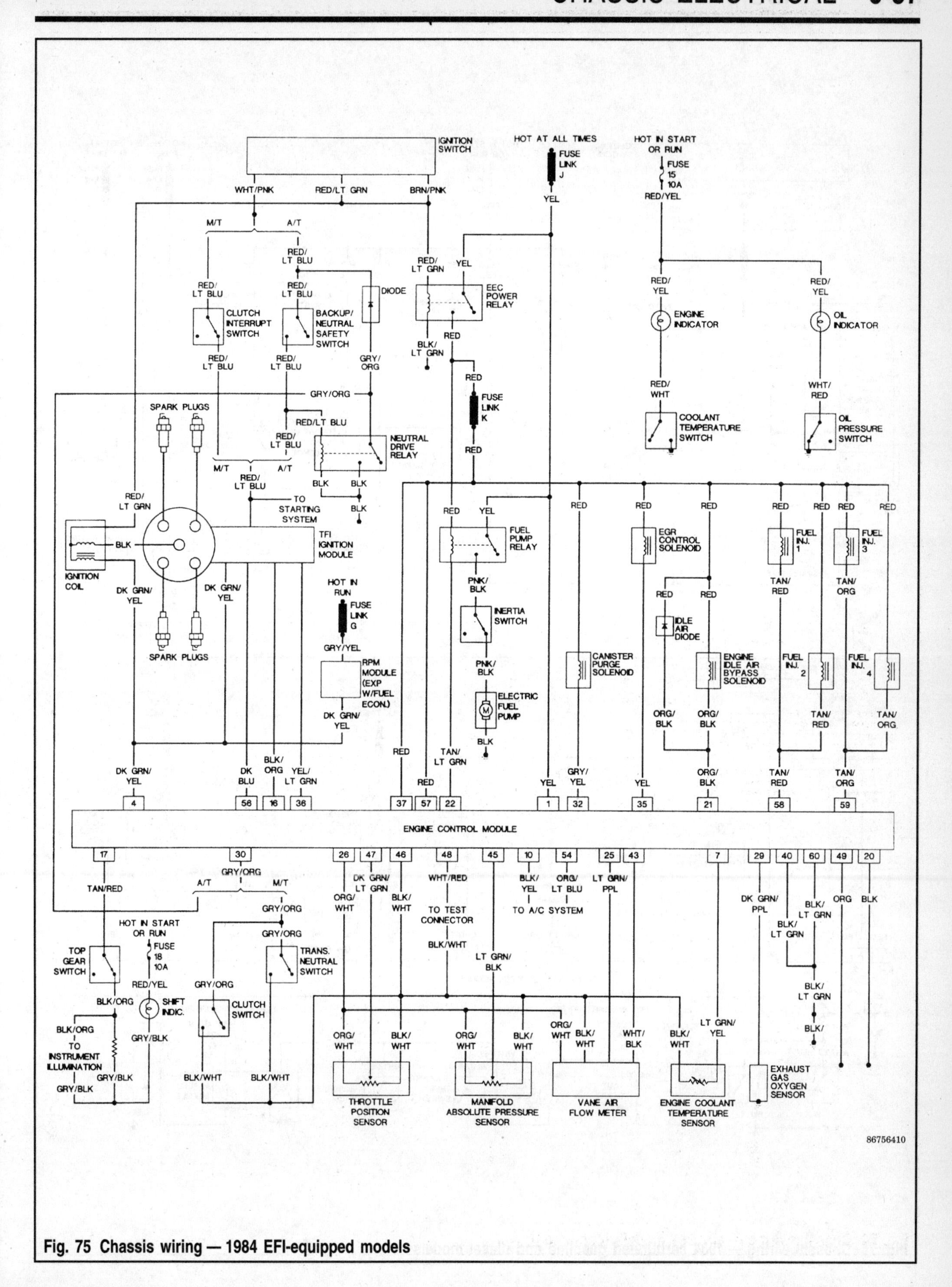

Fig. 75 Chassis wiring — 1984 EFI-equipped models

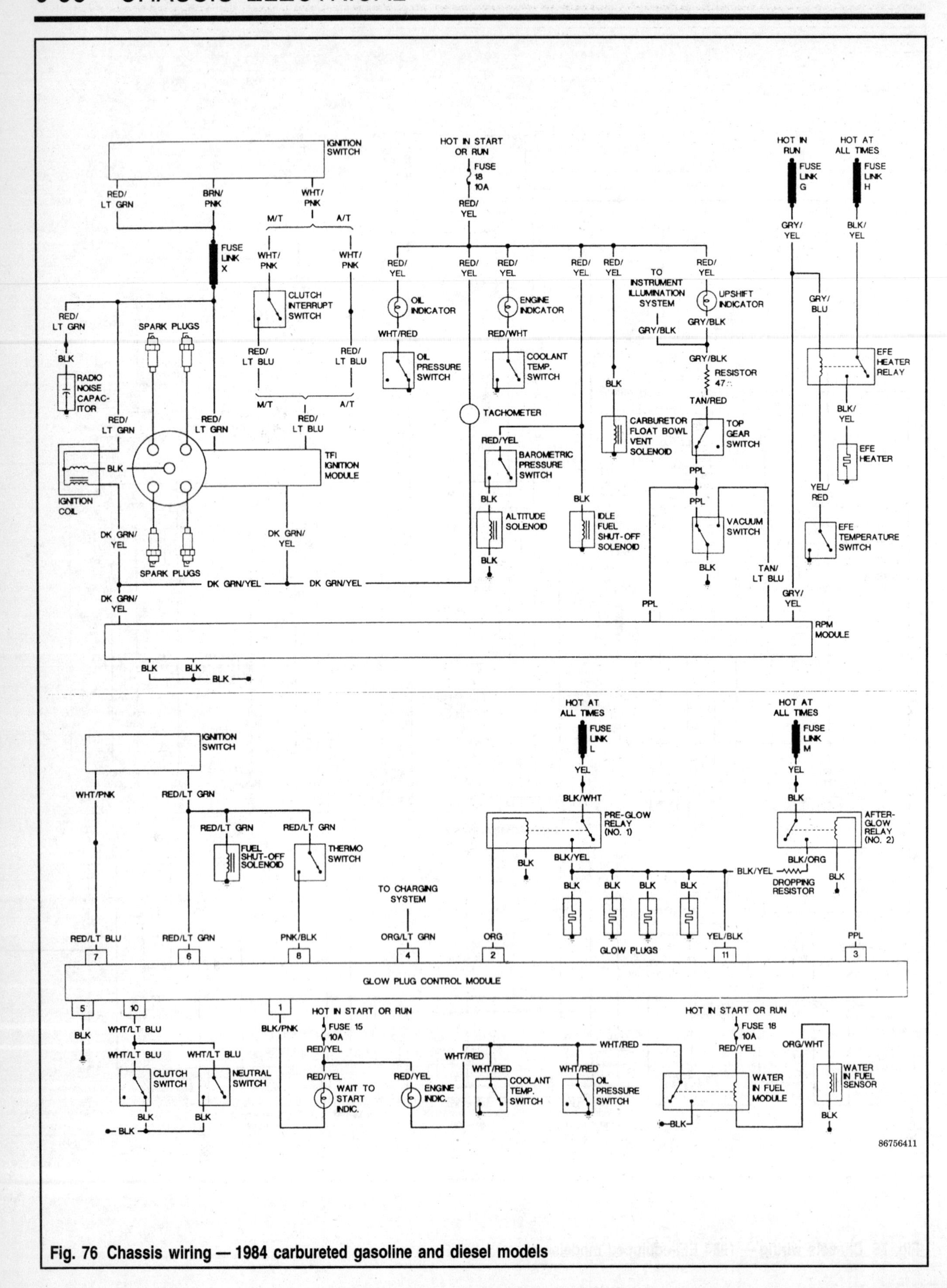

Fig. 76 Chassis wiring — 1984 carbureted gasoline and diesel models

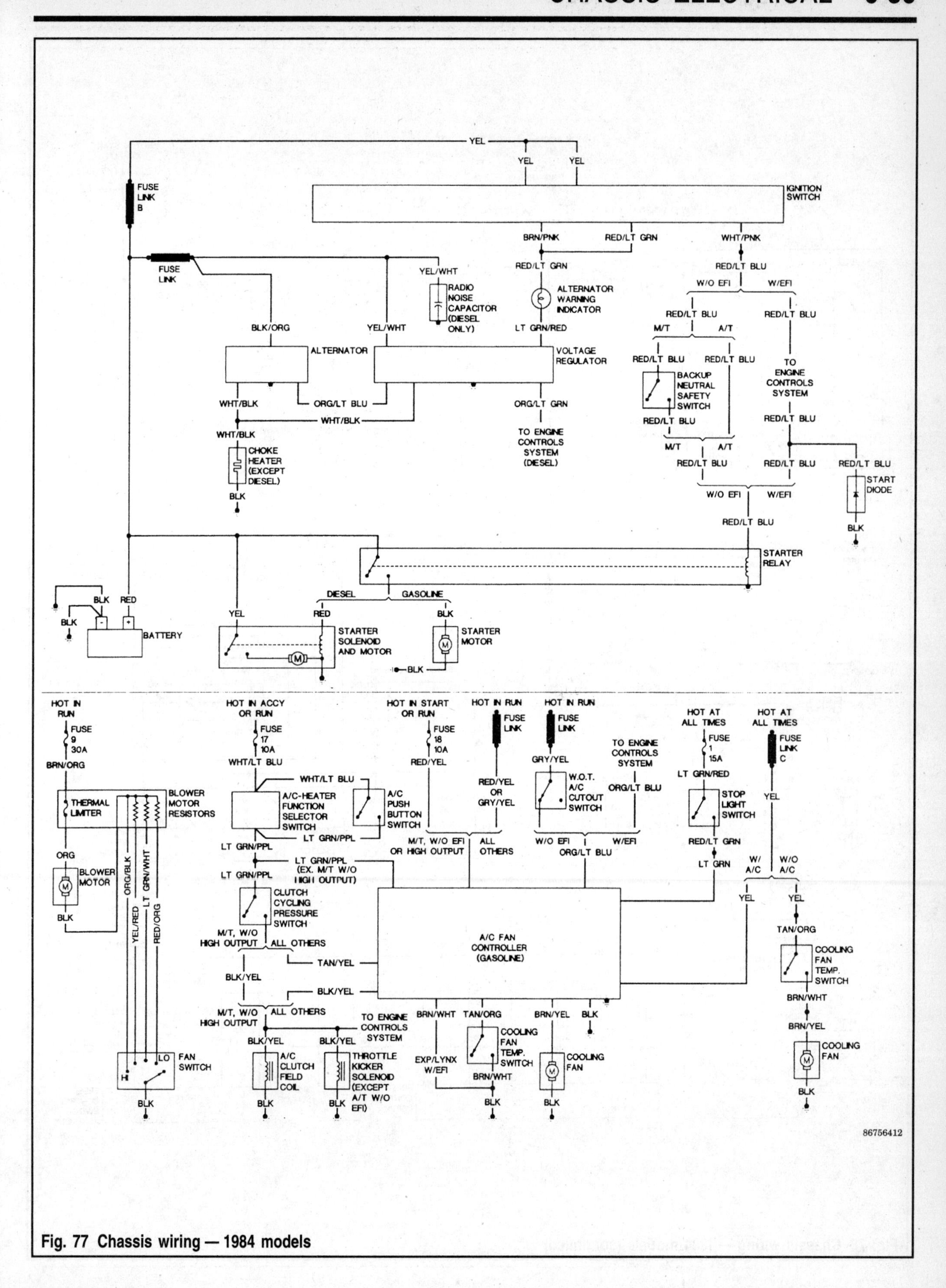

Fig. 77 Chassis wiring — 1984 models

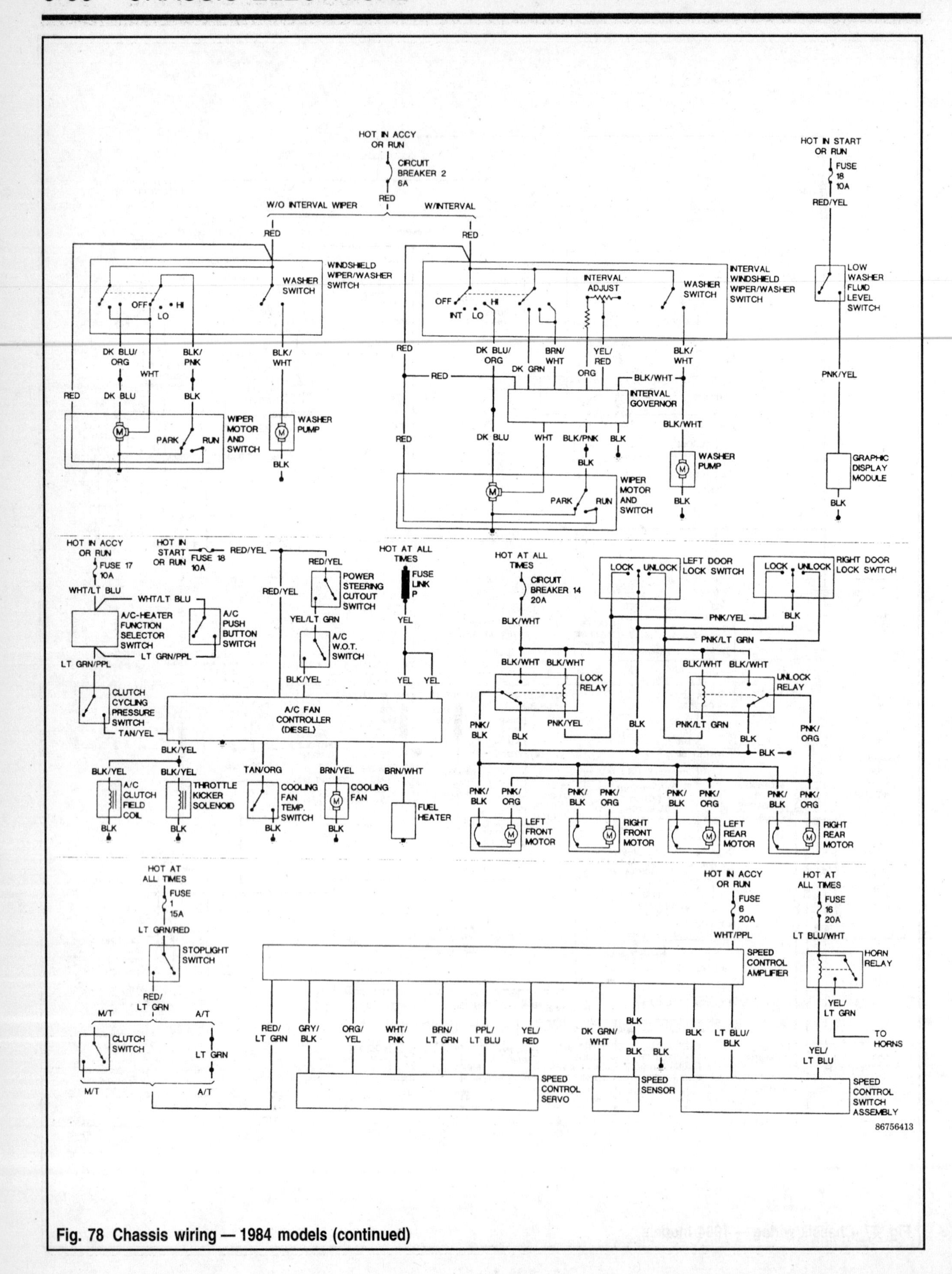

Fig. 78 Chassis wiring — 1984 models (continued)

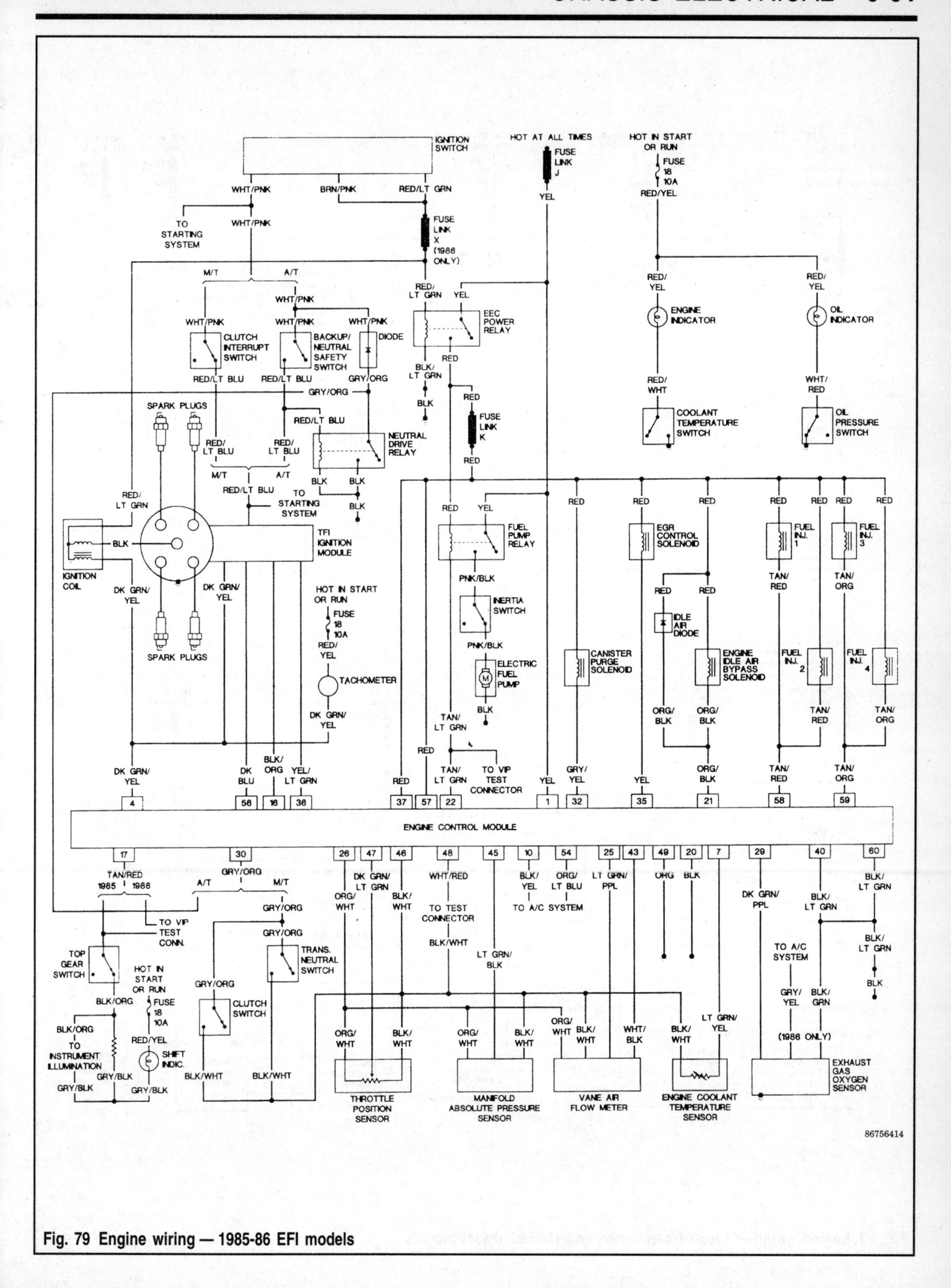

Fig. 79 Engine wiring — 1985-86 EFI models

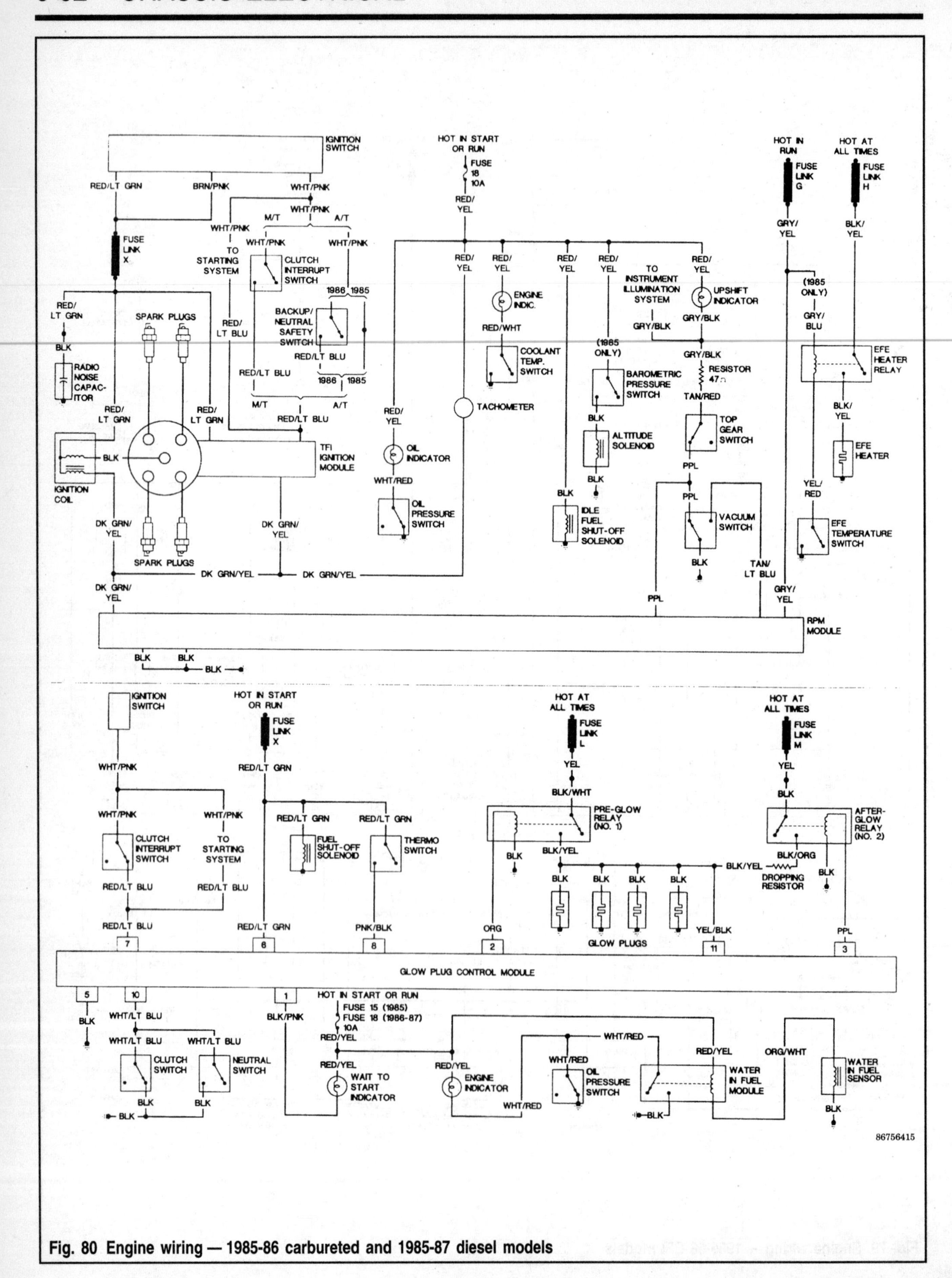

Fig. 80 Engine wiring — 1985-86 carbureted and 1985-87 diesel models

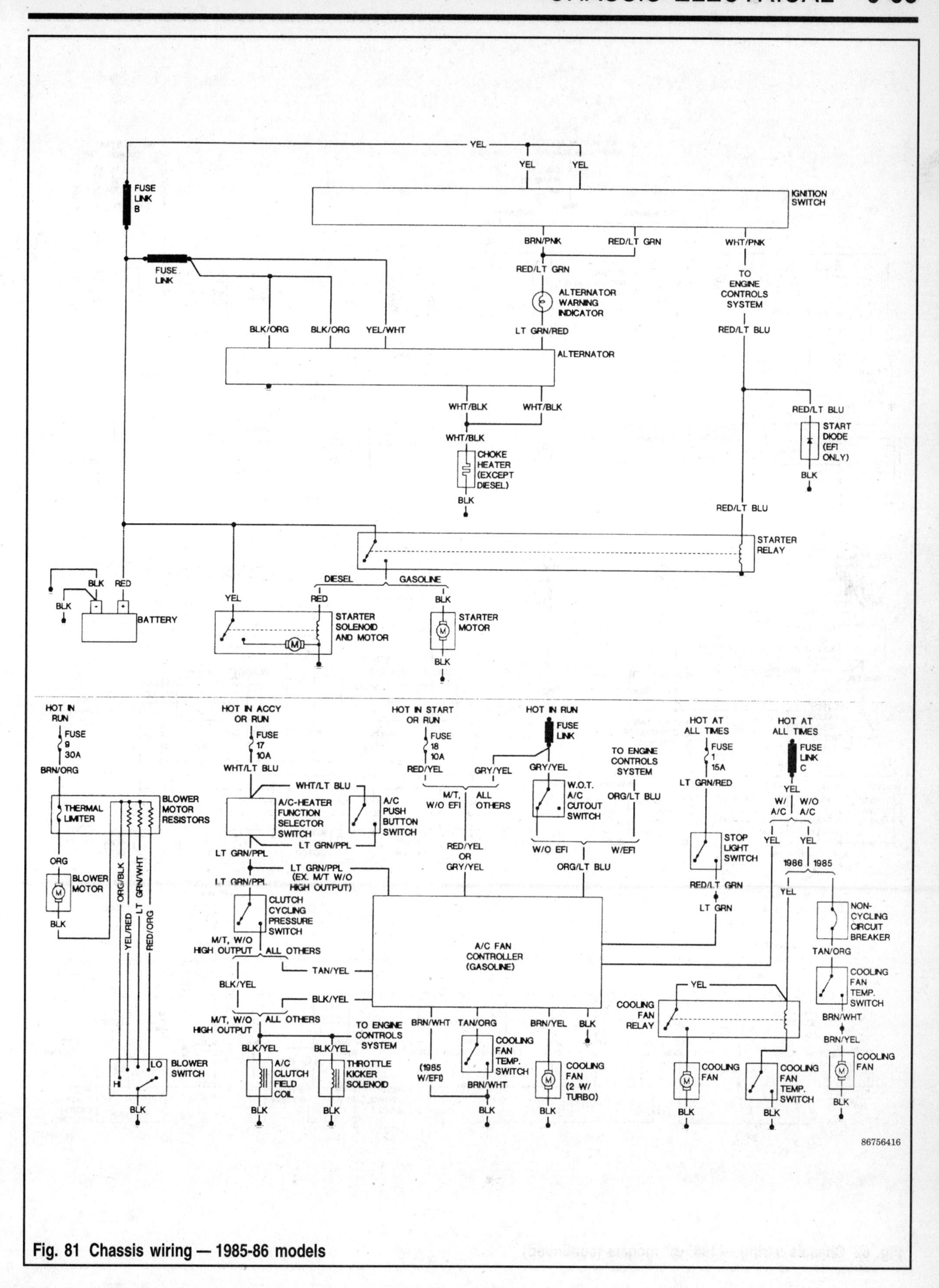

Fig. 81 Chassis wiring — 1985-86 models

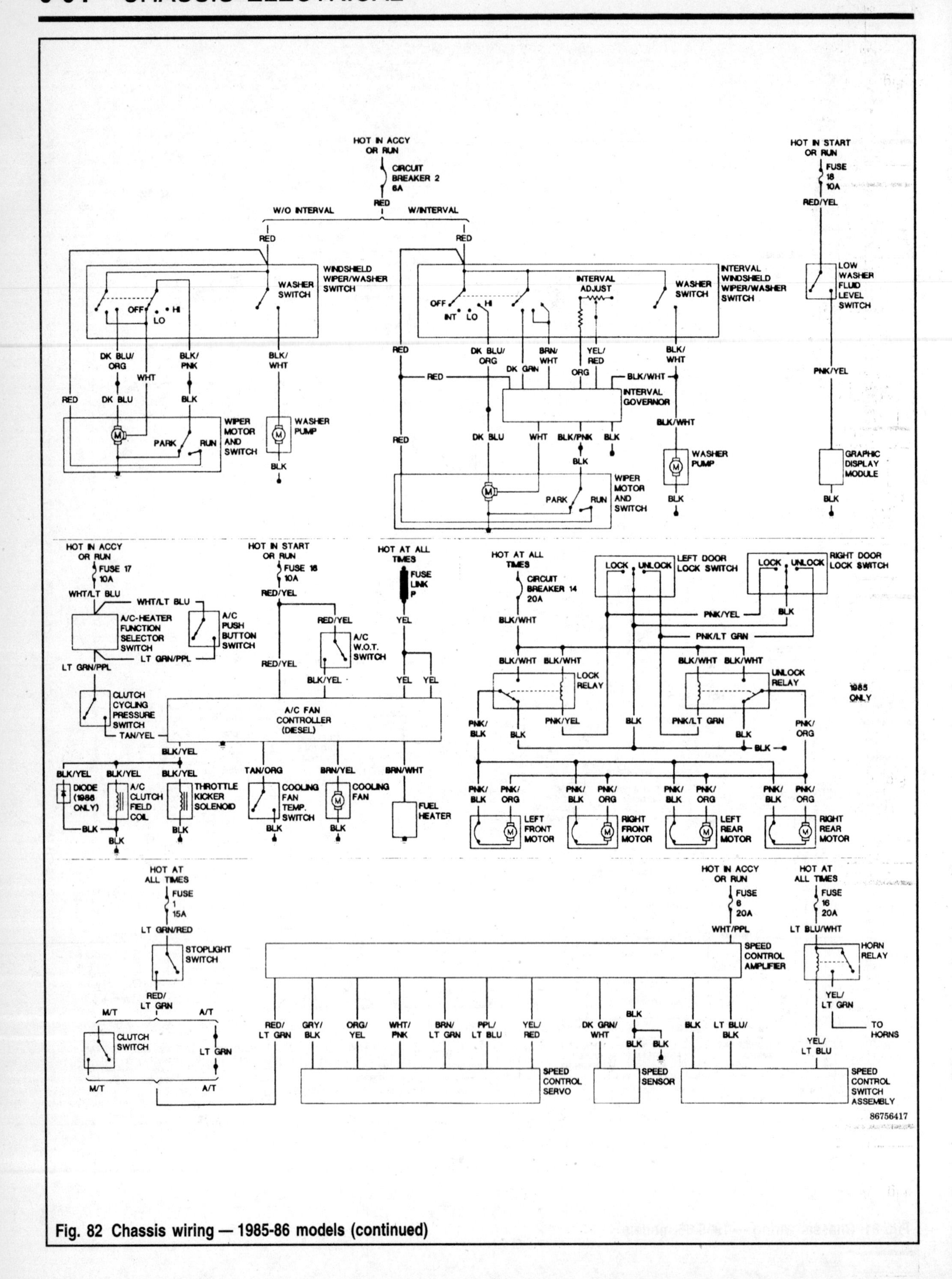

Fig. 82 Chassis wiring — 1985-86 models (continued)

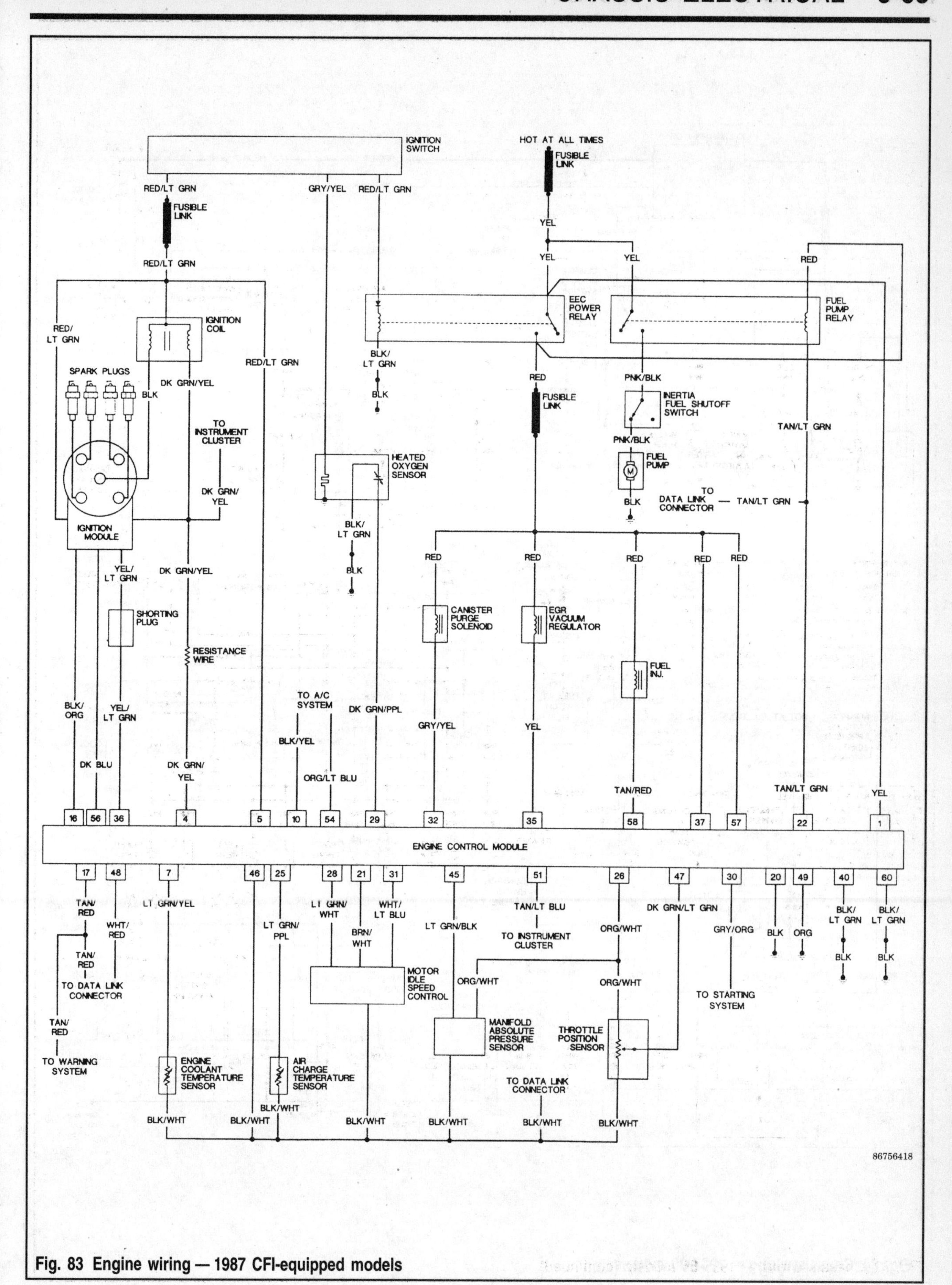

Fig. 83 Engine wiring — 1987 CFI-equipped models

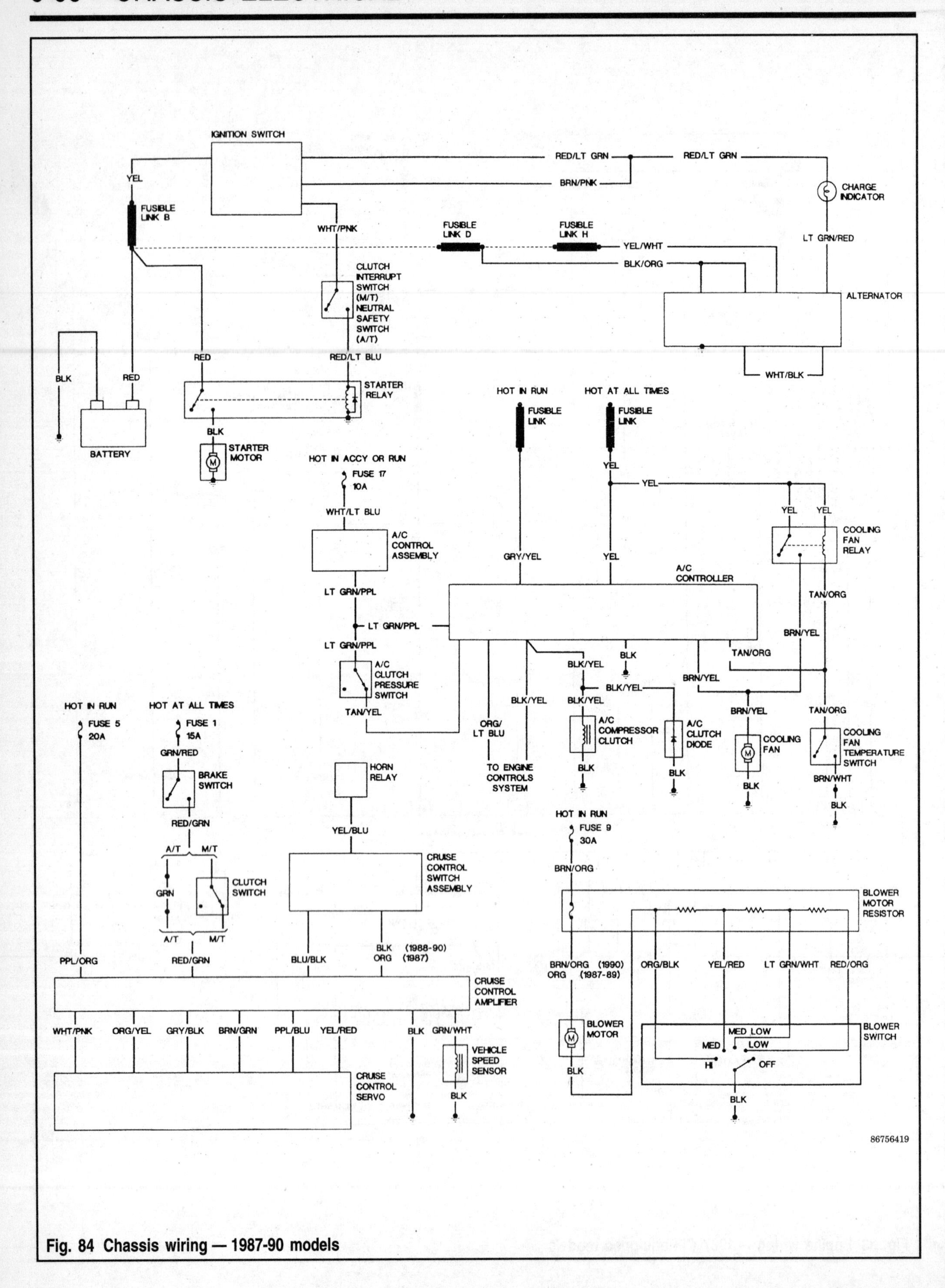

Fig. 84 Chassis wiring — 1987-90 models

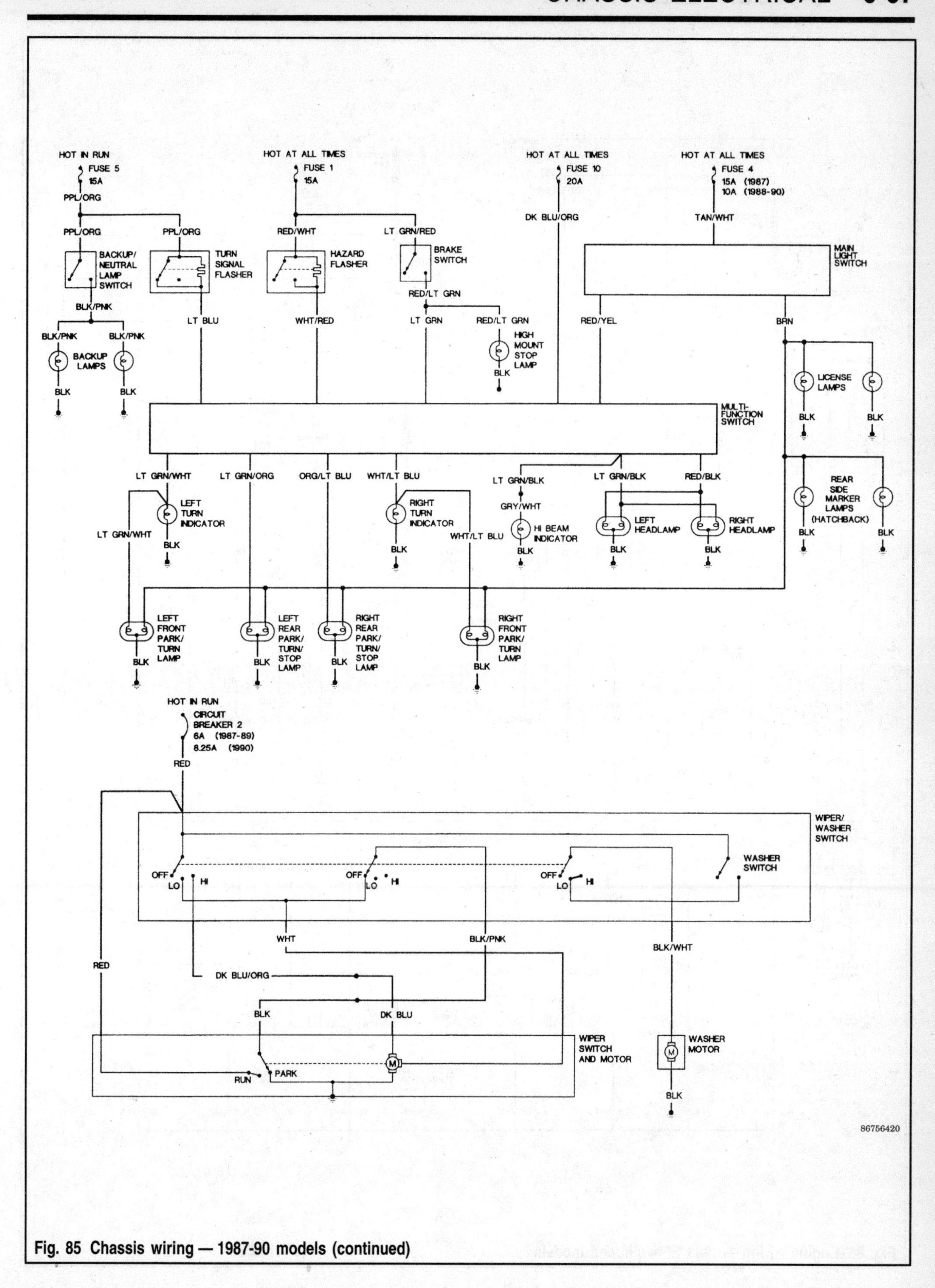

Fig. 85 Chassis wiring — 1987-90 models (continued)

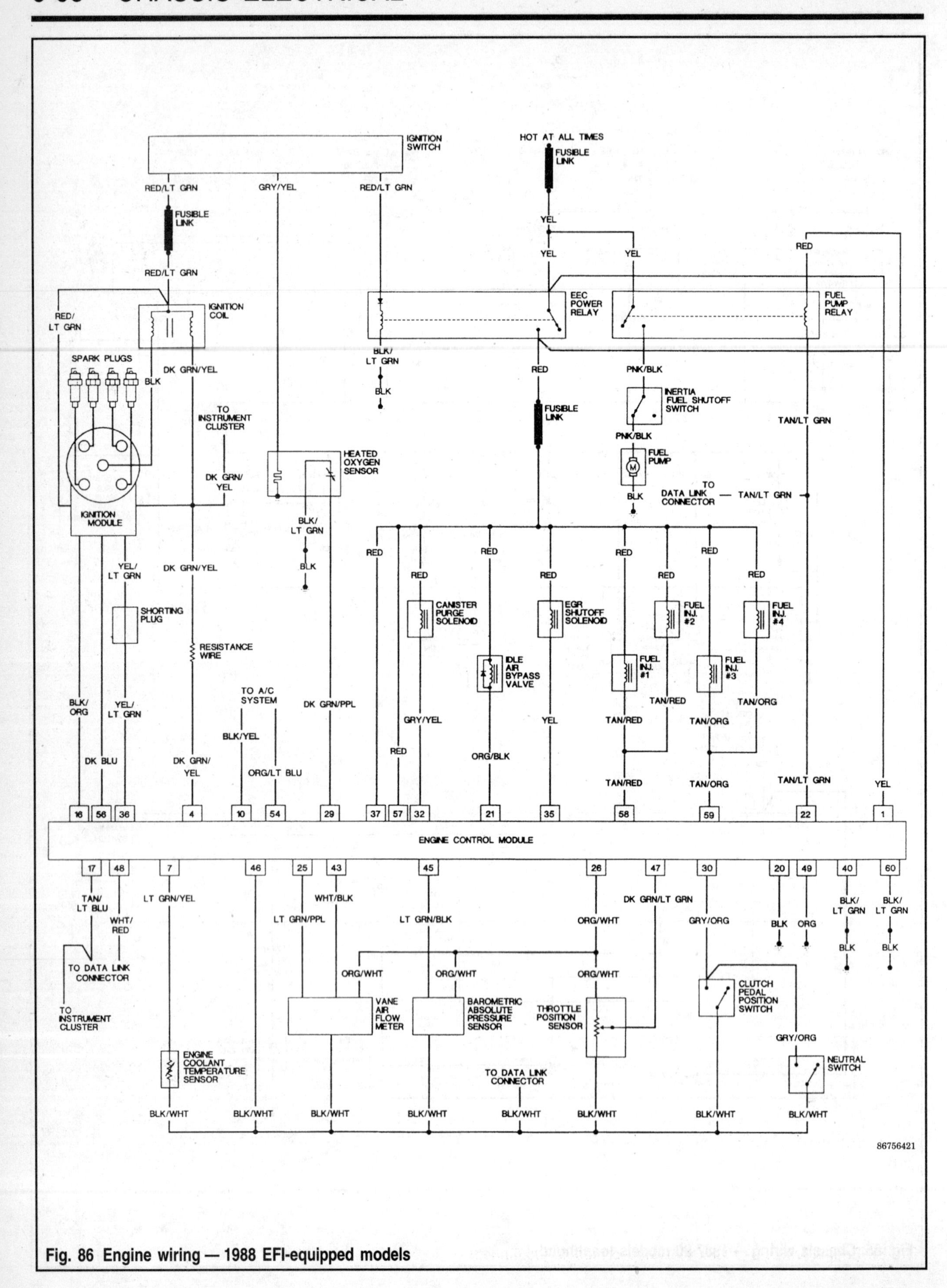

Fig. 86 Engine wiring — 1988 EFI-equipped models

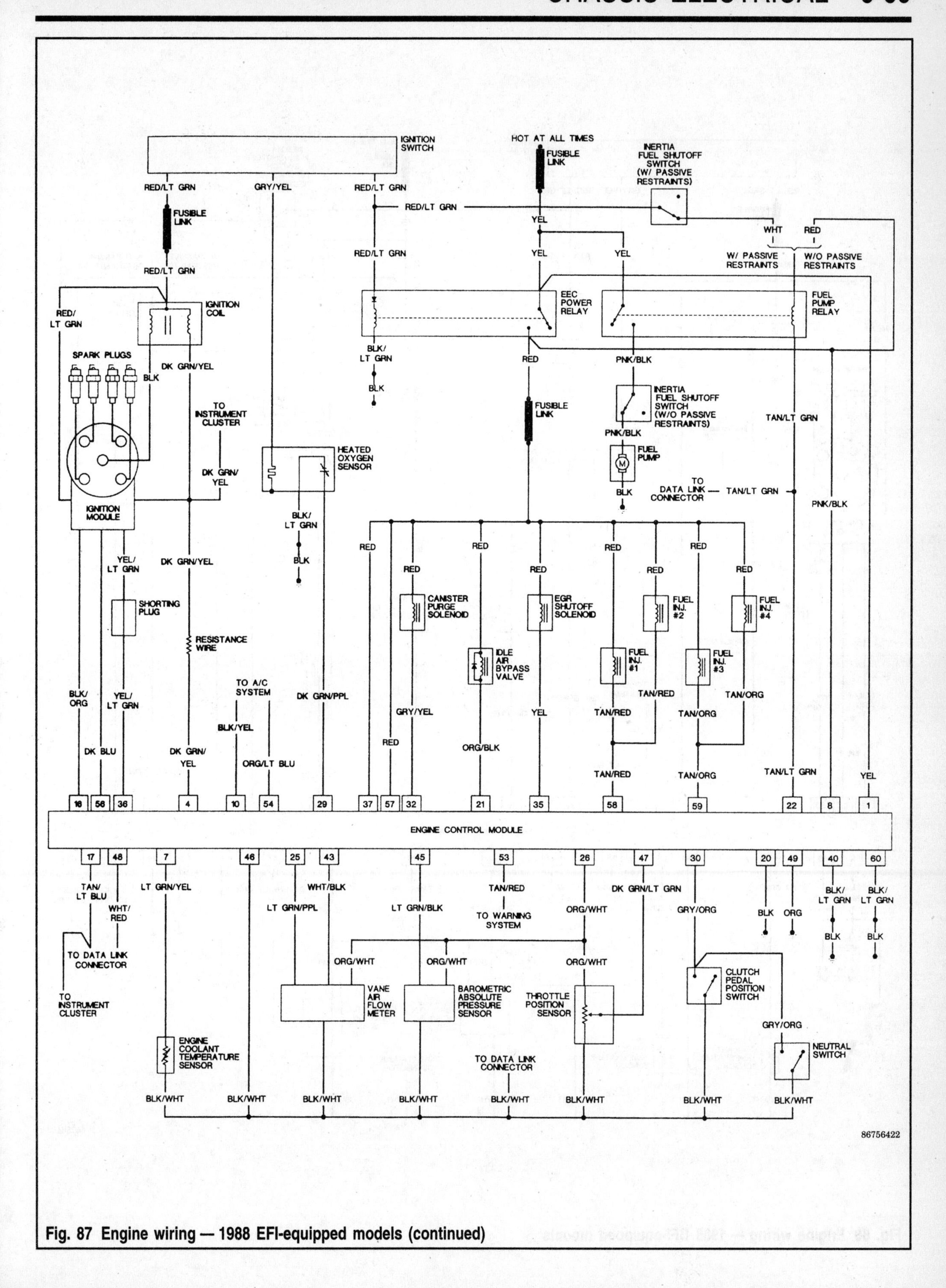

Fig. 87 Engine wiring — 1988 EFI-equipped models (continued)

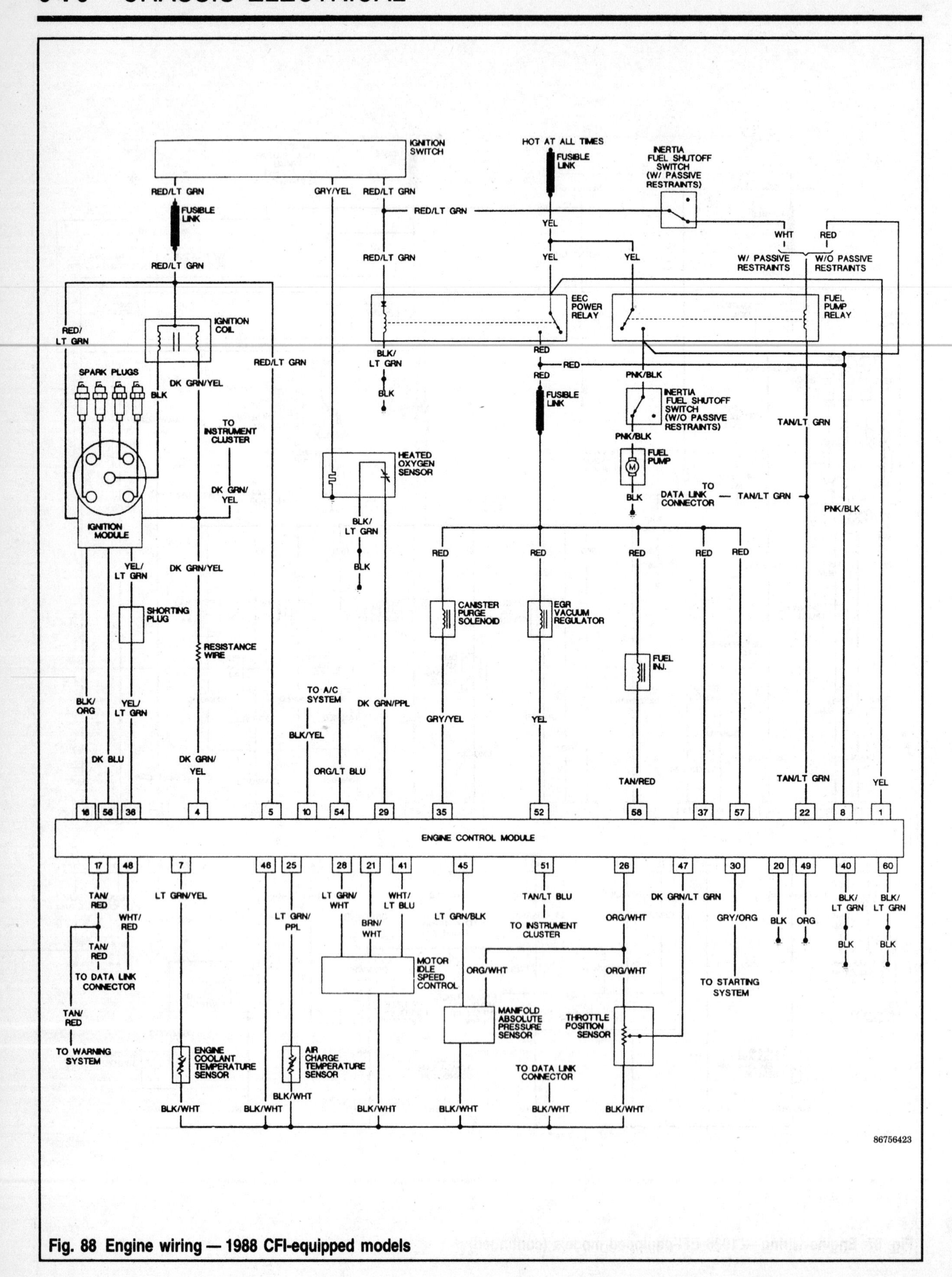

Fig. 88 Engine wiring — 1988 CFI-equipped models

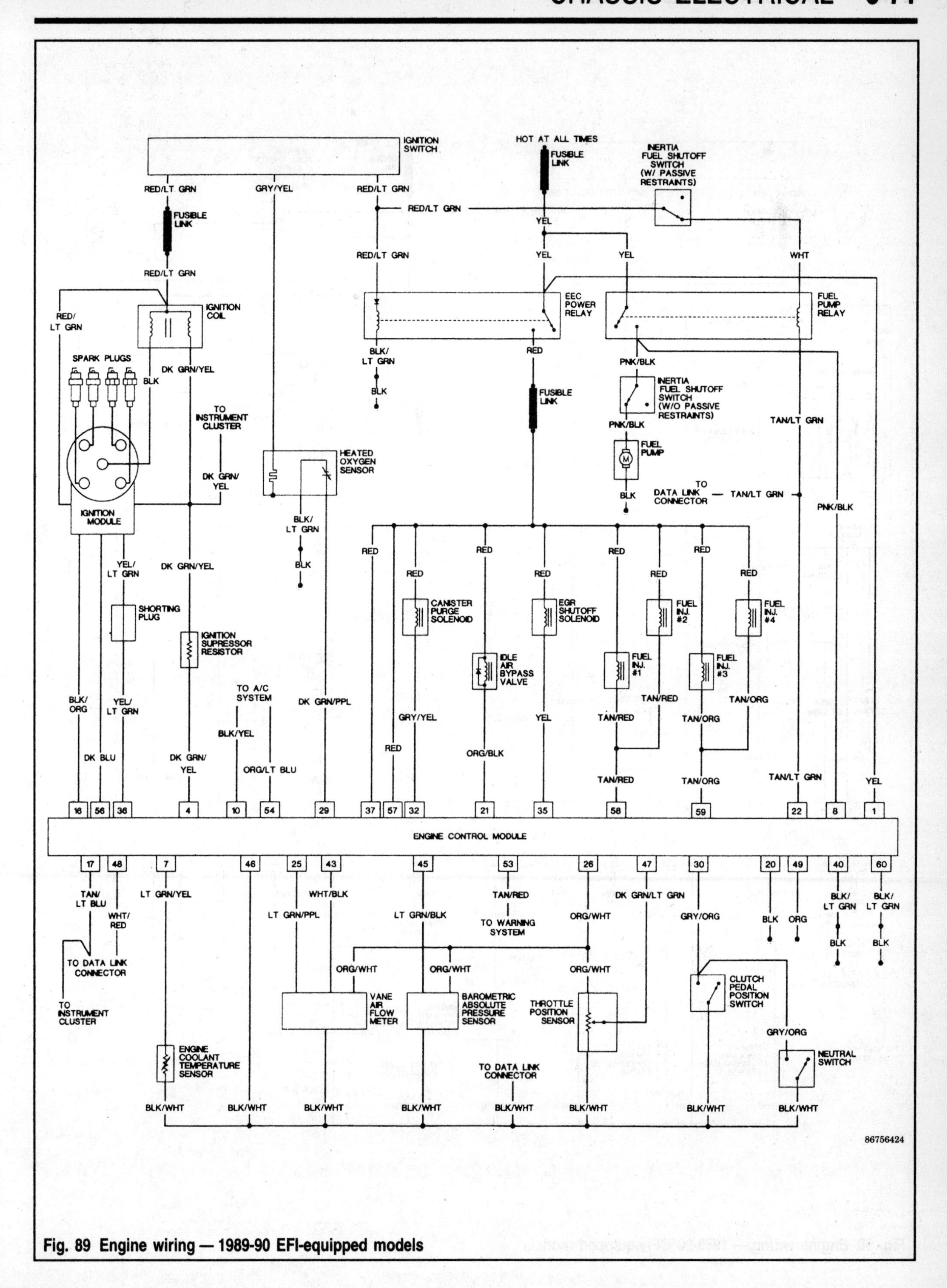

Fig. 89 Engine wiring — 1989-90 EFI-equipped models

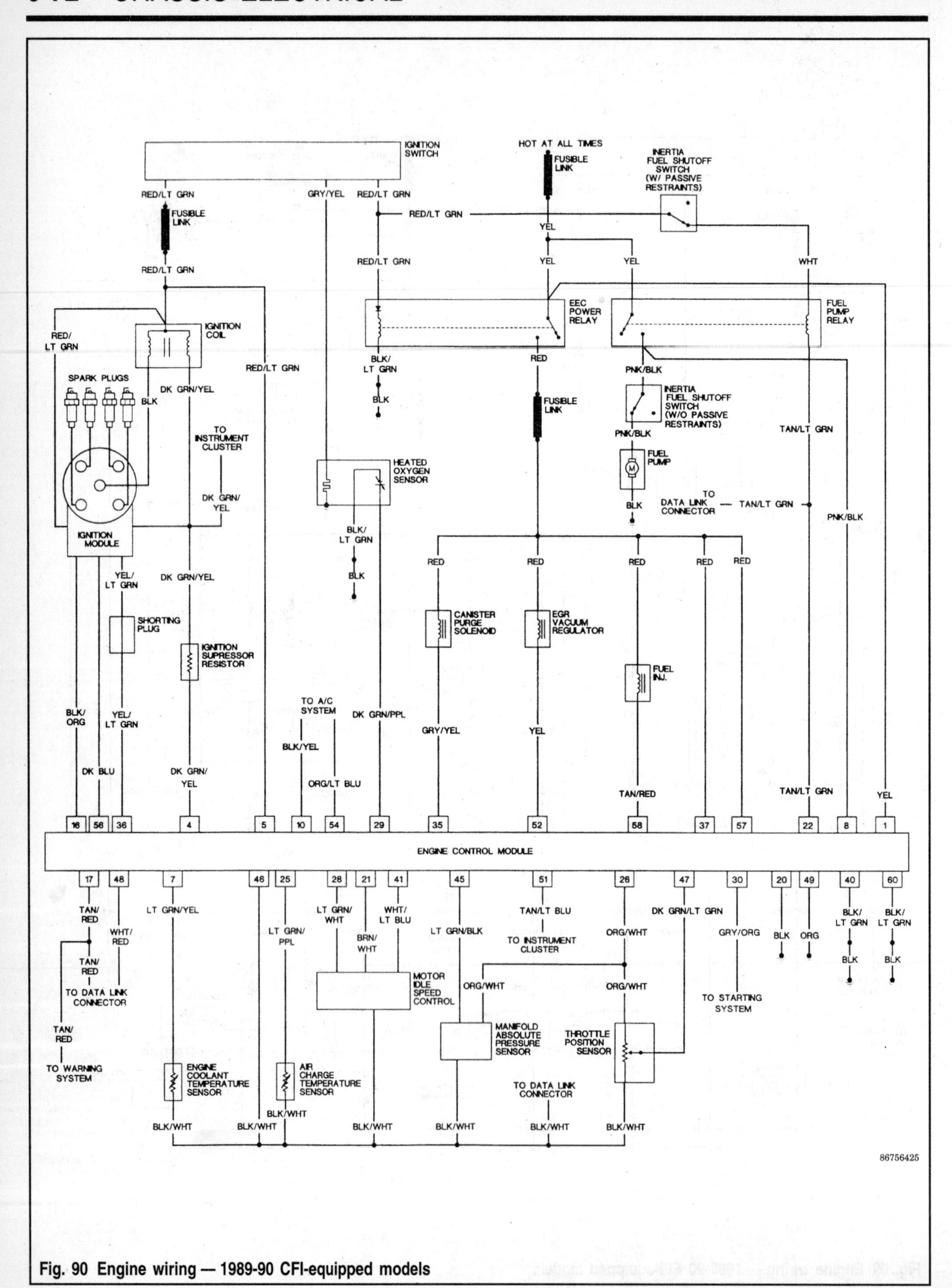

Fig. 90 Engine wiring — 1989-90 CFI-equipped models

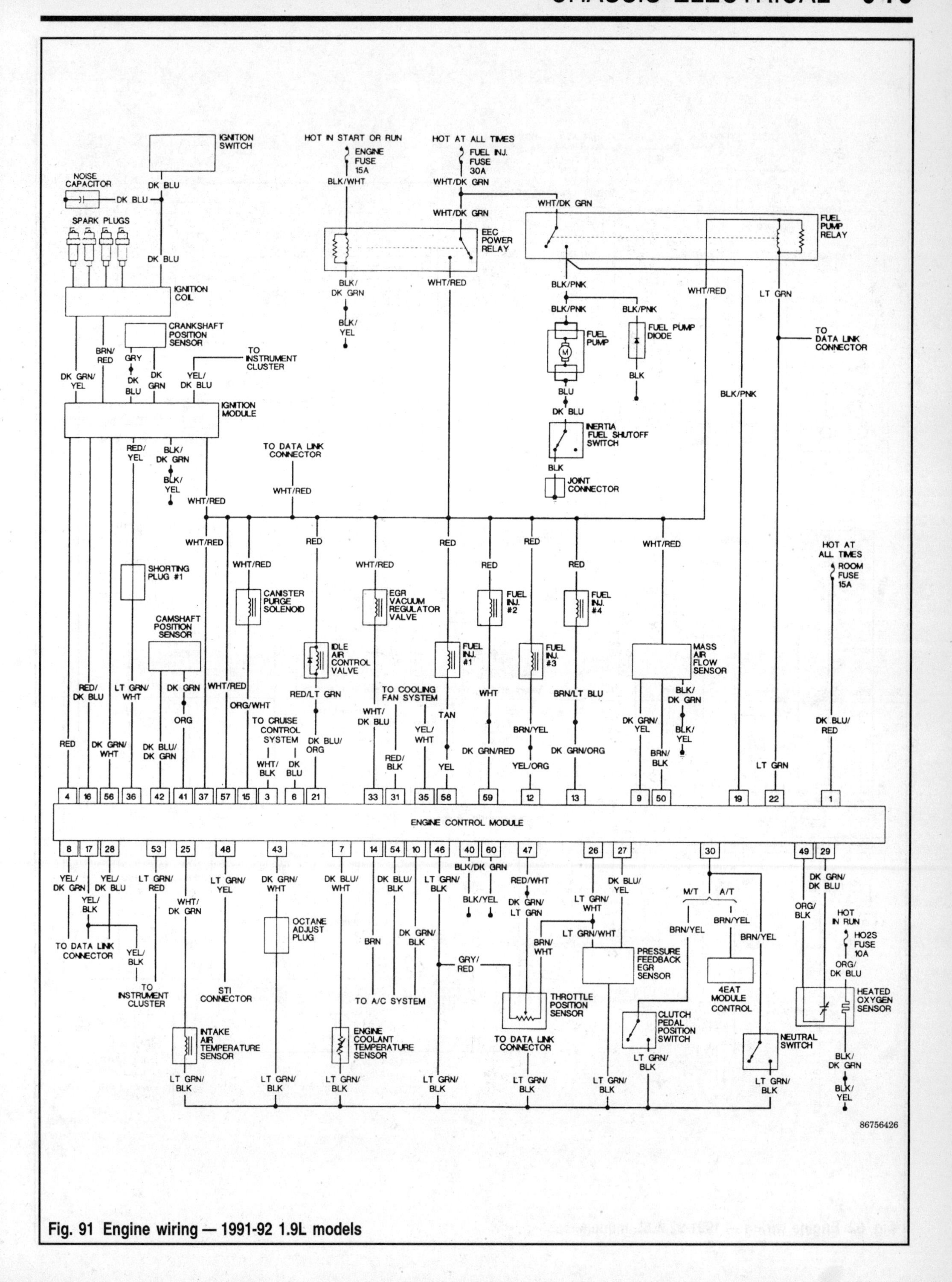

Fig. 91 Engine wiring — 1991-92 1.9L models

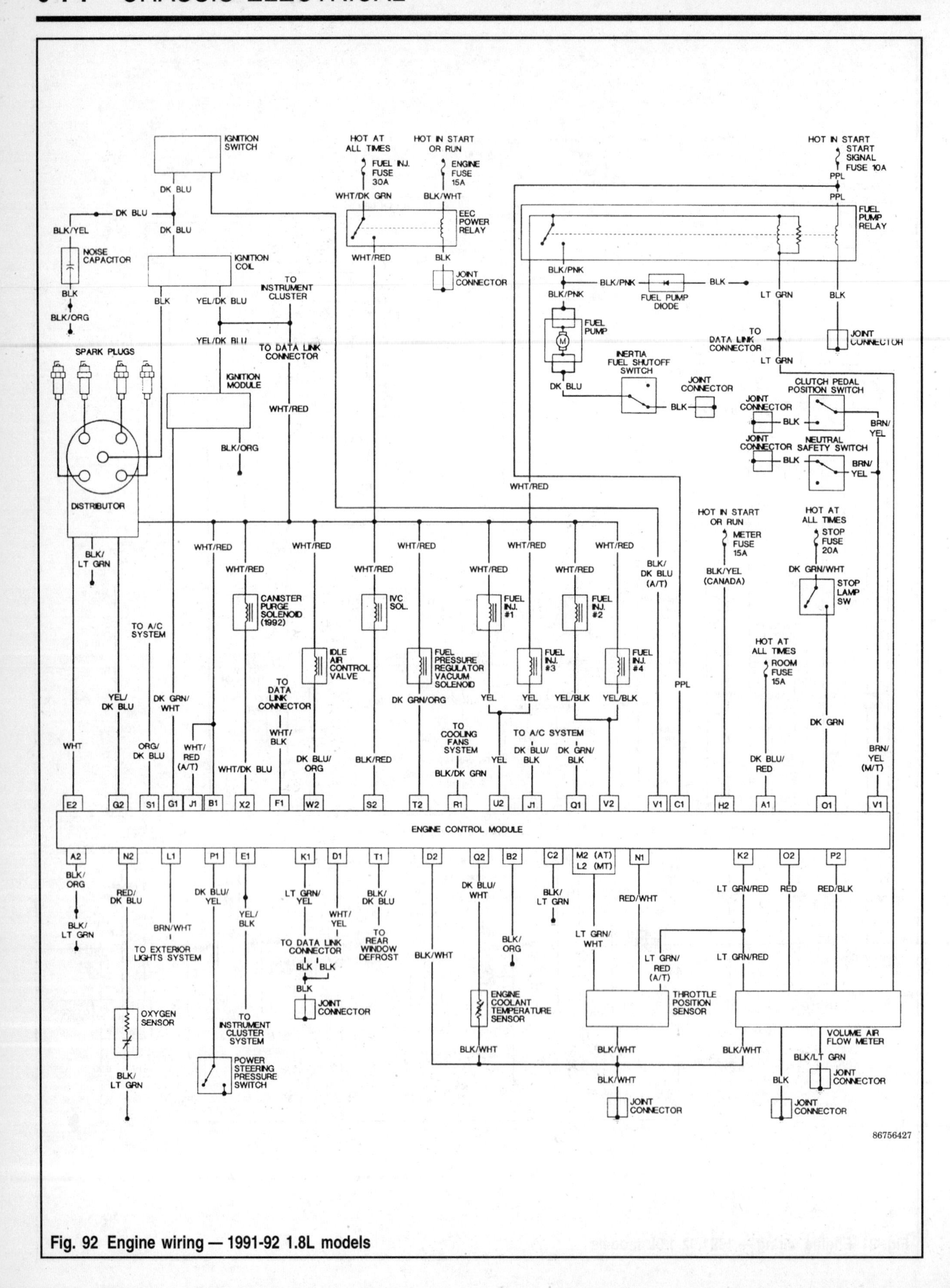

Fig. 92 Engine wiring — 1991-92 1.8L models

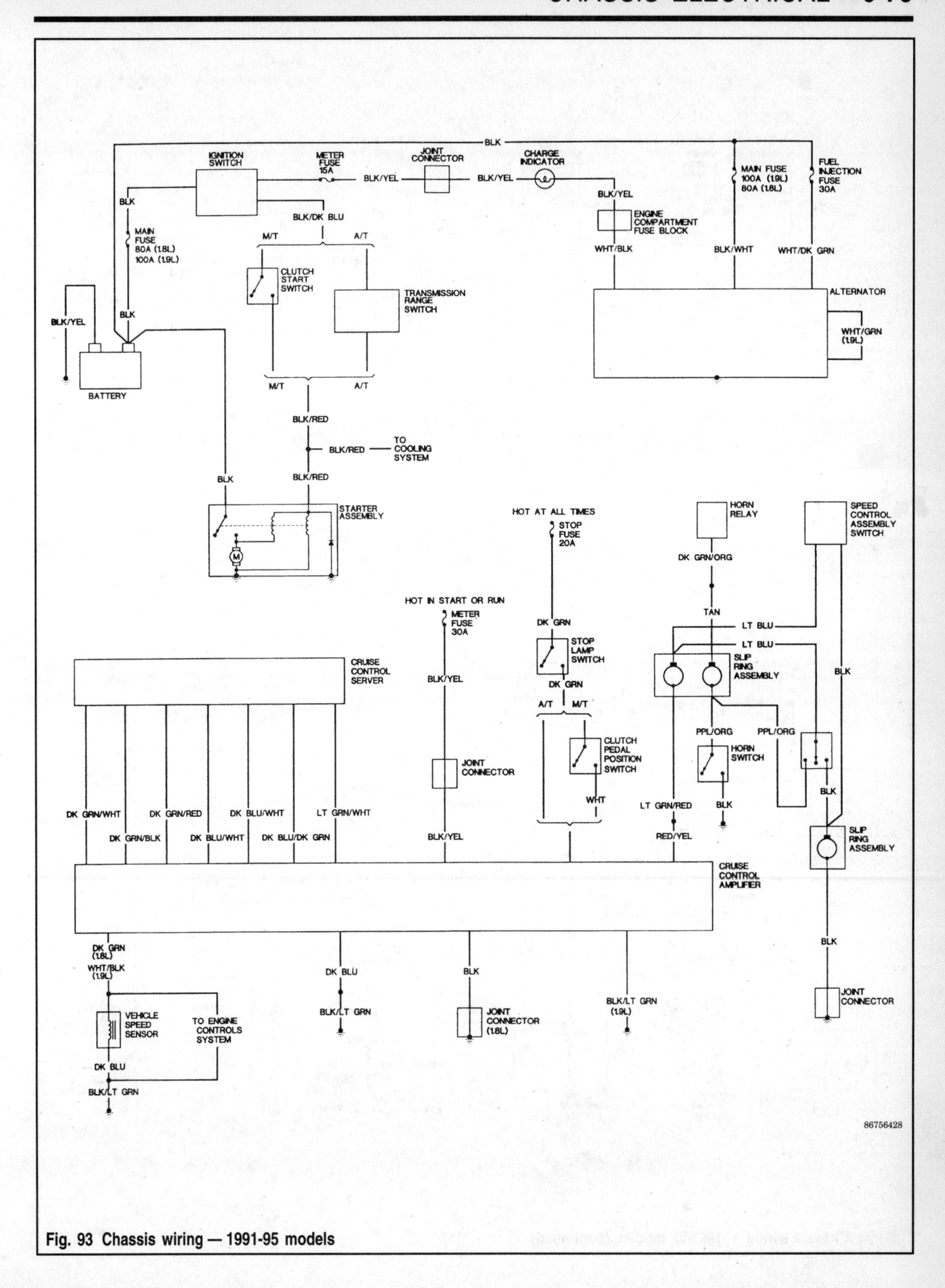

Fig. 93 Chassis wiring — 1991-95 models

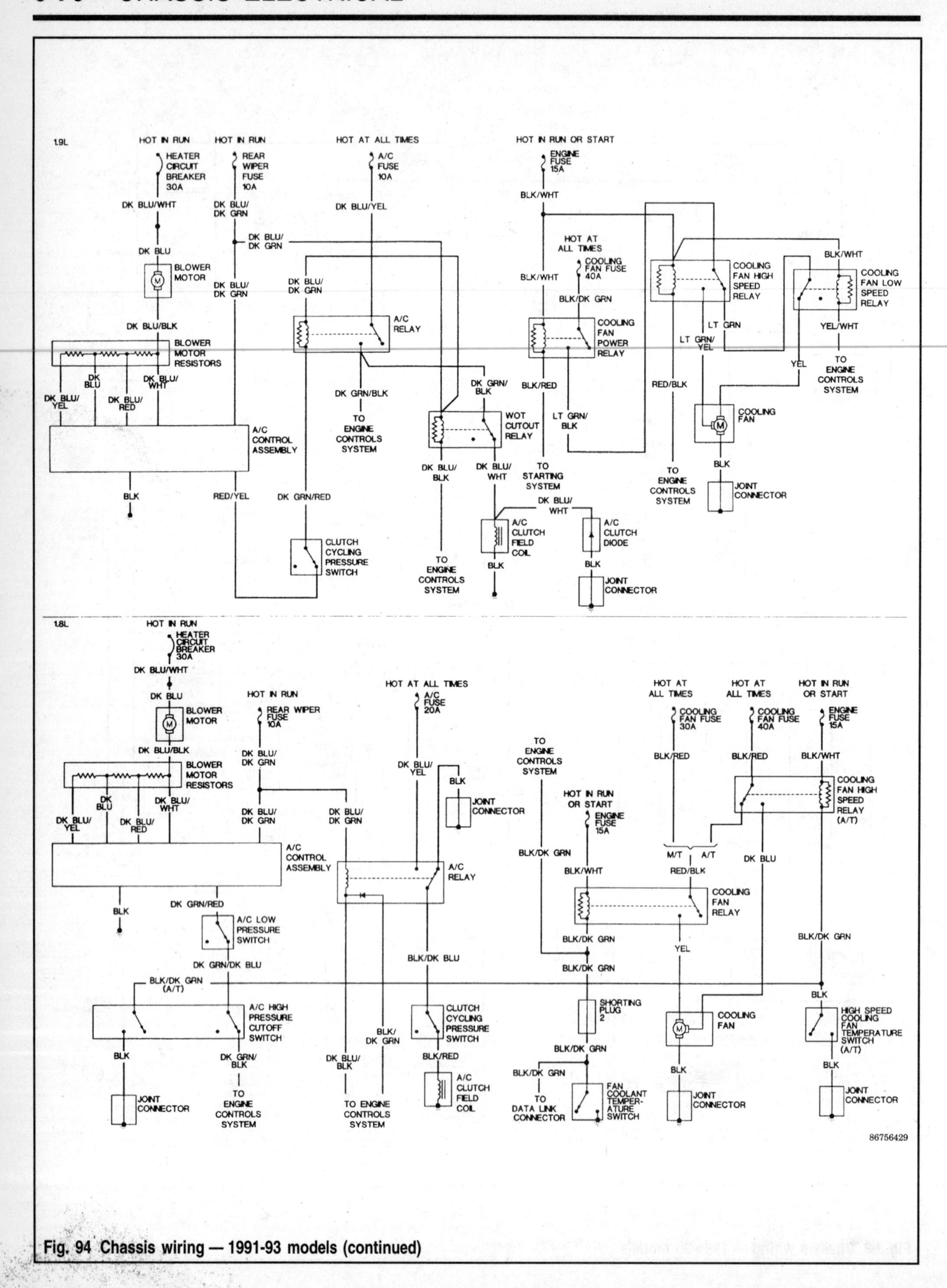

Fig. 94 Chassis wiring — 1991-93 models (continued)

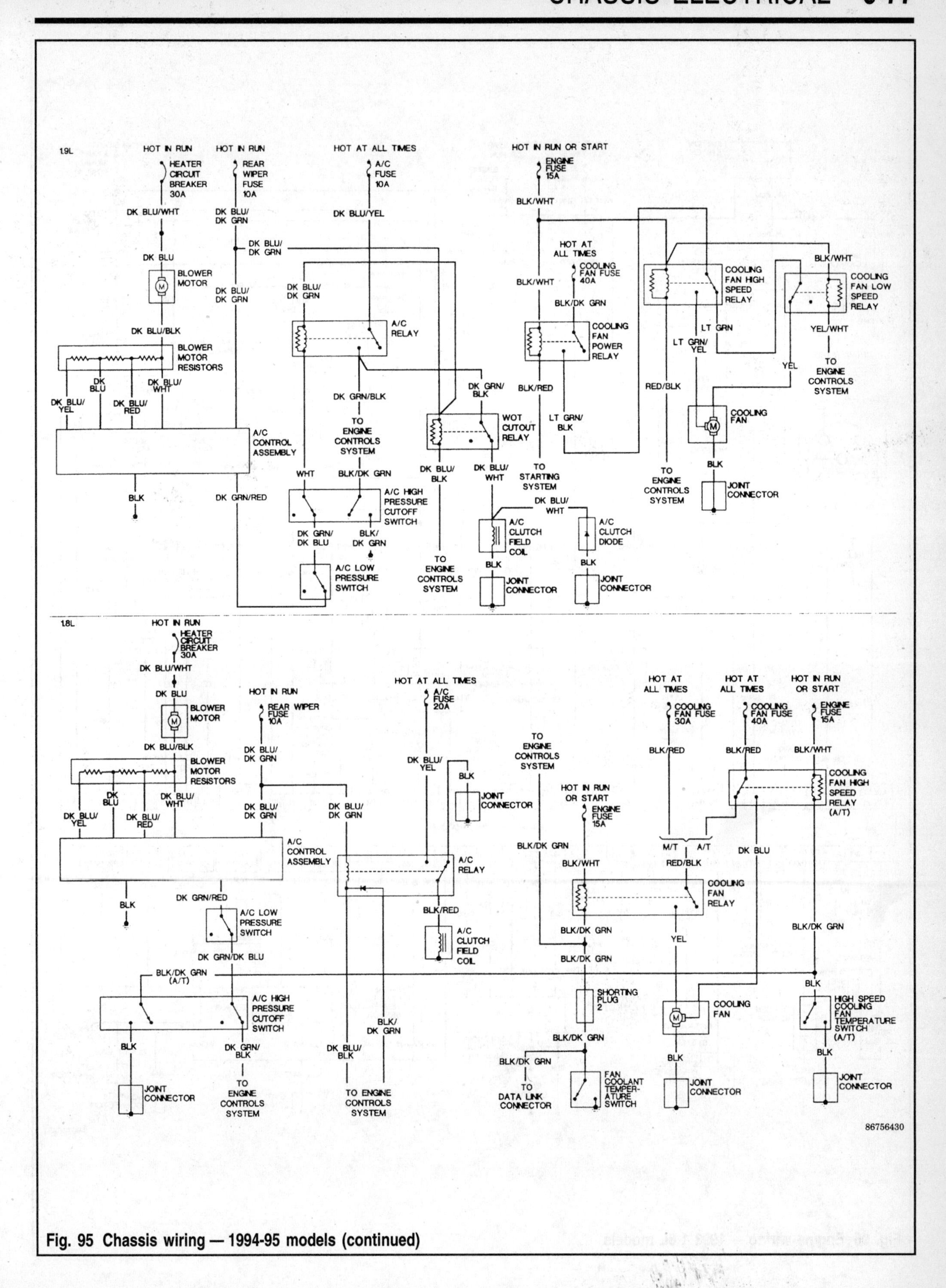

Fig. 95 Chassis wiring — 1994-95 models (continued)

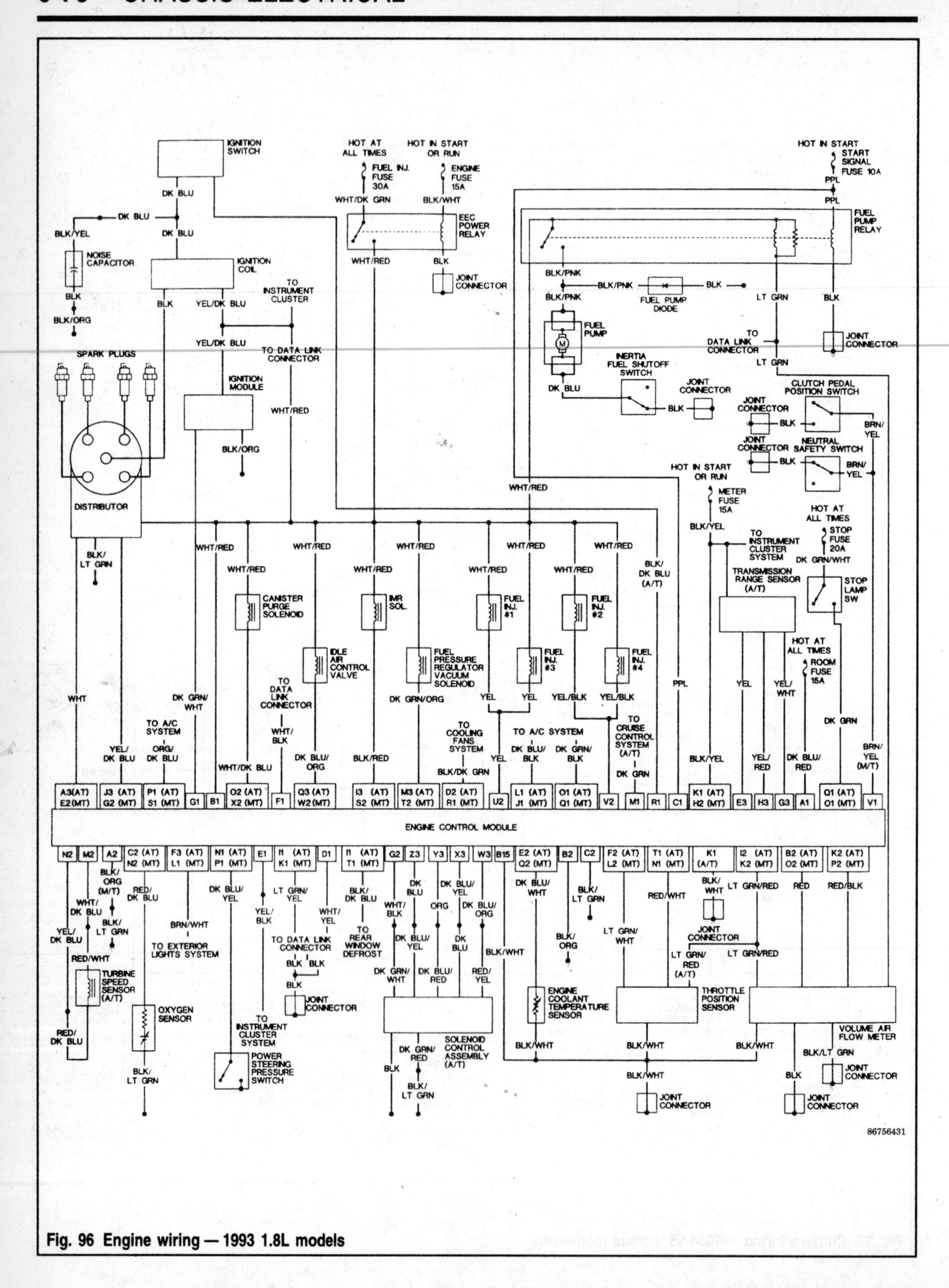

Fig. 96 Engine wiring — 1993 1.8L models

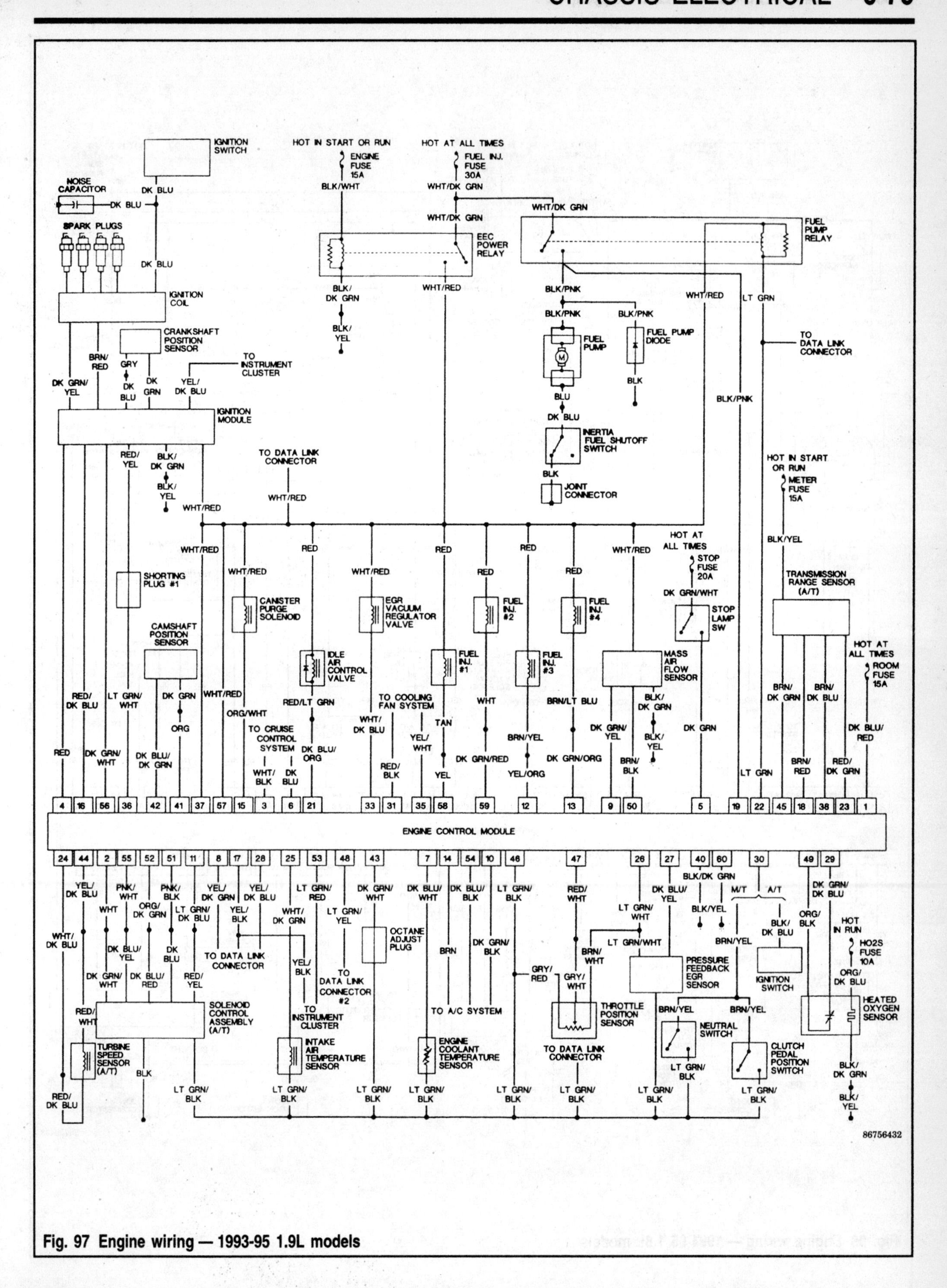

Fig. 97 Engine wiring — 1993-95 1.9L models

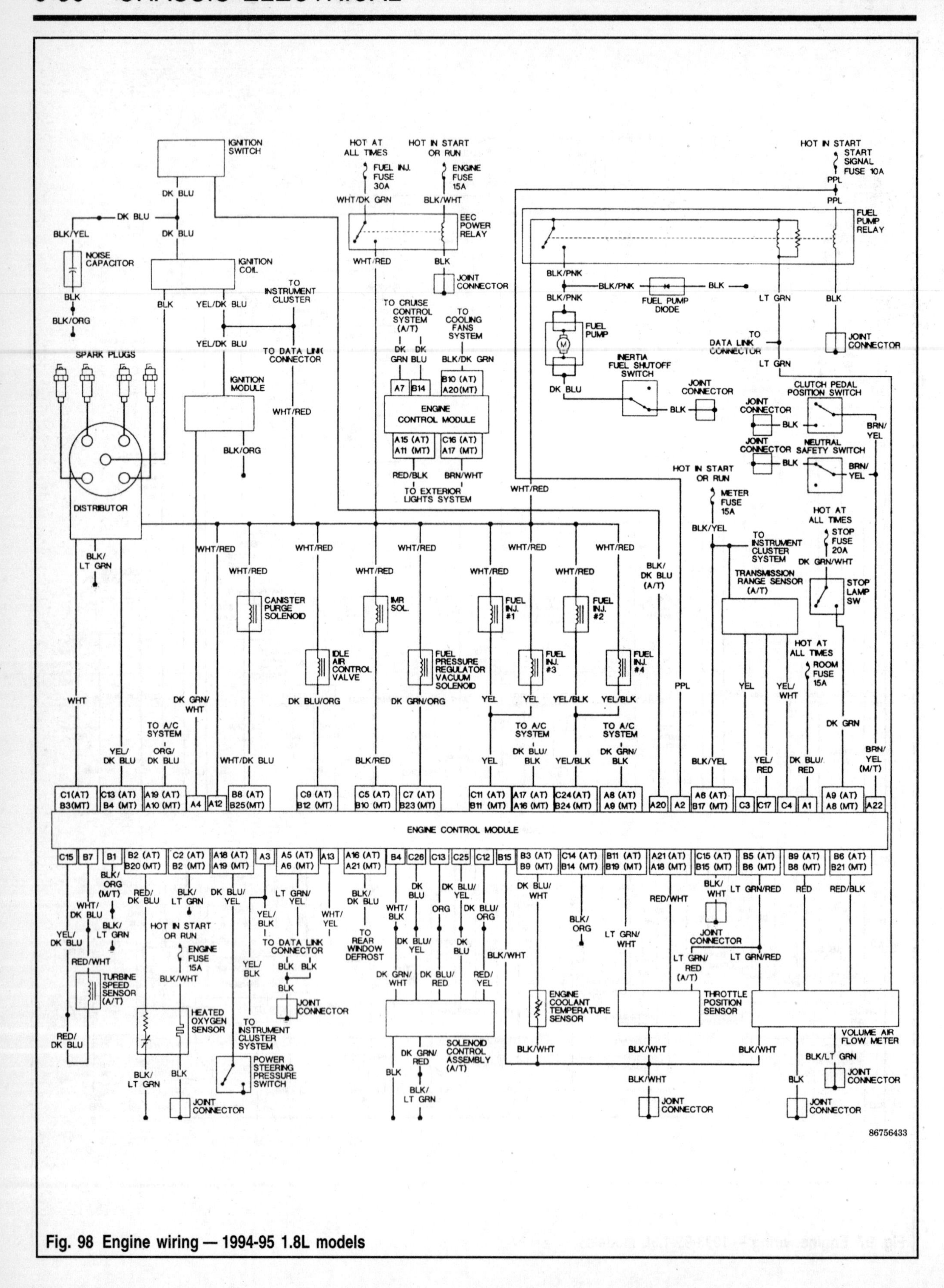

Fig. 98 Engine wiring — 1994-95 1.8L models

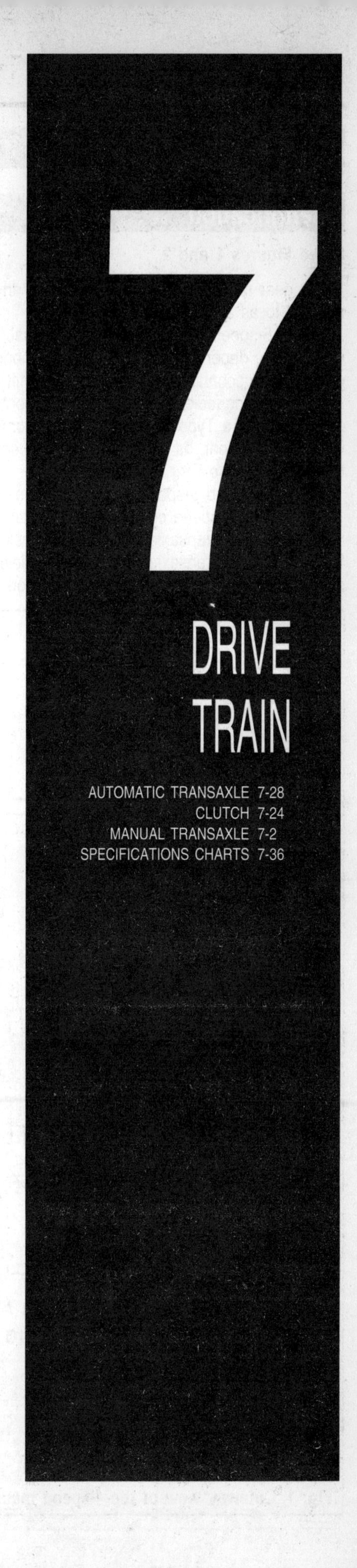

7 DRIVE TRAIN

MANUAL TRANSAXLE

Identification

➧ **See Figures 1 and 2**

The gear ratio unit used on front wheel drive vehicles, is referred to as a transaxle.

A 4 or 5-speed fully synchronized Manual Transaxle (MTX) is available, depending on the year and model. An internally gated shift mechanism and a single rail shift linkage eliminate the need for periodic shift linkage adjustments. The MTX is designed to use Type F or Dexron®II automatic transmission fluid, or equivalent, as a lubricant. Never use gear oil (GL) in the place of Type F or Dexron®II.

The MTX 4 and 5-speed transaxles have been used since 1981 with the 5-speed coming out in the later years. The 4-speed manual transaxle is similar in construction to the 5-speed manual transaxle except for the deletion of a 5th gear driveshaft assembly and a 5th gear shift fork assembly. Although similar in appearance, the gear set of the 4-speed transaxle cannot interchange with those of the 5-speed transaxle.

Power Flow

4-SPEED TRANSAXLE

From the clutch, engine torque is transferred to the mainshaft through the input cluster gear. Each gear on the input cluster is in constant mesh with a matching gear on the mainshaft. It is these matching gear sets which provide the four forward gear ratios. The transaxle gear ratio is determined by the number of teeth on the input cluster gear and the number of teeth on the mainshaft gear.

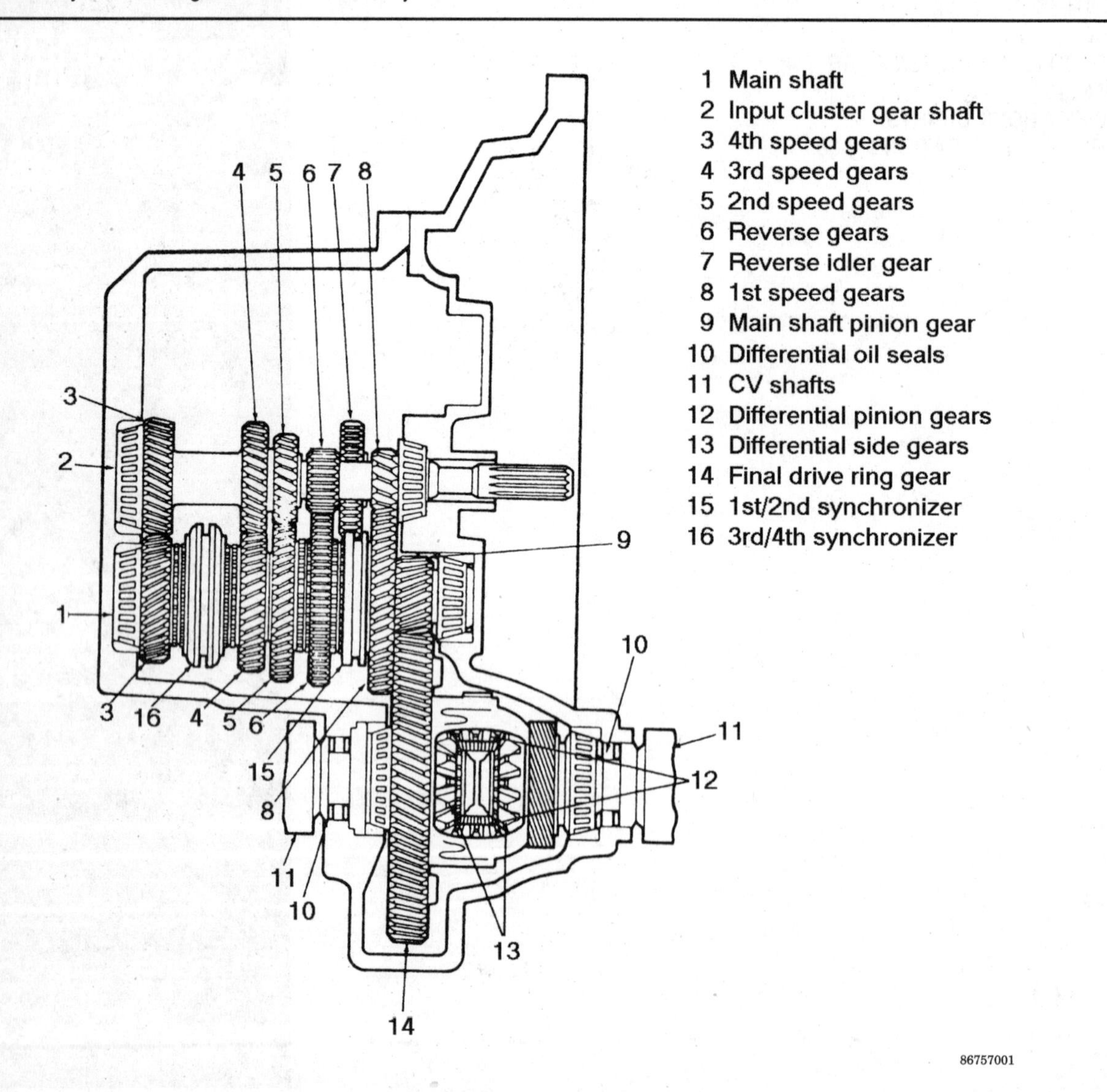

Fig. 1 Cutaway view of the 4-speed manual transaxle (MTX)

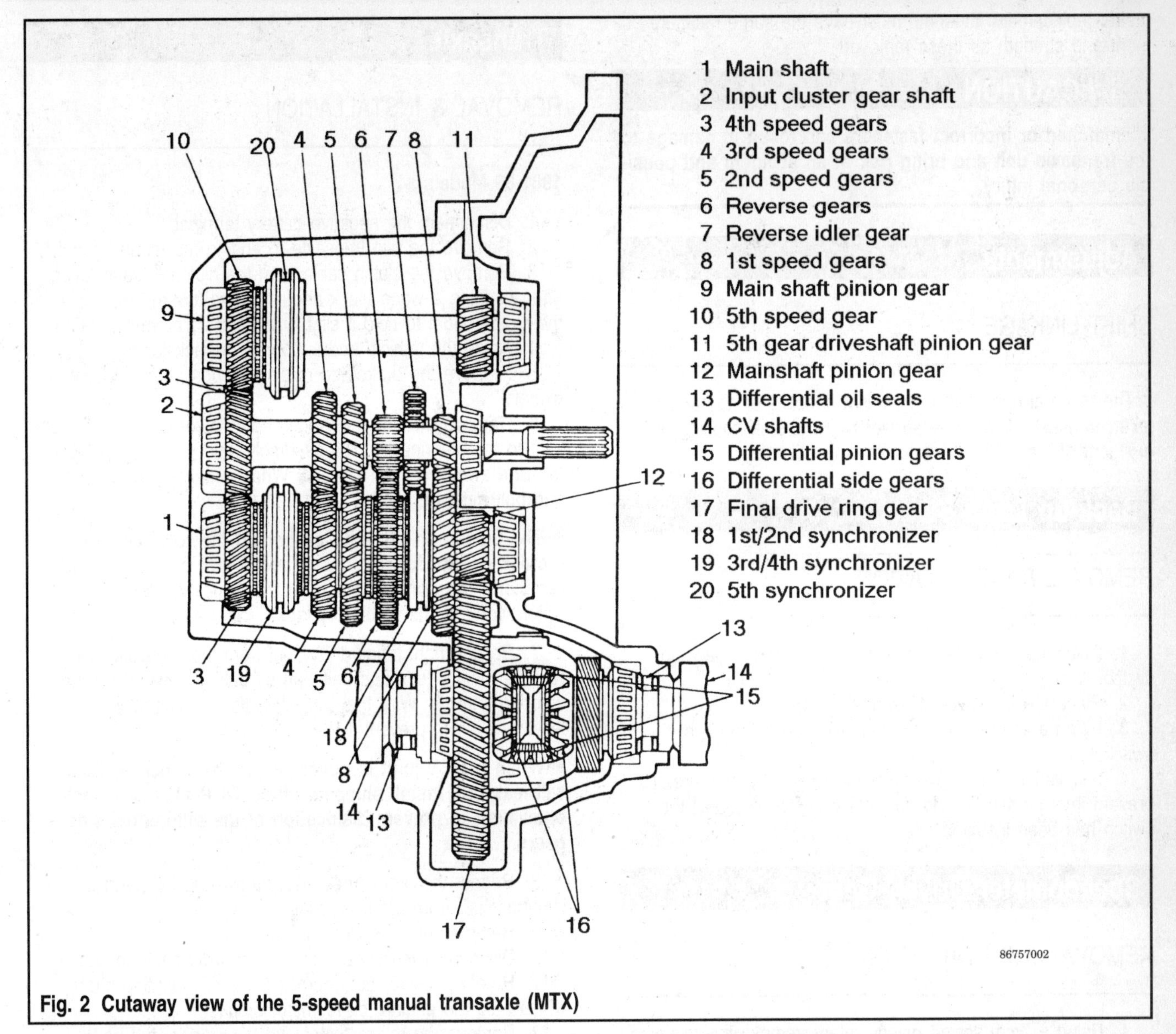

Fig. 2 Cutaway view of the 5-speed manual transaxle (MTX)

Reverse is accomplished by sliding a spur gear into mesh with the input cluster shaft gear and the reverse idler gear. The reverse idler gear, as its name implies, acts as an idler and serves to reverse the direction of mainshaft rotation. In neutral, none of the gears on the mainshaft are locked to their shafts. Then, no torque from the engine to the input cluster gear shaft is transferred to the differential assembly and to the wheels through the halfshafts.

5-SPEED TRANSAXLE

Engine torque is transferred from the clutch to the input cluster gear shaft. The four forward gears on the input cluster gear shaft are in constant mesh with a matching gear on the mainshaft. The 4th gear on the input cluster gear shaft is simultaneously meshed with the 5th speed gear on the 5th gear shaft. These meshed gearsets provide the five available forward gear ratios.

Both the mainshaft and the 5th gear shaft have a pinion gear, which is constantly engaged with the final drive ring gear of the differential assembly. If a single gear (1st through 4th) on the mainshaft is selected and that gear is locked to the shaft by its shift synchronizer, then the input cluster shaft gear will drive the mainshaft pinion gear; driving the differential final drive ring gear. If the 5th gear is selected, the input cluster shaft 4th gear will drive the 5th gear shaft pinion gear, driving the differential final drive ring gear. At this time, the mainshaft gears will rotate freely.

Reverse is accomplished by sliding a spur gear into mesh with the input cluster shaft gear and the reverse idler gear. The reverse idler gear acts as an idler and reverses the direction of mainshaft rotation.

Fasteners

Metric fasteners are used throughout the transaxles covered by this manual. They may appear very similar to the familiar inch system fasteners, but they are different and under no circumstances may the two types ever be interchanged. The metric replacement fasteners must have the same measurement and strength as those removed.

CAUTION

Mismatched or incorrect fasteners can result in damage to the transaxle unit and bring risk of an accident and possible personal injury.

Adjustments

SHIFT LINKAGE

The external gear shift mechanism consists of a gear shift lever, transaxle shift rod, stabilizer rod and shift housing. Adjustment of the external linkage is not necessary.

Back-up Light Switch

REMOVAL & INSTALLATION

1. Disconnect the electrical connector from the back-up switch.
2. Place the transaxle in reverse.
3. Using a suitable wrench, remove the back-up light switch.
4. Installation is the reverse of the removal procedure. To prevent internal damage do not shift the transaxle until the switch has been installed.

Speedometer Driven Gear

REMOVAL & INSTALLATION

1. Using a 7mm socket or equivalent, remove the retaining screw from the speedometer driven gear retainer assembly.
2. Using a prytool, carefully pry on the speedometer retainer to remove both the speedometer gear and retainer assembly from the clutch housing case bore. Be careful not to make contact with teeth on the speedometer gear.

To install:

3. Lightly grease the O-ring seal on the speedometer driven gear retainer.
4. Align the relief in the retainer with the attaching screw bore and using a tool, tap the assembly into its bore.
5. Tighten the retaining screw to 12-24 inch lbs. (1.35-2.8 Nm).

Transaxle

REMOVAL & INSTALLATION

1981-85 Models

1. Disconnect the negative battery terminal.
2. Remove the two transaxle to engine top mounting bolts.
3. Remove the clutch cable from the clutch release lever, after wedging a wood block about 7 in. (178mm) long under the clutch pedal to hold it slightly beyond its normal position.
4. Raise the vehicle and support it on jackstands.
5. Remove the brake line routing clamps from the front wheels.
6. Remove the bolt that secures the lower control arm ball joint to the steering knuckle assembly, and pry the lower control arm away from the knuckle. When installing, a new nut and bolt must be used.

➡The plastic shield installed behind the rotor contains a molded pocket for the lower control arm ball joint. When removing the control arm from the knuckle, bend the shield toward the rotor to provide clearance.

7. Pry the right inboard CV-joint from the transaxle, then remove the CV-joint and halfshaft by pulling outward on the steering knuckle. Wire the CV-joint/halfshaft assembly in a level position to prevent it from expanding.

➡When the CV-joint is pulled out of the transaxle fluid will leak out. Install shipping plugs T81P-1177-B or their equivalent to prevent dislocation of the differential side gears.

8. Repeat the procedures and remove the left-hand CV-joint/halfshaft from the transaxle.
9. Remove the stabilizer bar.
10. Disconnect the speedometer cable and back-up light.
11. Remove the (3) nuts from the starter mounting studs which hold the engine roll restrictor bracket.
12. Remove the roll restrictor and the starter stud bolts.
13. Remove the stiffener brace.
14. Remove the shift mechanism crossover spring.
15. Remove the shift mechanism stabilizer bar.
16. Remove the shift mechanism.
17. Place a transaxle jack under the transaxle.
18. Remove the rear transaxle mounts.
19. Remove the front transaxle mounts.
20. Lower the transaxle support jack until it clears the rear mount and support the engine with a jack, under the oil pan.
21. Remove the four remaining engine to transaxle bolts.

CAUTION

The transaxle case may have sharp edges. Wear protective gloves when handling the transaxle.

22. Remove the transaxle assembly.

To install:

23. Install the transaxle and leave it on the transaxle jack.
24. Install the four engine to transaxle bolts.
25. Install the front transaxle mounts.

TRANSAXLE

CONDITION	POSSIBLE SOURCE	ACTION
• Clicking Noise in Reverse Gear	• Damaged or rough gears.	• Replace damaged gears.
	• Damaged linkage preventing complete gear travel.	• Check for damaged or misaligned shift linkage or other causes of shift linkage travel restrictions.
• Gear Clash into Reverse	• Owner not familiar with manual transmission shift techniques.	• Instruct customer to refer to Owner's Guide on proper shifting and the time-lapse required before a shift into reverse.
	• Damaged linkage preventing complete gear travel.	• Check for damaged or misaligned shift linkage or other causes of shift linkage bind.
• Gears Clash When Shifting From One Forward Gear to Another	• Improper clutch disengagement.	
	• Clutch disc installed improperly with damper springs toward flywheel.	
	• Worn or damaged shift forks, synchro-teeth (usually high mileage phenomenon).	• Check for damage, and service or replace as required.
• Leaks	• Excessive amount of lubrication transaxle — wrong type.	• Check lube level and type. Fill to bottom of filler plug opening.
	• Other components leaking.	• Identify leaking fluid at engine, power steering, or transaxle.
	• False report. (Do not assume that lube on lower case surfaces is from gasket material leakage or seals).	• Remove all traces of lube on exposed transaxle surfaces. Operate transaxle and inspect for new leakage.
	• Worn or damaged internal components.	• Remove transaxle clutch housing lower dust cover and inspect for lube inside housing. Inspect for leaks at the shift lever shaft seal, differential seals and input shift shaft seal. Service as required.
	• Slight mist from vent.	• Normal condition that does not require service. If dripping, check lubricant level.
• Locked in One Gear — it cannot be shifted out of that gear	• Damaged external shift mechanism.	• Check external shift mechanism for damage. Service or replace as required.
	• Internal shift components worn or damaged.	• Disconnect external shift mechanism and verify problem by trying to shift input shift rail. Remove transaxle. Inspect the problem gear, shift rails, and fork and synchronizer assemblies for wear or damage, service or replace as required.
	• Synchronizer damaged by burrs which prevent sliding action.	• Replace synchronizer assembly.
• Noise in Neutral	• Neutral rollover rattle.	

86757003

Fig. 3 Manual transaxle diagnostic chart

TRANSAXLE — Continued

CONDITION	POSSIBLE SOURCE	ACTION
• Noisy in forward gears	• Low lubricant level.	• Fill to bottom of filler plug opening with proper lubricant (ATF). Type F.
	• Contact between engine/transaxle and chassis.	• Check for contact or for broken engine motor mounts.
	• Transaxle to engine block bolts loose.	• Tighten to specification.
	• Worn or damaged input/output bearings. Worn or damaged gear teeth (usually high mileage phenomenon).	• Remove transaxle. Inspect bearings and gear teeth for wear or damage. Replace parts as required.
	• Gear rattle.	
• Shifts hard	• Improper clutch disengagement.	
	• External shift mechanism binding.	
	• Clutch disc installed improperly with damper springs toward flywheel.	
	• Internal damage to synchronizers or shift mechanism.	• Check for damage to internal components.
	• Incorrect lubricant.	• Verify that ATF type lube is present. Do not use gear lube or hypoid type lubricants.
	• Sticking blocker ring.	
• Walks out of gear	• Damaged linkage preventing complete travel into gear.	• Check for damaged shift mechanism.
	• Floor shift stiff or improperly installed boot.	• Verify jumpout with boot removed, replace boot if necessary.
	• Floor shift interference between shift handle and console.	• Adjust console to eliminate interference.
	• Broken/loose engine mounts.	• Check for broken or loose engine mounts and service as required.
	• Loose shift mechanism stabilizer bar.	• Check stabilizer bar attaching bolt and torque to specification.
	• Worn or damaged internal components.	• Check shift forks, shift rails and shift rail detent system for wear or damage, synchronizer sliding sleeve and gear clutching teeth for wear or damage. Repair or replace as required.
	• Bent top gear locknut switch actuator.	• With shift lever in fourth gear, check actuator position with shift rod. Actuator should be positioned at a 90 degree angle to shift rod. Bend actuator to proper position, if required.

86757004

Fig. 4 Manual transaxle diagnostic chart

TRANSAXLE — Continued

CONDITION	POSSIBLE SOURCE	ACTION
• Will not shift into one gear — all other gears OK	• Damaged external shift mechanism.	• Check for damaged shift mechanism. Service or replace as necessary.
	• Floor shift. Interference between shift handle and console or floor cut out.	• Adjust console or cut out floor pan to eliminate interference.
	• Restricted travel of internal shift components.	• Disconnect external shift mechanism and shift the input shift rail through the gears to verify problem. Remove transaxle. Inspect fork system, synchronizer system and gear clutch teeth for restricted travel. Service or replace as required.
• Will not shift into reverse	• Damaged external shift mechanism.	• Check for damaged external shift mechanism. Remove shift mechanism at input shift rail and try shifting into reverse at the rail.
	• Worn or damaged internal components.	• Remove transaxle. Check for damaged reverse gear train, misaligned reverse relay lever, shift rail and fork system. Check the gear clutching teeth and synchronizer system for restricted travel or damage. Service or replace as required.
	• Normal blockout due to position of non-synchronized reverse gear components. **NOTE:** This condition may occur approximately 10 percent of the time.	• Condition is considered normal and requires "double-clutching" to engage into reverse.

86757005

Fig. 5 Manual transaxle diagnostic chart

26. Install the rear transaxle mounts.
27. Remove the transaxle jack from under the transaxle.
28. Install the shift mechanism.
29. Install the shift mechanism stabilizer bar.
30. Install the shift mechanism crossover spring.
31. Install the stiffener brace.
32. Install the roll restrictor and the starter stud bolts.
33. Install the (3) nuts to the starter mounting studs which hold the engine roll restrictor bracket.
34. Reconnect the speedometer cable and back-up light.
35. Install the stabilizer bar.
36. Install the left and right CV-joint/halfshafts to the transaxle.

➡When installing the CV-joint/halfshaft assemblies into the transaxle, install new circlips on the inner stub shaft, carefully install the assemblies into the transaxle to prevent damaging the oil seals, and insure that both joints are fully seated in the transaxle by lightly prying outward to confirm they are seated. If the circlips are not seated, the joints will move out of the transaxle.

37. Install the bolt that secures the lower control arm ball joint to the steering knuckle assembly. When installing, a new nut and bolt must be used.
38. Remove the brake line routing clamps from the front wheels.
39. Adjust the clutch. Lower the vehicle and remove the jackstands.
40. Install the two transaxle to engine top mounting bolts.
41. Reconnect the negative battery terminal.

1985½-90 Models

1. Disconnect the negative battery cable. Wedge a 7 in. (18cm) wooden block under the clutch pedal to hold the pedal up slightly beyond its normal position. Grasp the clutch cable, pull it forward and disconnect it from the clutch release shaft assembly. Remove the clutch casing from the rib on the top surface of the transaxle case.
2. Remove the upper two transaxle-to-engine bolts. Remove the air management valve bracket-to-transaxle upper bolt.
3. Raise and safely support the vehicle.

SHIFT LINKAGE

CONDITION	POSSIBLE SOURCE	ACTION
• Binding, sticking shift feel — difficult to find or engage gears, high shift efforts	• Worn, broken, missing bushings in shift rod U-joint.	• Replace shift rod.
	• Bent shift rod, U-joint or multi-piece bracket.	• Replace shift rod.
	• Bent or broken stabilizer.	• Replace support assembly.
	• Worn, missing stabilizer bushing.	• Replace stabilizer bushing.
	• Bolts holding control assembly to body J-nuts missing or loose.	• Tighten or replace bolts.
	• Bolt holding stabilizer bar to transaxle case missing or loose.	• Tighten or replace bolt.
	• Body J-nuts missing or broken.	• Replace J-nuts on seat track bracket.
	• Bolt, nut, and clamp washers loose at shift rod to transaxle connection.	• Tighten or replace bolt, nut and clamp washers.
	• Plastic control housing cracked or broken.	• Replace plastic control housing.
	• Plastic pivot housing on shift lever broken, cracked.	• Replace shift lever.
	• Shift lever pivot balls worn or loose.	• Replace shift lever.
	• Mounting insulators torn.	• Replace support assembly.
	• Shift lever loose on support assembly.	• Tighten or replace self-tapping screws.
	• Shift lever pivot balls worn, loose, or broken.	• Replace shift lever assembly.
	• Shift rod sealing boot torn.	• Replace shift rod assembly.
• Excessive noise, rattles, buzz or tizz	• Worn, broken, missing bushings in shift rod U-joint.	• Replace shift rod assembly.
	• Worn pivot balls on shift lever.	• Replace shift lever assembly.
	• Loose bolt, nut and clamp washers at shift rod to transaxle connection.	• Tighten or replace bolt, nut, and clamp washers.
	• Loose shift lever assembly.	• Tighten or replace self-tapping screws.
	• Loose control housing.	• Tighten self-tapping screws attaching housing to support assembly.
	• Loose control assembly.	• Tighten or replace bolts holding control assembly to body J-nuts.
	• Loose shift knob causes tizz.	• Drive knob further onto shift lever with rubber mallet. If still loose, replace boot/knob assembly.

86757006

Fig. 6 Manual transaxle shift linkage diagnostic chart

SHIFT LINKAGE — Continued

CONDITION	POSSIBLE SOURCE	ACTION
• Excessive Noise, Rattles, Buzz or Tizz (Continued)	• Mounting insulators torn.	• Replace support assembly.
	• Inner shift boot torn, split.	• Replace inner sealing boot.
	• Stabilizer bar bushing worn or split.	• Replace stabilizer bushing.
	• Pivot balls on shift lever chipped, cracked.	• Replace shift lever assembly.
	• Crimp on shift lever improperly placed allows loose pivot ball in pivot housing.	• Replace shift lever.
• Shifter is Inoperative — cannot shift gears	• Bolt, nut and clamp washers loose at shift rod to transaxle connection.	• Tighten or replace bolt, nut and clamp washers.
	• Shifter attachment to body weld bolts loose.	• Replace or tighten bolts on body J-nuts.
	• Shift lever loose on stabilizer mounting bracket.	• Replace or tighten self-tapping bolts.
	• Shift rod broken or bent.	• Replace shift rod.
	• Stabilizer bar is bent.	• Replace support assembly.
	• Mounting insulators torn or loose.	• Replace support assembly.
	• Crimp holding pivot ball tight in pivot housing inadequate.	• Replace shift lever assembly.
• Shift Lever Feels Sloppy or Loose	• Nuts holding control assemby to body weld bolts missing or loose.	• Tighten or replace nuts.
	• Body J-nuts missing or broken.	• Replace J-nuts on seat track bracket.
	• Worn, broken or missing anti-tizz bushing.	• Replace anti-tizz bushing in shift rod assembly.
	• Bolt holding stabilizer bar to transaxle case missing or loose.	• Tighten or replace bolt.
	• Bolt, nut and clamp washers loose at shift rod to transaxle connection.	• Tighten or replace bolt, nut and clamp washers.
	• Stabilizer bar broken.	• Replace mounting bracket and stabilizer assembly.
	• Plastic control housing cracked or broken.	• Replace plastic control housing.
	• Mounting insulators torn or improperly riveted.	• Replace mounting bracket and stabilizer assembly.
	• Shift lever attaching screw loose or missing.	• Tighten or replace shift lever attaching screws.
	• Shift lever pivot balls worn or loose.	• Replace shift lever assembly.
	• Shift knob is loose on shift lever.	• Drive knob further onto shift lever with rubber mallet. If still loose, replace boot/knob assembly.

86757007

Fig. 7 Manual transaxle shift linkage diagnostic chart (continued)

CONSIDER THE FOLLOWING FACTORS WHEN DIAGNOSING BEARING CONDITION:

1. GENERAL CONDITION OF ALL PARTS DURING DISASSEMBLY AND INSPECTION.
2. CLASSIFY THE PROBLEM WITH THE AID OF THE ILLUSTRATION.
3. DETERMINE THE CAUSE.
4. MAKE ALL SERVICES FOLLOWING RECOMMENDED PROCEDURES.

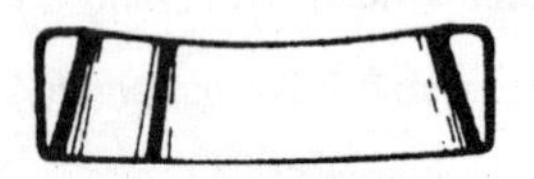

GOOD BEARING

BENT CAGE

CAGE DAMAGE DUE TO IMPROPER HANDLING OR TOOL USAGE.

REPLACE BEARING

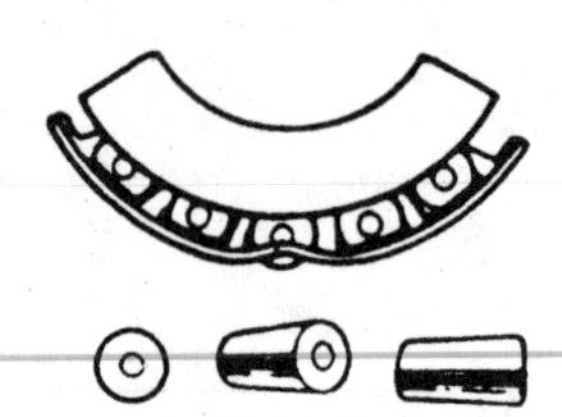

BENT CAGE

CAGE DAMAGE DUE TO IMPROPER HANDLING OR TOOL USAGE.

REPLACE BEARING.

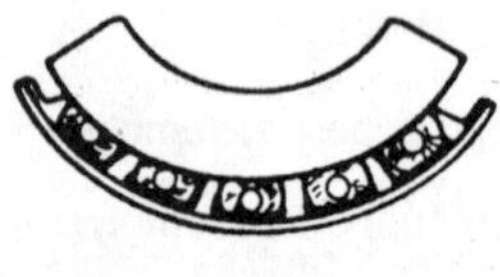

GALLING

METAL SMEARS ON ROLLER ENDS DUE TO OVERHEAT, LUBRICANT PROBLEM OR OVERLOAD.

REPLACE BEARING — CHECK SEALS AND CHECK FOR PROPER LUBRICATION.

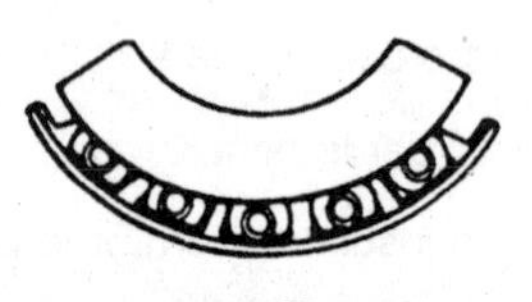

CRACKED INNER RACE

RACE CRACKED DUE TO IMPROPER FIT, COCKING, OR POOR BEARING SEATS.

ETCHING

BEARING SURFACES APPEAR GRAY OR GRAYISH BLACK IN COLOR WITH RELATED ETCHING AWAY OF MATERAIL USUALLY AT ROLLER SPACING.

REPLACE BEARINGS — CHECK SEALS AND CHECK FOR PROPER LUBRICATION.

BRINELLING

SURFACE INDENTATIONS IN RACEWAY CAUSED BY ROLLERS EITHER UNDER IMPACT LOADING OR VIBRATION WHILE THE BEARING IS NOT ROTATING.

REPLACE BEARING IF ROUGH OR NOISY.

HEAT DISCOLORATION

HEAT DISCOLORATION IS DARK BLUE RESULTING FROM OVERLOAD OR NO LUBRICANT (YELLOW OR BROWN COLOR IS NORMAL).

EXCESSIVE HEAT CAN CAUSE SOFTENING OF RACES OR ROLLERS.

TO CHECK FOR LOSS OF TEMPER ON RACES OR ROLLERS A SIMPLE FILE TEST MAY BE MADE. A FILE DRAWN OVER A TEMPERED PART WILL GRAB AND CUT METAL, WHEREAS, A FILE DRAWN OVER A HARD PART WILL GLIDE READILY WITH NO METAL CUTTING.

REPLACE BEARINGS IF OVER HEATING DAMAGE IS INDICATED. CHECK SEALS AND OTHER PARTS.

FATIGUE SPALLING

FLAKING OF SURFACE METAL RESULTING FROM FATIGUE.

REPLACE BEARING — CLEAN ALL RELATED PARTS.

86757008

Fig. 8 Manual transaxle bearing diagnostic chart

4. Remove the lower control arm ball joint-to-steering knuckle nut/bolt and discard the nut/bolt; repeat this procedure on the opposite side.

5. Using a large prybar, pry the lower control arm from the steering knuckle; repeat this procedure on the opposite side.

➡Be careful not to damage or cut the ball joint boot and do not contact the lower arm.

6. Using a large prybar, pry the left-side inboard CV-joint assembly from the transaxle.

➡Insert a shipping plug (tool number T81P-1177-B or equivalent) into the seal opening to prevent differential dislocation and lubricant leakage.

7. Grasp the left-hand steering knuckle and swing it and the halfshaft outward from the transaxle; this will disconnect the inboard CV-joint from the transaxle.

➡If the CV-joint assembly cannot be pried from the transaxle, insert a differential rotator tool through the left-side and tap the joint out; the tool can be used from either side of the transaxle.

8. Using a wire, support the halfshaft in a near level position to prevent damage to the assembly during the remaining operations; repeat this removal procedure on the opposite side.
9. Disengage the locking tabs and remove the back-up light switch connector from the transaxle back-up light switch.
10. Remove the starter bolts.
11. Remove the shift mechanism-to-shift shaft nut/bolt, the control selector indicator switch arm and the shift shaft.
12. Remove the shift mechanism stabilizer bar-to-transaxle bolt, control selector indicator switch and bracket assembly.
13. Using a crowfoot wrench, remove the speedometer cable from the transaxle.
14. Remove two stiffener brace retaining bolts.
15. Using a floor jack and a transaxle support, position it under the transaxle and secure the transaxle to it.
16. Remove both rear mount-to-floor pan bolts, loosen the nut at the bottom of the front mount and remove the front mount-to-transaxle bolts.
17. Lower the floor jack, until the transaxle clears the rear insulator. Support the engine by placing wood under the oil pan.
18. Remove the engine-to-transaxle bolts and lower the transaxle from the vehicle.

To install:

19. Raise the transaxle into position and engage the input shaft with the clutch plate. Install the lower engine-to-transaxle bolts and tighten to 28-31 ft. lbs. (38-42 Nm).

➡Never attempt to start the engine prior to installing the CV-joints or differential side gear dislocation and/or damage may occur.

20. Install the front mount-to-transaxle bolts and tighten to 25-35 ft. lbs. (34-47 Nm); also, tighten the nut on the bottom of the front transaxle mount.
21. Install the air management valve-to-transaxle upper bolt, finger-tight and the bottom bracket bolt to 28-31 ft. lbs. (38-42 Nm).
22. Install both rear mount-to-floor pan brace bolts to 40-51 ft. lbs. (55-70 Nm).
23. Remove the floor jack and adapter.
24. Using a crowfoot wrench, install the speedometer cable; be careful not to cross-thread the cable nut.
25. Install the two stiffener brace bolts and tighten to 15-21 ft. lbs. (21-28 Nm).
26. Install the shifter stabilizer bar/control selector indicator switch-to-transaxle bolt and tighten to 23-35 ft. lbs. (31-47 Nm).
27. Install the shift mechanism-to-shift shaft, the switch actuator bracket clamp and tighten the bolt to 7-10 ft. lbs. (9-13 Nm); be sure to shift the transaxle into 4th for 4-speed or 5th for 5-speed and align the actuator.
28. Install the starter bolts and tighten to 30-40 ft. lbs. (41-54 Nm).
29. Install the back-up light switch connector to the transaxle switch.
30. Install the new circlip onto both inner joints of the halfshafts, then insert the inner CV-joints into the transaxle and fully seat them; lightly pry outward to confirm that the retaining rings are seated.

➡When installing the halfshafts, be careful not to tear the oil seals.

31. Connect the lower ball joint to the steering knuckle, insert a new pinch bolt and tighten the new nut to 37-44 ft. lbs. (50-60 Nm); be careful not to damage the boot.
32. Refill the transaxle and lower the vehicle.
33. Install the upper air management valve bracket-to-transaxle bolt and tighten to 28-31 ft. lbs. (38-42 Nm).
34. Install the both upper transaxle-to-engine bolts and tighten to 28-31 ft. lbs. (38-42 Nm).
35. Connect the clutch cable to the clutch release shaft assembly and remove the wooden block from under the clutch pedal. Connect the negative battery cable.

➡Prior to starting the engine, set the hand brake and depress the clutch pedal several times to ensure proper clutch adjustment.

1991-95 Models

1. Disconnect the battery cables, then remove the battery and battery tray.
2. Remove the air hose and the resonance chamber.
3. Disconnect the speedometer cable at the transaxle.
4. Remove the retaining clip, then disconnect the slave cylinder line from the slave cylinder hose and plug the hose.
5. Disconnect the ground strap from the transaxle.
6. Remove the tie wrap and disconnect the three electrical connectors located above the transaxle. Remove the electrical connector support bracket.
7. Mount engine support bar D88L-6000-A or equivalent, and attach it to the engine hangers.
8. Remove the three nuts from the upper transaxle mount. Loosen the mount pivot nut and rotate the mount out of position. Remove the three bolts and the upper transaxle mount bracket.
9. Remove the two upper transaxle-to-engine bolts.
10. Raise and safely support the vehicle.
11. Remove the front wheel and tire assemblies.
12. Remove the inner fender splash shields.
13. Drain the transaxle fluid and install the drain plug.

14. Remove the halfshafts. Install two transaxle plugs between the differential side gears.

⁂WARNING

Failure to install the transaxle plugs may cause the differential side gears to become improperly positioned.

15. Remove the plenum support bracket and remove the starter.
16. Remove the nut and the extension bar and the bolt and nut and shift control rod from the transaxle.
17. Remove both lower splash shields.
18. Remove the two transaxle mount-to-crossmember nuts and remove the lower crossmember and the front transaxle mount.
19. Position and secure a suitable jack under the transaxle.
20. Remove the five lower engine-to-transaxle bolts and lower the transaxle out of the vehicle.

To install:

21. Apply a thin coating of synthetic grease to the spline of the input shaft.
22. Place the transaxle onto a suitable jack. Make sure the transaxle is secure.
23. Raise the transaxle into position on the engine.
24. Install the five lower engine-to-transaxle bolts and tighten to 27-38 ft. lbs. (37-52 Nm).
25. Install the front transaxle mount and tubing bracket. Tighten the bolts to 12-17 ft. lbs. (16-23 Nm).
26. Install the lower crossmember. Tighten the nuts and bolts to 47-66 ft. lbs. (64-89 Nm).
27. Install the two transaxle mount-to-crossmember nuts and tighten to 27-38 ft. lbs. (37-52 Nm).
28. Install both lower splash shields.
29. Install the shift control rod bolt and nut and tighten to 23-34 ft. lbs. (31-46 Nm).
30. Install the extension bar nut and tighten to 12-17 ft. lbs. (16-23 Nm).
31. Install the starter and the plenum support bracket.
32. Remove the transaxle plugs and install the halfshafts.
33. Install the inner fender splash shields.
34. Install the wheel and tire assemblies. Tighten the lug nuts to 65-87 ft. lbs. (88-118 Nm).
35. Lower the vehicle.
36. Install the two upper engine-to-transaxle bolts and tighten to 47-66 ft. lbs. (64-89 Nm).
37. Install the upper transaxle mount bracket and tighten the three bolts. Rotate the mount into position and tighten the pivot nut. Install and tighten the three upper mount nuts.
38. Remove the engine support bar.
39. Install the electrical connector support bracket. Connect the three electrical connectors and secure with the tie wrap.
40. Connect the ground strap to the transaxle.
41. Connect the slave cylinder line to the slave cylinder hose and install the retaining clip.
42. Add the proper type and amount of fluid to the transaxle.
43. Connect the speedometer cable.
44. Install the air hose and the resonance chamber.
45. Install the battery tray and the battery. Connect the battery cables.
46. Check for fluid leaks and proper operation.

Halfshafts

➧ See Figures 9 and 10

The front wheel drive halfshafts are a one-piece design. Constant velocity joint (CV) are used at each end. The left-hand (driver's side) halfshaft is solid steel and is shorter than the right side halfshaft. The right-hand (passenger's side) halfshaft is depending on year and model, constructed of tubular steel or solid construction. The automatic and manual transaxles use similar halfshafts.

The halfshafts can be replaced individually. The CV-joint or boots can be cleaned or replaced. Individual parts of the CV-joints are not available. The inboard and outboard joints differ in size. CV-joint parts are fitted and should never be mixed or substituted with a part from another joint.

Inspect the boots periodically for cuts or splits. If a cut or split is found, inspect the joint, repack it with grease and install a new boot.

REMOVAL & INSTALLATION

1981-90 Models

➧ See Figures 11, 12, 13, 14, 15, 16 and 17

Special tools are required for removing, installing and servicing halfshafts. They are listed by their descriptive names, with the Ford part numbers in parentheses: Front Hub Installer Adapter (T81P-1104-A), Wheel Bolt Adapters (T81P-1104-B or T83P-1104-BH), CV-Joint Separator (T81P-3514-A), Front Hub Installer/Remover (T81P-1104-C), Shipping Plug Tool (T81P-1177-B), Dust Deflector Installer (T83P-3425-AH), and Differential Rotator (T81P-4026-A).

It is necessary to have on hand new hub nuts and new lower control arm-to-steering knuckle attaching nuts and bolts. Once removed, these parts must not be reused, since their torque holding ability is destroyed during removal.

1. Loosen the front hub nut and the wheel lugs.
2. Raise and support the vehicle safely.
3. Remove the tire and wheel assembly. Remove and discard the front hub nut. Save the washers.

➡Halfshaft removal and installation are the same for manual and automatic transaxles, except that the right-hand halfshaft assembly must be removed first on automatic transaxle equipped models. The differential service tool (T81P-4026-A or equivalent) is then inserted to drive the left-hand halfshaft from the transaxle. If only the left-hand halfshaft is to be serviced, remove the right-hand halfshaft from the transaxle and support it with a length of wire. Drive the left-hand halfshaft assembly from the transaxle.

4. Remove the bolt that retains the brake hose to the strut.
5. Remove the nut and bolt securing the lower ball joint and separate the joint from the steering knuckle by inserting a

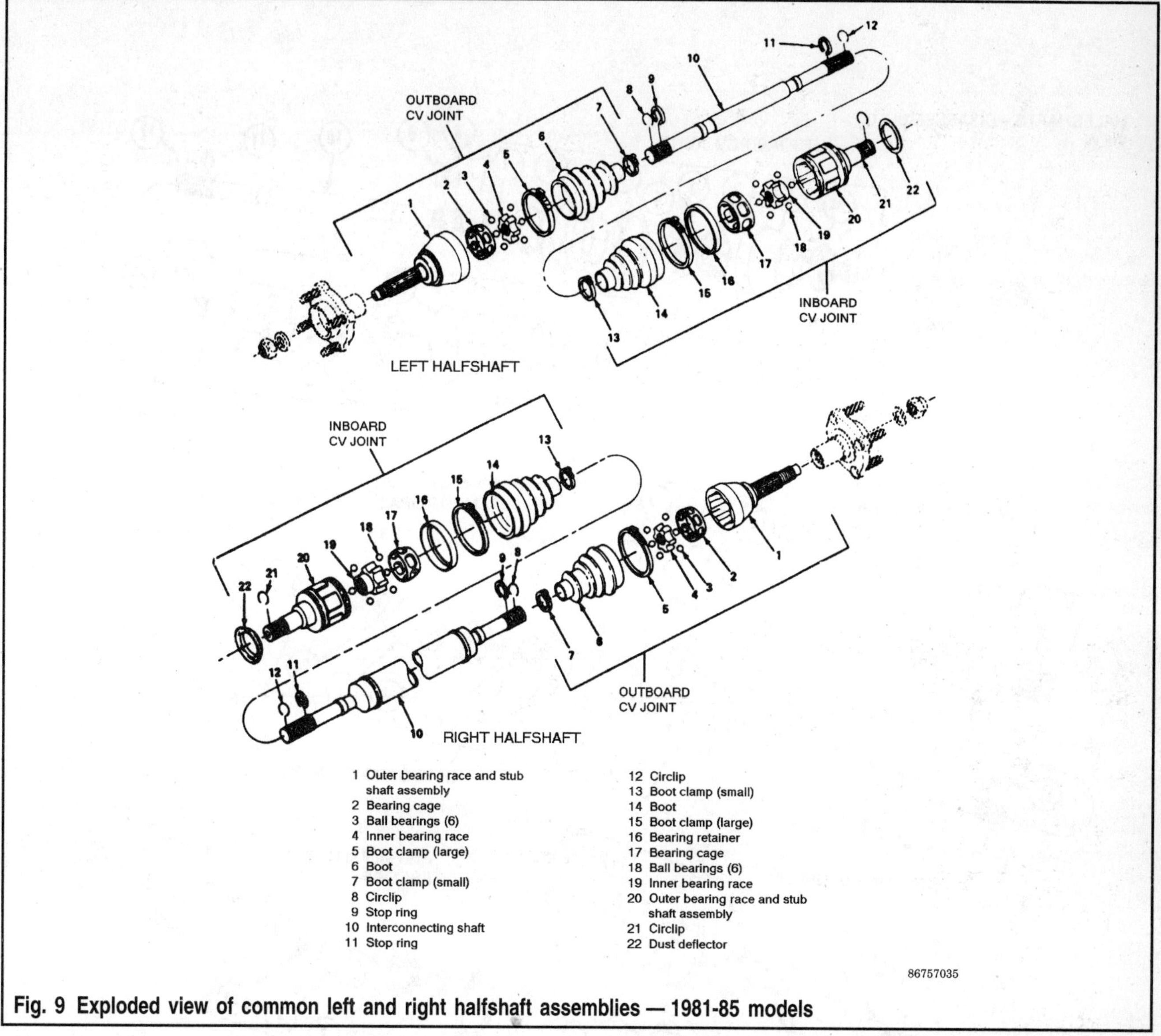

Fig. 9 Exploded view of common left and right halfshaft assemblies — 1981-85 models

prybar between the stabilizer and frame and pulling downward. Take care not to damage the ball joint boot.

➡On some models, the lower control arm ball joint fits into a pocket formed in a plastic disc rotor shield. The shield must be carefully bent back away from the ball joint while prying the ball joint out of the steering knuckle. Do not contact or pry on the lower control arm.

6. Remove the halfshaft from the differential housing using a prybar. Position the prybar between the case and the shaft and pry the joint away from the case. Do not damage the oil seal, the CV-joint boot or the dust deflector. Install a shipping plug (tool number T81P-1177-B or equivalent) to prevent fluid loss and differential side gear misalignment.

7. Support the end of the shaft with a piece of wire, suspending it from a chassis member.

8. Separate the shaft from the front hub using the special remover/installer tool and adapters.

✲✲WARNING

Never use a hammer to force the shaft from the wheel hub. Damage to the internal parts of the CV-joint may occur.

To install:

9. Install a new circlip on the inboard CV-joint stub shaft. Align the splines of the inboard CV-joint stub shaft with the splines in the differential. Push the CV-joint into the differential until the circlip seats on the side gear. Some force may be necessary to seat it.

10. Carefully align the splines of the outboard CV-joint stub shaft with the splines in the front wheel hub. Push the shaft into the hub as far as possible. Install the remover/installer tool and pull the CV-stub shaft through the hub.

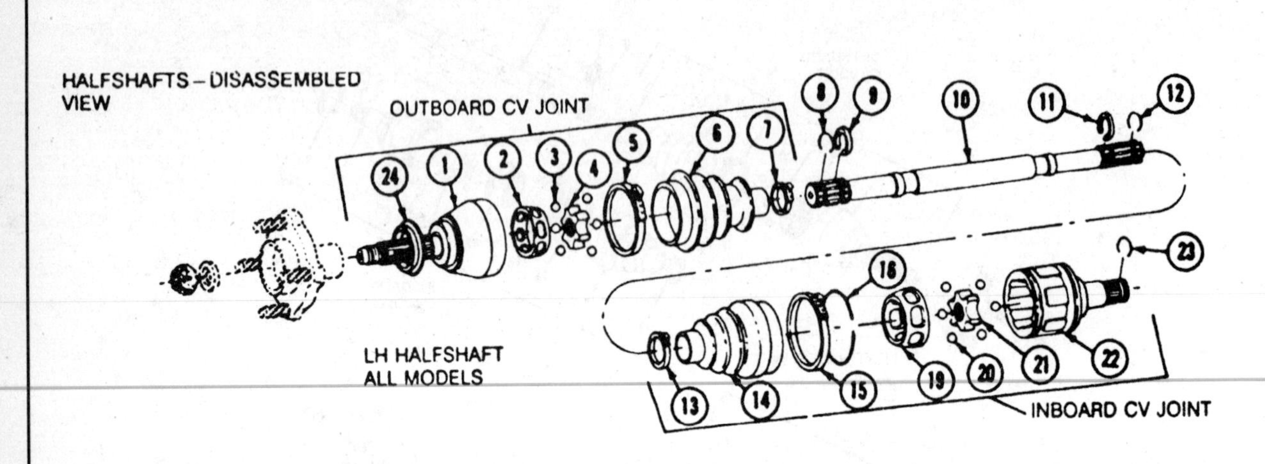

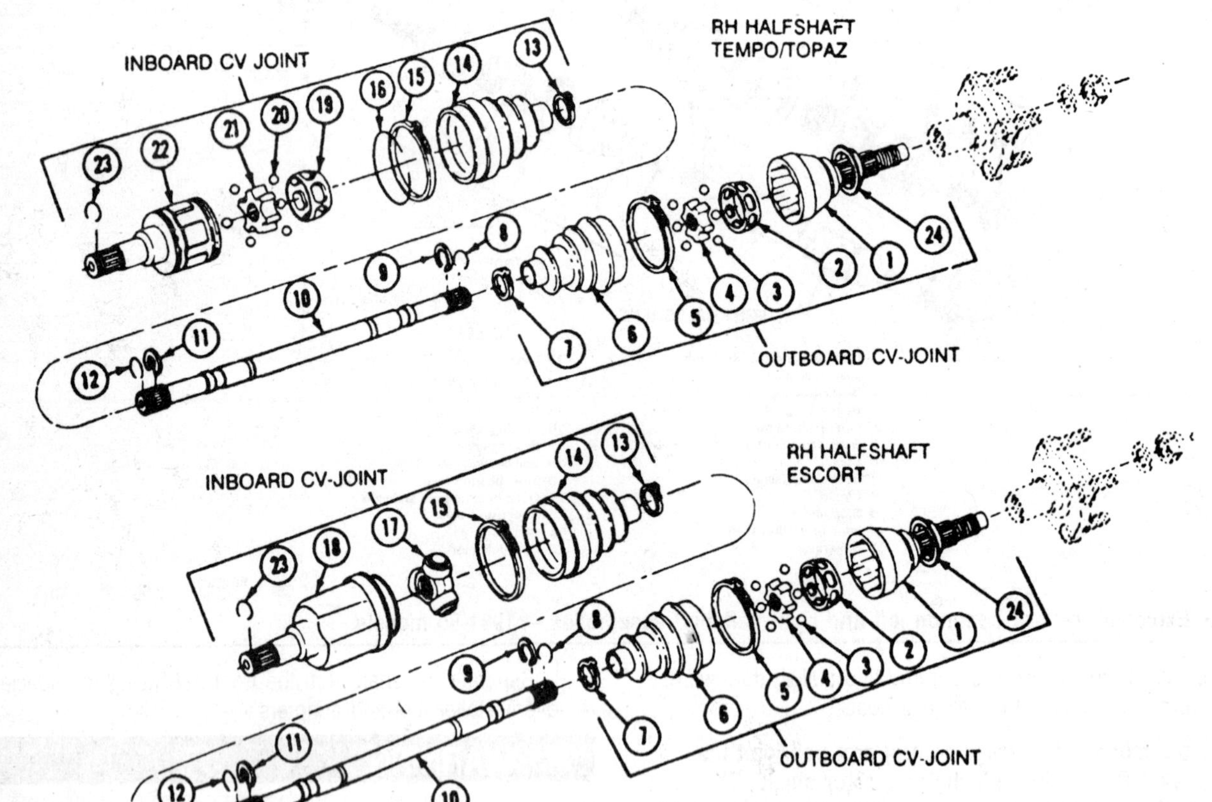

1. Outboard joint outer race and stub shaft
2. Ball cage
3. Balls (6)
4. Outboard joint inner race
5. Boot clamp (large)
6. Boot
7. Boot clamp (small)
8. Circlip
9. Stop ring
10. Interconnecting shaft
11. Stop ring
12. Circlip
13. Boot clamp (small)
14. Boot
15. Boot clamp (large)
16. Wire ring ball retainer
17. Tripod assy
18. Tripod outer race
19. Ball cage
20. Balls (6)
21. Inboard joint inner race
22. Inboard joint outer race and stub shaft
23. Circlip
24. Dust seal

86757036

Fig. 10 Exploded view of common left and right halfshaft assemblies — 1985½-90 models

Fig. 11 Loosen but do not remove the axle nut while the vehicle is still on the ground

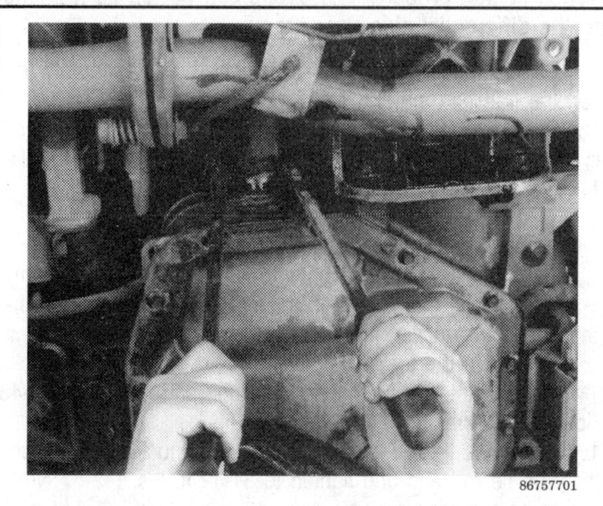

Fig. 12 Using a prybar, pry the halfshaft from the differential housing

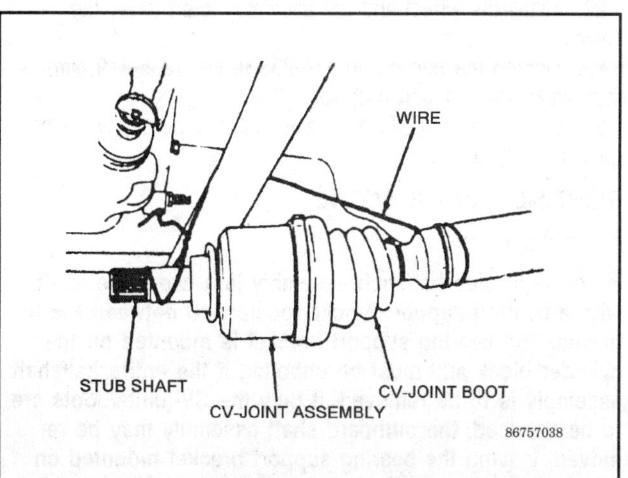

Fig. 13 When the halfshaft is detached, use a sturdy wire to support its weight as shown rather than allowing it to hang loose

Fig. 14 Using a front hub removal tool, press the halfshaft's outboard CV-joint from the hub

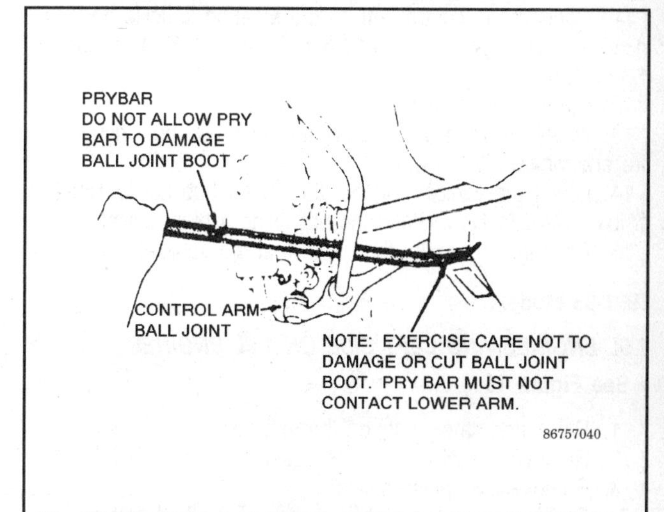

Fig. 15 Use a long prybar to separate the ball joint from the steering knuckle

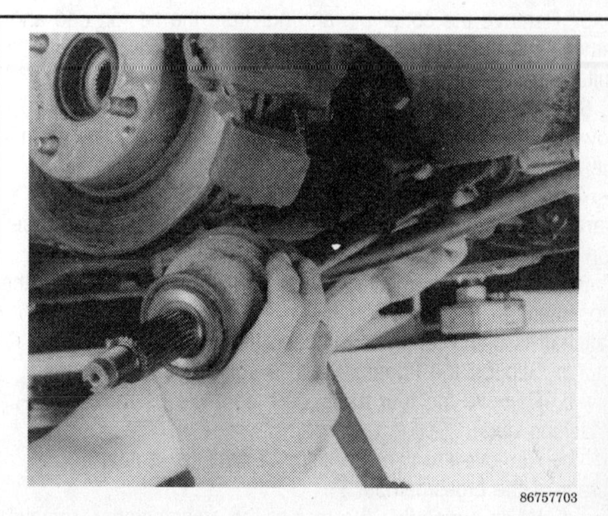

Fig. 16 Once completely detached, remove the halfshaft from the vehicle

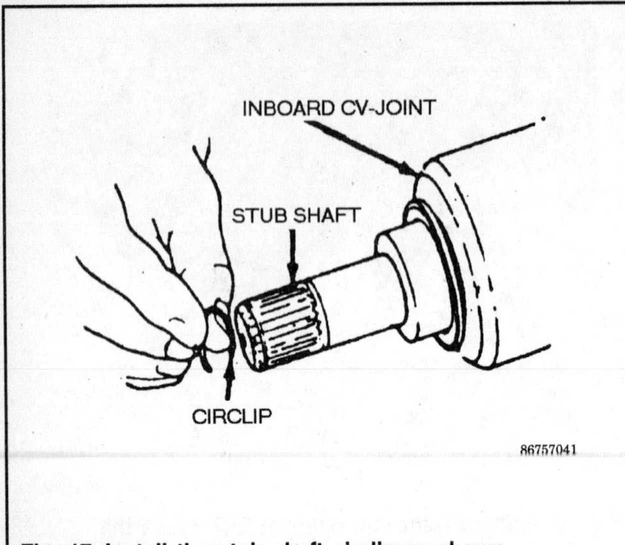

Fig. 17 Install the stub shaft circlip as shown

11. Connect the control arm to the steering knuckle and install a new mounting bolt and nut. Tighten to 37-44 ft. lbs. (50-60 Nm).
12. Connect the brake line to the strut.
13. Install the front hub washer and new hub nut. Install the tire and wheel assembly.
14. Lower the vehicle. Tighten the center hub nut to 180-200 ft. lbs. (244-271 Nm). Stake the nut using a blunt chisel.
15. Refill the transaxle, then road test the vehicle.

1991-95 Models

1.9L ENGINES AND LEFT SIDE ON 1.8L ENGINES

➧ See Figure 18

1. Raise and safely support the vehicle.
2. Remove the wheel and tire assembly.
3. Remove the splash shield.
4. Carefully raise the staked portion of the halfshaft retaining nut using a suitable small chisel. Remove and discard the retaining nut.
5. Remove the cotter pin and nut from the tie rod end and remove the tie rod end from the steering knuckle using a suitable removal tool.
6. Remove the lower ball joint clamp bolt. Carefully pry down on the lower control arm to separate the ball joint from the steering knuckle.
7. Pull outward on the steering knuckle/brake assembly. Carefully pull the halfshaft from the steering knuckle and position it aside.
8. Removal of the left side halfshaft requires removal of the crossmember to allow access with a prybar. If the left side halfshaft is being removed, proceed as follows:
   a. Support the transaxle with a suitable transaxle jack.
   b. Remove the four transaxle mount-to-crossmember attaching nuts.
   c. Remove the two crossmember attaching nuts at the rear of the crossmember.
   d. While supporting the rear of the crossmember, remove the two front mounting bolts. Remove the crossmember.
9. Position a drain pan under the transaxle.
10. Insert a prybar between the halfshaft and the transaxle case. Gently pry outward to release the halfshaft from the differential side gears. Be careful not to damage the transaxle case, oil seal, CV-joint or boot.
11. Remove the halfshaft.

➡Install shipping plugs (part no. T81P-1177-B or equivalent) after removing the halfshafts to prevent the differential side gears from becoming improperly positioned.

To install:

12. Position the circlip on the inner CV-joint spline so the circlip gap is at the top. Lubricate the splines lightly with grease.
13. Remove the plugs that were installed in the differential side gears.
14. Position the halfshaft so the CV-joint splines are aligned with the differential side gear splines. Push the halfshaft into the differential.

➡When seated properly, the circlip can be felt as it snaps into the differential side gear groove.

15. Pull outward on the steering knuckle/brake assembly and insert the halfshaft into the steering knuckle.
16. Pry downward on the control arm and position the lower ball joint in the steering knuckle.
17. For left side halfshaft installation, proceed as follows:
   a. Position the crossmember in place.
   b. Install the two mounting bolts and the two attaching nuts. Tighten the nuts and bolts to 47-66 ft. lbs. (64-89 Nm).
   c. Install the four transaxle mount-to-crossmember attaching nuts. Tighten the nuts to 27-38 ft. lbs. (37-52 Nm).
   d. Remove the transaxle jack.
18. Install the lower ball joint clamp bolt and tighten to 32-43 ft. lbs. (43-59 Nm).
19. Install the tie rod end in the steering knuckle. Install the nut to the tie rod end and tighten to 31-42 ft. lbs. (42-57 Nm). Install a new cotter pin.
20. Install a new halfshaft retaining nut.
21. Install the splash shield.
22. Install the wheel and tire assembly, then lower the vehicle.
23. Tighten the hub nut to 174-235 ft. lbs. (235-319 Nm), then stake the nut with a chisel.
24. Check and refill the transaxle with the proper type and quantity of fluid.

RIGHT SIDE ON 1.8L ENGINE

➧ See Figure 19

➡The right side halfshaft assembly is a two-piece shaft with a bearing support bracket positioned between the two halves. The bearing support bracket is mounted on the cylinder block and must be unbolted if the entire halfshaft assembly is to be removed. If only the CV-joints/boots are to be serviced, the outboard shaft assembly may be removed, leaving the bearing support bracket mounted on the engine cylinder block.

1. Raise and safely support the vehicle.
2. Remove the right front wheel and tire assembly.
3. Remove the splash shield.

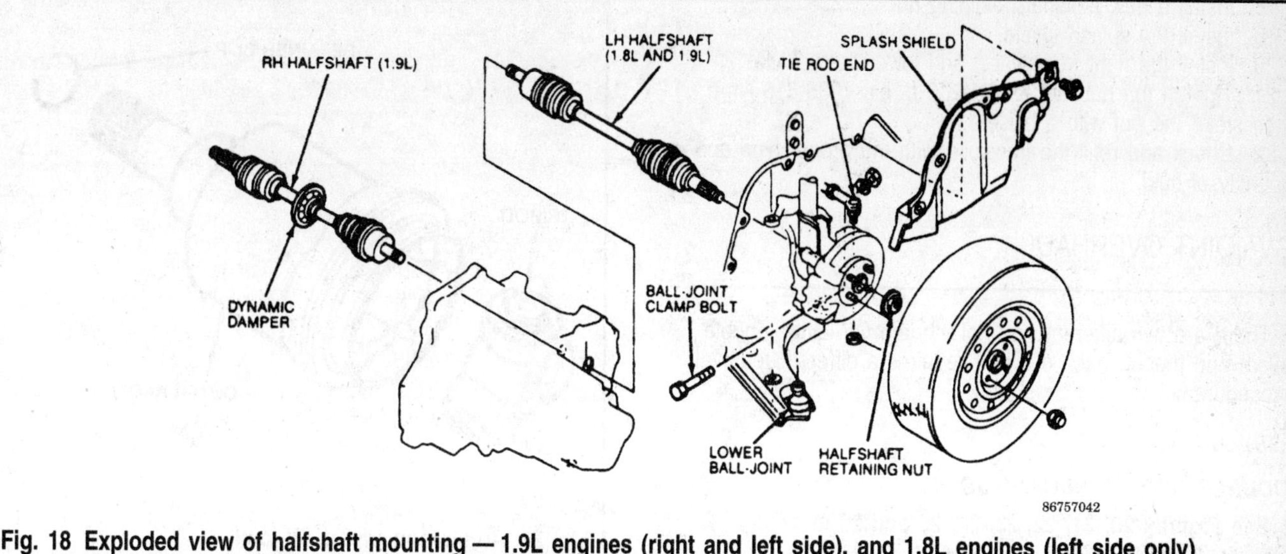

Fig. 18 Exploded view of halfshaft mounting — 1.9L engines (right and left side), and 1.8L engines (left side only)

4. Carefully raise the staked portion of the halfshaft retaining nut using a small chisel. Remove and discard the retaining nut.
5. Remove the cotter pin and nut from the tie rod end and separate the tie rod end from the steering knuckle.
6. Remove the lower ball joint clamp bolt. Carefully pry down on the lower control arm to separate the ball joint from the steering knuckle.
7. Pull outward on the steering knuckle/brake assembly. Carefully pull the halfshaft from the steering knuckle and position it aside.
8. Position a drain pan under the transaxle.
9. Remove the three bearing support bracket mounting bolts.
10. Insert a prybar between the bearing support bracket and the starter bracket. Gently pry outward on the damper until the halfshaft disengages from the differential side gear.
11. Remove the halfshaft assembly. Install a shipping plug (part no. T81P-1177-B or equivalent) in the differential side gear.

To install:

12. Position the circlip on the inner CV-joint spline so the circlip gap is at the top. Lubricate the splines lightly with grease.
13. Remove the plug from the side gear. Position the halfshaft assembly so the shaft splines are aligned with the differential side gear splines. Push the halfshaft into the differential.

➡When seated properly, the circlip can be felt as it snaps into the differential side gear groove.

14. Pull outward on the steering knuckle/brake assembly and insert the halfshaft into the steering knuckle.
15. Pry downward on the control arm and position the lower ball joint in the steering knuckle. Install the lower ball joint clamp bolt and tighten to 32-43 ft. lbs. (43-59 Nm).
16. Install the tie rod end in the steering knuckle. Install the nut to the tie rod end and tighten to 31-42 ft. lbs. (42-57 Nm). Install a new cotter pin.
17. Position the bearing support bracket and install the three mounting bolts. Tighten the bolts in the proper sequence to 31-46 ft. lbs. (42-62 Nm).

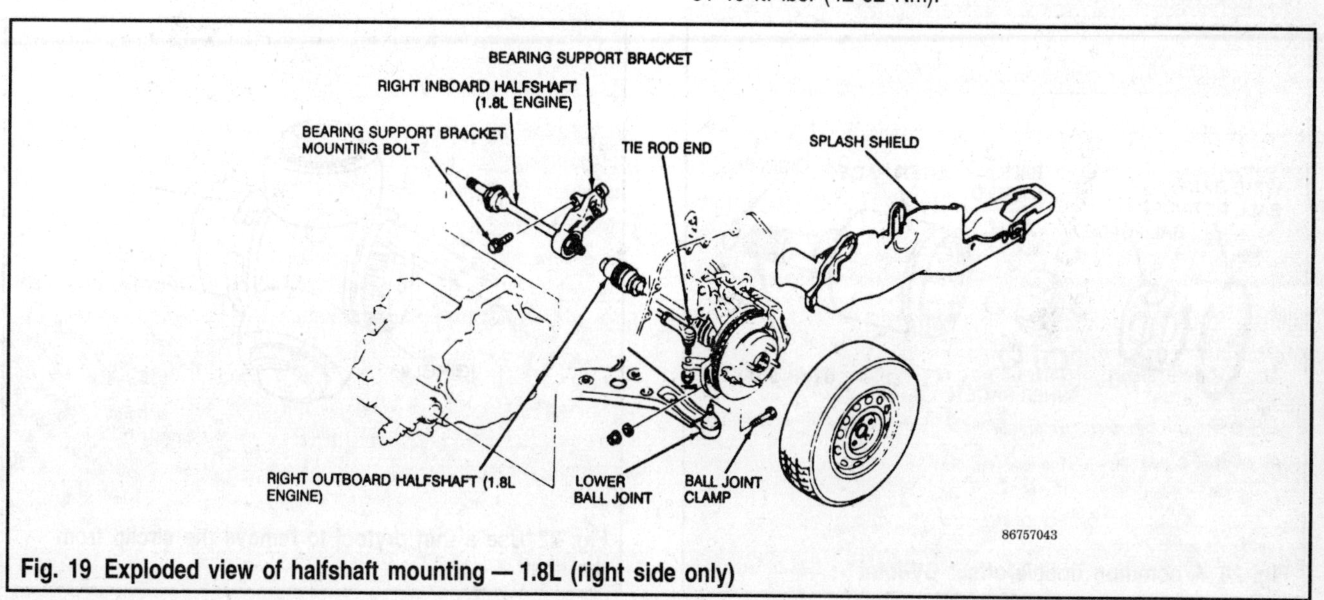

Fig. 19 Exploded view of halfshaft mounting — 1.8L (right side only)

18. Install a new halfshaft retaining nut.
19. Install the splash shield.
20. Install the right front wheel and lower the vehicle.
21. Tighten the hub nut to 174-235 ft. lbs. (235-319 Nm), then stake the nut with a chisel.
22. Check and refill the transaxle with the proper type and quantity of fluid.

CV-JOINT OVERHAUL

There are two different types of inboard CV-joints (double offset and tripod), each of which requires a different removal procedure.

1981-90 Models

DOUBLE OFFSET INBOARD JOINT

See Figures 20, 21, 22, 23, 24, 25 and 26

1. Disconnect the negative battery cable.
2. Remove halfshaft assembly from vehicle. Place the halfshaft in vise. Do not allow vice jaws to contact the boot or its clamp. The vise should be equipped with jaw caps to prevent damage to any machined surfaces.
3. Cut the large boot clamp using side cutters and peel away from the boot. After removing the clamp, roll the boot back over the shaft.
4. Remove the wire ring ball retainer.
5. Remove the outer race.
6. Pull inner race assembly out until it rests on the circlip. Using snapring pliers, spread the ring and move it back on the shaft.
7. Slide the inner race assembly down the shaft to allow access to the circlip. Remove circlip.
8. Remove the inner race assembly and boot.

Circlips must not be reused. Replace with new circlips before assembly.

9. When replacing damaged CV-boots, the grease should be checked for contamination. If the CV-joints were operating satisfactorily and the grease does not appear to be contaminated, add grease and replace the boot. If the lubricant appears contaminated, proceed with a complete CV-joint disassembly and inspection.

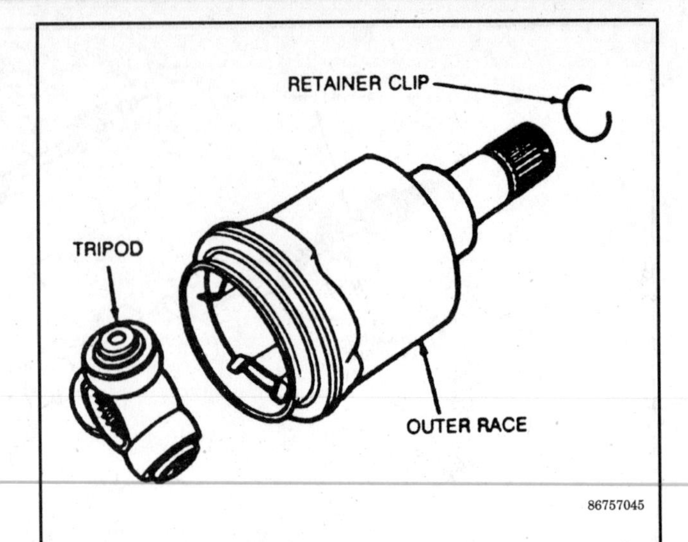

Fig. 21 A common tripod CV-joint

10. Remove balls by prying from cage.

Exercise care to prevent scratching or other damage to the inner race or cage.

11. Rotate inner race to align lands with cage windows. Lift inner race out through the wider end of the cage.

To assemble:

12. Clean all parts (except boots) in a suitable solvent.
13. Inspect all CV-joint parts for excessive wear, looseness, pitting, rust and cracks.

CV-joint components are matched during assembly. If inspection reveals damage or wear, the entire joint must be replaced as an assembly. Do not replace a joint merely because the parts appear polished. Shiny areas in ball races and on the cage spheres are normal.

14. Install a new circlip in groove nearest end of the shaft. Do not over-expand or twist circlip during installation.

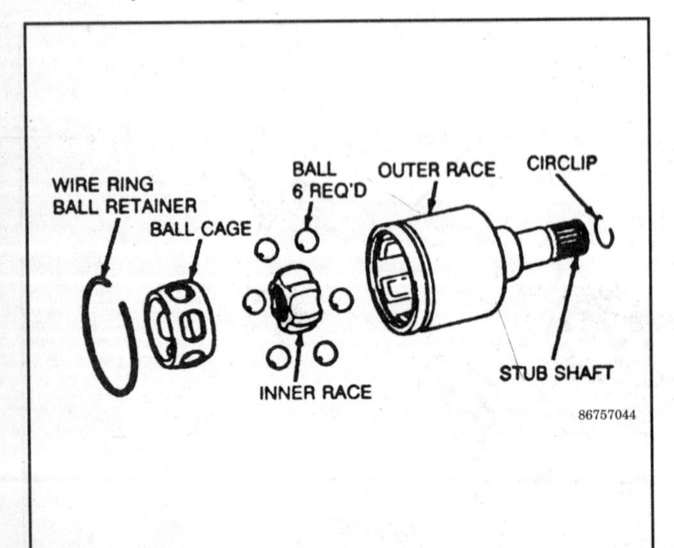

Fig. 20 A common double offset CV-joint

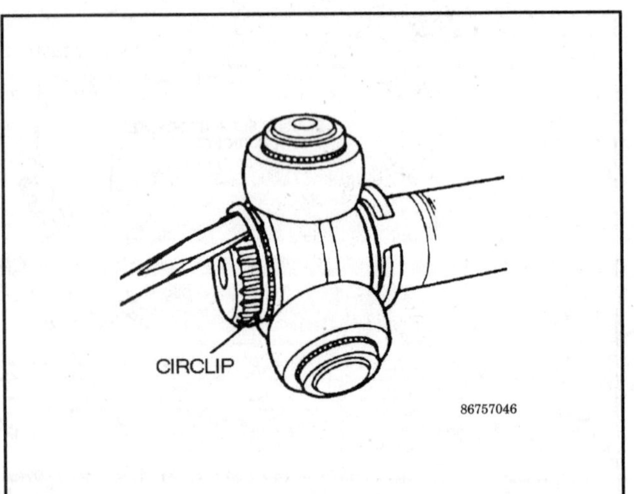

Fig. 22 Use a thin prytool to remove the circlip from the shaft

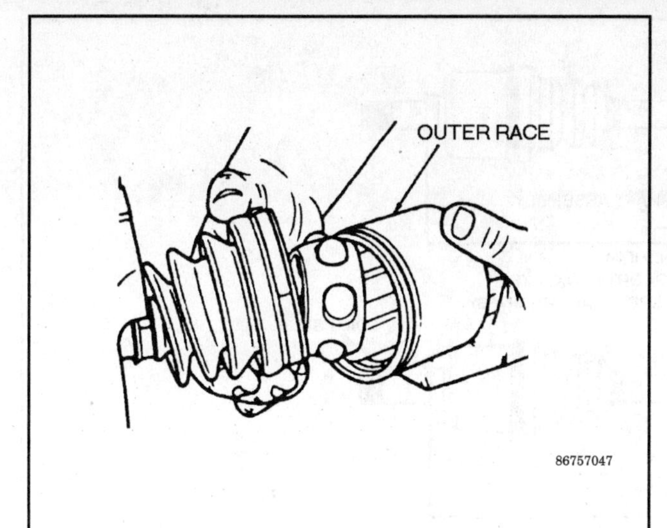

Fig. 23 The outer race assembly comes apart as shown

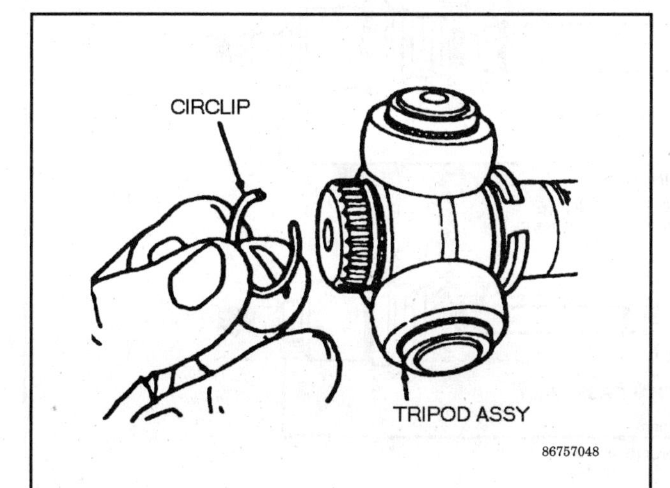

Fig. 24 When installing, use a new circlip on the end of the shaft

15. Install inner race in the cage. The race is installed through the large end of the cage with the circlip counterbore facing the large end of the cage.
16. With the cage and inner race properly aligned, install the balls by pressing through the cage windows with the heel of the hand.
17. Assemble inner race and cage assembly in the outer race.
18. Push the inner race and cage assembly by hand, into the outer race. Install with the inner race chamfer facing out.
19. Install the ball retainer into groove inside the outer race.
20. Install a new CV-boot.
21. Position the stop ring and new circlip into grooves on the shaft.
22. Fill the CV-joint outer race with 3.2 oz. (90 grams) of grease, then spread 1.4 oz. (40 grams) of grease evenly inside the boot for a total combined fill of 4.6 oz. (130 grams).
23. With the boot peeled back, install the CV-joint using a soft-faced hammer. Ensure that the splines are aligned prior to installing the CV-joint onto the shaft.
24. Remove all excess grease from the CV-joint external surfaces.
25. Position the boot over the CV-joint. Before installing the boot clamp, move the CV-joint in or out, as necessary, to adjust to the proper length.

➡Insert a suitable tool between the boot and outer bearing race and allow the trapped air to escape from the boot. The air should be released from the boot only after adjusting to the proper dimensions.

26. Ensure boot is seated in its groove and clamp in position.
27. Tighten the clamp securely, but not to the point where the clamp bridge is cut or the boot is damaged.
28. Install the halfshaft assembly in the vehicle.
29. Connect the negative battery cable.

INBOARD TRIPOD JOINT

See Figure 27

1. Disconnect the negative battery cable.
2. Remove the halfshaft assembly from the vehicle. Place the halfshaft in a vice. Do not allow the vise jaws to contact the boot or its clamp. The vise should be equipped with jaw caps to prevent damage to any machined surfaces.
3. Cut the large boot clamp using side cutters and peel away from the boot. After removing the clamp, roll the boot back over the shaft.
4. Bend the retaining tabs back slightly to allow for tripod removal.
5. Separate the outer race from the tripod.
6. Move the stop ring back on the shaft using snapring pliers.
7. Move the tripod assembly back on the shaft to allow access to the circlip.
8. Remove the circlip from the shaft.
9. Remove the tripod assembly from the shaft. Remove the boot.
10. When replacing damaged CV-boots, the grease should be checked for contamination. If the CV-joints were operating satisfactorily and the grease does not appear to be contaminated, add grease and replace the boot. If the lubricant ap-

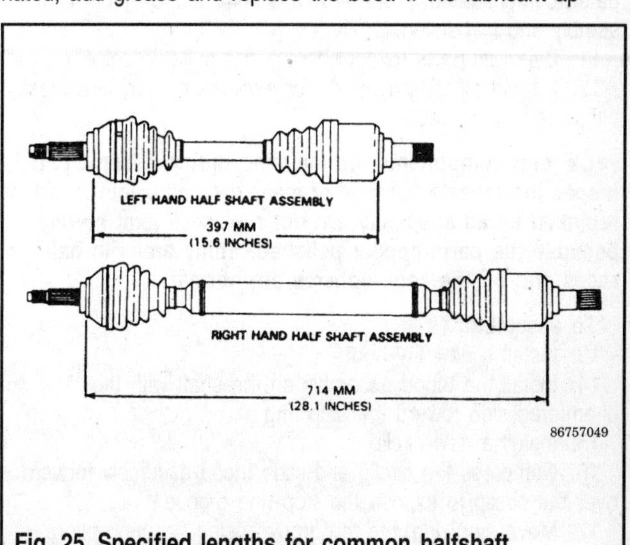

Fig. 25 Specified lengths for common halfshaft assemblies — 1981-83 models

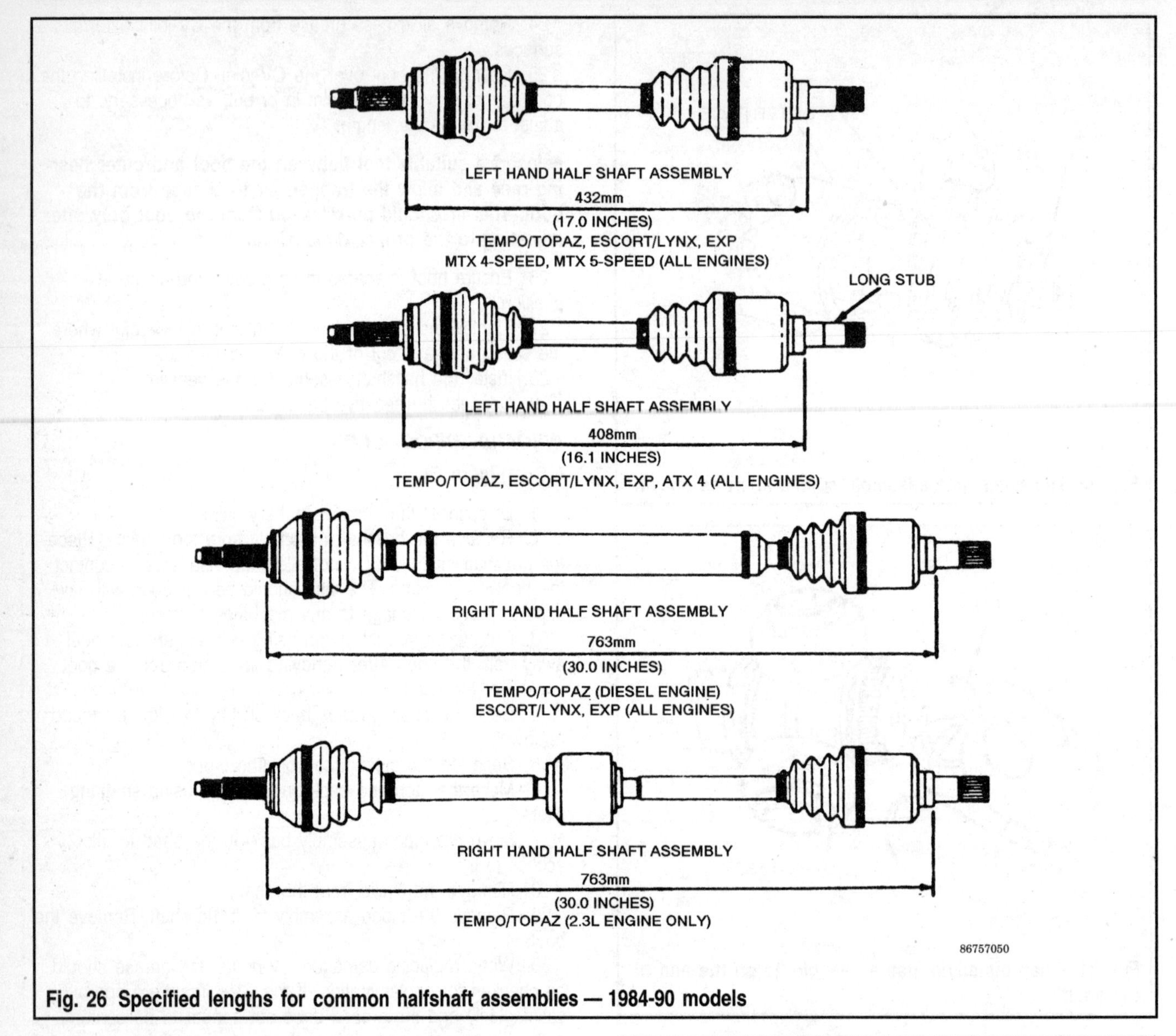

Fig. 26 Specified lengths for common halfshaft assemblies — 1984-90 models

pears contaminated, proceed with a complete CV-joint disassembly and inspection.

11. Clean all parts (except boots) in a suitable solvent.
12. Inspect all CV-joint parts for excessive wear, looseness, pitting, rust and cracks.

➡CV-joint components are matched during assembly. If inspection reveals damage or wear the entire joint must be replaced as an assembly. Do not replace a joint merely because the parts appear polished. Shiny areas in ball races and on the cage spheres are normal.

To assemble:

13. Install a new CV-boot.
14. Install the tripod assembly on the shaft with the chamfered side toward the stop ring.
15. Install a new circlip.
16. Compress the circlip and slide tripod assembly forward over the circlip to expose the stop ring groove.
17. Move stop ring into the groove using snapring pliers. Ensure that it is fully seated in the groove.

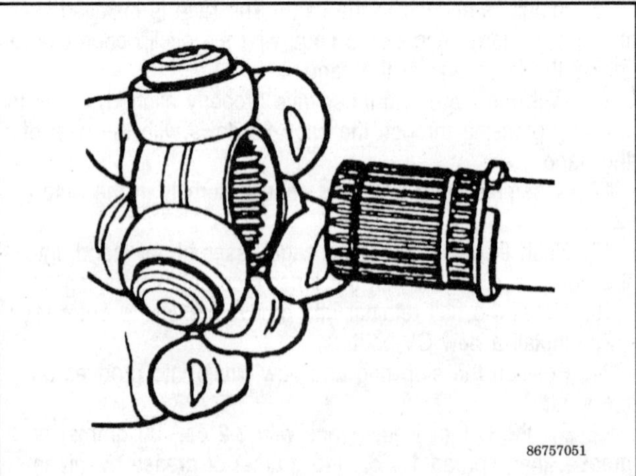

Fig. 27 Remove (and install) the the tripod assembly by matching the splines and pushing on until it seats on the shaft

18. Fill CV-joint outer race with 3.5 oz. (100 grams) of grease and fill CV-boot with 2.1 oz. (60 grams) of grease.
19. Install outer race over tripod assembly and bend the six retaining tabs back into their original position.
20. Remove all excess grease from CV-joint external surfaces. Position boot over the CV-joint. Move the CV-joint in and out as necessary, to adjust to proper length.

➡Insert a suitable tool between the boot and outer bearing race and allow the trapped air to escape from the boot. The air should be released from the boot only after adjusting to the proper dimensions.

21. Ensure boot is seated in its groove and clamp in position.
22. Tighten clamp securely, but not to the point where the clamp bridge is cut or the boot is damaged.
23. Install a new circlip in the groove nearest end of the shaft by starting one end in the groove and working clip over the stub shaft end and into the groove.
24. Install the halfshaft assembly in the vehicle.
25. Connect the negative battery cable.

OUTBOARD JOINT

See Figures 28, 29, 30 and 31

1. Disconnect the negative battery cable.
2. Remove the halfshaft assembly from the vehicle.
3. Place the halfshaft in a vice. Do not allow vise jaws to contact the boot or its clamp. The vise should be equipped with jaw caps or wood blocks to prevent the jaws from damaging any machined surfaces.
4. Cut the large boot clamp using side cutters and peel away from the boot. After removing the clamp, roll the boot back over shaft.
5. Support the interconnecting shaft in a soft jaw vise and angle the CV-joint to expose inner bearing race.
6. Using a brass drift and hammer, give a sharp tap to the inner bearing race to dislodge the internal circlip and separate the CV-joint from the interconnecting shaft. Take care not to drop the CV-joint at separation.
7. Remove the boot.
8. When replacing damaged CV-boots, the grease should be checked for contamination. If the CV-joints were operating satisfactorily and the grease does not appear to be contaminated, add grease and replace the boot. If the lubricant appears contaminated, proceed with a complete CV-joint disassembly and inspection.
9. Remove the circlip located near the end of the shaft. Discard the circlip.
10. Clamp CV-joint stub shaft in a vise with the outer face facing up. Care should be taken not to damage the dust seal. The vise must be equipped with jaw caps to prevent damage to the shaft splines.
11. Press down on the inner race until it tilts enough to allow removal of a ball. A tight assembly can be tilted by tapping the inner race with wooden dowel and hammer. Do not hit the cage.
12. With the cage sufficiently tilted, remove the ball from cage. Remove all 6 balls in this manner.
13. Pivot the cage and inner race assembly until it is straight up and down in outer race. Align cage windows with outer race lands while pivoting the bearing cage. With the cage pivoted and aligned, lift the assembly from the outer race.
14. Rotate the inner race up and out of the cage.

To assemble:

15. Clean all parts (except the boots) in a suitable solvent.
16. Inspect all CV-joint parts for excessive wear, looseness, pitting, rust and cracks.

➡CV-joint components are matched during assembly. If inspection reveals damage or wear the entire joint must be replaced as an assembly. Do not replace a joint merely because the parts appear polished. Shiny areas in ball races and on the cage spheres are normal.

17. Apply a light coating of grease on the inner and outer ball races. Install the inner race in the cage.
18. Install the inner race and cage assembly in the outer race.
19. Install the assembly vertically and pivot 90 degrees into position.

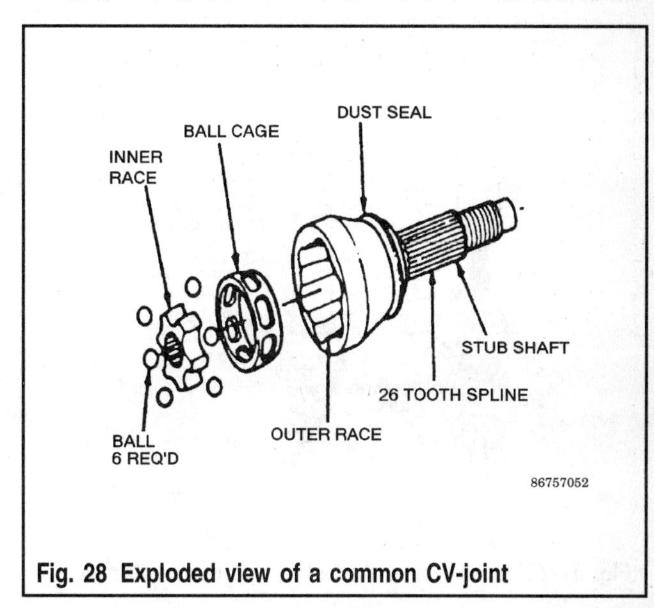

Fig. 28 Exploded view of a common CV-joint

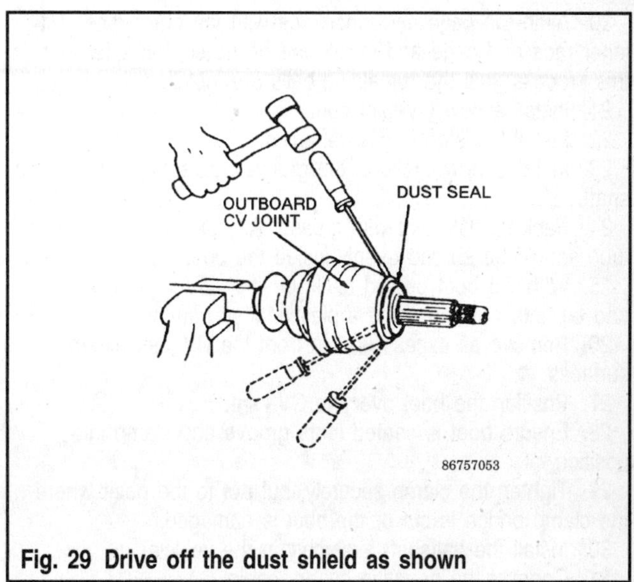

Fig. 29 Drive off the dust shield as shown

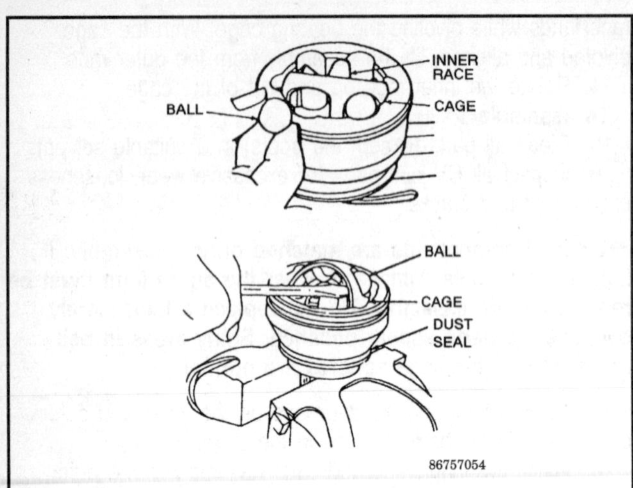

Fig. 30 With the shaft portion of the joint in a soft-jaw vise, remove the ball bearings for cleaning and inspection

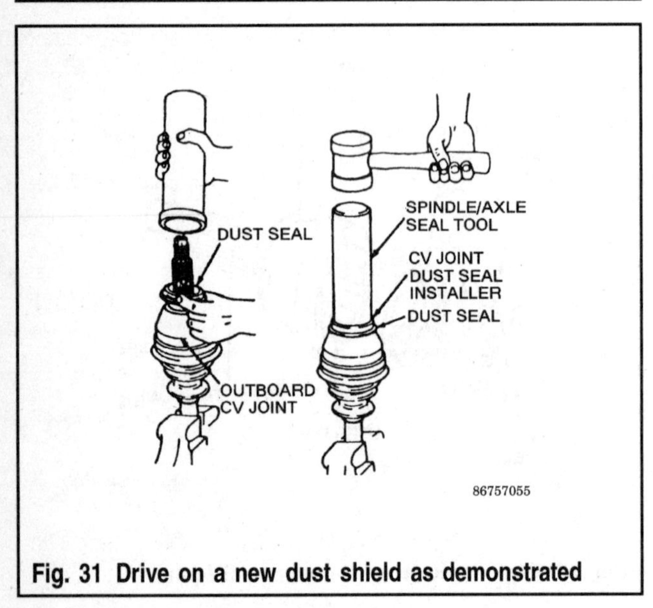

Fig. 31 Drive on a new dust shield as demonstrated

20. Align the cage and inner race with the outer race. Tilt inner race and cage and install one of the six balls. Repeat this process until the remaining balls are installed.
21. Install a new CV-joint boot.
22. Install the stop ring, if removed.
23. Install a new circlip in the groove nearest the end of the shaft.
24. Pack the CV-joint with grease. Any grease remaining in tube should be spread evenly inside the boot.
25. With the boot peeled back, position CV-joint on shaft and tap into position using a plastic-faced hammer.
26. Remove all excess grease from the CV-joint external surfaces.
27. Position the boot over the CV-joint.
28. Ensure boot is seated in its groove and clamp into position.
29. Tighten the clamp securely, but not to the point where the clamp bridge is cut or the boot is damaged.
30. Install the halfshaft assembly in the vehicle.
31. Connect the negative battery cable.

1991-95 Models

See Figures 32, 33, 34 and 35

1. Raise and safely support the vehicle.
2. Remove the halfshaft assembly from the vehicle.
3. Secure the halfshaft in a vise with protective jaw covers.
4. Using a suitable tool, pry up the locking tabs of the inner CV-boot bands. Remove the bands with pliers.
5. Slide the boot back to expose the tripod CV-joint. Mark the shaft and the CV-joint housing to ensure correct assembly.
6. Remove the retainer ring from the CV-joint housing and remove the CV-joint housing from the halfshaft.
7. Mark the tripod bearing and the shaft to ensure correct assembly. Using snapring pliers, remove the tripod snapring.
8. Using a soft-faced mallet, gently tap the tripod bearing from the shaft.
9. Wrap the shaft splines with tape to protect the CV-boot if the boot is to be reused.
10. Slide the inner CV-joint boot off the shaft. If the outer CV-joint boot is to be replaced, continue with the procedure.
11. On 1.9L right side halfshafts, pry up the rubber damper retaining band locking clip with a suitable tool. Remove the retaining band using pliers, then remove the rubber damper from the shaft.
12. Using a tool, pry up the outer CV-boot band locking tabs. Remove the bands with pliers.
13. Slide the outer CV-boot off the shaft.

➡When replacing a damaged boot, check the grease for contamination by rubbing it between two fingers. Any gritty feeling indicates a contaminated CV-joint. A contaminated inner CV-joint must be completely disassembled, cleaned and inspected. The outer CV-joint is not serviceable and should be replaced as an assembly, if necessary. If the grease is not contaminated and the CV-joint has been operating satisfactorily, replace only the boot and add the required lubricant.

To assemble:

14. Cover the halfshaft splines with a suitable tape for protection of the surfaces and install the outer CV-joint boot.

➡The outer and inner CV-joint boots are different. Failure to correctly install the boot on the proper end of the halfshaft could lead to premature boot and/or CV-joint wear.

15. Fill the outer CV-joint housing with the proper type and amount of lubricant.
16. Position the CV-boot. Make sure the boot is fully seated in the shaft grooves and the CV-joint housing.
17. Insert a suitable tool between the boot and the CV-joint housing to allow trapped air to escape.
18. Position new bands on the outer CV-joint boot.

➡Always use new bands. The bands should be mounted in the direction opposite the forward revolving direction of the halfshaft.

19. Wrap the bands around the boot in a clockwise direction, pull them tight with pliers and bend the locking tabs to secure the bands in position.
20. Work the CV-joint through its full range of travel at various angles. The CV-joint should flex, extend and compress smoothly.

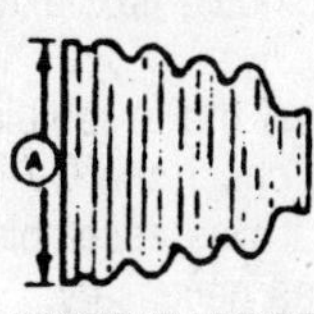

86757056

Fig. 32 Opening sizes for inner and outer CV-boots — 1991-95 models

	1.9L Engine		1.8L Engine	
	Right Side	Left Side	Right Side	Left Side
(A)	84.0 mm (3.31 in)	90.0 mm (3.54 in)	89.9 mm (3.54 in)	
(B)	89.0 mm (3.50 in)		85.2 mm (3.35 in)	

86757057

Fig. 33 CV-boot sizing chart — 1991-95 models

Halfshaft Assemblies	1.9L Engine		1.8L Engine	
	Right Side	Left Side	Right Side	Left Side
Differential Side	220 g (7.77 oz.) Lt. Yellow	140 g (4.94 oz.) Yellow	145 g (5.12 oz.) Yellow	
Wheel Side	140 g (4.94 oz.) Black		90 g (3.18 oz.) Black	

86757059

Fig. 35 CV-boot lubricant specifications

21. On 1.9L right side halfshafts, position the rubber damper on the halfshaft. Position a new band on the damper. Pull the band tight with pliers and fold it back. Lock the end of the band by bending the locking clip.
22. Position the inner CV-joint boot on the halfshaft.
23. Align the marks on the tripod bearing and the halfshaft. Install the tripod bearing on the halfshaft. If necessary, using a soft-faced mallet, tap the bearing into place.
24. Install the snapring.
25. Fill the inner CV-joint housing with the proper type and amount of lubricant. Coat the tripod bearing with the same lubricant.
26. Position the inner CV-joint housing over the tripod bearing, making sure to align the alignment marks. Install the retainer ring in the CV-joint housing.
27. Slide the inner CV-boot in place. Make sure the boot is fully seated in the shaft grooves and in the housing.
28. Insert a suitable tool between the boot and the CV-joint housing to allow trapped air to escape.

Item \ Model		1.8L Engine	1.9L Engine
Halfshaft			
Length of joint (between center of joint)	Right side	631.2 mm (24.85 in)	918.7 mm (36.16 in)
	Left side	621.7 mm (24.48 in)	640.7 mm (25.22 in)
Shaft diameter	Right side	23.0 mm (0.91 in)	
	Left side	23.0 mm (0.91 in)	

86757058

Fig. 34 Critical dimensions of CV-joints and halfshafts — 1991-95 models

29. Position new bands on the inner CV-joint boot.

➡**Always use new bands. The bands should be mounted in the direction opposite the forward revolving direction of the halfshaft.**

30. Wrap the bands around the boot in a clockwise direction, pull them tight with pliers and bend the locking tabs to secure the bands in position.

31. Work the CV-joint through its full range of travel at various angles. The CV-joint should flex, extend and compress smoothly.

32. Measure the length of the assembled halfshaft. If the length is not as specified, check the CV-joints for freedom of movement to ensure that it was assembled correctly. Repair or replace any components as necessary.

CLUTCH

See Figures 36, 37, 38 and 39

**CAUTION

The clutch driven disc may contain asbestos, which has been determined to be a cancer causing agent. Never clean clutch surfaces with compressed air! Do not inhale any dust from any clutch surface! When cleaning clutch surfaces, use a commercially available brake cleaning fluid.

The primary function of the clutch system is to couple and uncouple engine power to the transaxle as desired by the driver. The clutch system also allows engine torque to be applied to the transaxle input shaft gradually, due to mechanical slippage. The car can, consequently, be started smoothly from a full stop.

The transaxle changes the ratio between the rotating speeds of the engine and the wheels by the use of gears. The lower gears allow full engine power to be applied to the rear wheels during acceleration at low speeds.

The clutch driven plate is a thin disc, the center of which is splined to the transaxle input shaft. Both sides of the disc are covered with a layer of material which is similar to brake lining and which is capable of allowing slippage without roughness or excessive noise.

The clutch cover is bolted to the engine flywheel and incorporates a diaphragm spring which provides the pressure to engage the clutch. The cover also houses the pressure plate. The driven disc is sandwiched between the pressure plate and the smooth surface of the flywheel when the clutch pedal is released, thus forcing it to turn at the same speed as the engine crankshaft.

Adjustments

PEDAL HEIGHT

1981-90 Models

The pedal height and free-play are controlled by a self-adjusting feature.

1991-95 Models

To determine if the pedal height requires adjustment, measure the distance from the bulkhead to the upper center of the pedal pad. The distance should be 7.72-8.03 in. (196-204mm). If adjustment is necessary, proceed as follows:

1. Disconnect the clutch switch electrical connector.
2. Loosen the clutch switch locknut.
3. Turn the clutch switch until the correct height is achieved.
4. Tighten the locknut to 10-13 ft. lbs. (14-18 Nm).
5. Measure the pedal free-play.
6. Connect the electrical connector.

PEDAL FREE-PLAY

1981-90 Models

The pedal height and free-play are controlled by a self-adjusting feature. The self-adjusting feature should be checked every 5000 miles (8052 km). This is accomplished by insuring that the clutch pedal travels to the top of its upward position. Grasp the clutch pedal with hand or put foot under the clutch pedal, pull up on the pedal until it stops. Very little effort is required (about 10 lbs./4.5 kg). During the application of upward pressure, a click may be heard which means an adjustment was necessary and has been accomplished.

1991-95 Models

To determine if the pedal free-play requires adjustment, depress the clutch pedal by hand until clutch resistance is felt. Measure the distance between the upper pedal height and where the resistance is felt. Free-play should be 0.20-0.51 in. (5-13mm). If an adjustment is necessary, proceed as follows:

1. Loosen the pushrod locknut.
2. Turn the pushrod until the pedal free-play is within specification.
3. Check that the disengagement height is correct when the pedal is fully depressed. Minimum disengagement height is 1.6 in. (41mm).
4. Tighten the pushrod locknut to 9-12 ft. lbs. (12-17 Nm).

Clutch Cable

REMOVAL & INSTALLATION

1981-90 Models

1. Disconnect the negative battery cable.
2. Wedge a 7 in. (18cm) wood block under the clutch pedal to hold the pedal up slightly beyond its normal position.
3. Remove the air cleaner to gain access to the clutch cable.

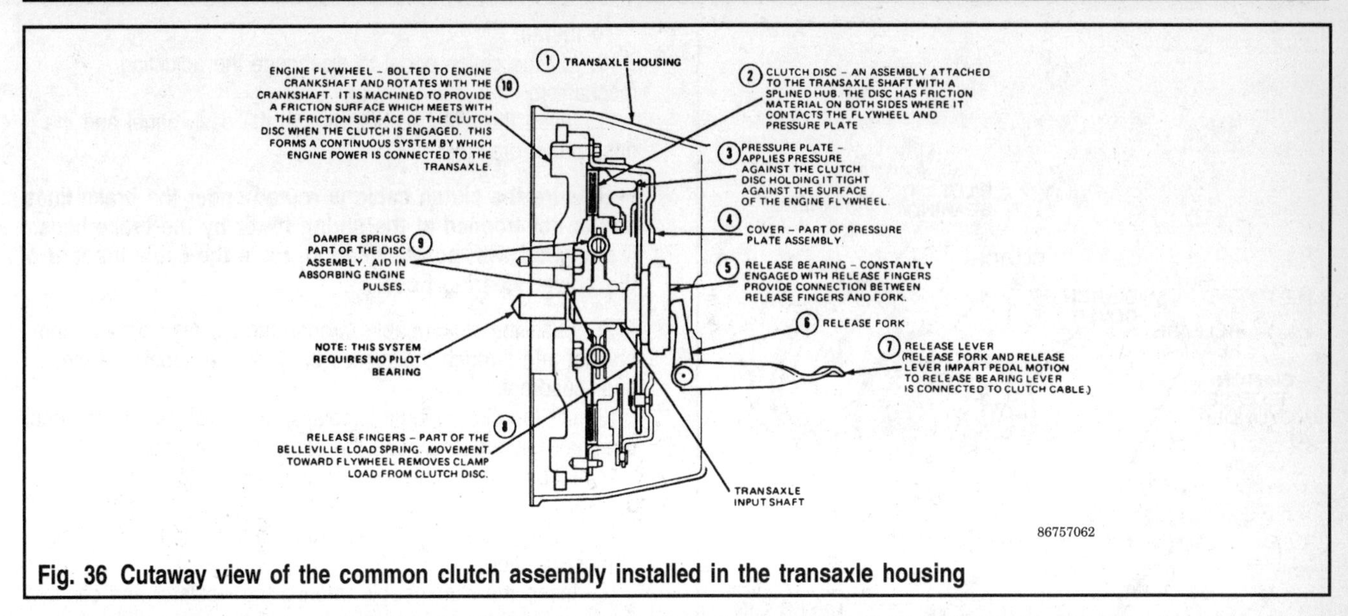

Fig. 36 Cutaway view of the common clutch assembly installed in the transaxle housing

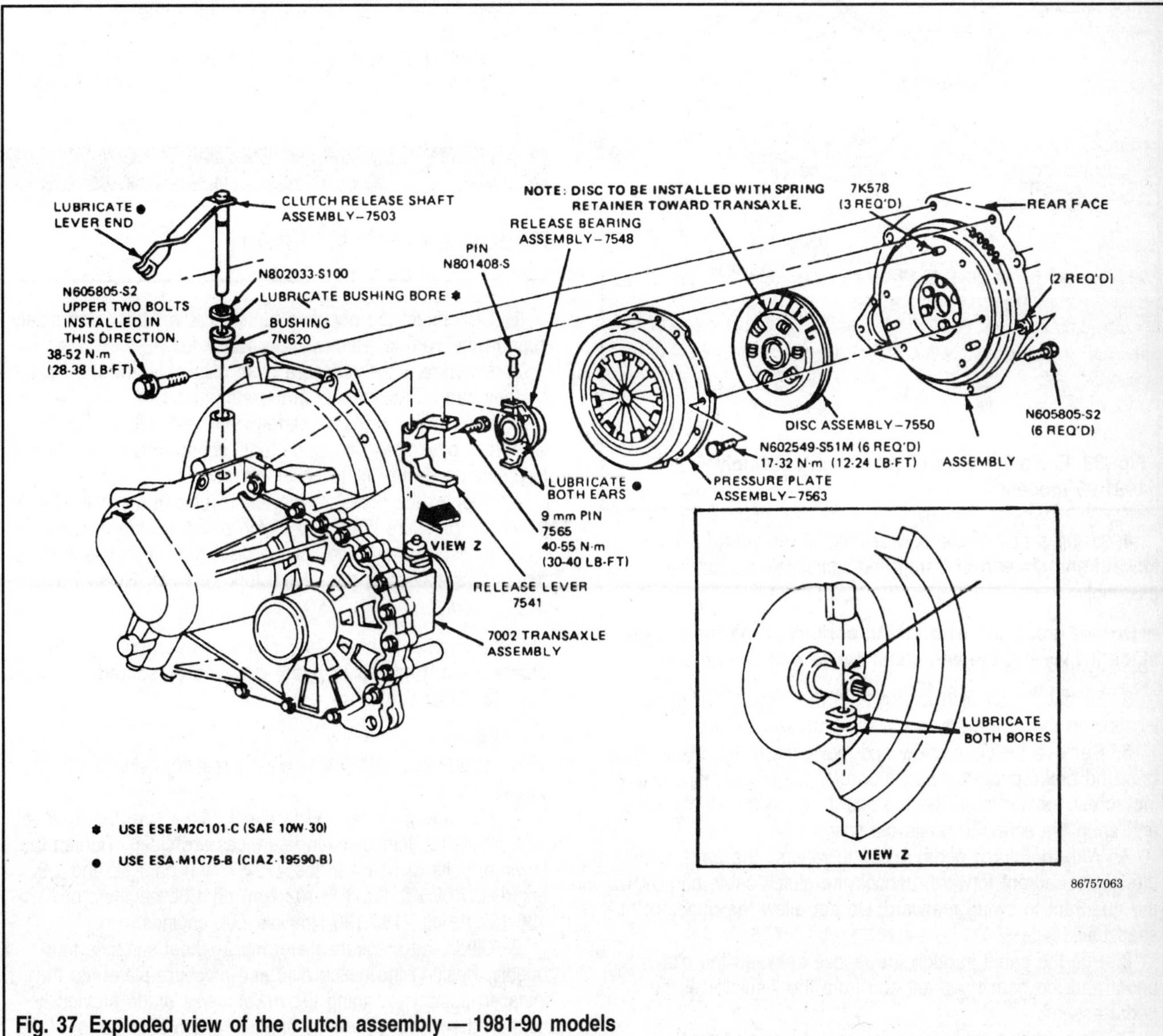

Fig. 37 Exploded view of the clutch assembly — 1981-90 models

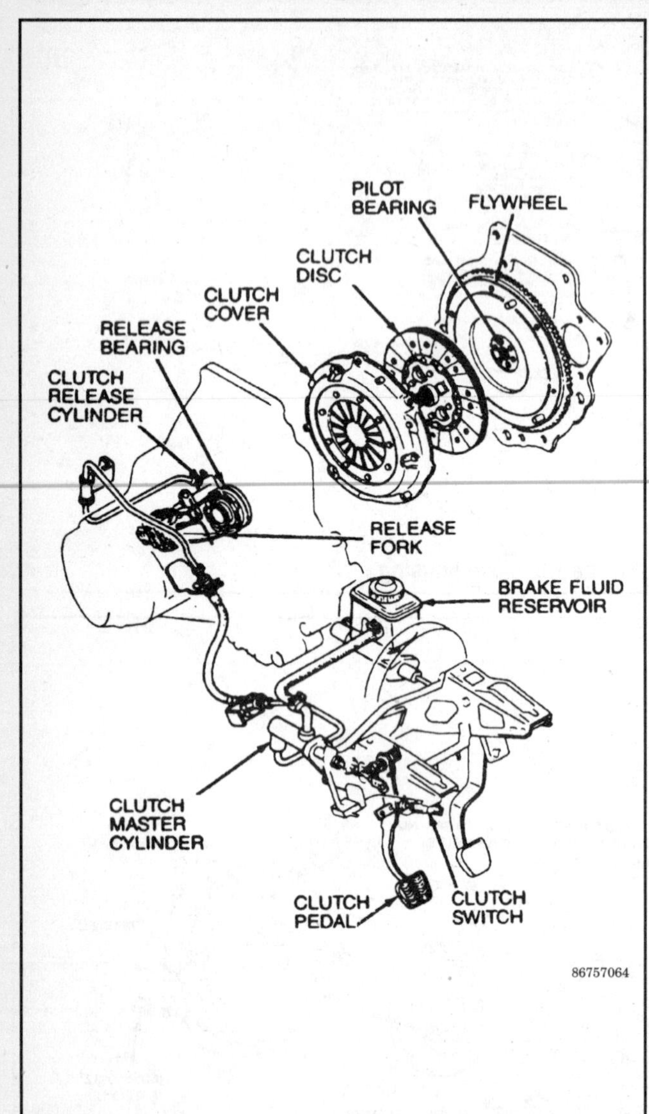

Fig. 38 Exploded view of the clutch assembly — 1991-95 models

4. Using a pair of pliers, grasp the clutch cable, pull it forward and disconnect it from the clutch release shaft assembly.

➡**Do not grasp the wire strand portion of the inner cable since it may cut the wires and cause cable failure.**

5. Remove the clutch casing from the insulator which is located on the rib on the top of the transaxle case.
6. Remove the rear screw and move the clutch shield away from the brake pedal support bracket. Loosen the front retaining screw, located near the toe board, rotate the shield aside and snug the screw to retain the shield.
7. With the clutch pedal raised to release the pawl, rotate the gear quadrant forward, unhook the clutch cable and allow the quadrant to swing rearward. Do not allow the quadrant to snap back.
8. Pull the cable through the recess between the clutch pedal and the gear quadrant and from the insulator of the pedal assembly.
9. Remove the cable from the engine compartment.

To install:

10. Lift the clutch pedal to disengage the adjusting mechanism.
11. Insert the clutch cable through the dash panel and the dash panel grommet.

➡**Be sure the clutch cable is routed under the brake lines and is not trapped at the spring tower by the brake lines. If equipped with power steering, route the cable inboard of the power steering hose.**

12. Push the clutch cable through the insulator on the stop bracket and through the recess between the pedal and the gear quadrant.
13. Lift the clutch pedal to release the pawl. Rotate the gear quadrant forward and hook the cable into the gear quadrant.
14. Install the clutch shield on the brake pedal support bracket.
15. Using a piece of wire or tape, secure the pedal in the upmost position.
16. Insert the clutch cable through the insulator and connect the cable to the clutch release lever in the engine compartment.
17. Remove the wooden block from under the clutch pedal.
18. Depress the clutch pedal several times. Install the air cleaner and connect the negative battery cable.

Driven Disc and Pressure Plate

REMOVAL & INSTALLATION

1. Disconnect the negative battery cable. Raise and safely support the vehicle. Remove the transaxle.
2. Matchmark the pressure plate assembly and the flywheel so they can be assembled in the same position.
3. Loosen the pressure plate-to-flywheel bolts one turn at a time, in a crisscross sequence, until spring tension is relieved to prevent pressure plate cover distortion.
4. Support the pressure plate and remove the bolts. Remove the pressure plate and clutch disc from the flywheel.
5. Inspect the flywheel, clutch disc, pressure plate, throwout bearing, pilot bearing and clutch fork for wear. Replace parts as required.

➡**If the flywheel shows any signs of overheating (blue discoloration) or if it is badly grooved or scored, it should be refaced or replaced.**

To install:

6. If removed, install a new pilot bearing using a suitable installation tool.
7. If removed, install the flywheel. Make sure the flywheel and crankshaft flange mating surfaces are clean. Tighten the flywheel bolts to 54-64 ft. lbs. (73-87 Nm) on 1.6L and 1.9L engines, 71-76 ft. lbs. (96-103 Nm) on 1.8L engines, or 130-137 ft. lbs. (180-190 Nm) on 2.0L engines.
8. Clean the pressure plate and flywheel surfaces thoroughly. Position the clutch disc and pressure plate into the installed position, aligning the matchmarks made previously; support them with a dummy shaft or clutch aligning tool.
9. Install the pressure plate-to-flywheel bolts. Tighten them gradually in a crisscross pattern to 12-24 ft. lbs. (17-32 Nm)

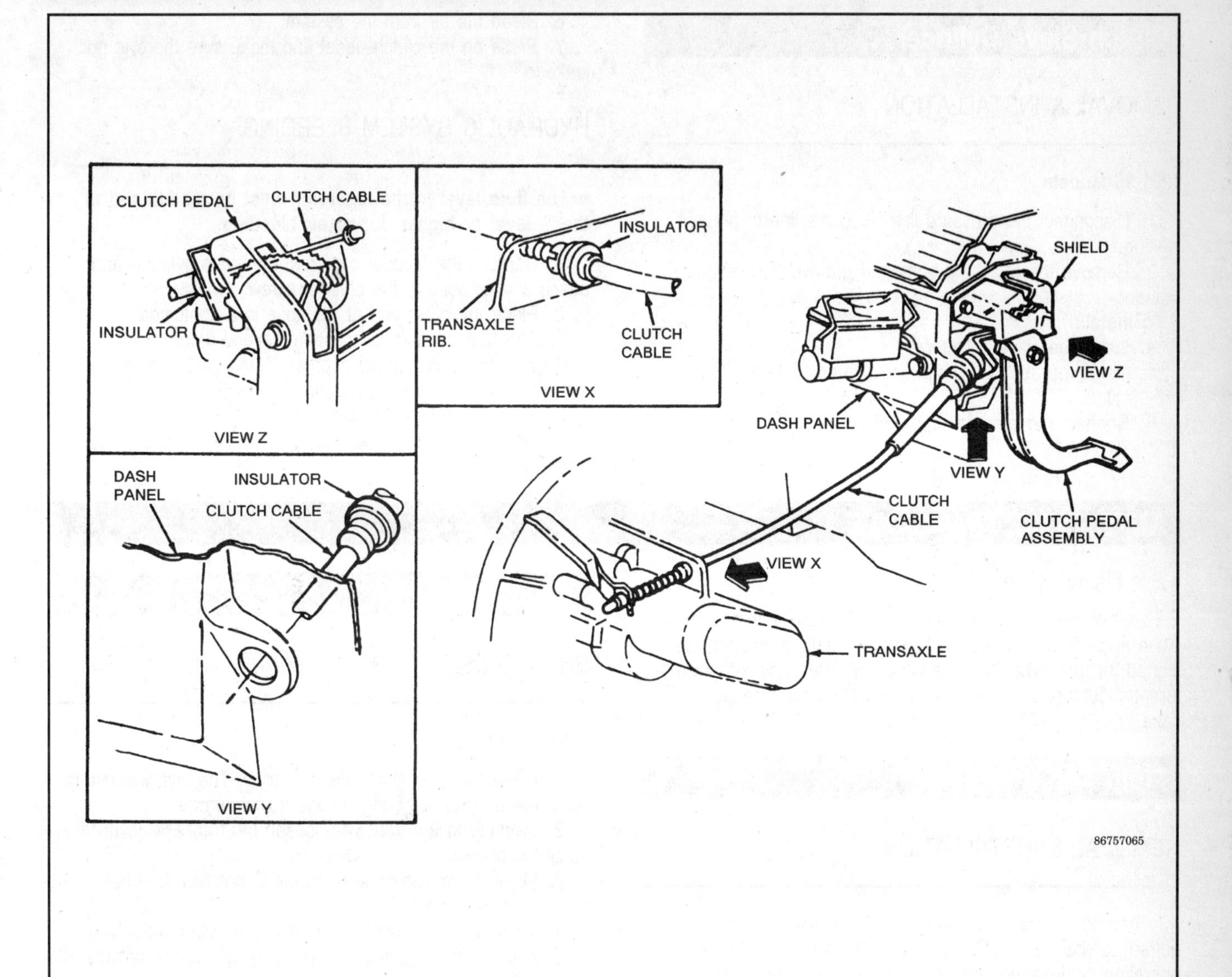

Fig. 39 Details of the clutch linkage — 1981-90 models

on all except 1991-95 models, where the torque should be 13-20 ft. lbs. (18-26 Nm). Remove the alignment tool.

10. Lubricate the release bearing and install it in the fork.
11. To complete the installation, reverse the removal procedures. Lower the vehicle and connect the negative battery cable.

Clutch Master Cylinder

REMOVAL & INSTALLATION

1991-95 Models

1. Disconnect the battery cables and remove the battery and battery tray.
2. Disconnect the clutch pipe from the master cylinder using a suitable line wrench.
3. Disengage the clamp and remove the master cylinder hose from the clutch master cylinder. Prevent excess fluid loss by plugging the hose.
4. Remove the external mounting nut.
5. Remove the internal mounting nut and remove the master cylinder.

To install:

6. Align the pushrod and install the clutch master cylinder.
7. Install the external and internal mounting nuts and tighten to 14-19 ft. lbs. (19-25 Nm).
8. Connect the clutch pipe and tighten the nut to 10-16 ft. lbs. (13-22 Nm).
9. Install the hose and the clamp to the master cylinder.
10. Install the battery and battery tray.
11. Bleed the air from the system.
12. Test the system and make sure there is no leakage.
13. Connect the negative battery cable.

Clutch Slave Cylinder

REMOVAL & INSTALLATION

1991-95 Models

1. Disconnect the pressure line. Plug the line to prevent leaking.
2. Remove the attaching bolts and remove the slave cylinder.

To install:

3. Install the slave cylinder.
4. Install the attaching bolts and tighten to 12-17 ft. lbs. (16-23 Nm).
5. Connect the pressure line and tighten the nut to 10-16 ft. lbs. (13-22 Nm).
6. Bleed the air from the system.
7. Press on the clutch pedal and make sure there is no leakage.

HYDRAULIC SYSTEM BLEEDING

➡The fluid level in the reservoir must be maintained at the ¾ level or higher during air bleeding.

1. Remove the bleeder cap from the slave cylinder and attach a vinyl hose to the bleeder screw.
2. Place the other end of the hose in a container.
3. Slowly pump the clutch pedal several times.
4. With the clutch pedal depressed, loosen the bleeder screw to release the fluid and air.
5. Tighten the bleeder screw.
6. Repeat the last three steps until no air bubbles appear in the fluid.

AUTOMATIC TRANSAXLE

➧ See Figures 40 and 41

The automatic transaxle (ATX) combines an automatic transaxle and differential into a single powertrain component designed for front wheel drive application. The transaxle and differential components are housed in a compact, one-piece case.

Fluid Pan and Filter

REMOVAL & INSTALLATION

In normal service it should not be necessary, nor is it required, to drain and refill the fluid. However, under severe operation or dusty conditions, the fluid should be changed every 20 months or 20,000 miles (32,206 km).

1. Raise and support the vehicle safely.
2. Place a suitable drain pan underneath the transaxle oil pan. Loosen the oil pan mounting bolts and allow the fluid to drain until it reaches the level of the pan flange. Remove the attaching bolts, leaving one end attached so that the pan will tip and the rest of the fluid will drain.
3. Remove the oil pan. Thoroughly clean the pan. Remove the old gasket. Make sure that the gasket mounting surfaces are clean.
4. Remove the transaxle filter screen retaining bolt. Remove the screen.
5. Install a new filter screen and O-ring. Place a new gasket on the pan and install the pan to the transaxle.
6. Lower the vehicle.
7. Fill the transaxle to the correct level. Refer to Section 1.

Adjustments

SHIFT LINKAGE

1981-90 Models

1. Place the gear shift selector into D. The shift lever must be in the D position during linkage adjustment.
2. Working at the transaxle, loosen the transaxle lever-to-control cable nut.
3. Move the transaxle lever to the D position, 2nd detent from the most rearward position.
4. Tighten the adjusting nut to 10-15 ft. lbs. (14-20 Nm).
5. Make sure all gears engage correctly and the vehicle will only start in P or D

1991-95 Models

➧ See Figure 42

1. Disconnect the negative battery cable. This will deactivate the shift-lock system.
2. Move the gear selector lever to P.
3. Remove the screw securing the gear selector knob to the gear selector lever. Remove the knob.
4. Remove the shift console as follows:
   a. Remove the rear seat ash tray and position both front seats to the rear-most position.
   b. Remove the two front retaining screws from the parking brake console and recline both front seats.
   c. Remove the two rear retaining screws from the parking brake console.
   d. With the parking brake engaged, remove the parking brake console.
   e. Remove the two front retaining screws from the shift console and remove the console.
5. Remove the position indicator mounting screws and disconnect the illumination bulb from the position indicator.

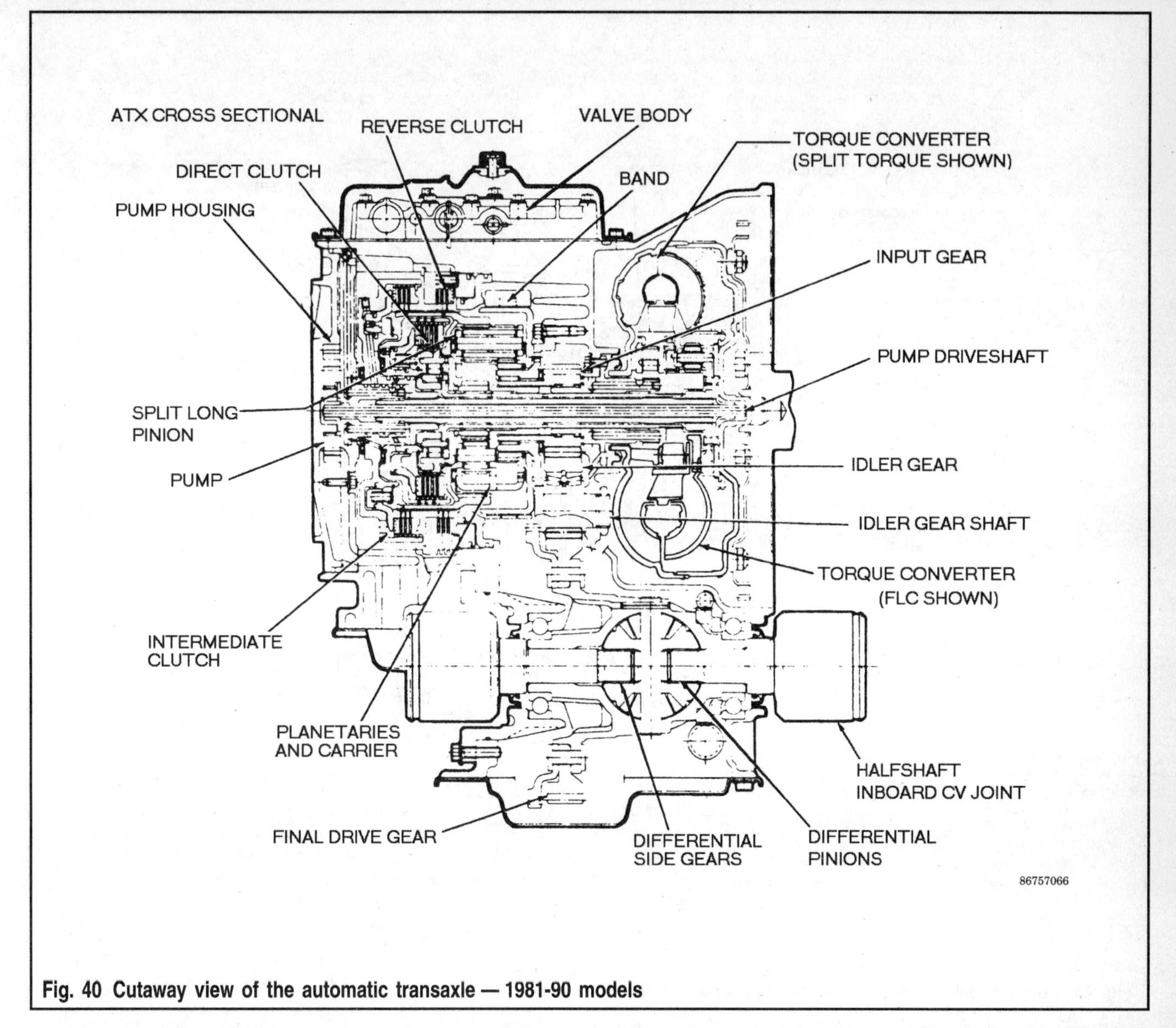

Fig. 40 Cutaway view of the automatic transaxle — 1981-90 models

6. Disconnect the shift-lock servo and park range switch electrical connectors.
7. Remove the position indicator.

➡Make sure the detent spring roller is in the P detent.

8. Loosen the shift control cable bracket mounting bolts.
9. Push the gear selector lever against the P range and hold it.
10. Tighten the shift control cable bracket mounting bolts to 69-95 inch lbs. (8-11 Nm).
11. Lightly press the gear selector pushrod and make sure the guide plate and guide pin clearances are within specifications.
12. Refer to the accompanying drawing and check that the guide plate and guide pin clearances are within 0.024 in. (0.6mm) when the selector lever is shifted to N and OD. If the clearances are not as specified, readjust the shift control cable.
13. Make sure the gear selector operates properly.
14. Connect the illumination bulb to the position indicator.
15. Connect the shift-lock servo and park range switch electrical connectors.
16. Install the position indicator and secure it with the mounting screws.
17. Install the shift console by reversing the removal procedure.
18. Position the gear selector knob onto the gear selector lever and secure the knob with the screw.
19. Connect the negative battery cable.

THROTTLE LINKAGE

➡The throttle valve (TV) linkage adjustment is set at the factory and is critical in establishing automatic transaxle upshift and downshift timing and feel. Any time the engine, transaxle or throttle linkage components are removed, it is recommended that the TV linkage adjustment be reset after the component installation or replacement

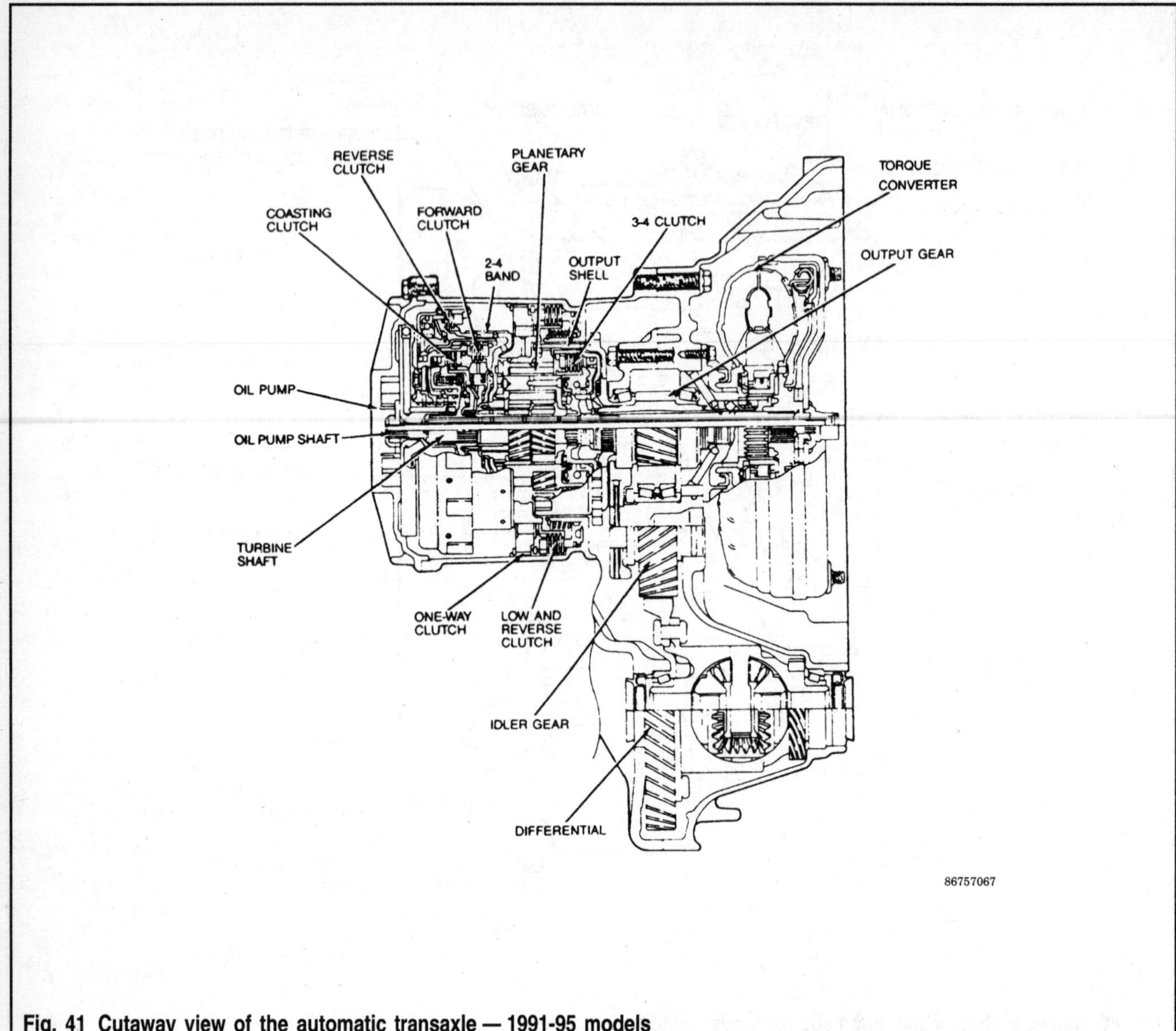

Fig. 41 Cutaway view of the automatic transaxle — 1991-95 models

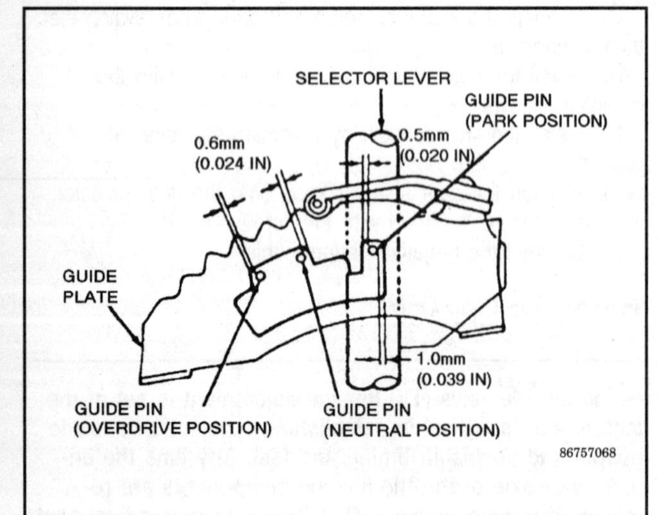

Fig. 42 Adjust the shift control cable according to the given tolerances

Carbureted Vehicles

➧ See Figure 43

The TV control linkage is adjusted at the sliding trunnion block.

1. Adjust the curb idle speed to specification as shown on the under hood decal.
2. After the curb idle speed has been set, shut off the engine. Make sure the choke is completely opened. Check the carburetor throttle lever to make sure it is against the hot engine curb idle stop.
3. Set the coupling lever adjustment screw at its approximate midrange. Make sure the TV linkage shaft assembly is fully seated upward into the coupling lever.

CAUTION

If adjustment of the linkage is necessary, allow the EGR valve to cool so you won't get burned.

4. To adjust, loosen the bolt on the sliding block on the TV control rod a minimum of one turn. Clean any dirt or corrosion

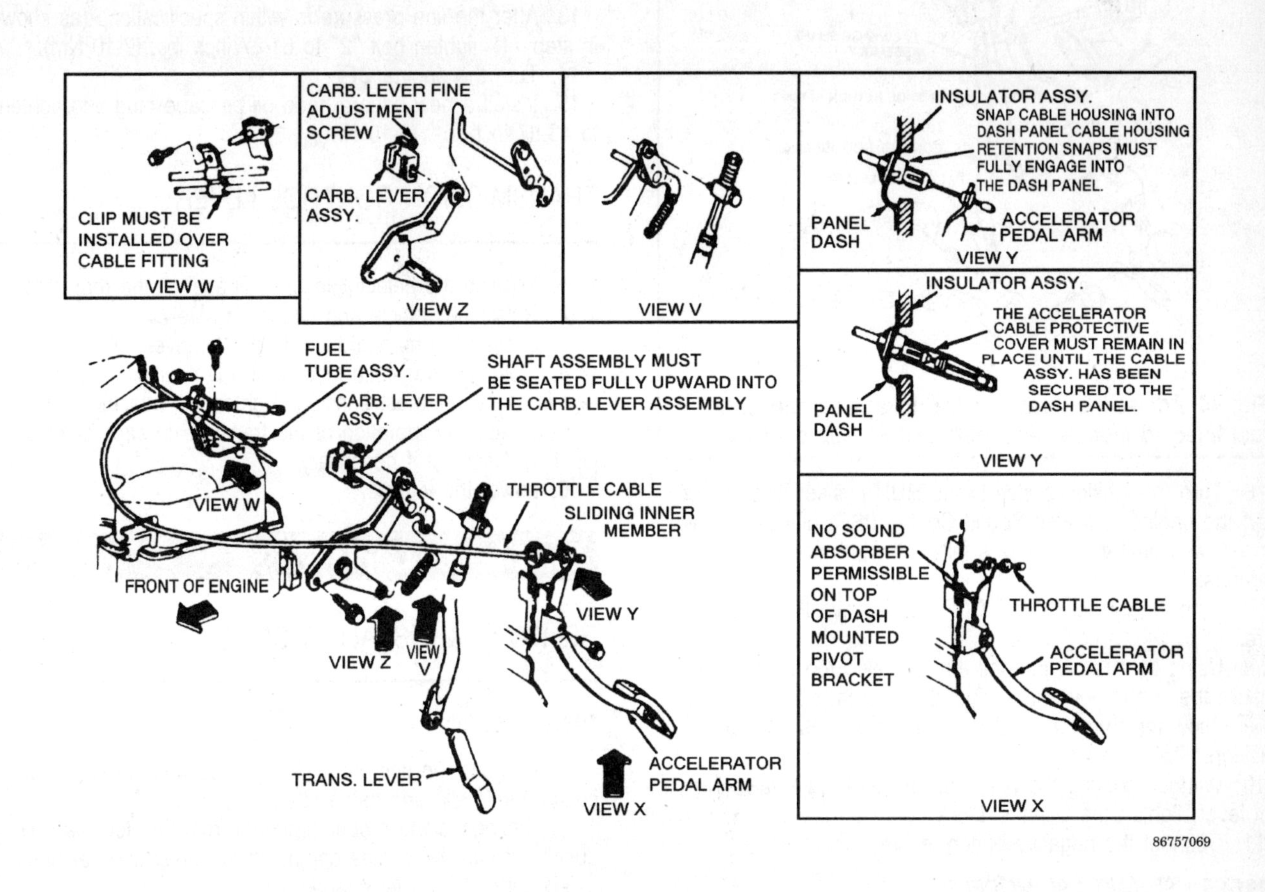

Fig. 43 Throtle linkage, cable and related components — carbureted models

from the control rod, free-up the trunnion block so that it will slide freely on the control rod.

5. Rotate the transaxle TV control lever up using a finger and light force, to insure that the TV control lever is against its internal stop. With reducing the pressure on the control lever, tighten the bolt on the trunnion block.

6. Check the carburetor throttle lever to be sure it is still against the hot idle stop. If not, repeat the adjustment steps.

Fuel Injected Vehicles

EXCEPT 1986-90 1.9L MODELS

➧ See Figure 44

1. Disconnect the negative battery cable.
2. Remove the splash shield from the cable retainer bracket.
3. Loosen the trunnion bolt at the throttle valve rod.
4. Install a plastic clip to bottom the throttle valve rod; be sure the clip does not telescope.
5. Be sure the return spring is connected between the throttle valve rod and the retaining bracket to hold the transaxle throttle valve lever at its idle position.
6. Make sure the throttle lever is resting on the throttle return control screw.
7. Tighten the throttle valve rod trunnion bolt and remove the plastic clip.
8. Install the splash shield. Connect the negative battery cable and check the vehicle's operation.

1986-90 1.9L MODELS

1. Disconnect the negative battery cable.
2. Set the parking brake and place the transaxle shift lever into P.
3. Loosen the sliding trunnion block bolt, located on the throttle valve control rod assembly, a minimum of one turn.
4. Make sure the trunnion block slides freely on the control rod.
5. Using a jumper wire, connect it between the STI connector and the signal return ground on the self-test connector.

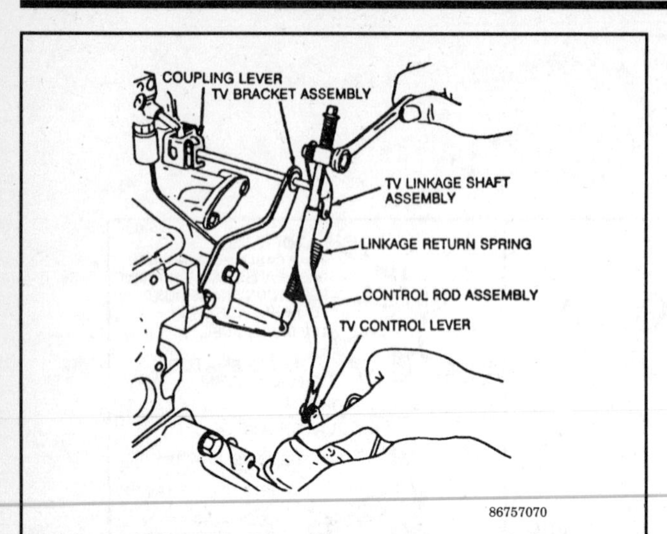

Fig. 44 Adjust the throttle valve linkage as shown on fuel injected models — except 1986-90 1.9L engines

6. Turn the ignition switch to the **RUN** position but do not start the engine. The Idle Speed Control (ISC) plunger should retract; wait until the plunger is fully retracted, about 10 seconds.
7. Turn the ignition switch **OFF** and remove the jumper wire.
8. Using light force, pull the throttle valve rod upward to ensure the control lever is against the internal stop.
9. Allow the trunnion to slide on the rod to its normal position.
10. Without relaxing the pressure on the throttle valve control lever, tighten the trunnion block bolt.
11. Connect the negative battery cable.

1991-95 1.8L AND 1.9L MODELS

➡The TV cable adjustment for the 4-speed Electronically Activated Transmission (4EAT) requires a transmission test adaptor, part No. D87C-77000-A, or equivalent and a line pressure gauge, part No. T57L-77820-A, or equivalent.

1. If necessary, install the ends of the TV control actuating cable to the transaxle and the throttle control lever.
2. If necessary, install the throttle cable bracket to the intake manifold bracket.
3. Tighten the hold-down bolt "1" at the bracket (closest to the throttle control lever) to 61-87 inch lbs. (7-10 Nm).
4. Remove the left front engine/transmission shields.
5. Remove the square head plug (marked "L") and install the transmission test adaptor, or equivalent, and a suitable line pressure gauge.
6. Warm-up the engine and let it run at idle.
7. Adjust the throttle valve control actuating cable until the line pressure reaches 71-74 psi (490-510 kPa).
8. Loosely tighten bolt "2" (closest to the transaxle).
9. Turn the engine and verify that the throttle valve control actuating cable operates smoothly.
10. Restart the engine and press the accelerator slightly, then run the engine at idle.
11. Verify that the line pressure is within 65-78 psi (448-537 kPa).
12. If the line pressure is not within specifications, repeat the procedure beginning with step 7.
13. After the line pressure is within specifications (as shown in step 11), tighten bolt "2" to 61-87 inch lbs. (7-10 Nm).
14. Turn the engine **OFF**.
15. Install a new square head oil passage plug and tighten it to 43-87 inch lbs. (5-10 Nm).

TRANSMISSION CONTROL LEVER

1. Position the selector lever in D against the rear stop.
2. Raise the vehicle and support it safely.
3. Loosen the manual lever-to-control lever nut.
4. Move the transaxle lever to the D position, second detent from the rearmost position. Tighten the attaching nut.
5. Check the operation of the transaxle in each selector position. Readjust if necessary.
6. Lower the vehicle.

Shift Lever Cable

REMOVAL & INSTALLATION

1981-90 Models

1. Remove the shift knob, locknut, console, bezel assembly, control cable clip and cable retaining pin.
2. Disengage the rubber grommet from the floor pan by pushing it into the engine compartment. Raise the car and safely support it on jackstands.
3. Remove the retaining nut and control cable assembly from the transaxle lever. Remove the control cable bracket bolts. Pull the cable through the floor.
4. To install the cable, feed the round end through the floor board. Press the rubber grommet into its mounting hole.
5. Position the control cable assembly in the selector lever housing and install the spring clip. Install the bushing and control cable assembly on the selector lever and housing assembly shaft and secure it with the retaining pin.
6. Install the bezel assembly, console, locknut and shift knob. Position the selector lever in the D position. The selector lever must be held in this position while attaching the other end of the control cable.
7. Position the control cable bracket on the retainer bracket and secure the tow mounting bolts.
8. Shift the control lever into the second detent from full rearward (D position).
9. Place the cable end on the transaxle lever stud. Align the flats on the stud with the slot in the cable. Make sure the transaxle selector lever has not moved from the second detent position and tighten the retaining nut.
10. Lower the car to the ground. Check the operation of the transaxle selector in all positions. Make sure the neutral safety switch is operating properly. (The engine should start only in P or N position).

Selector Indicator Bulb

REMOVAL & INSTALLATION

1981-90 Models

1. Remove the console and the four screws that mount the bezel.
2. Lift the bezel assembly and disconnect the indicator bulb harness.
3. Remove the indicator bulb.
4. Install a new bulb and reverse the removal procedure.

Neutral Safety Switch

REMOVAL & INSTALLATION

1981-90 Models

The mounting location of the neutral safety switch does not provide for adjustment of the switch position when installed. If the engine will not start in P or N, or if it will start in R or any of the D ranges, check the control linkage adjustment and/or replace with a known good switch.

1. Set the parking brake.
2. Disconnect the battery negative cable.
3. Disconnect the wire connector from the neutral safety switch.
4. Remove the two retaining screws from the neutral start switch and remove the switch.

To install:

5. Place the switch on the manual shift shaft and loosely install the retaining bolts.
6. Use a No. 43 drill (0.089 in. / 2.26mm) and insert it into the switch to set the contacts.
7. Tighten the retaining screws of the switch, remove the drill and complete the assembly by reversing the removal procedure.
8. Connect negative battery cable.
9. Check the ignition switch for proper starting in P or N. Also make certain that the start circuit cannot be actuated in the D or R position and that the column is locked in the **LOCK** position.

Transaxle

REMOVAL & INSTALLATION

1981-85 Models

1. Disconnect the negative battery cable.
2. From under the hood, remove the bolts that attach the air manage valve to the automatic transaxle valve body cover. Disconnect the wiring harness connector from the neutral safety switch.
3. Disconnect the throttle valve linkage and the manual control lever cable. Remove the two transaxle to engine upper attaching bolts. The bolts are located below and on either side of the distributor.
4. Loosen the front wheel lugs slightly. Jack up the front of the car and safely support it on jackstands. Remove the wheels.
5. Drain the transmission fluid. Disconnect the brake hoses from the strut brackets on both sides. Remove the pinch bolts that secure the lower control arms to the steering knuckles. Separate the ball joint from the steering knuckle. Remove the stabilizer bar attaching bracket. Remove the nuts that retain the stabilizer to the control arms. Remove the stabilizer bar. When removing the control arms from the steering knuckles, it will be necessary to bend the plastic shield slightly to gain ball joint clearance for removal.
6. Remove the tie rod ends from the steering knuckles. Use a special tie rod removing tool. Pry the right side halfshaft from the transaxle (see halfshaft removal section).
7. Remove the left side halfshaft from the transaxle. Support both right and left side halfshaft out of the way with wire.
8. Install sealing plugs or the equivalent into the transaxle halfshaft mounting holes.
9. Remove the starter support bracket. Disconnect the starter cable. Remove the starter mounting studs and the starter motor. Remove the transaxle support bracket.
10. Remove the lower cover from the transaxle. Turn the converter for access to the converter mounting nuts. Remove the nuts.
11. Remove the nuts that attach the left front insulator to the body bracket. Remove the bracket to body bolts and remove the bracket.
12. Remove the left rear insulator bracket attaching nut.
13. Disconnect the transaxle cooler lines. Remove the bolts that attach the manual lever bracket to the transaxle case.
14. Position a floor jack with a wide saddle under the transaxle and remove the four remaining transaxle to engine attaching bolts.
15. The torque converter mounting studs must be clear of the engine flywheel before the transaxle can be lowered from the car. Take a small prybar and place it between the flywheel and the converter. Carefully move the transaxle away from the engine. When the converter mounting studs are clear, lower the transaxle about 3 in. (76mm). Disconnect the speedometer cable from the transaxle.
16. Lower the transaxle to the ground.

➡When moving the transaxle away from the engine, watch the mount insulator. If it interferes with the transaxle before the converter mounting studs clear the flywheel, remove the insulator.

To install:

17. Installation is the reverse order of the removal procedure. Be sure to pay strict attention to the following:
    a. Before installing the halfshaft into the transaxle, replace the circlip on the CV-joint stub shaft. Carefully work the clip over the end of the shaft, spreading it as little as possible.
    b. To install the halfshaft into the transaxle, carefully align the splines of the CV-joint with the splines in the differential.

c. Exerting some force, push the CV-joint into the differential until the circlip is felt to seat the differential side gear. Be careful not to damage the differential oil seal.

➡A non-metallic, mallet may be used to aid in seating the circlip into the differential side gear groove. If a mallet is necessary, tap only on the outboard CV-joint stub shaft.

d. Attach the lower ball joint to the steering knuckle, taking care not to damage or cut the ball joint boot. Insert a new service pinch bolt and attach a new nut. Tighten the nut to 37-44 ft. lbs. (50-60 Nm). Do not tighten the bolt.

1985½-90 Models

1. Disconnect the negative battery cable.

➡Due to automatic transaxle case configuration, the right-side halfshaft assembly must be removed first. The differential rotator tool or equivalent, is then inserted into the transaxle to drive the left-side inboard CV-joint assembly from the transaxle.

2. Remove the air cleaner assembly.
3. Disconnect the electrical harness connector from the neutral safety switch.
4. Disconnect the throttle valve linkage and the manual lever cable from their levers.

➡Failure to disconnect the linkage and allowing the transaxle to hang, will fracture the throttle valve cam shaft joint, which is located under the transaxle cover.

5. To prevent contamination, cover the timing window in the converter housing. If equipped, remove the bolts retaining the thermactor hoses.
6. If equipped, remove the ground strap, located above the upper engine mount, and the coil and bracket assembly.
7. Remove both transaxle-to-engine upper bolts; the bolts are located below and on both ides of the distributor. Raise and safely support the vehicle. Remove the front wheels.
8. Remove the control arm-to-steering knuckle nut, at the ball joint.
9. Using a hammer and a punch, drive the bolt from the steering knuckle; repeat this step on the other side. Discard the nut and bolt.

➡Be careful not to damage or cut the ball joint boot. The prybar must not contact the lower arm.

10. Using a prybar, disengage the control arm from the steering knuckle; repeat this step on the other side.

➡Do not hammer on the knuckle to remove the ball joints. The plastic shield installed behind the rotor contains a molded pocket into which the lower control arm ball joint fits. When disengaging the control arm from the knuckle, clearance for the ball joint can be provided by bending the shield back toward the rotor. Failure to provide clearance for the ball joint can result in damage to the shield.

11. Remove the stabilizer bar bracket-to-frame rail bolts and discard the bolts; repeat this step on the other side.
12. Remove the stabilizer bar-to-control arm nut/washer and discard the nut; repeat this step on the other side.
13. Pull the stabilizer bar from of the control arms.
14. Remove the brake hose routing clip-to-suspension strut bracket bolt; repeat this step on the other side.
15. Remove the steering gear tie rod-to-steering knuckle nut and disengage the tie rod from the steering knuckle; repeat this step on the other side.
16. Using a halfshaft removal tool, pry the halfshaft from the right side of the transaxle and support the end of the shaft with a wire.

➡It is normal for some fluid to leak from the transaxle when the halfshaft is removed.

17. Using a differential rotator tool or equivalent, drive the left-side halfshaft from the differential side gear.
18. Pull the halfshaft from the transaxle and support the end of the shaft with a wire.

➡Do not allow the shaft to hang unsupported, as damage to the outboard CV-joint may result.

19. Install seal plugs into the differential seals.
20. Remove the starter support bracket and disconnect the starter cable. Remove the starter bolts and the starter. If equipped with a throttle body, remove the hose and bracket bolts on the starter and a bolt at the converter and disconnect the hoses.
21. Remove the transaxle support bracket and the dust cover from the torque converter housing.
22. Remove the torque converter-to-flywheel nuts by turning the crankshaft pulley bolt to bring the nuts into position.
23. Position a suitable transaxle jack under the transaxle and remove the rear support bracket nuts.
24. Remove the left front insulator-to-body bracket nuts, the bracket-to-body bolts and the bracket.
25. Disconnect the transaxle cooler lines.
26. Remove the manual lever bracket-to-transaxle case bolts.
27. Support the engine. Make sure the transaxle is supported and remove the remaining transaxle-to-engine bolts.
28. Make sure the torque converter studs will clear the flywheel. Insert a prybar between the flywheel and the converter, then, pry the transaxle and converter away from the engine. When the converter studs are clear of the flywheel, lower the transaxle about 2-3 in. (51-76mm).
29. Disconnect the speedometer cable and lower the transaxle.

➡When moving the transaxle away from the engine, watch the No. 1 insulator. If it contacts the body before the converter studs clear the flywheel, remove the insulator.

To install:

30. Raise the transaxle and align it with the engine and flywheel. Install the No. 1 insulator, if removed. Tighten the transaxle-to-engine bolts to 25-33 ft. lbs. (34-45 Nm) and the torque converter-to-flywheel bolts to 23-39 ft. lbs. (31-53 Nm).
31. Install the manual lever bracket-to-transaxle case bolts and connect the transaxle cooler lines.
32. Install the left front insulator-to-body bracket nuts and tighten the nuts to 40-50 ft. lbs. (55-70 Nm). Install the bracket-to-body and tighten the bolts to 55-70 ft. lbs. (75-90 Nm).
33. Install the transaxle support bracket and the dust cover to the torque converter housing.

34. If equipped with a throttle body, install the hose and bracket bolts on the starter and a bolt to the converter and connect the hoses. Install the starter and the support bracket; tighten the starter-to-engine bolts to 30-40 ft. lbs. (41-54 Nm). Connect the starter cable.

35. Remove the seal plugs from the differential seals and install the halfshaft by performing the following procedures:

a. Prior to installing the halfshaft in the transaxle, install a new circlip onto the CV-joint stub.

b. Install the halfshaft in the transaxle by carefully aligning the CV-joint splines with the differential side gears. Be sure to push the CV-joint into the differential until the circlip is felt to seat in the differential side gear. Use care to prevent damage to the differential oil seal.

c. Attach the lower ball joint to the steering knuckle, taking care not to damage or cut the ball joint boot. Insert a new pinch bolt and a new nut. While holding the bolt with a wrench, tighten the nut to 40-54 ft. lbs. (54-74 Nm).

36. Engage the tie rod with the steering knuckle and tighten the nut to 23-35 ft. lbs. (31-47 Nm).

37. Install the brake hose routing clip-to-suspension strut bracket and tighten the bolt to 8 ft. lbs. (11 Nm).

38. Install the stabilizer bar to control arm and using a new nut, tighten it to 98-125 ft. lbs. (133-169 Nm).

39. Install the stabilizer bar bracket-to-frame rail bolts and using new bolts, tighten them to 60-70 ft. lbs. (81-95 Nm).

40. Install the wheels and lower the vehicle. Install the upper transaxle-to-engine bolts and tighten to 25-33 ft. lbs. (34-45 Nm).

41. If equipped, install the ground strap, located above the upper engine mount, and the coil and bracket assembly.

42. If equipped, install the bolts retaining the thermactor hoses. Uncover the timing window in the converter housing.

43. Connect the throttle valve linkage and the manual lever cable to their levers.

44. Connect the electrical harness connector from the neutral safety switch.

45. Install the air cleaner assembly.

46. Connect the negative battery cable and road test the vehicle.

1991-95 Models

1. Disconnect the battery cables and remove the battery and battery tray.

2. Disconnect the wiring harness retaining clip from the battery tray.

3. Remove the air cleaner assembly.

4. Disconnect the shift control cable from the manual lever.

5. Disconnect the speedometer cable from the transaxle by unsnapping the cable at the speedometer driven gear.

6. Disconnect the transaxle electronic control electrical connectors and separate the harness from the transaxle clips.

7. Remove the manual lever position switch wiring brackets and disconnect the ground cables from the top of the transaxle.

8. Remove the starter.

9. Disconnect the manual lever position switch wiring connectors.

10. Install engine support D88L-6000-A or equivalent, to support the engine.

11. Disconnect the kickdown cable at the throttle cam.

12. Place a suitable drain pan under the transaxle and disconnect the transaxle cooler lines at the transaxle.

13. Remove the upper transaxle mount bolts, the mount and the upper transaxle housing bolts.

14. Disconnect the oxygen sensor electrical connector, the transaxle vent hose, and the electrical connector at the vehicle speed sensor.

15. Raise and safely support the vehicle.

16. Remove the front wheel and tire assemblies.

17. Remove the halfshafts.

18. Remove the three engine/transaxle lower splash shields and the torque converter inspection plate. Remove the nuts securing the torque converter to the flexplate.

19. Position the drain pan and remove the drainplug from the transaxle. Drain the fluid from the differential cavity. Remove the transaxle pan and drain the transaxle fluid.

20. Position a suitable transaxle jack under the transaxle. Secure the transaxle to the jack.

21. Remove the lower bolts securing the transaxle to the engine and carefully lower the transaxle out of the vehicle.

To install:

➡A pin is used for securing the throttle cam in a fixed position on new and rebuilt transaxles. This pin must be removed to allow proper transaxle operation. If the pin is not removed, the throttle lever will remain in a fixed position. After removing the pin, apply sealant to the bolt from the previous transaxle. Install the bolt and tighten to 69-95 inch lbs. (8-11 Nm).

22. Secure the transaxle on the transaxle jack.

23. Raise the transaxle into position and install the lower transaxle-to-engine bolts. Tighten the bolts to 41-59 ft. lbs. (55-80 Nm).

24. Position the torque converter to the flexplate and install the nuts. Tighten the nuts to 25-36 ft. lbs. (34-49 Nm).

25. Install the halfshafts.

26. Connect the crossmember to the transaxle mounts and the chassis. Tighten the crossmember-to-transaxle mount nuts to 27-38 ft. lbs. (37-52 Nm). Tighten the crossmember-to-chassis nuts and bolts to 47-66 ft. lbs. (64-89 Nm).

27. Install the engine/transaxle splash shields and the starter.

28. Position the lower ball joints into the steering knuckles and secure with the nuts and bolts. Tighten the nuts and bolts to 32-43 ft. lbs. (43-59 Nm).

29. Position the tie rod ends into the steering knuckles and install the nuts. Tighten to 31-42 ft. lbs. (42-57 Nm).

30. Install the wheel and tire assemblies. Tighten the lugs to 65-88 ft. lbs. (88-118 Nm).

31. Lower the vehicle.

32. Install the transaxle-to-engine bolts and tighten to 41-59 ft. lbs. (55-80 Nm).

33. Install the upper transaxle mount and tighten the nuts to 49-69 ft. lbs. (67-93 Nm).

34. Connect the transaxle vent hose, the electrical connector at the speed sensor, the speedometer cable and the oxygen sensor connector.

35. Connect the transaxle cooler lines and connect the kickdown cable at the throttle body.

36. Remove the engine support.

37. Connect the ground wires to the transaxle and connect the manual lever position switch bracket and wiring connectors.

38. Connect the shift control cable to the cable bracket and to the selector lever.
39. Install the battery tray and battery.
40. Install the air cleaner assembly.
41. Connect the battery cables.
42. Add the proper type and quantity of transaxle fluid.
43. Check the transaxle for proper operation.

Component	English	Metric
Clutch		
Transaxle-to-engine:	30–40 ft. lbs.	40–55 Nm
Pressure plate-to-flywheel:	12–24 ft. lbs.	17–32 Nm
Pin-to-release fork:	30–40 ft. lbs.	40–55 Nm
Manual Transaxle Assembly		
Case-to-clutch housing:	13–18 ft. lbs.	18–24 Nm
Reverse idler shaft-to-case:	15–20 ft. lbs.	21–27 Nm
Detent plunger retainer screw:	6–8 ft. lbs.	7.5–11 Nm
Filler plug:	9–15 ft. lbs.	12–20 Nm
Clutch release fork to shaft:	30–41 ft. lbs.	40–41 Nm
Manual Transaxle Installation		
Transaxle-to-engine bolts:	25–35 ft. lbs.	34–47 Nm
Control arm-to-steering knuckle:	37–44 ft. lbs.	50–60 Nm
Air manage valve bracket bolt-to-transaxle:	28–31 ft. lbs.	38–42 Nm
Rear mounting bolts:	35–50 ft. lbs.	47–68 Nm
Transaxle mounting stud:	38–41 ft. lbs.	52–56 Nm
Front mount bracket bolts:	25–35 ft. lbs.	34–47 Nm
Roll restrictor nuts:	25–35 ft. lbs.	34–47 Nm
Shift stablizer bar-to-transaxle case:	23–35 ft. lbs.	31–47 Nm
Automatic Transaxle Installation		
Transaxle-to-engine bolts:	25–33 ft. lbs.	34–45 Nm
Control arm to knuckle:	37–44 ft. lbs.	50–60 Nm
Stablizer to control arm:	98–125 ft. lbs.	133–169 Nm
Insulator-to-bracket:	55–70 ft. lbs.	75–90 Nm
Insulator bracket to frame:	40–50 ft. lbs.	55–70 Nm
Insulator mount-to-transmission:	25–33 ft. lbs.	34–45 Nm
Tie rod to knuckle*:	23–35 ft. lbs.	31–47 Nm

*Tighten to minimum specified torque. Continue tightening to nearest cotter pin slot.

86757C01

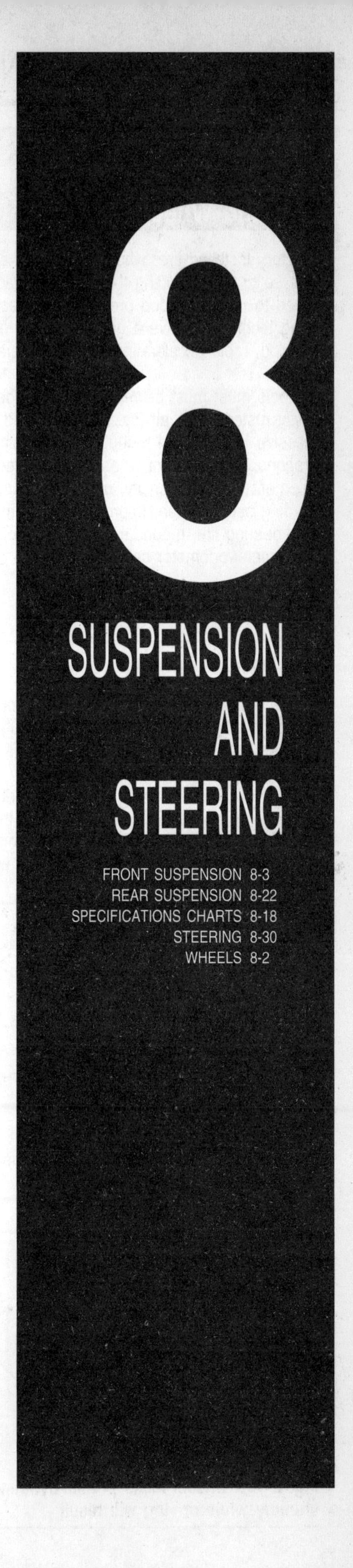

8 SUSPENSION AND STEERING

WHEELS

Tire and Wheel Assembly

Factory installed tires/wheels are designed to operate with loads up to and including the rated full-load capacity when inflated to recommended pressures. Correct tire pressures and driving techniques have a great influence on tire life. Heavy cornering, rapid acceleration, and sharp braking increases wear.

Wheels must must be replaced if they become, dented or heavily rusted, have air leaks or elongated bolt holes, or have excessive lateral/radial runout. Such conditions may cause vibrations. Replacement wheels must be equal to the original equipment in load capacity, diameter, width, offset and mounting configuration. Improper wheels may affect wheel/bearing life, ground/tire clearance, or speedometer/odometer calibrations.

TIRE AND WHEEL BALANCE

➧ **See Figures 1 and 2**

There are two types of wheel and tire balance:

- Static balance — is the equal distribution of weight around the wheel. If there is static imbalance, this condition causes a bouncing action called "wheel tramp."
- Dynamic balance — is the equal distribution of weight on each side of the centerline so that when the tire spins there is no tendency for the assembly to move from side-to-side. Improper dynamic balance will cause the wheel to shimmy.

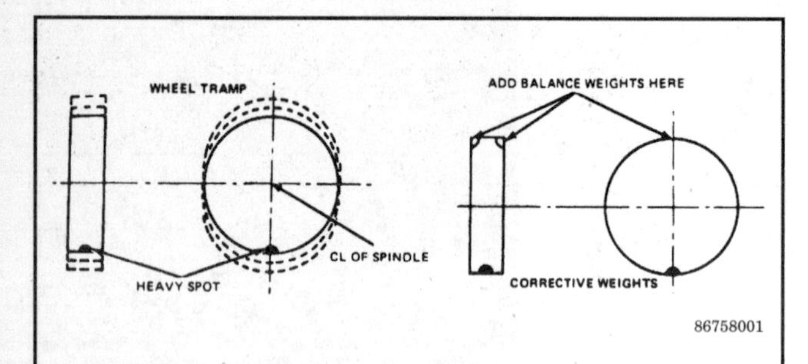

Fig. 1 Static imbalance condition causes a bouncing action called "wheel tramp"

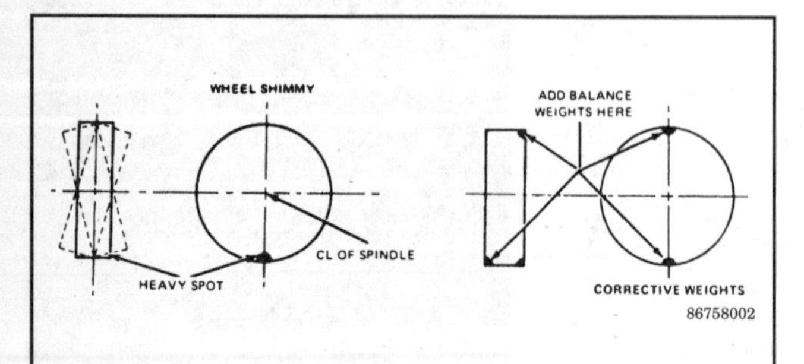

Fig. 2 If a wheels lacks proper dynamic balance, a shimmy while driving will result

REMOVAL & INSTALLATION

➧ **See Figures 3 and 4**

1. If equipped, remove the hub cap nuts and hub cap.
2. Loosen the nuts, then raise and support the vehicle safely.
3. Remove the lug nuts, then pull the wheel off the vehicle.

To install:

4. Clean the dirt from the hub or drum mounting surface, then install the wheel and tighten the nuts alternately until snug.
5. Lower the vehicle and tighten the nuts to 65-87 ft. lbs. (88-118 Nm). If equipped, install the hub cap and nuts.

Fig. 3 A common design wheel trim cover for 1980s models — remove by unscrewing the Phillips screws

Fig. 4 After the cap is removed, the car should be raised and safely supported for the wheel removal

FRONT SUSPENSION

➧ See Figures 5 and 6

The vehicles covered by this manual are equipped with a MacPherson strut front suspension. The strut acts upon a cast steering knuckle, which pivots on a ball joint mounted on a forged lower control arm. A stabilizer bar, which also acts as a locating link, is standard equipment. To maintain good directional stability, negative scrub radius is designed into the suspension geometry. This means that an imaginary line extended from the strut intersects the ground outside the tire patch. Caster and camber are present and nonadjustable. The front suspension fittings are "lubed-for-life"; no grease fittings are provided.

Lower Control Arm

REMOVAL & INSTALLATION

1981-90 Models

➧ See Figures 7, 8, 9, 10, 11, 12 and 13

1. Raise and safely support the vehicle.
2. Remove nut from stabilizer bar end. Pull off large dished washer.
3. Remove lower control arm inner pivot nut and bolt.
4. Remove lower control arm ball joint pinch bolt. Using a suitable prytool, slightly spread knuckle pinch joint and sepa-

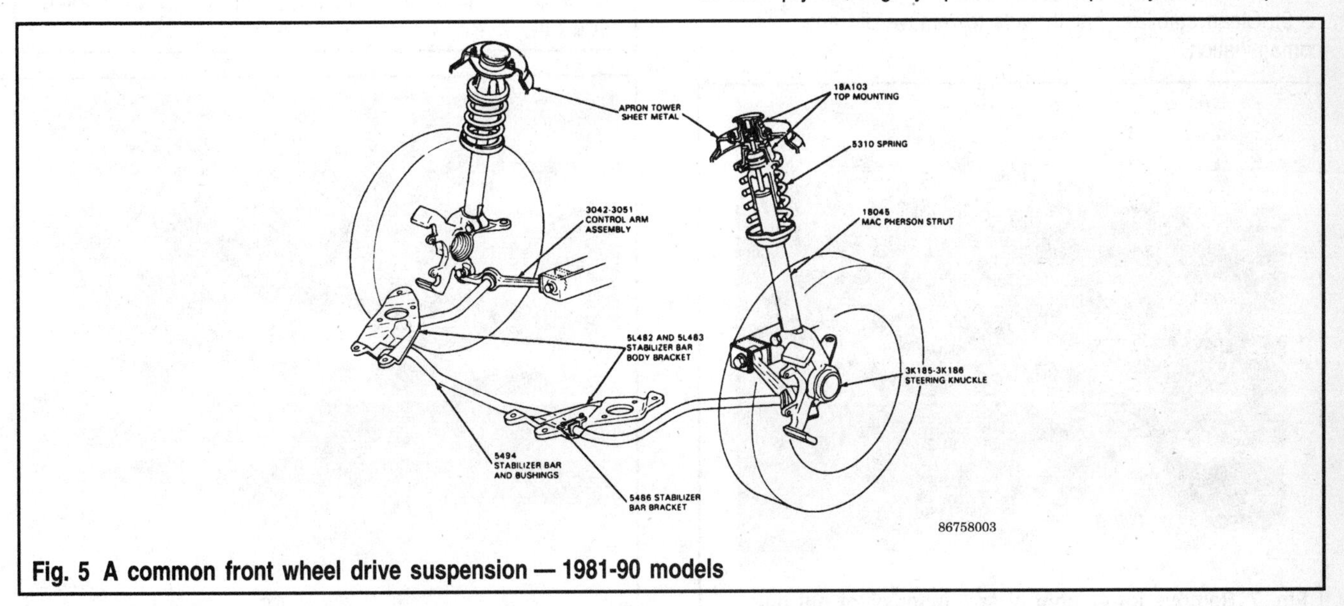

Fig. 5 A common front wheel drive suspension — 1981-90 models

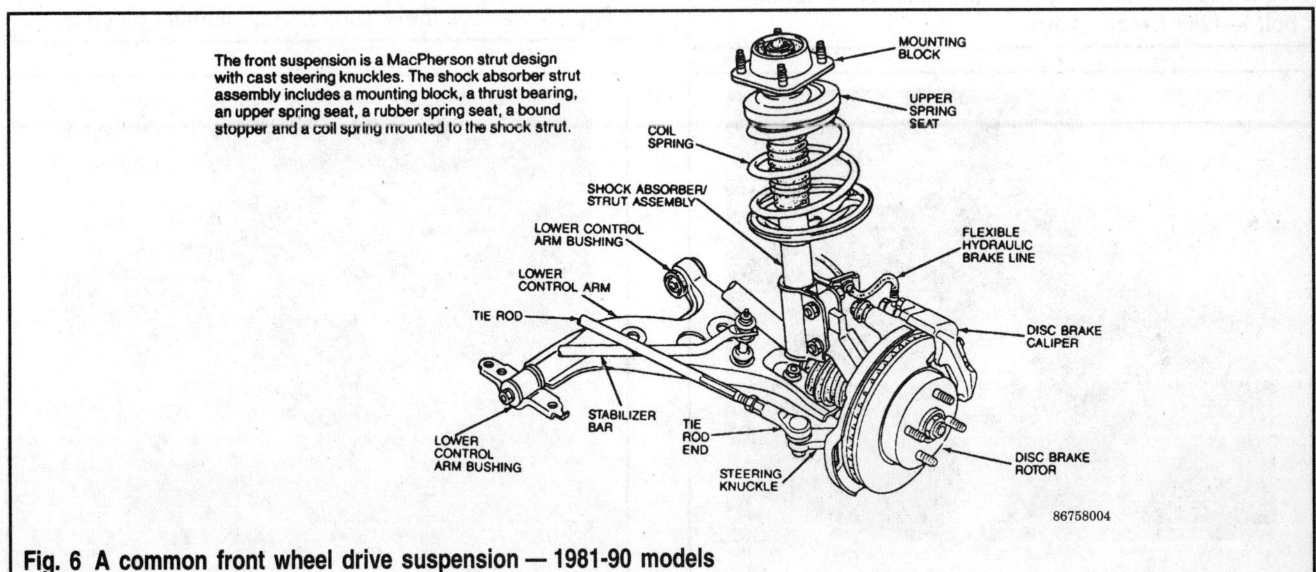

Fig. 6 A common front wheel drive suspension — 1981-90 models

rate control arm from steering knuckle. A drift punch may be used to remove the bolt.

➡Do not allow the steering knuckle/halfshaft to move outward. Over-extension of the tripod CV-joint could result in separation of internal parts, causing failure of the joint.

5. Remove the stabilizer bar spacer from the arm bushing.

➡Make sure the steering column is in the unlocked position. Do not use a hammer to separate the ball joint from knuckle.

To install:

6. Assemble the lower control arm ball joint stud to the steering knuckle, ensuring that the ball stud groove is properly positioned.
7. Insert a new pinch bolt and nut. Tighten to 38-45 ft. lbs. (52-60 Nm).
8. Insert stabilizer bar spacer into arm bushing.
9. Clean stabilizer bar threads to remove dirt and contamination.

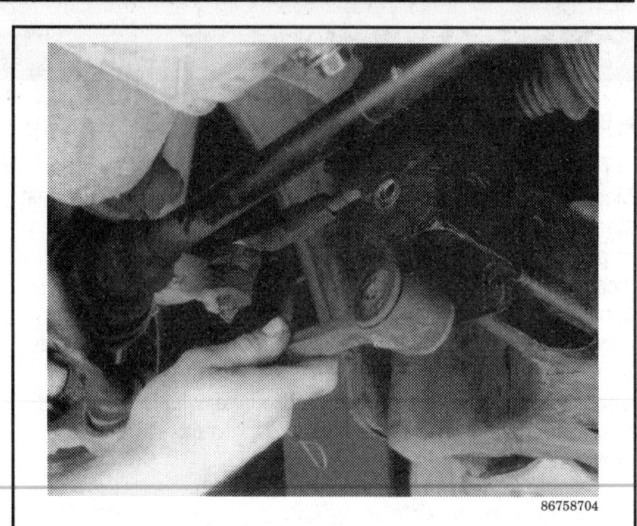

86758704

Fig. 9 Once the bolt is out, the pivoting portion should slide out

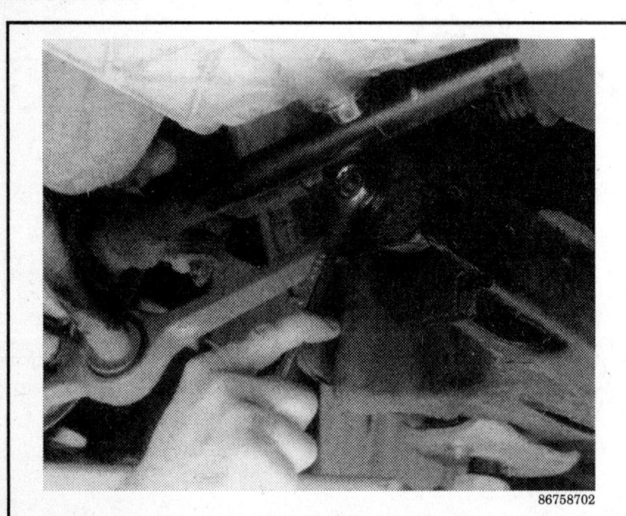

86758702

Fig. 7 Remove lower control arm inner pivot nut and bolt — 1988 Escort shown

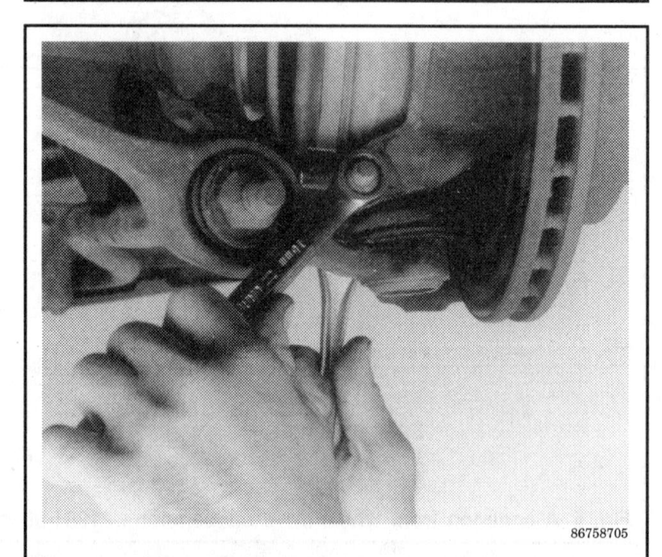

86758705

Fig. 10 Remove lower control arm ball joint pinch bolt

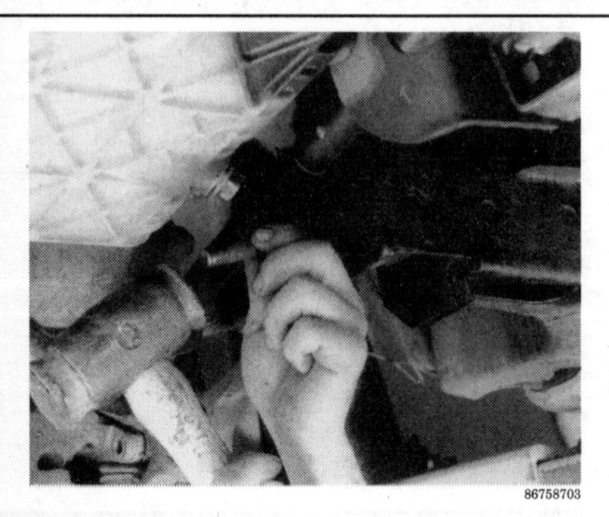

86758703

Fig. 8 A drift punch may be used to remove the pivot bolt

86758706

Fig. 11 A hammer and drift will probably be needed to push through the pinch bolt

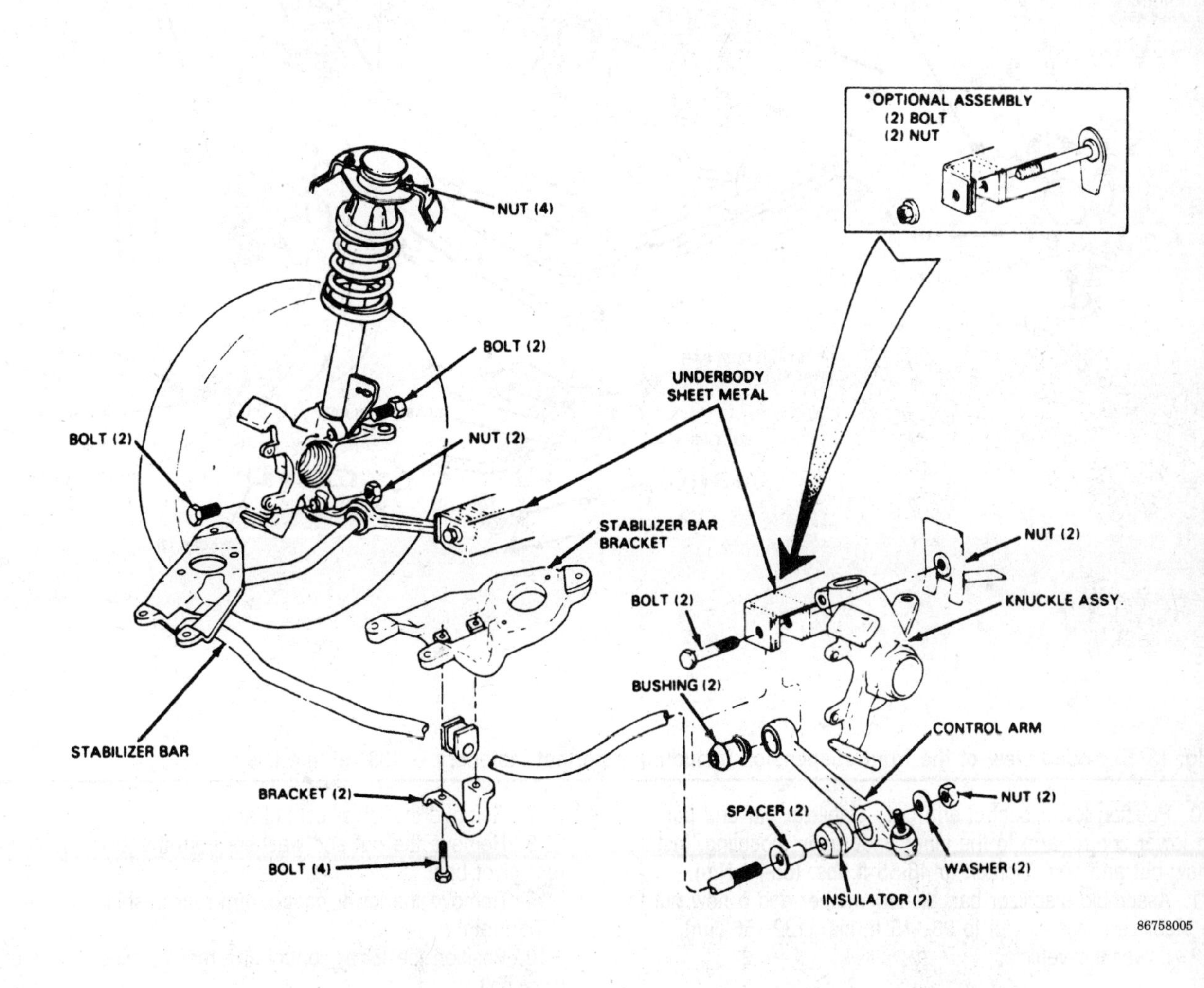

Fig. 12 Exploded view of the front suspension including important fasteners — 1981-83 models

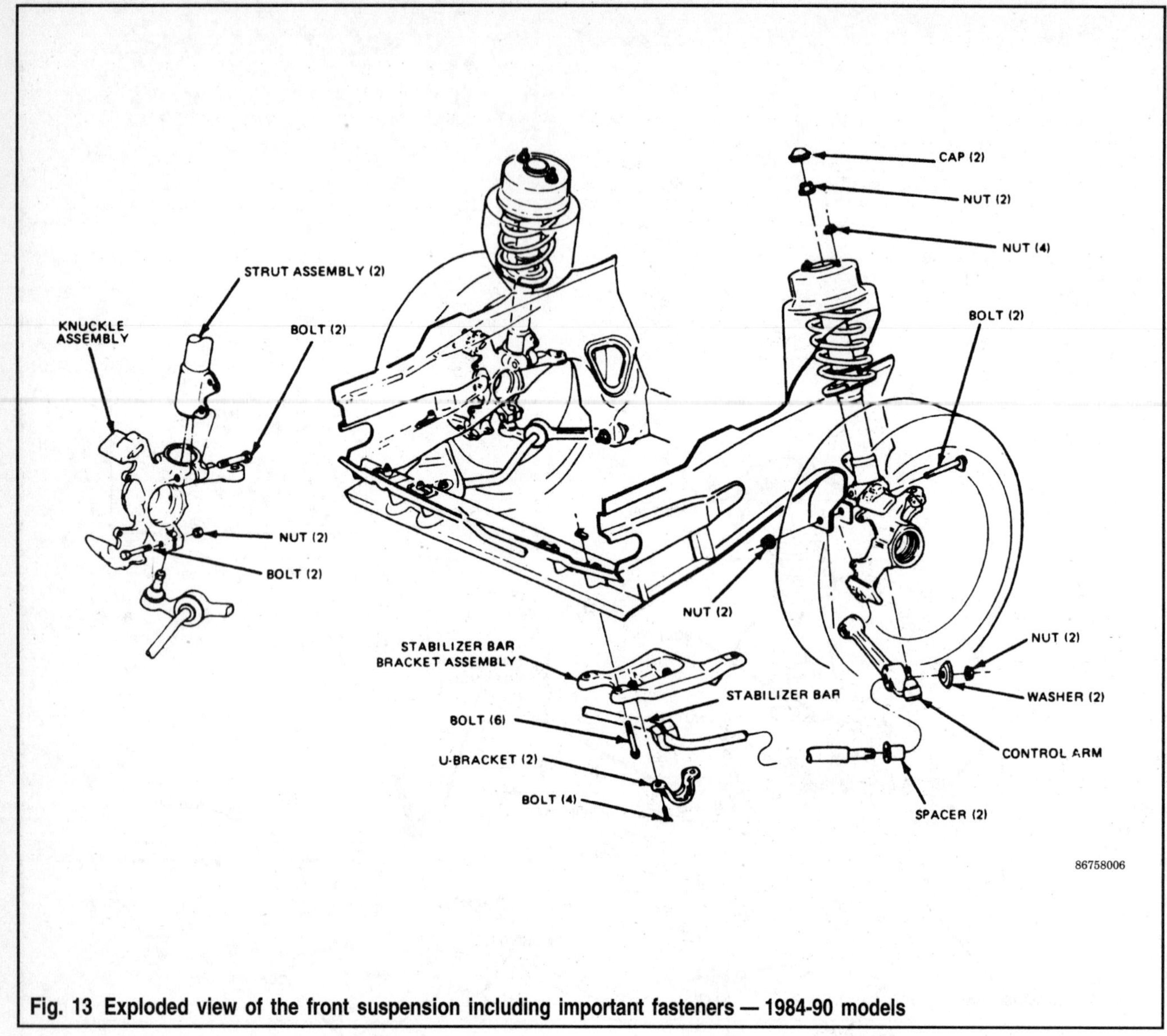

Fig. 13 Exploded view of the front suspension including important fasteners — 1984-90 models

10. Position lower control arm onto stabilizer bar and position lower control arm to the inner underbody mounting. Install a new nut and bolt. Tighten to 48-55 ft. lbs. (65-74 Nm).
11. Assemble stabilizer bar, dished washer and a new nut to the stabilizer. Tighten nut to 98-115 ft. lbs. (132-156 Nm).
12. Lower the vehicle.

1991-95 Models

See Figure 14

1. Loosen the lug nuts, then raise and support the vehicle safely.
2. Remove the front wheel and tire assembly.
3. Remove the front stabilizer nuts, washers, bushings, bolts and sleeves.
4. Remove the lower control arm front bushing bolt and washer.
5. Remove the bolts securing the lower control arm rear bushing retaining strap.
6. Remove the nut and bolt securing the lower ball joint to the steering knuckle. Separate the steering knuckle from the lower ball joint.
7. Remove the lower control arm.
8. Remove the nut and washers from the lower control arm rear pivot bolt.
9. Remove the lower control arm rear bushing.

To install:

10. Position the lower control arm rear bushing onto the rear pivot bolt.
11. Install the washers and nut onto the lower control arm pivot bolt. Tighten the nut to 69-86 ft. lbs. (93-117 Nm).
12. Install the ball joint into the steering knuckle. Install the ball joint retaining nut and bolt and tighten the nut to 32-43 ft. lbs. (43-59 Nm).
13. Install the lower control arm rear bushing retaining strap to the lower frame. Install the bolts and tighten to 69-86 ft. lbs. (93-117 Nm).
14. Install the lower control arm front pivot bolt and washer. Tighten the nut to 69-93 ft. lbs. (93-127 Nm).
15. Install the stabilizer bolts, washers, bushings, sleeves and nuts. Tighten the stabilizer nuts so 0.67-0.75 in. (17-19mm) of thread is exposed at the end of the bolt.

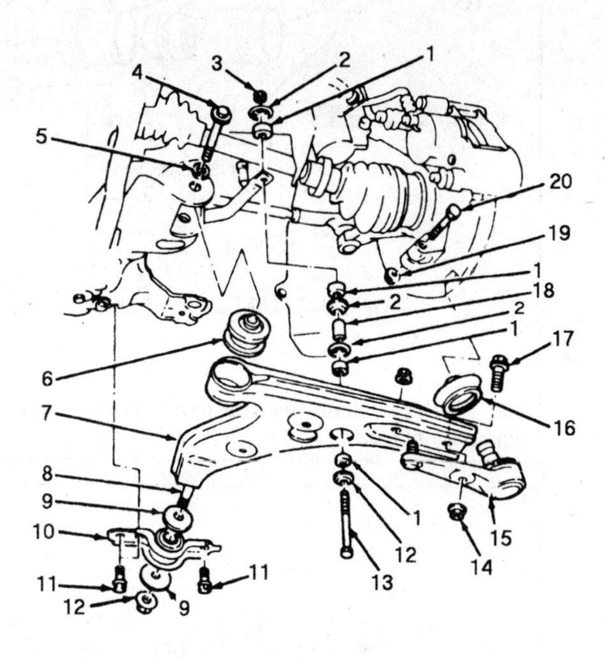

1 Raise the vehicle.
2 Remove the front wheel.
3 Remove the front stabilizer nuts, washers, bushings, bolts and sleeves.
4 Remove the lower control arm front bushing bolt and washer.

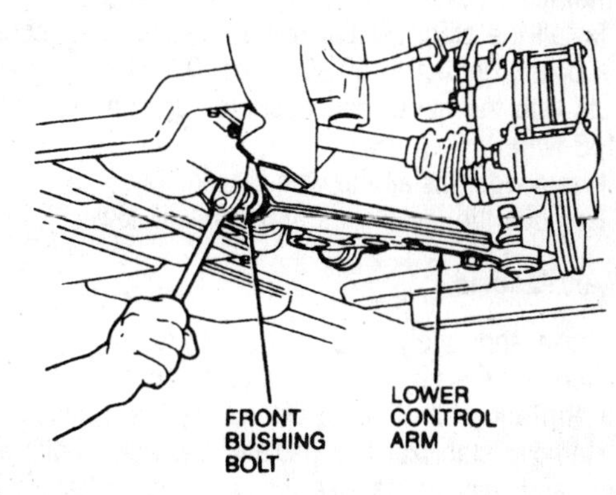

1 Bushings	7 Lower control arm	14 Nut
2 Washers	8 Pivot bolt	15 Ball joint
3 Nut	9 Washer	16 Dust cover
4 Bolt	10 Strap (rear bush assembly)	17 Bolt
5 Washer	11 Bolts	18 Sleeve
6 Lower control arm front bushing	12 Nut	19 Nut
	13 Bolt	20 Bolt

86758007

Fig. 14 Exploded view of the front lower control arm assembly — 1991-95 models

16. Install the wheel and tire assembly. Tighten the lug nuts to 65-87 ft. lbs. (88-118 Nm).
17. Lower the vehicle.

BUSHING REPLACEMENT

➧ See Figure 15

➡A C-clamp type remover/installer tool is necessary to replace the control arm to stabilizer mounting bushings. The Ford part number of this tool is T81P5493A and T74P-3044-A1.

1. Raise the front of the car and safely support it on jackstands.
2. Remove the lower control arm.
3. Carefully cut away the retaining lip of the bushing. Use the special clamp type tool and remove the bushing.
4. Saturate the new bushing with vegetable oil or soapy water and install the bushing using the special tool.
5. Install the lower control arm to the vehicle.

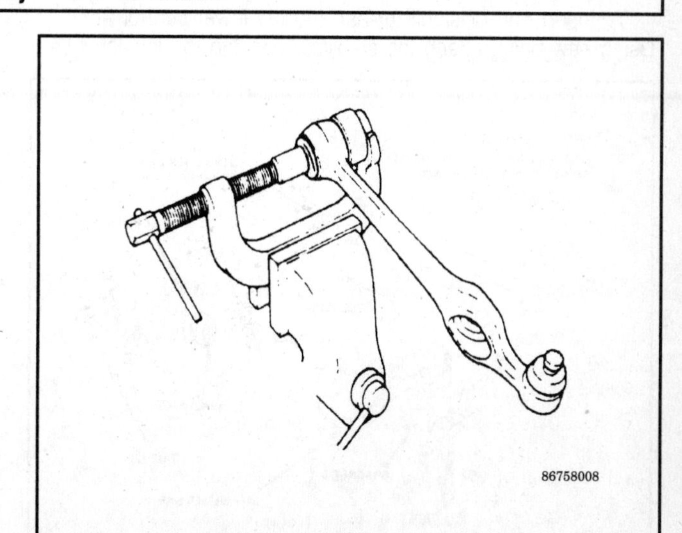

86758008

Fig. 15 Use the special C-clamp removal tool in a vise to press out the control arm bushing

Stabilizer Bar

REMOVAL & INSTALLATION

1981-85 Models

➧ See Figures 16, 17 and 18

1. Raise the vehicle and support it safely. The wheel(s) may be removed for convenience.
2. Remove the stabilizer bar insulator mounting bracket bolts, end nuts and washers. Remove the bar assembly.

To install:

3. Install the stabilizer bar using new insulator mounting bracket bolts. Tighten to 50-60 ft. lbs. (68-81 Nm). Install new end nuts with the old dished washers. Tighten to 75-80 ft. lbs. (102-108 Nm).
4. If removed, install the wheel assembly,
5. Remove the jackstands and carefully lower the vehicle.

1985½-90 Models

1. Raise and safely support the vehicle.
2. Remove the nut from the stabilizer bar at each lower control arm and pull off large dished washer. Discard nuts.
3. Remove stabilizer bar insulator U-bracket bolts and U-brackets and remove stabilizer bar assembly. Discard bolts.

➡Stabilizer bar U-bracket insulators can be serviced without removing the stabilizer bar assembly.

To install:

4. Slide new insulators onto the stabilizer bar and position them in the approximate location.
5. Clean stabilizer bar threads to remove dirt and contamination.
6. Install spacers into the control arm bushings from forward side of control arm so washer end of spacer will seat against stabilizer bar machined shoulder and push mounting brackets over insulators.
7. Insert end of stabilizer bar into the lower control arms. Using new bolts, attach the stabilizer bar and the insulator U-brackets to the bracket assemblies. Hand start all four U-bracket bolts. Tighten all bolts halfway, then tighten bolts to 85-100 ft. lbs. (115-135 Nm).
8. Using new nuts and the original dished washers (dished side away from bushing), attach the stabilizer bar to the lower control arm. Tighten nuts to 98-115 ft. lbs. (132-156 Nm).
9. Lower the vehicle.

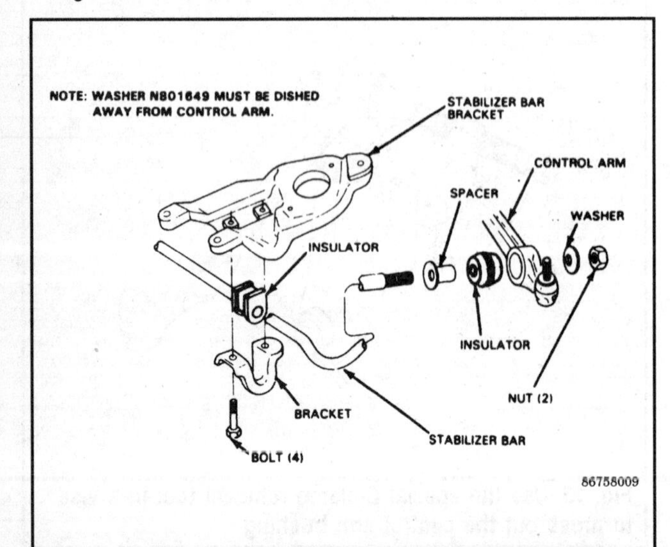

Fig. 16 Stabilizer bar components — 1981-90 models

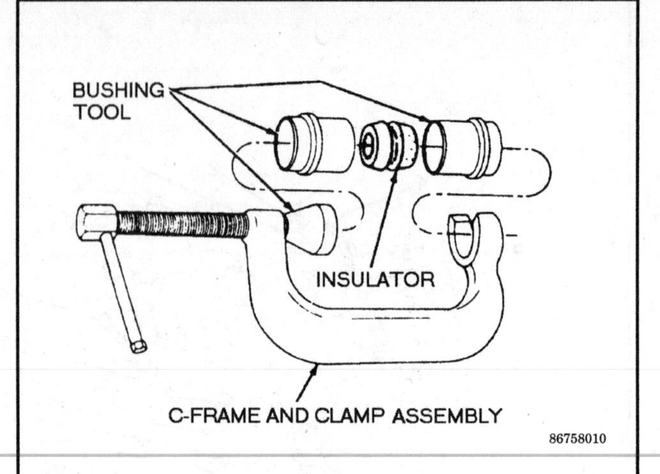

Fig. 17 The bushing removal tool utilizes a special C-clamp as shown

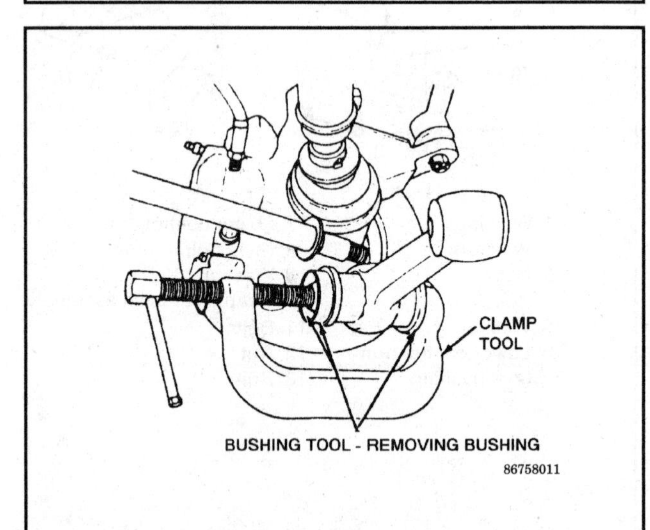

Fig. 18 Use the special C-clamp tool as shown to remove the stabilizer bar bushing — 1981-90 models

1991-95 Models

➧ See Figure 19

1. Support the engine with engine support D88L-6000-A or equivalent.
2. Raise and safely support the vehicle.
3. Remove the wheels.
4. Remove the nuts securing the steering gear mounting brackets and position the steering gear slightly forward.
5. Remove the stabilizer bar nuts, washers, bushings, sleeves and bolts from the lower control arm.
6. Remove the rear crossmember nuts from the rear transaxle mount and the vehicle frame.

7. Loosen the front crossmember bolts and nuts from the front transaxle mount and the vehicle frame. Lower the rear end of the crossmember.

8. Remove the nuts and bolts securing the chassis frame to the vehicle frame. Lower the chassis frame.

➡The engine and transaxle mounts will support the chassis frame when unbolting the chassis frame from the vehicle frame.

9. Unbolt the stabilizer bar from the chassis frame and remove the stabilizer bar from the vehicle.

To install:

10. Position the stabilizer bar into the vehicle.

11. Secure the stabilizer bar to the chassis frame with the bolts. Tighten the bolts to 32-43 ft. lbs. (43-59 Nm).

12. Install the chassis frame to the vehicle frame with the bolts and nuts. Tighten the bolts and nuts to 69-93 ft. lbs. (93-127 Nm).

13. Position the crossmember to the vehicle frame and the transaxle mounts. Tighten the bolts and nuts to the specified torque.

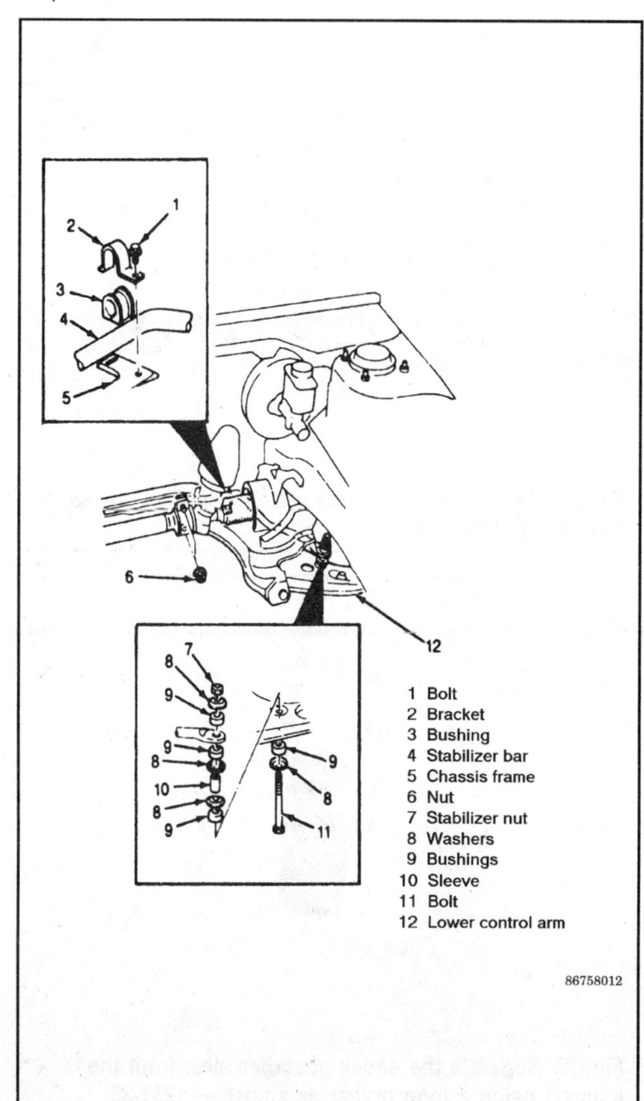

Fig. 19 Exploded view of the front stabilizer bar — 1991-95 models

14. Install the stabilizer bar bolts, sleeves, bushings, washers and nuts. Tighten the stabilizer bolts so 0.67-0.75 in. (17-19mm) of thread is exposed at the end of the bolt.

15. Position the steering gear and secure it with the brackets and nuts. Tighten the nuts to 28-38 ft. lbs. (37-52 Nm).

16. Install the wheels. Tighten the lug nuts to 65-87 ft. lbs. (88-118 Nm).

17. Lower the vehicle.

MacPherson Strut

REMOVAL & INSTALLATION

1981-85 Models

➧ See Figures 20, 21, 22, 23, 24, 25 and 26

➡A coil spring compressor (such as Ford Tool number T81P5310A, or equivalent) is required to compress the strut coil spring. DO NOT attempt to service the spring unless you are using a proper spring compressor tool.

1. Loosen the wheel lugs, raise the front of the car and safely support it on jackstands. Locate the jackstands under the frame jack pads, slightly behind the front wheels.

2. Remove the wheels.

3. Remove the brake line from the strut mounting bracket.

4. Place a floor jack or small hydraulic jack under the lower control arm. Raise the lower arm and strut as far as possible without raising the car.

5. Install the coil spring compressors. Place the top jaw of the compressors on the second coil from the top of the spring. Install the bottom jaw so that five coils will be gripped. Compress the spring evenly, from side to side, until there is about 1/8 in. (3mm) between any two spring coils. The coil spring must be compressed evenly. Always oil the compressor tool threads.

6. A pinch bolt retains the strut to the steering knuckle. Remove the pinch bolt.

7. Loosen, but do not remove, the two top mount to strut tower nuts. Lower the jack supporting the lower control arm.

8. Use a prybar and slightly spread the pinch bolt joint (knuckle to strut connection).

9. Place a piece of wood 2 in. x 4 in. x 7 1/2 in. long (51mm x 102mm x 191mm), against the shoulder on the steering knuckle. Use a short prybar between the wooden block and the lower spring seat to separate the strut from the knuckle.

10. Remove the two strut upper mounting nuts.

11. Remove the MacPherson strut, spring and top mount assembly from the car.

To install:

12. Install the assembled strut, spring and upper mount into the car. If you have installed a new coil spring, be sure it has been compressed enough.

13. Position the two top mounting studs through the holes in the tower and install two new mounting nuts. Do not tighten the nuts completely.

14. Install the bottom of the strut fully into the steering knuckle pinch joint.

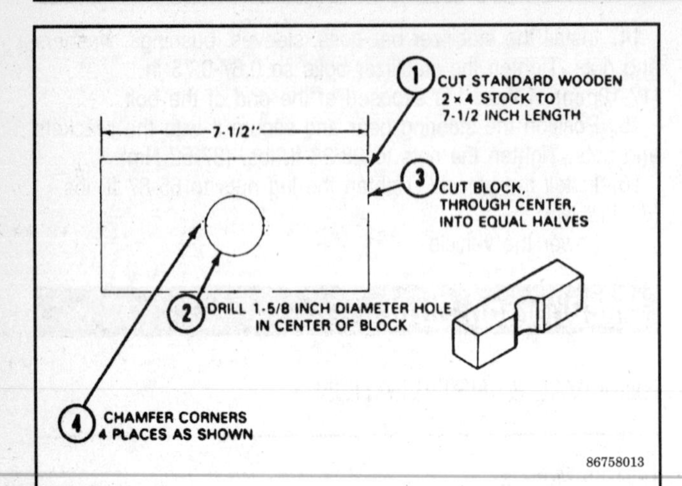

Fig. 20 Cut a piece of wood, 2 in. x 4 in. x 7½ in. long (51mm x 102mm x 191mm) and place it against the shoulder on the steering knuckle

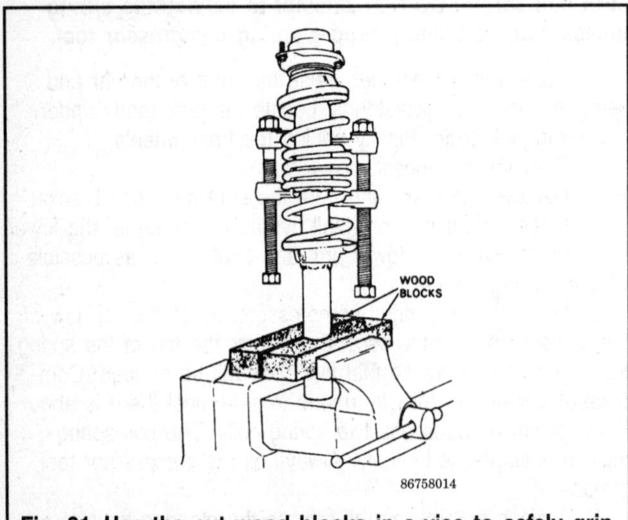

Fig. 21 Use the cut wood blocks in a vise to safely grip the damper unit — 1981-85 models

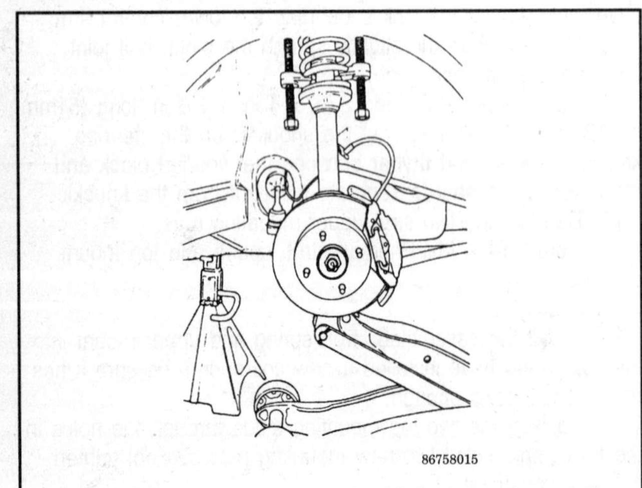

Fig. 22 With the car supported with jackstands and the wheel off, raise the strut with a jack into the shock tower

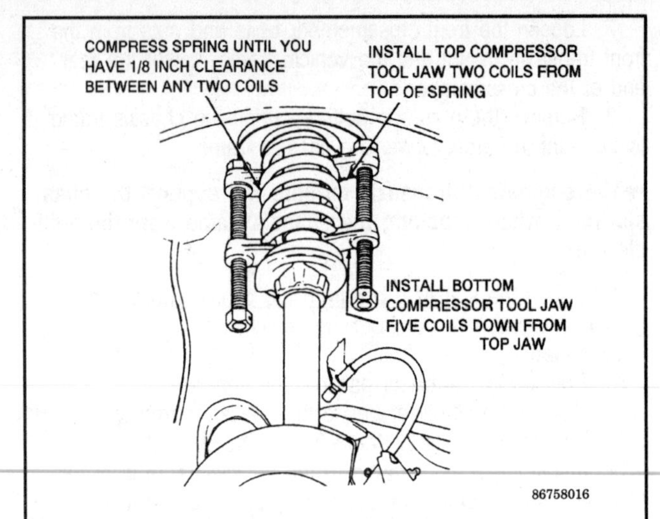

Fig. 23 Install the spring compressor as shown — 1981-85 models

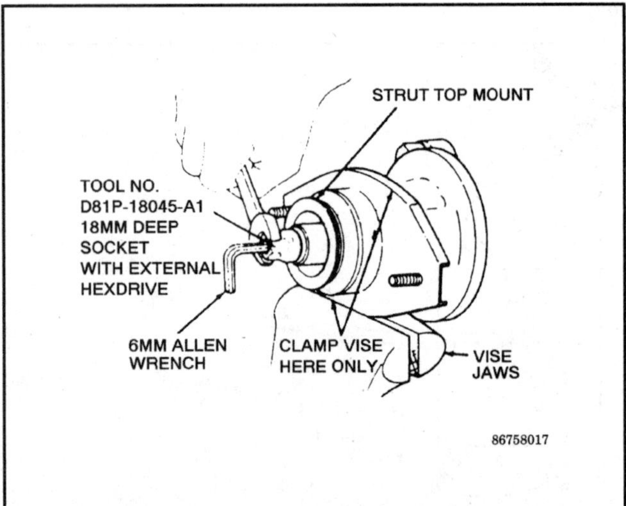

Fig. 24 Remove the top shaft retention nut as shown — 1981-85 models

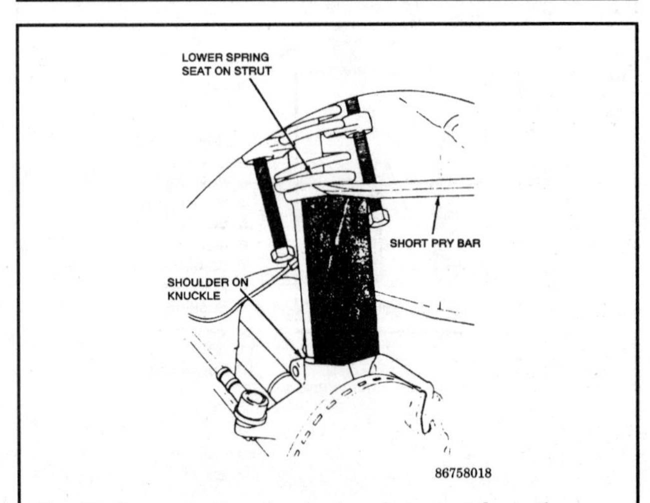

Fig. 25 Separate the shock absorber strut from the knuckle using a long prybar as shown — 1981-85 models

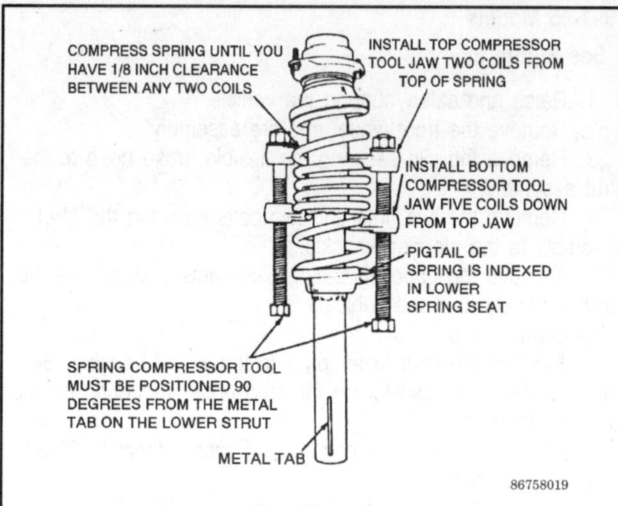

Fig. 26 A properly installed spring compression tool — 1981-85 models

15. Install a new pinch bolt and tighten it to 68-81 ft. lbs. (92-110 Nm). Tighten the tow upper mount nuts to 25-30 ft. lbs. (34-41 Nm).
16. Remove the coil spring compressor. Make sure the spring is fitting properly between the upper and lower seats.
17. Install the brake line to the strut bracket. Install the front wheel(s). Lower the car and tighten the lugs.
18. Have the alignment checked at a reputable repair facility.

1985½-90 Models

See Figures 27, 28, 29, 30, 31 and 32

1. Loosen but do not remove the two top mount-to-shock tower nuts.
2. Raise and safely support the vehicle. Raise the vehicle to a point where it is possible to reach the two top mount-to-shock tower nuts and the strut-to-knuckle pinch bolt.
3. Remove wheel and tire assembly.
4. Remove brake flex line-to-strut bolt.
5. Remove strut-to-knuckle pinch bolt.

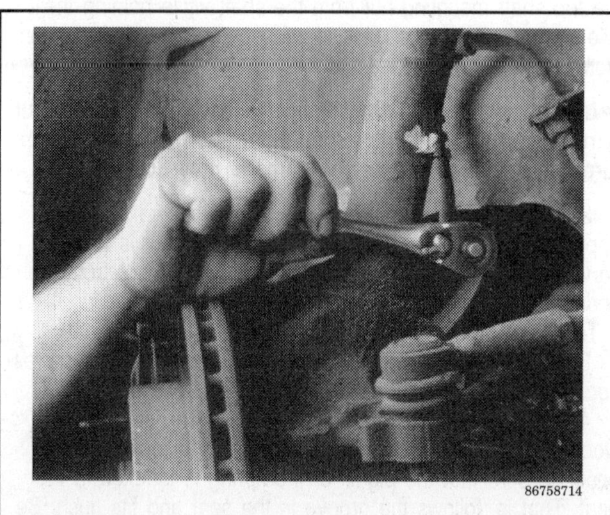

Fig. 27 Remove brake flex line-to-strut bolt with the correct wrench

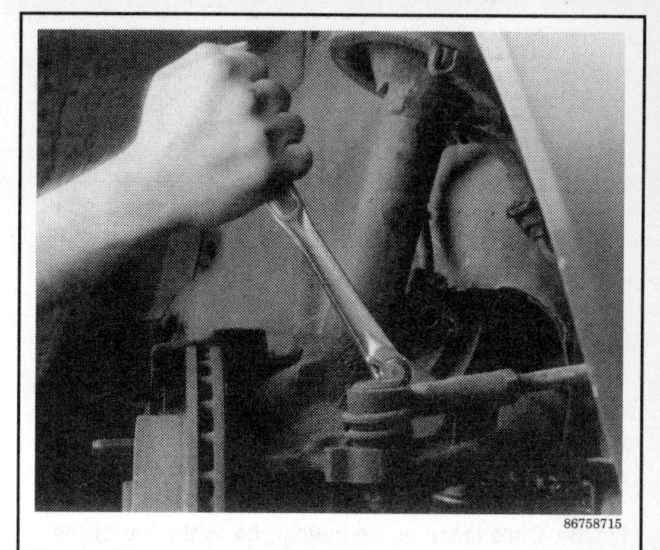

Fig. 28 Remove strut-to-knuckle pinch bolt

6. Using a suitable prytool, spread knuckle-to-strut pinch joint slightly.
7. Using a suitable prybar, place top of bar under fender apron and pry down on knuckle until strut separates from knuckle. Be careful not to pinch brake hose.

➡Do not pry against the caliper or brake hose bracket.

8. Remove the two top mount-to-shock tower nuts and remove strut from vehicle.

To install:

9. Install the strut assembly in vehicle. Install the two top mount-to-shock tower nuts. Tighten to 25-30 ft. lbs. (37-41 Nm).
10. Slide the strut mounting flange onto knuckle.
11. Install the strut-to-knuckle pinch bolt. Tighten to 68-80 ft. lbs. (92-110 Nm).
12. Install the brake flex line-to-strut bolt.
13. Install the wheel and tire assembly.
14. Lower the vehicle.
15. Have the alignment checked at a reputable repair facility.

Fig. 29 Place the top of a prybar under fender apron and pry down on the knuckle until strut separates from knuckle

86758717

Fig. 30 Once loose at the bottom, go to the top of the strut to unbolt it from its shock tower mounts

86758718

Fig. 31 Remove the two top mount-to-shock tower nuts and remove strut from vehicle

86758719

Fig. 32 Once detached, remove the strut from the vehicle for disassembly, inspection or replacement

1991-95 Models

➧ See Figure 33

1. Raise and safely support the vehicle.
2. Remove the front wheel and tire assembly.
3. Remove the clip securing the flexible brake hose to the strut assembly.
4. Remove the two nuts and two bolts securing the strut assembly to the steering knuckle.
5. Remove the upper mounting block nuts and remove the strut assembly from the vehicle.

To install:

6. Position the strut assembly into the wheel housing. Be sure the direction indicator on the strut upper mounting bracket is facing inboard.
7. Install the upper mount nuts and tighten them to 22-30 ft. lbs. (29-40 Nm).
8. Secure the strut to the front wheel knuckle using the mounting hardware. Tighten the nuts to 69-93 ft. lbs. (93-127 Nm).
9. Attach the front brake hose with the clip.
10. If equipped with ABS, install the front ABS harness clip on the strut.
11. Install the wheels and lower the vehicle.
12. Have the alignment checked at a reputable repair facility.

OVERHAUL

1981-85 Models

➧ See Figures 26 and 34

➡A coil spring compressor (such as Ford Tool number T81P5310A, or equivalent) is required to compress the strut coil spring. DO NOT attempt to service the spring unless you are using a proper spring compressor tool.

1. Place an 18mm deep socket that has an external hex drive top (Ford tool number D81P-18045-A1) over the strut shaft center nut. Insert a 6mm Allen wrench into the shaft end. With the edge of the strut mount clamped in a vise, remove the top shaft mounting nut from the shaft while holding the Allen wrench. Use vise grips, if necessary or a suitable extension to hold the Allen wrench.

➡Make a wooden holding device that will clamp the strut barrel into the bench vise (see illustration). Do not clamp directly onto the strut barrel, damage may occur.

2. Clamp the strut into a bench vise. Remove the strut upper mount and the coil spring. If only the strut is to be serviced, do not remove the coil spring compressor from the spring.

To assemble:

3. If the coil spring is to be replaced, remove the compressor from the old spring and install it on the new.
4. Mount the strut (if removed) in the vise using the wooden fixture. Position the coil spring in the lower spring seat. Be sure that the pigtail of the spring is indexed in the seat. That is, follows the groove in the seat and fits flush. Be sure that the spring compressors are positioned 90° from the metal tab on the lower part of the strut.

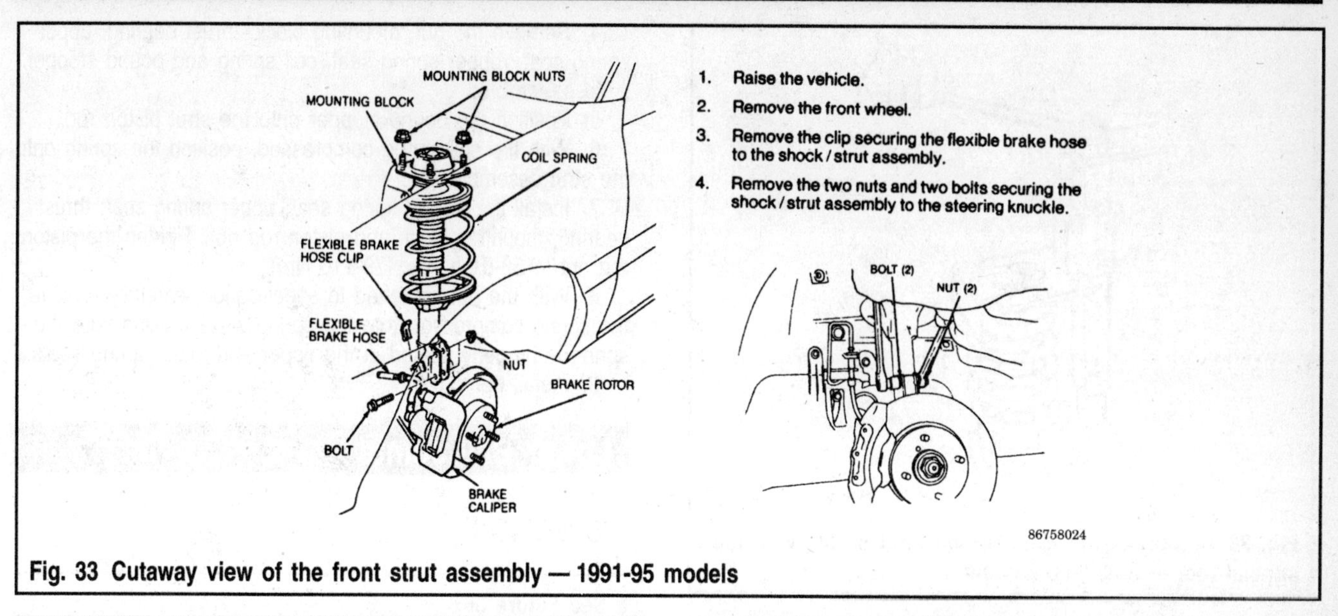

Fig. 33 Cutaway view of the front strut assembly — 1991-95 models

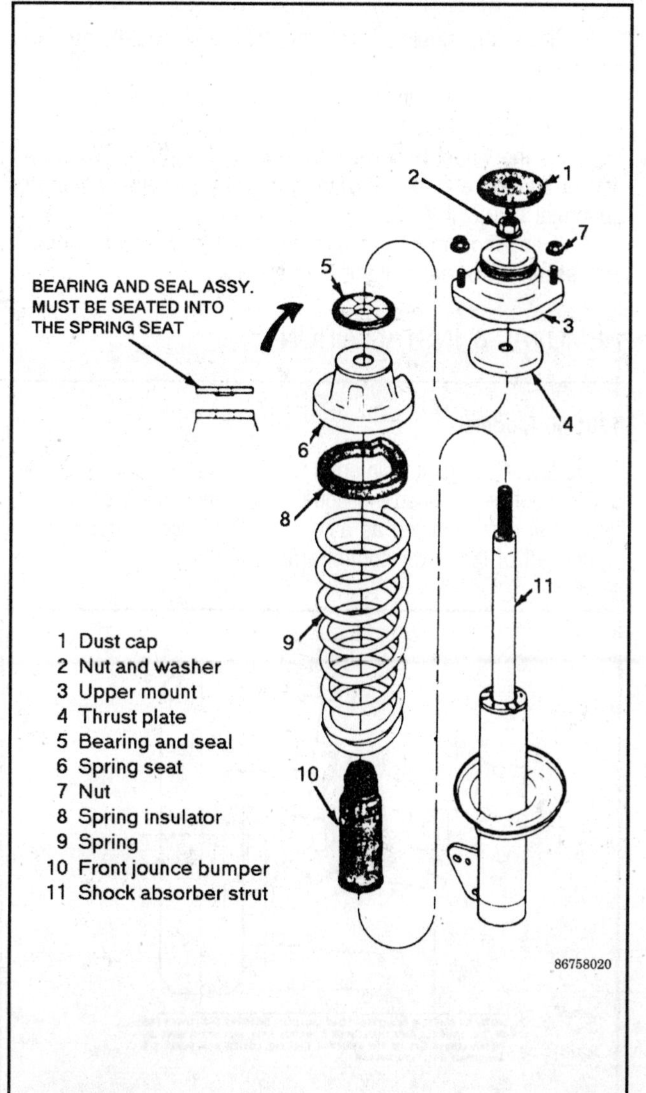

Fig. 34 Exploded view of the strut assembly — 1981-85 models

5. Use a new nut and assembly the top mount to the strut. Tighten the shaft nut to 48-62 ft. lbs. (65-84 Nm).

1985½-90 Models

➧ See Figures 35, 36 and 37

1. Install spring compressor in bench mount, install strut in compressor and compress spring.
2. Place a deep 18mm socket on strut shaft nut. Insert an 8mm deep socket with a ¼ in. drive wrench. Remove top shaft mounting nut from shaft while holding the ¼ in. drive socket with a suitable extension.

➡Do not attempt to remove shaft nut by turning shaft and holding nut. The nut must be turned and the shaft held to avoid possible damage to the shaft.

3. Loosen spring compressor tool and remove top mount bracket assembly, bearing, insulator and spring.

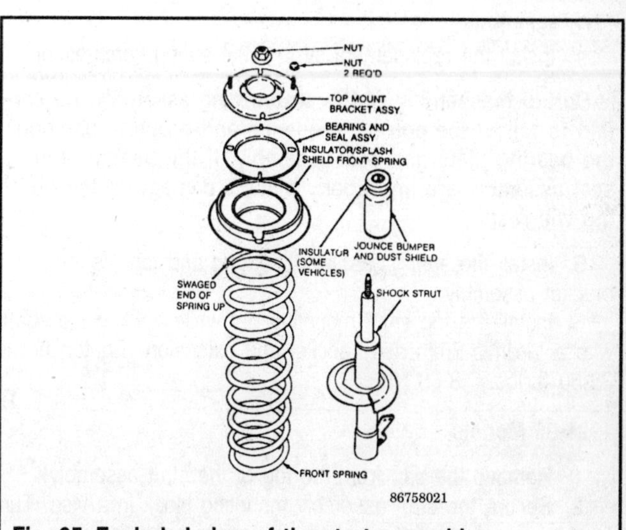

Fig. 35 Exploded view of the strut assembly — 1985½-90 models

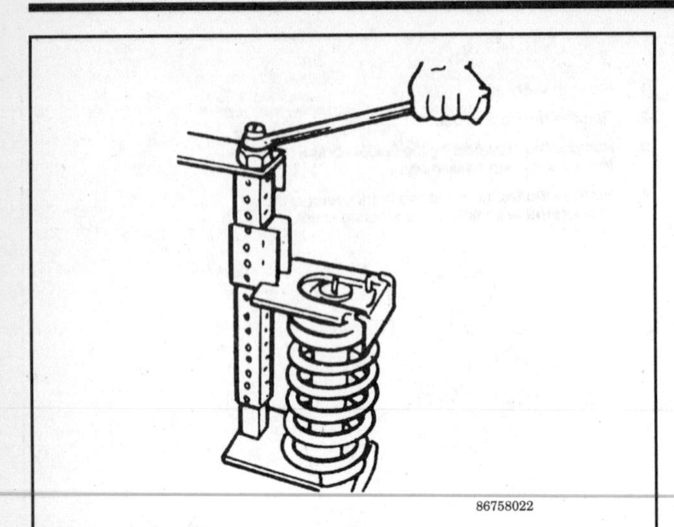

Fig. 36 Compress the MacPherson strut spring with the special tool — 1985½-90 models

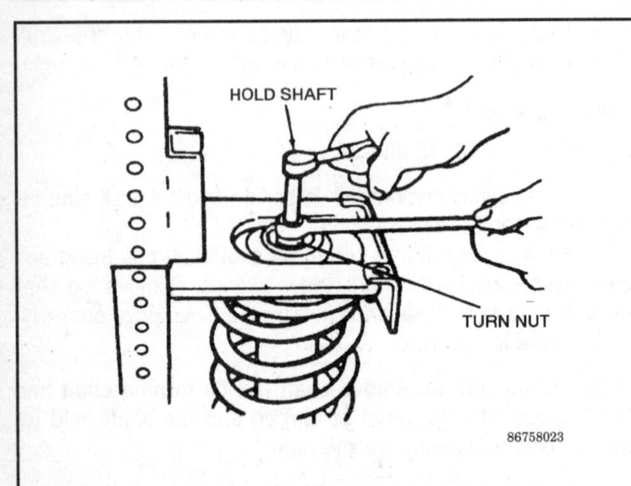

Fig. 37 Once safely compressed in the spring compressor, remove (or install) the retention nut and top mount bracket assembly

To assemble:

4. Install the replacement strut in the spring compressor.

➡**During reassembly of the strut/spring assembly, be certain to follow the correct sequence and properly position the bearing plate and seal assembly. If the bearing and seal assembly are improperly placed, damage to the bearing will result.**

5. Install the spring, insulator, bearing and top mount bracket assembly.
6. Install the top shaft mounting nut while holding the shaft with a ¼ drive 8mm deep socket and extension. Tighten nut to 35-50 ft. lbs. (48-68 Nm).

1991-95 Models

1. Remove the cap from the top of the strut assembly.
2. Secure the strut assembly mounting block in a vise. Turn the piston rod nut one revolution to loosen.
3. Install an appropriate spring compressor onto the strut spring and compress the spring.
4. Remove the nut, mounting block, thrust bearing, upper spring seat, rubber spring seat, coil spring and bound stopper.

To assemble:

5. Position the bound stopper onto the strut piston rod.
6. With the coil spring compressed, position the spring onto the strut assembly.
7. Install the rubber spring seat, upper spring seat, thrust bearing, mounting block and piston rod nut. Tighten the piston rod nut to 58-81 ft. lbs. (79-110 Nm).
8. With the nut tightened to specification, carefully remove the spring compressor from the spring while making sure the spring is properly seated in the upper and lower spring seats.
9. Install the cap.

Lower Ball Joints

INSPECTION

➧ See Figure 38

1. Raise and safely support the vehicle so wheels are fully extended.
2. Have an assistant grasp the lower edge of the tire and move the wheel and tire assembly in and out.
3. As the wheel is being moved in and out, observe lower end of knuckle and lower control arm. Any movement indicates abnormal ball joint wear.
4. If any movement is observed, install new lower control arm assembly or the ball joint, as required.

REMOVAL & INSTALLATION

1981-90 Models

The lower ball joint is integral to the lower control assembly and cannot be serviced individually. Any movement of the lower ball joint detected as a result of inspection requires replacement of the lower control arm assembly.

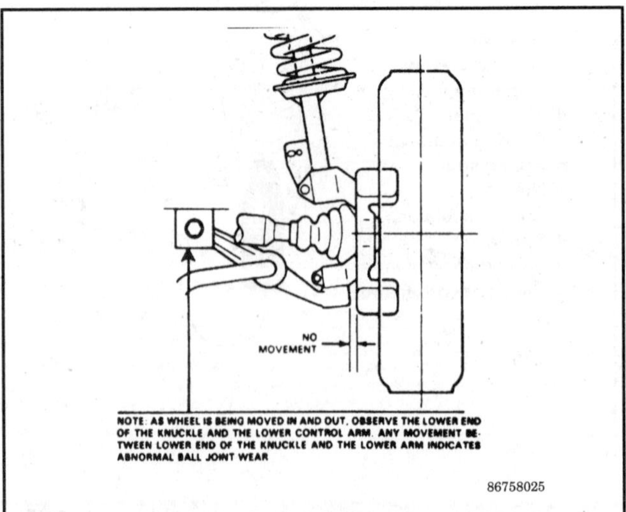

NO MOVEMENT
NOTE: AS WHEEL IS BEING MOVED IN AND OUT, OBSERVE THE LOWER END OF THE KNUCKLE AND THE LOWER CONTROL ARM. ANY MOVEMENT BETWEEN LOWER END OF THE KNUCKLE AND THE LOWER ARM INDICATES ABNORMAL BALL JOINT WEAR

Fig. 38 There should be no lateral play in the ball joint — if there is, it should be replaced

1991-95 Models

See Figure 39

1. Raise and safely support the vehicle.
2. Remove the wheel and tire assembly.
3. Remove the nut and bolt securing the ball joint to the steering knuckle.
4. Remove the nuts securing the lower ball joint to the lower control arm. Remove the lower ball joint.
5. Mount the lower ball joint in a vise.
6. Place a suitable chisel between the ball joint and the dust boot. Lightly tap on the chisel to separate the dust boot from the ball joint.

To install:

7. Position the dust boot over the ball joint and, using a suitable tool, press down on the tool to secure the dust boot to the ball joint.
8. Install the ball joint into the lower control arm and install the mounting nuts. Tighten the nuts to 69-86 ft. lbs. (93-117 Nm).
9. Install the lower ball joint into the steering knuckle and secure it with the nut and bolt. Tighten the nut to 32-43 ft. lbs. (43-59 Nm).
10. Install the wheel and tire assembly and lower the vehicle.

Front Wheel Hub, Knuckle and Bearings

REMOVAL & INSTALLATION

1981-85 Models

The wheel hub and knuckle must be removed for bearing replacement or servicing. A special puller is required to remove and install the hub. (Ford Part Number T81P-1104-A, T81P-1104-C and adapters T81P-1104-B or T83P-1104-AH). The adaptors screw over the lugs and attach to the puller, which uses a long screw attached to the end of the stub shaft to pull off or install the hub.

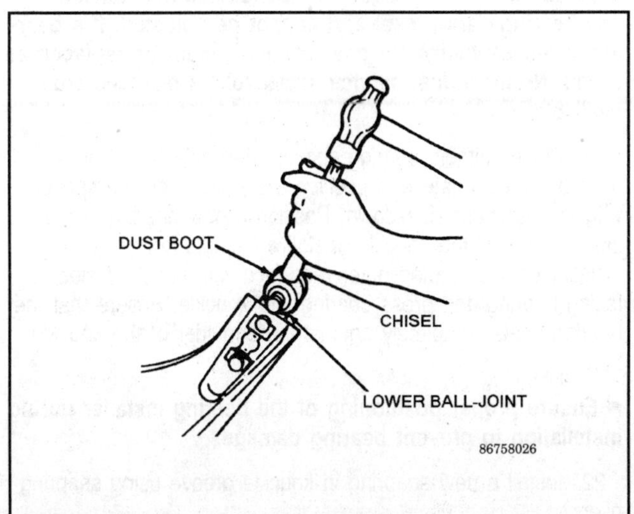

Fig. 39 Use a hammer and suitable chisel to remove the lower ball joint — 1991-95 models

1. Remove wheel cover and slightly loosen the lugs.
2. Remove the hub retaining nut and washer. The nut is crimped staked to the shaft. Use a socket and sufficient torque to overcome the locking force of the crimp.
3. Raise the front of the car and support safely with jackstands. Remove the wheel(s).
4. Remove the brake caliper and disc rotor.
5. Disconnect the lower control arm and tie rod from the steering knuckle. Loosen the two top strut mounting nuts, but do not remove them. Install the hub remover/installer tool and remove the hub. If the outer bearing is seized on the hub remove it with a puller.
6. Remove the front suspension knuckle.
7. On 1981-83 models:
   a. After the front knuckle is removed, pull out the inner grease shield, the inner seal and bearing.
   b. Remove the outer grease seal and bearing.
   c. If you hope to reuse the bearings, clean them in a safe solvent. After cleaning the bearings and races, carefully inspect them for damage, pitting and heat coloring, etc. If damage etc. has occurred, replace all components (bearings, cups and seals). Always replace the seals with new ones.
   d. If new bearings are to be used, remove the inner and outer races from the knuckle. A three jawed puller on a slide hammer will do the job.
   e. Clean the interior bore of the knuckle.
8. On 1984 and later models:
   a. Remove the snapring that retains the bearing in the steering knuckle.
   b. Position the knuckle, outboard side up under a hydraulic press with appropriate adapters in place, and press the bearing from the knuckle.
   c. Clean the interior bore of the knuckle.

To install:

9. On 1981-83 models:
   a. Install the new bearing cups using a suitable driver. Be sure the cups are fully seated in the knuckle bore.
   b. Pack the wheel bearings with multi-purpose lubricant (Ford part number C1AZ-19590-B or the equivalent). If a bearing packer is not available, place a large portion of grease into the palm of your hand and slide the edge of the roller cage through the grease with your other hand. Work as much grease as you can between the bearing rollers.
   c. Put a sufficient amount of grease between the bearing cups in the center of the knuckle. Apply a thin film of grease on the bearing cups.
   d. Place the outer bearing and new grease seal into the knuckle. Place a thin film of grease on all three lips of the new outer seal.
   e. Turn the knuckle over and install the inner bearing and seal. Once again, apply a thin film of grease to the three lips of the seal.
   f. Install the inner grease shield. A small block of wood may be used to tap the seal into the knuckle bore.
   g. Keep the knuckle in the vertical position or the inner bearing will fall out. Start the wheel hub into the outer

knuckle bore and push the hub as far as possible through the outer and inner bearings by hand.

➡Prior to installing the hub, make sure it is clean and free from burrs. Use crocus cloth to polish the hub if necessary. It is important to use only hand pressure when installing the hub, make sure the hub is through both the outer and inner bearings.

h. With the hub as fully seated as possible through the bearings, position the hub and knuckle to the front strut.

10. On 1984 and later models:

a. Position the knuckle. outboard side down on the appropriate adapter and press in the new bearing. Be sure the bearing is fully seated. Install a new retainer snapring.

b. Install the hub using tool T83T-1104-AH3 and press. Check that the hub rotates freely.

c. Lubricate the stub shaft splines with a thin film of SAE 20 motor oil. Use hand pressure only and insert the splines into the knuckle and hub as far as possible.

➡Do not allow the hub to back out of the bearings while installing the stub shaft, otherwise it will be necessary to start all over.

11. Complete the installation of the suspension parts.

12. Install the hub remover/installer tool and tighten the center adapter to 120 ft. lbs. (163 Nm) to ensure the hub is fully seated.

13. Remove the installer tool and install the hub washer and nut. Tighten the hub nut finger-tight.

14. Install the disc (rotor) and caliper, etc.

15. Install the wheel(s) and snug the wheel lugs.

16. Lower the car to the ground, set the parking brake and block the wheels.

17. Tighten the wheel lugs to 80-105 ft. lbs. (108-142 Nm).

18. Tighten the center hub nut to 180-200 ft. lbs. (244-271 Nm). Do not use an impact wrench to tighten the hub nut!

19. Stake the hub nut using a chisel.

20. Have the alignment checked at a reputable repair facility.

1985½-90 Models

1. Remove wheel cover/hub cover from wheel and tire assembly and loosen the wheel nuts.

2. Remove hub nut retainer and washer by applying sufficient torque to nut to break locking tab and remove hub nut retainer. The hub nut retainer must be discarded after removal.

3. Raise and safely support the vehicle. Remove wheel(s).

4. Remove brake caliper by loosening caliper locating pins and rotating caliper off rotor starting from lower end of caliper and lifting upward. Do not remove caliper pins from caliper assembly. Lift caliper off rotor and hang it free of rotor. Do not allow caliper assembly to hang from brake hose. Support caliper assembly with a length of wire.

5. Remove rotor from hub by pulling it off hub bolts. If rotor is difficult to remove from hub, strike rotor sharply between studs with a rubber or plastic hammer. If rotor will not pull off, apply rust penetrating fluid to inboard and outboard rotor hub mating surfaces. Install a three-jaw puller and remove the rotor by pulling on the rotor's outside diameter and pushing on the hub center. If excessive force is required for removal, check the rotor for lateral runout.

6. Remove the rotor splash shield.

7. Disconnect lower control arm and tie rod from knuckle (leave strut attached).

8. Loosen the two strut top mount-to-apron nuts.

9. Install a suitable hub removal tool and remove hub/bearing/knuckle assembly by pushing out CV-joint outer shaft until it is free of assembly.

10. Support knuckle with a length of wire, remove strut bolt and slide hub/knuckle assembly off strut.

11. Carefully remove support wire and transfer hub/bearing assembly to bench.

12. Install a suitable front hub puller with jaws of puller on the knuckle bosses and remove hub.

➡Ensure the shaft protector is centered, clears the bearing inside diameter and rests on the end face of the hub journal.

13. Remove the snapring which retains the bearing knuckle assembly and discard.

14. Using a hydraulic press, place a suitable front bearing spacer (step side up) on press plate and position knuckle on spacer with outboard side up. Install bearing removal tool on bearing inner race and press the bearing out of the knuckle.

15. Discard the bearing.

16. Remove the halfshaft.

17. Place halfshaft in vise. Remove the bearing dust seal by uniformly tapping on outer edge with a light-duty hammer and screwdriver. Discard the dust seal.

To install:

18. Place halfshaft in vise. Install a new dust seal using a suitable seal installer. Seal flange must face outboard.

19. Install the halfshaft.

20. On bench, remove all foreign material from the knuckle bearing bore and hub bearing journal to ensure correct seating of the new bearing.

➡If hub bearing journal is scored or damaged, replace the hub with a new one. Do not attempt to service it. The front wheel bearings are of a cartridge design and are pre-greased, sealed and require no scheduled maintenance. The bearings are preset and cannot be adjusted. If a bearing is disassembled for any reason, it must be replaced as a unit. No individual service seals, rollers or races are available.

21. Place suitable bearing spacer, step side down, on a hydraulic press plate and position the knuckle on the spacer with the outboard side down. Position a new bearing in the inboard side of the knuckle. Install a suitable front bearing installer on the bearing outer race face with undercut side facing bearing and press bearing into knuckle. Ensure that the bearing seats completely against the shoulder of the knuckle bore.

➡Ensure proper positioning of the bearing installer during installation to prevent bearing damage.

22. Install a new snapring in knuckle groove using snapring pliers.

23. Place a suitable front bearing spacer on a press plate and position the hub on the tool with lugs facing downward. Position the knuckle assembly on the hub barrel with the outboard side down. Place a suitable front bearing remover on

the inner race of the bearing and press down on the tool until the bearing moves freely in the knuckle after installation.

24. Suspend hub/knuckle/bearing assembly on vehicle with wire and attach strut loosely to knuckle. Lubricate the CV-joint stub shaft splines with SAE 30 weight motor oil and insert the shaft into the hub splines as far as possible using hand pressure only. Check that the splines are properly engaged.
25. Install suitable front hub installer and wheel bolt adapter to hub and stub shaft. Tighten the hub installer tool to 120 ft. lbs. (162 Nm) to ensure that hub is fully seated.
26. Remove tool and install washer and new hub nut retainer. Tighten hub nut retainer finger-tight.
27. Complete installation of front suspension components.
28. Install the disc brake rotor to hub assembly.
29. Install the disc brake caliper over rotor.
30. Ensure that the outer brake shoe spring end is seated under the upper arm of the knuckle.
31. Install the wheel and tire assembly, tightening the wheel nuts finger-tight.
32. Lower the vehicle and block wheels to prevent vehicle from rolling.
33. Tighten the wheel nuts to 85-105 ft. lbs. (115-142 Nm).
34. Manually thread the hub nut retainer assembly on the constant velocity output shaft as far as possible using a 30mm socket. Tighten the retainer nut assembly to 180-200 ft. lbs. (245-270 Nm).

➡Do not use power or impact tools to tighten the hub nut. Do not move the vehicle before the retainer is tightened.

35. During tightening, an audible click sound will indicate proper ratchet function of the hub nut retainer. As the hub nut retainer tightens, ensure that one of the three locking tabs is in the slot of the CV-joint shaft. If the hub nut retainer is damaged, or more than one locking tab is broken, replace the hub nut retainer.
36. Install the wheel, wheelcover or hub cover and lower vehicle completely to ground.
37. Remove the wheel blocks.
38. Have the alignment checked at a reputable repair facility.

1991-95 Models

1. Remove wheel cover/hub cover from wheel and tire assembly and loosen the wheel nuts.
2. Remove hub nut retainer and washer by applying sufficient torque to nut to break locking tab and remove hub nut retainer. The hub nut retainer must be discarded after removal.
3. Raise and safely support the vehicle. Remove the wheel(s).
4. Remove the front disc brake caliper and rotor.
5. Use a small chisel to raise the staked portion of the front wheel nut.
6. Remove the outer front wheel spindle connecting rod or end at the front wheel knuckle.
7. Remove the two shock absorber strut mounting studs and nuts that secure the spring and shock to the front knuckle.
8. Separate the spring and shock assembly from the front wheel knuckle.
9. Remove the ball joint bolt nut and the bolt that secures the front suspension lower arm ball joint to the front wheel knuckle.
10. Separate the front suspension lower arm ball joint from the front wheel knuckle.
11. Remove the front wheel hub/front wheel knuckle assembly from the front wheel driveshaft and joint.

To install:

➡Apply Loctite® 290, or equivalent thread locking compound to the ball joint bolt nut and bolt threads.

12. Install the front wheel hub/front wheel knuckle assembly onto the front suspension lower arm ball joint and secure it with the ball joint bolt nut and bolt. Tighten the nut to 32-43 ft. lbs. (43-59 Nm).
13. Install the connecting rod end.
14. Install the front wheel knuckle to the spring and shock assembly. Tighten the shock absorber strut mounting nuts and bolts to 69-93 ft. lbs. (93-127 Nm).
15. Install a new front axle wheel hub retainer to the front wheel halfshaft. Tighten to 174-235 ft. lbs. (235-319 Nm). Stake the retainer using a hammer and small chisel.
16. Install the front brake caliper and disc.
17. Install the wheel, wheelcover or hub cover and lower vehicle completely to ground.
18. Remove the wheel blocks.
19. Have the alignment checked at a reputable repair facility.

Front End Alignment

➧ See Figures 40, 41, 42, 43 and 44

The alignment of your vehicle's front wheels involves precise adjustments of their placement on the road in relation to the vehicle. The alignment determines how well your vehicle tracks down the road.

Caster and camber and toe angles are the three major factors that contribute to a properly aligned car. These three factors are preset at the factory and should not be adjusted in the field by a do-it-yourself mechanic without proper training and equipment. The setting of each has a critical affect on the cornering, steer-ability and straightline running of the vehicle.

If your car is handling poorly, or tends to consistently pull to one side or is wearing tires unevenly, it may or may not have need of a front wheel alignment check.

First ensure the tires for your vehicle are all the correct size, type and are properly inflated and balanced. If there is any significant variance in the wheels/tires, it is possible to simulate certain misalignment problems. If the wheels and tires are believed to be correct, and the vehicle does not operate properly on the road, then have the alignment checked by a qualified shop.

CASTER

The caster is the forward to rearward tilt of the top of the front wheel spindle. If the top of the spindle tilts to the rear, caster is positive. If the top of the spindle tilts to the front, caster is negative. Refer to the illustration to get a better grasp of caster.

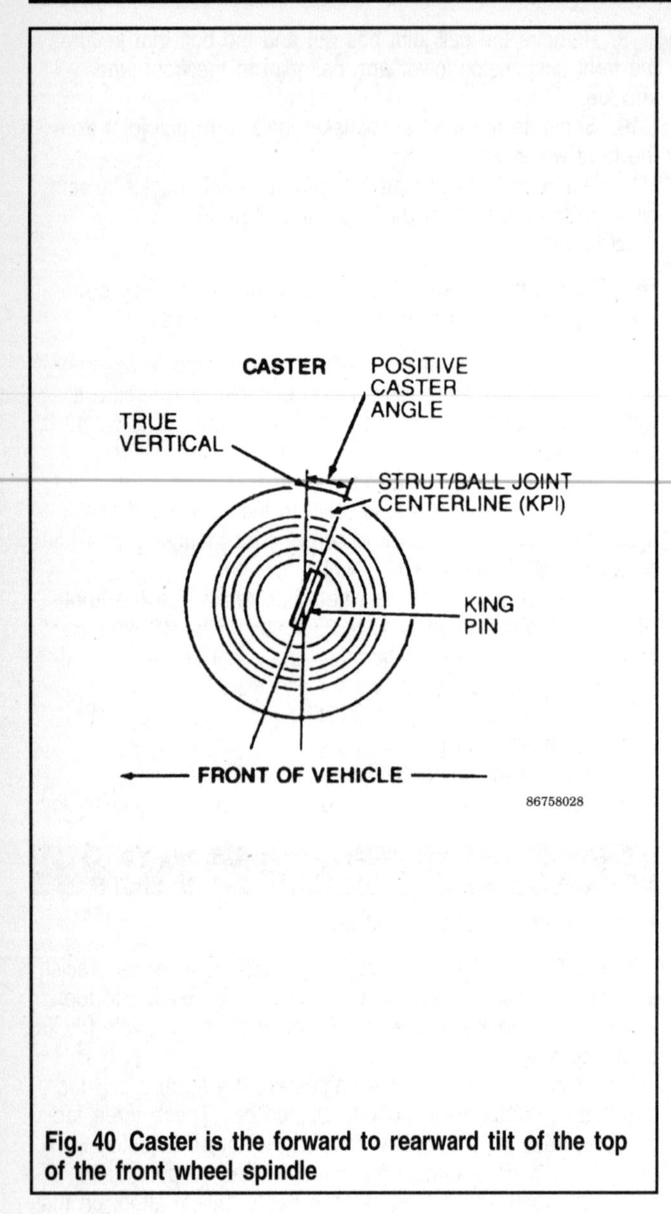

Fig. 40 Caster is the forward to rearward tilt of the top of the front wheel spindle

CAMBER

Camber is the amount that the centerline of the wheel is tilted inward or outward from the true vertical. If the top of the wheel is tilted outward, away from the vehicle's fender, the camber is positive. If the top of the wheel is tilted inward, toward the vehicle, the camber is negative.

TOE ADJUSTMENT

Technically, toe is the difference in distance between the front and rear of the front wheels when measured across the underside of the vehicle (perpendicular to the line of travel). A car with with a longer measurement between the rear of its front wheels will have the front of its wheels canted some degree inwards in relationship to the direction of travel, and vise versa.

If the vehicle's wheels are adjusted so that they point to any degree inwards, it is said to have "toe-in." A car adjusted so its wheels are pointed to any degree outwards (slightly splayed), is said to be adjusted for "toe-out." To give you a better picture of toe generally, the names"toe-in," and "toe-out" are metaphorical, and one could draw a relationship to a person's feet. If he is "pigeon toed," with his feet pointed in, then he would be like a car with toe-in.

Toe is adjusted by altering the length of the tie-rods by means of turning threaded adjustment collars on each of the rods. The tie-rod adjustments are locked in place by means of locknuts.

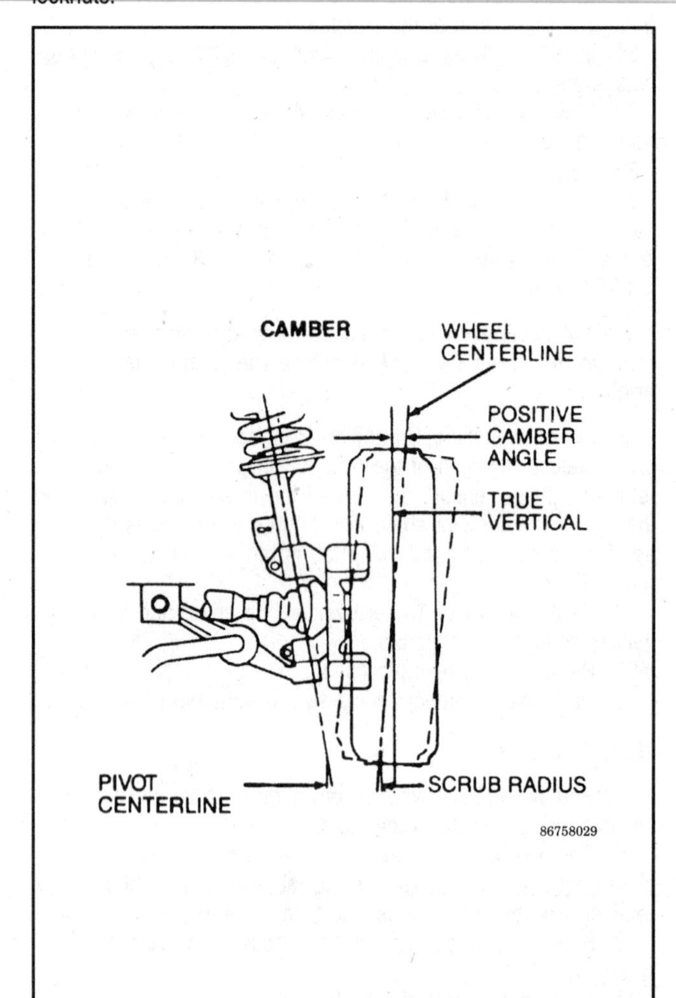

Fig. 41 Camber is the amount that the centerline of the wheel is tilted inward or outward from the true vertical

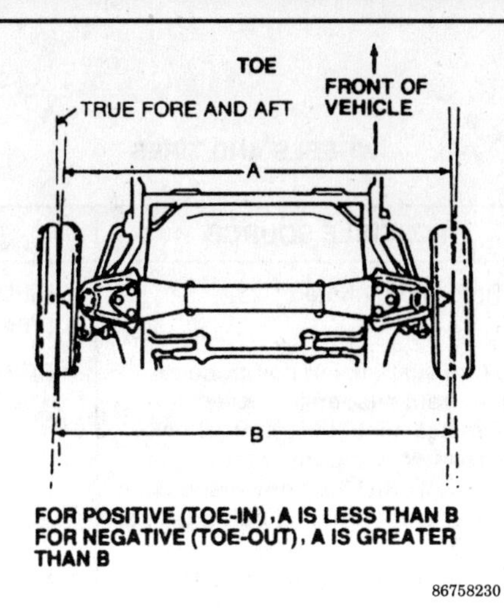

Fig. 42 Toe is the difference in distance between the front and rear of the front wheels when measured across the underside of the vehicle

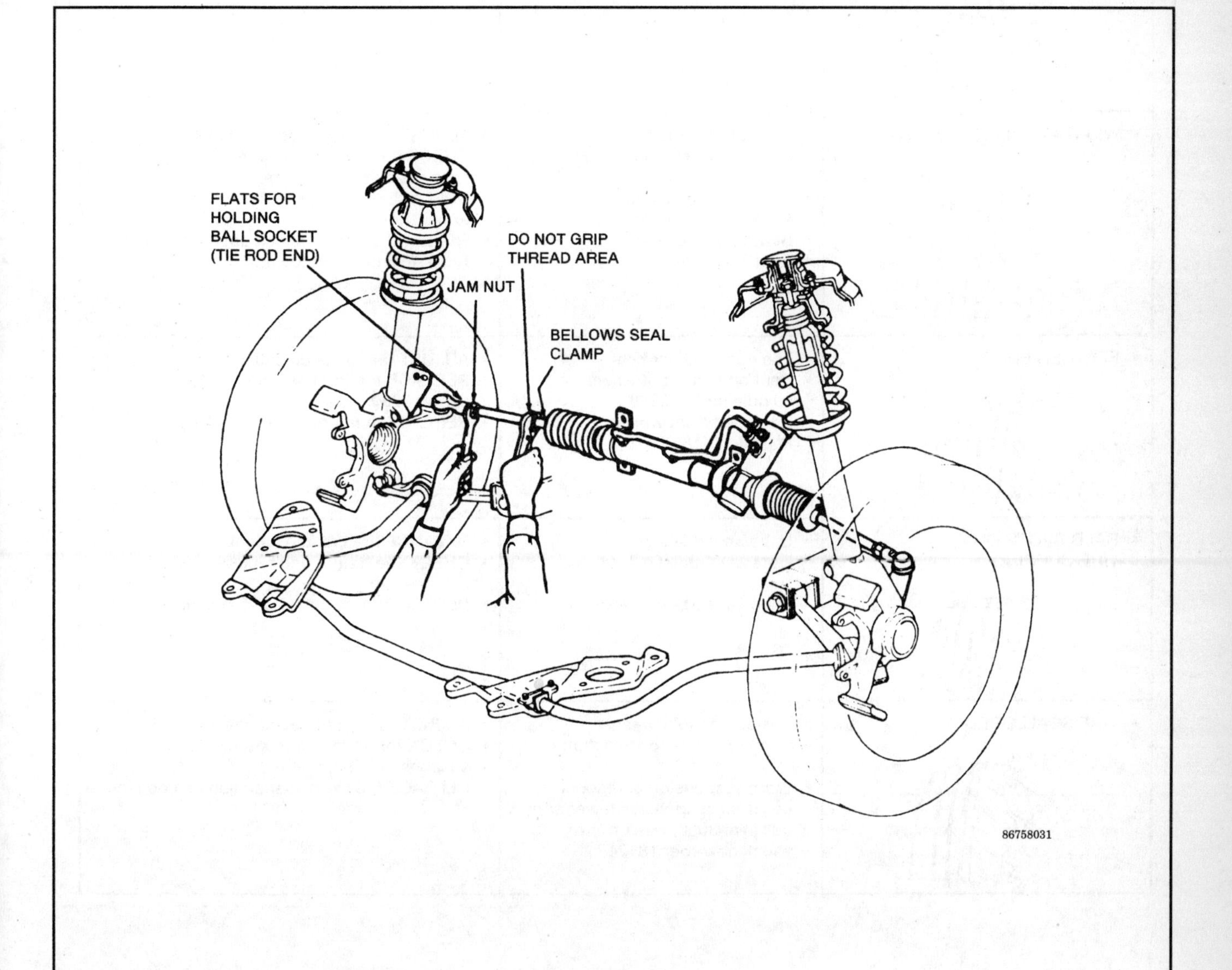

Fig. 43 Toe is altered by changing the length of the adjustable tie rod(s)

WHEELS AND TIRES

CONDITION	POSSIBLE SOURCE	ACTION
• RAPID WEAR AT THE SHOULDERS 	• Tires underinflated • Worn suspension components, i.e., front suspension lower arm ball joint 3050, front shock absorber upper mounting bracket 18A161, front suspension lower arm mounting bolt bushing 3069 • Excessive cornering speeds	• INFLATE the tires to the recommended pressure—rotate the tires. • REPLACE the worn components. • ROTATE the tires.
• RAPID WEAR AT CENTER OF TREAD 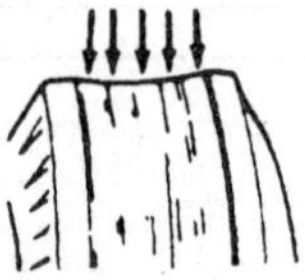	• Tires overinflated	• INFLATE the tires to the recommended pressure—rotate the tires.
• WEAR AT ONE SHOULDER 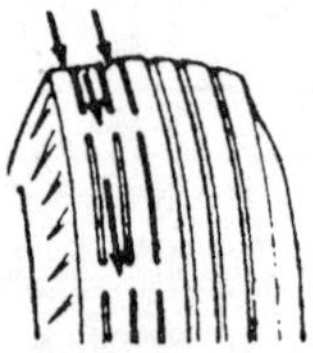	• Toe out of adjustment • Camber out of specification • Bent front suspension lower arm 3078 • Bent front shock absorber 18124 • Bent strut tower	• ADJUST the toe to specifications. • CHECK for worn or damaged suspension components. • REPLACE the front suspension lower arm 3078. • REPLACE the front shock absorber 18124. • REPLACE the strut tower.
• FEATHER EDGE 	• Toe out of adjustment • Bent or worn front wheel spindle tie rod 3280 • Damaged front wheel knuckle 3K185	• ADJUST toe to specifications. • REPLACE the front wheel spindle tie rod 3280. • REPLACE the front wheel knuckle 3K185.
• BALD SPOTS OR TIRE CUPPING 	• Unbalanced wheel • Excessive radial runout • Shock absorber(s) worn	• BALANCE the tire and wheel. • CHECK the runout and replace tire if necessary. • REPLACE the shock absorber(s) in question.
• TIRE SCALLOPED 	• Toe out of adjustment • Camber out of specification • Worn suspension components, i.e., front suspension lower arm ball joint 3050, weak front shock absorber 18124	• ADJUST the toe to specifications. • CHECK for worn or damaged suspension components. • REPLACE the worn suspension components.

86758027

Fig. 44 Refer to this tire wear condition chart to help assess whether an alignment check by a qualified shop is necessary

WHEEL ALIGNMENT

Year	Model		Caster Range (deg.)	Caster Preferred Setting (deg.)	Camber Range (deg.)	Camber Preferred Setting (deg.)	Toe-in (in.)	Steering Axis Inclination (deg.)
1981	Escort/Lynx	LF	9/16P-2 1/16P	1 5/16P	7/16P-1 15/16P	1 3/16P	1/8N	14 21/32
	Escort/lynx	RF	9/16P-2 1/16P	1 5/16P	0-1 1/2P	3/4P	1/8N	15 3/32
	Escort/Lynx	R	-	-	1 1/2N-5/8N	5/8N	1/16N	-
1982	Escort/Lynx	LF	9/16P-2 1/16P	1 5/16P	7/16P-1 15/16P	1 3/16P	1/8N	14 21/32
	Escort/lynx	RF	9/16P-2 1/16P	1 5/16P	0-1 1/2P	3/4P	1/8N	15 3/32
	Escort/Lynx	R	-	-	1 1/2N-5/8N	5/8N	1/16N	-
	EXP	LF	9/16P-2 1/16P	1 5/16P	7/16P-1 15/16P	1 3/16P	1/8N	14 21/32
	EXP	RF	9/16P-2 1/16P	1 5/16P	0-1 1/2P	3/4P	1/8N	15 3/32
	EXP	R	-	-	1 1/2N-5/8N	5/8N	1/16N	-
1983	Escort/Lynx	LF	9/16P-2 1/16P	1 5/16P	7/16P-1 15/16P	1 3/16P	1/8N	14 21/32
	Escort/lynx	RF	9/16P-2 1/16P	1 5/16P	0-1 1/2P	3/4P	1/8N	15 3/32
	Escort/Lynx	R	-	-	1 1/2N-5/8N	5/8N	1/16N	-
	EXP	LF	9/16P-2 1/16P	1 5/16P	7/16P-1 15/16P	1 3/16P	1/8N	14 21/32
	EXP	RF	9/16P-2 1/16P	1 5/16P	0-1 1/2P	3/4P	1/8N	15 3/32
	EXP	R	-	-	1 1/2N-5/8N	5/8N	1/16N	-
1984	Escort/Lynx ①	LF	9/16P-2 1/16P	1 5/16P	7/16P-1 15/16P	1 3/16P	1/8N	14 21/32
	Escort/lynx ①	RF	9/16P-2 1/16P	1 5/16P	0-1 1/2P	3/4P	1/8N	15 3/32
	Escort/Lynx ②	LF	1/4P-1 3/4P	1P	1 1/4P-2 5/8P	1 7/8P	1/8N	14 21/32
	Escort/Lynx ②	RF	1/4P-1 3/4P	1P	11/16P-2 3/16P	1 7/16P	1/8N	15 3/32
	Escort/Lynx	R	-	-	1 1/2N-5/8N	5/8N	1/16N	-
	EXP	LF	9/16P-2 1/16P	1 5/16P	7/16P-1 15/16P	1 3/16P	1/8N	14 21/32
	EXP	RF	9/16P-2 1/16P	1 5/16P	0-1 1/2P	3/4P	1/8N	15 3/32
	EXP	R	-	-	1 1/2N-5/8N	5/8N	1/16N	-
1985	Escort/Lynx ①	LF	9/16P-2 1/16P	1 5/16P	7/16P-1 15/16P	1 3/16P	1/8N	14 21/32
	Escort/lynx ①	RF	9/16P-2 1/16P	1 5/16P	0-1 1/2P	3/4P	1/8N	15 3/32
	Escort/Lynx ②	LF	1/4P-1 3/4P	1P	1 1/4P-2 5/8P	1 7/8P	1/8N	14 21/32
	Escort/Lynx ②	RF	1/4P-1 3/4P	1P	11/16P-2 3/16P	1 7/16P	1/8N	15 3/32
	Escort/Lynx	R	-	-	1 1/2N-5/8N	5/8N	1/16N	-
	Escort/Lynx ③	LF	1 11/16P-3 1/16P	2 7/16P	5/8P-2 1/8P	1 3/8P	3/32N	14 21/32
	Escort/Lynx ③	RF	1 11/16P-3 1/16P	2 7/16P	3/16P-1 11/16P	15/16P	3/32N	15 3/32
	Escort/Lynx ③	R	-	-	2 1/32N-11/32N	1 3/16P	3/16P	-
	EXP	LF	9/16P-2 1/16P	1 5/16P	7/16P-1 15/16P	1 3/16P	1/8N	14 21/32
	EXP	RF	9/16P-2 1/16P	1 5/16P	0-1 1/2P	3/4P	1/8N	15 3/32
	EXP	R	-	-	1 1/2N-5/8N	5/8N	1/16N	-
	EXP ③	LF	1 11/16P-3 1/16P	2 7/16P	5/8P-2 1/8P	1 3/8P	3/32N	14 21/32
	EXP ③	RF	1 11/16P-3 1/16P	2 7/16P	3/16P-1 11/16P	15/16P	3/32N	15 3/32
	EXP ③	R	-	-	2 1/32N-11/32N	1 3/16P	3/16P	-
1986	Escort/Lynx	LF	1 11/16P-3 1/16P	2 7/16P	5/8P-2 1/8P	1 3/8P	3/32N	14 21/32
	Escort/Lynx	RF	1 11/16P-3 1/16P	2 7/16P	3/16P-1 11/16P	15/16P	3/32N	15 3/32
	Escort/Lynx	R	-	-	2 1/32N-11/32N	1 3/16P	3/16P	-
	EXP	LF	1 11/16P-3 1/16P	2 7/16P	5/8P-2 1/8P	1 3/8P	3/32N	14 21/32
	EXP	RF	1 11/16P-3 1/16P	2 7/16P	3/16P-1 11/16P	15/16P	3/32N	15 3/32
	EXP	R	-	-	2 1/32N-11/32N	1 3/16P	3/16P	-
1987	Escort/Lynx	LF	1 5/8P-3 1/8P	2 3/8P	3/8P-1 7/8P	1 1/8P	1/8N	14 21/32
	Escort/Lynx	RF	1 5/8P-3 1/8P	2 3/8P	0-1 1/2P	3/4P	1/8N	15 3/32
	Escort/Lynx	R	-	-	1 3/16N-1/2P	5/16N	3/16P	-

86758C17

WHEEL ALIGNMENT

			Caster		Camber			Steering
Year	Model		Range (deg.)	Preferred Setting (deg.)	Range (deg.)	Preferred Setting (deg.)	Toe-in (in.)	Axis Inclination (deg.)
1988	Escort/Lynx	LF	1 5/8P-3 1/8P	2 3/8P	3/8P-1 7/8P	1 1/8P	1/8N	14 21/32
	Escort/Lynx	RF	1 5/8P-3 1/8P	2 3/8P	0-1 1/2P	3/4P	1/8N	15 3/32
	Escort/Lynx	R	-	-	1 3/16N-1/2P	5/16N	3/16P	-
1989	Escort/lynx	LF	1 5/8P-3 1/8P	2 3/8P	3/8P-1 7/8P	1 1/8P	1/8N	14 21/32
	Escort/Lynx	RF	1 5/8P-3 1/8P	2 3/8P	0-1 1/2P	3/4P	1/8N	15 3/32
	Escort/Lynx	R	-	-	1 3/16N-1/2P	5/16N	3/16P	-
1990	Escort/Lynx	LF	1 5/8P-3 1/8P	2 3/8P	3/8P-1 7/8P	1 1/8P	1/8N	14 21/32
	Escort/Lynx	RF	1 5/8P-3 1/8P	2 3/8P	0-1 1/2P	3/4P	1/8N	15 3/32
	Escort/lynx	R	-	-	1 3/16N-1/2P	5/16N	3/16P	-
1991	Escort/Lynx	LF	1 5/8P-3 1/8P	2 3/8P	3/8P-1 7/8P	1 1/8P	1/8N	14 21/32
	Escort/Lynx	RF	1 5/8P-3 1/8P	2 3/8P	0-1 1/2P	3/4P	1/8N	15 3/32
	Escort/Lynx	R	-	-	1 3/16N-1/2P	5/16N	3/16P	-
1992	Escort/Lynx	LF	1 5/8P-3 1/8P	2 3/8P	3/8P-1 7/8P	1 1/8P	1/8N	14 21/32
	Escort/Lynx	RF	1 5/8P-3 1/8P	2 3/8P	0-1 1/2P	3/4P	1/8N	15 3/32
	Escort/Lynx	R	-	-	1 3/16N-1/2P	5/16N	3/16P	-
1993	Escort/Tracer	LF	1 5/8P-3 1/8P	2 3/8P	3/8P-1 7/8P	1 1/8P	1/8N	14 21/32
	Escort/Tracer	RF	1 5/8P-3 1/8P	2 3/8P	0-1 1/2P	3/4P	1/8N	15 3/32
	Escort/Tracer	R	-	-	1 3/16N-1/2P	5/16N	3/16P	-
1994	Escort/Tracer	F	1.00P-2.88P	1.94P	0.84N-0.69P	0.09N	0.09P	23.81
	Escort/Tracer	R	-	-	1.09N-0.44P	0.34N	0.09P	-
1995	Escort/Tracer	F	1.00P-2.84P	1.92P	0.83N-0.67P	0.08N	0.30P	12.00
	Escort/Tracer	R	-	-	0.78N-0.12P	0.33N	0.30P	-

N - Negative
P - Positive
LF - Left Front
RF - Right Front
F- Front
R- Rear
(1) 1.6L non-turbo engine
(2) 1.6L turbo engine
(3) 1.9L engine

86758C18

REAR SUSPENSION

Coil Springs

REMOVAL & INSTALLATION

1981-90 Models

See Figures 45, 46, 47 and 48

1. Raise and support the vehicle safely. Position the jackstands on the frame pads slightly in front of the rear wheels.
2. Place a floor jack or small hydraulic jack under the rear control arm. Raise the control arm to its normal height with the jack, do not lift the car frame from the jackstands.

➡If a twin-post lift is used, vehicle must be supported on jackstands placed under the jack pads of the underbody.

3. Remove wheel(s).
4. Remove and discard nut, bolt and washers retaining lower control arm to spindle.
5. Slowly lower the jack under the control arm. The coil spring will relax as the control arm is lowered. Lower the control arm until the spring can be removed.

To install:

6. The spring insulator must be replaced when servicing the spring.
7. Index the insulator on the spring and press the insulator downward until it snaps into place. Check again to ensure the insulator is properly indexed against tip of the spring.
8. Install spring in control arm. Ensure spring is properly seated in control arm spring pocket.
9. Raise control arm and spring with a floor jack. Position the spring in the pocket on the underbody.

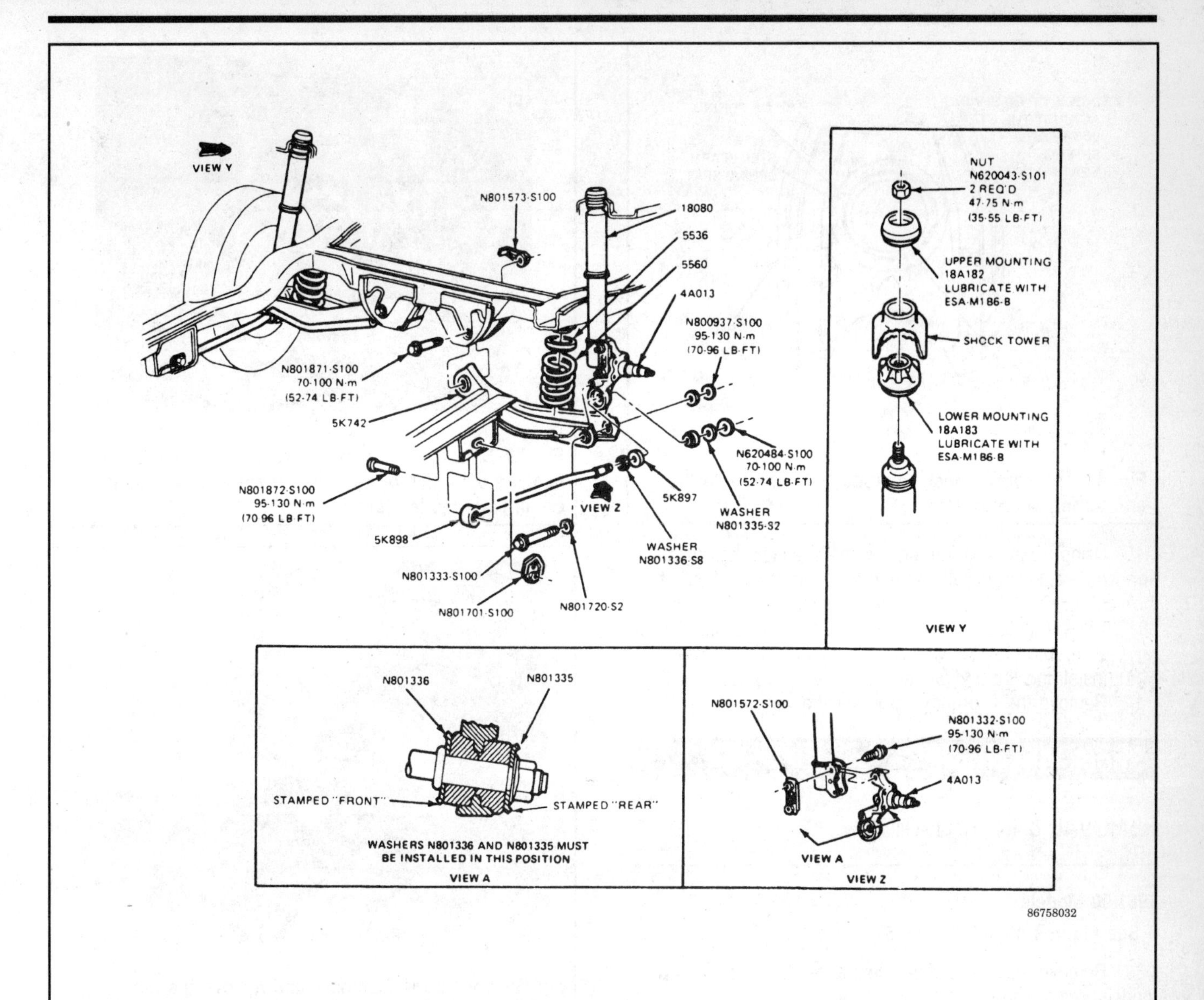

Fig. 45 Common rear suspension fasteners — 1981-85 models

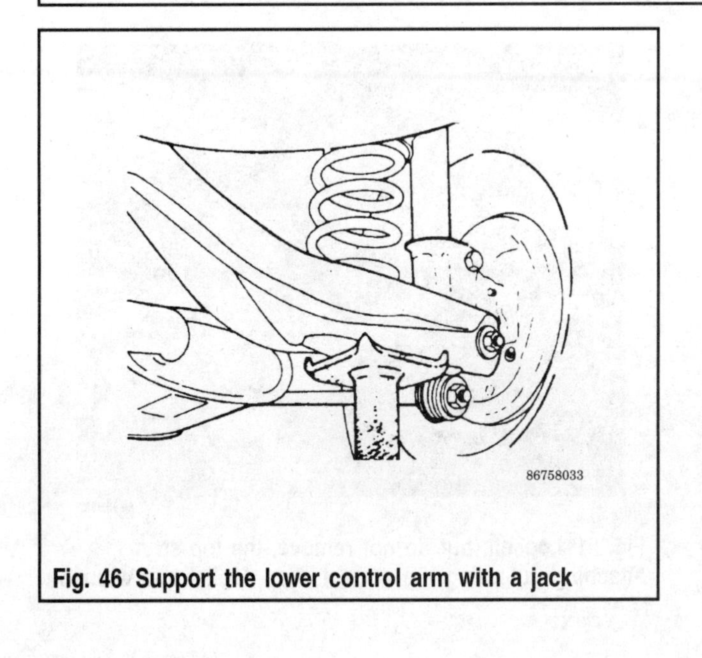

Fig. 46 Support the lower control arm with a jack

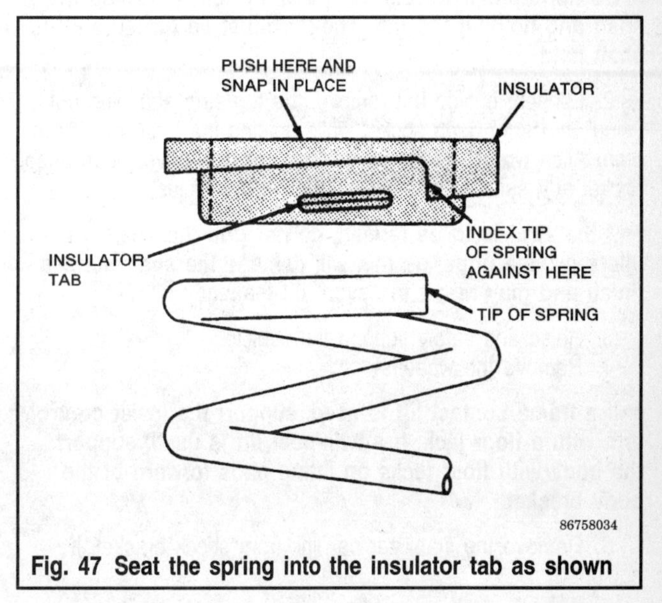

Fig. 47 Seat the spring into the insulator tab as shown

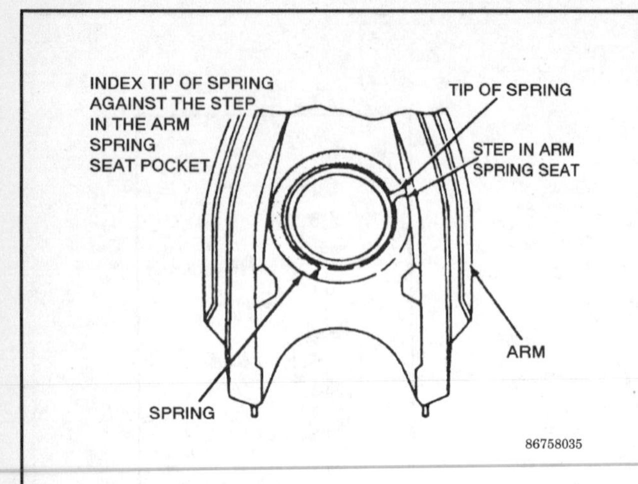

Fig. 48 The spring must be properly indexed into the arm spring seat pocket

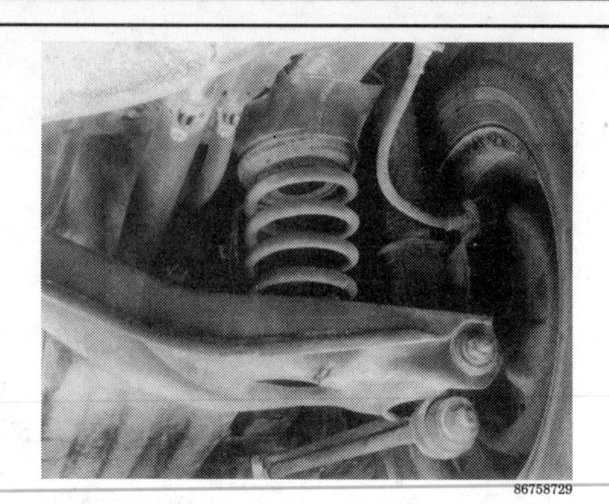

Fig. 49 Shock absorption and rebound damping are handled by a side-by-side spring and shock absorber on all early model Escorts

10. Using a new bolt, nut and washers, attach the control arm to the spindle. Install bolt with the head toward front of the vehicle. On the 1981-85 models, tighten the nut and bolt to 90-100 ft. lbs. (122-136 Nm). On the 1985½-90 models, tighten to 70-96 ft. lbs. (95-130 Nm).
11. Install the tire and wheel.
12. Remove the floor jack and lower the vehicle.

Shock Absorbers

REMOVAL & INSTALLATION

1981-90 Models

See Figures 49, 50, 51, 52, 53 and 54

1. Remove the rear compartment access panels. On 4-door models, remove the quarter trim panel.

Do not attempt to remove the shaft nut by turning the shaft and holding the nut. The nut must be turned and the shaft held.

2. Loosen, but do not remove, the top strut attaching nut using an 18mm deep socket while holding the strut rod with a 6mm Allen wrench (1981-85 vehicles) or a ¼ drive, 8mm deep socket and suitable extension (1985½-90 vehicles).

If the strut is to be reused, do not grip the shaft with pliers or vise grips, as this will damage the shaft surface finish and may result in severe oil leakage.

3. Raise and safely support the vehicle.
4. Remove the wheel(s).

If a frame contact lift is used, support the lower control arm with a floor jack. If a twin-post lift is used, support the body with floor jacks on lifting pads forward of the body bracket.

5. Remove the stabilizer bar link from shock bracket, if equipped.

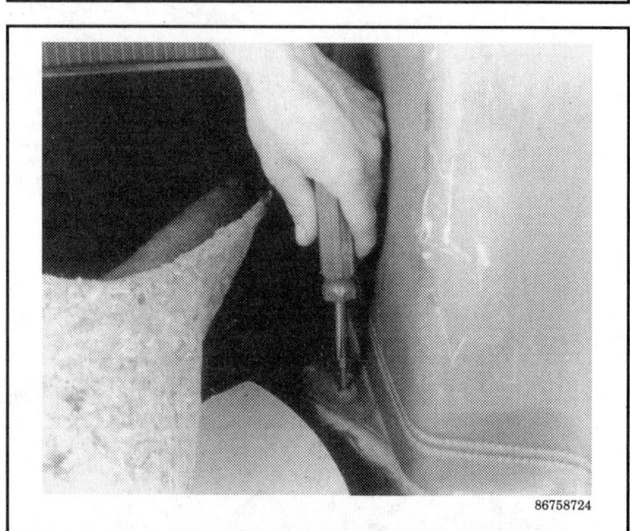

Fig. 50 Locate the fasteners and remove the rear compartment access panels — 1988 wagon shown

Fig. 51 Loosen, but do not remove, the top strut attaching nut using the correct deep socket and wrench

86758726

Fig. 52 If a frame contact lift is used, support the lower control arm with a floor jack

6. Remove the clip retaining the brake line flexible hose to the rear shock and move it aside.
7. Loosen the two nuts and bolts retaining the shock to the spindle. Do not remove the bolts at this time.
8. Remove and discard the top mounting nut, washer and rubber insulator.
9. Remove and discard the two bottom mounting bolts and remove the shock from the vehicle.

To install:

10. Extend shock absorber to its maximum length.
11. Install a new lower washer and insulator assembly, using tire mounting lubricant, or equivalent, to ease insertion into the quarter panel shock tower.
12. Position the upper part of the shock absorber shaft into the shock tower opening in the body and push slowly on the lower part of the shock until the mounting holes are lined up with the mounting holes in the spindle.
13. Install new lower mounting bolts and nuts. Do not tighten at this time.

➡The heads of both bolts must be to the rear of the vehicle.

86758727

Fig. 53 Remove the clip retaining the brake line flexible hose to the rear shock strut and move it aside

86758728

Fig. 54 Loosen the nuts/bolts retaining the shock to the spindle — but do not remove until the top mounting nuts are off

14. Place a new upper insulator and washer assembly and nut on the upper shock absorber shaft. Tighten the nut to 35-55 ft. lbs. (48-75 Nm). Do not grip the shaft with pliers or vise grips.
15. Tighten the two lower mounting bolts to 70-96 ft. lbs. (95-130 Nm).
16. Install stabilizer bar link to bracket on strut, if equipped. Tighten bolts to 40-55 ft. lbs. (55-75 Nm).
17. Install brake line flex hose and retaining clip.
18. Install the wheel and tire assembly.
19. Install quarter trim and access panels, as required.

MacPherson Strut

REMOVAL & INSTALLATION

1991-95 Models

See Figure 55

1. Raise and safely support the vehicle.
2. Remove the wheel and tire assembly.
3. Remove the clip securing the flexible brake hose to the rear strut assembly.
4. Remove the nuts and bolts securing the rear strut assembly to the rear wheel spindle assembly.
5. On hatchback and wagon models, remove the quarter lower trim panel.
6. Remove the mounting block nuts and remove the rear strut assembly from the vehicle.

To install:

7. Position the strut assembly into the vehicle wheel housing.
8. Install the mounting block nuts and tighten to 22-27 ft. lbs. (29-40 Nm).
9. On hatchback and wagon, install the quarter lower trim panel.
10. Install the nuts and bolts securing the strut assembly to the rear spindle assembly. Tighten the lower strut bolts to 69-93 ft. lbs. (93-127 Nm).

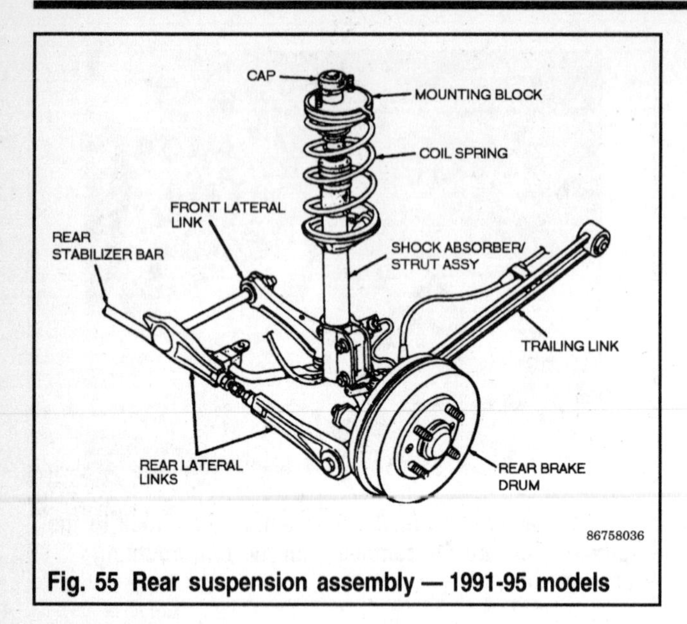

Fig. 55 Rear suspension assembly — 1991-95 models

11. Install the wheel and tire assembly. Tighten the lug nuts to 65-87 ft. lbs. (88-118 Nm).
12. Check the rear alignment and lower the vehicle.

OVERHAUL

1991-95 Models

See Figures 56 and 57

1. Position the strut assembly into a vise and secure the assembly at the mounting block.
2. Remove the cap and loosen the piston rod nut one turn. Do not remove the piston rod nut at this time.
3. Install a suitable coil spring compressor onto the coil spring and compress the coil spring.
4. Remove the piston rod nut, washer, retainer and mounting block.
5. Remove the coil spring.
6. Remove the bound stopper seat and stopper from the strut piston.

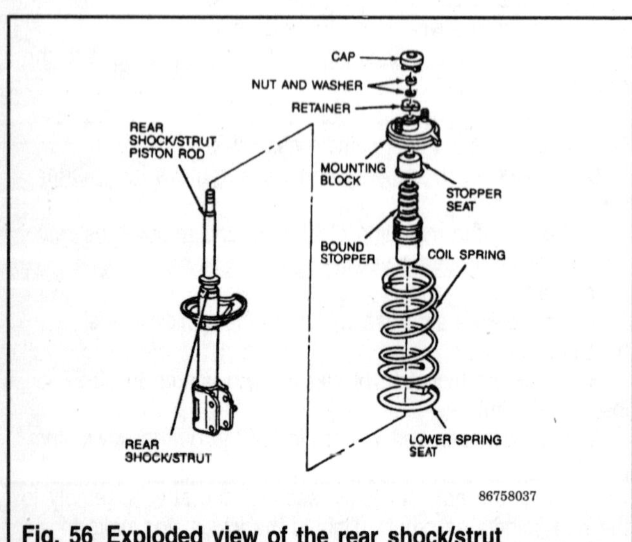

Fig. 56 Exploded view of the rear shock/strut assembly — 1991-95 models

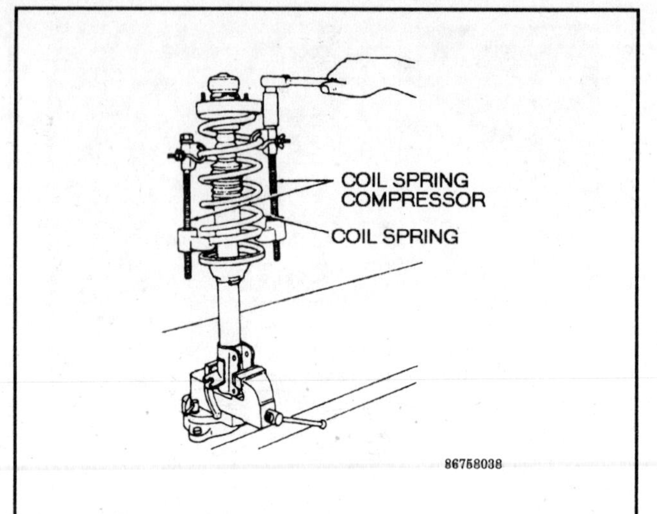

Fig. 57 Tighten the spring compression tool to remove the spring from the strut — 1991-95 models

To assemble:

7. Position the strut assembly into a vise and secure.
8. Install the bound stopper seat and stopper onto the strut piston rod.
9. Install the coil spring onto the strut assembly.
10. Install the mounting block, then align the mounting block studs and the lower bracket of the strut assembly.
11. Install the retainer, washer and piston rod nut. Tighten the nut to 41-50 ft. lbs. (55-68 Nm).
12. Make sure the spring is properly aligned and carefully release the spring into the seats of the strut.
13. Remove the spring compressor from the coil spring and install the cap.

Rear Control Arms

REMOVAL & INSTALLATION

1981-90 Models

1. Raise and safely support the vehicle.
2. Place a floor jack under the lower control arm. Raise lower control arm to curb position.

➡If a twin-post lift is used, vehicle must be supported on jackstands placed under the jack pads of the underbody.

3. Remove the wheel(s).
4. Remove the nuts from the control arm-to-body mounting and control arm-to-spindle mounting. Do not remove the bolts at this time.
5. Remove and discard spindle end mounting bolt. Slowly lower control arm with floor jack until spring can be removed.
6. Remove and discard bolt from the body end and remove control arm from vehicle.

To install:

7. Attach lower control arm-to-body bracket using a new bolt and nut. Head of the bolt should face the front of the vehicle. Do not tighten at this time.
8. The spring insulator must be replaced when servicing spring.

9. Index the insulator on the spring and press insulator downward until it snaps into place. Place spring in spring pocket in lower control arm. Make sure spring is properly indexed.
10. Using a floor jack, raise lower control arm until it is in line with mounting hole in the spindle.
11. Install lower control arm to spindle using a new bolt, nut and washers. Do not tighten at this time. Bolt head should face the front of the vehicle.
12. Using the floor jack, raise lower control arm to curb height.
13. Tighten control arm-to-spindle bolt to 60-80 ft. lbs. (81-109 Nm).
14. Tighten control arm-to-body bolt to 52-74 ft. lbs. (70-100 Nm).
15. Install the tire and wheel.
16. Remove the floor jack and lower the vehicle.

1991-95 Models

1. Raise and safely support the vehicle.
2. Remove the wheel and tire assembly.
3. Remove the stabilizer nuts, washers, bushings, sleeves and bolts.
4. Remove the bolts securing the stabilizer bar brackets and grommets to the rear suspension crossmember.
5. Remove the stabilizer bar.
6. Remove the cap covering the front and rear lateral link pivot bolts.
7. Position a floor jack stand under the rear suspension crossmember.
8. Remove the bolts securing the rear suspension crossmember to the vehicle frame.
9. Lower the floor jack stand to allow the rear suspension crossmember to be lowered from the vehicle frame.
10. Remove the front and rear lateral link pivot nut, washer and bolt from the rear suspension crossmember.
11. Remove the front and rear lateral links from the rear suspension crossmember.
12. Remove the bolt, washers and nut securing the front and rear lateral links to the rear wheel spindle and remove the lateral links.
13. Remove the nuts securing the parking brake cable and cable bracket to the trailing link.
14. Remove the rear trailing link bolts and washers from the vehicle frame and rear wheel spindle. Remove the rear trailing link.

To install:

15. Position the rear trailing link and install the bolts and washers. Tighten the trailing link front bolt to 46-69 ft. lbs. (63-93 Nm) and the rear bolt to 69-93 ft. lbs. (93-127 Nm).
16. Position the parking brake cable and bracket to the trailing link and secure it with the nuts.
17. Position the front and rear lateral links to the rear wheel spindle and install the washers, bolt and nut. Tighten the front and rear lateral link nut at the rear wheel spindle to 63-86 ft. lbs. (85-117 Nm).
18. Position the front and rear lateral links to the rear suspension crossmember. Tighten the front and rear lateral link nut at the rear suspension crossmember to 50-70 ft. lbs. (68-95 Nm).
19. Install the cap.
20. Raise the floor jack stand to position the rear suspension crossmember to the vehicle frame. Install and tighten the bolts. Remove the floor jack stand from under the vehicle.
21. Position the grommets onto the stabilizer bar and align the grommets to the positions painted on the bar.
22. Position the stabilizer bar to the rear suspension crossmember and secure it in place with the straps and bolts. Tighten the bolts to 32-43 ft. lbs. (43-59 Nm).
23. Install the stabilizer bolts, washers, grommets, sleeves and nuts. Tighten the stabilizer nuts so 0.64-0.72 in. (16.2-17.0mm) of thread is exposed at the end of the bolt.
24. Install the wheel and tire assembly. Tighten the lug nuts to 65-87 ft. lbs. (88-118 Nm).
25. Check the wheel alignment and lower the vehicle.

Rear Wheel Bearings

REMOVAL & INSTALLATION

1981-90 Models

1. Raise and safely support the vehicle.
2. Remove the wheel and tire assembly. Remove the grease cap from the hub.
3. Remove the cotter pin, nut retainer, adjusting nut and flatwasher from spindle. Discard the cotter pin.
4. Pull the hub and drum assembly off the spindle being careful not to drop outer bearing assembly.
5. Remove the outer bearing assembly.
6. Using a seal remover, remove and discard grease seal. Remove the inner bearing assembly from the hub.
7. Wipe all lubricant from the spindle and inside of the hub. Cover the spindle with a clean cloth and vacuum all loose dust and dirt from the brake assembly. Carefully remove cloth to prevent dirt from falling on spindle.
8. Clean both bearing assemblies and cups using solvent. inspect bearing assemblies and cups for excessive wear, scratches, pits or other damage. Replace all worn or damaged parts as required.

➡Allow the solvent to dry before repacking bearings. Do not spin-dry bearings with air pressure.

9. If cups are replaced, remove them with wheel hub cup remover D80L-927-A and bearing cup puller T77F-1102-A or equivalent.

To install:

10. If inner or outer bearing cups were removed, install replacement cups using driver handle T80T-4000-W and bearing cup replacers T77F-1202-A and T73T-1217-A or equivalent. Support drum hub on wood block to prevent damage. Insure cups are properly seated in hub.

➡Do not use cone and roller assembly to install cup as this will cause damage to bearing cup and cone and roller assembly.

11. Ensure all spindle and bearing surfaces are clean.
12. Using a bearing packer, pack bearing assemblies with a suitable wheel bearing grease. If a packer is not available, work in as much grease as possible between the rollers and the cages. Grease the cup surfaces.

13. Place inner bearing cone and roller assembly in the inner cup. Apply a light film of grease to the lips of a new grease seal and install seal with rear hub seal replacer T81P-1249-A or equivalent. Ensure the retainer flange is seated all around.
14. Apply a light film of grease on the spindle shaft bearing surfaces.
15. Install a hub and drum assembly on the spindle. Keep the hub centered on the spindle to prevent damage to the grease seal and spindle threads.
16. Install the outer bearing assembly and keyed flat washer on the spindle. Install adjusting nut finger-tight. Adjust wheel bearings. Install a new cotter pin.
17. Install the wheel and tire on drum.
18. Lower the vehicle.

1991-95 Models

1. Loosen the rear lug nuts and the rear hub nut.
2. Raise and safely support the vehicle.
3. Remove the wheel and tire assembly.
4. Remove the brake drum or brake caliper and rotor, as necessary.
5. Remove the nut securing the rear wheel hub to the spindle and remove the hub and bearing assembly.

To install:

6. Install the rear wheel hub and bearing assembly onto the spindle.
7. Install the hub nut onto the spindle and tighten to 130-174 ft. lbs. (177-235 Nm).
8. Stake the hub nut and install the cap.
9. Install the brake drum or the brake caliper and rotor, as necessary.
10. Install the wheel and tire assembly.
11. Lower the vehicle. Tighten the lug nuts to 65-87 ft. lbs. (88-118 Nm).

ADJUSTMENT

➡The rear wheel bearings are adjustable only on 1981-90 models.

1. Raise and safely support the vehicle.
2. Remove the wheel covers or ornament and nut covers. Remove grease cap from hub.
3. Remove the cotter pin and nut retainer. Discard cotter pin.
4. Back-off adjusting nut one full turn. Ensure nut turns freely on the spindle threads. Correct any binding condition.
5. Tighten the adjusting nut to 17-25 ft. lbs. (23-34 Nm) while rotating hub and drum assembly to seat bearings. Loosen the adjusting nut ½ turn and tighten adjusting nut to 24-28 inch lbs. (2.7-3.2 Nm).
6. Position adjusting nut retainer over adjusting nut so the slots in the nut retainer flange are in line with the cotter pin hole in the spline.
7. Install a new cotter pin and bend ends around retainer flange.
8. Check hub rotation. If the hub rotates freely, install the grease cap. If not, check bearings for damage and replace as necessary.
9. Install the wheel and tire assembly, wheel cover or ornaments, and nut covers as required.
10. Lower the vehicle.

Rear End Alignment

CHECKING

➧ See Figures 58, 59 and 60

The rear caster, camber and toe angles on these vehicles are preset at the factory and should not be adjusted without the proper equipment and training.

There is a method; however, of checking whether the vehicle is "dog tracking." Dog tracking is a condition where the rear wheels do not follow the front wheels and the vehicle does not travel squarely down the road.

1. Pour water on flat dry pavement and drive the vehicle over the water, keeping the vehicle as straight as possible.
2. Measure the total width of each overlapping imprint on the left and right sides.
3. If the width of one rear imprint is more than 1½ in. (38mm) greater than one front imprint, this means the vehicle is not tracking properly.

ADJUSTMENT

Rear end alignment requires expensive special equipment and experience. If inspection reveals evidence of mis-alignment, have the vehicle serviced by a qualified technician.

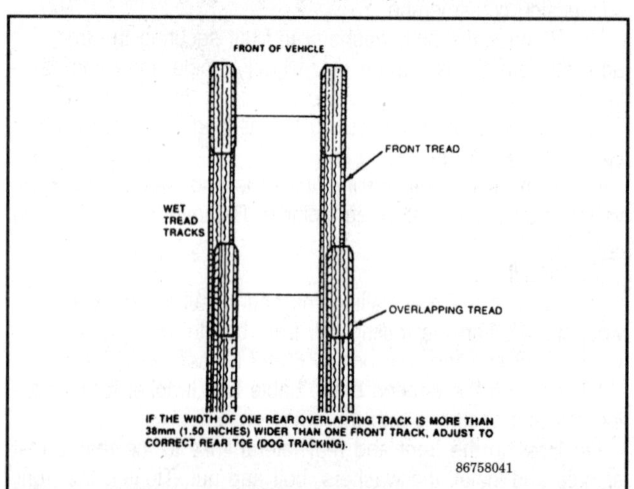

Fig. 58 Dog tracking occurs when the rear wheels are not following the front correctly — a rear toe alignment often corrects this condition

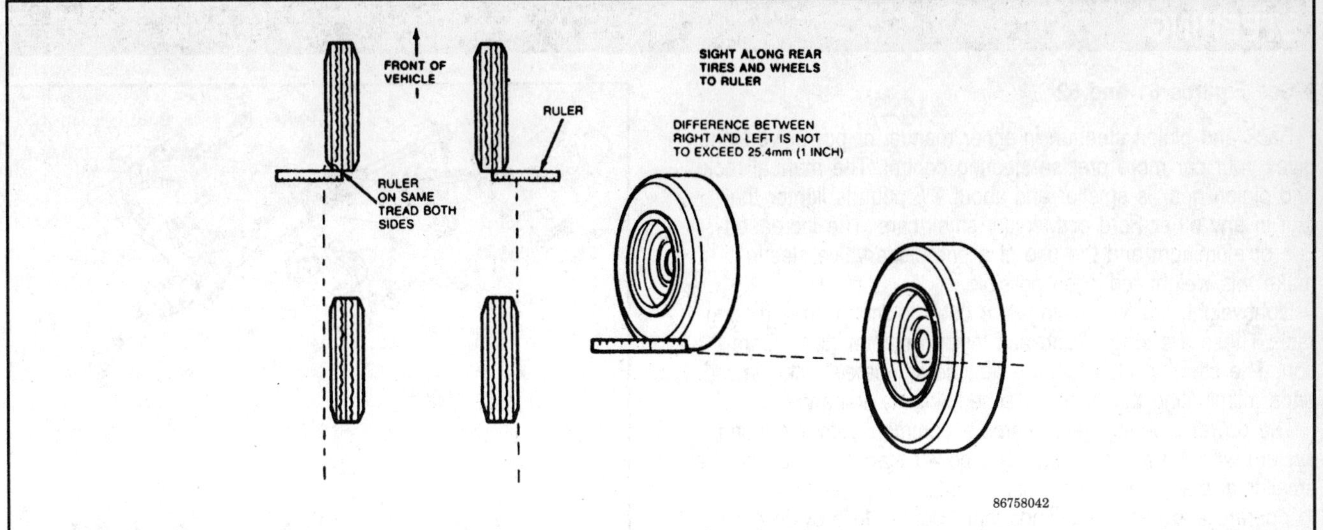

Fig. 59 To determine whether the car is dog tracking excessively, measure the difference between the right and left side

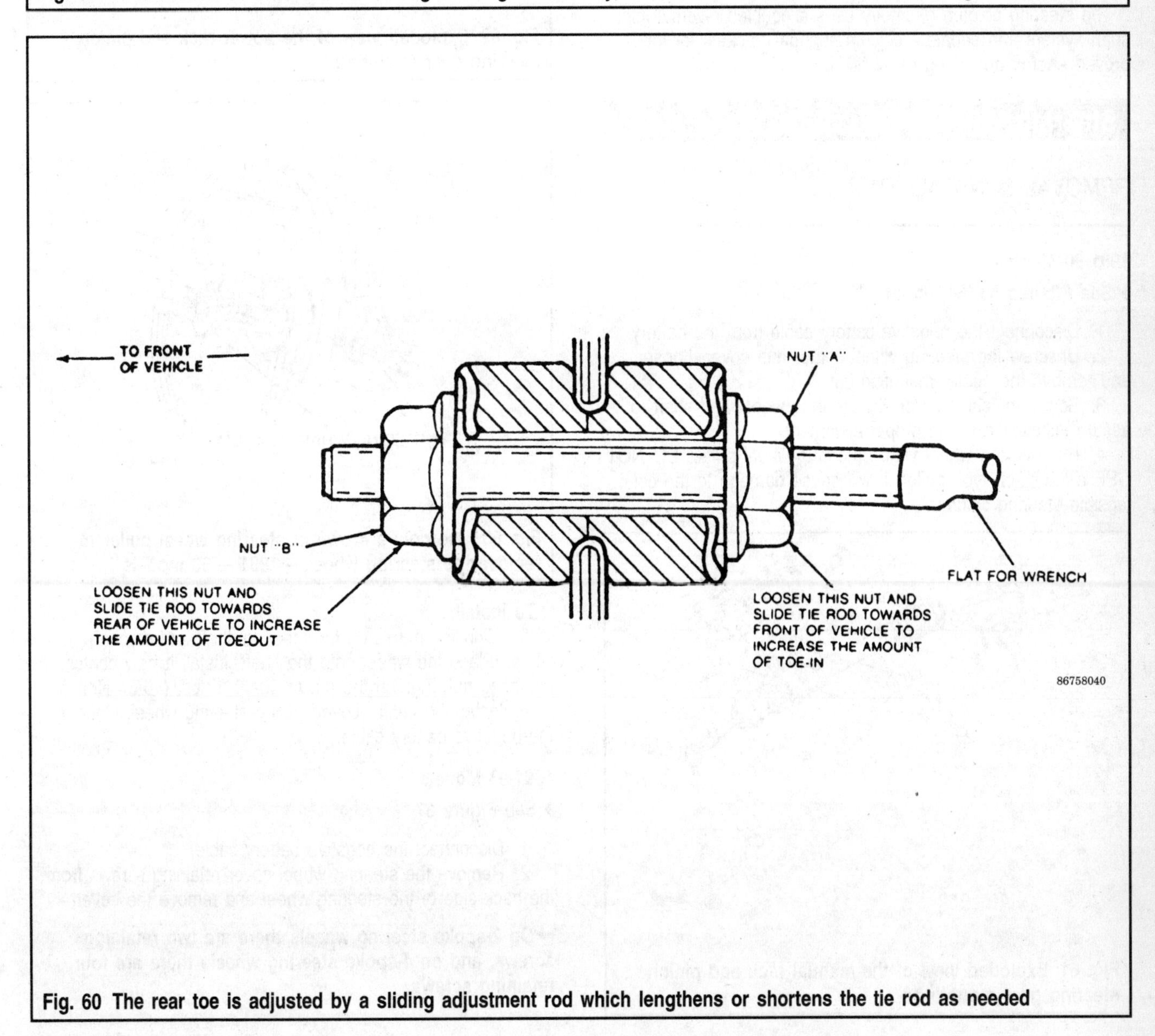

Fig. 60 The rear toe is adjusted by a sliding adjustment rod which lengthens or shortens the tie rod as needed

STEERING

➧ See Figures 61 and 62

Rack and pinion steering in either manual or power versions gives your car more precise steering control. The manual rack and pinion gear is smaller and about 7½ pounds lighter than that in any other Ford or Mercury small cars. The increased use of aluminum and the use of a one-piece valve sleeve make this weight reduction possible.

Lightweight, sturdy bushings are used to mount the steering rack. These are long lasting and lend to quieter gear operation. The steering also features lifetime lubricated outer tie rod ends, eliminating the need for scheduled maintenance.

The power steering gear shares a common body mounting system with the manual gear. The power steering pump is of a smaller displacement than most pumps. It requires less power to operate and has streamlined inner porting to provide more efficient fluid flow characteristics.

The steering column geometry uses a double universal joint shaft system and separate column support brackets for improved energy absorbing capabilities.

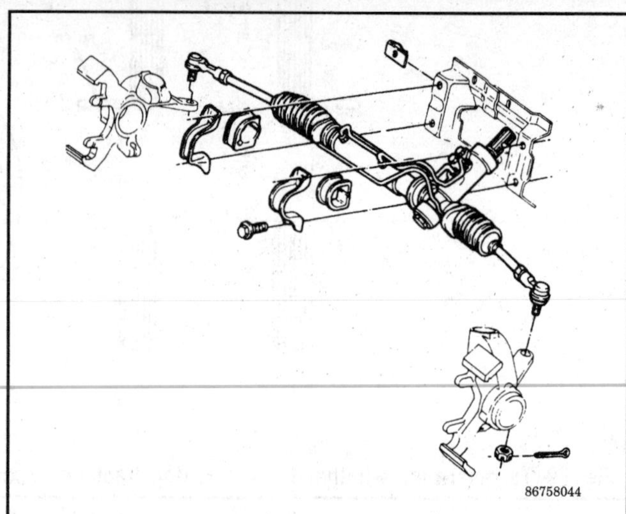

Fig. 62 Exploded view of the power rack and pinion steering gear mounting

Steering Wheel

REMOVAL & INSTALLATION

1981-90 Models

➧ See Figures 63, 64, 65 and 66

1. Disconnect the negative battery cable from the battery.
2. Unscrew the steering wheel center hub cover. Loosen and remove the center mounting nut.
3. Scribe matchmarks on the steering wheel and shaft to assure installation in the proper alignment.
4. Remove the wheel with a steering wheel puller. DO NOT USE a knock-off type puller. It will cause damage to the collapsible steering column.

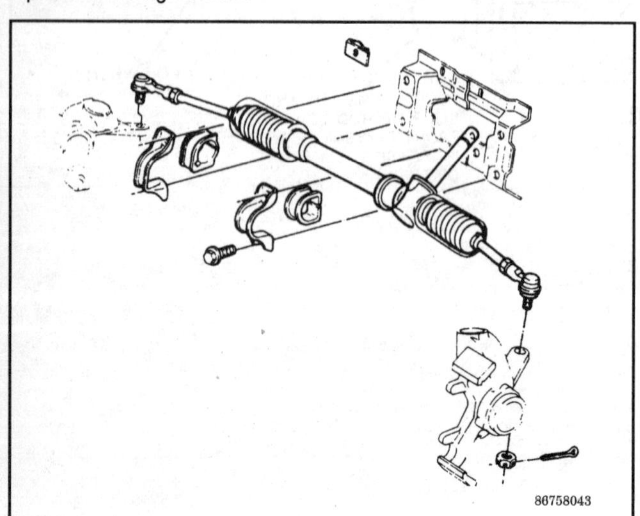

Fig. 61 Exploded view of the manual rack and pinion steering gear mounting

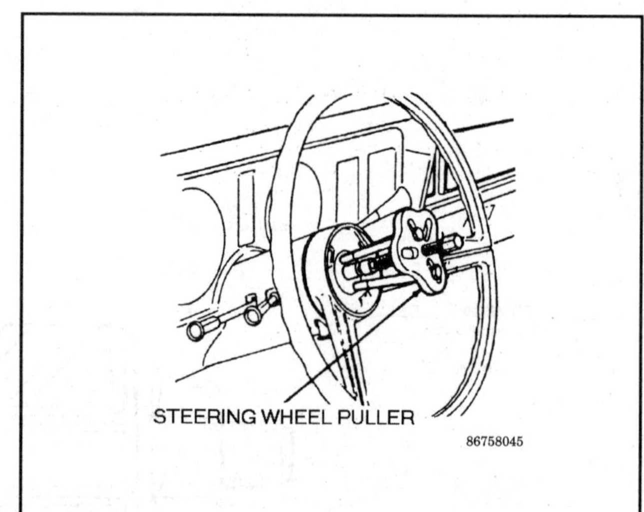

Fig. 63 Use only a crowfoot steering wheel puller to remove the steering wheel — 1981 — 93 models

To install:

5. Align the marks on the steering shaft and steering wheel. Place the wheel onto the shaft. Install a new center mounting nut. Tighten the nut to 30-40 ft. lbs. (40-54 Nm)
6. Install the center cover on the steering wheel. Connect the negative battery cable.

1991-93 Models

➧ See Figure 67

1. Disconnect the negative battery cable.
2. Remove the steering wheel cover retaining screws from the back side of the steering wheel and remove the cover.

➡On 2-spoke steering wheels there are two retaining screws, and on 4-spoke steering wheels there are four retaining screws.

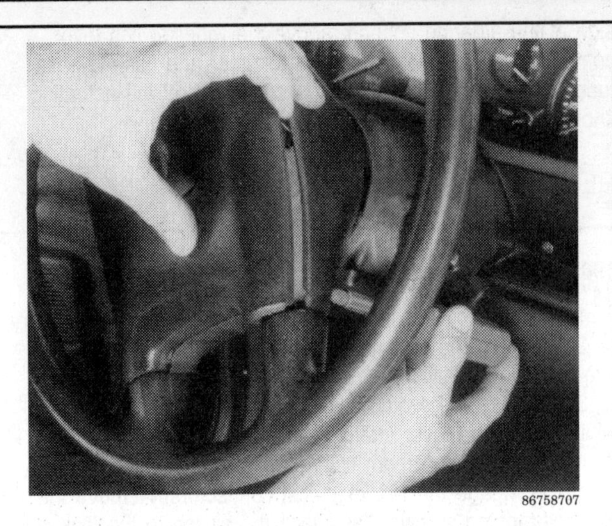
86758707

Fig. 64 Remove the steering wheel center hub by unscrewing it from the back of the wheel

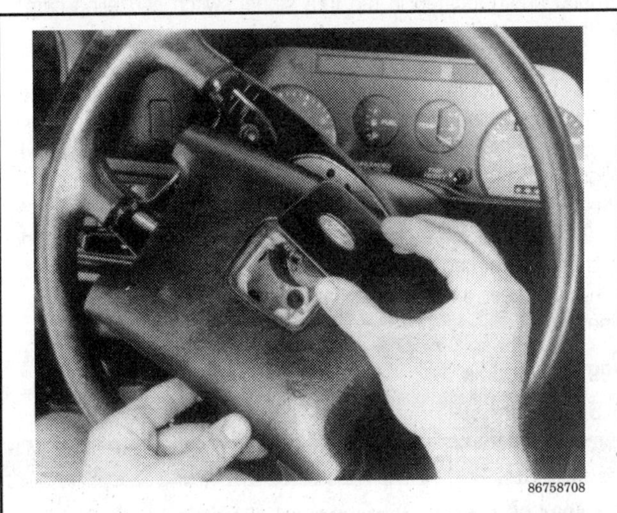
86758708

Fig. 65 Remove the cover, once unscrewed, to expose the wheel retaining nut

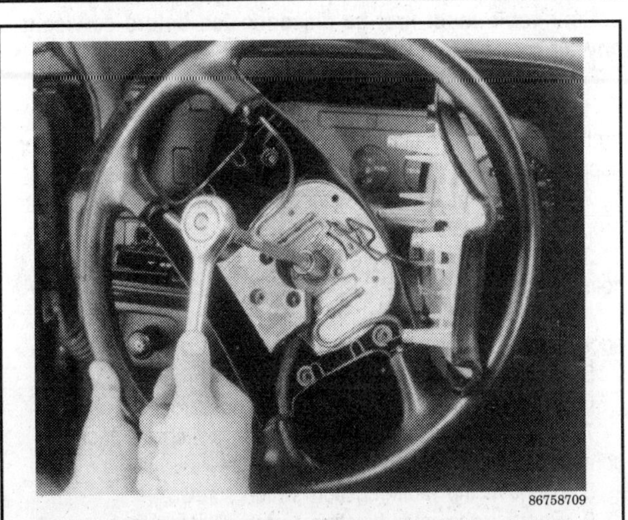
86758709

Fig. 66 Unbolt the retaining nut in order to pull the steering wheel

3. Disengage the horn electrical connector and the speed control electrical connector, if equipped.
4. Remove the steering wheel mounting nut, then scribe matchmarks on the steering wheel and shaft to assure installation in the proper alignment.
5. Remove the steering wheel with a suitable puller. DO NOT USE a knock-off type puller. It will cause damage to the collapsible steering column.

To install:

6. Position the steering wheel, aligning the matchmarks made earlier, then install the mounting nut. Tighten the nut to 29-36 ft. lbs. (39-49 Nm).
7. Connect the horn electrical connector and the speed control electrical connector, if equipped.
8. Position the steering wheel cover and install the retaining screws.
9. Connect the negative battery cable.

1994-95 Models

See Figure 68

➡These models are equipped with a driver's side Supplemental Restraint System (SRS) or air bag assembly. Consult the SRS precautions in Section 6 before proceeding.

1. Make sure the wheels are straight ahead (to ensure alignment of the air bag sliding contact).

****CAUTION**

The backup power supply energy must be depleted before servicing the air bag. To deplete the power supply energy, disconnect the negative battery cable and wait one minute.

2. Disconnect the negative battery cable and wait one minute before proceeding.
3. Remove the two air bag module bolts from behind the steering wheel.

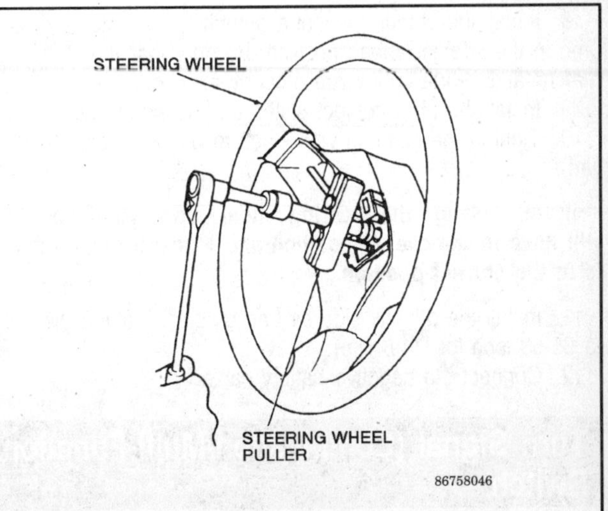

86758046

Fig. 67 Use a steering wheel puller to remove the steering wheel — 1991-93 models

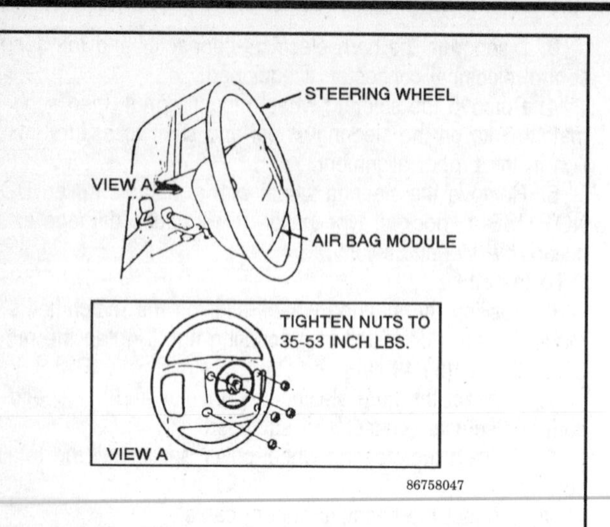

Fig. 68 The air bag assembly is held in place by four nuts — 1993-95 models

4. Pull the air bag module up and disconnect the wiring from the air bag sliding contact. Remove the module from the vehicle.

****WARNING**

When carrying a live air bag, make sure the bag and trim cover are pointed away from your body. If the bag deploys accidently, this will reduce the chance of injury. Also, when placing the air bag on any surface, always face the bag and trim cover UP, away from the surface. This will prevent the air bag from launching in the event of an accidental deployment.

5. Remove the driver's side air bag module.
6. Remove the steering wheel bolt. Scribe matchmarks on the steering wheel and shaft to assure installation in the proper alignment.
7. Remove the wheel using a steering wheel puller such as T67L-3600-A, or equivalent.

To install:

8. Install the steering wheel assembly on the steering column in the straight ahead position. Be sure that the matchmarks made earlier are properly aligned.
9. Install the horn contact plates and screw in place.
10. Tighten the steering wheel bolt to 34-46 ft. lbs. (46-63 Nm).

➡If you misalign the steering wheel upon installation, you will have to remove, re-position and install it again until it is in the correct position.

11. Install the driver's side air bag module. Tighten the bolts to 35-53 inch lbs. (4-6 Nm).
12. Connect the negative battery cable.

Turn Signal (Combination/Multi-Function) Switch

The combination switch assembly is a multi-function switch comprising the controls for turn signals, hazard, headlight dimmer and flash-to-pass functions. The switch lever on the left side of the steering column, above the wiper switch lever, controls the turn signal, headlight dimmer and flash-to-pass functions. The hazard function is controlled by the actuating knob on the bottom part of the steering column.

REMOVAL & INSTALLATION

1981-90 Models

1. Disconnect the negative (ground) cable from the battery.
2. Remove the steering column shroud by taking out the five mounting screws. Remove both halves of the shroud.
3. Remove the switch lever by using a twisting motion while pulling the lever straight out from the switch.
4. Peel back the foam cover to expose the switch.
5. Disengage the two electrical connectors. Remove the two self-tapping screws that attach the switch to the lock cylinder housing. Disengage the switch from the housing.
6. If your car is equipped with speed control, transfer the ground brush located in the turn signal switch canceling cam to the new switch.

To install:

7. To install the new switch, align the switch with the holes in the lock cylinder housing. Install the two self-tapping screws.
8. Install the foam covering the switch. Install the handle by aligning the key on the lever with the keyway in the switch. Push the lever into the switch until it is fully engaged.
9. Reconnect the two electrical connectors. Install the upper and lower steering column shrouds.
10. Connect the negative battery cable. Test the switch operation.

1991-95 Models

➧ See Figure 69

****CAUTION**

On 1994-95 models, the electrical circuit for air bag deployment is powered directly from the battery. To avoid accidental deployment and possible injury, the negative battery cable must first be disconnected before servicing any air bag system components.

1. Disconnect the negative battery cable. On air bag equipped models, wait one minute for the SRS backup power supply to deplete (disabling the air bag system).
2. Remove the steering wheel according to the appropriate procedure.
3. Remove the four screws that retain the lower steering column shroud.
4. Remove the ignition lock cylinder illumination lamp socket from the lower shroud.
5. Remove the lower steering column shroud.
6. Remove the upper steering column shroud.
7. Disengage the three multi-function switch electrical connectors.
8. Remove the multi-function switch screws.
9. Remove the multi-function switch electrical connectors and the multi-function switch.

To install:

10. Install the multi-function switch and fasten in place.

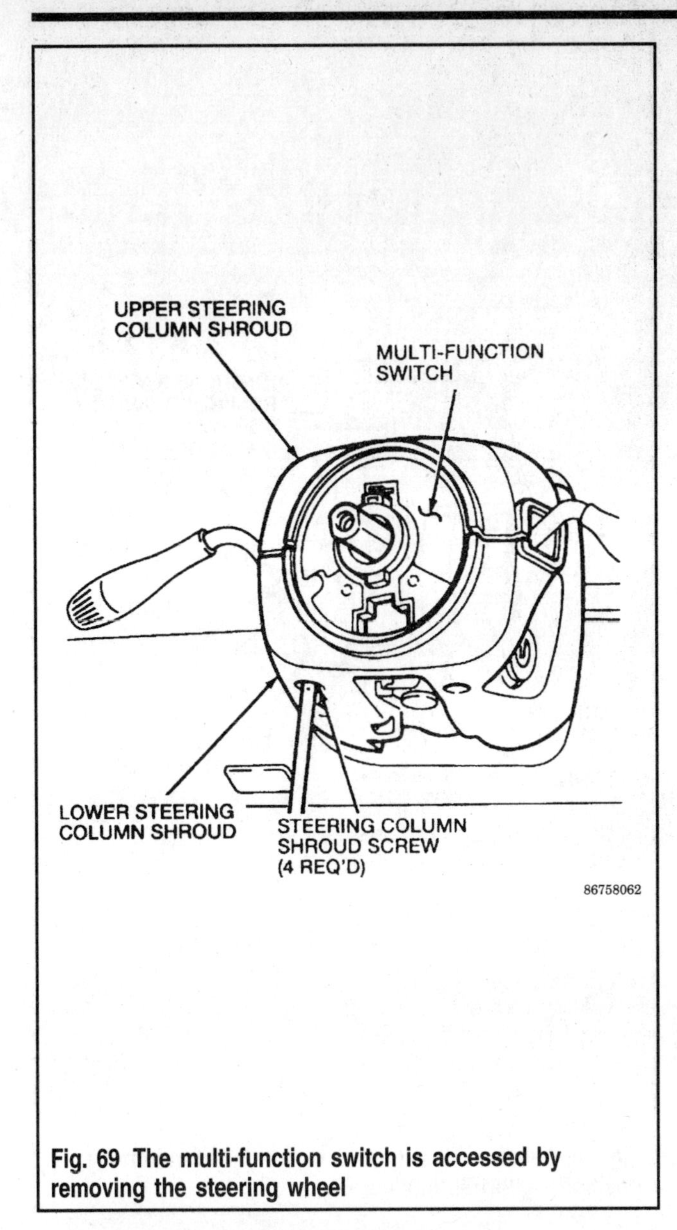

Fig. 69 The multi-function switch is accessed by removing the steering wheel

11. Plug in the electrical connector.
12. Install the upper and lower steering column shroud. Install the ignition lock in the lower shroud.
13. Install the steering wheel.
14. Connect the negative battery cable.

Ignition Switch

REMOVAL & INSTALLATION

1981-85 Models

1. Disconnect the negative (ground) battery cable from the battery.

➡This procedure will require special break-off bolts which should be available from your Ford/Mercury dealer.

2. Remove the upper and lower steering column shrouds by taking out the five retaining screws.
3. Disconnect the electrical harness at the ignition switch.
4. Remove the nuts and bolts retaining the steering column mounting brackets and lower the steering wheel and column to the front seat.
5. Use an 1/8 in. (3mm) drill bit and drill out the break-off head bolts mounting the ignition switch.
6. Take a small screw extractor and remove the bolts.
7. Remove the ignition switch by disconnecting it from the actuator pin.

To install:

➡If reinstalling the old switch, it must be adjusted to the LOCK or RUN (depending on year and model) position. Slide the carrier of the switch to the required position and insert a 1/16 in. (1.6mm) drill bit or pin through the switch housing into the carrier. This keeps the carrier from moving when the switch is connected to the actuator. It may be necessary to wiggle the carrier back and forth to line up the holes when installing the drill or pin. New switches come with a pin in place.

8. When installing the ignition switch, rotate the key lock cylinder to the required position.
9. Install the ignition switch by connecting it to the actuator and loosely installing the two new mounting screws.
10. Move the switch up the steering column until it reaches the end of its elongated screw slots. Hold the switch in position, tighten the mounting screws until the heads break off. Tighten to 15-25 ft. lbs. (20-34 Nm) if non-break off head bolts are used.
11. Remove the pin or drill bit that is locking the actuator carrier in position.
12. Raise the steering column and secure the mounting brackets.
13. Connect the wiring harness to the ignition switch. Install the upper and lower steering column shrouds.
14. Connect the negative battery cable.
15. Check the ignition for operation. Make sure the car will start in N and P, if equipped with an automatic transaxle, but be sure it will not start in D or R. Make sure the steering (wheel) locks when the key switch is in the **LOCK** position.

1985½-90 Models

1. Disconnect the negative battery cable.
2. Remove the steering column upper and lower trim shroud by removing the self-tapping screws. The steering column attaching nuts may have to be loosened enough to allow removal of the upper shroud.
3. Remove the two bolts and nuts holding the steering column assembly to the steering column bracket assembly and lower the steering column to the seat.
4. Remove the steering column shrouds.
5. Disengage electrical connector from ignition switch.
6. Rotate ignition lock cylinder to the **RUN** position.
7. Remove the two screws attaching switch to the lock cylinder housing.
8. Disengage the ignition switch from the actuator pin.

To install:

9. Check to see that the actuator pin slot in ignition switch is in the **RUN** position.

➡A new switch assembly will be pre-set in the RUN position.

10. Make certain that the ignition key lock cylinder is in approximately the **RUN** position. The **RUN** position is achieved by rotating the key lock cylinder approximately 90° from the **LOCK** position.

11. Install the ignition switch onto the actuator pin. It may be necessary to move the switch slightly back and fourth to align the switch mounting holes with the column lock housing threaded holes.

12. Install the new screws and tighten to 50-70 inch lbs. (5.6-7.9 Nm).

13. Plug in the electrical connector to the ignition switch.

14. Connect the negative battery cable.

15. Check the ignition switch for proper function including **START** and **ACC** positions. Also make certain that the steering column is locked when in the **LOCK** position.

16. Position the top half of the shroud on the steering column.

17. Install the two bolts and nuts attaching the steering column assembly to the steering column bracket assembly.

18. Position lower shroud to upper shroud and install five self-tapping screws.

1991-95 Models

See Figure 70

1. Remove the multi-function switch.
2. Unplug the ignition switch electrical connector.

The ignition key reminder switch is an integral part of the ignition switch and is not able to be separately serviced.

3. Remove the two ignition key reminder switch screws.
4. Remove the ignition switch screws and remove the ignition switch.

To install:

5. Install the ignition switch and screw in place.
6. Plug in the ignition switch electrical connector.
7. Install the multi-function switch.

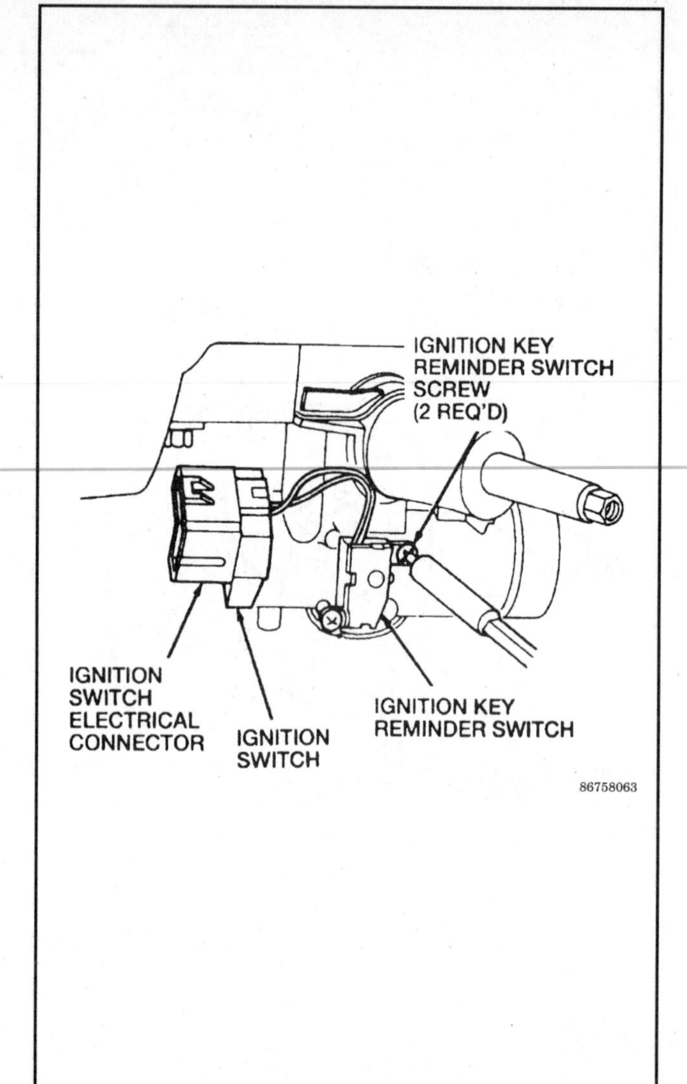

Fig. 70 Details of the ignition switch in its mounted position — 1991-95 models

Ignition Lock Cylinder Assembly

REMOVAL & INSTALLATION

1981-90 Models

1. Disconnect the negative battery cable.
2. If equipped with a tilt steering column, remove the upper extension shroud by unsnapping the shroud from the retaining clip at the 9 o'clock position.
3. Remove the steering column lower shroud.
4. Disengage the warning buzzer electrical connector. With the lock cylinder key, rotate the cylinder to the **RUN** position.
5. Take a 1/8 in. (3mm) diameter pin or small wire punch and push on the cylinder retaining pin. The pin is visible through a hole in the mounting surrounding the key cylinder. Push on the pin and withdraw the lock cylinder from the housing.
6. Install the lock cylinder by turning it to the **RUN** position and depressing the retaining pin. Be sure the lock cylinder is fully seated and aligned in the interlocking washer before turning the key to the **OFF** position. This action will permit the cylinder retaining pin to extend into the cylinder housing hole.
7. Rotate the lock cylinder, using the lock cylinder key, to ensure correct mechanical operation in all positions.
8. Install the electrical connector for the key warning buzzer.
9. Install the lower steering column shroud.
10. Connect the negative battery cable to battery terminal.
11. Check for proper start in P or N. Also, make certain that that the start circuit cannot be actuated in the D and R positions and that the column is locked in the **LOCK** position.

1991-95 Models

If the vehicle you are working on is equipped with a driver's side Supplemental Restraint System (SRS) or air bag assembly, consult the SRS precautions in Section 6 before proceeding.

1. For 1994-95 models, disconnect the negative battery cable and wait at least one minute to deplete the power reserve for the air bag.

2. Remove the steering wheel. For details, please refer to the procedure in this section.
3. Remove the turn signal and windshield wiper switch.
4. Disengage the ignition switch electrical connector.
5. Remove the ignition/shifter interlock cable mounting bracket bolt and position the bracket and ignition/shifter interlock cable aside.
6. Remove the four steering column upper mounting bolts and lower the steering column.

➡You will need two new ignition lock cylinder bracket bolts (with heads that shear off when tightened to the correct torque) in order to re-install the lock cylinder correctly.

7. Use a hammer and chisel to make a groove in the heads of the two ignition lock cylinder bracket bolts.
8. Remove the bolts with a screwdriver and discard the bolts.
9. Remove the ignition lock cylinder and mounting bracket.

To Install:

10. Position the ignition lock cylinder and bracket and install two new bolts. Tighten them only enough to hold the ignition lock cylinder in position.
11. With the key in the ignition, verify the operation of the ignition lock cylinder. If necessary, reposition until it operates properly.
12. Tighten the ignition lock cylinder bracket bolts until the heads break off.
13. Position the steering column and install the four upper mounting bracket bolts. Tighten the bolts to 80-124 inch lbs. (9-14 Nm).
14. On vehicles equipped with a tilt column, remove the upper mounting bracket retaining pin.
15. Position the ignition/shifter interlock cable mounting bracket and install the bolt. Tighten the bolt to 35-53 inch lbs. (4-6 Nm).
16. Engage the ignition switch electrical connector.
17. Install the turn signal and wiper switch.
18. Install the steering wheel.
19. Connect the negative battery cable.
20. On models equipped with an automatic transaxle, inspect the shift interlock system for correct function. If problems are suspected, please refer to the shift interlock system inspection procedure in this section.

Shift Interlock System

The ignition/shifter interlock cable prevents the operator of vehicles equipped with automatic transaxles from shifting out of the PARK position unless the ignition switch is in the **RUN** position.

TROUBLESHOOTING

➧ See Figures 71, 72, 73 and 74

1. Visually inspect the mechanical components of the shift-lock system, look for problems such as:
   - Kinked or bound ignition/shifter interlock cable
   - Kinked or bound transmission shift cable and bracket
   - Damaged selector linkage
   - Shift control selector lever and housing out of adjustment
2. Check the selector lever and ignition/shifter interlock cable for damage or a binding condition.
3. Check the shift button on the shift control selector lever knob for ease of movement throughout the gears.
4. If the problem with the ignition/shifter interlock is not found among the mechanical checks listed, inspect the electrical system by looking for for the following symptoms:
   - Blown fuses: 15A METER, 10A ROOM, 20A STOP
   - Damaged ignition switch
   - Poor connections
   - Damaged or disconnected Brake On/Off (BOO) switch
   - Damaged shift lock actuator
5. If the concern is not found during the visual inspection, proceed to the Symptom Chart accompanying this procedure, and if necessary, continue from the Symptom Chart to the Pinpoint Tests.

Symptom Chart — Shift Interlock System

SHIFT INTERLOCK SYSTEM

CONDITION	POSSIBLE SOURCE	ACTION
• Selector Lever Cannot Be Moved From PARK (Key ON, Brake Pedal Depressed)	• Fuse. • Circuit. • Shift lock actuator. • Brake On / Off (BOO) switch . • Park range switch. • Gear selector lever adjustment. • Gear selector lever linkage binding.	• GO to Pinpoint Test A1.
• Shift Lock Actuator Operates Whenever Brake Pedal Is Depressed	• Shift lock actuator. • Park range switch.	• GO to Pinpoint Test B1.
• Manual Override Lever Does Not Work	• Manual override lever.	• REPLACE the transmission control selector dial bezel.
• Ignition Key Can Be Removed When Shift Control Selector Lever Is Out of PARK Range	• Ignition / shifter interlock cable. • Ignition switch lock cylinder.	• GO to Pinpoint Test C1.
• Ignition Key Cannot Be Removed or Turned to Lock Position	• Ignition / shifter interlock cable. • Ignition switch lock cylinder.	• GO to Pinpoint Test C1.

Pinpoint Tests — Shift Interlock System

Interior Fuse Junction Panel Connector Locations

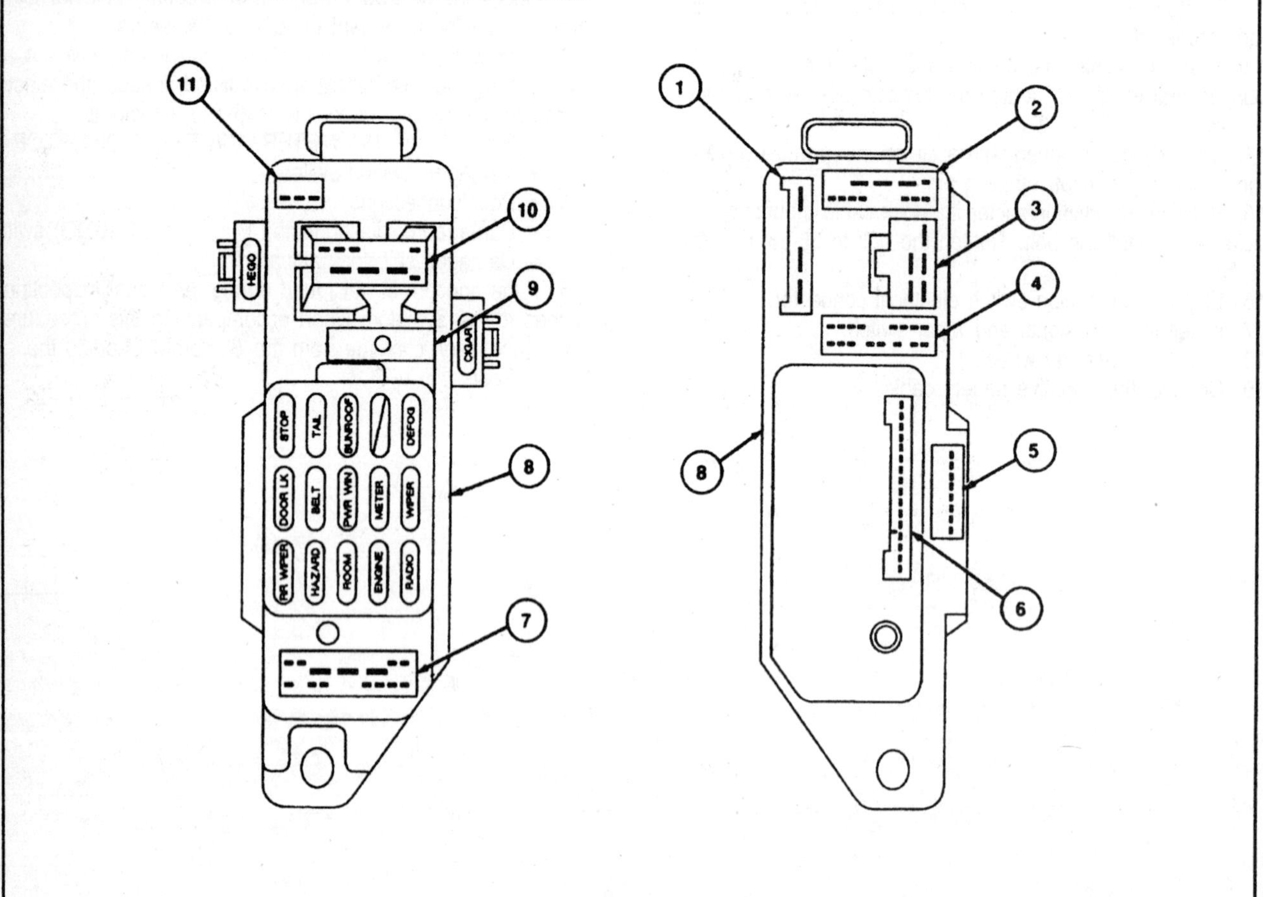

86758900

Fig. 71 Shift Interlock System (SIS) Symptom and Pinpoint Tests diagnostic charts

Item	Part Number	Description	Item	Part Number	Description
1	—	3-Pin Interior Fuse Junction Panel Connector A	6	—	6-Pin Interior Fuse Junction Panel Connector B
2	—	13-Pin Interior Fuse Junction Panel Connector	7	—	15-Pin Interior Fuse Junction Panel Connector
3	—	6-Pin Interior Fuse Junction Panel Connector A	8	14A068	Interior Fuse Junction Panel
			9	—	HEATER (c.b.)
4	—	18-Pin Interior Fuse Junction Panel Connector	10	—	11-Pin Interior Fuse Junction Panel Connector
5	—	8-Pin Interior Fuse Junction Panel Connector	11	—	3-Pin Interior Fuse Junction Panel Connector B

(Continued)

PINPOINT TEST A: SELECTOR LEVER CANNOT BE MOVED FROM PARK (KEY ON, BRAKE PEDAL DEPRESSED)

TEST STEP		RESULT	ACTION TO TAKE
A1	CHECK FUSES		
	• Key OFF. • Check the 15A METER fuse, 10A ROOM fuse, and 20A STOP fuse located in the interior fuse junction panel. • **Are the fuses OK?**	Yes ▶ No ▶	GO to **A4**. GO to **A2**.
A2	CHECK SYSTEM		
	• Key OFF. • Replace the blown fuse(s). • Key ON. • **Did the fuse(s) fail again?**	Yes ▶ No ▶	GO to **A3**. GO to **A4**.
A3	CHECK FOR SHORT TO GROUND		
	• Key OFF. • Locate and disconnect the shift lock actuator. • Locate and disconnect the 6-pin interior fuse junction panel connector A and the 15-pin interior fuse junction panel connector. • Measure the resistance from the wire in question at the interior fuse junction panel connector to ground. • **Is the resistance less than 5 ohms?**	Yes ▶ No ▶	SERVICE the wire in question. GO to **A4**.
A4	CHECK POWER TO SERVO		
	• Key OFF. • Locate and disconnect the shift lock actuator assembly connector. • Key ON. • Measure the voltage on the "BL/R" and "BK/Y" wires at the shift lock actuator connector. • **Are both of the voltages greater than 10 volts?**	Yes ▶ No ▶	GO to **A5**. SERVICE the wire in question.
A5	CHECK BRAKE ON/OFF (BOO) SWITCH		
	• Depress the brake pedal. • Measure the voltage on the "GN" wire at the Brake On/Off (BOO) switch connector (leave the connector connected). Brake Pedal Position: Pedal Released — Voltage: 0 volts Brake Pedal Position: Pedal Depressed — Voltage: 10-12 volts • **Are the voltages OK?**	Yes ▶ No ▶	GO to **A6**. REPLACE the BOO switch.
A6	CHECK FOR SHORT TO GROUND		
	• Key OFF. • Disconnect the shift lock actuator and the BOO switch connectors. • Measure the resistance of the "GN" wire between the BOO switch connector and ground. • **Is the resistance greater than 10,000 ohms?**	Yes ▶ No ▶	GO to **A7**. SERVICE the "GN" wire for a short to ground.

Brake Pedal Position	Voltage
Pedal Released	0 volts
Pedal Depressed	10-12 volts

86758901

Fig. 72 Shift Interlock System (SIS) diagnostic troubleshooting charts (continued)

PINPOINT TEST A: SELECTOR LEVER CANNOT BE MOVED FROM PARK (KEY ON, BRAKE PEDAL DEPRESSED) (Continued)

	TEST STEP	RESULT ▶	ACTION TO TAKE
A7	CHECK FOR CONTINUITY		
	• Key OFF. • Disconnect the shift lock actuator and BOO switch connectors. • Measure the resistance of the "GN" wire between the BOO switch and the shift lock actuator connectors. • **Is the resistance less than 5 ohms?**	Yes ▶ No ▶	GO to **A8**. SERVICE the "GN" wire.
A8	CHECK PARK RANGE SWITCH GROUND		
	• Key OFF. • Disconnect the park range switch connector. • Measure the resistance between the "BK" wire at the park range switch connector (ground side) and ground. • **Is the resistance less than 5 ohms?**	Yes ▶ No ▶	GO to **A9**. SERVICE the "BK" wire.
A9	CHECK PARK RANGE SWITCH		
	• Key OFF. • Disconnect the park range switch from the shift lock actuator. • Measure the resistance between the "BK" wire terminals at the park range switch under the following conditions. (see table below) • **Are the resistances OK?**	Yes ▶ No ▶	REPLACE the shift lock actuator. CHECK the "BK" wires from the shift lock actuator to the park range switch for opens — SERVICE as required. If the "BK" wires are OK, REPLACE the shift control selector lever and housing.

Range	Resistance
Park Release Button Out	Less than 5 ohms
Park Release Button In	Greater than 10,000 ohms
R, Ⓓ, D, and L	Greater than 10,000 ohms

PINPOINT TEST B: SHIFT LOCK ACTUATOR OPERATES WHENEVER BRAKE PEDAL IS DEPRESSED

	TEST STEP	RESULT ▶	ACTION TO TAKE
B1	CHECK PARK RANGE SWITCH		
	• Key OFF. • Locate and disconnect the park range switch connector. • Place the shift control selector lever in the PARK range. • Measure the resistance between the "BK" wire terminals of the park range switch. • Move the shift control selector lever out of the PARK range. • Measure the resistance between the terminals of the park range switch. • **Is the resistance less than 5 ohms when the shift control selector lever is in the PARK range, and greater than 10,000 ohms when the shift control selector lever is out of the Park range?**	Yes ▶ No ▶	REPLACE the shift lock actuator. REPLACE the shift control selector lever and housing.

PINPOINT TEST C: SHIFT CONTROL LINKAGE

	TEST STEP	RESULT ▶	ACTION TO TAKE
C1	CHECK IGNITION / SHIFTER INTERLOCK CABLE		
	• Inspect the ignition / shifter interlock cable for damage or binding conditions. • **Is the ignition / shifter interlock cable damaged or binding?**	Yes ▶ No ▶	REPAIR or REPLACE the ignition / shifter interlock cable. GO to **C2**.

86758902

Fig. 73 Shift Interlock System (SIS) diagnostic troubleshooting charts (continued)

PINPOINT TEST C: SHIFT CONTROL LINKAGE (Continued)

	TEST STEP	RESULT	▶	ACTION TO TAKE
C2	CHECK SHIFT CONTROL LINKAGE			
	• Disconnect the transmission shift cable from the manual lever position switch. • Is the concern corrected?	Yes	▶	ADJUST or REPLACE the ignition / shifter interlock cable.
		No	▶	REPLACE the ignition switch lock cylinder.

86758903

Fig. 74 Shift Interlock System (SIS) diagnostic troubleshooting charts (continued)

Tie Rod Ends

REMOVAL & INSTALLATION

See Figures 50, 51, 75, 76, 77 and 78

1. Remove and discard cotter pin and nut from the worn tie rod end ball stud.

➡Although it is possible to remove the tie rod end first, loosening the jam nut is easier when the rod is still held in place.

2. Holding the tie rod end with a suitable wrench, loosen the tie rod jam nut.
3. Disconnect the tie rod end from spindle, using a tie rod end remover tool such as 3290-D and adapter T81P-3504-W or suitable equivalents.

86758721

Fig. 76 Holding the tie rod end with a suitable wrench (or locking pliers), loosen the tie rod jam nut

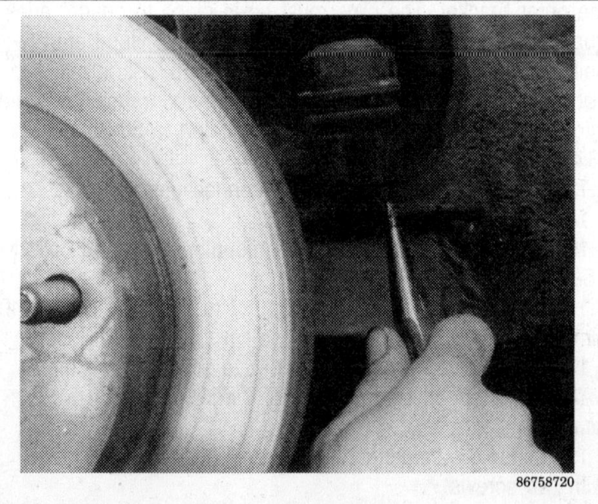
86758720

Fig. 75 Remove and discard cotter pin and nut from the worn tie rod end ball stud

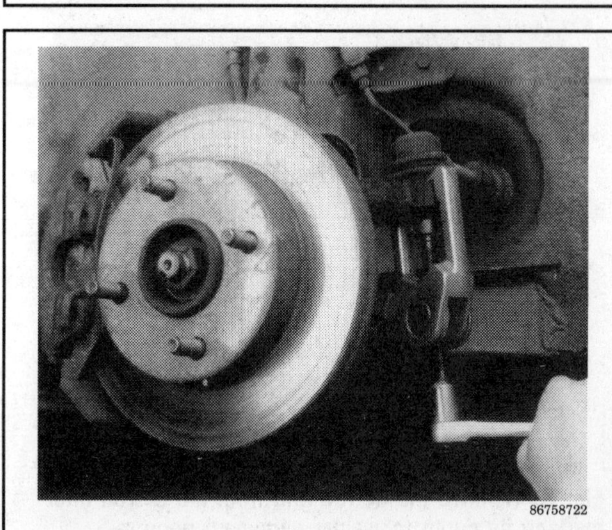
86758722

Fig. 77 Disconnect the tie rod end from spindle, using a suitable tie rod end remover tool

4. Grip the tie rod hex flats with a pair of locking pliers, and remove the tie rod end from the tie rod. Note the depth to which tie rod was located, using jam nut as a marker.

To install:

5. Clean tie rod threads. Apply a light coating of disc brake caliper slide grease D7AZ-19590-A or equivalent, to tie rod threads. Thread new tie rod end to same depth as removed tie rod end. Tighten jam nut.
6. Place the tie rod end stud into the steering spindle.
7. Install a new nut on tie rod end stud. Tighten nut to minimum specification. The continue tightening the nut to align the next castellation with the cotter pin hole in the stud. Install a new cotter pin.
8. Set the toe to specification and tighten the jam nuts to specification. Do not twist the bellows. Have the front end alignment (specifically the toe) checked by a reputable repair facility..

CHECKING

Tie Rod Articulation/Steering Effort

1981-90 MODELS

The yoke clearance is not adjustable except when overhauling the steering gear assembly. Pinion bearing preload is not adjustable because of the non-adjustable bearing usage. Tie rod articulation is preset and is not adjustable. If articulation is out of specification, replace the tie rod assembly. To check tie rod articulation, proceed as follows:

1. With the tie rod end disconnected from the steering knuckle, loop a piece of wire through the hole in the tie rod end stud.
2. Insert the hook of spring scale T74P-3504-Y or equivalent, through the wire loop. Effort to move the tie rod after initial breakaway should be 0.7-5.0 lbs. (0.3-2.25 Nm).

➡Do not damage tie rod neck.

3. Replace ball joint/tie rod assembly if effort falls outside this range. Save the tie rod end for use on the new tie rod assembly.

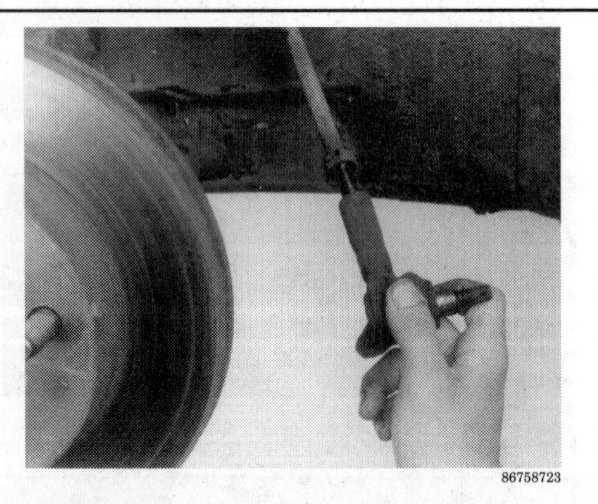

86758723

Fig. 78 Remove the tie rod end from the tie rod after marking its depth for easier alignment upon reinstallation

Steering Column

REMOVAL & INSTALLATION

1981-90 Models

➧ See Figure 79

1. Disconnect the negative battery cable.
2. Remove the steering column cover on lower portion of instrument panel (two screws).
3. Remove speed control module, if equipped (two screws).
4. Remove lower steering column shroud (five screws).
5. Loosen, but do not remove, the two nuts and two bolts retaining the steering column to support bracket and remove upper shroud.
6. Disengage all steering column electrical connections. On console shift automatic transaxles, remove the interlock cable retaining screw and disconnect cable from the steering column.
7. Loosen the steering column to intermediate shaft clamp connection and remove bolt or nut.
8. Remove the two nuts and two bolts retaining the steering column to support bracket.
9. Pry open the steering column shaft in area of clamp on each side of bolt groove with the steering column locked. Open enough to disengage the shafts with minimal effort. Do not use excessive force.
10. Inspect the two steering column bracket clips for damage. If the clips have been bent or excessively distorted, they must be replaced.

To install:

11. Engage the lower steering shaft to intermediate shaft and hand start clamp bolt and nut.
12. Align the two bolts on the steering column support bracket assembly with the outer tube mounting holes and hand start the two nuts. Check for the presence of the two clips on the outer bracket. The clips must be in place to ensure adequate performance of vital parts and systems. Hand start two bolts through outer tube upper bracket and clip and into support bracket nuts. On console shift automatic transaxles, install interlock cable and retaining screw. Tighten to 30-38 inch lbs. (3.4-4.3 Nm).
13. Engage all column electrical connections.
14. Install the upper shroud.
15. Tighten the steering column mounting nuts and bolts to 15-25 ft. lbs. (20-34 Nm).
16. Tighten steering shaft clamp nut to 20-30 ft. lbs. (27-40 Nm).
17. Install lower trim shroud with five screws.
18. Install speed control module, if equipped, with two screws.
19. Install the steering column cover on instrument panel with two screws.
20. Connect the battery ground cable.
21. Check the steering column for proper operation.

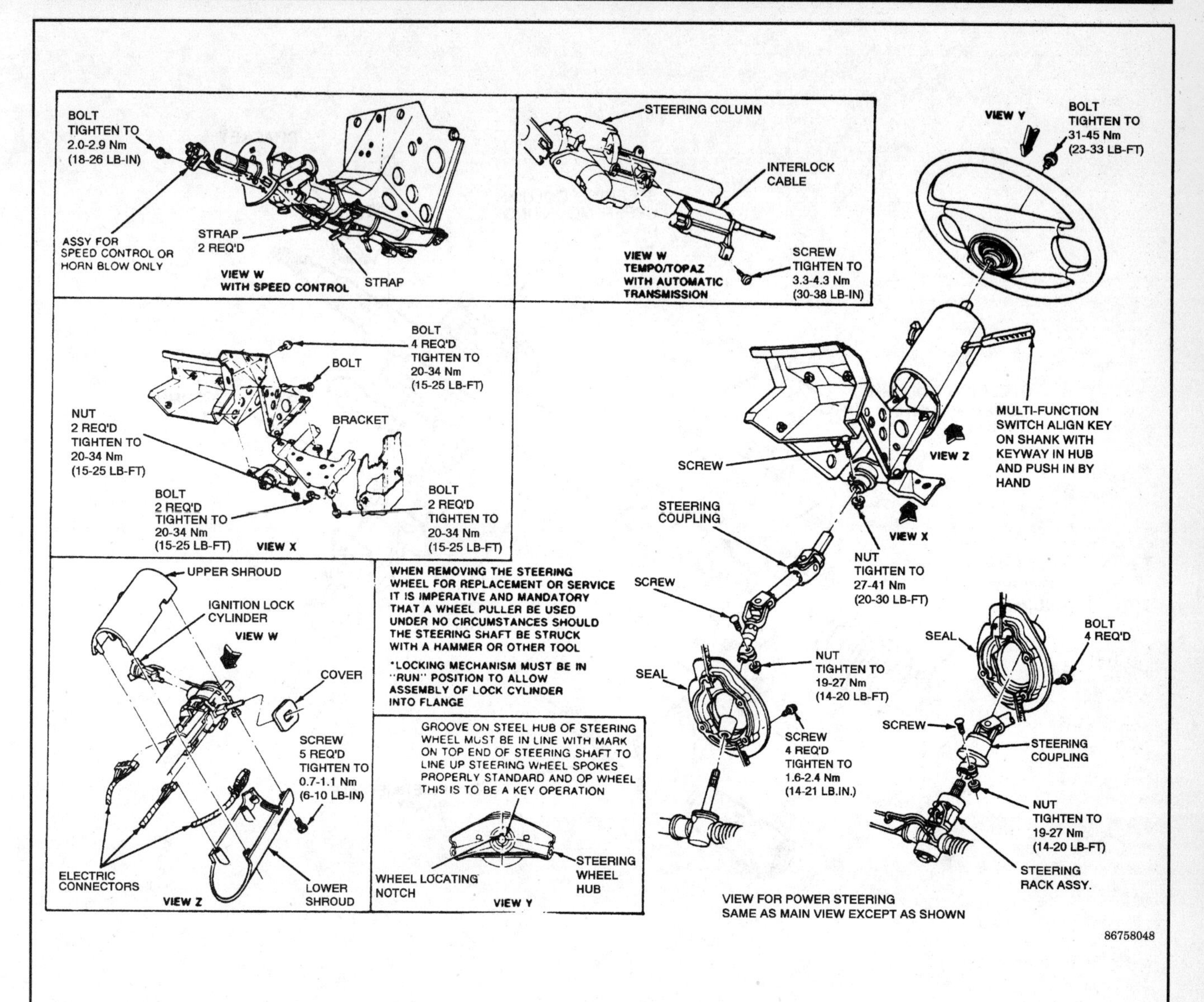

Fig. 79 Detailed views of the fixed steering column — 1981-90 models

1991-95 Models

See Figure 80

1. Disconnect the negative battery cable. If equipped with an air bag, properly disable the system as directed in Section 6.

CAUTION

The backup power supply energy must be depleted before servicing the air bag. To deplete the power supply energy, disconnect the negative battery cable and wait one minute.

2. Remove the steering wheel.
3. Remove the combination switch and unplug the ignition switch electrical connector.
4. Remove the shift-lock cable mounting bracket bolt and place the bracket and cable aside.
5. Remove the four steering column upper mounting bracket bolts and lower the column.
6. Remove the five set plate mounting nuts and remove the set plate.
7. Remove the intermediate shaft-to-pinion shaft bolt.
8. Remove the two steering column lower mounting bracket nuts and remove the column.

To install:

9. Position the steering column and install the two lower mounting bracket nuts.
10. Install the intermediate shaft-to-pinion shaft bolt and tighten to 30-36 ft. lbs. (40-50 Nm).
11. Position the set plate and install the five mounting nuts.
12. Install the four steering column upper mounting bracket bolts and tighten to 80-123 inch lbs. (9-14 Nm).
13. Position the shift-lock cable mounting bracket and install the bolt. Tighten the bolt to 37-55 inch lbs. (4-6 Nm).
14. Plug in the ignition switch electrical connector and install the combination switch.
15. Install the steering wheel.
16. Connect the negative battery cable and inspect the shift-lock system.

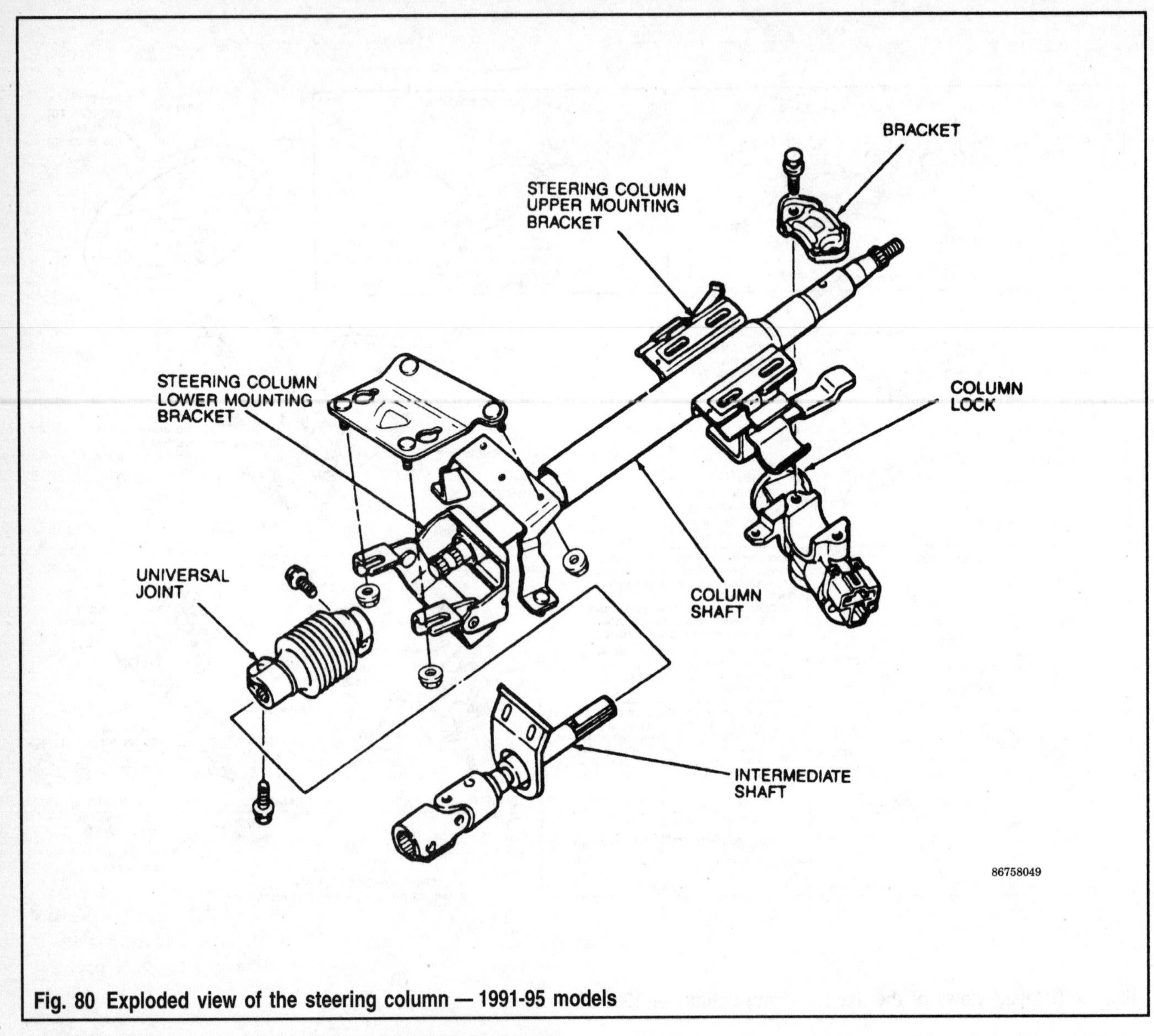

Fig. 80 Exploded view of the steering column — 1991-95 models

Manual Rack and Pinion

If your vehicle is equipped with manual steering, it is of the rack and pinion type. The gear input shaft is connected to the steering shaft by a double U-joint. A pinion gear, machined on the input shaft, engages the rack. The rotation of the input shaft pinion causes the rack to move laterally. The rack has two tie rods with ends connected to the front wheels. When the rack moves, so do the front wheel knuckles. Toe adjustment is made by turning the outer tie rod ends in or out equally as required.

REMOVAL & INSTALLATION

1981-90 Models

1. Disconnect the negative battery cable.
2. Turn the ignition key to the **RUN** position.
3. Remove the access trim panel from below the steering column.
4. Remove the intermediate shaft bolts at the rack and pinion input shaft and the steering column shaft.
5. Spread the slots enough to loosen the intermediate shaft at both ends. They cannot be separated at this time.
6. Raise the vehicle and support it safely.
7. Separate the tie rod ends from the steering knuckles, using a suitable tool. Turn the right wheel to the full left turn position.
8. Disconnect the speedometer cable at the transaxle on automatic transaxles only.
9. Disconnect the secondary air tube at the check valve. Disconnect the exhaust system at the manifold and remove the system.
10. Remove the gear mounting brackets and insulators. Keep them separated as they are not interchangeable.
11. Turn the steering wheel full left so the tie rod will clear the shift linkage during removal.

12. Separate the gear intermediate shaft, with an assistant pulling upward on the shaft from the inside of the vehicle.

➡Care should be taken during steering gear removal and installation to prevent tearing or damaging the steering gear bellows.

13. Rotate the gear forward and down to clear the input shaft through the dash panel opening.
14. With the gear in the full left turn position, move the gear through the right (passenger side) apron opening until the left tie rod clears the shift linkage and other parts so it may be lowered.
15. Lower the left side of the gear assembly and remove from the vehicle.

To install:

16. Rotate the input shaft to a full left turn stop. Position the right wheel to a full left turn.
17. Start the right side of the gear through the opening in the right apron. Move the gear in until the left tie rod clears all parts so it may be raised up to the left apron opening.
18. Raise the gear and insert the left side through the apron opening. Rotate the gear so the joint shaft enters the dash panel opening.
19. With an assistant guiding the intermediate shaft from the inside of the vehicle, insert the input shaft into the intermediate shaft coupling. Insert the intermediate shaft clamp bolts finger-tight. Do not tighten at this time.
20. Install the gear mounting insulators and brackets in their proper places. Ensure the flat in the left mounting area is parallel to the dash panel. Tighten the bracket bolts to 40-55 ft. lbs. (54-75 Nm) in the sequence as described below:
    a. Tighten the left (driver's side) upper bolt halfway.
    b. Tighten the left side lower bolt.
    c. Tighten the left side upper bolt.
    d. Tighten the right side bolts.
    e. Do not forget that the right and left side insulators and brackets are not interchangeable side to side.
21. Attach the tie rod ends to the steering knuckles. Tighten the castellated nuts to 27-32 ft. lbs. (36-43 Nm), then tighten the nuts until the slot aligns with the cotter pin hole. Insert a new cotter pin.
22. Install the exhaust system. Install the speedometer cable, if removed.
23. Tighten the gear input shaft to intermediate shaft coupling clamp bolt first. Then, tighten the upper intermediate shaft clamp bolt. Tighten both bolts to 20-37 ft. lbs. (28-50 Nm).
24. Install the access panel below the steering column. Turn the ignition key to the **OFF** position.
25. Check and adjust the toe. Tighten the tie rod end jam nuts, check for twisted bellows.

1991-95 Models

1. Disconnect the negative battery cable. If equipped with an air bag, properly disable the system as directed in Section 6.

⁂CAUTION

For 1994-95 models equipped with a driver's side Supplemental Restraint System (SRS) or air bag assembly, consult the SRS precautions in Section 6.

2. Working inside the vehicle, remove the nuts securing the set plate and remove the set plate.
3. Remove the intermediate shaft-to-pinion shaft bolt from inside the vehicle.
4. Raise and safely support the vehicle.
5. Remove the front wheels.
6. Remove the cotter pins and nuts securing the tie rod ends to the steering knuckles. Separate the tie rod ends from the steering knuckles using a suitable tool.
7. If equipped with a manual transaxle, disconnect the extension bar.
8. Remove the nuts securing the steering gear brackets to the bulkhead. Remove the brackets.
9. Remove the steering gear from the vehicle.

To install:

10. Position the steering gear into its mounting position and install the brackets and nuts. Tighten the nuts to 27-38 ft. lbs. (37-52 Nm).
11. If equipped with a manual transaxle, connect the extension bar. Tighten the nut to 23-34 ft. lbs. (31-46 Nm).
12. Attach the tie rod ends to the steering knuckles. Install the nuts and tighten to 31-42 ft. lbs. (42-57 Nm). Install new cotter pins.
13. Install the front wheels.
14. Lower the vehicle.
15. Install the intermediate shaft-to-pinion shaft bolt and tighten to 13-20 ft. lbs. (18-27 Nm).
16. Position the set plate and secure it with the nuts.

Power Steering Rack

A rotary design control valve uses the relative rotational motion of the input shaft and valve sleeve to direct fluid flow. When the steering wheel is turned, the resistance of the wheels and the weight of the car cause a torsion bar to twist. The twisting causes the valve to move in the sleeve and aligns fluid passages for right/left and straight ahead position. The pressure forces the valve and helps move the rack to assist in the turning effort. The piston is attached directly to the rack. The housing tube functions as the power cylinder. The hydraulic areas of the gear assembly are always filled with fluid. The mechanical gears are filled with grease which makes periodic lubrication unnecessary. The fluid and grease act as a cushion to absorb road shock.

REMOVAL & INSTALLATION

1981-90 Models

See Figures 81, 82, 83 and 84

1. Disconnect the negative battery cable.
2. Turn the ignition key to the **RUN** position.
3. Remove the access panel from the dash below the steering column.
4. Remove the screws from the steering column boot at the dash panel and slide the boot up the intermediate shaft.
5. Remove the intermediate shaft bolt at gear input shaft and loosen the bolt at the steering column shaft joint.

6. With a suitable tool, spread the slots enough to loosen intermediate shaft at both ends. The intermediate shaft and gear input shaft cannot be separated at this time.

7. Remove the air cleaner, if necessary.

8. On vehicles equipped with air conditioning, secure the air conditioner liquid line above the dash panel opening. Doing so provides clearance for gear input shaft removal and installation.

9. Separate the pressure and return lines at the intermediate connections.

10. Disconnect the exhaust secondary air tube at check valve. Raise the vehicle and support it safely. Disconnect the exhaust system at the exhaust manifold.

11. Separate the tie rod ends from the steering knuckles.

➡Mark the location of the tie rod end prior to removal.

12. Remove the left tie rod end from the tie rod on manual transaxle vehicles. This will allow the tie rod to clear the shift linkage.

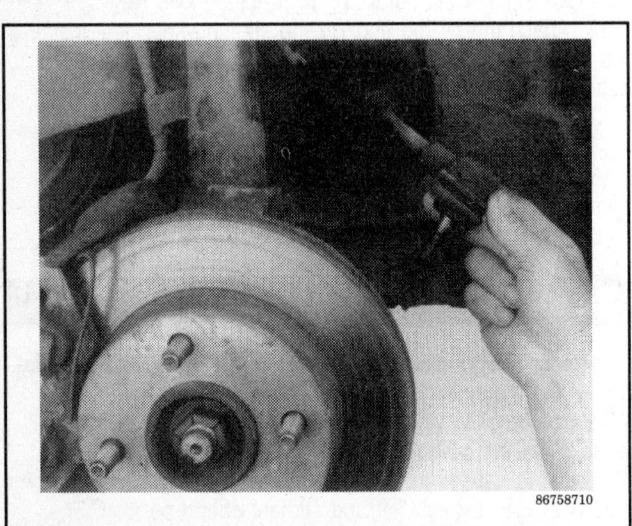

86758710

Fig. 81 Separate the tie rod ends from the steering knuckles

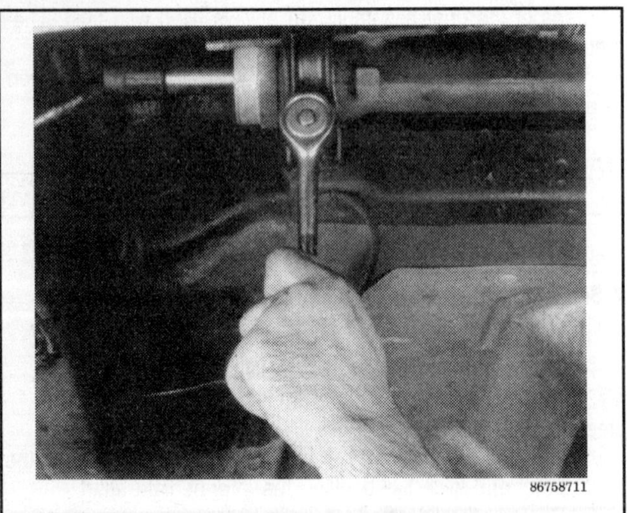

86758711

Fig. 82 Remove the gear mounting brackets with the correct size socket

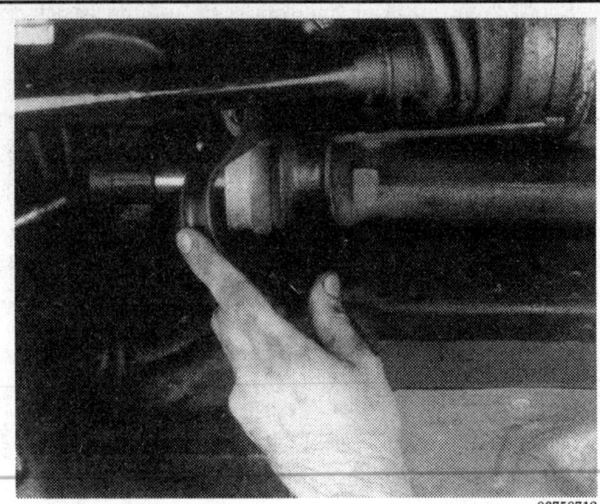

86758712

Fig. 83 Once the mounting bracket is free, remove the insulator behind it

13. Disconnect the speedometer cable at the transaxle, if equipped with automatic transaxle. Remove the vehicle speed sensor.

14. Remove the transaxle shift cable assembly at the transaxle on vehicles equipped with automatic transaxle.

15. Turn the steering wheel to full left turn stop for easier gear removal.

16. Remove the screws holding the heater water tube to the shake brace below the oil pan.

17. Remove the nut from the lower of two bolts holding the engine mount support bracket to transaxle housing. Tap the bolt out as far as it will go.

18. Remove the gear mounting brackets and insulators.

19. Drape a cloth towel over both apron opening edges to protect bellows during gear removal.

20. Separate the gear from the intermediate shaft by either pushing up on the shaft with a bar from underneath the vehicle while pulling the gear down or with an assistant removing the shaft from inside the vehicle.

21. Rotate the gear forward and down to clear the input shaft through the dash panel opening.

22. Make sure the input shaft is in full left turn position. Move the gear through the right (passenger) side apron opening until left tie rod clears left apron opening and other parts so it may be lowered. Guide the power steering hoses around the nearby components as the gear is being removed.

23. Lower the left side of the gear and remove the gear out of the vehicle. Use care not to tear the bellows.

To install:

24. Rotate the input shaft to a full left turn stop. Position the right road wheel to a full left turn.

25. Start the right side of the gear through the opening in the right apron. Move the gear in until the left tie rod clears all parts so it may be raised up to the left apron opening.

26. Raise the gear and insert the left side through the apron opening. Move the power steering hoses into their proper position at the same time. Rotate the gear so the joint shaft enters the dash panel opening.

27. With an assistant guiding the intermediate shaft from the inside of the vehicle, insert the input shaft into the intermediate

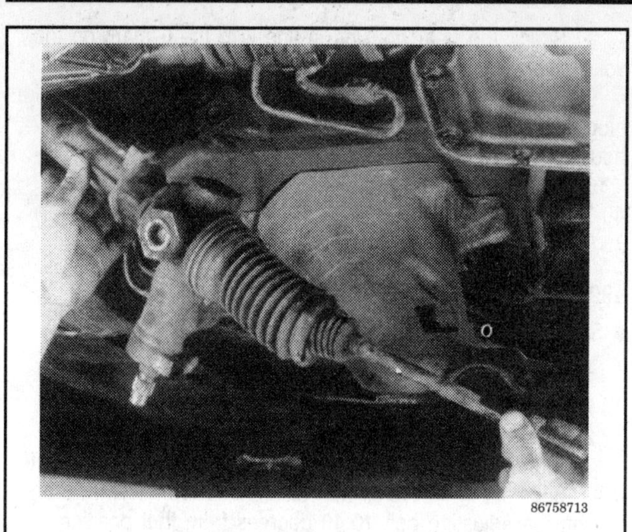

Fig. 84 Lower the left side of the gear and remove the gear out of the vehicle

shaft coupling. Insert the intermediate shaft clamp bolts finger-tight. Do not tighten at this time.

28. Install the gear mounting insulators and brackets in their proper places. Ensure the flat in the left mounting area is parallel to the dash panel. Tighten the bracket bolts to 40-55 ft. lbs. (54-75 Nm) in the sequence as described below:
   a. Tighten the left (driver's side) upper bolt halfway.
   b. Tighten the left side lower bolt.
   c. Tighten the left side upper bolt.
   d. Tighten the right side bolts.
   e. Do not forget that the right and left side insulators and brackets are not interchangeable side to side.
29. Attach the tie rod ends to the steering knuckles. Tighten the castellated nuts to 27-32 ft. lbs. (36-43 Nm), then tighten the nuts until the slot aligns with the cotter pin hole. Insert a new cotter pin.
30. Install the engine mount nut.
31. Install the heater water tube to the shake brace.
32. Install the exhaust system. Install the speedometer cable, if removed. Install the vehicle speed sensor and the transaxle shift cable.
33. Connect the secondary air tube at the check valve. Connect the pressure and return lines at the intermediate connections or steering gear.
34. Install the air cleaner.
35. Tighten the gear input shaft to intermediate shaft coupling clamp bolt first. Then, tighten the upper intermediate shaft clamp bolt. Tighten to 20-30 ft. lbs. (27-40 Nm).
36. Install the access panel below the steering column. Turn the ignition key to the **OFF** position.
37. Fill the system. Check and adjust the toe, then have the alignment checked by a qualified shop as soon as possible. Tighten the tie rod end jam nuts to 40-50 ft. lbs. (54-68 Nm), check for twisted bellows.
38. Connect the negative battery cable.

1991-95 Models

1. Disconnect the negative battery cable. If equipped with an air bag, properly disable the system as directed in Section 6.

****CAUTION**

For 1994-95 models equipped with a driver's side Supplemental Restraint System (SRS) or air bag assembly, consult the SRS precautions in Section 6.

2. From inside the passenger compartment, remove the five set plate nuts and remove the set plate.
3. Remove the intermediate shaft-to-pinion shaft bolt.
4. Raise and safely support the vehicle.
5. Remove the front wheels.
6. Remove the cotter pins and attaching nuts from the tie rod ends. Using a suitable tool, separate the tie rod ends from the steering knuckles.
7. If equipped with the 1.8L engine, remove the two screws from the power steering line retaining bracket and remove the bracket from the steering gear housing. If equipped with the 1.9L engine, remove the strap that holds the power steering lines to the steering gear housing and discard the strap.
8. Disconnect the high-pressure and return lines from the steering gear and plug the lines.
9. If equipped with a manual transaxle, disconnect the extension bar and shift control rod from the transaxle.
10. Remove the nuts from the two steering gear mounting brackets.
11. Remove the splash shield from the left wheel well.
12. Remove the steering gear from the left side of the vehicle.

To install:

13. Position the steering gear in its mounting location and install the splash shield in the left wheel well.
14. Position the two steering gear mounting brackets and install the two nuts to each bracket. Tighten the nuts to 27-38 ft. lbs. (37-52 Nm).
15. If equipped with a manual transaxle, connect the extension bar and shift control rod. Tighten the extension bar nut to 23-34 ft. lbs. (31-46 Nm) and the shift control rod nut to 12-17 ft. lbs. (16-23 Nm).
16. Remove the plugs and connect the pressure and return lines to the steering gear. Tighten the flare nuts to 22-28 ft. lbs. (29-39 Nm).
17. If equipped with 1.8L engine, position the power steering line retaining bracket and install the two screws. If equipped with 1.9L engine, install a new strap to hold the power steering lines to the steering gear housing.
18. Position the tie rod ends in the steering knuckles and install the attaching nuts. Tighten the nuts to 31-42 ft. lbs. (42-57 Nm). Install new cotter pins.
19. Install the wheels and lower the vehicle.
20. From inside the vehicle, install the intermediate shaft-to-pinion shaft bolt. Tighten the bolt to 13-20 ft. lbs. (18-27 Nm).
21. Position the set plate and install the five set plate nuts.
22. Fill the system with steering fluid.

ADJUSTMENTS

The power rack and pinion steering gear provides for only rack yoke plug preload adjustment. This adjustment can be performed only with the gear out of the vehicle:

1981-90 Models

ONE-PIECE HOUSING

1. Disconnect the negative battery cable.
2. Raise and safely support the vehicle.
3. Remove power rack and pinion assembly from vehicle.
4. Clean the exterior of the steering gear thoroughly.
5. Mount the steering gear in a suitable rack housing holding fixture.

➡Do not mount the gear in a vice.

6. Do not remove external pressure lines, unless they are leaking or damaged. If these lines are removed, they must be replaced with new lines.
7. Drain the power steering fluid by rotating the input shaft lock-to-lock twice using input shaft torque adapter T81P-3504-R or equivalent. Position adapter and wrench on input shaft.
8. Loosen yoke plug locknut with yoke locknut wrench T81P-3504-G or equivalent.
9. Loosen yoke plug using yoke plug adapter T87P-3504-G or equivalent.
10. With rack at center of travel, tighten yoke plug to 44-50 inch lbs. (5.0-5.7 Nm). Clean the threads of yoke plug prior to tightening to prevent a false reading.
11. Install yoke plug adapter T87P-3504-G or equivalent. Mark the location of zero degree mark on housing. Back off adjuster so 48 degree mark lines up with zero degree mark.
12. Place yoke locknut wrench T81P-3504-G or equivalent, on yoke plug locknut. While holding yoke plug, tighten locknut to 40-50 ft. lbs. (54-68 Nm). Do not allow yoke plug to move while tightening or preload will be affected. Check input shaft torque after tightening locknut.
13. If external pressure lines were removed, the Teflon® seal rings must be replaced. Clean out Teflon® seal shreds from housing ports prior to installation of new lines.
14. Install power rack assembly in vehicle.
15. Lower the vehicle.
16. Connect the negative battery cable.

TWO-PIECE HOUSING

➧ See Figure 85

1. Disconnect the negative battery cable.
2. Raise and safely support the vehicle.
3. Remove the power rack and pinion assembly from the vehicle.
4. Clean the exterior of the gear in the yoke plug area and mount the gear in a vise, gripping it near the center of the tube. Do not overtighten.
5. Loosen and remove the yoke plug locknut.
6. Back off the yoke plug one turn.
7. Tighten the yoke plug to 45 inch lbs. (5.8 Nm) using a yoke plug adapter such as T81P-3504-U or equivalent.
8. Scribe the gear housing in line with the 0 mark on the yoke plug adapter tool.
9. Back off the yoke plug so the second mark on the yoke plug adapter tool aligns with the scribe mark on the gear housing.
10. Hold the plug, and install and tighten the locknut to 40-50 ft. lbs. (54-68 Nm) using a yoke locknut wrench T81P-3504-G or equivalent.

1991-95 Models

➧ See Figures 86 and 87

1. Remove the rack and pinion assembly from the vehicle and mount it in a suitable vice.
2. Loosen the locknut.
3. Tighten the adjusting bolt using yoke adjustment adapter T90P-3504-JH in the yoke plug to 8.7 inch lbs. (1 Nm), then loosen the adjusting bolt 10-40 degrees from that position.
4. Measure the pinion turning torque using a pinion shaft adapting tool T86P-3504-K. The correct torque at the neutral position (plus or minus 90°) should be 9-12 inch lbs. (1.0-1.3 Nm). At any other position the torque should be 14.7 inch lbs. (1.6 Nm) or less.
5. If the pinion torque is not within specification, turn the adjusting bolt to achieve the correct pinion torque. Tighten the adjusting bolt locknut.

Power Steering Pump

REMOVAL & INSTALLATION

1981-85 Gasoline Engines

1. Remove the air cleaner, air pump and belt. Remove the reservoir extension and plug the hole with a clean rag.
2. From under the car, loosen the pump adjusting bolt. Remove the pump to bracket mounting bolt and disconnect the fluid return line. Be prepared to catch any spilled fluid in a suitable container.

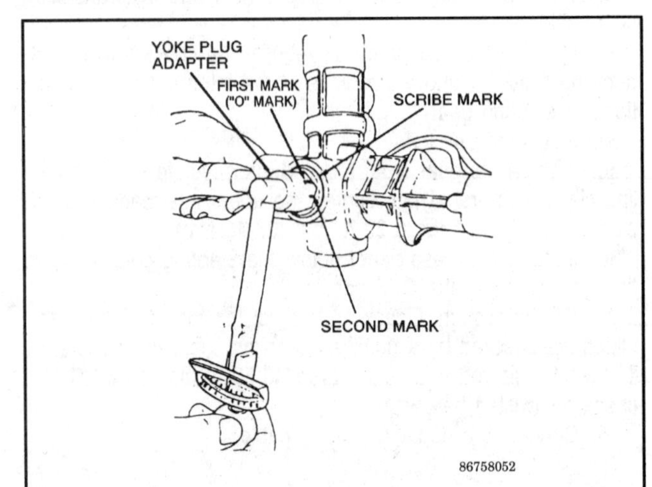

Fig. 85 Tighten the yoke plug to 45 inch lbs. (5.8 Nm) using a yoke plug adapter T81P-3504-U or equivalent, and a suitable inch-pound torque wrench

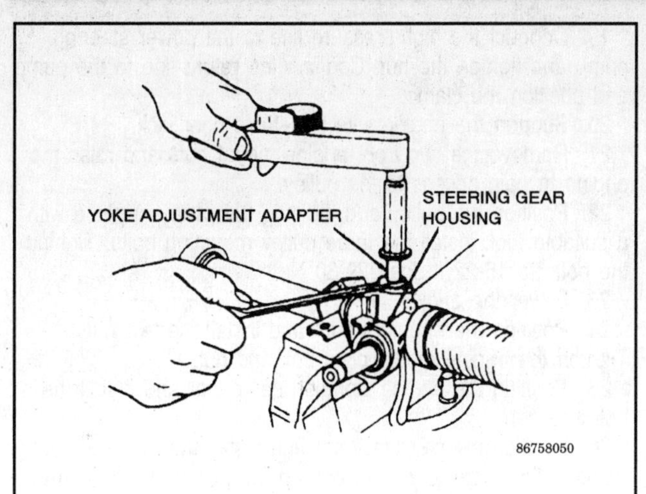

Fig. 86 Tighten the adjusting bolt using yoke adjustment adapter T90P-3504-JH — 1991-95 manual steering rack

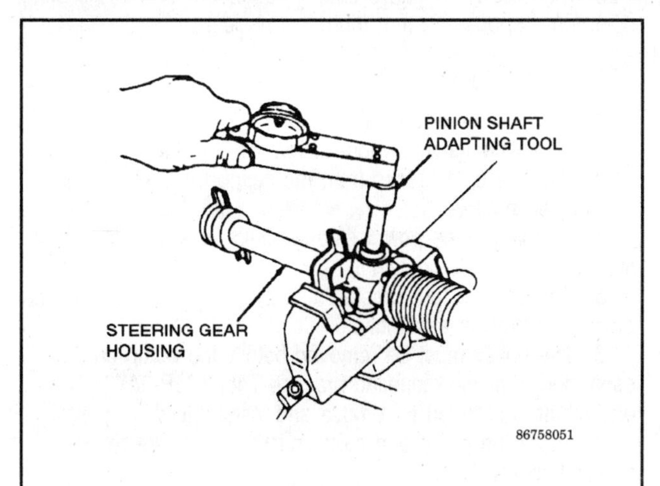

Fig. 87 Measure the pinion turning torque using a pinion shaft adapting tool T86P-3504-K — 1991-95 manual steering rack

3. From above, loosen the adjusting bolt and remove the drive belt. Remove the two remaining mounting bolts. Remove the adjusting bolts.

4. Remove the pump by passing the pulley end through the adjusting bracket opening.

5. Remove the pressure hose from the pump.

6. Installation is in the reverse order. Fill the pump with fluid and check for proper operation.

1985½-90 Gasoline Engines

1. Disconnect the negative battery cable. Remove the air cleaner, thermactor air pump and belt. Remove the reservoir filler extension and cover the hole to prevent dirt from entering.

2. If equipped with a remote reservoir, remove the reservoir supply hose at the pump, drain the fluid and plug or cap the opening at the pump to prevent entry of contaminants during removal.

3. From under the vehicle, loosen 1 pump adjusting bolt. Remove 1 pump-to-bracket mounting bolt and disconnect the fluid return line.

4. From above the vehicle, loosen 1 adjusting bolt and the pivot bolt. Remove the drive belt and the two remaining pump to bracket mounting bolts.

5. Remove the pump by passing the pulley through the adjusting bracket opening. Remove the pressure hose from the pump assembly.

To install:

6. From under the vehicle, connect the pressure hose to the pump. Pass the pulley through the opening in the adjusting bracket. Install the mounting bolts and tighten to 30-45 ft. lbs. (40-62 Nm).

7. If applicable, make sure the air pump belt is on the inner power steering pump pulley groove. Install the power steering pump belt and adjust. Tighten all bolts to 30-45 ft. lbs. (40-62 Nm).

➡When adjusting belt tension, never pry on the pump or surrounding aluminum parts or brackets.

8. If not equipped with a remote reservoir, install the return line to the pump.

9. From above the vehicle, install the reservoir filler neck extension, if applicable. Install the air cleaner.

10. If applicable, install the remote reservoir supply to the pump.

11. Fill pump or remote reservoir with fluid and check operation.

1991-95 Models

1.8L ENGINE

1. Disconnect the negative battery cable.

2. Loosen the power steering fluid reservoir-to-pump hose clamp and pull the hose from the reservoir. Plug the hose.

3. Remove the two reservoir mounting bolts and lift the reservoir from its mounting position.

4. Loosen the return hose clamp and pull the return hose from the reservoir. Plug the hose and remove the reservoir.

5. Disengage the electrical connector from the power steering pressure switch.

6. Loosen the high-pressure line flare nut and disconnect the line from the pump. Plug the line.

7. Raise and safely support the vehicle.

8. Remove the five right front undercover bolts and remove the undercover.

9. Remove the belt tensioner adjustment bolt and remove the accessory drive belt from the pulley.

10. Lower the vehicle.

11. Remove the three pump mounting bracket bolts and remove the pump and the bracket.

12. Remove the bolt that attaches the pump to the mounting bracket.

13. Remove the nut and bolt that attaches the tensioner to the pump mounting bracket and remove the nut and bolt that attaches the tensioner to the pump.

To install:

14. Position the tensioner to the pump and install the bolt and nut. Tighten the nut to 14-19 ft. lbs. (19-25 Nm).

15. Position the tensioner to the pump mounting bracket and install the bolt and nut. Tighten the nut to 23-34 ft. lbs. (31-46 Nm).

16. Install the bolt that attaches the pump to the mounting bracket and tighten to 27-40 ft. lbs. (36-54 Nm).

17. Position the pump and bracket and install the three pump mounting bracket bolts. Tighten the bolts to 27-38 ft. lbs. (37-54 Nm).
18. Raise and safely support the vehicle.
19. Position the accessory drive belt on the pulley and install the belt tensioner adjustment bolt.
20. Position the right front undercover and install the five bolts.
21. Lower the vehicle.
22. Unplug the high-pressure line and connect the line to the pump. Tighten the flare nut to 12-17 ft. lbs. (16-24 Nm).
23. Connect the power steering pressure switch electrical connector.
24. Unplug the return hose and connect the hose to the reservoir. Tighten the clamp.
25. Position the reservoir and install the two mounting bolts.
26. Unplug the reservoir-to-pump hose and connect the hose to the reservoir. Tighten the clamp.
27. Fill the system with power steering fluid and adjust the accessory drive belt tension.

1.9L ENGINE

1. Disconnect the negative battery cable and drain the cooling system.
2. Loosen the belt tensioner and remove the drive belt from the pulley. Remove the belt tensioner bolt and remove the tensioner.
3. Support the engine with a suitable floor jack.
4. Remove the engine vibration dampener nut and bolt and remove the dampener.
5. Remove the two front engine mount nuts. Loosen the engine mount pivot bolt and nut and position the engine mount aside.
6. Raise the engine to gain access to the power steering pump pulley.
7. Hold the pulley in position with a suitable tool and remove the three pulley mounting bolts. Remove the pulley and lower the engine.
8. Position the engine mount and install the two nuts.
9. Loosen the clamp and disconnect the return line from the pump. Loosen the flare nut from the high-pressure line and disconnect the line from the pump.
10. Raise and safely support the vehicle.
11. Remove the two passenger side splash shields.
12. If equipped, remove the four compressor mounting bolts and position the air conditioning compressor aside.
13. Remove the lower radiator hose.
14. Remove the three power steering pump mounting bolts and remove the pump.

To install:

15. Position the power steering pump and install the three mounting bolts. Tighten the bolts to 30-45 ft. lbs. (40-62 Nm).
16. Install the lower radiator hose.
17. If equipped, position the air conditioning compressor and install the four mounting bolts. Tighten the bolts to 30-40 ft. lbs. (40-55 Nm).
18. Install the two passenger side splash shields and lower the vehicle.
19. Connect the high-pressure line to the power steering pump and tighten the nut. Connect the return line to the pump and position the clamp.
20. Support the engine with a suitable floor jack.
21. Remove the two front engine mount nuts and raise the engine to gain access to the pulley.
22. Position the pulley and, holding the pulley in place with a suitable tool, install the three pulley mounting bolts. Tighten the bolts to 15-22 ft. lbs. (20-30 Nm).
23. Lower the engine.
24. Position the engine mount and install the two nuts. Tighten the engine mount pivot bolt and nut.
25. Position the engine vibration dampener and install the bolt and nut.
26. Position the belt tensioner and install the bolt loosely. Position the accessory drive belt on the pulley and tighten the tensioner mounting bolt to 30-41 ft. lbs. (40-55 Nm).
27. Fill the cooling system.
28. Add the proper type and quantity of power steering fluid.
29. Connect the negative battery cable. Check that the pump operates properly and that there are no leaks.

2.0L Diesel Engines

1. Remove the drive belts.
2. On air conditioned models, remove the alternator.
3. Remove both braces from the support bracket on air conditioned models.
4. Disconnect the power steering fluid lines and drain the fluid into a suitable container.
5. Remove the four bracket mounting bolts and remove the pump and bracket assembly.
6. The pulley must be removed before the pump can be separated from the mounting bracket. Tool T65P-3A733-C or equivalent is required to remove and install the drive pulley.
7. Install the pump and mounting bracket in the reverse order of removal.

SYSTEM BLEEDING

1981-90 Models

If air bubbles are present in the power steering fluid, bleed the system by performing the following:

1. Fill the reservoir to the proper level.
2. Operate the engine until it reaches normal operating temperature.
3. Turn the steering wheel all the way to the left then all the way to the right several times. Do not hold the steering wheel in the far left or far right position stops.
4. Check the fluid level and recheck the fluid for the presence of trapped air. If it is apparent that air is still in the system, fabricate or obtain a vacuum tester and purge the system as follows:
   a. Remove the pump dipstick cap assembly.
   b. Check and fill the pump reservoir with fluid to the COLD FULL mark on the dipstick.
   c. Disconnect the ignition wire and raise the front of the vehicle and support safely.

d. Crank the engine with the starter and check the fluid level. Do not turn the steering wheel at this time.

WARNING

DO NOT operate the starter for more than a few seconds at a time without stopping to allow the motor to cool down. Severe damage to the starter may occur if it is allowed to overheat by constant cranking.

e. Fill the pump reservoir to the COLD FULL mark on the dipstick. Crank the engine with the starter while cycling the steering wheel lock-to-lock. Check the fluid level.

f. Tightly insert a suitable size rubber stopper and air evacuator pump into the reservoir fill neck. Connect the ignition coil wire.

g. With the engine idling, apply a 15 in. Hg (50.6 kPa) vacuum to the reservoir for three minutes. As air is purged from the system, the vacuum will drop off. Maintain the vacuum on the system as required throughout the three minutes.

h. Remove the vacuum source. Fill the reservoir to the COLD FULL mark on the dipstick.

i. With the engine idling, re-apply 15 in. Hg (50.6 kPa) vacuum source to the reservoir. Slowly cycle the steering wheel to lock-to-lock stops for approximately five minutes. Do not hold the steering wheel on the stops during cycling. Maintain the vacuum as required.

j. Release the vacuum and disconnect the vacuum source. Add fluid, as required.

k. Start the engine and cycle the wheel slowly and check for leaks at all connections.

l. Lower the front wheels.

5. In cases of severe aeration, repeat the procedure.

1991-95 Models

1. Check the fluid level in the power steering pump auxiliary reservoir. If necessary, fill the power steering cylinder seal kit with the proper power steering fluid to the FULL mark.
2. Raise and safely support the front of the vehicle on jackstands.
3. Turn the ignition key to the **ON** position.
4. With the engine off, turn the steering wheel fully to the left, then fully to the right several times.
5. Check the fluid level again. If the level has dropped, add fluid.
6. Repeat steps 4 and 5 until the fluid level stabilizes.
7. Start the engine and let it idle.

WARNING

Do not hold the steering wheel against the stop for more than three to five seconds.

8. Turn the steering wheel fully to the left and to the right several times.
9. Verify that the fluid is not foamy and that the fluid level has not dropped.
10. Add fluid if necessary and repeat steps 8 and 9.

TORQUE SPECIFICATIONS - 1981-90 MODELS

Component	English	Metric
Front Suspension		
Strut top mount-to-body:	25–30 ft. lbs.	34–41 Nm
Strut-to-top mount:	35–50 ft. lbs.	48–68 Nm
Strut-to-knuckle:	55–81 ft. lbs.	75–110 Nm
Control arm-to-body:	48–55 ft. lbs.	65–74 Nm
Control arm-to-knuckle:	38–45 ft. lbs.	51–61 Nm
Stablizer bar-to-control arm:	98–115 ft. lbs.	132–156 Nm
Stablizer bar bracket assembly-to-body:	48–55 ft. lbs.	65–74 Nm
Tie rod end-to-steering knuckle:	28–32 ft. lbs.	38–43 Nm
Left hand front engine mount-to-stablizer bar to body bracket:	55–65 ft. lbs.	75–88 Nm
Rear Suspension		
Shock absorber-to-body:	35–55 ft. lbs.	48–75 Nm
Shock absorber-to-spindle:	70–96 ft. lbs.	95–130 Nm
Control arm-to-body:	52–74 ft. lbs.	70–100 Nm
Control arm-to-spindle:	60–80 ft. lbs.	81–109 Nm
Tie rod-to-body nut, front:	52–74 ft. lbs.	70–100 Nm
Tie rod-to-body nut, rear:	6–12 ft. lbs.	8–16 Nm
Tie rod-to-spindle:	35–50 ft. lbs.	47–68 Nm
Stabilizer bar link-to-shock bracket:	41–55 ft. lbs.	55–75 Nm
Steering Column		
Steering wheel bolt:	23–33 ft. lbs.	31–45 Nm
Column-to-support bracket bolt:	15–25 ft. lbs.	20–34 Nm
Intermediate shaft-to-steering gear nut and bolt:	14–20 ft. lbs.	19–27 Nm
Air bag module-to-steering wheel nuts		
1994-95:	36–49 inch lbs.	4–6 Nm
Steering Gear – Rack-and-Pinion Manual		
Pinion plug:	52–73 ft. lbs.	70–100 Nm
Steering gear mounting bolts:	40–55 ft. lbs.	54–75 Nm
Tie rod end-to-spindle arm*:	27–32 ft. lbs.	36–43 Nm
Tie rod end-to-inner tie rod jam nut:	35–50 ft. lbs.	47–68 Nm
Pinion shaft-to-intermediate shaft bolts:	20–37 ft. lbs.	28–50 Nm
Ball housing-to-rack:	50–60 ft. lbs.	68–81 Nm
Yoke plug prior to 30 degrees back-off:	40 inch lbs.	4.5 Nm
*Tighten to nearest cotter pin slot after tightening to minimum specifications.		
Steering Gear – Power Rack-and-Pinion TRW 2-piece Housing		
Pinion locknut:	20–35 ft. lbs.	27–47 Nm
Pinion cap:	35–45 ft. lbs.	47–61 Nm
Yoke plug locknut:	40–50 ft. lbs.	54–68 Nm
Tie rod ball housing:	50–55 ft. lbs.	68–75 Nm
Tie rod end-to-spindle arm*:	27–32 ft. lbs.	36–43 Nm
Steering gear mounting bolt:	40–55 ft. lbs.	54–75 Nm
Flex coupling-to-steering gear input shaft clamp bolt:	20–30 ft. lbs.	27–40 Nm
Tie rod-to-tie rod end jam nut:	42–50 ft. lbs.	57–68 Nm
*Tighten to nearest cotter pin slot after tightening to minimum specifications.		

86758C01

TORQUE SPECIFICATIONS - 1981-90 MODELS (CONT.)

Component	English	Metric
Steering Gear – Power Rack-and-Pinion Corporate 1-piece Housing		
Pinion locknut:	20–35 ft. lbs.	27–47 Nm
Pinion cap:	35–45 ft. lbs.	47–61 Nm
Yoke plug locknut:	40–50 ft. lbs.	54–68 Nm
Tie rod ball housing:	40–50 ft. lbs.	54–68 Nm
Tie rod end-to-spindle arm*:	27–32 ft. lbs.	36–43 Nm
Steering gear mounting bolt:	40–55 ft. lbs.	54–75 Nm
Flex coupling-to-steering gear input shaft clamp bolt:	20–30 ft. lbs.	27–40 Nm
Tie rod-to-tie rod end jam nut:	42–50 ft. lbs.	57–68 Nm
*Tighten to nearest cotter pin slot after tightening to minimum specifications.		

86758C02

TORQUE SPECIFICATIONS - 1991-95 MODELS

Component	English	Metric
Steering wheel nut:	29–36 ft. lbs.	39–49 Nm
Intermediate shaft-to-pinion shaft bolt:	29–36 ft. lbs.	39–49 Nm
Upper mounting bracket bolts:	80–123 inch lbs.	9–14 Nm
Steering Gear – Rack-and-Pinion Manual		
Rack preload/support yoke adjustment bolt:	8–7 inch lbs.	1 Nm
Pinion pull torque from neutral position:	9–12 inch lbs.	1–1.3 Nm
Tie rod stud-to-steering knuckle:	31–42 ft. lbs.	42–57 Nm
Tie rod end jam nut:	25–29 ft. lbs.	34–49 Nm
Pinion pull torque from any position other than neutral:	14.7 inch lbs.	1.6 Nm
Steering gear bracket nuts:	27–38 ft. lbs.	37–52 Nm
Intermediate shaft-to-pinion shaft bolt:	13–20 ft. lbs.	18–27 Nm
Steering Gear – Power Rack-and-Pinion 1.8L Engine		
Pinion torque:	9–10 inch lbs.	1.0–2.0 Nm
Tie rod end attaching nuts:	31–42 ft. lbs.	42–57 Nm
Intermediate shaft-to-pinion shaft bolt:	13–20 ft. lbs.	18–27 Nm
Pump mounting bracket bolt:	27–38 ft. lbs.	37–54 Nm
Yoke adjustment nut:	43 inch lbs.	5 Nm
Yoke plug locknut:	29–36 ft. lbs.	39–49 Nm
Tie rod end jam nut:	26–86 inch lbs.	3–9 Nm
Steering gear mounting bracket nuts:	27–38 ft. lbs.	37–54 Nm
Tensioner-to-pump bolt and nut:	14–19 ft. lbs.	19–25 Nm
Tensioner-to-pump bracket bolt and nut:	23–34 ft. lbs.	31–46 Nm
Pump-to-mounting bracket bolt:	27–40 ft. lbs.	36–54 Nm
Steering Gear – Power Rack-and-Pinion 1.9L Engine		
Pinion shaft locknut:	20–35 ft. lbs.	28–47 Nm
Yoke plug locknut:	40–50 ft. lbs.	54–68 Nm
Tie rod end jam nut:	25–37 ft. lbs.	34–50 Nm
Tie rod-to-rack:	40–50 ft. lbs.	54–68 Nm

86758C03

Troubleshooting the Turn Signal Switch

Problem	Cause	Solution
Turn signal will not cancel	· Loose switch mounting screws · Switch or anchor bosses broken · Broken, missing or out of position detent, or cancelling spring	· Tighten screws · Replace switch · Reposition springs or replace switch as required
Turn signal difficult to operate	· Turn signal lever loose · Switch yoke broken or distorted · Loose or misplaced springs · Foreign parts and/or materials in switch · Switch mounted loosely	· Tighten mounting screws · Replace switch · Reposition springs or replace switch · Remove foreign parts and/or material · Tighten mounting screws

86758053

Troubleshooting the Turn Signal Switch (cont.)

Problem	Cause	Solution
Turn signal will not indicate lane change	• Broken lane change pressure pad or spring hanger • Broken, missing or misplaced lane change spring • Jammed wires	• Replace switch • Replace or reposition as required • Loosen mounting screws, reposition wires and retighten screws
Turn signal will not stay in turn position	• Foreign material or loose parts impeding movement of switch yoke • Defective switch	• Remove material and/or parts • Replace switch
Hazard switch cannot be pulled out	• Foreign material between hazard support cancelling leg and yoke	• Remove foreign material. No foreign material impeding function of hazard switch—replace turn signal switch.
No turn signal lights	• Inoperative turn signal flasher • Defective or blown fuse • Loose chassis to column harness connector • Disconnect column to chassis connector. Connect new switch to chassis and operate switch by hand. If vehicle lights now operate normally, signal switch is inoperative • If vehicle lights do not operate, check chassis wiring for opens, grounds, etc.	• Replace turn signal flasher • Replace fuse • Connect securely • Replace signal switch • Repair chassis wiring as required
Instrument panel turn indicator lights on but not flashing	• Burned out or damaged front or rear turn signal bulb • If vehicle lights do not operate, check light sockets for high resistance connections, the chassis wiring for opens, grounds, etc. • Inoperative flasher • Loose chassis to column harness connection • Inoperative turn signal switch • To determine if turn signal switch is defective, substitute new switch into circuit and operate switch by hand. If the vehicle's lights operate normally, signal switch is inoperative.	• Replace bulb • Repair chassis wiring as required • Replace flasher • Connect securely • Replace turn signal switch • Replace turn signal switch
Stop light not on when turn indicated	• Loose column to chassis connection • Disconnect column to chassis connector. Connect new switch into system without removing old.	• Connect securely • Replace signal switch

86758054

Troubleshooting the Turn Signal Switch (cont.)

Problem	Cause	Solution
Stop light not on when turn indicated (cont.)	Operate switch by hand. If brake lights work with switch in the turn position, signal switch is defective.	
	• If brake lights do not work, check connector to stop light sockets for grounds, opens, etc.	• Repair connector to stop light circuits using service manual as guide
Turn indicator panel lights not flashing	• Burned out bulbs	• Replace bulbs
	• High resistance to ground at bulb socket	• Replace socket
	• Opens, ground in wiring harness from front turn signal bulb socket to indicator lights	• Locate and repair as required
Turn signal lights flash very slowly	• High resistance ground at light sockets	• Repair high resistance grounds at light sockets
	• Incorrect capacity turn signal flasher or bulb	• Replace turn signal flasher or bulb
	• If flashing rate is still extremely slow, check chassis wiring harness from the connector to light sockets for high resistance	• Locate and repair as required
	• Loose chassis to column harness connection	• Connect securely
	• Disconnect column to chassis connector. Connect new switch into system without removing old. Operate switch by hand. If flashing occurs at normal rate, the signal switch is defective.	• Replace turn signal switch
Hazard signal lights will not flash—turn signal functions normally	• Blow fuse	• Replace fuse
	• Inoperative hazard warning flasher	• Replace hazard warning flasher in fuse panel
	• Loose chassis-to-column harness connection	• Conect securely
	• Disconnect column to chassis connector. Connect new switch into system without removing old. Depress the hazard warning lights. If they now work normally, turn signal switch is defective.	• Replace turn signal switch
	• If lights do not flash, check wiring harness "K" lead for open between hazard flasher and connector. If open, fuse block is defective	• Repair or replace brown wire or connector as required

86758055

Troubleshooting the Power Steering Pump

Problem	Cause	Solution
Chirp noise in steering pump	• Loose belt	• Adjust belt tension to specification
Belt squeal (particularly noticeable at full wheel travel and stand still parking)	• Loose belt	• Adjust belt tension to specification
Growl noise in steering pump	• Excessive back pressure in hoses or steering gear caused by restriction	• Locate restriction and correct. Replace part if necessary.
Growl noise in steering pump (particularly noticeable at stand still parking)	• Scored pressure plates, thrust plate or rotor • Extreme wear of cam ring	• Replace parts and flush system • Replace parts
Groan noise in steering pump	• Low oil level • Air in the oil. Poor pressure hose connection.	• Fill reservoir to proper level • Tighten connector to specified torque. Bleed system by operating steering from right to left—full turn.
Rattle noise in steering pump	• Vanes not installed properly • Vanes sticking in rotor slots	• Install properly • Free up by removing burrs, varnish, or dirt
Swish noise in steering pump	• Defective flow control valve	• Replace part
Whine noise in steering pump	• Pump shaft bearing scored	• Replace housing and shaft. Flush system.
Hard steering or lack of assist	• Loose pump belt • Low oil level in reservoir **NOTE:** Low oil level will also result in excessive pump noise • Steering gear to column misalignment • Lower coupling flange rubbing against steering gear adjuster plug • Tires not properly inflated	• Adjust belt tension to specification • Fill to proper level. If excessively low, check all lines and joints for evidence of external leakage. Tighten loose connectors. • Align steering column • Loosen pinch bolt and assemble properly • Inflate to recommended pressure
Foaming milky power steering fluid, low fluid level and possible low pressure	• Air in the fluid, and loss of fluid due to internal pump leakage causing overflow	• Check for leaks and correct. Bleed system. Extremely cold temperatures will cause system aeriation should the oil level be low. If oil level is correct and pump still foams, remove pump from vehicle and separate reservoir from body. Check welsh plug and body for cracks. If plug is loose or body is cracked, replace body.

86758056

Troubleshooting the Power Steering Pump (cont.)

Problem	Cause	Solution
Low pump pressure	• Flow control valve stuck or inoperative • Pressure plate not flat against cam ring	• Remove burrs or dirt or replace. Flush system. • Correct
Momentary increase in effort when turning wheel fast to right or left	• Low oil level in pump • Pump belt slipping • High internal leakage	• Add power steering fluid as required • Tighten or replace belt • Check pump pressure. (See pressure test)
Steering wheel surges or jerks when turning with engine running especially during parking	• Low oil level • Loose pump belt • Steering linkage hitting engine oil pan at full turn • Insufficient pump pressure	• Fill as required • Adjust tension to specification • Correct clearance • Check pump pressure. (See pressure test). Replace flow control valve if defective.
Steering wheel surges or jerks when turning with engine running especially during parking (cont.)	• Sticking flow control valve	• Inspect for varnish or damage, replace if necessary
Excessive wheel kickback or loose steering	• Air in system	• Add oil to pump reservoir and bleed by operating steering. Check hose connectors for proper torque and adjust as required.
Low pump pressure	• Extreme wear of cam ring • Scored pressure plate, thrust plate, or rotor • Vanes not installed properly • Vanes sticking in rotor slots • Cracked or broken thrust or pressure plate	• Replace parts. Flush system. • Replace parts. Flush system. • Install properly • Freeup by removing burrs, varnish, or dirt • Replace part

86758057

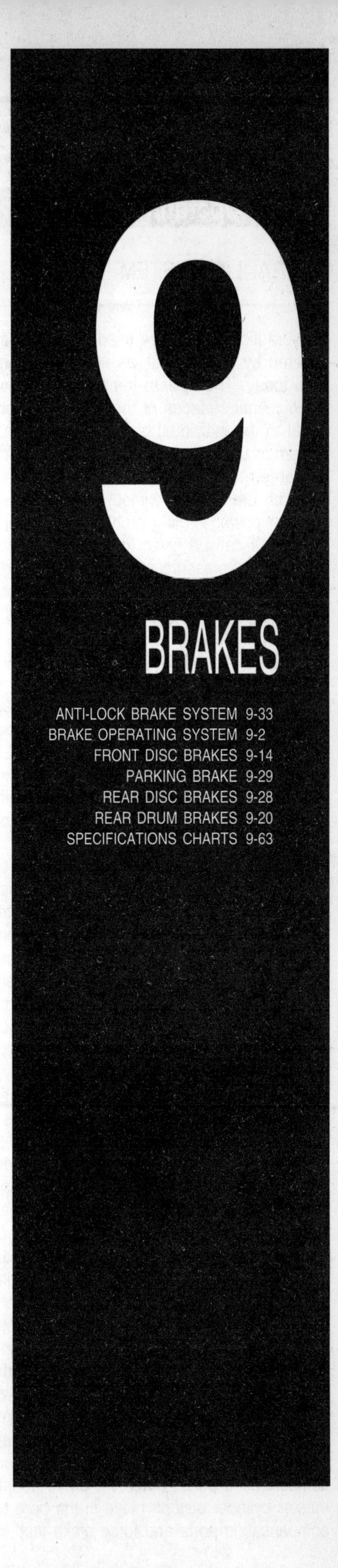

9 BRAKES

BRAKE OPERATING SYSTEM

Basic Operating Principles

HYDRAULIC SYSTEM

Hydraulic systems are used to actuate the brakes of all cars covered by this manual, as well as most motor vehicles on the road today. The system transports the power required to force the frictional surfaces of the braking system together from the pedal to the individual brake units at each wheel. A hydraulic system is used for two reasons. First, fluid under pressure can be carried to all parts of an automobile by small hoses, some of which are flexible, without taking up a significant amount of room or posing routing problems. Second, a great mechanical advantage can be given to the brake pedal end of the system, and the foot pressure required to actuate the brakes can be reduced by making the surface area of the master cylinder pistons smaller than that of any of the pistons in the wheel cylinders or calipers.

The master cylinder consists of a double reservoir and piston assembly as well as other springs, fittings, etc. Double (dual) master cylinders are designed to separate two wheels from the other two. Your car's braking system is separated diagonally. That is, the right front and left rear use one reservoir and the left front and right rear use the other.

Steel lines carry the brake fluid to a point on the car's frame near each wheel. A flexible hose usually carries the fluid from the steel line to the disc caliper or wheel cylinder. The flexible line allows for suspension and steering movements.

The rear wheel cylinders contain two pistons each, one at either end, which push outward in opposite directions. The front disc brake calipers contain one piston each.

All pistons employ some type of seal, usually made of rubber, to minimize fluid leakage. A rubber dust boot seals the outer end of the cylinder against dust and dirt. The boot fits around the outer end of the piston on disc brake calipers, and around the brake actuating rod on wheel cylinders.

The hydraulic system operates as follows: When at rest, the entire system, from the piston(s) in the master cylinder to those in the wheel cylinders or calipers, is full of brake fluid. Upon application of the brake pedal, fluid trapped in front of the master cylinder piston(s) is forced through the lines to the wheel cylinders. Here, it forces the pistons outward, in the case of drum brakes, or inward toward the disc, in the case of disc brakes. The motion of the pistons is opposed by return springs mounted outside the cylinders in drum brakes, and by internal springs or a spring seal, in disc brakes.

Upon release of the brake pedal, a spring located inside the master cylinder immediately returns the master cylinder pistons to the normal position. The pistons contain check valves and the master cylinder has compensating ports drilled in it. The piston check valves allow fluid to flow toward the wheel cylinders or calipers as the pistons withdraw. Then, as the return springs force the brake pads or shoes into the released position, the excess fluid flows to the reservoir through the compensating ports. When the brake pedal is depressed, the master cylinder pistons move in the bore to block the compensating ports and force brake fluid into the line. When the brakes are released, the pistons retract and expose the compensating ports, allowing a pressure equalization. It is while the pedal is in the released position that any fluid which has leaked out of the system will be replaced from the reservoirs through the compensating ports.

The dual master cylinder has two pistons, located one behind the other. The primary piston is actuated directly by mechanical linkage from the brake pedal. The secondary piston is actuated by fluid trapped between the two pistons. If a leak develops in front of the secondary piston, it moves forward until it bottoms against the front of the master cylinder. The fluid trapped between the piston will operate one side of the diagonal system. If the other side of the system develops a leak, the primary piston will move forward until direct contact with the secondary piston takes place, and it will force the secondary piston to actuate the other side of the diagonal system. In either case the brake pedal drops closer to the floor board and less braking power is available.

The brake system uses a switch to warn the driver when only half of the brake system is operational. This switch is located in a valve body which is mounted on the firewall or to the frame below the master cylinder. A hydraulic piston receives pressure from both circuits, with each circuit's pressure being applied to one end of the piston. When the pressures are in balance, the piston remains stationary. When one circuit has a leak, however, the greater pressure in the circuit during application of the brakes will push the piston to one side, closing the switch and activating the brake warning light.

In disc brake systems, this valve body contains a metering valve and, in some cases, a proportioning valve or valves, The metering valve keeps pressure from traveling to the disc brakes on the front wheels until the brake shoes on the rear wheels have contacted the drums, ensuring that the front brakes will never be used alone. The proportioning valve controls the pressure to the rear brakes to avoid rear wheel lock-up during very hard braking.

Warning lights may be tested by depressing the brake pedal and holding it while opening one of the wheel cylinder bleeder screws. If this does not cause the light to go on, substitute a new lamp, make continuity checks, and if necessary, replace the switch.

The hydraulic system may be checked for leaks by applying pressure to the pedal gradually and steadily. If the pedal sinks very slowly to the floor, the system has a leak. This is not to be confused with a springy or spongy feel due to the compression of air within the lines. If the system leaks, there will be a gradual change in the position of the pedal with a constant pressure. Check for leaks along all lines and at wheel cylinders or calipers. If no external leaks are apparent, the problem is inside the master cylinder.

DISC BRAKES

Instead of the traditional expanding brakes that press outward against a circular drum, disc brake systems utilize a disc (rotor) with brake pads positioned on either side of it. Braking effect is achieved in a manner similar to the way modern bicycle brake pads grip a spinning bicycle wheel. In the example of the bike, as its rubber pads clamp inward, friction is created to slow or stop the wheel. On the car with disc brakes, the same principle operates between the pads and the disc which is bolted to the wheel. The disc is a casting with cooling fins between the two braking surfaces. This enables air to circulate between the braking surfaces making them less sensitive to heat buildup and more resistant to fade. Dirt and water do not significantly affect braking action since contaminants are thrown off by the centrifugal action of the rotor or scraped off by the pads. Also, the equal clamping action of the two brake pads tends to ensure uniform, straight line stops. Disc brakes are inherently self-adjusting.

Your car uses a pin slider front wheel caliper. The brake pad on the inside of the brake rotor is moved in contact with the rotor by hydraulic pressure. The caliper, which is not held in a fixed position, moves slightly, bringing the outside brake pad into contact with the disc rotor.

DRUM BRAKES (REAR)

Drum brakes employ two brake shoes mounted on a stationary backing plate. These shoes are positioned inside a circular drum which rotates with the wheel assembly. The shoes are held in place by springs. This allows them to slide toward the drums (when they are applied) while keeping the linings and drums in alignment. The shoes are actuated by a wheel cylinder which is mounted at the top of the backing plate. When the brakes are applied, hydraulic pressure forces the wheel cylinder's actuating links outward. Since these links bear directly against the top of the brake shoes, the tops of the shoes are then forced against the inner side of the drum. This action forces the bottoms of the two shoes to contact the brake drum by rotating the entire assembly slightly (know as servo action). When pressure within the wheel cylinder is released, return springs pull the shoes back away from the drum.

The rear drum brakes on your car are designed to self-adjust themselves during application. Motion causes both shoes to rotate very slightly with the drum, rocking an adjusting lever, thereby causing rotation of the adjusting screw or lever.

POWER BRAKE BOOSTERS

Power brakes operate just like standard brake systems except in the actuation of the master cylinder pistons. A vacuum diaphragm is located on the front of the master cylinder and assists the driver in applying the brakes, reducing both the effort and travel he must put into moving the brake pedal.

The vacuum diaphragm housing is connected to the intake manifold by a vacuum hose. A check valve is placed at the point where the hose enters the diaphragm housing, so that during periods of low manifold vacuum brake assist vacuum will not be lost.

Depressing the brake pedal closes off the vacuum sources and allows atmospheric pressure to enter on one side of the diaphragm. This causes the master cylinder pistons to move and apply the brakes. When the brake pedal is released, vacuum is applied to both sides of the diaphragm, and return springs restore the diaphragm and master cylinder pistons to the released position. If the vacuum fails, the brake pedal rod will butt against the end of the master cylinder actuating rod, and direct mechanical application will occur as the pedal is depressed.

The hydraulic and mechanical problems that apply to conventional brake systems also apply to power brakes.

Adjustments

FRONT DISC BRAKES

The conventional hydraulic front disc brakes require no periodic adjustments and in fact are not adjustable, but are instead self-adjusting. The proper pad-to-disc contact is maintained at all times by the hydraulic line pressure. The only service procedure that could be considered an "adjustment" is the bleeding of the hydraulic lines which involves purging any air or contaminating substances (water, dirt, etc.). If your believe this may be necessary, refer to the section entitled "Bleeding the Brake System" for information on bleeding the brakes.

REAR DRUM BRAKES

See Figure 1

The rear drum brakes are self-adjusting. The only adjustments necessary should be an initial adjustment, which is performed after new brake shoes have been installed or some type of service work has been done on the rear brake system.

➡After any brake service, obtain a firm brake pedal before moving the vehicle. Adjusted brakes must not drag. The wheel must turn freely. Be sure the parking brake cables (rear brakes only) are not adjusted too tightly. A special brake shoe gauge, tool No. D81L-1103-A or equivalent size (for brake measuring) vernier caliper, is necessary for making an accurate adjustment after installing new brake shoes. The special gauge measures both the drum diameter and the brake shoe setting.

1. Measure and set the special brake gauge, tool No. D81L-1103-A or equivalent size vernier caliper, to the inside diameter of the brake drum.
2. Manipulate the adjuster mechanism until the brake shoes are set to the same diameter measurement as the rear brake drum. To adjust the brake shoe outside diameter for 1981-90 models with 7 in. brakes, pivot the adjuster quadrant until it reaches the correct notch. For 1981-90 models with 8 in. brakes, turn the starwheel for the correct shoe diameter. For 1991-95 models, insert a prytool into the knurled quadrant of the rear quad operating lever stopper to adjust the brake shoe outside diameter.

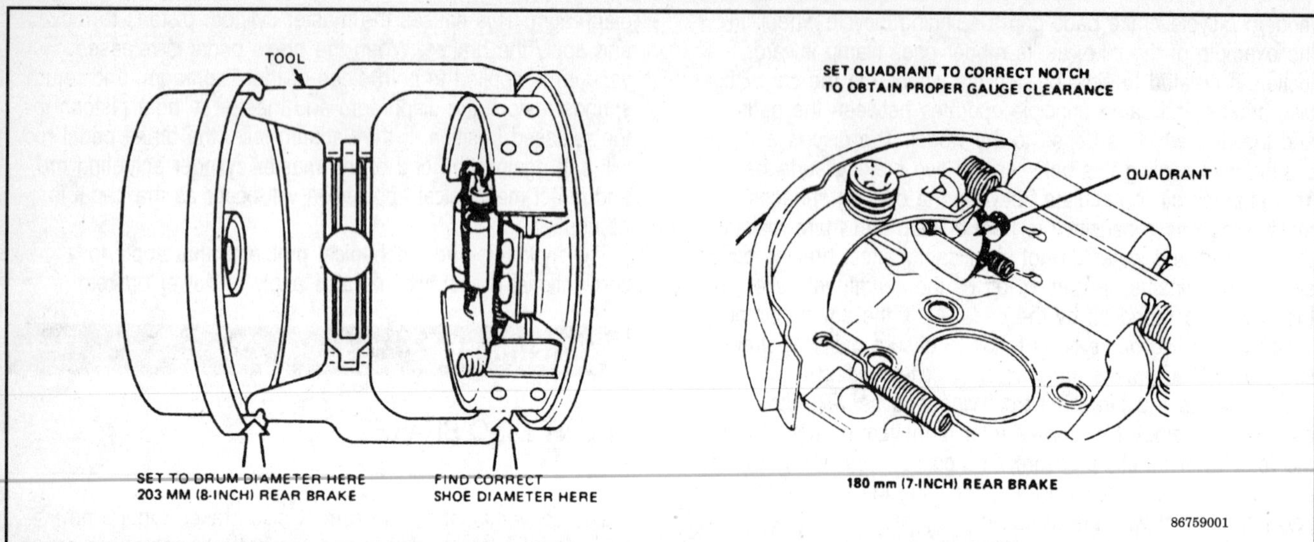

Fig. 1 Use this special gauge to take the guesswork out of adjusting your rear drum brakes

3. When a good brake shoe-to-drum fit is achieved, install the hub, the drum and wheel(s).

➡**Complete the adjustment by applying the brakes several times. After the brakes have been properly adjusted, check their operation by making several stops from varying forward speeds.**

Brake Light Switch

REMOVAL & INSTALLATION

1. Disconnect the negative battery cable.
2. Unplug the wire harness at the connector from the switch.

➡**The locking tab must be lifted before the connector can be removed.**

3. Remove the hairpin retainer and white nylon washer. Slide the brake light switch and the pushrod away from the pedal. Remove the switch by sliding the switch up/down.

➡**Since the switch side plate nearest the brake pedal is slotted, it is not necessary to remove the brake master cylinder pushrod black bushing and one white spacer washer nearest the pedal arm from the brake pedal pin.**

To install:

4. Position the switch so that the U-shaped side is nearest the pedal and directly over/under the pin. The black bushing must be in position in the push rod eyelet with the washer face on the side closest to the retaining pin.
5. Slide the switch up/down, trapping the master cylinder pushrod and black bushing between the switch side plates. Push the switch and pushrod assembly firmly towards the brake pedal arm. Assemble the outside white plastic washer to pin and install the hairpin retainer to trap the whole assembly.

➡**Do not substitute other types of pin retainer. Replace only with a production type hairpin retainer.**

6. Plug in the wire harness connector to the switch.
7. Connect negative battery cable.
8. Check the brake light switch for proper operation. Stoplights should illuminate with less than 6 lbs. (2.7 kg) applied to the brake pedal at the pad.

➡**The brake light switch wire harness must have sufficient length to travel with the switch during full stroke at the pedal.**

Master Cylinder

REMOVAL & INSTALLATION

➡**Brake fluid acts like a paint remover. Be certain not to spill brake fluid on the vehicle's painted surfaces. If any is spilled, wipe it off completely, then, if necessary, wet a cloth and re-wipe to completely remove any residue. If brake fluid falls on a difficult to reach place, wash it off with low pressure water. Cap the master cylinder reservoir to make sure you do not splash any water into it.**

1981-90 Models

See Figures 2, 3, 4, 5, 6, 7, 8, 9 and 10

1. Disconnect the negative battery cable.
2. Disconnect the brake lines from the primary and secondary outlet ports of the master cylinder and pressure control valves. Be sure to plug all openings to prevent excessive fluid loss or system contamination.
3. Disconnect the brake warning light wire.
4. Remove the nuts attaching the master cylinder to the brake booster assembly.
5. Slide the master cylinder forward and upward from the vehicle.

To install:

6. Before installation, bench bleed the new master cylinder as follows:
   a. Mount the new master cylinder in a suitable holding fixture. Be careful not to damage the housing.
   b. Fill the master cylinder reservoir with brake fluid.

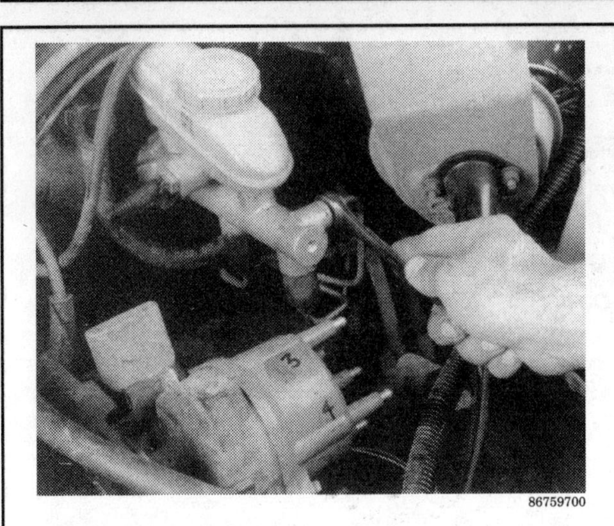

Fig. 2 Disconnect and plug the brake lines from master cylinder ports — 1988 Escort shown

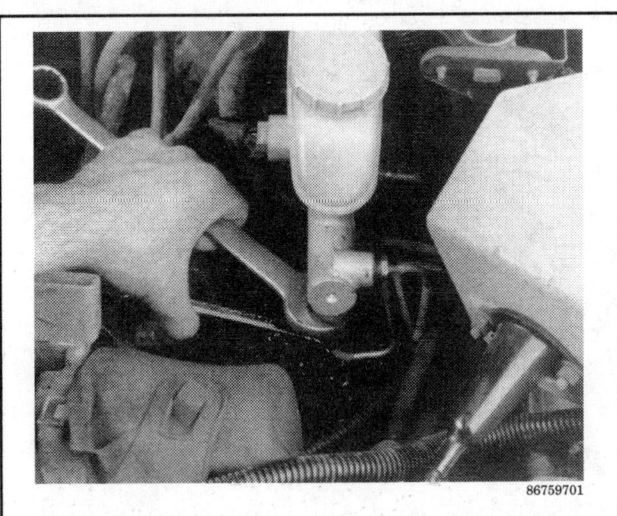

Fig. 3 Use the correct size wrenches to disconnect the brake line fittings

Fig. 4 Disconnect the brake warning light wire

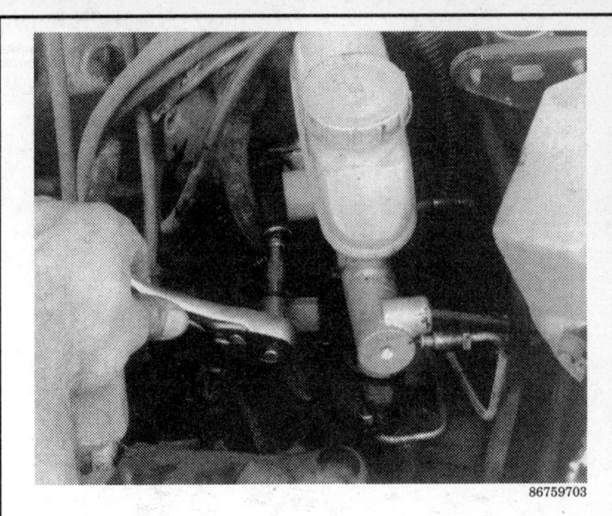

Fig. 5 Remove the nuts attaching the master cylinder to the brake booster assembly

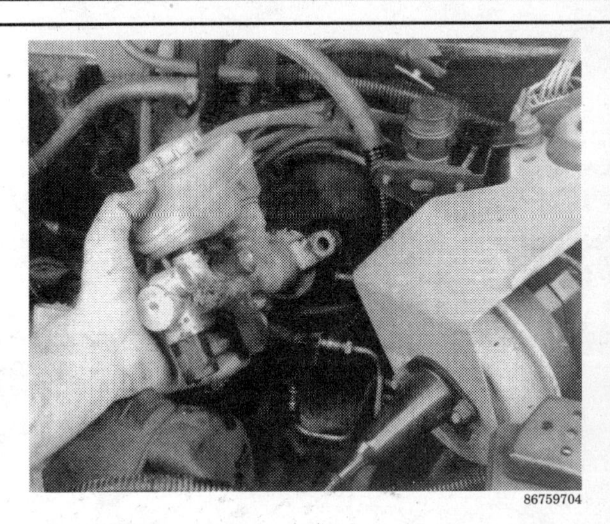

Fig. 6 Slide the master cylinder forward and upward from the vehicle

c. Using a wooden dowel inserted into the booster pushrod cavity, push the master cylinder piston in slowly. Place a suitable container under the master cylinder to catch the fluid being expelled from the outlet ports.

d. Place a finger tightly over each outlet port and allow the master cylinder piston to return.

e. Repeat the procedure until clear fluid only is expelled from the master cylinder. Plug the outlet ports and remove the master cylinder from the holding fixture.

7. Position the master cylinder over the booster pushrod and mounting studs. Install the nuts and tighten to 13-25 ft. lbs. (18-33 Nm).

8. Remove the plugs and connect the brake lines. Tighten the fittings.

9. Make sure the master cylinder reservoir is full. Have an assistant push down on the brake pedal. When the pedal is all the way down, crack open the brake line fittings, one at a time, to expel any remaining air in the master cylinder and brake lines. Tighten the fittings, then have the assistant allow the brake pedal to return.

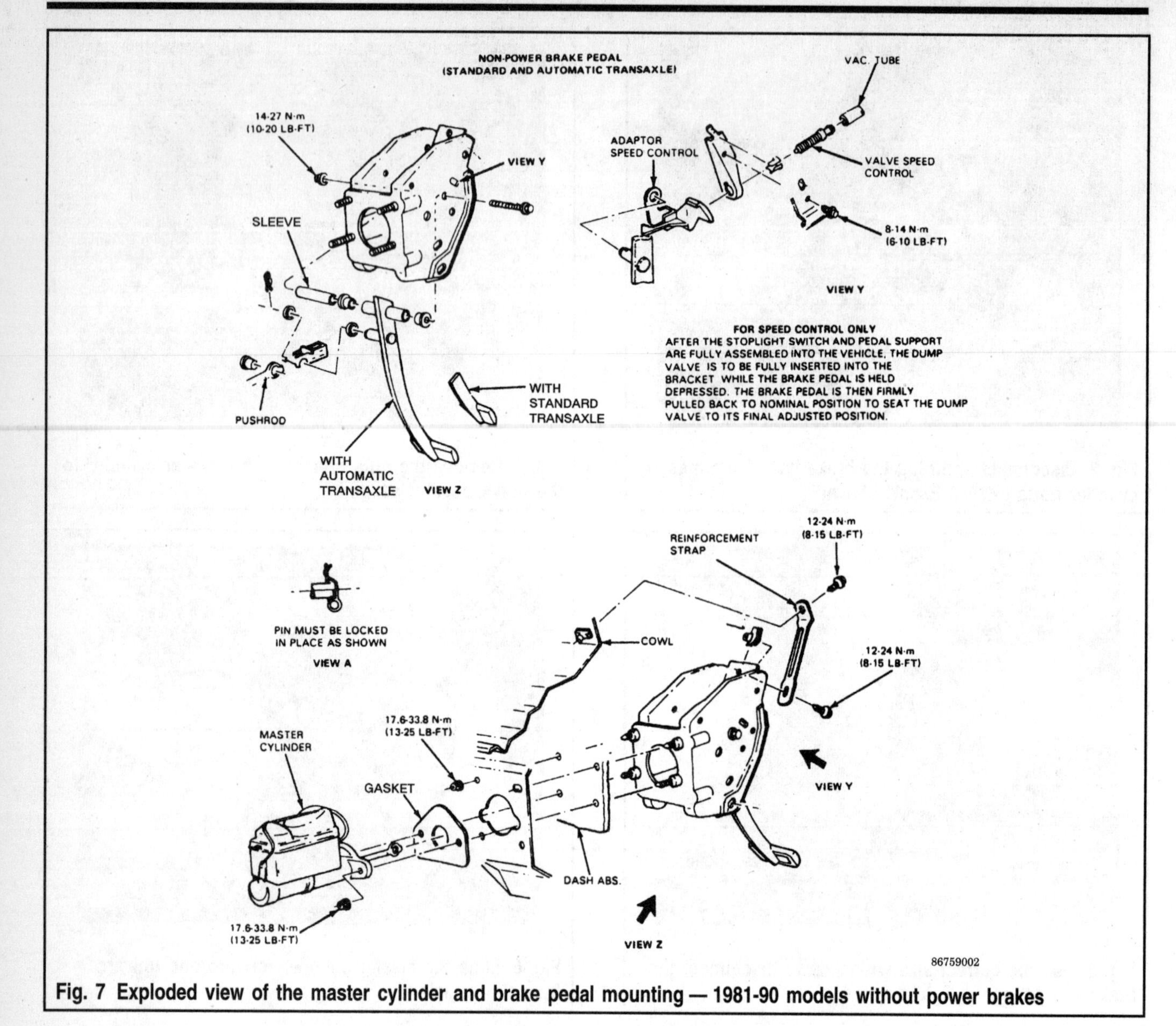

Fig. 7 Exploded view of the master cylinder and brake pedal mounting — 1981-90 models without power brakes

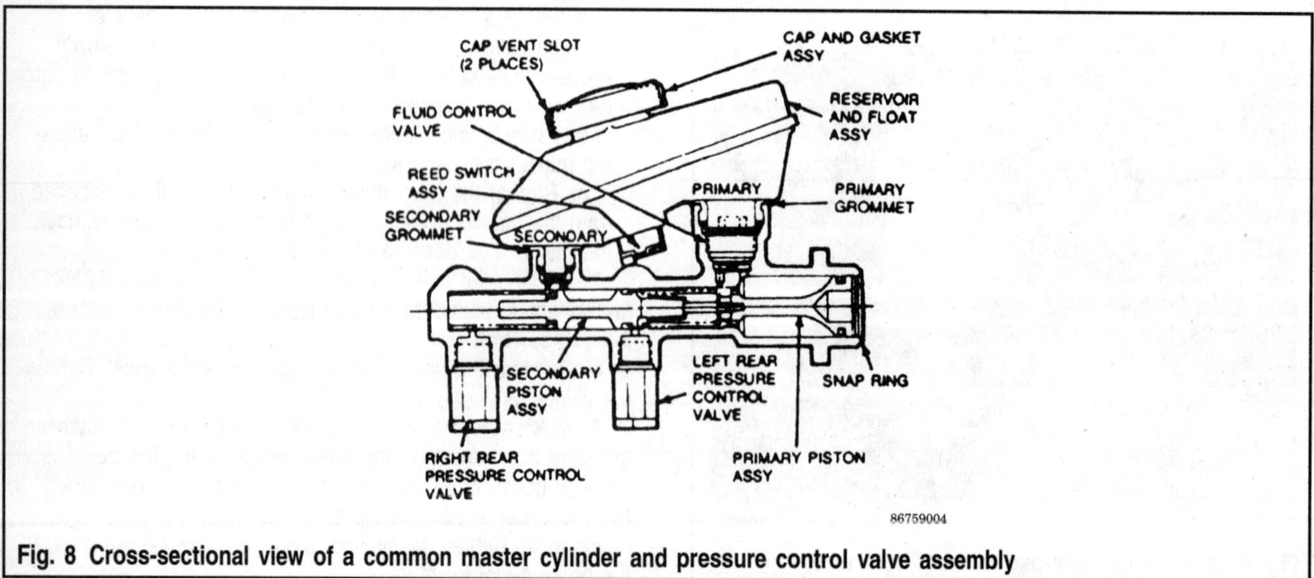

Fig. 8 Cross-sectional view of a common master cylinder and pressure control valve assembly

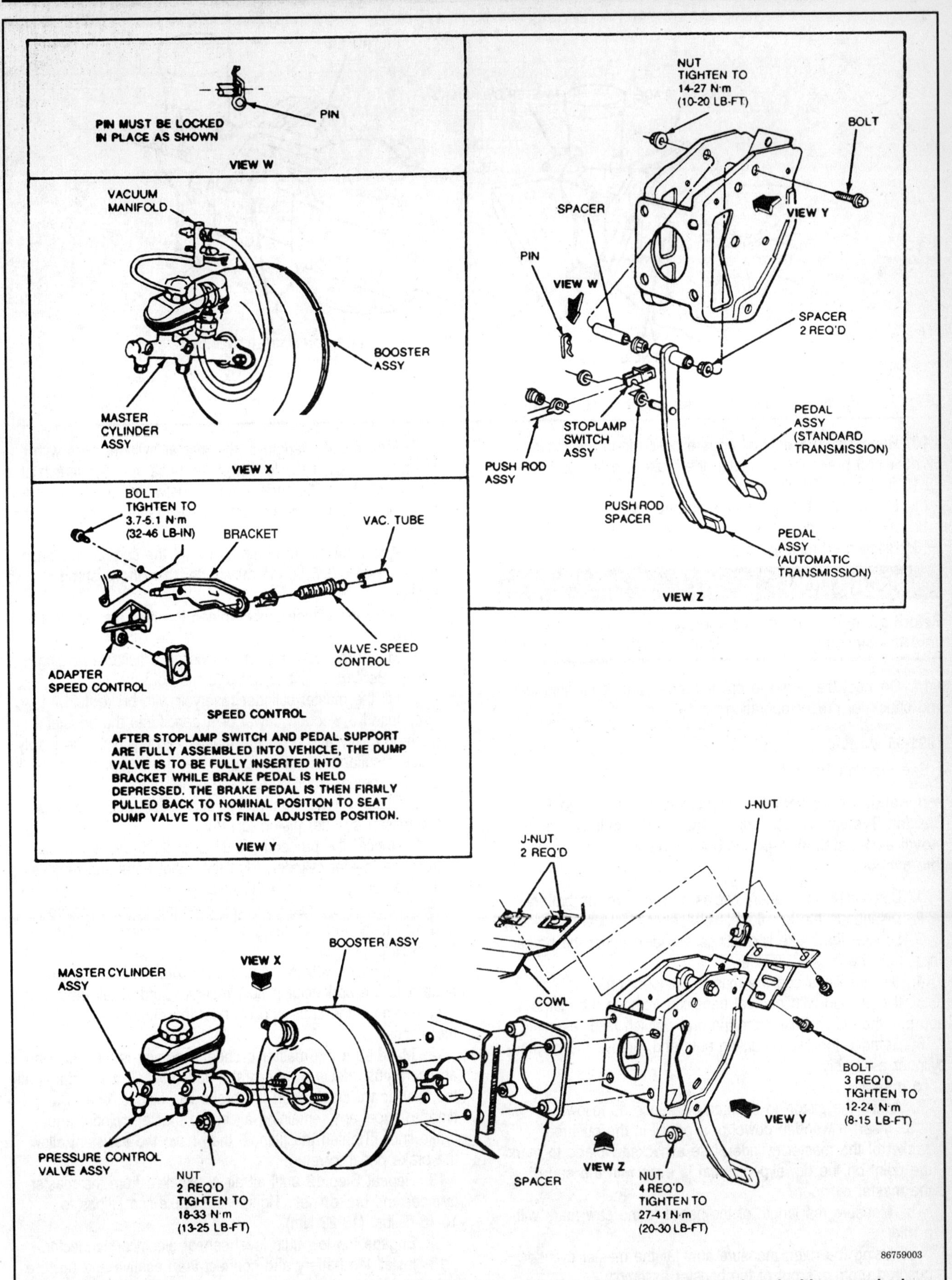

Fig. 9 Exploded view of the master cylinder and brake pedal mounting for 1981-90 vehicles equipped with power brakes

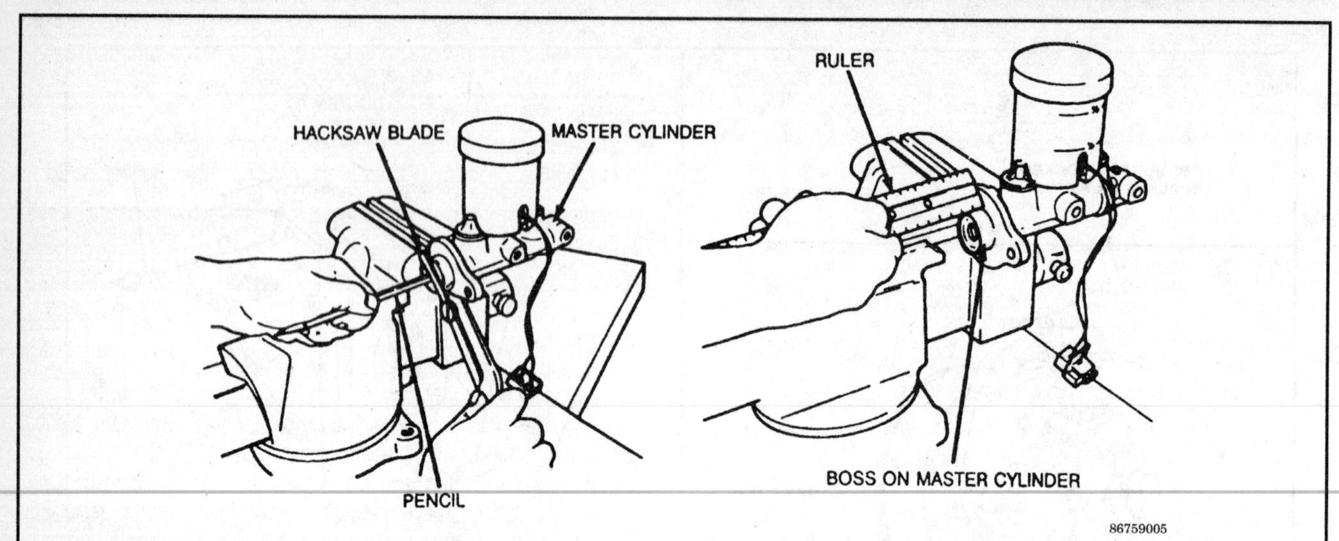

Fig. 10 Adjust the master cylinder pushrod as shown

10. Repeat step 8 until all air is expelled from the master cylinder and brake lines. Tighten the brake line fittings to 10-18 ft. lbs. (14-24 Nm).
11. Engage the brake warning indicator connector.
12. Make sure the master cylinder reservoir is full.
13. Bleed the brake system.

CAUTION

Before attempting to test or operate the vehicle, make sure the bleeding procedure achieves a firm brake pedal.

14. Connect the negative battery cable. Check for fluid leaks and check for proper operation.

1991-95 Models

See Figures 10 and 11

If working on a vehicle equipped with the Anti-lock Braking System (ABS), refer to the master cylinder removal and installation procedure in the ABS portion of this section.

1. Disconnect the battery cables and remove the battery.
2. Disengage the low fluid level sensor electrical connector.
3. Loosen the brake line fittings and disconnect the brake lines from the master cylinder.
4. Cap the lines and the master cylinder ports.
5. If equipped with manual transaxle, remove the clamp and pull the clutch hose from the brake/clutch fluid reservoir.
6. Remove the two mounting nuts and remove the master cylinder assembly.

To install:

7. Adjust the piston to pushrod clearance as follows:
   a. Insert a wooden dowel or a pencil in the pushrod socket of the master cylinder. Use a hacksaw blade to mark the point on the dowel/pencil that is even with the end of the master cylinder.
   b. Measure the length of the pencil to the saw mark with a ruler.
   c. Using the ruler, measure how far the master cylinder pushrod protrudes out of the booster assembly.
   d. Measure the length of the master cylinder boss with the ruler. Subtract the length of the boss from the length of the pencil. The difference in length between the master cylinder pushrod and the corrected pencil length is equal to the pushrod clearance.
   e. Adjust the pushrod length to get the correct clearance. It should be 0.025 in. (1mm) shorter than the pushrod socket.
8. Before installation, bench bleed the new master cylinder as follows:
   a. Mount the new master cylinder in a suitable holding fixture. Be careful not to damage the housing.
   b. Fill the master cylinder reservoir with brake fluid.
   c. Insert a wooden dowel or a pencil into the booster pushrod cavity and push the master cylinder piston in slowly. Place a suitable container under the master cylinder to catch the fluid being expelled from the outlet ports.
   d. Place a finger tightly over each outlet port and allow the master cylinder piston to return.
   e. Repeat the procedure until clear fluid only is expelled from the master cylinder. Plug the outlet ports and remove the master cylinder from the holding fixture.
9. Position the master cylinder over the booster pushrod and mounting studs. Install the nuts and tighten to 8-12 ft. lbs. (10-16 Nm).
10. If equipped with a manual transaxle, connect the clutch hose onto the brake/clutch fluid reservoir and install the clamp.
11. Remove the caps and connect the brake lines. Tighten the fittings.
12. Make sure the master cylinder reservoir is full. Have an assistant push down on the brake pedal. When the pedal is all the way down, crack open the brake line fittings, one at a time, to expel any remaining air in the master cylinder and brake lines. Tighten the fittings, then have the assistant allow the brake pedal to return.
13. Repeat Step 12 until all air is expelled from the master cylinder and brake lines. Tighten the brake line fittings to 10-16 ft. lbs. (13-22 Nm).
14. Engage the low fluid level sensor electrical connector.
15. Install the battery and connect the negative and positive battery cable.

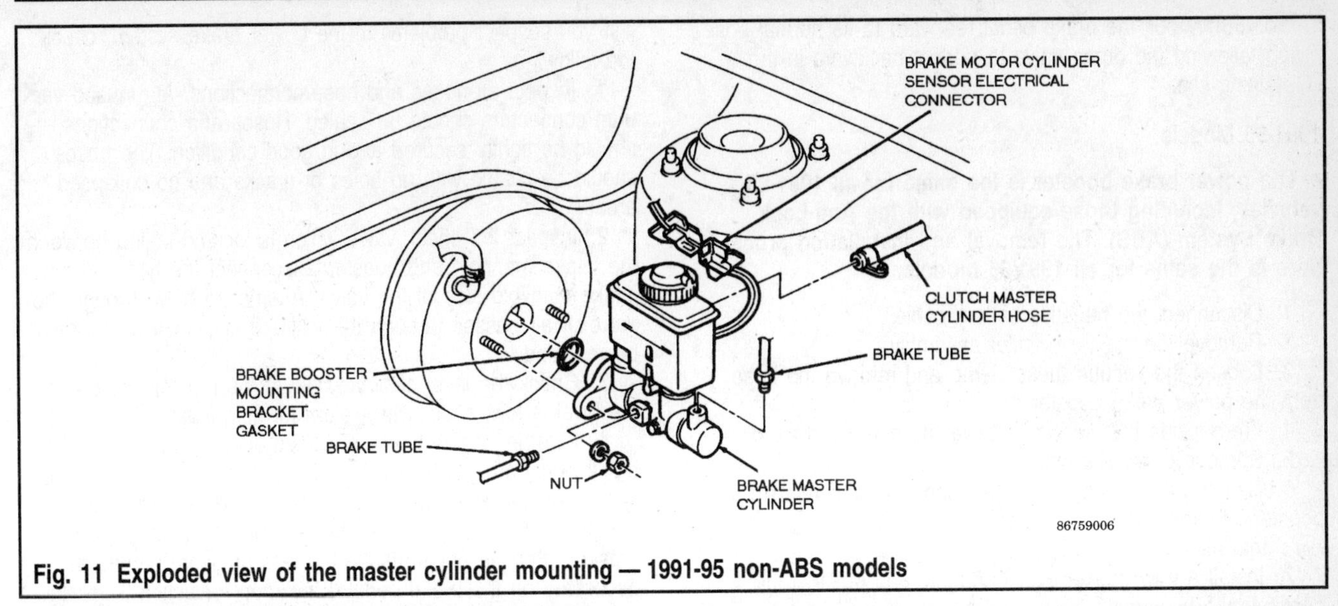

Fig. 11 Exploded view of the master cylinder mounting — 1991-95 non-ABS models

16. Make sure the master cylinder reservoir is full. Bleed the brakes.

CAUTION

Before attempting to test or operate the vehicle, make sure the bleeding procedure achieves a firm brake pedal.

17. Check for brake fluid leaks and for proper brake operation.

Power Brake Booster

REMOVAL & INSTALLATION

1981-85 Models

1. Disconnect the negative battery cable.
2. Working from inside the car, beneath the instrument panel, remove the booster pushrod from the brake pedal.
3. Disconnect the brake light switch wires and remove the switch from the brake pedal. Use care not to damage the switch during removal.
4. Raise the hood and remove the master cylinder from the booster.
5. Remove the manifold vacuum hose from the booster.
6. Remove the booster-to-firewall attaching nuts and remove the booster from the vehicle.

To install:

7. Position the booster to the firewall and install the mounting nuts.
8. Connect the manifold vacuum hose to the booster.
9. Install the booster pushrod and brake light switch.
10. Connect the negative battery cable.

1985½-90 Models

1. Disconnect the battery ground cable.
2. Remove the brake lines from the master cylinder.
3. Remove the retaining nuts and remove the master cylinder.
4. From under the instrument panel, remove the brake light switch wiring connector from the switch. Remove the pushrod retainer and outer nylon washer from the brake pin, slide the switch along the brake pedal pin, far enough for the outer hole to clear the pin.
5. Remove the switch by sliding it upward. Remove the booster to dash panel retaining nuts. Slide the booster pushrod and pushrod bushing off the brake pedal pin.
6. Disconnect the manifold vacuum hose from the booster check valve and move the booster forward until the studs clear the dash panel, then remove the booster.

To install:

7. Align the pedal support and support spacer inside the vehicle, then place the booster in position on the dash panel. Hand-start the retaining nuts.
8. Working inside the vehicle, install the pushrod and pushrod bushing on the brake pedal pin. Tighten the booster-to-dash panel retaining nuts to 13-25 ft. lbs. (18-33 Nm).
9. Position the brake light switch so it straddles the booster pushrod with the switch slot toward the pedal blade and the hole just clearing the pin. Slide the switch down onto the pin. Slide the assembly toward the pedal arm, being careful not to bend or deform the switch. Install the nylon washer on the pin and secure all parts to the pin with the hairpin retainer. Make sure the retainer is fully installed and locked over the pedal pin. Install the brake light switch connector on the switch.
10. Connect the manifold vacuum hose to the booster check valve using a hose clamp.
11. Install the master cylinder according to the proper procedure.
12. Bleed the brake system.
13. Connect the negative battery cable and start the engine. Check the power brake function.
14. If equipped with speed control, adjust the dump valve as follows:
   a. Firmly depress and hold the brake pedal.
   b. Push in the dump valve until the valve collar bottoms against the retaining clip.
   c. Place a 0.050-0.100 in. (1.27-2.54mm) shim between the white button of the valve and the pad on the brake pedal.

d. Firmly pull the brake pedal rearward to its normal position, allowing the dump valve to ratchet backward in the retaining clip.

1991-95 Models

➡**The power brake booster is the same for all 1991-95 vehicles, including those equipped with the Anti-Lock Brake System (ABS). The removal and installation procedure is the same for all 1991-95 models.**

1. Disconnect the negative battery cable.
2. Remove the master cylinder assembly.
3. Loosen the vacuum hose clamp and remove the hose from the power brake booster.
4. From inside the vehicle, remove the pin and discard.
5. Remove the clevis pin.
6. Remove the four booster mounting nuts and remove the booster. Remove and discard the gasket.

To install:

7. Install a new gasket over the studs and position the power brake booster.
8. From inside the vehicle, install the four mounting nuts and tighten to 14-19 ft. lbs. (19-25 Nm).
9. Lubricate a new clevis pin with white lithium grease and install.
10. Position the vacuum hose to the booster and install the clamp.
11. Install the master cylinder, making sure to check the master cylinder pushrod clearance.
12. Adjust the brake pedal as follows:
    a. Press the brake pedal several times to eliminate the vacuum in the booster.
    b. Carefully press the pedal and measure the amount of free-play until resistance is felt. If the free-play is 0.16-0.28 in. (4-7mm), the pedal free-play is within specification. If the free-play is not within specification, proceed to Step c.
    c. Loosen the rod locknut and rotate the rod either in or out, as necessary, to obtain the specified free-play.
    d. While holding the rod in position, tighten the rod locknut.
    e. Measure the distance from the center of the brake pedal to the floor. If the distance measures 7.60-7.72 in. (193-196mm), the pedal height is within specification. If the pedal height is not within specification, proceed to Step f.
    f. Disengage the brake light switch electrical connector, loosen the switch locknut and turn the switch until it does not contact the brake pedal.
    g. Loosen the rod locknut and turn the rod until the brake pedal height is within specification.
    h. Turn the brake light switch until it contacts the brake pedal, then turn it an additional ½ turn. Tighten the brake light locknut and the rod locknut.
    i. Connect the brake light switch electrical connector and check the operation of the brake lights and brake system.

TESTING

The power brake booster utilizes engine vacuum the engine to assist with braking power and lighten the pedal effort needed.

If you suspect problems in the power brake system, check the following:

1. Inspect all hoses and hose connections. All unused vacuum connectors should be sealed. Hoses and connections should be tightly secured and in good condition. The hoses should be pliable with no holes or cracks and no collapsed areas.
2. Inspect the check valve which is located in-line between the intake manifold and booster. Disconnect the hose on the intake manifold side of the valve. Attempt to blow through the valve. If air passes through the valve, it is defective and must be replaced.
3. Check the level of brake fluid in the master cylinder. If the level is low, check the system for fluid leaks.
4. Idle the engine briefly and then shut it **OFF**. Pump the brake pedal several times to exhaust all of the vacuum stored in the booster. Keep the brake pedal depressed and start the engine. The brake pedal should drop slightly, if vacuum is present after the engine is started less pressure should be necessary on the brake pedal. If no drop, or action is felt the power brake booster should be suspect.
5. With the parking brake applied and the wheels blocked, start the engine and allow to idle in Neutral (Park if automatic). Disconnect the vacuum line to the check valve on the intake manifold side. If vacuum is felt, connect the hose and repeat Step 4. Once again, if no action is felt on the brake pedal, suspect the booster.
6. Operate the engine at a fast idle for about ten seconds, shut **OFF** the engine. Allow the car to sit for about ten minutes. Depress the brake pedal with moderate force (about 20 lbs./9 kg). The pedal should feel about the same as when the engine was running. If the brake pedal feels hard (no power assist) suspect the power booster.

Pressure Differential Valve

➧ **See Figure 12**

If a loss of brake fluid occurs on either side of the diagonally split system when the brakes are applied, a piston mounted in the valve moves off center allowing the brakes on the non-leaking side of the split system to operate. When the piston moves off center a brake warning switch, located in the center of the valve body, will turn on a dash mounted warning light indicating brake problems.

After repairs are made on the brake system and the system is bled, the warning switch will reset itself, once you pump the brake pedal. The dash light should also turn OFF.

Pressure Control Valves

➡**On some early models, this valve was called the brake control valve assembly. Integral with this early unit was the proportioning valve and together, they are the same unit as the pressure control valve on later cars.**

There are two pressure control valves housed in the master cylinder assembly. The valves reduce rear brake system hydraulic pressure when the pressure exceeds a preset value. The rear brake hydraulic pressure is limited in order to minimize rear wheel skidding during hard braking.

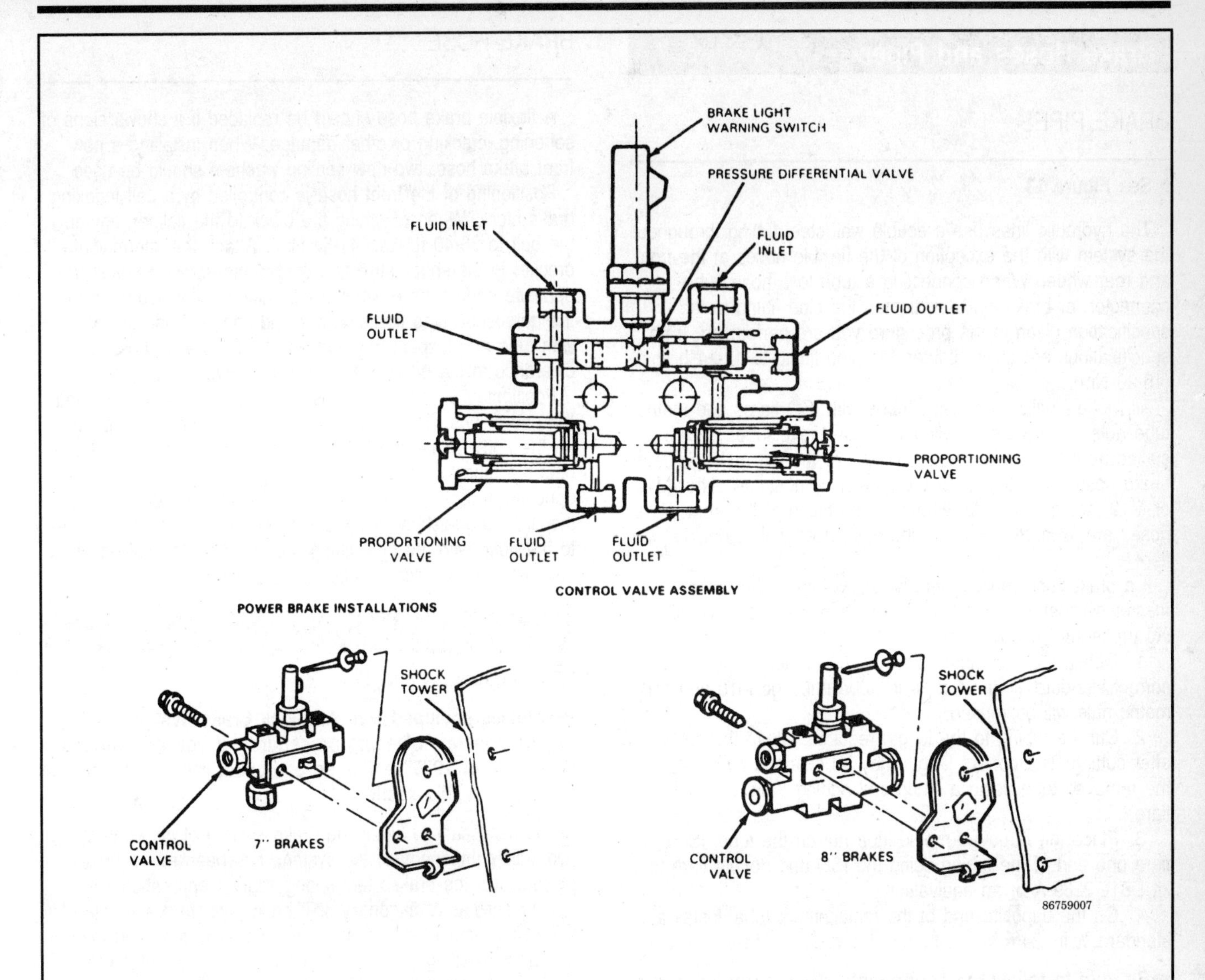

Fig. 12 Cross-sectional of the pressure differential valve assembly — exploded views of mounting are very similar for 7 and 8 inch brakes

TROUBLESHOOTING

If the rear brakes lock-up during light brake application or do not lock-up under heavy braking the problem could be with the dual proportioning valve.

1. Check tires and tire pressures.
2. Check the brake linings for thickness, and for contamination by fluid, grease etc.
3. Check the brake system hoses, steel lines, calipers and wheel cylinders for leaks.
4. If none of the proceeding checks have uncovered any problems, suspect the proportioning ability of the pressure control valve.

➡Take the car to a qualified service center and ask them to do a pressure test on the valve. If a pressure test is not possible, replace the control valve.

REMOVAL & INSTALLATION

1. Disconnect the primary or secondary brake line, as necessary.
2. Loosen and remove the pressure control valve from the master cylinder housing.

To install:

3. Install the pressure control valve in the master cylinder housing port and tighten to 10-18 ft. lbs. (14-24 Nm).
4. Connect the brake line and tighten the fitting to 10-18 ft. lbs. (14-24 Nm).
5. Fill and bleed the brake system.

Brake Hoses and Pipes

BRAKE PIPES

➧ **See Figure 13**

The hydraulic lines use a double wall steel tubing throughout the system with the exception of the flexible hoses at the front and rear wheel. When connecting a tube to a hose, tube connector, or brake cylinder, tighten the pipe fitting to the specification given in the procedure you are performing. If no specifications are given, tighten the pipe fitting to 12-14 ft. lbs. (16-20 Nm).

All models utilize the brake tubes with ISO flares and metric tube nuts at the master cylinder. These brake tubes are installed from the brake master cylinder to the left and right front brake hoses. The fittings at the master cylinder are either M10 or M12 metric tube nuts, where as the fitting at the front brake hoses are 3/8 in.-24 x 3/16 in. tube nuts, used with a double flare.

If a brake tube replacement is required from the brake master cylinder to the left or right front brake hose, the following procedure must be used.

1. Obtain the recommended bulk 3/16 in. steel tubing and correct standard 3/8 in.-24 x 3/16 in. tube nut. The M10 and M12 metric nuts will be reused.
2. Cut the tubing to the length required. Clean the burrs after cutting. The correct length may be obtained by measuring the removed tube using a string and adding 1/8 in. for each flare.
3. Place the removed metric tube nut on the tube. ISO flare one end of the tubing using the ISO and double flare tool kit D81L-2269-A or an equivalent.
4. On the opposite end of the replacement tube, install a standard 3/8 in.-24 x 3/16 in. tube nut and double flare tube end.

➡Be sure to follow the flaring instructions included in the ISO and double flare tool kit D81L-2269-A or equivalent.

5. Bend the replacement brake tube to match the removed tube using a suitable tube bender. When the replacement brake tube is installed, maintain adequate clearance to all moving or vibrating parts.

➡If a section of brake tubing becomes damaged, the entire section should be replaced with tubing of the same size, shape, length and material. Copper tubing should not be used in a hydraulic system. When bending the brake tubing to fit the body contours, be careful not to kink or crack the tubing.

All brake tubing should be flared properly to provide a good leakproof connection. Clean the brake tubing by flushing it with clean brake fluid before installation. When connecting a tube to a hose, tube connector or brake cylinder, tighten the tube fitting nut to specifications with a suitable torque wrench.

Always bleed the applicable primary or secondary brake system after the hose or line replacement

BRAKE HOSE

A flexible brake hose should be replaced if it shows signs of softening, cracking or other damage. When installing a new front brake hose, two new sealing washers should be used.

Positioning of the front hose is controlled by a self indexing brass block. When attaching the block to the caliper, tighten the bolt to 30-40 ft. lbs. (41-54 Nm). Attach the intermediate bracket to the shock strut and tighten the screw. Engage the opposite end of the hose to the bracket on the body. Install the horseshoe type retaining clip and connect tube to hose with tube nut. Inspect the position of the installed hose for clearance to the other chassis components.

Positioning of rear brake hose is controlled by self-indexing the end fittings. Engage either end of the hose to the bracket on the body. Install the horseshoe type retaining clip and connect the tube to the hose with the tube fitting nut. Engage the opposite end of the hose to the bracket on the rear spindle. Install the horseshoe type retaining clip and connect the tube to the hose with the tube fitting nut. Inspect the position of the installed hose for contact with other chassis parts.

Bleeding the Brake System

➧ **See Figures 14 and 15**

➡Vehicles equipped with Anti-lock Brake Systems (ABS) require separate bleeding procedures. If you are working on a 1994 or 1995 vehicle so equipped, refer to the procedure later in this section.

It is necessary to bleed the brake system of air whenever a hydraulic component, of the system, has been rebuilt or replaced, or if the brakes feel spongy during application.

Your car has a diagonally split brake system. Each side of this system must be bled as an individual system, and there is a correct bleeding sequence to be followed. First bleed the right rear brake, second, bleed the left front brake, then follow with the left rear brake and lastly, bleed the right front brake.

✱✱CAUTION

When bleeding the system(s) never allow the master cylinder to run completely out of brake fluid. Always use DOT 3 heavy duty brake fluid, or the equivalent. Never reuse brake fluid that has been drained from the system or that has been allowed to stand in an opened container for an extended period of time. If your car is equipped with power brakes, remove the reserve vacuum stored in the booster by pumping the pedal several times before bleeding.

1. Clean all dirt away from the master cylinder filler cap.
2. Start bleeding by filling the master cylinder reservoir to the MAX or FULL line with fresh brake fluid from a sealed container and keep it at least half full throughout the bleeding procedure.
3. Raise and support the car on jackstands. You may remove the wheel from the brake to be bled if this gives better access.
4. It is strongly recommended that any time bleeding is to be performed all wheels be bled rather than just one or two.

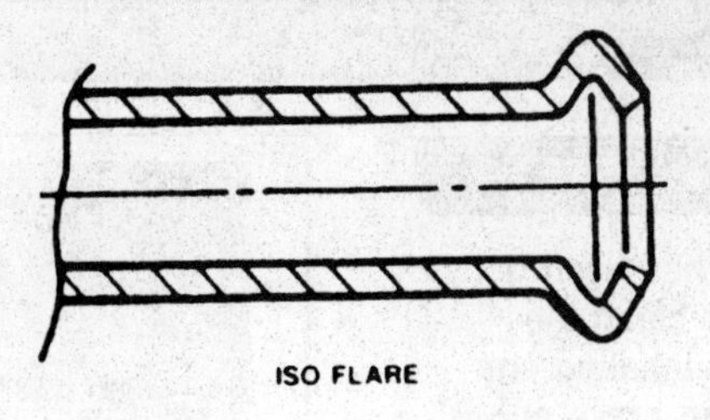

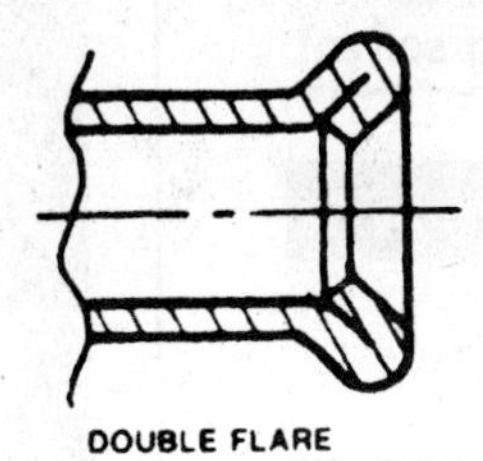

Fig. 13 Common ISO and double flared ends as found on hydraulic brake lines

5. Starting with the right rear wheel cylinder. Remove the dust cover from the bleeder screw. Place the proper size box wrench over the bleeder fitting and attach a piece of rubber tubing (about three feet long and snug) over the end of the fitting.
6. Submerge the free end of the rubber tube into a container half filled with clean brake fluid.
7. Have a friend pump up the brake pedal and then push down to apply the brakes while you loosen the bleeder screw. When the pedal reaches the bottom of its travel close the bleeder fitting before your friend releases the brake pedal.
8. Repeat Step 5 until air bubbles cease to appear in the container in which the tubing is submerged. Tighten the fitting, remove the rubber tubing and install the dust cover.
9. Repeat Steps 5 through 6 to the left front wheel, then to the left rear and right front.

➡Refill the master cylinder after each wheel cylinder or caliper is bled. Be sure the master cylinder top gasket is mounted correctly and the brake fluid level is within 1/4 in. (6mm) of the top.

10. After bleeding the brakes, pump the brake pedal several times, this ensures proper seating of the rear linings and the front caliper pistons.

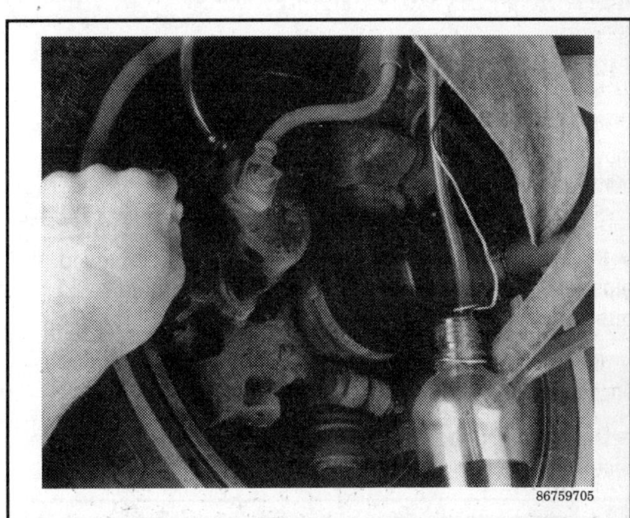

Fig. 14 Bleed the front caliper as shown — note the hanging plastic bottle of brake fluid

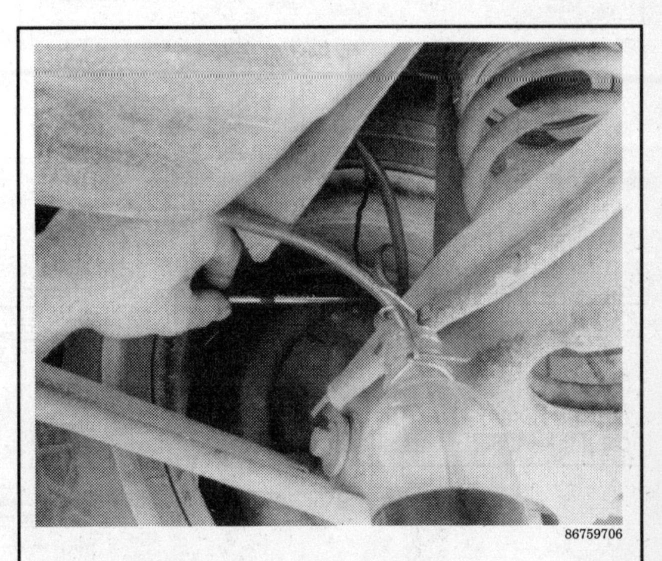

Fig. 15 Bleed the rear caliper as shown

FRONT DISC BRAKES

✲✲CAUTION

Brake shoes may contain asbestos, which has been determined to be a cancer causing agent. Never clean the brake surfaces with compressed air! Avoid inhaling any dust from any brake surface! When cleaning brake surfaces, use a commercially available brake cleaning solvent.

Brake Caliper

REMOVAL & INSTALLATION

1981-90 Models

See Figures 16, 17, 18, 19, 20, 21 and 22

1. Disconnect the negative battery cable.
2. Raise and safely support the vehicle.
3. Remove the wheel.
4. Disconnect the flexible brake hose from the caliper. Remove the hollow banjo bolt that connects hose fitting to caliper. Remove hose assembly from caliper and plug hose.
5. Remove the caliper locating pins using a Torx® T40 bit.

➡Do not remove the pins all the way. If fully removed, the pins are difficult to install and require new guide bushings.

6. Lift the caliper off the rotor and integral knuckle and anchor plate using a rotating motion.

➡Do not pry directly against plastic piston or damage to piston will occur.

86759707

Fig. 16 Remove the front wheel for access to the caliper — 1988 Escort shown

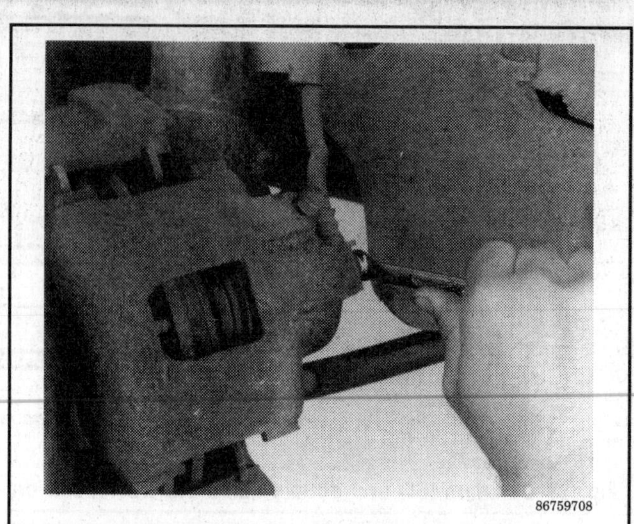

86759708

Fig. 17 Disconnect the flexible brake hose from the caliper

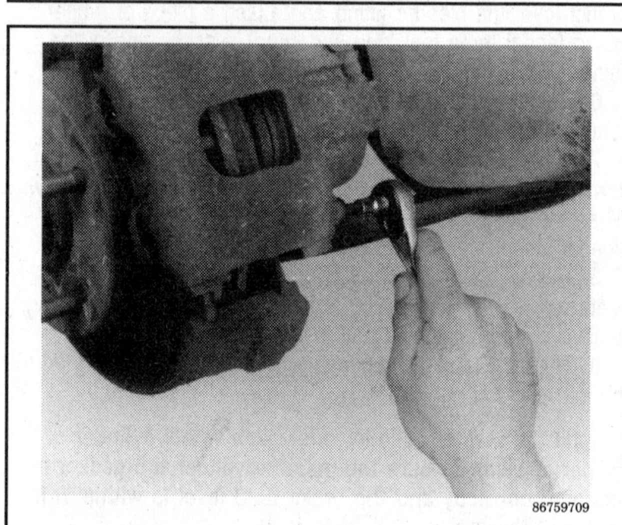

86759709

Fig. 18 Remove the caliper locating pins using the correct size and type of wrench

To install:

7. Position the caliper assembly above the rotor with the anti-rattle spring under the upper arm of the knuckle. Install the caliper over the rotor with a rotating motion. Ensure the inner shoe is properly positioned.

➡Ensure that the correct caliper assembly is installed on the correct knuckle. The caliper bleed screw should be positioned on top of the caliper when assembled on the vehicle.

8. Lubricate the locating pins and inside of insulators with silicone grease. Install the locating pins through the caliper insulators and into the knuckle attaching holes. The caliper

86759710

Fig. 19 Lift the caliper off the rotor and integral knuckle/anchor plate using a rotating motion

locating pins must be inserted and the threads started by hand.

CAUTION

Do not allow grease to come in contact with the braking surface or braking ability will be reduced and possible accident and personal injury may result.

9. Using the correct wrench and a Torx® T40 bit to tighten the caliper locating pins to 18-25 ft. lbs. (24-34 Nm).
10. Remove the plug or cap and install brake hose on caliper with a new gasket on each side of fitting outlet. Insert the attaching bolt through washers and fittings. Tighten bolts to 30-40 ft. lbs. (40-54 Nm).
11. Bleed the brake system. Always install the rubber bleed screw cap after bleeding.
12. Top off the master cylinder, as required.
13. Install the wheel(s). Tighten the wheel nuts to 80-105 ft. lbs. (109-142 Nm).
14. Connect negative battery cable.

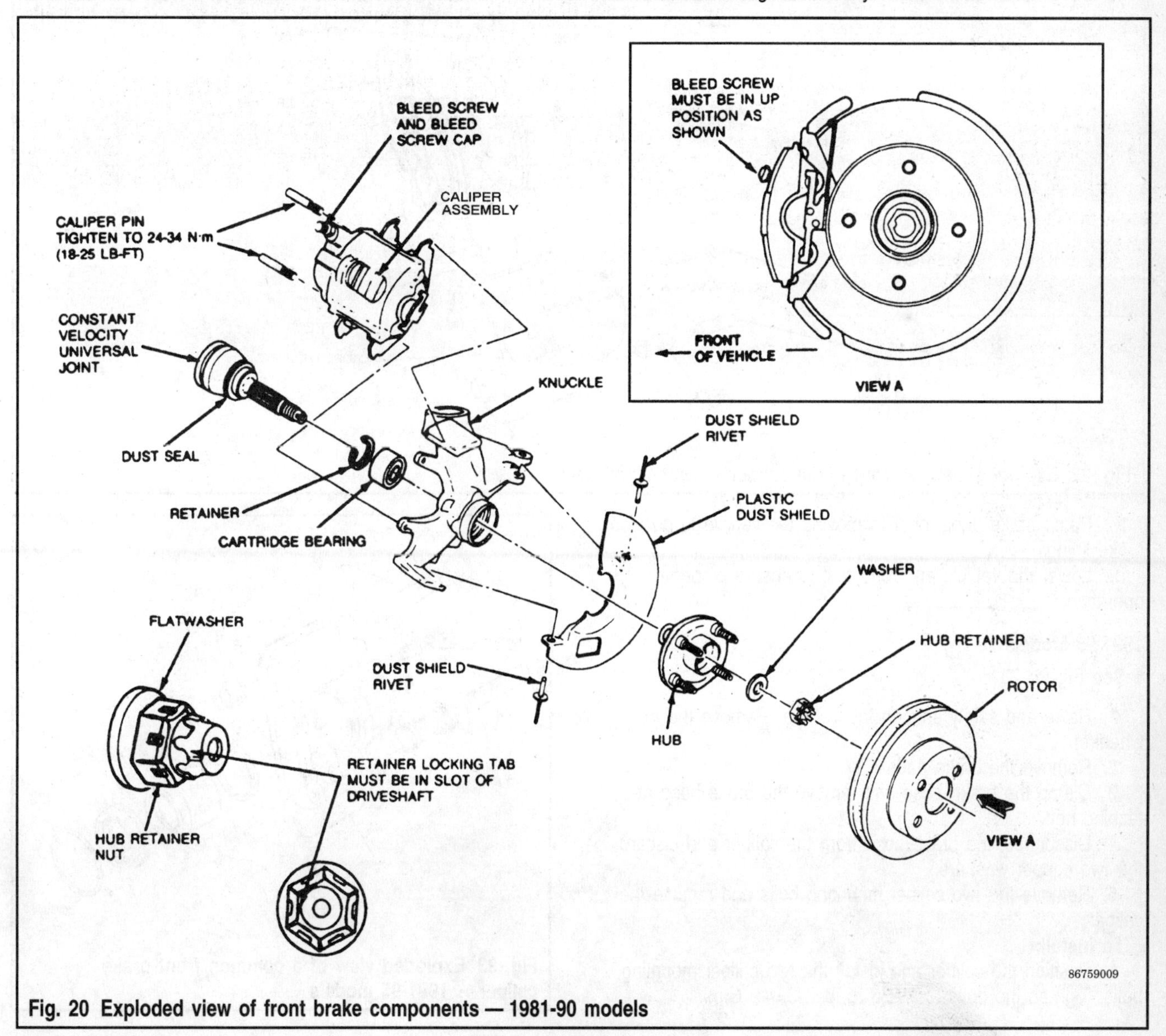

86759009

Fig. 20 Exploded view of front brake components — 1981-90 models

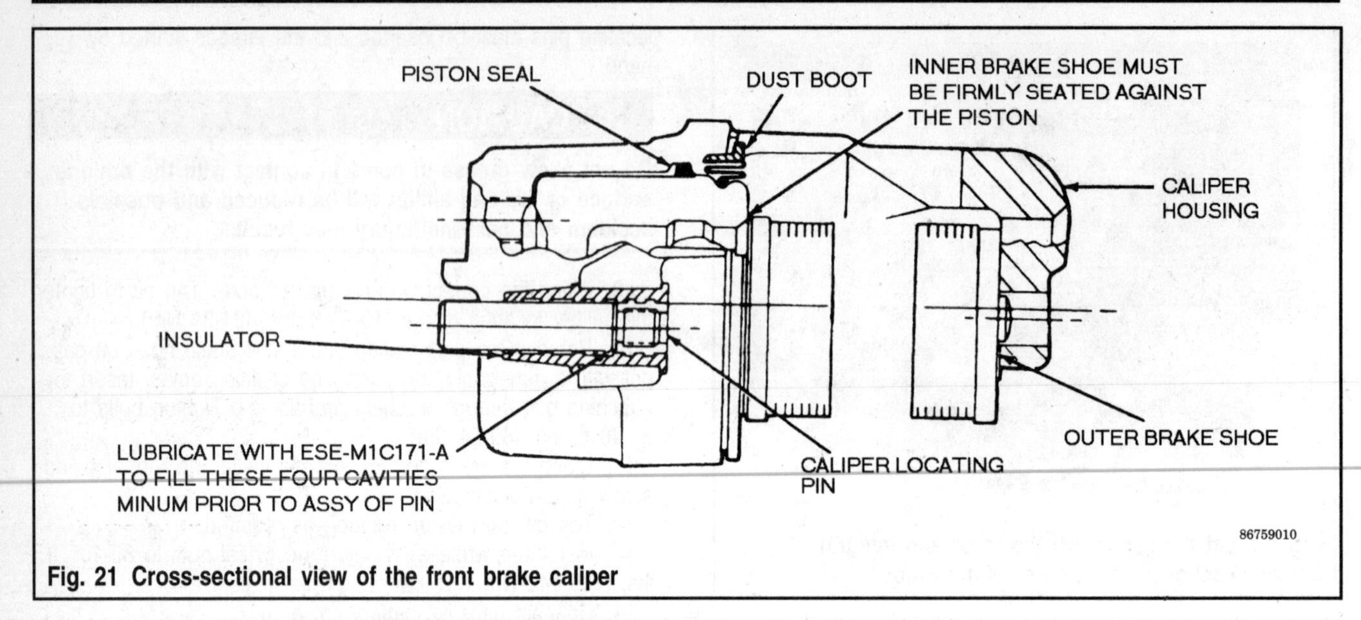

Fig. 21 Cross-sectional view of the front brake caliper

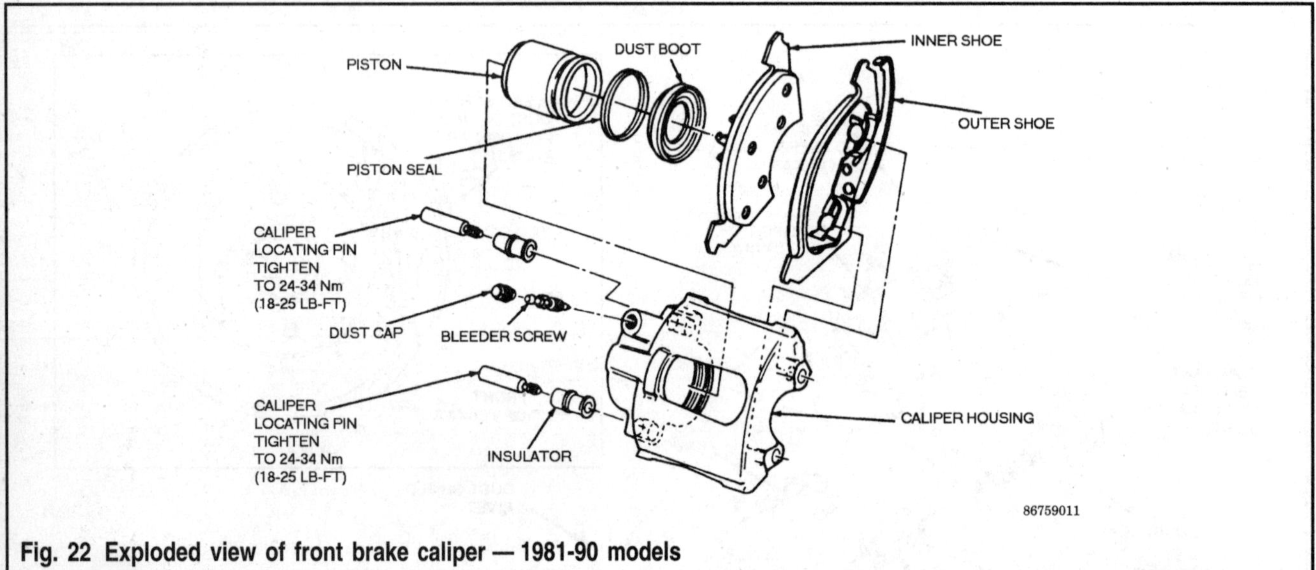

Fig. 22 Exploded view of front brake caliper — 1981-90 models

15. Pump brake pedal prior to moving the vehicle to position brake linings.
16. Lower the vehicle and road test to ensure proper operation.

1991-95 Models

➧ See Figure 23

1. Raise and safely support the vehicle. Remove the front wheel(s).
2. Remove the brake pads.
3. Clamp the brake hose and remove the brake hose attaching bolt.
4. Disconnect the brake hose from the caliper and discard the two copper washers.
5. Remove the two caliper mounting bolts and remove the caliper.

To install:

6. Position the caliper and install the two caliper mounting bolts. Tighten the bolts to 29-36 ft. lbs. (39-49 Nm).

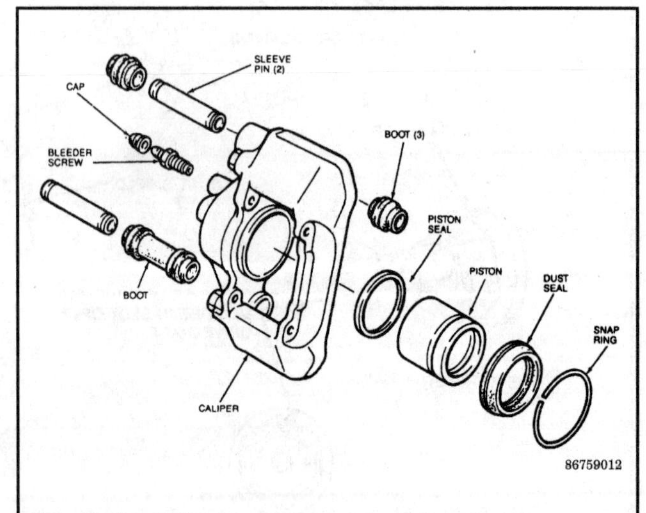

Fig. 23 Exploded view of a common front brake caliper — 1991-95 models

7. Install two new copper washers to the brake hose. Position the brake hose onto the caliper and install the attaching bolt. Tighten the bolt to 16-22 ft. lbs. (22-29 Nm).
8. Remove the clamp from the brake hose.
9. Install the brake pads.
10. Bleed the brake system.
11. Install the wheel(s).
12. Lower the vehicle and road test to ensure proper operation.

OVERHAUL

See Figures 24, 25, 26, 27, 28 and 29

This procedure calls for the use of compressed air and a rubber tipped air nozzle.

1. Remove the master cylinder cap and check the fluid level in the reservoir. Remove the brake fluid until reservoir is ½ full. Discard the removed fluid.
2. Raise and safely support the vehicle.
3. Remove the wheel(s).
4. Remove the brake caliper, then remove the pads.

The next step requires a controllable air source. If you have one fine, if not take the caliper(s) to your local service station and ask them to do this procedure for you.

5. For 1991-95 models, remove the snap ring and dust seal.
6. Place a folded cloth, shop rag, etc. over the caliper piston and place a wood block in the caliper to control the piston removal. Apply air pressure through the brake line fitting hole with a rubber tipped compressed air nozzle. The air pressure will force the caliper piston from its bore. If the piston is seized, tap lightly on the caliper with a plastic hammer while applying air pressure.

CAUTION

Apply air pressure slowly. Pressure can built up inside the caliper and the piston may come out with considerable force.

7. Remove the dust boot and piston seal from the caliper. Clean all parts with alcohol or clean brake fluid. Blow out the passage ways in the caliper. Check the condition of the caliper bore and piston. If they are pitted or scored or show excessive wear, replacement is necessary. Slight scoring in the caliper bore may be cleaned up by light honing. Replace the piston if it is scored.

To install:

8. Apply a coating of brake fluid to the new caliper piston seal and caliper bore. Some rebuilding kits provide a lubricant for this purpose. Install the seal in the caliper bore, make sure it is not twisted and that it is firmly seated in the groove.

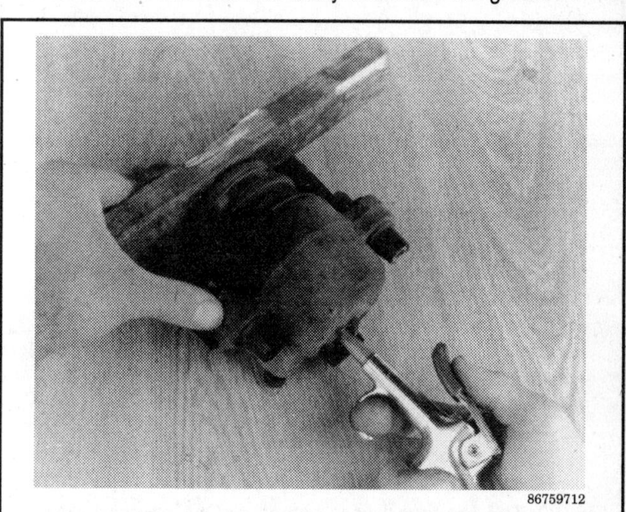

86759712

Fig. 25 Apply air pressure through the brake line fitting hole with a rubber tipped compressed air nozzle

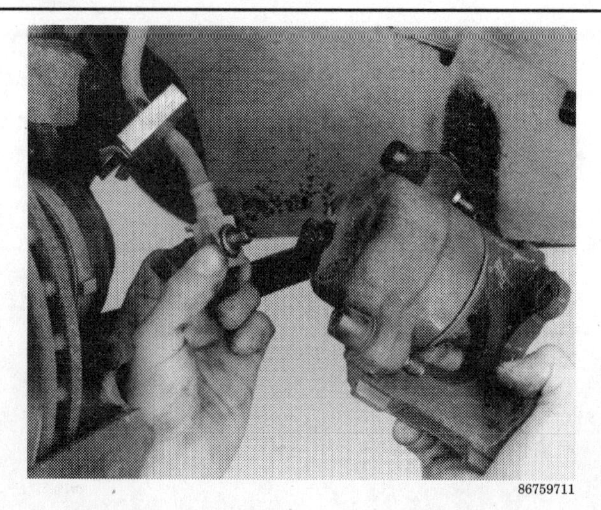

86759711

Fig. 24 Remove the caliper from the vehicle — note the special clamp to shut off fluid flow

86759713

Fig. 26 Pull out the piston from the caliper

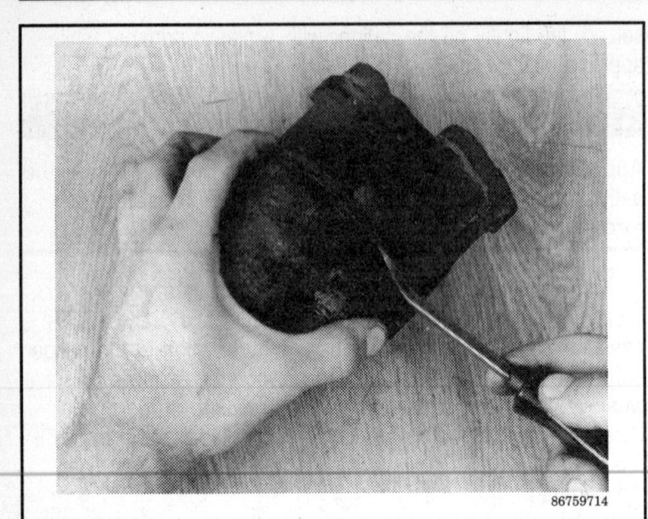

Fig. 27 Use a suitable prytool to remove the dust boot and piston seal from the caliper

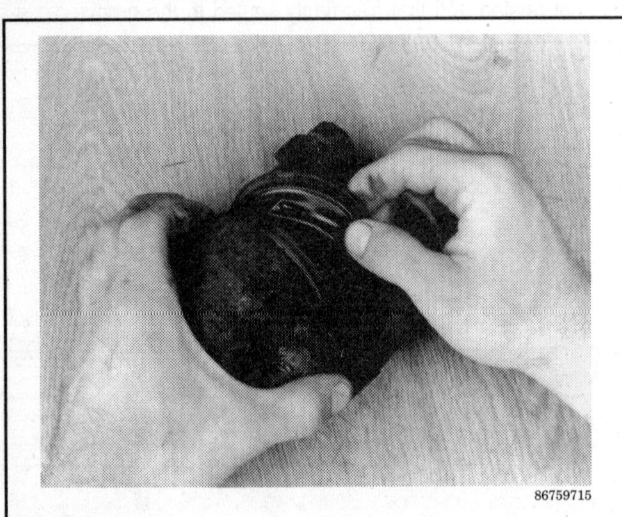

Fig. 28 The loosened seal comes out as shown — do not pry into the bore with sharp tools

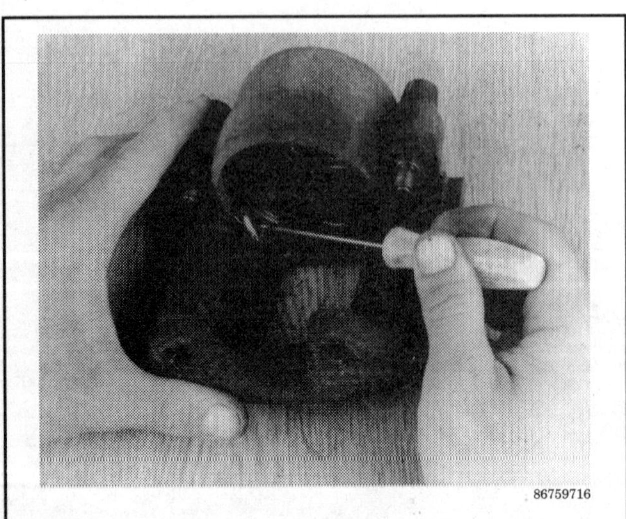

Fig. 29 With a thin prytool, carefully pull out the inner seal

9. Coat the piston with clean brake fluid, then install it in the caliper bore, make sure it is properly seated in the bottom of the caliper bore. Lubricate a new dust seal with clean brake fluid and seat it in the piston groove.
10. For 1991-95 models, install the snapring.
11. Install the bleeder screw and cap.
12. Install the brake pads/caliper.
13. Install the wheel(s) and lower the vehicle.

➡**Do not attempt to operate the vehicle until a firm brake pedal is achieved.**

14. Road test the vehicle.

Brake Pads

REMOVAL & INSTALLATION

1981-90 Models

➧ **See Figures 30 and 31**

1. Remove the master cylinder cap and check fluid level in reservoir. Remove the brake fluid until reservoir is ½ full. Discard the removed fluid.
2. Raise and safely support the vehicle.
3. Remove the front wheel(s).
4. Back out but do not remove caliper locating pins.

➡**A large C-clamp may be used to force the piston back into the caliper prior to the pad removal.**

5. Lift the caliper assembly from the rotor/integral knuckle and anchor plate using a rotating motion. Do not pry directly against plastic piston or damage will occur.
6. Remove the outer brake pad.
7. Remove the inner brake pad.
8. Inspect both rotor braking surfaces. Minor scoring or buildup of lining material does not require machining or replacement of rotor. Sand any glaze from both rotor braking surfaces using garnet paper 100-A (medium grit) or aluminum oxide 150-J (medium).

Fig. 30 A large C-clamp may be used to force the piston back into the caliper prior to the pad removal

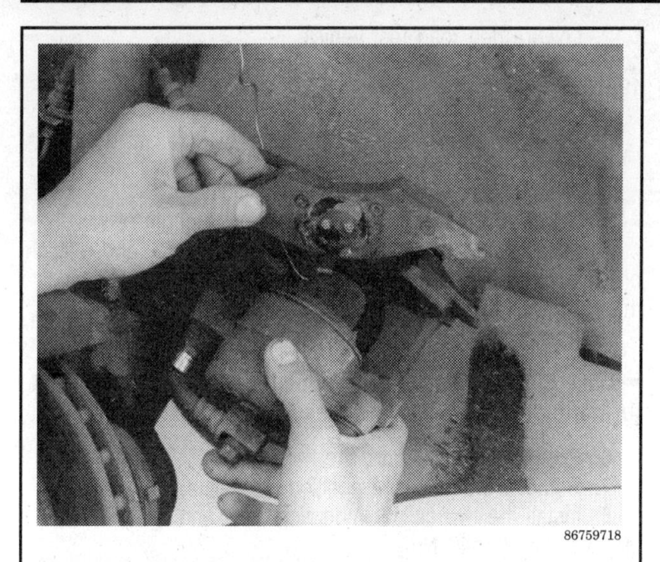

Fig. 31 Remove the inner and outer brake pads

9. Suspend the caliper inside fender housing with a sturdy length of wire. Use care not to damage caliper or stretch the brake hose.

To install:

➡Extra care must be taken during this procedure to prevent damage to the plastic piston. Metal or sharp objects cannot come into direct contact with the piston surface or damage will result.

10. Remove all rust buildup from inside of caliper legs where the outer shoe makes contact.
11. Install inner shoe and lining assembly in caliper piston(s). Do not bend shoe clips during installation in piston.
12. Install correct outer shoe and lining assembly. Ensure clips are properly seated.
13. Install caliper over rotor.
14. Install the wheel(s). Tighten the wheel nuts to 80-105 ft. lbs. (109-142 Nm).
15. Lower the vehicle.
16. Pump the brake pedal prior to moving the vehicle to position the brake linings. Check the fluid level in the master cylinder.
17. Connect the negative battery cable.
18. Road test to ensure correct operation.

1991-95 Models

1. Remove the master cylinder cap and check the fluid level in reservoir. Remove brake fluid until the reservoir is 1/2 full. Discard the removed fluid.
2. Raise and safely support the vehicle.
3. Remove the front wheel(s).
4. Remove the two brake pad pins, then remove the M-spring and the W-spring.
5. Remove the brake pads and shims from the caliper.

To install:

6. Use a large C-clamp to push the piston into the caliper bore.
7. Apply brake caliper grease between the shims and the brake pad guide plates and position the brake pads and shims into the caliper.

****CAUTION**

Do not allow grease to come in contact with the braking surface or braking ability will be reduced and possible accident and personal injury may result.

8. Install the W-spring and the M-spring. Install the two brake pad pins.
9. Install the wheel(s) and lower the vehicle.
10. Pump brake pedal prior to moving vehicle to position brake linings. Check the fluid level in the master cylinder.
11. Road test to ensure correct operation.

INSPECTION

1. Loosen the front wheel lugs slightly, then raise the front of the car and safely support it on jackstands.
2. Remove the front wheel(s).
3. The cut out in the top of the front brake caliper allows visual inspection of the disc brake pad. If the lining is worn to within 3mm (1/8 in.) of the metal disc shoe (check local inspection requirements) replace all four pads (both sides).
4. While you are inspecting the brake pads, visually inspect the caliper for hydraulic fluid leaks. If a leak is visible the caliper will have to be rebuilt or replaced.

Front Brake Disc (Rotor)

REMOVAL & INSTALLATION

1981-90 Models

➧ See Figure 32

1. Raise and safely support the vehicle.
2. Remove the wheel(s).
3. Using a the correct wrench and Torx® T40 bit, unthread, but do not slide all the way out the caliper locating pins.
4. Lift the caliper assembly from the rotor/integral knuckle and anchor plate using a rotating motion. Do not pry directly against plastic piston or damage will occur.
5. Position the caliper aside and support it with a length of wire to avoid damage to the line or fitting.
6. Remove the rotor from hub assembly by pulling it off the hub studs. Inspect the rotor and refinish or replace, as necessary. If refinishing, check the minimum thickness specification.

To install:

7. If the rotor is being replaced, remove protective coating from new rotor with carburetor degreaser. If original rotor is being installed, make sure rotor braking and mounting surfaces are clean.
8. Install the rotor on the hub assembly.
9. Install the caliper assembly on the rotor.
10. Install the wheel(s). Tighten the wheel nuts to 80-105 ft. lbs. (109-142 Nm).

86759719

Fig. 32 Remove the rotor from hub assembly by pulling it off the hub studs

11. Pump the brake pedal prior to moving vehicle to position brake linings.
12. Lower, then road test vehicle.

1991-95 Models

1. Raise and safely support the vehicle.
2. Remove the front wheel(s).
3. Remove the two caliper mounting bolts.
4. Secure the caliper aside with a sturdy length of wire.
5. Pull the rotor from the hub. Inspect the rotor and refinish or replace, as necessary. If refinishing, check the minimum thickness specification.

To install:

➡Make sure to use a non-residue, brake cleaning solvent to thoroughly degrease the brake rotor surface.

6. Position the rotor onto the hub.
7. Remove the wire and position the caliper.
8. Install the two caliper mounting bolts and tighten to 29-36 ft. lbs. (39-49 Nm).
9. Install the wheel(s) and lower the vehicle.
10. Pump the brake pedal prior to moving vehicle to position brake linings.
11. Road test vehicle.

REAR DRUM BRAKES

✻✻CAUTION

Brake shoes may contain asbestos, which has been determined to be a cancer causing agent. Never clean the brake surfaces with compressed air! Avoid inhaling any dust from any brake surface! When cleaning brake surfaces, use a commercially available brake cleaning solvent.

Brake Drums

REMOVAL & INSTALLATION

1981-90 Models

➧ See Figures 33, 34, 35, 36 and 37

1. Raise and safely support the vehicle.
2. Remove the rear wheel(s).
3. With a small prytool, remove the grease cap from the hub. Remove the cotter pin with needle nose pliers, then remove the nut and keyed flat washer from the spindle. Remove the outer bearing.
4. Remove the hub and drum assembly as a unit.

➡If the hub/drum assembly will not come off, pry the rubber plug from the backing plate inspection hole. On vehicles with 7 in. brakes, insert a long, thin prytool in the hole until it contacts the adjuster assembly pivot. Apply side pressure on this pivot point to allow the adjuster quadrant to ratchet and release the brake adjustment. On vehicles with 8 in. brakes, remove the brake line-to-axle retention bracket. This will allow sufficient room for insertion of a long thin screwdriver to disengage the adjuster lever and back-off the adjusting screw.

86759720

Fig. 33 With a small prytool, carefully remove the grease cap from the hub — 1988 Escort shown

5. Inspect the brake drum and refinish or replace, as necessary. If refinishing, check the maximum inside diameter specification.

To install:

6. Inspect and lubricate bearings, as necessary. Replace grease seal if any damage is visible.
7. Clean spindle stem and apply a thin coat of wheel bearing grease.
8. Install the hub and drum assembly on spindle.
9. Install the outer bearing into hub on spindle.
10. Install the keyed flat washer and adjusting nut. Finger tighten the nut.
11. Adjust the wheel bearing (refer to Section 8). Install the nut retainer and a new cotter pin.
12. Install the grease cap.

Fig. 34 Remove the cotter pin with needle nose pliers, then remove the nut and washer from the spindle

Fig. 35 With the bearing assembly removed, carefully pull off the hub and drum assembly as a unit

13. Install the wheel(s). Tighten wheel nuts to 80-105 ft. lbs. (109-142 Nm).
14. Pump brake pedal prior to moving vehicle to position brake linings.
15. Road test the vehicle.

1991-95 Models

1. Raise and safely support the vehicle.
2. Remove the rear wheel(s).
3. Remove the spring nut or attaching screws, if necessary.
4. Pull the brake drum from the hub. Inspect the drum and refinish or replace, as necessary. If refinishing, check the maximum inside diameter specification.

To install:

5. Position the brake drum on the hub.
6. Install the outer bearing into hub on spindle.
7. Install the keyed flat washer and adjusting nut. Finger tighten the nut.
8. Adjust the wheel bearing (refer to Section 8). Install the nut retainer and a new cotter pin.
9. Install the grease cap.
10. Install the two drum attaching screws, if applicable.
11. Install the wheel(s) and lower the vehicle.

Brake Shoes

REMOVAL & INSTALLATION

1981-90 Models

7-INCH BRAKE SHOES

See Figure 38

1. Raise and safely support the vehicle.
2. Remove the rear wheel(s).
3. Remove the hub and drum assembly.
4. Remove the hold-down spring and pins.
5. Lift the brake shoe and adjuster assembly up and away from the anchor block and shoe guide. Do not damage the boots when rotating shoes off the wheel cylinder.
6. Remove the lower shoe-to-shoe spring from the leading and trailing shoe slots.
7. Hold the brake shoe/adjuster assembly, remove the leading shoe-to-adjuster strut retracting spring. This can be done by rotating shoe over adjuster quadrant until spring is slack and then disconnecting spring. The leading shoe should now be free.
8. Remove the trailing shoe-to-parking brake strut retracting spring by pivoting the strut downward until it disengages from the trailing shoe.
9. Disassemble the adjuster, if necessary, by pulling the quadrant away from the knurled pin in strut and rotating quadrant in either direction until its teeth are no longer meshed with the pin. Remove spring and slide quadrant out of slot. Do not overstress spring during disassembly.
10. Remove parking brake lever from trailing shoe and lining assembly by removing horeshoe retaining clip and spring washer, then lifting lever off pin on brake shoe.

To install:

11. Apply light coating of high temperature grease at points where brake shoes contact the backing plate.

****CAUTION**

Do not allow grease to come in contact with the braking surface or braking ability will be reduced and possible accident or personal injury may result.

12. Apply light uniform coating of multi-purpose lubricant to strut at contact surface between strut and adjuster quadrant.
13. Install adjuster quadrant pin into slot in strut and install adjuster spring. Pivot quadrant until it meshes with knurled pin in third and fourth notch of outboard end of quadrant.
14. Assemble parking brake lever to trailing shoe. Install spring washer and new horseshoe clip. Crimp clip until lever is securely fastened.
15. Install trailing shoe-to-parking brake strut retracting spring by attaching spring to slots in each part and pivoting strut into position to tension spring. Make sure the end of the spring with the hook that is parallel to the center line of the coils is

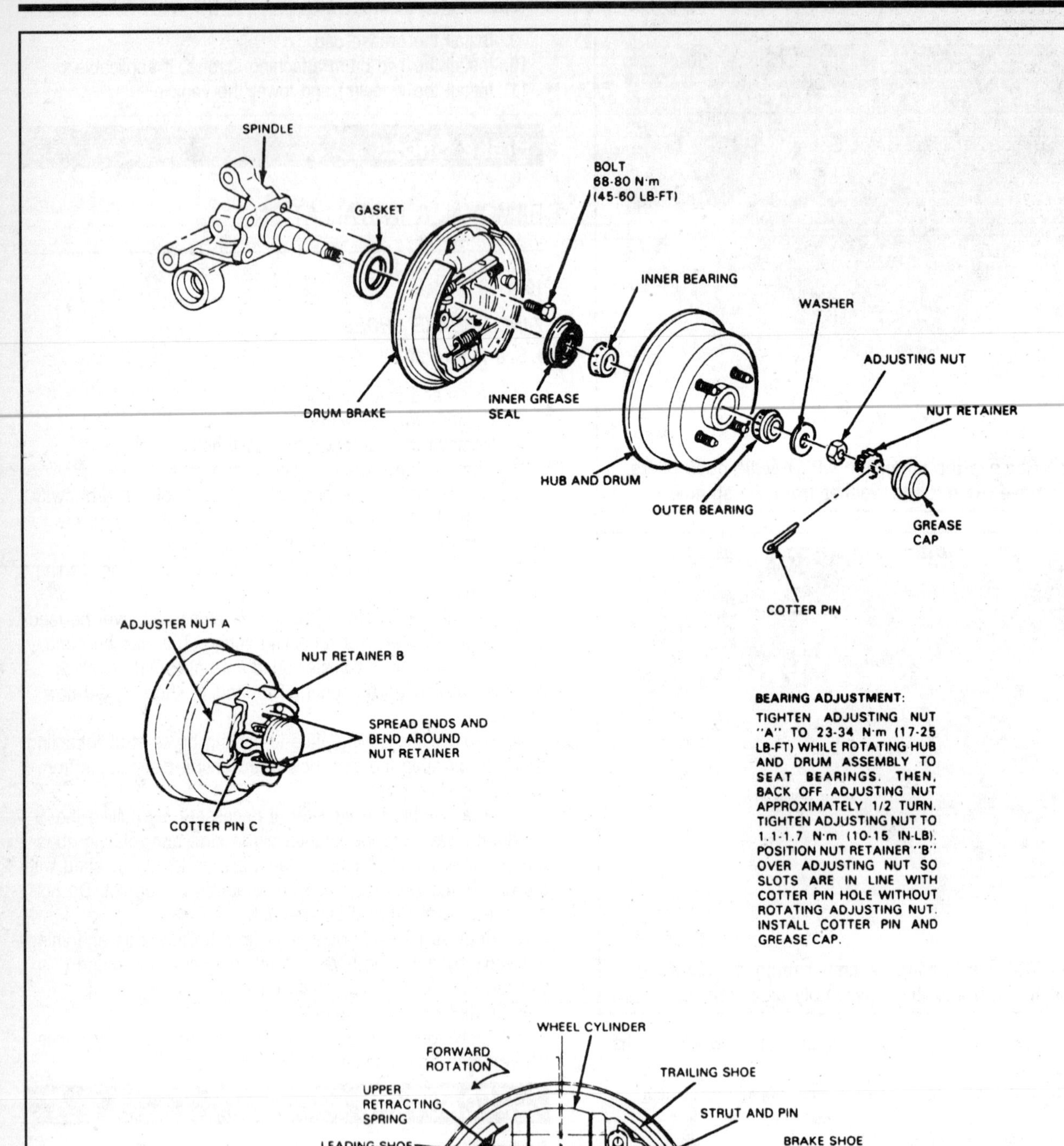
SPINDLE
BOLT
68-80 N·m
(45-60 LB-FT)
GASKET
INNER BEARING
WASHER
ADJUSTING NUT
INNER GREASE
SEAL
DRUM BRAKE
NUT RETAINER
HUB AND DRUM
OUTER BEARING
GREASE
CAP
COTTER PIN
ADJUSTER NUT A
NUT RETAINER B
SPREAD ENDS AND
BEND AROUND
NUT RETAINER
COTTER PIN C
BEARING ADJUSTMENT:
TIGHTEN ADJUSTING NUT "A" TO 23-34 N·m (17-25 LB-FT) WHILE ROTATING HUB AND DRUM ASSEMBLY TO SEAT BEARINGS. THEN, BACK OFF ADJUSTING NUT APPROXIMATELY 1/2 TURN. TIGHTEN ADJUSTING NUT TO 1.1-1.7 N·m (10-15 IN-LB). POSITION NUT RETAINER "B" OVER ADJUSTING NUT SO SLOTS ARE IN LINE WITH COTTER PIN HOLE WITHOUT ROTATING ADJUSTING NUT. INSTALL COTTER PIN AND GREASE CAP.

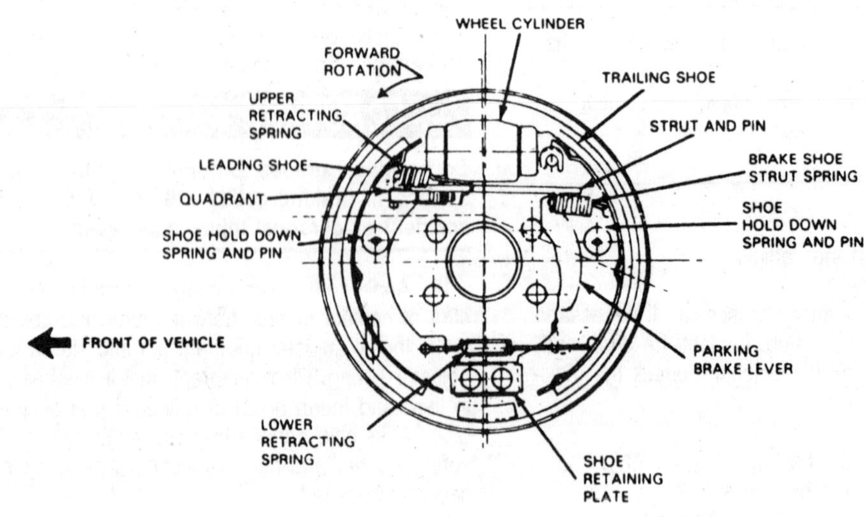
WHEEL CYLINDER
FORWARD
ROTATION
TRAILING SHOE
UPPER
RETRACTING
SPRING
STRUT AND PIN
LEADING SHOE
BRAKE SHOE
STRUT SPRING
QUADRANT
SHOE
HOLD DOWN
SPRING AND PIN
SHOE HOLD DOWN
SPRING AND PIN
FRONT OF VEHICLE
PARKING
BRAKE LEVER
LOWER
RETRACTING
SPRING
SHOE
RETAINING
PLATE
86759013

Fig. 36 Exploded view and cutaway of a rear 7 in. drum brake — 1981-90 models

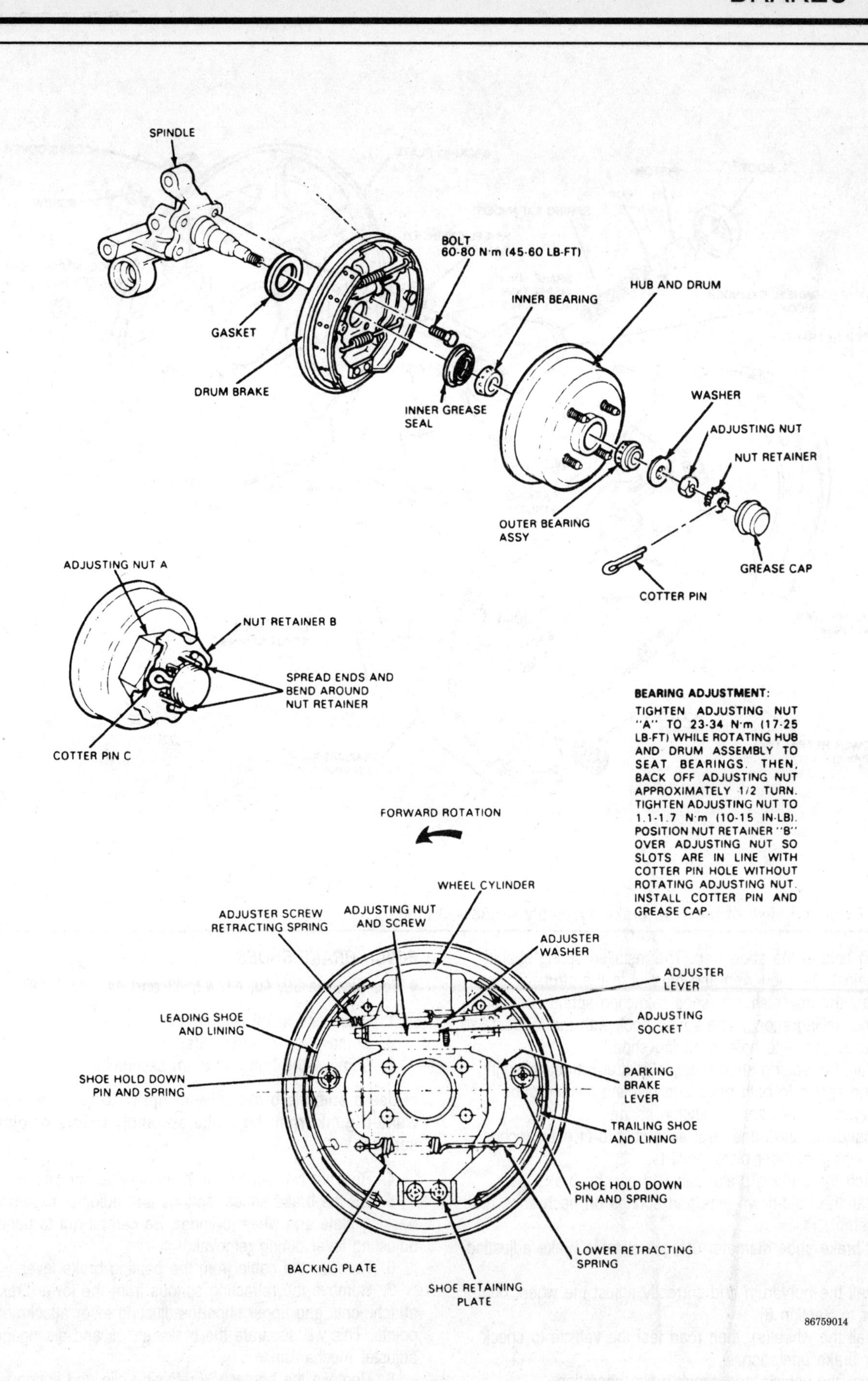
SPINDLE
BOLT
60-80 N·m (45-60 LB-FT)
HUB AND DRUM
INNER BEARING
GASKET
DRUM BRAKE
INNER GREASE
SEAL
WASHER
ADJUSTING NUT
NUT RETAINER
OUTER BEARING
ASSY
GREASE CAP
COTTER PIN
ADJUSTING NUT A
NUT RETAINER B
SPREAD ENDS AND
BEND AROUND
NUT RETAINER
COTTER PIN C
BEARING ADJUSTMENT:
TIGHTEN ADJUSTING NUT "A" TO 23-34 N·m (17-25 LB-FT) WHILE ROTATING HUB AND DRUM ASSEMBLY TO SEAT BEARINGS. THEN, BACK OFF ADJUSTING NUT APPROXIMATELY 1/2 TURN. TIGHTEN ADJUSTING NUT TO 1.1-1.7 N·m (10-15 IN-LB). POSITION NUT RETAINER "B" OVER ADJUSTING NUT SO SLOTS ARE IN LINE WITH COTTER PIN HOLE WITHOUT ROTATING ADJUSTING NUT. INSTALL COTTER PIN AND GREASE CAP.
FORWARD ROTATION
WHEEL CYLINDER
ADJUSTER SCREW
RETRACTING SPRING
ADJUSTING NUT
AND SCREW
ADJUSTER
WASHER
ADJUSTER
LEVER
ADJUSTING
SOCKET
LEADING SHOE
AND LINING
SHOE HOLD DOWN
PIN AND SPRING
PARKING
BRAKE
LEVER
TRAILING SHOE
AND LINING
SHOE HOLD DOWN
PIN AND SPRING
LOWER RETRACTING
SPRING
BACKING PLATE
SHOE RETAINING
PLATE
86759014

Fig. 37 Exploded view and cutaway of a rear 8 in. drum brake — 1981-90 models

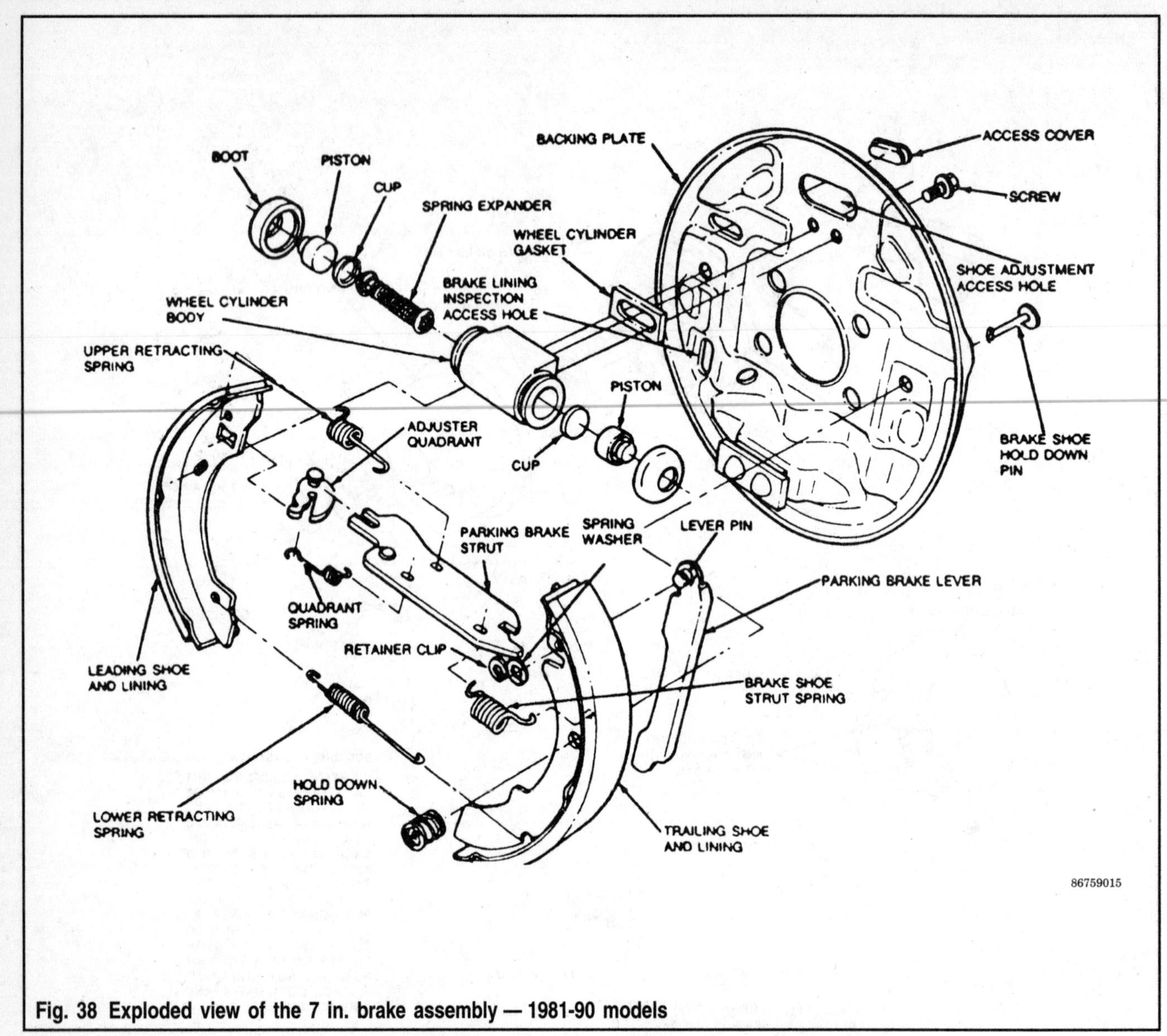

Fig. 38 Exploded view of the 7 in. brake assembly — 1981-90 models

installed in hole in the shoe web. The installed spring should be flat against the shoe web and parallel to the strut.

16. Install the lower shoe-to-shoe retracting spring between leading and trailing shoes. The spring hook with the longest straight section fits into hole in trailing shoe.
17. Install the leading shoe-to-adjuster/strut retracting spring by installing spring to both parts and pivoting leading shoe over quadrant into position to tension spring.
18. Expand the shoe and strut assembly to fit over anchor plate and wheel cylinder piston inserts.
19. Attach the parking brake cable to parking brake lever.
20. Install the hold-down pins and springs on each shoe and lining assembly.
21. Set brake shoe diameter using a suitable brake adjusting gauge.
22. Install the hub/drum and correctly adjust the wheel bearings (refer to Section 8).
23. Install the wheel(s), then road test the vehicle to check for proper brake operation.
24. Lower the vehicle and check brake operation.

8-INCH BRAKE SHOES

See Figures 39, 40, 41, 42, 43 and 44

1. Raise and safely support the vehicle.
2. Remove the rear wheel(s).
3. Remove the hub and drum assembly.

Use a suitable brake cleaner spray to remove any unwanted gunk from the brake assembly before or during service.

4. Remove two shoe hold-down springs and pins.
5. Lift the brake shoes, springs and adjuster assembly off backing plate and wheel cylinder. Be careful not to bend the adjusting lever during removal.
6. Remove the cable from the parking brake lever.
7. Remove the retracting springs from the lower brake shoe attachments and upper shoe-to-adjusting lever attachment points. This will separate the brake shoes and disengage the adjuster mechanism.
8. Remove the horseshoe retaining clip and spring washer, then slide the lever off the pin on the trailing shoe.

Fig. 39 Use a suitable brake cleaner spray to remove any unwanted gunk from the brake assembly

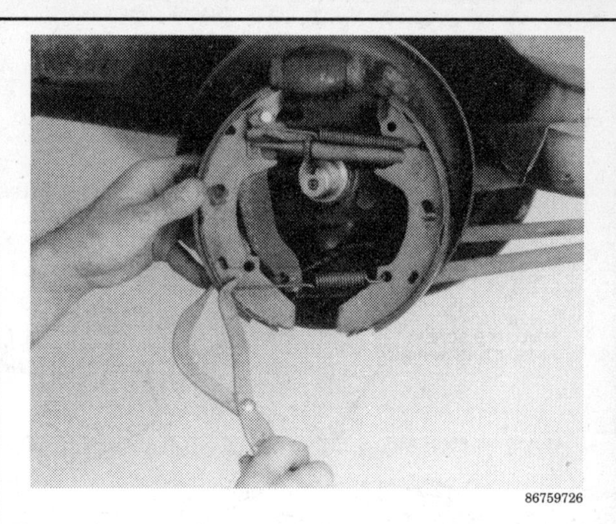

Fig. 42 Use a spring plier tool to remove the retracting springs from the brake shoe attachments

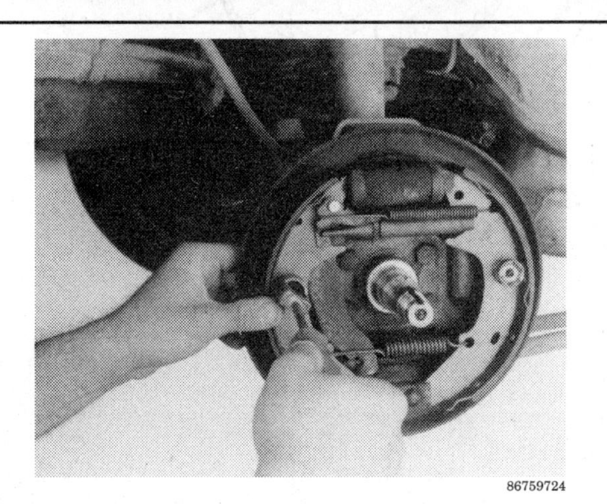

Fig. 40 Use the special removal tool that grips the diameter of the spring retainer to remove the hold-down springs

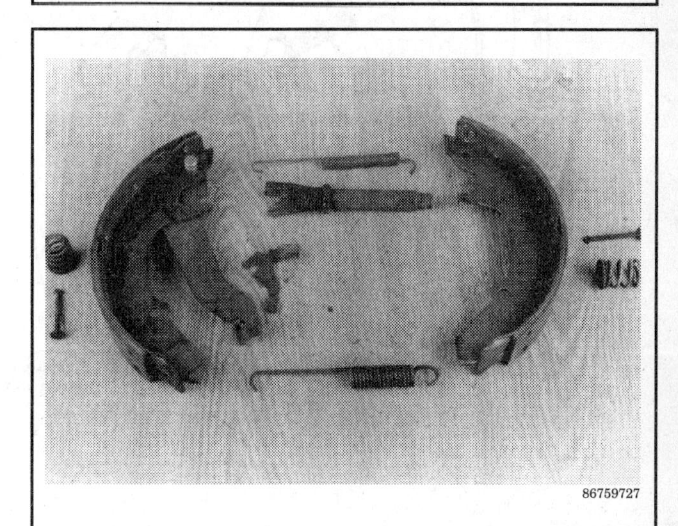

Fig. 43 As you remove the components, display then to remind yourself of their proper positions for installation

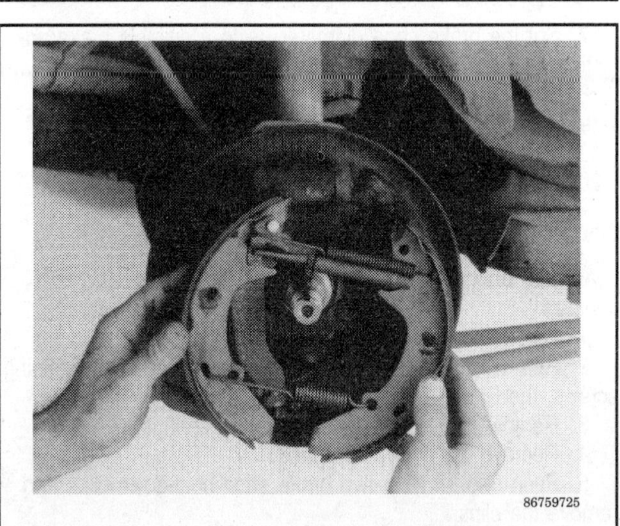

Fig. 41 Be careful not to bend the adjusting lever when you are removing the assembly

To install:

9. Apply a light coating of high temperature grease at the points where the brake shoes contact the backing plate.
10. Apply a light coating of lubricant to the adjuster screw threads and the socket end of the adjusting screw. Install the stainless steel washer over the socket end of the adjusting screw and install the socket. Turn the adjusting screw into the adjusting pivot nut to the limit of the threads and then back-off $^{1}/_{2}$ turn.
11. Assemble the parking brake lever to the trailing shoe by installing the spring washer and a new horseshoe retaining clip. Crimp the clip until it retains the lever to the shoe securely.
12. Attach the cable to the parking brake lever.
13. Attach the lower shoe retracting spring to the leading and trailing shoes and install them to the backing plate. It will be necessary to stretch the retracting spring (as the shoes are installed) downward over the anchor plate to the inside of shoe retaining plate.

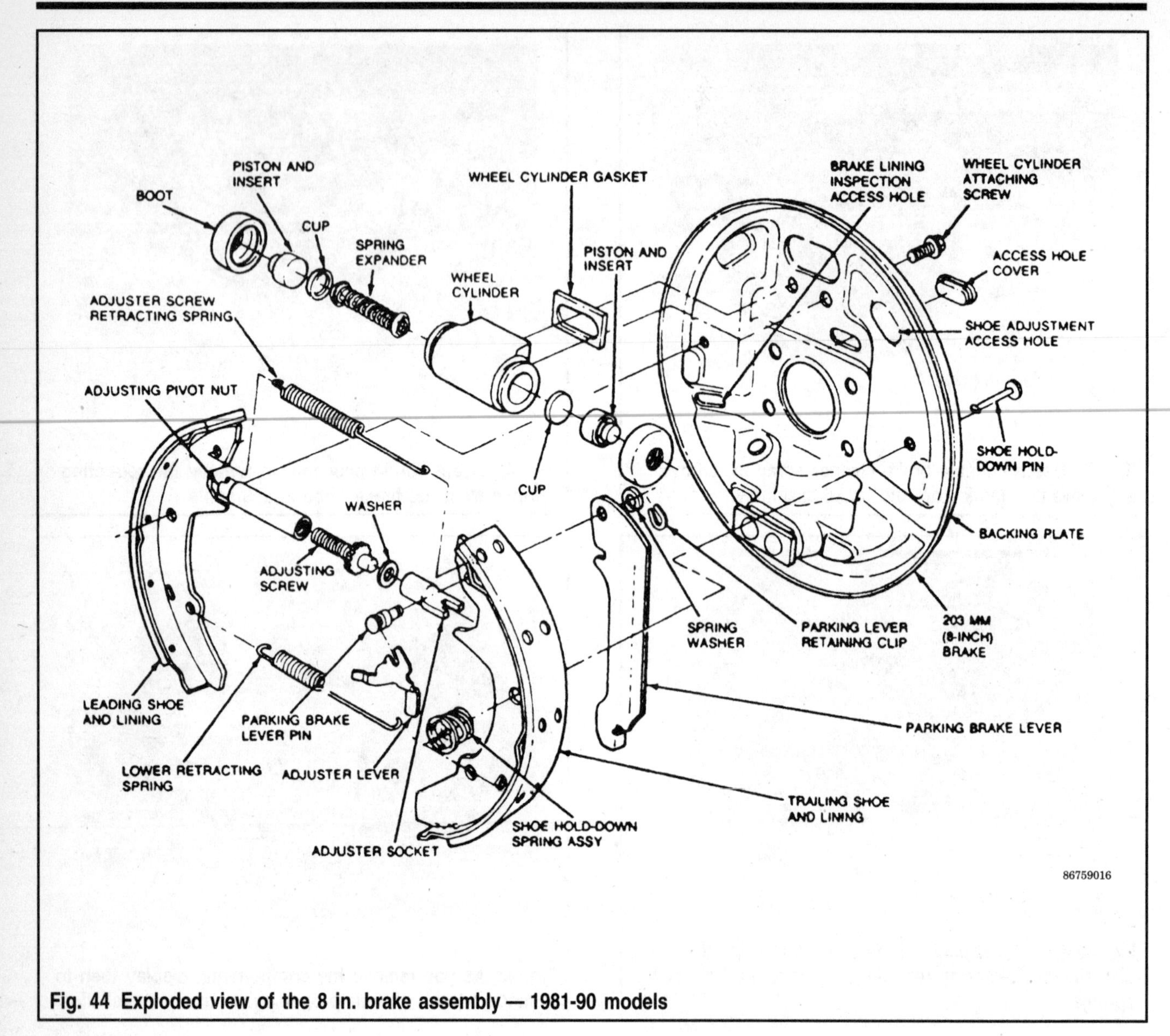

Fig. 44 Exploded view of the 8 in. brake assembly — 1981-90 models

14. Install the adjuster screw assembly between the leading shoe slot and the slot in the trailing shoe and parking brake lever. The adjuster socket end slot must fit into the trailing shoe parking brake lever.

➡The adjuster socket blade is marked R or L for the right or left brake assemblies. The R or L adjuster blade must be installed with the letter R or L in the upright position, facing the wheel cylinder, on the correct side to ensure that the deeper of the two slots in the adjuster sockets fits into the parking brake lever.

15. Assemble the adjuster lever in the groove located in the parking brake lever pin and into the slot of the adjuster socket that fits into the trailing shoe web.
16. Attach the upper retracting spring to the leading shoe slot. Using a suitable spring tool, stretch the other end of the spring into the notch on the adjuster lever. If the adjuster lever does not contact the star wheel after installing the spring, it is possible that the adjuster socket is installed incorrectly.
17. Set the brake shoe diameter using a suitable brake adjusting gauge.
18. Install the hub/drum. Refer to Section 8 to adjust the wheel bearing(s).
19. Install the wheel(s).
20. Lower the vehicle and check brake operation.

1991-95 Models

An 8-in. brake drum assembly is utilized on the 1991-95 vehicles.

1. Raise and safely support the vehicle.
2. Remove the wheel, remove the two brake drum retaining screws, then remove the brake drum.
3. Remove the two brake shoe return springs.
4. Remove the anti-rattle spring.
5. Push and turn the two brake shoe hold-down clips and remove the clips.
6. Remove the leading and trailing shoes from the backing plate.

To install:

7. Use a suitable high temperature grease to lubricate the brake shoe contact points on the backing plate.

✱✱CAUTION

Do not allow grease to come in contact with the braking surface or braking ability will be reduced and possible accident or personal injury may result.

8. Position the trailing brake shoe on the backing plate and install one of the brake shoe hold-down clips.
9. Position the leading brake shoe on the backing plate and install the other brake shoe hold-down clip.
10. Install the anti-rattle spring.
11. Install the two brake shoe return springs.
12. Press the brake pedal to position the brake shoes.
13. Install the brake drum and the wheel(s). Lower the vehicle.

Wheel Cylinders

REMOVAL & INSTALLATION

1981-90 Models

See Figures 45, 46 and 47

1. Raise and safely support the vehicle. Remove the wheel(s), then the hub/drum assemblies.
2. Remove the brake shoe assembly.
3. Disconnect the brake tube from the wheel cylinder.
4. Remove the wheel cylinder attaching bolts and remove wheel cylinder.

➡Use caution to prevent brake fluid from contacting brake linings and drum braking surface. Contaminated linings must be replaced.

To install:

5. Ensure ends of hydraulic fittings are free of foreign matter before making connections.
6. Position wheel cylinder and foam seal on backing plate, then finger-tighten brake tube to cylinder.
7. Secure cylinder to backing plate by installing attaching bolts. Tighten bolts to 8-10 ft. lbs. (10-14 Nm).
8. Tighten the tube nut fitting.
9. Install and adjust the brakes.
10. Install the hub/drum assemblies and the wheel(s).
11. Bleed the brake system and lower the vehicle.
12. Road test the vehicle.

1991-95 Models

1. Raise and safely support the vehicle.
2. Remove the wheel, then remove the brake drum.
3. Remove the upper brake shoe return spring.
4. Clamp the wheel cylinder brake hose.
5. Using a suitable nut wrench, loosen the wheel cylinder-to-brake line flare nut.
6. Pull the clip from the brake hose bracket and remove the brake hose from the retaining bracket.
7. Disconnect the brake line from the wheel cylinder.

86759728

Fig. 45 A special clamp makes it a simple matter to prevent fluid leakage

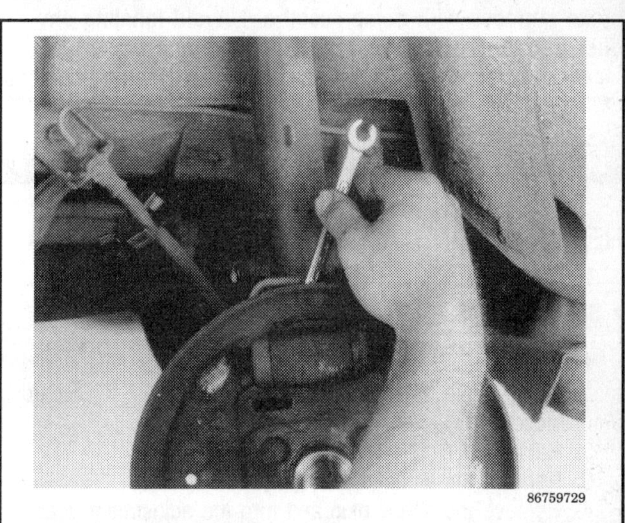

86759729

Fig. 46 Remove the line flange from the wheel cylinder using the correct wrench

86759730

Fig. 47 Remove the disconnected wheel cylinder from the vehicle

8. Remove the two wheel cylinder mounting bolts and remove the wheel cylinder from the backing plate.
9. Remove and discard the wheel cylinder gasket.

To install:

10. Install a new wheel cylinder gasket onto the backing plate.
11. Position the wheel cylinder onto the backing plate and install the two mounting bolts. Tighten the bolts to 89-115 inch lbs. (10-13 Nm).
12. Position the brake line into the wheel cylinder fitting and tighten the wheel cylinder-to-brake line flare nut to 12-16 ft. lbs. (16-22 Nm).
13. Position the brake hose into the retaining bracket and install the clip. Remove the clamp from the wheel cylinder brake hose.
14. Install the brake shoe return spring.
15. Install the brake drum and the wheel.
16. Press the brake pedal to verify the operation of the automatic brake adjuster.
17. Bleed the brake system and lower the vehicle.
18. Road test the vehicle.

REAR DISC BRAKES

CAUTION

Brake shoes may contain asbestos, which has been determined to be a cancer causing agent. Never clean the brake surfaces with compressed air! Avoid inhaling any dust from any brake surface! When cleaning brake surfaces, use a commercially available brake cleaning solvent.

Disc Brake Pads

REMOVAL & INSTALLATION

See Figure 48

1. Remove the master cylinder cap and check fluid level in reservoir. Remove brake fluid until reservoir is ½ full. Discard the removed fluid.
2. Raise and safely support the vehicle.
3. Remove the wheel(s).
4. Remove the screw plug and turn the adjustment gear counterclockwise with a hex wrench to pull the piston fully inward.
5. Remove the caliper lock bolt.
6. Using a suitable tool, pivot the caliper on its mounting bracket to access the brake pads. If the upper lock bolt requires lubrication or service, remove it and suspend the caliper with mechanics wire.
7. Remove the brake pads, shims, spring and guides.

To install:

8. Apply a high-temperature grease formulated for use between the shims and the brake pads.

CAUTION

Do not allow grease to come in contact with the braking surface or braking ability will be reduced and possible accident and personal injury may result.

9. Using a prytool, if necessary, pivot the caliper on its mounting bracket and position the brake pads, shims, spring and guides to the rotor.
10. Lubricate and install the lock bolt. Tighten the bolt to 33-43 ft. lbs. (45-59 Nm).
11. If necessary, turn the adjustment gear clockwise with an Allen wrench until the brake pads just touch the rotor, then loosen the gear ⅓ of a turn. Install the screw plug and tighten to 9-12 ft. lbs. (12-16 Nm).
12. Install the wheel(s) and lower the vehicle.
13. Pump brake pedal prior to moving vehicle to position brake linings. Check the fluid level in the master cylinder.
14. Road test the vehicle.

Brake Caliper

REMOVAL & INSTALLATION

See Figures 49 and 50

1. Raise and safely support the vehicle. Remove the wheel(s).
2. Remove the brake pads.
3. Remove the parking brake cable bracket bolt and position the bracket aside.
4. Disconnect the parking brake cable from the operating lever.
5. Clamp the brake hose, then disconnect the brake line attaching bolt and remove the two washers. Discard the washers.
6. Disconnect the brake line and slide the caliper off the mounting bracket.

To install:

7. Position the caliper on the mounting bracket.
8. Install two new washers to the brake line. Position the brake line to the caliper and install the attaching bolt. Tighten the bolt to 16-22 ft. lbs. (22-29 Nm).
9. Remove the clamp from the brake hose.
10. Attach the parking brake cable to the operating lever, then position the bracket and install the bracket bolt.
11. Install the brake pads.
12. Bleed the brake system.
13. Install the wheel(s) and lower the vehicle.

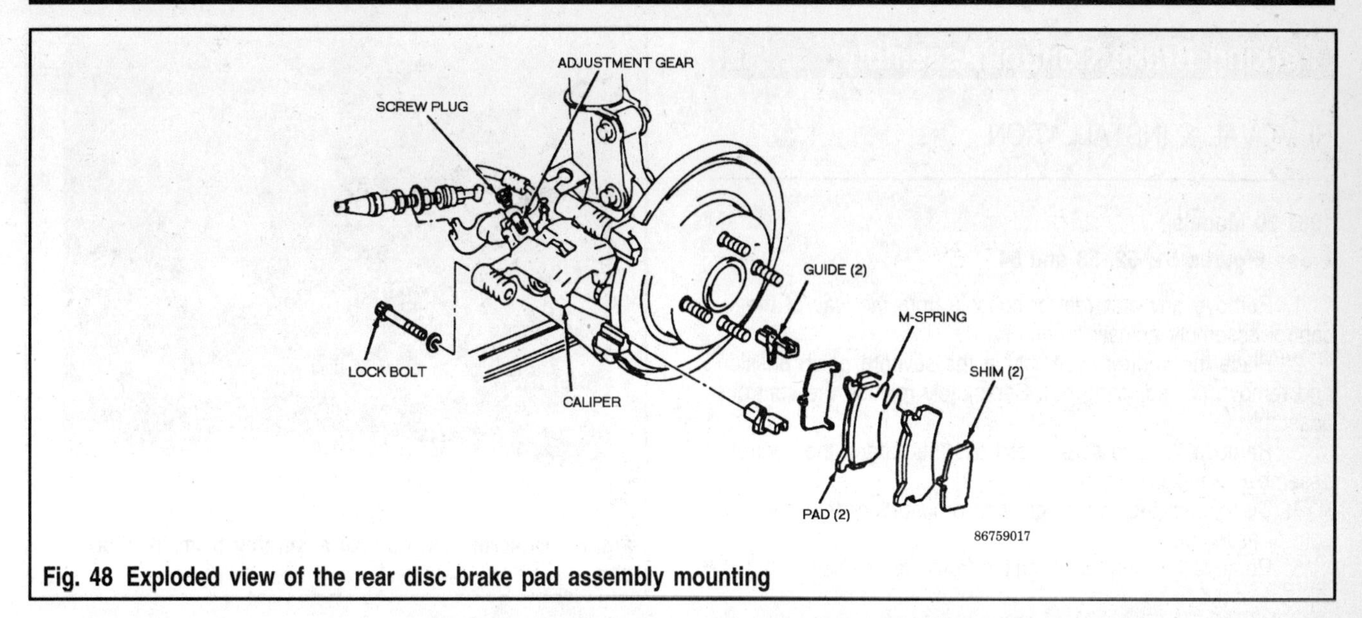

Fig. 48 Exploded view of the rear disc brake pad assembly mounting

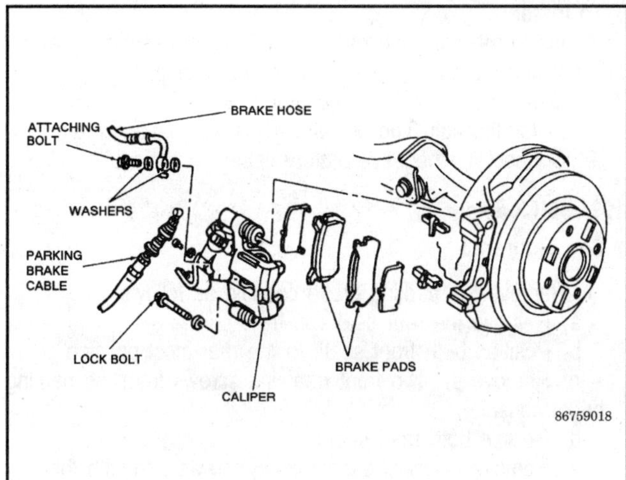

Fig. 49 Exploded view of the rear disc brake caliper and pad assemblies

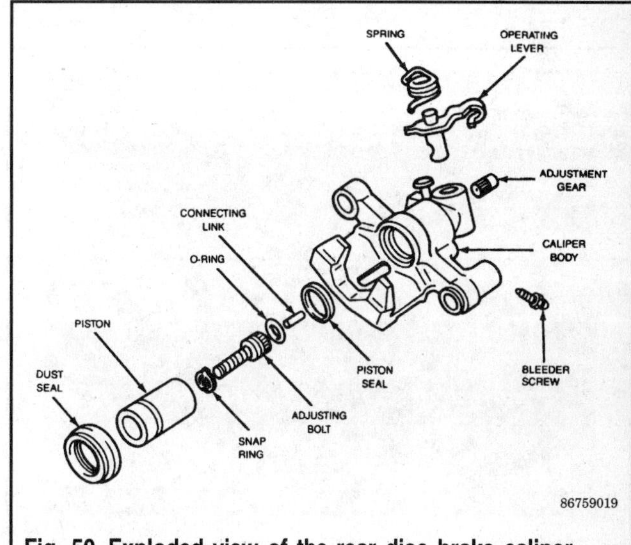

Fig. 50 Exploded view of the rear disc brake caliper

Brake Rotor

REMOVAL & INSTALLATION

1. Raise and safely support the vehicle.
2. Remove the wheel(s).
3. Remove the brake pads.
4. Remove the two rotor mounting screws.
5. Using a suitable tool, pivot the caliper on its mounting bracket and remove the rotor. Inspect the rotor and refinish or replace, as necessary. If refinishing, check the minimum thickness specification.

To install:

6. Using a prytool, pivot the caliper on its mounting bracket and position the rotor.
7. Install the two mounting screws.
8. Install the brake pads.
9. Install the wheel(s), lower the vehicle.
10. Pump the brakes to seat the pads.

PARKING BRAKE

The parking brake control is hand operated and mounted on the floor between the front seats. When the control lever is pulled up (from the floor) an attached cable applies the rear brakes.

Parking Brake Control Assembly

REMOVAL & INSTALLATION

1981-90 Models

➧ See Figures 51, 52, 53 and 54

1. Remove any arm rest or console from the way of the control assembly adjusting nut.
2. Place the control assembly in the seventh notch position and remove the adjusting nut. Completely release the control assembly.
3. Remove the two screws or bolts that attach the control assembly to the floor pan.
4. Disconnect the brake light and ground wire from the control assembly.
5. Remove the control assembly from the vehicle.

86759731

Fig. 51 Remove the arm rest if it obstructs the adjuster mechanism

86759732

Fig. 52 Place the control assembly in the seventh notch position and remove the adjusting nut. Completely release the control assembly

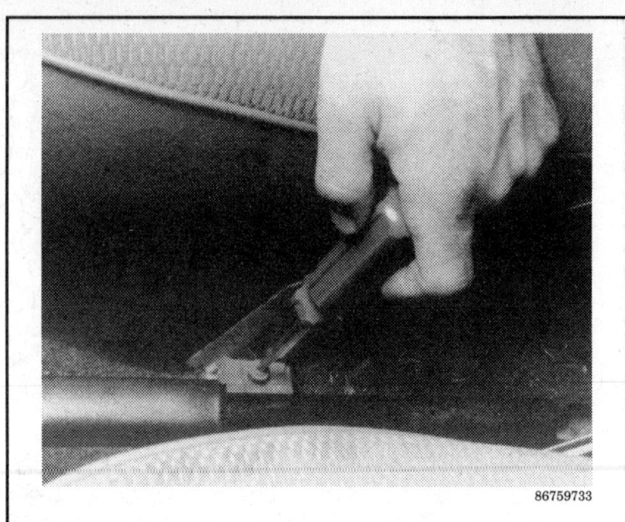

86759733

Fig. 53 Unscrew the control assembly from the floor pan

To install:

6. Install the adjusting rod into the control assembly clevis and position the control assembly on the floor pan.
7. Install the brake light and ground wire.
8. Install the adjusting nut and adjust the parking brake.
9. Connect the negative battery cable.

1991-95 Models

➧ See Figure 55

1. Remove the parking brake console as follows:
   a. Remove the rear seat ash tray.
   b. Position both front seats to the rear-most position.
   c. Remove the two front retaining screws from the parking brake console.
   d. Recline both front seats.
   e. Remove the two rear retaining screws and with the parking brake engaged, remove the parking brake console.
2. Disengage the warning light switch electrical connector.
3. Remove the adjusting nut.
4. Remove the two mounting bolts and remove the control lever.

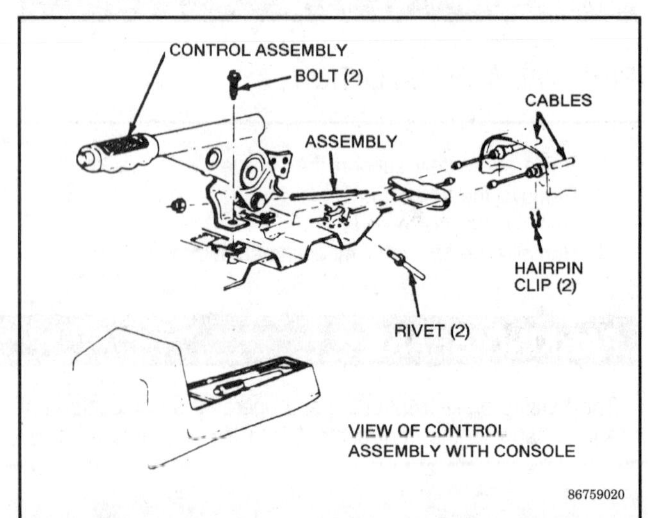

86759020

Fig. 54 Exploded view of the parking brake assembly — 1981-90 models

5. Pull the front parking brake cable and conduit out of the cable guide.

To install:

6. Install the parking cable into the cable guide.
7. Place the control lever into position and install the mounting bolts.
8. Install the adjusting nut.
9. Connect the warning light switch electrical connector.
10. Adjust the parking brake.
11. Install the parking brake console.
12. Connect the negative battery cable.

Cables

REMOVAL & INSTALLATION

1981-85 Models

➧ See Figures 56 and 57

1. Pull up slowly on the control lever and stop at the seventh notch position, count the clicks as you pull up on the handle. The adjusting nut is now accessible. Remove the adjusting nut. Completely release the control handle (push the release button and lower the lever to the floor.
2. Raise the car and safely support on jackstands.
3. Disconnect the parking brake cables from the front equalizer and rod assembly.
4. If the front equalizer and rod assembly is to be replaced, drill out the rivets that hold the cable guide to the floor pan. Remove the equalizer and rod assembly from the brake control lever and withdraw it through the floor pan.
5. To install the front equalizer and rod assembly, feed the adjusting rod end of the assembly through the floor pan and into the parking control lever clevis. Attach the cable guide to the floor pan using new pop rivets. If necessary, borrow a pop rivet gun from a friend.
6. If the rear parking brake cable is to be replaced, perform the following
   a. Disconnect it from the front equalizer and rod assembly.

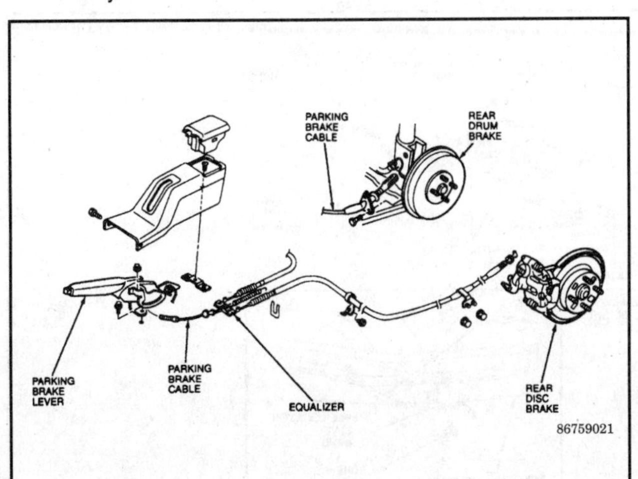

Fig. 55 Exploded view of the parking brake assembly — 1991-95 models

Fig. 56 Disconnect the parking brake cable from the trailing shoe parking brake levers

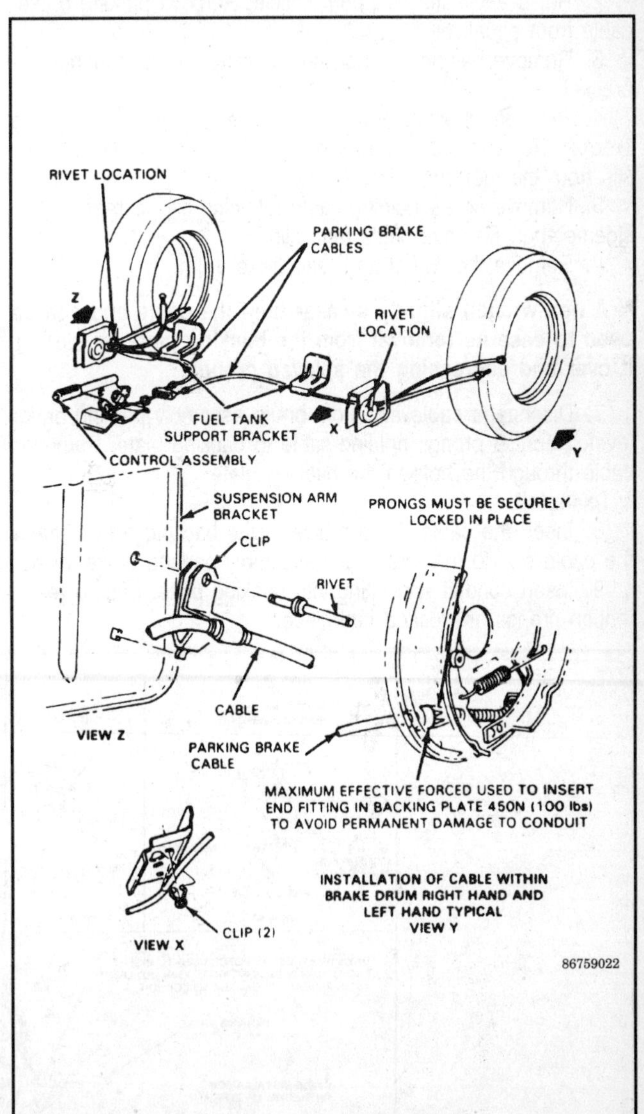

Fig. 57 Common parking brake cable routing along with specialized brackets and hardware — 1981-85 models

b. Remove the hairpin clip that holds the cable to the floor pan tunnel bracket.

7. Remove the wire retainer that holds the cable to the fuel tank mounting bracket.

8. Remove the cable from the retaining clip.

9. Remove the rear tire and wheel assemblies and the brake drums.

10. Disconnect the parking brake cable from the trailing shoe parking brake levers. Depress the cable prongs that hold the cable in the backing plate hole. Remove the cable through the holes.

11. Installation is in the reverse order of removal.

12. Adjust the parking brake cable.

1985½-90 Models

➧ See Figure 58

1. Place the control assembly in the seventh applied notch position and loosen the adjusting nut, then completely release control assembly.

2. Raise and safely support vehicle. Remove parking brake cable from equalizer.

3. Remove hairpin clip holding cable to floor pan tunnel bracket.

4. Remove wire retainer holding cable to fuel tank mounting bracket. Remove cable from wire retainer. Remove cable and clip from the fuel pump bracket.

5. Remove screw holding cable retaining clip to rear sidemember. Remove cable from clip.

6. Remove the wheel and rear brake drum.

➡A box wrench slightly smaller than the cable end can be used to ease its removal from the backing plate by sliding it over and depressing the splayed prongs.

7. Disengage cable end from brake assembly parking brake lever. Depress prongs holding cable to backing plate. Remove cable through the hole in the backing plate.

To install:

8. Insert the cable through hole in the backing plate. Attach the cable end to the rear brake assembly parking brake lever.

9. Insert conduit end fitting into backing plate. Ensure retention prongs are locked into place.

10. Insert cable into rear attaching clip and attach clip to rear sidemember with screw.

11. Route cable through bracket in floor pan tunnel and install hairpin retaining clip.

12. Install cable end into equalizer.

13. Insert cable into wire retainer and snap retainer into hole in fuel tank mounting bracket. Insert cable and install clip into fuel pump bracket.

14. Install rear drum, wheel and wheel cover.

15. Lower vehicle.

16. Adjust parking brake.

1991-95 Models

1. Remove the parking brake console as follows:
   a. Remove the rear seat ash tray.
   b. Position both front seats to the rear-most position.
   c. Remove the two front retaining screws from the parking brake console.
   d. Recline both front seats.
   e. Remove the two rear retaining screws and with the parking brake engaged, remove the parking brake console.
   f. Release the parking brake lever.

2. Remove the cable adjusting nut.

3. Raise and safely support the vehicle.

4. Remove the rear exhaust pipe and resonator heat shields.

5. Disconnect the equalizer return spring and remove the cables from the equalizer.

6. Remove the clip that attaches the cable to the retaining bracket located near the equalizer. Remove the cable from the bracket.

7. Remove the cable routing bracket bolt from the floor pan and remove the bracket.

8. Remove the two cable routing bracket nuts from the trailing link and remove the bracket.

9. Remove the two cable retaining bracket bolts from the backing plate and remove the bracket.

10. Remove the cable from the parking brake actuating lever.

To install:

11. Position the cable onto the parking brake actuating lever.

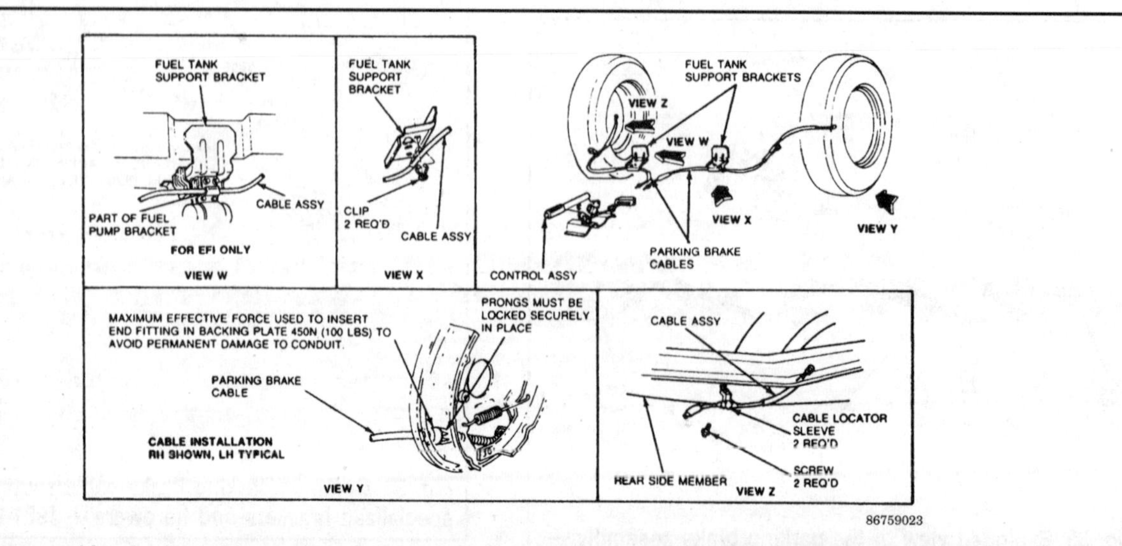

Fig. 58 Common parking brake cable routing and specialized brackets and hardware — 1985 1/2-90 models

12. Position the parking brake cable bracket onto the backing plate and install the two bolts. Tighten the bolts to 14-19 ft. lbs. (19-25 Nm).
13. Position the cable routing bracket onto the trailing link and install the two nuts. Tighten the nuts to 12-17 ft. lbs. (16-23 Nm).
14. Position the cable routing bracket to the floor pan and install the mounting bolt. Tighten the bolt to 14-19 ft. lbs. (19-25 Nm).
15. Position the cable into the retaining bracket near the equalizer and install the clip.
16. Install the cables into the equalizer and install the cable return spring.
17. Install the rear exhaust pipe and resonator heat shields.
18. Lower the vehicle.
19. Install the adjusting nut.
20. Adjust the parking brake cable, then install the parking brake console in the reverse order of removal.

ADJUSTMENTS

1981-90 Models

➡The rear brake shoes should be properly adjusted before adjusting the parking brake. Although ordinarily the shoes are only adjusted initially upon setup, if you believe you may have disturbed the adjustment, refer to the brake shoe removal and installation procedure in this section.

1. With the engine running, apply approximately 100 lbs. (45 kg) pedal effort to the hydraulic service brake three times before adjusting the parking brake.
2. Block the front wheel(s) and place the transaxle in Neutral. Raise and safely support the rear of the vehicle just enough to rotate the wheel.
3. Place the parking brake control assembly in the 12th notch position, just two notches from full application. Tighten the adjusting nut until approximately 1 in. (25mm) of threaded rod is exposed beyond the nut. Release the parking brake control and rotate the rear wheels by hand. There should be no brake drag.
4. If the brakes drag when the control assembly is fully released, or the handle travels too far upward on full, repeat the procedure and adjust the nut accordingly.

1991-95 Models

1. Start the engine and place the transaxle in Reverse.
2. With the vehicle moving in reverse, depress the brake pedal several times.
3. Stop the vehicle and place the transaxle in Park. Stop the engine.
4. Remove the parking brake console as follows:
   a. Remove the rear seat ash tray.
   b. Position both front seats to the rear-most position.
   c. Remove the two front retaining screws from the parking brake console.
   d. Recline both front seats.
   e. Remove the two rear retaining screws and with the parking brake engaged, remove the parking brake console.
   f. Release the parking brake lever.
5. Turn the adjusting nut until the parking brake lever stroke is 5-7 notches when pulled with a force of 22 lbs. (10 kg).
6. Install the parking brake console by reversing the removal procedure.

ANTI-LOCK BRAKE SYSTEM

Description

➧ See Figures 59 and 60

The Anti-Lock Brake System (ABS) was made available as an option on certain 1994-95 Escort and Tracer models. The ABS is an answer to the real-world problem of panic stops and braking on slippery or uneven pavement. The need for brakes that can use what traction is available to stop the car without locking-up becomes apparent during hazardous braking situations. These situations can cause the front, rear or all four wheels to skid or lock on a conventional brake system. If the rear wheels skid, stability is lost or compromised and if the front wheels skid, it is maneuverability that is affected. Beyond theory, what often happens when braking under such hazardous conditions is simply an out-of-control four-wheel lock-up.

Ford's ABS is a computer-controlled system that augments otherwise conventional hydraulic brakes by monitoring each wheel's rotational speed as compared to vehicle road speed. When (during braking) it detects that one or more wheels are rotating slower than the rate of travel, it compensates by modulating the brakes, allowing the car to slow but preventing the impending lock-up. In many cases, the goal to maximize stability and maneuverability under adverse braking conditions is met.

There are conditions, however, for which the ABS system provides no benefit. Hydroplaning is possible when the tires ride on a film of water, losing contact with the paved surface. And the same is possible on snow, ice and loose terrain. This renders the vehicle totally uncontrollable until road contact is regained. Extreme steering maneuvers at high speed or cornering beyond the limits of tire adhesion can result in skidding which is independent of vehicle braking. For this reason, the system is named "anti-lock" rather than "anti-skid."

Under normal conditions, the ABS system functions in the same manner as a conventional brake system and is not noticed by the operator. The system is a combination of electrical, mechanical and hydraulic components, working together to control the flow of brake fluid to the wheels when necessary.

During ABS operation, the driver will sense brake pedal pulsation, along with a slight up-and-down movement in the pedal height and a clicking sound; this is normal.

Power Brake Booster

The power brake booster is a conventional vacuum-assisted device designed to reduce the effort required to push the brake pedal and apply the brakes.

The booster is a self-contained unit that is mounted on the engine compartment side of the dash panel. If it is damaged

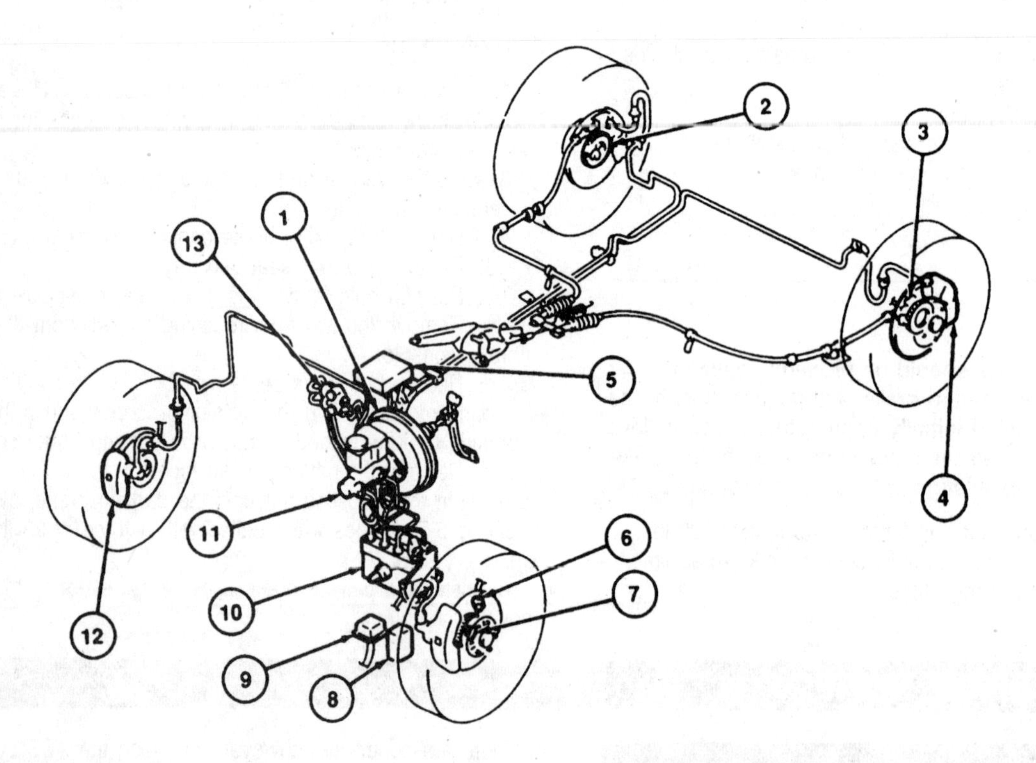

1 Power brake booster
2 Rear brake anti-lock sensor indicator (2)
3 Rear brake anti-lock sensor (2)
4 Rear disc brake caliper
5 Anti-lock brake control module
6 Front anti-lock sensor and bracket (2)
7 Front brake anti-lock sensor indicator (2)
8 Anti-lock relay
9 Data link connector
10 Hydraulic anti-lock actuator assembly
11 Brake master cylinder
12 Front disc brake caliper
13 Brake pressure control valve

86759031

Fig. 59 Locations on the vehicle for the ABS system components

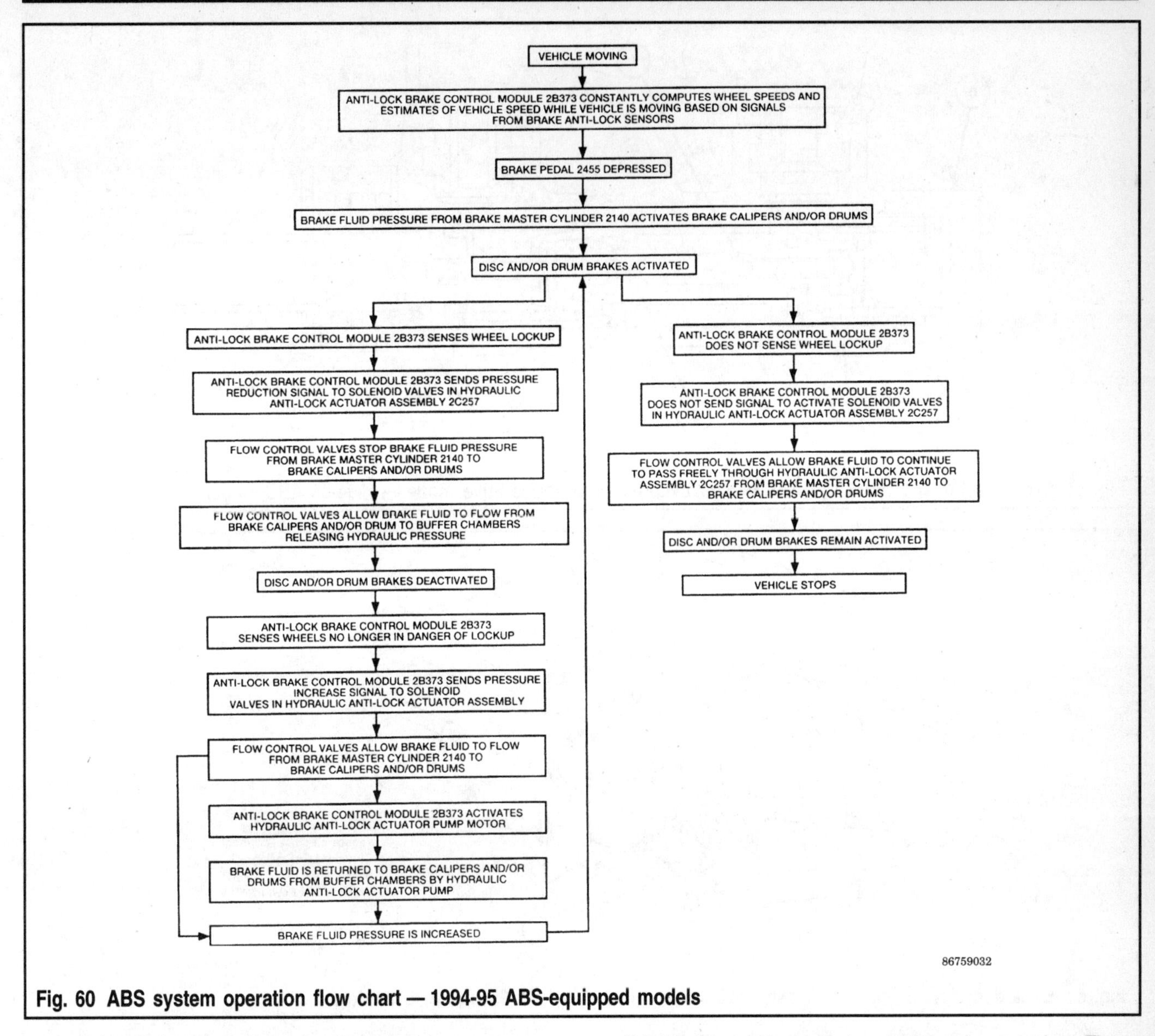

Fig. 60 ABS system operation flow chart — 1994-95 ABS-equipped models

or stops functioning properly, it must be replaced as an assembly, except for the power brake booster check valve.

REMOVAL & INSTALLATION

The power brake booster for ABS-equipped vehicles is a conventional design, and is the same as supplied with 1991-95 non-ABS cars. Please refer to the 1991-95 removal and installation procedure under "Power Brake Booster" found in this section.

Brake Master Cylinder

➧ See Figure 61

The brake master cylinder is different from the master cylinders used in vehicles not equipped with ABS. The relief port has been eliminated, and a center valve with a center port has been included in the secondary piston. The primary (rear) circuit feeds the right-hand front and left-hand rear brakes. The secondary (front) circuit feeds the left-hand front and right-hand rear brakes. The master cylinder is serviced as a complete assembly.

REMOVAL & INSTALLATION

➧ See Figure 62

1. If equipped, remove the speed control wire from its bracket.
2. Disengage the low fluid level sensor electrical connector.
3. Loosen the brake line fittings and disconnect the brake lines from the master cylinder.
4. Remove the clamp and pull the clutch hose from the brake/clutch fluid reservoir.
5. Cap the lines and the master cylinder ports.
6. Remove the mounting nuts and remove the master cylinder assembly.

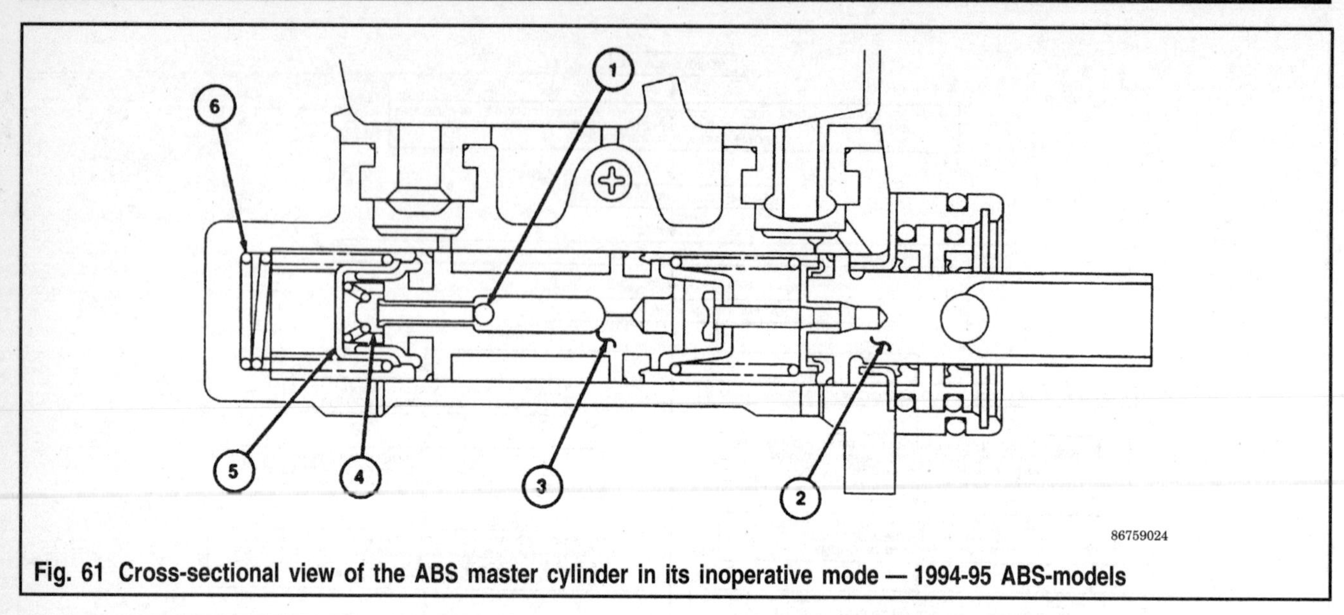

Fig. 61 Cross-sectional view of the ABS master cylinder in its inoperative mode — 1994-95 ABS-models

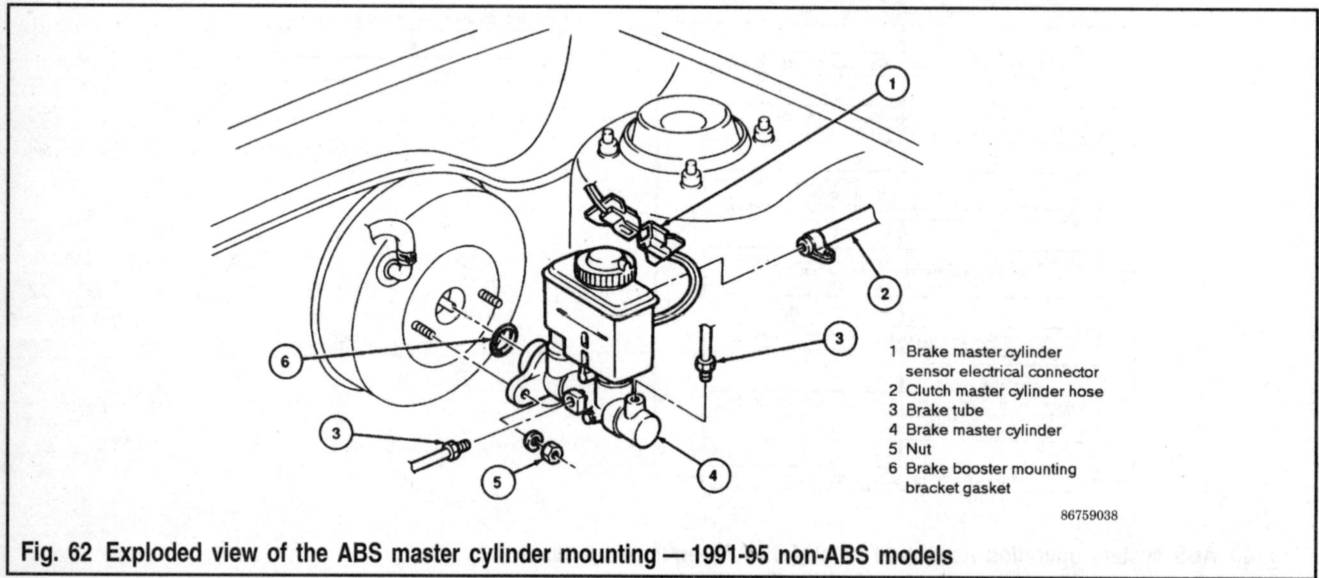

Fig. 62 Exploded view of the ABS master cylinder mounting — 1991-95 non-ABS models

To install:

7. Adjust the piston-to-pushrod clearance as follows:

a. Insert a pencil in the pushrod socket of the master cylinder. Mark the point on the pencil that is even with the end of the master cylinder with a hacksaw blade.

b. Measure the length of the pencil to the saw mark with a ruler.

c. Using the ruler, measure how far the master cylinder pushrod protrudes out of the booster assembly.

d. Measure the length of the master cylinder boss with the ruler. Subtract the length of the boss from the length of the pencil. The difference in length between the master cylinder pushrod and the corrected pencil length is equal to the pushrod clearance.

e. Adjust the pushrod length to get the correct clearance. It should be 0.025 in. (1mm) shorter than the pushrod socket.

8. Before installation, bench bleed the new master cylinder as follows:

a. Mount the new master cylinder in a suitable holding fixture. Be careful not to damage the housing.

b. Fill the master cylinder reservoir with brake fluid.

c. Using a pencil or wooden dowel inserted into the booster pushrod cavity, push the master cylinder piston in slowly. Place a plastic tray or container under the master cylinder to catch the fluid being expelled from the outlet ports.

d. Place a finger tightly over each outlet port and allow the master cylinder piston to return.

e. Repeat the procedure until only clear fluid is expelled from the master cylinder. Plug the outlet ports and remove the master cylinder from the holding fixture.

9. Position the master cylinder over the booster pushrod and booster mounting studs. Install the nuts and tighten to 8-12 ft. lbs. (10-16 Nm).

10. Connect the clutch hose onto the brake/clutch fluid reservoir and install the clamp.

11. Remove the caps and connect the brake lines. Tighten the fittings.

12. Make sure the master cylinder reservoir is full. Have an assistant push down on the brake pedal. When the pedal is all the way down, crack open the brake line fittings, one at a time, to expel any remaining air in the master cylinder and brake lines. Tighten the fittings, then have the assistant allow the brake pedal to return.

13. Repeat Step 12 until all air is expelled from the master cylinder and brake lines. Tighten the brake line fittings to 10-16 ft. lbs. (13-22 Nm).

14. Engage the low fluid level sensor electrical connector.

15. Make sure the master cylinder reservoir is full. Bleed the brakes.

****CAUTION**

Before attempting to test or operate the vehicle, make sure the bleeding procedure achieves a firm brake pedal.

16. Check for brake fluid leaks and for proper brake operation.

Brake Pressure Control Valve

See Figure 63

The ABS utilizes a brake pressure control valve that regulates hydraulic pressure in the rear brake circuit. It is located on the dash panel. When the brake pedal is applied, full rear circuit pressure passes through the brake pressure control valve until the split point of the brake pressure control valve is reached. Above the split point, the brake pressure control valve begins to reduce hydraulic pressure to the rear brake circuit. This creates a balanced braking condition between the front and the rear wheels while maintaining balanced hydraulic pressure at each rear wheel.

REMOVAL & INSTALLATION

See Figure 64

1. Use a tubing wrench to loosen the four brake tubes connected to the brake pressure control valve.
2. Loosen the brake tubes at the master cylinder with a tubing wrench.
3. Remove the tubes between the master cylinder and the control valve.
4. Disconnect all tubes to the control valve.
5. Remove the two bolts and remove the valve.

To install:

6. Position the valve in place on the dash panel and loosely install one bolt. Make sure the "R" marks face the driver's side.
7. Loosely install the brake tubes between the master cylinder and the control valve.
8. Install the other bolt into the brake pressure control valve and tighten both bolts to 14-17 ft. lbs. (19-23 Nm).
9. Tighten all of the brake tube fittings to 10-16 ft. lbs. (13-22 Nm).
10. Bleed the brakes

Hydraulic Anti-Lock Actuator Assembly

See Figure 65

The hydraulic anti-lock actuator assembly contains solenoid valves, flow control valves, a pump motor and buffer chambers. The solenoid valves open and close by signals sent from the the anti-lock brake control module. The flow control valves move according to the solenoid valve condition and control the hydraulic pressure in the brake calipers (pressure reduction or pressure increase). The hydraulic anti-lock actuator assembly has four solenoid valves which operate the three-channel system.

During normal braking, there is no current flow to the solenoid valve and the solenoid valve needle is held closed by spring pressure. The flow control valve does not move because the fluid pressure above and below the spool orifice is

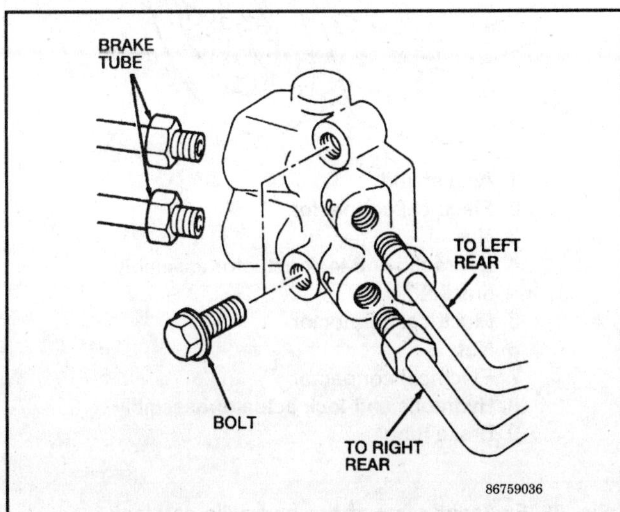

Fig. 63 Exploded view of the brake pressure control valve tube mounting

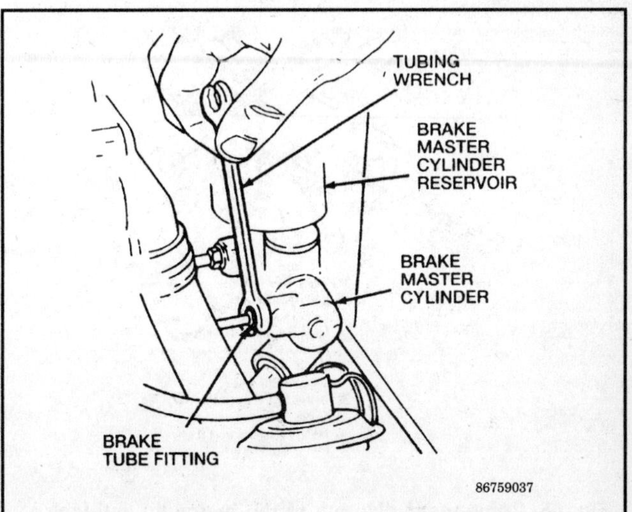

Fig. 64 Use a tube wrench to loosen and tighten the fittings to the brake pressure control valve

equal. In this condition, the master cylinder pressure passes through the flow control valve to the brakes.

When the hydraulic pressure increases and the wheel is about to lock, the anti-lock control module sends a command for pressure reduction to the solenoid valve. As a result, current flows to the solenoid and opens the solenoid needle valve. The pressure balance inside the flow control valve changes (upper: high, lower: low), and the flow control spool valve moves down and closes the fluid passage from the brake master cylinder to the brake caliper.

As the pressure above the spool orifice increases, the flow control spool valve moves farther down and the brake fluid in the brake caliper begins to flow through it to the buffer chamber (reservoir). The fluid from the brake caliper depresses the buffer chamber piston and is temporarily held in the chamber, releasing the hydraulic pressure in the brake caliper and allowing the wheel speed to increase.

When the wheel speed recovers, the anti-lock brake control module determines that the wheel is no longer in danger of locking up, and sends a command to increase brake pressure which deactivates the solenoid valve. As a result, the solenoid needle valve closes (moves up). The anti-lock brake control module also activates the pump motor and the brake fluid held in the buffer chamber returns to the caliper through the flow control valve passage. The flow is controlled by the position of the spool valve and increases the fluid pressure to the brake caliper.

The hydraulic anti-lock actuator assembly is located in the front of the engine compartment on the left-hand side of the vehicle. It attaches to a bracket that is mounted to the left-hand front inside rail inside the engine compartment. The battery and battery tray sit atop the hydraulic control bracket.

REMOVAL & INSTALLATION

See Figure 66

1. Disconnect the battery cables, remove the battery and the battery tray.

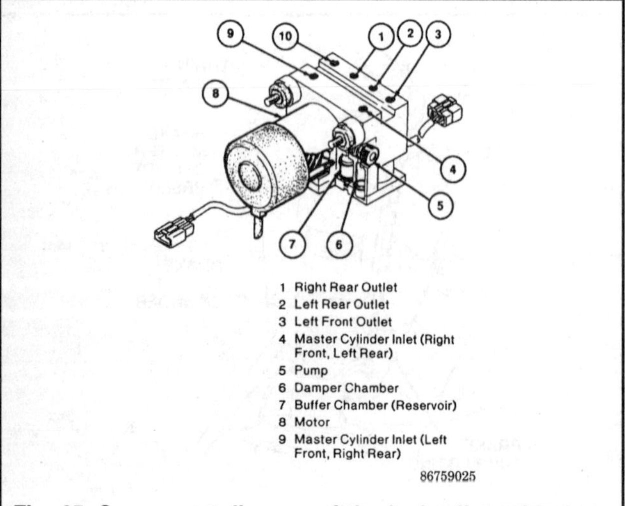

Fig. 65 Component diagram of the hydraulic anti-lock actuator assembly

2. Remove the acid shield.
3. Tag and unfasten the electrical connectors.
4. Tag the brake tubes and mark the corresponding ports. Remove the six brake tubes from the hydraulic anti-lock actuator assembly. Plug each port to prevent brake fluid from spilling onto the paint and wiring.
5. Loosen the nut on the front and the two nuts on the back of the assembly, then remove the assembly from the vehicle.

To install:

6. Place the hydraulic anti-lock actuator assembly in the correct mounting position. Make sure the electrical wires/connectors are properly routed.
7. Tighten the nuts.
8. Connect the six brake tubes. Tighten the fittings to 10-16 ft. lbs. (13-22 Nm).
9. Fasten the electrical connector.
10. Install the acid shield. Install the battery tray, then install the battery and connect the cables.
11. Bleed the brake system, then check for fluid leaks.

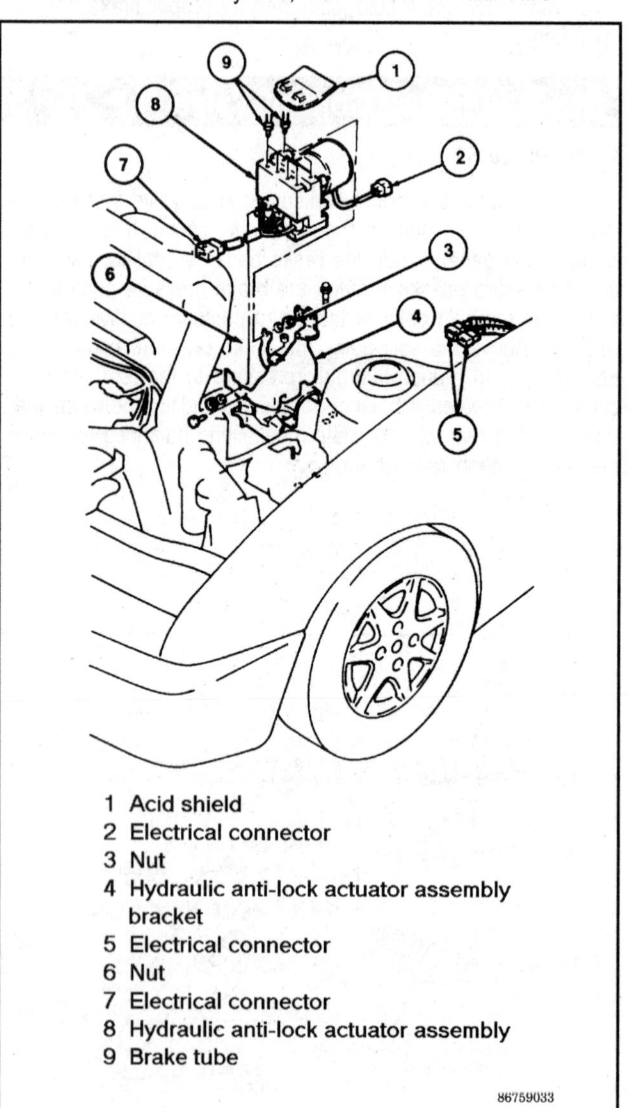

Fig. 66 Exploded view of the hydraulic anti-lock actuator assembly mounting

Anti-Lock Brake (ABS) Control Module

➧ **See Figure 67**

The Anti-lock Brake System (ABS) control module is an on-board diagnostic, non-serviceable unit. The module monitors system operation during normal driving, as well as during anti-lock braking. Through its preprogramming, the anti-lock brake control module decides which wheel's brake pressure requires modulation based on feedback from the wheel sensors. Once the decision is made, the ABS control module sends appropriate signals to the solenoid valves in the hydraulic anti-lock actuator assembly. These solenoid valves allow adjoining flow control valves to modulate fluid pressure, resulting in a pressure reduction at the calipers to prevent lockup.

The ABS control module continuously calculates wheel speed and thus vehicle speed. The module activates the ABS only when it senses wheel lockup under severe braking conditions. If the ABS control module senses lockup, it sends a pressure reduction signal through the ABS relay to the hydraulic anti-lock actuator assembly. The solenoid controls the flow of hydraulic fluid into a buffer chamber located in the hydraulic anti-lock actuator assembly.

When the wheel is no longer in danger of lockup, the anti-lock brake control module sends pressure increase signals through the anti-lock relay to the hydraulic anti-lock actuator assembly. one signal tells the solenoid to allow hydraulic fluid pressure to increase while the other signal activates the pump motor to further increase pressure by returning fluid from the buffer chamber. This operation continues for all wheels until the wheels are no longer in danger of lockup.

➡**The anti-lock relay is located in the engine compartment behind the driver's side headlight.**

A fail-safe function is programmed into the ABS control module that reverts the system to normal braking if a malfunction is detected. A self-diagnosis function checks for problems within the ABS. The ABS control module stores service codes in its memory to aid in diagnosing problems. The ABS warning indicator on the dash panel is illuminated while the engine is on to notify the driver of a present failure.

REMOVAL & INSTALLATION

⁂WARNING

The ignition key must be in the OFF position when disconnecting the negative battery cable. It is possible that an electrical surge could kickback through the wiring to the module thus damaging or destroying it.

The ABS control module is located under the front passenger's seat.

1. Disconnect the negative battery cable.
2. Unplug the electrical connector.
3. Remove the three bolts and remove the module.
4. To install, reverse the removal procedure. Tighten the bolts to 61-86 inch lbs. (7-10 Nm).

Anti-Lock Brake Sensor

➧ **See Figures 68 and 69**

Four sets of variable-reluctance brake anti-lock sensors and sensor indicators which determine the rotational speed of each wheel are used in the ABS system. The sensors operate on the magnetic induction principle. As the teeth on the ABS sensor indicators rotate past the sensors, a signal proportional to the speed of rotation is generated and sent to the ABS control module.

The front brake anti-lock sensors are attached to the front wheel spindles. The front brake anti-lock sensor indicators are pressed into the outer CV-joints. The rear brake anti-lock sensors are attached to the right and left-hand rear disc brake adapters. The rear brake anti-lock sensor indicators are pressed into the wheel hub assemblies.

REMOVAL & INSTALLATION

➧ **See Figure 70**

Front

1. Disconnect the negative battery cable.
2. If necessary, remove the battery for access to the LH front sensor electrical connector and grommet. Unplug the electrical connector.
3. Pinch the sides of the grommet and push it through the hole in the shock tower.
4. Raise and safely support the vehicle.
5. Remove the wheel.
6. Remove the wiring harness clip from the bracket on the wheel well.
7. Remove the upper wiring harness bracket from the wheel well bracket and remove the clip from the bracket on the shock absorber.
8. Remove the lower wiring harness bracket.
9. Remove the two anti-lock sensor bolts and remove the front anti-lock sensor and bracket.

To install:

10. Align the sensor with its mounting holes on the front wheel spindle. Using a feeler gauge, adjust clearance to 0.012-0.043 in. (0.3-1.1mm).
11. Tighten the retaining screws to 12-17 ft. lbs. (16-23 Nm).
12. Install the grommets at the height sensor bracket, then install the retainer clip at the shock absorber.
13. Thread the wire through the holes in the fender apron. Install the retainer clips. Secure the splash shield with the plastic push studs.
14. Engage the sensor connector to the wiring harness from the engine compartment.
15. If the battery was removed for LH sensor electrical connector access, re-install it at this time.
16. Connect the negative battery cable.
17. Install the wheel, tightening the lug nuts to 65-87 ft. lbs. (88-118 Nm).

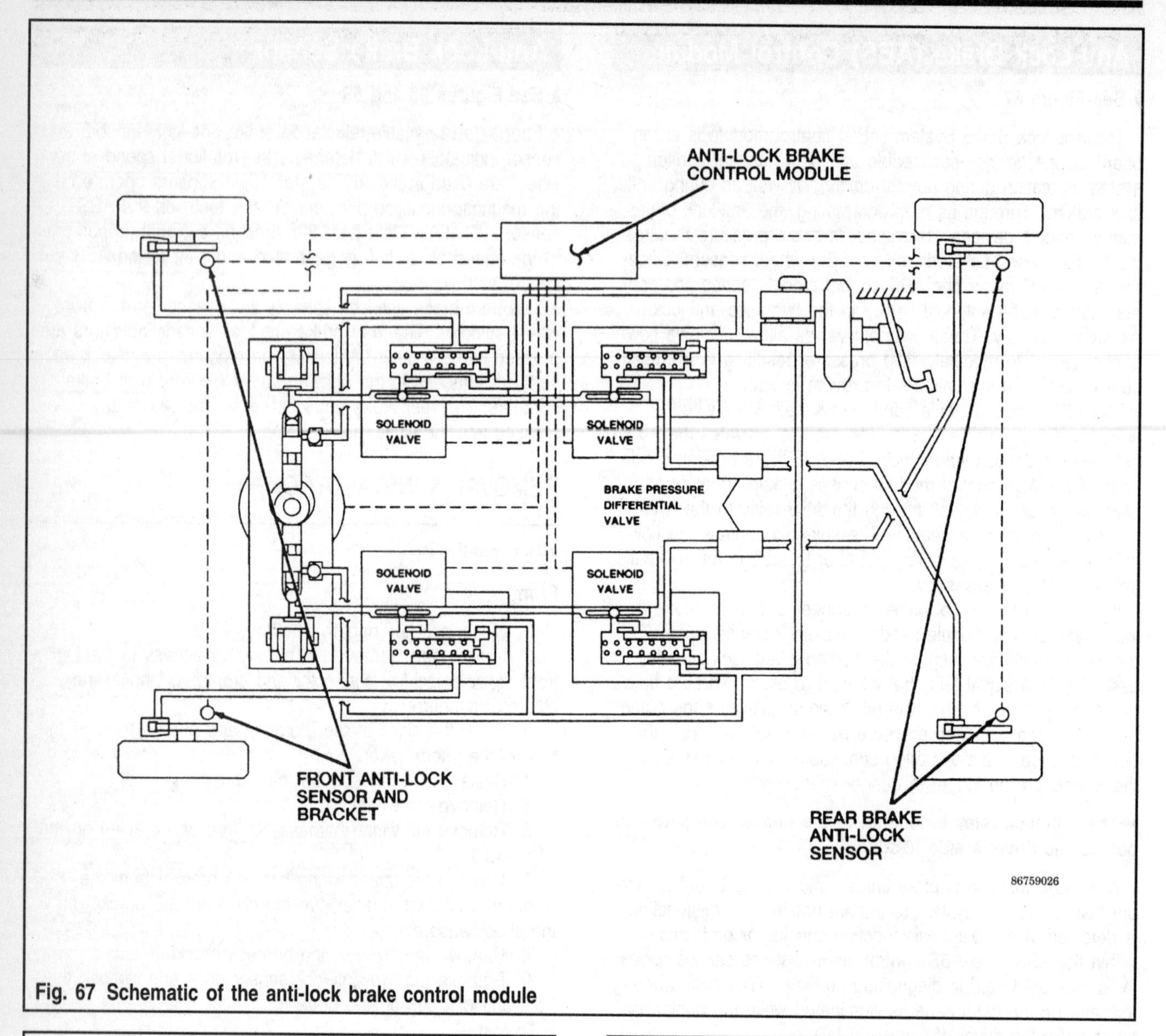

Fig. 67 Schematic of the anti-lock brake control module

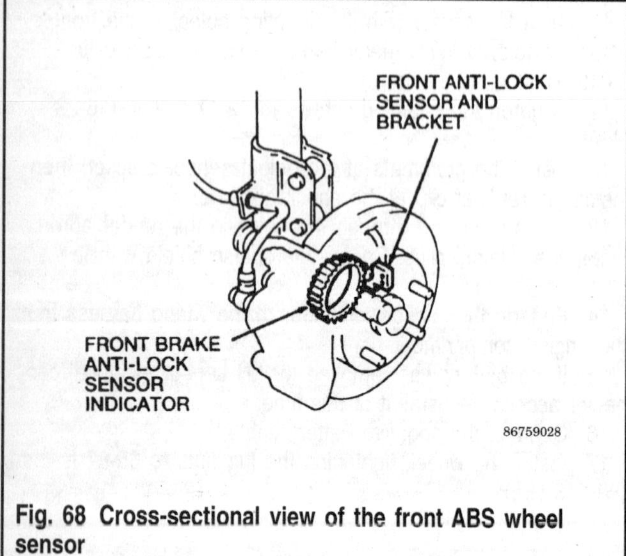

Fig. 68 Cross-sectional view of the front ABS wheel sensor

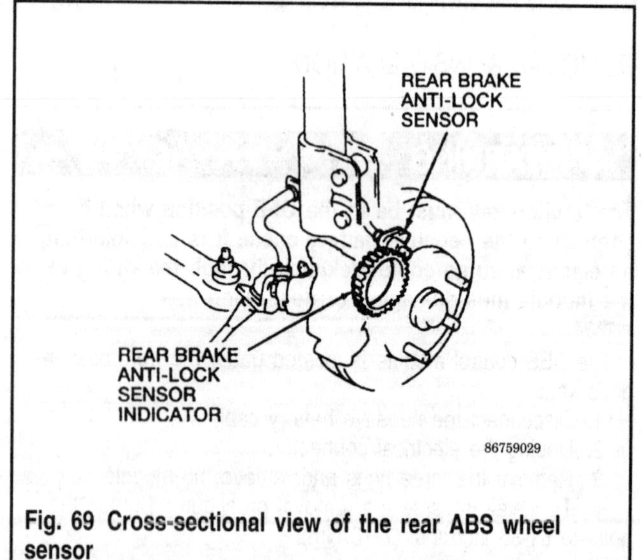

Fig. 69 Cross-sectional view of the rear ABS wheel sensor

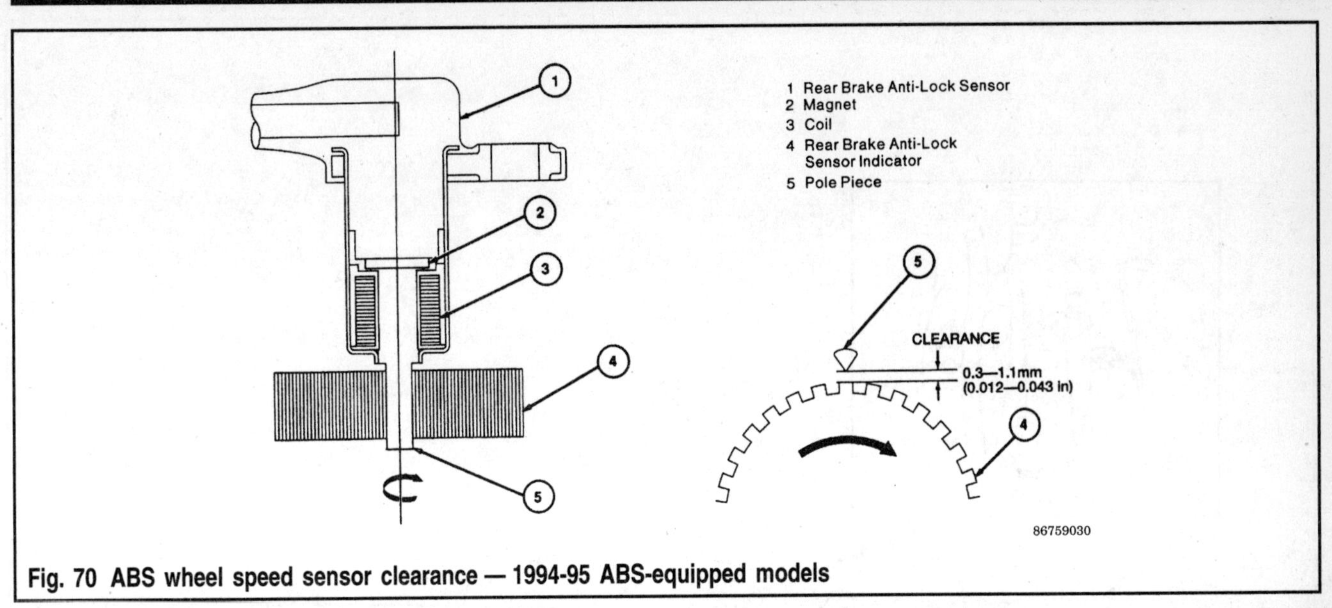

Fig. 70 ABS wheel speed sensor clearance — 1994-95 ABS-equipped models

Rear

➧ See Figure 71

1. Disconnect the negative battery cable.
2. Remove the quarter trim panel.
3. Disengage the sensor electrical connector from the harness.
4. Remove the sensor wire with the attached grommet from the hole in the chassis.
5. Raise and safely support the vehicle.
6. Remove the wheel.
7. Remove the upper and lower clips, then unfasten the sensor retaining bolt and remove the sensor from the vehicle.

To install:

8. Install the sensor, then secure using the retaining bolt. Using a feeler gauge, adjust clearance to 0.012-0.043 in. (0.3-1.1mm).
9. Tighten the bolt to 12-17 ft. lbs. (16-23 Nm).
10. Route the sensor wire, then install the clips.
11. Engage the sensor electrical connector to the wiring harness, then push the grommet through the hole in the chassis and into position.
12. Install the quarter trim panel.
13. Lower the vehicle, then connect the negative battery cable.

Filling and Bleeding

The ABS brake master cylinder for 1994-95 Escort and Tracer models does not require special bleeding or filling procedures beyond those required for the conventional brake system found on non-ABS cars of the same years. If you have opened the system and have air (spongy pedal), or you wish to perform routine filling and/or flushing, refer to the appropriate portion of this section for bleeding the brakes.

System Testing

In the event of an ABS failure, the warning indicator will come on and stay on while the engine is running, although normal brake system operation will remain. However, the wheels will lock up under a hard stop until the failure is corrected. At the same time, Diagnostic Trouble Codes (DTCs) will be stored in the control module's memory.

To diagnose an apparent failure, always begin with a visual inspection (refer to the inspection chart). This section will cover two specialized tests, the "Key ON-Engine Running (KOER) Test," and the "Continuous Test."

To retrieve diagnostic trouble codes, you may use any of the following tools or methods:

- Analog voltmeter to identify voltage fluctuations
- Count flashes of the ABS warning indicator
- Read a digital or audible code from the Rotunda Super Star II Tester 007-0041B using the Rotunda Super MECS Adapter 007-00052, or an equivalent scan tool

➡The test connector for obtaining DTCs is the Data Link Connector, located near the battery.

The DTC may indicate different failures, so parting from the Quick Test may result in code identification error. If you begin the Quick Test procedures, follow it to its entirety. ABS warning indicator mode inspection and DTC retrieval are covered in the quick test.

The KOER Test checks the ABS control module and system circuitry by testing its integrity and processing capability. The test also verifies that the various sensors and actuators are connected and operating properly.

The Continuous Test is intended as an aid in diagnosing intermittent failures in the ABS. It is identical to the KOER Test, but also allows you to enter this mode of the test and to attempt to recreate the intermittent failure by tapping, moving, and wiggling the harness and/or the suspected sensor. Faults will be indicated using a digital multimeter such as the Rotunda Model 73, part No. 105-00051, or the Rotunda Super STAR II Tester 007-0041B, or an equivalent scan tool. With the knowledge of the affected circuits, a close check of the associated harnesses can be made.

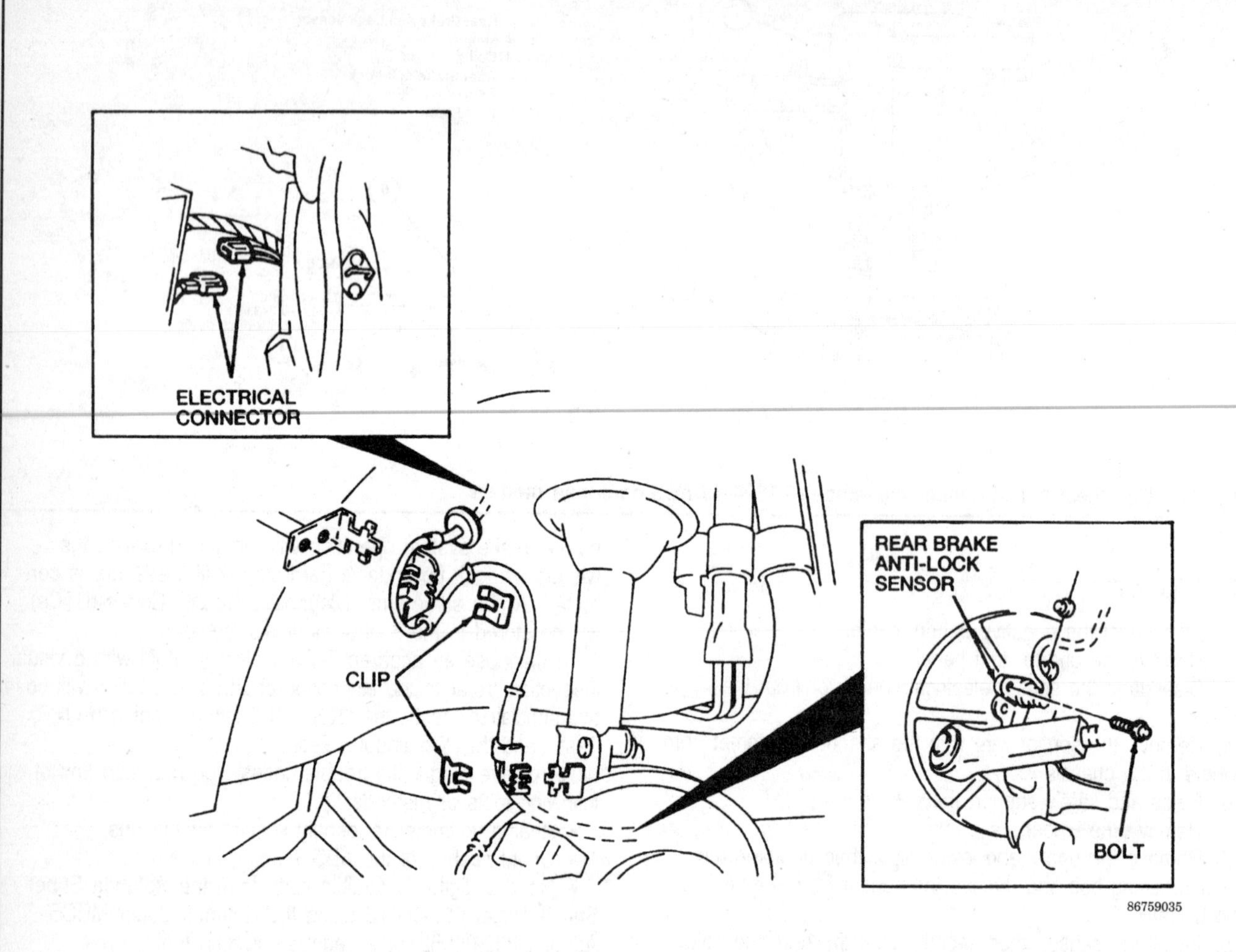

Fig. 71 Rear wheel sensor connections and mounting location

READING & ERASING DTCs

Using Analog Voltmeter (VOM)

➧ See Figure 72

1. Connect pins TBS and GND at the data link connector with a jumper wire (refer to the accompanying drawing).
2. Key **ON**.
3. Output DTCs using the VOM.
4. After the first code is repeated, depress the brake pedal 10 times quickly (less than one second between each).
5. Key **OFF**.
6. Disconnect the jumper wire.

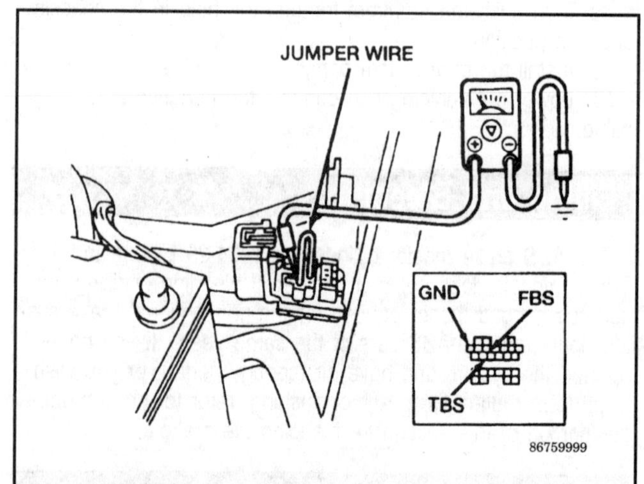

Fig. 72 Connect pints TBS and GND with a jumper wire, then read the DTCs of a voltmeter connected between terminal FBS and ground

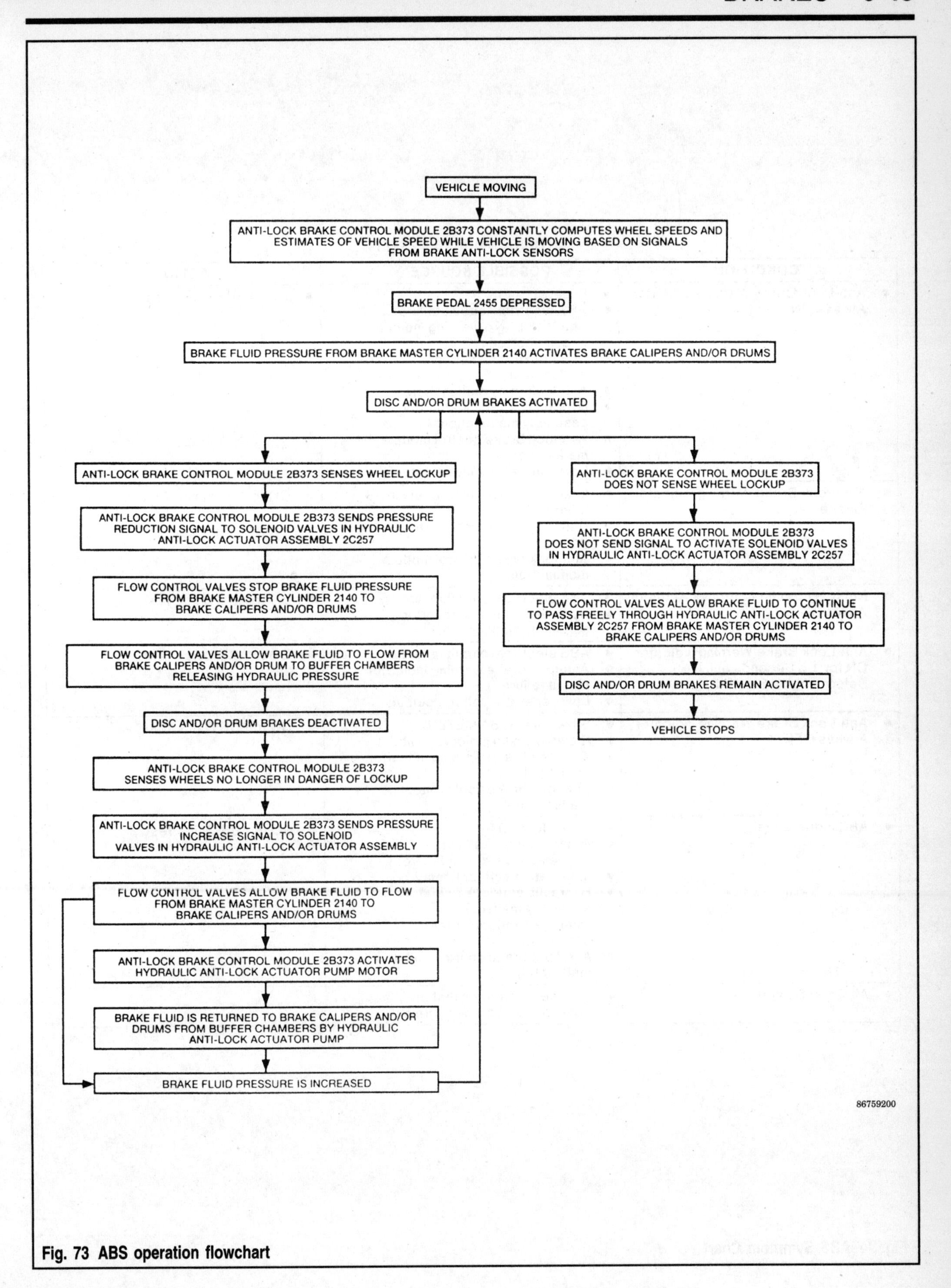

Fig. 73 ABS operation flowchart

ANTI-LOCK BRAKE SYSTEM

CONDITION	POSSIBLE SOURCE	ACTION
• Anti-Lock Brake Warning Indicator Always ON	• Fuse(s). • ABS electrical circuit failure. • Anti-lock brake warning indicator circuit shorted. • Anti-Lock brake sensor malfunction. • Anti-lock relay malfunction. • Hydraulic anti-lock actuator assembly malfunction. • Anti-lock brake control module malfunction. • Low generator voltage output.	• GO to ABS Quick Test.
• Anti-Lock Brake Warning Indicator Flashes	• Intermittent ABS electrical circuit failure. • Data link connector shorted to ground. • Anti-lock brake control module malfunction.	• GO to ABS Quick Test.
• Noisy Hydraulic Anti-Lock Actuator Assembly	• ABS electrical circuit failure. • Hydraulic anti-lock actuator assembly malfunction.	• GO to ABS Quick Test.
• Anti-Lock Brake Warning Indicator ON for 1.5 Seconds and OFF Before Engine Started	• ABS electrical circuit failure. • Anti-lock brake warning indicator circuit failure. • Low generator voltage output.	• GO to ABS Quick Test.
• Anti-Lock Brake Warning Indicator Always OFF	• Blown fuse (15A METER). • Blown warning indicator bulb. • Anti-lock brake warning indicator circuit failure. • Anti-lock brake control module malfunction.	• GO to ABS Quick Test.
• ABS Inoperative	• Blown fuse(s). • Insufficient brake fluid. • ABS electrical circuit failure. • Inoperative anti-lock relay. • Hydraulic anti-lock actuator assembly malfunction. • Damaged anti-lock brake sensor(s). • Anti-lock brake control module malfunction.	• GO to ABS Quick Test.
• All Other Symptoms	• All other symptoms that are common to all brake systems.	

86759201

Fig. 74 ABS Symptom Chart

	TEST STEP	RESULT ▶	ACTION TO TAKE
QT1	PERFORM VISUAL CHECK		
	• Check for sufficient hydraulic brake fluid, damaged anti-lock sensors, leaks, and damaged hydraulic anti-lock actuator assembly. • Check the ABS wiring harness for proper connections, bent or broken pins, corrosion, loose wires, and proper routing. • Check all of the fuses for proper connection or damage. • Check the anti-lock brake control module for physical damage. • **Are all of the components OK?** NOTE: It may be necessary to disconnect or disassemble harness connector assemblies to do some of the inspections. Note pin locations before disassembly. Disconnect assemblies with key OFF.	Yes ▶ No ▶	DRIVE vehicle to verify Anti-Lock Brakes symptom and PROCEED to Test Step **QT2**. SERVICE fault(s) in system and then PROCEED to Test Step QT2.
QT2	PERFORM VEHICLE PREPARATION		
	• Perform all of the following safety steps required to run ABS Quick Test. • Apply the parking brake. • Place the shift control selector lever firmly into the PARK position (NEUTRAL on MTX). • Block the drive wheels. • Turn off all of the electrical loads. — Radios — Indicators — A/C-heater blower fans, etc. • **Have all of the safety steps been performed and all of the electrical loads turned OFF?**	Yes ▶ No ▶	PROCEED to Test Step **QT3**. Personal safety and correct diagnostic results are dependent on Test Step **QT2**. Do not PROCEED with Quick Test if vehicle preparation cannot be performed.

86759202

Fig. 75 ABS Quick Test

	TEST STEP	RESULT ▶	ACTION TO TAKE
QT3	CHECK ANTI-LOCK BRAKE WARNING INDICATOR		
	• Turn the ignition switch ON without starting the engine. • **Does the anti-lock brake warning indicator illuminate continuously?**	Yes (Warning indicator illuminates continuously) ▶	Normal operation. PROCEED to Quick Test Step **QT4**.
		No (Warning indicator not illuminated) ▶	CHECK anti-lock brake warning indicator circuit, 15A METER fuse and miniature bulb. GO to Pinpoint Test **H1**.
		No (Warning indicator flashing) ▶	VERIFY that the data link connector is not jumped (or shorted to ground) between pins "TBS" and "GND."
		No (Warning indicator illuminates for 1.5 seconds and goes out before engine is started) ▶	Low generator output. GO to Pinpoint Test **G1**.
QT4	CHECK ANTI-LOCK BRAKE WARNING INDICATOR WITH ENGINE RUNNING		
	• Start the engine. • Drive the vehicle if necessary (read note). NOTE: Certain ABS faults require that the vehicle be driven in order for the warning indicator to come on. Other faults will cause the warning indicator to turn on each time the engine is started. • **Does the anti-lock brake warning indicator illuminate?**	Yes (Retrieve codes using Super STAR II Tester) ▶	Indicates a present failure. PROCEED to Quick Test Step **QT5**.
		Yes (Retrieve codes using VOM) ▶	Indicates a present failure. PROCEED to Quick Test Step **QT6**.
		No (Warning indicator not illuminated) ▶	Normal operation. If ABS symptom exists, GO to Pinpoint Test **G1**.

86759203

Fig. 76 Quick Test (continued)

TEST STEP		RESULT	▶	ACTION TO TAKE
QT5	PERFORM SUPER STAR II HOOKUP			
	• Verify that a failure has been detected in the ABS. (An illuminated anti-lock brake warning indicator in the KOER mode indicates a present failure. If the anti-lock brake warning indicator is not illuminated in KOER mode, but symptom exists, it may indicate a past or intermittent problem.) • Turn the ignition switch OFF. • Access the data link connector located in the engine compartment. • Connect Rotunda Super STAR II Tester 007-0041B to the data link connector using Rotunda Super MECS Adapter 007-00052. 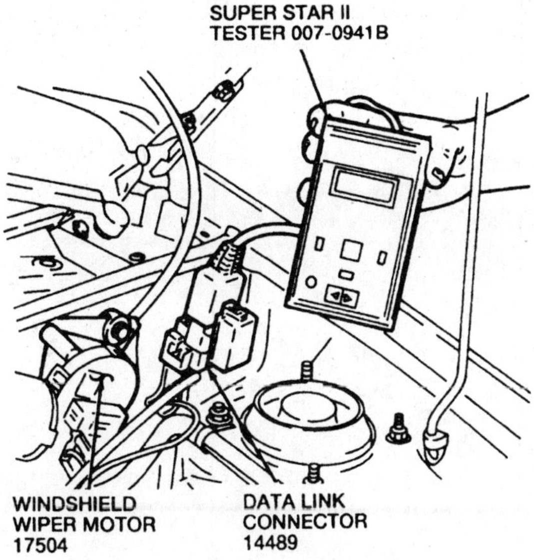 SUPER STAR II TESTER 007-0941B WINDSHIELD WIPER MOTOR 17504 DATA LINK CONNECTOR 14489 • Place the adapter in the "ABS" position. • Place the tester in the "MECS" position. • Latch the tester to the "Test" position. • **Is the tester hooked up properly?**	Yes	▶	PROCEED to **QT7**, ABS Diagnostic Trouble Code Retrieval.
		No	▶	RE-ATTEMPT Step **QT5**, Super STAR II Hookup. SERVICE any faults if necessary.

86759204

Fig. 77 Quick Test (continued)

TEST STEP		RESULT ▶	ACTION TO TAKE
QT6	PERFORM VOM HOOKUP		
	• Verify that a failure has been detected in the ABS. (An illuminated anti-lock brake warning indicator in the KOER mode indicates a present failure. If the anti-lock brake warning indicator is not illuminated in KOER mode but symptom exists, it may indicate a past or intermittent problem). • Turn the ignition switch OFF. • Access the data link connector located in the engine compartment. • Connect a jumper wire at data link connector from "TBS" (Test Brake System) to "GND" terminals (see illustration). • Connect an analog VOM between "FBS" (Failure Brake System) terminal and engine ground (see illustration). • Set the VOM on a DC voltage range to read from 0 to 20 volts. • **Is the jumper wire and VOM hooked up properly as shown in illustration?** 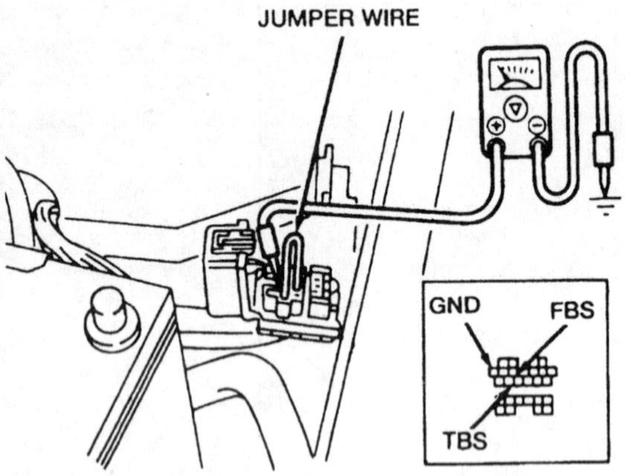 JUMPER WIRE GND FBS TBS	Yes ▶ No ▶	PROCEED to **QT7**, ABS Diagnostic Trouble Code Retrieval. RE-ATTEMPT Step **QT6**, VOM Hookup. SERVICE any faults if necessary.

86759205

Fig. 78 Quick Test (continued)

	TEST STEP	RESULT ▶	ACTION TO TAKE
QT7	PERFORM ABS DIAGNOSTIC TROUBLE CODE RETRIEVAL		
	• Verify that the anti-lock brake warning indicator illuminated (prior to equipment hookup) in the KOEO test before continuing. • Key ON. If using Rotunda Super STAR II Tester 007-0041B, turn the key ON, wait two seconds, then turn the tester ON. • **Does the anti-lock brake warning indicator flash briefly then go out?** NOTE: When a diagnostic trouble code is reported on the analog VOM, it will represent itself as a pulsing or sweeping movement of the voltmeter's needle across the dial face. Codes will be repeated after all memory codes have been displayed once.	Yes ▶	ABS OK. GO to Section 06-00 for non-ABS related symptoms.
		No (Warning indicator illuminates constantly) ▶	RECORD VOM or tester diagnostic trouble codes. ERASE diagnostic trouble codes from memory as explained in Erasing Diagnostic Trouble Codes in this section. RE-ATTEMPT diagnostic trouble code retrieval. RECORD all re-created diagnostic trouble codes and REFER to Code Identification Chart. SERVICE re-created codes as necessary. If the problem still exists or if no codes were re-created, PROCEED to **QT8**. (Codes that were not re-created indicate past or intermittent faults.)
		No (Warning indicator flashes service codes) ▶	Indicates past or intermittent fault(s). Be sure to RECORD the diagnostic trouble codes before erasing faults. ERASE diagnostic trouble codes from the memory as explained in Erasing Diagnostic Trouble Codes in this section, then PROCEED to **QT8**.
QT8	PERFORM CONTINUOUS TEST		
	• Hook up the Rotunda 73 Digital Multimeter 105-00051 or equivalent and jumper wire, or the Rotunda Super STAR II Tester 007-0041B, as in Test Step QT5 or QT6. • Key ON. NOTE: Use the audible warning function on the tester by turning the "SPKR" switch ON. You will be alerted of a continuous test fault without having to visually check the tester. • Tap, move, and wiggle the suspected sensor and/or harness working with short sections from the sensor to dash panel and to anti-lock brake control module. Drive vehicle, if necessary. • **Does the indicator illuminate continuously or is an audible warning heard from Super STAR II Tester?** NOTE: With the key ON, any coded fault re-created during continuous test will illuminate the warning indicator constantly. If the key is turned OFF, then back On without clearing codes from memory, the warning indicator will flash codes along with the VOM or the Super STAR II Tester indicating a past or intermittent fault.	Yes ▶	RECORD VOM or tester diagnostic trouble codes and REFER to Code Identification Chart. SERVICE only the codes re-created in this test step.
		No ▶	Normal operation. If intermittent fault cannot be re-created, turn key OFF. DISCONNECT suspect sensor and anti-lock brake control module from harness very carefully. Visually INSPECT all terminals for corrosion, bad crimps, improperly seated terminals, etc. RECONNECT harness connectors and RE-ATTEMPT continuous test.

86759206

Fig. 79 Quick Test (continued)

Diagnosis Indication				
ABS Warning Indicator	VOM	Diagnostic Trouble Code	Possible Failure Location	Action To Take
• Illuminated Constantly for Present Failure • Flashes According to VOM Indication for Past or Intermittent Failure	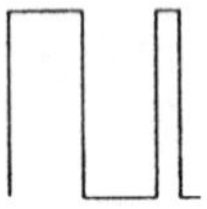	11	RH Front Brake Anti-Lock Sensor and Bracket 2C179 RH Front Brake Anti-Lock Sensor Indicator 2C182	GO to Pinpoint Test A1.
	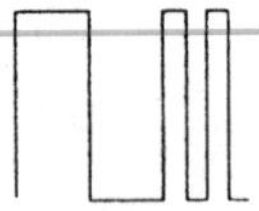	12	LH Front Brake Anti-Lock Sensor and Bracket 2C179 LH Front Brake Anti-Lock Sensor Indicator 2C182	
	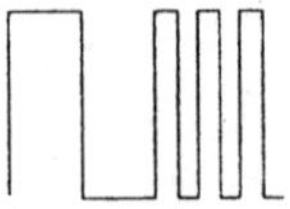	13	RH Rear Brake Anti-Lock Sensor 2C190 RH Rear Brake Anti-Lock Sensor Indicator 2C189	
	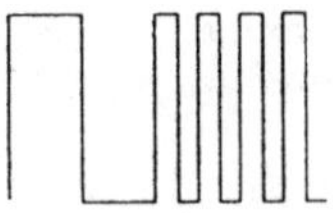	14	LH Rear Brake Anti-Lock Sensor 2C190 LH Rear Brake Anti-Lock Sensor Indicator 2C189	
	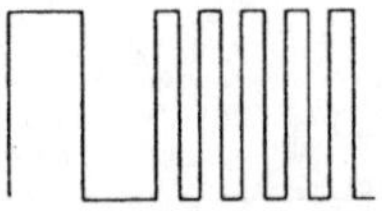	15	Front and Rear Brake Anti-Lock Sensors	GO to Pinpoint Test B1.
	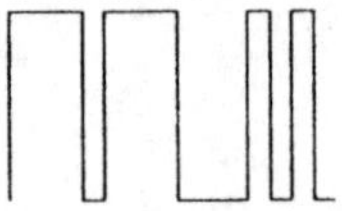	22	Solenoid Valve	GO to Pinpoint Test C1.
	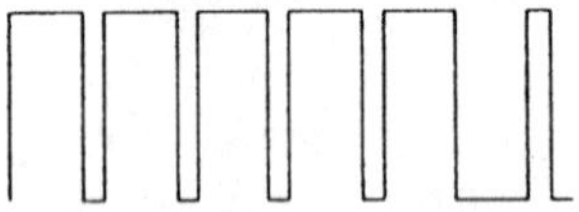	51	Fail-Safe Relay	GO to Pinpoint Test D1.
	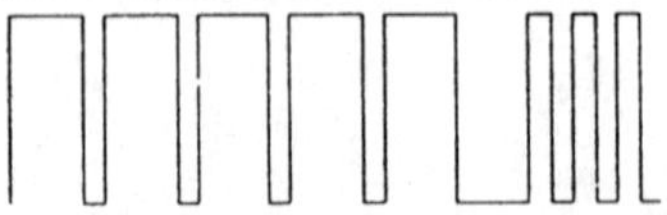	53	Motor Relay Motor	GO to Pinpoint Test E1.
	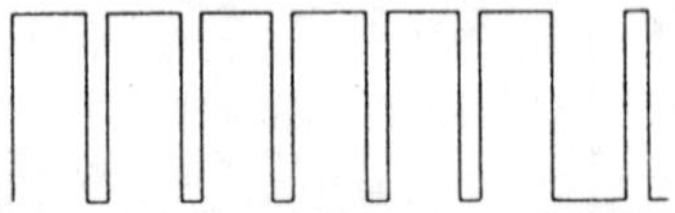	61	Anti-Lock Brake Control Module 2B373	REPLACE Anti-Lock Brake Control Module.
• Illuminated Constantly	No Indication	No Code	Generator	GO to Pinpoint Test F1.
	No Indication	No Code	ABS Warning Indicator	GO to Pinpoint Test G1.

86759207

Fig. 80 ABS diagnostic trouble code (DTC) identification chart

Diagnostic Trouble Code	Possible Failure Location	Diagnostic Trouble Code Logic Specifications				Warning Indicator	Failure Mode		
		ABS Initialized (KOEO)	Starting Up or Slowing Down	Normal Driving	Driving with ABS Operating		Open	Short	Other
11	RH Front Anti-Lock Sensor 2C204 and Front Brake Anti-Lock Sensor Indicator 2C182	—	No pulse from Anti-Lock Sensor when actual vehicle speed reaches 7 mph.	—		ON	X	X	Incorrect voltage from Anti-Lock Sensor (Excessive gap between Brake Anti-Lock Sensor Indicator and Pickup Coil)
		—	No pulse from Anti-Lock Sensor but Anti-Lock Brake Control Module 2B373 receives signal from other Anti-Lock Sensor for 20 sec.	—		ON	X	X	
12	LH Front Anti-Lock Sensor 2C204 and Anti-Lock Sensor Indicator 2C182	—		Incorrect pulse or no pulse from Anti-Lock Sensor when vehicle speed is above 6.25 mph without braking	—	ON	X	X	
		—		Incorrect pulse or no pulse from Anti-Lock Sensor when vehicle speed is above 18.75 mph without braking	—	ON	X	X	
13	RH Rear Brake Anti-Lock Sensor 2C190 and Rear Brake Anti-Lock Sensor Indicator 2C189	—		No pulse from Anti-Lock Sensor without braking	—	ON	X	X	
		—		No pulse from Anti-Lock Sensor without braking.	—	ON	X	X	
14	LH Rear Brake Anti-Lock Sensor 2C190 and Rear Brake Anti-Lock Sensor Indicator 2C189	—		Incorrect pulse from Anti-Lock Sensor	—	ON	—	—	Broken Brake Anti-Lock Sensor Indicator Tooth

86759208

Fig. 81 ABS control module logic specifications for DTCs

<table>
<tr><th rowspan="2">Diagnostic Trouble Code</th><th rowspan="2">Possible Failure Location</th><th colspan="4">Diagnostic Trouble Code Logic Specifications</th><th rowspan="2">Warning Indicator</th><th colspan="3">Failure Mode</th></tr>
<tr><th>ABS Initialized (KOEO)</th><th>Starting Up or Slowing Down</th><th>Normal Driving</th><th>Driving with ABS Operating</th><th>Open</th><th>Short</th><th>Other</th></tr>
<tr><td>11</td><td>RH Front Anti-Lock Sensor 2C179</td><td rowspan="2">—</td><td rowspan="2">Front Anti-Lock Sensor sends anti-lock brake requirement signal to Anti-Lock Brake Control Module 2B373 before vehicle speed reaches 9.3 mph without braking</td><td colspan="2" rowspan="2">—</td><td rowspan="2">ON</td><td rowspan="2">—</td><td rowspan="2">—</td><td rowspan="2">Incorrect Anti-Lock Sensor output, Broken Front Brake Anti-Lock Sensor Indicator Tooth</td></tr>
<tr><td>12</td><td>LH Front Anti-Lock Sensor 2C179</td></tr>
<tr><td>15</td><td>Anti-Lock Sensor</td><td colspan="4">Current does not flow when output from Anti-Lock Brake Control Module 2B373 to Anti-Lock Sensor — Anti-Lock Brake Control Module 2B373 detects open circuit in Anti-Lock Sensor</td><td>ON</td><td>X</td><td>—</td><td>—</td></tr>
<tr><td rowspan="5">22</td><td rowspan="4">Solenoid</td><td>Power Transistor failure in Anti-Lock Brake Control Module 2B373</td><td colspan="3" rowspan="2">—</td><td>ON</td><td>X</td><td>X</td><td rowspan="4">—</td></tr>
<tr><td>All solenoids are OFF and Fail-Safe Relay is OFF even though Anti-Lock Brake Control Module 2B373 sends ON signal to all solenoids</td><td>ON</td><td>X</td><td>—</td></tr>
<tr><td colspan="4">Solenoid is not OFF even though Anti-Lock Brake Control Module 2B373 sends OFF Signal to solenoid after Fail-Safe Relay is ON</td><td>ON</td><td>X</td><td>X</td></tr>
<tr><td colspan="3">—</td><td>Solenoid is not ON even though Anti-Lock Brake Control Module 2B373 sends ON signal to solenoid</td><td>ON</td><td>X</td><td>X</td></tr>
<tr><td>Hydraulic Anti-Lock Actuator Assembly 2C257</td><td colspan="3">—</td><td>Vehicle needs more than 2 sec. for pressure reduction periods when slippage is more than 50% and/or coeff. of friction is 0.4 or more after 2 sec. of pressure reduction control</td><td>ON after ABS operation</td><td>—</td><td>—</td><td>Hydraulic Anti-Lock Actuator Assembly 2C257 cannot reduce pressure</td></tr>
</table>

86759209

Fig. 82 DTC identification (continued)

Diagnostic Trouble Code	Possible Failure Location	Diagnostic Trouble Code Logic Specifications				Warning Indicator	Failure Mode		
		ABS Initialized (KOEO)	Starting Up or Slowing Down	Normal Driving	Driving with ABS Operating		Open	Short	Other
51	Fail-Safe Relay	1K terminal voltage does not stay 0 volts for 48 msec. after key ON		—		ON	—	X	Fail-Safe Relay stays ON
		1K terminal voltage does not stay 12 volts for 48 msec. after Anti-Lock Brake Control Module 2B373 sends ON signal to Fail-Safe Relay				ON	X	X	Fail-Safe Relay stays OFF
		—	1K terminal voltage is 0 volts for 0.2 to 2 seconds			ON	X	X	—
53	Motor Relay	—	1L terminal voltage is 0 volts even though 2H terminal voltage is 0 volts			ON	X	X	—
			1L terminal voltage is battery voltage even though 2H terminal voltage is battery voltage			ON	—	—	Motor Relay stays ON
	Motor	No self-generated voltage from motor after motor turned OFF		—		ON	—	—	Motor Locked
61	Anti-Lock Brake Control Module 2B373	Failure of IC (Integrated Circuit) in Anti-Lock Brake Control Module 2B373				ON	—	—	—
—		Failure of ROM, RAM, or timer to Anti-Lock Brake Control Module 2B373				ON	—	—	—

86759210

Fig. 83 DTC identification (continued)

PINPOINT TEST A: ANTI-LOCK SENSORS AND SENSOR INDICATORS

	TEST STEP	RESULT ►	ACTION TO TAKE
A1	CHECK SYSTEM INTEGRITY		
	• Visually inspect all wiring, wiring harnesses, connectors, brake tubes, and components for evidence of overheating, insulation damage, looseness, shorting, or other damage. • **Is there any cause for concern?**	Yes ► No ►	SERVICE as required. GO to **A2**.
A2	CHECK FOR SHORT TO GROUND		
	• Key OFF. • Locate and disconnect the anti-lock brake control module connector. • Measure the resistance between the following anti-lock brake control module connector wire(s) in question and ground:	Yes ► No ►	GO to **A3**. SERVICE short to ground from sensor(s) to anti-lock brake control module.

Brake Anti-Lock Sensor	Wire Color
LH Front Anti-Lock Sensor	"BK/W" and ground
RH Front Anti-Lock Sensor	"BK/R" and ground
LH Rear Anti-Lock Sensor	"BK/BL" and ground
RH Rear Anti-Lock Sensor	"BK/O" and ground

• **Is the resistance greater than 10,000 ohms?**

	TEST STEP	RESULT ►	ACTION TO TAKE
A3	CHECK RESISTANCE AT ANTI-LOCK BRAKE CONTROL MODULE CONNECTOR		
	• Key OFF. • Anti-lock brake control module disconnected. • Measure the resistance between the following wire(s) in question at the anti-lock brake control module connector leading to the anti-lock sensor(s):	Yes ► No ►	GO to **A5**. GO to **A4**.

Brake Anti-Lock Sensor	Wires
LH Front Anti-Lock Sensor	"BK/W" and "O/W"
RH Front Anti-Lock Sensor	"BK/R" and "O"
LH Rear Anti-Lock Sensor	"BK/BL" and "R/BL"
RH Rear Anti-Lock Sensor	"BK/O" and "W"

• **Is the resistance reading 1600-2000 ohms?**

86759211

PINPOINT TEST A: ANTI-LOCK SENSORS AND SENSOR INDICATORS (Continued)

TEST STEP	RESULT ▶	ACTION TO TAKE
A4 CHECK RESISTANCE AT SENSOR(S)		
• Locate and disconnect the anti-lock sensor(s) in question. • Measure the resistance between the following sensor pins at the connector(s) leading to the anti-lock sensor(s) in question:	Yes ▶	SERVICE wire(s) from sensor(s) to anti-lock brake control module.
	No ▶	REPLACE anti-lock sensor(s).

Brake Anti-Lock Sensor	Sensor Pins
LH Front Anti-Lock Sensor	"BK/W" and "O/W"
RH Front Anti-Lock Sensor	"BK/R" and "O"
LH Rear Anti-Lock Sensor	"BK/BL" and "R/BL"
RH Rear Anti-Lock Sensor	"BK/O" and "W"

• **Is the resistance reading 1600-2000 ohms?**

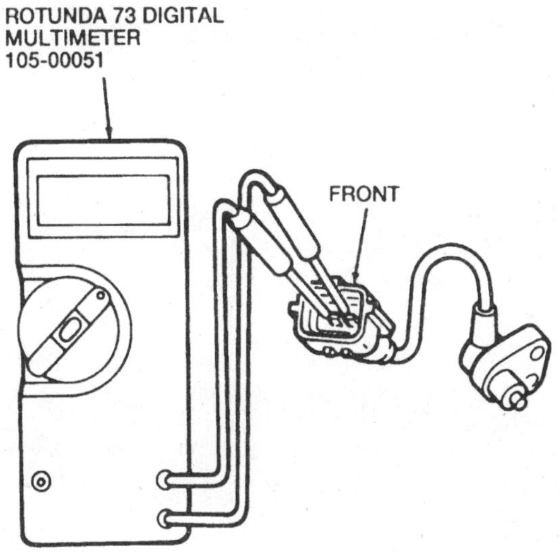

ROTUNDA 73 DIGITAL MULTIMETER 105-00051

FRONT

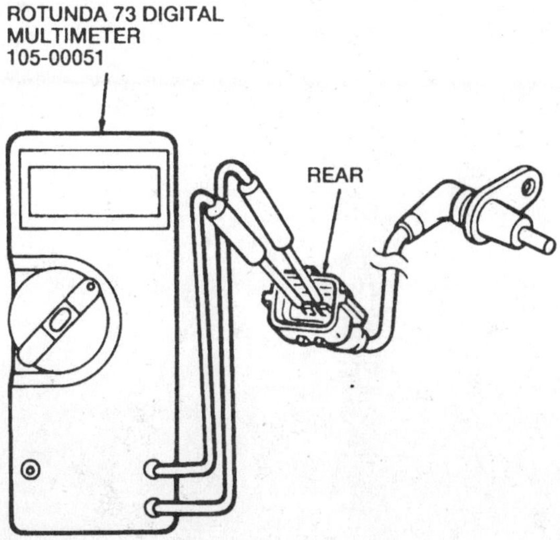

ROTUNDA 73 DIGITAL MULTIMETER 105-00051

REAR

86759212

PINPOINT TEST A: ANTI-LOCK SENSORS AND SENSOR INDICATORS (Continued)

TEST STEP		RESULT ▶	ACTION TO TAKE
A5	CHECK SIGNAL AT ANTI-LOCK BRAKE CONTROL MODULE CONNECTOR		
	• Key OFF. • Anti-lock brake control module disconnected. • Multimeter on AC scale. • Measure the voltage between the following wires at the anti-lock brake control module connector leading to the anti-lock sensor(s) in question while rotating wheel approximately 60 rpm (approximately one wheel turn per second):	Yes ▶ No ▶	GO to **A7**. GO to **A6**.

Brake Anti-Lock Sensor	Wires
LH Front Anti-Lock Sensor	"BK/W" and "O/W"
RH Front Anti-Lock Sensor	"BK/R" and "O"
LH Rear Anti-Lock Sensor	"BK/BL" and "R/BL"
RH Rear Anti-Lock Sensor	"BK/O" and "W"

- **Is the voltage reading between 0.25 and 3.0 volts AC?**

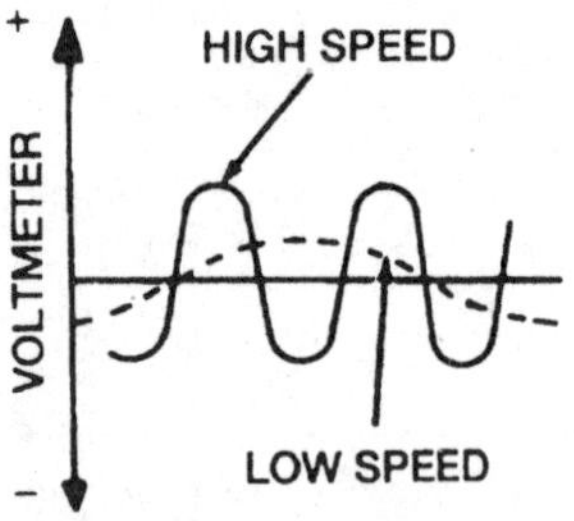

+
HIGH SPEED
VOLTMETER
LOW SPEED
−

86759213

PINPOINT TEST A: ANTI-LOCK SENSORS AND SENSOR INDICATORS (Continued)

TEST STEP		RESULT ▶	ACTION TO TAKE
A6	INSPECT ANTI-LOCK SENSOR(S) AND BRAKE ANTI-LOCK SENSOR INDICATOR(S)		
	• Remove the wheel and tire assembly for the anti-lock sensor(s) or brake anti-lock sensor indicators in question. • Check for damage to the anti-lock sensor(s) or brake anti-lock sensor indicators. • Check for objects sticking to the anti-lock sensor(s) or brake anti-lock sensor indicators. • Check the anti-lock sensor bolt(s) tightening torque: 16-23 N·m (12-17 lb-ft). • Check the clearance between anti-lock sensor(s) and brake anti-lock sensor indicators: 0.3-1.1mm (0.012-0.043 inch). • **Are the conditions OK?**	Yes ▶ No ▶	REPLACE anti-lock sensor(s). REPLACE anti-lock sensor(s) or brake anti-lock sensor indicator(s).

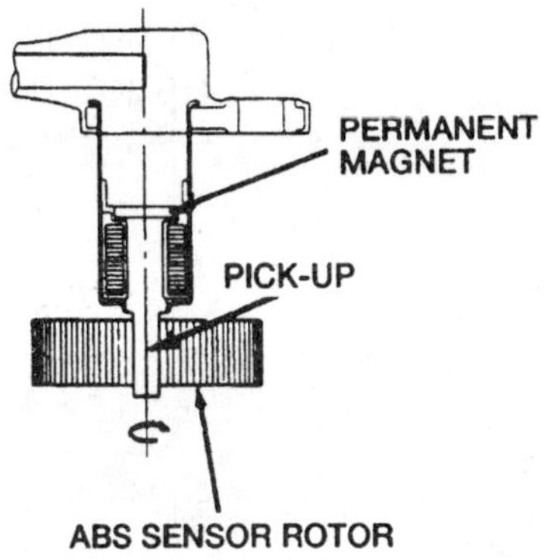

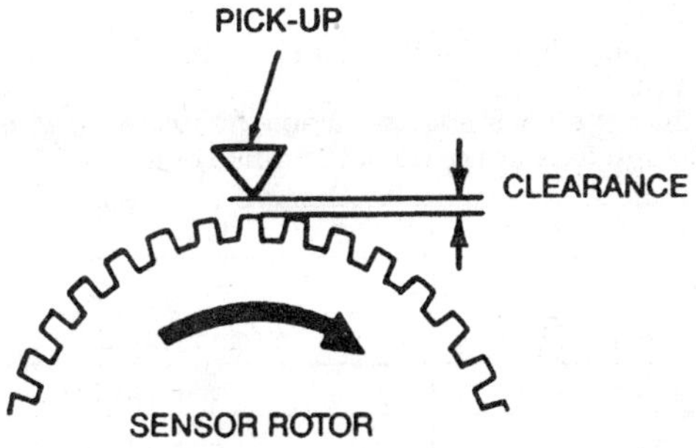

TEST STEP		RESULT ▶	ACTION TO TAKE
A7	CHECK BRAKE ON/OFF (BOO) SWITCH CIRCUIT		
	• Depress the brake pedal. • Check to see that the stoplamps illuminate. • **Do the stoplamps operate properly?**	Yes ▶ No ▶	GO to **A8**. SERVICE BOO switch as required. REFER to Section 17-01.
A8	CHECK BOO SWITCH VOLTAGE		
	• Key OFF. • Disconnect the anti-lock brake control module. • Key ON. • Measure the voltage on the "GN" wire at the anti-lock brake control module connector for the following conditions:	Yes ▶ No ▶	GO to Pinpoint Test **H1**. SERVICE the "GN" wire between Brake On/Off (BOO) switch and anti-lock brake control module.

Brake Pedal Position	Voltage
Depressed	Above 10 volts
Released	0-2 volts

• **Are the voltage readings OK?**

PINPOINT TEST B: ANTI-LOCK SENSOR OPEN CIRCUIT

TEST STEP		RESULT ▶	ACTION TO TAKE
B1	CHECK OPEN CIRCUIT		
	• Drive the vehicle at 10 km/h (6 mph). • Recheck the malfunction codes. Refer to the Quick Test in this section. • **Is a Code 11, 12, 13, or 14 obtained?**	Yes ▶ No (No codes) ▶ No (Code 15 reappears) ▶	GO to Pinpoint Test **A1**. Intermittent fault. REFER to Continuous Test in this section. SUBSTITUTE a known good anti-lock brake control module. PERFORM Test Step **B1** again.

86759214

PINPOINT TEST C: SOLENOID VALVE

	TEST STEP	RESULT ▶	ACTION TO TAKE
C1	CHECK SYSTEM INTEGRITY		
	• Visually inspect all wiring, wiring harnesses, connectors, brake tubes, and components for evidence of overheating, insulation damage, looseness, shorting, or other damage. • **Is there any cause for concern?**	Yes ▶ No ▶	SERVICE as required. GO to **C2**.
C2	CHECK SOLENOID SIGNAL		
	• Key ON. • Measure the voltage at 1K ("Y") terminal of the anti-lock brake control module. (Anti-lock brake control module must be connected.) • **Does the voltage reading momentarily read above 10 volts?**	Yes ▶ No ▶	GO to **C3**. SERVICE "Y" wire between anti-lock relay and anti-lock brake control module.
C3	CHECK SOLENOID AT ANTI-LOCK BRAKE CONTROL MODULE		
	• Key OFF. • Locate and disconnect the anti-lock brake control module. • Measure the resistance between the following wires at the anti-lock brake control module connector. (see table below) • **Are the resistances about 3 ohms?**	Yes ▶ No ▶	GO to Pinpoint Test **H1**. GO to **C4**.
C4	CHECK SOLENOID AT HYDRAULIC ANTI-LOCK ACTUATOR ASSEMBLY		
	• Perform the Hydraulic Anti-Lock Actuator Assembly component test in this section. • **Is the hydraulic anti-lock actuator assembly OK?**	Yes ▶ No ▶	SERVICE wire(s) between anti-lock brake control module and hydraulic anti-lock actuator assembly. REPLACE hydraulic anti-lock actuator assembly.

Solenoid	Wires
Left Front	"Y" and "Y/BL"
Right Front	"Y" and "BL/O"
Left Rear	"Y" and "BR"
Right Rear	"Y" and "PK"

PINPOINT TEST D: FAIL-SAFE RELAY

	TEST STEP	RESULT ▶	ACTION TO TAKE
D1	CHECK SYSTEM INTEGRITY		
	• Visually inspect all wiring, wiring harnesses, connectors, brake tubes, and components for evidence of overheating, insulation damage, looseness, shorting, or other damage. • **Is there any cause for concern?**	Yes ▶ No ▶	SERVICE as required. GO to **D2**.
D2	CHECK FUSES		
	• Check the 60A ABS fuse in the main fuse junction panel and the 10A ABS fuse in the interior fuse junction panel. • **Are the fuses OK?**	Yes ▶ No ▶	GO to **D3**. REPLACE fuse(s).
D3	CHECK ANTI-LOCK RELAY OPERATION		
	• Key OFF. • Locate and disconnect the anti-lock brake control module. • Key ON. • Connect the "BK/BL" wire at the anti-lock brake control module connector to ground. • **Does the anti-lock relay click when wire is grounded?**	Yes ▶ No ▶	GO to **D4**. INSPECT "BK/BL" wire from anti-lock relay to anti-lock brake control module. If OK, GO to **D6**.

86759215

PINPOINT TEST D: FAIL-SAFE RELAY (Continued)

	TEST STEP	RESULT	ACTION TO TAKE
D4	CHECK ANTI-LOCK BRAKE WARNING INDICATOR DIODE		
	• Anti-lock brake control module disconnected. • Key ON. • Connect the "BK/BL" wire at the anti-lock brake control module connector to ground. • Check to see that the anti-lock brake warning indicator does not illuminate when grounded. • **Does the anti-lock brake warning indicator illuminate?**	Yes No	GO to **D6**. GO to **D5**.
D5	CHECK VOLTAGE FROM ANTI-LOCK RELAY		
	• Anti-lock brake control module disconnected. • Key ON. • Connect the "BK/BL" wire at the anti-lock brake control module connector to ground. • Measure the voltage at the "Y" wire at the anti-lock brake control module connector. • **Is the voltage reading greater than 10 volts?**	Yes Yes, if directed to this Pinpoint Test from Step F1 No	GO to Pinpoint Test **G1**. GO to **E2**. GO to **D6**.
D6	CHECK ANTI-LOCK RELAY		
	• Perform the Anti-Lock Relay component test in this section. • **Is the anti-lock relay OK?**	Yes No	SERVICE the "Y" wire between the anti-lock relay and the anti-lock brake control module. REPLACE the anti-lock relay.

PINPOINT TEST E: HYDRAULIC ANTI-LOCK ACTUATOR MOTOR AND ANTI-LOCK RELAY

	TEST STEP	RESULT	ACTION TO TAKE
E1	CHECK FAIL-SAFE RELAY		
	• Go to the Pinpoint Test D1 and check the operation of the fail-safe relay. • **Does the fail-safe relay operate properly?**	Yes No	GO to **E2**. REPLACE the anti-lock relay.
E2	CHECK SYSTEM INTEGRITY		
	• Visually inspect all wiring, wiring harnesses, connectors, brake tubes, and components for evidence of overheating, insulation damage, looseness, shorting, or other damage. • **Is there any cause for concern?**	Yes No	SERVICE as required. GO to **E3**.
E3	CHECK MOTOR RELAY OPERATION		
	CAUTION: While performing this test step, do not allow motor to operate for more than two seconds. • Key OFF. • Locate and disconnect the anti-lock brake control module. • Key ON. • Connect the "BK/BL" wire to ground at the anti-lock brake control module harness connector. • Connect the "BL" wire to ground at the anti-lock brake control module harness connector for no more than two seconds. • **Does the motor relay click and the motor operate when wires are grounded?**	Yes No (Motor relay clicks but motor does not operate) No (Motor relay does not click and motor does not operate)	GO to **E8**. GO to **E5**. GO to **E4**.
E4	CHECK ANTI-LOCK RELAY		
	• Perform the Anti-Lock Relay component test in this section. • **Is the anti-lock relay OK?**	Yes No	GO to **E5**. REPLACE the anti-lock relay.

86759A16

PINPOINT TEST E: HYDRAULIC ANTI-LOCK ACTUATOR MOTOR AND ANTI-LOCK RELAY (Continued)

TEST STEP		RESULT	▶	ACTION TO TAKE
E5	CHECK MOTOR RESISTANCE			
	• Key OFF. • Locate and disconnect the hydraulic anti-lock actuator assembly 2-pin motor connector. • Measure the resistance between the "R / Y" and "BK" terminals of the motor. R/Y BK HYDRAULIC ACTUATOR MOTOR H9144-A • **Is the resistance less than 1 ohm?**	Yes No	▶ ▶	GO to **E6**. REPLACE the hydraulic anti-lock actuator assembly.
E6	CHECK MOTOR OPERATION			
	CAUTION: While performing this test step, do not allow motor to operate for more than two seconds. • Disconnect the hydraulic anti-lock actuator assembly 2-pin motor connector. • Apply battery voltage to the "R / Y" terminal and ground the "BK" terminal at the hydraulic anti-lock actuator assembly 2-pin motor connector. • **Does the motor operate when voltage is applied?**	Yes No	▶ ▶	GO to **E7**. REPLACE hydraulic anti-lock actuator assembly.
E7	CHECK MOTOR GROUND			
	• Hydraulic anti-lock actuator assembly 2-pin motor connector disconnected. • Measure the resistance between the "BK" wire at the hydraulic anti-lock actuator assembly 2-pin motor connector (harness side) and ground. • **Is the resistance less than 5 ohms?**	Yes No	▶ ▶	SERVICE "R / Y" wire between anti-lock relay and hydraulic anti-lock actuator assembly. SERVICE "BK" wire to ground.
E8	CHECK RESISTANCE AT ANTI-LOCK BRAKE CONTROL MODULE			
	• Key OFF. • Hydraulic anti-lock actuator assembly connected. • ABS control module disconnected. • Measure the resistance between the "R / Y" wire at the anti-lock brake control module and ground. • **Is the resistance less than 1 ohm?**	Yes No	▶ ▶	GO to Pinpoint Test **F1**. SERVICE "R / Y" wire between anti-lock brake control module and hydraulic anti-lock actuator assembly.

PINPOINT TEST F: GENERATOR

TEST STEP		RESULT	▶	ACTION TO TAKE
F1	CHECK BATTERY VOLTAGE			
	• Measure the voltage at the battery. Refer to Section 14-00. • **Is the voltage reading as specified?**	Yes No	▶ ▶	GO to **F2**. CHARGE or REPLACE the battery as necessary. REFER to Section 14-01.

86759216

PINPOINT TEST F: GENERATOR (Continued)

	TEST STEP	RESULT	ACTION TO TAKE
F2	CHECK BATTERY VOLTAGE AT ANTI-LOCK BRAKE CONTROL MODULE		
	• Locate and disconnect the ABS control module connectors. • Measure the voltage at the anti-lock brake control module 1H ("BK/O") terminal under the following conditions: **Ignition Switch** / **Voltage**: OFF — 0 Volts; ON — Above 10 Volts • **Are the voltage readings as specified?**	Yes No	▶ GO to **F3**. ▶ SERVICE the "BK/O" wire.
F3	CHECK VOLTAGE AT GENERATOR		
	• Measure the voltage at the B ("BK/W"), L ("W/BK"), and S ("W/R") terminals at the generator with the engine idling. Refer to Section 14-00 for testing procedures and voltage specifications. • **Are the voltage readings as specified?**	Yes No	▶ GO to **F4**. ▶ SERVICE or REPLACE generator. REFER to Section 14-00.
F4	CHECK GENERATOR VOLTAGE AT ANTI-LOCK BRAKE CONTROL MODULE		
	• Measure the voltage at the 2F ("W/BK") terminal of the anti-lock brake control module under the following conditions: **Condition** / **Voltage**: Key ON Engine Off — 0.8-3 Volts; Engine Idling — Above 10 Volts • **Are the voltages as specified?**	Yes No	▶ GO to Pinpoint Test **G1**. ▶ SERVICE "W/BK" wire.

PINPOINT TEST G: WARNING INDICATOR

	TEST STEP	RESULT	ACTION TO TAKE
G1	CHECK ANTI-LOCK BRAKE WARNING OPERATION		
	• Key OFF. • Locate and disconnect the anti-lock brake control module. • Key ON. • **Does the anti-lock brake warning indicator illuminate?**	Yes No	▶ GO to **G2**. ▶ REPLACE the 15A METER fuse and/or warning indicator miniature bulb if burned out. REFER to Section 13-01. If OK, SERVICE "Y/R" wire from instrument cluster to anti-lock relay.
G2	CHECK FOR SHORT TO GROUND		
	• Key ON. • Anti-lock brake control module disconnected. • Locate and disconnect the anti-lock relay. • **Does the anti-lock brake warning indicator go off?**	Yes No	▶ GO to **G3**. ▶ SERVICE the "Y/R" wire between the instrument cluster and anti-lock relay for short to ground.

86759217

PINPOINT TEST G: WARNING INDICATOR (Continued)

	TEST STEP	RESULT	►	ACTION TO TAKE
G3	CHECK ANTI-LOCK BRAKE WARNING INDICATOR SIGNAL			
	• Key ON. • Anti-lock brake control module disconnected. • ABS relay disconnected. • Connect the "Y/R" wire at the anti-lock brake control module and the "Y/R" wire at the anti-lock relay to ground. • **Does the anti-lock brake warning indicator illuminate when both wires are connected to ground?**	Yes	►	GO to **G4**.
		No (Does not illuminate at all)	►	REPLACE the 15A METER fuse and/or warning indicator bulb if burned out. If OK, SERVICE "Y/R" wire from instrument cluster to anti-lock relay and/or anti-lock brake control module.
		No (Illuminates only when grounded at anti-lock brake control module)	►	SERVICE "Y/R" wire to anti-lock relay.
		No (Illuminates only when grounded at anti-lock relay)	►	SERVICE "Y/R" wire to anti-lock brake control module.
G4	CHECK GROUNDS AT ABS CONTROL MODULE			
	• Key OFF. • Anti-lock brake control module disconnected. • Measure the resistance between the 1E ("BK") terminal and ground and the 1F ("BK") terminal and ground at the anti-lock brake control module. • **Are the resistances less than 5 ohms?**	Yes	►	REPLACE anti-lock brake control module.
		No	►	SERVICE the "BK" wire(s) to ground.

PINPOINT TEST H: HYDRAULIC SYSTEM

	TEST STEP	RESULT	►	ACTION TO TAKE
H1	CHECK SYSTEM INTEGRITY			
	• Visually inspect all wiring, wiring harnesses, connectors, brake tubes, and components for evidence of overheating, insulation damage, looseness, shorting, or other damage. • **Is there any cause for concern?**	Yes	►	SERVICE as required.
		No	►	GO to **H2**.

86759218

PINPOINT TEST H: HYDRAULIC SYSTEM (Continued)

	TEST STEP	RESULT	▶ ACTION TO TAKE
H2	CHECK HYDRAULIC PRESSURE		
	NOTE: This test requires an assistant. The pressure reduction operation occurs within a 2 second period. • Jack up the vehicle so that all the wheels are clear off the ground and the vehicle is properly supported. • Shift the transaxle to NEUTRAL. • Release the parking brake. • Check to see that there is no brake drag while rotating the wheels by hand. • Use a jumper wire to connect the "TBS" and "GND" terminals at the data link connector. • Depress the brake pedal and have an assistant verify that the wheels will not rotate. • With the brake pedal still depressed, turn the key ON and verify that the brake pressure is released momentarily (approximately 0.5 seconds) and that each wheel rotates when pressure reduction operates as shown:  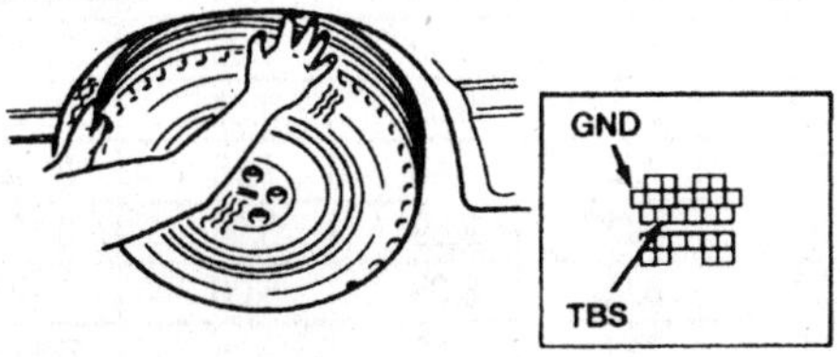 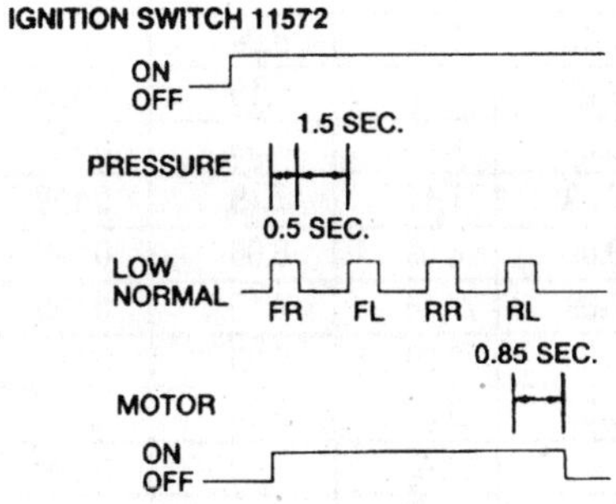 GND TBS IGNITION SWITCH 11572 ON OFF 1.5 SEC. PRESSURE 0.5 SEC. LOW NORMAL FR FL RR RL 0.85 SEC. MOTOR ON OFF • **Does the pressure reduction operate properly?**	Yes (If directed to this Pinpoint Test from Quick Test Step QT4)	▶ ABS functioning properly.
		Yes (If directed to this Pinpoint Test from Step A8)	▶ Intermittent fault. GO to Continuous Test in this section.
		Yes (If directed to this Pinpoint Test from Step C3)	▶ GO to Pinpoint Test **G1**.
		No	▶ INSPECT hydraulic system piping and wiring. If OK, REPLACE hydraulic anti-lock actuator assembly.

86759219

BRAKE SPECIFICATIONS

All measurements in inches unless noted

		Master	Brake Disc			Brake Drum Diameter			Minimum Lining Thickness	
Year	Model	Cylinder Bore	Original Thickness	Minimum Thickness	Maximum Run-out	Original Inside Diameter	Max. Wear Limit	Maximum Machine Diameter	Front	Rear
1981	Escort/Lynx	0.828	0.945	0.882	0.002	7.09	7.18	7.15	0.125	①
1982	Escort/Lynx	0.828	0.945	0.882	0.002	7.09	7.18	7.15	0.125	①
	EXP/LN7	0.828	0.945	0.882	0.002	8.00	8.09	8.06	0.125	①
1983	Escort/Lynx ②	0.828	0.945	0.882	0.002	7.09	7.18	7.15	0.125	①
	Escort/Lynx ③	0.828	0.945	0.882	0.002	8.00	8.09	8.06	0.125	①
	EXP/LN7	0.828	0.945	0.882	0.002	8.00	8.09	8.06	0.125	①
1984	Escort/Lynx ②	0.828	0.945	0.882	0.002	7.09	7.18	7.15	0.125	①
	Escort/Lynx ③	0.828	0.945	0.882	0.002	8.00	8.09	8.06	0.125	①
	EXP/LN7	0.828	0.945	0.882	0.002	8.00	8.09	8.06	0.125	①
1985	Escort/Lynx ②	0.828	0.945	0.882	0.002	7.09	7.18	7.15	0.125	①
	Escort/Lynx ③	0.828	0.945	0.882	0.002	8.00	8.09	8.06	0.125	①
	EXP	0.828	0.945	0.882	0.002	8.00	8.09	8.06	0.125	①
1986	Escort/Lynx ②	0.828	0.945	0.882	0.002	7.09	7.18	7.15	0.125	①
	Escort/Lynx ③	0.828	0.945	0.882	0.002	8.00	8.09	8.06	0.125	①
	EXP	0.828	0.945	0.882	0.002	8.00	8.09	8.06	0.125	①
1987	Escort/Lynx ②	0.828	0.945	0.882	0.002	7.09	7.18	7.15	0.125	①
	Escort/Lynx ③	0.828	0.945	0.882	0.002	8.00	8.09	8.06	0.125	①
1988	Escort ②	0.828	0.945	0.882	0.002	7.09	7.18	7.15	0.125	①
	Escort ③	0.828	0.945	0.882	0.002	8.00	8.09	8.06	0.125	①
1989	Escort ②	0.828	0.945	0.882	0.002	7.09	7.17	7.15	0.125	①
	Escort ③	0.828	0.945	0.882	0.002	8.00	8.09	8.06	0.125	①
1990	Escort ②	0.828	0.945	0.882	0.002	7.09	7.18	7.15	0.125	①
	Escort ③	0.828	0.945	0.882	0.002	8.00	8.09	8.06	0.125	①
1991	Escort/Tracer ④	⑥	0.870	0.820	0.004	9.00	9.06	9.04	0.080	0.040
	Escort/Tracer ⑤	⑥	⑦	⑧	0.004	-	-	-	0.080	0.300
1992	Escort/Tracer ④	⑥	0.870	0.820	0.004	9.00	9.06	9.04	0.080	0.040
	Escort/Tracer ⑤	⑥	⑦	⑧	0.004	-	-	-	0.080	0.300
1993	Escort/Tracer ④	⑥	0.870	0.820	0.004	7.87	7.95	7.91	0.080	0.040
	Escort/Tracer ⑤	⑥	⑦	⑧	0.004	-	-	-	0.080	0.300
1994	Escort/Tracer ④	⑥	0.870	0.790	0.004	7.87	7.95	7.91	0.080	0.040
	Escort/Tracer ⑤	⑥	⑦	⑧	0.004	-	-	-	0.080	0.300
1995	Escort/Tracer ④	⑥	0.870	0.790	0.004	7.87	7.95	7.91	0.080	0.040
	Escort/Tracer ⑤	⑥	⑦	⑧	0.004	-	-	-	0.080	0.300

① 0.030 in. over rivet head; 0.062 in. if bonded lining
② 7 inch rear drum
③ 8 inch rear drum
④ Rear drum-equipped models
⑤ Rear disc-equipped models
⑥ Primary bore: 1.12
Secondary bore: 0.776
⑦ Front: 0.870
Rear: 0.350
⑧ Front: 0.820
Rear: 0.200

86759C16

Troubleshooting the Brake System

Problem	Cause	Solution
Low brake pedal (excessive pedal travel required for braking action.)	• Excessive clearance between rear linings and drums caused by inoperative automatic adjusters	• Make 10 to 15 alternate forward and reverse brake stops to adjust brakes. If brake pedal does not come up, repair or replace adjuster parts as necessary.
	• Worn rear brakelining	• Inspect and replace lining if worn beyond minimum thickness specification
	• Bent, distorted brakeshoes, front or rear	• Replace brakeshoes in axle sets
	• Air in hydraulic system	• Remove air from system. Refer to Brake Bleeding.
Low brake pedal (pedal may go to floor with steady pressure applied.)	• Fluid leak in hydraulic system	• Fill master cylinder to fill line; have helper apply brakes and check calipers, wheel cylinders, differential valve tubes, hoses and fittings for leaks. Repair or replace as necessary.
	• Air in hydraulic system	• Remove air from system. Refer to Brake Bleeding.
	• Incorrect or non-recommended brake fluid (fluid evaporates at below normal temp).	• Flush hydraulic system with clean brake fluid. Refill with correct-type fluid.
	• Master cylinder piston seals worn, or master cylinder bore is scored, worn or corroded	• Repair or replace master cylinder
Low brake pedal (pedal goes to floor on first application—o.k. on subsequent applications.)	• Disc brake pads sticking on abutment surfaces of anchor plate. Caused by a build-up of dirt, rust, or corrosion on abutment surfaces	• Clean abutment surfaces
Fading brake pedal (pedal height decreases with steady pressure applied.)	• Fluid leak in hydraulic system	• Fill master cylinder reservoirs to fill mark, have helper apply brakes, check calipers, wheel cylinders, differential valve, tubes, hoses, and fittings for fluid leaks. Repair or replace parts as necessary.
	• Master cylinder piston seals worn, or master cylinder bore is scored, worn or corroded	• Repair or replace master cylinder
Spongy brake pedal (pedal has abnormally soft, springy, spongy feel when depressed.)	• Air in hydraulic system	• Remove air from system. Refer to Brake Bleeding.
	• Brakeshoes bent or distorted	• Replace brakeshoes
	• Brakelining not yet seated with drums and rotors	• Burnish brakes
	• Rear drum brakes not properly adjusted	• Adjust brakes

86759400

Troubleshooting the Brake System (cont.)

Problem	Cause	Solution
Decreasing brake pedal travel (pedal travel required for braking action decreases and may be accompanied by a hard pedal.)	• Caliper or wheel cylinder pistons sticking or seized	• Repair or replace the calipers, or wheel cylinders
	• Master cylinder compensator ports blocked (preventing fluid return to reservoirs) or pistons sticking or seized in master cylinder bore	• Repair or replace the master cylinder
	• Power brake unit binding internally	• Test unit according to the following procedure: (a) Shift transmission into neutral and start engine (b) Increase engine speed to 1500 rpm, close throttle and fully depress brake pedal (c) Slow release brake pedal and stop engine (d) Have helper remove vacuum check valve and hose from power unit. Observe for backward movement of brake pedal. (e) If the pedal moves backward, the power unit has an internal bind—replace power unit
Grabbing brakes (severe reaction to brake pedal pressure.)	• Brakelining(s) contaminated by grease or brake fluid	• Determine and correct cause of contamination and replace brakeshoes in axle sets
	• Parking brake cables incorrectly adjusted or seized	• Adjust cables. Replace seized cables.
	• Incorrect brakelining or lining loose on brakeshoes	• Replace brakeshoes in axle sets
	• Caliper anchor plate bolts loose	• Tighten bolts
	• Rear brakeshoes binding on support plate ledges	• Clean and lubricate ledges. Replace support plate(s) if ledges are deeply grooved. Do not attempt to smooth ledges by grinding.
	• Incorrect or missing power brake reaction disc	• Install correct disc
	• Rear brake support plates loose	• Tighten mounting bolts
Chatter or shudder when brakes are applied (pedal pulsation and roughness may also occur.)	• Brakeshoes distorted, bent, contaminated, or worn	• Replace brakeshoes in axle sets
	• Caliper anchor plate or support plate loose	• Tighten mounting bolts
	• Excessive thickness variation of rotor(s)	• Refinish or replace rotors in axle sets
Noisy brakes (squealing, clicking, scraping sound when brakes are applied.)	• Bent, broken, distorted brakeshoes	• Replace brakeshoes in axle sets
	• Excessive rust on outer edge of rotor braking surface	• Remove rust

86759401

Troubleshooting the Brake System (cont.)

Problem	Cause	Solution
Hard brake pedal (excessive pedal pressure required to stop vehicle. May be accompanied by brake fade.)	• Loose or leaking power brake unit vacuum hose	• Tighten connections or replace leaking hose
	• Incorrect or poor quality brake-lining	• Replace with lining in axle sets
	• Bent, broken, distorted brakeshoes	• Replace brakeshoes
	• Calipers binding or dragging on mounting pins. Rear brakeshoes dragging on support plate.	• Replace mounting pins and bushings. Clean rust or burrs from rear brake support plate ledges and lubricate ledges with molydisulfide grease. **NOTE:** If ledges are deeply grooved or scored, do not attempt to sand or grind them smooth—replace support plate.
	• Caliper, wheel cylinder, or master cylinder pistons sticking or seized	• Repair or replace parts as necessary
	• Power brake unit vacuum check valve malfunction	• Test valve according to the following procedure: (a) Start engine, increase engine speed to 1500 rpm, close throttle and immediately stop engine (b) Wait at least 90 seconds then depress brake pedal (c) If brakes are not vacuum assisted for 2 or more applications, check valve is faulty
	• Power brake unit has internal bind	• Test unit according to the following procedure: (a) With engine stopped, apply brakes several times to exhaust all vacuum in system (b) Shift transmission into neutral, depress brake pedal and start engine (c) If pedal height decreases with foot pressure and less pressure is required to hold pedal in applied position, power unit vacuum system is operating normally. Test power unit. If power unit exhibits a bind condition, replace the power unit.

86759402

Troubleshooting the Brake System (cont.)

Problem	Cause	Solution
Hard brake pedal (excessive pedal pressure required to stop vehicle. May be accompanied by brake fade.)	• Master cylinder compensator ports (at bottom of reservoirs) blocked by dirt, scale, rust, or have small burrs (blocked ports prevent fluid return to reservoirs).	• Repair or replace master cylinder **CAUTION:** Do not attempt to clean blocked ports with wire, pencils, or similar implements. Use compressed air only.
	• Brake hoses, tubes, fittings clogged or restricted	• Use compressed air to check or unclog parts. Replace any damaged parts.
	• Brake fluid contaminated with improper fluids (motor oil, transmission fluid, causing rubber components to swell and stick in bores	• Replace all rubber components, combination valve and hoses. Flush entire brake system with DOT 3 brake fluid or equivalent.
	• Low engine vacuum	• Adjust or repair engine
Dragging brakes (slow or incomplete release of brakes)	• Brake pedal binding at pivot	• Loosen and lubricate
	• Power brake unit has internal bind	• Inspect for internal bind. Replace unit if internal bind exists.
	• Parking brake cables incorrrectly adjusted or seized	• Adjust cables. Replace seized cables.
	• Rear brakeshoe return springs weak or broken	• Replace return springs. Replace brakeshoe if necessary in axle sets.
	• Automatic adjusters malfunctioning	• Repair or replace adjuster parts as required
	• Caliper, wheel cylinder or master cylinder pistons sticking or seized	• Repair or replace parts as necessary
	• Master cylinder compensating ports blocked (fluid does not return to reservoirs).	• Use compressed air to clear ports. Do not use wire, pencils, or similar objects to open blocked ports.
Vehicle moves to one side when brakes are applied	• Incorrect front tire pressure	• Inflate to recommended cold (reduced load) inflation pressure
	• Worn or damaged wheel bearings	• Replace worn or damaged bearings
	• Brakelining on one side contaminated	• Determine and correct cause of contamination and replace brakelining in axle sets
	• Brakeshoes on one side bent, distorted, or lining loose on shoe	• Replace brakeshoes in axle sets
	• Support plate bent or loose on one side	• Tighten or replace support plate
	• Brakelining not yet seated with drums or rotors	• Burnish brakelining
	• Caliper anchor plate loose on one side	• Tighten anchor plate bolts
	• Caliper piston sticking or seized	• Repair or replace caliper
	• Brakelinings water soaked	• Drive vehicle with brakes lightly applied to dry linings
	• Loose suspension component attaching or mounting bolts	• Tighten suspension bolts. Replace worn suspension components.
	• Brake combination valve failure	• Replace combination valve

86759403

Troubleshooting the Brake System (cont.)

Problem	Cause	Solution
Noisy brakes (squealing, clicking, scraping sound when brakes are applied.) (cont.)	• Brakelining worn out—shoes contacting drum of rotor	• Replace brakeshoes and lining in axle sets. Refinish or replace drums or rotors.
	• Broken or loose holdown or return springs	• Replace parts as necessary
	• Rough or dry drum brake support plate ledges	• Lubricate support plate ledges
	• Cracked, grooved, or scored rotor(s) or drum(s)	• Replace rotor(s) or drum(s). Replace brakeshoes and lining in axle sets if necessary.
	• Incorrect brakelining and/or shoes (front or rear).	• Install specified shoe and lining assemblies
Pulsating brake pedal	• Out of round drums or excessive lateral runout in disc brake rotor(s)	• Refinish or replace drums, re-index rotors or replace

86759404

TORQUE SPECIFICATIONS

1981-90 MODELS

Component	English	Metric
Master cylinder mounting nuts:	13–25 ft. lbs.	18–33 Nm
Booster-to-dash panel:	13–25 ft. lbs.	18–33 Nm
Rear Drum Brakes		
Wheel cylinder bleeder screws:	7.5–15 ft. lbs.	10–20 Nm
Wheel cylinder-to-backing plate screws:	9–13 ft. lbs.	12–18 Nm
Rear brake backing plate-to-spindle:	45–60 ft. lbs.	60–80 Nm
Wheel to hub and drum:	85–105 ft. lbs.	115–142 Nm
Front Disc Brakes		
Caliper bleeder screws:	7.5–15 ft. lbs.	10–20 Nm
Caliper locating pin:	18–25 ft. lbs.	24–34 Nm
Wheel nuts:	85–105 ft. lbs.	115–142 Nm
1991-95 MODELS		
Master cylinder mounting nuts:	8–12 ft. lbs.	10–16 Nm
Booster mounting nuts:	14–19 ft. lbs.	19–25 Nm
Bleeder screws:	53–77 inch lbs.	6–8 Nm
Proportioning valve mounting bolts:	14–17 ft. lbs.	19–23 Nm
Rear Drum Brakes		
Wheel cylinder-to-brake line flare nut:	12–16 ft. lbs.	16–22 Nm
Wheel cylinder mounting bolts:	7–9 ft. lbs.	10–13 Nm
Front Disc Brakes		
Brake hose attaching bolts:	16–20 ft. lbs.	22–29 Nm
Caliper mounting bolt:	29–36 ft. lbs.	39–49 Nm
Rear Disc Brakes		
Brake line-to-caliper attaching bolts:	16–22 ft. lbs.	22–29 Nm
Caliper lock bolt:	33–43 ft. lbs.	45–59 Nm
Adjustment screw plug:	9–12 ft. lbs.	12–16 Nm

86759C01

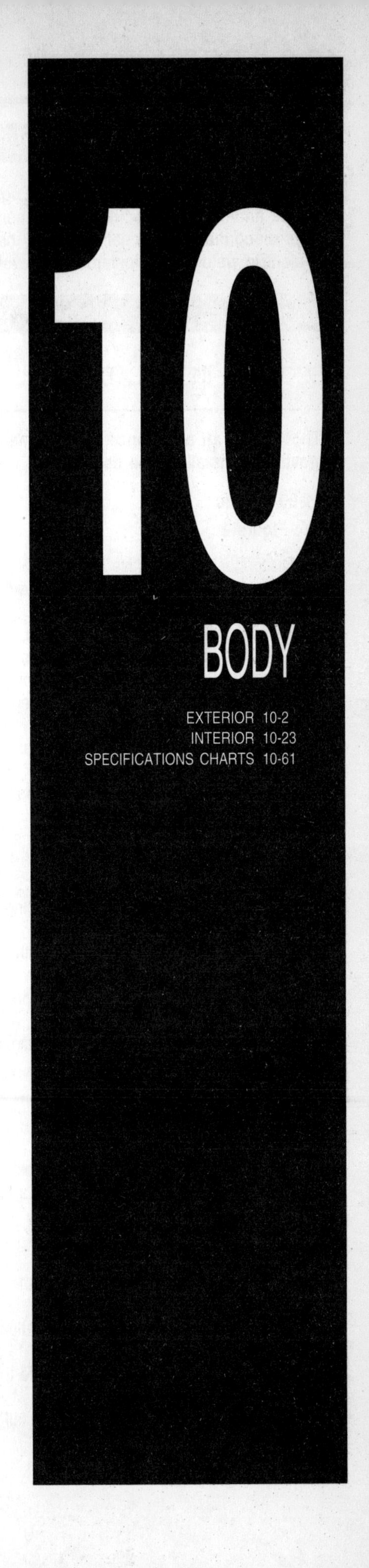

10

BODY

EXTERIOR

➡**To avoid damage to the Electronic Engine Control (EEC) modules and/or other electrical components or wiring, always disconnect the negative battery cable before using any electric welding equipment on the vehicle.**

Doors

REMOVAL & INSTALLATION

➡**The help of an assistance is recommended, when removing or installing the door(s).**

1981-90 Models

➧ **See Figure 1**

1. Disconnect the negative battery cable.
2. Open the door and support it with a Rotunda Door Rack 103-00027 or equivalent for door service.
3. Remove the trim panel, watershield, and all usable outside mouldings and clips (if the door is to be replaced).
4. Remove all usable window and door latch components from the door (if the door is to be replaced).
5. Support the door.
6. Scribe marks around the hinge locations for reference during installation.
7. Remove the door hinge attaching bolts from the door and remove the door.
8. Disconnect any wiring harness connectors, if so equipped.

To install:

9. Drill holes, as necessary, for attaching the outside moulding.
10. Position the door hinges and partially tighten the bolts.
11. Install the latch mechanism, window mechanism, glass and glass weatherstripping. Adjust the window mechanism.
12. Install the exterior trim, watershield, and the interior trim.
13. Adjust the door and tighten the retaining bolts.
14. Connect the negative battery cable.

1991-95 Models

➧ **See Figures 2, 3 and 4**

1. Disconnect the negative battery cable.
2. Remove the door checker pin with a hammer and punch, or suitable tool.
3. Detach the rubber electrical conduit from the vehicle body.
4. Pry the electrical connector out of the body and disconnect.
5. Scribe marks around the hinge locations for reference during installation.
6. Remove the hinge bolts and remove the door.

To install:

7. Place the door into position and install the hinge bolts.
8. Align the hinges with the marks made previously.
9. Adjust the door.
10. Install the electrical conduit.
11. Install the door checker pin.
12. Connect the negative battery cable.

ADJUSTMENTS

Adjusting the hinge affects the positioning of the outside surface of the door frame. Adjusting the latch striker affects the alignment of the door relative to the weatherstrip and the door closing characteristics.

1981-90 Models

➧ **See Figure 5**

The door latch striker pin can be adjusted laterally and vertically as well as for and aft. The latch striker should not be adjusted to correct the door sag.

The latch striker should be shimmed to get the clearance shown in the illustration, between the striker and the latch. To check this clearance, clean the latch jaws and striker area. Apply a thin layer of dark grease to the striker. As the door is closed and opened, a measurable pattern will result on the latch striker.

➡**Use a maximum of two shims under the striker.**

The door hinges provide sufficient adjustment to correct most door misalignment conditions. The holes of the hinge and/or the hinge attaching points are enlarged or elongated to provide for hinge and door alignment.

➡**DO NOT cover up a poor alignment with a latch striker adjustment.**

1. Refer to the illustration to determine which hinge screws must be loosened to move the door in the desired direction.
2. Loosen the hinge screws just enough to permit movement of the door with a padded pry bar.
3. Move the door the distance estimated to be necessary for a correct fit. Tighten the hinge bolts and check the door fit to be sure there is no bind or interference with the adjacent panel.

1991-95 Models

➧ **See Figures 6 and 7**

1. Loosen the hinge bolts just enough to permit movement of the door.
2. Move the door to the desired position and tighten the hinge bolts to 13-22 ft. lbs. (18-29 Nm).
3. Check the door fit to be sure the clearances are within the specifications shown.
4. Repeat Steps 1 and 2 until the desired fit is obtained, then check the striker plate for proper door closing.

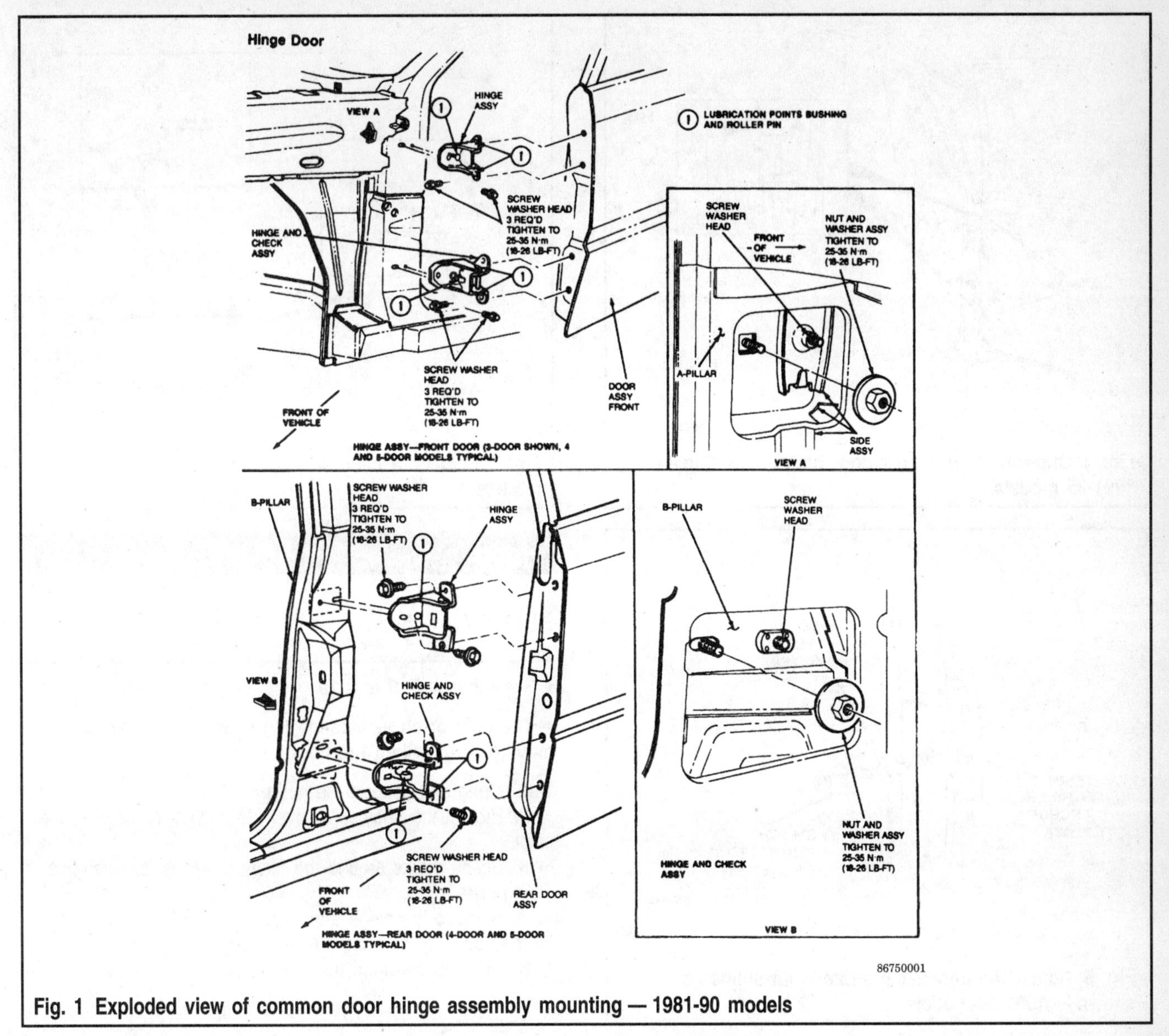

Fig. 1 Exploded view of common door hinge assembly mounting — 1981-90 models

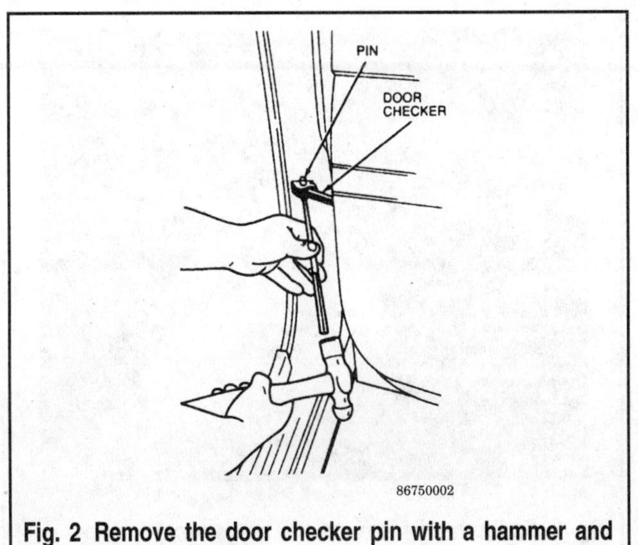

Fig. 2 Remove the door checker pin with a hammer and punch — 1991-95 models

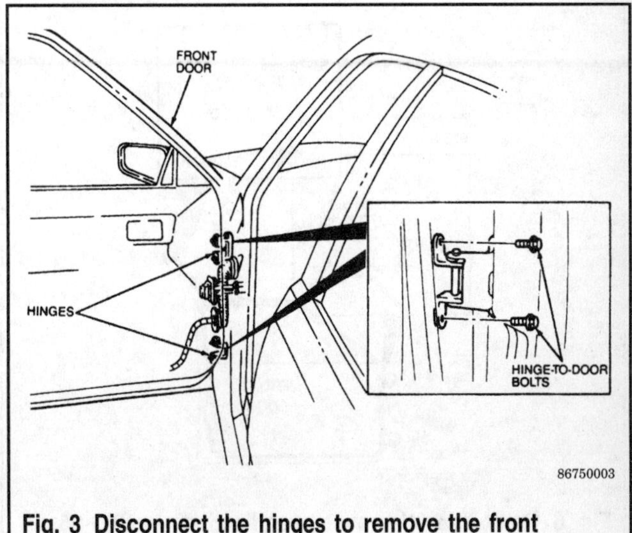

Fig. 3 Disconnect the hinges to remove the front door — 1991-95 models

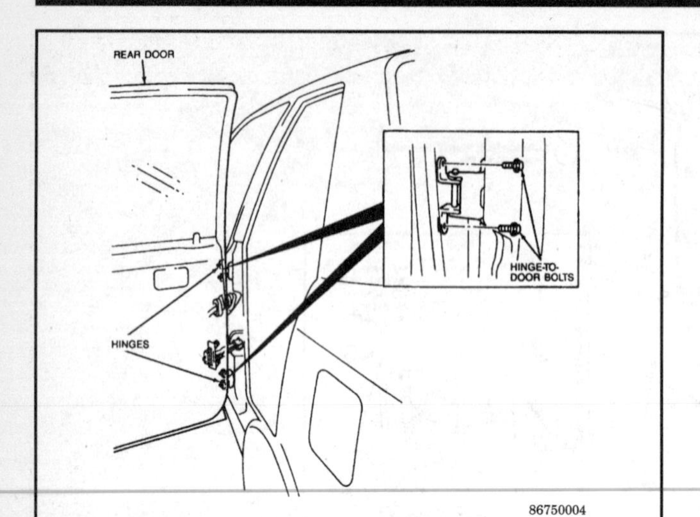

Fig. 4 Cutaway view of rear door hinge mounting — 1991-95 models

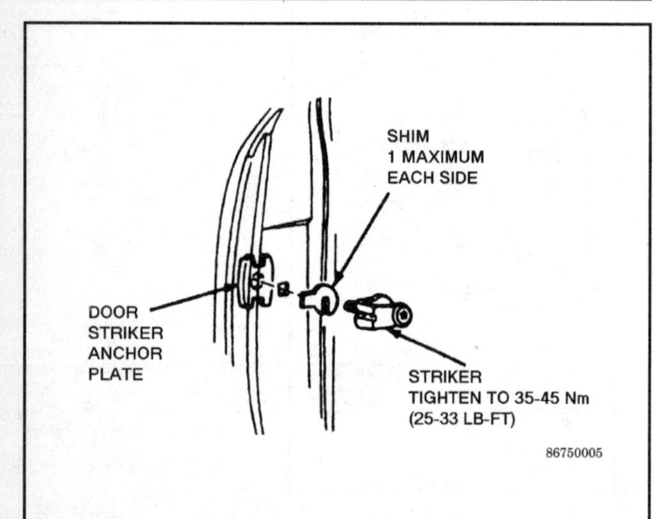

Fig. 5 Adjust the door latch striker with shims as shown — 1981-90 models

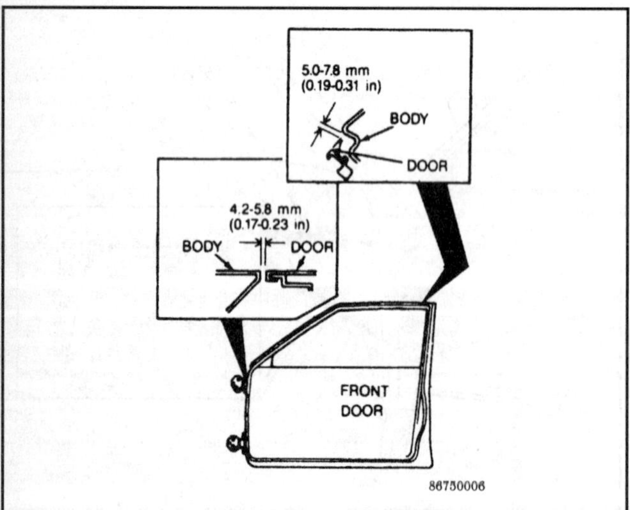

Fig. 6 Front door clearance specifications — 1991-95 models

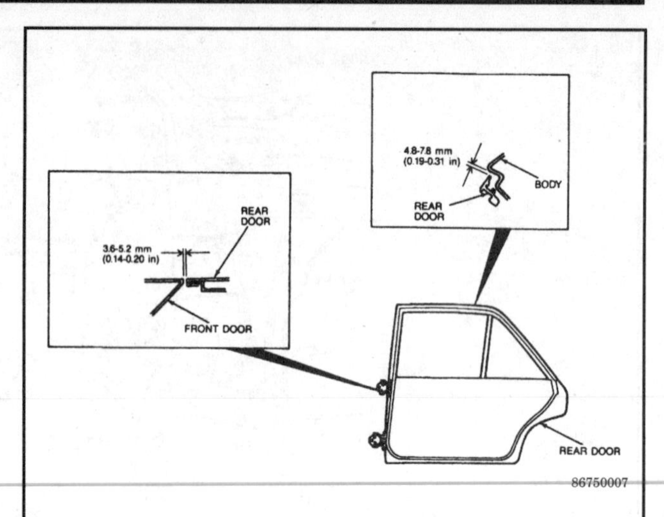

Fig. 7 Rear door clearance specifications — 1991-95 models

Hood

REMOVAL & INSTALLATION

➧ See Figures 8, 9 and 10

➡The help of an assistance is recommended, when removing or installing the hood.

1. Open and support the hood.
2. Protect the body with covers to prevent damage to the paint.
3. Scribe marks around the hinge locations for reference during installation.
4. Remove the hinge attaching bolts, being careful not to let the hood slip as bolts are removed.
5. Remove the hood from the vehicle.

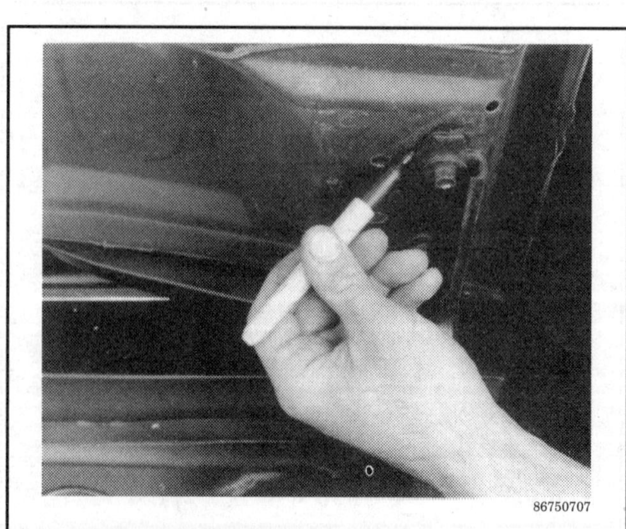

Fig. 8 Scribe marks around the hinge locations for reference during installation

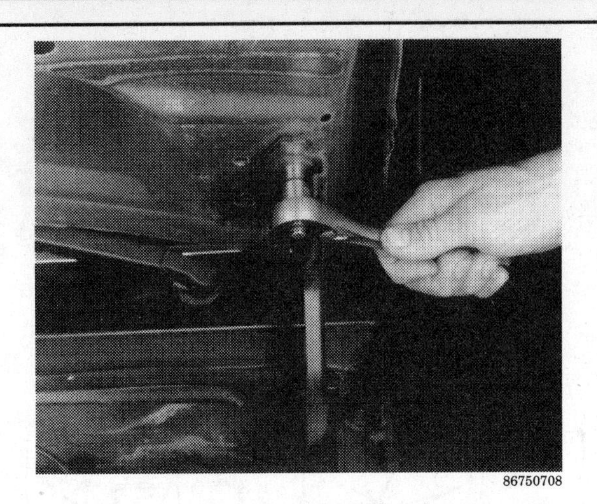

Fig. 9 Carefully remove the hinge attaching bolts. Be careful not to let the hood slip when the bolts are removed

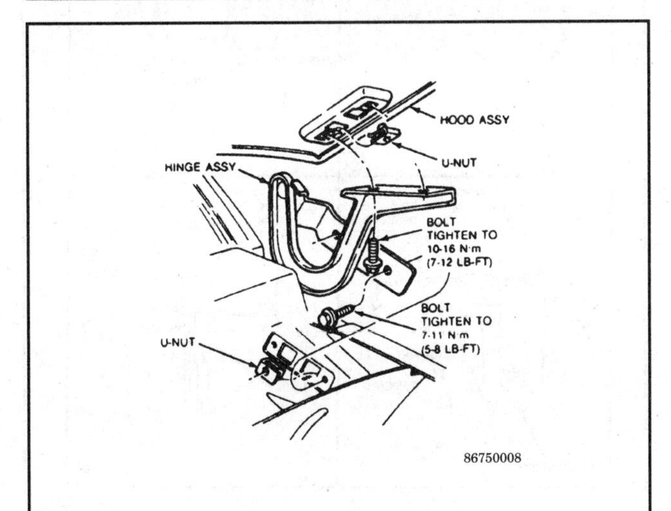

Fig. 10 Common hood hinge alignment and torque specifications

To install:

6. Place the hood into position. Install and partially tighten attaching bolts. Adjust the hood with the reference marks and tighten the attaching bolts.
7. Check the hood for an even fit between the fenders and for flush fit with the front of the fenders. Also, check for a flush fit with the top of the cowl and fenders. If necessary, adjust the hood latch.

ALIGNMENT

The hood can be adjusted fore and aft and side to side by loosening the hood-to-hinge attaching bolts and reposition the hood. To raise or lower the hood, loosen the hinge hood on body attaching bolts and raise or lower the hinge as necessary.

The hood lock can be moved from side-to-side and up and down and laterally to obtain a snug hood fit by loosening the lock attaching screws and moving as necessary.

Hatchback and Liftgate

REMOVAL & INSTALLATION

Hatchback

1. Open the hatchback assembly.
2. Remove the weatherstripping along the top of the hatchback opening and remove the headlining covering attaching screw.
3. Support the hatchback in an open position and remove the support cylinder from the hatchback.
4. Remove the hinge to roof frame attaching screw and washer assembly, then remove the hatchback.
5. Installation is the reverse of removal. Check and perform alignment as necessary.

Liftgate

1. Open the liftgate assembly.
2. Remove the weatherstripping along the top of the liftgate opening and remove the headlining covering attaching screw.
3. Support the liftgate in an open position and remove the support cylinder from the liftgate.
4. Remove the hinge to roof frame attaching screw and washer assembly, then remove the liftgate.
5. Installation is the reverse of removal. Check and perform alignment as necessary.

ALIGNMENT

Hatchback Hinge

ESCORT/LYNX, EXP/LN-7 — 3-DOOR HATCHBACK

The hatchback can be adjusted fore-and-aft, and side-to-side by loosening the hinge to roof frame attaching screw at each hinge.

To adjust the hinge, pull down on the weatherstrip across the entire top edge of the hatchback opening. Carefully loosen and pull down the headlining to expose the access holes to the hinge screws. Adjust the hinge as necessary. Seal the hinge after adjustment with clear silicone sealer. Apply trim cement to the sheet metal flange, and install the headlining and smooth out any wrinkles. Install the weatherstrip.

The hatchback can be adjusted in and out by shimming the hinge at the header roof frame.

The hatchback should be adjusted for an even and parallel fit with the hatchback opening and shrouding panels.

Liftgate hinge

ESCORT/LYNX — 4-DOOR LIFTGATE

On the four-door liftgate models the liftgate can be adjusted up and down and side to side by loosening the header roof frame attaching screw and washer assembly. The liftgate can be adjusted in and out by shimmering the hinges at the header roof frame.

The liftgate should be adjusted for an even parallel fit with the liftgate opening and surrounding panels.

To adjust a hinge, or hinges, remove the weatherstrip and pull down the headliner to gain access to the hinge attachment(s). Adjust the hinge(s) as necessary. Seal the hinge after adjustment with clear silicone sealer. Apply trim cement to the sheet metal flange, and install the headlining and smooth out any wrinkles. Install the weatherstrip.

Bumpers

REMOVAL & INSTALLATION

Front Bumper

➧ See Figures 11, 12, 13, 14, 15, 16 and 17

1981-85 MODELS

1. Remove all necessary trim moulding and guards from the bumper in order to gain access to the bumper retaining bolts.
2. If the vehicle is equipped with the optional (long) bumper extension assemblies with attachments to the fender, remove the two screws through the tab on the inside surface of the extension assemblies.
3. Remove the isolator to reinforcement screws and retaining nut and remove the bumper assembly from the vehicle.

To install:

4. Transfer the bumper guards, rub strip, extension assemblies, pads and license plate bracket and bumper mounting brackets to replacement bumper.
5. To install, position the bumper assembly to the isolators and install the attaching screws and retaining nuts, but do not tighten.
6. Adjust the bumper height so that the distance from the top edge to the ground meets the specifications given in the illustration.
7. Then, adjust the bumper to body clearance so that the vertical and horizontal body to bumper dimensions meet the specifications in the illustration provided. Tighten the isolator to bumper bolts to 26-40 ft. lbs. (35-55 Nm).
8. On vehicle equipped with optional extension assemblies, secure the extension assembly to the fender with the retaining screws. New holes may have to be drilled through the tab in the extension housing.

1985½-90 MODELS EXCEPT ESCORT GT

➧ See Figures 18 and 19

1. Remove all necessary trim moulding and guards from the bumper in order to gain access to the bumper retaining bolts.
2. Support the bumper and remove the six bumper to isolator attaching bolts.
3. Lower the front of the bumper assembly slightly and pull the bumper away from the vehicle to disengage the side attachments.

To install:

4. Transfer the bumper guards, rub strip, extension assemblies, pads and license plate bracket and bumper mounting brackets to replacement bumper.
5. To install, position the bumper assembly to the vehicle while sliding the ends over the side attachments.

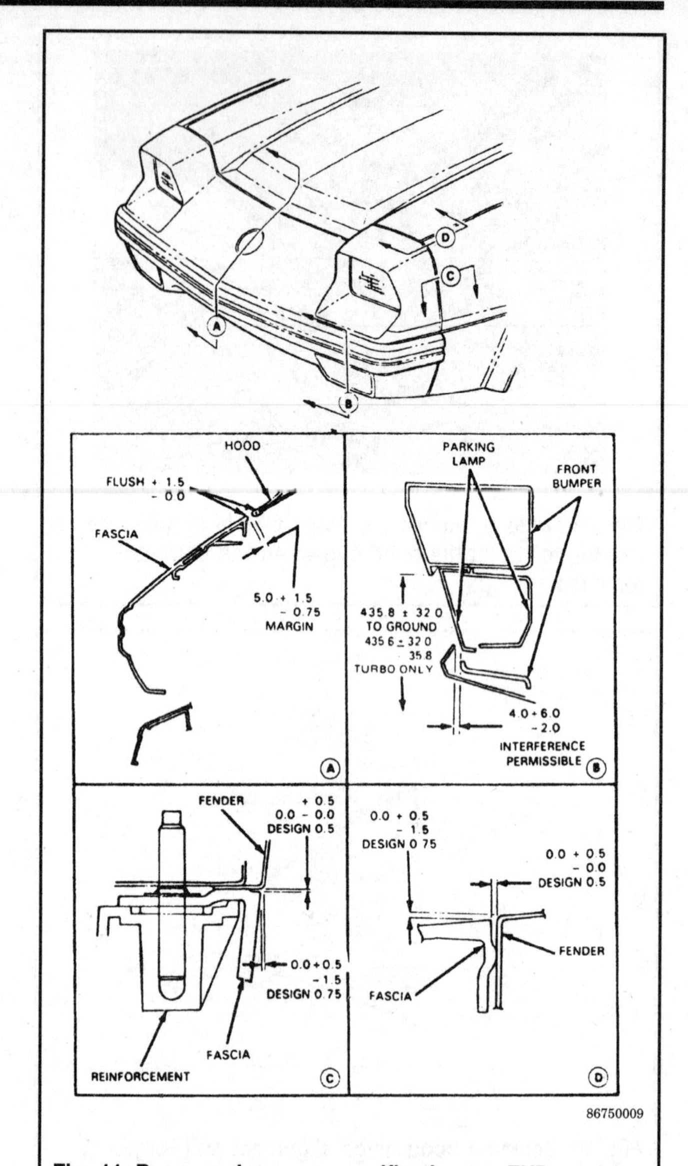

Fig. 11 Bumper clearance specifications — EXP models

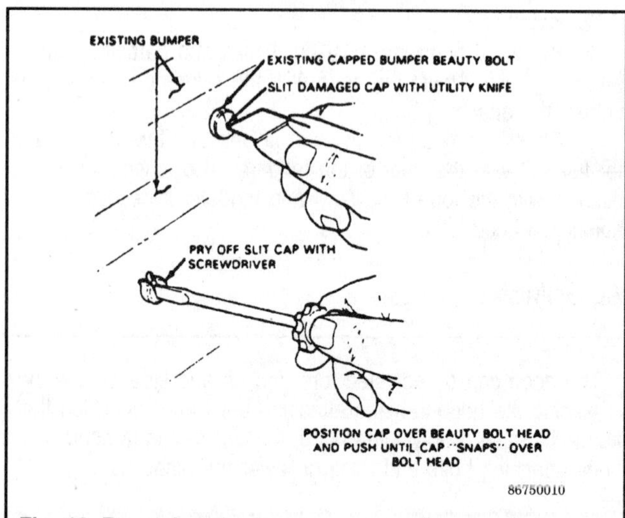

Fig. 12 Removing the bumper caps will necessitate acquiring new replacements

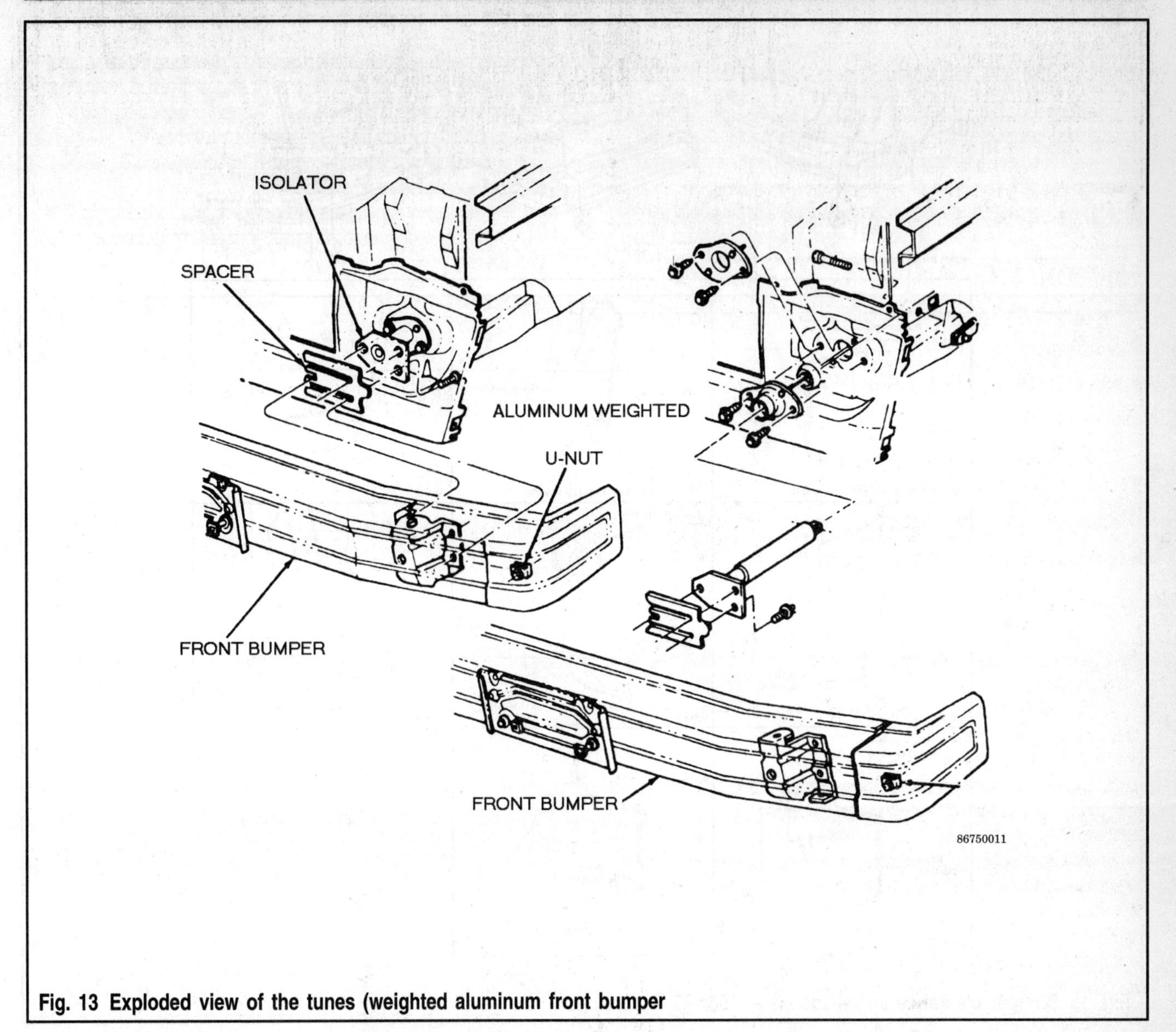

Fig. 13 Exploded view of the tunes (weighted aluminum front bumper

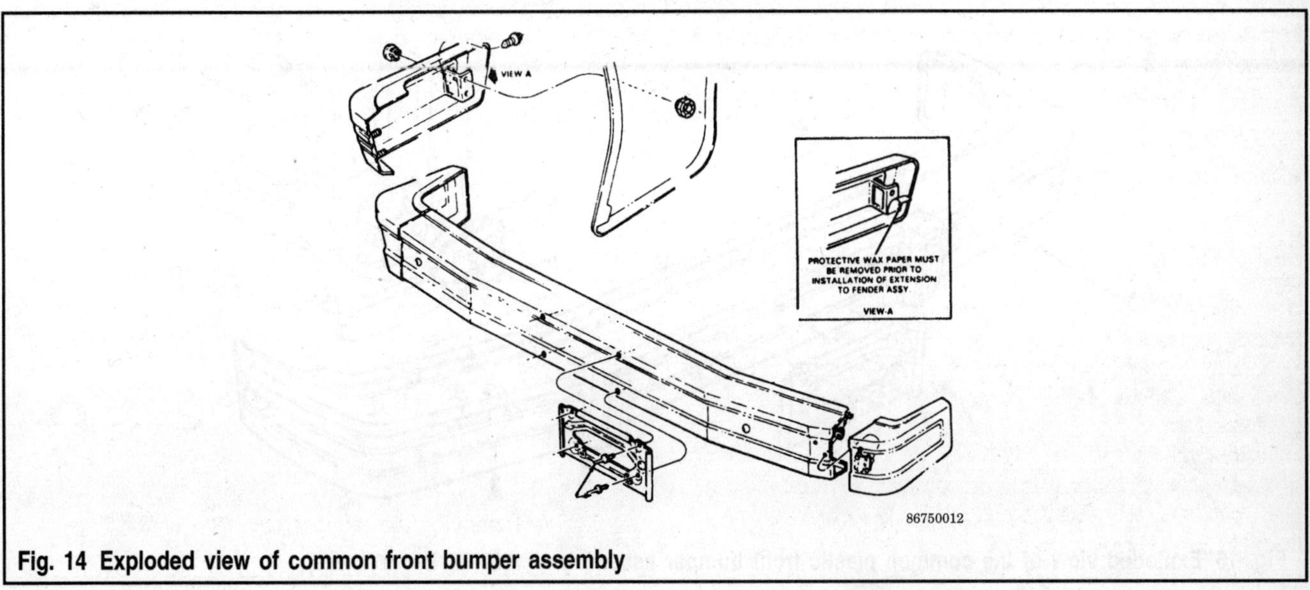

Fig. 14 Exploded view of common front bumper assembly

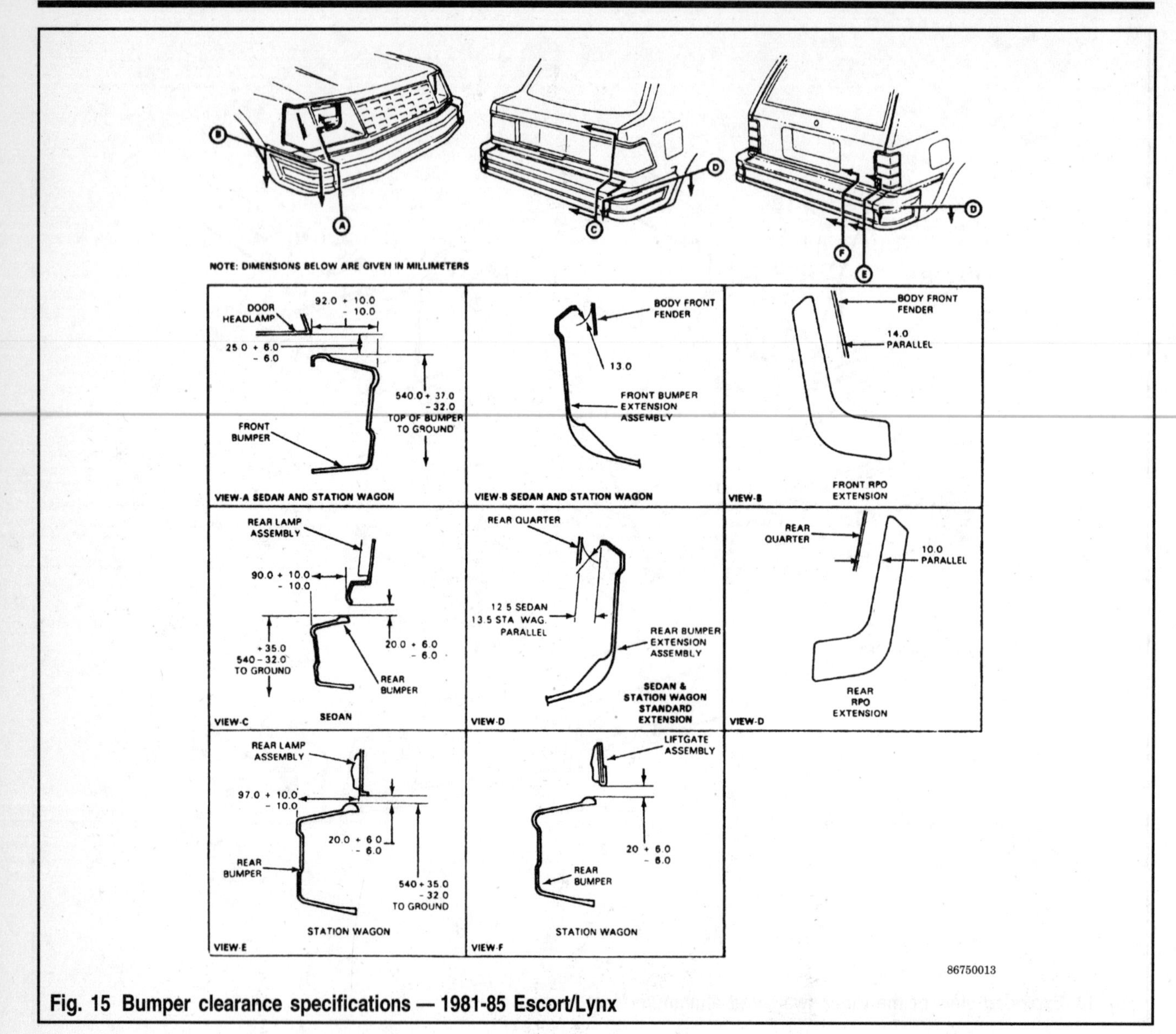

Fig. 15 Bumper clearance specifications — 1981-85 Escort/Lynx

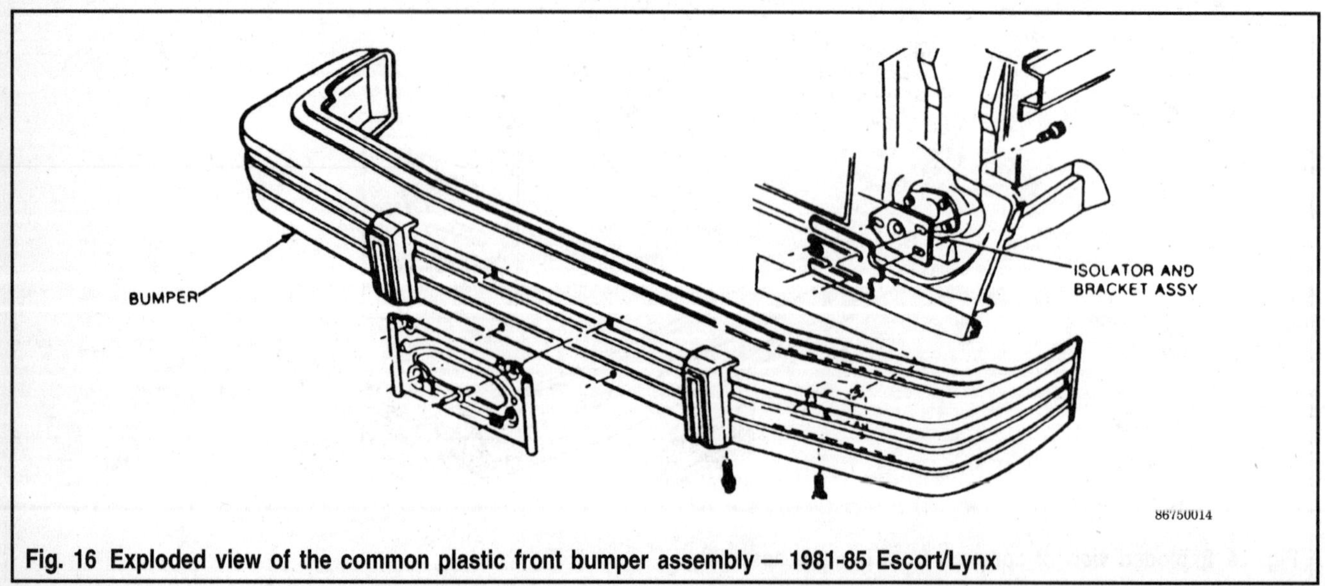

Fig. 16 Exploded view of the common plastic front bumper assembly — 1981-85 Escort/Lynx

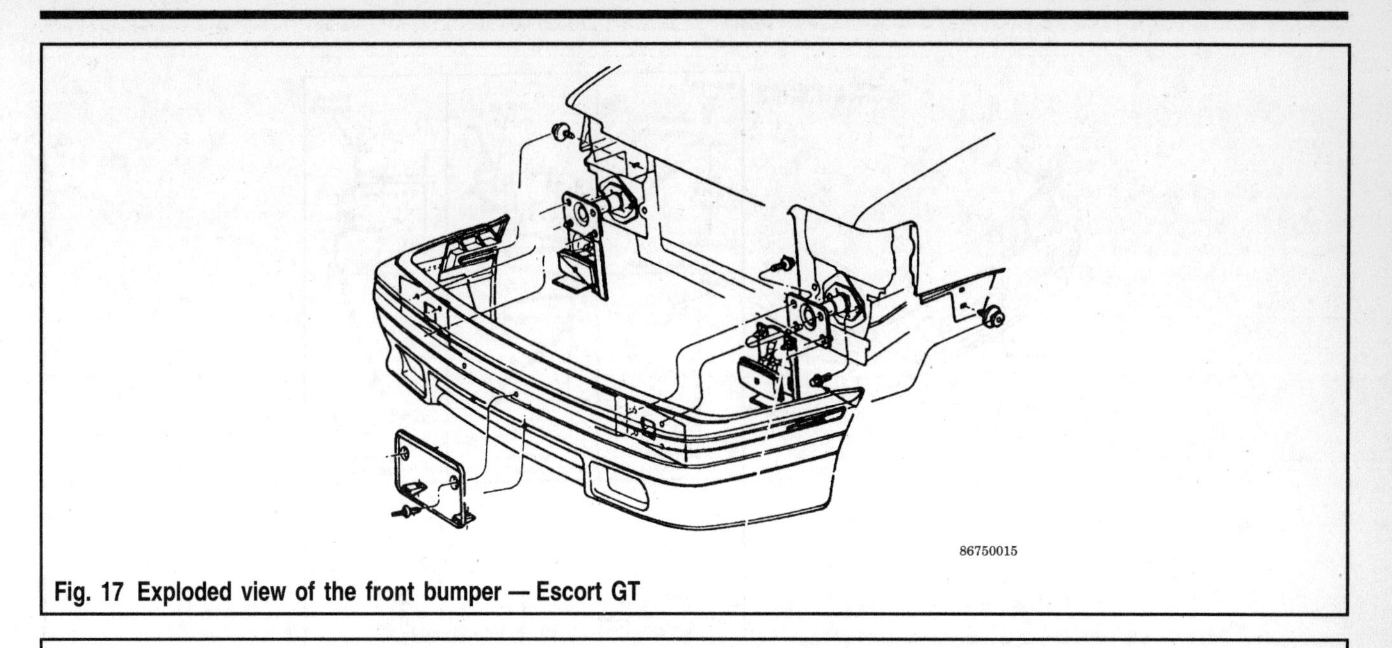

Fig. 17 Exploded view of the front bumper — Escort GT

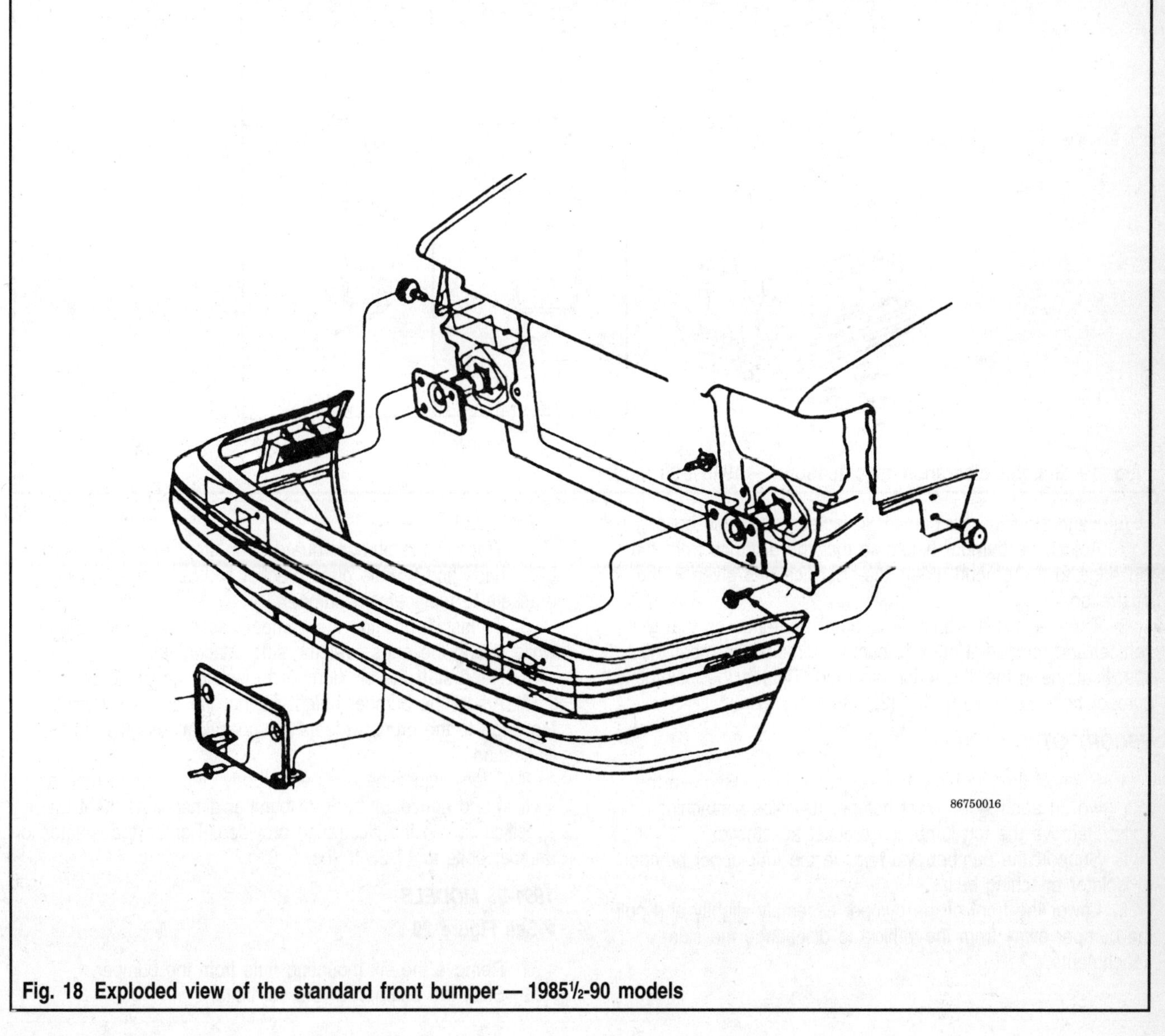

Fig. 18 Exploded view of the standard front bumper — 1985½-90 models

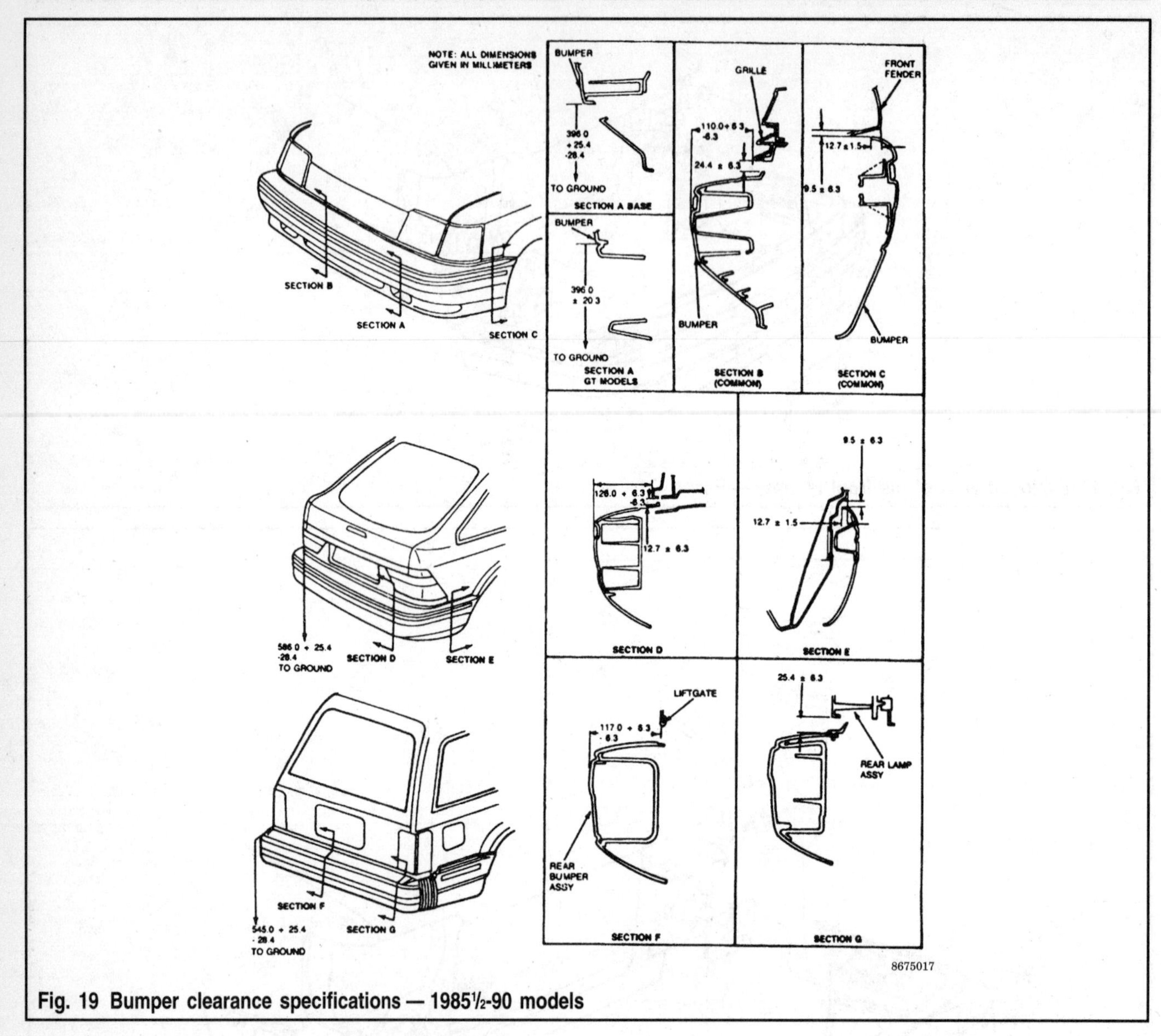

Fig. 19 Bumper clearance specifications — 1985½-90 models

6. Hand start the six bumper to isolator attaching bolts.
7. Adjust the bumper height so that the distance from the top edge to the ground meets the specifications given in the illustration.
8. Then, adjust the bumper to body clearance so that the vertical and horizontal body to bumper dimensions meet the specifications in the illustration provided. Tighten the isolator to bumper bolts to 17-25 ft. lbs. (22-33 Nm).

ESCORT GT

1. Support the fog lamp bracket assemblies. Remove the four (two on each side) lower bumper to isolator attaching bolts. Remove the fog lamp and bracket assemblies.
2. Support the bumper and remove the four upper bumper to isolator attaching bolts.
3. Lower the front of the bumper assembly slightly and pull the bumper away from the vehicle to disengage the side attachments.

To install:

4. Transfer the bumper guards, rub strip, extension assemblies, pads and license plate bracket and bumper mounting brackets to replacement bumper.
5. To install, position the bumper assembly to the vehicle while sliding the ends over the side attachments.
6. Hand start the six bumper to isolator attaching bolts.
7. Adjust the bumper height so that the distance from the top edge to the ground meets the specifications given in the illustration.
8. Then, adjust the bumper to body clearance so that the vertical and horizontal body to bumper dimensions meet the specifications in the illustration provided. Tighten the isolator to bumper bolts to 17-25 ft. lbs.

1991-95 MODELS

➧ **See Figure 20**

1. Remove the six mounting nuts from the bumper.
2. Slide the bumper off the set bolts.

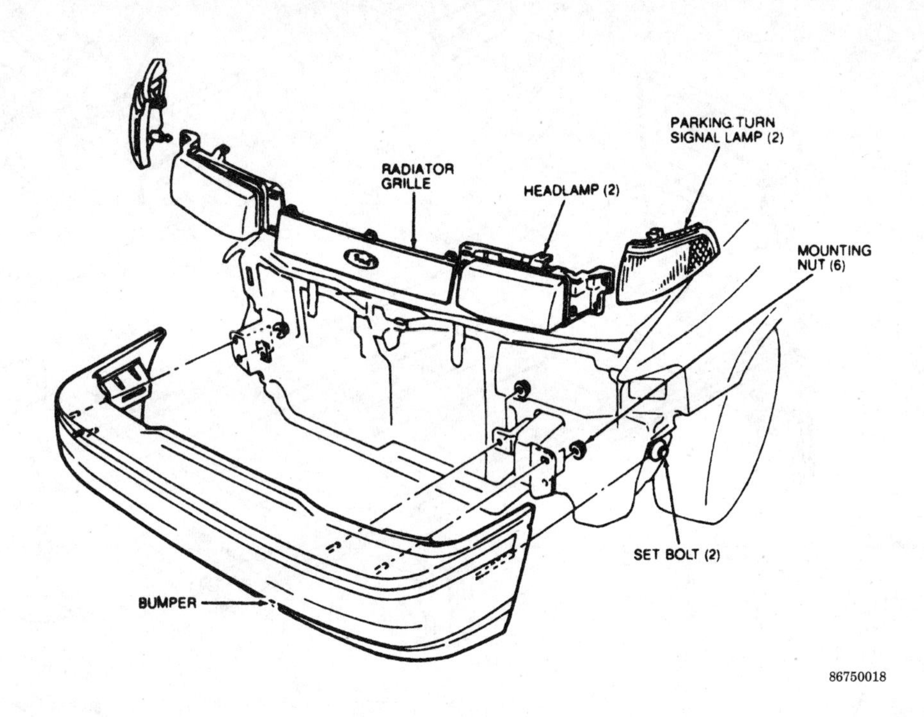

Fig. 20 Exploded view of the standard front bumper mounting — 1991-95 models

To install:

3. Position the bumper and engage the set bolts with the slots in the bumper side supports.
4. Install the six mounting nuts and tighten to 12-17 ft. lbs. (16-23 Nm).

Rear Bumper

1981-85 MODELS

➧ See Figures 21, 22 and 23

1. Remove all necessary trim moulding and guards from the bumper in order to gain access to the bumper retaining bolts.
2. If the vehicle is equipped with the optional (long) bumper extension assemblies with attachments to the fender, remove the two screws through the tab on the inside surface of the extension assemblies.
3. Remove the isolator to reinforcement screws and retaining nut and remove the bumper assembly from the vehicle.

➡Steel and aluminum bumpers have four screws and retaining nuts at each isolator, light weight aluminum bumpers have three screws and retaining nuts at each isolator.

To install:

4. Transfer the bumper guards, rub strip, extension assemblies, pads and license plate bracket and bumper mounting brackets to replacement bumper.
5. To install, position the bumper assembly to the isolators and install the attaching screws and retaining nuts, but do not tighten.
6. Adjust the bumper height so that the distance from the top edge to the ground meets the specifications given in the illustration.
7. Then, adjust the bumper to body clearance so that the vertical and horizontal body to bumper dimensions meet the specifications in the illustration provided. Tighten the isolator to bumper bolts to 26-40 ft. lbs. (35-55 Nm).

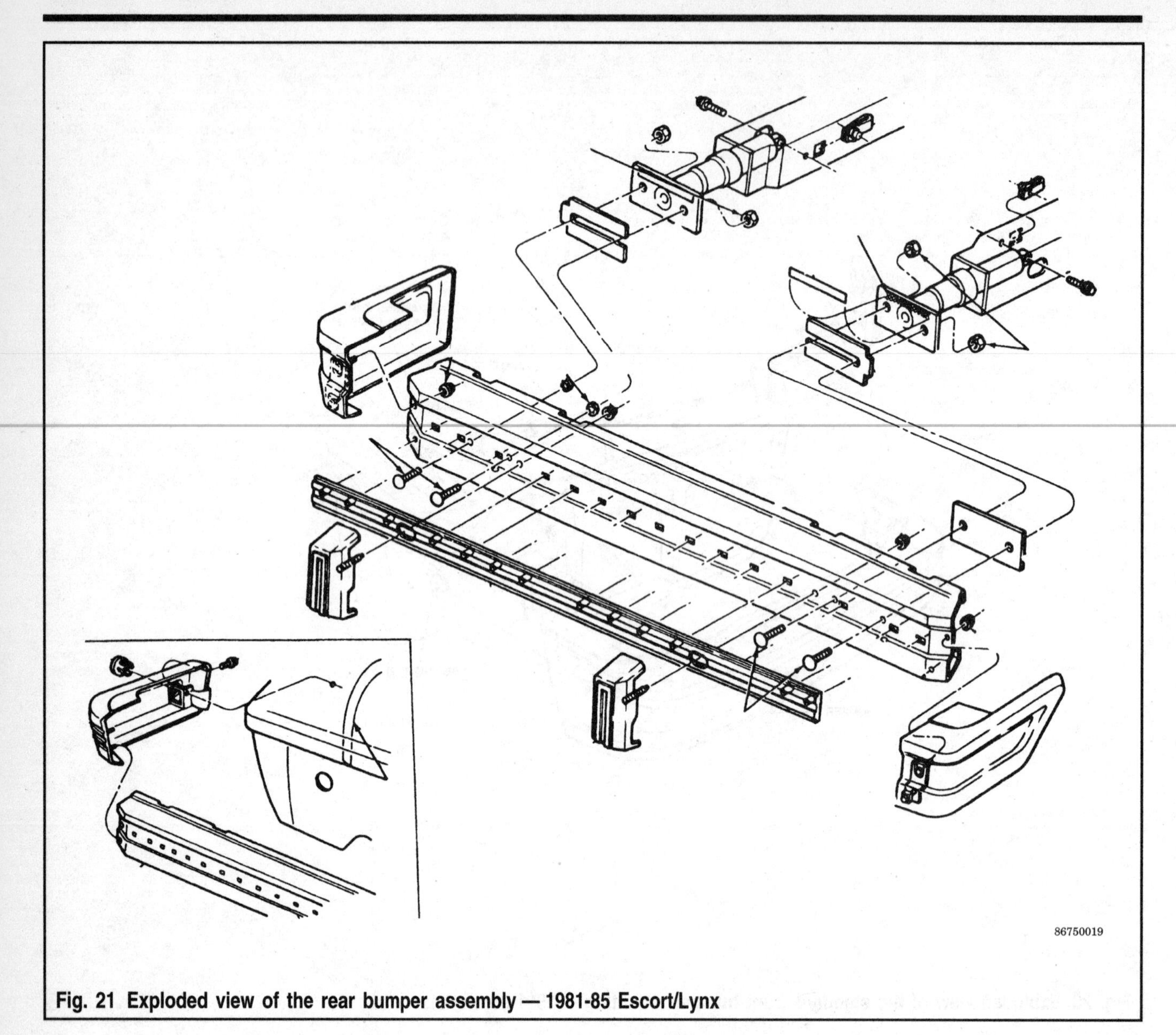

Fig. 21 Exploded view of the rear bumper assembly — 1981-85 Escort/Lynx

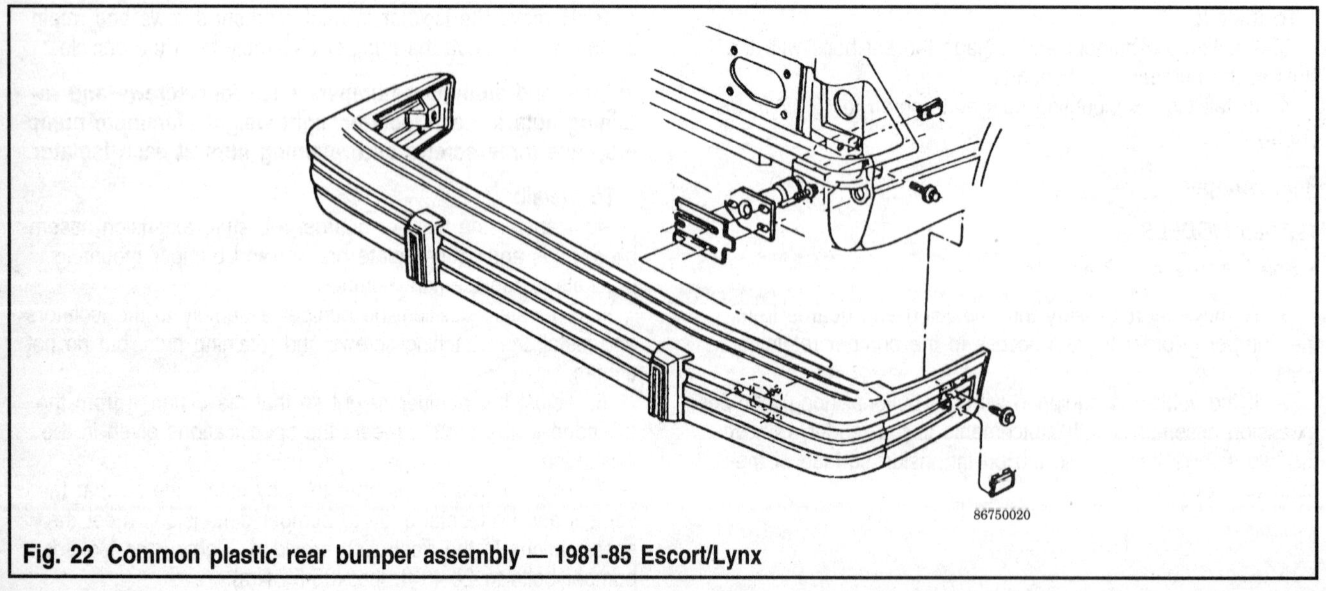

Fig. 22 Common plastic rear bumper assembly — 1981-85 Escort/Lynx

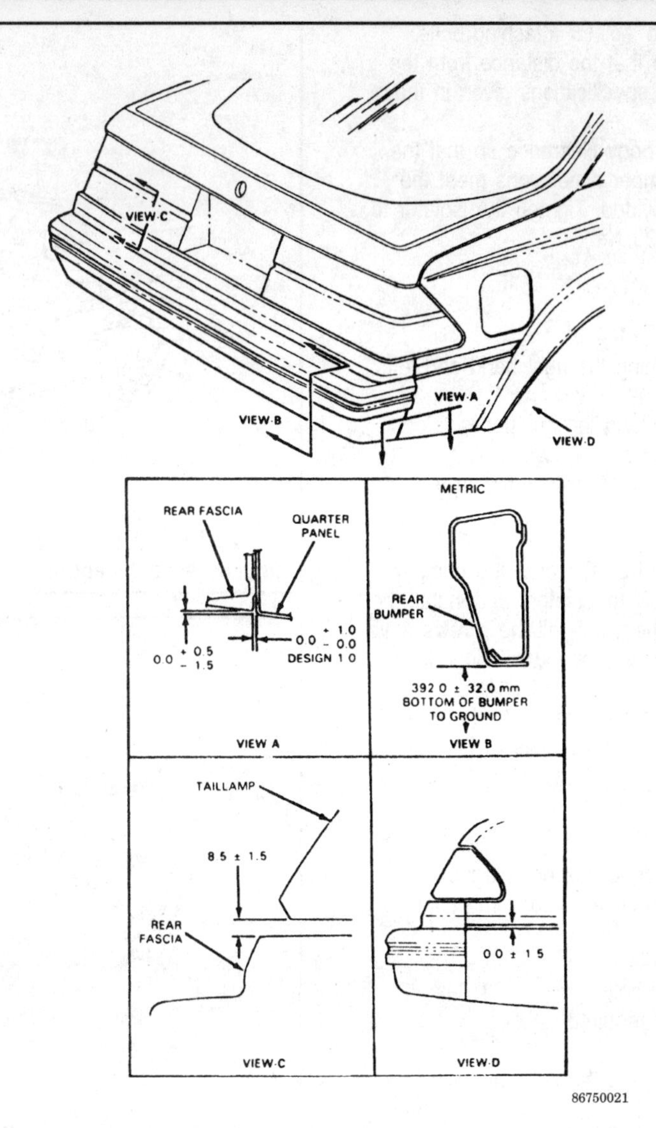

Fig. 23 Rear bumper alignment specifications — EXP

8. On vehicle equipped with optional extension assemblies, secure the extension assembly to the fender with the retaining screws. New holes may have to be drilled through the tab in the extension housing.

1985½-90 MODELS (EXCEPT ESCORT WAGON)

See Figure 24

1. Remove all necessary trim moulding and guards from the bumper in order to gain access to the bumper retaining bolts.
2. Support the bumper and remove the six bumper to isolator attaching bolts.
3. Lower the front of the bumper assembly slightly and pull the bumper away from the vehicle to disengage the side attachments.

To install:

4. Transfer the bumper guards, rub strip, extension assemblies, pads and license plate bracket and bumper mounting brackets to replacement bumper.
5. To install, position the bumper assembly to the vehicle while sliding the ends over the side attachments.

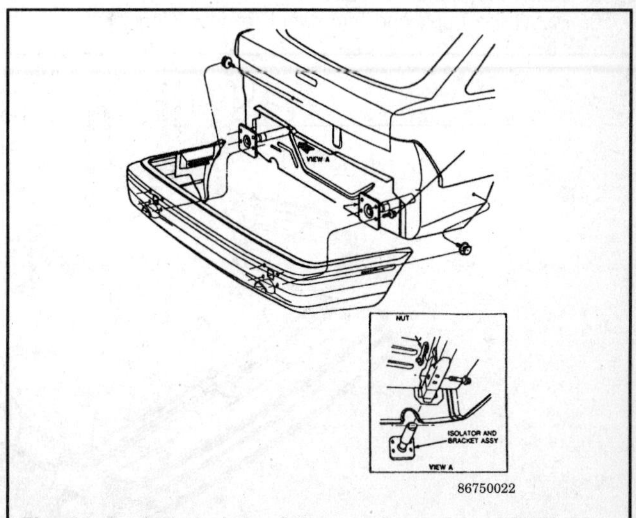

Fig. 24 Exploded view of the rear bumper — 1985½-90 models

6. Hand start the six bumper to isolator attaching bolts.
7. Adjust the bumper height so that the distance from the top edge to the ground meets the specifications given in the illustration.
8. Then, adjust the bumper to body clearance so that the vertical and horizontal body to bumper dimensions meet the specifications in the illustration provided. Tighten the isolator to bumper bolts to 17-25 ft. lbs. (22-33 Nm).

1985½-90 ESCORT WAGON

See Figure 25

1. Remove the four bolts attaching the right hand and left hand extensions to the bumper.
2. Remove the six screws attaching the bumper isolators. Remove the bumper from the vehicle.
3. Remove the eight clips and stone deflector from the bumper.

To install:

4. Install the stone deflector and 8 clips onto the bumper.
5. Position the bumper assembly to isolators and install the attaching screws. Do not tighten them until all the screws have been hand started and the bumper is properly positioned.
6. Tighten the screws to 17-25 ft. lbs. (22-34 Nm).
7. Install the four bolts attaching the bumper to the right hand and left hand extensions. Tighten the bolts to 7-10 ft. lbs.

1991-95 MODELS

See Figures 26 and 27

1. Remove the trunk end trim panel (except Wagon).
2. On Wagon models, remove the rear floor trim panel.
3. Remove the splash shields.
4. Remove the six mounting nuts.
5. Slide the bumper off the set bolts.
6. Remove the bumper filler, if required.

To install:

7. Position the bumper and engage the set bolts with the slots in the bumper side support.
8. Install the six mounting bolts and tighten to 12-17 ft. lbs. (16-23 Nm).
9. Install the splash shields.
10. Install the trunk end trim panel (except Wagon).

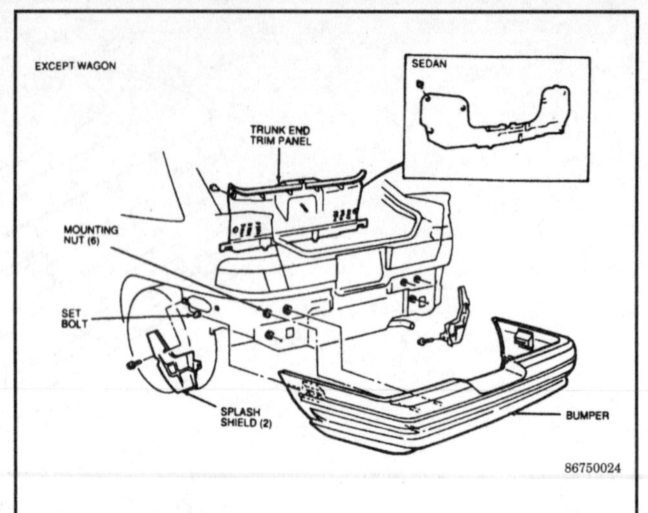

Fig. 26 Exploded view of the rear bumper — 1991-95 models (except wagon)

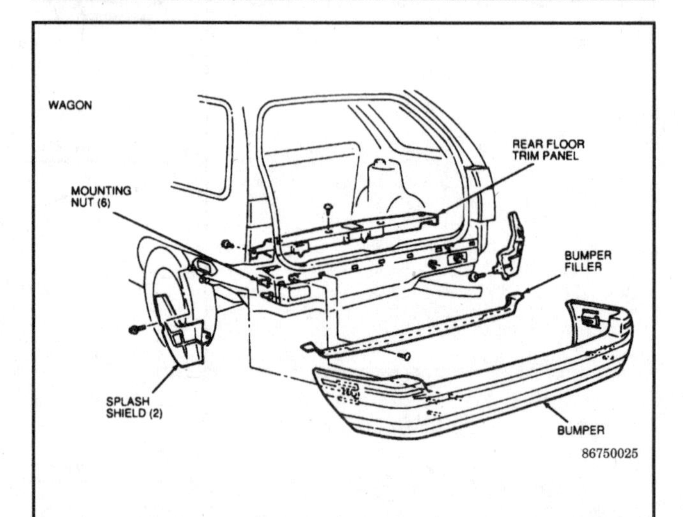

Fig. 27 Exploded view of the rear bumper — 1991-95 wagon

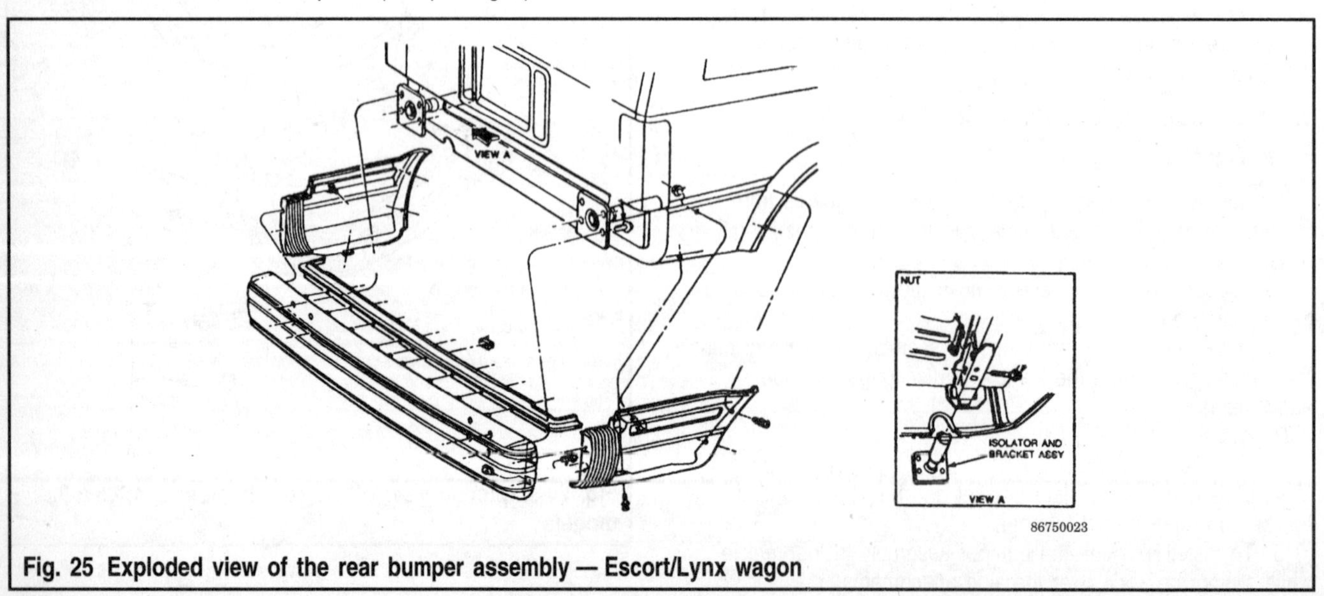

Fig. 25 Exploded view of the rear bumper assembly — Escort/Lynx wagon

11. On Wagon models, install the rear floor trim panel.

Radiator Grille

REMOVAL & INSTALLATION

1981-85 Models

See Figure 28

1. Remove the radiator grille attaching screws and remove the grille from the mounting brackets on the radiator support.

To install:

2. Position the grille to the vehicle and loosely install the grille attaching screws. The grille should rest on the locating tabs that extend from the headlamp doors.
3. Adjust the grille side to side so there is a uniform gap between the grille and the headlamp doors. Tighten the retaining bolts.

1985½-90 Escort/Lynx

See Figure 29

1. Push down on the top side of lower snap-in retainer at both sides of grille and pull the grille out at the bottom.
2. Push up on the bottom side of the upper snap-in retainer at both sides of the grille out at the top.
3. Put grille forward out of the grille opening panel.

To install:

4. Position the grille to the vehicle and align the snap-in retainers with appropriate slots and push in on the grille until all the retainers are seated.

1985½-88 GT

See Figure 30

1. Remove the retaining screw on the top of the grille assembly at both sides and pull the grille out at the top.
2. Push up on the bottom side of the upper snap-in retainer at both sides of the grille out at the top.
3. Put grille forward out of the grille opening panel.

To install:

4. Position the grille to align the lower snap-in retainers and upper tabs over the U-nuts at both sides.
5. Align the snap-in retainers with appropriate slots and push in on the grille until all the retainers are seated.
6. Install the upper retaining screw at both sides.

1988-90 Escort GT

See Figure 31

1. Remove lower grille bar by pushing up on the three retaining tabs located on the back side of the grille. Pull the grille bar forward to remove.
2. Remove the two screws retaining grille at top ends to mounting brackets.
3. Pull grille forward to remove.
4. Remove the mounting brackets from the headlamp housing by pushing down on the top side of the lower snap-in retainers at both sides and push up on the bottom of the top snap-in retainers.

To install:

5. Position the grille to align the upper and lower snap-in retainers.
6. Push the grille in, to the seat retainers.
7. Align grille bar retainers with the holes in the grille and push in until seated.
8. Install the retaining screws. Tighten the screws to 6-14 ft.lbs. (8-19 Nm).

1991-95 Models

See Figure 32

1. Remove the grille retaining screws.
2. Release the five locking clips and remove the radiator grille.
3. Install the radiator grille by positioning the grille and pressing into place.
4. Install the retaining screws.

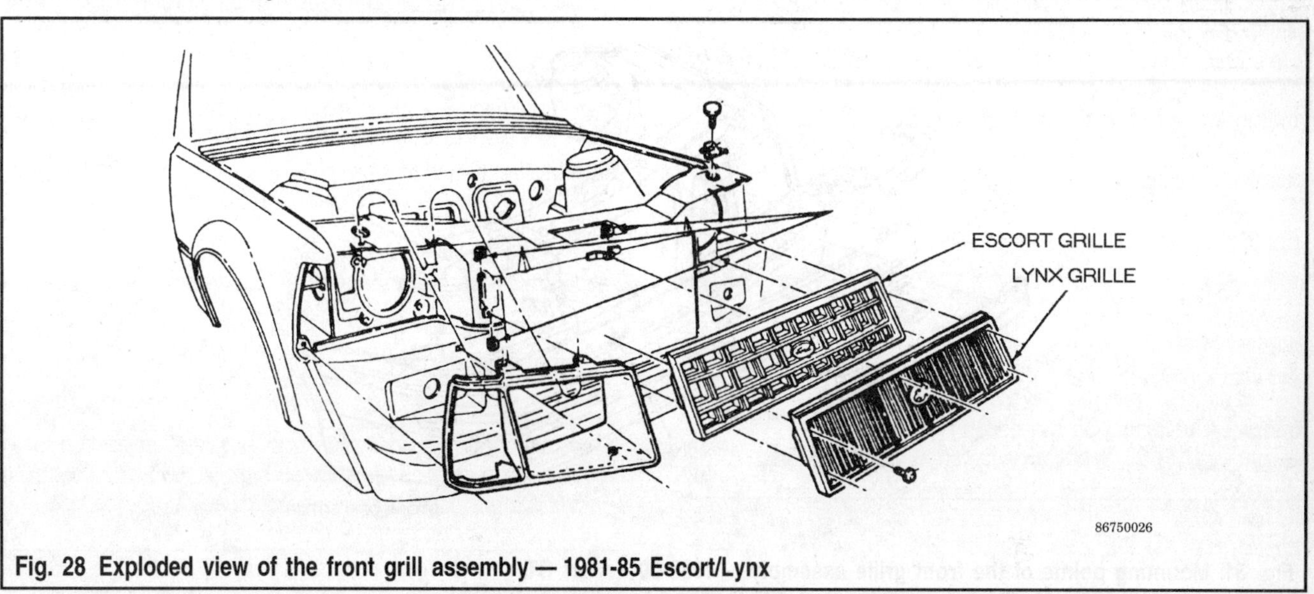

Fig. 28 Exploded view of the front grill assembly — 1981-85 Escort/Lynx

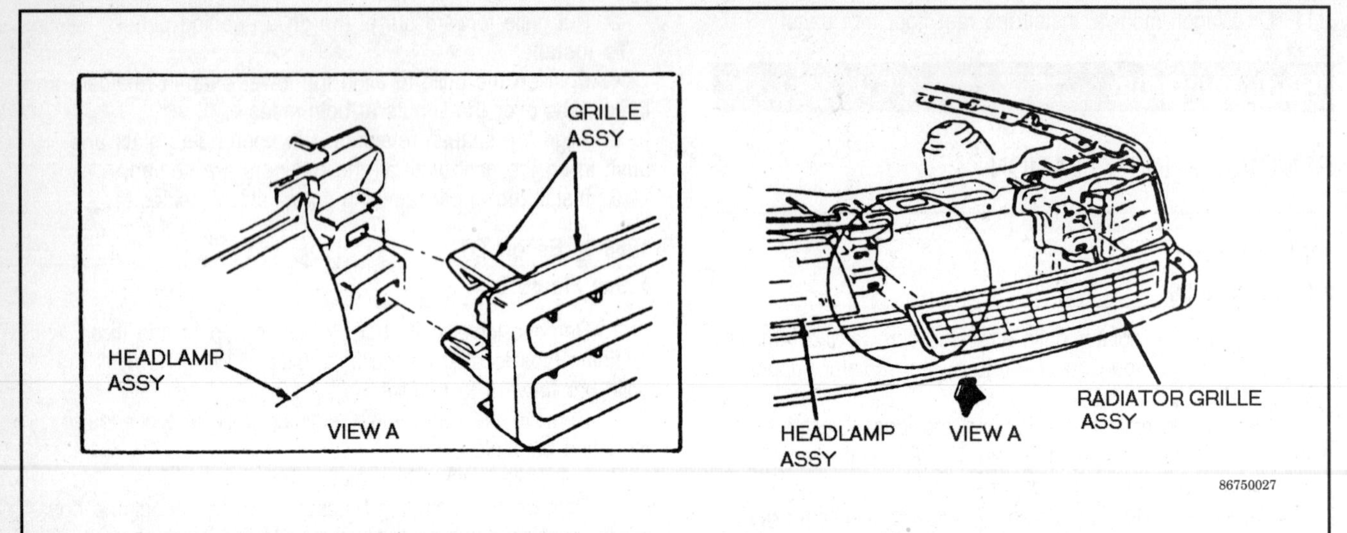

Fig. 29 Mounting points of the front grille assembly — 1985½-90 models

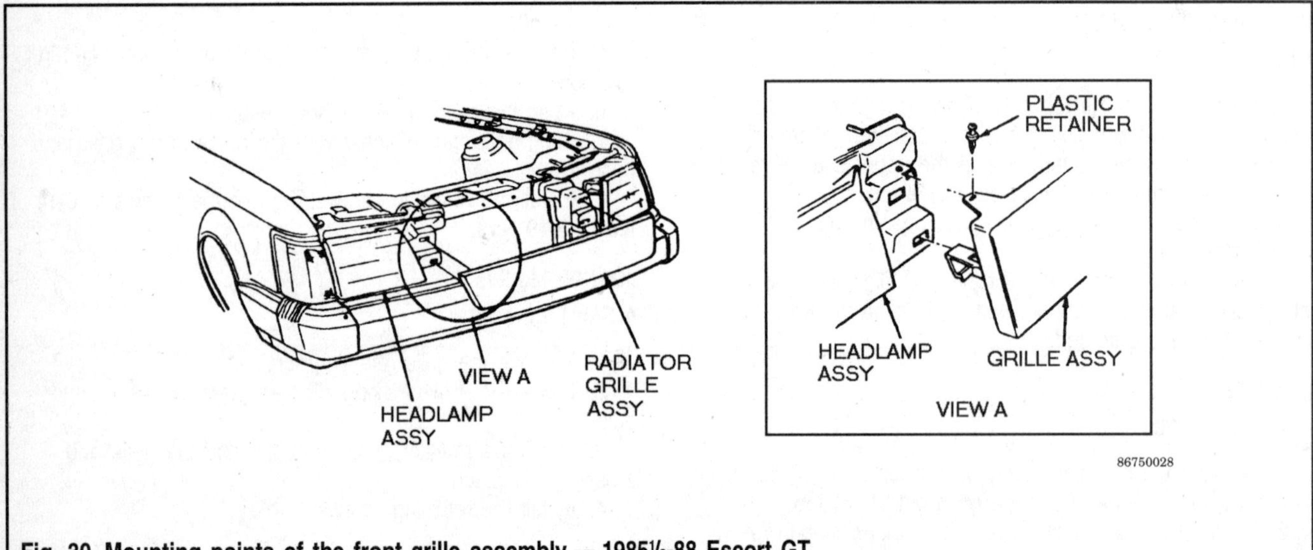

Fig. 30 Mounting points of the front grille assembly — 1985½-88 Escort GT

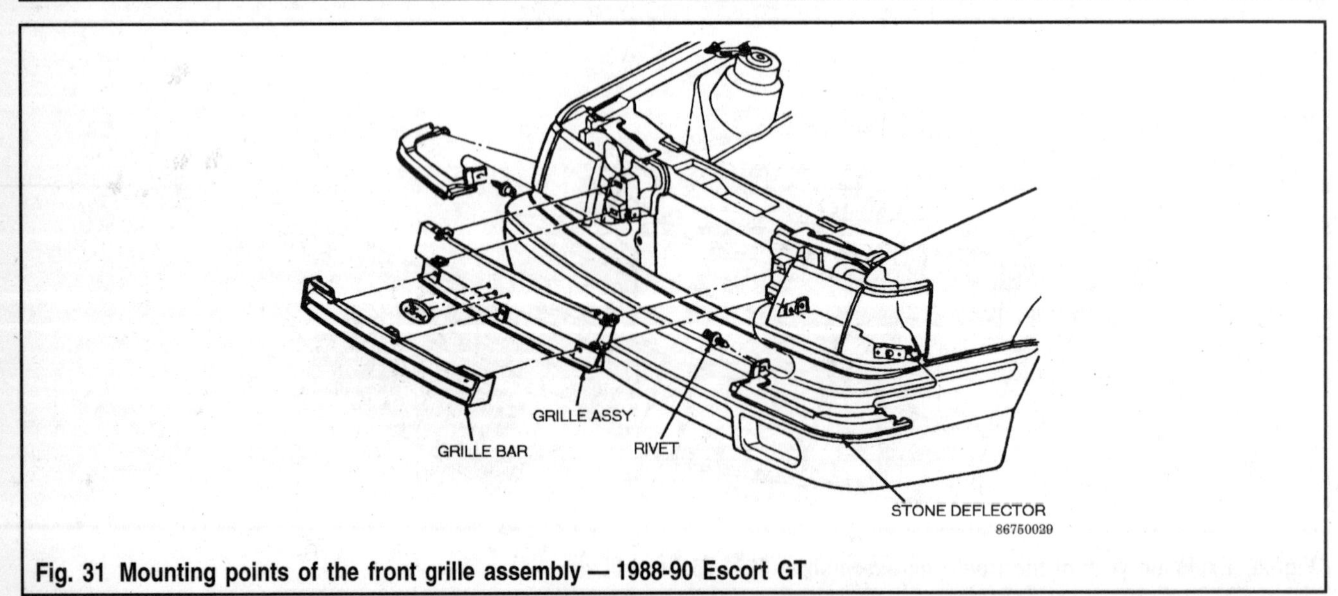

Fig. 31 Mounting points of the front grille assembly — 1988-90 Escort GT

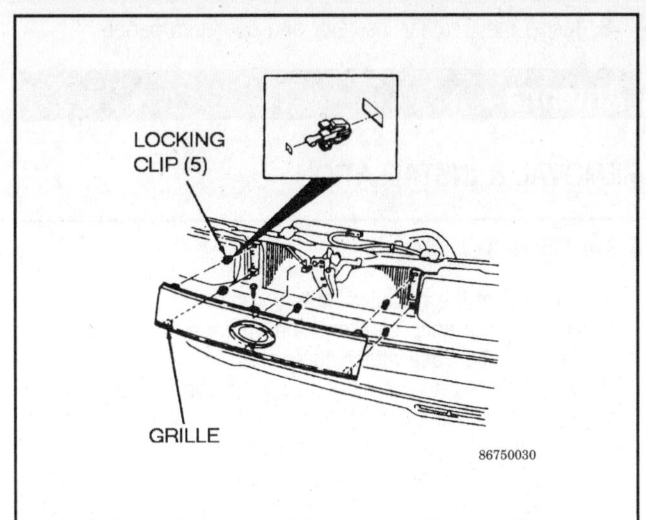

Fig. 32 Exploded view of the front radiator grille mounting — 1991-95 models

Outside Mirrors

REMOVAL & INSTALLATION

Manual Mirrors

See Figure 33

1. Remove the inside door trim panel from the door in which the mirror is to be taken from.
2. Remove the retaining nuts and washers from the mirror.
3. Lift the mirror up and out of the door and discard the gasket.

To install:

4. Install the mirror and gasket onto the door.
5. Install the nuts and washers and tighten the nuts to 25-36 inch lbs.
6. Reinstall the door trim panel.

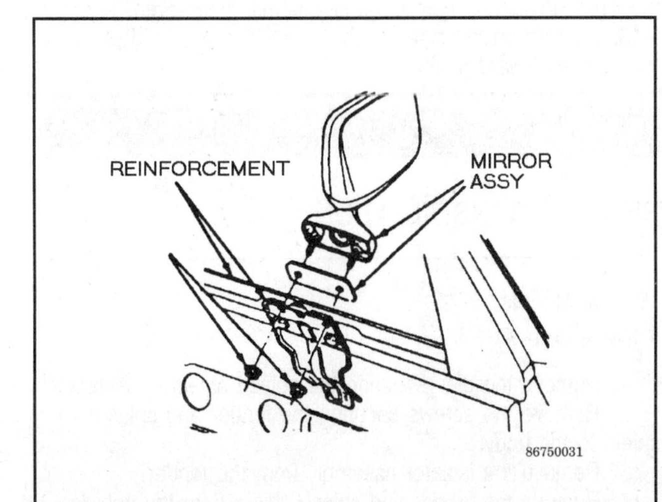

Fig. 33 Exploded view of a common manually operated mirror

Remote Control Mirrors

EXCEPT 1991-95 MODELS

See Figures 34 and 35

1. Remove the set screw fastening the control lever end of the cable assembly to the control lever bezel on the door trim panel.
2. Remove the inside door trim panel and weather insulator from the door in which the mirror is to be taken from.
3. Disengage the cable from the routing clips and guides located inside the door.
4. Remove the mirror attaching nuts and washers. Remove the mirror and cable assembly from the door.

To install:

5. Place the remote cable into the hole and the door and position the mirror to the door. Install the nuts and washers and tighten them to 21-39 inch lbs. (2.3-4.4 Nm).
6. Route the cable through the door into the cable guides and engage the cable into the locating clips.

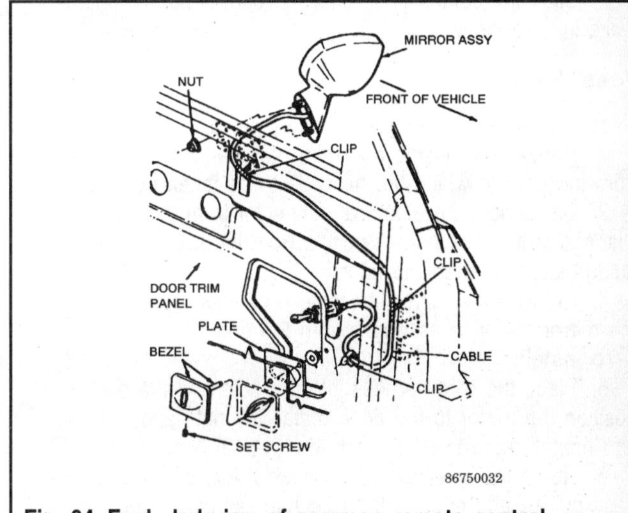

Fig. 34 Exploded view of common remote control mirrors

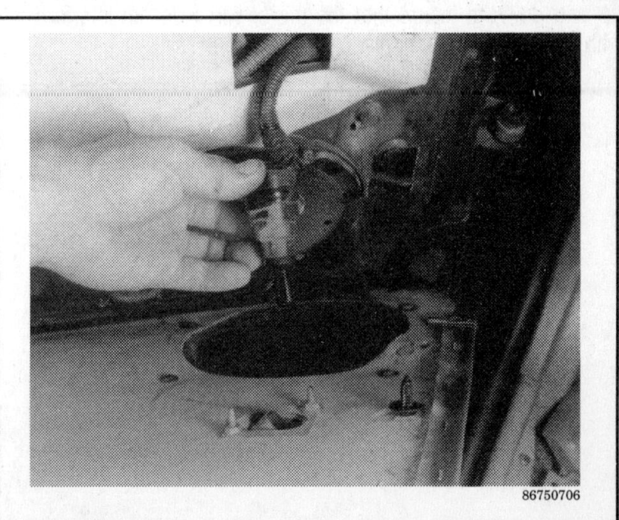

Fig. 35 The mirror control is accessible once the door panel is removed

7. Check the operation of the mirror and operate the mirror up and down to insure that the mirror cables do not interfere with the window mechanism.
8. Install the weather insulator and door trim panel.
9. Place the control lever bezel onto the door trim panel and install the set screw.

1991-95 MODELS

➧ See Figure 36

1. Using a small, flat-bladed tool, pry the control knob inside the locking tab slightly away from the control handle and slide the control knob OFF.
2. Remove the mirror trim bezel from the door.
3. Remove the three retaining screws.
4. Remove the mirror.

To install:

5. Place the mirror into position and install the retaining screws.
6. Install the mirror trim bezel.
7. Slide the control knob onto the control handle until it locks into position.

Power Mirrors

1. Disconnect the negative battery cable.
2. Remove the inside door trim panel and weather insulator from the door in which the mirror is to be taken from.
3. Disconnect the electrical connector from the mirror unit. Disengage the wire harness cable from the routing clips and guides located inside the door.
4. Remove the mirror attaching nuts and washers. Remove the mirror and wire assembly from the door.

To install:

5. Place the wire harness into the hole and the door and position the mirror to the door. Install the nuts and washers and tighten them to 35-51 inch lbs. (4-5.75 Nm).
6. Route the wire harness through the door into the harness guides and engage the wire harness connector into the mirror unit. Reconnect the negative battery cable.
7. Check the operation of the mirror and operate the mirror up and down to insure that the mirror wires do not interfere with the window mechanism.

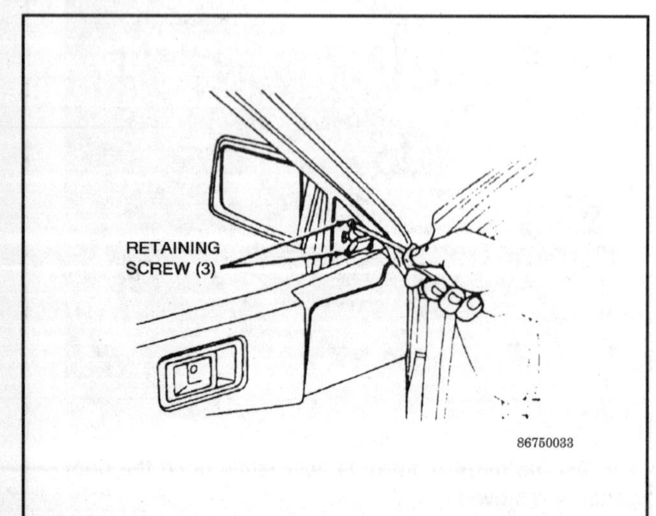

Fig. 36 Unscrew the fasteners from the inside to remove the outside mirror — 1991-95 models

8. Install the weather insulator and door trim panel.

Antenna

REMOVAL & INSTALLATION

➧ See Figure 37

1. Disconnect the negative battery cable.
2. Remove the snap cap from the antenna, if so equipped.
3. Remove the base attaching screws.
4. Pull (do not pry) the antenna up through the fender.
5. Push in on the sides of the glove box door and place the door in the hinged downward position.
6. Disconnect the antenna lead from the rear of the radio and remove the antenna cable from the heater or air conditioning cable retaining clips.

➡On some models it may be necessary to remove the right hand side kick panel in order to gain access to some of the antenna cable retaining clips.

7. Pull the antenna cable through the hole in the door hinge pillar and fender and remove the antenna assembly from the vehicle.

To install:

8. With the right front door open, put the gasket on the antenna and position the antenna base and wire harness assembly into the fender opening. Install the antenna base onto the fender using the retaining screws.
9. Install the antenna base cap and antenna mast assembly, if so equipped.
10. Pull the antenna lead through the door hinge pillar opening. Seat the grommet by pulling the antenna wiring harness cable through the hole from the inside of the vehicle.
11. Route the antenna cable behind the glove box, along the instrument panel and install the cable in the retaining clips from which they were removed.
12. Connect the antenna wiring connector into the back of the radio. Install the right hand kick panel, if removed.
13. Push in on the sides of the glove box door and place in the hinged upward position.

Fenders

REMOVAL & INSTALLATION

1981-90 Models

➧ See Figure 38

1. Remove the pins securing the splash shield to the body.
2. Remove the screws securing the fender and splash shield to the body.
3. Remove the isolator assembly from the fender.
4. Remove the fender and splash shield from the vehicle.

To install:

5. Place the splash shield and fender into position. Install the retaining screws.
6. Install the splash shield and fender to the body. Secure with the retaining screws and pushpins.

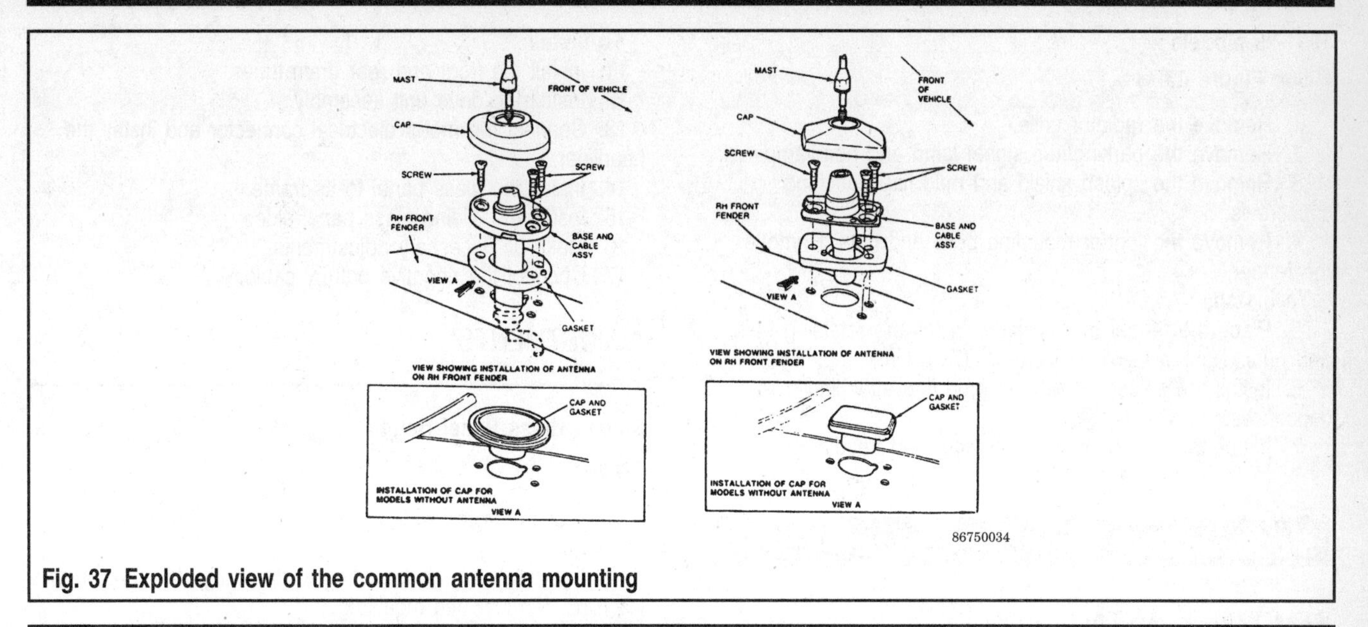

Fig. 37 Exploded view of the common antenna mounting

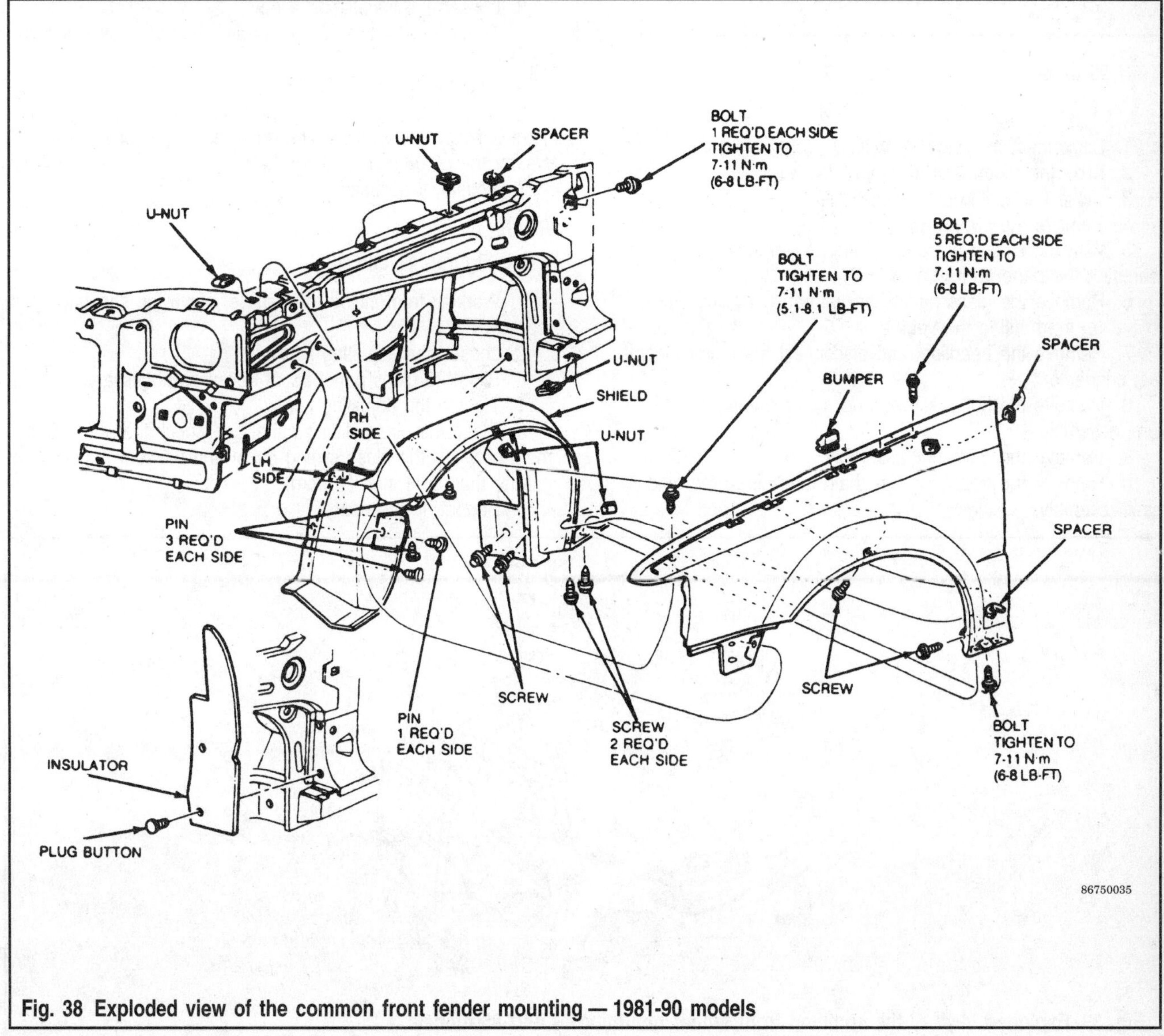

Fig. 38 Exploded view of the common front fender mounting — 1981-90 models

1991-95 Models

➧ See Figure 39

1. Remove the radiator grille.
2. Remove the parking/turn signal lamp and headlamp.
3. Remove the splash shield and mud flap attaching capscrews.
4. Remove the fender mounting bolts and nuts. Remove the fender.

To install:

5. Place the fender into position. Install the retaining bolts and nuts. Tighten to 61-87 inch lbs. (7-10 Nm).
6. Install the splash shield and mud flap attaching capscrews.
7. Install the parking/turn signal lamp and headlamp.
8. Install the radiator grille.

Moon Roof

REMOVAL & INSTALLATION

1991-95 Models

➧ See Figure 40

1. Disconnect the negative battery cable.
2. Slide the moon roof sunshade rearward.
3. Close the sliding glass panel.
4. Remove the sliding glass panel side.
5. With the sliding glass panel closed, remove the nuts securing the panel to its frame.
6. Remove the glass panel from its frame, by lifting the panel up from inside the vehicle.
7. Remove the headliner and disconnect the motor electrical connector.
8. Remove the bolts, screws and nuts retaining the drive unit assembly.
9. Remove the drive unit assembly.
10. Remove the front and rear drain tubes from the guide unit assembly.

To install:

11. Install the front and rear drain tubes.
12. Install the drive unit assembly.
13. Connect the motor electrical connector and install the headliner.
14. Install the glass panel to its frame.
15. Install the sliding glass panel side.
16. Make all necessary adjustments.
17. Connect the negative battery cable.

ADJUSTMENTS

Sliding Glass Panel Height

FRONT

1. Working from inside the vehicle, move the sunshade rearward.
2. Pull down on the moulding to disengage the three retaining clips. Remove the moulding.
3. Loosen the installation screw.
4. Turn the adjusting screw, as necessary, to raise or lower the glass panel.
5. Tighten the installation screw.
6. Close the glass sliding panel and check that the adjustment between the glass sliding panel and the roof is not greater than 0.06 inch (1.5mm).
7. Repeat, if necessary.

REAR

➧ See Figures 41 and 42

1. Working from inside the vehicle, move the sunshade rearward.
2. Loosen the adjusting screw.
3. Slide the glass panel up or down, as necessary.
4. Tighten the adjusting screw.
5. Close the glass sliding panel and check that the adjustment between the glass sliding panel and the roof is not greater than 0.06 inch (1.5mm).
6. Repeat, if necessary.

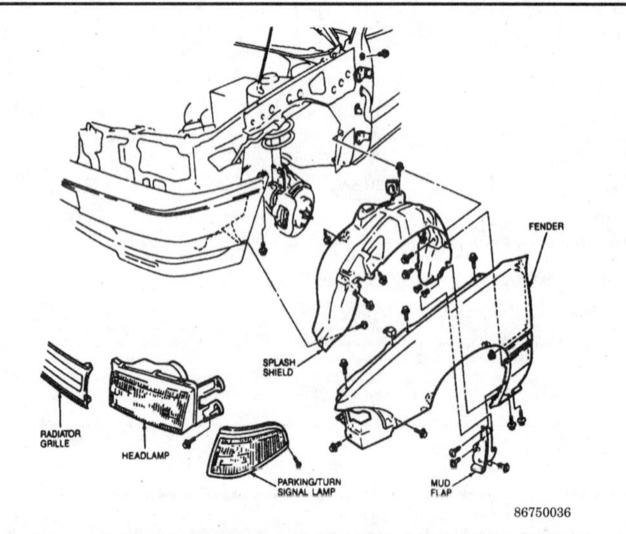

Fig. 39 Exploded view of the common front fender mounting — 1991-95 models

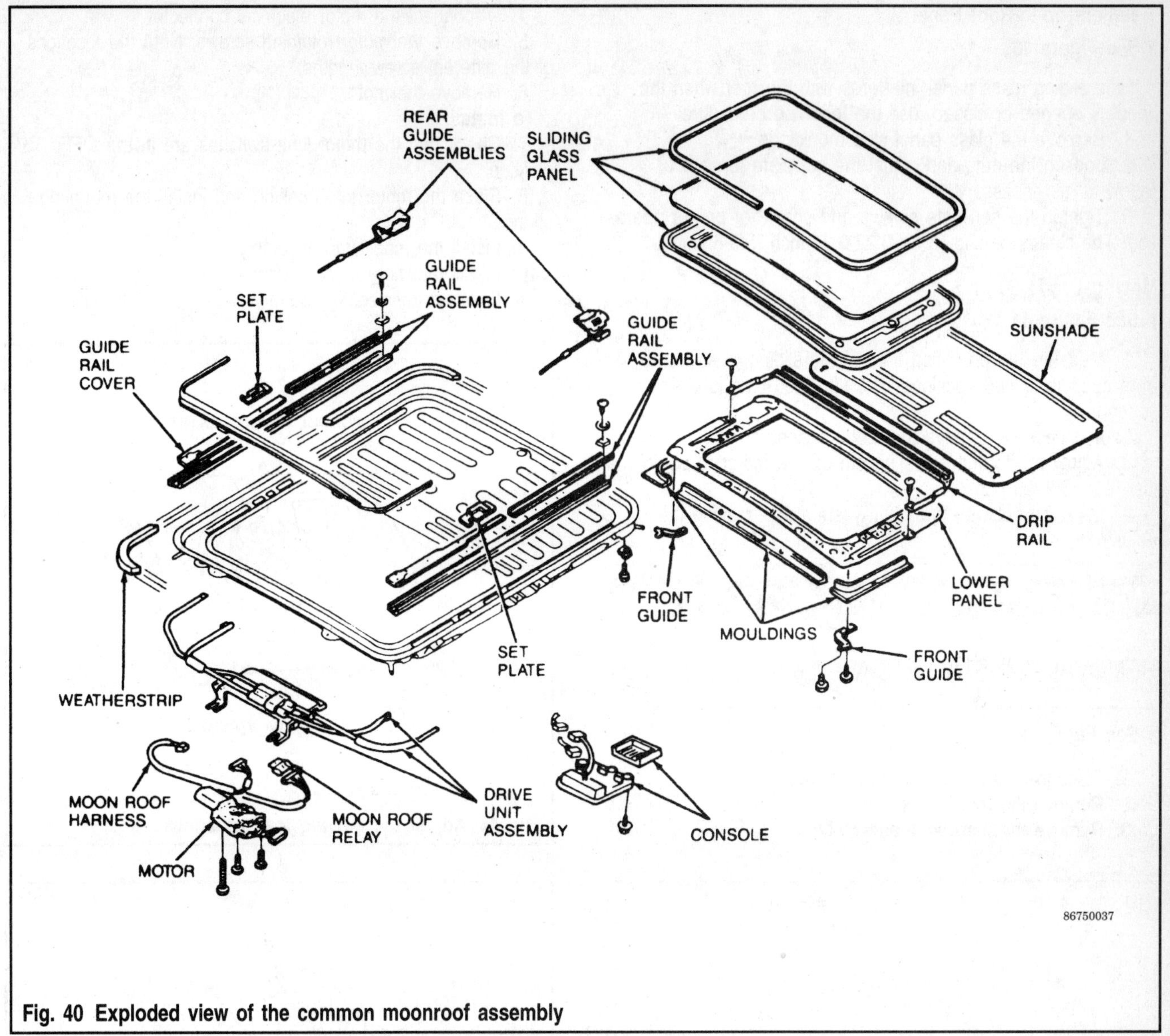

Fig. 40 Exploded view of the common moonroof assembly

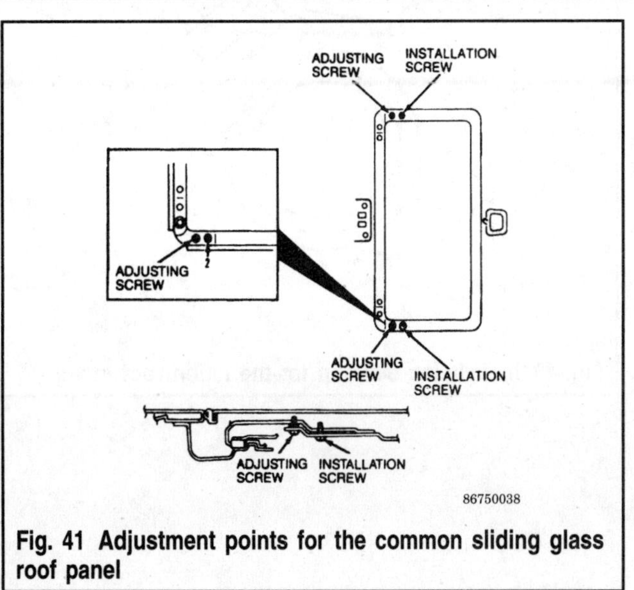

Fig. 41 Adjustment points for the common sliding glass roof panel

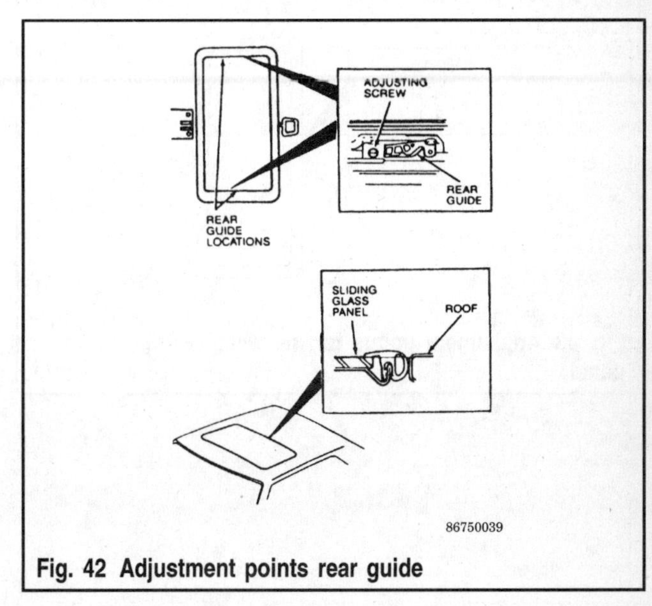

Fig. 42 Adjustment points rear guide

Weatherstrip-to-Roof Panel

See Figure 43

If the sliding glass panel interferes with the roof when the panel is opened or closed, use the following procedure:

1. Remove the glass panel side mouldings.
2. Loosen the nuts and adjust the set plate forward or rearward, as necessary.
3. Tighten the set plate screws and check for proper operation. The clearance should be 0.22-0.24 inch (5.5-6.1mm).

Moving Load

See Figure 44

1. Measure the operation time of the sliding glass panel from open to closed positions. The specified time is 4-7 seconds.
2. If necessary, remove the motor access cover.
3. Adjust the torque adjusting nut on the motor to 35-43 inch lbs. (3.9-4.9 Nm).
4. Lock the nut with the pawl washer after making the adjustment.

Moon Roof Motor

REMOVAL & INSTALLATION

See Figure 45

1. Disconnect the negative battery cable.
2. Remove the motor access door.
3. Remove the map lamp assembly.
4. Disconnect the motor electrical connector.
5. Remove the motor retaining screws. Note the locations of the different screw lengths.
6. Remove the motor.

To install:

7. Check that the motor limit switches are in the OFF position.
8. Place the motor into position and install the mounting screws.
9. Install the map lamp assembly.
10. Install the motor access door.
11. Connect the negative battery cable.

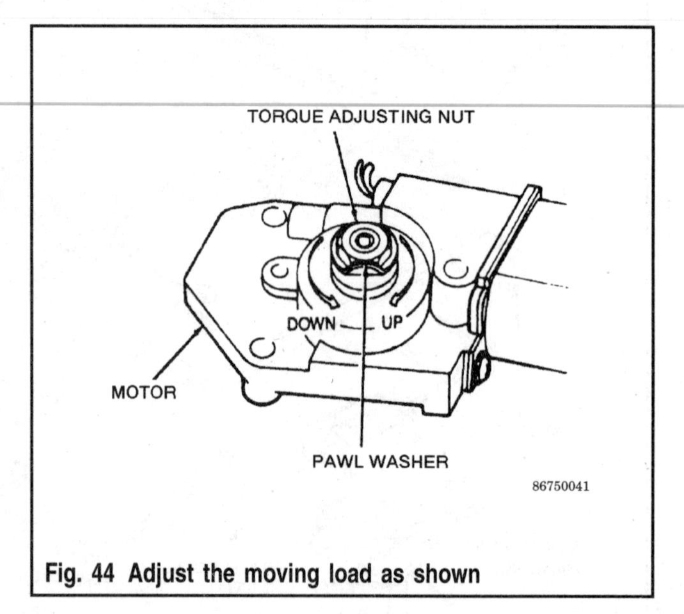

Fig. 44 Adjust the moving load as shown

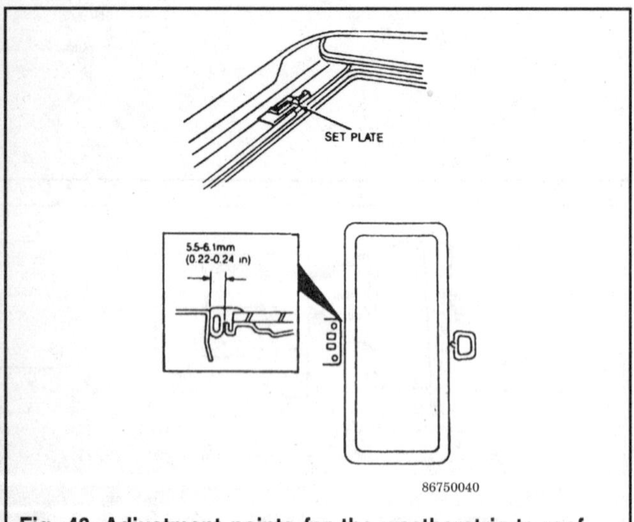

Fig. 43 Adjustment points for the weatherstrip-to-roof panel

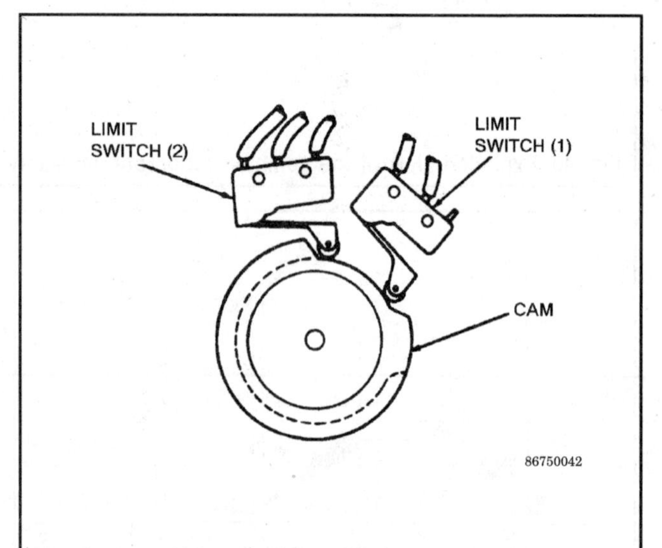

Fig. 45 Installation position for the moon roof motor

INTERIOR

Instrument Panel and Pad

REMOVAL & INSTALLATION

1981-90 Models

➧ See Figures 46, 47, 48 and 49

1. Disconnect the negative battery cable.
2. Remove the steering column opening cover retaining screws and remove the cover.
3. Remove the sound insulator, if equipped.
4. On 1988-89 vehicles, remove the snap-in lower cluster finish panel(s) to expose the retaining screws.
5. Remove the steering column trim shrouds.
6. Disengage all electrical connections.
7. To remove the steering column, remove the bolt and nut at the lock collar U-joint and screws at steering column bracket.
8. On 1988-89 vehicles, disconnect the speedometer at the transaxle.
9. Remove the cluster.
10. Disconnect the speedometer cable by reaching up under the instrument panel and pressing on the flat surface of the plastic connector.
11. Remove the glove box hinge support screws. Depress the sides of the glove box bin and remove the glove box assembly.
12. Disconnect all vacuum hoses and electrical connectors, heater, A/C control cables and radio antenna cable.
13. Disconnect all necessary under hood electrical connectors to the main wire loom. Disengage the rubber grommet from the dash panel and feed wire and connectors into the instrument panel area.
14. Remove the steering column support bracket retaining nut.
15. Remove the speaker covers.
16. Remove the instrument panel tubular brace retaining screw.
17. Remove the upper and lower instrument panel to cowl side retaining screws and remove the instrument panel from the vehicle.
18. Transfer all attaching components to the replacement panel.

To install:

19. Place the instrument panel in the vehicle and into position. Install the upper and lower instrument panel to cowl side retaining screws.
20. Install the instrument panel tubular brace retaining screw.
21. Install the speaker covers.
22. Push the wiring harness and connectors through the dash panel into the engine compartment.
23. Connect all necessary under hood electrical connectors.
24. Connect all vacuum hoses and electrical connectors, heater, A/C control cables and radio antenna cable. Connect the speedometer cable.
25. Install the glove box assembly.

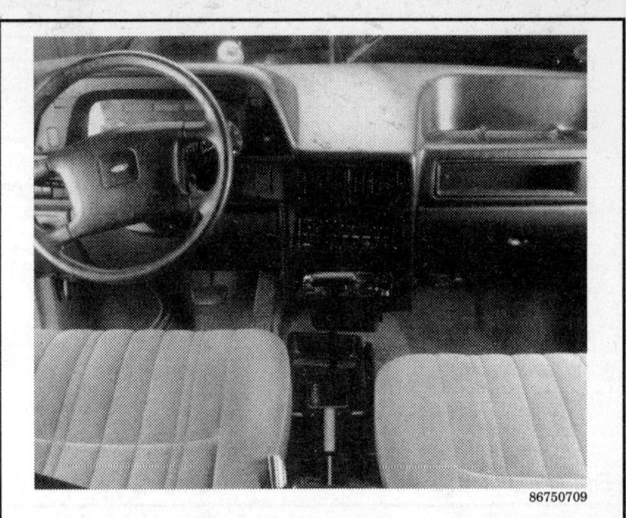

86750709

Fig. 46 A common instrument panel and pad — 1988 Escort shown

26. Install the cluster.
27. Connect the speedometer to the transaxle, if required.
28. Install the steering column trim shrouds.
29. Install the sound insulator, if equipped.
30. Install the steering column opening cover.
31. Connect the negative battery cable.

1991-95 Models

➧ See Figure 50

1. Disconnect the negative battery cable.
2. Remove the instrument cluster. Refer to Section 6 of this manual.
3. Remove the hood release cable from the lower dash trim panel.
4. Carefully pry out both dash side panels.
5. Remove the lower dash trim side panels.
6. Remove the glove box retaining screws and remove the glove box.
7. Remove the climate control assembly.
8. Remove the accessory console retaining screws.
9. Disconnect all electrical connectors and radio antenna.
10. Remove the steering column support bolts and lower the steering column.
11. Disconnect the amplifier connectors.
12. Remove the instrument panel to floor pan attaching bolts (4).
13. Remove the bolts from the lower and upper instrument panel mounts.
14. Remove the defroster duct bezel retaining screw.
15. Remove the mounting bolts that attach the upper instrument panel to the cowl.
16. Carefully remove the instrument panel from the vehicle.
17. Transfer all attaching components to the replacement panel.

To install:

18. While holding the instrument panel close to installed position and route all wire harness and connectors to their proper locations.

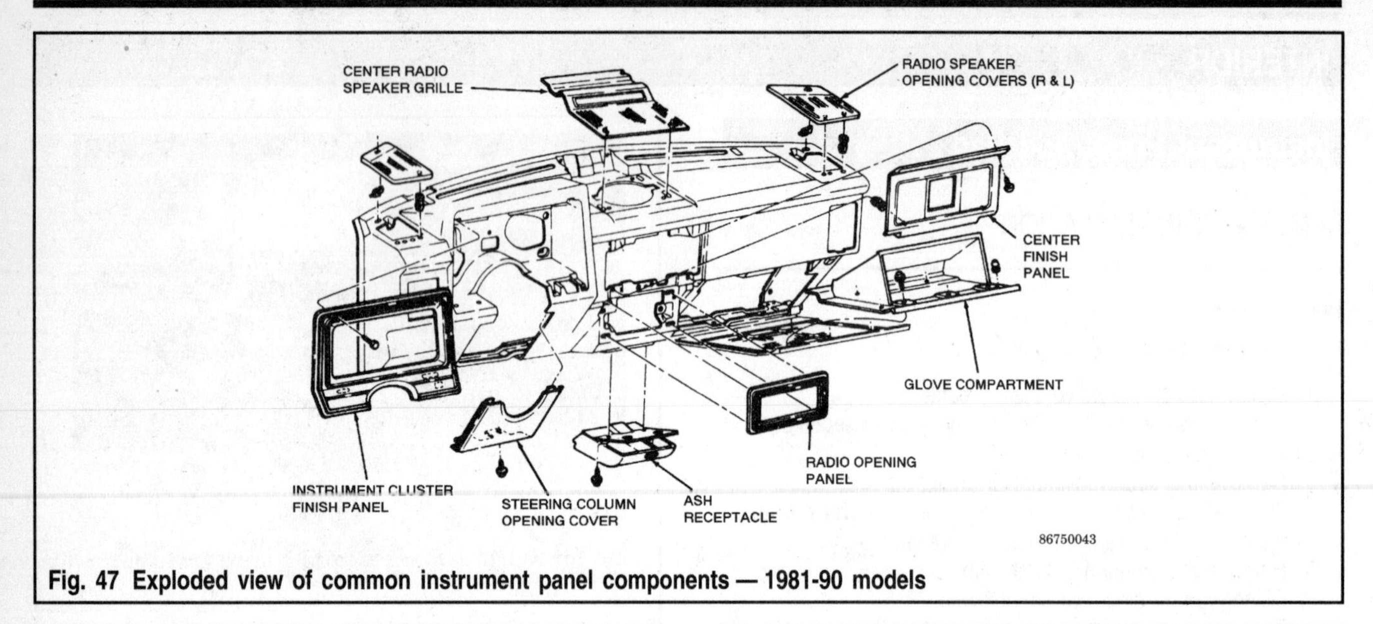

Fig. 47 Exploded view of common instrument panel components — 1981-90 models

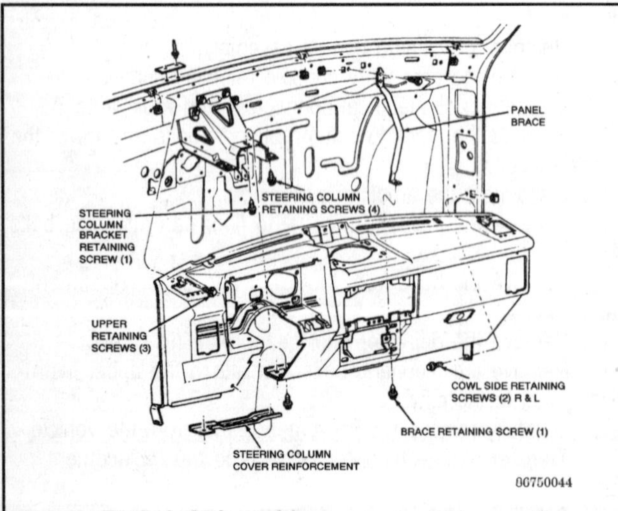

Fig. 48 Exploded view of common instrument panel mounting — 1981-90 models

Fig. 49 Exploded view of instrument panel mounting — 1988 shown

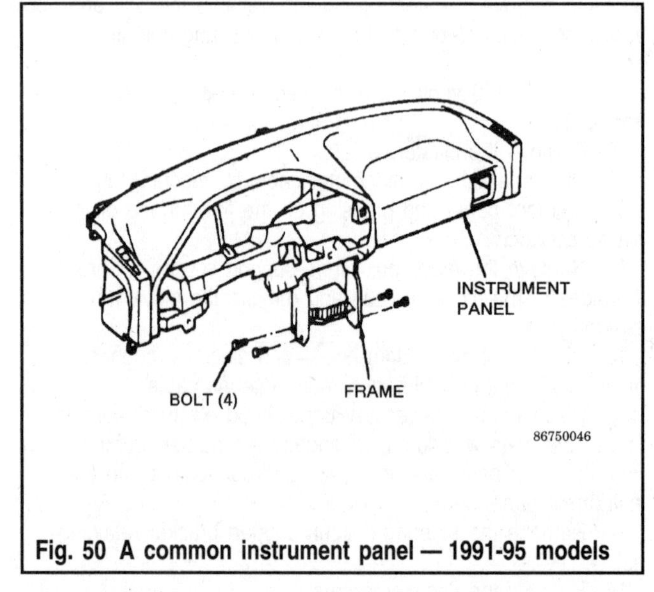

Fig. 50 A common instrument panel — 1991-95 models

19. Place the instrument panel into position and install the retaining bolts.
20. Install the defroster duct bezel retaining screw.
21. Install the bolts to the lower and upper instrument panel mounts.
22. Install the instrument panel to floor pan attaching bolts (4).
23. Disconnect the amplifier connectors.
24. Install the steering column.
25. Plug in all electrical connectors and radio antenna.
26. Install the climate control assembly and glove box.
27. Install the hood release cable.
28. Install the instrument cluster. Refer to Section 6 of this manual.
29. Connect the negative battery cable.

Door Panel

REMOVAL & INSTALLATION

1981-90 Models

See Figures 51, 52, 53, 54, 55, 56, 57 and 58

1. Remove the window regulator handle retaining screw and the handle.
2. Remove the door handle pull cup.
3. Remove the retaining screws from the armrest assembly. Remove the armrest. On vehicles with power door locks, disconnect the wiring connector.
4. Remove the trim panel retaining screws from the bottom of the map compartment, if so equipped.
5. Remove the retaining set screw from the remote control mirror bezel, if so equipped.

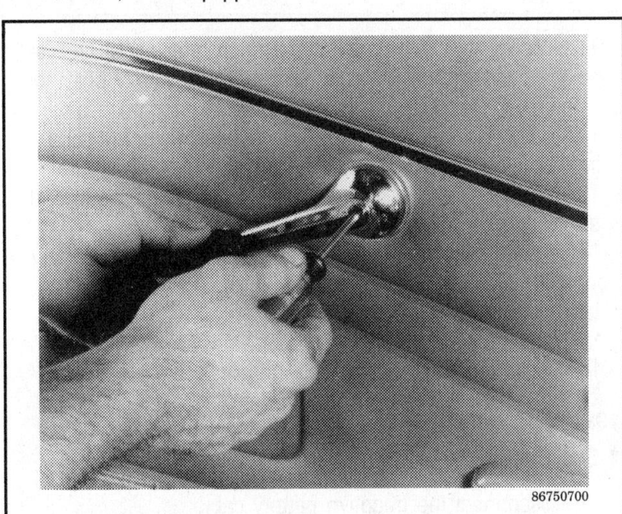
86750700

Fig. 51 Use a Phillips screwdriver to remove the window regulator handle retaining screw and the handle

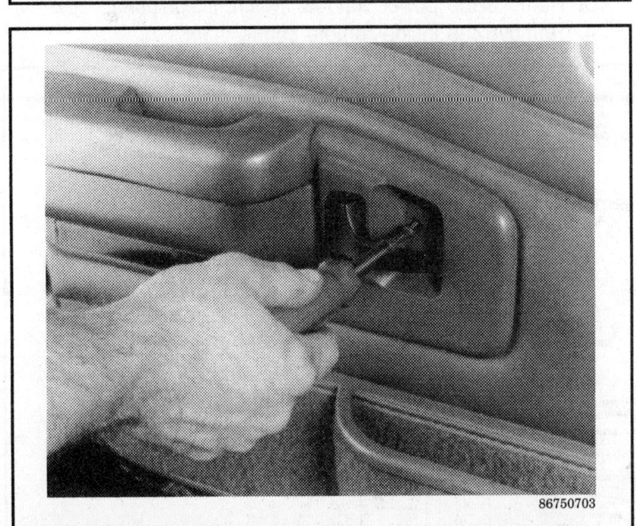
86750703

Fig. 52 Remove the Phillips screw and remove door handle pull cup

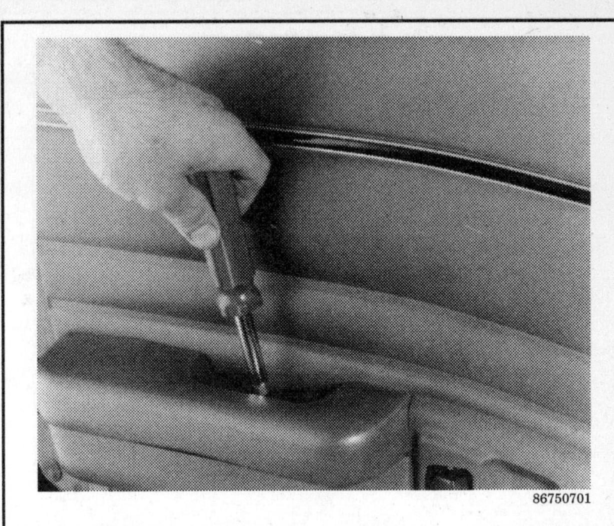
86750701

Fig. 53 Remove the retaining screws from the armrest assembly, then remove the armrest

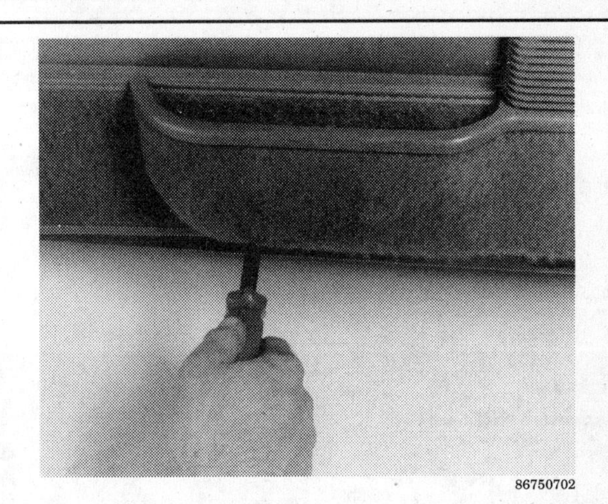
86750702

Fig. 54 Remove the trim panel retaining screws from the bottom of the map compartment, then remove the map compartment

6. Using a suitable push pin tool, pry the trim panel retaining push pins from the door interior panel.

Do not use the trim panel to pull the push pins from the door inner panel holes.

7. If the trim panel is to be replaced, transfer the trim panel retaining push pins to the new panel assembly.

To install:

8. Replace any bent, broken or missing push pins.

If the watershield has been removed, be sure to position it correctly before installing the trim panel.

9. Be sure that the armrest retaining clips are properly positioned on the door inner panel. If they have been dislodged, they must be installed before installing the watershield.
10. Position the trim panel to the door inner panel. Route the remote control outside mirror cable through the bezel, if so equipped.

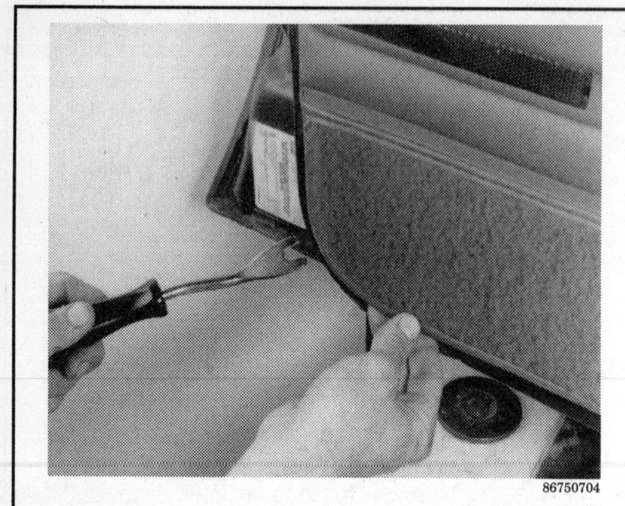

Fig. 55 Use a suitable push pin tool to pry the trim panel retaining push pins from the door interior panel

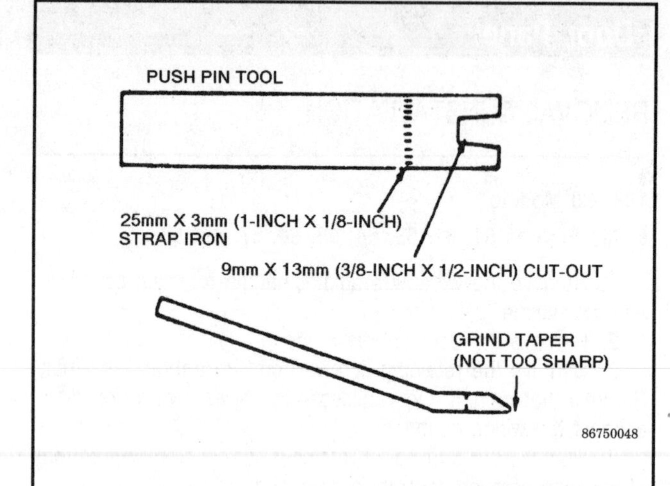

Fig. 58 Construct a push pin tool to the dimensions shown

Fig. 56 When fully detached, remove the door panel

11. Position the trim panel to the door inner panel and locate the push pins in the countersunk holes. Firmly push the trim panel at the push pin locations to set each push pin.
12. Install the set screw from the remote control outside mirror bezel, if so equipped.
13. Install the trim panel retaining screws at the bottom of the map pocket, if so equipped.
14. On vehicles with power door locks, connect the wiring connector. Position the armrest to the trim panel and install the retaining screws.
15. Install the door handle pull cup.
16. Install the window regulator handle.

1991-95 Models

➧ **See Figures 59 and 60**

1. Disconnect the negative battery cable.
2. Remove the window regulator handle, using a suitable tool.
3. Remove the power window switch, if equipped.
4. Remove the inside remote control handle.

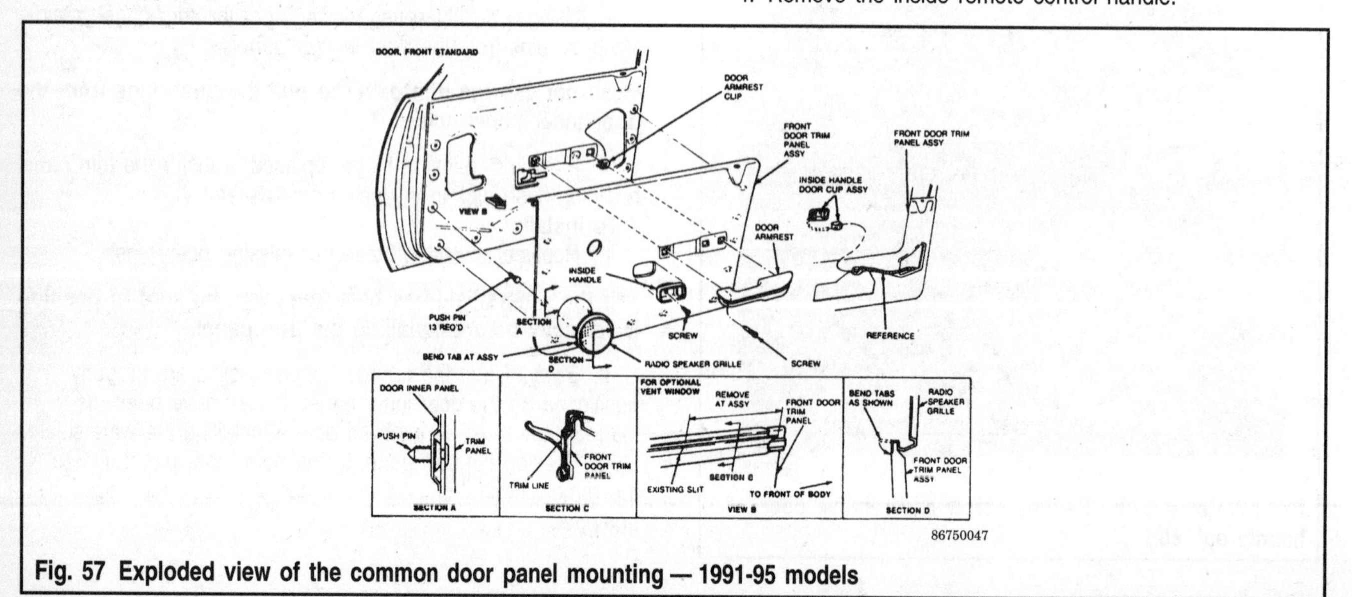

Fig. 57 Exploded view of the common door panel mounting — 1991-95 models

5. Slide a flat-bladed tool behind each of the retaining clips and twist to disengage the clips from the door shell.
6. Remove the trim panel by lifting it up and sliding it rearward to clear the sheet metal.

To install:

7. Replace all damaged trim panel retainers.
8. If removed, install the weathersheet.
9. Place the trim panel into position on the door and insert the remote control handle through the opening.
10. Install the inside remote control handle.
11. Install the power window switch, if equipped.
12. Install the window regulator handle.
13. Connect the negative battery cable.

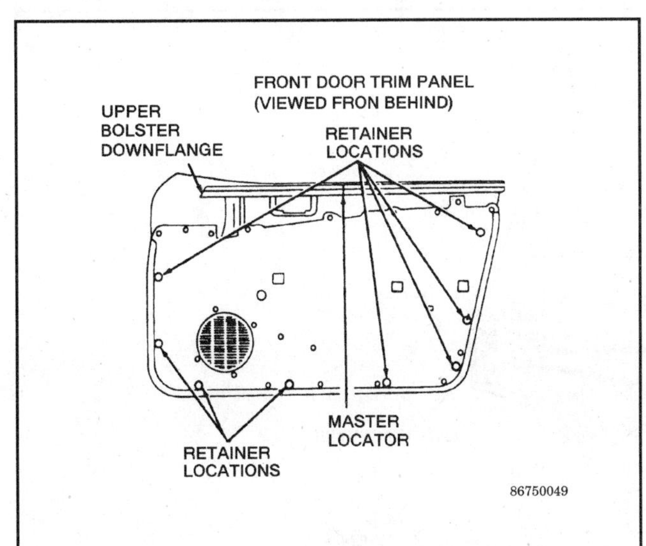

Fig. 59 Common door trim panel — 1991-95 models

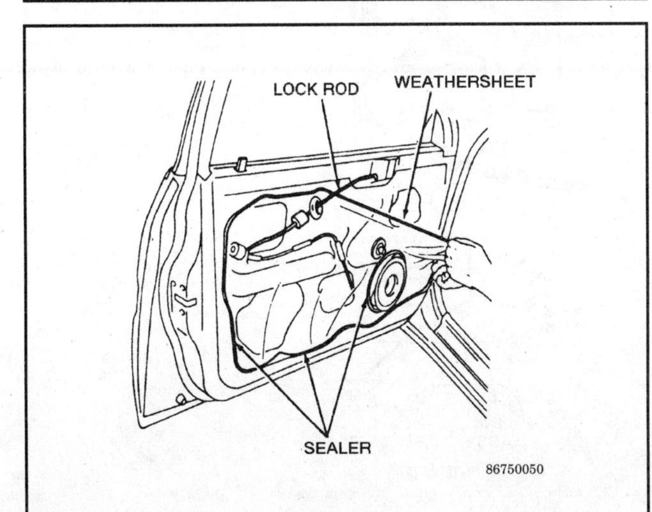

Fig. 60 The weathersheet is a piece of plastic cut to fit between the door and door panel

Door Lock Cylinder

REMOVAL & INSTALLATION

See Figures 61, 62, 63, 64, 65, 66 and 67

➡When a lock cylinder must be replaced, replace both locks in the set to avoid carrying an extra key which fits only one lock.

1. Remove the door trim panel and the watershield.
2. Remove the clip attaching the lock cylinder rod to the lock cylinder.
3. Pry the lock cylinder retainer out of the slot in the door.
4. Remove the lock cylinder from the door.
5. Work the cylinder lock assembly into the outer door panel.
6. Install the cylinder retainer into its slot and push the retainer onto the lock cylinder.
7. Install the lock cylinder rod with the clip onto the lock assembly.
8. Lock and unlock the door to check the lock cylinder operation.
9. Install the watershield and door trim panel.

Power Door Lock Actuator Motor

REMOVAL & INSTALLATION

1. Disconnect the negative battery cable.
2. Remove the door trim panel and the watershield.
3. Using a 1/4 in. (6mm) diameter drill bit, remove the pop rivet attaching the actuator motor to the door. Disconnect the wiring at the connector.
4. Disconnect the actuator motor link from the door latch and remove the motor.

To install:

5. Connect the actuator motor link to the door latch.
6. Connect the wiring at the connector.
7. Install the door lock actuator motor to the door with a pop rivet, using a suitable rivet gun.

➡Make sure that the actuator boot is not twisted during installation. The pop rivet must be installed with the bracket base tight to the inner panel.

8. Install the door trim panel and water shield.
9. Reconnect the negative battery cable.

Door Glass

REMOVAL & INSTALLATION

1981-90 Models

See Figures 68, 69 and 70

1. Remove the door trim panel and watershield.

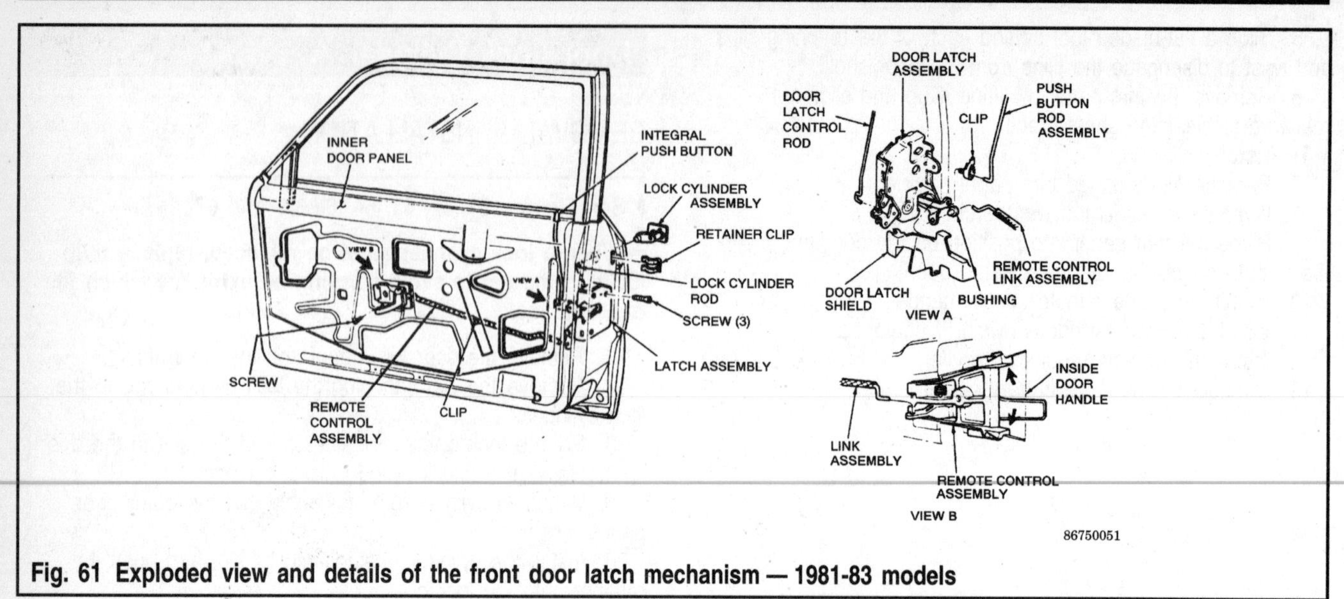

Fig. 61 Exploded view and details of the front door latch mechanism — 1981-83 models

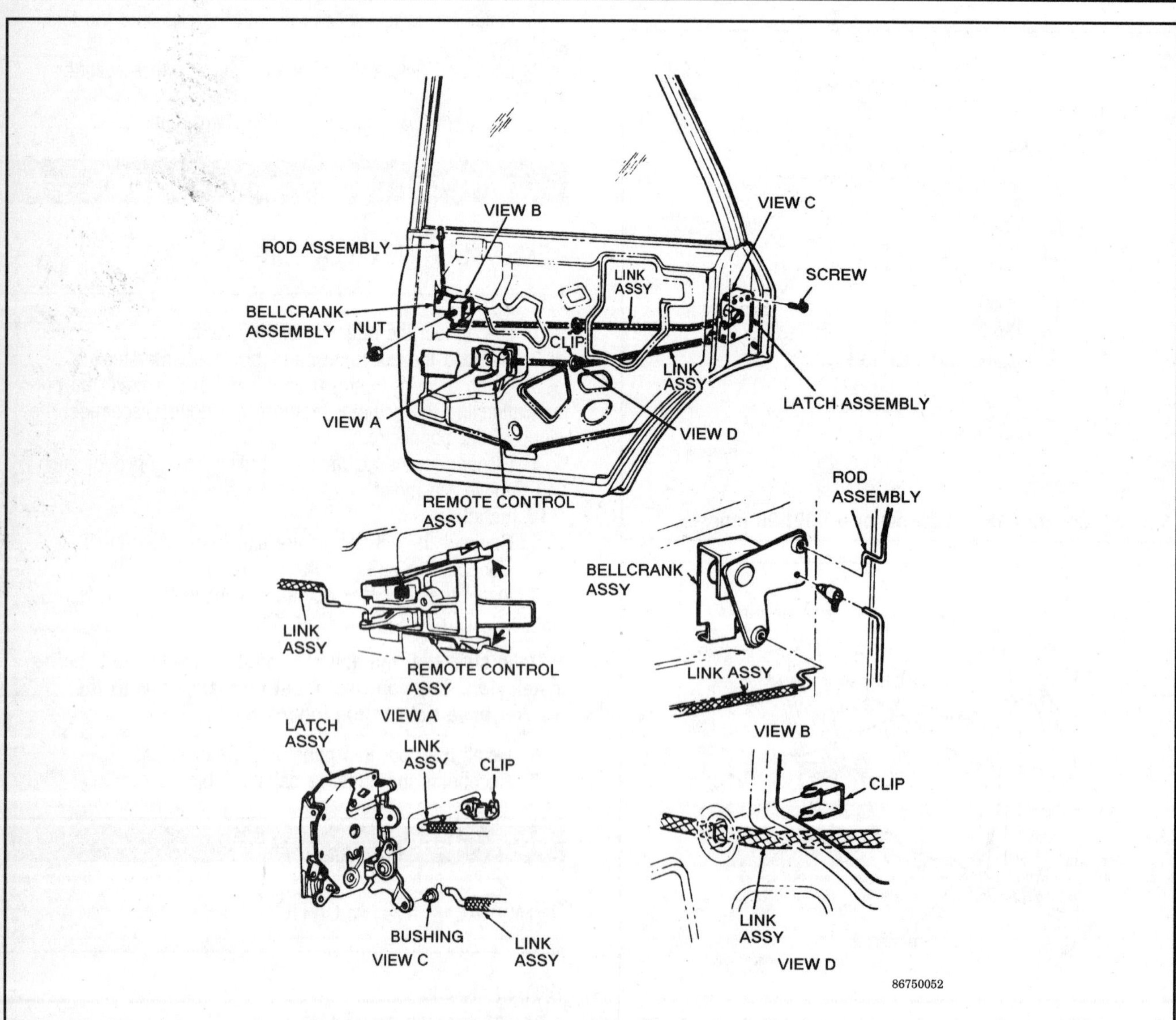

Fig. 62 Exploded view of the rear door latch and remote control assembly — 1981-83 models

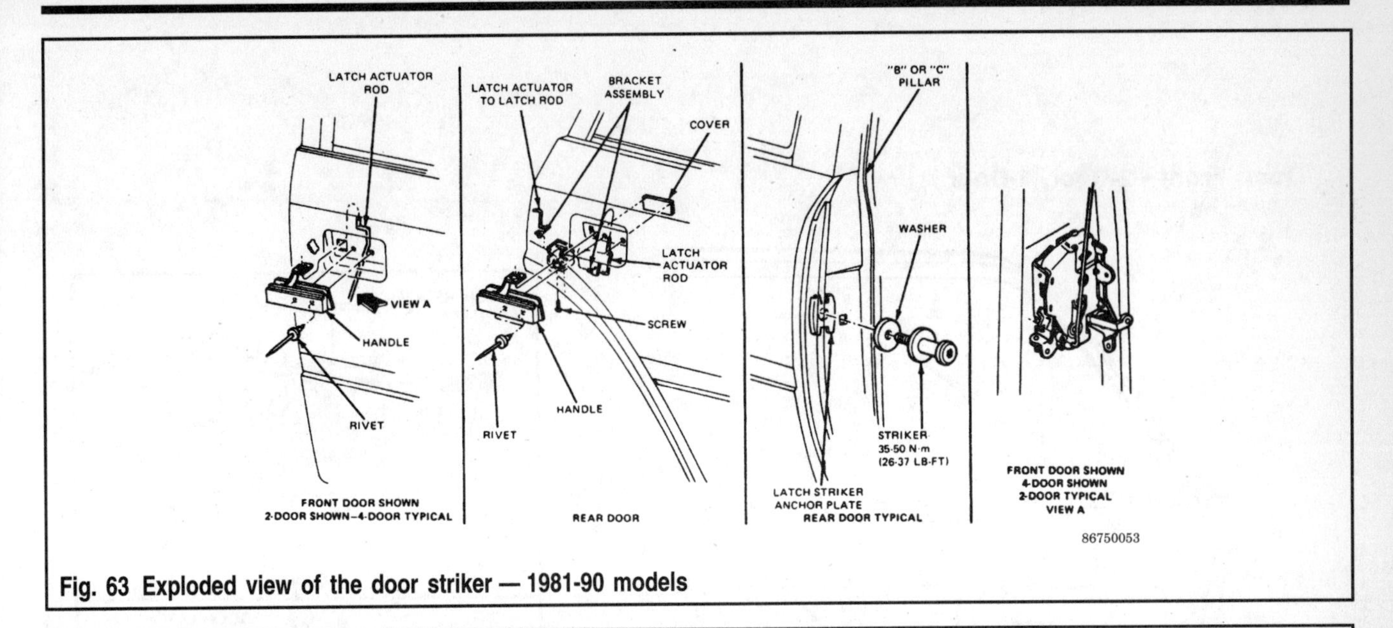

Fig. 63 Exploded view of the door striker — 1981-90 models

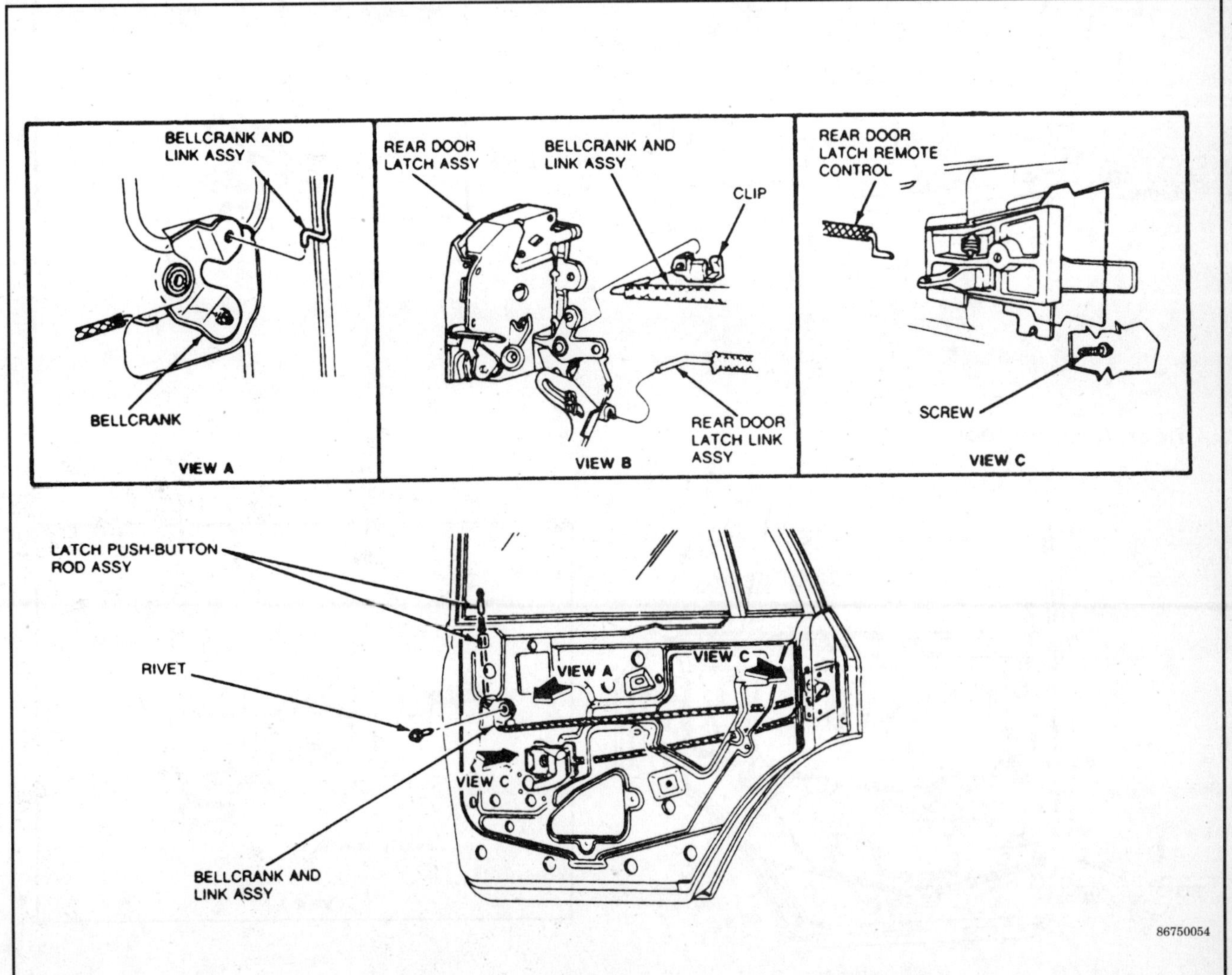

Fig. 64 Exploded view of the door latch and remote control assembly — 1984-90 Escort/Lynx

Door, Front—2-Door, 4-Door

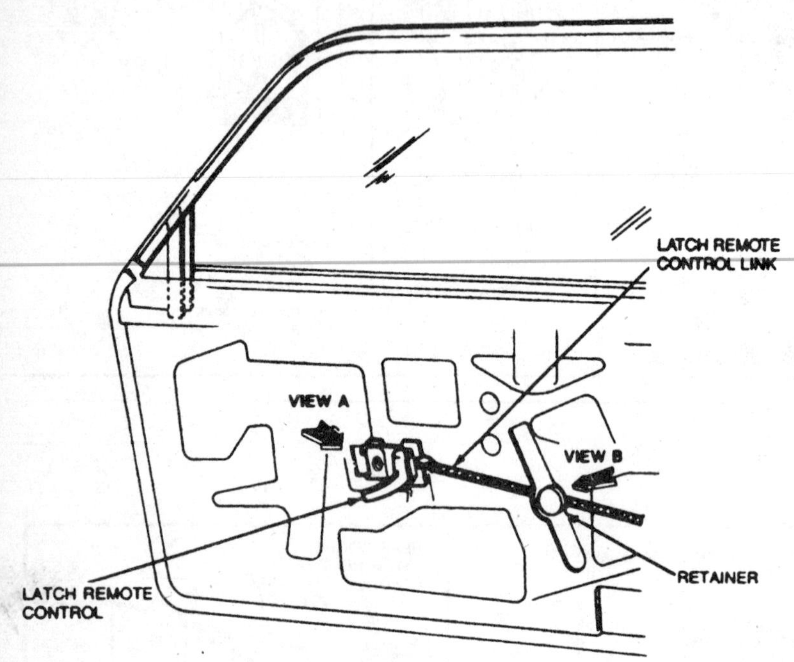

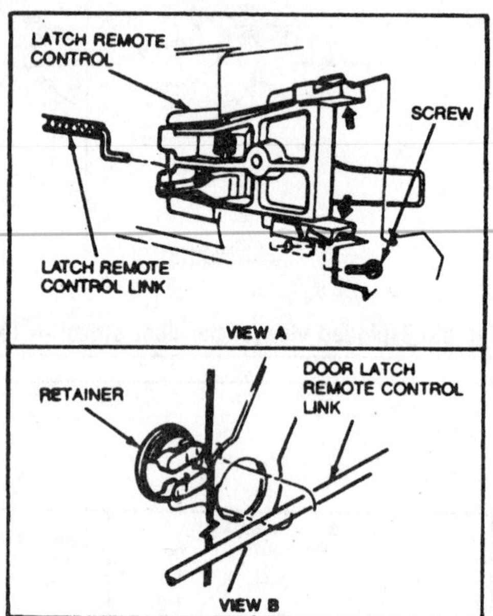

Door, Rear—4-Door

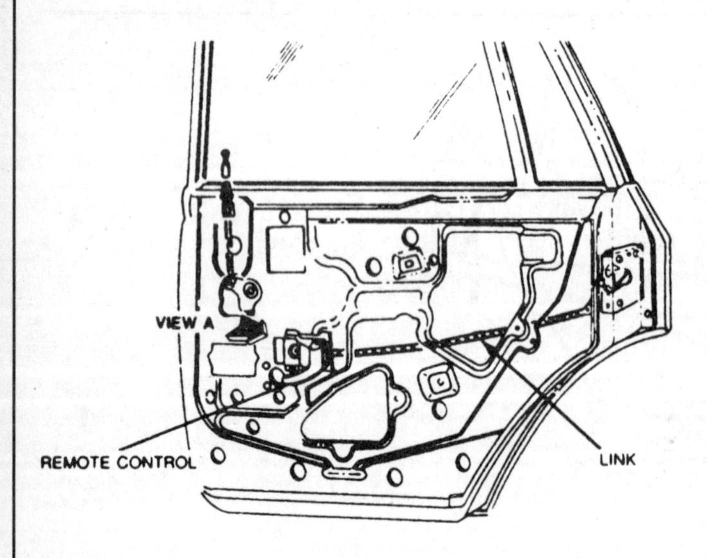

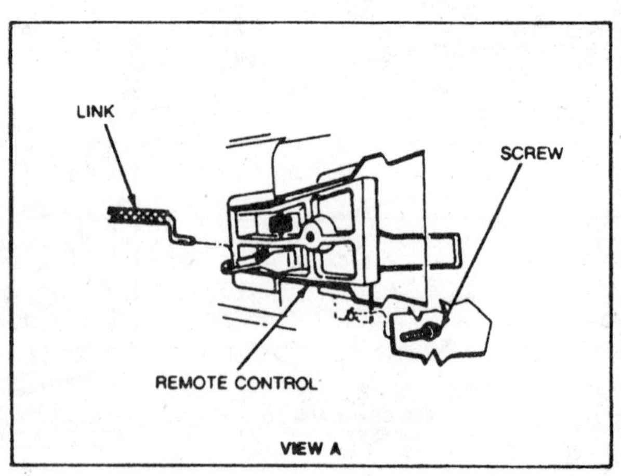

86750055

Fig. 65 Exploded view of the door latch and remote control assembly — 1984-90 Escort/Lynx

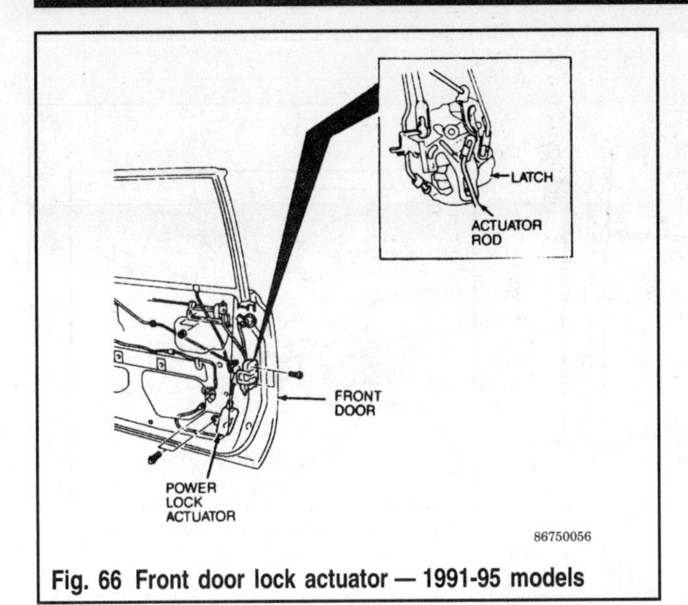

Fig. 66 Front door lock actuator — 1991-95 models

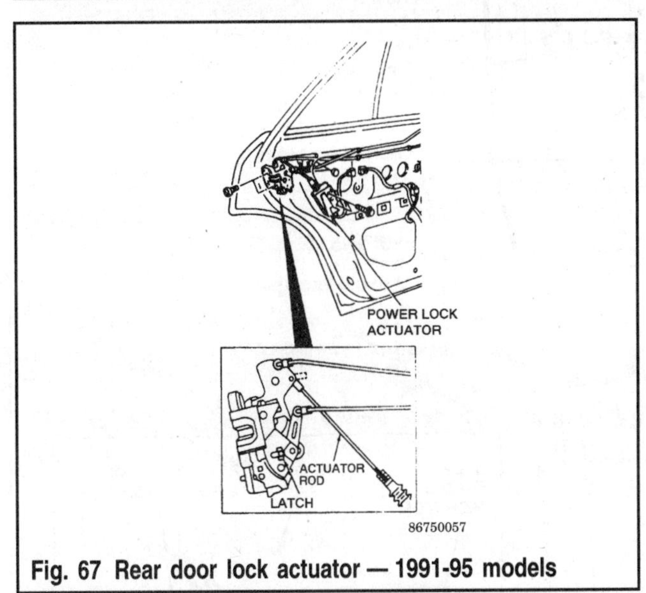

Fig. 67 Rear door lock actuator — 1991-95 models

2. Remove the two rivets attaching the glass to the run and bracket assembly.

➡Prior to the removing center pins from the rivet, it is recommended that a suitable block support be inserted between the door outer panel and the glass bracket to stabilize the glass during the rivet removal. Remove the center pin from each rivet with a drift punch. Then, using a ¼ in. (6mm) diameter drill carefully drill out the remainder of each rivet as damage to the plastic glass retainer and spacer could result.

3. Remove the glass.
4. Remove the drillings and pins from the bottom of the door.

To install:

5. Snap the plastic retainer and spacer into the two glass retainer holes. Make certain that the metal washer in the retainer assembly is on the outboard side of the glass.
6. Insert the glass into the door.

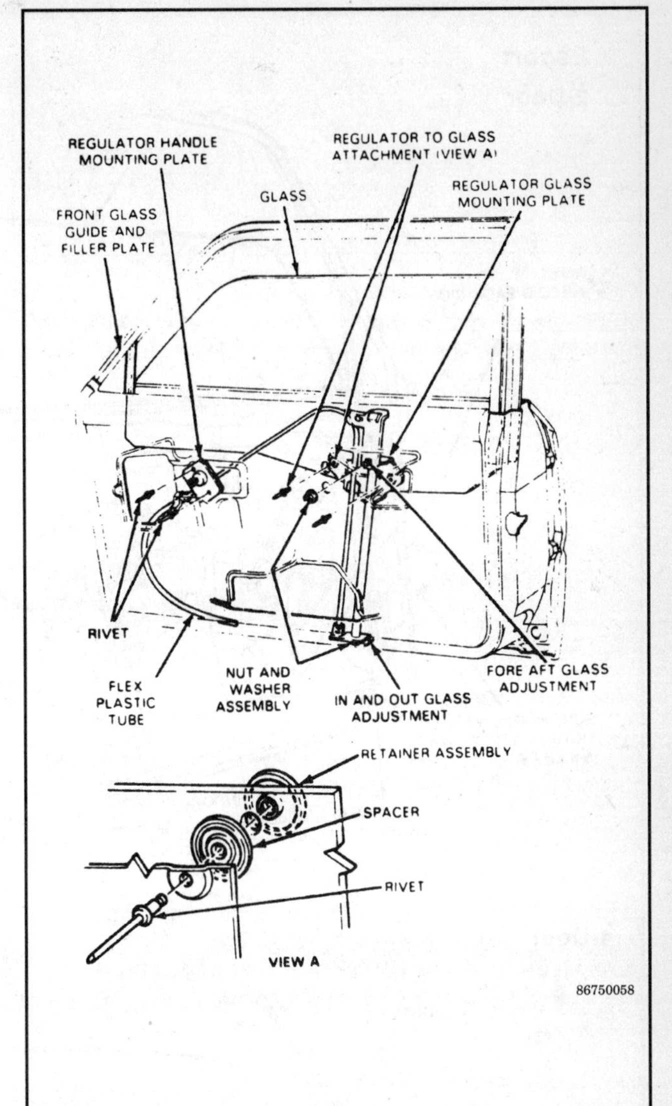

Fig. 68 Exploded view of the front window mechanism and cable drive system

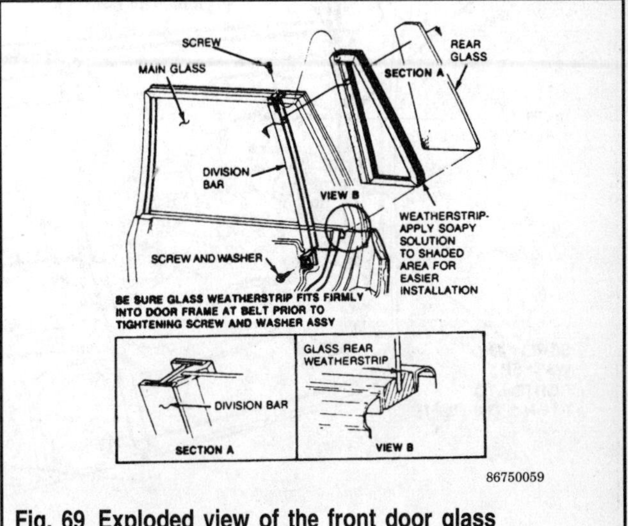

Fig. 69 Exploded view of the front door glass mounting — 1991-95 models

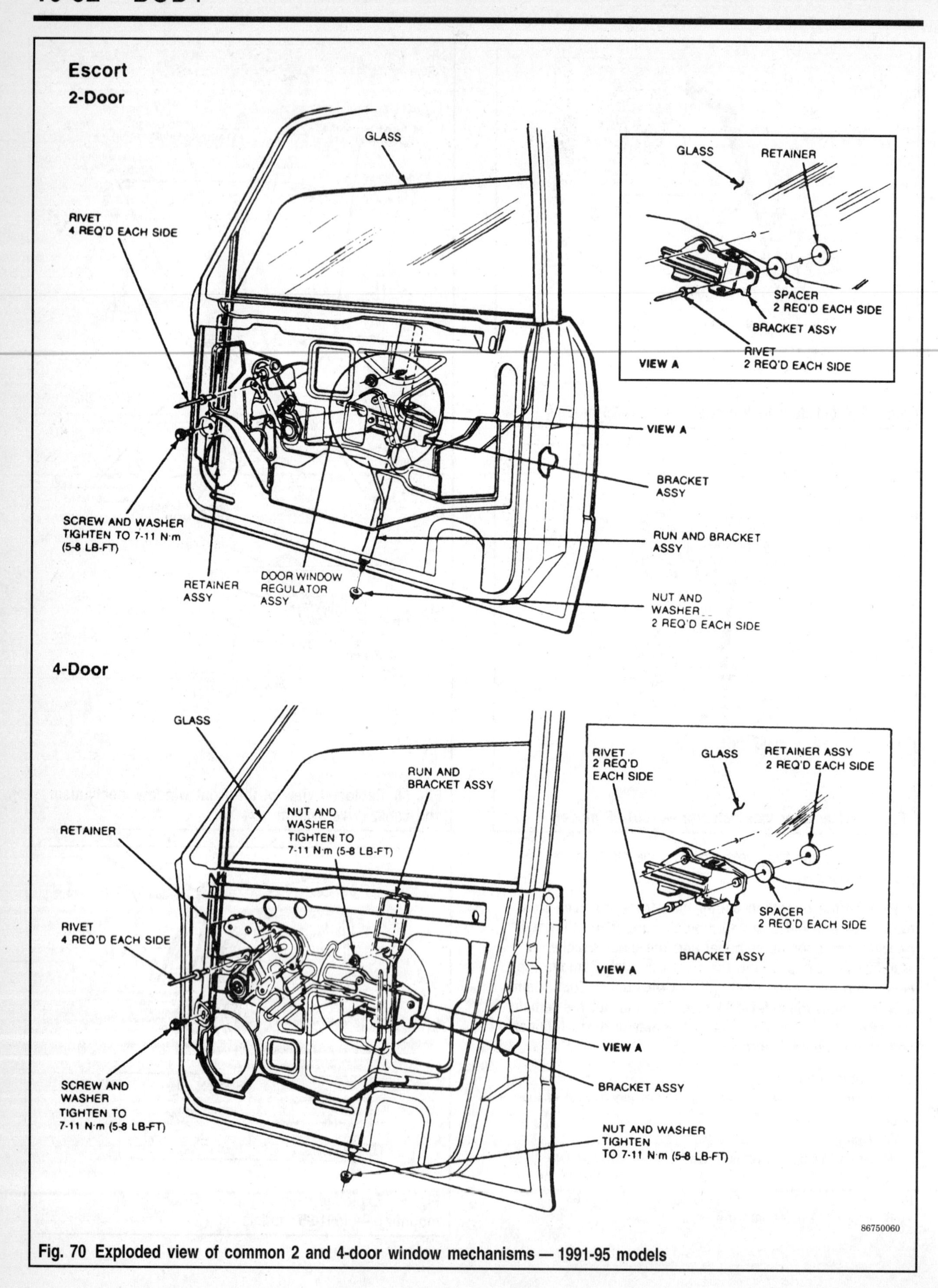

Fig. 70 Exploded view of common 2 and 4-door window mechanisms — 1991-95 models

7. Position the door glass to the door glass bracket and align the glass and glass bracket retaining holes
8. Install the retaining rivets.
9. Raise the glass to the full UP position.
10. Install the rear glass run retainer and rear glass run.
11. Check the operation of the window.
12. Install the trim panel and watershield.

1991-95 Models

FRONT

1. Raise the front door glass 4.3 inch (110mm) from the fully open position.
2. Disconnect the negative battery cable.
3. Remove the door trim panel and watershield.
4. Remove the two glass retaining bolts. Allow the glass to remain supported on the glass plastic clips.
5. Tilt the front of the door glass downward to disengage if from the channel and pull the glass up and out of the door.
6. Place the glass on a protected surface.

To install:

7. Place the glass in the door and tilt the front end downward.
8. Engage the rear edge of the glass into the channel.
9. Bring the front edge of the glass upward and engage it into the channel.
10. Support the glass on the slider with the plastic clips and install the two glass retainer bolts.
11. Install the trim panel and watershield.
12. Connect the negative battery cable. Check that the window operates properly.

REAR

1. Open the rear door glass fully.
2. Disconnect the negative battery cable.
3. Remove the door trim panel and watershield.
4. Remove the two glass retainers, retaining the center channel and channel protector.
5. Remove the window regulator roller through the large hole in the lift bracket and remove the rear door glass. Pull the fixed glass out of the channel.

To install:

6. Install the fixed glass to the door channel.
7. Install the rear door glass and engage the regulator roller into the large hole.
8. Install the center channel, channel protector and retainers.
9. Attach the weatherstrips.
10. Install the door trim panel.
11. Connect the negative battery cable. Check that the window operates properly.

ADJUSTMENTS

1. Remove the door trim panel and watershield.
2. Loosen the nut and washer assemblies retaining the glass run and bracket assembly.
3. Move the glass fore and/or aft (or IN and/or OUT), as required. Tighten the nut and washer assemblies.
4. Check the operation of the window.
5. Install the trim panel and watershield.

Window Regulator

REMOVAL & INSTALLATION

1981-90 Models

FRONT

➧ **See Figure 71**

1. Remove the door trim panel and watershield.
2. Prop the glass if the full-up position.
3. Remove the four pop rivets attaching the regulator mounting plate assembly to the inner door panel. Remove the center pin from each rivet with a drift punch. Using a 1/4 in. (6mm) diameter drill, drill out the remainder of the rivet, using care not to enlarge the sheet metal retaining holes.
4. Remove the two nut and washer assemblies attaching the regulator tube to the inner panel and door sill.
5. Slide the tube up between the door belt and glass.
6. Remove the window regulator arm slide/roller from the glass bracket C-channel and remove the regulator.

To install:

7. With glass in full position, install the window regulator through the access hole in the door and insert the slide roller into the glass bracket channel.
8. Slide the tube assembly forward into position, loosely install the two nut and washer assemblies to the regulator tube guide.
9. Install the four rivets or four, 1/4 in.-20 x 1/2 in. screws and washer assemblies and two, 1/4 in.-20 nut/washer assemblies to secure the regulator handle mounting plate to door inner panel. Equivalent metric retainers may be used.
10. Tighten loosely assembled nut and washer assemblies from Step 9.
11. Cycle the glass to ensure smooth operation. Install the watershield and door trim panel.

REAR

1. Remove the door trim panel and watershield.
2. Remove the two rivets attaching the main glass-to-glass bracket.
3. Remove the three rivets attaching the regulator mounting plate assembly to the inner door panel.
4. Remove the two nut and washer assemblies retaining the run and bracket assembly to the inner panel.
5. Disconnect the door latch remote rods at the door latch.
6. Remove the window regulator from the door. Be sure to use the access hole in the inner door panel for removal and installation of the regulator.

To install:

7. Install the window regulator through the access hole in the rear door.
8. Loosely assemble the two nut and washer assemblies to the run and bracket assembly studs on the door inner panel.
9. Install three rivets or three equivalent screw, washer and nut assemblies to secure the regulator mounting plate to the inner door panel.
10. Install the rear door window glass bracket. Position the glass in the full up position and tighten loosely assembles nut from Step 8.

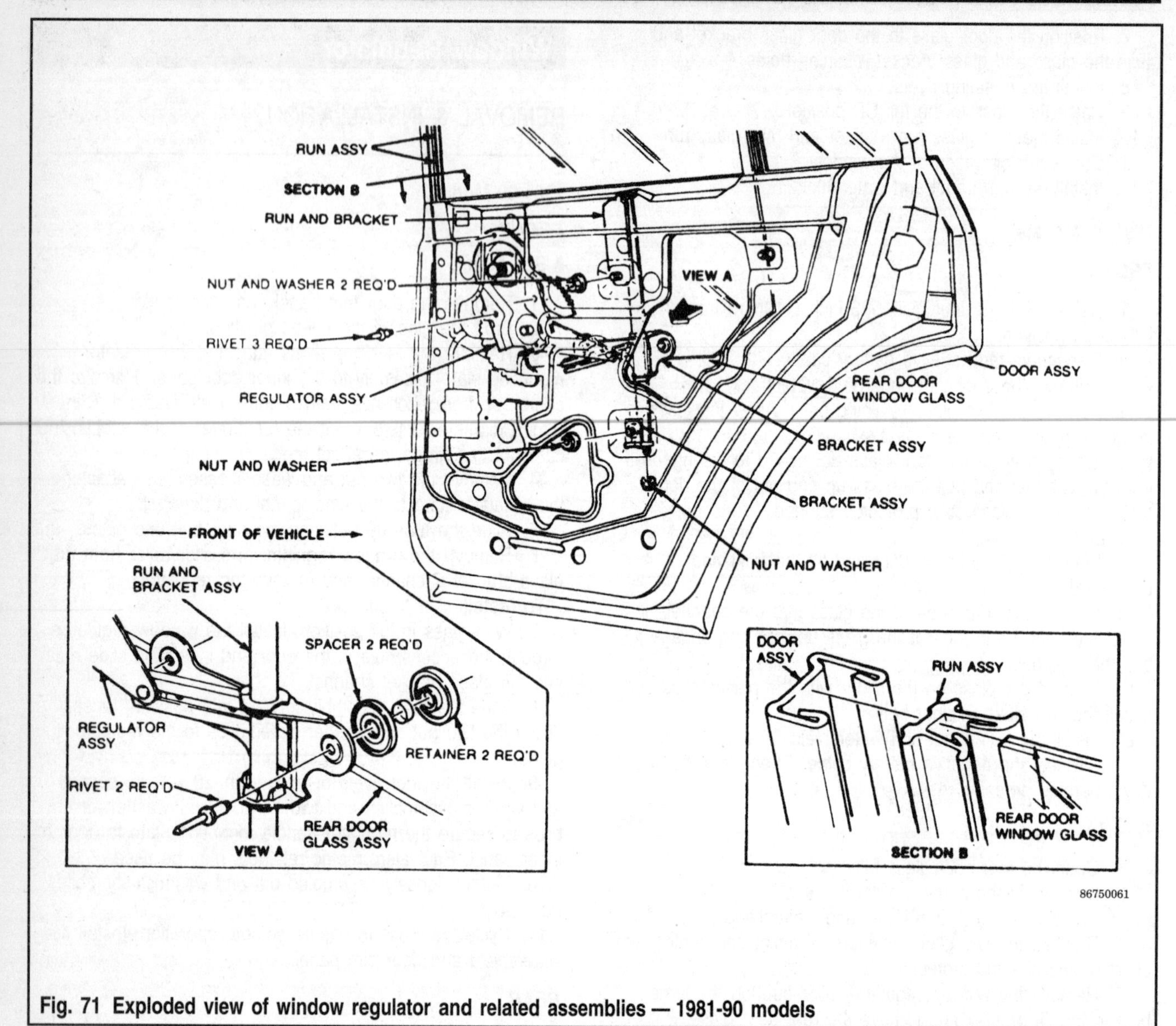

Fig. 71 Exploded view of window regulator and related assemblies — 1981-90 models

11. Connect the door latch remote rods at the door latch.
12. Cycle the glass up and down to check for smooth operation. Install the watershield and trim panel.

1991-95 Models

MANUAL FRONT REGULATOR

➧ **See Figure 72**

1. Remove the front door glass.
2. Remove the two regulator retaining nuts and one regulator retaining screw.
3. Remove the regulator drive retaining nuts.
4. Remove the regulator through the large opening in the bottom of the door.

To install:

5. Rotate the regulator dive unit 180° to install, so that the gray cable is toward the glass and the black cable is toward the inner door panel.
6. Install the regulator through the large opening in the bottom of the door.

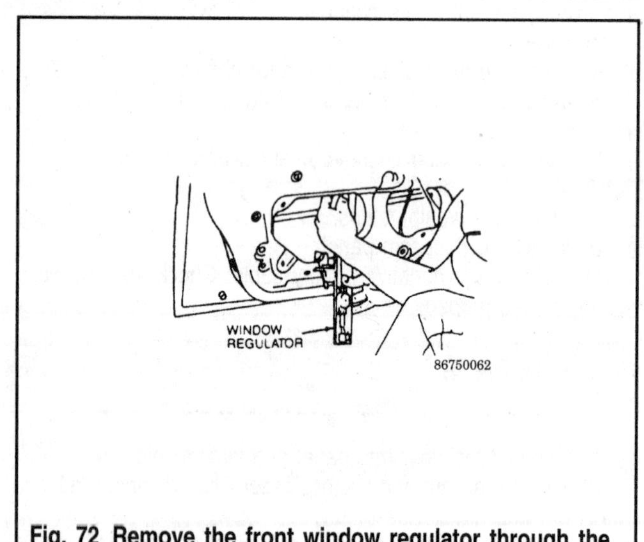

Fig. 72 Remove the front window regulator through the bottom of the door — 1991-95 models

7. Install the regulator drive retaining nuts. Tighten to 61-87 inch lbs. (7-9 Nm).
8. Install the two regulator retaining nuts and one regulator retaining screw.
9. Install the front door glass.

MANUAL REAR REGULATOR

1. Remove the rear door glass.
2. Disconnect the electrical connector and remove the three retaining bolts.
3. Remove the regulator through the large opening in the bottom of the door.
4. Install the regulator in the reverse order of removal. Tighten the bolts to 61-87 inch lbs. (7-9 Nm).

POWER FRONT REGULATOR

See Figure 73

1. Remove the front door glass.
2. Twist the retainers to release the conduit from the door.
3. Disconnect the electrical connector.
4. Remove the two upper regulator mounting nuts.
5. Remove the three lower regulator mounting bolts.
6. Remove the regulator through the large opening in the bottom of the door.

To install:

7. Install the regulator through the large opening in the bottom of the door.
8. Install the lower and upper regulator retaining nuts and bolts. Tighten to 61-87 inch lbs. (7-9 Nm).
9. Connect the electrical connector.
10. Twist the retainers to secure the conduit from the door.
11. Install the front door glass. Cycle the glass up and down to check for smooth operation.

POWER REAR REGULATOR

1. Remove the rear door glass.
2. Disconnect the electrical connector and remove the four retaining bolts.
3. Remove the regulator through the large opening in the bottom of the door.
4. Install the regulator in the reverse order of removal. Tighten the bolts to 61-87 inch lbs. (7-9 Nm).

Electric Window Motor

REMOVAL & INSTALLATION

1981-90 Models

2-DOOR MODELS

See Figure 74

1. Raise the window to the full up position, if possible. If the glass cannot be raised and is partially down or in the full down position, it must be supported so that it will not fall into the door well during motor removal.
2. Disconnect the negative battery cable.
3. Remove the door trim panel and watershield.
4. Disconnect the electric window motor wire from the wire harness connector and move the motor away from the area to be drilled.
5. Using a 3/4 in. hole saw with a 1/4 in. pilot, drill the hole at point A and point B dimples. Remove the drillings.

Before the removal of the motor drive assembly, make certain that the regulator arm is in a fixed position to prevent counterbalance spring unwind.

6. Remove the three window motor mounting screws and disengage the motor and drive assembly from the regulator quadrant gear.
7. Install the new motor and drive assembly. Tighten the three motor mounting screws to 50-85 inch lbs. (5.5-9.5 Nm).
8. Connect window motor wiring harness leads.
9. Connect the negative battery cable.
10. Check the power window for proper operation.
11. Install the door trim panel and watershield. Check that all drain holes at the bottom of the doors are open to prevent water accumulation over the motor.

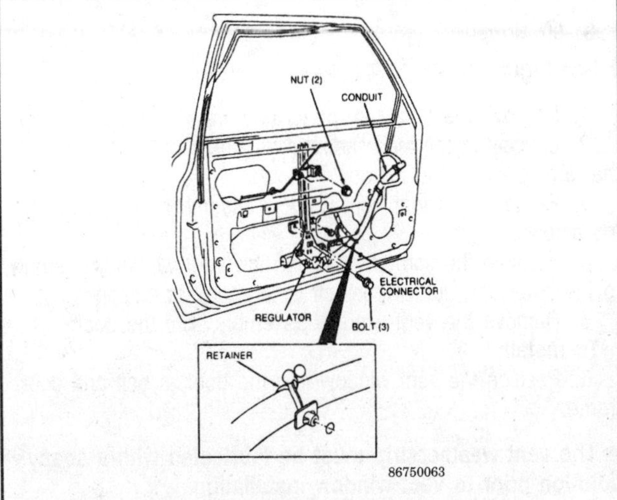

Fig. 73 Exploded view of the power front window regulator — 1991-95 models

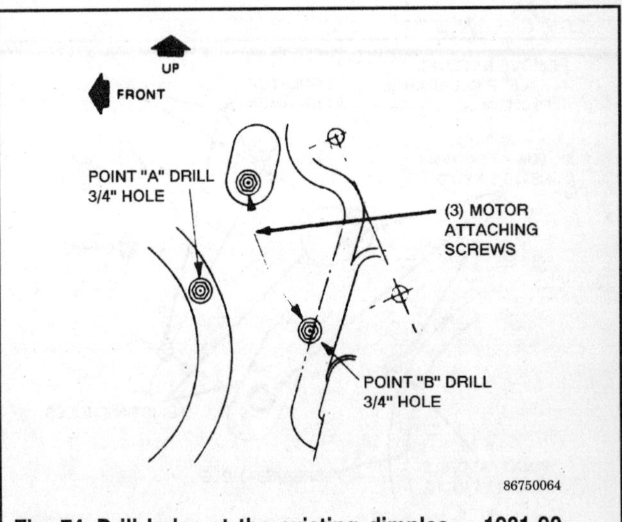

Fig. 74 Drill holes at the existing dimples — 1981-90 2-door models

4-DOOR MODELS — FRONT

➧ See Figure 75

1. Raise the window to the full up position, if possible. If the glass cannot be raised and is partially down or in the full down position, it must be supported so that it will not fall into the door well during motor removal.
2. Disconnect the negative battery cable.
3. Remove the door trim panel and watershield.
4. Disconnect the electric window motor wire from the wire harness connector and move the motor away from the area to be drilled.
5. Using a 3/4 in. hole saw with a 1/4 in. pilot, drill the hole at the existing dimple (point A) adjacent to the radio speaker opening. Remove the drillings.
6. At the upper motor mount screw head, the sheet metal interference can be removed by grinding out the inner panel surface sufficiently to clear the screw head for easy removal. Remove the drillings.

➡Before the removal of the motor drive assembly, make certain that the regulator arm is in a fixed position to prevent counterbalance spring unwind.

7. Remove the three window motor mounting screws and disengage the motor and drive assembly from the regulator quadrant gear.
8. Install the new motor and drive assembly. Tighten the three motor mounting screws to 50-85 inch lbs. (5.5-9.5 Nm).
9. Connect window motor wiring harness leads.
10. Connect the negative battery cable.
11. Check the power window for proper operation.
12. Install the door trim panel and watershield. Check that all drain holes at the bottom of the doors are open to prevent water accumulation over the motor.

4-DOOR MODELS — REAR

1. Raise the window to the full up position, if possible. If the glass cannot be raised and is partially down or in the full down position, it must be supported so that it will not fall into the door well during motor removal.
2. Disconnect the negative battery cable.

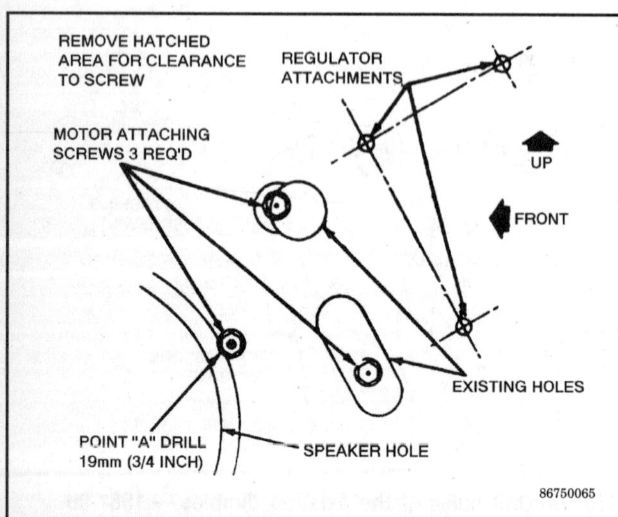

Fig. 75 Drill holes at the existing dimples — 1981-90 4-door models

3. Remove the door trim panel and watershield.
4. Disconnect the electric window motor wire from the wire harness connector and move the motor away from the area to be drilled.
5. Using a 3/4 in. hole saw with a 1/4 in. pilot, drill three holes in the door inner panel at the three existing dimples to gain access to the three motor and drive attaching screws. Remove the drillings.

➡Before the removal of the motor drive assembly, make certain that the regulator arm is in a fixed position to prevent counterbalance spring unwind.

6. Remove the three window motor mounting screws and disengage the motor and drive assembly from the regulator quadrant gear.
7. Install the new motor and drive assembly. Tighten the three motor mounting screws to 50-85 inch lbs. (5.5-9.5 Nm).
8. Connect window motor wiring harness leads.
9. Connect the negative battery cable.
10. Check the power window for proper operation.
11. Install the door trim panel and watershield. Check that all drain holes at the bottom of the doors are open to prevent water accumulation over the motor.

Windshield and Rear Window Glass

REMOVAL & INSTALLATION

Ford cars use a Butyl/Urethane type sealed windshield and rear window which requires the use of special tools for removal and installation. It is advised that if the windshield needs replacement the vehicle be taken to a professional auto glass repair shop.

Door Vent

REMOVAL & INSTALLATION

1981-90 Models

➧ See Figure 76

1. Remove the door trim panel and watershield.
2. Loosely install the window regulator handle and move the door glass to the full-down position.
3. Remove the door vent window assembly to door retaining screws.
4. Remove the screws attaching the vent window assembly to the inner and outer door belt (one each), is equipped.
5. Remove the vent window assembly from the door.

To install:

6. Position the vent window into the door at belt and door frame.

➡The vent weatherstrip must be lubricated with a soapy solution prior to vent window installation.

7. Loosely install all attaching screws, then tighten until snug.
8. Install the trim panel.

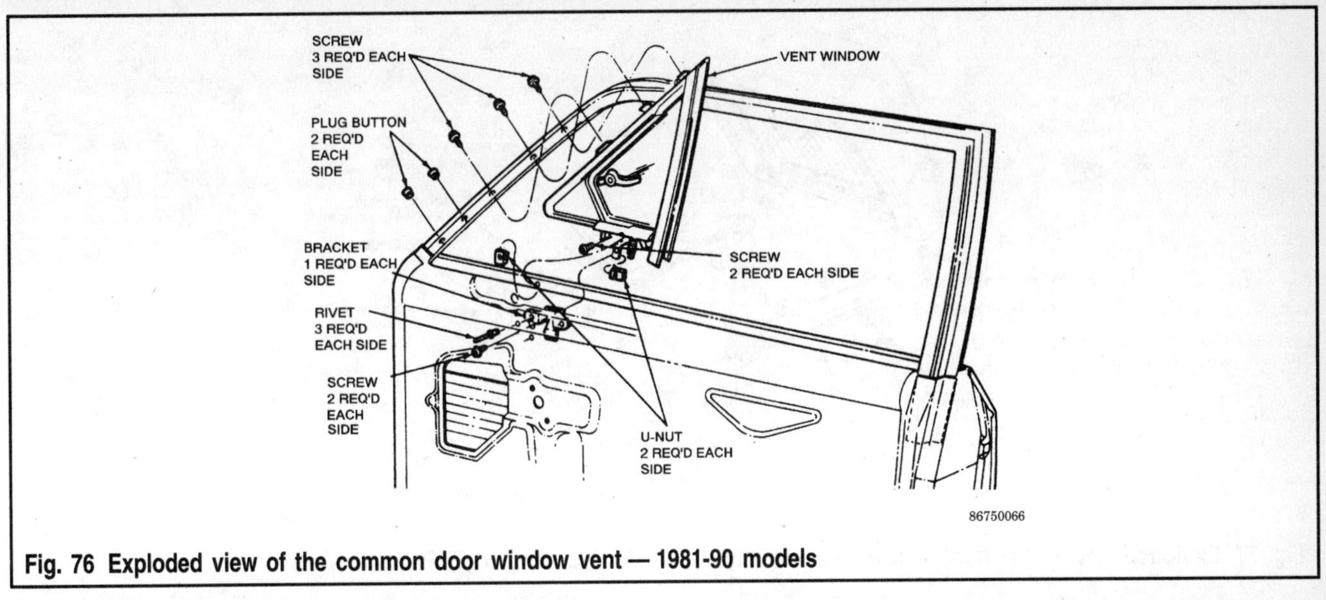

Fig. 76 Exploded view of the common door window vent — 1981-90 models

9. Check the operation of the window.

Inside Mirror

REMOVAL & INSTALLATION

1. Loosen the mirror assembly-to-mounting bracket set screw.
2. Remove the mirror assembly by sliding upward and away from the mounting bracket.
3. Install it by attaching the mirror assembly to the mounting bracket and tighten the set screw to 10-20 inch lbs. (1-2 Nm)
4. If the mirror bracket pad has to be removed from the windshield (or if it has fallen off), it will be necessary to use a suitable heat gun to heat the vinyl pad until vinyl softens. Peel the vinyl off the windshield and discard. Install the new one as follows:
    a. Make sure that the glass, bracket and adhesive kit (Rearview mirror adhesive D9AZ-19554-CA or equivalent) are at least at room temperature 65-75°F (18-24°C).
    b. Locate and mark the mirror mounting bracket location on the outside surface of the windshield.
    c. Thoroughly clean the bonding surfaces of the glass and bracket to remove old adhesive if reusing the old mirror bracket pad. Use a mild abrasive cleaner on the glass and fine sandpaper on the bracket to lightly roughen the surface. Wipe clean with a alcohol moistened cloth.
    d. Crush the accelerator vial (part of the Rearview mirror adhesive kit D9AZ-19554-CA) and apply the accelerator to the bonding surface of the bracket and windshield. Let it dry for 3 minutes.
    e. Apply two drops of adhesive (part of the rearview mirror adhesive kit D9AZ-19554-CA) to the mounting surface of the bracket and windshield. Using a clean toothpick or a wooden match, quickly spread the adhesive evenly over the mounting surface of the bracket.
    f. Quickly position the mounting bracket on the windshield. The ⅜ in. (9.5mm) circular depression in the bracket must be toward the inside of the passengers compartment. Press the bracket firmly against the windshield for one minute.
    g. Allow the bond to set for five minutes. Remove any excess bonding material from the windshield with an alcohol dampened cloth.

Seats

REMOVAL & INSTALLATION

Manual Seats

FRONT

➧ **See Figures 77, 78, 79 and 80**

The manual front seats are installed on a metal track that is retained to the floorpan by studs with nut and washer assemblies or screws with a washer type head. Nuts and/or screws retaining the seat tracks are removed from inside and/or underneath the vehicle.

1. Remove the seat track plastic shield retaining pins, screws and/or nuts and washers from inside or underneath the vehicle. If the screws and/or nuts have to be removed from underneath the vehicle, be sure to raise the vehicle and support with the proper jack stands. Lift the seat and seat track assembly from the vehicle.

➡Be sure not to drop the seat and seat tracking assembly and do not sit on the seat if it is not secured in the vehicle because it may result in damaged components.

2. Place the seat and seat track assemblies on a clean working area and disconnect the adjusting springs, assist spring and latch tie wire from the tracks.
3. Remove the seat track-to-seat cushion attaching screws and remove the seat cushion from the tracks.

➡To ease in the assist spring removal and installation, adjust the seat to the full forward position.

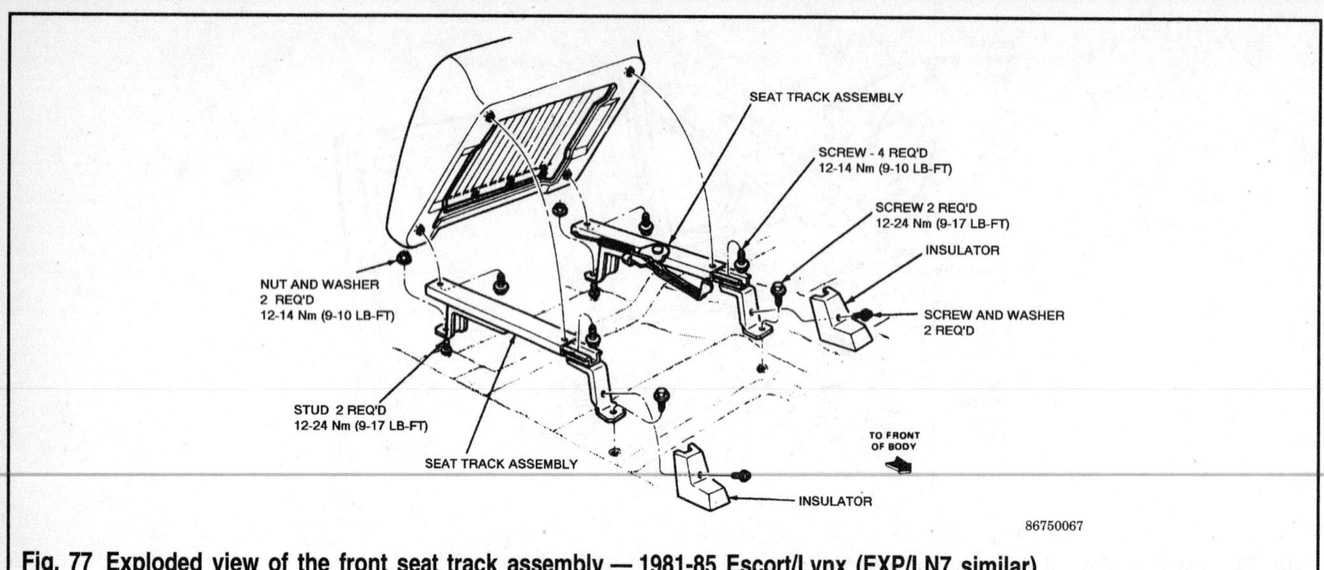

Fig. 77 Exploded view of the front seat track assembly — 1981-85 Escort/Lynx (EXP/LN7 similar)

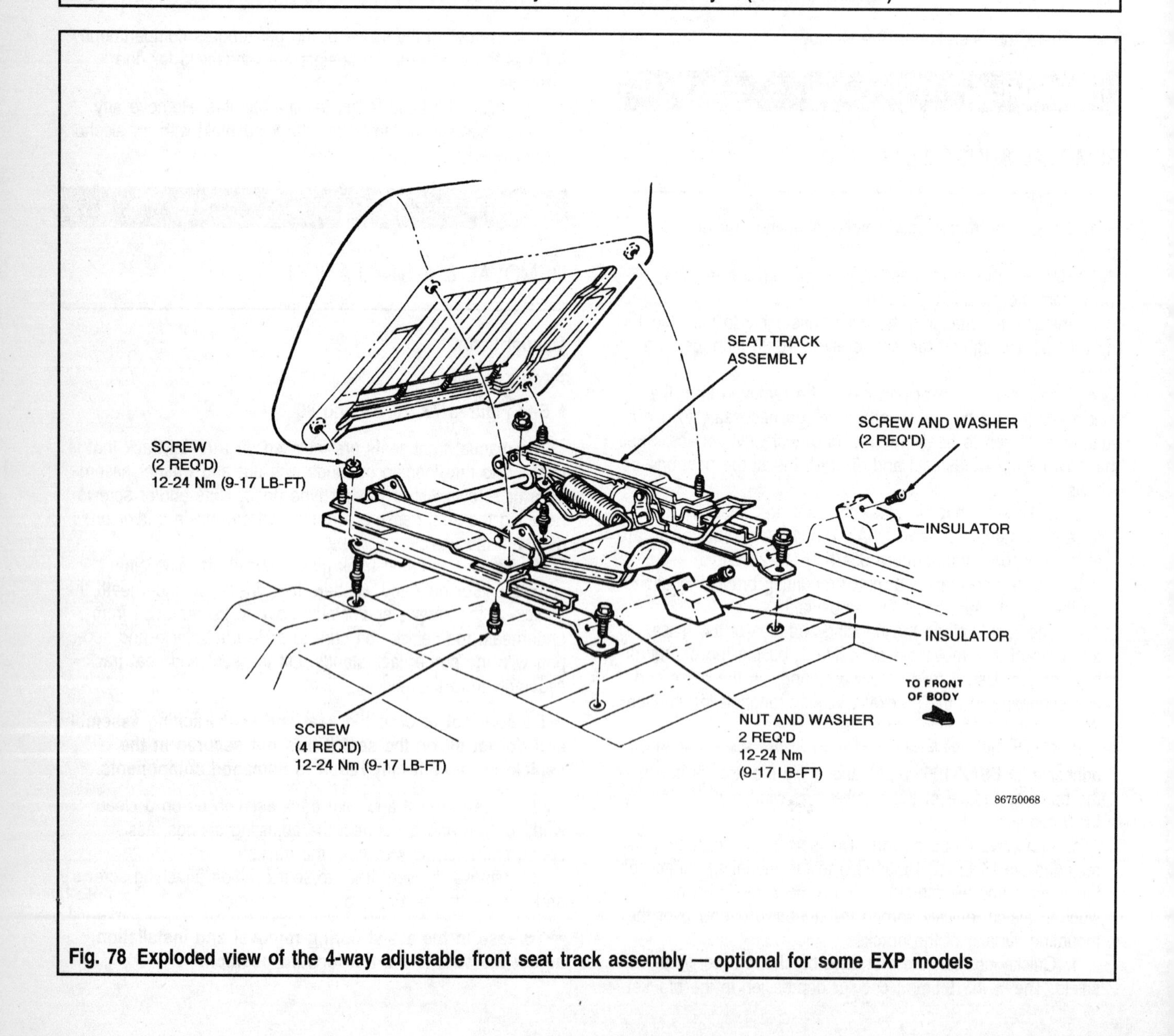

Fig. 78 Exploded view of the 4-way adjustable front seat track assembly — optional for some EXP models

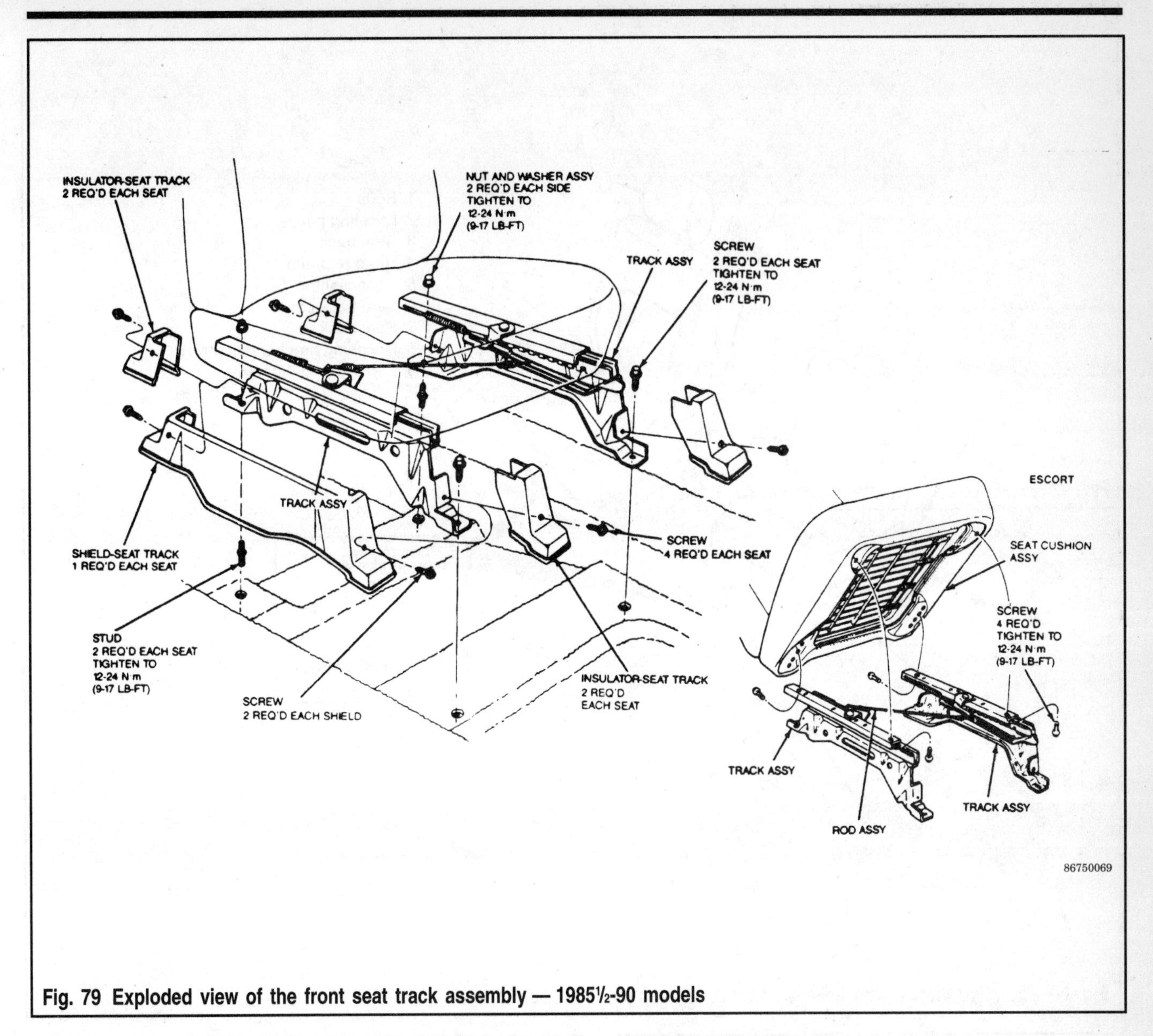

Fig. 79 Exploded view of the front seat track assembly — 1985½-90 models

4. If the seat tracks are being replaced, transfer the retracting springs and spacers (anti-squeak) to the new track assembly.

To install:

5. Mount the seat tracks to the seat cushion.
6. Install the seat-track-to-seat cushion retaining screws and tighten them to 9-18 ft. lbs. (12.2-24.5 Nm). Install the tie wire to the track and install the assist springs.
7. Place the seat assembly into the vehicle and insure proper alignment.
8. Install the screws, studs and/or nuts and washer assemblies. Tighten them to 9-18 ft. lbs. (12.2-24.5 Nm). Install the plastic shield.

REAR FOLD DOWN TYPE

See Figures 81, 82 and 83

1. When removing the seat cushion portion of the rear split folding seat, remove the articulating arm mounting bolt, bushing, spacer and washer from the seat cushion. Fold the seat cushion forward.
2. On the full folding seat only, remove the retaining strap attaching screw.
3. Remove the hinge attaching screws.
4. Remove the seat cushion from the vehicle. On the split folding seat only, slide the seat cushion pivot pin out of the bushing and bracket.
5. To remove the seat back portion of the rear fold down seat, detach the luggage compartment cover from the seat back.
6. Remove the carpeting from the seat back.
7. Disengage the inboard safety belts from the guides and outboard safety belts from the strap retainers. Pull the strap retainers through the holes in the seat back from the rear.
8. Fold the seat back forward. Remove the two screws attaching each hinge to the floor.
9. Remove the seat back from the vehicle. For split folding seat only, slide the seat back off the pivot assembly to remove.

To install:

10. Install the seat back into the vehicle. For the spilt folding seats only, slide the seat back over the pivot assembly.

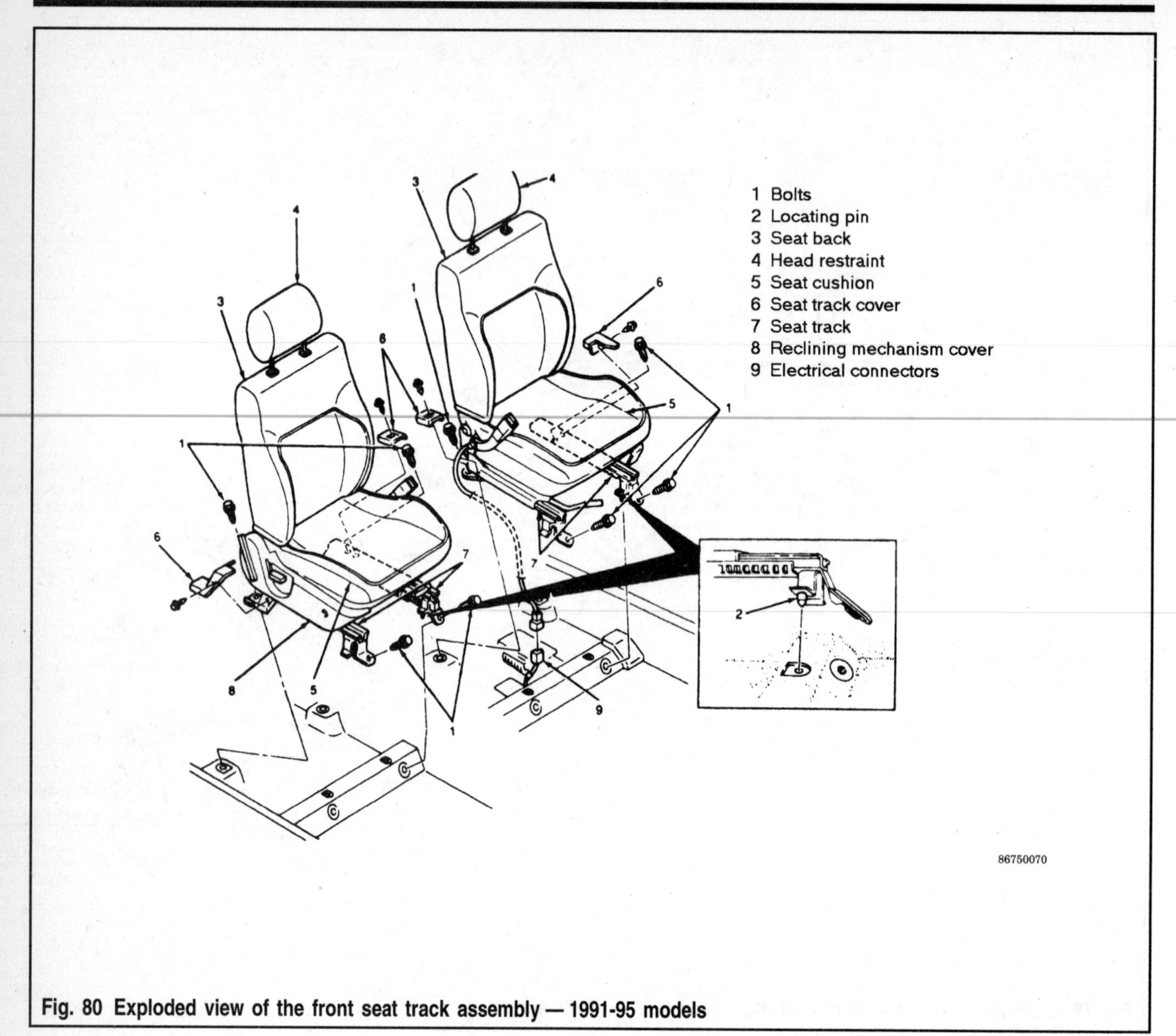

Fig. 80 Exploded view of the front seat track assembly — 1991-95 models

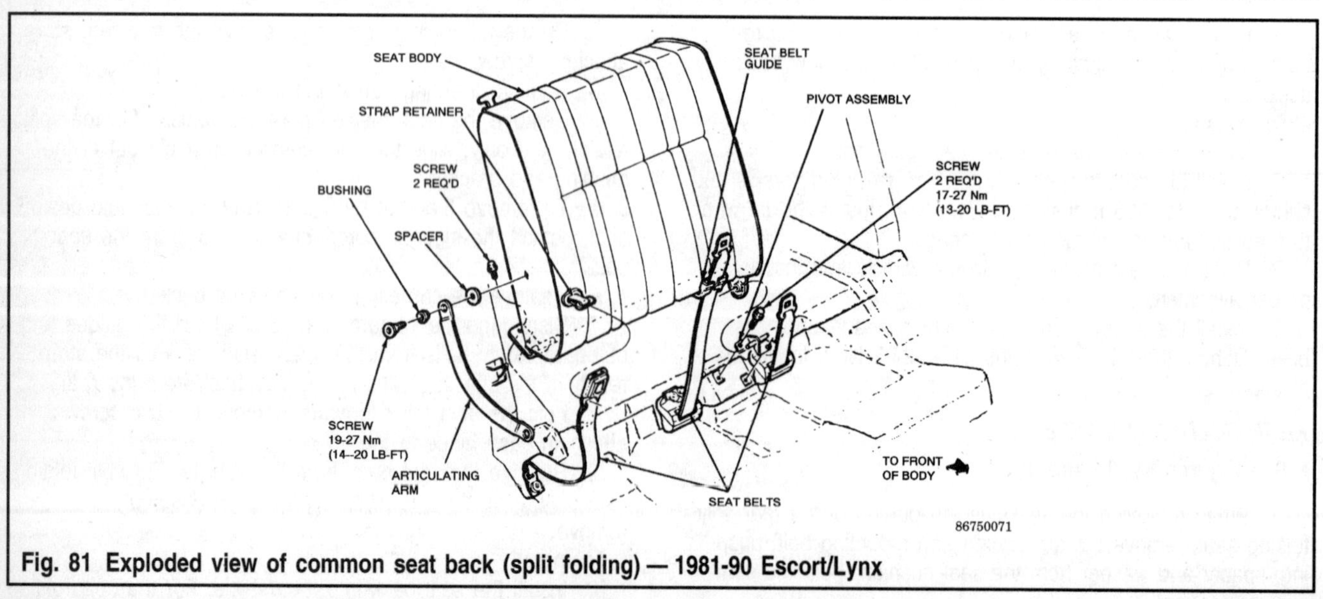

Fig. 81 Exploded view of common seat back (split folding) — 1981-90 Escort/Lynx

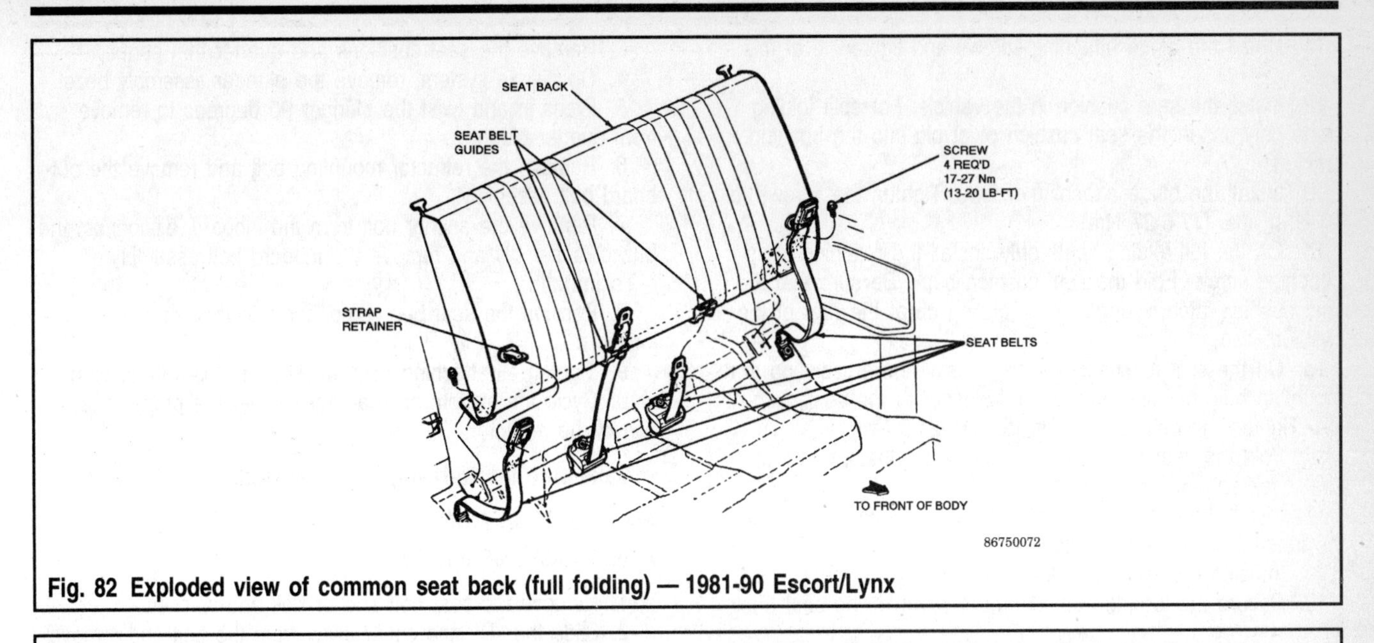

Fig. 82 Exploded view of common seat back (full folding) — 1981-90 Escort/Lynx

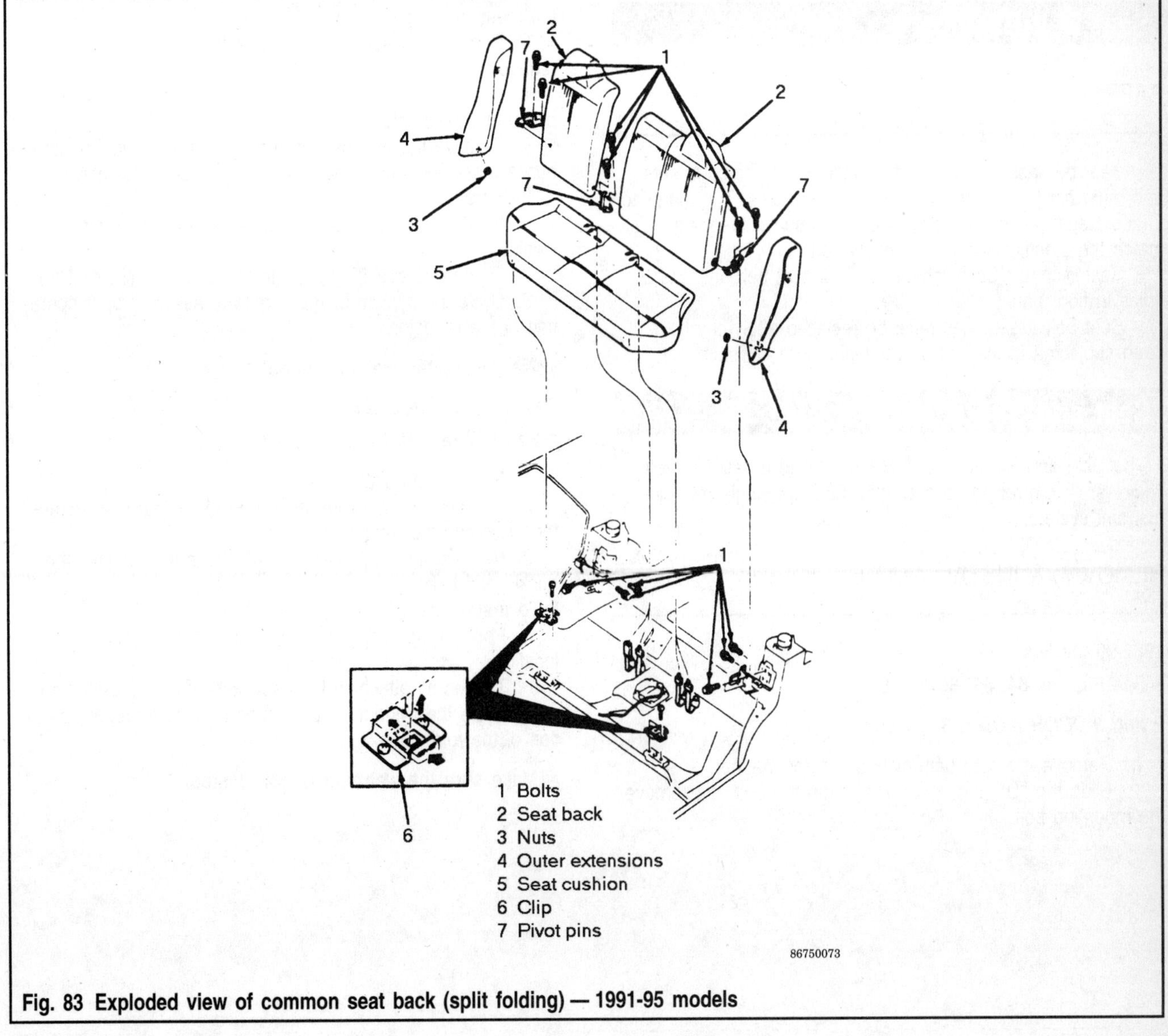

Fig. 83 Exploded view of common seat back (split folding) — 1991-95 models

11. Install the hinge attaching screws and tighten to at this time.

12. Install the seat cushion in the vehicle. For split folding seats only, insert the seat cushion pivot pin into the bushing bracket.

13. Install the hinge attaching screws. Tighten the screws to 13-20 ft. lbs. (17.6-27 Nm).

14. On the full folding seats only, install the retaining strap attaching screw. Fold the seat cushion back. Be sure that the seat cushion latch is engaged by pulling up at the rear of the cushion.

15. On the split folding seats only, install the articulating arm mounting bolt, bushing, spacer and washer to the seat cushion. Tighten the bolt to 14-16 ft. lbs. (19-21.5 Nm).

16. Fold the seat back and cushion back. Check that both seat back engage properly.

17. Install the outboard safety belt strap retainers and install the inboard safety belts guides.

18. Install the carpeting to the seat back.

19. Secure the luggage compartment cover to the seat back.

Seat Belt Systems

SAFETY PRECAUTIONS

- Seat belt assemblies must be installed in matched sets and must not be interchanged between vehicles. The manufacturer's identification on the label of the retractor webbing must match the identification on the buckle base.
- Sealer should be placed around all seat belt anchor bolt holes in floor pan.
- Seat belt assemblies must be replaced after they have been subjected to loading by occupants in a collision.

Seat and Shoulder Belts

The Seat and Shoulder Belt System, used on all 1981-90 vehicles, is referred to as a continuous loop, single retractor restraint system.

REMOVAL & INSTALLATION

1981-90 Models

See Figures 84, 85, 86 and 87

2 and 3-DOOR MODELS — FRONT

1. Remove the seat belt anchor bolt and washer.
2. Slide the "D" ring cover away from the bolt and remove the mounting bolt.
3. Remove the seat cushions and quarter trim panel.
4. On deluxe system, remove the plunger assembly bezel.
5. Press in and twist the plunger 90 degrees to remove from quarter plunger.
6. Remove the retractor mounting bolt and remove the outboard belt assembly.
7. Remove the anchor bolt from the inboard, disconnect the buzzer assembly and remove the inboard belt assembly.

To install:

8. Position the seat belt components in their proper location.
9. Tighten all attaching bolts to 22-32 ft. lbs. (30-45 Nm).
10. Cycle the system several times to assure proper operation of the retractor.

Make sure the webbing is not twisted.

4 AND 5-DOOR MODELS — FRONT

See Figures 88 and 89

1. Remove the seat belt anchor bolt and washer.
2. Slide the "D" ring cover away from the bolt and remove the mounting bolt.
3. Remove the seat cushions and trim panel(s), as required.
4. Remove the retractor mounting bolt and remove the outboard belt assembly.
5. Remove the anchor bolt from the inboard, disconnect the buzzer assembly and remove the inboard belt assembly.

To install:

6. Position the seat belt components in their proper location.
7. Tighten all attaching bolts to 22-32 ft. lbs. (30-45 Nm).
8. Cycle the system several times to assure proper operation of the retractor.

Make sure the webbing is not twisted.

REAR — ALL MODELS

See Figures 90, 91, 92 and 93

1. Remove the seat cushions.
2. Remove the mounting bolts from both rear seat retractors. Remove the retractors.
3. Remove the buckle end anchor bolts and remove the buckle end belts.

To install:

4. Position the seat belt components in their proper location.
5. Tighten all attaching bolts to 22-32 ft. lbs. (30-45 Nm).
6. Cycle the system several times to assure proper operation of the retractor.

Make sure the webbing is not twisted.

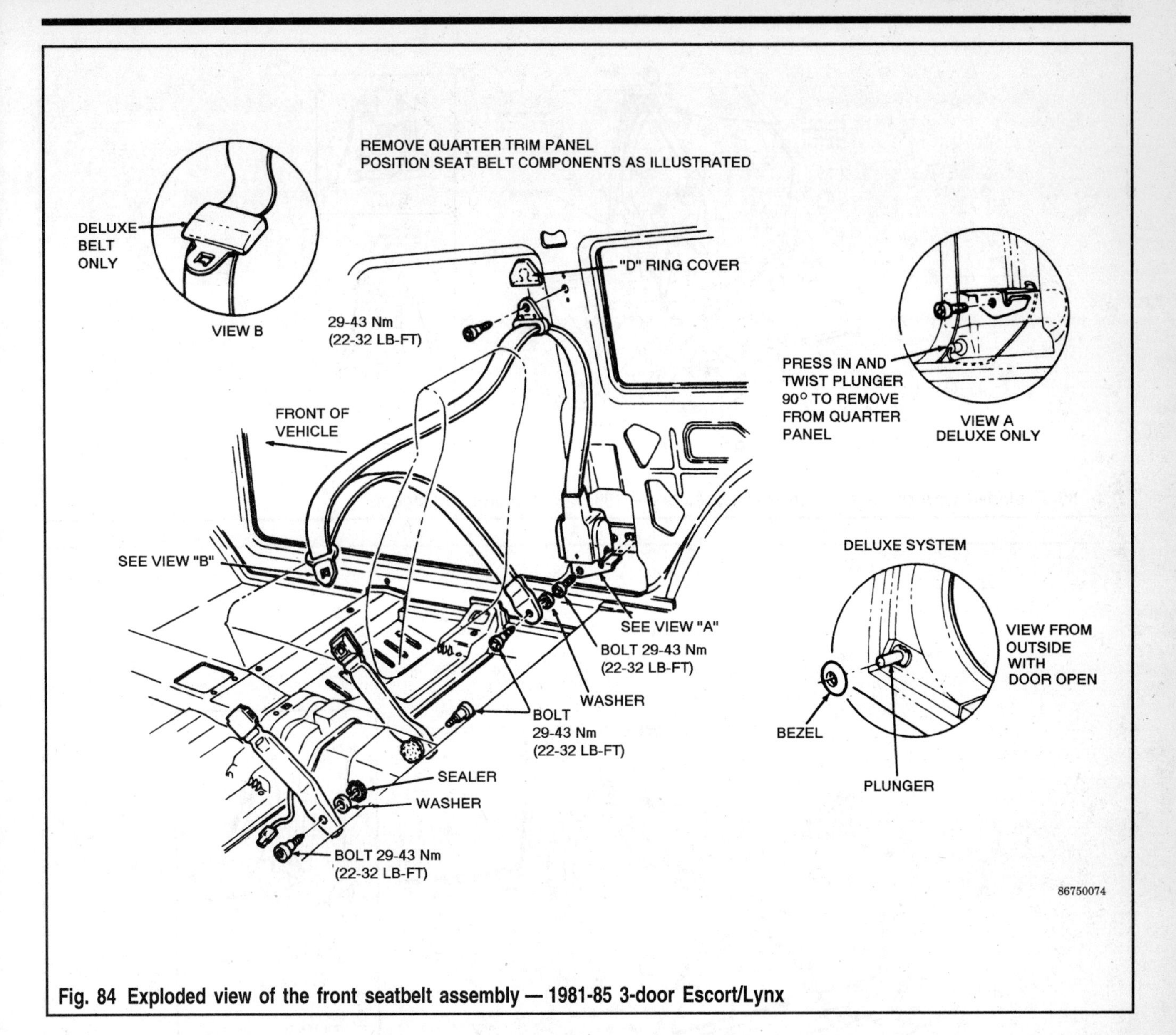

Fig. 84 Exploded view of the front seatbelt assembly — 1981-85 3-door Escort/Lynx

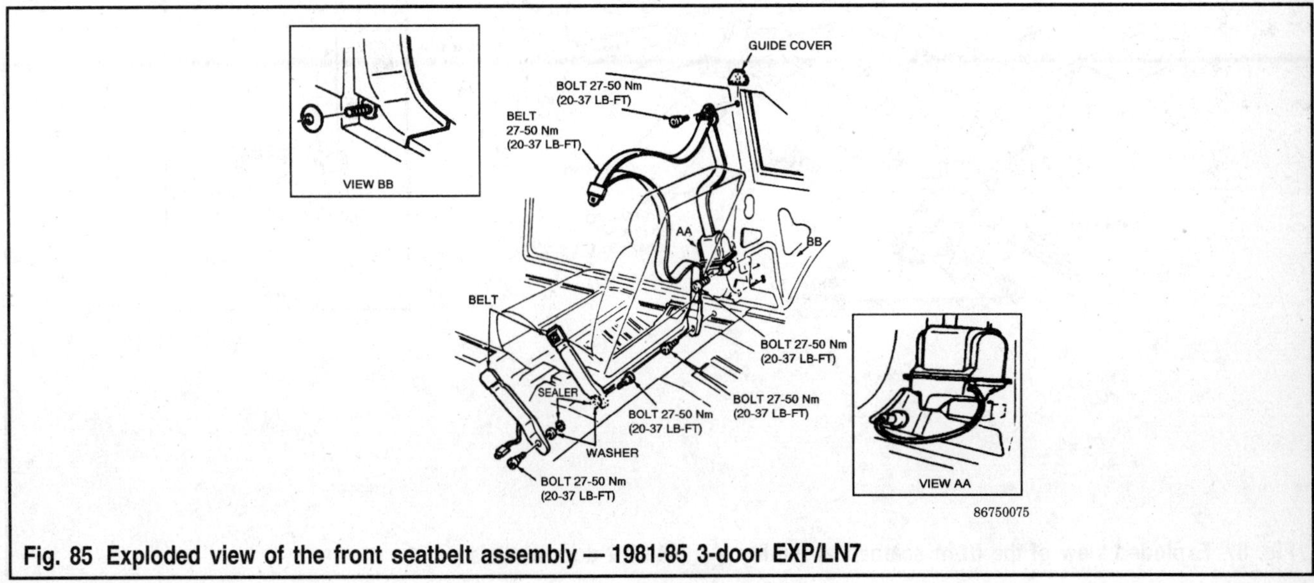

Fig. 85 Exploded view of the front seatbelt assembly — 1981-85 3-door EXP/LN7

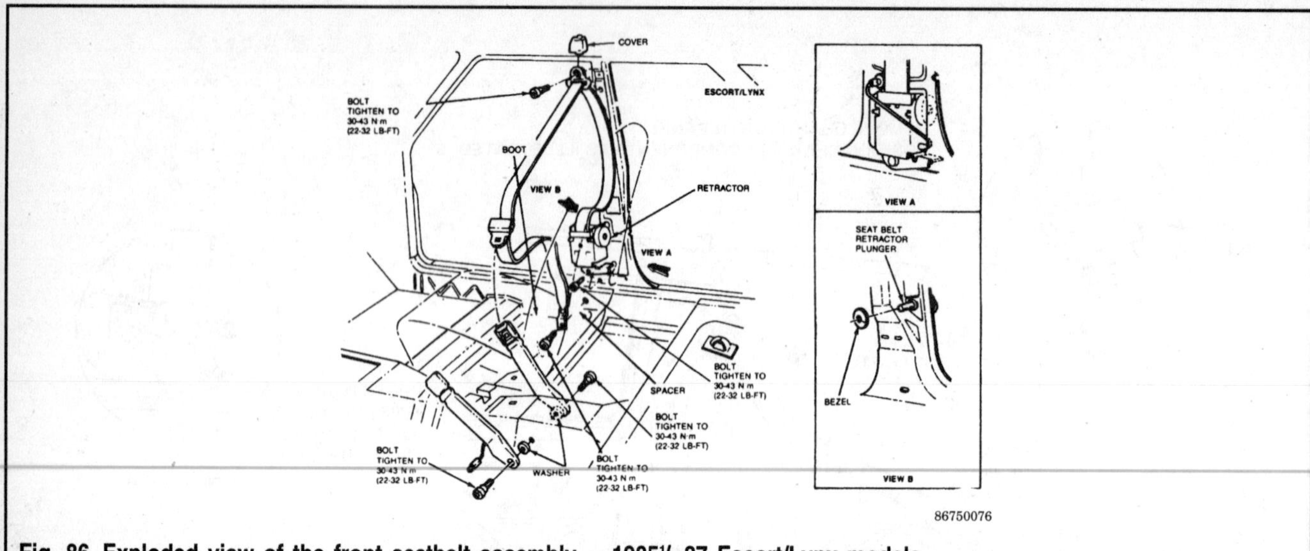

Fig. 86 Exploded view of the front seatbelt assembly — 1985½-87 Escort/Lynx models

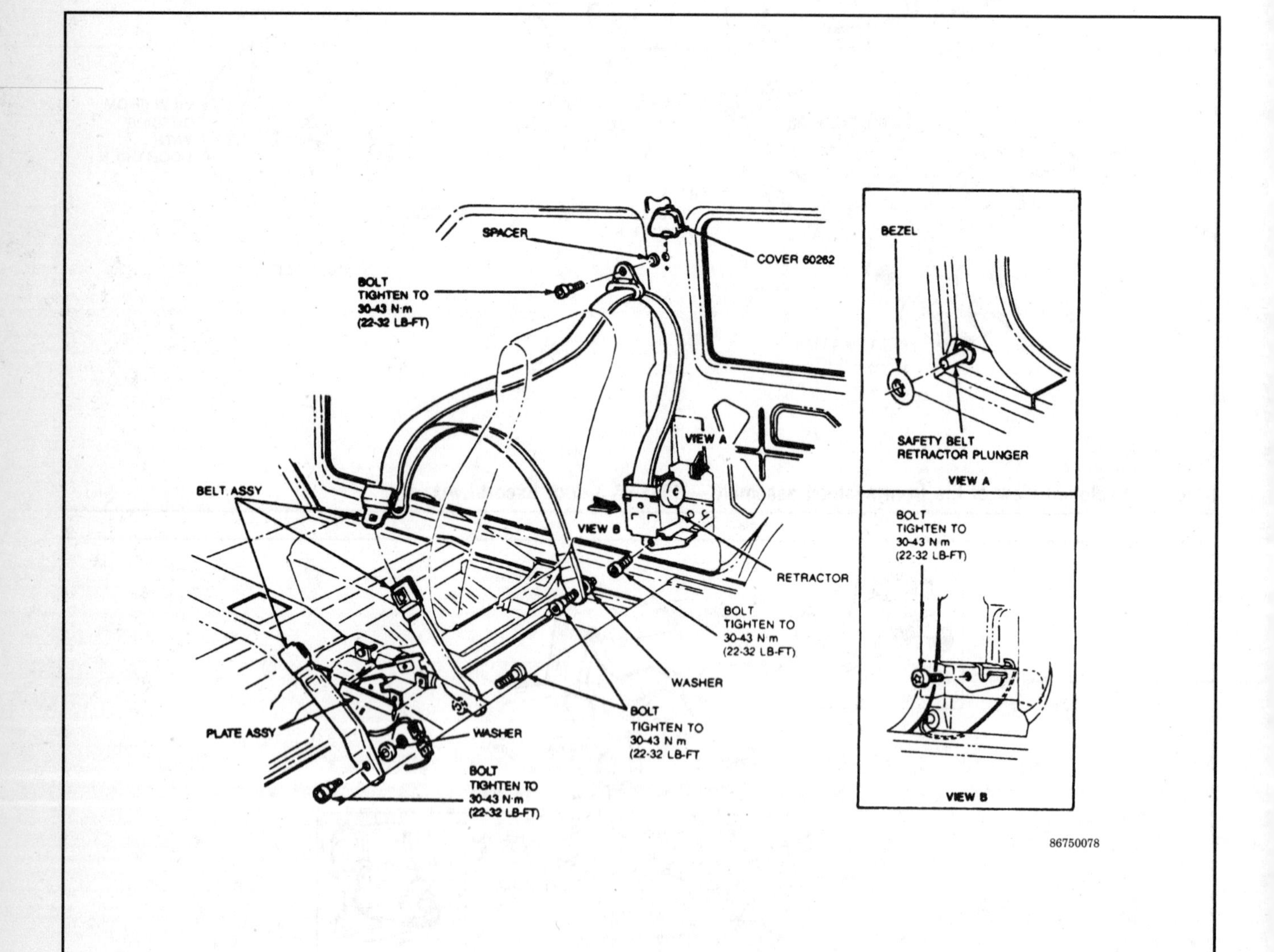

Fig. 87 Exploded view of the front seatbelt assembly — 1988-90 2-door models

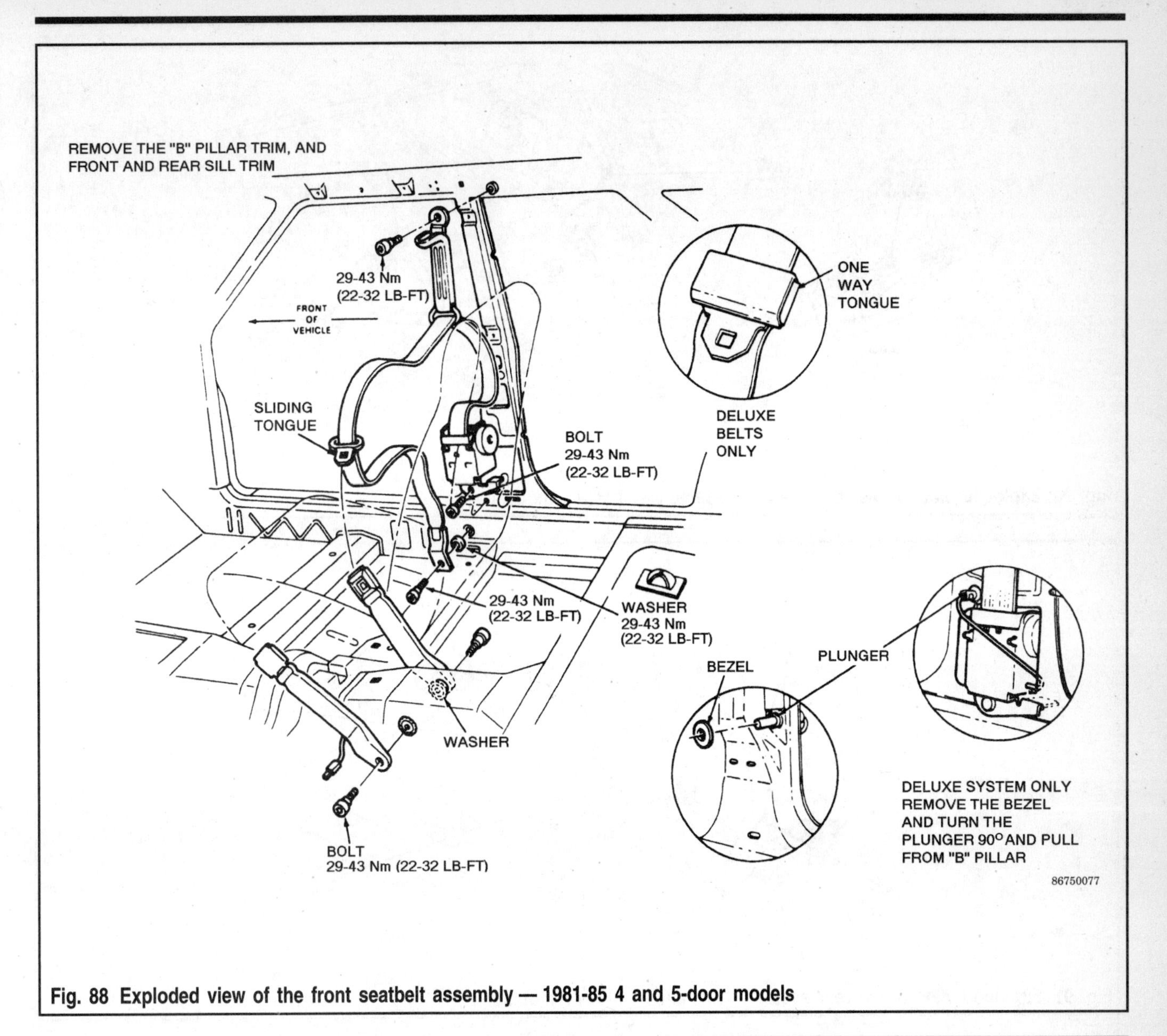

Fig. 88 Exploded view of the front seatbelt assembly — 1981-85 4 and 5-door models

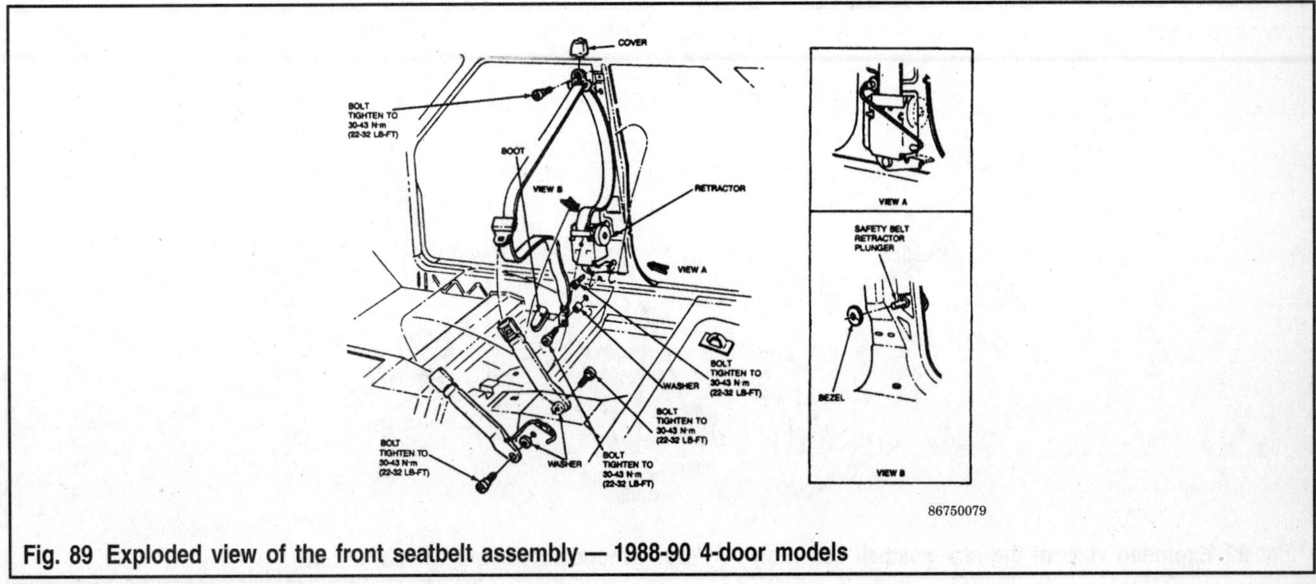

Fig. 89 Exploded view of the front seatbelt assembly — 1988-90 4-door models

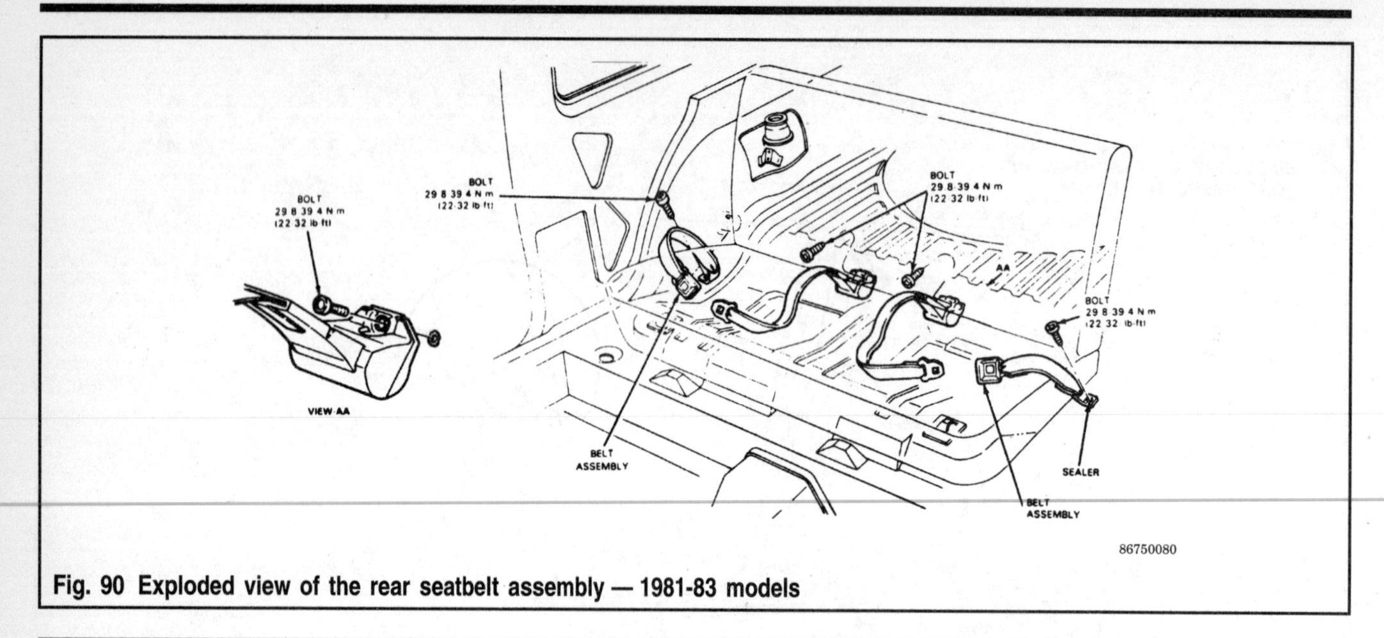

Fig. 90 Exploded view of the rear seatbelt assembly — 1981-83 models

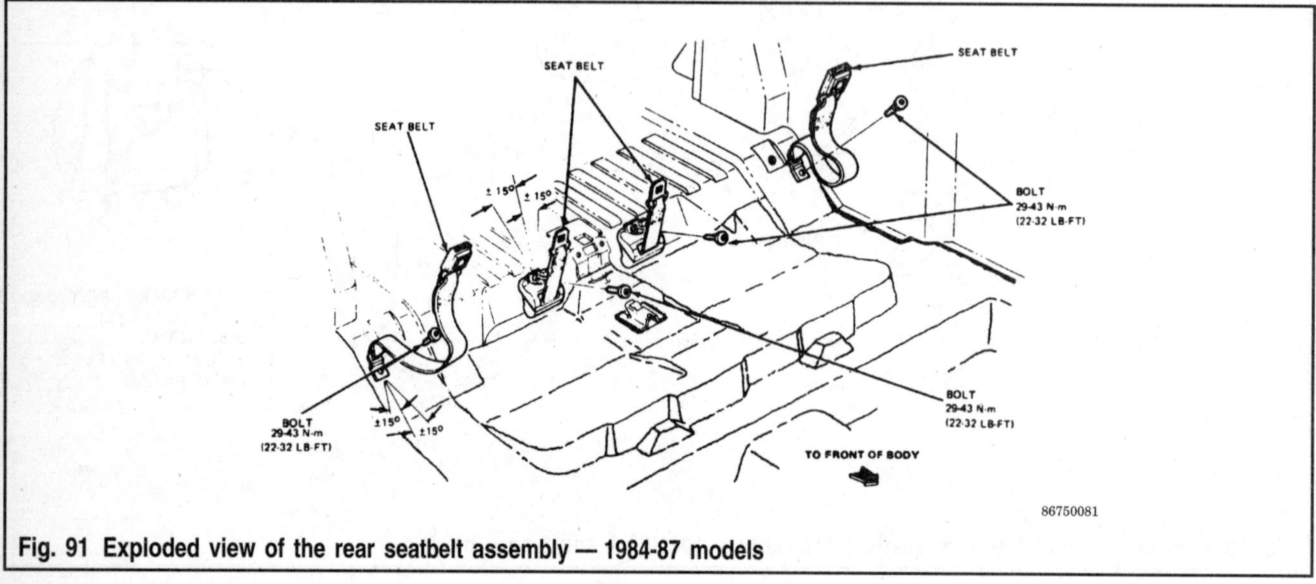

Fig. 91 Exploded view of the rear seatbelt assembly — 1984-87 models

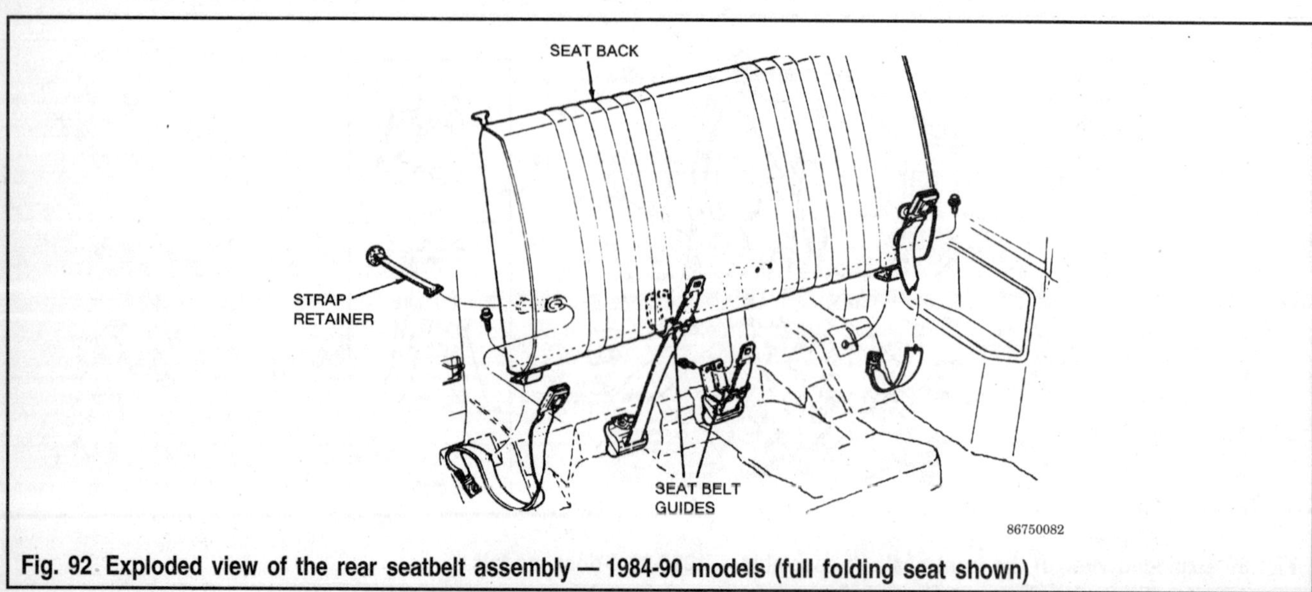

Fig. 92 Exploded view of the rear seatbelt assembly — 1984-90 models (full folding seat shown)

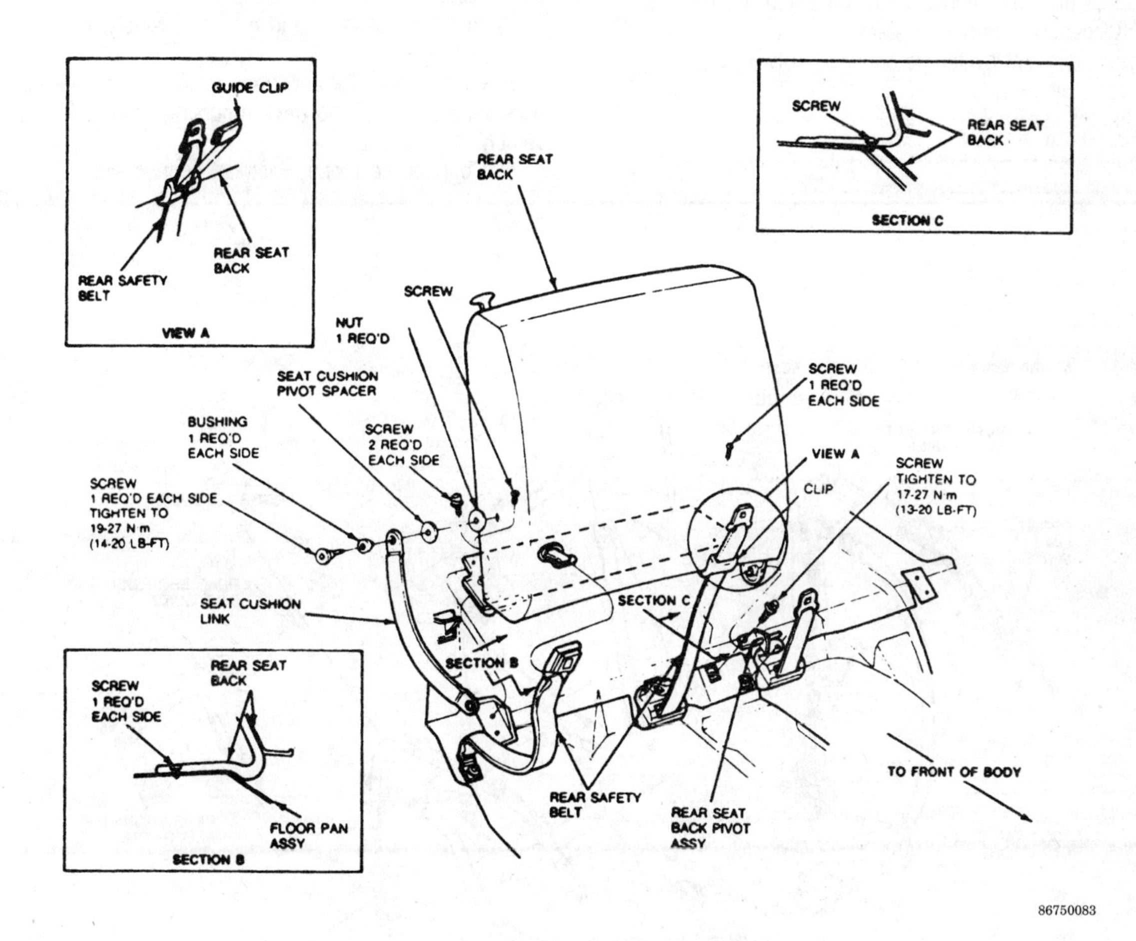

Fig. 93 Exploded view of the rear seatbelt assembly — 1988-90 models (with split folding seat)

Passive Restraint System

1991-95 MODELS

➧ **See Figures 94, 95, 96, 97, 98, 99, 100, 101, 102, 103 and 104**

The passive restraint system consists of an outboard rear 3-point lap shoulder belt, a center rear passenger lap belt, manual front lap belts and the passive restraint system that controls the front shoulder belts.

The front lap belts, rear lap shoulder belts and center passenger lap belt are conventionally mounted and are not controlled by the passive restraint system.

The passive restraint system is serviced in two parts:

- "A" pillar limit switch
- Track/motor assembly

Track and Motor Assembly

REMOVAL & INSTALLATION

1. Unbuckle the shoulder belt from the carrier.
2. Cycle the carrier to the retracted position.
3. Disconnect the negative battery cable.
4. Remove the "A-B" pillar and "B" pillar trim panels.
5. Disconnect the front limit switch electrical connector and two motor connectors.
6. Remove all track and motor assembly mounting bolts and capscrews.
7. Remove the track and motor assembly.

To install:

8. Place the motor and track assembly into its mounting position. Install 1 of the track mounting bolts to hold the assembly in place.
9. Connect the motor electrical connectors.

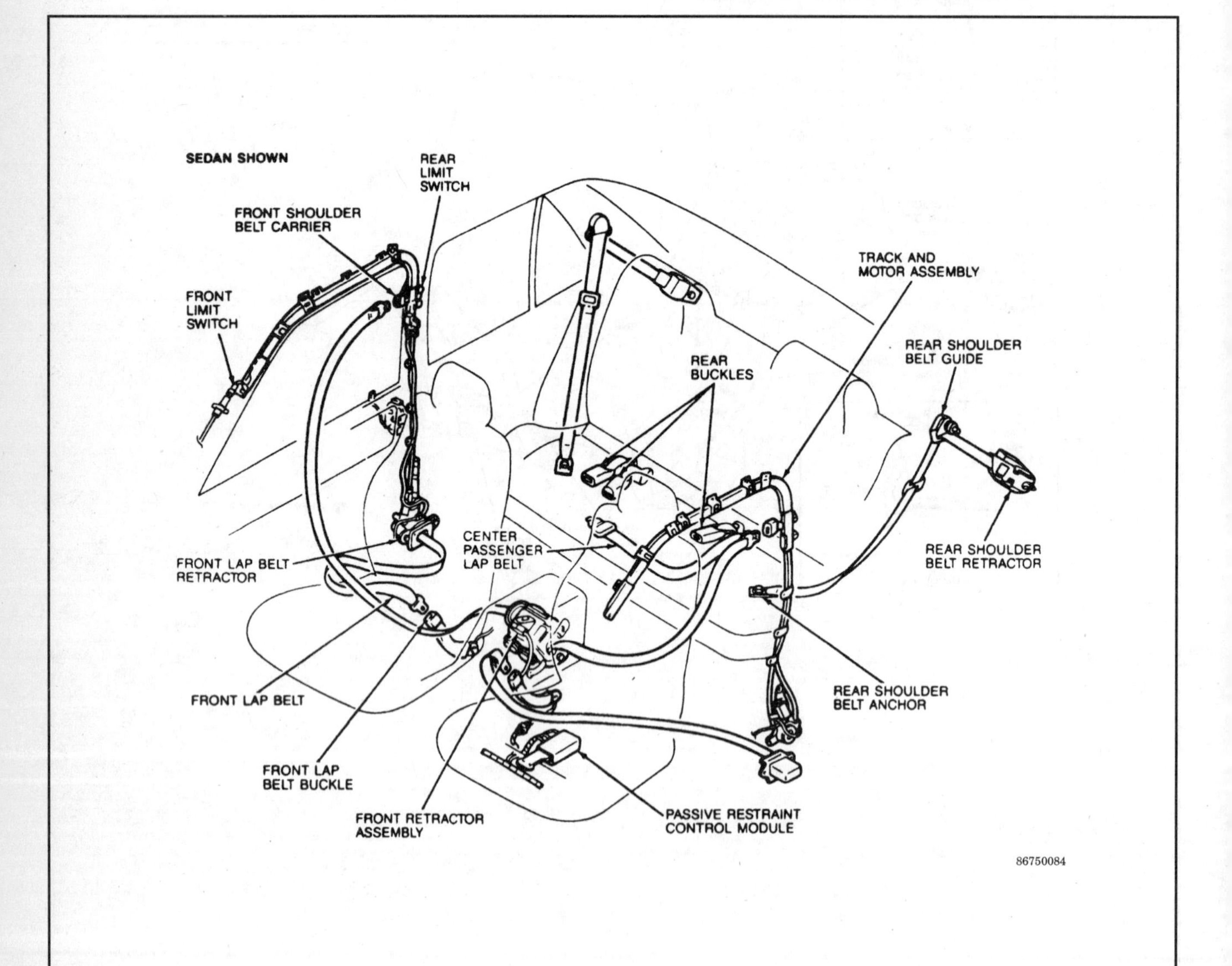

Fig. 94 Exploded view of the complete seatbelt system — 1991-95 models

CONDITION	POSSIBLE SOURCE	ACTION
• Passive Restraint Does Not Work	• Passive restraint control module. • Passive restraint circuit. • Electrical system.	• GO to OR1.
• Belt Transport Will Not Move to "B" Pillar	• Door catch switch. • Rear limit switch. • Passive restraint control module. • Track and motor assembly. • Passive restraint circuit.	• GO to OR7.
• Belt Transport Will Not Move to "A" Pillar	• Door catch switch. • Front limit switch. • Passive restraint control module. • Track and motor assembly. • Passive restraint circuit.	• GO to OR7.
• Passive Restraint Stops at "A" Pillar	• Front limit switch.	• REPLACE switch.
• Passive Restraint Carrier Stops at "B" Pillar, Fasten Belts Indicator remains On	• Track and motor assembly.	• REPLACE track and motor assembly.
• Passive Restraint Carrier Stops at "B" Pillar, Motor Continues to Run. Noise is heard from the motor and / or module	• Track and motor assembly (rear limit switch).	• REPLACE track and motor assembly.
• Seat Belt Light and Chime Turn On Intermittently	• Seat belt retractor assembly (shoulder belts).	• GO to OR20.
• Both Belts will not Leave the "B" Pillar	• Inertia switch. • Wire between module and inertia switch.	• GO to OR21.

86750086

Fig. 95 Passive restraint system diagnosis — 1991-95 models

10. Install the motor mounting bolts. On 3-door models tighten the bolts to 28-58 ft. lbs. (38-78 Nm). On all other models, tighten the bolts to 69-104 inch lbs. (8-12 Nm).
11. Install the track mounting bolts (rear of limit switch) and tighten to 13-19 ft. lbs. (18-25 Nm).
12. Install the track mounting capscrews. Tighten the capscrews to 16-32 inch lbs. (2-3.5 Nm).
13. Install the remaining track mounting bolts. Tighten the capscrews to 69-104 inch lbs. (8-12 Nm).
14. Install the "A-B" pillar and "B" pillar trim panels.
15. Connect the shoulder belt to carrier.
16. Connect the negative battery cable.
17. Check the system for proper operation.

Limit Switches

REMOVAL & INSTALLATION

Front

1. Remove the track and motor assembly.
2. Remove the roll pin from the track and motor assembly.
3. Slide the switch out of the track.

To install:

4. Slide the limit switch into the track and align the holes for the roll pin. Install the roll pin.
5. Install the track and motor assembly.
6. Check the system for proper operation.

Rear

The rear limit switch is service with the track and motor as an assembly.

TEST STEP		RESULT ►	ACTION TO TAKE
OR1	OCCUPANT RESTRAINT FUSE CHECK		
• Access the interior fuse panel. • Check the 30 amp "belt" fuse and 15 amp "meter" fuse. • Are the fuses OK?		Yes ► No ►	GO to **OR4**. Go to **OR2**.

TEST STEP		RESULT ►	ACTION TO TAKE
OR2	CHECK SYSTEM		
• Replace the fuse. • Key ON. • Did the fuse(s) blow again?		Yes ► No ►	GO to **OR3**. GO to **OR4**.

TEST STEP		RESULT ►	ACTION TO TAKE
OR3	CHECK FOR SHORT TO GROUND		
• Replace the blown fuse(s). • Disconnect the "Y" and "BK/Y" wires at the fuse panel and the passive restraint module. • Measure the resistance of each wire to ground. • Is either resistance less than 5 ohms?		Yes ► No ►	SERVICE wire in question. REPAIR/REPLACE passive restraint control module.

86750087

Fig. 96 Passive restraint system diagnosis — 1991-95 models (continued)

TEST STEP		RESULT ►	ACTION TO TAKE
OR4	**PASSIVE RESTRAINT MODULE SUPPLY CHECK**		
• Measure voltage on "Y" wires at passive restraint module. • Is the voltage greater than 10 volts?		Yes ► No ►	GO to **OR5**. REPAIR/REPLACE wires.

TEST STEP		RESULT ►	ACTION TO TAKE
OR5	**PASSIVE RESTRAINT MODULE SUPPLY CHECK**		
• Ignition ON. • Measure the voltage on the "BK/Y" wire. • Is the voltage greater than 10 volts?		Yes ► No ►	GO to **OR6**. REPAIR/REPLACE "BK/Y" wire to passive restraint module.

TEST STEP		RESULT ►	ACTION TO TAKE
OR6	**PASSIVE RESTRAINT MODULE GROUND CHECK**		
• Measure the resistance of "BK" wires from passive restraint module connector to ground. • Is the resistance less than 5 ohms?		Yes ► No ►	GO to **OR7**. REPAIR/REPLACE "BK" wire.

86750088

Fig. 97 Passive restraint system diagnosis — 1991-95 models (continued)

TEST STEP		RESULT ►	ACTION TO TAKE
OR7	DOOR CATCH SWITCH SUPPLY CHECK		
	• Disconnect passive restraint module connections. • Measure the resistance between door catch switch and passive restraint module. —driver's side - "BL/Y" wire —passenger's side - "BL/O" wire • Is the resistance less than 5 ohms?	Yes ► No ►	GO to OR8 . REPAIR/REPLACE wires as necessary.

TEST STEP		RESULT ►	ACTION TO TAKE
OR8	DOOR CATCH SWITCH GROUND CHECK		
	• Measure the resistance of "BK" wire (driver's and passenger's side) at door catch switch to ground. • Is the resistance less than 5 ohms?	Yes ► No ►	GO to OR9 . REPAIR/REPLACE "BK" wire.

TEST STEP		RESULT ►	ACTION TO TAKE
OR9	CHECK DOOR CATCH SWITCH		
	• Open the door. • Measure the resistance of the following wires to ground: —driver's side - "BL/Y" wire —passenger's side - "BL/O" wire • Is the resistance less than 5 ohms?	Yes ► No ►	Belt will not move to Pillar B - GO to OR10 . Belt will not move to Pillar A - GO to OR15 . REPAIR/REPLACE door catch switch.

86750089

Fig. 98 Passive restraint system diagnosis — 1991-95 models (continued)

TEST STEP		RESULT ►	ACTION TO TAKE
OR10	REAR LIMIT SWITCH SUPPLY CHECK		
	• Measure the resistance of rear limit switch circuit between passive restraint module and passive restraint motor. —driver's side - "Y/R" wire —passenger's side - "W" wire • Is the resistance less than 5 ohms?	Yes ► No ►	GO to OR11 . REPAIR/REPLACE wire.

TEST STEP		RESULT ►	ACTION TO TAKE
OR11	REAR LIMIT SWITCH GROUND CHECK		
	• Measure the resistance of "BK" wire (driver's and passenger's side) between passive restraint motor and ground. • Is the resistance less than 5 ohms?	Yes ► No ►	GO to OR12 . REPAIR/REPLACE "BK" wire.

TEST STEP		RESULT ►	ACTION TO TAKE
OR12	REAR LIMIT SWITCH CHECK		
	• Key ON. • Door closed. • Measure resistance of the following wires to ground: —driver's side - "Y/R" wire —passenger's side - "W" wire • Is the resistance less than 5 ohms?	Yes ► No ►	GO to OR13 . REPLACE motor and track assembly.

86750090

Fig. 99 Passive restraint system diagnosis — 1991-95 models (continued)

TEST STEP		RESULT ►	ACTION TO TAKE
OR13	PASSIVE RESTRAINT MOTOR SUPPLY CHECK		
• Measure the resistance of passive restraint motor supply between passive restraint module and passive restraint motor. —driver's side - "BL/GN" wire "BR" wire —passenger's side - "Y/GN" wire "W/BK" wire • Is the resistance less than 5 ohms?		Yes ► No ►	GO to OR14 . REPAIR/REPLACE wires as necessary.

TEST STEP		RESULT ►	ACTION TO TAKE
OR14	PASSIVE RESTRAINT MOTOR FEED CHECK		
• Key ON, door open. Belt at "A" pillar. • Close door. Belt is traveling to "B" pillar. • Measure the voltage on the following wires at the passive restraint motor.		Yes ► No ►	REPLACE track and motor assembly. REPLACE passive restraint control module or call (313) 390-8420.

Vehicle Side	Wire Color	Voltage
Driver	"BL/GN"	greater than 10 volts
	"BR"	less than 1 volt
Passenger	"W/BK"	greater than 10 volts
	"Y/GN"	less than 1 volt

- Open door. Belt is traveling to the "A" pillar.
- Measure the voltage on the following wires at the passive restraint motor.

Vehicle Side	Wire Color	Voltage
Driver	"BR"	greater than 10 volts
	"BL/GN"	less than 1 volt
Passenger	"Y/GN"	greater than 10 volts
	"W/BK"	less than 1 volt

- Are the voltage readings OK?

86750091

Fig. 100 Passive restraint system diagnosis — 1991-95 models (continued)

TEST STEP	RESULT ►	ACTION TO TAKE
OR15 FRONT LIMIT SWITCH SUPPLY CHECK		
• Measure resistance of the front limit switch circuit between passive restraint control module and passive restraint motor. —driver's side - "Y/BL" wire —passenger's side - "BL/W wire • Is the resistance less than 5 ohms?	Yes ► No ►	GO to **OR16** . REPAIR/REPLACE wires as necessary.

TEST STEP	RESULT ►	ACTION TO TAKE
OR16 FRONT LIMIT SWITCH GROUND CHECK		
• Measure the resistance of "BK" wire (driver's and passenger's side) between passive restraint motor and ground. • Is the resistance less than 5 ohms?	Yes ► No ►	GO to **OR17** . REPAIR/REPLACE wire.

TEST STEP	RESULT ►	ACTION TO TAKE
OR17 FRONT LIMIT SWITCH CHECK		
• Key ON. • Open door. • Measure the resistance of the following wires from the passive restraint module to ground. —driver's side - "Y/BL" wire —passenger's side - "BL/W" wire • Is the resistance less than 5 ohms?	Yes ► No ►	GO to **OR18** . REPLACE front limit switch.

86750092

Fig. 101 Passive restraint system diagnosis — 1991-95 models (continued)

TEST STEP		RESULT ►	ACTION TO TAKE
OR18	PASSIVE RESTRAINT MOTOR SUPPLY CHECK		
• Measure the resistance of supply wires between passive restraint control module and passive restraint motor. —driver's side - "BL/GN" wire "BR" wire —passenger's side - "Y/GN" wire "W/BK" wire • Is the resistance less than 5 ohms?		Yes ► No ►	GO to OR19 . REPAIR/REPLACE wires as necessary.

TEST STEP		RESULT ►	ACTION TO TAKE
OR19	PASSIVE RESTRAINT MOTOR FEED CHECK		
• Key ON, door open. Belt at "A" pillar. • Close door. Belt is traveling to "B" pillar. • Measure the voltage on the following wires at the passive restraint motor.		Yes ► No ►	REPLACE track and motor assembly. REPLACE passive restraint control module or call (313) 390-8420.

Vehicle Side	Wire Color	Voltage
Driver	"BL/GN"	greater than 10 volts
	"BR"	less than 1 volt
Passenger	"W/BK"	greater than 10 volts
	"Y/GN"	less than 1 volt

- Open door. Belt is traveling to the "A" pillar.
- Measure the voltage on the following wires at the passive restraint motor.

Vehicle Side	Wire Color	Voltage
Driver	"BR"	greater than 10 volts
	"BL/GN"	less than 1 volt
Passenger	"Y/GN"	greater than 10 volts
	"W/BK"	less than 1 volt

- Are the voltage readings OK?

86750093

Fig. 102 Passive restraint system diagnosis — 1991-95 models (continued)

TEST STEP		RESULT ►	ACTION TO TAKE
OR20	SEAT BELT RETRACTOR SWITCHES (BUCKLE SWITCHES)		
• Key ON. • Both carries at "B" pillar and belts buckled. • Measure the voltage on the following wires at the passive restraint module.		Yes ► No ►	GO to OR9 . REPLACE the retractor assembly.

Vehicle Side	Wire Color	Voltage
Driver	"O/GN"	less than .75 volt
Passenger	"P"	less than .75 volt

• Are the voltage readings OK?

TEST STEP		RESULT ►	ACTION TO TAKE
OR21	INERTIA INPUT TO PASSIVE RESTRAINT CONTROL MODULE		
• Disconnect both passive restraint control module connectors. • Measure the voltage between passive restraint module "GN/R" wire and passive restraint module "BK" wire. • Is the voltage reading above 10V?		Yes ► No ►	GO to OR4 . RESET the fuel pump interia switch. If OK, CHECK the "GN/R" wire for short.

86750094

Fig. 103 Passive restraint system diagnosis — 1991-95 models (continued)

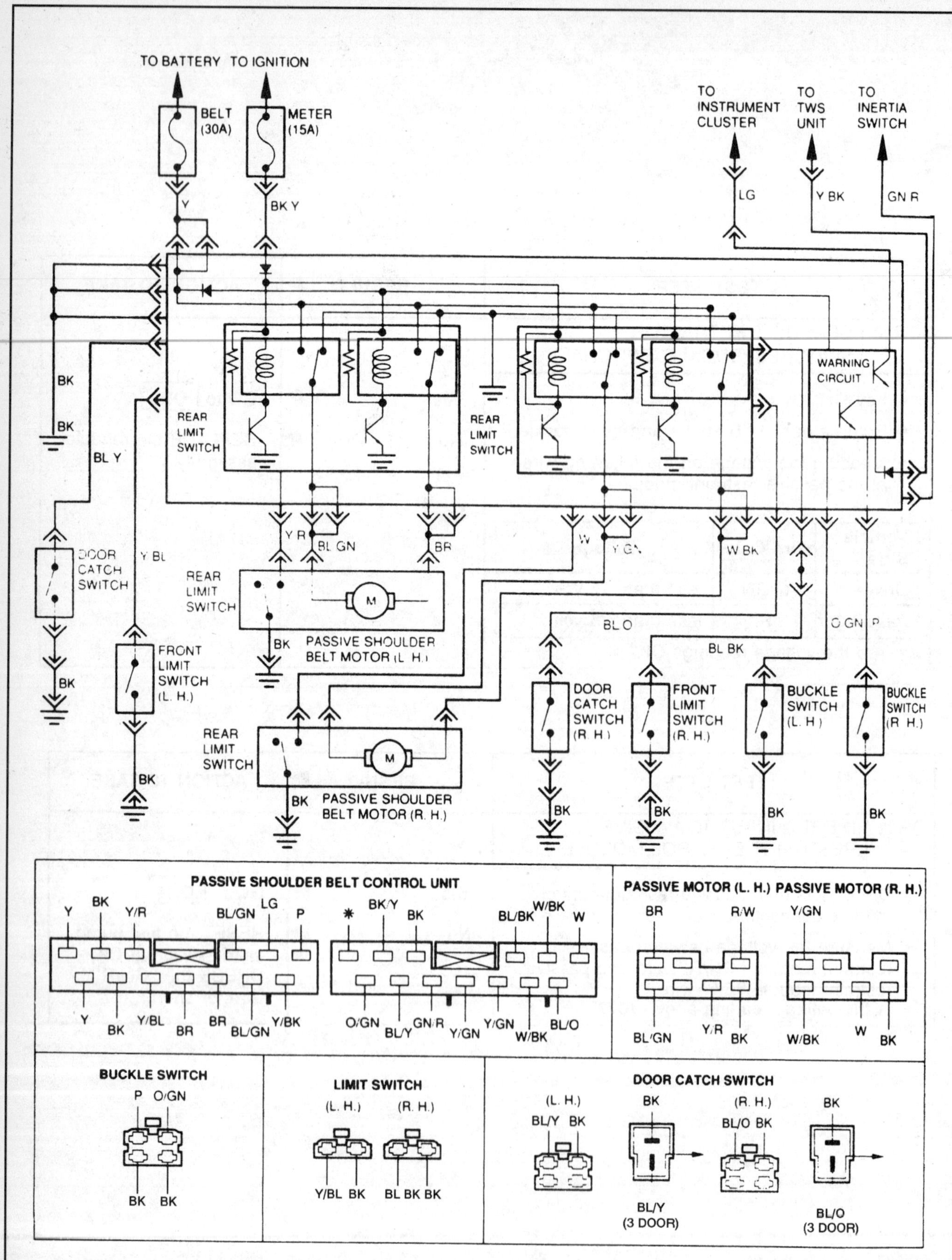

Fig. 104 Passive restraint system, electrical schematic — 1991-95 models

Warning Switch

REMOVAL & INSTALLATION

The warning switch is serviced with the retractor as an assembly.

Headliner

REMOVAL & INSTALLATION

Before removing the headlining on the Escort/Lynx, EXP/LN-7, the hatchback or liftgate weatherstrip, door weatherstrip, and the quarter window glass and the weatherstrip assemblies must be removed. When installing the headlining, start at the hatchback, or the liftgate and move toward the front of the vehicle.

If the vehicle is equipped with assist handles, they must be removed during the replacement procedure.

Escort/Lynx, EXP/LN-7

2-DOOR, 3-DOOR HATCHBACK

➧ See Figure 105

1. Remove the right and left sun visors and the visor center clips.

➡If the vehicle is equipped with illuminated sun visors, disconnect the electrical leads.

2. Remove the header garnish moulding.
3. Remove the windshield side garnish mouldings.
4. Remove the dome light.
5. Remove the roof rail assist handles and coat hooks.
6. Remove the roof rail weatherstrip assemblies.
7. Detach the liftgate gas cylinders at body opening.
8. Detach the ground wire for the heated rear window, if so equipped.
9. Remove the folding rear seat assembly including the luggage cover.
10. Remove the quarter window and weatherstrip assemblies.
11. Remove the headlining.

To install:

12. Unpackage the new headlining and lay it out on a flat surface. Mark and trim the new headlining using the old one as a pattern.
13. Trim the listings, pockets, on the new headlining to the approximate length of the old one. Remove the support rods from the old headlining and install them in the same relative rod positions of the new headliner. The roof headlining support rods are color coded at each end. When ordering new rods, be sure to note the color at each end of the rod.
14. Position the headliner in the vehicle, connect the bows.
15. Starting at the rear window area, apply trim cement and align the rear bow to the vertical position.
16. Working from the center to the outboard side, stretch and cement the headliner to the rear window opening flange.
17. Apply cement to the windshield opening flange, door opening weatherstrip flange, quarter glass and hatchback opening flanges. Align the bows and pull the headlining forward and cement into position at the windshield opening.
18. Working from the front to the rear, stretch and cement the headlining to the door(s), quarter window and hatchback opening.
19. Trim all excess material, leaving approximately ½ in. (13mm) to wrap into the pinch weld areas.
20. Apply cement to the pinch weld areas.
21. To install the trim items, reverse the removal procedures.

4-DOOR HATCHBACK AND 4-DOOR WAGON

➧ See Figure 106

1. Remove the right and left sun visors and the visor center clips.

➡If the vehicle is equipped with illuminated sun visors, disconnect the electrical leads.

2. Remove the header garnish moulding.
3. Remove the windshield side garnish mouldings.
4. Remove the dome light.
5. Remove the roof rail assist handles and coat hooks.
6. Remove the roof rail weatherstrip assemblies.
7. Detach the liftgate gas cylinders at body opening.
8. Remove the folding seat assembly.
9. Remove the luggage compartment cover.
10. Remove the center body pillar trim panels.
11. Remove the lower back trim panel.
12. Remove the quarter trim panels.
13. Remove the side window assemblies and seats.
14. Remove the headlining.

To install:

15. Unpackage the new headlining and lay it out on a flat surface. Mark and trim the new headlining using the old one as a pattern.
16. Trim the listings, pockets, on the new headlining to the approximate length of the old one. Remove the support rods from the old headlining and install them in the same relative rod positions of the new headliner. The roof headlining support rods are color coded at each end. When ordering new rods, be sure to note the color at each end of the rod.
17. Position the headliner in the vehicle, connect the bows.
18. Starting at the rear window area, apply trim cement and align the rear bow to the vertical position.
19. Working from the center to the outboard side, stretch and cement the headliner to the rear window opening flange.
20. Apply cement to the windshield opening flange, door opening weatherstrip flange, quarter glass and hatchback opening flanges. Align the bows and pull the headlining forward and cement into position at the windshield opening.
21. Working from the front to the rear, stretch and cement the headlining to the door(s), quarter window and hatchback opening.
22. Trim all excess material, leaving approximately ½ in. (13mm) to wrap into the pinch weld areas.
23. Apply cement to the pinch weld areas.
24. To install the trim items, reverse the removal procedures.

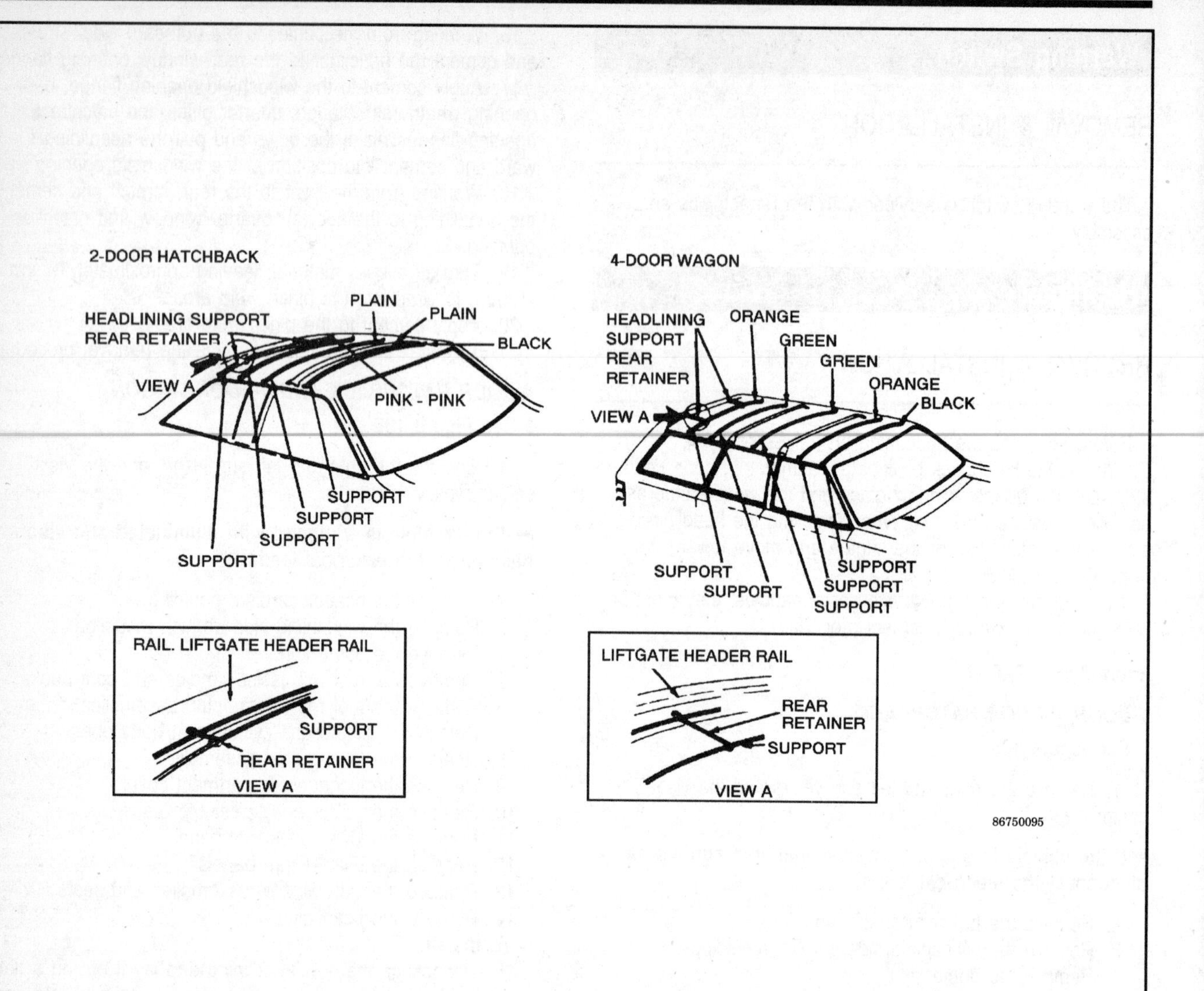

Fig. 105 Location of common headliner support rods — 2 models and 4-door wagon

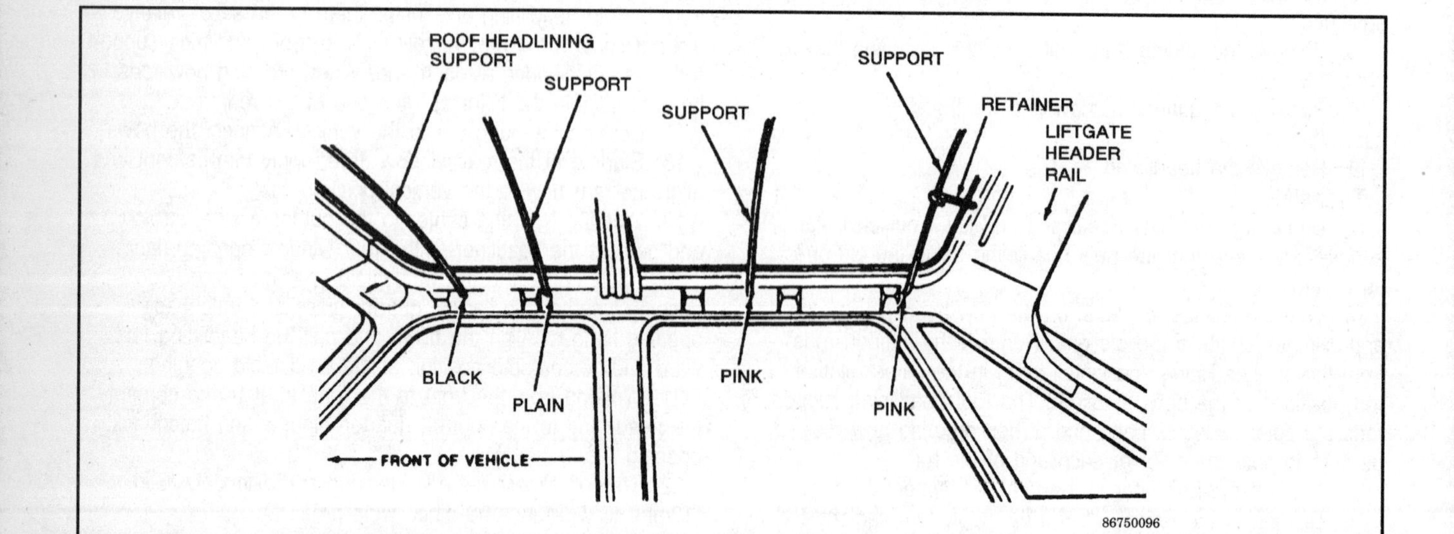

Fig. 106 Interior view of headliner support rods — Escort/Lynx models

1991-95 Models

➧ See Figures 107, 108 and 109

1. Remove the rear seat assist straps, if equipped.
2. Remove the coat hooks, if equipped.
3. Remove the interior lamp assembly.
4. Remove the sun visor retaining screws and remove the sun visors.
5. Disconnect all electrical connectors.
6. Remove the seaming welt from the moon roof opening, if equipped.
7. Remove the overhead console door and remove the overhead console.
8. Remove the "A-B" pillar trim panels.
9. Detach the seaming welts from the upper door openings.
10. Remove the rear header panel and quarter trim panels.
11. Remove the black push-pin fastener from the interior door lamp area.
12. Carefully remove the white master locating clip from the passenger visor retainer clip area. If necessary, break the clip, then remove all broken pieces.
13. Carefully detach the headliner at the two-side tape area above the rear door openings.
14. While supporting the headliner, slide it forward to release it from the rear retaining tabs.
15. Remove the headliner through the rear of the vehicle.

To install:

16. Position the headliner in the vehicle and slide it rearward onto the rear retaining tabs. Center the headliner on the tabs.
17. Install the passenger visor locating clip.
18. Install the black push-pin fastener to the interior door lamp area.
19. Install the rear header panel and quarter trim panels.
20. Install sun visors, interior lamp assembly and coat hooks.
21. Attach all electrical connectors.

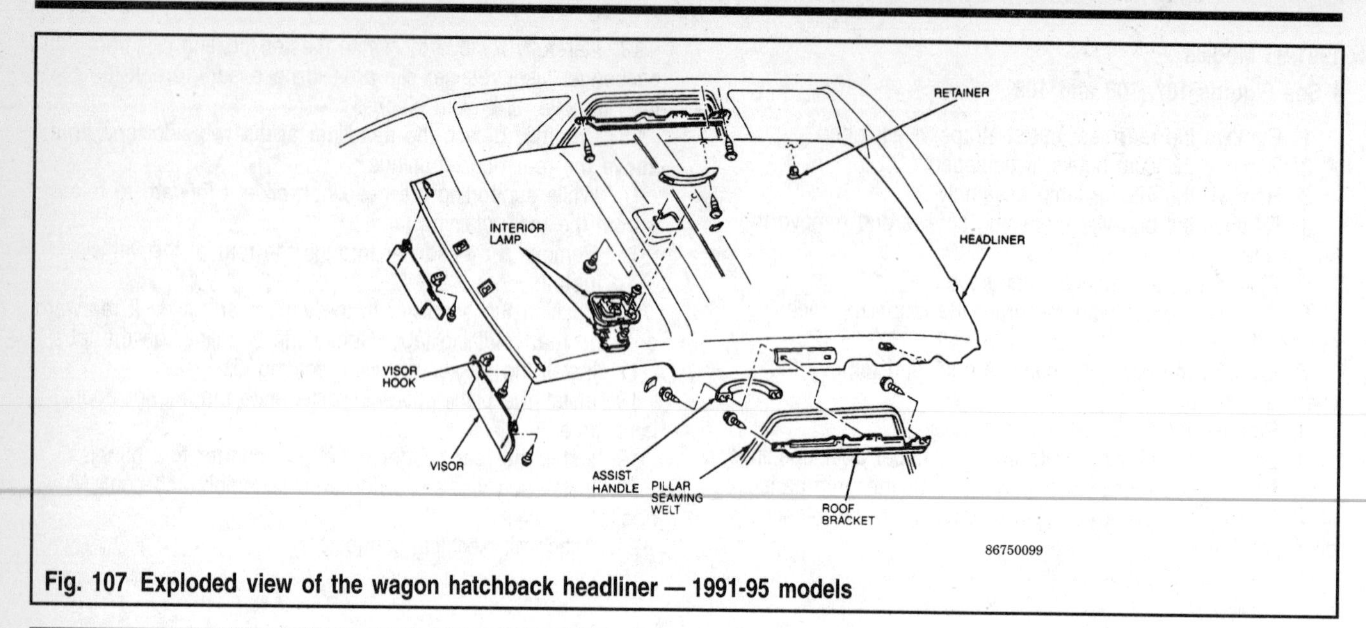

Fig. 107 Exploded view of the wagon hatchback headliner — 1991-95 models

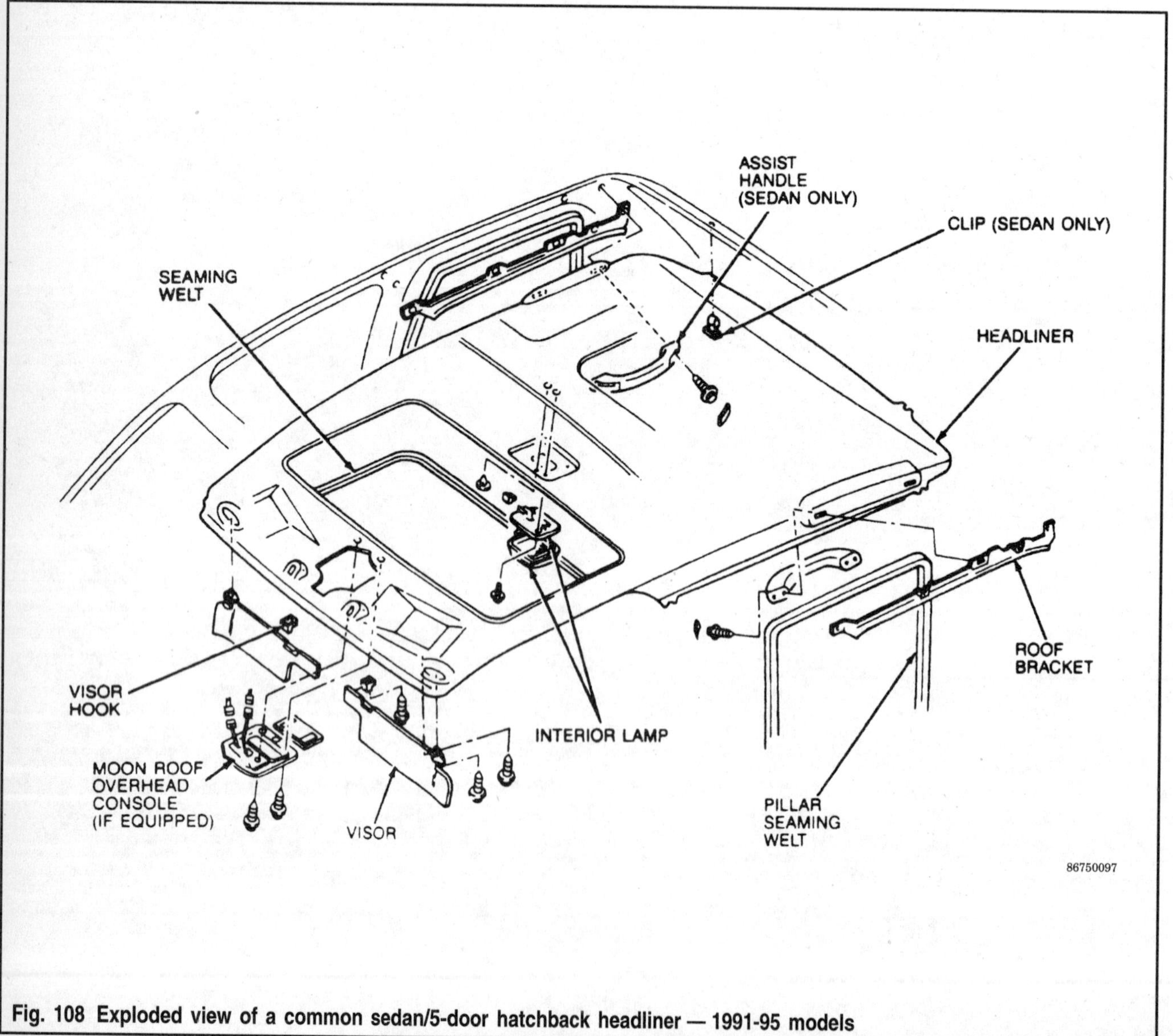

Fig. 108 Exploded view of a common sedan/5-door hatchback headliner — 1991-95 models

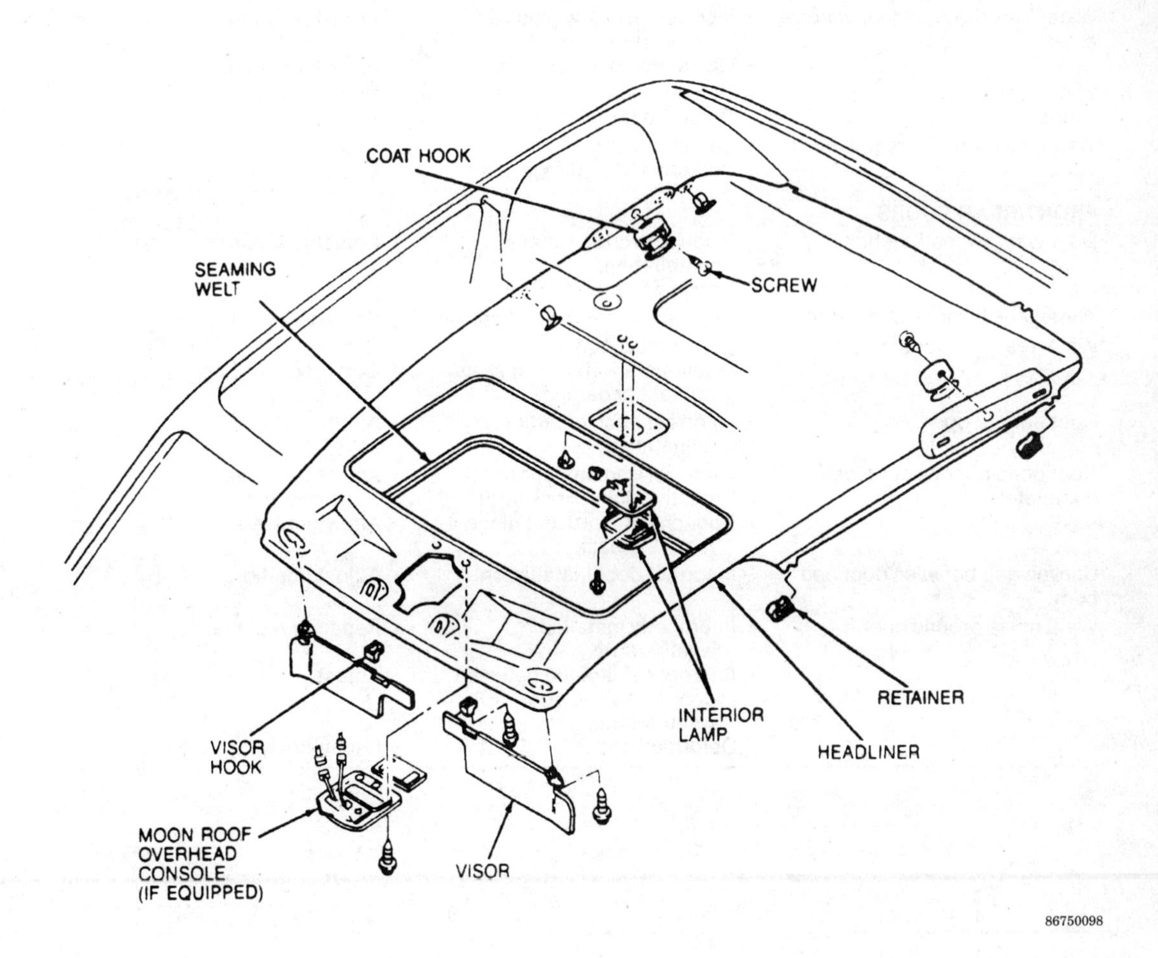

Fig. 109 Exploded view of a common 3-door hatchback headliner — 1991-95 models

Hood, Trunk Lid, Hatch Lid, Glass and Doors

Problem	Possible Cause	Correction
HOOD/TRUNK/HATCH LID		
Improper closure.	• Striker and latch not properly aligned.	• Adjust the alignment.
Difficulty locking and unlocking.	• Striker and latch not properly aligned.	• Adjust the alignment.
Uneven clearance with body panels.	• Incorrectly installed hood or trunk lid.	• Adjust the alignment.
WINDOW/WINDSHIELD GLASS		
Water leak through windshield	• Defective seal. • Defective body flange.	• Fill sealant • Correct.
Water leak through door window glass.	• Incorrect window glass installation. • Gap at upper window frame.	• Adjust position. • Adjust position.
Water leak through quarter window.	• Defective seal. • Defective body flange.	• Replace seal. • Correct.
Water leak through rear window.	• Defective seal. • Defective body flange.	• Replace seal. • Correct.
FRONT/REAR DOORS		
Door window malfunction.	• Incorrect window glass installation. • Damaged or faulty regulator.	• Adjust position. • Correct or replace.
Water leak through door edge.	• Cracked or faulty weatherstrip.	• Replace.
Water leak from door center.	• Drain hole clogged. • Inadequate waterproof skeet contact or damage.	• Remove foreign objects. • Correct or replace.
Door hard to open.	• Incorrect latch or striker adjustment.	• Adjust.
Door does not open or close completely.	• Incorrect door installation. • Defective door check strap. • Door check strap and hinge require grease.	• Adjust position. • Correct or replace. • Apply grease.
Uneven gap between door and body.	• Incorrect door installation.	• Adjust position.
Wind noise around door.	• Improperly installed weatherstrip. • Improper clearance between door glass and door weatherstrip. • Deformed door.	• Repair or replace. • Adjust. • Repair or replace.

86750100

How to Remove Stains from Fabric Interior

For best results, spots and stains should be removed as soon as possible. Never use gasoline, lacquer thinner, acetone, nail polish remover or bleach. Use a 3′ x 3″ piece of cheesecloth. Squeeze most of the liquid from the fabric and wipe the stained fabric from the outside of the stain toward the center with a lifting motion. Turn the cheesecloth as soon as one side becomes soiled. When using water to remove a stain, be sure to wash the entire section after the spot has been removed to avoid water stains. Encrusted spots can be broken up with a dull knife and vacuumed before removing the stain.

Type of Stain	How to Remove It
Surface spots	Brush the spots out with a small hand brush or use a commercial preparation such as K2R to lift the stain.
Mildew	Clean around the mildew with warm suds. Rinse in cold water and soak the mildew area in a solution of 1 part table salt and 2 parts water. Wash with upholstery cleaner.
Water stains	Water stains in fabric materials can be removed with a solution made from 1 cup of table salt dissolved in 1 quart of water. Vigorously scrub the solution into the stain and rinse with clear water. Water stains in nylon or other synthetic fabrics should be removed with a commercial type spot remover.
Chewing gum, tar, crayons, shoe polish (greasy stains)	Do not use a cleaner that will soften gum or tar. Harden the deposit with an ice cube and scrape away as much as possible with a dull knife. Moisten the remainder with cleaning fluid and scrub clean.
Ice cream, candy	Most candy has a sugar base and can be removed with a cloth wrung out in warm water. Oily candy, after cleaning with warm water, should be cleaned with upholstery cleaner. Rinse with warm water and clean the remainder with cleaning fluid.
Wine, alcohol, egg, milk, soft drink (non-greasy stains)	Do not use soap. Scrub the stain with a cloth wrung out in warm water. Remove the remainder with cleaning fluid.
Grease, oil, lipstick, butter and related stains	Use a spot remover to avoid leaving a ring. Work from the outisde of the stain to the center and dry with a clean cloth when the spot is gone.
Headliners (cloth)	Mix a solution of warm water and foam upholstery cleaner to give thick suds. Use only foam—liquid may streak or spot. Clean the entire headliner in one operation using a circular motion with a natural sponge.
Headliner (vinyl)	Use a vinyl cleaner with a sponge and wipe clean with a dry cloth.
Seats and door panels	Mix 1 pint upholstery cleaner in 1 gallon of water. Do not soak the fabric around the buttons.
Leather or vinyl fabric	Use a multi-purpose cleaner full strength and a stiff brush. Let stand 2 minutes and scrub thoroughly. Wipe with a clean, soft rag.
Nylon or synthetic fabrics	For normal stains, use the same procedures you would for washing cloth upholstery. If the fabric is extremely dirty, use a multi-purpose cleaner full strength with a stiff scrub brush. Scrub thoroughly in all directions and wipe with a cotton towel or soft rag.

86750101

GLOSSARY

AIR/FUEL RATIO: The ratio of air-to-gasoline by weight in the fuel mixture drawn into the engine.

AIR INJECTION: One method of reducing harmful exhaust emissions by injecting air into each of the exhaust ports of an engine. The fresh air entering the hot exhaust manifold causes any remaining fuel to be burned before it can exit the tailpipe.

ALTERNATOR: A device used for converting mechanical energy into electrical energy.

AMMETER: An instrument, calibrated in amperes, used to measure the flow of an electrical current in a circuit. Ammeters are always connected in series with the circuit being tested.

AMPERE: The rate of flow of electrical current present when one volt of electrical pressure is applied against one ohm of electrical resistance.

ANALOG COMPUTER: Any microprocessor that uses similar (analogous) electrical signals to make its calculations.

ARMATURE: A laminated, soft iron core wrapped by a wire that converts electrical energy to mechanical energy as in a motor or relay. When rotated in a magnetic field, it changes mechanical energy into electrical energy as in a generator.

ATMOSPHERIC PRESSURE: The pressure on the Earth's surface caused by the weight of the air in the atmosphere. At sea level, this pressure is 14.7 psi at 32°F (101 kPa at 0°C).

ATOMIZATION: The breaking down of a liquid into a fine mist that can be suspended in air.

AXIAL PLAY: Movement parallel to a shaft or bearing bore.

BACKFIRE: The sudden combustion of gases in the intake or exhaust system that results in a loud explosion.

BACKLASH: The clearance or play between two parts, such as meshed gears.

BACKPRESSURE: Restrictions in the exhaust system that slow the exit of exhaust gases from the combustion chamber.

BAKELITE: A heat resistant, plastic insulator material commonly used in printed circuit boards and transistorized components.

BALL BEARING: A bearing made up of hardened inner and outer races between which hardened steel balls roll.

BALLAST RESISTOR: A resistor in the primary ignition circuit that lowers voltage after the engine is started to reduce wear on ignition components.

BEARING: A friction reducing, supportive device usually located between a stationary part and a moving part.

BIMETAL TEMPERATURE SENSOR: Any sensor or switch made of two dissimilar types of metal that bend when heated or cooled due to the different expansion rates of the alloys. These types of sensors usually function as an on/off switch.

BLOWBY: Combustion gases, composed of water vapor and unburned fuel, that leak past the piston rings into the crankcase during normal engine operation. These gases are removed by the PCV system to prevent the buildup of harmful acids in the crankcase.

BRAKE PAD: A brake shoe and lining assembly used with disc brakes.

BRAKE SHOE: The backing for the brake lining. The term is, however, usually applied to the assembly of the brake backing and lining.

BUSHING: A liner, usually removable, for a bearing; an anti-friction liner used in place of a bearing.

CALIPER: A hydraulically activated device in a disc brake system, which is mounted straddling the brake rotor (disc). The caliper contains at least one piston and two brake pads. Hydraulic pressure on the piston(s) forces the pads against the rotor.

CAMSHAFT: A shaft in the engine on which are the lobes (cams) which operate the valves. The camshaft is driven by the crankshaft, via a belt, chain or gears, at one half the crankshaft speed.

CAPACITOR: A device which stores an electrical charge.

CARBON MONOXIDE (CO): A colorless, odorless gas given off as a normal byproduct of combustion. It is poisonous and extremely dangerous in confined areas, building up slowly to toxic levels without warning if adequate ventilation is not available.

CARBURETOR: A device, usually mounted on the intake manifold of an engine, which mixes the air and fuel in the proper proportion to allow even combustion.

CATALYTIC CONVERTER: A device installed in the exhaust system, like a muffler, that converts harmful byproducts of combustion into carbon dioxide and water vapor by means of a heat-producing chemical reaction.

CENTRIFUGAL ADVANCE: A mechanical method of advancing the spark timing by using flyweights in the distributor that react to centrifugal force generated by the distributor shaft rotation.

CHECK VALVE: Any one-way valve installed to permit the flow of air, fuel or vacuum in one direction only.

CHOKE: A device, usually a moveable valve, placed in the intake path of a carburetor to restrict the flow of air.

CIRCUIT: Any unbroken path through which an electrical current can flow. Also used to describe fuel flow in some instances.

CIRCUIT BREAKER: A switch which protects an electrical circuit from overload by opening the circuit when the current flow exceeds a predetermined level. Some circuit breakers must be reset manually, while most reset automatically.

COIL (IGNITION): A transformer in the ignition circuit which steps up the voltage provided to the spark plugs.

COMBINATION MANIFOLD: An assembly which includes both the intake and exhaust manifolds in one casting.

COMBINATION VALVE: A device used in some fuel systems that routes fuel vapors to a charcoal storage canister instead of venting them into the atmosphere. The valve relieves fuel tank pressure and allows fresh air into the tank as the fuel level drops to prevent a vapor lock situation.

COMPRESSION RATIO: The comparison of the total volume of the cylinder and combustion chamber with the piston at BDC and the piston at TDC.

CONDENSER: 1. An electrical device which acts to store an electrical charge, preventing voltage surges. 2. A radiator-like device in the air conditioning system in which refrigerant gas condenses into a liquid, giving off heat.

CONDUCTOR: Any material through which an electrical current can be transmitted easily.

CONTINUITY: Continuous or complete circuit. Can be checked with an ohmmeter.

COUNTERSHAFT: An intermediate shaft which is rotated by a mainshaft and transmits, in turn, that rotation to a working part.

CRANKCASE: The lower part of an engine in which the crankshaft and related parts operate.

CRANKSHAFT: The main driving shaft of an engine which receives reciprocating motion from the pistons and converts it to rotary motion.

CYLINDER: In an engine, the round hole in the engine block in which the piston(s) ride.

CYLINDER BLOCK: The main structural member of an engine in which is found the cylinders, crankshaft and other principal parts.

CYLINDER HEAD: The detachable portion of the engine, usually fastened to the top of the cylinder block and containing all or most of the combustion chambers. On overhead valve engines, it contains the valves and their operating parts. On overhead cam engines, it contains the camshaft as well.

DEAD CENTER: The extreme top or bottom of the piston stroke.

DETONATION: An unwanted explosion of the air/fuel mixture in the combustion chamber caused by excess heat and compression, advanced timing, or an overly lean mixture. Also referred to as "ping".

DIAPHRAGM: A thin, flexible wall separating two cavities, such as in a vacuum advance unit.

DIESELING: A condition in which hot spots in the combustion chamber cause the engine to run on after the key is turned off.

DIFFERENTIAL: A geared assembly which allows the transmission of motion between drive axles, giving one axle the ability to turn faster than the other.

DIODE: An electrical device that will allow current to flow in one direction only.

DISC BRAKE: A hydraulic braking assembly consisting of a brake disc, or rotor, mounted on an axle, and a caliper assembly containing, usually two brake pads which are activated by hydraulic pressure. The pads are forced against the sides of the disc, creating friction which slows the vehicle.

DISTRIBUTOR: A mechanically driven device on an engine which is responsible for electrically firing the spark plug at a predetermined point of the piston stroke.

DOWEL PIN: A pin, inserted in mating holes in two different parts allowing those parts to maintain a fixed relationship.

DRUM BRAKE: A braking system which consists of two brake shoes and one or two wheel cylinders, mounted on a fixed backing plate, and a brake drum, mounted on an axle, which revolves around the assembly.

DWELL: The rate, measured in degrees of shaft rotation, at which an electrical circuit cycles on and off.

ELECTRONIC CONTROL UNIT (ECU): Ignition module, module, amplifier or igniter. See Module for definition.

ELECTRONIC IGNITION: A system in which the timing and firing of the spark plugs is controlled by an electronic control unit, usually called a module. These systems have no points or condenser.

END-PLAY: The measured amount of axial movement in a shaft.

ENGINE: A device that converts heat into mechanical energy.

EXHAUST MANIFOLD: A set of cast passages or pipes which conduct exhaust gases from the engine.

FEELER GAUGE: A blade, usually metal, of precisely predetermined thickness, used to measure the clearance between two parts.

FIRING ORDER: The order in which combustion occurs in the cylinders of an engine. Also the order in which spark is distributed to the plugs by the distributor.

FLOODING: The presence of too much fuel in the intake manifold and combustion chamber which prevents the air/fuel mixture from firing, thereby causing a no-start situation.

FLYWHEEL: A disc shaped part bolted to the rear end of the crankshaft. Around the outer perimeter is affixed the ring gear. The starter drive engages the ring gear, turning the flywheel, which rotates the crankshaft, imparting the initial starting motion to the engine.

FOOT POUND (ft. lbs. or sometimes, ft.lb.): The amount of energy or work needed to raise an item weighing one pound, a distance of one foot.

FUSE: A protective device in a circuit which prevents circuit overload by breaking the circuit when a specific amperage is present. The device is constructed around a strip or wire of a lower amperage rating than the circuit it is designed to protect. When an amperage higher than that stamped on the fuse is present in the circuit, the strip or wire melts, opening the circuit.

GEAR RATIO: The ratio between the number of teeth on meshing gears.

GENERATOR: A device which converts mechanical energy into electrical energy.

HEAT RANGE: The measure of a spark plug's ability to dissipate heat from its firing end. The higher the heat range, the hotter the plug fires.

HUB: The center part of a wheel or gear.

HYDROCARBON (HC): Any chemical compound made up of hydrogen and carbon. A major pollutant formed by the engine as a byproduct of combustion.

HYDROMETER: An instrument used to measure the specific gravity of a solution.

INCH POUND (inch lbs.; sometimes in.lb. or in. lbs.): One twelfth of a foot pound.

INDUCTION: A means of transferring electrical energy in the form of a magnetic field. Principle used in the ignition coil to increase voltage.

INJECTOR: A device which receives metered fuel under relatively low pressure and is activated to inject the fuel into the engine under relatively high pressure at a predetermined time.

INPUT SHAFT: The shaft to which torque is applied, usually carrying the driving gear or gears.

INTAKE MANIFOLD: A casting of passages or pipes used to conduct air or a fuel/air mixture to the cylinders.

JOURNAL: The bearing surface within which a shaft operates.

KEY: A small block usually fitted in a notch between a shaft and a hub to prevent slippage of the two parts.

MANIFOLD: A casting of passages or set of pipes which connect the cylinders to an inlet or outlet source.

MANIFOLD VACUUM: Low pressure in an engine intake manifold formed just below the throttle plates. Manifold vacuum is highest at idle and drops under acceleration.

MASTER CYLINDER: The primary fluid pressurizing device in a hydraulic system. In automotive use, it is found in brake and hydraulic clutch systems and is pedal activated, either directly or, in a power brake system, through the power booster.

MODULE: Electronic control unit, amplifier or igniter of solid state or integrated design which controls the current flow in the ignition primary circuit based on input from the pick-up coil. When the module opens the primary circuit, high secondary voltage is induced in the coil.

NEEDLE BEARING: A bearing which consists of a number (usually a large number) of long, thin rollers.

OHM:(Ω) The unit used to measure the resistance of conductor-to-electrical flow. One ohm is the amount of resistance that limits current flow to one ampere in a circuit with one volt of pressure.

OHMMETER: An instrument used for measuring the resistance, in ohms, in an electrical circuit.

OUTPUT SHAFT: The shaft which transmits torque from a device, such as a transmission.

OVERDRIVE: A gear assembly which produces more shaft revolutions than that transmitted to it.

OVERHEAD CAMSHAFT (OHC): An engine configuration in which the camshaft is mounted on top of the cylinder head and operates the valve either directly or by means of rocker arms.

OVERHEAD VALVE (OHV): An engine configuration in which all of the valves are located in the cylinder head and the camshaft is located in the cylinder block. The camshaft operates the valves via lifters and pushrods.

OXIDES OF NITROGEN (NOx): Chemical compounds of nitrogen produced as a byproduct of combustion. They combine with hydrocarbons to produce smog.

OXYGEN SENSOR: Used with the feedback system to sense the presence of oxygen in the exhaust gas and signal the computer which can reference the voltage signal to an air/fuel ratio.

PINION: The smaller of two meshing gears.

PISTON RING: An open-ended ring which fits into a groove on the outer diameter of the piston. Its chief function is to form a seal between the piston and cylinder wall. Most automotive pistons have three rings: two for compression sealing; one for oil sealing.

PRELOAD: A predetermined load placed on a bearing during assembly or by adjustment.

PRIMARY CIRCUIT: The low voltage side of the ignition system which consists of the ignition switch, ballast resistor or resistance wire, bypass, coil, electronic control unit and pick-up coil as well as the connecting wires and harnesses.

PRESS FIT: The mating of two parts under pressure, due to the inner diameter of one being smaller than the outer diameter of the other, or vice versa; an interference fit.

RACE: The surface on the inner or outer ring of a bearing on which the balls, needles or rollers move.

REGULATOR: A device which maintains the amperage and/or voltage levels of a circuit at predetermined values.

RELAY: A switch which automatically opens and/or closes a circuit.

RESISTANCE: The opposition to the flow of current through a circuit or electrical device, and is measured in ohms. Resistance is equal to the voltage divided by the amperage.

RESISTOR: A device, usually made of wire, which offers a preset amount of resistance in an electrical circuit.

RING GEAR: The name given to a ring-shaped gear attached to a differential case, or affixed to a flywheel or as part of a planetary gear set.

ROLLER BEARING: A bearing made up of hardened inner and outer races between which hardened steel rollers move.

ROTOR: 1. The disc-shaped part of a disc brake assembly, upon which the brake pads bear; also called, brake disc. 2. The device mounted atop the distributor shaft, which passes current to the distributor cap tower contacts.

SECONDARY CIRCUIT: The high voltage side of the ignition system, usually above 20,000 volts. The secondary includes the ignition coil, coil wire, distributor cap and rotor, spark plug wires and spark plugs.

SENDING UNIT: A mechanical, electrical, hydraulic or electromagnetic device which transmits information to a gauge.

SENSOR: Any device designed to measure engine operating conditions or ambient pressures and temperatures. Usually electronic in nature and designed to send a voltage signal to an on-board computer, some sensors may operate as a simple on/off switch or they may provide a variable voltage signal (like a potentiometer) as conditions or measured parameters change.

SHIM: Spacers of precise, predetermined thickness used between parts to establish a proper working relationship.

SLAVE CYLINDER: In automotive use, a device in the hydraulic clutch system which is activated by hydraulic force, disengaging the clutch.

SOLENOID: A coil used to produce a magnetic field, the effect of which is to produce work.

SPARK PLUG: A device screwed into the combustion chamber of a spark ignition engine. The basic construction is a conductive core inside of a ceramic insulator, mounted in an outer conductive base. An electrical charge from the spark plug wire travels along the conductive core and jumps a preset air gap to a grounding point or points at the end of the conductive base. The resultant spark ignites the fuel/air mixture in the combustion chamber.

SPLINES: Ridges machined or cast onto the outer diameter of a shaft or inner diameter of a bore to enable parts to mate without rotation.

TACHOMETER: A device used to measure the rotary speed of an engine, shaft, gear, etc., usually in rotations per minute.

THERMOSTAT: A valve, located in the cooling system of an engine, which is closed when cold and opens gradually in response to engine heating, controlling the temperature of the coolant and rate of coolant flow.

TOP DEAD CENTER (TDC): The point at which the piston reaches the top of its travel on the compression stroke.

TORQUE: The twisting force applied to an object.

TORQUE CONVERTER: A turbine used to transmit power from a driving member to a driven member via hydraulic action, providing changes in drive ratio and torque. In automotive use, it links the driveplate at the rear of the engine to the automatic transmission.

TRANSDUCER: A device used to change a force into an electrical signal.

TRANSISTOR: A semi-conductor component which can be actuated by a small voltage to perform an electrical switching function.

TUNE-UP: A regular maintenance function, usually associated with the replacement and adjustment of parts and components in the electrical and fuel systems of a vehicle for the purpose of attaining optimum performance.

TURBOCHARGER: An exhaust driven pump which compresses intake air and forces it into the combustion chambers at higher than atmospheric pressures. The increased air pressure allows more fuel to be burned and results in increased horsepower being produced.

VACUUM ADVANCE: A device which advances the ignition timing in response to increased engine vacuum.

VACUUM GAUGE: An instrument used to measure the presence of vacuum in a chamber.

VALVE: A device which control the pressure, direction of flow or rate of flow of a liquid or gas.

VALVE CLEARANCE: The measured gap between the end of the valve stem and the rocker arm, cam lobe or follower that activates the valve.

VISCOSITY: The rating of a liquid's internal resistance to flow.

VOLTMETER: An instrument used for measuring electrical force in units called volts. Voltmeters are always connected parallel with the circuit being tested.

WHEEL CYLINDER: Found in the automotive drum brake assembly, it is a device, actuated by hydraulic pressure, which, through internal pistons, pushes the brake shoes outward against the drums.

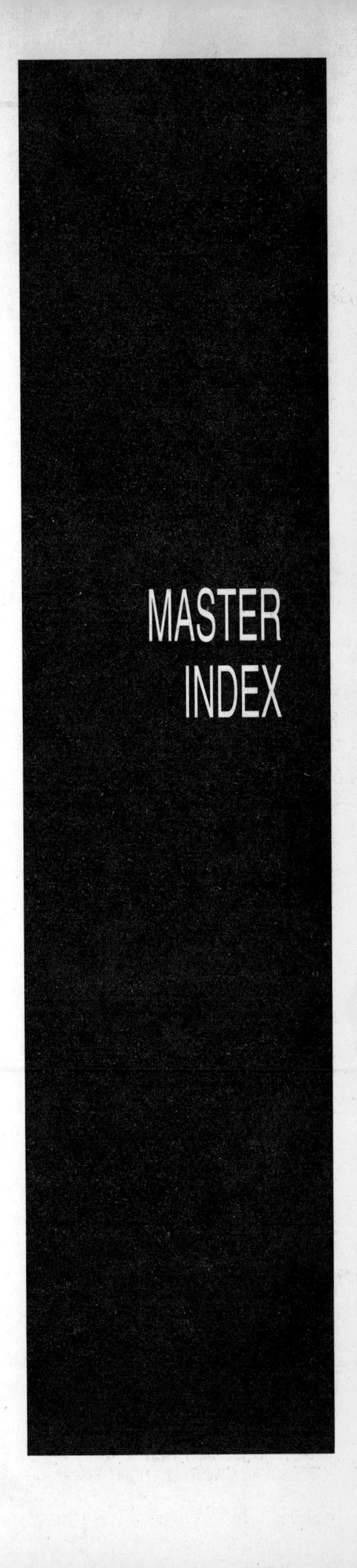
MASTER
INDEX